CHAMBERS

PRIMARY
DICTIONARY

CHAMBERS

CHAMBERS
An imprint of Chambers Harrap Publishers Ltd
7 Hopetoun Crescent
Edinburgh, EH7 4AY

First published by Chambers Harrap Publishers Ltd 2002

A CIP catalogue record for this book is available from the British Library.

ISBN 0550 10046 6

Designed and typeset by Chambers Harrap Publishers Ltd, Edinburgh
Printed in Italy by Rotolito Lombarda SpA

Contents

Contributors

Project Editor
Mary O'Neill

Compilers
Sandra Anderson   Pat Bulhosen
Kay Cullen   Lucy Hollingworth
Megan Thomson

Panels written by
Ruth Thomson

Editorial Assistance
Rosalind Fergusson

Publishing Manager
Patrick White

Prepress
Clair Good

*The editors would like to acknowledge with thanks the assistance
and advice of the following:*

Briar Hill Lower School, Northampton
Chirnside Primary School, Chirnside, Scottish Borders
Hatherleigh County Primary School, Hatherleigh, Devon
Ide First School, Ide, Exeter
St Patrick's Primary School, Coatbridge, Lanarkshire
Woodlands CP Junior School, Tonbridge, Kent

Preface

Chambers Primary Dictionary has been specially written for use by primary school pupils aged 7-11, taking into consideration the requirements of Key Stage 2 of the English and Welsh National Curriculum and levels C and D of Curriculum and Assessment in Scotland. It has been compiled with the benefit of advice from a number of primary school teachers, ensuring that the book will be useful for most pupils in this age group.

The aim of the dictionary is to provide all the information a pupil at this level needs in the most straightforward terms, while still providing more challenging material for older or more able primary pupils. Over 10,000 look-up words give wide coverage, including definitions of words used in subjects such as mathematics and science at Key Stage 2. Labelled pictures have been chosen not just to lend attractiveness to the page, but to illustrate, for example, the parts of a flower and the planets in the solar system.

To encourage young dictionary users, the entry words are picked out in colour. The alphabet is printed down the side of the page, showing the reader where they are. The vocabulary used in the definitions has been kept deliberately simple, and the tone friendly. Examples of the word in context are included in many entries, helping to identify both the meaning and how the word is used. In many cases, these examples have been taken directly from our corpus of children's literature, another resource which has helped the editors to make informed decisions about the words a child is likely to meet in his or her reading.

Further assistance with language is provided by clear, coloured part of speech labels (noun, verb, etc), designed to increase pupils' awareness and understanding of the concepts. The inclusion of full-out forms such as the plurals of nouns and past tenses of verbs makes such inflections easy to identify and spell. Extra pieces of important and interesting information, such as homophones that can be confused, pronunciations and word histories, are included in short, eye-catching boxes. As well as making the page attractive, this ensures that the main entry itself remains uncluttered and easy to follow.

Particularly useful is the series of larger panels, each dealing with a language topic that teachers expressed a wish to see more fully covered, such as verbs, prefixes, synonyms etc. These panels have been specially written to provide full but simple explanations of concepts that children often find difficult to learn, but which are essential to their understanding of language. It is such features which make *Chambers Primary Dictionary* an invaluable resource for primary school pupils, for dictionary work and everyday reference.

www

To help make best use of *Chambers Primary* titles, teachers can download photocopiable versions of the panels, along with language exercises, from our website at www.chambers.co.uk

Panels in this book

Panels explaining an important language topic are given on the following pages. These panels tell you what the terms mean and give many examples to help make it clear.

Illustrations in this book

Word histories in this book

Aboriginal
agoraphobia
alphabet
angel
animal
April
arena
atlas
audio
August

banquet
bazaar
beret
biblio-
binoculars
blancmange
bog
boil
braille

Caesarean
cardigan
castanets
chauvinism
circus
clan
cobra
comedy
cot
crescent

daisy
dandelion
December
dinosaur
disease
doctor
dormitory

easel
echo
eerie
electricity
encyclopedia
enormous

fang
feast
February
flour
fowl
Friday

galore
garage
gentle
gossip
graffiti
gravity
gypsy

Hallowe'en
hamburger
harbour
hippopotamus
holiday
hospital

idiot
idle
index
infant

January
jaywalking
JCB
jinx
jubilee
July
June

karate
khaki

lens
limerick
lion
lolly
lunatic

magazine

manufacture
marathon
March
May
meander
midwife
millennium
Monday

nasal
naval
neighbour
nightmare
noise
nostril
November

October
octopus
OK
ooze
orang-utan
origami
oval

panda car
panic
parole
pasteurize
pelican crossing
photograph
pyjamas

rabbi
radius
Ramadan
restaurant
rhinoceros
rucksack
rugby

safari
sandwich
Saturday
science
September

sequin
shampoo
sinister
sky
soap opera
solar
squad
stanza
steeplechase
Sunday
swindle

thump
Thursday
ticket
town
trade
trapezium
Tuesday
tulip

umbrella
unicorn

vacuum
ventriloquism
video
virus
volcano

walrus
waltz
Wednesday
wellingtons
wisdom tooth

Xmas
xylophone

yawn

zany
zoo

How do I use my Primary Dictionary?

A **dictionary** is a book that contains a list of words and their meanings, in alphabetical order.

You can use a dictionary to find out what a word means, but also to check that you have spelt or used a word properly.

How do I find a word?
Imagine that you want to look up the word **balloon**.

1 The alphabet down the side of the page will show you the letter that begins the words on that page, so you look for the pages where **Bb** is marked.

> **Aa**
>
> **Bb**
>
> **Cc**
>
> **Dd**

2 The blue words at the top of the page show you which words appear in alphabetical order on that page, for example on page 46:

bale → bandage

Because the word **balloon** comes between these two words in alphabetical order, you know to look for it on that page.

3 The first words in an entry are the main words that you look up, so these words are large and coloured blue so it is easy to find them.

ballet

balloon

Each main word and and the block of information below it is called a dictionary **entry**.

4 You may find the word you want marked with a blue diamond (♦)

A word in **blue** after a blue diamond is part of the **word family** of the main word, and is usually in alphabetical order after the main word.

> **absolute** . ADJECTIVE . complete: *absolute rubbish*
> ◆ **absolutely** . ADVERB . 1 completely: *absolutely ridiculous* 2 yes, certainly: *'Please can I have one of those?' 'Absolutely.'*

When you see and arrow like this ⇒ , it tells you that the word after the arrow is also part of the family, but it has its own entry nearby that you can look up using alphabetical order.

> **collide** . VERB . **collides, colliding, collided**
> moving objects collide when they hit each other
> ⇒ **collision**

5 What if the word you are looking for is part of a **phrase**? A phrase is a group of words that always appear together and have a single meaning. For example, *better off* and *keep count* are phrases.

Some of these phrases are **idioms**. These are phrases that you use in speaking with a very special meaning that you cannot work out from the meanings of the words themselves. For example, *bury the hatchet* and *the apple of my eye* are idioms.

> **apple** . NOUN . **apples** a hard, round fruit with red, green or yellow skin
> • **the apple of someone's eye** a person that someone is very proud of

Phrases and idioms like these come after a black dot (•), so all you need to do is look up the main word in the phrase, and if the phrase is there you will spot it right away and find the meaning.

What will the dictionary tell me about the word?

1 The **BLUE** word in capital letters with dots around it tells you the **part of speech** the main word is. This simply tells you the type of word it is, and the job it does.

•NOUN•	A noun names people or things.
•VERB•	A verb is used to tell what people are doing or what is happening.
•ADJECTIVE•	An adjective describes people or things.
•ADVERB•	An adverb describes the way something is done.
•PRONOUN•	A pronoun is used to replace a noun so that you do not repeat the noun over and over again.
•PREPOSITION•	A preposition is placed before a noun to tell you where something is or where it is moving to.
•CONJUNCTION•	A conjunction joins two parts of a sentence together.

You can learn more about these words and what they mean from the panels with these headings in the dictionary.

2 A word in bold after •NOUN• is the **plural**, which is the word you use when you are talking about more than one of something.

draft •NOUN• **drafts**

3 Words in bold after •VERB• are the different **forms** of the verb. The one you use depends on who did the action or when it happened.

drag •VERB• **drags, dragging, dragged**

4 Words in bold after •ADJECTIVE• are the ones you use when you are making a comparison and you want to say something is *more* or *the most…*

calm •ADJECTIVE• **calmer, calmest**

⑤ Numbers show you that there are different meanings of the main word. Each one has a different number.

> **bed.** NOUN. **beds 1** a piece of furniture or place to sleep on: *Each night, chimpanzees make beds of twigs high up in the trees.* ● *Time to get ready for bed.*
> **2** the bottom of a river, a lake or the sea
> **3** an area in a garden that contains flowers and other plants: *a bed of lilies*

⑥ The meaning of the word is explained after this. This is called the **definition** of the word.

⑦ The phrases or sentences in *italics* after some of the meanings are **examples** to show you how you might use the main word, and to help explain the meaning even more.

> **bedraggled.** ADJECTIVE. untidy and dirty:
> *The kitten had been caught in the rain and its fur was all bedraggled.*

What else can I find in my Primary Dictionary?

❶ Sometimes after an entry there will be a small box that starts like this:

> ⓘ

The ⓘ sign tells you that there is extra information in the box.

These information boxes might tell you how to say a word:

> ⓘ The word **dough** sounds the same as the word **doe** (a female deer), and rhymes with **slow.**

xi

They might tell you where the word comes from:

> ⓘ **Dinosaur** comes from Greek words which mean 'terrible lizard'.

They might tell you how to use the word properly, for example by not getting the word mixed up with another one that sounds the same:

> ⓘ You have to be careful not to confuse **affect**, which is a verb, with **effect**, which is a noun.
> ✓ One thing **affects** another.
> ✗ One thing has an **effect** on another.

2 If there is a lot more to say about a word and what it means, there may be a panel nearby with more explanation of the topic in it. A large box like this will give you extra information about things you might need to know more about, like **nouns** and **verbs**, or **commas** and **apostrophes**.

⌐ *Apostrophes* ────────────────────────────────⌐

The dictionary entry will tell you if there is a panel like this, and the word you look up will be white in a blue box:

apostrophe

3 There are some pictures in the dictionary. These give you lots more information about things like birds, flowers, and the solar system by showing you what the different parts of them are and what they are called.

a *or* **an** • ADJECTIVE • **1** one: *a hundred miles* **2** any: *I need a pen.* **3** each: *He gets $5 a week.*

ⓘ **A** is used before words beginning with a consonant, for example *a horse*. It is also used before words beginning with **u** if they are pronounced like 'you', for example *a uniform*. **An** is used before words beginning with a vowel (**a**, **e**, **i**, **o**, **u**) or **h** when it is not pronounced, for example *an eye*, *an hour*.

aback • ADVERB • if someone is **taken aback**, they are rather shocked: *I was taken aback by the change in Dad. He was really pale and he was shaking.*

abacus • NOUN • **abacuses** a frame with rows of beads that can be used for counting and doing sums

abandon • VERB • **abandons, abandoning, abandoned 1** to go away, leaving something or someone behind on purpose: *He'll abandon the getaway car as soon as possible.* **2** to give up something such as an idea or plan: *If it rains, we'll just abandon the whole trip.*

abashed • ADJECTIVE • shy and embarrassed

abattoir • NOUN • **abattoirs** a place where animals are killed for food

abbess • NOUN • **abbesses** a nun who is in charge of an abbey

abbey • NOUN • **abbeys 1** the home of a group of Christian monks or nuns **2** a church that was built for monks or nuns to use

abbot • NOUN • **abbots** a monk who is in charge of an abbey

abbreviate • VERB • **abbreviates, abbreviating, abbreviated** to abbreviate a word or phrase is to make it shorter: *Everyone abbreviates Alistair John's name to A.J.*

♦ **abbreviation** • NOUN • **abbreviations** a short form of a word or phrase. For example, **UK** is an abbreviation for *United Kingdom*.

See the box called **Abbreviations**

abdicate • VERB • **abdicates, abdicating, abdicated** if a king or queen abdicates, they give up their position to someone else
♦ **abdication** • NOUN • **abdications** an abdication is when someone gives up a position of power or responsibility

abdomen • NOUN • **abdomens 1** the part of an animal's body that contains the stomach **2** the back part of an insect's body
♦ **abdominal** • ADJECTIVE • in the area of the stomach

abduct • VERB • **abducts, abducting, abducted** to take someone away by using force: *Two more tourists have been abducted from their hotel room.*
♦ **abduction** • NOUN • **abductions** taking someone away using force: *in prison for abduction and murder*

abhor • VERB • **abhors, abhorring, abhorred** to abhor someone or something is to hate them: *The politicians will abhor this idea.*

abide • VERB • **abides, abiding, abode** *or* **abided 1** if you cannot abide something or someone, you cannot put up with them: *I can't abide people who smoke in restaurants.* **2** to abide by a rule or decision is to keep to it: *Please abide by the rules of the game.*
♦ **abiding** • ADJECTIVE • an abiding feeling or memory lasts for a long time

ability • NOUN • **abilities 1** someone who has the ability to do something is able to do it: *Not everyone has the ability to keep a secret.* **2** talent: *a pupil with great ability*

abject • ADJECTIVE • sad or miserable

ablaze • ADJECTIVE AND ADVERB • **1** on fire: *The bomb set several buildings ablaze.* **2** shining very brightly: *The children's eyes were ablaze with excitement.*

able • ADJECTIVE • **abler, ablest 1** if you are able to do something, you can do it: *He wasn't able to run fast enough.* • *Will you be able to help me?* **2** an able person is good at

⌐Abbreviations

An **abbreviation** is a shortened version of a word or a group of words, for example:

Units of measurement

C	Celsius, Centigrade
cc	cubic centimetres
cm	centimetre
F	Fahrenheit
ft	foot
g	gram
in	inch
kg	kilogram
km	kilometre
kmph	kilometres per hour
kw	kilowatt
l	litre
m	metre
mg	milligram
ml	millilitre
mm	millimetre
mph	miles per hour
sq	square
w	watt

People's titles

Dr	Doctor
Jr	Junior
Prof	Professor
Rev *or* Revd	Reverend
Sr	Senior

Compass points

N	north
S	south
E	east
W	west
NE	north-east
NW	north-west
SE	south-east
SW	south-west

In letters

PTO	please turn over
RSVP	répondez s'il vous plaît — French for *please reply*
sae	stamped addressed envelope

Addresses

Ave	Avenue
Co	County
Cres	Crescent
Dr	Drive
Mt	Mount
Rd	Road
Sq	Square
St	Street

Time

am *or* a.m.	ante meridiem — Latin for *before noon*
h *or* hr	hour
min	minute
pm *or* p.m.	post meridiem — Latin for *after noon*
sec	second

In books

ch	chapter
eg	for example
esp	especially
etc	and so on
ie	that is
no	number
p	page
pp	pages

Aa Bb Cc Dd Ee Ff Gg Hh Ii Jj Kk Ll Mm Nn Oo Pp Qq Rr Ss Tt Uu Vv Ww Xx Yy Zz

doing something: *a very able singer*
⇒ **ability**

◆ **able-bodied** • ADJECTIVE• **1** fit and healthy **2** able-bodied is sometimes used to describe people who are not disabled

ably • ADVERB• if you do something ably, you do it well

abnormal • ADJECTIVE• not normal, especially in a worrying way: *abnormal behaviour for a five-year-old*

◆ **abnormality** • NOUN• **abnormalities** something that is not normal

◆ **abnormally** • ADVERB• unusually: *an abnormally fast heartbeat*

aboard • PREPOSITION• on a bus, train, ship or aeroplane: *the team aboard the shuttle*
• ADVERB• on or on to a bus, train, ship or aeroplane: *Everyone should go aboard now.*

abode • NOUN• an old word for the place where someone lives

abolish • VERB• to abolish a rule or a way of doing something is to get rid of it: *a plan to abolish fishing licences*

◆ **abolition** • NOUN• getting rid of something such as a law or system of doing something: *the abolition of free eye tests*

abominable • ADJECTIVE• very bad

Aboriginal *or* **Aborigine** • NOUN• one of the people who lived in Australia before anyone arrived from other countries

ⓘ This word comes from the Latin words **ab**, which means *from*, and **origo**, which means *the beginning*.

abort • VERB• **aborts, aborting, aborted** to abort a plan or process is to stop it after it has already started: *We were seen by a security guard and decided to abort the whole mission.*

abound • VERB• **abounds, abounding, abounded** if things abound, there are a lot of them: *Stories abound of boys running away to sea to seek their fortunes.*

about • PREPOSITION• **1** on the subject of: *a book about bats* • *a talk about Spain*
2 not exactly but nearly the number given: *about five years ago* • *about four centimetres*

3 around: *books scattered about the room*
• ADVERB• **1** in or to one place and then another: *move things about* • *running about all day* **2** in the opposite direction: *He turned about and walked away.*
• **about to** just going to: *I was about to leave when the phone rang.* • *I think it's about to rain.*
• **about turn** an order to turn around to face the opposite direction

above • PREPOSITION• **1** over: *the shelf above the sink* • *two degrees above zero* • *in the class above me* **2** if someone feels they are above a feeling or action, they think it is not worth their time: *James was above asking for his ten pence back.*
• ADVERB• **1** higher up: *clouds in the sky above* **2** earlier in a piece of writing: *See instruction 5 above.*
• **above all** more than anything else: *We were, above all, hungry.*

abrasion • NOUN• **abrasions** a graze on the skin
◆ **abrasive** • ADJECTIVE• scratchy: *Rub the dirt off with abrasive paper.*

abreast • ADVERB• side by side: *walking three abreast*
• ADJECTIVE• if someone keeps abreast of events or developments, they make sure they know about any changes that happen

abridge • VERB• **abridges, abridging, abridged** to make a book or story shorter
◆ **abridgement** *or* **abridgment** • NOUN• **abridgements** a book or story that has been made shorter

abroad • ADVERB• **1** in or to a foreign country: *travel abroad* **2** out and about: *creatures that go abroad at night*

abrupt • ADJECTIVE• **1** sudden: *an abrupt change of direction*
2 an abrupt person speaks sharply
3 an abrupt statement or question is sudden and short
◆ **abruptly** • ADVERB• **1** suddenly: *He abruptly stopped speaking and left.* **2** if someone speaks abruptly, they say something sharply

abscess • NOUN• **abscesses** a lump inside the body that is painful and filled with liquid

Aa **Bb** **Cc** **Dd** **Ee** **Ff** **Gg** **Hh** **Ii** **Jj** **Kk** **Ll** **Mm** **Nn** **Oo** **Pp** **Qq** **Rr** **Ss** **Tt** **Uu** **Vv** **Ww** **Xx** **Yy** **Zz**

abseil •VERB• **abseils, abseiling, abseiled** to let yourself down a rope with your feet against a wall or cliff

absence •NOUN• **absences** being away from a place: *Your absence from the meeting was noticed.*

absent •ADJECTIVE• away for a short time: *Is anyone absent today?* • *Two people were absent from the rehearsal.*
  ♦ **absently** •ADVERB• in a dreamy way: *'Mmm…' he replied absently.*
  ♦ **absent-minded** •ADJECTIVE• an absent-minded person often forgets things

absolute •ADJECTIVE• complete: *absolute rubbish*
  ♦ **absolutely** •ADVERB• **1** completely: *absolutely ridiculous* **2** yes, certainly: *'Please can I have one of those?' 'Absolutely.'*

absolve •VERB• **absolves, absolving, absolved** to forgive someone for doing something bad

absorb •VERB• **absorbs, absorbing, absorbed 1** to soak up liquid: *The bath mat will absorb the splashes.* **2** if you are **absorbed in** something, you are giving it all your attention: *We were so absorbed in our game, we didn't hear the bell.*
  ♦ **absorbency** •NOUN• **absorbencies** how absorbent something is
  ♦ **absorbent** •ADJECTIVE• able to soak up liquid: *absorbent kitchen cloths*
  ♦ **absorbing** •ADJECTIVE• very interesting and taking all your attention: *an absorbing puzzle*

abstain •VERB• **abstains, abstaining, abstained 1** to refuse to vote: *If you can't make up your mind, why don't you just abstain?* **2** to stop yourself from doing something: *Would you please abstain from shouting so loudly?*
  ♦ **abstention** •NOUN• **abstentions** when a person refuses to vote: *Three said 'yes', two said 'no', and there were two abstentions.*
  ♦ **abstinence** •NOUN• when you stop yourself from doing something, especially eating or drinking

abstract •ADJECTIVE• something that is abstract cannot be seen or touched, for example *honesty* and *an argument*

ⓘ The opposite of **abstract** is **concrete**.

absurd •ADJECTIVE• ridiculous: *What an absurd idea!*
  ♦ **absurdity** •NOUN• **absurdities** something that is ridiculous: *I can't listen to any more of these absurdities!*
  ♦ **absurdly** •ADVERB• in a ridiculous way: *That was an absurdly easy question.*

abundance •NOUN• **1** an abundance of something is a lot of it: *an abundance of information on the subject* **2** if something is **in abundance**, there is plenty of it: *There was food in abundance.*
  ♦ **abundant** •ADJECTIVE• existing in large amounts: *an abundant harvest* • *abundant hair*
  ♦ **abundantly** •ADVERB• **1** in large amounts: *Fruit is abundantly available in the market.* **2** very: *It is abundantly clear that you are very angry.*

abuse •NOUN• **abuses 1** using something the wrong way on purpose: *alcohol abuse* **2** bad treatment: *child abuse* **3** insults: *shouting abuse at us in the street* •VERB• **abuses, abusing, abused 1** to use something the wrong way on purpose: *a bank manager who abused people's trust and stole their money* **2** to treat someone or something badly: *people who abuse animals*
  ♦ **abusive** •ADJECTIVE• rude or insulting

ⓘ The verb **abuse** ends with the sound 'z'. The noun **abuse** ends with the sound 's'.

abysmal •ADJECTIVE• very bad: *abysmal exam results*
  ♦ **abysmally** •ADVERB• very badly: *The team played abysmally.*

abyss •NOUN• **abysses** a very deep or bottomless hole

academic •ADJECTIVE• to do with studying and education: *academic qualifications* •NOUN• **academics** a teacher at a college or university
  ♦ **academically** •ADVERB• to do with studying and learning: *an academically bright pupil*

academy •NOUN• **academies** a school or college

accelerate •VERB• **accelerates, accelerating, accelerated** to go faster
♦ **acceleration** •NOUN• **1** acceleration is increasing speed: *You'll be pushed back into your seat during acceleration.* **2** a vehicle's acceleration is its power to go faster: *This car has amazing acceleration!*
♦ **accelerator** •NOUN• **accelerators** the pedal or lever that makes a vehicle go faster: *Press the accelerator gently and move off.*

accent •NOUN• **accents 1** the way people from a certain area pronounce words: *I have a Scottish accent.* • *I speak German with a strong English accent.*
2 a mark over a letter in a foreign language that shows how to pronounce it, for example over *e* in the word *café*
3 a stress that makes one part of a word or a sentence, or one note in music, stand out more than the others: *Put the accent on the third syllable in the word 'preparation'.*

accentuate •VERB• **accentuates, accentuating, accentuated** to make something more obvious

accept •VERB• **accepts, accepting, accepted 1** to take something that someone offers you
2 you accept an invitation when you say 'yes' to it
3 you accept something like an idea if you agree that it is true: *I accept that I was wrong and I'm sorry.*
♦ **acceptable** •ADJECTIVE• good enough: *This kind of behaviour is just not acceptable!*
♦ **acceptance** •NOUN• taking something that is given to you: *Most actors make an acceptance speech when they win an Oscar.*

access •NOUN• **accesses** a way of getting to or into a place: *The builders will need access to the house while you're out at work.*
•VERB• **accesses, accessing, accessed** to get and be able to use information on a computer: *This file was last accessed yesterday.*
♦ **accessible** •ADJECTIVE• easy to get to: *The house is not very accessible.*

accessory •NOUN• **accessories 1** an extra part that can be used with something bigger: *a hairdrier with lots of accessories*
2 something like a bag, a scarf or jewellery, that goes with your clothes

3 a person who helps someone to do something bad: *an accessory to murder*

accident •NOUN• **accidents 1** a bad thing that happens by chance: *We had an accident with the glue and now it's everywhere.*
2 a road accident is when a vehicle crashes into something on a road
3 something happens **by accident** when it happens by chance: *I dropped the glass by accident and it smashed.*
♦ **accidental** •ADJECTIVE• if something is accidental, it happens by mistake.
♦ **accidentally** •ADVERB• by accident: *I accidentally shut the car door and locked my keys inside.*

acclaim •NOUN• praise
♦ **acclaimed** •ADJECTIVE• if something is acclaimed, it has had a lot of praise: *an acclaimed television show*

accommodate •VERB• **accommodates, accommodating, accommodated 1** to find space for someone: *The whole group can be accommodated on the top floor.* **2** to do what you can to help someone
♦ **accommodating** •ADJECTIVE• being helpful
♦ **accommodation** •NOUN• somewhere to stay or live: *We'll look for accommodation as soon as we arrive.*

accompaniment •NOUN• **accompaniments** the music that someone plays for a person to sing or play an instrument to: *a love song with a guitar accompaniment*

accompany •VERB• **accompanies, accompanying, accompanied 1** to go with someone to where they are going: *Would you mind accompanying me to the station, sir?* **2** to play an instrument, especially the piano, while someone else sings a song or plays music: *Her sister usually accompanies her on the piano.*

accomplice •NOUN• **accomplices** someone who helps a person to do something bad

accomplish •VERB• **accomplishes, accomplishing, accomplished** to manage to do something: *Most children accomplished the task in a few minutes.*
♦ **accomplished** •ADJECTIVE• **1** completed:

Aa Bb Cc Dd Ee Ff Gg Hh Ii Jj Kk Ll Mm Nn Oo Pp Qq Rr Ss Tt Uu Vv Ww Xx Yy Zz

Mission accomplished! **2** talented: *an accomplished goalkeeper*

♦ **accomplishment** • NOUN• **accomplishments** something you are very good at: *Cooking is just one of her accomplishments.*

accord • NOUN• if you do something **of your own accord** you do it without being asked or told: *I was surprised that he thanked me of his own accord.*

according to • PREPOSITION• **1** information according to someone is what that person says: *Hannah's ill, according to Lucy.* **2** if one thing is measured according to another, they are compared with each other: *You'll be paid according to how much work you have done.* • *Did everything go according to plan?*

♦ **accordingly** • ADVERB• in a way that suits what has just been said or what is happening: *The sun was shining and Jake dressed accordingly.*

accordion • NOUN• **accordions** a musical instrument with a small keyboard like a piano on the side of a big folding box that you squeeze in and out

account • NOUN• **accounts** **1** a description of something that happened: *His account of the journey made us laugh.*

2 money that someone keeps in a bank: *Which account do you want to pay this cheque into?*

3 a bill showing how much someone has paid and how much they must still pay

4 to take something into account is to consider it: *Will they take my age into account when they decide who can go?* • VERB• **accounts, accounting, accounted** to account for something is to explain it: *The fact that it's her birthday accounts for all the visitors she's had today.*

• **on account of** because of: *I can't run very well on account of my bad leg.*

• **on no account** definitely not: *You are on no account to stay out after ten o'clock.*

accountancy • NOUN• the job of organizing and keeping records of a person's or a company's money

accountant • NOUN• **accountants** someone whose job is to write and keep in order a

person's or company's money accounts

accumulate • VERB• **accumulates, accumulating, accumulated** **1** you have accumulated things if you have collected a lot of them **2** things accumulate when they pile up: *A pile of bills had accumulated on my desk.*

♦ **accumulation** • NOUN• **accumulations** a lot of things that have come together in one place: *an accumulation of empty boxes in the hall*

accuracy • NOUN• being exactly right: *Please check the accuracy of this measurement.*

accurate • ADJECTIVE• exactly right: *an accurate guess*

♦ **accurately** • ADVERB• exactly: *Copy the shape as accurately as possible.*

accusation • NOUN• **accusations** a statement saying that a person has done something wrong: *Jude has made a very serious accusation against you.*

accuse • VERB• **accuses, accusing, accused** you accuse someone when you say they have done something wrong: *Are you accusing me of lying?*

♦ **accused** • NOUN• **the accused** is the person in a court who is supposed to have committed a crime: *Do you recognize the accused?*

① **The accused** can mean more than one person: *The accused are all pupils at the same school.*

accustomed • ADJECTIVE• used to: *We've all become accustomed to his strange way of talking.*

ace • NOUN• **aces** **1** a playing-card with one symbol on it and an **A** in the corner: *the ace of spades*

2 an expert: *a Brazilian soccer ace*

3 in tennis, a serve that the other player cannot reach • ADJECTIVE• very good: *The food was ace.* • *an ace detective*

ache • NOUN• **aches** a pain that goes on and on: *an ache behind my eyes* • VERB• **aches, aching, ached** to hurt for a long time, especially in a dull, heavy sort of way: *My arm aches from playing too much tennis.*

achieve •VERB• **achieves, achieving, achieved 1** to succeed in doing something: *We have achieved everything we set out to do.* **2** to get something, especially by trying hard: *She has achieved a very high standard.*
✦ **achievement** •NOUN• **achievements 1** an achievement is a success or good result: *a list of his achievements so far* **2** achievement is having success: *a high level of achievement in this class*

acid •NOUN• **acids** a type of chemical. Strong acids can dissolve metals
✦ **acidic** •ADJECTIVE• **1** containing acid **2** with a sharp, sour taste
✦ **acidity** •NOUN• how acid something is

acid rain •NOUN• rain that contains pollution that factories and cities have released into the air

acknowledge •VERB• **acknowledges, acknowledging, acknowledged 1** to admit that something is true: *I acknowledge that you were right.* **2** to tell someone that you have received something they sent you: *They never acknowledge my letters.*
✦ **acknowledgement** •NOUN• **acknowledgements** a note to tell someone that you have received something: *I sent two letters but only got one acknowledgement.*

acne •NOUN• a skin problem that causes spots, usually on someone's face

acorn •NOUN• **acorns** a kind of nut that grows on oak trees

acoustic •ADJECTIVE• **1** to do with sound and hearing: *an acoustic signal* **2** an acoustic musical instrument does not need electrical equipment to work
✦ **acoustics** •PLURAL NOUN• the way a room can make music or speech sound better or worse: *The Tudor Hall has wonderful acoustics.*

acquaint •VERB• **acquaints, acquainting, acquainted 1** to acquaint someone with something is to tell them about it: *Let me acquaint you with the facts of the case.* **2** if you acquaint yourself with something, you find out about it: *I tried to acquaint myself with what had been going on.*

3 if you are acquainted with something or someone, you have met them
✦ **acquaintance** •NOUN• **acquaintances 1** someone you have met **2** to **make someone's acquaintance** is to meet them for the first time

ⓘ This is a formal word.

acquire •VERB• **acquires, acquiring, acquired** to get something: *I see you've acquired a new jacket.*

acquit •VERB• **acquits, acquitting, acquitted 1** to acquit someone of a crime is to decide in a court that they did not do it **2** to **acquit yourself well** or **badly** is to do well or badly

acre •NOUN• **acres** an area of land of about 4047 square metres

acrobat •NOUN• **acrobats** someone who performs gymnastic tricks like somersaults and tightrope-walking
✦ **acrobatic** •ADJECTIVE• to do with gymnastic movements, especially jumping
✦ **acrobatics** •PLURAL NOUN• clever physical movements like skilful jumping and balancing

acronym •NOUN• **acronyms** a word made from the first letters of other words. For example, the second part of *CD-ROM* is an acronym for *Read Only Memory*

across •ADVERB• **1** from one side of something to the other: *Don't run, but walk across quickly.* • *clouds moving across the sky* **2** on or to the other side: *I ran across the road.*
•PREPOSITION• **1** on the other side: *Their house is across the river from ours.* **2** from one side of something to the other: *a bridge across the river*

acrylic •NOUN• a substance used for making some paints, fabrics and different kinds of plastic materials
•ADJECTIVE• made with acrylic

act •VERB• **acts, acting, acted 1** to perform in a play or film
2 to behave in a certain way: *Do stop acting like a baby.*
3 to do something: *We must act now to save the planet!*
4 to **act up** is to behave badly

Aa
Bb
Cc
Dd
Ee
Ff
Gg
Hh
Ii
Jj
Kk
Ll
Mm
Nn
Oo
Pp
Qq
Rr
Ss
Tt
Uu
Vv
Ww
Xx
Yy
Zz

• NOUN• **acts** 1 something that someone does: *a brave act*
2 a law
3 a section of a play
♦ **acting** • NOUN• performing in plays or films ⇒ **actor, actress**

action • NOUN• **actions** 1 an action is a movement someone or something makes: *Hit the ball with a swinging action.*
2 action is moving or doing something: *Let's see some action around here!*
3 the action of a film, book or play is what happens in the story: *Most of the action takes place in America.*
4 action is fighting in a war: *a soldier killed in action*
♦ **action replay** • NOUN• **action replays** a repeat of a bit of film, especially part of a sports match, often shown in slow-motion
♦ **action stations** • PLURAL NOUN• the positions soldiers take up when they get ready to fight
• **out of action** not working

activate • VERB• **activates, activating, activated** to make something start working: *Activate all emergency systems now!*

active • ADJECTIVE• 1 busy doing a lot of things: *Her mum's very active in the drama club.*
2 moving around a lot: *Try to keep active in order to to keep fit.*
3 in grammar, an active verb is one that the subject of the sentence performs, for example in the sentence *The cat chased the mouse.* See the box called **Active and Passive**
♦ **actively** • ADVERB• in a way that involves doing a lot of things: *actively helping people with problems*
♦ **activity** • NOUN• **activities** 1 an activity is something you do, especially something you do for fun, in an organized way: *a variety of sporting activities* 2 activity is doing something, especially in a busy way

actor • NOUN• **actors** a person who performs in a play or film

actress • NOUN• **actresses** a woman who performs in plays or films

actual • ADJECTIVE• real: *We guessed there*

were about 100 people but the actual number was 110.
♦ **actually** • ADVERB• in fact: *Actually, there are a lot of things you don't know.*

acupuncture • NOUN• a treatment for pain and illness where the points of very thin needles are put into the skin at different places on your body

acute • ADJECTIVE• 1 an acute problem, especially a pain or illness, is very bad
2 quick to realize or understand something: *an acute mind* • *acute eyesight*
3 an acute accent is a line that slopes up over a letter in some languages, for example over *e* in the French word *café*, to show how it is pronounced
♦ **acutely** • ADVERB• extremely: *I felt acutely embarrassed.*

acute angle • NOUN• **acute angles** an angle that is less than 90 degrees

AD • ABBREVIATION• short for **Anno Domini**, which is Latin for 'in the year of our Lord'. **AD** is added after a date to show that the date was after the birth of Jesus Christ, for example *2000AD*

ⓘ **BC** is the abbreviation used with dates before the birth of Christ.

ad • NOUN• **ads** an informal word for an advertisement

adamant • ADJECTIVE• very firm and not likely to give in: *Her father was adamant about going home immediately.*

Adam's apple • NOUN• **Adam's apples** the lump you can see at the front of a man's neck

adapt • VERB• **adapts, adapting, adapted**
1 to change something to make it more suitable: *Can you adapt your wedding speech for Jody's birthday?* 2 if you adapt to something, you get used to it: *It didn't take long to adapt to the heat when we moved south.*
♦ **adaptable** • ADJECTIVE• an adaptable person can easily fit in with new or different situations
♦ **adaptation** • NOUN• **adaptations** an old story that is told in a new way: *a television adaptation of Roald Dahl's fantastic novel*
♦ **adaptor** • NOUN• **adaptors** a kind of plug

Active and passive

You can use many verbs in two different ways, known as the **active voice** and the **passive voice**.

The active voice
This sentence is in the **active** voice.

> **The car hit a wall.**

The **car** does the action.

Hit is an active verb.

The **wall** receives the action.

The passive voice
This sentence is in the **passive** voice.

> **The wall was hit by a car.**

The **wall** is on the receiving end of the action.

Was hit is a passive verb.

The **car** is the doer of the action, and is shown using the word **by**.

Both the sentences above give you the same information, but their focus is different. The first one is about what the car *did*. The second is about what *happened to* the wall.

Using the passive voice
The passive voice brings more attention to a person or thing that an action is being done to.

Active	Passive
We saw them.	They were seen.
He has mended it.	It has been mended.
A snake bit Ben.	Ben was bitten by a snake.

Aa
Bb
Cc
Dd
Ee
Ff
Gg
Hh
Ii
Jj
Kk
Ll
Mm
Nn
Oo
Pp
Qq
Rr
Ss
Tt
Uu
Vv
Ww
Xx
Yy
Zz

you can use to connect up electrical equipment

add •VERB• 1 to put things together: *Add two and two.* • *Add the milk and sugar to the mixture.*
2 to say or write something else: *'If you don't mind?' he added.*
3 to **add up** is to find the total of numbers put together: *Can you add these numbers up in your head?*
4 if things **add up**, they grow into a large amount: *£1 a week soon adds up.*
⇒ **addition**

adder •NOUN• **adders** a poisonous snake with a black zigzag pattern on its back which is found in the north of Europe and Asia

addict •NOUN• **addicts** someone who cannot stop taking something: *a drug addict*

♦ **addicted** •ADJECTIVE• if you are addicted to something, you cannot manage without it
♦ **addiction** •NOUN• **addictions** not being able to stop taking something
♦ **addictive** •ADJECTIVE• if something is addictive, it makes you want to do it more and more

addition •NOUN• **additions** 1 addition is adding up numbers: *some addition exercises*
2 an addition is something that has been added: *I noticed a new addition to the collection.*
♦ **additional** •ADJECTIVE• extra: *We're having three additional classrooms built on the back of the school.*
♦ **additionally** •ADVERB• as well as that: *Additionally, you have to pay to get in.*
• **in addition** as well

address •NOUN• **addresses** 1 your address

Aa
Bb
Cc
Dd
Ee
Ff
Gg
Hh
Ii
Jj
Kk
Ll
Mm
Nn
Oo
Pp
Qq
Rr
Ss
Tt
Uu
Vv
Ww
Xx
Yy
Zz

is the name or number of the house, street and town where you live **2** a speech
• VERB• **addresses, addressing, addressed 1** to speak to: *Were you addressing me?* **2** to write an address on something like an envelope

adept • ADJECTIVE• very clever at something

adequate • ADJECTIVE• enough: *Three rooms should be adequate for our family.*

adhesive • NOUN• glue
• ADJECTIVE• sticky: *adhesive tape*

Adi Granth • NOUN• the holy book of the Sikh religion

adjacent • ADJECTIVE• next to: *The school is adjacent to the hospital.* • *A policeman was in the adjacent room.*

adjective • PART OF SPEECH• **adjectives** a word that tells you something about a noun. For example, *difficult*, *good* and *stupid* are adjectives. See the boxes called **Adjectives** and **Comparison of adjectives**

adjoin • VERB• **adjoins, adjoining, adjoined** a formal word that means to be joined to: *The bathroom adjoins the bedroom.*
♦ **adjoining** • ADJECTIVE• an adjoining room is the next room along

adjust • VERB• **adjusts, adjusting, adjusted 1** to change something a little bit: *I adjusted the clock by two minutes.* **2** to get used to something: *It was difficult to adjust to living in a flat.*
♦ **adjustable** • ADJECTIVE• something adjustable can be changed to fit: *adjustable seat belts*
♦ **adjustment** • NOUN• **adjustments 1** an adjustment is a slight change: *We've made a few adjustments to the timetable this week.* **2** adjustment is making changes to suit a new situation: *You'll be fine after a short period of adjustment.*

administer • VERB• **administers, administering, administered** to administer a medicine is to give it to someone

administrate • VERB• **administrates, administrating, administrated** to run an organization
♦ **administration** • NOUN• **administrations 1** administration is running an organization

2 the administration in the USA is the government
♦ **administrative** • ADJECTIVE• to do with running a business or country: *an administrative job*
♦ **administrator** • NOUN• **administrators** a person who runs or helps to run an organization

admirable • ADJECTIVE• if something is admirable, a lot of people think it is very good: *The way he behaved was admirable.*
♦ **admirably** • ADVERB• very well: *I thought you spoke admirably.*

admiral • NOUN• **admirals** one of the most important officers in the navy

admiration • NOUN• a feeling of liking someone or something very much because you think they are good: *He looked at the boy with admiration.*

admire • VERB• **admires, admiring, admired 1** to like someone or something very much **2** to enjoy looking at something: *I've been admiring your new hat.*
♦ **admirer** • NOUN• **admirers** a person who likes someone or something very much
⇒ **admiration**

admission • NOUN• **admissions 1** being allowed into a place: *A sign on the door said 'No admission'.* **2** the cost of getting in: *We don't charge admission here.* **3** an admission is when you agree that something bad is true: *We were surprised by his admission that he had done it.*

admit • VERB• **admits, admitting, admitted 1** to agree that you have done something bad: *I admit that I should have told you sooner.* **2** to agree that something is true: *I admit that this is a difficult exercise, but do your best.* **3** to let someone in: *They won't admit anyone not wearing trainers.*
♦ **admittance** • NOUN• being allowed to go in somewhere: *No admittance for anyone under 18.*

ado • NOUN• without further ado means without any more fuss

adolescence • NOUN• the time between childhood and being an adult

Adjectives

An **adjective** adds extra information and meaning to a noun.

Some adjectives give information about the qualities of people or things.

The **tall** man wore a **red** jacket, **furry** gloves and a **pointed** hat.

The **Chinese** girl put the **valuable** box on to the **dusty** table.

Some adjectives express a personal opinion about what someone, something or somewhere is like.

He is a **wonderful** teacher.

She lives in a **beautiful** house.

Using adjectives
An adjective usually comes before a noun.

The **happy** boy smiled.

The **fierce** dog growled.

However, adjectives can be separated from their nouns and come after verbs such as *be, become, feel, get, look,* and *seem.*

The policeman *was* **angry.**

The dog *seems* **friendly.**

When you use two adjectives this way, use a linking word between them.

The room was **shabby** *and* **smelly.**

The cat was **old** *but* **healthy.**

If you use three or more adjectives, join the last two with a linking word and put commas between the others.

They were **cold, tired** *and* **hungry.**

Aa Bb Cc Dd Ee Ff Gg Hh Ii Jj Kk Ll Mm Nn Oo Pp Qq Rr Ss Tt Uu Vv Ww Xx Yy Zz

✦ **adolescent** .NOUN. **adolescents** someone older than a child, but not yet an adult

adopt .VERB. **adopts, adopting, adopted**
1 to adopt a child is to take them into your own family and legally become their parent **2** to adopt a way of doing something is to start to do it that way: *We must adopt new methods of fighting crime.*

✦ **adoption** .NOUN. **1** taking a child into a new family: *Adoption can take a long time.* **2** taking on something new: *the adoption of*

a new homework timetable
✦ **adoptive** .ADJECTIVE. adoptive parents are the new parents of a child who goes into a new family

adorable .ADJECTIVE. a thing or person is adorable if you cannot help liking them very much

adoration .NOUN. loving very much: *a look of adoration*

adore .VERB. **adores, adoring, adored** to think something or someone is wonderful:

She just adores her father.

adorn •VERB• **adorns, adorning, adorned**
to decorate: *Their hair was adorned with flowers.*

adrenalin *or* **adrenaline** •NOUN• a chemical in your body that is produced when you are afraid, angry or excited

adrift •ADJECTIVE• a boat that is adrift is not tied up and is probably moving in the wind •ADVERB• if a boat goes adrift it floats too far from the shore

adulation •NOUN• a lot of praise from people

adult •NOUN• **adults** a grown-up
•ADJECTIVE• to do with or for grown-ups: *adult sizes*
✦ **adulthood** •NOUN• the period of time in your life when you are an adult: *the duties of adulthood*

advance •VERB• **advances, advancing, advanced** to move forwards: *a crowd advancing towards us*
•ADJECTIVE• happening before an event: *an advance booking for the show*
• **in advance** earlier: *I arrived in advance to make sure everything was ready.*
✦ **advanced** •ADJECTIVE• high level: *an advanced Spanish course*

advantage •NOUN• **advantages** 1 if you have an advantage over someone else, things are better for you for some reason: *Her long legs give her an advantage in the high jump.*
2 to take advantage of a situation is to use it well: *We took advantage of the sunshine to get the clothes dry.*
3 to take advantage of a person is to take more of their kindness than you really should
4 in tennis scoring, advantage is the point after deuce (40-40)

advent •NOUN• 1 the arrival of something: *the advent of the steam engine* 2 Advent, with a capital *A*, is the four weeks before Christmas

adventure •NOUN• **adventures** something exciting that happens or is going to happen to you: *A jungle visit would be a real adventure for us.*
✦ **adventurous** •ADJECTIVE• an

adventurous person likes to do exciting new things

adverb •PART OF SPEECH• **adverbs** a word that you use to describe verbs, adjectives or other adverbs. For example, *really, badly, abroad* and *often* are adverbs. See the box called **Adverbs**

adversary •NOUN• **adversaries** an enemy or somebody who is against you in a competition

adverse •ADJECTIVE• harmful or bad

advert •NOUN• **adverts** an advertisement

advertise •VERB• **advertises, advertising, advertised** to tell as many people as possible about something: *Nobody will come unless we advertise the concert.*
✦ **advertisement** •NOUN• **advertisements** a notice or short film about something that somebody is trying to sell: *I saw an advertisement for a new chocolate bar.*

advice •NOUN• someone who gives you advice tells you what they think you should do: *If I follow her advice, I won't have any money left!*

ⓘ Remember that **advice** with a **c** is a noun: *Can you give me some advice?*
Advise with an **s** is a verb: *Can you advise me?*

advisable •ADJECTIVE• something that is advisable is probably a sensible thing to do

advise •VERB• **advises, advising, advised** to tell someone what you think they should do
✦ **adviser** *or* **advisor** •NOUN• **advisers** *or* **advisors** a person who tries to tell people the best thing to do
✦ **advisory** •ADJECTIVE• telling people the best thing to do

advocate •VERB• **advocates, advocating, advocated** to recommend
•NOUN• **advocates** 1 a person who supports an idea: *He's an advocate of higher taxes.* 2 a lawyer in Scotland

aeon *or* **eon** •NOUN• **aeons** *or* **eons** a very long time

aerate •VERB• **aerates, aerating, aerated** to put air into something like soil or a liquid

Adverbs

An **adverb** tells you more about a verb, an adjective or another adverb.

The following sentence makes sense on its own, but it gives you very little information:
Ranjit ran.

You can explain *how, where, when* and *why* Ranjit ran, by using adverbs.
Ranjit ran **home** *(where)* **eagerly** *(how)* **at noon** *(when)*.
Ranjit ran **around** *(where)* **worriedly** *(how)* **all day** *(when)*.

Adverbs can tell you *how* something happens.
The explorers plodded **slowly, silently** and **wearily**.

They are useful for showing how people speak.
He asked **anxiously**, 'When can I go home?'
He said **cheerfully**, 'You can go soon.'

Adverbs can tell you *where* something happens.
They went **outside** and looked **up** at the sky.

Adverbs can tell you *when* something happens.
They arrived **late** and left **early**.

Adverbs can tell you *how often* something happens.
I **often** watch TV, but I **never** watch horror films.

Other adverbs that tell you how often something happens are **always, often, frequently, usually, regularly, normally, sometimes, occasionally, seldom, rarely, hardly ever, never**.

Adverbs can also tell you *how much* or *to what extent* something happens. They give more information about other adverbs or adjectives.
I woke up **fairly** early.
The shelf was **too** high to reach.

---

aerial • NOUN • **aerials** equipment made of metal, especially wire, for getting or sending radio or television signals: *a TV aerial on the roof*
• ADJECTIVE • from up in the air: *an aerial photo*

aero- • PREFIX • if a word starts with **aero-** it is to do with air or flying

aerobatics • PLURAL NOUN • flying stunts in an aeroplane

aerobics • PLURAL NOUN • exercises for the whole body that make your heart and lungs work hard

aerodrome • NOUN • **aerodromes** a place where aeroplanes are kept, with an airfield for taking off and landing

aeroplane • NOUN • **aeroplanes** a machine for flying that has fixed wings. Look at the illustration on the next page

aerosol • NOUN • **aerosols** a container with a

Aa
Bb
Cc
Dd
Ee
Ff
Gg
Hh
Ii
Jj
Kk
Ll
Mm
Nn
Oo
Pp
Qq
Rr
Ss
Tt
Uu
Vv
Ww
Xx
Yy
Zz

Aa
Bb
Cc
Dd
Ee
Ff
Gg
Hh
Ii
Jj
Kk
Ll
Mm
Nn
Oo
Pp
Qq
Rr
Ss
Tt
Uu
Vv
Ww
Xx
Yy
Zz

an aeroplane

fin

rudder

wings

tailplane

fuselage

cockpit

jet engine

button on top that you press to let out a spray of liquid

afar . ADVERB . a long way away: *The visitors had travelled from afar.*

affair . NOUN . **affairs** 1 a group of events that make up a situation: *We need to investigate this affair of the missing ticket money.* 2 your affairs are your own business: *I'm not going to tell you because it's my own affair.*

affect . VERB . **affects, affecting, affected** to change a thing or person in some way or cause them some harm: *The accident affected his eyesight.* • *Were you affected by the floods?*

ⓘ You have to be careful not to confuse **affect**, which is a verb, with **effect**, which is a noun.
✓ *One thing **affects** another.*
✗ *One thing has an **effect** on another.*

affection . NOUN . a strong feeling of liking someone
♦ **affectionate** . ADJECTIVE . an affectionate person shows that they like or love someone: *Her mother gave her an affectionate kiss.*
♦ **affectionately** . ADVERB . in a kind, loving sort of way: *Gramp smiled at Lisa affectionately.*

affiliated . ADJECTIVE . if one organization is affiliated to another, they are connected in some kind of partnership: *The school is affiliated to the local technical college.*
♦ **affiliation** . NOUN . **affiliations** a connection between two or more organizations

affinity . NOUN . **affinities** a feeling that different things or people in fact have a close connection: *Flo had always had a deep affinity with horses.*

affix . VERB . **affixes, affixing, affixed** to attach: *Affix stamp here.*

afflict . VERB . **afflicts, afflicting, afflicted** if an illness afflicts someone, they suffer from it: *This is a disease that can afflict anyone.*
♦ **affliction** . NOUN . **afflictions** a great problem that makes a person miserable

affluence . NOUN . having lots of money to spend: *There was greater affluence after the war.*

affluent . ADJECTIVE . having a lot of money and possessions: *an affluent lifestyle*

afford . VERB . **affords, affording, afforded** 1 to have enough money to pay for something: *I can't afford a new dress.* • *We couldn't afford to go abroad.* 2 to have enough time to do something: *I can't afford to stay any longer or I'll be late.*

affordable • ADJECTIVE• at a low enough price to buy

affront • VERB• **affronts, affronting, affronted** if you are affronted, you are offended and cross
• NOUN• **affronts** a remark or action that offends someone: *Mary sees being left out of the school team as an affront.*

afloat • ADVERB• floating: *Donny held on to a piece of wood to stay afloat.*

afoot • ADJECTIVE• if something is afoot, it is happening

afraid • ADJECTIVE• 1 frightened: *There's no need to be afraid.* • *Small children are often afraid of dogs.* • *I was afraid that I'd fall.*
2 sorry: *I'm afraid I don't know.*

afresh • ADVERB• once again: *Throw that away and begin afresh.*

after • PREPOSITION• 1 following: *I'll do it after dinner.* • *Your name's after mine on the list.* • *It rained day after day.*
2 if you were named after someone, you were given their name: *Gordon was named after his uncle.*
3 to ask after someone is ask how they are: *Mrs Young was asking after you.*
• ADVERB• later: *Can you come the week after?*
• CONJUNCTION• following in time: *Mrs Shaw died after we moved.* • *After we'd said goodbye, we felt awfully sad.*
• **after all** anyway: *I went after all.*

after- • PREFIX• later: *an afterthought*

afternoon • NOUN• **afternoons** the time between midday and the evening
• ADJECTIVE• happening in the afternoon: *afternoon classes*

aftershave • NOUN• a liquid for men to put on their skin after shaving

afterwards • ADVERB• later on: *He's busy now but I'll speak to him afterwards.*

again • ADVERB• 1 once more: *Do it again!*
2 to the place you started from: *Can we go back home again now?*
3 on the other hand: *Again, I could be wrong.*
• **again and again** lots of times

against • PREPOSITION• 1 leaning on, touching or hitting something: *throwing the ball against the wall* • *sitting against a tree*
2 competing with someone: *We're playing against you next.*
3 if you are against something, you do not like or want it: *We're against starting any earlier than 8.30.*

age • NOUN• **ages** 1 a person's age is how old they are
2 an age is a very long time: *We had to wait an age for him to come out.* • *You took ages to finish.*
3 a time in history: *the Stone Age*
• VERB• **ages, aging** *or* **ageing, aged** to look older or to make someone look older: *She's aged a lot recently.* • *We'll age you with make-up for your part in the play.*
• **come of age** to become an adult
• **under age** too young to legally do something: *You can't get married – you're under age.*

agency • NOUN• **agencies** an office or business that organizes things

agenda • NOUN• **agendas** a list of things that will be discussed at a meeting: *What's on the agenda today?*

agent • NOUN• **agents** 1 a spy: *a secret agent*
2 a person whose job is arranging things for someone else or an organization: *The travel agent will send you the tickets before you leave.*
3 a cleaning agent is a substance that you use to clean things

aggravate • VERB• **aggravates, aggravating, aggravated** to make something worse: *Don't scratch or you'll simply aggravate the infection.*
• **aggravating** • ADJECTIVE• annoying: *a very aggravating situation*
• **aggravation** • NOUN• irritating kind of trouble: *That man has caused a lot of aggravation today.*

aggregate • NOUN• **aggregates** a total

aggression • NOUN• a way of behaving that is angry and threatening

aggressive • ADJECTIVE• angry and ready to attack
• **aggressively** • ADVERB• in a threatening

Aa
Bb
Cc
Dd
Ee
Ff
Gg
Hh
Ii
Jj
Kk
Ll
Mm
Nn
Oo
Pp
Qq
Rr
Ss
Tt
Uu
Vv
Ww
Xx
Yy
Zz

Aa

way: *'What do you think you're looking at?'* he asked aggressively.

Bb

aggrieved •ADJECTIVE• feeling that someone has been unfair to you

Cc

aghast •ADJECTIVE• horrified

Dd

agile •ADJECTIVE• good at moving about quickly and easily: *These children were as agile as monkeys.*

Ee

◆ **agility** •NOUN• being able to move about and change direction quickly

Ff

agitate •VERB• **agitates, agitating, agitated**
Gg
1 something agitates you if it makes you nervous and worried: *That news will*
Hh
agitate her. 2 to **agitate for** something is to try to get something or make something
Ii
happen: *He is agitating for a new bicycle.*
• *We must agitate for a change in the law.*
Jj
◆ **agitated** •ADJECTIVE• nervous and worried: *I started to get agitated when*
Kk
nobody answered the door.
◆ **agitation** •NOUN• getting nervous and
Ll
upset: *She tried to hide her agitation.*

Mm

agnostic •NOUN• **agnostics** a person who believes nobody can tell if God exists or not

Nn

ago •ADVERB• in the past: *Lily was born ten*
Oo
years ago.

agog •ADJECTIVE• excited and interested

Pp

agony •NOUN• very great pain: *You could see he was in agony.*

Qq

agoraphobia •NOUN• people who have
Rr
agoraphobia may be afraid of being in open spaces or of going outside at all
◆ **agoraphobic** •ADJECTIVE• afraid of
Ss
leaving a place that feels safe

Tt

ⓘ The word **agoraphobia** comes from the
Uu
Greek words **agora**, which means *market place*, and **phobia**, which means *fear*.
Vv

agree •VERB• **agrees, agreeing, agreed 1** to
Ww
agree with someone is to think the same as them about something: *Don't you agree?*
Xx
• *She never agrees with him about anything.*
• *I agree with everything you've said.*
Yy
2 to agree to do something is to say that you will do what someone has asked you to: *I*
Zz
only agreed to come if you came too.
3 if some food or drink does not agree with you, it upsets your stomach

◆ **agreeable** •ADJECTIVE• **1** an agreeable experience is one you enjoy **2** someone who is agreeable will agree to something: *If you're agreeable, we'll leave at about 3.*

◆ **agreement** •NOUN• **agreements 1** when you make an agreement, you and someone else decide to do something: *These countries now have an agreement to work together for peace.* **2** agreement is when things such as opinions or answers are the same: *I am happy to say that we are in complete agreement about this.*

agriculture •NOUN• growing crops
◆ **agricultural** •ADJECTIVE• to do with growing crops

ahead •ADVERB• in front: *Run on ahead and tell them we're coming.* • *Our house is straight ahead.* • *We've got a long journey ahead of us.*

aid •NOUN• help: *He can walk with the aid of a stick.* • *Mr Oliver came to our aid.* • *Many countries will send aid workers to the disaster area.*
• **in aid of** to get money to help: *a collection in aid of the crash victims*
•VERB• **aids, aiding, aided** to help someone

AIDS •NOUN• a condition that makes every illness very dangerous to the person that has it. AIDS stands for Acquired Immune Deficiency Syndrome

ailment •NOUN• **ailments** something wrong with you, like an illness

aim •VERB• **aims, aiming, aimed 1** to aim something like a gun is to decide where to fire it: *Paul was aiming at the target but missed it completely.* **2** to aim to do something is to intend to do it: *We aim to help all our customers.*
•NOUN• **aims1** your aim is the reason you are trying to do something: *Here's a list of our aims for the year.* **2** if your aim is good, you can hit a target well
◆ **aimless** •ADJECTIVE• having no goal or purpose: *an aimless stroll!*
◆ **aimlessly** •ADVERB• without a reason: *walking aimlessly around the house*

air •NOUN• **1** the gases around us that we breathe in: *Kelly left the room to get some air.* • *The air carries the seeds for miles.*

2 an air of secrecy or mystery is a feeling that there is a secret or mystery
3 a tune
• VERB• **airs, airing, aired 1** to air washing is to make it completely dry
2 to air a room is to let some fresh air into it
3 to air your views or opinions is to tell people what you think
• **by air** in a plane or helicopter
• **on the air** broadcasting a radio or television programme
• **up in the air** not yet definite or decided: *Our holiday plans are still up in the air.*

airbag • NOUN• **airbags** a bag that blows up like a balloon in front of a driver or passenger to protect them if their vehicle crashes

airbed • NOUN• **airbeds** a mattress filled with air

airborne • ADJECTIVE• moving in the air: *airborne seeds*

air conditioning • NOUN• a system of keeping a room at a certain temperature

aircraft • NOUN• **aircraft** a vehicle that you can fly in

aircraft carrier • NOUN• **aircraft carriers** a warship that aircraft can take off from and land on

air force • NOUN• **air forces** the part of an army that uses aircraft

airgun • NOUN• **airguns** a gun that fires using the power of compressed air

airless • ADJECTIVE• an airless room is stuffy

airline • NOUN• **airlines** a company that takes people places by plane: *an airline ticket*

airlock • NOUN• **airlocks 1** a bubble in a pipe that stops liquid flowing through it **2** a compartment with two doors for getting in and out of a spaceship or submarine

airport • NOUN• **airports** a place where passengers can get on and off aircraft

air raid • NOUN• **air raids** an attack by aircraft

airship • NOUN• **airships** a large balloon with engines for carrying things or people

airtight • ADJECTIVE• made so that air cannot pass in or out

airy • ADJECTIVE• **airier, airiest 1** with lots of fresh air: *an airy balcony* **2** not very serious: *an airy way of talking*

aisle • NOUN• **aisles** the space that you can walk along between rows of seats or shelves

ajar • ADVERB• slightly open: *David left the door ajar on purpose.*

aka • ABBREVIATION• short for **also known as**

akimbo • ADVERB• if you stand with your arms akimbo, you have your hands on your hips and your elbows pointing outwards

akin • ADJECTIVE• similar: *Lara had something akin to a smile on her face.*

alarm • NOUN• **alarms 1** an alarm is a way of warning people: *the fire alarm* **2** alarm is a sudden feeling of fear: *Freddie jumped back in alarm.*
• VERB• **alarms, alarming, alarmed** to frighten someone, especially suddenly
✦ **alarming** • ADJECTIVE• scary: *an alarming sight*

alas • INTERJECTION• an old word that a person said when they were sad

albatross • NOUN• **albatrosses** a large white seabird

albino • NOUN• **albinos** a person or animal with no natural colour in their hair, skin or eyes

album • NOUN• **albums 1** a book for keeping a collection of something like photos or autographs **2** a collection of songs or pieces of music put on a CD, tape or record and given a title: *an old Beatles album*

albumen • NOUN• the white part of an egg

alcohol • NOUN• a kind of liquid that burns easily. It is contained in wine, beer and other drinks, and in substances such as paint and perfume
✦ **alcoholic** • ADJECTIVE• containing alcohol: *alcoholic drinks*
• NOUN• **alcoholics** an alcoholic is a person who cannot stop drinking alcohol

alcove • NOUN• **alcoves** a space where part of a wall is further back than the rest: *an alcove filled with shelves*

Aa
Bb
Cc
Dd
Ee
Ff
Gg
Hh
Ii
Jj
Kk
Ll
Mm
Nn
Oo
Pp
Qq
Rr
Ss
Tt
Uu
Vv
Ww
Xx
Yy
Zz

Aa

Bb

Cc

Dd

Ee

Ff

Gg

Hh

Ii

Jj

Kk

Ll

Mm

Nn

Oo

Pp

Qq

Rr

Ss

Tt

Uu

Vv

Ww

Xx

Yy

Zz

ale •NOUN• **ales** a kind of beer

alert •ADJECTIVE• wide awake and ready for action
•VERB• **alerts, alerting, alerted** to warn someone about a danger
•NOUN• **alerts** an alarm
• **on the alert** ready to deal with possible problems

algae •NOUN• a group of plants that grow near or in water and which do not have stems, leaves or flowers, for example seaweed

ⓘ **Algae** is the plural of **alga**. The singular, **alga**, is not often used.

algebra •NOUN• a type of mathematics that has letters and signs instead of numbers

alias •ADVERB• also known as: *Norman Cook, alias Fatboy Slim*
•NOUN• **aliases** another name that a person uses: *She uses an alias when she travels abroad.*

alibi •NOUN• **alibis** proof that a person could not have committed a particular crime, because they were somewhere else: *Taylor has a great alibi – he was in prison when the robbery took place.*

alien •NOUN• 1 a foreigner 2 a creature from another planet
•ADJECTIVE• strange: *an alien idea*

alight •ADJECTIVE• on fire: *eyes alight with excitement*
•ADVERB• on fire: *She set the building alight.*
•VERB• **alights, alighting, alighted** 1 to get off a train or bus 2 to settle or land: *A seagull will always alight on the highest point.*

align •VERB• to bring things into line with each other: *Align the words down the left side of the page.* • *Align the buttons with the holes before you do them up.*
♦ **alignment** •NOUN• the arrangement of things in a straight line: *The wheels need to be in alignment to work properly.*

alike •ADJECTIVE• like one another: *The twins aren't alike.*
•ADVERB• the same way: *He treats us both alike.*

alive •ADJECTIVE• 1 living: *the greatest ballerina alive*
2 lively: *The town comes alive on Friday nights.*
3 if you are **alive to** something, you know about it: *We are all alive to the dangers of the situation.*

alkali •NOUN• the type of chemical that behaves in the opposite way to acids and can cancel it out. It is used in substances such as soap and dye
♦ **alkaline** •ADJECTIVE• containing an alkali

all •ADJECTIVE• 1 every one: *All the children stood up.* 2 every part: *We ate all the cake.*
•PRONOUN• 1 every one: *I want to see them all.* 2 every part of something: *Don't spend it all.*
•ADVERB• completely: *all dirty*
• **all in** tired out: *We were all in after the race.*
• **all over** 1 finished: *Is it all over yet?*
2 everywhere: *clothes all over the place*

Allah •NOUN• the Muslim name for the creator of the world

allegation •NOUN• **allegations** to make an allegation against someone is to claim that they have done something wrong

allege •VERB• **alleges, alleging, alleged** to say that a person has done something wrong: *The boys allege that they are being bullied.*
♦ **allegedly** •ADVERB• something that is allegedly true is only what people say, without any proof: *He allegedly stole money out of the till but he still works there.*

allegiance •NOUN• loyalty: *The soldiers all swear allegiance to their country.*

allegory •NOUN• **allegories** a story, play, poem or picture where the characters stand for real people in real situations

allergy •NOUN• **allergies** a condition where your body reacts badly to something you touch, breathe, eat or drink: *a peanut allergy*
♦ **allergic** •ADJECTIVE• to be allergic to something is to become uncomfortable or ill because your body is sensitive to it: *an allergic reaction* • *I'm allergic to citrus fruit.*

alley •NOUN• **alleys** 1 a narrow passage in between buildings 2 a place where you can play games like skittles: *a bowling alley*

alliance • NOUN• **alliances** an agreement between people or countries to be on the same side if there is an argument

alligator • NOUN• **alligators** a large reptile like a crocodile, with thick skin, a long tail and large jaws

alliteration • NOUN• using the same sound to begin two or more words that are close together, for example *sing a song of sixpence*
♦ **alliterative** • ADJECTIVE• with the same sound at the beginning of words that are close together

allocate • VERB• **allocates, allocating, allocated** to give someone their part of something: *Now we'll allocate the rooms you will be staying in.*
♦ **allocation** • NOUN• **1** allocation is giving or sharing something out **2** an allocation is something that has been given out: *Both teams have the same allocation of tickets for the cup final.*

allot • VERB• **allots, allotting, allotted** to allot something is to share something out: *The money was allotted to the winners.*
♦ **allotment** • NOUN• **allotments 1** allotment is giving out shares of something
2 an allotment is a share of something
3 an allotment is a small piece of land that a person can rent for growing plants

allow • VERB• **allows, allowing, allowed 1** to allow someone to do something is to let them do it: *Will you allow me to come in now?*
2 to allow something is to let it happen: *We do not allow smoking in the house.*
3 to allow someone something is to give it to them: *Len's parents allowed him £40 a week while he was a student.*
♦ **allowance** • NOUN• **allowances 1** an amount of money that someone is given regularly: *My parents have promised to give me an allowance when I'm a teenager.* **2** the amount that anyone can have of something: *There's a baggage allowance that you mustn't go over.*
• **make allowances for** to make allowances for something is to expect less from someone for that reason: *We'll make allowances for the fact that you've never*

done anything like this before.

alloy • NOUN• **alloys** a mixture of two or more metals

all right • ADVERB• **1** reasonably good: *The party was all right I suppose.*
2 safe: *I'm glad you're all right – we heard there had been an accident.*
3 satisfactory: *Is it all right if I go out tonight?*
• INTERJECTION• you can say 'all right' when you agree to something: *All right, I'll go then.*

ⓘ Some people think it is wrong to write *alright*, so it is best to write it this as two words: **all right**.

allure • NOUN• something that you find attractive about a thing or person: *the allure of life at sea*
♦ **alluring** • ADJECTIVE• tempting: *an alluring idea*

ally • NOUN• **allies** a country, business or person that is joined to or supports another
• VERB• **allies, allying, allied** if a country or business is allied to another, they are joined as partners
⇒ **alliance**

almighty • ADJECTIVE• **1** very powerful: *almighty God* **2** very big: *There was an almighty row.*
• **the Almighty** God

almond • NOUN• **almonds** a long narrow nut with a hard shell

almost • ADVERB• very nearly but not quite: *She is almost ten years old.*

alms • PLURAL NOUN• money that is given to the poor

aloft • ADVERB• high up: *banners waving aloft*

alone • ADJECTIVE• without anyone else: *I was alone in the house.*
• ADVERB• **1** not with others: *I live alone.* **2** without other things: *The ticket alone will use up all my money.*

along • PREPOSITION• **1** from one end to the other: *Shona walked along the street.* **2** on the length of: *Harry's house is somewhere along this street.*

Aa
Bb
Cc
Dd
Ee
Ff
Gg
Hh
Ii
Jj
Kk
Ll
Mm
Nn
Oo
Pp
Qq
Rr
Ss
Tt
Uu
Vv
Ww
Xx
Yy
Zz

•ADVERB• **1** onwards: *Move along please.*
2 to a particular place: *I'll come along later.*
• **along with** together with: *We'd packed drinks along with the sandwiches.*

alongside •PREPOSITION• beside: *The hat was alongside the coat on the bench.*

aloof •ADJECTIVE• staying apart from other people and not being interested in them

aloud •ADVERB• if you do something aloud, you do it so that someone can hear you: *It's much slower to count aloud.*

alphabet •NOUN• **alphabets** all the letters of a language arranged in a particular order
♦ **alphabetical** •ADJECTIVE• with the first letters in the order of the alphabet: *an alphabetical index*
♦ **alphabetically** •ADVERB• with the letters in the order of the alphabet: *The list has been arranged alphabetically.*
• **alphabetical order** something that is arranged in alphabetical order is arranged so that words beginning with **A** come first, then **B** and so on: *This dictionary is in alphabetical order.*

ⓘ **Alphabet** comes from the Greek word **alphabetos**, which is made up of the first two Greek letters – **alpha** (a) and **beta** (b).

alp •NOUN• **alps** a high mountain, especially one in or near Switzerland
♦ **alpine** •ADJECTIVE• to do with high parts of mountains: *alpine meadow*

already •ADVERB• **1** before a particular time: *I had already gone when Bob arrived.*
2 now, before the expected time: *Is he here already?*

ⓘ If you write *all ready* as two words, then it means 'completely prepared', for example: *Are you all ready to go?*

alright •ADVERB• another spelling of **all right**

ⓘ It is best to write this as two words, as many people think the spelling *alright* is wrong.

alsatian •NOUN• **alsatians** a large breed of dog with a short brown and black coat. An alsatian can also be called a **German shepherd dog**

also •ADVERB• in addition: *Bernie speaks French and also some Italian.* • *My sister also attends this school.*

altar •NOUN• **altars** a raised place or table for offerings to a god

alter •VERB• **alters, altering, altered 1** to alter something is to change it: *Can you alter this skirt to fit me?* **2** to alter is to change: *The town has altered a lot recently.*
♦ **alteration** •NOUN• **alterations 1** an alteration is a change: *There have been a few alterations to our plans.* **2** alteration is change: *Alteration work is being carried out on the gym.*

alternate •VERB• **alternates, alternating, alternated** to do or happen in turn: *Rain and sun alternated throughout the day.*
•ADJECTIVE• alternate things are in turn, first one then the other: *a fence with alternate stripes of red and green*

alternative •ADJECTIVE• giving you another choice or possibility: *If you cannot come on Tuesday you can suggest an alternative day.*
•NOUN• **alternatives** another possibility: *Is there an alternative to chips on the menu?*

alternator •NOUN• **alternators** an electricity generator that produces an electric current that keeps changing its direction

although •CONJUNCTION• in spite of the fact that: *He was late for school although he'd hurried.*

altitude •NOUN• **altitudes** the altitude something has is its height above the level of the sea: *We are flying at an altitude of 20 000 metres.*

alto •NOUN• **altos 1** the lowest singing voice for a woman **2** the highest singing voice for a man

altogether •ADVERB• **1** completely: *I'm not altogether happy.* **2** in total: *We raised £100 altogether.*

ⓘ If you write *all together* as two words, it has the different meaning of 'together in a group', for example, *It's good that we're all together again.*

aluminium • NOUN • a very light metal that is silver-coloured

(i) **Aluminium** is spelled *aluminum* in the United States, and pronounced a-**loom**-in-um.

always • ADVERB • **1** at all times: *I always work hard.*
2 continually: *I'm always getting this wrong.*
3 forever: *I'll always remember that day.*

am[1] • VERB • **1** the form of the verb **be** in the present tense that you use with **I**: *I am happy.* **2** am is also used as a helping verb along with a main verb: • *I am going out.*

am[2] *or* **a.m.** • ABBREVIATION • short for **ante meridiem**, which is Latin for 'before midday'. **am** is added after the time to show that the time is in the morning, for example *7am*. Look up and compare **pm**

amalgamate • VERB • **amalgamates, amalgamating, amalgamated** to join with something else: *The two firms amalgamated last year.*
♦ **amalgamation** • NOUN • **1** amalgamation is the joining of two or more things, especially organizations **2** an amalgamation is two or more things joined together

amass • VERB • **amasses, amassing, amassed** to collect a large quantity of something: *The family has amassed a lot of furniture over the years.*

amateur • NOUN • **1** someone who takes part in a sport without being paid for it **2** someone who does something because they enjoy it, not because they are paid for it: *Holly's an excellent actress even though she's an amateur.*
• ADJECTIVE • **1** not paid: *an amateur disc-jockey* **2** not involving payment: *amateur athletics*

amaze • VERB • **amazes, amazing, amazed** to surprise very much: *It amazes me how stupid you can be.*
♦ **amazed** • ADJECTIVE • very surprised: *We were all amazed.*
♦ **amazement** • NOUN • great surprise: *To my amazement, Dad agreed with me.*

♦ **amazing** • ADJECTIVE • very surprising: *an amazing sight*
♦ **amazingly** • ADVERB • very surprisingly: *The cake was amazingly good.* • *Amazingly, it didn't rain for our picnic.*

ambassador • NOUN • **ambassadors** an official who represents their own government in a foreign country

amber • NOUN • a clear yellowish-brown liquid that has gone hard, and that may contain fossils. Amber is sometimes used to make jewellery

ambi- • PREFIX • if a word starts with **ambi-** it is to do with both parts or two of something. For example, if you are *ambivalent* you have two different feelings at the same time about something

ambidextrous • ADJECTIVE • an ambidextrous person can use either of their hands equally well

ambience • NOUN • the ambience of a place is the atmosphere it has: *The garden has a pleasant ambience.*
• **ambient** • ADJECTIVE • to do with the atmosphere in a place: *The ambient temperature is twenty degrees Celsius.*

ambiguous • ADJECTIVE • with two possible meanings: *This question is ambiguous.*
♦ **ambiguity** • NOUN • **ambiguities 1** an ambiguity is something with more than one meaning **2** ambiguity is uncertainty
♦ **ambiguously** • ADVERB • without one clear meaning: *The book ends ambiguously – we have to decide ourselves what really happened.*

ambition • NOUN • **ambitions 1** an ambition is something that you have wanted to do for a long time: *I have an ambition to see the pyramids.* **2** ambition is wanting to be very successful
♦ **ambitious** • ADJECTIVE • **1** an ambitious person wants to be very successful in life **2** an ambitious project is one that you know will be difficult for you

amble • VERB • **ambles, ambling, ambled** to walk slowly in a relaxed way

ambulance • NOUN • **ambulances** a vehicle for taking sick or injured people to hospital

Aa
Bb
Cc
Dd
Ee
Ff
Gg
Hh
Ii
Jj
Kk
Ll
Mm
Nn
Oo
Pp
Qq
Rr
Ss
Tt
Uu
Vv
Ww
Xx
Yy
Zz

ambush • NOUN• ambushes an ambush is when a person hides so that they can make a surprise attack on someone
•VERB• ambushes, ambushing, ambushed to attack someone from a hiding place

amend •VERB• amends, amending, amended to improve something you have said or written by making small changes
♦ **amendment • NOUN• amendments** a slight change to something like a law
• **make amends** to make up for having done something wrong: *Now we'll see if he can make amends for letting in that goal.*

amenity • NOUN• amenities something such as a shop or park that makes life easier or more pleasant for people in that area

amethyst • NOUN• a precious purple or violet stone: *a necklace of amethysts*

amiable • ADJECTIVE• friendly and relaxed
♦ **amiability • NOUN•** friendliness
♦ **amiably • ADVERB•** in an easy-going, friendly way

amicable • ADJECTIVE• you reach an amicable agreement without any argument
♦ **amicably • ADVERB•** in a friendly way

amid or **amidst • ADVERB•** in the middle of: *a moment of calm amid great excitement*

amiss • ADVERB• if something is amiss, there is something wrong

ammonia • NOUN• a substance that can be a gas or a liquid and has a very strong smell

ammunition • NOUN• something like bullets or bombs, that you can fire from a weapon

amnesia • NOUN• amnesia is losing your memory

amnesty • NOUN• a period of time when the usual punishments for crimes do not apply: *an amnesty for people who owe parking fines*

amoeba • NOUN• amoebas or **amoebae** a microscopic creature that is made up of only one cell and usually lives in water

amok • ADVERB• if someone **runs amok**, they go mad and do a lot of damage

among or **amongst • PREPOSITION•**
1 surrounded by or in the middle of: *You are among friends.*
2 one of a group of: *Among all my books, this is my favourite.*
3 in shares or parts: *Divide the chocolate among yourselves.*

ⓘ If you are talking about more than two people, you should use **among** or **amongst**, for example *The work was divided **among** the pupils.*
If you are talking about two people, you should use **between**, for example *Carl and Sue divided the sweets **between** them.*

amount • NOUN• amounts a quantity: *a small amount of money* • *large amounts of land*
•VERB• amounts, amounting, amounted
1 to amount to a particular number is to add up to that much: *What I've spent amounts to exactly $10.* 2 if one thing amounts to another, it is the just about the same thing: *His speech amounted to a description of how clever he was.*

amp • NOUN• amps 1 the usual word for an **ampere**. Amps are used to measure how strong an electric current is 2 a short form of the word **amplifier**

ampersand • NOUN• ampersands the sign &, which means 'and'

amphibian • NOUN• amphibians 1 an animal that lives on land and in water 2 a vehicle that can travel on land and on water
♦ **amphibious • ADJECTIVE•** able to go or live on land and in water

amphitheatre • NOUN• amphitheatres a theatre that has seats in a circle around an area in the centre

ample • ADJECTIVE• plenty or more than enough: *We had ample opportunity to ask questions.*
♦ **amply • ADVERB•** very well or even more than necessary: *We were amply rewarded with tea and chocolate cake.*

amplifier • NOUN• amplifiers a machine that makes sounds louder

amplify •VERB• amplifies, amplifying, amplified to make something louder
♦ **amplification • NOUN•** making sounds louder: *It was impossible to hear the singer without amplification.*

amputate •VERB• **amputates, amputating, amputated** to cut off a part of the body
  ♦ **amputation** •NOUN• **amputations**
  1 amputation is cutting off part of the body
  2 an amputation is an operation to cut off part of the body
  ♦ **amputee** •NOUN• **amputees** a person who has had part of their body cut off

amrit •NOUN• a Sikh ceremony where someone drinks amrit, a special mixture of water and sugar, as a sign that they are joining the body of Sikhs

amuse •VERB• **amuses, amusing, amused**
  1 to make someone laugh 2 to keep someone happy for a while: *Would you amuse the children for half an hour?*
  ♦ **amusement** •NOUN• **amusements**
  1 amusement is the feeling that makes you laugh
  2 amusement is entertainment: *What did you do for amusement on holiday?*
  3 an amusement is a machine or activity that you enjoy: *There were amusements, food stalls and talent shows.*

an •ADJECTIVE• you use **an** instead of **a** before words beginning with a vowel or **h** when it is not pronounced: *an elephant* • *an honest person*

anaemia •NOUN• a condition where someone does not have enough red blood cells and looks pale
  ♦ **anaemic** •ADJECTIVE• 1 suffering from anaemia 2 looking pale or ill

anaesthesia •NOUN• giving someone a drug to stop them feeling any pain

anaesthetic •NOUN• **anaesthetic** a drug that stops you feeling pain
  ♦ **anaesthetist** •NOUN• **anaesthetists** a doctor whose job is to help control the pain of people in hospital

anagram •NOUN• **anagrams** a word or sentence that has the same letters as another word or sentence, but in a different order. For example, *live* is an anagram of *evil*

analogue •ADJECTIVE• an analogue watch or clock has hands that move around a clockface to show the time

analogy •NOUN• **analogies** something that is similar and so helps to explain the thing you started with

analyse •VERB• **analyses, analysing, analysed** to examine the different parts of something: *His quick brain analysed and summed up the evidence.*
  ♦ **analysis** •NOUN• **analyses** an examination of the different parts of something
  ♦ **analyst** •NOUN• **analysts** 1 a person who examines the different parts of something
  2 a person whose job is to talk to a person and examine what is making them unhappy

anarchy •NOUN• a situation where people do not obey laws and there is no organization

anatomy •NOUN• all the parts of the body

ancestor •NOUN• **ancestors** your ancestors are all the past members of your family
  ♦ **ancestral** •ADJECTIVE• belonging to a person's family in the past: *the Duke's ancestral home*
  ♦ **ancestry** •NOUN• your ancestry is your family's past: *We can trace our ancestry back to the twelfth century.*

anchor •NOUN• **anchors** a heavy piece of metal on a rope or chain that is attached to a boat or ship and that stops it from moving away
  •VERB• **anchors, anchoring, anchored** 1 to drop the anchor of a boat or ship to stop it moving away 2 to fix something firmly to the spot
  ♦ **anchorage** •NOUN• **anchorages** a place where ships can stop

anchovy •NOUN• **anchovies** a type of small fish with a very salty taste

ancient •ADJECTIVE• 1 belonging to a very long time ago: *the ancient people who once lived here* 2 very old

and •CONJUNCTION• 1 a word that is used to join parts of sentences: *We'll have bread and butter.* • *Red and green striped paper.* • *Go and get ready.* 2 plus: *2 and 2 make 4*

android •NOUN• **androids** a robot that looks like a human being

anecdote •NOUN• **anecdotes** a short story that someone tells, often about something

Aa
Bb
Cc
Dd
Ee
Ff
Gg
Hh
Ii
Jj
Kk
Ll
Mm
Nn
Oo
Pp
Qq
Rr
Ss
Tt
Uu
Vv
Ww
Xx
Yy
Zz

angles

acute angle

right angle

obtuse angle

that happened to them: *a very funny speech, full of anecdotes about his journey*

anemone • NOUN• **anemones** a kind of flower that often grows in woodland

angel • NOUN• **angels** 1 a messenger from God 2 a very good person
◆ **angelic** • ADJECTIVE• very beautiful and good
◆ **angelically** • ADVERB• very sweetly

ⓘ **Angel** comes from the Greek word **angelos**, which means *messenger*.

anger • NOUN• the bad feeling you get about someone or something that annoys you
• VERB• **angers, angering, angered** to make someone feel angry

angle • NOUN• 1 the shape that is made at the point where two straight lines meet 2 a point of view: *What's your angle on this?*
• VERB• **angles, angling, angled** to try to get something by making hints: *Did you hear her angling to borrow my new coat?*
◆ **angler** • NOUN• **anglers** a person who enjoys fishing

Anglican • ADJECTIVE• to do with or belonging to the Church of England
• NOUN• **Anglicans** a member of the Church of England

angling • NOUN• the sport of fishing with a fishing-rod

Anglo-Saxon • NOUN• 1 the peoples who came to live in England and parts of Scotland in the 5th century 2 Old English, the English language before about 1150
• ADJECTIVE• belonging to or to do with the Anglo-Saxon people or their language, Old English

angry • ADJECTIVE• **angrier, angriest** cross or very cross: *Then Mum got very angry.*
• *an angry crowd* • *The second article made us even angrier.*
◆ **angrily** • ADVERB• in an angry way: *A young woman came in, crying angrily.*

anguish • NOUN• a terrible feeling of unhappiness and suffering
◆ **anguished** • ADJECTIVE• miserable and suffering: *an anguished look*

angular • ADJECTIVE• an angular body or face is thin and pointed

animal • NOUN• **animals** 1 a living being that can feel and move: *Humans and insects – we're all animals.* 2 a living being that is not a human: *an animal hospital* • *an animal lover*

ⓘ This word comes from the Latin word **anima**, which means *life*.

animated •ADJECTIVE• 1 in an animated film, things appear to move and be alive when they are really only pictures or objects 2 moving in a lively way: *He had never seen them so animated and it gave him a real lift.*
♦ **animatedly** •ADVERB• in a lively way

animation •NOUN• **animations** 1 an animation is a film where pictures or objects appear to move by themselves 2 animation is energy and liveliness
♦ **animator** •NOUN• **animators** a person who makes films from drawings or objects that are moved around

animosity •NOUN• **animosities** a feeling of strong dislike towards someone

aniseed •NOUN• a seed that tastes like liquorice and is used in making sweets, drinks and medicines

ankle •NOUN• **ankles** the place where your foot joins your leg

annex *or* **annexe** •NOUN• **annexes** an extra part of a building that may be added on to it or in a separate place
•VERB• **annexes, annexing, annexed** to annex something such as land is to take it and use it like your own

ⓘ The spelling **annexe**, with an **e** at the end, can only be used for the *noun*. The verb is **to annex**.

annihilate •VERB• **annihilates, annihilating, annihilated** to destroy somebody or something completely
♦ **annihilation** •NOUN• destroying somebody or something completely

anniversary •NOUN• **anniversaries** a day that has the same date as an event in the past: *a wedding anniversary* • *Today is the anniversary of the King's death.*

announce •VERB• **announces, announcing, announced** to tell everyone something: *Have they announced their engagement yet?* • *The minister has announced that he is retiring.*
♦ **announcement** •NOUN• **announcements** something that everybody is told, either in a special speech or on a notice: *Listen everyone; I want to make an announcement.* • *the wedding announcements in the daily paper*

♦ **announcer** •NOUN• **announcers** a person who introduces programmes on television or the radio

annoy •VERB• **annoys, annoying, annoyed** to annoy someone is to make them feel rather angry: *The way she never listens to me really annoys me.*
♦ **annoyance** •NOUN• **annoyances** 1 annoyance is a feeling of irritation: *a look of annoyance* 2 an annoyance is something that irritates you
♦ **annoyed** •ADJECTIVE• rather angry: *annoyed that it was raining* • *feeling annoyed about being kept waiting*

annual •ADJECTIVE• an annual event happens once every year: *an annual meeting of headteachers*
•NOUN• **annuals** 1 a book that is published every year 2 a plant that lives for only one year
♦ **annually** •ADVERB• happening once every year

anoint •VERB• **anoints, anointing, anointed** to put oil on someone's head in a ceremony as a sign that they are specially chosen for something

anon •ABBREVIATION• a short form of the word **anonymous**

anonymous •ADJECTIVE• 1 an anonymous letter or book is written by an unknown writer 2 an anonymous telephone call is made by someone who does not give their name
♦ **anonymously** •ADVERB• by a person who does not give their name: *The money has been given anonymously.*

anorak •NOUN• **anoraks** a waterproof jacket, usually with a hood

anorexia •NOUN• an illness that makes a person very thin because they do not want to eat
♦ **anorexic** •ADJECTIVE• suffering from anorexia and perhaps very thin

another •ADJECTIVE• 1 one more: *Have another piece of chocolate.* 2 a different one: *Another day we'll walk further.*
•PRONOUN• 1 one more: *He had two gold medals and now he has another.* 2 a different one: *If that's broken, use another.*

answer • NOUN• **answers** 1 an answer is what you reply when someone asks you a question 2 the answer to a problem is the solution

•VERB• **answers, answering, answered** 1 to reply when someone asks you a question: *Aren't you going to answer?* • *Answer each question on a different page.* • *Answer me now please.*
2 to pick up the phone when it rings: *A child answered the telephone.*
3 to open the door when someone rings or knocks: *Would you answer the door please?*
4 if you **answer back**, you are cheeky or rude to someone who has told you off

ant • NOUN• **ants** a tiny insect that usually has no wings

antagonism • NOUN• a feeling of wanting to fight against someone or an idea
♦ **antagonistic** • ADJECTIVE• wanting to fight with someone or something
♦ **antagonize** or **antagonise** • VERB• **antagonizes, antagonizing, antagonized** to make a person want to fight or argue with you

ante- • PREFIX• if a word starts with **ante-** it often means 'before something'. For example, an *anteroom* is a room you go into before you enter a larger room

anteater • NOUN• **anteaters** an animal with a long nose and no teeth, that mainly eats ants

antelope • NOUN• **antelope** or **antelopes** an animal like a deer, that has long horns and runs very fast

antenna • NOUN• **antennae** or **antennas** 1 a long thin feeler on the head of an insect or shellfish 2 an aerial, for example, for a television

ⓘ The plural of **antenna** when it means 'a feeler' is **antennae** (pronounced an-**ten**-ee). The plural form when it means 'an aerial' is **antennas**.

anthem • NOUN• **anthems** a song that praises someone or something, for example a national anthem, which praises a country or its ruler

ant-hill • NOUN• **ant-hills** a pile of earth that ants build up over their nest

anthology • NOUN• **anthologies** a book of stories, poems or songs by different writers

anthropology • NOUN• the study of the way human beings live
♦ **anthroplogist** • NOUN• **anthroplogists** a person who studies the development of humans and the way they live

anti- • PREFIX• against: *anti-aircraft weapons*

antibiotic • NOUN• **antibiotics** a medicine that fights bacteria that can cause infections: *Penicillin is an antibiotic.*

antibody • NOUN• **antibodies** a substance that the body produces in the blood to fight harmful bacteria

anticipate • VERB• **anticipates, anticipating, anticipated** to anticipate something is to expect it to happen and even to do something about it before it happens: *We anticipate having a quiet evening at home.* • *A couple of reporters had anticipated his early arrival.*
♦ **anticipation** • NOUN• 1 if you act in anticipation of something, you do it because you expect that thing to happen: *The school has closed in anticipation of the heavy snow forecast for tomorrow.* 2 anticipation is excitement about something that is going to happen: *There was cheering in anticipation of the team's entrance.*

anticlimax • NOUN• **anticlimaxes** 1 an anticlimax is a dull end to an exciting story 2 you get a feeling of anticlimax when some excitement is over and things calm down again

anticlockwise • ADVERB• going in the opposite direction to the hands of a clock: *Turn the top of the bottle anticlockwise.*
• ADJECTIVE• in the opposite direction to the hands of a clock: *an anticlockwise movement*

antics • PLURAL NOUN• someone's antics are the funny things that they do

antidote • NOUN• **antidotes** a medicine that stops a poison being harmful

antifreeze .NOUN. a chemical that you can add to a liquid to stop it from freezing, especially the water in a car radiator

antiperspirant .NOUN. **antiperspirants** a substance that stops skin sweating

antiquated .ADJECTIVE. old-fashioned

antique .NOUN. **antiques** an object that is old and valuable: *a collector of antiques* .ADJECTIVE. old and valuable

♦ **antiquity** .NOUN. a long time ago, especially the times of the ancient Greeks and Romans

antiseptic .NOUN. **antiseptics** a substance that kills germs

antisocial .ADJECTIVE. 1 antisocial behaviour is unpleasant or harmful to other people 2 antisocial people do not enjoy being with other people

antler .NOUN. **antlers** a horn that divides like branches and grows on the head of a deer, especially a **stag**

antonym .NOUN. **antonyms** a word that means the opposite of another word. For example, *big* is an antonym of *small*. Look up and compare **synonym**. See the box called **Opposites**

anus .NOUN. the opening in a bottom that lets out the solid matter that the body does not need

anvil .NOUN. **anvils** a heavy metal block that a blacksmith holds hot metal against when it is being hammered into shape

anxiety .NOUN. **anxieties** 1 anxiety is worrying, especially about what may happen 2 an anxiety is something you are worried about

anxious .ADJECTIVE. 1 worried: *an anxious face*
2 nervous and uncomfortable: *an anxious time*
3 keen: *I'm anxious to get there on time to get a good seat.*
♦ **anxiously** .ADVERB. in a worried way: *He looked anxiously at his watch.*

any .ADJECTIVE. 1 every: *Any child would know that answer.*
2 one, but not a particular one: *It'll be here any day now.*

3 some: *Have we got any sweets?*
.ADVERB. at all: *I can't go on any longer.*
.PRONOUN. 1 one: *Ask any of them.* 2 some: *We haven't got any left.*

anybody .PRONOUN. 1 any person at all: *Anybody is allowed to enter.* 2 an important person: *Don't listen to her – she isn't anybody.*

anyhow .ADVERB. 1 anyway: *I missed lunch but I wasn't hungry anyhow.* 2 in an untidy, careless way: *The books had been left anyhow all over the floor.*

anyone .PRONOUN. any person at all: *There isn't anyone left.*

anything .PRONOUN. something of any kind: *He hasn't eaten anything.* • *Did Louise say anything?* • *Has anything happened?*

anyway .ADVERB. 1 in any case: *Leon couldn't go with me but I enjoyed the party anyway.* 2 a word you use to change the subject in a conversation: *Anyway, how have you been lately?*

anywhere .ADVERB. in or to any place: *I'm not going anywhere.* • *I can't find my keys anywhere.*
.PRONOUN. any place: *Anywhere would be better than this.*

ⓘ **Any place** (two words) is used in American English instead of **anywhere**.

apart .ADVERB. 1 separated by distance or time: *with your feet apart* • *two classes, a week apart* 2 into pieces: *Take the lamp apart.*
.PREPOSITION. except for: *Apart from us, nobody's interested.*

apartheid .NOUN. the system that used to operate in South Africa, where black and white people were treated differently

apartment .NOUN. 1 a set of rooms on one level of a building 2 a room in a building

apathy .NOUN. someone who suffers from apathy is not interested in anything

ape .NOUN. **apes** a kind of monkey that is large and has no tail
.VERB. **apes, aping, aped** to copy what someone else does

apex .NOUN. **apexes** or **apices** the top point

Aa Bb Cc Dd Ee Ff Gg Hh Ii Jj Kk Ll Mm Nn Oo Pp Qq Rr Ss Tt Uu Vv Ww Xx Yy Zz

of something, especially a triangle

aphid • NOUN• **aphids** a small insect, for example a greenfly, that feeds on plants

apiary • NOUN• **apiaries** a place where bees are kept

apiece • ADVERB• an old-fashioned word for **each**: *five packets at £1 apiece*

apologetic • ADJECTIVE• if you are apologetic, you show that you are sorry for something you have done
♦ **apologetically** • ADVERB• showing that you are sorry

apologize or **apologise** • VERB• **apologizes, apologizing, apologized** to say sorry for doing something wrong: *I had to apologize to the rest of the family for being so rude.*
♦ **apology** • NOUN• **apologies** an apology is when you say you are sorry for something you have done: *The headmaster sat waiting for our apology.*

apostle • NOUN• **apostles** one of the first twelve followers of Jesus Christ

apostrophe • NOUN• **apostrophes** the mark (') that shows where a letter or letters have been missed out, for example in *don't* or *he's*. It also shows who owns something when it is used with *s* as in *Nicky's desk*. See the box called **Apostrophes**

appal • VERB• **appals, appalling, appalled** if you are appalled, you are shocked because something is so bad: *I was appalled by her language.*
♦ **appalling** • ADJECTIVE• 1 shocking: *an appalling accident* 2 very bad: *appalling weather*

apparatus • NOUN• the equipment that you need for a particular task: *breathing apparatus for the divers*

apparent • ADJECTIVE• 1 easy to see: *Then, for no apparent reason, he began to cry.* 2 appearing to be true: *Make a list of the apparent problems.*
♦ **apparently** • ADVERB• it appears or seems: *David is apparently off sick today.*

appeal • VERB• **appeals, appealing, appealed** 1 to appeal for something is to ask everyone for what you badly need: *The*

police have appealed to the public for more information.
2 to appeal to someone is to be attractive to them: *Bungee jumping doesn't appeal to me one bit.*
3 to appeal against a decision is to ask someone to change their mind
• NOUN• **appeals** 1 an appeal is a request for something you want very much
2 appeal is what makes a thing or person attractive and interesting: *I don't understand the appeal of stamp collecting.*
3 an appeal is asking someone to change a decision, especially in a court of law

appear • VERB• **appears, appearing, appeared** 1 a thing or person appears when you can suddenly see them: *Then Greta appeared round the corner.* • *A black mark has appeared on the wall.*
2 to seem: *Jill appeared to be getting very cross.* • *You don't appear to be ready yet.*
3 to have to be in front of other people, for example in a court of law or on the stage: *Tom is appearing as Hamlet at the Globe Theatre.* • *The president had to apppear before the finance committee.*
♦ **appearance** • NOUN• **appearances** 1 arriving: *Until Linda's appearance, the evening had been very dull.*
2 the way a thing or person looks: *Change your appearance with a new hairstyle.*
3 being in front of people for a performance or interview: *This is Mel's second appearance in a comedy.*
4 appearances are the way things seem to be, but possibly not the way they really are

appease • VERB• **appeases, appeasing, appeased** to make someone feel better by giving them what they want

appendicitis • NOUN• an illness where the appendix is painful and usually has to be removed

appendix • NOUN• **appendices** or **appendixes** 1 a small tube on the right side of the body that is a useless part of the human intestines 2 an extra section at the end of a book or document that gives more details about something

Apostrophes

An **apostrophe** is a punctuation mark that looks like this '. It has two main uses.

Showing missing letters
An apostrophe takes the place of the missing letter, or letters, when two words are shortened.

I'll

you've

he'd

she's

don't

Look at the panel called **Short forms** for a full list.

Showing ownership
An apostrophe plus **s** added to a noun shows ownership. It makes the noun **possessive.**
  my mother's purse = the purse *belonging to* my mother.

Just because a word ends with an **s** does not mean that it needs an apostrophe.

Do not add apostrophes to plural nouns that end in **s** *unless* they are possessive.

  ✗ The **cat's** and **dog's** fight.

  ✓ The **cats** and **dogs** fight.

  ✗ The **cats** food and the **dogs** bones are in the kitchen.

  ✓ The **cat's** food and the **dogs'** bones are in the kitchen.

Remember...
These words do not have apostrophes even though they show who owns something:

  his   hers   its   ours   theirs   yours

ⓘ The plural of **appendix** when it is a part of the body is **appendixes**: *The doctor removed two appendixes that day.*
The plural when it is part of a book is **appendices**: *The appendices begin on page 430.*

appetite • NOUN• **appetites** your appetite, usually for food, is how much you want any: *Elly has lost her appetite since she's been ill.*
  ✦ **appetizer** or **appetiser** • NOUN• **appetizers** something small to eat or drink before a meal
  ✦ **appetizing** or **appetising** • ADJECTIVE• making you want to eat: *an appetizing smell*

applaud • VERB• **applauds, applauding,**
applauded to praise someone, especially by clapping: *The audience applauded Nancy loudly.* • *For a moment we didn't think anyone would applaud.*
  ✦ **applause** • NOUN• clapping

apple • NOUN• **apples** a hard, round fruit with red, green or yellow skin
  • **the apple of someone's eye** a person that someone is very proud of

appliance • NOUN• **appliances** a piece of equipment: *kitchen appliances*

applicable • ADJECTIVE• **1** a rule that is applicable to you applies to you **2** a question that is not applicable to you is one that you do not have to answer

Aa Bb Cc Dd Ee Ff Gg Hh Ii Jj Kk Ll Mm Nn Oo Pp Qq Rr Ss Tt Uu Vv Ww Xx Yy Zz

applicant .NOUN . **applicants** a person who applies for something like a job or university place

application .NOUN . **applications** 1 an application is a letter or a form asking for something like a job
2 application is an effort to do something well: *He could pass the exam with a little more application.*
3 an application is when you put something such as paint or cream on a surface: *Let the paint dry between applications.*
4 an application is a computer program that does a particular kind of job, for example, a word processing program

applicator .NOUN . **applicators** a tool or device that helps you to use a product in exactly the right place: *Spread the glue with the applicator on the top.*

applied .ADJECTIVE . an applied science is one that has a practical use

apply .VERB . **applies, applying, applied**
1 to ask for something like a job, usually by a letter or a form: *Martin's applying to university this year.*
2 to apply something to a surface is to put or spread it on: *Apply the cream to your skin three times a day.*
3 if something applies to you, it affects you: *Do these rules apply to all of us?*
4 to apply yourself is to try hard

appoint .VERB . **appoints, appointing, appointed** 1 to give someone a job: *The committee appointed Mrs Burns as manager?* 2 an appointed time or place is one arranged in advance: *Lizzie was the only one there at the appointed time.*
♦ **appointment** .NOUN . **appointments** 1 an appointment is a time and place that you must meet someone: *I have a doctor's appointment at 2 o'clock tommorow.*
2 an appointment is a job
3 appointment is giving someone a job: *the appointment of a new music teacher*

appreciate .VERB . **appreciates, appreciating, appreciated** 1 to think that something is valuable, useful, important or kind: *Rosie appreciated the card we sent her.*
2 to understand: *Martha appreciates that she won't live forever.*
3 to become more valuable
♦ **appreciation** .NOUN . 1 understanding: *the appreciation of art*
2 thanks: *a gift in appreciation of your help*
3 increasing value
♦ **appreciative** .ADJECTIVE . an appreciative person shows that they are grateful or pleased by something: *an appreciative audience*

apprehension .NOUN . 1 worry about the future: *in a state of apprehension* 2 catching someone, such as a criminal

apprehensive .ADJECTIVE . nervous and afraid: *apprehensive about the future*
♦ **apprehensively** .ADVERB . in a nervous way

apprentice .NOUN . **apprentices** a person who is learning how to do a skilled job from someone who can already do it
♦ **apprenticeship** .NOUN . the time when someone is learning their job

approach .VERB . **approaches, approaching, approached** 1 to come towards a place, person or thing: *approach the animals very slowly* • *a plane approaching Paris from the south* 2 to go to a person with a suggestion: *If you want more money you'll have to approach the manager.*
.NOUN . **approaches** 1 coming near: *the approach of summer*
2 the way up to a building: *a tree-lined approach*
3 a way of trying to deal with something: *the cheap approach*
♦ **approachable** .ADJECTIVE . an approachable person is easy to talk to

appropriate .ADJECTIVE . suitable: *Please wear appropriate clothing.*

approval .NOUN . approval is when someone thinks something is good or satisfactory: *We need your approval before we can send the money.*

approve .VERB . **approves, approving, approved** 1 to **approve of** something is to think it is good: *He did not approve of children dreaming.* 2 to approve something is to agree to it

approximate • ADJECTIVE• not exact: *Can you tell me the approximate number of chairs we'll need?*
  ◆ **approximately** • ADVERB• more or less: *approximately one thousand people*

apricot • NOUN• **apricots** 1 a small orange-coloured fruit with a soft peachy skin and a stone inside 2 a soft orange colour

April • NOUN• the fourth month of the year, after March and before May

ⓘ **April** comes from the Latin word **aperire**, which means *to open*, because the spring flowers start to open around this time.

apron • NOUN• **aprons** you wear an apron if you want to keep the front of your clothes clean or dry

apt • ADJECTIVE• 1 likely to: *apt to fly into a temper* 2 suitable: *an apt description*
  ◆ **aptly** • ADVERB• suitably: *a house by the river, very aptly named 'River's Edge'*

aptitude • NOUN• talent: *Sylvia shows plenty of aptitude for maths.*

aqua- • PREFIX• if a word starts with **aqua-**, it has something to do with water. For example, an *aqualung* is a piece of equipment that lets you breathe under water

aquamarine • ADJECTIVE• bluish-green

aquarium • NOUN• **aquariums** *or* **aquaria** a glass tank or a building, for example in a zoo, for keeping fish or water animals

aquatic • ADJECTIVE• to do with water: *aquatic sports* • *Aquatic plants live in water.*

aqueduct • NOUN• **aqueducts** a bridge that carries a river or canal across a valley

arable • ADJECTIVE• arable land is farming land where crops grow

arbitrary • ADJECTIVE• an arbitrary decision or choice is one that you make without a good reason: *Just make an arbitrary choice: red or blue?*

arbitrate • VERB• **arbitrates, arbitrating, arbitrated** to be a judge when people are arguing
  ◆ **arbitration** • NOUN• trying to settle an argument between other people

arc • NOUN• **arcs** a curve that is like part of a circle

arcade • NOUN• **arcades** a covered walk, especially with shops along the side

arch • NOUN• **arches** 1 the curved top of a doorway or between the supports of a bridge 2 the curved underneath part of your foot
  • VERB• **arches, arching, arched** to curve over: *a cat arching its back*

arch- • PREFIX• if a word starts with **arch-** it means 'most important'. For example, your *arch-enemy* is your main enemy

archaeology • NOUN• the study of what is on or in the ground, left there by people in the past
  ◆ **archaeological** • ADJECTIVE• to do with studying the things left by people in the past
  ◆ **archaeologist** • NOUN• a person who studies things left in the ground by people in the past

archaic • ADJECTIVE• dating from a very long time ago

archangel • NOUN• **archangels** a chief angel

archbishop • NOUN• **archbishops** a chief bishop

archer • NOUN• **archers** a person who shoots with a bow and arrow

archery • NOUN• the sport of shooting with a bow and arrow

archipelago • NOUN• **archipelagoes** *or* **archipelagos** a group of small islands

architect • NOUN• **architects** a person whose job is to design buildings
  ◆ **architectural** • ADJECTIVE• to do with the way buildings are designed: *architectural features like pillars and arches*
  ◆ **architecturally** • ADVERB• to do with building design: *Architecturally, the city is very interesting.*
  ◆ **architecture** • NOUN• 1 designing buidings: *Len had given up architecture to become an artist.* 2 a style of building: *Roman architecture*

archives • PLURAL NOUN• the historical records of a place or organization: *Search the archives for some information about the fire in 1900.*

ardent •ADJECTIVE• having strong feelings: *an ardent football fan*
♦ **ardently** •ADVERB• passionately: *arguing ardently about the election*

arduous •ADJECTIVE• difficult or hard-going: *an arduous climb to the top of the hill*

are •VERB• 1 the form of the verb **be** in the present tense that is used with **you**, **we**, **they** and plural nouns: *We are all here today.* • *Where are the best places to visit?* 2 **are** is also used as a helping verb along with a main verb: *We are leaving tomorrow.*

area •NOUN• **areas** 1 a part or region: *a children's play area* • *There are a lot of farms in this area.*
2 a part of a subject or activity: *Drama is an area that Gavin knows a lot about.*
3 the size of a surface, that you measure in **square** units: *A carpet that is 5m by 5m has an area of 25 square metres.*

arena •NOUN• **arenas** a large space for sports or other entertainments with seats all around it

ⓘ **Arena** means *sand* in Latin. In ancient times an arena would have been the part of a theatre covered with sand.

aren't •SHORT FORM• a short way to say and write **are not**: *These aren't my boots.*

arguable •ADJECTIVE• if something is arguable, some people say that it is true: *It is arguable that he is the best player we've ever had.*
♦ **arguably** •ADVERB• something is arguably true if it is possible to believe it: *It is arguably a very good thing that Kevin lost his job.*

argue •VERB• **argues, arguing, argued**
1 to **argue with** someone is to tell them how you disagree with what they have said: *The children never stop arguing with each other.*
2 to argue a point of view is to give reasons for having it: *The manager argued that the shop would have to close.*
♦ **argument** •NOUN• **arguments** 1 a discussion where people do not agree with each other: *There was a heated argument going on next door.* 2 the reasons for a point of view: *My argument against the plan is*

that we just don't have the money.
♦ **argumentative** •ADJECTIVE• an argumentative person often has disagreements with other people

arid •ADJECTIVE• very dry: *the arid deserts of Arizona*

arise •VERB• **arises, arising, arose, arisen**
1 to happen: *A small problem has arisen.*
2 to move upwards: *A wonderful smell arose from the basement.*

aristocracy •NOUN• people from a country's oldest families that were often close to the royal families of the past: *Only members of the aristocracy are invited to these occasions.*
♦ **aristocrat** •NOUN• **aristocrats** a person from an old family who often has a title like *Lord* or *Lady*
♦ **aristocratic** •ADJECTIVE• 1 belonging to a country's upper class 2 looking like a member of the upper class

arithmetic •NOUN• adding, subtracting, dividing and multiplying numbers
♦ **arithmetical** •ADJECTIVE• to do with calculating numbers

ark •NOUN• **arks** the boat that carried Noah, his family and two of every animal during the flood in the Bible story

arm [1] •NOUN• **arms** 1 your arm is between your shoulder and your hand: *Alan slowly folded his arms.*
2 the arm of a piece of clothing is a sleeve
3 a part of something that sticks out of its side, usually with a bend or angle in it: *the arm of a chair*

arm [2] •VERB• **arms, arming, armed** to arm someone is to give them a weapon to fight with
♦ **armed** •ADJECTIVE• someone who is armed has a weapon with them: *When the burglar was arrested, the police found that he had been heavily armed.*

armada •NOUN• a fleet of ships going to war

armadillo •NOUN• **armadillos** a small animal from America that has a kind of protective shell made of small pieces of bone

armaments •PLURAL NOUN• weapons and other war equipment

armchair • NOUN• **armchairs** a chair with sides for resting your arms on

armistice • NOUN• a time when enemies agree stop fighting for a while, especially to talk about stopping for ever

armour • NOUN• a hard cover, usually made from metal, that protects someone or something in a battle: *a knight wearing a suit of armour*
♦ **armoured** • ADJECTIVE• protected by a hard layer of something such as metal: *an armoured vehicle*

armpit • NOUN• **armpits** the angle where your arm joins your body under your shoulder

arms • PLURAL NOUN• weapons

army • NOUN• **armies** an organization of a lot of people, usually soldiers, who will fight against an enemy

aroma • NOUN• **aromas** a nice smell, especially of food
♦ **aromatherapy** • NOUN• using the oils of plants and flowers that have different smells to treat people who are not well
♦ **aromatic** • ADJECTIVE• having a good smell: *aromatic plants*

arose • VERB• a way of changing the verb **arise** to make a past tense: *The council arose when the president entered the room.*

around • PREPOSITION• 1 on all sides: *sitting around the table*
2 in a circle: *hold hands around the tree*
3 at or to different parts of a place: *walking around the city*
4 about: *at around 4 o'clock* • *around sixty kilos* • *She lives somewhere around here.*
• ADVERB• all about in different places: *clothes lying all around* • *children running around*

arouse • VERB• **arouses, arousing, aroused**
1 to arouse someone is to wake them up 2 to arouse a feeling in someone is to make them have that feeling

arrange • VERB• **arranges, arranging, arranged** 1 to set things out carefully: *Arrange the knives and forks on the table.*
2 to make plans so that something happens: *Who is arranging the wedding?*

♦ **arrangement** • NOUN• **arrangements**
1 arrangement is putting or planning things the way you want them: *classes in flower arrangement*
2 an arrangement is the position that things are put in: *a flower arrangement*
3 an arrangement is a plan or set of plans that are made so that something can happen the way you want it to: *The arrangement was that we should meet back at the car.*

array • NOUN• **arrays** a lot of things set out for people to see: *The table was full with an array of different salads.*

arrears • PLURAL NOUN• to be **in arrears** is to be behind with payments that should have been made: *I don't like being in arrears with the rent.*

arrest • VERB• **arrests, arresting, arrested**
1 to arrest someone is to catch them and take them to be charged with a crime 2 to arrest something is to stop it from continuing: *to arrest the progress of the illness*
• NOUN• **arrests** 1 an arrest is when the police take a person to be charged with a crime
2 an arrest is a stopping of something
• **under arrest** a person is under arrest when the police hold them before charging them with a crime

arrival • NOUN• **arrivals** 1 an arrival is when someone reaches a place: *We are all looking forward to Alice's arrival.* 2 an arrival is a person or thing that has come to a place: *Come and meet the new arrivals to the school.*

arrive • VERB• **arrives, arriving, arrived**
1 to arrive at a place is to reach it: *Please arrive at the station by 5.30.* • *I they don't arrive soon, we'll have to go without them.*
2 when a time or event arrives, it happens: *Would her birthday ever arrive?*
3 to arrive at a decision is to finally make a decision

arrogance • NOUN• a feeling of being more important or better than other people

arrogant • ADJECTIVE• an arrogant person thinks they are better than other people

arrow • NOUN• **arrows** 1 a pointed stick that you can shoot from a bow 2 a pointed shape that shows a particular direction

Aa
Bb
Cc
Dd
Ee
Ff
Gg
Hh
Ii
Jj
Kk
Ll
Mm
Nn
Oo
Pp
Qq
Rr
Ss
Tt
Uu
Vv
Ww
Xx
Yy
Zz

arsenal .NOUN. **arsenals** a weapons store

arsenic .NOUN. a strong poison

arson .NOUN. the crime of setting fire to a building on purpose
♦ **arsonist** .NOUN. **arsonists** a person who sets fire to a building on purpose

art .NOUN. **arts** 1 art is the beautiful things that people do and invent in painting, sculpture, music and literature
2 an art is a skill that you use to do or make something beautiful
3 arts are subjects that you can study that are not sciences

artery .NOUN. **arteries** a tube that takes blood around the body from the heart

artful .ADJECTIVE. clever in a sneaky, dishonest way
♦ **artfully** .ADVERB. in a way that gets what you want, but not obviously

arthritis .NOUN. swollen joints that are painful and make moving difficult
♦ **arthritic** .ADJECTIVE. swollen and painful because of arthritis

artichoke .NOUN. **artichokes** a vegetable that grows on a long stem and looks like a bit like a pineapple

article .NOUN. **articles** 1 a thing or item: *articles of clothing*
2 a piece of writing in a magazine or newspaper: *an article about farming*
3 the words **a** and **the**

articulate .VERB. **articulates, articulating, articulated** to say something clearly
♦ **articulated** .ADJECTIVE. an articulated lorry has a joint between the cab and the trailer that makes turning easier
♦ **articulation** .NOUN. speaking very clearly

artificial .ADJECTIVE. looking natural, but actually made by humans or by a machine: *artificial fur*
♦ **artificially** .ADVERB. not naturally

artillery .NOUN. big guns that an army uses

artist .NOUN. **artists** 1 a person who paints, draws or makes sculptures 2 a person who does something very skilfully, especially some kind of performing
♦ **artistic** .ADJECTIVE. 1 an artistic person is creative and enjoys art 2 something artistic is creative and skilful: *a very artistic arrangement*
♦ **artistically** .ADVERB. skilfully done in a way that is pleasing to look at: *an artistically arranged room*

artiste .NOUN. **artistes** a stage performer such as a dancer, singer or actor

as .CONJUNCTION. 1 a word you use when you compare things or people: *Are you as tall as me?* • *This one's not as cheap as that one.*
2 while: *As we climbed, the air got colder.*
3 because: *I went first as I was the youngest.*
4 like: *As I thought, most people had already left.*

asbestos .NOUN. a greyish-white material that does not burn and is used in buildings and clothes as protection against fire

ascend .VERB. **ascends, ascending, ascended** 1 to ascend something like a hill is to climb it 2 to ascend is to go upwards: *a bird ascending into the sky*
♦ **ascent** .NOUN. **ascents** an upward movement or climb: *The plane will now begin its ascent to 50 000 feet.*

ash 1 .NOUN. **ashes** the white powder that remains after something is burnt

ash 2 .NOUN. **ashes** a tree with a silvery-grey bark

ashamed .ADJECTIVE. 1 to be ashamed of yourself is to feel bad about something that you have done: *I'm ashamed of my behaviour today.* 2 to be ashamed of a thing or person is to feel bad because they are not good enough: *I'm ashamed of my Dad's rotten old car but he likes it.*

ashore .ADVERB. on or on to dry land: *We went ashore for dinner and returned to the ship later.*

ashtray .NOUN. **ashtrays** a small dish for the ash from people's cigarettes

aside .ADVERB. to or on one side: *Please stand aside and let us through.*
.NOUN. **asides** an aside is a remark that someone makes that not everyone present is supposed to hear

ask .VERB. **asks, asking, asked** 1 to ask a

question is to say it so that you get an answer from someone: *They asked us about our families.*

2 to ask someone for something is to tell them that you want them to give it to you: *I've no idea what the time is – ask Joanne.*

3 to ask someone to an event like a party is to invite them: *We've asked twenty people but they won't all turn up.*

4 to ask something of someone is to expect it *I think you're asking too much of these children.*

5 to **ask after someone** is to ask how they are
• **ask for it** to do something that will definitely get you into trouble
• **ask for trouble** to do something stupid that will probably end badly

askew • ADVERB• not straight: *Dom's collar was open and his tie was askew.*

asleep • ADJECTIVE• **1** sleeping: *Don't wake her if she's asleep.* **2** if your arm or leg is asleep, you cannot feel it because it's been in the same position for too long
• ADVERB• into sleep: *I fell asleep after a while.*

asp • NOUN• **asps** a small, poisonous snake

asparagus • NOUN• a plant with fat, pale green stems that can be cooked and eaten as a vegetable

aspect • NOUN• **aspects 1** a part of a situation or problem: *Many aspects of this plan bother me.* **2** the direction a building faces: *a house with a northern aspect*

asphalt • NOUN• a surface for roads and paths that looks like gravel mixed with tar

aspire • VERB• **aspires, aspiring, aspired** to aspire to something is to hope that you will have it
♦ **aspiration** • NOUN• **aspirations** a hope that you will have or achieve something

aspirin • NOUN• **aspirins** a medicine for stopping pain, usually made into tablets

ass • NOUN• **asses 1** a donkey **2** a stupid person

assail • VERB• **assails, assailing, assailed** to attack
♦ **assailant** • NOUN• **assailants** an attacker

assassin • NOUN• **assassins** a person who kills someone on purpose
♦ **assassinate** • VERB• **assassinates, assassinating, assassinated** to kill someone, especially a politician
♦ **assassination** • NOUN• **assassinations** a planned killing

assault • NOUN• **assaults** an attack
• VERB• **assaults, assaulting, assaulted** to attack someone

assault course • NOUN• **assault courses** a set of obstacles in a row that people, especially soldiers, have to climb, jump or crawl over in order to get fit, or prove that they are fit

assemble • VERB• **asssembles, assembling, assembled 1** to get several things or people together: *We've assembled a choir for the concert.*
2 to put something together from several parts: *instructions for assembling the bookcase*
3 to come together in a group: *Please assemble in the hall after the show.*
♦ **assembly** • NOUN• **assemblies 1** putting something together from different parts: *assembly instructions*
2 coming together to form a group: *notices for morning assembly at school*
3 an assembly is a group of important people such as politicians, who make decisions for other people: *the General Assembly of the United Nations*

assembly line • NOUN• **assembly lines** a conveyor belt in a factory which a line of products travels down. People standing beside it add a different part to each product until it is complete

assent • VERB• **assents, assenting, assented** to agree
• NOUN• agreement

assert • VERB• **asserts, asserting, asserted 1** to claim that something is true **2** to **assert yourself** is to act or speak out confidently
♦ **assertion** • NOUN• **assertions** something that someone claims as true: *We know Nigel did it in spite of his assertions that he didn't.*
♦ **assertive** • ADJECTIVE• confident and not afraid to speak out

assess •VERB• **assesses, assessing, assessed** to consider and decide how good, valuable or important something is: *Now we'll have to assess how much damage has been done.*
♦ **assessment** •NOUN• **assessments** an opinion about something from someone who has considered it carefully: *What is your assessment of the situation now?*

asset •NOUN• **assets 1** an asset is something that is useful: *Our team's chief asset is Tom.* • *Philippa's voice is her best asset.* **2** someone's assets are the valuable things they own: *The company must sell some of its assets.*

assign •VERB• **assigns, assigning, assigned** to assign a job or task to someone is to give it to them to do
♦ **assignment** •NOUN• **assigments** a job or task for a particular person to do: *I've got three homework assigments to finish by Friday.*

assist •VERB• **assists, assisting, assisted** to help someone to do something
♦ **assistance** •NOUN• help for someone who is trying to do something
♦ **assistant** •NOUN• **assistants 1** a person whose job is to help someone else: *My assistant will take some notes.* **2** a shop assistant

associate •VERB• **associates, associating, associated 1** to associate with someone is to spend time with them: *Frank associates with a lot of very important people.* **2** to associate things like words is to make connections between them in your mind
•NOUN• **associates** your associates are the people you mix with
♦ **associated** •ADJECTIVE• connected in some way: *a disease with associated problems*

association •NOUN• **associations 1** an association is a club or society **2** association is putting things or people together: *a word association game*

assorted •ADJECTIVE• mixed: *assorted flavours*
♦ **assortment** •NOUN• **assortments** a mixture: *a strange assortment of people*

assume •VERB• **assumes, assuming,**

assumed 1 to suppose something: *Oh sorry, I assumed that you had met each other before.* **2** to assume something like a look or attitude is to begin to have it: *He assumed a puzzled look but of course he knew the answer.* **3** to assume a new name is to change your name
♦ **assumption** •NOUN• **assumptions** something you suppose

assurance •NOUN• **assurances 1** assurance is being confident: *Tim plays tennis with complete assurance.* **2** an assurance is similar to a promise: *I had his assurance that it would be done.*

assure •VERB• **assures, assuring, assured** to try to make someone feel certain about what you are telling them: *I'd like to assure you we are doing all we can.* • *Mr Harris has assured us that the car will be ready tomorrow.*
♦ **assured** or **self-assured** •ADJECTIVE• confident: *an assured manner*
• **rest assured** to be confident of something: *Pupils can rest assured that the school will be open soon.*

asterisk •NOUN• **asterisks** a star (*) in a written text that usually means there is another star beside a note, probably at the bottom of the page

asteroid •NOUN• **asteroids** one of the rocky objects that circle the sun, mostly between Jupiter and Mars

asthma •NOUN• an illness that people may suffer from for a long time and that makes breathing difficult
♦ **asthmatic** •ADJECTIVE• a person who is asthmatic sometimes finds it very difficult to breathe and usually has medicine with them in case this happens suddenly
•NOUN• **asthmatics** a person who has trouble breathing because they suffer from asthma

astonish •VERB• **astonishes, astonishing, astonished** to surprise someone very much: *What he said simply astonished me!*
♦ **astonished** •ADJECTIVE• you are astonished when you are extremely surprised: *I'm astonished that you think that about me.*
♦ **astonishing** •ADJECTIVE• extremely

surprising: *an astonishing outburst* • *It was astonishing just how easy the exercise was.*

astound •VERB• **astounds, astounding, astounded** to surprise or shock someone very much: *The information astounded us all.*

♦ **astounded** •ADJECTIVE• you are astounded when you are very surprised and shocked

♦ **astounding** •ADJECTIVE• amazing: *an astounding announcement*

astray •ADVERB• 1 to **go astray** is to go to the wrong place or in the wrong direction: *Your letter must have gone astray because it hasn't arrived yet.* 2 to **be led astray** is to start behaving badly because other people do: *Tom was led astray by a boy he met on holiday.*

astride •PREPOSITION• with one leg on each side: *sitting astride a horse*

astro- •PREFIX• if a word starts with **astro-**, it has something to do with the stars or space. For example, *astronautics* is the science of travelling in space

astrologer •NOUN• **astrologers** a person who studies the stars and suggests how their movements might affect our lives

astrology •NOUN• the study of how the stars and the way they move may affect our lives

astronaut •NOUN• **astronauts** a member of the crew of a spacecraft

astronomer •NOUN• **astronomers** a person who studies the stars

astronomical •ADJECTIVE• 1 to do with the stars: *the American Astronomical Society* 2 very large: *an astronomical number*

♦ **astronomically** •ADVERB• very much: *Prices have risen astronomically.*

astronomy •NOUN• the study of the stars and the way they move

astute •ADJECTIVE• clever in getting the best out of a situation: *We need astute players like him.*

♦ **astutely** •ADVERB• cleverly, often in a tricky situation

asylum •NOUN• 1 asylum is safety and protection, especially for people who do not feel safe in their own country: *people who seek asylum in this country* 2 an old-fashioned word for a home for people with mental illnesses

asymmetrical •ADJECTIVE• something asymmetrical has two sides of different shapes. Asymmetrical is the opposite of **symmetrical**

at •PREPOSITION• 1 showing where or when you mean: *Look at me!* • *Meet at the station.* • *School finishes at 4 o'clock.* 2 costing: *four bottles at 75p each*

ate •VERB• a way of changing the verb **eat** to make a past tense: *The dog ate most of my dinner last night.*

atheist •NOUN• **atheists** a person who does not believe in a god

♦ **atheism** •NOUN• the belief that there is no god

athlete •NOUN• **athletes** a person who is very fit and good at sport

♦ **athletic** •ADJECTIVE• 1 fit and strong in a sporty way 2 to do with the sports of running, jumping and throwing

♦ **athletics** •PLURAL NOUN• the group of sports that include running, jumping and throwing

atlas •NOUN• **atlases** a book of maps

ⓘ This word comes from the name of a character in Greek mythology, **Atlas**. He was forced by the Greek gods to carry the universe on his shoulders as a punishment.

atmosphere •NOUN• **atmospheres** 1 the air around a planet: *the Earth's atmosphere* 2 a feeling around where you are: *There was an atmosphere of excitement in the town.*

♦ **atmospheric** •ADJECTIVE• 1 to do with the air 2 with a very strong feeling in the air: *a very atmospheric experience*

atoll •NOUN• **atolls** an island made of coral

atom •NOUN• **atoms** the tiniest possible part of a substance. More than one atom can make up a **molecule**

♦ **atom bomb** or **atomic bomb** •NOUN• **atom bombs** another word for a **nuclear bomb**

♦ **atomic** •ADJECTIVE• using the power that

is created when atoms are broken: *atomic weapons*

atrocious • ADJECTIVE• very bad
♦ **atrocity** • NOUN• **atrocities** a terrible, violent crime

attach • VERB• **attaches, attaching, attached**
to attach one thing to another is to fix it there: *attached to the wall with a nail*
♦ **attached** • ADJECTIVE• if you are attached to someone, you are very fond of them
♦ **attachment** • NOUN• **attachments** 1 a friendship
2 an extra part that you can add to a machine to make it do something different: *a cutting attachment on the food mixer*
3 something like a document or picture that you send with an email message: *Save the attachment before opening it.*

attack • VERB• **attacks, attacking, attacked**
1 to attack a person is to suddenly try to hurt them: *A man was attacked and robbed on Friday.*
2 to attack a person or thing is to say bad things about them: *The newspapers have all attacked the minister's story.*
3 to attack a place is to fire at it or drop bombs on it: *The airfield is being attacked by enemy bombers.*
• NOUN• **attacks** 1 an violent act against a place or person: *an attack on the west of the city*
2 an attempt to hurt someone by writing or saying bad things about them: *an attack in the newspapers*
3 a sudden pain or illness: *an attack of hay fever*
♦ **attacker** • NOUN• **attackers** a person who tries to hurt someone violently: *He said he didn't know his attackers.*

attain • VERB• **attains, attaining, attained** to achieve something: *Penny has attained Level D this term.*
♦ **attainment** • NOUN• **attainments** 1 attainment is how much you have achieved: *an attainment test* 2 an attainment is something you have achieved

attempt • VERB• **attempt, attempting, attempted** to attempt something or to attempt to do something is to try to do it: *attempting a very steep climb to the top*

• *Nobody has ever attempted to do this before.*
• NOUN• **attempts** 1 when you make an attempt, you try to do something: *an attempt to break the record* 2 to make an attempt on someone's life is to try to kill them

attend • VERB• **attends, attending, attended**
1 to attend an event is to go to it: *Thousands of people attended the concert in the park.*
2 to **attend to** a thing is to deal with it: *I've got a lot of jobs to attend to this morning.*
3 to **attend to** a person is to do what they need you to do for them: *The doctor will attend to the children first.*
♦ **attendance** • NOUN• 1 being present somewhere: *the attendance register* 2 the number of people who are present somewhere: *poor attendance*
• **in attendance** going or being with someone: *a general with two other officers in attendance*
♦ **attendant** • NOUN• **attendants** a person whose job is to help: *a petrol pump attendant*

attention • NOUN• 1 you pay attention to something when you think about it, listen to it or look at it 2 attention is care or concentration: *medical attention* • *I found it difficult to hold the audience's attention for long.*
• **stand to attention** to stand up straight like a soldier
♦ **attentive** • ADJECTIVE• giving a lot of thought and care: *an attentive student*
♦ **attentively** • ADVERB• carefully, with a lot of consideration: *Graeme looked after me very attentively when I was ill.*

attic • NOUN• **attics** the space in the roof of a house

attitude • NOUN• **attitudes** 1 the way a person thinks about something: *John's attitude to work is not helpful.*
2 if someone has attitude, they are very confident, sometimes in a rude way
3 an attitude is a position you hold your body in: *an attitude of deep concentration*

attract • VERB• **attracts, attracting, attracted** 1 to be attracted to someone or something is to be interested in them and to like them: *The children are always attracted* to the big dipper first.

2 to attract someone's attention is to get them to look or listen: *trying to attract his attention from the other side of the room*

3 things are attracted to each other when they move towards each other without any help: *The dust is attracted to the shiny surfaces first.*

♦ **attraction** .NOUN. **attractions 1** attraction is the way things seem to pull together without any help **2** an attraction is something that you want to see or do: *What do you think are the main attractions here?*

♦ **attractive** .ADJECTIVE. **1** an attractive thing or person looks nice **2** an attractive idea sounds like a good idea

♦ **attractively** .ADVERB. in a pleasant way

aubergine .NOUN. **aubergines** an oval vegetable with a smooth, shiny, dark purple skin

auburn .ADJECTIVE. auburn hair is reddish-brown

auction .NOUN. **auctions** a sale where the person who offers the highest price for something is able to buy it
.VERB. **auctions, auctioning, auctioned** to auction something is to sell it to the person who offers the most money for it

♦ **auctioneer** .NOUN. **auctioneers** a person whose job is to sell things to the person who offers the most money for them

audacious .ADJECTIVE. brave and daring: *an audacious plan* • *an audacious young man*

♦ **audaciously** .ADVERB. in a bold, daring way

♦ **audacity** .NOUN. boldness

audible .ADJECTIVE. an audible sound can be heard easily

♦ **audibility** .NOUN. how easy something is to hear

♦ **audibly** .ADVERB. in a way that people can hear: *Douglas gulped audibly.*

audience .NOUN. **audiences 1** the people who listen to or watch a performance: *Henry was right in the audience tonight.* • *a television audience of millions* **2** an interview with an important person: *an audience with the Queen*

audio .ADJECTIVE. to do with hearing: *an audio cassette*

ⓘ **Audio** is Latin for *I hear.*

audio- .PREFIX. if a word starts with **audio-**, it has something to do with hearing. For example, an *audiologist* studies how people hear

audio-visual .ADJECTIVE. to do with both hearing and seeing: *an audio-visual presentation at the start of the museum tour*

audition .NOUN. **auditions** a short performance in front of one or more people to show what you can do: *Mum and Dad took my sister to an audition to choose the best dancers to go to ballet school.*
.VERB. **auditions, auditioning, auditioned 1** to try to get a place in a show or a musical group by showing how well you can do **2** to listen to performers and try to choose the best ones for something like a choir or play

auditorium .NOUN. **auditoriums** the part of a theatre where the audience sits

August .NOUN. the eighth month of the year, after July and before September

ⓘ **August** comes from the Latin word for this month, **Augustus**, which was named after the Roman emperor *Augustus Caesar.*

aunt .NOUN. **aunts 1** the sister of one of your parents **2** your uncle's wife

au pair .NOUN. **au pairs** a person, usually a young woman, who lives with a family in another country and works for them in return for some pocket money

aural .ADJECTIVE. to do with your ears or hearing: *We're going to have an aural comprehension test.*

♦ **aurally** .ADVERB. by hearing

austere .ADJECTIVE. **1** something that is austere looks plain, hard and dull: *an austere waiting-room* **2** a person who is austere is hard and unfriendly

♦ **austerely** .ADVERB. in a hard, cold way

♦ **austerity** .NOUN. **1** a plain, hard appearance **2** strictness

authentic .ADJECTIVE. real: *an authentic wartime uniform*

Aa Bb Cc Dd Ee Ff Gg Hh Ii Jj Kk Ll Mm Nn Oo Pp Qq Rr Ss Tt Uu Vv Ww Xx Yy Zz

♦ **authentically** • ADVERB• using real methods or equipment

♦ **authenticity** • NOUN• how real or true something is: *It's difficult to prove the authenticity of this story.*

author • NOUN• **authors** a writer of something such as a book: *Who was the author of this novel?*

authority • NOUN• **authorities** 1 authority is power and control: *You have no authority in this building.*
2 an authority is the group of people who control an activity or area: *The local authority is the district council.*
3 an authority on a subject is an expert: *She's a world authority on butterflies.*

♦ **authorize** or **authorise** • VERB• **authorizes, authorizing, authorized** 1 to give someone permission to do something: *Can you authorize us to continue?* 2 to officially allow something to happen: *The chief has authorized the use of riot police.*

♦ **authorization** or **authorisation** • NOUN• official permission for someone to do something: *You must ask the United Nations for authorization to start bombing.*

autism • NOUN• a condition where someone finds it very difficult to communicate and mix with other people and the world outside themselves

♦ **autistic** • ADJECTIVE• an autistic person suffers from autism

auto- • PREFIX• **auto-** at the start of a word means it has something to do with yourself. For example, an *autobiography* is a book about yourself that you write yourself

autobiography • NOUN• **autobiographies** the story of a person's own life

♦ **autobiographical** • ADJECTIVE• to do with a person's own life: *Many of the events in Barrie's story are autobiographical.*

autograph • NOUN• **autographs** someone's name that they wrote themselves: *Please can I have your autograph?*
• VERB• **autographs, autographing, autographed** to sign your name on something like your photograph or a book that you have written

automatic • ADJECTIVE• 1 an automatic

machine only needs to be switched on and then it works by itself: *an automatic washing machine* 2 an automatic action is something you do without thinking: *When I saw the stone coming I automatically ducked.*
• NOUN• **automatics** a machine such as a car or a rifle, that does certain things by itself

♦ **automatically** • ADVERB• working or happening without being controlled all the time

♦ **automation** • NOUN• using machines to do things instead of people

automobile • NOUN• **automobiles** the American word for a car

autopsy • NOUN• **autopsies** an examination of a dead person's body, usually to find out why they died

autumn • NOUN• **autumns** the season of the year between summer and winter when the leaves change colour and fall, and it gets dark earlier

♦ **autumnal** • ADJECTIVE• happening after summer and before winter: *trees in their autumnal colours*

auxiliary • NOUN• **auxiliaries** 1 a helper: *He's a hospital auxiliary.* 2 an auxiliary verb
• ADJECTIVE• helping, additional: *an auxiliary worker*

auxiliary verb • PART OF SPEECH• **auxiliary verbs** a short verb like *should, will* or *can* that you use with a main verb to make slight differences of meaning, for example a past tense in *Have you finished?* These words are sometimes called **helping verbs**

avail • VERB• **avails, availing, availed** if you avail yourself of something, you make good use of it: *Make sure you avail yourself of every opportunity that comes your way.*
• **to no avail** no use: *Our attempt to hide was to no avail – they spotted us immediately.*

available • ADJECTIVE• 1 if something is available, you can get it, usually by buying it
2 if someone is available, they are free to do something: *I'm sorry, Mr Wright isn't available just now.*

♦ **availability** • NOUN• 1 how possible it is to get something: *Please can you check the availablity of tickets for Thursday?* 2 how free a person is to do something

avalanche •NOUN• **avalanches** a huge amount of snow and ice sliding down the side of a mountain

avarice •NOUN• another word for greed
✦ **avaricious** •ADJECTIVE• greedy

avenge •VERB• **avenges, avenging, avenged** to punish a person for something they did to someone you care about

avenue •NOUN• **avenues** a street, usually with trees on both sides

average •NOUN• **averages** 1 the number you get if you add amounts together and then divide that total by the number of amounts: *The average of 4, 6 and 8 is 6.* 2 the normal level or standard: *We spend an average of £100 a week on food.* •ADJECTIVE• usual or ordinary: *How much do you do in an average day?*

avert •VERB• **averts, averting, averted** 1 to turn away: *Avert your eyes for a moment please.* 2 to manage to stop something happening: *desperately trying to avert war*

aviary •NOUN• **aviaries** a large cage or building for keeping birds

aviation •NOUN• flying in aircraft: *aviation fuel*

avid •ADJECTIVE• keen: *an avid reader*

avocado •NOUN• **avocados** or **avocadoes** 1 a pear-shaped fruit with dark green skin and a large stone in the middle 2 a light green colour

avoid •VERB• **avoids, avoiding, avoided** to keep out of the way of a thing or person: *avoid being seen* • *Have you been avoiding me for some reason?*
✦ **avoidable** •ADJECTIVE• something that is avoidable is not necessary or does not need to happen

await •VERB• **awaits, awaiting, awaited** to wait for a thing or person: *A surprise was awaiting me at home.*

awake •ADJECTIVE• not sleeping: *Are you still awake?*
•VERB• **awakes, awaking, awoke, awoken** to wake up: *Gloria awoke early.* • *Grandma awoke the whole family in the night.*

✦ **awaken** •VERB• **awakes, awaking, awakened** to wake up: *We were awakened by the bombs.*

award •NOUN• **awards** a prize: *Joe has won an award for being so good at basketball.* •VERB• **awards, awarding, awarded** to award someone something is to give it to them because they deserve it: *We have been awarded the title of 'School of the Year'.*

aware •ADJECTIVE• if you are **aware of** something, you know about it or know that it exists: *Derek became aware of someone else in the room.* • *I'm perfectly aware that you've been waiting a long time.*
✦ **awareness** •NOUN• realizing and understanding: *safety awareness week*

away •ADVERB• 1 somewhere else: *Go away!* • *Throw that away.*
2 at a distance: *How far away is the school?* • *only a week away*
3 in the opposite direction: *Peter turned away.* • *Remember what you take out and please make sure you put everything away again.*
4 continuously: *working away all night*
•ADJECTIVE• an away game or match is one your team has to travel to. Look up and compare **home**.
• **right away** immediately

awe •NOUN• a feeling that a thing or person is wonderful but a little frightening: *Freddie and Bob looked at their hero in awe.*
✦ **awesome** •ADJECTIVE• 1 very good or impressive 2 making you feel very small and scared: *the awesome possibility of war*
✦ **awestruck** •ADJECTIVE• filled with feelings of wonder mixed with fear

awful •ADJECTIVE• 1 very bad: *an awful headache* 2 very great: *That won't make an awful lot of difference.*
✦ **awfully** •ADVERB• 1 very: *It's an awfully long way.* 2 very badly: *We played awfully.*

awkward •ADJECTIVE• 1 difficult to manage or use: *That's an awkward question.* • *I find this keyboard a bit awkward.*
2 someone who is being awkward is not being helpful: *Just stop being awkward and say you'll come.*
3 if you feel awkward, you feel

awl → azure

uncomfortable or embarrassed: *I began to feel awkward when they started to talk about me.*

♦ **awkwardly** • ADVERB• in a difficult or uncomfortable way

awl • NOUN• **awls** a small metal tool with a point for making holes, for example, in leather

awning • NOUN• **awnings** a cover like a soft roof that protects something from rain or sun

awoke • VERB• a way of changing the verb **awake** to make a past tense: *I awoke next morning to the sound of birds singing.*

axe • NOUN• **axes** a tool for chopping wood • VERB• **axes, axing, axed** 1 if a plan or service is axed, it is stopped 2 if jobs are axed, the people doing them are no longer needed

axis • NOUN• **axes** 1 the line through something like a planet that it seems to spin around 2 in a graph, the line up the side or along the bottom that you measure against

axle • NOUN• **axles** in a vehicle, an axle is a rod that has a wheel at each end

aye • INTERJECTION• another word for **yes**

ayatollah • NOUN• **ayatollahs** a Muslim religious leader in Iran

azalea • NOUN• **azaleas** a bush that has bright white, cream or pink flowers

azure • NOUN• the blue colour of the sky

babble .VERB. **babbles, babbling, babbled**
1 to talk or say something quickly without making very much sense: *Carol babbled something about having to be somewhere, and hurried off.* **2** running water babbles when it makes a pleasant bubbling sound: *The stream babbled and sparkled as it flowed over the rocks.*

baboon .NOUN. **baboons** a type of large monkey with a long pointed nose and long teeth, found in Africa and parts of Asia

baby .NOUN. **babies 1** a very young child **2** an older child or an adult who is crying or behaving like a baby: *Don't be such a baby, it's only a little spider.*
.ADJECTIVE. very young: *a baby elephant*
◆ **babyish** .ADJECTIVE. **1** like a baby: *He had a smooth babyish face.* **2** suitable for babies or younger children: *This game is probably too babyish for ten-year-olds.*

babysit .VERB. **babysits, babysitting, babysat** to look after a baby or a child when its parents are out: *My older cousin sometimes babysits for Mum in the evenings.* • *Would you babysit the boys next Saturday?*
◆ **babysitter** .NOUN. **babysitters** someone who looks after a baby or a child when its parents are out

bachelor .NOUN. **bachelors** a man who has never married

ⓘ Remember there is no **t** before the **c** in **bachelor**.

back .NOUN. **backs 1** the back of something is the side that is opposite to or furthest away from its front: *She hid her diary at the back of a drawer.*
2 the part of your body that stretches from the back of your neck to your bottom: *I always sleep on my back.*
3 in football and hockey, a back is a player who mostly tries to stop the other team scoring a goal. Look up and compare **forward**

• **put someone's back up** to put someone's back up is to annoy them: *Don't be so cheeky. You'll put Dad's back up and he won't let us go out.*
.ADJECTIVE. behind or opposite the front: *He's had one of his back teeth out.*
.ADVERB. **1** farther away in distance: *Stand back and make more room.*
2 to the place, person or state from which someone or something came: *We won't be able to get there and back in a day.* • *I lent him my book and he hasn't given it back yet.*
3 in or to an earlier time: *Think back and try to remember exactly what happened.*
.VERB. **backs, backing, backed 1** to move backwards: *When he saw what was in the box, he backed away in fear.*
2 to back someone is to give them support or help, often money: *It's a great invention and I'm sure you'll soon find someone to back you.*
3 someone **backs down** when they admit they are beaten or have lost an argument: *He knows he can't win, but he's still refusing to back down.*
4 to **back up** computer information is to make a separate copy of it so that the information is not lost if the computer breaks down

backbone .NOUN. **backbones** the row of bones down the middle of your back that forms your spine

backfire .VERB. **backfires, backfiring, backfired 1** if a motor vehicle backfires, its fuel burns too soon and causes a loud bang in its exhaust pipe **2** if a plan backfires, it goes wrong

backgammon .NOUN. a game where you throw dice and move round pieces on a patterned board

background .NOUN. **backgrounds 1** the part of a picture behind the main figures: *white flowers on a green background*

Aa

Bb

Cc

Dd

Ee

Ff

Gg

Hh

Ii

Jj

Kk

Ll

Mm

Nn

Oo

Pp

Qq

Rr

Ss

Tt

Uu

Vv

Ww

Xx

Yy

Zz

• *Here's a photo of us with Ben Nevis in the background.*
2 a person's background is their family, the kind of life they have had, and the things they have done in the past: *children from poorer backgrounds* • *He has an army background.*
3 the background of an event is anything that happened before that helps to explain how the event came about: *the background to the English Civil War*

backhand • NOUN• in games like tennis or squash, a way of hitting the ball by holding the racket across the front of the body with the back of the hand facing towards the ball

backstroke • NOUN• a way of swimming where you lie on your back, kick your legs and swing your arms backwards over your shoulders

backward • ADJECTIVE• **1** facing or aimed towards the back: *a backward look* **2** slow to learn or develop
• ADVERB• backwards: *She was looking backward over her shoulder.*

backwards • ADVERB• **1** in the direction opposite to the one you are facing: *Stepping backwards without looking, he fell down the manhole.*
2 towards the past: *If we move further backwards in time, we come to the age of the dinosaurs.*
3 in the opposite way to the usual way: *He can say the alphabet backwards.*

bacon • NOUN• salted meat from a pig, usually eaten in thin strips called rashers

bacteria • NOUN• very small creatures living in air, water, living animals and plants, and in dead and decaying things. Some types of bacteria can cause diseases or illness in humans and animals

ⓘ **Bacteria** is the plural of **bacterium**. The singular, **bacterium**, is not often used. Because **bacteria** is the plural it should be used with a plural verb:
✓ *The bacteria* **have** *not been identified.*
✗ *The bacteria* **has** *not been identified.*

bad • ADJECTIVE• **worse, worst 1** wicked or naughty: *Tony and Harry have been very*

bad boys today. • *Don't jump up on me, you bad dog!*
2 not of a good standard: *His handwriting is bad, and his spelling is worse.*
3 nasty or upsetting: *a bad storm* • *very bad news*
4 harmful to your health: *Eating too many fatty foods can be bad for you.*
5 if someone is bad at doing something they do not do it well: *I'm very bad at maths.*
6 something is bad or has gone bad if it is rotten or decaying: *Don't eat that pear – it's bad.* • *Your teeth will go bad if you don't brush them regularly.*
• **not bad** or **not too bad** you say 'not bad' or 'not too bad' to mean quite good: *'How are you feeling today?' 'Not too bad, thanks.'*
⇒ **badly**

ⓘ Comparing how **bad** things are: *The weather was* **bad** *yesterday, but it was* **worse** *the day before, and last Friday was* **worst** *of all.*

bade • VERB• a way of changing the verb **bid²** to make a past tense

badge • NOUN• **badges** a small object with words or pictures printed on it that you pin or sew on to your clothing to show, for example, that you are a member of a group or club

badger • NOUN• **badgers** an animal with a pointed black-and-white striped face and grey fur on the rest of its body. Badgers live underground and come out at night to feed

badly • ADVERB• **1** not well: *The work was done very badly.*
2 seriously: *The car was badly damaged in the crash.*
3 very much: *I badly wanted a new pair of trainers.*

badminton • NOUN• a game in which two or four players use rackets to hit a light object called a shuttlecock across a net

bad-tempered • ADJECTIVE• speaking or behaving angrily or rudely: *Perhaps you wouldn't be so bad-tempered in the morning if you got more sleep.*

baffle • VERB• **baffles, baffling, baffled** if a problem baffles you, you cannot work out what it is about or how to solve it : *The robbers tried to baffle the local police by leaving false clues.*

◆ **baffling** •ADJECTIVE• puzzling: *a baffling problem*

bag •NOUN• **bags** an object made of paper, plastic, cloth or leather used to carry things in • **bags of** an informal way of saying there is a lot of something: *We've got bags of time before the bus comes.*
•VERB• **bags, bagging, bagged** to put things into a bag or bags: *We helped Dad bag all the garden rubbish.*

bagful •NOUN• **bagfuls** the amount that a bag holds: *He's eaten four or five bagfuls of crisps.*

baggage •NOUN• the cases and bags that a person takes with them when they travel: *The passengers' baggage is carried in the back of the bus.*

baggy •ADJECTIVE• **baggier, baggiest** baggy clothes are too big for the person wearing them and hang loosely from their body: *I like wearing baggy jumpers because they're comfortable.*

bagpipes •PLURAL NOUN• bagpipes are a musical instrument made up of a cloth or leather bag with pipes attached to it

baguette •NOUN• **baguettes** a long narrow loaf of French bread, also called a **French stick**

ⓘ This word is said as **bag-ett**.

bail[1] •NOUN• money that has to be paid to a court so that someone who has been arrested for a crime can be let out of prison until their trial
•VERB• **bails, bailing, bailed** a prisoner is bailed or **bailed out** when a sum of money is paid to the court and they are set free until their trial

ⓘ Be careful not to confuse the spellings or meanings of **bail** and **bale**.

bail[2] •NOUN• **bails** on a cricket wicket, the bails are the short pieces of wood that lie across the top of the stumps

bairn •NOUN• **bairns** a Scottish word for child

bait •NOUN• food put on a hook to catch fish or put in a trap to catch animals
•VERB• **baits, baiting, baited** to bait a hook or trap is to put food on it to attract and catch fish or animals

bake •VERB• **bakes, baking, baked** 1 to cook something such as a cake or bread in an oven: *Mum does a lot of cooking but she doesn't bake very often.*
2 to bake food is to cook it in an oven: *Bake the lasagne in a medium oven until it is golden brown.*
3 to bake things that are soft is to harden them in the sun or in an oven: *The bricks have to be baked before they can be used to build with.*

baker •NOUN• **bakers** 1 someone who bakes bread and cakes: *My grandma is a brilliant baker.* 2 a baker's is a shop selling freshly baked bread and cakes

bakery •NOUN• **bakeries** a shop or factory where bread and cakes are made

balaclava or **balaklava** •NOUN• **balaclavas** or **balaklavas** a kind of knitted hat that covers the head and neck but not the top half of the face

balance •NOUN• 1 you have your balance if you are in a steady enough position not to fall: *I lost my balance and fell over.* 2 the balance of a bank or building society account is the amount of money in it
•VERB• **balances, balancing, balanced** 1 to balance something is to make or keep it steady: *She balanced it on her head.* 2 to balance the books is to make sure that the amount of money spent isn't bigger than the amount received

balcony •NOUN• **balconies** 1 a platform built out from the wall of a building, usually with a railing around it 2 the balcony in a theatre or cinema is an area upstairs where the seats are above the rest of the audience

bald •ADJECTIVE• **balder, baldest** 1 someone who is bald has very little or no hair: *His uncle is completely bald.* 2 something that is bald has very little covering: *We'll have to hide that bald patch in the middle of the rug somehow.*
◆ **balding** •ADJECTIVE• going bald: *a*

Aa

balding elderly gentleman
* **baldness** .NOUN. being bald

Bb

bale¹ .NOUN. **bales** a bundle of hay, cloth or paper that has been tied up tightly

Cc

.VERB. **bales, baling, baled** to bale hay, cloth or paper is to tie it tightly in bundles

Dd

bale² .VERB. **bales, baling, baled** to **bale out** of a dangerous place or an emergency situation is to escape from it: *The pilot had to bale out of the burning aeroplane and parachute to the ground.*

Ee

Ff

Gg

ball¹ .NOUN. **balls 1** a round object that you use for playing games like football, hockey, cricket and tennis **2** anything that has a round or roundish shape: *a ball of string* * *The hedgehog had rolled itself into a tight ball.*

Hh

Ii

Jj

* **on the ball** if someone is on the ball they are alert and quick to act

Kk

ball² .NOUN. **balls** a big formal party where people dance: *Cinderella couldn't go to the ball.*

Ll

Mm

* **have a ball** to have a ball is to have a very good time

Nn

ballad .NOUN. **ballads** a poem or song that tells a story, often about love

Oo

ball bearings .PLURAL NOUN. small metal balls that are placed in grooves in some machine parts and allow the parts to move easily over each other

Pp

Qq

ballerina .NOUN. **ballerinas** a female ballet dancer

Rr

ballet .NOUN. **ballets 1** a type of dancing that uses graceful steps and movements: *Emily prefers ballet to tap dancing.* **2** a ballet is a story told using dance: *My favourite ballets are The Nutcracker and Swan Lake.*

Ss

Tt

Uu

balloon .NOUN. **balloons** a very light object made of thin rubber that expands and floats when it is filled with air or gas
.VERB. **balloons, ballooning, ballooned** to balloon is to expand or swell like a balloon does when it is filled with air or gas: *The sail ballooned out in the breeze.*

Vv

Ww

Xx

Yy

ballot .NOUN. **ballots** a way of voting in secret by marking a paper and putting it into a special box
.VERB. **ballots, balloting, balloted** to ballot

Zz

a group of people is to get votes from them by ballot: *The workers were balloted and voted to strike.*

ballpoint or **ballpoint pen** .NOUN. **ballpoints** or **ballpoint pens** a pen with a small circular metal tip

balm .NOUN. a soothing ointment used to help heal burns and damaged skin
* **balmy** .ADJECTIVE. **balmier, balmiest** warm and soothing: *hot days followed by balmy nights*

balsa or **balsa wood** .NOUN. a very light wood that is often used to make model boats and aircraft

bamboo .NOUN. **bamboos** a type of Asian grass that can grow very tall and has hard round hollow stems

bamboozle .VERB. **bamboozle, bamboozling, bamboozled** to bamboozle someone is to confuse or trick them: *The instructions for the video completely bamboozled me.*

ban .VERB. **bans, banning, banned** to ban something is to not allow it: *Cycling is banned in the park.*
.NOUN. **bans** an order that something is not allowed: *a ban on smoking.*

banana .NOUN. **bananas** a long, yellow, very soft fruit that you peel to eat and that grows in hot countries

band .NOUN. **bands 1** a strip of material to put round something: *a rubber band* * *a headband*
2 a stripe: *a broad band of colour*
3 a group: *a band of robbers*
4 a group of musicians who play together: *My big brother has formed a rock band with some of his school friends.*
.VERB. **bands, banding, banded** to **band together** is to join together to do something as a group: *All the parents banded together to campaign for a new school crossing.*

bandage .NOUN. **bandages** a strip of cloth for wrapping round a part of your body that has been cut or hurt
.VERB. **bandages, bandaging, bandaged** to bandage a part of the body is to wrap it in a bandage

bandit • NOUN• **bandits** an armed criminal who attacks and robs travellers

bandwagon • NOUN• people who **jump** or **climb on the bandwagon** join something only because it is fashionable or successful, not because it is right or worthwhile

bandy • ADJECTIVE• **bandier, bandiest** bandy legs curve outwards at the knees

bane • NOUN• the **bane of your life** is the thing that most annoys you or that causes you the most trouble: *Hay fever is the bane of my life.*

bang • NOUN• **bangs 1** a sudden loud noise: *There was a loud bang and all the lights went out.* **2** a hard knock: *She's had a bang on the head and is feeling a bit dizzy.*
• **go with a bang** if a party or other event goes with a bang everyone there has a very good time
• VERB• **bangs, banging, banged 1** a door or window bangs when it closes or is shut roughly so that it makes a loud noise: *The door banged shut in the wind.* **2** to bang something is to knock it hard against something else: *Neil banged his books down on the table.*

banger • NOUN• **bangers 1** a type of firework that makes loud banging noises when it is set off
2 a sausage: *bangers and mash*
3 a rusty car that is falling to pieces

bangle • NOUN• **bangles** a ring of metal, wood or plastic that you wear on your wrist

banish • VERB• **banishes, banishing, banished 1** to banish someone is to make them leave the country or their home as a punishment **2** to banish a feeling is to make it go away: *His exam results banished any doubts about his ability.*
♦ **banishment** • NOUN• being banished

banisters • PLURAL NOUN• the rail and its supports that you hold on to as you go up and down stairs

banjo • NOUN• **banjos** or **banjoes** an instrument with a round body and a long neck which you play by plucking the strings

bank • NOUN• **banks 1** a business that looks after and lends money: *Most people keep* their money in a bank for safety. • *I have to go to the bank this morning.*
2 a place where a particular thing is stored so that it can be used later: *a computer data bank* • *a blood bank*
3 the banks of a river or a lake are the areas of ground beside it: *We camped on the banks of Loch Lomond.*
4 a mound or a raised area of ground: *There's a steep wooded bank behind the house.*
• VERB• **banks, banking, banked 1** to bank money is to put it in a bank: *I'm going to spend half this £20 and bank the rest.*
2 if you **bank on** something you depend on it: *You can't bank on the weather staying dry, so take an umbrella.*
3 an aeroplane banks when it tips over to one side as it changes direction

banker • NOUN• **bankers** someone who runs a business that looks after and lends money

bank holiday • NOUN• **bank holidays** a public holiday when the banks are closed

banking • NOUN• the business that banks do

banknote • NOUN• **banknotes** a piece of paper money issued by a bank

bankrupt • ADJECTIVE• a person or a business is bankrupt or goes bankrupt if they are not able to pay the money they owe: *The business went bankrupt when it started to sell less.*
♦ **bankruptcy** • NOUN• **bankruptcies** being bankrupt: *The business is facing bankruptcy.* • *The number of bankruptcies went up last year.*

banner • NOUN• **banners** a large piece of cloth with printing or writing on it which is carried on poles

banquet • NOUN• **banquets** a formal dinner that is attended by a lot of people and where guests often make speeches and toasts

ⓘ **Banquet** is a French word, which in turn comes from an Italian word which means a *little bench.* This is because of the benches which people put around a table when they were eating a meal.

ⓘ This word is pronounced **bang**-kwit.

banter •NOUN• banter is talk where people tease each other in fun or make funny remarks to each other

baptism •NOUN• **baptisms** a Christian ceremony where someone has water sprinkled on their head as a sign they are to become part of the Church

baptize or **baptise** •VERB• **baptizes, baptizing, baptized** to baptize someone is to make them part of the Christian Church by the ceremony of sprinkling water on their head

bar •NOUN• **bars** 1 a piece of hard material: *an iron bar* 2 a bar of something is a solid piece of it: *a bar of soap* 3 a broad line or band: *a brown bird with black bars on its wings* 4 a room or counter serving drinks or food: *a burger bar* 5 one of the sections of equal time into which a piece of music is divided: *four beats to the bar* •VERB• **bars, barring, barred** 1 to bar a door, a window or a gate is to put metal or wooden bars across it so that no one can get in or out 2 if people are barred from a place or from doing something they are not allowed in or are not allowed to do it: *Anyone over the age of 12 is barred from the competition.*

barb •NOUN• **barbs** a point on an arrowhead or a fish hook that faces backwards and makes the arrow or hook stick firmly

barbarian •NOUN• **barbarians** a savage or uncivilized person

barbaric •ADJECTIVE• cruel or uncivilized: *a barbaric custom*

barbecue •NOUN• **barbecues** 1 a grill used for cooking food outdoors 2 an outdoor party where food is grilled on a barbecue •VERB• **barbecues, barbecuing, barbecued** to barbecue food is to grill it on a barbecue

barbed wire •NOUN• wire that has sharp spikes twisted round it. Barbed wire is used on walls and fences to stop people and animals climbing over

barber •NOUN• **barbers** 1 a man who cuts men's hair 2 a barber's is a shop where men have their hair cut: *Dad's just been to the barber's.*

bar chart •NOUN• **bar charts** a diagram in which various amounts are shown using coloured or shaded blocks of different heights

bar code •NOUN• **bar codes** a code made up of lines and spaces which is printed on an item for sale so that it can be identified by a computer

bare •ADJECTIVE• **barer, barest** naked or without any covering: *It's a bit too cold to be going out with bare legs.* • *Without the posters on the walls the bedroom looks really bare.*

barefaced •ADJECTIVE• something that is barefaced is done without feeling any guilt or embarrassment: *a barefaced lie*

barely •ADVERB• hardly or almost not: *They had barely arrived when they had to leave again.* • *The truck barely avoided hitting us when it skidded across the road.*

bargain •NOUN• **bargains** 1 an agreement people make between themselves 2 if something is a bargain it is cheap or cheaper than usual: *These jeans were a real bargain.* • **into the bargain** as well or besides: *It's a good warm jacket and waterproof into the bargain.* •VERB• **bargains, bargaining, bargained** to bargain is to argue about the price you will pay for something • **get more than you bargain for** if you get more than you bargain for, you get something extra, usually something bad, that you didn't expect

barge •NOUN• **barges** a flat-bottomed boat used on canals and rivers •VERB• **barges, barging, barged** 1 to barge into a place or a person is to rush, push or bump into them clumsily: *He barged into the room knocking all the books over as he came.* 2 to barge against people or barge through a crowd is to push against or through them roughly and rudely: *He barged past us to get to the front of the queue.*

baritone •NOUN• **baritones** 1 a male singing voice between the lowest and highest pitch 2 a man with this singing voice

bark¹ • NOUN• **barks** the short loud sound that a dog or fox makes
• VERB• **barks, barking, barked** 1 animals bark when they make this sound 2 if a person barks they speak loudly and sharply: *'Hurry up, you lot!' he barked.*
• **bark up the wrong tree** if someone barks up the wrong tree they make a mistake that leads them to think something that is not correct

bark² • NOUN• the bark of a tree is the rough outer covering of its trunk and branches

barley • NOUN• a grain used for food and for making beer

barman • NOUN• **barmen** a man who serves drinks at a bar

bar mitzvah • NOUN• **bar mitzvahs** a religious ceremony for Jewish boys to mark the time, at about age 13, when they are expected to take some of the responsibilities of an adult

barn • NOUN• **barns** a large building on a farm for storing grain or hay

barnacle • NOUN• **barnacles** a type of small shellfish that fastens itself on to rocks and the bottoms of boats

barometer • NOUN• **barometers** an instrument for measuring the pressure of air and showing changes in the weather

baron • NOUN• **barons** a type of nobleman

baroness • NOUN• **baronesses** a female baron or a baron's wife: *Baroness Thatcher*

barracks • NOUN• **barracks** a place where soldiers live or are based

barracuda • NOUN• **barracudas** a large fierce sea fish with big teeth, found in the Caribbean and other warm seas

barrel • NOUN• **barrels** 1 a wooden or metal container with curved sides used for holding liquids like beer and wine 2 the barrel of a gun is the metal tube through which the shot or bullet is fired

barren • ADJECTIVE• a barren landscape has very little or nothing growing on it

barricade • NOUN• **barricades** a barrier put up in a street to stop people passing through
• VERB• **barricades, barricading, barricaded** to barricade a place is to put up a barrier to stop people getting in or passing through

barrier • NOUN• **barriers** 1 a gate or fence used to stop people getting past 2 a barrier is anything that stops you getting ahead: *Nowadays, being a girl isn't any barrier to a career in the navy.*

barrister • NOUN• **barristers** a lawyer who presents people's cases in court

barrow • NOUN• **barrows** a type of small cart

barter • VERB• **barters, bartering, bartered** to give one thing in exchange for another, without using any money

base • NOUN• **bases** 1 the surface or part on which a thing rests: *a bronze statue on a black marble base* 2 the lowest part of something: *the base of the mountain*
• VERB• **bases, basing, based** to base one thing on another is to create it using the other thing as a foundation: *a story based on fact*

ⓘ Though the words **base** and **bass** sound the same, remember that they have different spellings.

baseball • NOUN• **baseballs** 1 a game played with a long rounded bat and a ball by two teams of nine players 2 a baseball is a small ball used in the game of baseball

bases • NOUN• the plural form of **basis** and **base**

bash • VERB• **bashes, bashing, bashed** to bash something is to hit it hard: *The door closed suddenly and bashed me on the nose.*
• NOUN• **bashes** a hard hit: *He gave the nail a couple of good bashes.*
• **have a bash** to have a bash is to have a try: *I don't know exactly how to do it, but I'll have a bash at it anyway.*

basic • ADJECTIVE• 1 basic describes things that are at the most essential or simple: *basic driving skills*
2 something is basic if it does not include anything unnecessary or too fancy: *The cottage was pretty basic – it didn't even have a proper bath.*
• **the basics** the basics are the most essential

Aa
Bb
Cc
Dd
Ee
Ff
Gg
Hh
Ii
Jj
Kk
Ll
Mm
Nn
Oo
Pp
Qq
Rr
Ss
Tt
Uu
Vv
Ww
Xx
Yy
Zz

or important facts, skills or knowledge you need to have about a subject: *To be a good writer you need to know the basics of grammar and punctuation.*

basically .ADVERB. in the most important or essential way: *He's basically a good person.*

ⓘ Remember the correct spelling:
✓ basic**ally**
✗ basicly

basil .NOUN. a herb with sweet-smelling leaves that are used in cookery

basin .NOUN. **basins** 1 a sink for washing your hands and face in 2 a bowl used in the kitchen for holding liquids or food: *a pudding basin* 3 an area of land from which water flows into a river: *the Amazon basin*

basis .NOUN. **bases** the basis of something is what it is built on or what it is based on: *They've always been on a very friendly basis until now.*

bask .VERB. **basks, basking, basked** 1 to bask is to sit or lie enjoying warmth: *We basked in the warm sunshine.* 2 to bask in other people's praise or attention is to enjoy it: *He'd scored the winning goal and was basking in the admiration of his friends.*

basket .NOUN. **baskets** a container made of strips of wood or canes woven together

basketball .NOUN. **basketballs** 1 a game played by two teams who try to score points by throwing a ball through a hoop fixed high above the ground on a post 2 a basketball is a large ball used to play basketball

bass .NOUN. **basses** 1 in music, the bass is the lowest range of notes 2 a musical instrument with a low tone, such as a bass guitar or double bass 3 a man with the deepest kind of singing or speaking voice .ADJECTIVE. of or making the lowest range of musical notes: *singing the bass part*

bass clef .NOUN. **bass clefs** a musical sign that shows you that the pitch of the following notes should be bass

bassoon .NOUN. **bassoons** a long wooden

instrument that makes a low sound when it is blown into

bat[1] .NOUN. **bats** a shaped piece of wood that you use to hit the ball in games like cricket and baseball • **off your own bat** if you do something off your own bat you do it without anyone telling you that you have to do it .VERB. **bats, batting, batted** to bat is to use the bat in games like cricket and rounders: *It's Gary to bat next.*

bat[2] .NOUN. **bats** a flying animal that comes out at night to feed

batch .NOUN. **batches** 1 a number of things, especially pieces of food, all made at one time: *a batch of scones* 2 a group of people that arrive or are dealt with at one time: *A new batch of hotel guests arrives tomorrow.*

bated .ADJECTIVE. if you are waiting **with bated breath** you are excited or anxious to find out what will happen next: *We were all waiting with bated breath to see how the film would end.*

ⓘ Try not to confuse the spelling of **bated** with **baited**, the past tense form of **bait**.

bath .NOUN. **baths** 1 a bath is a large container that you fill with water and sit in to wash yourself: *You're filthy! When did you last have a bath?* 2 baths are a building which contains a public swimming pool: *I learnt to swim in the local baths.* .VERB. **baths, bathing, bathed** to bath someone is to wash them in a bath: *Will you bath the baby for me, please?*

bathe .VERB. **bathes, bathing, bathed** 1 to wash yourself in a bath 2 to swim in water: *They always bathe in the sea before breakfast.* 3 you bathe a sore part of your body when you wash it gently with water or some other liquid: *I'm going to bathe my aching feet as soon as I get home.*

bathroom .NOUN. **bathrooms** a room for washing yourself in, usually containing a bath or a shower, a washbasin and a lavatory

bat mitzvah .NOUN. **bat mitzvahs** a religious ceremony for Jewish girls to mark the time, at about age 12, when they are

50

expected to start taking some of the responsibilites of an adult

baton • NOUN• **batons** a short thin stick used, for example, by someone who is conducting music or by runners in a relay race

batsman • NOUN• **batsmen** a man who bats in cricket

battalion • NOUN• **battalions** a large group of soldiers that are part of a regiment

batten • VERB• **battens, battening, battened** to **batten something down** is to fasten it down firmly and make it secure: *He'd battened down the edges of the tent to stop them flapping in the wind.*

batter • VERB• **batters, battering, battered** to hit something hard over and over again: *The rain battered down on the metal roof.*
• NOUN• batter is a mixture of flour, milk and eggs used to coat fish and other food before it is fried in oil

battering ram • NOUN• **battering rams** a large heavy log hit against a door or gate to break it down

battery • NOUN• **batteries** 1 a device used to supply electrical power to things like watches, cameras and car engines: *Did you remember to buy new batteries for the torch? • The car wouldn't start because its battery was flat.* 2 a set of cages that hens are kept in so that their eggs can be collected easily

battle • NOUN• **battles** 1 a fight between two armies: *the Battle of Hastings* 2 any fight or struggle: *It's always been a bit of a battle to get him to do his homework.*
• VERB• **battles, battling, battled** to battle is to fight or struggle: *The ship battled bravely through the storm.*

battlements • PLURAL NOUN• a wall around the top of a castle or fort that has spaces cut in it for the people inside to shoot at people outside

battleship • NOUN• **battleships** a very large ship that has big guns and is used in naval battles

bauble • NOUN• **baubles** a shiny or glittery decoration

bawl • VERB• **bawls, bawling, bawled** to cry or shout very loudly: *You'll have to bawl at*

him to make him hear you.

ⓘ Try not to confuse **bawl** and **ball**, which sound the same when you say them.

bay • NOUN• **bays** 1 a piece of land on the coast or on the shore of a lake that bends inwards: *the Bay of Biscay* 2 an area that is marked out for a particular use: *a loading bay*
• **at bay** If you keep something at bay you do not let it come near you or harm you: *Vitamin C helps to keep colds at bay.*

bayonet • NOUN• **bayonets** a long sharp blade that can be fixed on to the end of a soldier's rifle

bazaar • NOUN• **bazaars** 1 an event when goods are sold to raise money, especially for a good cause 2 a type of Middle Eastern market, usually with small shops or stalls selling different goods

ⓘ This word comes from the Persian word **bazar**, which means *market*.

BC • ABBREVIATION• short for **before Christ**. BC is added after a date to show that the date was before the birth of Jesus Christ, for example, *450 BC*

ⓘ **AD** is the abbreviation used with dates after the birth of Christ.

be • VERB• 1 to be is to exist: *There may be a very good reason for it.*
2 to be something is to have that position or to do that job: *What do you want to be when you grow up?*
3 to be a particular thing is to have that feeling or quality: *Try to be happy.* • *We can't all be as clever as you.*

ⓘ There are many different forms of the verb **be**.
If you are talking about something that is happening at this very time, you use the present tense forms. These are *I* **am**, *you* or *they* **are**, *he*, *she*, or *it* **is**.
You can also say *I* **am being**, *you*, *we*, or *they* **are being**, *he*, *she*, or *it* **is being**.
If you are talking about something that was the case in the past, you use the past tense forms. These are *I*, *he*, *she*, or *it* **was**, *you*, *we*,

Aa

Bb

Cc

Dd

Ee

Ff

Gg

Hh

Ii

Jj

Kk

Ll

Mm

Nn

Oo

Pp

Qq

Rr

Ss

Tt

Uu

Vv

Ww

Xx

Yy

Zz

or *they* **were**.
You can also say *I, you, we,* or *they* **have been**, *he, she,* or *it* **has been**.

beach •NOUN• **beaches** the shore of the sea, especially an area of sand or pebbles that have been left on the shore by the waves

beacon •NOUN• **beacons** a light or a fire that can be seen from a long distance away and acts as a warning or a signal

bead •NOUN• **beads 1** a small round piece of glass, plastic or wood with a hole through the middle, used to make necklaces or sewn on to clothes as decoration **2** a round drop of liquid: *There were beads of sweat on his forehead.*

beady •ADJECTIVE• **beadier, beadiest** beady eyes are round and shiny

beagle •NOUN• **beagles** a type of dog with a black, white and brown coat and long ears

beak •NOUN• **beaks** a bird's beak is the hard, pointed part of its mouth that it uses to pick up food

beaker •NOUN• **beakers 1** a straight glass or plastic container, used in laboratories **2** a type of drinking cup, usually without a handle

beam •NOUN• **beams 1** a long thick piece of wood or metal used to support a building or bridge **2** a line of light
•VERB• **beams, beaming, beamed 1** to shine: *The sun beamed down all day.* **2** if someone beams they smile broadly

bean •NOUN• **beans** a type of seed that grows in a pod and is eaten as a vegetable
• **full of beans** if someone is full of beans they have lots of energy

bear[1] •NOUN• **bears** a large heavy animal with a thick coat and hooked claws

bear[2] •VERB• **bears, bearing, bore, born** *or* **borne 1** to bear something is to put up with it: *She couldn't bear the cold winters.*
• *Stephen just can't bear to part with his old toys.*
2 to bear something is to carry it or have it: *Hassan appeared, bearing a steaming cup.*
• *The door bore the family's name.*
3 women bear children and animals bear young when they give birth to them

• **bear in mind** if you bear something in mind you remember that it is important: *Please bear in mind that you only have an hour to write your essay.*
◆ **bearable** •ADJECTIVE• if something is bearable you are able to put up with it: *'Is the pain bad?' 'Just now it's bearable.'*

ⓘ If you are talking about the birth of a child or young animal, you use the spelling **born**: *He was born at midnight on New Year's Eve.* If you mean that something is carried, or someone has put up with something, or a woman has given birth to a child, you use the spelling **borne**: *She had borne five children.*
• *I couldn't have borne much more of the heat.*
• *The seeds are borne on the wind.*

beard •NOUN• **beards** the hair that grows on a man's chin and cheeks: *He'd shaved off his beard.*
◆ **bearded** •ADJECTIVE• having a beard: *a tall bearded man*

bearing •NOUN• **bearings 1** a person's bearing is the way they behave, especially the way they stand and walk: *a old gentleman with a dignified bearing* **2** something that has a bearing on a situation affects it in some way: *His age will have a bearing on how quickly he recovers from his illness.*
• **get your bearings** to get your bearings is to find your way or to find out where you are
• **lose your bearings** if you lose your bearings you lose your way and don't know where you are

beast •NOUN• **beasts 1** a four-footed animal: *the beasts of the field* **2** a cruel or nasty person: *Don't do that, you beast!*
◆ **beastly** •ADJECTIVE• **beastlier, beastliest** horrible or nasty: *Stop being so beastly to your little brother.*

beat •VERB• **beats, beating, beat, beaten**
1 to hit over and over again: *He beat his fists on the table.*
2 to **beat someone up** is to injure them by hitting them over and over again
3 to beat someone is to defeat them or win against them: *Do you think Manchester United can beat Real Madrid?*

4 to make a regular sound or movement: *He could hear his heart beating.*

5 to beat food is to stir or mix it by making quick regular movements through it with a spoon, fork or whisk

•NOUN• **beats 1** a beat is a regular sound or movement like that made by your heart or your pulse: *A low moan from nearby made my heart skip a beat.*

2 music with a beat has a regular rhythm

3 a police officer's beat is the regular route he or she takes around an area

beautiful •ADJECTIVE• **1** a beautiful person is very pretty or handsome

2 very pleasant to see, hear or smell: *a beautiful sunset • a beautiful voice • a rose with a beautiful scent*

3 the weather is beautiful when it is very pleasant, especially if it is bright, dry and sunny: *It's a beautiful morning.*

♦ **beautifully** •ADVERB• in a beautiful way: *She is always beautifully dressed.*

ⓘ Remember that beautiful starts **b-e-a-u**.

beauty •NOUN• **beauties 1** beauty is the quality of being very attractive, and pleasant to see or hear: *the beauty of the alpine scenery*

2 a person who is beautiful to look at: *Her grandmother was a famous beauty.*

3 something you think is excellent: *Just look at the fish he caught. Isn't it a beauty?*

beaver •NOUN• **beavers 1** an animal with a soft brown coat and a large flat tail that lives in dams built across rivers using tree branches **2** a beaver is a member of the most junior branch of the Scout Association

•VERB• **beavers, beavering, beavered** to **beaver away** is to work very hard: *Sanjay's been beavering away at that science project for days now.*

became •VERB• a way of changing the verb **become** to make a past tense

because •CONJUNCTION• for the reason that: • *You can't borrow my bike because there's something wrong with the brakes.* • *Just because it's raining, it doesn't mean you should do nothing all day.* • **because of** as a result of: *Because of the school holidays, the return match*

will be delayed for a fortnight.

beckon •VERB• **beckons, beckoning, beckoned** to beckon to someone is to make a sign with your hand to show them that you want them to come nearer: *The teacher beckoned to the pupil to come to her desk.*

become •VERB• **becomes, becoming, became 1** to come to be: *She'd become old and frail.* • *Tony Blair became prime minister in 1997.* **2** if something becomes you it suits you

♦ **becoming** •ADJECTIVE• something that is becoming looks nice on the person wearing it

bed •NOUN• **beds 1** a piece of furniture or place to sleep on: *Each night, chimpanzees make beds of twigs high up in the trees.* • *Time to get ready for bed.*

2 the bottom of a river, a lake or the sea

3 an area in a garden that contains flowers and other plants: *a bed of lilies*

•VERB• **beds, bedding, bedded** you **bed down** somewhere when you get ready to go to sleep there

bedclothes •PLURAL NOUN• things like sheets, blankets or a quilt used to cover a bed

bedding •NOUN• anything used to make a bed with, such as a mattress, sheets, and pillows, or for animals, straw or hay

bedlam •NOUN• a place full of confusion and noise: *The railway station was bedlam with thousands of people stranded.*

bedraggled •ADJECTIVE• untidy and dirty: *The kitten had been caught in the rain and its fur was all bedraggled.*

bedridden •ADJECTIVE• someone who is bedridden stays in bed all the time, usually because they are too ill or frail to get up

bedroom •NOUN• **bedrooms** a room with a bed or beds used for sleeping in

bedspread •NOUN• **bedspreads** a cover that goes over the top of the other bedclothes on a bed

bedstead •NOUN• **bedsteads** the metal or wooden framework of a bed

bee •NOUN• **bees** a small winged insect that can sting you. Bees fly from flower to flower collecting nectar to make honey

Aa
Bb
Cc
Dd
Ee
Ff
Gg
Hh
Ii
Jj
Kk
Ll
Mm
Nn
Oo
Pp
Qq
Rr
Ss
Tt
Uu
Vv
Ww
Xx
Yy
Zz

Aa
Bb
Cc
Dd
Ee
Ff
Gg
Hh
Ii
Jj
Kk
Ll
Mm
Nn
Oo
Pp
Qq
Rr
Ss
Tt
Uu
Vv
Ww
Xx
Yy
Zz

• **have a bee in your bonnet** if you have a bee in your bonnet about something you believe it is so important that you think or talk about it all the time

beech • NOUN• **beeches** a tree with grey smooth bark and rounded leaves

beef • NOUN• meat from a cow

beefburger • NOUN• **beefburgers** a flattened cake of minced beef that is fried or grilled and eaten in a bread roll

beefeater • NOUN• **beefeaters** one of the guards at the Tower of London, who wear an old-fashioned red uniform

beehive • NOUN• **beehives** a box or container where bees are kept so that the honey they make can be collected

beeline • NOUN• if you **make a beeline for something** you go straight towards it: *As soon as the doors opened we made a beeline for the sale rail.*

been • VERB• a form of the verb **be** that is used with a helping verb to show that something happened in the past: *My brother has been very good today.*

beer • NOUN• **beers** an alcoholic drink made from barley and often flavoured with hops

beetle • NOUN• **beetles** an insect with two pairs of wings. Its front wings are hard and cover its back wings when the beetle is not flying

beetroot • NOUN• **beetroots** a small round dark red vegetable that grows under the ground

befall • VERB• **befalls, befalling, befell** if something befalls you it happens to you: *If some accident should befall me, please get in touch with my relatives in Australia.*

ⓘ **Befall** is a word that isn't used very often nowadays, but you might come across it in older stories.

before • PREPOSITION• earlier than something: *Let's go for a walk before lunch.* • *I sent the letter the day before yesterday.* • ADVERB• at an earlier time: *I don't think we've met before.* • *We had all been to the beach the day before.* • CONJUNCTION• 1 earlier than the time when something will happen: *Wash your hands before you come to the table.* 2 rather than: *Ali would die before he would admit he was wrong.*
• **before long** soon: *If you can wait a while, the boss will be back before long.*

beforehand • ADVERB• before the time when something else happens: *If you're coming to the party next week, would you let me know beforehand.*

beg • VERB• **begs, begging, begged** 1 if someone begs they ask other people to give them money or food, because they are poor or have no job: *children begging in the streets* 2 if you beg for something you ask someone very eagerly for it because you want it very much: *Kitty begged her father to buy her the shoes.*

began • VERB• a way of changing the verb **begin** to make a past tense: *It began to rain and we stayed in.*

beggar • NOUN• **beggars** someone who lives by begging for money or food from people who pass by

begin • VERB• **begins, beginning, began, begun** to begin is to start: *The concert began at 7.30 and finished at about 9.30.* • *Marie had begun to enjoy being at the new school.*
• **to begin with** at first: *She hadn't liked her new school to begin with.*
✦ **beginner** • NOUN• **beginners** someone who has only just started to do or to learn something: *a guitar class for beginners*
✦ **beginning** • NOUN• **beginnings** 1 the start of something: *He led from the beginning of the race.* 2 the early part of a period of time: *In the beginning, I didn't like her much.* • *My birthday is at the beginning of July.* 3 the beginnings of something are the first things that happen before it gets bigger: *the beginnings of a really successful company*

beguile • VERB• **beguiles, beguiling, beguiled** to beguile someone is to persuade them to do something by making it seem attractive
✦ **beguiling** • ADJECTIVE• seeming to be attractive: *Winning millions on the lottery is a very beguiling idea, but it isn't very likely to happen.*

begun •VERB• a form of the verb **begin** that is used with a helping verb to show that something happened in the past: *I had just begun my homework when James phoned.*

behalf •NOUN• you do something **on behalf of** a person or an organization when you act as their representative: *I'm here on behalf of the Premium Insurance Company.*
• **on someone's behalf** is to do it for them or because of them: *Please don't go to any trouble on my behalf.*

behave •VERB• **behaves, behaving, behaved** 1 to behave in a certain way is to act in that way: *If you behave badly today, you won't get sweets.* • *They were all behaving very strangely.* 2 if you behave or behave yourself, you are good and don't do anything that you shouldn't

behaviour •NOUN• 1 the way you behave: *Gold stars are awarded for good behaviour.* • *His behaviour was really awful that day.* 2 the way an animal or other living thing normally behaves: *He wants to study the behaviour of gorillas.*

behead •VERB• **beheads, beheading, beheaded** to behead someone is to cut their head off: *King Charles I was beheaded in 1649.*

behind •PREPOSITION• 1 at or to the back of something: *Look behind the sofa.* • *Shut the door behind you, please.*
2 staying after someone or something: *The steam train left a trail of sooty smoke behind it.*
3 not as far ahead as other people: *He's fallen behind the rest of the class.*
4 helping or encouraging someone or something: *The crowd really got behind him and cheered and clapped as he ran to the finishing line.*
5 responsible for something: *We want to find out who was behind the robbery.*
6 an experience is behind you when it happened in the past: *That's all behind him now.*
• **behind someone's back** if something is done behind your back, it is done without you knowing about it: *I don't like people talking about me behind my back.*
• ADVERB• 1 at or to the back: *a steam engine with six carriages behind*
2 late or not up to date: *She's fallen behind with her work.*
3 if you stay behind or remain behind you do not leave when other people leave: *My sister left. I stayed behind to pack her things along with mine.*
• NOUN• **behinds** your bottom: *Get up off your behind and do some work!*

behold •VERB• **beholds, beholding, beheld** to behold something is to see it: *He beheld a huge, tawny lion, with great glistening white teeth.*

ⓘ **Behold** is an old-fashioned word.

beige •NOUN• a very light pinkish brown colour, like the colour of milky coffee or tea

ⓘ This word is pronounced **bayj**.

being •VERB• the form of the verb **be** that is used to make certain tenses: *I am being good today.* • *He was just being kind.*
• NOUN• **beings** a being is something that lives or exists: *a science fiction story about beings from other planets*

belated •ADJECTIVE• arriving late: *a belated birthday present*
♦ **belatedly** •ADVERB• late: *He did it rather belatedly, but at least he did thank me.*

belch •VERB• **belches, belching, belched** to belch is to let air from your stomach come out of your mouth with a loud noise
• NOUN• **belches** this noise

belfry •NOUN• **belfries** a tower, especially on a church, where a bell is hung

belief •NOUN• **beliefs** something you believe, especially something that you think is true or exists

believe •VERB• **believes, believing, believed** 1 to be sure that something is true or real: *I believed his story.* • *Do you believe in ghosts?* 2 to think that something is true though you are not completely sure: *I believe he was once a famous film star.*
• **make believe** if you make believe you pretend something is real when it isn't
♦ **believable** •ADJECTIVE• if something is

Aa
Bb
Cc
Dd
Ee
Ff
Gg
Hh
Ii
Jj
Kk
Ll
Mm
Nn
Oo
Pp
Qq
Rr
Ss
Tt
Uu
Vv
Ww
Xx
Yy
Zz

believable it can be believed: *a believable excuse*

♦ believer •NOUN• **believers** someone who believes something, especially someone who believes in a particular religion

bell •NOUN• **bells 1** a hollow metal object with a long piece of metal inside that swings and hits the sides of the bell making a ringing sound **2** any device that makes a ringing sound: *a doorbell • a bicycle bell*

bellow •VERB• **bellows, bellowing, bellowed** to bellow is to roar like a bull: *He bellowed at us to stop what we were doing.*
• NOUN• **bellows** a roar

belly •NOUN• **bellies 1** the front part of your body between your chest and the tops of your legs
2 your stomach
3 the part underneath an animal's body between its front legs and its back legs

belly-button •NOUN• **belly-buttons** your navel

belly-flop •NOUN• **belly-flops** someone diving does a belly-flop when they hit the surface of the water with the front of their body

belong •VERB• **belongs, belonging, belonged 1** if something belongs to you, you own it: *Who does this suitcase belong to?*
2 you belong to the place where you feel at home: *She felt as if she didn't belong there.*
3 if you belong to a club or organization you are a member: *Peter belongs to the local tennis club.*
4 something belongs in a particular place if that is where it is usually kept: *That big chair belongs over there by the fireplace.*
5 people or things that belong with each other match each other, fit together or make a pair: *These socks don't belong together.*
♦ belongings •PLURAL NOUN• your belongings are the things you own: *He just packed up all his belongings and moved out.*

beloved •ADJECTIVE• loved very much: *her beloved old teddy bear*
• NOUN• the person that someone is in love with: *He sent a red rose to his beloved.*

ⓘ This word is pronounced be-**luv**-id.

below •PREPOSITION• lower than or under something: *the cupboard below the stairs • Simon was below me in school.*
•ADVERB• at or to a lower place: *We climbed to the top of the hill and looked down on the valley below. • Fill in this section of the form and then sign your name in the box below.*

belt •NOUN• **belts 1** a band of leather, cloth or plastic that you wear around your waist **2** a loop of material in a machine that moves round and round: *a conveyor belt • a fan belt*
•VERB• **belts, belting, belted 1** to belt someone is to hit them hard: *The branch sprang back and belted him on the nose.* **2** to belt is to go very fast: *The boys came belting down the hill on their bikes.*

bench •NOUN• **benches 1** a long seat: *We sat on a wooden bench in the park.* **2** a table used to make things on: *a carpenter's bench*

bend •VERB• **bends, bending, bent 1** you bend or bend down when you lower your body by making your back curve: *She bent down to look more closely at the tiny insects.* **2** to bend is to curve: *He bent the wire around the post.*
• NOUN• **bends** a curve: *a bend in the road*
• **bend over backwards** if you bend over backwards to do something you try your hardest to it
• **bend the rules** if someone bends the rules, they break the rules in a way that will not be noticed or is not very important

beneath •PREPOSITION• below or under something: *Atlantis, the lost city beneath the sea*
•ADVERB• below or under: *the sky above and the earth beneath • I hadn't realized there was a second layer of chocolates beneath.*

benefit •NOUN• **benefits 1** a benefit is something that helps you: *Having a mobile phone can be a real benefit in an emergency.* **2** people on benefit get money from the government to help them with their living expenses
•VERB• **benefits, benefiting** or **benefitting, benefited** or **benefitted** if you benefit from something, or if something benefits you, it helps you: *I think you'll benefit from the extra lessons.*

benevolent •ADJECTIVE• full of kindness:

The old man gave the children a benevolent smile.

bent •VERB• a way of changing the verb **bend** to make a past tense, either with or without a helping verb: *The striker bent the ball round the defenders.* • *I have bent this fork.*
•ADJECTIVE• not straight: *a bent pin*
• **bent on** if someone is bent on doing something they are determined to do it

bequeath •VERB• bequeaths, bequeathing, bequeathed to bequeath your money or property to someone is to arrange for them to be given it after you die

bequest •NOUN• bequests a gift of money or property to be made after the person who has given it has died

bereaved •ADJECTIVE• someone is bereaved if one of their close relatives or friends has died: *the bereaved families of the accident victims*
•PLURAL NOUN• the bereaved are the close relatives or friends of someone who has died: *an organization offering counselling to the bereaved*
• **bereavement** •NOUN• bereavements someone suffers a bereavement when a relative or close friend dies

beret •NOUN• berets a flat round hat made of felt or some other kind of soft fabric

ⓘ Beret is a French word which in turn comes from the Latin word **birretum**, which means *cap*.

ⓘ This word is pronounced **ber**-ay.

berry •NOUN• berries a small fruit containing lots of seeds that grows on certain types of plant: *Holly has red berries.*

ⓘ Do not confuse the spellings of **berry**, **beret** and **bury**, which can sound the same.

berserk •ADJECTIVE• to go berserk is to become very angry or violent: *My big sister will go berserk if she finds out I've been wearing her T-shirt.*

berth •NOUN• berths 1 a bed on a boat or a train 2 a place in a harbour where a boat or ship can tie up or anchor
•VERB• berths, berthing, berthed a ship berths when it reaches the end of a journey and ties up or anchors in a harbour

beside •PREPOSITION• 1 next to or at the side of someone or something: *We do like to be beside the sea.* • *Go and stand beside Billy.* 2 compared with: *Beside that tiny kitten the dog looks enormous.*
• **beside the point** if something is beside the point, it has nothing to do with the thing being talked about or dealt with
• **beside yourself** terribly upset: *She's beside herself with grief.*

ⓘ Be careful not to use **besides** when you should use **beside**:
✓ *That's beside the point.*
✗ *That's besides the point.*

besides •PREPOSITION• as well as: *He isn't really interested in anything besides football.*
•ADVERB• also: *It's too wet to go out. Besides, I have a lot of homework to do.*

besiege •VERB• besieges, besieging, besieged to surround a place so that no one or nothing can get out: *The castle was besieged for three weeks by the English army.*

best •ADJECTIVE• better than all the rest: *the best film they'd ever seen*
•ADVERB• in the most suitable or pleasing way: *I know it's difficult but just do it as best you can.* • *The city is best seen at night when all the skyscrapers are lit up.*
•NOUN• the most excellent things: *Parents want the best for their children.*
• **do your best** to do as well as you can
• **make the best of** to make the best of something is to enjoy it or do as well as you can with it, even if it is not very good: *Although it was raining, we made the best of our trip to the seaside.*

best man •NOUN• the best man at a wedding is the man who helps the bridegroom and stands beside him during the ceremony

bet •NOUN• bets a bet is money that you risk on the result of something before the result is known. If the result is the way you have said it would be you win more money, but if the result is different you lose the money you bet

•VERB• **bets, betting, bet** or **betted** 1 to make a bet 2 to bet is to say that something will happen because you are pretty sure that it will: *I bet that Jackie will be late again.*

betray •VERB• **betrays, betraying, betrayed** to betray someone who trusts you is to do something to harm them: *He betrayed his country by selling secrets to the enemy.*

♦ **betrayal** •NOUN• **betrayals** betrayal is harm done to a person who trusts you

betrothed •ADJECTIVE• one person is betrothed to another when they are engaged to be married

better •ADJECTIVE• 1 of a higher standard or more excellent: *This is a better way to do it.* 2 not as bad or as ill: *My cold's much better today.* • *Don't go back to work until you're better.*
• **ADVERB•** in a more pleasing or more suitable way: *Which do you like better, the green one or the blue one?* • *Try to do better next time.*
• **NOUN•** something of a higher standard than others: *Of the two tennis players, Sampras was definitely the better.*
• **better off** in a better position: *We'd be better off taking the plane. We'd get there quicker.*
• **get the better of** to defeat: *You'll never get the better of him, no matter how long you argue.*
• **had better** must or ought to: *I had better hurry, or I'll be late.*

between • PREPOSITION• 1 in the area or space that divides two people, things or places: *What letter comes between Q and S in the alphabet?* • *the road between San Francisco and Los Angeles* 2 giving each a part or a piece: *Colin and Russell divided the work between them.* 3 including or involving each one: *They'll have to sort it out between them. We're not getting mixed up in it.* 4 one and not the other: *I had to decide between going to the concert or staying to watch the fireworks.*
• **ADVERB•** things between or in between are in the middle: *He'd had a big breakfast, an enormous lunch and lots of snacks in between.*

beverage •NOUN• **beverages** a drink

beware •VERB• to tell someone to beware or beware of something is to warn them tha there is danger: *The sign on the gate said 'Beware of the dog'.*

ⓘ The verb **beware** does not have differen forms or tenses like other verbs, because it is only used when you are telling people what t do or giving them a warning.

bewilder •VERB• **bewilders, bewildering, bewildered** to bewilder someone is to confuse them
♦ **bewildering** •ADJECTIVE• confusing
♦ **bewilderment** •NOUN• being bewildered: *'What is this?' exclaimed Lucy in bewilderment.*

bewitch •VERB• **bewitches, bewitching, bewitched** to bewitch someone is to put a magic spell on them
♦ **bewitching** •ADJECTIVE• so attractive that you feel as if you are under a magic spell *a bewitching smile*

beyond • PREPOSITION• 1 on the far side of something: *Turn right just beyond the bridge.* 2 more than or greater than something: *The noise level was beyond anything I'd eve experienced before.* 3 if something is beyond someone it is too difficult or confusing for them to understand: *It's beyond me why he didn't grab the opportunity when he had it.*
• ADVERB• further away: *We could see right across the valley to the mountains beyond.*

bi- • PREFIX• 1 if a word starts with **bi-**, it sometimes means *two*. For example, a *bicycle* is so called because it has two whee 2 if a word starts with **bi-**, it sometimes means *twice*. For example, *bimonthly* mean twice a month.

bias • NOUN• **biases** to have a bias towards person or thing is to prefer them, often without thinking about whether someone c something else may be just as good: *There a definite bias against change of any sort in the local council.*
♦ **biased** or **biassed** • ADJECTIVE• favouring one person or thing unfairly: *a biased point of view*

a bicycle

saddle — handlebars — pedal — crossbar — fork — reflector — gear wheels — chain — spokes — derailleur — tyres

bib •NOUN• **bibs** a piece of cloth or plastic tied under a baby's chin to protect its clothes while it is eating

Bible •NOUN• **Bibles** the holy book of the Christian and Jewish religions
• **biblical** •ADJECTIVE• to do with or in the Bible: *a biblical character*

biblio- •PREFIX• if a word starts with **biblio-**, it means it has something to do with books. For example, a *bibliography* is a list of books

ⓘ This has come into English from the Greek word **biblion**, which means *book*.

biceps •NOUN• **biceps** the big muscles at the top of your arms that bulge when you bend your arms upwards

bicker •VERB• **bickers, bickering, bickered** to bicker is to argue about things that are not very important: *Let's not waste time bickering about who will pay for it. It's only 10p.*

bicycle •NOUN• **bicycles** a machine you ride on, made up of a metal frame with two wheels which are moved by pressing down on pedals with your feet

bid[1] •NOUN• **bids** 1 a bid is an offer of the price you are prepared to pay for something at an auction 2 a bid is a try: *They made a*

final desperate bid for freedom.
•VERB• **bids, bidding, bid** to make an offer of a price: *Will someone bid £5 for this beautiful old chair?*

bid[2] •VERB• **bids, bidding, bid** or **bade, bidden** or **bid** 1 to make a greeting to someone: *He bade me goodnight.* 2 to tell someone to do something: *The headmaster bade them come to his office next morning.*

bidet •NOUN• **bidets** a bidet is a small low washbasin that you sit on to wash your bottom

ⓘ This word is pronounced **bee**-day.

big •ADJECTIVE• **bigger, biggest** 1 large: *a big lorry • It was the biggest fish he'd ever seen.*
2 older: *My big brother is 15. • You won't be allowed to walk to school on your own until you're a lot bigger.*
3 important: *Are you going to watch the big match on TV?*
4 successful, popular or famous: *He used to be big in the United States.*

bigot •NOUN• **bigots** a person who thinks people with different beliefs or who belong to a different group are wrong
• **bigoted** •ADJECTIVE• prejudiced against anyone with different beliefs or from a different group

♦ **bigotry** •NOUN• being bigoted

bike •NOUN• **bikes** a bicycle

bikini •NOUN• **bikinis** a kind of swimsuit for girls and women made up of a bra top and pants

bile •NOUN• a liquid made in the liver that helps to digest food

bilingual •ADJECTIVE• using, knowing or dealing with two different languages: *Many children in Wales are bilingual: they can speak Welsh as well as English.*

bill¹ •NOUN• **bills** 1 a piece of paper showing how much is owed for something, such as a meal in a restaurant or the supply of goods or services: *an electricity bill*
2 a poster or printed sheet listing or advertising something
3 a suggestion for a new law that people in parliament discuss and vote for or against

bill² •NOUN• **bills** a bird's beak

billiards •NOUN• a game you play by hitting three balls on a large cloth-covered table with the tip of a long stick called a cue

billion •NOUN• **billions** a thousand million, written in numbers as 1,000,000,000 or 1 000 000 000: *The government gets billions of pounds a year from taxes.*

billow •VERB• **billows, billowing, billowed** to billow is to rise in curving shapes like waves: *storm clouds billowing landward from the west*
•NOUN• **billows** a wave

billy-goat •NOUN• **billy-goats** a male goat

bin •NOUN• **bins** a container for putting rubbish in or for storing food or wine
•VERB• **bins, binning, binned** to bin something is to get rid of it

binary •ADJECTIVE• made up of two parts: *a binary star*

binary number •NOUN• **binary numbers** a number that is made up of the digits 0 and 1 only, used to stand for the amount of units, twos, fours and so on in the number. Computers use these numbers to operate

bind •VERB• **binds, binding, bound** to tie or fasten together: *They'd bound his hands and feet with tape.*

•NOUN• a nuisance: *It was a bit of a bind having to take two buses to get to work.*

binge •VERB• **binges, bingeing** or **binging, binged** to eat or drink too much, especially in a short time
•NOUN• **binges** a spell of eating or drinking too much

bingo •NOUN• a gambling game where you match the numbers on your card against numbers picked out at random and called out

binoculars •PLURAL NOUN• an instrument that is like a telescope but has a lens for each eye: *a pair of binoculars*

ⓘ **Binoculars** comes from the Latin words **bini**, which means *two at a time*, and **oculus**, which means *an eye*, because both eyes are used at the same time to look through binoculars.

bio- •PREFIX• If a word starts with **bio-** it has something to do with life or living things. For example, *biology* is the study of living things

biodegradable •ADJECTIVE• a biodegradable substance can be broken down by bacteria or in other natural ways

biographical •ADJECTIVE• about a person's life: *biographical details* • *a biographical film*

biography •NOUN• **biographies** a story about a real person's life

biological •ADJECTIVE• to do with living things and the way they grow and behave: *a biological process*

biologist •NOUN• **biologists** a person who studies biology

biology •NOUN• the study of living things

bionic •ADJECTIVE• something that is bionic acts like a living thing, but works electronically

bionics •NOUN• making electronic devices that work like living things. Bionics is short for **biological electronics**

biosphere •NOUN• the area on and above the Earth where living things exist

birch •NOUN• **birches** a kind of tree with grey or silvery bark and small leaves

Aa Bb Cc Dd Ee Ff Gg Hh Ii Jj Kk Ll Mm Nn Oo Pp Qq Rr Ss Tt Uu Vv Ww Xx Yy Zz

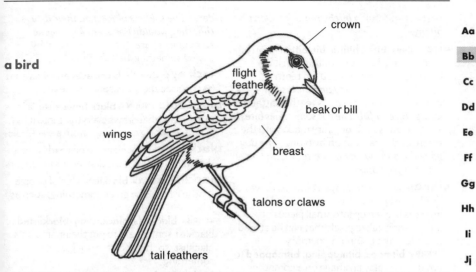

a bird

crown

flight
feathers

beak or bill

wings

breast

talons or claws

tail feathers

bird •NOUN• **birds** a creature with feathers growing on its body and which lays eggs: *Penguins are flightless birds.*

bird of prey •NOUN• **birds of prey** a bird which kills and eats small animals or birds

birdwatching •NOUN• the hobby of looking at birds in their natural surroundings

Biro •NOUN• **Biros** a kind of ballpoint pen. This word is a trademark

birth •NOUN• **births** 1 birth is the process of being born: *Life is the time between birth and death.* • *the birth of nations* 2 a birth is the time when a particular person or animal is born

birthday •NOUN• **birthdays** your birthday is the anniversary of the date when you were born

birthmark •NOUN• **birthmarks** a mark on someone's body which they have had since they were born

biscuit •NOUN• **biscuits** a kind of hard, baked cake made from dough

bisect •VERB• **bisects, bisecting, bisected** a line bisects something when it cuts it into two parts

bishop •NOUN• **bishops** 1 in some Christian churches such as the Catholic Church and the Church of England, a bishop is a member

of the clergy in charge of a district 2 in the game of chess, a bishop is a piece which has a bishop's hat

bison •NOUN• **bison** or **bisons** a kind of wild ox with a long shaggy coat

bistro •NOUN• **bistros** a kind of small restaurant

bit¹ •NOUN• **bits** 1 a piece or a part: *There were some bits of the book that I really enjoyed.*
2 a small amount: *I need a bit of help with this sum.*
3 a short time: *Let's wait a bit longer.*
4 a metal bar on a horse's bridle that the horse holds in its mouth
5 the smallest piece of computer information
• **bit by bit** to do something bit by bit is to do it gradually
• **do your bit** if you do your bit you do your share of work that has to be done
• **to bits** if something comes to bits or falls to bits, it breaks into pieces or falls apart: *The toy came to bits in my hand.* • *This car is falling to bits.*

bit² •VERB• a way of changing the verb **bite** to make a past tense

bitch •NOUN• **bitches** a female dog
♦ **bitchy** •ADJECTIVE• **bitchier, bitchiest**

nasty or spiteful: *a bitchy remark* • *Don't be bitchy.*

bite •VERB• **bites, biting, bit, bitten 1** you bite something when you cut through it by bringing your top and bottom teeth together: *He stumbled and bit his tongue.* **2** if an animal bites it uses its teeth to attack or injure: *Be careful! The cat sometimes bites.* •NOUN• **bites** a cut or injury made with the teeth, or the part cut off by biting: *The dog gave the postman a nasty bite.* • *Can I have a bite of your apple?*

bitmap •NOUN• **bitmaps** a bitmap is a way of displaying an image on a computer. The image is broken up into small pieces of information called pixels that can be stored as units in the computer memory •VERB• **bitmaps, bitmapping, bitmapped** to create or display an image on a computer in this way

bitter •ADJECTIVE• **1** bitter things have a sour rather than a sweet taste: *Lemon juice is bitter.*
2 if the weather is bitter it is uncomfortably cold: *a bitter winter's night*
3 to be bitter is to be angry and resentful because of disappointment: *He turned into a bitter old man who hated the world.*

bizarre •ADJECTIVE• very odd or strange

black •NOUN• the darkest colour, the colour of coal or a dark night •VERB• **blacks, blacking, blacked** if someone **blacks out** they become unconscious for a short time

black-and-blue •ADJECTIVE• badly bruised or covered with bruises: *The forwards are often black-and-blue the day after a rugby match.*

blackberry •NOUN• **blackberries** a small, very dark purple or black fruit that grows on a plant with prickly stems

blackbird •NOUN• **blackbirds** a bird with black feathers and an orange beak. Female blackbirds are dark brown

blackboard •NOUN• **blackboards** a dark board for writing on with chalk

blacken •VERB• **blackens, blackening, blackened 1** to make something black or

dark: *The soldiers blackened their faces so that they wouldn't be seen.* **2** to blacken someone's character is to damage it by saying something bad about it

black eye •NOUN• **black eyes** an injury that has bruised the skin around the eye

black hole •NOUN• **black holes** an area in outer space that draws everything into it by gravity. Nothing can escape from a black hole

black ice •NOUN• clear ice on roads that is difficult to see and so is dangerous for drivers

blacklist •NOUN• **blacklists** a list of people who are not to be given something, such as jobs •VERB• **blacklists, blacklisting, blacklisted** to blacklist someone is to put their name on a blacklist, so that they are not given something

black magic •NOUN• magic which is meant to do harm

blackmail •VERB• **blackmails, blackmailing, blackmailed** to blackmail someone is to threaten them with something bad such as hurting one of their friends or relatives or telling one of their secrets, if they do not pay money •NOUN• the crime of blackmailing someone • **blackmailer** •NOUN• **blackmailers** a criminal who blackmails someone

black market •NOUN• something bought or sold on the black market is bought or sold illegally or dishonestly

blackout •NOUN• **blackouts 1** if there is a blackout somewhere it is in total darkness with no lights on or to be seen **2** if someone has a blackout they become unconscious for a short time and don't remember anything from that time

black pudding •NOUN• **black puddings** a kind of sausage made from animal's blood mixed with spices

black sheep •NOUN• **black sheep** a member of a family or group who gets into trouble a lot or is a failure

blacksmith •NOUN• **blacksmiths** someone who makes and repairs things made of iron, especially horseshoes

black widow •NOUN• **black widows** a kind

of very poisonous spider found in America

bladder •NOUN• **bladders** the organ in your body where urine is collected

blade •NOUN• **blades 1** the cutting part of a knife, sword or razor that has a thin sharp edge **2** a long thin leaf of grass

blame •VERB• **blames, blaming, blamed 1** to say that something is someone's fault: *It's not my fault so don't try to blame me.* • *He's been made to look silly, so you can't blame him for being angry.* **2** you are to blame for something bad if you are responsible for it: *Who is to blame for this mess?* •NOUN• blame is fault or responsibility for something bad that has happened: *They were made to take the blame.*
♦ **blameless** •ADJECTIVE• with no faults or having done nothing wrong: *She has led a blameless life.*

blancmange •NOUN• **blancmanges** a soft jelly-like pudding made with milk

ⓘ This word is pronounced **bla-monj**. It comes from the French words **blanc**, which means *white*, and **manger**, which means *to eat*. In the past, blancmange was always white.

bland •ADJECTIVE• **blander, blandest 1** bland food is mild and doesn't have any strong flavours or spices **2** bland means mild and not causing any offence or annoyance: *a bland smile*

blank •ADJECTIVE• **blanker, blankest 1** if something, like a sheet of paper, is blank it has nothing marked or written on it **2** if someone's face is blank, their face or eyes show nothing, either because they don't understand or they don't want to show any feeling: *He gave me a blank stare.* •NOUN• **blanks 1** an empty space: *I can't remember anything. The whole of last week is a complete blank.* **2** a cartridge for a gun that contains an explosive but no bullet: *The actors used blanks in their rifles when the battle scenes were being filmed.*

blanket •NOUN• **blankets 1** a covering for a bed, usually made of wool or some other warm fabric **2** a layer that covers everything: *a blanket of snow*

blare •VERB• **blares, blaring, blared** to blare is to sound loudly: *music blaring from the loudspeakers* •NOUN• **blares** a loud sound like the sound made by a trumpet or horn

blaspheme •VERB• **blasphemes, blaspheming, blasphemed 1** to blaspheme is to curse using words that offend people, especially people who believe in God or a god
♦ **blasphemous** •ADJECTIVE• using curses or swearwords, especially ones that are disrespectful to God or a god
♦ **blasphemy** •NOUN• **blasphemies** cursing or swearing that is disrespectful, especially to God or a god

blast •NOUN• **blasts 1** a loud violent explosion: *The bomb went off and many people were injured in the blast.* **2** a strong wind or gust of wind: *They stood shivering in the icy blast.* **3** a loud sound from a trumpet or horn: *The lorry driver gave a couple of blasts on his horn.* •VERB• **blasts, blasting, blasted 1** to blast is to use explosives or an explosion to break up or destroy something solid, such as rock: *They were blasting in the quarry again yesterday.* **2** to blast is to make a loud noise: *music blasting out of the open windows* **3** to blast something is to strongly criticize it: *He made a speech blasting all his opponents.* **4** a rocket **blasts off** when its fuel is ignited and it starts to rise into the air
• **at full blast** as strongly or loudly as possible: *David was playing his stereo at full blast.*

blast-off •NOUN• **blast-offs** the moment when a rocket is launched

blatant •ADJECTIVE• bad behaviour is blatant when it is very obvious and the person doing it doesn't seem to care that it is obvious: *It was a blatant lie.*
♦ **blatantly** •ADVERB• in a very obvious way: *They were quite blatantly dropping litter all over the park.*

blaze •NOUN• **blazes 1** the bright flames from a fire: *The firemen put out the blaze.*

Aa Bb Cc Dd Ee Ff Gg Hh Ii Jj Kk Ll Mm Nn Oo Pp Qq Rr Ss Tt Uu Vv Ww Xx Yy Zz

Aa
Bb
Cc
Dd
Ee
Ff
Gg
Hh
Ii
Jj
Kk
Ll
Mm
Nn
Oo
Pp
Qq
Rr
Ss
Tt
Uu
Vv
Ww
Xx
Yy
Zz

2 something that glows like a fire: *a blaze of colour* • *a blaze of glory*
•VERB• **blazes, blazing, blazed** to glow brightly with, or as if with, flames: *She was blazing with anger.*

blazer •NOUN• **blazers** a kind of jacket worn as part of a school uniform or by members of a club

bleach •NOUN• a chemical used to whiten or lighten fabrics or as a household cleaner
•VERB• **bleaches, bleaching, bleached** to lighten or whiten by bleach or by sunlight
♦ **bleached** •ADJECTIVE• made white or blond by bleach or sunlight: *bleached hair*

bleak •ADJECTIVE• **bleaker, bleakest 1** cold, bare and miserable: *a bleak winter landscape* **2** hopeless and miserable: *Our chances of winning the football match looked bleak.*
♦ **bleakly** •ADVERB• in a cold or miserable way: *He smiled bleakly.*
♦ **bleakness** •NOUN• being bleak: *the bleakness of the dark hills*

bleary •ADJECTIVE• **blearier, bleariest** if your eyes are bleary they are tired and you aren't able to see clearly
♦ **blearily** •ADVERB• in a bleary way
♦ **bleariness** •NOUN• being bleary

bleat •NOUN• **bleats** the sound a sheep or goat makes
•VERB• **bleats, bleating, bleated 1** a sheep or goat bleats when it makes its usual sound **2** to speak in an annoying complaining way: *She was bleating on about how unfair it all was.*

bleed •VERB• **bleeds, bleeding, bled 1** you bleed when you lose blood, especially from a cut or injury **2** if a person's heart bleeds, they are feeling very sad
♦ **bleeding** •NOUN• a flow of blood: *First try to stop the bleeding and then ring for an ambulance.*

bleep •NOUN• **bleeps** a short high-pitched sound made by an electronic device as a signal
•VERB• **bleeps, bleeping, bleeped 1** to make this sound **2** to signal to someone using an electronic device: *If you need to get in touch, you can have me bleeped.*

♦ **bleeper** •NOUN• **bleepers** an electronic device used to contact someone by signalling them with a bleeping sound

blemish •NOUN• **blemishes 1** a mark that spoils something's appearance: *an apple covered with blemishes* **2** something that spoils someone's good reputation: *a blemish on his character*

blend •VERB• **blends, blending, blended 1** to put things together so that they are mixed in with each other: *blend the butter and the sugar* **2** if people or things **blend in** somewhere they fit in well with the people or things around them
•NOUN• **blends 1** a mixture of two or more things: *Banana milkshake is a blend of milk, banana and ice cream.* **2** two or more sounds joined together
♦ **blender** •NOUN• **blenders** a machine with a blade that turns quickly, used for mixing foods or liquids together

bless •VERB• **blesses, blessing, blessed 1** if someone is blessed they are made happy or they have good luck: *They've been blessed with two beautiful children.* **2** to bless someone or something is to make them or it holy: *The cardinal blessed the poor.*
♦ **blessing** •NOUN• **blessings 1** a wish for happiness: *He gave the young couple his blessing.* **2** something that brings happiness or relief: *The rain will be a blessing for everyone who has been suffering in the drought.*
• **a blessing in disguise** something that doesn't seem to be good but which has a good or useful effect

blew •VERB• a way of changing the verb **blow** to make a past tense

blind •ADJECTIVE• not able to see: *New-born kittens are blind.*
•VERB• **blinds, blinding, blinded** to make blind: *He was blinded in the war.* • *The light blinded me for a moment.*
•NOUN• **blinds** a covering for a window used instead of curtains or to keep out strong sunlight: *pull down the blinds*
⇒ **blinding**

blindfold •NOUN• **blindfolds** a cover put over someone's eyes to stop them seeing

•VERB• **blindfolds, blindfolding, blindfolded** to put a blindfold on someone

blinding •ADJECTIVE• something blinding is dazzling or causes blindness for a short time: *a blinding flash*

blindman's buff •NOUN• a game where one of the players is blindfolded and tries to catch the other players

blink •VERB• **blinks, blinking, blinked** to close your eyes for a short time: *blinking in the strong sunlight* • *It will all be over before you can blink.*
•NOUN• **blinks** 1 the short time taken to close and open your eyes: *It was all over in a blink of the eye.* 2 a light that shows for a very short time: *a blink of sunshine*

blinkers •PLURAL NOUN• blinkers are two pieces of leather put over a horse's eyes to stop it seeing in any direction except to the front

bliss •NOUN• bliss is a feeling of very great happiness: *It was bliss not to have to go to school for a couple of days.*
♦ **blissful** •ADJECTIVE• lovely: *We spent a blissful day at the seaside.*
♦ **blissfully** •ADVERB• happily: *He was blissfully unaware of the trouble he had caused.*

blister •NOUN• **blisters** a thin bubble on the skin that is caused by burning or rubbing the skin
•VERB• **blisters, blistering, blistered** to form blisters
♦ **blistering** •ADJECTIVE• 1 a blistering pace is a very fast pace 2 blistering weather is uncomfortably hot

blithe •ADJECTIVE• happy and carefree
♦ **blithely** •ADJECTIVE• happily and without worry or care: *He blithely imagines he can pass the exam without doing any work.*

blitz •NOUN• **blitzes** 1 an attack made by many military aircraft dropping bombs 2 a quick attack, for example, to get through tidying or other work that needs to be done

blizzard •NOUN• **blizzards** a storm with wind and heavy snow

bloated •ADJECTIVE• swollen: *His stomach felt bloated after the huge meal.*

blob •NOUN• **blobs** a round lump of something soft or liquid: *blobs of paint*

block •NOUN• **blocks** 1 a solid lump of something: *Cut the wood into blocks.* • *a block of ice cream*
2 a group of buildings or houses that are joined together: *a block of flats* • *Go down a couple of blocks and turn the corner.*
3 a barrier or obstacle that stops people or things getting through: *a road block*
•VERB• **blocks, blocking, blocked** 1 to block something which things usually pass through, like a road or a pipe, is to make a barrier on or in it so that nothing can get through: *The fallen leaves had blocked the drain.* 2 to block something is to get in its way: *There were lots of taller people in front blocking our view.*

blockade •NOUN• **blockades** the surrounding of a place by soldiers or ships to stop people or things getting in and out: *a blockade of French ports*
•VERB• **blockades, blockading, blockaded** to surround a place to stop people or things getting in and out

block capitals •PLURAL NOUN• you use block capitals when you use capital letters to write every letter in every word, LIKE THIS

block graph •NOUN• **block graphs** a graph with piles of blocks that show the number of things in different groups

blond *or* **blonde** •ADJECTIVE• **blonder, blondest** fair-haired
•NOUN• **blonds** *or* **blondes** a person with fair hair

ⓘ The spelling **blonde**, with an **e**, is used for girls and women.
The spelling **blond**, without an **e**, is used for boys and men.

blood •NOUN• the red liquid that carries nutrients, oxygen and other substances round your body in veins

blood donor •NOUN• **blood donors** someone who gives some of their blood to be used for other people who have lost blood in an accident or operation and need a blood transfusion

blood group •NOUN• **blood groups** your

Aa
Bb
Cc
Dd
Ee
Ff
Gg
Hh
Ii
Jj
Kk
Ll
Mm
Nn
Oo
Pp
Qq
Rr
Ss
Tt
Uu
Vv
Ww
Xx
Yy
Zz

bloodhound → blue

blood group is the type of blood you have. If you ever need a blood transfusion the blood used will come from someone with the same blood group

bloodhound •NOUN• **bloodhounds** a kind of hunting dog with long ears, a wrinkled face and a very good sense of smell

bloodshed •NOUN• bloodshed is violence in which people are injured or killed

bloodshot •ADJECTIVE• if your eyes are bloodshot the white parts are red

bloodstream •NOUN• your bloodstream is the blood moving round your body inside a system of veins: *If the infection gets into the bloodstream it is carried quickly round the body.*

bloodthirsty •ADJECTIVE• **bloodthirstier, bloodthirstiest** a bloodthirsty person is eager to kill or enjoys seeing people or animals being killed

blood vessel •NOUN• **blood vessels** one of the tubes that carry blood around the body such as an artery, vein or capillary, and that form a network throughout the whole body

bloody •ADJECTIVE• **bloodier, bloodiest** covered in or full of blood: *a bloody nose*

bloom •NOUN• **blooms** a flower: *a rose bush with many blooms* •VERB• **blooms, blooming, bloomed** to flower: *Many plants in the garden have bloomed early this year.*

blossom •NOUN• **blossoms** the flowers that appear on a fruit tree before the fruit •VERB• **blossoms, blossoming, blossomed** 1 a tree or bush blossoms when it flowers before producing fruit 2 a person blossoms when they become more successful or attractive: *Under the teacher's guidance, his musical talent blossomed.*

blot •NOUN• **blots** 1 an inky stain 2 a stain: *a blot on his character* •VERB• **blots, blotting, blotted** 1 to make an inky stain on paper 2 to dab at wet ink on paper to dry it and prevent it smearing 3 if you **blot out** an unpleasant thought or memory you put it out of your mind

completely: *Jackson had blotted the accident out because it upset him to think of it.*

blotch •NOUN• **blotches** a spot or patch of a different colour: *Madeleine had an allergy and her skin was covered with red blotches.* •VERB• **blotches, blotching, blotched** to mark with blotches ♦ **blotchy** •ADJECTIVE• **blotchier, blotchiest** marked with blotches

blouse •NOUN• **blouses** a loose top with sleeves

blow •NOUN• **blows** 1 a hard knock: *a blow to the face* 2 a sudden piece of bad luck: *It was a bit of a blow not being able to go to the concert.* •VERB• **blows, blowing, blew, blown** 1 wind blows when it moves around: *a breeze blowing from the west* 2 to blow something is to force air on to it or into it: *Blow on the hot soup so that you don't burn your mouth.* • *He huffed and he puffed and he blew their house down.* 3 to blow a musical instrument is to breathe into it to make a sound: *blow a horn* 4 when something unpleasant **blows over**, it passes and is forgotten: *They had been arguing, but that's blown over now.* 5 to **blow something up** is to destroy it with an explosion: *Guy Fawkes plotted to blow up the Houses of Parliament.*

blowtorch •NOUN• **blowtorches** a tool for aiming a very hot flame at something to heat it up and melt it

blubber •NOUN• the fat from whales and other sea animals •VERB• **blubbers, blubbering, blubbered** to cry in a way that other people think is weak

blue •NOUN• **blues** the colour of the sky in the day time if there are no clouds • **out of the blue** if something comes out of the blue it happens without anyone expecting it • **have the blues** if someone has the blues they are feeling unhappy or depressed •ADJECTIVE• 1 of the colour blue: *a blue jersey* 2 unhappy or depressed: *Poor Brendan is feeling a bit blue today.*

66

bluebell •NOUN• **bluebells** a flower with blue bell-shaped flowers

bluebottle •NOUN• **bluebottle** a large fly with a shiny blue body

Blue Peter •NOUN• the Blue Peter is a blue flag with a white centre that a ship flies when it is about to sail

blueprint •NOUN• **blueprints** a plan of work that is to be done, especially of something that is to be built

bluff •VERB• **bluffs, bluffing, bluffed** to bluff is to make people think that you know something when you don't, or that you are going to do something that you have no intention of doing
•NOUN• **bluffs** a trick or deception: *They weren't going to attack. It was only a bluff.*

blunder •NOUN• **blunders** a bad or embarrassing mistake
•VERB• **blunders, blundering, blundered**
1 to make a bad or embarrassing mistake
2 to move around in an awkward or clumsy way: *He couldn't see where he was going and blundered into a ditch.*

blunt •ADJECTIVE• **blunter, bluntest** 1 with an edge or point that is not sharp: *This knife is blunt.* 2 saying what you think without trying to be polite: *He is always blunt and to the point.*
♦ **bluntly** •ADVERB• without trying to be polite: *'I hate it,' she said bluntly.*

blur •NOUN• **blurs** 1 something with edges that can't be seen clearly: *a blur of faces* 2 something that you can't remember clearly: *I don't really know what happened. It was all a blur.*
•VERB• **blurs, blurring, blurred** to become fuzzy or indistinct: *His vision blurred as he became more and more exhausted.*

blurt •VERB• **blurts, blurting, blurted** to blurt **something out** is to say it suddenly without thinking: *Kenny told us about the party. He just blurted it out and totally spoiled the surprise.*

blush •NOUN• **blushes** 1 a bright pink glow on the face from embarrassment 2 a soft red or pink glow: *a white flower with a blush of pink*
•VERB• **blushes, blushing, blushed** to go pink

in the face with embarrassment: *Everyone turned to look at Philip, who blushed.*

bluster •NOUN• loud angry talk or boasting
♦ **blustery** •ADJECTIVE• if the weather is blustery the wind is blowing in strong gusts

boa constrictor •NOUN• **boa constrictors** a very large South American snake that kills its prey by coiling round it and crushing it

boar •NOUN• **boars** 1 a male pig 2 a wild pig

board •NOUN• **boards** 1 a flat piece of cut wood
2 a flat piece of material with a pattern or divisions marked on it, used to play a game: *a backgammon board*
3 if board is provided somewhere where people stay they are given their meals there: *He pays £25 a day for board.*
4 a group of people who manage a business company or other organization: *She's on the school's board of governors.*
•VERB• **boards, boarding, boarded** 1 if someone boards they are provided with their meals and lodging somewhere: *The boys will board during term time while their parents are away.* 2 to board a ship or an aircraft is to get on it to make a journey: *The astronauts boarded the spaceship.*
• **on board** on a ship or aircraft
♦ **boarder** •NOUN• **boarders** 1 someone who stays in a boarding house 2 a pupil who stays at a boarding school: *The school has both day pupils and boarders.*

boarding house •NOUN• **boarding houses** a house where guests pay a fixed price for meals and their room

boarding school •NOUN• **boarding schools** a school where pupils stay during term time and are given food and lodging

boast •VERB• **boasts, boasting, boasted** to boast is to talk proudly about things you own or things you have done, in a way that other people find annoying: *He's always boasting about his big house and his fancy car.*
•NOUN• **boasts** something you say when you boast: *It was her proud boast that she always got the highest mark in her class.*
♦ **boastful** •ADJECTIVE• a boastful person is in the habit of talking proudly about what they own or what they have done

Aa Bb Cc Dd Ee Ff Gg Hh Ii Jj Kk Ll Mm Nn Oo Pp Qq Rr Ss Tt Uu Vv Ww Xx Yy Zz

Aa
Bb
Cc
Dd
Ee
Ff
Gg
Hh
Ii
Jj
Kk
Ll
Mm
Nn
Oo
Pp
Qq
Rr
Ss
Tt
Uu
Vv
Ww
Xx
Yy
Zz

a boat

mast
mainsail
boom
stern
bow
rudder
keel
cabin

boat •NOUN• **boats** a vehicle for travelling over the surface of water. A boat is smaller than a ship
• **in the same boat** if two or more people are in the same boat, they have the same problems or face the same difficulties

bob •VERB• **bobs, bobbing, bobbed** to bob is to move up and down quickly above the surface or top of something: *little boats bobbing on the lake* • *I saw their heads bob up from behind the hedge*.

bobbin •NOUN• **bobbins** a round object on which thread is wound, often so that it can be used in a sewing machine

bobble •NOUN• **bobbles 1** a small round piece of soft material used for decoration on clothing, especially on hats **2** a small round object used to tie up or decorate hair

bobby •NOUN• **bobbies** in Britain, an informal name for a policeman

bobsleigh •NOUN• **bobsleighs** a kind of long sledge which has a compartment for the riders and is used for racing down ice slopes

bode •VERB• **bodes** if something bodes well, or bodes ill, it shows that something good, or something bad, is likely to happen

bodice •NOUN• **bodices** the part of a dress that fits tightly on the body above the waist

bodily •ADJECTIVE• bodily means of the body: *Blood and saliva are bodily fluids*.
•ADVERB• entirely: *He was carried bodily down the river by the current*.

body •NOUN• **bodies 1** the whole of a human being or an animal: *I had a rash all over my body*. **2** a dead person or animal: *They found the bodies of hundreds of dead birds on the shore*.

bodyguard •NOUN• **bodyguards** someone whose job is to protect an important or famous person

bog •NOUN• **bogs** an area of land that is very wet and where the ground is so soft that you sink into it
•VERB• **bogs, bogging, bogged** you get **bogged down** in something if it stops you making good progress: *She got bogged down in her sums and couldn't finish the exercise*.
⇒ **boggy**

ⓘ This word comes from the Gaelic word **bogach**, which means *swamp*.

boggle •VERB• **boggles, boggling, boggled** your mind boggles when you are not able to understand or imagine something

boggy •ADJECTIVE• **boggier, boggiest** boggy ground is wet and sinks under you when you step on it

bogus •ADJECTIVE• **1** pretending to be something they are not: *Old people must be careful of bogus salesmen.* **2** false: *The documents turned out to be bogus.*

boil[1] •VERB• **boils, boiling, boiled 1** something boils when it is heated until it bubbles and turns into gas or vapour: *Is the water boiling yet?*
2 to boil a liquid is to heat it until it bubbles : *Boil some water in a saucepan and add the pasta.*
3 to boil food is to cook it in boiling water: *Are you going to boil or fry the potatoes?*
•NOUN• a state of boiling: *Bring the water to the boil.*
⇒ **boiling**

ⓘ This word comes from a French word, **boillir.** The French word comes from the Latin word for *bubble*, with is **bulla.**

boil[2] •NOUN• **boils** a boil is a red painful swelling on the skin caused by an infection

boiling •ADJECTIVE• very hot: *It's boiling in here.*

boiling point •NOUN• **boiling points** the temperature at which a particular liquid boils: *The boiling point of water is 100 degrees Celsius.*

boisterous •ADJECTIVE• very active and full of energy, especially playing roughly and noisily: *The children are excited and are very boisterous.*

bold •ADJECTIVE• **bolder, boldest 1** daring or fearless: *a bold leader* • *It was rather bold of him to ask that question.*
2 standing out clearly: *a bold swirly pattern*
3 heavy printing, like this **bold type**
♦ **boldly** •ADJECTIVE• **1** fearlessly: *He walked boldly into the room, which was full of strangers.* **2** clearly: *The bright red flowers stood out boldly against the green leaves.*

bollard •NOUN• **bollards** a short post placed on a road to stop cars from driving into or on an area

bolster •VERB• **bolsters, bolstering, bolstered** to bolster something, or to bolster it up, is to do something to support or strengthen it: *We were bolstered up by the people cheering us on along the route.*

•NOUN• **bolsters** a long pillow

bolt •NOUN• **bolts 1** a metal bar that slides across to fasten a door
2 a kind of heavy screw that is held in place by a nut
3 a streak of lightning
•VERB• **bolts, bolting, bolted 1** to bolt a door is to fasten it securely with a bolt **2** to bolt is to run away very fast: *There was a loud bang and Beth's pony bolted.*

bomb •NOUN• **bombs** a hollow metal case containing explosives that can be set off
•VERB• **bombs, bombing, bombed** to bomb a place is to drop bombs on it

bombard •VERB• **bombard, bombarding, bombarded 1** an army bombards a place when it attacks it with lots of missiles **2** if you are bombarded with things they come at you very quickly all together or one after the other: *His parents bombarded him with questions.*

bombshell •NOUN• **bombshells** a piece of news that takes you completely by surprise: *Lily dropped a bombshell the other day when she said she was going to another school.*

bond •NOUN• **bonds 1** something that brings or keeps people together: *a bond of friendship*
2 something used for tying someone up or taking away their freedom: *the bonds of slavery*
3 a bond is the strong force that holds two atoms together: *a chemical bond*
•VERB• **bonds, bonding, bonded 1** to bond one thing to another is to make the first thing stick firmly to the second thing: *Use glue to bond the two pieces together.* **2** if two people bond they feel close to each other, usually because they have something in common

bone •NOUN• **bones 1** bone is the hard substance that forms a skeleton and supports the flesh and muscle in the body
2 a bone is one of the pieces of a skeleton: *He broke a bone in his arm.*
⇒ **bony**

bonfire •NOUN• **bonfires** a large fire built outside: *We made a bonfire of all the garden rubbish.*

Aa
Bb
Cc
Dd
Ee
Ff
Gg
Hh
Ii
Jj
Kk
Ll
Mm
Nn
Oo
Pp
Qq
Rr
Ss
Tt
Uu
Vv
Ww
Xx
Yy
Zz

Aa
Bb
Cc
Dd
Ee
Ff
Gg
Hh
Ii
Jj
Kk
Ll
Mm
Nn
Oo
Pp
Qq
Rr
Ss
Tt
Uu
Vv
Ww
Xx
Yy
Zz

bonnet • NOUN• **bonnets** 1 a hat that ties under the chin 2 the piece at the front of a car that covers the engine

bonny • ADJECTIVE• **bonnier, bonniest** pretty: *a bonny baby*

bonsai • NOUN• **bonsai** a very small tree grown in a pot

bonus • NOUN• **bonuses** something extra that is good to get: *We were lucky enough to see the whales and as a bonus one of them jumped right out of the water.*

bony • ADJECTIVE• **bonier, boniest** 1 so thin that the shape of the bones can be seen through the skin: *long bony fingers* 2 full of bones: *a bony piece of fish*

boo • VERB• **boos, booing, booed** people in an audience boo when they make loud rude noises because they don't like what they have seen or heard: *He was booed off the stage.*
• NOUN• **boos** a word that people in an audience shout when they are not pleased

booby prize • NOUN• **booby prizes** the booby prize is a prize sometimes given to the person who has come last

booby trap • NOUN• **booby traps** a booby trap is a trap or bomb that people don't know is there until it is too late

book • NOUN• **books** pages joined together and given a cover
• VERB• **books, booking, booked** you book a table in a restaurant or tickets for an event or a holiday when you tell the restaurant or the company selling the tickets that you want them kept for you: *We've booked a family holiday in France in July.*

book-keeping • NOUN• book-keeping is the keeping of records that show all the money that a business or organization makes and spends

◆ **book-keeper** • NOUN• **book-keepers** someone whose job is to keep a record of the money a business or organization makes or spends

booklet • NOUN• **booklets** a small book, usually with only a few pages, that gives information about something

bookmaker • NOUN• **bookmakers** 1 some-one who takes bets on things like horseraces and pays back money to the people who have won 2 a bookmaker's is a shop where people can make bets

bookmark • NOUN• **bookmarks** a strip of paper or other material that you put between the pages of a book so that you can go back later to the place where you had stopped reading

bookworm • NOUN• **bookworms** someone who likes reading lots of books

boom • NOUN• **booms** 1 a boom is a loud noise like the sound a big drum makes: *We could hear the boom of thunder in the distance.* 2 if there is a boom in business or in a country a lot more things are bought and sold, and more money is made
• VERB• **booms, booming, boomed** 1 to boom is to make a loud sound 2 business booms when a lot more things are sold

boomerang • NOUN• **boomerangs** a boomerang is a curved piece of wood that you throw away from you and which turns in the air and comes back towards you

boon • NOUN• **boons** a boon is something good that happens that you are grateful for: *It would be a real boon if we got hot weather for the barbecue next Saturday.*

boor • NOUN• **boors** a person with no manners, who behaves rudely
◆ **boorish** • ADJECTIVE• rude and coarse: *boorish behaviour*

boost • NOUN• **boosts** something that helps to improve something or raise it to a higher or better level: *The school funds got a boost from the money raised at the summer fair.*
• VERB• **boosts, boosting, boosted** to boost something is to help raise it to a higher or better level: *Playing in the school concert will boost her confidence.*

boot • NOUN• **boots** a kind of shoe that covers the ankle and often part of the leg
• VERB• **boots, booting, booted** 1 to boot something is to kick it: *Georgie booted the ball right over the bar.*
2 to **boot someone out** is to force them to leave: *He was booted out of the club for breaking the rules.*
3 to **boot up** a computer is to start its

operating system, the program that controls all the other programs

booth •NOUN• **booths** a small enclosed compartment used for a particular purpose, for example, to make a phone call, where you can have your photo taken, or where people mark their voting paper in an election

booty •NOUN• booty is the things that thieves, pirates or invading soldiers steal or take by force and keep for themselves: *The thieves were sharing out their booty when the police burst in.*

border •NOUN• **borders 1** the border between two countries or areas is the line on the map which separates them: *They settled near the Canadian and United States border.* **2** an edge of something or a strip round its edge: *a pillowcase with a lace border*
•VERB• **borders, bordering, bordered** one thing **borders on** another when the first thing is very close to the second thing: *Jumping off that wall borders on stupidity.*

borderline •NOUN• **borderlines 1** a line that separates two places or things **2** something that is **on the borderline** is very close to the line or division between two things
•ADJECTIVE• something that is borderline is so close to two different things that it is difficult to decide which it is: *Your work is borderline. You might get a pass or a fail.*

bore¹ •VERB• **bores, boring, bored** if something bores you it makes you feel tired and fed-up because it doesn't interest you: *The speech bored him.*
•NOUN• **bores** someone or something that makes you feel tired and fed-up: *It was a real bore having to sort all the papers.*
⇒ **bored, boredom, boring**

ⓘ Be careful not to confuse the spellings of the noun **boar** meaning a male pig, and the verb and noun **bore**.

bore² •VERB• **bores, boring, bored** to bore something is to use a drill, or something that works like a drill, to make a hole in or through that thing: *The insect bores a tiny hole in the fruit.*

bore³ •VERB• a way of changing the verb **bear** to make a past tense

bored •ADJECTIVE• if you are bored you feel tired and fed-up because you are doing something that isn't interesting, or because you have nothing to do: *I'm bored. Let's go out and play.*

boredom •NOUN• being bored

boring •ADJECTIVE• not at all interesting: *a long boring journey*

born •VERB• **1** a form of the verb **bear** that you use if you are talking about the birth of a baby or animal: *My sister was born three years ago.* **2** to be born is to come into existence: *A new star was born.*
•ADJECTIVE• having a talent you seem to have been born with: *She's a born entertainer.*

borne •VERB• a form of the verb **bear** that is used with a helping verb to show that something happened in the past: *He had borne the hardships of his life without complaining.*

borough •NOUN• **boroughs 1** historically, a borough was a town with special privileges that were granted by the king or queen of the time **2** nowadays, a borough is a town that elects members of parliament

borrow •VERB• **borrows, borrowing, borrowed** to borrow something is to take it with the owner's permission and give it back to them later: *Can I borrow your pencil for a minute, please?*
♦ **borrower** •NOUN• **borrowers** a person who borrows something

ⓘ Try not to confuse **borrowing** and **lending**. If you **borrow** something *from* someone you get it from them, and if you **lend** something *to* someone you give it to them.

bosom •NOUN• **bosoms** someone's bosom is their breast
•ADJECTIVE• a bosom friend is a very close friend

boss •NOUN• **bosses 1** a manager in a workplace who is charge of other people working there: *Her boss gave her a pay rise.* **2** the most important person in a group, who orders the others about: *I'm the boss, so*

you've got to do what I tell you.
•VERB• **bosses, bossing, bossed** to boss people, or to **boss them around**, is to tell them what to do

bossy •ADJECTIVE• **bossier, bossiest** someone who is bossy likes telling other people what to do: *Stop being so bossy. You're not in charge here.*
◆ **bossily** •ADVERB• in a bossy way
◆ **bossiness** •NOUN• being bossy

botanic or **botanical** •ADJECTIVE• to do with plants or the study of plants: *We visited the city's botanic gardens.* • *a botanical specimen*

botanist •NOUN• **botanists** someone who studies plants

botany •NOUN• the study of plants

botch •VERB• **botches, botching, botched** to botch something is to make a mess of it or to do it wrongly: *Carrie was really worried that she'd botched the exam.*

both •ADJECTIVE• both is used to refer to two people or things when you mean the one and also the other: *She ate both cakes, and I didn't get one.* • *Both the boys are good at tennis.*
•PRONOUN• you can say both to talk about two people or things together: *I bought both because they were so pretty.* • *Both of you are good at tennis.*

bother •VERB• **bothers, bothering, bothered 1** if you bother someone, you do something that annoys them or interrupts them: *Stop bothering me, I'm busy.*
2 if something bothers you, it makes you feel unhappy or worried: *He said it didn't bother him that he hadn't won.*
3 to bother to do something is to take the time or trouble to do it: *Don't bother tidying up yet.*
•NOUN• nuisance or trouble: *The address book saves you the bother of having to remember e-mail addresses.* • *It was no bother to help you out.*

bottle •NOUN• **bottles** a container with a narrow neck used for holding liquids like milk, lemonade or wine
•VERB• **bottles, bottling, bottled 1** to bottle a liquid is to put it in a bottle **2** if someone

bottles up unpleasant memories or feelings they aren't able to talk about them to anyone even though it would probably make them feel better if they did

bottle bank •NOUN• **bottle banks** a container where empty glass bottles can be put so that the glass can be recycled

bottleneck •NOUN• **bottlenecks** a place where traffic cannot move properly because the passage has been blocked and is too narrow

bottom •NOUN• **bottoms 1** the lowest part of something: *the bottom of the stairs* • *the bottom of the sea* **2** the part of your body that you sit on
•ADJECTIVE• in the lowest position, with other things above: *the bottom shelf*
◆ **bottomless** •ADJECTIVE• very deep, as if having no bottom: *a bottomless pit*

bough •NOUN• **boughs** one of the bigger branches that grows from the trunk of a tree

ⓘ This word rhymes with **cow**.

bought •VERB• a way of changing the verb **buy** to make a past tense. It can be used with or without a helping verb: *She bought me an ice cream.* • *He has bought the land on which his shop stands.*

boulder •NOUN• **boulders** a big piece of stone or rock

ⓘ Be careful not to confuse the spellings of **bolder** meaning 'more bold' and **boulder** meaning 'a large rock'.

bounce •VERB• **bounces, bouncing, bounced 1** to bounce is to jump up and down quickly on a springy surface: *We bounced on the trampoline.*
2 a ball bounces when it hits something hard and moves away again in another direction
3 if someone **bounces back** they recover quickly from a failure or disappointment
◆ **bouncing** •ADJECTIVE• a bouncing baby is strong and healthy
◆ **bouncy** •ADJECTIVE• springy and able to move up and down: *a bouncy castle*

bound[1] •NOUN• **bounds** a leap or jumping

Aa
Bb
Cc
Dd
Ee
Ff
Gg
Hh
Ii
Jj
Kk
Ll
Mm
Nn
Oo
Pp
Qq
Rr
Ss
Tt
Uu
Vv
Ww
Xx
Yy
Zz

movement: *The deer was over the fence in a single bound.*

•VERB• **bounds, bounding, bounded** to run with jumping movements: *The dogs bounded into the room, barking excitedly.*

bound² •VERB• **bounds, bounding, bounded** the place where one area bounds another is the place which marks the boundary between them: *The farm is bounded in the east by a forest and in the west by a large lake.*

• **out of bounds** if a place is out of bounds you are not allowed to go there: *The riverbank is out of bounds for the younger children.*
⇒ **boundless**

bound³ •ADJECTIVE• **1** going in a particular direction: *We were homeward bound.*

2 to be bound for a place is to be on your way there or planning to go there: *ships bound for the Far East*

3 to be bound to do something is to be certain or very likely to do it: *The plants are bound to grow if you keep them well watered.*

bound⁴ •VERB• a way of changing the verb **bind** to make a past tense. It can be used with or without a helping verb: *He has bound the ropes tight.*

boundary •NOUN• **boundaries** a line that divides a place or thing from what is next to it: *the boundary between the city and the countryside*

boundless •ADJECTIVE• having no limit: *Granny still has boundless energy.*

bountiful •ADJECTIVE• giving generously: *a bountiful harvest*

bounty •NOUN• **bounties 1** bounty is generosity: *The harvest festival is a celebration of nature's bounty.* **2** a bounty is money paid as a reward, especially for capturing or killing a person or animal

bouquet •NOUN• **bouquets** a bunch of flowers

ⓘ This word is pronounced boo-kay.

bout •NOUN• **bouts** a period of something unpleasant, especially illness: *a bout of flu*

boutique •NOUN• **boutiques** a small shop selling fashionable clothes

bovine •ADJECTIVE• to do with cattle: *The full name of the cattle disease BSE is bovine spongiform encephalopathy.*

bow¹ •VERB• **bows, bowing, bowed 1** if you bow to someone you bend your head or the top half of your body forward to greet them or show them respect: *Everyone bowed to the king and queen.*

2 to bow is to bend: *He walked with his head bowed in shame.*

3 if someone **bows to** something they give in to it: *We all had to bow to his demands.*

4 to **bow out** of something that you have been doing before, or that you have said you would do, is to stop doing it or not to take part in it: *He may bow out of politics altogether.*

•NOUN• **bows** a bending of the head or body: *The pianist took a bow when the audience clapped.*

bow² •NOUN• **bows 1** a weapon for shooting arrows

2 a wooden rod with horsehair stretched along it, used for playing a musical instrument such as a violin or cello

3 a knot made with loops on either side: *She wore bows in her hair.*

•VERB• **bows, bowing, bowed 1** to use a bow to play a stringed musical instrument **2** to bend: *The shelf bowed under the weight of the books.*

•ADJECTIVE• bent: *bow legs* • *bow-legged*

bow³ •NOUN• **bows** the pointed front part of a ship or boat: *The anchor is stored in the bow.* • *The bows of the ship hit the pier.*

ⓘ **bow¹** and **bow³** rhyme with **cow**. **bow²** is pronounced **bo**.

bowels •PLURAL NOUN• a long tube inside the lower part of your body that food goes through after leaving your stomach

bowl •NOUN• **bowls 1** a wide container open at the top and used for holding various things: *a soup bowl*

2 anything round and hollow that is shaped like this kind of container, such as a sports stadium

Aa
Bb
Cc
Dd
Ee
Ff
Gg
Hh
Ii
Jj
Kk
Ll
Mm
Nn
Oo
Pp
Qq
Rr
Ss
Tt
Uu
Vv
Ww
Xx
Yy
Zz

Brackets

Brackets ( ) are used in pairs, before and after an extra piece of information in a sentence. You put them round information that does not fit into the flow of a sentence, but which you still want to include, for example:

The policemen turned in the wrong direction (left instead of right).

Sometimes, information in brackets may make a sentence clearer.

Tomorrow (April 30), the new school term begins.

Sometimes, it may help explain something.

Bivalves are molluscs with two (bi) shells (or valves).

The information inside brackets is usually not essential, or not as important as the other information. It could be left out of a sentence, and the meaning of the sentence would not change.

3 a heavy ball used in games like bowls and skittles
•VERB• **bowls, bowling, bowled 1** to bowl is to throw the ball towards the person batting in cricket and rounders
2 to bowl is to play the game of bowls
3 if something **bowls you over**, it overwhelms you: *Wendy was bowled over by their generosity.*

bowler[1] •NOUN• **bowlers 1** someone who bowls in cricket and rounders **2** someone who plays the game of bowls

bowler[2] *or* **bowler hat** •NOUN• **bowlers** *or* **bowler hats** a kind of smart hat worn by men, especially businessmen, that has a rounded top and a narrow brim

bowling •NOUN• **1** the game of tenpin bowling, played with skittles **2** the game of bowls, played on a bowling green

bowls •NOUN• a game in which heavy balls are rolled along a special flat surface called a bowling green

bow tie •NOUN• **bow ties** a tie that is shaped like a small bow and is worn by men

box •NOUN• **boxes** a container, sometimes with a lid, used for holding or storing things
•VERB• **boxes, boxing, boxed 1** to box something is to put it in a box or boxes **2** people box when they hit each other with their fists
• **boxing** •NOUN• a sport in which two

people hit each other with their fists, usually while wearing heavy leather gloves
♦ **boxer** •NOUN• **boxers** someone who does the sport of boxing

Boxing Day •NOUN• the day after Christmas Day

box office •NOUN• a theatre box office is the place where you can buy tickets for shows

boy •NOUN• **boys** a male child

boycott •VERB• **boycotts, boycotting, boycotted** to boycott something or someone is to refuse to buy it or do any sort of business with them
•NOUN• **boycotts** a refusal to buy or sell things or do any sort of business

boyfriend •NOUN• **boyfriends** a male friend, especially someone you are having a special relationship with

boyhood •NOUN• the period of time in your life when you are a boy

boyish •ADJECTIVE• **1** behaving like a boy: *She's always been boyish and full of mischief.* **2** looking like a young boy: *He has a charming boyish grin.*

bra •NOUN• **bras** a piece of underwear that women wear to support their breasts

brace •NOUN• **braces 1** a device that forces or holds two things together tightly **2** a piece of wire put on teeth to straighten them

bracelet •NOUN• **bracelets** a piece of jewellery that you wear around your wrist

braces •PLURAL NOUN• 1 two pieces of elastic or stretchy fabric that are fastened to the back and front of the waistband of trousers to hold the trousers up 2 two sets of wires used to straighten the top and bottom teeth

bracing •ADJECTIVE• healthy and fresh: *a bracing walk by the sea*

bracken •NOUN• a wild plant like a fern that grows in clumps in woods and on hillsides

bracket •NOUN• **brackets** 1 a punctuation symbol usually written or printed in pairs to show that the words, letters, or numbers inside them are separated from the writing coming before or after. See the box called **Brackets**
2 a grouping or category: *Holidays to the Caribbean are in a much higher price bracket than holidays to Spain.*
3 a piece of metal used to attach things to walls

brag •VERB• **brags, bragging, bragged** to brag is to boast: *She's always bragging about her fashionable clothes.*

Brahman or **Brahmin** •NOUN• **Brahmans** or **Brahmins** a person who belongs to the highest ranking group of Hindus

braid •NOUN• **braids** 1 braid is a thick kind of fancy ribbon used to trim things with 2 a plait of hair
•VERB• **braids, braiding, braided** to plait hair

braille •NOUN• a writing system for blind people which instead of printed letters has groups of raised dots which can be read by touching them

ⓘ **Braille** was named after the man who invented it, Louis *Braille*, who was a teacher in France.

brain •NOUN• **brains** the organ inside your skull that controls all the other parts of your body and with which you think

brainwash •VERB• **brainwashes, brainwashing, brainwashed** to brainwash someone is to make them believe something by telling them over and over again that it is true

brainwave •NOUN• **brainwaves** if you have a brainwave you suddenly have a very good idea

brainy •ADJECTIVE• **brainier, brainiest** clever: *Caitlin is definitely brainy enough to be a doctor.*

brake •NOUN• **brakes** a device or system in a vehicle that is used for stopping or slowing down: *Always check your brakes before you go out on a long bike ride.*
•VERB• **brakes, braking, braked** to use a brake to slow down or stop: *He braked suddenly and we were all thrown forward.*

bramble •NOUN• **brambles** a blackberry plant

bran •NOUN• the brown parts that cover wheat grains

branch •NOUN• **branches** 1 any of the parts of a tree that grow out from the trunk: *Rooks build their nests high in the branches of trees.*
2 one of the shops or businesses that belong to a larger organization: *the local branch of the bank*
•VERB• **branches, branching, branched** 1 to form branches or to separate into different parts like the branches of a tree: *The road branches to the north and west.* 2 to **branch out** is to develop in different ways: *He's trying to branch out into selling on the Internet.*

brand •NOUN• **brands** a name given to a particular product by the company that makes it: *This isn't my usual brand of shampoo, but it's just as good as the one I used to buy.*

brandish •VERB• **brandishes, brandishing, brandished** to brandish a weapon is to wave it about in a threatening way: *The robbers burst in brandishing guns.*

brand-new •ADJECTIVE• completely new: *a brand-new bike*

brandy •NOUN• **brandies** a kind of very strong alcoholic drink

brass •NOUN• 1 a metal made by mixing copper and zinc 2 musical instruments made of brass, like trumpets and tubas, that form

part of a bigger orchestra or are used in a brass band
•ADJECTIVE• made of brass: *a brass name plate*
⇒ **brassy**

brass band •NOUN• **brass bands** a musical group in which wind instruments made of brass are played

brassy •ADJECTIVE• **brassier, brassiest** 1 yellowish in colour like brass: *brassy blonde hair* 2 having a loud harsh sound like a musical instrument made of brass: *a brassy voice*

brat •NOUN• **brats** a child who is rude or naughty

bravado •NOUN• behaviour intended to make people believe that you are brave and confident, but which is only done for show

brave •ADJECTIVE• **braver, bravest** able to face danger without fear or able to suffer pain without complaining: *It was brave of you to chase away that bull.*
•NOUN• **braves** a young warrior belonging to a Native American tribe
✦ **bravery** •NOUN• being brave: *an award for bravery*
✦ **bravely** •ADVERB• courageously: *She smiled bravely, though she was in pain.*

bravo •INTERJECTION• a word that people say or shout when they think something is well done: *'I got a prize for my science project.' 'Bravo, that's excellent!'*

brawl •NOUN• **brawls** a noisy fight or quarrel, especially in a public place
•VERB• **brawls, brawling, brawled** to brawl is to fight or quarrel noisily, especially in a public place

brawn •NOUN• big strong muscles or the strength these give
✦ **brawny** •ADJECTIVE• **brawnier, brawniest** having strong muscles: *A brawny young man lifted the boxes out of the van.*

bray •NOUN• **brays** the loud harsh sound a donkey or ass makes
•VERB• **brays, braying, brayed** 1 a donkey or ass brays when it makes this sound 2 a person brays when they speak in a loud harsh-sounding voice

brazen •ADJECTIVE• bold and impudent
• **brazen it out** if someone brazens it out they keep on doing something that other people would find too embarrassing or difficult to continue with
✦ **brazenly** •ADVERB• boldly and impudently

brazier •NOUN• **braziers** a metal container in which coal is burnt to warm people who are standing outside in cold weather

breach •NOUN• **breaches** 1 a gap or hole made in something solid like a wall: *A breach in the dam caused flooding in the valley below.* 2 a breaking of an agreement or a relationship: *a breach of the peace agreement*
•VERB• **breaches, breaching, breached** to break or make a hole in: *The explosion breached the castle wall.*

bread •NOUN• a food whose main ingredient is flour. Bread is baked in an oven and is often cut into slices for making sandwiches and toast

breadth •NOUN• **breadths** the size of something measured from one side to the other: *Measure the length and the breadth and multiply the two to get the area.*

breadwinner •NOUN• **breadwinners** the person in a family who earns the money

break •VERB• **breaks, breaking, broke, broken** 1 something breaks when it falls to pieces: *The vase fell over and broke.*
2 to break something is to cause it to fall to pieces, usually by dropping it or hitting it against something: *Careful, or you'll break that glass.*
3 to break a law is to do something that law forbids
4 to break news is to tell it: *I didn't want to break the bad news to them before they had finished their holiday.*
5 a boy's voice breaks when it gets deeper and becomes like a man's
6 if a machine **breaks down** it stops working
7 if you **break off** what you are doing, you stop doing it for a while
8 fire, fighting or a disease **breaks out** when it starts suddenly
9 school **breaks up** when the term finishes

and the teachers and pupils go on holiday
•NOUN• **breaks** 1 a opening or crack in
something: *a break in the clouds* • *Colin had
a bad break in his leg.*
2 a pause: *a break in her studies*
3 a piece of good luck: *It was a lucky break
finding someone to buy your old bike.*
✦ **breakable** •ADJECTIVE• something
breakable can be broken if you don't handle it
carefully

ⓘ Be careful not to confuse the spellings of
break meaning 'to damage' and **brake**
meaning 'to slow down or stop'.

---

breakdown •NOUN• **breakdowns** 1 a
breakdown happens when a machine breaks
or stops working: *We had a breakdown on
the motorway.* **2** someone has a breakdown
if they become depressed and anxious and
can't cope with everyday life

breaker •NOUN• **breakers** a large wave that
breaks on the shore

breakfast •NOUN• **breakfasts** a meal
people eat in the morning soon after getting
out of bed

break-in •NOUN• **break-ins** an illegal entry
to a house or other building by someone who
intends to cause damage or steal things

breakthrough •NOUN• **breakthroughs** a
sudden success after working for a long
time: *a breakthrough in the treatment of the
disease*

breakwater •NOUN• **breakwaters** a
barrier built in or near the sea that stops the
force of the waves

breast •NOUN• **breasts** 1 the part of the
front of your body between your neck and
your waist **2** either of the two organs on the
front of a woman's body that are used to feed
milk to her baby
• **make a clean breast of it** someone makes a
clean breast of it when they tell the whole
truth, especially about something they have
done wrong

breastbone •NOUN• **breastbones** the bone
that goes down the front of your chest
between your ribs

breaststroke •NOUN• a way of swimming
where you hold your hands together in front

of you and then push forwards and sideways
with your arms, while moving your legs like a
frog

breath •NOUN• **breaths** 1 you take a breath
when you fill your lungs with air and then let
the air out again: *Take a few deep breaths.*
2 your breath is the air that comes out of
your mouth: *We could see our breath in the
freezing air.*
• **under your breath** if you say something
under your breath you say it very quietly

breathe •VERB• **breathes, breathing,
breathed** to take in air through your mouth
or nose into your lungs so that your body
gets the oxygen it needs, and to blow air back
out through your mouth or nose to get rid of
carbon dioxide: *He was so quiet I thought he
wasn't breathing.*

ⓘ Remember that the verb **breathe** has an **e**
at the end, while the noun **breath** does not.
Be careful not to confuse the spellings of the
verb **breathes** and the noun plural **breaths**.

---

breathless •ADJECTIVE• if you are
breathless you are finding it difficult to
breathe, usually because of hard exercise or
an illness like asthma

breathtaking •ADJECTIVE• very
impressive, surprising or exciting: *The
scenery was breathtaking.*

breeches •PLURAL NOUN• breeches are
short trousers that fit or are tied tightly
around the knees

breed •VERB• **breeds, breeding, bred**
1 animals breed when they mate and have
babies or young **2** to breed animals is to
allow them to mate and have young: *a
farmer who breeds rare types of cattle*
•NOUN• **breeds** a particular type of animal:
*The Aberdeen Angus is a famous Scottish
breed of cattle.*
✦ **breeder** •NOUN• **breeders** someone who
breeds animals: *a dog breeder*

breeze •NOUN• **breezes** a light wind
✦ **breezy** •ADJECTIVE• **breezier, breeziest**
1 if the weather is breezy there is a light wind
blowing **2** someone who is breezy is cheerful
and light-hearted: *He's always bright and
breezy in the mornings.*

Aa
Bb
Cc
Dd
Ee
Ff
Gg
Hh
Ii
Jj
Kk
Ll
Mm
Nn
Oo
Pp
Qq
Rr
Ss
Tt
Uu
Vv
Ww
Xx
Yy
Zz

brethren .PLURAL NOUN. an old-fashioned word meaning 'brothers'

brevity .NOUN. shortness: *Aim for brevity when you are e-mailing people.*

brew .VERB. brews, brewing, brewed 1 to make beer
2 to make tea by letting tea leaves soak in boiling water
3 if there is a storm or trouble brewing, then it is just about to begin
◆ **brewer** .NOUN. brewers a person or business that makes beer
◆ **brewery** .NOUN. breweries a factory where beer is made

briar *or* **brier** .NOUN. briars *or* briers a wild rose bush with prickly stems

bribe .NOUN. bribes a bribe is money or a gift offered to someone to get them to do something: *He was accused of taking bribes.*
.VERB. bribes, bribing, bribed to bribe someone is to offer them money or a gift to get them to do something: *You shouldn't have to be bribed with sweets to do your homework.*
◆ **bribery** .NOUN. offering or taking bribes

bric-a-brac .NOUN. small ornaments that are interesting or attractive but which aren't worth very much

brick .NOUN. bricks a block of baked clay used for building

bricklayer .NOUN. bricklayers a worker whose job is to build things with bricks, especially walls

bridal .ADJECTIVE. used by a bride or having to do with brides: *a bridal bouquet* • *a white bridal car*

bride .NOUN. brides a bride is a woman on her wedding day

bridegroom .NOUN. bridegrooms a bridegroom is a man on his wedding day

bridesmaid .NOUN. bridesmaids a bridesmaid is a girl or unmarried woman who helps a bride on her wedding day

bridge .NOUN. bridges 1 a structure built over a river, road or valley, to allow people or vehicles to cross from one side to the other
2 a platform on a ship where the captain usually stands
3 the bridge of your nose is the bony part

bridle .NOUN. bridles a horse's bridle is the part of its harness that goes around its head: *She attached the reins to the horse's bridle.*

brief .ADJECTIVE. briefer, briefest short: *The lesson was much briefer than Malcolm thought it was going to be.*
.VERB. briefs, briefing, briefed to brief someone is to give them information or instructions about something: *Our coach always briefs us before a match on the other team's strengths.*
.NOUN. briefs someone, especially a lawyer, is given a brief when they are given the information or instructions they need to do their work
◆ **briefly** .ADVERB. in a short form or for a short time: *Tell us briefly what you want us to do.* • *They stopped briefly to get more petrol.*

briefcase .NOUN. briefcases a flat case for carrying business papers in

briefs .PLURAL NOUN. briefs are short underpants

brier .NOUN. briers another spelling of **briar**

brigade .NOUN. brigades 1 a group of soldiers that form part of an army division 2 a group of people who do a special job: *the fire brigade*

brigadier .NOUN. brigadiers an army officer in command of a brigade

bright .ADJECTIVE. brighter, brightest
1 giving out a lot of light or having a lot of light: *the bright lights of the city* • *a nice bright bedroom*
2 a bright colour is strong and clear: *His eyes were bright blue.*
3 to feel bright is to feel cheerful and happy, and to be interested in what is going on around you: *Grandad was a lot brighter this morning when I saw him.*
4 a bright person is clever: *She's bright but she's a bit lazy.*
◆ **brighten** .VERB. brightens, brightening, brightened 1 to make or become lighter or sunnier: *The weather brightened up and we went out for a walk* 2 to make or become more cheerful and happy: *Jack brightened a bit when I suggested a game of cricket.*

♦ **brightly** •ADVERB• in a bright way: *The sun shone brightly.*

♦ **brightness** •NOUN• being bright

brilliance •NOUN• **1** being very bright or giving out strong light: *the brilliance of the crown jewels* **2** impressiveness or cleverness: *She shows brilliance as an actress.*

brilliant •ADJECTIVE• **1** very bright or giving out strong light: *brilliant sunshine* **2** very clever or impressive: *Fiona gave a brilliant speech.*

♦ **brilliantly** •ADVERB• **1** very brightly: *The arena was brilliantly lit.* **2** very cleverly or impressively: *In the school play, Sanjay plays the bad-tempered old king brilliantly.*

brim •NOUN• **brims 1** the edge of a container: *His glass was filled right up to the brim.* **2** the lower part of a hat that sticks out: *She wore a big felt hat with the brim turned up.* •VERB• **brims, brimming, brimmed** a container brims when it is full up to its top edge

♦ **brimming** •ADJECTIVE• full to the brim: *a brimming mug of hot soup*

brine •NOUN• water with salt in it, often used to keep food in

bring •VERB• **brings, bringing, brought 1** to bring is to take, lead or carry a person or thing with you: *You can bring all your friends to the party.* • *He'd brought a couple of jigsaws out of the cupboard.*
2 if one thing brings another the first thing causes the second to come: *The drought brought famine to the area.*
3 if one event **brings about** another the first causes the second: *The changes in climate were thought to have been brought about by global warming.*
4 if someone **brings something off**, they manage to do it successfully
5 if you **bring someone round**, you persuade them to change their opinion and agree with you: *We have to bring him round to our point of view.*
6 to **bring someone round** when they are unconscious is to make them wake up
7 to **bring up** a subject is to mention it: *You shouldn't have brought up the subject of money.*
8 to **bring up** children or young animals is to look after them until they are old enough to look after themselves: *Oliver Twist was brought up in an orphanage.*
9 if someone **brings up** their food, they vomit

brink •NOUN• **1** the edge of something high or deep, like a cliff or river: *The boat stopped right on the brink of a waterfall.* **2** if you are on the brink of something, it is about to happen: *We could see that Noreen was on the brink of tears.*

brisk •ADJECTIVE• **brisker, briskest** quick and lively: *walking at a brisk pace*
♦ **briskly** •ADVERB• quickly
♦ **briskness** •NOUN• being brisk

bristle •NOUN• **bristles** a short stiff hair: *This brush is losing its bristles.*
♦ **bristly** •ADJECTIVE• **bristlier, bristliest** having or covered with bristles: *Dad had a bristly chin because he hadn't shaved.*

brittle •ADJECTIVE• hard but easily broken: *Eggshells are brittle.*

broach •VERB• **broaches, broaching, broached** to broach a subject or question is to begin to talk about it

broad •ADJECTIVE• **broader, broadest**
1 having a relatively large width: *a broad avenue* • *My feet are small but broad.*
2 a broad accent or dialect is strong or noticeable: *He wrote poetry in broad Scots.*
♦ **broaden** •VERB• **broadens, broadening, broadened** to make wider: *They'd broadened the road and made two lanes.*
♦ **broadly** •ADVERB• **1** widely: *He was smiling broadly, so we knew everything was okay.* **2** generally: *Your essay is broadly right, but not detailed enough.*
♦ **broadness** •NOUN• how broad something is

broadcast •VERB• **broadcasts, broadcasting, broadcast 1** a TV or radio station broadcasts when it sends out programmes which people can receive on their televisions or radios **2** to broadcast something is to tell it to a lot of people: *Someone's been broadcasting lies about him.* •NOUN• **broadcasts** a programme sent out by a TV or radio station

Aa
Bb
Cc
Dd
Ee
Ff
Gg
Hh
Ii
Jj
Kk
Ll
Mm
Nn
Oo
Pp
Qq
Rr
Ss
Tt
Uu
Vv
Ww
Xx
Yy
Zz

✦ **broadcaster** •NOUN• **broadcasters** someone whose job is presenting programmes on TV or radio

✦ **broadcasting** •NOUN• the work or business of TV and radio stations

broad-minded •ADJECTIVE• someone who is broad-minded thinks other people should be free to think or act as they want to

broadsheet •NOUN• **broadsheets** a newspaper printed on large sheets of paper folded in the middle, especially a newspaper that deals with news in a serious way

broccoli •NOUN• a vegetable with lots of tiny tightly-packed green or purple flowerheads growing from a thick stalk

brochure •NOUN• **brochures** a booklet with information about a particular range of products, often with pictures: *a holiday brochure*

brogue¹ •NOUN• **brogues** a heavy kind of leather shoe with laces and often a pattern punched in the leather

brogue² •NOUN• **brogues** a strong accent: *an Irish brogue*

broke¹ •VERB• a way of changing the verb **break** to make a past tense: *She always broke their toys, but she didn't mean to.*

broke² •ADJECTIVE• having no money: *I can't afford a holiday, I'm completely broke.*

broken •VERB• a form of the verb **break** that is used with a helping verb to show that something happened in the past: *A curious crack sounded, as if something had broken.* •ADJECTIVE• 1 with a break or breaks: *a broken window* 2 a broken home is a home in which one of the parents has left to live somewhere else

bronchitis •NOUN• a lung disease which makes breathing difficult

bronco •NOUN• **broncos** a wild horse from the west of the United States

brontosaurus •NOUN• **brontosauruses** *or* **brontosauri** a kind of huge dinosaur with a small head and a very long neck and tail, which ate plants

bronze •NOUN• 1 a metal that is a mixture of copper and tin: *The statue was cast in*

bronze. 2 a yellowish-brown colour like this metal
•ADJECTIVE• made of, or the colour of, bronze: *a bronze medal*

✦ **bronzed** •ADJECTIVE• covered with bronze or of a yellowish-brown colour like bronze: *bronzed skin*

bronze medal •NOUN• **bronze medals** a medal made of bronze awarded to the person who comes third in sporting events

brooch •NOUN• **brooches** a piece of jewellery with a pin or clasp that you fasten on to your collar or near the shoulder of your dress or jacket

ⓘ This word rhymes with **coach**.

brood •NOUN• **broods** a brood is several young birds or reptiles with the same mother that hatch out of their eggs at the same time •VERB• **broods, brooding, brooded** 1 a bird broods when it sits on its eggs to hatch them 2 to **brood over** or **about** something is to think hard or worry about it for a long time: *Gabriel's brooding over the goal he gave away in the final.*

✦ **broody** •ADJECTIVE• 1 a broody hen is sitting on eggs to hatch them 2 if someone is broody they are thinking long and hard about something

brook •NOUN• **brooks** a small stream

broom •NOUN• **brooms** a brush with a long handle, used for sweeping floors

broomstick •NOUN• **broomsticks** a long handle with thin sticks tied to one end that witches are supposed to ride on

broth •NOUN• **broths** a kind of soup made with vegetables and sometimes meat

brother •NOUN• **brothers** your brother is a boy or man who has the same parents as you do

✦ **brotherhood** •NOUN• **brotherhoods** 1 brotherhood is a feeling of friendship among boys and men 2 a brotherhood is a group or society for men

brother-in-law •NOUN• **brothers-in-law** your sister's husband, or your husband or wife's brother, or your husband or wife's sister's husband

brought •VERB• a way of changing the verb **bring** to make a past tense. It can be used with or without a helping verb: *Jeremy brought me a cup of hot tea.* • *I have brought a box of chocolates for you.*

brow •NOUN• **brows 1** your brow is your forehead
2 your brows are your eyebrows
3 the brow of a hill is the point at the top from where it slopes down

browbeat •VERB• **browbeats, browbeating, browbeat, browbeaten** to browbeat someone is to bully them with words

brown •NOUN• the colour of soil and most kinds of wood, made by mixing red, yellow and blue

brownie •NOUN• **brownies 1** a good helpful fairy who is described in fairy stories as wearing a brown costume and hat **2** a Brownie is a member of the Brownie Guides, the junior branch of the Guide Association

browse •VERB• **browses, browsing, browsed** to browse is to look quickly through a range of different things, such as the books in a bookshop, to see if there is anything you want or like
♦ **browser** •NOUN• **browsers** a browser is a computer program that lets you search and move around the Internet

bruise •NOUN• **bruises** a mark on the skin caused by a knock or blow: *He's got a big bruise just under his eye.*
•VERB• **bruises, bruising, bruised** to make a bruise on someone or something's skin: *Daniel bruised his knees when he fell.* • *Be careful not to bruise the peaches when you handle them.*

brunette •ADJECTIVE• having brown hair
•NOUN• **brunettes** someone with brown hair

brunt •NOUN• to **bear** or **take the brunt of** something is to take its full force: *The side of the bus bore the brunt of the impact.*

brush •NOUN• **brushes 1** a device with tufts of bristles used to smooth hair, paint with, or clean dirt or dust away **2** to have a brush with something is to have a short meeting with it: *a brush with the law*
•VERB• **brushes, brushing, brushed 1** to move a brush over: *Have you brushed your hair?* **2** to **brush against** something is to touch it lightly with part of your body

Brussels sprout •NOUN• **Brussels sprouts** a vegetable that looks like a tiny cabbage

brutal •ADJECTIVE• very cruel: *a brutal murder*
♦ **brutality** •NOUN• violent cruelty
♦ **brutally** •ADVERB• cruelly, savagely: *The poor horses had been brutally beaten.*

brute •NOUN• **brutes 1** an animal, especially a big strong animal like a bull or a horse **2** a very cruel or savage man

BSE •ABBREVIATION• short for *bovine spongiform encephalopathy*, a disease that affects the brains of cattle. Many people call it mad cow disease

bubble •NOUN• **bubbles 1** a very thin light ball of liquid filled with air: *soap bubbles* **2** a small ball of air inside a liquid: *We could see the air bubbles in the water.*
•VERB• **bubbles, bubbling, bubbled 1** something bubbles when small balls of air form in it: *A big pot of soup was bubbling on the stove.* **2** if something bubbles up it is forced up to the surface like bubbles rising in a liquid: *Excitement was bubbling up inside her.*
♦ **bubbly** •ADJECTIVE• **bubblier, bubbliest 1** full of bubbles: *The paint had gone all bubbly in the heat of the sun.* **2** full of energy and life: *She has a bubbly personality.*

buccaneer •NOUN• **buccaneers** someone who attacks ships while they are at sea and steals things from them: *an adventure story about pirates and buccaneers*

buck •NOUN• **bucks 1** a male rabbit, hare or deer **2** an informal word for an American dollar: *It cost twenty bucks.*
•VERB• **bucks, bucking, bucked** a horse bucks when it jumps into the air kicking its back legs outwards

bucket •NOUN• **buckets 1** a container, usually with a handle, used for carrying water or things like earth, sand or cement **2** the amount that a bucket will hold: *four buckets of water*

bucketful •NOUN• **bucketfuls** the amount that a bucket will hold: *We'll need a couple*

Aa
Bb
Cc
Dd
Ee
Ff
Gg
Hh
Ii
Jj
Kk
Ll
Mm
Nn
Oo
Pp
Qq
Rr
Ss
Tt
Uu
Vv
Ww
Xx
Yy
Zz

Aa

more bucketfuls of sand to finish the castle.

Bb

buckle •NOUN• **buckles** a clip for fastening a belt or a strap
•VERB• **buckles, buckling, buckled 1** to buckle something is to fasten it with a buckle: *one, two, buckle my shoe* **2** to **buckle down** is to start working hard or with determination: *You'll have to buckle down to work when you go back to school.*

Cc

Dd

Ee

Ff

bud •NOUN• **buds** the part of a tree or plant from which a leaf or flower develops
•VERB• **buds, budding, budded** a plant buds when its buds start to show

Gg

Hh

Buddhism •NOUN• a religion, practised in many parts of the world, that follows the teachings of Buddha
♦ **Buddhist** •NOUN• **Buddhists** someone who follows the teachings of Buddha
•ADJECTIVE• to do with Buddhism or Buddhists

Ii

Jj

Kk

Ll

budding •ADJECTIVE• in the early stages of becoming something: *Henry's a budding scientist.*

Mm

budge •VERB• **budges, budging, budged** to budge means to move slightly: *We all tried to turn the key in the lock, but it wouldn't budge.*

Nn

Oo

Pp

budgerigar •NOUN• **budgerigars** a small bird with brightly coloured feathers that is often kept as a pet

Qq

Rr

budget •NOUN• **budgets** a plan for spending, usually for a certain time period: *We had a monthly budget of £200 for food and bus fares.*
•VERB• **budgets, budgeting, budgeted** to budget is to decide what you are able to spend money on: *We'll have to budget very carefully to make our money last a fortnight.*

Ss

Tt

Uu

Vv

budgie •NOUN• **budgies** a budgerigar: *We've taught our budgie to talk.*

Ww

Xx

buff •NOUN• **1** a light yellowish-brown colour: *buff envelopes* **2** someone who is interested in a particular subject and knows a lot about it: *a film buff • a computer buff*
•VERB• **buffs, buffing, buffed** to buff a surface, or to **buff it up**, is to rub it with a soft dry cloth to make it shiny

Yy

Zz

buffalo •NOUN• **buffalos** or **buffaloes 1** a large ox with big curved horns, found in Asia and Africa **2** a bison

buffer •NOUN• **buffers** something designed to reduce the force of a collision, especially the metal posts on a railway barrier that help bring a moving train to a stop

buffet[1] •NOUN• **buffets 1** a compartment on a train where food and drinks are served **2** various types of food set out on a table at a party for people to help themselves

buffet[2] •VERB• **buffets, buffeting, buffeted** to buffet something is to knock it about roughly: *The little boat was buffeted by the storm.*

ⓘ **buffet**[1] is pronounced **boof**-ay, with a silent t a the end.
buffet[2] is pronounced **buf**-it.

---

buffoon •NOUN• **buffoons** a clown or a fool

bug •NOUN• **bugs 1** a small insect, especially one that bites
2 a germ that causes illness: *She had a tummy bug.*
3 a tiny hidden microphone used to record secretly what people say
4 a fault in a computer program that stops it working properly
•VERB• **bugs, bugging, bugged 1** to bug someone is to annoy them **2** to bug a room or a telephone is to put a hidden microphone in it to record what people say

buggy •NOUN• **buggies** a baby's pushchair

bugle •NOUN• **bugles** a instrument like a small trumpet, used for military signals

build •VERB• **builds, building, built 1** to build something is to put together its parts bit by bit: *He's building a wall. • Milk builds healthy teeth and bones.* **2** if something **builds you up** it makes you stronger
•NOUN• your build is the shape of your body: *He's got a strong, muscular build.*

builder •NOUN• **builders** someone who builds and repairs houses

building •NOUN• **buildings 1** building is the trade or action of making houses and other structures: *There is a lot of building going on in this street.* **2** a building is a house or other structure: *New York has lots of tall buildings.*

building society •NOUN• **building societies** an organization, rather like a bank, whose main business is lending money so that people can buy houses

bulb • NOUN• **bulbs 1** the rounded part of plants like onions or tulips that the rest grows out of: *daffodil bulbs* **2** a glass globe with an electrical part inside that gives out light: *The bulb's gone in my bedside lamp.*

bulge • NOUN• **bulges** a swelling or lump: *I knew the cat was in the bed when I saw the bulge in the duvet.*
•VERB• **bulges, bulging, bulged** to bulge is to stick out: *His eyes bulged in horror.*

bulk • NOUN• **1** something's bulk is its size, especially if it is large and heavy: *Wrestlers use their bulk to throw their opponents.*
2 the bulk of something is most of it: *The bulk of his pocket money was spent on computer games.*
3 if you buy **in bulk**, you buy large quantities at one time: *It's much cheaper to buy household goods in bulk.*
♦ **bulky** • ADJECTIVE• **bulkier, bulkiest** large or taking up a lot of space: *a bulky package*

bull • NOUN• **bulls 1** the male of a type of cattle or ox: *Don't go into that field. There's a bull in it.* **2** a male elephant or a male whale
• **a bull in a china shop** a clumsy person
• **take the bull by the horns** to deal with a difficult problem in a very determined way

bulldog • NOUN• **bulldogs** a kind of dog with short legs, a strong body and a wrinkled face

bulldozer • NOUN• **bulldozers** a large machine with a heavy triangular metal device at the front used to move big amounts of earth and stones

bullet • NOUN• **bullets** a piece of shaped metal fired from a gun
• **bite the bullet** if you bite the bullet, you make a decision to do something that you don't really want to do

bulletin • NOUN• **bulletins** a report of the latest news: *The next bulletin will be at 6 p.m.*

bullet-proof • ADJECTIVE• specially

strengthened so that bullets cannot go through: *a bullet-proof vest*

bullfight • NOUN• **bullfights** a kind of entertainment held in Spain and some other countries, in which a bull charges at men on horseback or on foot, and is usually killed with a sword by a man called a matador
♦ **bullfighter** • NOUN• **bullfighters** someone who fights bulls as part of this entertainment

bullion • NOUN• brick-shaped bars of gold or silver

bullock • NOUN• **bullocks** a young bull

bull's-eye • NOUN• **bull's-eyes** the mark in the centre of an archery target or dartboard that scores very high points if you hit it

bully • NOUN• **bullies** a person who is cruel to people smaller or weaker than they are
•VERB• **bullies, bullying, bullied** to be cruel to smaller or weaker people
♦ **bullying** • NOUN• what bullies do to people smaller or weaker than they are

bum [1] • NOUN• **bums** a very informal word for your bottom

bum [2] • NOUN• **bums** a tramp or beggar

bumbag • NOUN• **bumbags** a small bag that hangs from a strap tied around your waist

bumblebee • NOUN• **bumblebees** a kind of bee with a fat yellow and black striped body

bump • NOUN• **bumps 1** a knock or blow: *He got a bump on the head and was knocked unconscious.* **2** a raised or swollen part on the surface of something: *a road with speed bumps to slow the traffic down*
•VERB• **bumps, bumping, bumped 1** to bump something is to knock it by accident: *Try not to bump my arm when I'm writing.*
• *The baby bumped her head on the table.*
2 if you **bump into** someone you meet them by chance: *I bumped into Helen in the street yesterday.*

bumper • NOUN• **bumpers** a car's bumper is the piece of metal or plastic around the front or back that protects it from knocks
• ADJECTIVE• a bumper crop or a bumper harvest is bigger than usual

bumpy • ADJECTIVE• **bumpier, bumpiest** full of bumps: *a very bumpy ride across the fields*

bun •NOUN• **buns** a kind of cake made with sweet dough: *a currant bun*

bunch •NOUN• **bunches** a group of things tied or growing together: *a bunch of grapes* • *He carried a big bunch of keys.*
•VERB• **bunches, bunching, bunched** to **bunch together**, or to **bunch up**, is to be or move close together: *The sheep bunched together and the sheepdog couldn't separate them.*

bundle •NOUN• **bundles** a number of things fastened or tied up together: *a bundle of newspapers*
•VERB• **bundles, bundling, bundled 1** to bundle things is to tie them up in a bundle **2** to bundle someone into something is to push them roughly into it: *He was bundled into a taxi before the photographers could see him.*

bung •NOUN• **bungs** something used to block a hole so that liquid does not get in or out
•VERB• **bungs, bunging, bunged** to **bung something up** is to block it: *His voice sounded funny because his nose was all bunged up.*

bungalow •NOUN• **bunglalows** a house with only one storey

bungee jumping •NOUN• a sport where you jump from a high place with strong rubber ropes attached to your ankles so that you bounce back up again before you reach the ground

bungle •VERB• **bungles, bungling, bungled** to bungle something is to do it badly or clumsily
♦ **bungler** •NOUN• **bunglers** someone who makes a mess of doing something
♦ **bungling** •ADJECTIVE• making mistakes or clumsy

bunk •NOUN• **bunks** a narrow bed fitted against a wall like the bed in a ship's cabin
• **do a bunk** if someone does a bunk they run away, usually to escape something unpleasant

bunk bed •NOUN• **bunk beds** two or more beds built one above the other

bunker •NOUN• **bunkers 1** a sandpit on a golf course that players try to avoid because it is difficult to hit the ball out of

2 a large box or container for storing coal **3** an underground shelter used to escape from bombs during a war

bunny •NOUN• **bunnies** a rabbit

Bunsen burner •NOUN• **Bunsen burners** a gas burner with an open flame used to heat things up in science laboratories

bunting •NOUN• a row of little flags tied to a length of rope and used to decorate ships or streets during celebrations

buoy •NOUN• **buoys** a large floating object anchored to the seabed and used to mark a shipping channel or to warn ships that there is shallow water

ⓘ Lots of people get the spelling of **buoy** wrong. Remember the **u**, which comes before the **o**, not after it.

buoyant •ADJECTIVE• able to float

bur •NOUN• **burs** another spelling of **burr**

burden •NOUN• **burdens** something that has to be carried: *donkeys with heavy burdens on their backs*
•VERB• **burdens, burdening, burdened** to burden someone is to give them a load to carry: *I was burdened with all the suitcases.*

bureau •NOUN• **bureaux 1** an office where you can get information: *a travel bureau* **2** a writing desk with drawers

burglar •NOUN• **burglars** a criminal who breaks into a house or other building to steal things
♦ **burglary** •NOUN• **burglaries** the crime of breaking into houses to steal things

burial •NOUN• **burials** putting a dead person in the ground

burly •ADJECTIVE• **burlier, burliest** a burly person is big, strong and heavy

burn •VERB• **burns, burning, burnt 1** to burn something is to set fire to it: *Be careful with that wok or you'll burn the house down.* **2** to burn is to be on fire: *We could see the grass burning from miles away.* **3** if something burns you it injures you by burning or being very hot: *The soup burnt his tongue.*
•NOUN• **burns** an injury or mark left after touching fire or something very hot

burp •VERB• **burps, burping, burped** to burp is to make a rude sound by letting air come out of your stomach through your mouth •NOUN• **burps** this sound

burr or **bur** •NOUN• **burrs** or **burs** the small prickly case full of seeds that some plants have

burrow •NOUN• **burrows** a hole in the ground made by a rabbit or other animal •VERB• **burrows, burrowing, burrowed** to burrow is to make a hole in the ground

burst •VERB• **bursts, bursting, burst 1** to break or tear, especially from being put under too much pressure: *He blew and blew until the balloon burst.* **2** to **burst in** is to come in suddenly and noisily: *He burst in just as I was falling asleep.* •ADJECTIVE• having burst: *a burst tyre*

bury •VERB• **buries, burying, buried 1** to bury a dead person is to put their body in the ground **2** to bury something is to cover or hide it: *She buried her face in her hands.* • **bury the hatchet** people who have been fighting or quarrelling bury the hatchet when they make up

bus •NOUN• **buses** a large vehicle with lots of seats for passengers

busby •NOUN• **busbies** a tall fur hat worn by certain soldiers

bush •NOUN• **bushes** a plant that has many leaves and is smaller than a tree: *a rose bush* • **bushy** •ADJECTIVE• **bushier, bushiest** **1** covered with bushes **2** growing thickly: *a long bushy tail*

business •NOUN• **businesses 1** business is buying and selling, and the work of producing things that people want to buy: *He went into business with his brother.* **2** a business is any company that makes and sells goods, or that sells services **3** someone's business is their work or trade: *What business are you in?* • **go out of business** a company goes out of business when it stops trading • **mind your own business** to mind your own business is to pay attention only to your own personal affairs or things that concern you directly

businesslike •ADJECTIVE• someone who is businesslike deals with things in a practical and efficient way

businessman •NOUN• **businessmen** a man whose work is in a business

businesswoman •NOUN• **businesswomen** a woman whose work is in a business

busker •NOUN• **buskers** a musician who plays in the street and gets money from passers-by

bus stop •NOUN• **bus stops** a place where a bus stops on its route to let passengers get on and off

bust •NOUN• **busts 1** a woman's bust is her breasts **2** a bust is a sculpture of a person's head and shoulders •ADJECTIVE• **1** broken: *The video's bust.* **2** bankrupt: *The business is almost bust.*

bustle •VERB• **bustles, bustling, bustled** to bustle is hurry or make yourself busy: *She was bustling around trying to make lunch.*

busy •ADJECTIVE• **busier, busiest 1** someone is busy when they have a lot to do: *You'll need something to keep you busy during the school holidays.* **2** if a place or a road is busy there are lots of people or a lot of traffic in it: *London's busy streets* • **busily** •ADVERB• in a busy, hard-working way: *He was busily trying to persuade all his friends to join the club.*

busybody •NOUN• **busybodies** a nosy person who tries to find out everyone else's business

but •CONJUNCTION• **1 but** is used between parts of a sentence to show that there is a difference between the first part and the second part: *I can cycle but I can't drive.* • *He'd like to have gone to the pictures but he doesn't have any money.* **2 but** is also used between parts of a sentence to mean 'except': *You are nothing but a liar.* •PREPOSITION• except: *No one but me turned up.*

butcher •NOUN• **butchers 1** someone whose job is to carve up raw meat **2** a butcher's is a shop that sells meat

butler •NOUN• **butlers** a male servant who looks after a rich person or who is in charge of the other servants in a rich person's house

Aa
Bb
Cc
Dd
Ee
Ff
Gg
Hh
Ii
Jj
Kk
Ll
Mm
Nn
Oo
Pp
Qq
Rr
Ss
Tt
Uu
Vv
Ww
Xx
Yy
Zz

butt •NOUN• **butts** 1 the butt of a gun or rifle is the thick part furthest away from the barrel 2 if you are the butt of other people's jokes, they all make jokes about you or laugh at you •VERB• **butts, butting, butted** 1 to butt something is to hit it using the head: *The goat butted me when I tried to stroke it.* 2 to **butt in** is to interrupt other people while they are talking together

butter •NOUN• a yellow fatty food made from milk and used to spread on bread or for cooking •VERB• **butters, buttering, buttered** 1 to spread butter on bread or toast: *Mum buttered and filled about two hundred sandwiches for the party.* 2 if you **butter someone up** you say flattering things to them so that they will help you or be nice to you ◆ **buttery** •ADJECTIVE• tasting or looking like butter

buttercup •NOUN• **buttercups** a common wild flower with yellow petals

butterfly •NOUN• **butterflies** a kind of insect with brightly coloured patterned wings

buttermilk •NOUN• the part of milk that is left after making butter

butterscotch •NOUN• a type of hard toffee made with butter

buttocks •PLURAL NOUN• your buttocks are your bottom

button •NOUN• **buttons** 1 a round object used to fasten clothes 2 something you press to make a machine work •VERB• **buttons, buttoning, buttoned** to fasten with buttons

buttonhole •NOUN• **buttonholes** a hole that you push a button through to fasten your clothes

buttress •NOUN• **buttresses** a support built against a wall

buy •VERB• **buys, buying, bought** to buy something is to give money so that it becomes yours: *I've bought all their albums.* ◆ **buyer** •NOUN• **buyers** someone who buys something: *We couldn't find a buyer for our old computer.*

buzz •VERB• **buzzes, buzzing, buzzed** 1 to make a sound like a bee: *Flies buzzed round* our heads. 2 to **buzz about** or **around** is to move about busily and quickly: *He was buzzing about trying to organize everyone.* •NOUN• **buzzes** 1 the sound a bee makes when it is flying 2 a murmuring sound made by lots of people talking at once: *a buzz of excitement* 3 a pleasant feeling you get when you do something exciting or successful: *I always get a buzz out of performing on stage.* 4 a call using the telephone: *Give me a buzz tomorrow.*

buzzard •NOUN• **buzzards** a large bird which kills and eats small animals

buzzer •NOUN• **buzzers** a device that makes a buzzing noise

by •PREPOSITION• 1 near to or next to something: *the big house by the station* 2 past someone or something: *He ran by me.* 3 through, along or across something: *We came by the north road.* 4 something is by someone when they are the person who has created it: *a painting by Turner* 5 something happens or is done by a certain time when it happens or is done no later than that time: *I'll be home by 7.30.* 6 by means of something: *go by train* 7 to the extent of something: *He won by a whisker.* 8 by is used when giving measurements of length and width: *The room is 5 metres by 3 metres.* 9 by is used to say how much or how often: *Will he be paid by the week or by the month?* •ADVERB• 1 near: *They all stood by, watching but doing nothing to help.* 2 past: *The cars went whizzing by.* 3 aside: *Try to put some money by for an emergency.* • **by and by** after some time: *By and by, they came to a little house in the middle of the wood.* • **by the way** something you say when you want to add something to what you have just said: *I've made soup for later, I've fed the cat, and by the way, there's no milk left.*

by- •PREFIX• **by-** is put in front of some words where it adds the meaning 'at or to the side': *bystander* • *bypass*

bye •NOUN• **byes** 1 a short way of saying **goodbye** 2 in competitions, you get a bye if you have no opponent in a round and automatically go into the next round

bye-bye •INTERJECTION• a more informal way of saying **goodbye**

by-election •NOUN• **by-elections** an election to vote in a new member of parliament that happens between general elections

bygone •ADJECTIVE• bygone days are in the past: *In bygone days, when there were no telephones or computers.*

by-law •NOUN• **by-laws** a law made by a local council rather than by a national parliament

bypass •NOUN• **bypasses** a road built around a town or city so that traffic does not need to pass through the town or city •VERB• **bypasses, bypassing, bypassed** to go round something rather than through it

by-product •NOUN• **by-products** something useful that is produced when making something else

bystander •NOUN• **bystanders** someone who watches something happening but isn't involved in it

byte •NOUN• **bytes** a unit used to measure computer memory or data

ⓘ Remember that a computer **byte** is spelt with a **y**.

Aa
Bb
Cc
Dd
Ee
Ff
Gg
Hh
Ii
Jj
Kk
Ll
Mm
Nn
Oo
Pp
Qq
Rr
Ss
Tt
Uu
Vv
Ww
Xx
Yy
Zz

Cc

C • ABBREVIATION • short for **Celsius** or **centigrade**

cab • NOUN • **cabs** 1 a taxi: *We took a cab to the airport.* 2 a compartment at the front of a lorry or bus where the driver sits

cabaret • NOUN • **cabarets** a show in a club or restaurant, which usually includes singers, dancers and comedians

ⓘ This word is pronounced **cab**-a-ray.

cabbage • NOUN • **cabbages** a large round green vegetable with layers of leaves packed close together

cabin • NOUN • **cabins** 1 a wooden hut or house: *a log cabin*
2 one of the small rooms in a ship used by passengers or crew members to sleep in
3 the part of an aeroplane where the passengers sit

cabin crew • NOUN • **cabin crews** the people whose job it is to look after the passengers on an aeroplane

cabinet • NOUN • **cabinets** 1 a cupboard with shelves and doors used for storing things: *a bathroom cabinet* 2 a group of government members who decide what the government will do

cable • NOUN • **cables** 1 strong metal rope used for tying up ships or for supporting heavy loads: *Miles of cable were used to build the bridge.* • *The tent collapsed when a cable snapped.*
2 a tube with wires inside that carry electronic signals or electric current: *a telephone cable*
3 cable television: *We can't get cable or satellite here.*
4 a telegram: *He sent a cable saying he would be arriving home at midnight the next day.*

cable car • NOUN • **cable cars** a vehicle used to carry people up mountains. The cable car hangs in the air from strong wires and is moved by pulleys

cable television • NOUN • a television service in which programmes are transmitted along underground cables to people's houses

cackle • NOUN • **cackles** 1 a loud sound made by a hen or a goose 2 a loud harsh-sounding laugh
• VERB • **cackles, cackling, cackled** 1 a hen or goose cackles when it makes this sound 2 if someone cackles they laugh loudly and harshly: *The witch cackled, rubbing her bony hands together in glee.*

cactus • NOUN • **cactuses** or **cacti** a kind of prickly plant that grows mainly in deserts and very dry places. Cactuses store water in their thick leaves

CAD • ABBREVIATION • short for **computer-aided design**, where computers are used to help draw plans for things like buildings or machines: *a new CAD program*

caddie • NOUN • **caddies** someone whose job is to carry a golfer's clubs around the golf course

caddy • NOUN • **caddies** a box for keeping tea in

cadence • NOUN • **cadences** 1 cadence is the way your voice goes down as you speak, especially at the end of a sentence 2 a cadence is a group of notes or chords that comes at the end of a piece of music

cadet • NOUN • **cadets** 1 a young person training to be an officer in the armed forces or the police 2 a school pupil who is doing military training

cadge • VERB • **cadges, cadging, cadged** to cadge something from someone is to get it by begging or asking them for it: *He missed the bus so had to cadge a lift from his neighbour.*
✦ **cadger** • NOUN • **cadgers** someone who begs for things

Caesarean section or **Caesarean**
• NOUN • **Caesarean sections** or **Caesareans**

a surgical operation in which a pregnant woman's stomach is cut so that the baby inside her womb can be taken out

ⓘ The word **Caesarean** is used because the Roman emperor Julius *Caesar* was supposed to have been born this way.

café •NOUN• **cafés** a small restaurant that serves drinks and snacks

cafeteria •NOUN• **cafeterias** a restaurant where the customers serve themselves from a counter

caffeine •NOUN• caffeine is a substance that makes you feel more alert and active. Tea and coffee and some fizzy drinks contain caffeine

caftan •NOUN• **caftans** a loose long-sleeved piece of clothing that comes down to the ankles, worn in some Middle Eastern countries

cage •NOUN• **cages** a box or enclosure with bars where a bird or animal is kept so that it can't escape
•VERB• **cages, caging, caged** to cage an animal or bird is to put it in a cage
♦ **caged** •ADJECTIVE• kept in a cage: *caged birds*

cagoule •NOUN• **cagoules** a hooded waterpoof jacket like a light anorak but without an opening all the way down the front

cajole •VERB• **cajoles, cajoling, cajoled** to cajole someone is to get them to do something by being nice to them
♦ **cajolery** •NOUN• persuasion by flattery

cake •NOUN• **cakes** a food made from flour, eggs, sugar and other ingredients mixed together and baked in an oven until they are firm: *Do you like cake?* • *a Christmas cake*

calamine •NOUN• a pink powder used in a lotion that soothes burns or sore skin

calamity •NOUN• **calamities** something terrible that happens, a disaster

calcium •NOUN• a chemical found in chalk and lime and in bones and teeth

calculate •VERB• **calculates, calculating, calculated 1** to calculate something is to count it up or work it out using numbers or

mathematics: *One apple costs 13p. Calculate the cost of 174 apples.* **2** if you calculate something you make a guess about it using all the facts that you have: *The robbers had calculated that no one would realize that anything was missing until they were long gone.*
♦ **calculating** •ADJECTIVE• a calculating person works out what is going to benefit them
♦ **calculation** •NOUN• **calculations** something you work out, either using numbers or what you know: *By my calculation, we should be finished by Tuesday.*
♦ **calculator** •NOUN• **calculators** an electronic machine that you use to do mathematical calculations quickly

calendar •NOUN• **calendars** a table or list that shows the days of the year with their dates, divided into weeks and months

calf¹ •NOUN• **calves 1** a young cow or ox: *a bull calf* **2** a young elephant, whale or deer: *a red deer calf*

calf² •NOUN• **calves** the back part of your leg just below the knee where there is a big muscle

call •VERB• **calls, calling, called 1** to call is to shout: *I heard him calling my name.*
2 to call someone is to ask them to come to you: *Call the children in from the garden.*
3 to call someone is to speak to them on the telephone: *Have you called your mother yet?*
4 to call someone something is to give them that name: *He's called Jonathan James.* • *How dare you call me a liar.*
5 to **call at** a place is to stop there for a short time: *We drove to Ipswich, calling at my sister's house on the way.*
•NOUN• **calls 1** a shout: *calls for help*
2 a telephone conversation: *I had a call from David yesterday.*
3 a short visit: *I've got a couple of calls to make on the way home.*

callous •ADJECTIVE• cruel or unkind to other people: *a callous murderer*
♦ **callousness** •NOUN• being callous: *the shocking callousness of the murder*

Aa Bb Cc Dd Ee Ff Gg Hh Ii Jj Kk Ll Mm Nn Oo Pp Qq Rr Ss Tt Uu Vv Ww Xx Yy Zz

ⓘ Do not confuse the spelling of the adjective **callous** with the noun **callus**.

callus •NOUN• **calluses** an area of hard skin on the hands or feet, caused by constant rubbing

calm •ADJECTIVE• **calmer, calmest** 1 still and quiet: *a calm sea* 2 not anxious, excited or upset
•VERB• **calms, calming, calmed** 1 to calm or to **calm down** is to become quiet and still again after being noisy or disturbed: *The boats can sail when the weather calms down.* 2 to calm someone, or to **calm someone down**, is to stop them being so excited or upset: *She took a couple of deep breaths to calm herself down.*
♦ **calmly** •ADVERB• without showing any anxiety or excitement: *Grace walked calmly on to the stage.*
♦ **calmness** •NOUN• being calm: *We were impressed by his calmness under pressure.*

calorie •NOUN• **calories** a unit of heat used to measure how much energy a food gives

calypso •NOUN• **calypsos** a type of West Indian popular song, usually with words that are made up as it is sung

camber •NOUN• **cambers** a curve on the surface of a road which slopes down on each side from a high point in the middle

camcorder •NOUN• **camcorders** a video camera that also records sound

came •VERB• a way of changing the verb **come** to make a past tense: *They came downstairs, laughing and shouting.*

camel •NOUN• **camels** a desert animal with a long neck and one or two humps on its back for storing water

cameo •NOUN• **cameos** a stone, usually part of a piece of jewellery, with a pattern cut out of a different coloured background so that it stands out

camera •NOUN• **cameras** a device for taking photographs, or for making television programmes or films

camisole •NOUN• **camisoles** a woman's light vest or top with thin shoulder straps

camomile •NOUN• a kind of plant with yellow flowers, used to make herbal tea and medicines

camouflage •NOUN• **camouflages** a way of disguising things so that they are not easily seen, especially by making them blend in with their background
•VERB• **camouflages, camouflaging, camouflaged** to camouflage something is to disguise it so that it will not be noticed easily: *The stick insect camouflages itself by sitting very still on a twig.*

camp •NOUN• **camps** a place where people live in tents, huts or caravans, usually for a short time: *a refugee camp*
•VERB• **camps, camping, camped** to camp is to stay somewhere for a short time in a tent, hut or caravan: *We camped in a clearing in the woods.*
♦ **camper** •NOUN• **campers** someone who stays in a tent or hut, usually while they are on holiday
♦ **camping** •NOUN• if you go camping you go somewhere where you stay in a shelter like a tent, hut or caravan

campaign •NOUN• **campaigns** a campaign is a series of activities to try to achieve a particular thing, such as selling a product or getting a political party elected: *an advertising campaign*
•VERB• **campaigns, campaigning, campaigned** to campaign for something is to organize support for it: *They've been campaigning to have a new school built.*
♦ **campaigner** •NOUN• **campaigners** someone who organizes support for something

campsite •NOUN• **campsites** a place where people camp in tents

campus •NOUN• **campuses** the buildings and grounds of a college or university

can¹ •VERB• 1 to be able to: *Can you swim? Yes, I can.* 2 to be allowed to: *Can I go swimming? Yes, you can.*

ⓘ **Can** is the present tense form. You use **could** for the past tense.

can² •NOUN• **cans** a container made of tin or some other metal, especially one that is sealed to keep a food or drink from going bad

•VERB• **cans, canning, canned** to can food is to seal it in cans

canal •NOUN• **canals** a long channel filled with water and built so that boats can travel across an area of land: *the Panama Canal*

canary •NOUN• **canaries** a small singing bird with yellow feathers, often kept as a pet

cancel •VERB• **cancels, cancelling, cancelled** 1 to cancel an arrangement is to say that it will not happen: *The match was cancelled because of the snow.* 2 to cancel a cheque or a payment is to stop it being paid
♦ **cancellation** •NOUN• **cancellations** a cancellation is something that had been booked in advance and has then been cancelled: *You'll get a seat on the flight if there are any last-minute cancellations.*

cancer •NOUN• **cancers** a serious disease in which some cells in the body start to grow very quickly and form lumps

candid •ADJECTIVE• honest and truthful: *She was very candid about her past mistakes.*
♦ **candidly** •ADVERB• openly and truthfully: *He spoke candidly about what had gone wrong.*

candidate •NOUN• **candidates** 1 someone who is taking an exam 2 someone who is trying for a job or position

candle •NOUN• **candles** a stick of wax with a piece of string called a wick through the middle, which is lit so that it burns and gives out light

candlestick •NOUN• **candlesticks** a holder for keeping a candle upright

candy •NOUN• **candies** 1 candy is sugar that has been boiled and then become solid 2 a candy is a sweet

candyfloss •NOUN• candyfloss is sugar that has been heated and spun into fluff which you eat off a stick

cane •NOUN• **canes** 1 the hollow woody stem of bamboo and some other plants 2 a walking stick: *He carried a silver-topped cane*
•VERB• **canes, caning, caned** to cane someone is to hit them with a long stick as a punishment

canine •ADJECTIVE• 1 to do with dogs or like a dog: *canine behaviour* 2 canine teeth are sharp and pointed. Humans have four canine teeth

canister •NOUN• **canisters** a container, often made of metal, used for storing things: *a canister of tea*

cannibal •NOUN• **cannibals** a person who eats other people, or an animal that eats animals of the same species
♦ **cannibalism** •NOUN• eating other people, or eating other animals of the same species

cannon •NOUN• **cannons** a type of large gun that fires cannonballs or heavy shells

cannonball •NOUN• **cannonballs** a heavy ball of metal or stone fired from a cannon

cannot •VERB• 1 cannot is used with another verb to say that you are not able to do something: *I cannot read your writing.* 2 cannot is used with another verb when you are not giving permission for something: *No, you cannot have another slice of cake.*

canny •ADJECTIVE• **cannier, canniest** a canny person does not do things without thinking about them very carefully first

canoe •NOUN• **canoes** a light boat that is pointed at both ends and that you move through the water using a paddle
•VERB• **canoes, canoeing, canoed** to canoe is to paddle, or to travel in, a canoe

canon •NOUN• **canons** 1 a rule or law 2 a title given to some Christian priests, especially a priest that works in a cathedral

canopy •NOUN• **canopies** a covering that is hung above something: *a canopy over a bed*

can't •SHORT FORM• a short way to say and write cannot: *I can't hear you.*

canteen •NOUN• **canteens** a restaurant in a school, office or factory where pupils or workers can get meals and snacks

canter •NOUN• **canters** a gentle running pace of a horse that is faster than a trot and slower than a gallop
•VERB• **canters, cantering, cantered** to canter is to go at a pace between a trot and a gallop

Aa
Bb
Cc
Dd
Ee
Ff
Gg
Hh
Ii
Jj
Kk
Ll
Mm
Nn
Oo
Pp
Qq
Rr
Ss
Tt
Uu
Vv
Ww
Xx
Yy
Zz

canvas •NOUN• **canvases** 1 canvas is a strong cloth used to make tents and sails 2 a canvas is a piece of this cloth stretched and used for painting on

canvass •VERB• **canvasses, canvassing, canvassed** to canvass opinion or support is to go round asking people for it: *He's canvassing for the Green Party.*

ⓘ Notice the different spellings of the noun **canvas** and the verb **canvass**.

canyon •NOUN• **canyons** a deep river valley with steep sides

cap •NOUN• **caps** 1 a soft hat that often has a peak at the front 2 a small top for a bottle, tube or pen
•VERB• **caps, capping, capped** 1 to cap something is to put a covering or lid on it: *mountains capped with snow* 2 a sportsman is capped when he or she is chosen to play in the team representing their country

capable •ADJECTIVE• 1 a capable person is able to deal with problems or difficulties without help 2 if you are capable of something you are able to do it or achieve it: *The old lady isn't capable of looking after herself any more.*
♦ **capably** •ADVERB• to do something capably is to deal with it well or efficiently: *I'm sure you'll do the job very capably.*

capacity •NOUN• **capacities** 1 the capacity of a container or building is the total amount that it will hold: *a barrel with a capacity of 100 litres*
2 someone's capacity to do something is their ability to do it: *He has the capacity to be a great leader.*
3 to do something in your capacity as something is to do it as part of a job you have: *Mrs Jones came to the meeting in her capacity as head teacher.*

cape¹ •NOUN• **capes** a kind of coat with no sleeves which is tied at the neck

cape² •NOUN• **capes** a piece of land that sticks out into the sea: *He sailed round the Cape of Good Hope and Cape Horn.*

caper •VERB• **capers, capering, capered** to caper is to leap and dance about in an amusing way: *The clown capered round the stage.*

•NOUN• **capers** 1 a leap: *Simon jumped up, did a little caper of joy and hugged everyone.* 2 an informal word for an adventure or an amusing activity: *He's off on one of his climbing capers.*

capital •ADJECTIVE• 1 most important: *a capital city* 2 punishable by death: *Murder is still a capital crime in some states in the US.*
•NOUN• **capitals** 1 the capital of a country or state is the city where its government is based: *What's the capital of Sweden?*
• *Sacramento is the state capital of California.*
2 a capital is a capital letter: *Write your name in capitals at the top of the page.*
3 capital is money that can be invested, for example in a business or a savings account, to make more money

capital city •NOUN• **capital cities** a city in a state or country where its government is based

capitalism •NOUN• a system in which businesses are owned and run by individuals rather than being controlled by the government of a country
♦ **capitalist** •NOUN• **capitalists** someone who believes in capitalism
•ADJECTIVE• having a system of capitalism: *capitalist countries*

capitalize or **capitalise** •VERB• **capitalizes, capitalizing, capitalized** 1 to capitalize a letter is to write or print it as a capital letter 2 to **capitalize on** something is to use it to your advantage or benefit

capital letter •NOUN• **capital letters** a letter like the larger one you write at the start of your name, as in CAPITAL LETTERS

capital punishment •NOUN• capital punishment is being killed as a punishment for a crime, such as murder

cappuccino •NOUN• **cappuccinos** coffee made with frothy hot milk and often served with powdered chocolate on the top

capsize •VERB• **capsizes, capsizing, capsized** when a boat capsizes it turns upside down: *The little sailing boat capsized.*

capsule •NOUN• **capsules** 1 a small pill filled

a car

rearview mirror
steering wheel
door mirror
bonnet
boot
headlights
radiator
numberplate
indicator
tyres
exhaust pipe

with a dose of medicine **2** a part of a spacecraft, especially the part that the astronauts live and work in, that can be separated from the rest of the spacecraft

captain •NOUN• **captains 1** an officer in charge of a ship, an aircraft or a company of soldiers **2** the leader of a sports team or a sports club
•VERB• **captains, captaining, captained** to captain a ship or an aircraft, or a sports team, is to be its captain

caption •NOUN• **captions** a piece of writing above, below or beside a picture or photograph that explains or describes what is in it

captivate •VERB• **captivates, captivating, captivated** to captivate someone is to charm or fascinate them
✦ **captivating** •ADJECTIVE• charming or fascinating: *a captivating smile*

captive •NOUN• **captives** a person who has been caught and is being held prisoner
•ADJECTIVE• **1** caught and held prisoner: *a captive bird* **2** not able to escape: *The other passengers were a captive audience when she started singing on the train.*
✦ **captivity** •NOUN• **1** being a prisoner **2** animals in captivity are kept in a zoo or some other enclosed space, rather than living in the wild

capture •VERB• **captures, capturing, captured 1** to capture someone is to take

them prisoner: *Many soldiers were captured by the enemy.* **2** to capture something belonging to someone else is to take it from them by force: *He captured many Spanish ships loaded with gold and silver.*

car •NOUN• **cars** a vehicle with an engine and seats for a small number of passengers

caramel •NOUN• **caramels 1** caramel is sugar that has been heated until it goes brown **2** a caramel is a sweet made with browned sugar

carat •NOUN• **carats** a measurement of the weight of gems and of the purity of gold

caravan •NOUN• **caravans** a vehicle for living in which can be towed behind a car

carbohydrate •NOUN• **carbohydrates** a mixture of sugar, hydrogen and oxygen that is found in certain foods and gives the body energy

carbon •NOUN• a chemical element found in all living things as well as in substances like coal, oil, charcoal and diamond
✦ **carbonated** •ADJECTIVE• a carbonated drink has carbon dioxide gas added to it to make it fizzy

carbon dioxide •NOUN• a gas found in air and breathed out by humans and animals

carbon monoxide •NOUN• a poisonous gas with no smell which is made when carbon is burned

carbon paper •NOUN• a special type of

paper coated with ink on one side that is used to make copies of documents as they are being written or typed

carbuncle •NOUN• **carbuncles** a painful swelling under the skin

carburettor •NOUN• **carburettors** the part inside an engine where air and the fuel are mixed to produce a gas that will burn to give power to the engine

carcass •NOUN• **carcasses** a dead body of an animal

card •NOUN• **cards**1 card is thick stiff paper
2 a card is a piece of this used to give a greeting or information to someone: *a birthday card* • *a business card*
3 cards or playing cards are a set of rectangular pieces of card with numbers and symbols printed on one side, that are used for playing games
4 cards or card games are games like whist and bridge that are played with a set of playing cards
• **on the cards** something that is on the cards is likely to happen

cardboard •NOUN• cardboard is very thick paper used to make boxes and packaging

cardiac •ADJECTIVE• to do with the heart: *a cardiac surgeon*

cardigan •NOUN• **cardigans** a piece of knitted clothing worn on the top of the body, which has buttons down the front

ⓘ Cardigans were named after the Earl of *Cardigan*, whose soldiers wore woollen jackets with buttons.

cardinal •NOUN• **cardinals**1 a high ranking priest in the Roman Catholic Church 2 a cardinal number

cardinal number •NOUN• **cardinal numbers** a cardinal number is any number used to represent a number or quantity, such as 1, 2, 3, 9, 16, 47, 102. Look up and compare **ordinal number**

care •NOUN• **cares**1 care is worry or anxiety: *We all want a life with as little care and trouble as possible.*
2 a care is a cause for worry or anxiety: *She was humming to herself as if she didn't*

have a care in the world.
3 care is close attention paid to something: *Meg does her school work with great care.*
•VERB• **cares, caring, cared**1 to care is to be concerned or interested: *He said he didn't care what happened.*
2 to care for a child or an ill person is to look after them: *She wants to be a vet so that she can care for sick animals.*
3 if you say you care for something it is a way of saying that you like it or want it: *I don't care much for fish.*
♦ **carer** •NOUN• **carers** someone who looks after an old or ill person, especially in their home

career •NOUN• **careers** a person's career is the job or profession they have trained for and which they can move up in as they go through their working life: *He wants a career in the police force.*
•VERB• **careers, careering, careered** to career is to move very quickly and without proper control: *The car careered into a lamp-post.*

carefree •ADJECTIVE• having no worries: *a carefree life*

careful •ADJECTIVE• making sure that you do something properly without making a mistake or causing an accident: *Dad is always careful to lock all the doors.* • *Be careful when you cross the road.*
♦ **carefully** •ADVERB• without making mistakes or causing damage: *She wrapped up the ornament carefully in tissue paper.*
♦ **carefulness** •NOUN• being careful

careless •ADJECTIVE• not being careful or not paying close attention: *a careless mistake* • *He is a bit careless with his money.*
♦ **carelessly** •ADVERB• in a careless way
♦ **carelessness** •NOUN• being careless

caress •VERB• **caresses, caressing, caressed** to caress something is to touch it or stroke it lovingly: *A gentle breeze caressed her face.*

caretaker •NOUN• **caretakers** someone whose job is to look after a building

cargo •NOUN• **cargoes** the things carried by a ship or aeroplane: *a cargo of iron ore*

caricature •NOUN• **caricatures** a caricature of a person is a drawing of them that makes

their features look funny or ridiculous
•VERB• **caricatures, caricaturing, caricatured** to caricature someone is to draw them or describe them to make them seem funny or ridiculous

caries •NOUN• the medical name for decayed parts of the teeth: *Brushing your teeth will help to prevent caries.*

carnage •NOUN• carnage is killing, especially the killing or injuring of a lot of people

carnation •NOUN• **carnations** a garden plant that has long stems and brightly coloured pink, red or white flowers with lots of petals

carnival •NOUN• **carnivals** carnival or a carnival is a celebration for which people get dressed up in costumes and sing and dance outdoors

carnivore •NOUN• **carnivores** any animal that eats meat. Look up and compare **herbivore** and **omnivore**
♦ **carnivorous** •ADJECTIVE• eating meat: *Tyrannosaurus rex was a huge carnivorous dinosaur.*

carol •NOUN• **carols** a song sung at Christmas time
♦ **caroller** •NOUN• **carollers** someone, often part of a group, who sings carols at Christmas time
♦ **carolling** •NOUN• singing carols at Christmas time, usually going from one house to another

carp •NOUN• **carp** or **carps** a kind of fish with a wide body, often kept in ponds

car park •NOUN• **car parks** a place where cars can be left for a short time

carpenter •NOUN• **carpenters** someone who works at making things from wood
♦ **carpentry** •NOUN• making things from wood

carpet •NOUN• **carpets** 1 a covering for a floor made of wool or some other soft strong fabric 2 anything that forms a covering on the ground: *a carpet of primroses and bluebells*
•VERB• **carpets, carpeting, carpeted** to carpet something is to cover it, either with a

carpet or with something that covers like a carpet

carriage •NOUN• **carriages** 1 one of the long sections of a train where passengers sit or sleep
2 a vehicle that can carry passengers and is pulled by horses
3 carriage is carrying anything or the cost of carrying something

carrion •NOUN• carrion is rotting flesh from animals that have died, which is often eaten by other animals or birds such as foxes and crows

carrot •NOUN• **carrots** a long orange vegetable that grows under the ground

ⓘ Be careful not to confuse the spellings of the words **carat** and **carrot**.

carry •VERB• **carries, carrying, carried** 1 if you carry something you pick it up and take it somewhere: *This bag is too heavy for me to carry.*
2 when sound carries, travels over a long distance: *He has the sort of voice that carries.*
3 to **carry on** is to continue: *Carry on with your work while I go and see the headmaster.*
4 to **carry on** is to behave in a certain way, especially badly: *Will you two stop carrying on like babies, please.*
5 to **carry something out** is to do it: *The surgeon will carry out the operation tomorrow morning.*
• **get carried away** if someone gets carried away they get too excited by something: *He got a bit carried away by the music and started jumping up and down.*

carry-on •NOUN• **carry-ons** a fuss

carry-out •NOUN• **carry-outs** a meal or alcoholic drink that is bought in a shop or restaurant and taken away to be eaten or drunk somewhere else

cart •NOUN• **carts** 1 a vehicle pulled by a horse and used for carrying loads 2 a small vehicle with wheels that is pushed by hand

cartilage •NOUN• **cartilages** cartilage is a strong stretchy type of body tissue found between certain bones and in the nose and ears

cartographer •NOUN• **cartographers** someone who makes maps and charts

cartography •NOUN• making maps and charts

carton •NOUN• **cartons** a box or container made of cardboard

cartoon •NOUN• **cartoons** 1 a drawing or a series of drawings printed in a newspaper or magazine, often making fun of someone famous 2 a film made by drawing the characters and action

♦ **cartoonist** •NOUN• **cartoonists** someone who draws cartoons

cartridge •NOUN• **cartridges** a small case holding, for example, film for a camera, ink for a pen, or the bullet for a gun. A cartridge can be removed and replaced easily

cartwheel •NOUN• **cartwheels** a movement in which you take your weight on your hands and turn your whole body sideways in a circle through the air to land on your feet

carve •VERB• **carves, carving, carved** 1 to carve something is to make or shape it using a cutting tool: *The faces of the presidents are carved out of the rock.* 2 to carve meat is to cut it into slices or pieces using a sharp knife

cascade •NOUN• **cascades** a waterfall •VERB• **cascades, cascading, cascaded** to cascade is to tumble downwards like water in a waterfall

case¹ •NOUN• **cases** 1 a suitcase: *Have you unpacked your cases yet?* 2 a container or covering: *The crown jewels are kept in a glass case.*

case² •NOUN• **cases** 1 a particular example of something happening: *It was a case of having to wait until the train arrived.* 2 a problem that is dealt with by a lawyer, a doctor or the police: *a court case* • *There had been no cases of smallpox for many years.*
• **in case** because a certain thing might happen: *Take an umbrella in case it rains.*

casement •NOUN• **casements** a type of window frame in which the window opens sideways by swinging on hinges

cash •NOUN• cash is banknotes and coins: *I didn't have enough cash to pay the fare, so I had to go to the bank.*
•VERB• **cashes, cashing, cashed** 1 to cash a cheque is to change it for banknotes or coins 2 to **cash in on** something is to profit from it

cashew •NOUN• **cashews** a kind of kidney-shaped nut with a buttery taste

cashier •NOUN• **cashiers** someone whose job is to take in and pay out money, for example in a bank

cash register •NOUN• **cash registers** a machine used in a shop that records and stores the money paid by customers

casino •NOUN• **casinos** a building where people can gamble

cask •NOUN• **casks** a barrel for holding wine or beer

casket •NOUN• **caskets** 1 a wooden or metal box for keeping things in, especially jewels 2 a coffin

casserole •NOUN• **casseroles** 1 a dish with a cover for cooking and serving food 2 the food cooked in a casserole: *a beef casserole* •VERB• **casseroles, casseroling, casseroled** to casserole food is to cook it in the oven in a covered dish

cassette •NOUN• **cassettes** a small case holding a long piece of recording tape or film that moves around a spool when it is fitted into a tape recorder or camera

cassock •NOUN• **cassocks** a long-sleeved robe that goes from the shoulders down to the ankles and is worn by priests

cast •VERB• **casts, casting, cast** 1 to cast is to throw: *They'd been cast into prison.*
2 to cast an object in metal or plaster is to shape it in a mould
3 to cast a play or a film is to choose the actors who will be in it
•NOUN• **casts** 1 an object formed in a mould: *The policeman made a plaster cast of the footprints.* 2 the cast of a play or film are the actors in it

castanets •PLURAL NOUN• castanets are two shells made of hard wood that are held in the hand and hit together to make a loud clicking sound

ⓘ This word comes from a Spanish word for *chestnuts*, because they have a rounded shape.

---

castaway •NOUN• **castaways** someone who has been left in a lonely place, such as a desert island, usually after a shipwreck

caste •NOUN• **castes** a class or rank of people

caster •NOUN• another spelling of **castor**

castle •NOUN• **castles** a type of large house with thick high walls and usually towers and battlements, which was built to protect the people inside from attack

castor *or* **caster** •NOUN• **castors** *or* **casters** one of a set of small wheels attached to the legs of a piece of furniture so that it can be moved about easily

castor oil •NOUN• a yellowish oil from a kind of palm that is used as medicine

castor sugar •NOUN• a kind of sugar in the form of very fine granules that is used in cooking and baking

casual •ADJECTIVE• 1 not suitable for formal occasions: *casual clothes* 2 not serious, not caring or not taking much interest: *She's a bit too casual in her attitude to her schoolwork.*
♦ **casually** •ADVERB• in a casual way: *casually dressed*

casualty •NOUN• **casualties** 1 a casualty is someone who has been injured or killed: *ambulances ferrying the casualties to hospital* 2 casualty is a hospital department that deals with people who have been injured and need medical attention

cat •NOUN• **cats** 1 an animal, often kept as a pet, that has soft fur and claws 2 any animal that belongs to the family of animals that includes cats, lions, leopards and tigers
• **let the cat out of the bag** if you let the cat out of the bag you tell people something that they aren't supposed to know

catalogue •NOUN• **catalogues** a book showing a company's products or a list in a library giving details of all the books available
•VERB• **catalogues, cataloguing, catalogued** to catalogue things is to put details about them in a list

catalyst •NOUN• **catalysts** 1 a substance

which starts a chemical reaction but which does not itself react or change 2 something that results in change

catalytic converter •NOUN• **catalytic converters** a device in a car that stops harmful substances getting into the air from the car's exhaust

catamaran •NOUN• **catamarans** a type of sailing boat with two hulls beside each other

catapult •NOUN• **catapults** a small weapon made up of a forked stick with a piece of elastic stretched between them, used for firing small stones
•VERB• **catapults, catapulting, catapulted** to be catapulted is to be thrown forward forcefully: *The bike hit a rock and he was catapulted over the handlebars.*

cataract •NOUN• **cataracts** an eye disease in which the lens at the front of the eye becomes gradually thicker so that it becomes more and more difficult to see

catastrophe •NOUN• **catastrophes** a sudden terrible disaster
♦ **catastrophic** •ADJECTIVE• absolutely terrible: *the catastrophic effects of the earthquake*

ⓘ **Catastrophe** is pronounced cat-**as**-tro-fi. **Catastrophic** is pronounced cat-as-**trof**-ik.

catch •VERB• **catches, catching, caught** 1 to catch something is to hold it and stop it from escaping: *Throw the ball and I'll try to catch it.* • *He caught a fish but let it go again.*
2 to catch an illness is to get it: *Be careful not to catch a cold.*
3 to catch a bus or train is to be in time to get on to it: *Dad left early so that he would catch the 8.30 bus.*
4 to catch someone doing something, especially something bad, is to surprise or discover them while they are doing it: *My sister caught me making faces at her.*
5 if you catch part of your body or your clothing you injure or damage it on something: *He caught his head on the door as he was coming in.*
6 to **catch up**, or **catch up with** people who are ahead of you, is to reach the place where they are
• **catch fire** to start to burn and produce flames

Aa

Bb

Cc

Dd

Ee

Ff

Gg

Hh

Ii

Jj

Kk

Ll

Mm

Nn

Oo

Pp

Qq

Rr

Ss

Tt

Uu

Vv

Ww

Xx

Yy

Zz

•NOUN• **catches1** a fastening: *The catch on my bracelet has broken.*
2 a fisherman's catch is the number of fish he has caught
3 something that seems good at first has a catch if it has a disadvantage that you didn't know about: *The holiday was supposed to be free, but there was a catch, of course.*
◆ **catching** •ADJECTIVE• if an illness or disease is catching it is infectious: *I hope that sore throat you have isn't catching.*

catchment area •NOUN• **catchment areas**
1 an area from which a particular school gets its pupils **2** an area from which water drains into a particular river

catchphrase •NOUN• **catchphrases** a phrase that is used by someone again and again, especially an entertainer or comedian, so that you remember it

catchy •ADJECTIVE• **catchier, catchiest** a catchy tune is one that you remember easily

categorize or **categorise** •VERB• **categorizes, categorizing, categorized** to categorize people or things is to group them together according to what type, size or age they are

category •NOUN• **categories** a grouping of people or things of the same type: *different categories of trees*

cater •VERB• **caters, catering, catered 1** to cater is to prepare and supply food **2** to cater for something or someone is to provide what is wanted or needed: *an exhibition that caters for every type of gardener*
◆ **caterer** •NOUN• **caterers** a person or business whose job is to prepare and provide food for people, for example at a conference or wedding

caterpillar •NOUN• **caterpillars** a small creature with a soft body that feeds on plants and leaves and which turns into a moth or butterfly

caterwaul •VERB• **caterwauls, caterwauling, caterwauled** to caterwaul is to make a horrible howling or screeching noise like a cat

cat flap •NOUN• **cat flaps** a small door cut in a door through which a pet cat can come in or go out

cathedral •NOUN• **cathedrals1** a church where a bishop preaches **2** the main church in an area

catherine wheel •NOUN• **catherine wheels** a firework that spins round and round as it burns

catholic •ADJECTIVE• covering a wide range: *His musical taste is catholic; he likes all kinds.*
◆ **Catholic** •ADJECTIVE• having to do with, or belonging to, the Roman Catholic Church
•NOUN• **Catholics** a Roman Catholic

catkin •NOUN• **catkins** a small tightly-packed flower that hangs from a short stem and grows on some trees, like willow and hazel

cat's cradle •NOUN• cat's cradle is a game played with a loop of string, with the string being wound round the fingers to make complicated patterns

catseye •NOUN• **catseyes** catseyes are small objects fixed in a road surface which reflect light and guide drivers at night. This word is a trademark

cattle •PLURAL NOUN• cows, bulls and oxen and any other grass-eating animals of this family

caught •VERB• a way of changing the verb **catch** to make a past tense. It can be used with or without a helping verb: *Emily caught a cold.* ◆ *She must have caught it from Sophie.*

cauldron •NOUN• **cauldrons** a big pot heated over a fire and used to cook things in

cauliflower •NOUN• **cauliflowers** a round vegetable related to the cabbage and made up of tightly packed whitish flowers or florets

cause •VERB• **causes, causing, caused** to cause something is to make it happen: *The leak in the roof caused damp in the bedroom.*
•NOUN• **causes 1** a cause of something is what makes it happen: *the causes of poverty* **2** a cause is something that people support because they believe it is right: *She supports many good causes.*

causeway •NOUN• **causeways** a causeway is a raised road over shallow water or wet ground

caustic •ADJECTIVE• a caustic substance burns or causes rust

cauterize or **cauterise** •VERB• **cauterizes, cauterizing, cauterized** to cauterize a wound is to burn it with hot metal so that it heals well

caution •NOUN• **cautions 1** caution is taking care to avoid danger or risk: *Please drive with caution*. **2** a caution is a warning
♦ **cautionary** •ADJECTIVE• a cautionary story or tale is one that gives a warning
♦ **cautious** •ADJECTIVE• to be cautious is to be very careful to avoid danger or risk

cavalcade •NOUN• **cavalcades** a long line of people on horseback or in vehicles moving along a route to celebrate something

Cavalier •NOUN• **Cavaliers** one of the King's supporters in the English Civil War

cavalry •NOUN• cavalry or the cavalry are soldiers on horseback: *He joined the cavalry.*

cave •NOUN• **caves** a large hole in the side of a hill, cliff or mountain or under the ground

caveman •NOUN• **cavemen** a male human from prehistoric times who lived in a cave

cavern •NOUN• **caverns** a large cave
♦ **cavernous** •ADJECTIVE• deep and wide, like a cavern: *inside the whale's cavernous mouth*

cavewoman •NOUN• **cavewomen** a female human from prehistoric times who lived in a cave

caviare or **caviar** •NOUN• an expensive food from fish eggs

cavity •NOUN• **cavities 1** a hollow space or hole **2** a hollow in a tooth caused by decay

caw •VERB• **caws, cawing, cawed** a crow caws when it makes a loud harsh sound •NOUN• **caws** the sound a crow makes

cc •ABBREVIATION• short for **cubic centimetre** or **cubic centimetres**

CD •ABBREVIATION• **CD's** or **CDs** short for **compact disc**: *I got two CD's for my birthday.*

CD-ROM •ABBREVIATION• **CD-ROMs** short for **compact disc read-only memory**, a system by which optical information on a compact disc can be viewed on the visual display unit of a computer, but cannot be altered: *This game is available on CD-ROM.*

cease •VERB• **ceases, ceasing, ceased** to cease is to stop

ceasefire •NOUN• **ceasefires 1** a order given to stop firing weapons **2** an agreement made between two armies or fighting groups to stop fighting for a time

ceaseless •ADJECTIVE• not stopping: *a ceaseless thump, thump, thump*

cedar •NOUN• **cedars** a kind of tall evergreen tree

ceilidh •NOUN• **ceilidhs** a social event with Scottish dancing and music

ⓘ This word is pronounced **kay**-li.

ceiling •NOUN• **ceilings 1** the inner roof of a room **2** an upper limit: *They'd set a ceiling of 7% on pay rises.*

celebrate •VERB• **celebrates, celebrating, celebrated** to celebrate something is to have a party or do something special because of it: *Everyone was celebrating the New Year.*
♦ **celebrated** •ADJECTIVE• a celebrated person or event is famous
♦ **celebration** •NOUN• **celebrations** celebration or a celebration is something done to celebrate an event: *They've won money on the lottery and are having a celebration.*

celebrity •NOUN• **celebrities 1** celebrity is fame **2** a celebrity is someone who has become famous

celery •NOUN• a kind of vegetable with long light-green ridged stalks with leaves growing at the top

cell •NOUN• **cells 1** the smallest part of a living thing. The cells in most living things divide so that the animal or plant can grow or repair any part that has been damaged or injured
2 a small room that a prisoner is kept in or that a monk lives in
3 a device in a battery that produces electrical energy using chemicals

cellar •NOUN• **cellars** an underground room used for storing things

Aa
Bb
Cc
Dd
Ee
Ff
Gg
Hh
Ii
Jj
Kk
Ll
Mm
Nn
Oo
Pp
Qq
Rr
Ss
Tt
Uu
Vv
Ww
Xx
Yy
Zz

cellist •NOUN• **cellists** someone who plays the cello

cello •NOUN• **cellos** an instrument like a large violin that is held upright on the floor and played with a bow.

ⓘ This word is pronounced **chel**-o.

cellophane •NOUN• cellophane is a thin transparent material used for wrapping things in. This word is a trademark

cellular •ADJECTIVE• **1** made up of or having cells: *the cellular structure of a honeycomb* **2** a cellular phone uses a system of radio transmitters called cells. A phone message is sent between the transmitters until it reaches the one nearest the phone that is to receive the message

cellulose •NOUN• a substance that makes up the cell walls of plants and is used to make paper and textiles

Celsius •ADJECTIVE• of the temperature scale at which water freezes at 0 degrees and boils at 100 degrees, or measured using this scale: *57 degrees Celsius*

Celtic •ADJECTIVE• of or having to do with the ancient European people, the Celts, whose modern descendants live in Ireland, Scotland, Wales and parts of Cornwall and northern France

cement •NOUN• **1** a grey powder that is mixed with sand and water and used to stick bricks together in a wall or to make concrete **2** any type of strong glue that bonds things together firmly: *plastic cement* •VERB• **cements, cementing, cemented 1** to cement things is to join or bond them with cement **2** to cement something is to fix it or bond it firmly: *an exchange of gifts to cement their new friendship*

cemetery •NOUN• **cemeteries** a place where dead people are buried

cenotaph •NOUN• **cenotaphs** a monument to people who are buried somewhere else, especially soldiers, sailors and airmen who have died in a war

censor •NOUN• **censors** someone whose job is to cut any unsuitable parts out of books and films before they are seen by the public •VERB• **censors, censoring, censored** to censor something is stop it being sold or shown to the public

census •NOUN• **censuses** an official survey carried out every few years to find out how many people are living in a particular country: *The last census in Britain was in 2001.*

cent •NOUN• **cents** a unit of money worth one hundredth of a larger unit of money, such as the American or Australian dollar

centaur •NOUN• **centaurs** a creature from old stories or myths which was half man and half horse

centenary •NOUN• **centenaries** the hundredth anniversary of an event: *a special edition to celebrate the centenary of Beatrix Potter's birth*

centennial •ADJECTIVE• **1** having lasted for a hundred years **2** happening every hundred years •NOUN• **centennials** a centenary

centi- *or* **cent-** •PREFIX• if a word starts with **centi-** or **cent-** it means a hundred or a hundredth part of: *centimetre • century*

centigrade •ADJECTIVE• **1** of temperature or a temperature scale that is measured in or made up of a hundred degrees **2** Celsius

centigram *or* **centigramme** •NOUN• **centigrams** *or* **centigrammes** a measurement of weight that is a hundredth part of a gram. This is often shortened to **cg**

centilitre •NOUN• **centilitres** a measurement used for liquids that is a hundredth part of a litre. This is often shortened to **cl**

centimetre •NOUN• **centimetres** a measurement of length that is a hundredth part of a metre. This is often shortened to **cm**

centipede •NOUN• **centipedes** a crawling insect with a long body and lots of pairs of legs

central •ADJECTIVE• near or at the centre

central heating •NOUN• a system used for heating houses where water is heated in a boiler and sent through pipes to radiators in each room

central locking •NOUN• a system in a car

Aa Bb Cc Dd Ee Ff Gg Hh Ii Jj Kk Ll Mm Nn Oo Pp Qq Rr Ss Tt Uu Vv Ww Xx Yy Zz

where all the locks on the doors are locked or unlocked by turning a key in one lock

centre •NOUN• **centres** 1 the centre of something is its middle point or part: *the centre of a circle* • *chocolates with soft centres* 2 a centre is a building or group of buildings used for a particular activity: *a sports centre*
•VERB• **centres, centring, centred** to centre something is to put it or place it in the centre
⇒ **central**

centurion •NOUN• **centurions** a soldier in the ancient Roman army who was in command of a hundred soldiers

century •NOUN• **centuries** 1 a hundred years 2 if a cricketer scores a century he or she scores a hundred runs in a match

ceramic •ADJECTIVE• made of clay that is baked until hard in a very hot oven called a kiln: *a ceramic dish*
•NOUN• **ceramics** an object made of pottery: *She makes beautiful sculptures and ceramics.*
◆ **ceramics** •NOUN• ceramics is the art or craft of making things with clay which is then baked in a kiln

cereal •NOUN• **cereals** 1 a cereal is a grain that is used as food, for example wheat, maize, oats, barley and rice 2 cereal or a cereal is this food, especially one that is eaten for breakfast

---

ⓘ Be careful not to confuse the spellings of **cereal** and **serial**.

---

ceremonial •ADJECTIVE• to do with ceremony or a particular ceremony: *Opening Parliament is one of the monarch's ceremonial duties.*
•NOUN• **ceremonials** an action that forms part of an official or traditional ceremony

ceremonious •ADJECTIVE• ceremonious behaviour is very correct and polite: *He gave a ceremonious bow.*
◆ **ceremoniously** •ADVERB• with grand gestures or actions: *A huge cake was placed ceremoniously in the centre of the table.*

ceremony •NOUN• **ceremonies** 1 ceremony is formal behaviour at a grand or important occasion: *all the ceremony of a coronation* 2

a ceremony is an event where special forms or customs are used: *a wedding ceremony*
⇒ **ceremonial, ceremonious**

certain •ADJECTIVE• 1 if something is certain it will definitely happen or be the case: *There's certain to be someone there who can help you.* 2 if you are certain about something you are sure about it: *I'm almost certain I saw a light in the old mill.*
• **for certain** for certain means definitely or surely: *How can you say for certain that this is a dinosaur bone?*
• **make certain** to make certain is to make sure: *Make certain that rope is tied tightly.*
◆ **certainly** •ADVERB• definitely: *Joe certainly impressed us with his acting.*
◆ **certainty** •NOUN• **certainties** 1 certainty is feeling or being certain 2 a certainty is something that will definitely happen

certificate •NOUN• **certificates** an official piece of paper that gives written details of something, such as a person's birth or death, or an exam they have passed: *Peter got first prize for English and Sheila got a certificate of merit.*
◆ **certify** •VERB• **certifies, certifying, certified** to certify something is to put it down in writing as an official statement or promise

CFC •ABBREVIATION• **CFCs** short for **chlorofluorocarbon**, a chemical that can damage the Earth's ozone layer and which was used in the past in refrigerators

cg •ABBREVIATION• short for **centigram** or **centigrams**

chador or **chadar** or **chudder** •NOUN• **chadors** or **chadars** or **chudders** a thick veil worn by Muslim women that covers the head and shoulders

chafe •VERB• **chafes, chafing, chafed** to chafe is to make sore or warm by rubbing, or to wear away by rubbing: *Toby's wellington boots were chafing his legs.*

chaff •NOUN• chaff is the husks from corn left after the corn has been threshed

chaffinch •NOUN• **chaffinches** a small singing bird with black, white and brown stripes on its wings

chain •NOUN• **chains** 1 chain, or a chain, is

several rings that are linked together

2 a chain of things is several things that are linked or connected: *a chain of events*

3 a chain of shops is several similar shops owned by the same person or company

chain letter • NOUN • **chain letters** a letter that asks the person receiving it to send a copy to several other people, promising or threatening that something will happen if they do or do not

chain mail • NOUN • chain mail is armour made up of small iron links

chain reaction • NOUN • **chain reactions** a chain reaction happens when one event causes another event to happen and so on

chain saw • NOUN • **chain saws** a motorized saw that has cutting teeth on the edge of a chain which rotates very quickly

chain store • NOUN • **chain stores** a shop or store that is part of a group of similar stores, all owned by the same company

chair • NOUN • **chairs** a chair is a piece of furniture with a back on which one person sits

• VERB • **chairs, chairing, chaired** someone chairs a meeting when they act as its chairperson

chairlift • NOUN • **chairlifts** a system that has chairs or seats hanging from a moving wire, used to carry skiers and walkers up mountains

chairperson • NOUN • **chairpeople** a person who is in charge of a meeting. If it is a man, he may be called a **chairman**, and if it is a woman, she may be called a **chairwoman**

chalet • NOUN • **chalets** a small wooden house

ⓘ This word is pronounced **shal**-ay.

chalice • NOUN • **chalices** a cup for wine used in church services, for example when taking communion

chalk • NOUN • **chalks 1** chalk is a kind of soft white limestone **2** a chalk is a piece of this, often with a colour mixed through it, that is used to draw with

• **chalky** • ADJECTIVE • **chalkier, chalkiest**
1 tasting or feeling like chalk **2** pale or white

like chalk: *unhealthy-looking chalky skin*

challenge • VERB • **challenges, challenging, challenged 1** to challenge a person or their actions is to question whether they are right: *The border guards challenged anyone who they thought was trying to get into the country.*

2 to challenge someone is to ask them to compete or fight: *He challenged his enemy to a duel.*

3 if something challenges you, you have to work hard or use all your abilities to get it done: *This exam will challenge even the most able pupil.*

• NOUN • **challenges 1** a challenge is something that needs all your ability to do it **2** a challenge is an invitation to fight or compete with someone

• **challenger** • NOUN • **challengers** someone who invites another person to compete with them, especially a sportsman who wants to compete against a champion

• **challenging** • ADJECTIVE • something challenging is difficult to do

chamber • NOUN • **chambers 1** an old-fashioned word for a room: *in my lady's chamber*

2 a large room for meetings

3 an enclosed space: *a dark underground chamber*

chamber music • NOUN • music for a small group of players that is performed in a room rather than a large hall

chameleon • NOUN • **chameleons** a small lizard that can change its colour to match its surroundings.

chamois • NOUN • **chamois 1** a small goat-like mountain deer that is found in Europe and parts of Asia **2** soft thin leather made from the skin of this animal, used to make gloves or for polishing things

ⓘ When you are talking about the deer this word is pronounced **shamwah**. When you are talking about the leather it is pronounced **shammy**.

champ • VERB • **champs, champing, champed** to champ is to chew noisily

champagne • NOUN • a type of sparkling

wine produced in the Champagne area of France

champion •NOUN• **champions 1** someone who has beaten all the others in a contest or competition: *the world boxing champion* **2** someone who is a champion of a cause is a strong supporter of that cause: *Mrs Pankhurst, the champion of women's right to vote*
•VERB• **champions, championing, championed** to champion something is to support it strongly
• **championship** •NOUN• **championships** a competition or contest to decide the champion

chance •NOUN• **chances 1** a possibility: *Is there any chance that we'll be picked for the team, do you think?*
2 to take a chance is to take a risk: *We took a chance that we would find accommodation when we got there.*
3 an opportunity: *You didn't give me a chance to answer.*
4 something that happens by chance happens by accident: *I saw him quite by chance parking his van up the street.*
•VERB• **chances, chancing, chanced** to chance is to take a risk: *It would probably have been all right, but we didn't want to chance it.*
•ADJECTIVE• happening by accident: *a chance meeting*

chancellor •NOUN• **chancellors** a high-ranking government official or minister: *the Chancellor of the Exchequer*

chancy •ADJECTIVE• **chancier, chanciest** rather risky: *It was a bit chancy taking a route we didn't know well.*

chandelier •NOUN• **chandeliers** a light fitting that hangs from the ceiling and holds several lights

change •VERB• **changes, changing, changed 1** to change is to make or become different: *The leaves changed from green to golden brown.*
2 if you change, you put on different clothes
3 if you change schools, jobs or houses you leave one and go to another

4 to change money is exchange one type of money for another
5 if you change your mind, you think differently from the way you thought before about something
•NOUN• **changes 1** a change is a difference
2 a change of clothes is a different set of clothes
3 change is money in the form of coins
4 change is any extra money that you have given to a seller that is more than the price of the item you want to buy and which the seller gives back to you

changeable •ADJECTIVE• the weather is changeable when it changes often or is likely to change

changeling •NOUN• **changelings** in stories, a fairy child that was secretly exchanged for a real one by the fairies

channel •NOUN• **channels 1** a groove or passage that water can travel along, or part of a sea or river that is deep enough for ships to travel along: *a drainage channel* • *a shipping channel*
2 a narrow sea or part of a sea: *the English Channel*
3 a television or radio station that is broadcast on a particular frequency: *Let's turn over to the other channel.*
•VERB• **channels, channelling, channelled** to channel something is to make it go in a particular direction: *They should channel their energies into something more useful.*

Channukah •NOUN• another spelling of **Hannukah**, a Jewish festival

chant •VERB• **chants, chanting, chanted** to chant something is to say it or repeat it as if you were singing
•NOUN• **chants** a chant is something that is repeated again and again in a singing voice

chaos •NOUN• great disorder and confusion
• **chaotic** •ADJECTIVE• completely disorganized: *The traffic was chaotic.*

chap •NOUN• **chaps** an informal word for a man

chapatti •NOUN• **chapattis** a kind of flat Indian bread

chapel •NOUN• **chapels 1** a small church or a small part of a larger church **2** a room inside

Aa
Bb
Cc
Dd
Ee
Ff
Gg
Hh
Ii
Jj
Kk
Ll
Mm
Nn
Oo
Pp
Qq
Rr
Ss
Tt
Uu
Vv
Ww
Xx
Yy
Zz

Aa

Bb

Cc

Dd

Ee

Ff

Gg

Hh

Ii

Jj

Kk

Ll

Mm

Nn

Oo

Pp

Qq

Rr

Ss

Tt

Uu

Vv

Ww

Xx

Yy

Zz

a building that is used for worship

chaperone • NOUN• **chaperones** a woman who accompanies an unmarried girl or young woman when she is out in public

chaplain • NOUN• **chaplains** someone, often a priest or minister of the church, who conducts religious services in an organization such as the army, a hospital or a school

chapped • ADJECTIVE• chapped skin is dry, red and sore

chapter • NOUN• **chapters** one of the sections of a book: *Turn to chapter three in your history books.*

char [1] •VERB• **chars, charring, charred** if something chars or is charred it is burnt black

char [2] • NOUN• **chars** a woman who cleans other people's houses

character • NOUN• **characters** 1 your character is the type of nature you have or the good and bad points that make you the way you are 2 a person that a writer creates for a story, film or play: *Sam Weller, Mr Micawber and other Dickens characters*
 ◆ **characteristic** • NOUN• **characteristics** a person's or thing's characteristics are the features or qualities that you notice or that make them what they are
 • ADJECTIVE• a characteristic feature or quality is one that is typical of a particular person or thing
 ◆ **characterize** or **characterise** •VERB• **characterizes, characterizing, characterized** 1 a quality or feature that characterizes someone or something is the one that is typical of them or by which they can be recognized 2 to characterize someone in a certain way is to describe them in that way: *He'd been characterized as a villain.*
 ◆ **characterization** • NOUN• characterization is the creation of different characters by a writer and the way the writer makes these characters change and develop during the story

charade • NOUN• **charades** a pretence
 ◆ **charades** • NOUN• charades is a game where players have to guess the title of a book, film or television programme from acting it out

charcoal • NOUN• charcoal is wood that has been burnt until it is black. Charcoal is used to draw with and as fuel

charge •VERB• **charges, charging, charged**
 1 to charge someone with a crime is to accuse them of it: *He was charged with murder.*
 2 to charge a certain price for something is to ask that amount of money for it: *The shopkeeper charged me $20 too much.*
 3 to charge is to move forward in a sudden rush: *'Forward, the Light Brigade! Charge for the guns!' he said.*
 • NOUN• **charges** 1 an accusation: *arrested on a charge of robbery*
 2 a price or fee: *There will be a small extra charge for postage and packing.*
 3 a sudden rush to attack: *The forwards should have reached the ten-yard line with that last charge.*
 4 an amount of electricity in something
 • **in charge** to be in charge is to be the person controlling or managing something: *Miss Handy is in charge of the younger children.*

charger • NOUN• **chargers** a charger was a type of large horse ridden in battles by a knight or cavalry officer

chariot • NOUN• **chariots** a chariot was a two-wheeled open vehicle pulled by one or more horses. Chariots were used by ancient people, like the ancient Egyptians, Greeks and Romans

charisma • NOUN• charisma is a personal quality that charms and impresses people: *a politician with lots of charisma*
 ◆ **charismatic** • ADJECTIVE• a charismatic person attracts or impresses people by the way they speak or act: *a charismatic leader*

charitable • ADJECTIVE• 1 a charitable person or a charitable act is kind and generous without asking anything in return 2 a charitable organization is one that gives money or help to the poor

charity • NOUN• **charities** 1 charity is giving to the poor and needy without asking anything in return 2 a charity is an organization that raises money to give to the poor

charm • NOUN• **charms** 1 charm is a quality

some people have that attracts and delights other people **2** a charm is a magic spell or something that is believed to have magical powers

•**VERB**• **charms, charming, charmed 1** to charm someone is to attract and delight them **2** to charm someone or something is to put a magic spell on them: *The Pied Piper charmed the rats with his playing.*
♦ **charming** •**ADJECTIVE**• delightful: *What a charming young man your son is.*

chart •**NOUN**• **charts 1** a chart is a table or diagram showing various measurements usually taken at different times: *A chart showing the rate of population growth.*
2 a chart is a map of the sea or the coast used by sailors
3 a chart is a list of the most popular CDs, tapes and records

charter •**NOUN**• **charters** an official document listing rights that people have
•**VERB**• **charters, chartering, chartered** to charter a boat or an aeroplane is to hire it

charwoman •**NOUN**• **charwomen** a woman who cleans other people's houses

chase •**VERB**• **chases, chasing, chased** to chase someone or something is to run after them
•**NOUN**• **chases** a chase is a hunt or pursuit

chasm •**NOUN**• **chasms** a deep narrow opening between rocks

chassis •**NOUN**• **chassis** a vehicle's chassis is the frame and wheels that support its body

ⓘ This word is pronounced **shass**-i, with a silent *s* at the end.

chaste •**ADJECTIVE**• a chaste person is very good and virtuous

chat •**VERB**• **chats, chatting, chatted** people chat when they talk to each other in a friendly way about everyday things
•**NOUN**• **chats** a friendly talk
⇒ **chatty**

chateau •**NOUN**• **chateaux** a castle or large house in France

chatter •**VERB**• **chatters, chattering, chattered 1** if animals or birds chatter they make loud cries quickly one after the other:

monkeys chattering in the treetops
2 to chatter is to talk about silly or unimportant things: *Stop chattering, you two, and get on with your work.*
3 if your teeth chatter they rattle against each other, usually because you are cold or frightened

chatty •**ADJECTIVE**• **chattier, chattiest** if someone is chatty they like to talk or chat to other people: *At first she was shy, but now she's become quite chatty.*

chauffeur •**NOUN**• **chauffeurs** someone whose job is to drive a car, especially a big expensive car belonging to a rich person

chauvinism •**NOUN**• chauvinism is a belief that your own country or your own sex is the best or the most important
♦ **chauvinist** •**NOUN**• **chauvinists** someone who believes that their own sex or their own country is superior
•**ADJECTIVE**• showing chauvinism: *a chauvinist attitude*

ⓘ **Chauvinism** is named after Nicholas Chauvin, a French soldier who was very proud of his country.

cheap •**ADJECTIVE**• **cheaper, cheapest**
1 something cheap does not cost a lot: *a cheap fare* **2** something that is cheap is of little value: *a cheap imitation diamond*
♦ **cheapen** •**VERB**• **cheapens, cheapening, cheapened** to cheapen something is to make it be or appear shoddy or worthless
♦ **cheaply** •**ADVERB**• inexpensively: *You can eat quite cheaply at these cafés.*

cheat •**VERB**• **cheats, cheating, cheated 1** to cheat someone is to deceive them: *The man cheated the old lady out of all her savings.* **2** to cheat in a game or exam is to act dishonestly so that you gain an advantage: *It's cheating to look at someone else's cards.*
•**NOUN**• **cheats** a cheat is someone who deceives people or tries to gain an advantage by behaving dishonestly

check¹ •**VERB**• **checks, checking, checked**
1 to check something is to make sure that it is correct or that it is working properly: *Can you check these sums, please.*
2 to check something is to hold it back or bring it to a stop: *He tried to check the*

Aa

Bb

Cc

Dd

Ee

Ff

Gg

Hh

Ii

Jj

Kk

Ll

Mm

Nn

Oo

Pp

Qq

Rr

Ss

Tt

Uu

Vv

Ww

Xx

Yy

Zz

bleeding by tying a handkerchief round his leg.

3 if you **check something out** you find out about it: *Can you check out the times of the trains for me, please?*

•NOUN• **checks** a test to see that something is correct or is working properly: *a health check*

check² •NOUN• **checks** a pattern of squares: *trousers with a bold check*

♦ **checked** •ADJECTIVE• having a pattern of squares: *a checked skirt*

checkmate •NOUN• checkmate is a position in chess from which the king cannot escape

checkout •NOUN• **checkouts** a checkout is the place where you pay at a supermarket or self-service shop

cheek •NOUN• **cheeks** 1 your cheeks are the two areas of your face that stretch from below your eyes to your chin 2 cheek, or a cheek, is rudeness to someone who should be given more respect: *He said I was the worst goalie he'd ever seen. What a cheek!*

♦ **cheekily** •ADVERB• rudely and disrespectfully

♦ **cheeky** •ADJECTIVE• **cheekier, cheekiest** rude and showing lack of respect: *Don't be cheeky to your father!*

cheer •NOUN• **cheers** 1 a cheer is a loud shout to someone to give them encouragement or to show that you think they are doing well 2 cheer is happiness and fun

•VERB• **cheers, cheering, cheered** 1 to cheer is to shout encouragement or approval: *They cheered each runner as he ran into the stadium.* 2 to cheer someone, or to **cheer them up**, is to make them feel happier

⇒ **cheers, cheery**

cheerful •ADJECTIVE• 1 a cheerful person behaves in a happy way 2 if a place is cheerful it is bright and pleasant and makes you feel comfortable or happy

cheerio •INTERJECTION• a word people use instead of 'goodbye' when they want to sound informal or friendly: *Cheerio, see you tomorrow.*

cheers •INTERJECTION• 1 a word people use as a toast: *Cheers, everyone. Happy New*

Year! 2 a word people use when they want to say 'thank you': *'Here's your book back.' 'Cheers.'*

cheery •ADJECTIVE• **cheerier, cheeriest** a cheery person or thing is bright and merry: *He gave me a cheery smile as he drove away.*

cheese •NOUN• **cheeses** a white or yellow food made from milk, which can be solid or soft

•ADJECTIVE• made with or containing cheese: *a cheese sandwich*

⇒ **cheesy**

cheesecake •NOUN• **cheesecakes** a dessert which has a crisp biscuit base with a sweet mixture containing cream cheese on top

cheesecloth •NOUN• a kind of loosely-woven cotton that was originally used to wrap cheeses in, but is now often used to make clothing

cheesy •ADJECTIVE• **cheesier, cheesiest** 1 tasting or smelling of cheese 2 a cheesy grin is a very broad smile

cheetah •NOUN• **cheetahs** a spotted African animal, related to the cat, that can run very fast over short distances

chef •NOUN• **chefs** a person with special training who cooks in the kitchen of a restaurant or hotel

chemical •NOUN• **chemicals** a chemical is a substance formed by or connected with chemistry

•ADJECTIVE• formed by, using, or containing a chemical or chemicals: *a chemical reaction*

chemist •NOUN• **chemists** 1 someone who studies chemistry

2 someone who makes up medicines and medical prescriptions

3 a chemist's is a shop where medicines and toiletries are sold

chemistry •NOUN• 1 chemistry is the study of chemical elements and the way they combine and react with each other 2 the chemistry between people is the way they act or react to each other

chemotherapy •NOUN• a treatment for cancer using powerful chemicals or combinations of chemicals

cheque •NOUN• **cheques** a piece of printed

paper used to pay for things with money from a bank account

(i) In North America, the spelling of this word is **check**.

chequered or **checkered** •ADJECTIVE• having a pattern of different coloured squares, like a chessboard

chequers or **checkers** •PLURAL NOUN• 1 black and white squares like those on a chessboard 2 another name for the game of **draughts**

cherish •VERB• **cherishes, cherishing, cherished** to cherish someone or something is to care for and look after them

cherry •NOUN• **cherries** 1 a kind of small round red fruit with a large stone inside 2 the tree that this fruit grows on

cherub •NOUN• **cherubs** or **cherubim** an angel that looks like a plump baby with wings

chess •NOUN• a game played on a chequered board by two players. Each player has a set of chess pieces, or chessmen, which are moved in various ways to capture the other player's pieces

chest •NOUN• **chests** 1 your chest is the area of your body from the bottom of your neck to your stomach 2 a large box for storing or carrying things: *a treasure chest*

chestnut •NOUN• **chestnuts** 1 a shiny reddish-brown nut that grows inside a prickly skin
2 a tree that chestnuts grow on
3 a reddish-brown colour

chew •VERB• **chews, chewing, chewed** 1 to chew is to break up food with the teeth before swallowing it 2 to **chew on** something, or to **chew something over**, is to think about it carefully for a while

chick •NOUN• **chicks** a baby bird

chicken •NOUN• **chickens** 1 a chicken is a hen, especially a young hen
2 chicken is the meat from a hen: *roast chicken*
3 a coward: *Jump! Don't be such a chicken.*
• **count your chickens before they're hatched** if you count your chickens before they are hatched you expect something that

you might not actually get

chickenpox •NOUN• an infectious disease which causes large itchy spots to appear on your skin

chickpea •NOUN• **chickpeas** a type of light brown pea that can be boiled and eaten in sauces or salads

chicory •NOUN• a plant with bitter-tasting leaves that are eaten in salads

chide •VERB• **chides, chiding, chided** to chide someone is to scold or criticize them: *He chided me about my forgetfulness.*

chief •NOUN• **chiefs** 1 a ruler or leader: *the chief of an African tribe* 2 a boss: *the chiefs of industry*
•ADJECTIVE• main or most important: *the chief city of the region*
♦ **chiefly** •ADVERB• mainly: *They ate some meat but chiefly their diet consisted of roots and berries.*

chieftain •NOUN• **chieftains** a leader or ruler of a tribe or clan: *a Scottish Highland chieftain*

chiffon •NOUN• a thin transparent material made of silk or nylon

chihuahua •NOUN• **chihuahuas** a tiny breed of dog, originally from Mexico

child •NOUN• **children** 1 a young human being: *a child's view of the world* 2 a son or daughter: *Their children are grown up.*
♦ **childhood** •NOUN• the period of time in your life when you are a child: *memories of childhood*

childlike •ADJECTIVE• typical of or behaving like a child: *childlike innocence*

childminder •NOUN• **childminders** someone who looks after a child or children when their parents are at work

children •NOUN• the plural of **child**: *One child was late and the rest of the children had to wait.*

chill •NOUN• **chills** 1 if there is a chill in the air it feels cold 2 if you get a chill you suffer from a fever and shivering
•ADJECTIVE• cold: *a chill wind blowing from the mountains*
•VERB• **chills, chilling, chilled** to chill

Aa Bb Cc Dd Ee Ff Gg Hh Ii Jj Kk Ll Mm Nn Oo Pp Qq Rr Ss Tt Uu Vv Ww Xx Yy Zz

something is to make it cold
⇒ **chilly**

chilli •NOUN• **chillis** a pod from a type of pepper that has a hot fiery taste and is used in cooking

chilly •ADJECTIVE• **chillier, chilliest** cold: *Shut the window. It's a bit chilly in here.*

chime •NOUN• **chimes** a chime is the sound of a bell or bells ringing
•VERB• **chimes, chiming, chimed 1** bells chime when they make ringing sounds **2** a clock chimes when it makes a ringing or musical sound as it strikes the hour or any part of the hour

chimney •NOUN• **chimneys** a passage above a fire that allows smoke to escape

chimneysweep •NOUN• **chimneysweeps** someone who sweeps the soot out of chimneys

chimpanzee •NOUN• **chimpanzees** a small African ape with black fur, a flat face and large brown eyes

chin •NOUN• **chins** your chin is the part of your face that sticks out below your mouth

china •NOUN• china is porcelain, a high quality material used to make things like cups, plates and ornaments

chink •NOUN• **chinks 1** a small gap: *a shaft of sunlight coming through a chink in the curtains* **2** a sound made when coins or other small metal objects hit each other

chip •VERB• **chips, chipping, chipped 1** to chip something is to break a small piece off it: *Roy chipped one of his teeth playing rugby.* **2** if someone **chips in**, they contribute to a discussion, usually with a suggestion or comment
•NOUN• **chips 1** a small piece broken off a hard object, or the place where a small piece has been broken off: *The bowl had a few chips and cracks, but it was still worth a lot of money.*
2 chips are potatoes cut into strips and fried: *chips with everything*
3 in the United States, chips are potato crisps
• **a chip off the old block** if someone is a chip off the old block, they look like or behave like

one of their parents, especially their father

chipmunk •NOUN• **chipmunks** a small North American animal with a long bushy tail and stripes on its back

chiropodist •NOUN• **chiropodists** someone who treats problems and diseases of the feet
♦ **chiropody** •NOUN• the care and treatment of people's feet, especially problems like corns and verrucas

chirp or **chirrup** •VERB• **chirps, chirping, chirped** or **chirrups, chirruping, chirruped** to chirp is to make a short shrill sound or sounds: *sparrows chirping*
•NOUN• **chirps** a short shrill sound: *the chirp of baby birds*
♦ **chirpy** •ADJECTIVE• **chirpier, chirpiest** happy and cheerful: *You sound very chirpy this morning.*

chisel •NOUN• **chisels** a very sharp tool used for cutting pieces off wood, stone or metal
•VERB• **chisels, chiselling, chiselled** to chisel something is to cut it using a chisel: *He chiselled his name in the stone.*

chive •NOUN• **chives** a herb with long thin hollow shoots that have a flavour like a mild-tasting onion

chlorinate •VERB• **chlorinates, chlorinating, chlorinated** to chlorinate water is to add chlorine to it to kill any bacteria

chlorine •NOUN• a yellowish-green gas with a harsh smell which is used as a bleach and disinfectant

chloroform •NOUN• a liquid that makes you become unconscious if you inhale its vapour

chlorophyll •NOUN• green substance in the leaves of a plant that allows the plant to use energy from the sun in a process called photosynthesis

chock-a-block •ADJECTIVE• if something is chock-a-block it is very full or crowded: *All the roads into the city were chock-a-block with rush-hour traffic.*

chocolate •NOUN• **chocolates 1** chocolate is a sweet food or drink made from the beans of the cacao tree: *a bar of chocolate* • *He always has a cup of hot chocolate before going to bed.* **2** a chocolate is a sweet or a drink made with chocolate

Aa
Bb
Cc
Dd
Ee
Ff
Gg
Hh
Ii
Jj
Kk
Ll
Mm
Nn
Oo
Pp
Qq
Rr
Ss
Tt
Uu
Vv
Ww
Xx
Yy
Zz

choice •NOUN• **choices** there is choice, or a choice, when you are able to decide which thing you will have because there is more than one thing available or on offer: *We were given a choice of meat or fish.* • *He had to do it; he had no choice in the matter.*
• ADJECTIVE• **choicer, choicest** choice things are of the best quality available: *the choicest vegetables*

choir •NOUN• **choirs** 1 a group of singers: *He sings in the church choir.* 2 part of a church where the choir sings
⇒ **choral, chorus**

choke •VERB• **chokes, choking, choked** 1 to choke on something is to have your breathing tubes blocked, especially by a piece of food that has got stuck in your throat: *She choked on a fish bone.*
2 if someone chokes they cough and gasp because they can't breathe properly: *This collar's far too tight; it's choking me.*
3 if a drain or something similar is choked it is blocked up with things: *gutters choked with leaves*

cholesterol •NOUN• a substance found in the body that helps to carry fats in the blood to the body tissues

chomp •VERB• **chomps, chomping, chomped** to chomp is to chew noisily

choose •VERB• **chooses, choosing, chose, chosen** to choose a person or thing from a group of people or things is to decide that you want that particular person or thing: *If you could have only one of them, which would you choose?*

chop •VERB• **chops, chopping, chopped** 1 to chop something is to cut it with an axe or a sharp tool like an axe: *Mr Willis was busy chopping a tree down.* 2 to chop something up is to cut it into small pieces: *He chopped the wood up to put on the fire.*
• **chop and change** to chop and change is to keep changing things
• NOUN• **chops** a chop is a piece of meat, usually with a bit of bone, that has been cut off a larger piece of meat

chopper •NOUN• **choppers** 1 a small axe used for chopping wood 2 an informal word for a helicopter

choppy •ADJECTIVE• **choppier, choppiest** if the sea is choppy, it is rough with lots of little waves

chopsticks •PLURAL NOUN• chopsticks are two thin pieces of wood or plastic held in one hand and used to pick up food and put it in your mouth. Chopsticks are used in the Far East, in places like China and Japan

choral •ADJECTIVE• sung by or written for a choir: *choral music*

chord •NOUN• **chords** 1 a musical sound made by playing several notes together: *Andy can play a few chords on the guitar.* 2 a straight line joining two points on a curve

chore •NOUN• **chores** a job, often one that is difficult or boring and has to be done regularly

choreographer •NOUN• **choreographers** someone who designs and arranges dances and dance steps, especially for a ballet or musical
• **choreography** •NOUN• the design and arrangement of dances and dance steps

chortle •VERB• **chortles, chortling, chortled** to chortle is to laugh or chuckle happily

chorus •NOUN• **choruses** 1 the part of a song that is repeated after every verse
2 the chorus in a play or musical is a group of singers that perform together on the stage
3 a choir
4 lots of people speaking or shouting together: *a chorus of protest*
• VERB• **choruses, chorusing, chorused** to chorus is to speak or sing all together: *'Happy birthday to you,' they chorused.*

chose •VERB• a way of changing the verb **choose** to make a past tense: *I wasn't made to do it; I chose to do it.*

chosen •VERB• a form of the verb **choose** that is used with a helping verb to show that something happened in the past: *Banking was the career he had chosen.*
• ADJECTIVE• being your choice: *your chosen career*

christen •VERB• **christens, christening, christened** to christen a child is to baptize it and give it a name
• **christening** •NOUN• **christenings** a ceremony at which a child is baptized

Aa
Bb
Cc
Dd
Ee
Ff
Gg
Hh
Ii
Jj
Kk
Ll
Mm
Nn
Oo
Pp
Qq
Rr
Ss
Tt
Uu
Vv
Ww
Xx
Yy
Zz

Aa
Bb
Cc
Dd
Ee
Ff
Gg
Hh
Ii
Jj
Kk
Ll
Mm
Nn
Oo
Pp
Qq
Rr
Ss
Tt
Uu
Vv
Ww
Xx
Yy
Zz

Christian •NOUN• **Christians** someone who is a believer in Christianity and follows the teachings of Jesus Christ
•ADJECTIVE• to do with Christianity or Christians
✦ **Christianity** •NOUN• a religion, practised in many parts of the world, that follows the teachings of Jesus Christ

Christian name •NOUN• **Christian names** a first name or personal name. Look up and compare **surname**

Christmas •NOUN• a Christian festival celebrating the birth of Christ and held on 25 December each year
•ADJECTIVE• for or to do with Christmas: *a Christmas tree*

Christmas Eve •NOUN• 24 December, the day before Christmas Day

chromosome •NOUN• **chromosomes** a rod-shaped part found in every body cell of living things. Chromosomes contain the special chemical patterns, or genes, that control what an individual living thing is like

chronic •ADJECTIVE• **1** a chronic disease is one that goes on for a long time **2** an informal way of saying that something is very bad: *The smell from the gasworks was really chronic.*

chronicle •NOUN• **chronicles** a record of things in the order that they happened
•VERB• **chronicles, chronicling, chronicled** to chronicle events is to write them down in the order that they happen

chronological •ADJECTIVE• if a record of events is chronological, or in chronological order, it is arranged in the order in which the events happened
✦ **chronology** •NOUN• **chronologies** **1** chronology is ordering events according to when they happened **2** a chronology is a list of events ordered in this way

chrysalis •NOUN• **chrysalises** an insect, such as a moth or butterfly, at the stage of its life when it covers itself with a case

chrysanthemum •NOUN• **chrysanthemums** a garden plant which either has clusters of small flowers or one or two large flowers with lots of petals

chubby •ADJECTIVE• **chubbier, chubbiest** rather fat, but in an attractive way: *the baby's chubby little legs*

chuck •VERB• **chucks, chucking, chucked** to chuck something is to throw it or toss it: *He'd chucked his schoolbag down on the floor.*

chuckle •VERB• **chuckles, chuckling, chuckled** to chuckle is to laugh softly: *The story made me chuckle to myself.*
•NOUN• **chuckles** a low or quiet laugh

chug •VERB• **chugs, chugging, chugged** to chug is to make a noise like a slowly moving engine, or to move along slowly: *The little steam train came chugging up the hill.*

chum •NOUN• **chums** a friend: *Have you made any chums at your new school?*

chump •NOUN• **chumps** a fool: *I felt such a chump when I found out I'd been tricked.*

chunk •NOUN• **chunks 1** a thick or uneven lump of something: *a chunk of cheese* • *pineapple chunks* **2** a large part of something: *He had to use quite a chunk of his savings to pay for the damage to the car.*
✦ **chunky** •ADJECTIVE• **chunkier, chunkiest** **1** thick and heavy: *a warm chunky sweater* **2** broad and heavy: *a chunky body*

church •NOUN• **churches** a building where people, especially Christians, go to worship

churchyard •NOUN• **churchyards** the area of land around a church, where people are buried

churlish •ADJECTIVE• bad-mannered or rude: *It would be churlish to refuse his generous offer.*

churn •NOUN• **churns** a special container for making butter from milk. The milk inside is moved about quickly by paddles until the fat separates
•VERB• **churns, churning, churned 1** to churn milk is to make it into butter inside a churn **2** if something churns it moves about violently: *I was so nervous my stomach was churning.*

chute •NOUN• **chutes 1** a long sloping channel that water, objects or people slide down **2** a piece of playground equipment with a sloping part that children can slide down

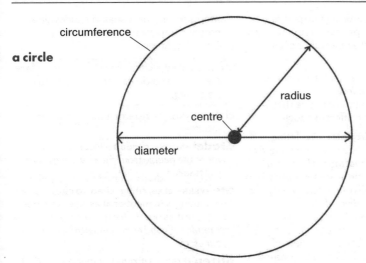

a circle

circumference

radius

centre

diameter

3 a short form of the word **parachute**

chutney •NOUN• chutney is a thick sauce made from fruit or vegetables, vinegar and spices and eaten with meat or cheese

cider •NOUN• cider is an alcoholic drink made from apples

cigar •NOUN• **cigars** a thick tube made from tobacco leaves that people smoke

cigarette •NOUN• **cigarettes** a tube of thin paper filled with chopped tobacco that people smoke

cinder •NOUN• **cinders** a small piece of burnt coal or wood that is left at the bottom of a fire

cine camera •NOUN• **cine cameras** a type of camera for making films

cinema •NOUN• **cinemas 1** a cinema is a place where films are shown on a big screen **2** cinema is films as an industry or an art form: *a career in cinema*

cinnamon •NOUN• a yellowish-brown sweet-tasting spice used in puddings and cakes

cipher •NOUN• **ciphers** a secret written code: *They wrote messages to each other in cipher.*

circa •PREPOSITION• if circa is used before a

date it means 'about' or 'approximately': *circa 1850*

circle •NOUN• **circles 1** a shape whose outside edge is an endless curving line which is always the same distance away from a central point: *Draw one circle for the head and another for the body.* • *Form a circle in the centre of the room.*
2 a circle of people is a group of people who know each other, have something in common or do a particular thing together: *a sewing circle* • *He's not part of my circle of friends.*
3 the circle in a theatre is the seats in one of the upper floors
• **come full circle** if something comes full circle it returns to the point where it began
•VERB• **circles, circling, circled 1** to circle is to go round and round: *vultures circling overhead* **2** to circle something is draw a circle round it: *She circled the area on the map with a red marker.*
⇒ **circular**

circuit •NOUN• **circuits 1** if you do a circuit of something you go right round it, often arriving back at or near the place where you started
2 a racing circuit is a track that racing cars and motorbikes race round
3 an electrical circuit is the path that

electricity follows between two points

4 a connected group of events, especially of a particular sport: *the international golf circuit*

circular •ADJECTIVE• round, in the shape of a circle: *a circular window*
•NOUN• **circulars** a letter or notice that is sent round to a lot of different people

circulate •VERB• **circulates, circulating, circulated 1** to circulate is to move round or through: *water circulating in the central heating system* **2** to circulate something is to send it round: *Details of the meeting will be circulated to all members of staff.*
♦ **circulation** •NOUN• **1** circulation is movement round or through something **2** your circulation is the movement of blood round your body, pumped by your heart through your veins and arteries **3** a particular newspaper's or magazine's circulation is the number of copies that are sold

circumcision •NOUN• **circumcisions** an operation to cut away the part covering the end of a boy's penis called the foreskin, either for medical or religious reasons
♦ **circumcise** •VERB• **circumcises, circumcising, circumcised** to cut away the foreskin from the penis

circumference •NOUN• **circumferences 1** the length of the outside edge of a circle: *What's the circumference of this coin?* **2** the outside edge of a circle: *Mark a point on the circumference of the circle and draw a line through it.*

circumstance •NOUN• **circumstances 1** an event or fact: *Is there any circumstance that might alter your decision?* **2** the circumstances of a situation is the state or condition that affects or led up to that situation **3** your circumstances are the condition of your life, especially how much money or wealth you have
♦ **circumstantial** •ADJECTIVE• circum-stantial evidence is evidence that makes you believe something though there is no actual proof

circus •NOUN• **circuses** a type of travelling entertainment that usually includes clowns, acrobats, trapeze artistes, and often performing animals

(i) It is called a **circus** because it takes place inside a ring, and **circus** is the Latin word for a *circle* or *ring*.

cistern •NOUN• **cisterns** a tank for storing water

citadel •NOUN• **citadels** a fort inside a city where the people from the city can go if they are attacked

cite •VERB• **cites, citing, cited** to cite something is to mention it as an example or to quote it as proof: *Try to cite some examples of good environmental schemes in your essay*

citizen •NOUN• **citizens 1** someone who lives in a particular town, state or country: *citizens of Paris* **2** someone who belongs officially to a particular country: *He lives in Singapore but he's an Australian citizen.*
♦ **citizenship** •NOUN• **1** to have citizenship of a country is to belong officially to that country: *He's applied for Canadian citizenship.* **2** citizenship is the responsibilities and duties you have by being a citizen of a particular state or country: *Children should be taught good citizenship.*

citrus fruit •NOUN• **citrus fruits** fruits with a thick skin and a sharp flavour, such as oranges, lemons, limes and grapefruit

city •NOUN• **cities** a large important town, especially one that has a cathedral: *What's the biggest city in Europe?*

civic •ADJECTIVE• to do with a city or citizens: *civic pride* • *a civic centre*

civil •ADJECTIVE• **1** if a person is civil they talk or behave in a polite way **2** civil means involving or having to do with the citizens of a country: *a civil war* **3** civil means having to do with ordinary people or civilians, not the military or the church: *civil life* • *a civil marriage ceremony*
⇒ **civilian, civilization, civilize**

civil engineer •NOUN• **civil engineers** someone whose job is to plan and build public buildings and things like roads and bridges

civilian •NOUN• **civilians** a person who is not in the armed forces

civilization •NOUN• **civilizations** 1 civilization is being or becoming civilized 2 a civilization is a particular society or culture at a particular period in time: *He spent his life studying ancient civilizations in Central and South America.*

civilize *or* **civilise** •VERB• **civilizes, civilizing, civilized** 1 to civilize primitive people is to teach them how things are done in more advanced cultures or societies, so that their society becomes more developed 2 to civilize someone is to teach them good behaviour
♦ **civilized** •ADJECTIVE• behaving well or politely, without arguing or being aggressive: *Let's try and have a civilized discussion instead of all shouting at once.*

civil rights •PLURAL NOUN• civil rights are your rights to be treated fairly in society no matter what sex, colour or religion you are

civil servant •NOUN• **civil servants** someone who works in the civil service of a country
♦ **civil service** •NOUN• the civil service is all the departments of the government that organize the running of the country, rather than the law-making or military branches of the government

civil war •NOUN• **civil wars** a war between two groups within the same country

cl •ABBREVIATION• short for **centilitre** or **centilitres**

clad •ADJECTIVE• clothed or covered: *Robin Hood and his merry men, all clad in Lincoln green* • *mountains clad in snow*

claim •VERB• **claims, claiming, claimed** 1 to claim that something is true is to state that it is a fact, even though there is no real proof: *He claims he saw a flying saucer.* 2 to claim something is to demand it as your right or to state that it is yours: *You'll need to fill in this form to claim unemployment benefit.* • *If no one claims any of the lost items they will be sold for charity.*
•NOUN• **claims** 1 a statement that something is a fact: *No one listened to his repeated claims that he was innocent.* 2 a demand or request for something that you have a right to or that you say you own: *an insurance claim* • *the family's historical claim to the land*
♦ **claimant** •NOUN• **claimants** someone who makes a claim

clairvoyant •ADJECTIVE• able to see into the future
•NOUN• **clairvoyants** someone who claims that they can see things that will happen in the future

clam •NOUN• **clams** a large shellfish with two shells that are joined at one side and which can be closed tightly for protection
•VERB• **clams, clamming, clammed** if someone **clams up** they stop talking or won't give any more information

clamber •VERB• **clambers, clambering, clambered** to clamber is to climb up or over things using your hands and feet: *They tried to clamber up the steep and slippery slope.*

clammy •ADJECTIVE• **clammier, clammiest** damp in a sticky unpleasant way: *His hands became clammy and his hair stood on end with fear.*

clamour •VERB• **clamours, clamouring, clamoured** to clamour for something is to try to get it by making noisy demands: *All the children were clamouring to see what was in the box.*
•NOUN• clamour, or a clamour, is noisy shouts or demands

clamp •NOUN• **clamps** a device for holding things together tightly or a device attached tightly to something to stop it moving: *a wheel clamp*
•VERB• **clamps, clamping, clamped** 1 to clamp something is to put a clamp on it: *Clamp the two pieces of wood together until the glue dries.* 2 to **clamp down** on something is to stop it happening by controlling it more strictly: *We will have to clamp down on litter if we want to clean up the city.*

clan •NOUN• **clans** a group of families all descended from the same family and usually all having the same name

ⓘ This word comes from the Scottish Gaelic word **clann**, which means *children* or *family*.

clandestine •ADJECTIVE• if something is clandestine it is kept secret or hidden, especially because it is not allowed: *The plotters held a series of clandestine meetings.*

clang •VERB• **clangs, clanging, clanged** to clang is to make a loud ringing sound, like a heavy piece of metal hitting against a hard material: *The prison gate clanged shut behind them.*
•NOUN• **clangs** a loud ringing sound

clank •VERB• **clanks, clanking, clanked** to make a loud dull sound, like metal hitting metal: *Strange machines were clanking in the gloomy shed.*
•NOUN• **clanks** a loud dull sound: *the clank of heavy chains*

clap •VERB• **claps, clapping, clapped** 1 you clap when you hit the palms of your hands together making a slapping sound: *The audience clapped and cheered.* • *We all clapped in time to the music.* 2 to hit lightly with a slapping movement: *He clapped his friend on the back.*
•NOUN• **claps** 1 a short slapping sound made when you hit your hands together or when you hit someone lightly with the flat of your hand 2 a sudden very loud sound made by thunder
♦ **clapper** •NOUN• **clappers** the part of a bell that strikes against the inside to make the ringing sound

claptrap •NOUN• nonsense or meaningless talk

clarify •VERB• **clarifies, clarifying, clarified** to clarify something is to make it clearer or easier to understand

clarinet •NOUN• **clarinets** an instrument made of wood that you play by blowing through it and pressing keys with your fingers
♦ **clarinettist** •NOUN• **clarinettists** someone who plays the clarinet

clarity •NOUN• clearness: *the clarity of the image*

clash •VERB• **clashes, clashing, clashed** 1 if two pieces of hard material clash they make a loud sound as they hit each other: *cymbals clashing*
2 if two people clash they disagree or argue

angrily with each other
3 if two colours clash they do not go well together: *The purple clashes with the red.*
•NOUN• **clashes** 1 a sound made when two things hit against each other: *the clash of cymbals* 2 an angry disagreement between people: *They've had a few clashes over the years.*

clasp •VERB• **clasps, clasping, clasped** to clasp something is to hold it tightly or closely: *She was clasping a little child in her arms.*
•NOUN• **clasps** 1 a hook or pin for holding things together: *a hair clasp* 2 a grasp

class •NOUN• **classes** 1 a group of schoolchildren or students who are taught together, or a period of time during which a particular subject is taught: *It was Maureen's first day in Miss Smith's class.*
• *Mum is going to her aerobics class tonight.*
2 a grouping of people who have similar backgrounds or who belong to the same rank in society: *the working class*
3 a division of things according to how good they are: *He's a first class student.*
4 a grouping of animals or plants that are related to each other or have something in common
•VERB• **classes, classing, classed** to class people or things is to put them in a grouping with others of the same type or rank: *Anyone under 16 is classed as a junior member.*
⇒ **classify, classy**

classic •NOUN• **classics** a great book or other work of art that goes on being admired long after it was written or made
•ADJECTIVE• 1 recognized as great for all time: *classic children's stories* 2 a classic example of something is typical: *He made the classic mistake of thinking that he could do all his studying in the week before the exam.*
♦ **classical** •ADJECTIVE• 1 belonging to the style or culture of ancient Greece or Rome: *classical architecture* 2 traditional: *classical ballet*

classical music •NOUN• high quality or serious music that goes on being played or listened to for a long time after it has been composed

classics •NOUN• the study of the ancient Greek and Latin languages, and the work of ancient Greek and Roman writers

classify •VERB• **classifies, classifying, classified** to classify people or things is to put them into groups or classes according to what type they are
♦ **classified** •ADJECTIVE• classified information is information that the government keeps secret from the public
♦ **classification** •NOUN• **classifications** 1 classification is putting things into groups of different types 2 a classification is a group that includes people or things of the same type

classmate •NOUN• **classmates** your class-mates are the people in your school or college class

classroom •NOUN• **classrooms** a room where lessons are given in a school or college

classy •ADJECTIVE• **classier, classiest** stylish and expensive: *He's always worn classy clothes.*

clatter •VERB• **clatters, clattering, clattered** to clatter is to make a loud noise like hard objects falling or hitting each other: *He came clattering downstairs in his ski boots.*
•NOUN• a sound made when hard objects fall or hit against each other: *the clatter of dishes being washed*

clause •NOUN• **clauses** 1 a group of words that make up a sentence or part of a sentence 2 a part of an official document or contract

claustrophobia •NOUN• people who have claustrophobia are afraid of small, enclosed or crowded spaces
♦ **claustrophobic** •ADJECTIVE• afraid of small, enclosed or crowded spaces

claw •NOUN• **claws** 1 one of the long pointed nails on some animals' paws 2 a part on the end of a crab's or lobster's leg that it uses for gripping things
•VERB• **claws, clawing, clawed** to claw something is to scratch it with claws or fingernails

clay •NOUN• soft sticky material found in the ground and used for making pottery

clean •ADJECTIVE• **cleaner, cleanest** 1 if something is clean it has no dirt or germs on or in it: *a clean face and hands* • *There was no clean water to drink.*
2 complete: *She wanted a clean break from her past.*
3 straight, without any jagged or rough edges: *It is a clean break so the bone should heal well.*
4 unused: *Take a clean sheet of paper and start again.*
5 fair and honest: *a clean game of football*
•ADVERB• completely: *It went clean through and out the other side.* • *He's gone clean mad.*
• **come clean** if someone comes clean they tell the truth
•VERB• **cleans, cleaning, cleaned** 1 to clean something is to remove the dirt from it 2 to **clean up** is to tidy a place, removing any dirt and rubbish
♦ **cleaner** •NOUN• **cleaners** 1 a person whose job is to clean houses, offices or other buildings 2 a product for cleaning things: *lavatory cleaner*
♦ **cleanliness** •NOUN• being clean: *Cleanliness helps prevent germs spreading.*

cleanse •VERB• **cleanses, cleansing, cleansed** to cleanse something is to make it clean: *cleanse the wound with an antiseptic*
♦ **cleanser** •NOUN• **cleansers** a product that cleanses something, especially your skin

clear •ADJECTIVE• **clearer, clearest** 1 easy to see, hear or understand: *a clear view* • *She spoke in a clear voice.* • *His explanation wasn't very clear.*
2 see-through: *clear glass*
3 not blocked or marked by anything: *a clear sky* • *The road was clear.*
4 without meeting any difficulties or obstacles: *The way is clear for him to win the title.*
•ADVERB• not touching, away from: *Stand clear of the gates.*
•VERB• **clears, clearing, cleared** 1 to clear is to make or become clear: *The sky cleared and the sun came out.*
2 to clear things is to move them or tidy

Aa
Bb
Cc
Dd
Ee
Ff
Gg
Hh
Ii
Jj
Kk
Ll
Mm
Nn
Oo
Pp
Qq
Rr
Ss
Tt
Uu
Vv
Ww
Xx
Yy
Zz

cleave → climax

them away: *Whose turn is it to clear the dirty supper dishes?*

3 if someone is cleared of something, they are found to be not guilty or not to blame

4 to clear something is to jump over it without touching it: *Janey's pony cleared all the fences.*

5 to **clear off** is to go right away from somewhere: *We had wandered on to his land and he told us to clear off.*

6 if something, such as a rash, **clears up** it goes away

♦ **clearance** •NOUN• **clearances 1** clearing something away: *the clearance of the land to make room for housing*

2 the amount of space between one thing and another passing beside it or under it: *There isn't enough clearance for the lorry to go through that gap.*

3 if someone or something has clearance to do something they have permission to do it: *Air traffic controllers give aeroplanes clearance to land.*

♦ **clearing** •NOUN• **clearings** a gap in a forest where there are no trees

♦ **clearly** •ADVERB• **1** in a clear way: *I can't see it very clearly.* **2** obviously: *Clearly, we couldn't continue without proper equipment.*

♦ **clearness** •NOUN• being clear
⇒ **clarify, clarity**

cleave •VERB• **cleaves, cleaving, clove** *or* **cleft** *or* **cleaved, cloven** *or* **cleft** *or* **cleaved**
to cleave something is to split it

♦ **cleaver** •NOUN• **cleavers** a cutting tool with a large square blade fitted to a handle

clef •NOUN• **clefs** a symbol used at the beginning of a piece of music to show how high or low the notes should be

cleft •NOUN• **clefts** a split or opening: *A jagged cleft had opened up in the rocks.*
•ADJECTIVE• split: *a cleft stick*

cleft palate •NOUN• **cleft palates** a split in the roof of the mouth that some people have when they are born

clench •VERB• **clenches, clenching, clenched**
to clench something is to hold it tightly or press it tightly together: *Clenching his teeth, he jumped out of the plane.*

clergy •PLURAL NOUN• the clergy are priests or ministers in the Christian church

clergyman •NOUN• **clergymen** a man who is a priest or minister of the church

clergywoman •NOUN• **clergywomen** a woman who is a priest or minister of the church

cleric •NOUN• **clerics** a member of the clergy
♦ **clerical** •ADJECTIVE• **1** of or used by the clergy: *The man was wearing a clerical collar.* **2** to do with office work: *a clerical assistant*

clerk •NOUN• **clerks** an office worker whose job is to write letters, do filing, or keep accounts

clever •ADJECTIVE• **cleverer, cleverest**
1 quick to learn and understand things: *He's the cleverest boy in his class.* **2** skilful: *He's clever with his hands.*

cliché •NOUN• **clichés** a phrase that has been used so often it no longer has the effect it once had

ⓘ This word is pronounced klee-shay.

click •NOUN• **clicks** a short sharp sound like the sound made when a door lock is closed gently
•VERB• **clicks, clicking, clicked 1** to make this sound: *We could hear her heels clicking on the stone floor.* **2** if you **click on** something that appears on a computer screen, you choose it by pressing the button on the mouse

client •NOUN• **clients 1** someone who uses the services of a person like a lawyer or accountant **2** a customer

cliff •NOUN• **cliffs** a high steep rocky slope, usually facing the sea

cliffhanger •NOUN• **cliffhangers** a situation or story that is exciting because you don't know how it will turn out until the very end

climate •NOUN• **climates** the usual sort of weather there is in a region or area: *The Earth's climate is getting warmer.* • *plants that only grow in warmer climates*

climax •NOUN• **climaxes** the most important, most exciting or most interesting point in a story or situation

climb •VERB• **climbs, climbing, climbed** 1 to climb is to go up, or to go towards the top: *He likes to climb mountains.* 2 if someone involved in an argument or disagreement **climbs down** they eventually admit that they were wrong
•NOUN• **climbs** an act of climbing: *We had a steep climb to the top.*
♦ **climber** •NOUN• **climbers** 1 someone who climbs, often as a pastime or sport 2 a plant that climbs up things like walls and fences

clinch •VERB• **clinches, clinching, clinched** to clinch a bargain or argument is to settle it

cling •VERB• **clings, clinging, clung** to cling to something is to stick to it or hang on to it tightly: *shellfish clinging to the rocks*

clingfilm •NOUN• clingfilm is a very thin sheet of plastic that is used to cover food

clinic •NOUN• **clinics** a place where people can be seen by doctors to get treatment and advice: *an eye clinic*

clink •NOUN• **clinks** a sharp ringing sound like the sound made when glasses or coins are hit together
•VERB• **clinks, clinking, clinked** to clink is to make this sound

clip •VERB• **clips, clipping, clipped** 1 to clip something is to cut small or short parts off it: *clipping the hedge with shears* 2 to clip something is to fasten it with a clip: *a badge clipped on to his lapel*
•NOUN• **clips** a small fastening device: *a paper clip*

clipper •NOUN• **clippers** 1 a type of fast sailing ship 2 clippers are an instrument used for clipping things: *nail clippers*

clique •NOUN• **cliques** a small group of people who are friendly to each other but keep other people out of the group
♦ **cliquey** •ADJECTIVE• **cliquier, cliquiest** to do with a clique or forming cliques

cloak •NOUN• **cloaks** 1 a piece of clothing without sleeves that is worn over other clothing and hangs down loosely from the shoulders 2 anything that covers or hides: *the cloak of darkness*
•VERB• **cloaks, cloaking, cloaked** to cloak something is to cover or hide it: *hills cloaked in mist*

cloakroom •NOUN• **cloakrooms** a room or area in a building where visitors can leave their coats, hats and bags

clobber •VERB• **clobbers, clobbering, clobbered** to clobber someone is to hit them hard

ⓘ This is an informal word.

clock •NOUN• **clocks** a machine for measuring time
•VERB• **clocks, clocking, clocked** to **clock up** a certain number of points, for example, is to achieve that number over a period of time

clockwise •ADJECTIVE• turning or moving in the same direction as the hands of a clock

clockwork •NOUN• the machinery of an old-fashioned clock with a spring that you wind up
• **like clockwork** if something goes or works like clockwork it goes or works smoothly without any problems

clod •NOUN• **clods** a solid lump of earth

clog •NOUN• **clogs** a shoe with a wooden sole
•VERB• **clogs, clogging, clogged** to clog something, or to **clog it up**, is to block it: *drains clogged up with fallen leaves and litter*

cloister •NOUN• **cloisters** a covered passageway that is open on one side and goes round a courtyard in a monastery, cathedral or college

clone •NOUN• **clones** an exact copy of a plant or animal, made artificially by taking cells from it
•VERB• **clones, cloning, cloned** to make an exact copy of a plant or animal in this way

close¹ •ADJECTIVE• 1 near in distance or time: *They are quite close in age.*
2 very dear or intimate: *a close friendship*
3 tight: *a close fit*
4 thorough or careful: *Pay close attention.*
5 having no fresh air: *a close atmosphere*
•ADVERB• **closer, closest** near: *He came close to winning.* • *She stood close by.*
♦ **closely** •ADVERB• 1 at a close distance: *He came into the room, closely followed by his two friends.* 2 tightly: *closely packed sardines*

Aa Bb Cc Dd Ee Ff Gg Hh Ii Jj Kk Ll Mm Nn Oo Pp Qq Rr Ss Tt Uu Vv Ww Xx Yy Zz

Aa
Bb
Cc
Dd
Ee
Ff
Gg
Hh
Ii
Jj
Kk
Ll
Mm
Nn
Oo
Pp
Qq
Rr
Ss
Tt
Uu
Vv
Ww
Xx
Yy
Zz

close [2] • VERB• **closes, closing, closed** 1 to shut: *Close the door behind you.* 2 to finish: *They closed the concert by singing the national anthem.*
• NOUN• **closes** 1 the end of something: *at the close of day* 2 a street that is blocked at one end
⇒ **closure**

ⓘ If you are talking about the **close** of something, you pronounce it **cloze**. If you are talking about a street, you pronounce **close** with an **ss** sound.

closet • NOUN• **closets** a cupboard

close-up • NOUN• **close-ups** a photograph or a shot in a film that has been taken very close to something so that all the details can be seen

closure • NOUN• **closures** an act of closing: *school closures*

clot • NOUN• **clots** a lump or clump that forms in liquids, especially in cream or blood
• VERB• **clots, clotting, clotted** to form clots

cloth • NOUN• **cloths** 1 cloth is material made by weaving threads of wool, silk, cotton or some other fibre 2 a cloth is a piece of fabric

clothe • VERB• **clothes, clothing, clothed** to put clothes on or to provide with clothes: *They need money to feed and clothe themselves.*
♦ **clothes** • PLURAL NOUN• clothes are the things people wear to cover their bodies
♦ **clothing** • NOUN• clothing is clothes

cloud • NOUN• **clouds** 1 clouds are masses of tiny water drops floating in the sky 2 a cloud of something is a mass of it in the air: *a cloud of flies*
• **on cloud nine** if you are on cloud nine you are very happy
• VERB• **clouds, clouding, clouded** to become cloudy: *The sky clouded over and it started to rain.*
⇒ **cloudy**

cloudburst • NOUN• **cloudbursts** a sudden spell of very heavy rain

cloudy • ADJECTIVE• **cloudier, cloudiest** 1 filled with clouds: *a cloudy sky* 2 not clear: *a cloudy liquid*

clout • NOUN• **clouts** a blow with the hand
• VERB• **clouts, clouting, clouted** to hit with the hand

ⓘ This is an informal word.

clove [1] • NOUN• **cloves** a small dried flower-bud of a tropical plant, used in cooking as a spice

clove [2] • NOUN• **cloves** one of the sections into which a plant bulb splits: *a clove of garlic*

cloven hoof • NOUN• **cloven hooves** a hoof divided into two parts, like that of cows, sheep, pigs and goats

clover • NOUN• a small flowering plant that grows amongst grass

clown • NOUN• **clowns** someone who works in a circus and does funny acts dressed up in ridiculous clothes
• VERB• **clowns, clowning, clowned** to clown or **clown around** is to act in a funny or silly way

cloying • ADJECTIVE• sweet in a sickly way

club • NOUN• **clubs** 1 an organized group of people who meet regularly to take part in an activity, or the place where they meet
2 one of the metal sticks used in golf to hit the ball
3 a heavy piece of wood or metal used as a weapon
4 clubs is one of the four suits of playing cards, which have the symbol (♣) printed on them
• VERB• **clubs, clubbing, clubbed** if people **club together** they each put some money in to buy something

cluck • NOUN• **clucks** a sound made by a hen
• VERB• **clucks, clucking, clucked** to make this sound

clue • NOUN• **clues** 1 a sign or piece of evidence that helps solve a riddle, mystery or crime 2 if someone doesn't have a clue, they don't know anything or they don't know how to do something

clump • NOUN• **clumps** a group of plants growing close together: *a clump of bluebells*

clumsy • ADJECTIVE• **clumsier, clumsiest** a clumsy person is awkward in the way they move or act, especially by dropping things or bumping into things

clung •VERB• a way of changing the verb **cling** to make a past tense. It can be used with or without a helping verb: *Barnacles and mussels clung to the rocks.* • *She had clung on to her teddy bear all day.*

cluster •NOUN• **clusters** several things placed or growing very close together: *roses growing in clusters*
•VERB• **clusters, clustering, clustered** to cluster is to move or be very close together: *The children clustered round the teacher.*

clutch •VERB• **clutches, clutching, clutched**
1 to clutch something is to hold it tightly in your hand or hands 2 to clutch at something is to try to get hold of it
• **clutch at straws** to clutch at straws is to try hard to find a way out of a bad situation or to think of a way of solving it, even though it has very little chance of being successful
•NOUN• **clutches** 1 to be in someone's clutches is to be in their grasp, especially if they have control or power over you 2 the part of a car's engine that you operate with a pedal to control the gears

clutter •NOUN• clutter is lots of things that cover or fill a space so that it looks untidy or disorganized
•VERB• **clutters, cluttering, cluttered** to clutter, or to **clutter up**, a space is to fill it with lots of things and make it untidy: *Books cluttered up the shelves.*

cm •ABBREVIATION• short for **centimetre** or **centimetres**

Co. •ABBREVIATION• short for **Company** when it is part of a business name: *Reginald Bloggs & Co., Ironmongers*

co- •PREFIX• if a word starts with **co-** it adds the meaning 'working with' or 'together with'. For example, a *co-author* is someone who has written a book with another writer

coach •NOUN• **coaches** 1 a single-decker bus used to carry passengers over long distances 2 a type of large four-wheeled carriage pulled by horses and used to carry passengers 3 a railway carriage for passengers 4 a person who trains someone in a

particular skill or prepares them for a competition or performance: *a rugby coach* • *a singing coach*
•VERB• **coaches, coaching, coached** to coach someone is to prepare them for a competition or performance

coal •NOUN• a hard black substance containing carbon that is dug out of the ground and burnt as fuel

coal gas •NOUN• a mixture of gases that come from coal, used as a fuel for lighting and heating

coalmine •NOUN• **coalmines** a mine where coal is dug out of the earth

coarse •ADJECTIVE• **coarser, coarsest**
1 feeling rough or harsh: *coarse cloth*
2 vulgar: *coarse language*
• **coarsen** •VERB• **coarsens, coarsening, coarsened** to make rough or vulgar

coast •NOUN• **coasts** the coast is the area of land next to the sea
• **the coast is clear** if the coast is clear there is no one around to see you or stop you doing something
•VERB• **coasts, coasting, coasted** to coast, or to **coast along**, is to go along without making much effort

coastguard •NOUN• **coastguards** someone whose job is to guard the coast of a country against smugglers and to help ships in danger

coat •NOUN• **coats** 1 a piece of clothing with sleeves that usually reaches to your knees and that you wear over your other clothes 2 a layer: *three coats of paint*
•VERB• **coats, coating, coated** to coat something is to cover it with a layer of something: *They'd coated their bodies with mud.*

coat of arms •NOUN• **coats of arms** a coat of arms is the badge or crest used by a particular family

coax •VERB• **coaxes, coaxing, coaxed** to coax someone to do something is to persuade them gently to do it

cob •NOUN• **cobs** a long round solid part of a corn plant that the seeds grow on

cobble •NOUN• **cobbles** cobbles are rounded stones set into a road

Aa
Bb
Cc
Dd
Ee
Ff
Gg
Hh
Ii
Jj
Kk
Ll
Mm
Nn
Oo
Pp
Qq
Rr
Ss
Tt
Uu
Vv
Ww
Xx
Yy
Zz

♦ **cobbled** . ADJECTIVE. covered with cobbles

cobbler . NOUN. **cobblers** someone whose job is making and repairing shoes

cobblestone . NOUN. **cobblestones** one of the rounded stones laid side by side on some roads

cobra . NOUN. **cobras** a type of poisonous snake that raises itself up before it bites

ⓘ The word **cobra** is Portuguese and means **snake**.

cobweb . NOUN. **cobwebs** a criss-cross pattern of thin threads that a spider makes to catch insects

cock . NOUN. **cocks** a male bird • VERB. **cocks, cocking, cocked** 1 an animal cocks its ears when it makes its ears stand upright so that it can hear better 2 you cock your head when you tilt it to one side

cockatoo . NOUN. **cockatoos** a type of large parrot with a crest on top of its head that it can raise and lower

cockerel . NOUN. **cockerels** a male chicken

cocker spaniel . NOUN. **cocker spaniels** a breed of small dog with a long silky coat and ears that hang down

cockle . NOUN. **cockles** a type of small round edible shellfish that lives in the sea

cockney . NOUN. **cockneys** 1 someone who comes from the east end of London 2 the accent or way of speaking of people who come from around the east end of London

cockpit . NOUN. **cockpits** the space in an aeroplane where the pilot sits

cockroach . NOUN. **cockroaches** a large crawling insect usually found in damp or dirty places

cocktail . NOUN. **cocktails** 1 a drink made with one or more alcoholic drinks that are often also mixed with fruit juice and ice 2 a mixture made with several different ingredients: *a fruit cocktail*

cocky . ADJECTIVE. **cockier, cockiest** a cocky person is cheeky and confident

cocoa . NOUN. **cocoas** a hot drink made with the powdered seeds of the cacao plant, which are also used to make chocolate

coconut . NOUN. **coconuts** a large hairy nut from a tropical palm tree that has white firm flesh and a thin liquid called coconut milk inside

cocoon . NOUN. **cocoons** a case made by a caterpillar inside which it changes into an adult moth or butterfly

cod . NOUN. **cod** a large sea fish found in northern seas of the world and caught for food

coddle . VERB. **coddles, coddling, coddled** to coddle someone is to protect them and treat them like a baby

code . NOUN. **codes** 1 code, or a code, is a set of signs or letters used for signalling or writing: *a message written in secret code* 2 a set of rules or laws: *a code of honour* • VERB. **codes, coding, coded** to code something is to put it in a particular code of letters or signs: *All messages were coded before being sent.*

coed . ADJECTIVE. a short form of the word **coeducational**

coeducation . NOUN. the teaching of boys and girls in the same school or college ♦ **coeducational** . ADJECTIVE. teaching both male and female students: *a coeducational school*

coexist . VERB. **coexists, coexisting, coexisted** if two or more people or things coexist they live or exist together at the same time and sometimes also in the same place

coffee . NOUN. **coffees** 1 coffee is a drink made from the roasted and ground-up beans of a tropical plant 2 a coffee is a cup of this drink

coffer . NOUN. **coffers** 1 a coffer is a large strong box used to store things in, especially money or valuables 2 a company's or organization's coffers is the store of money it has

coffin . NOUN. **coffins** a long wooden box that a dead body is put into

cog . NOUN. **cogs** one of the pointed parts, looking rather like teeth, that are round the edge of a cogwheel in an engine or machine

cognac •NOUN• cognac is a kind of French brandy

cogwheel •NOUN• **cogwheels** a metal disc with cogs cut out of its edge, used to turn other cogwheels or parts inside a machine, such as a clock or watch

cohere •VERB• **coheres, cohering, cohered** if things cohere they stick together
♦ **coherence** •NOUN• connection between things, especially thoughts or ideas
♦ **coherent** •ADJECTIVE• **1** coherent speech is clear and easy to understand **2** coherent thoughts or ideas are connected in a logical way
♦ **coherently** •ADVERB• clearly or logically: *He argued forcibly and coherently against the changes.*

cohesion •NOUN• sticking together
♦ **cohesive** •ADJECTIVE• closely linked or connected

cohort •NOUN• **cohorts** in the ancient Roman army, a cohort was a tenth part of a legion

coil •VERB• **coils, coiling, coiled** to coil is to twist or wind to form rings or loops: *The huge snake coiled itself round the branch.*
•NOUN• **coils** a loop or series of loops in something long, such as rope or hair: *a coil of thin wire*

coin •NOUN• **coins** a piece of metal money
•VERB• **coins, coining, coined 1** to make metal into money **2** to coin a new word or phrase is to invent it

coinage •NOUN• **coinages 1** a country's coinage is all the coins used in its particular money system **2** a coinage is a newly invented word or phrase

coincide •VERB• **coincides, coinciding, coincided** events coincide with each other when they happen at the same time: *The carnival will coincide with the beginning of the school holidays.*

coincidence •NOUN• **coincidences** a coincidence is when two things happen at the same time, without being planned: *Both families booked holidays at the same resort by sheer coincidence.*
♦ **coincidental** •ADJECTIVE• happening at the same time by chance

coke •NOUN• a type of fuel made from coal

cola •NOUN• **colas** a dark brown fizzy drink

colander •NOUN• **colanders** a container with holes in the bottom used to drain water from food

cold •ADJECTIVE• **colder, coldest 1** low in temperature: *a cold drink* • *It's too cold to go outside.* **2** unfriendly: *a cold stare*
•NOUN• **colds 1** coldness: *Granny doesn't like the cold.* **2** an illness caused by a virus which makes you sneeze and cough, and makes your nose run
♦ **coldly** •ADVERB• in an unfriendly way: *She treated them coldly.*
♦ **coldness** •NOUN• being cold

cold-blooded •ADJECTIVE• **1** a cold-blooded animal is not able to store heat in its body. Reptiles and snakes are cold-blooded **2** a cold-blooded person is unfeeling and cruel

cold sore •NOUN• **cold sores** a blister, usually somewhere on the lip or mouth, caused by a virus

coleslaw •NOUN• a salad made from sliced raw cabbage mixed with mayonnaise

colic •NOUN• a sudden and severe pain in the stomach

collaborate •VERB• **collaborates, collaborating 1** if two or more people collaborate they help each other by sharing information and ideas **2** if someone collaborates they give an enemy information or help
♦ **collaboration** •NOUN• sharing information or ideas
♦ **collaborator** •NOUN• **collaborators** someone who shares information with another person

collage •NOUN• **collages** a picture or design made by sticking different materials, such as bits of paper, photographs or small objects, on to a sheet of card or wood

ⓘ This word is pronounced col-**aj**.

collapse •VERB• **collapses, collapsing, collapsed** to fall down from being under too much weight or because of lack of strength: *The bridge collapsed under the lorry's weight.* • *The runner collapsed, exhausted,*

Aa
Bb
Cc
Dd
Ee
Ff
Gg
Hh
Ii
Jj
Kk
Ll
Mm
Nn
Oo
Pp
Qq
Rr
Ss
Tt
Uu
Vv
Ww
Xx
Yy
Zz

collar → colony

just before the finish line.
•NOUN• **collapses** a falling down or caving in
♦ **collapsible** •ADJECTIVE• collapsible furniture or equipment can be folded or broken down so that it fits into a smaller space

collar •NOUN• **collars** 1 a band of material on a shirt or other piece of clothing that fits round your neck 2 a band of leather or other material fastened round an animal's neck
•VERB• **collars, collaring, collared** to collar someone or something is to get hold of them

collarbone •NOUN• **collarbones** one of two bones in your body that stretch from your shoulder to just under the front of your neck

collate •VERB• **collates, collating, collated** to collate different pieces of information or pieces of paper is to bring them together and arrange them in order

colleague •NOUN• **colleagues** a person's colleagues are the people they work with

collect •VERB• **collects, collecting, collected** 1 to collect things is to find them and gather them together: *He collects unusual postcards.* 2 to collect someone or something from a place is to go there and pick them up: *George's dad usually collects him from school.*
♦ **collection** •NOUN• **collections** a number of things that have been gathered together by one person or in one place: *a stamp collection*
♦ **collective** •ADJECTIVE• done by several people or groups, not just one: *a collective decision*
⇒ **collector**

collective noun •NOUN• **collective nouns** a collective noun is a word used to refer to a group or collection of people or things. The words *family, team, staff, government, police, herd, flock, cattle, luggage* and *furniture* are examples of collective nouns

collector •NOUN• **collectors** someone who finds and gathers several things of the same type to make a collection: *a collector of antiques*

college •NOUN• **colleges** a place where people go to learn or be trained after leaving school: *He's going to engineering college.*

collide •VERB• **collides, colliding, collided** moving objects collide when they hit each other
⇒ **collision**

collie •NOUN• **collies** a kind of sheepdog

colliery •NOUN• **collieries** a coal mine

collision •NOUN• **collisions** a crash between moving vehicles or objects: *a collision between two lorries on the motorway*

colloquial •ADJECTIVE• colloquial language is used in everyday speech but not in formal speaking or writing. For example, *ta-ta* is a colloquial expression for 'goodbye'
♦ **colloquially** •ADVERB• informally

collude •VERB• **colludes, colluding, colluded** if people collude they make agreements with each other in secret
♦ **collusion** •NOUN• collusion is secret cooperation between people

cologne •NOUN• cologne is a kind of light perfume

colon[1] •NOUN• **colons** a colon is a punctuation mark (:) used to separate parts of a sentence or used before items in a list: *There are three things you will need: paper, scissors, and glue.*

colon[2] •NOUN• **colons** your colon is part of your bowel

colonel •NOUN• **colonels** a high-ranking officer in the army or air force

ⓘ This word is pronounced kir-nil.

colonial •ADJECTIVE• having to do with a country's colonies abroad

colonize or **colonise** •VERB• **colonizes, colonizing, colonized** 1 people, animals or plants colonize an area when they move into it and begin to live or grow there 2 if a country colonizes another part of the world it takes it over and controls it
♦ **colonist** •NOUN• **colonists** someone who goes to another country to set up a colony

colony •NOUN• **colonies** 1 a group of people who have settled in another part of the world, or the new settlement they have made: *The Pilgrim Fathers set up colonies on the east coast of America.*
2 a group of people, animals or plants of the

Aa Bb Cc Dd Ee Ff Gg Hh Ii Jj Kk Ll Mm Nn Oo Pp Qq Rr Ss Tt Uu Vv Ww Xx Yy Zz

same type living together: *a colony of ants*
3 a country's foreign colonies were the parts of the world that it controlled: *Hong Kong used to be a British colony.*
⇒ **colonial, colonize**

colossal •ADJECTIVE• enormous: *a colossal appetite*

colour •NOUN• **colours** 1 colour, or a colour, is a quality that shows up when light hits an object, for example, redness, blueness, yellowness, and so on: *What colour are your eyes?* • *The sea was a lovely greenish-blue colour.* 2 a person's colour is the shade of their skin
• **off colour** if someone is off colour they are not feeling very well
• **with flying colours** when you pass a test or exam with flying colours you get a high mark or you do very well in it
•ADJECTIVE• having or using colour: *colour TV*
•VERB• **colours, colouring, coloured** to colour a picture is to add colours to it with paints or crayons
♦ **coloured** •ADJECTIVE• having colour: *a brightly coloured scarf*
⇒ **colouring**

colour blind •ADJECTIVE• not able to tell the difference between certain colours, especially red and green

colourful •ADJECTIVE• 1 having lots of bright colours: *colourful clothing* 2 interesting or exciting: *He's a colourful character.*

colouring •NOUN• **colourings** 1 colouring is a substance used to give something a colour: *red food colouring* 2 someone's colouring is the colour of their skin and hair: *That shade of green suits her dark colouring.*

colourless •ADJECTIVE• 1 having no colour: *Water is a colourless liquid.* 2 dull and uninteresting: *She had a flat colourless voice.*

colt •NOUN• **colts** a young horse

column •NOUN• **columns** 1 a stone or wooden pillar
2 something with a long or tall narrow shape: *Columns of smoke and dust rose from the erupting volcano.*

3 a long line of people one behind the other or things one below the other: *a column of marching soldiers* • *a column of figures*
4 a part in a newspaper that appears regularly and is usually written by the same person
♦ **columnist** •NOUN• **columnists** a person who writes an article in a newspaper

coma •NOUN• **comas** if someone is in a coma they are unconscious for a long period of time
♦ **comatose** •ADJECTIVE• in a coma or seeming to be in a coma

comb •NOUN• **combs** 1 an object with a row of teeth along one side that you use to make your hair tidy 2 a part that sticks up on the top of some birds' heads
•VERB• **combs, combing, combed** 1 to comb hair is to make it tidy using a comb 2 to comb a place is to search it carefully and thoroughly: *Detectives were combing the area for clues.*

combat •NOUN• combat is fighting: *soldiers in combat*
•VERB• **combats, combatting, combatted** to combat something is to fight or struggle against it: *a superhero who combats crime*
♦ **combative** •ADJECTIVE• a combative person tends to get involved in quarrels or fights

combination •NOUN• **combinations** 1 combination is the joining or mixing of two or more things 2 a combination is several things that have been joined or mixed

combination lock •NOUN• **combination locks** a lock that can only be opened when a certain sequence of numbers is selected on a keypad or by turning a dial

combine •VERB• **combines, combining, combined** to combine things is to join or mix them together: *Combine all the ingredients in a mixing bowl.*
⇒ **combination**

combine harvester •NOUN• **combine harvesters** a large farm machine that both cuts and threshes crops

combustible •ADJECTIVE• a combustible substance will burn or catch fire: *a highly combustible gas found in coal mines*

Aa
Bb
Cc
Dd
Ee
Ff
Gg
Hh
Ii
Jj
Kk
Ll
Mm
Nn
Oo
Pp
Qq
Rr
Ss
Tt
Uu
Vv
Ww
Xx
Yy
Zz

combustion • NOUN• burning: *the combustion of gases*

come • VERB• **comes, coming, came** 1 to move towards the person speaking or to move to the place where they are: *Are you coming with us or not?* • *They came by boat and train.*
2 to arrive or happen: *Has my parcel come yet?* • *The mountains came into view.* • *People come in all shapes and sizes.*
3 to **come about** is to happen: *How did this disagreement come about?*
4 to **come across** a person or thing is to meet or find them by accident: *I came across a letter I had written on 28 June, 1944.*
5 to **come by** something is to get it: *Work was becoming harder and harder to come by.*
6 someone who has been unconscious or has fainted **comes round** or **comes to** when they wake up

comedian • NOUN• **comedians** a performer who tells jokes and funny stories or who acts in comedies

comedy • NOUN• **comedies** 1 comedy is the art of making people laugh 2 a comedy is a funny play or film
⇒ **comic**

ⓘ This comes from a French word, **comedie**. The French word comes from the Greek words **komos**, which means *merrymaking*, and **aoidos**, which means *a singer*.

comet • NOUN• **comets** a kind of star that travels across the sky trailing a tail of light behind it

comfort • NOUN• **comforts** 1 comfort is a pleasant feeling you get if you are relaxed, happy, warm or secure 2 comforts are luxuries or pleasant surroundings: *a hotel with all the comforts of home*
• VERB• **comforts, comforting, comforted** to comfort someone who is sad or upset is to make them feel happier by saying or doing nice things

comfortable • ADJECTIVE• having no pain, worry or trouble
♦ **comfortably** • ADVERB• in a comfortable way: *Are you all sitting comfortably?*

comfy • ADJECTIVE• **comfier, comfiest** an informal word for **comfortable**: *a comfy chair*

comic • ADJECTIVE• 1 having to do with or involved in comedy: *a comic actor* 2 funny, amusing: *His face had a really comic expression.*
• NOUN• **comics** 1 a magazine, especially for children, that has funny stories told in pictures 2 someone who is funny, especially a comedian
♦ **comical** • ADJECTIVE• funny: *His antics were comical.*

comic strip • NOUN• **comic strips** a series of drawings that tell a funny story

comma • NOUN• **commas** a punctuation mark (,) used to show a slight pause in a sentence or to separate off parts of a sentence to make it easier to read and understand. See the box called **Commas**

command • VERB• **commands, commanding, commanded** 1 to command someone to do something is to order them to do it: *'I command you to kneel before me,'* shouted the king. 2 to command something is to be in control or in charge of it: *He commanded the Roman legions.*
• NOUN• **commands** 1 a command is an order: *by royal command* 2 to be in command is to be in charge or in control: *Who's the officer in command?*
♦ **commandeer** • VERB• **commandeers, commandeering, commandeered** if something is commandeered it is taken especially by an army for their use
♦ **commander** • NOUN• **commanders** someone who commands or is in command, especially an officer in the police or navy
♦ **commandment** • NOUN• **commandments** a command or order, especially one of the ten commandments given to Moses by God

commando • NOUN• **commandos** or **commandoes** a soldier who works with others in a small group and is specially trained to do difficult or dangerous tasks

commemorate • VERB• **commemorates, commemorating, commemorated** to

Commas

A **comma** is a punctuation mark that separates parts of a sentence.

Use a comma before *and, but, or, for, nor, so, yet* when they join two complete sentences.

We wanted to go to the cinema, *but* it was shut.

Joe couldn't do his homework, *so* he asked his sister for help.

Use commas to separate three or more words or phrases in a list.

Max put on his hat, his gloves, his coat and his scarf.

Max went upstairs, brushed his teeth, got into bed and put out the light.

When you do this, you do not put a comma before *and*.

Use a pair of commas around any information or comment that is not essential to the meaning of your sentence. You can test for this by leaving it out of the sentence and seeing if the sentence still makes sense.

Ben found our cat in his cellar.

Ben, *captain of the local football team*, found our cat in his cellar.

Use a comma to separate the words from the speaker when you are writing direct speech.

'I'm going to make a chocolate cake today,' *said Mum.*

Fay replied, 'What a good idea.'

Use commas to separate dates and the different parts of addresses.

He died on *13 January, 1999.*

Carpets can be ordered from *Floorstuffs, 44 Bridgeman Road, Buttleford.*

Aa
Bb
Cc
Dd
Ee
Ff
Gg
Hh
Ii
Jj
Kk
Ll
Mm
Nn
Oo
Pp
Qq
Rr
Ss
Tt
Uu
Vv
Ww
Xx
Yy
Zz

commemorate something, such as a battle or some other famous event, is to remember it by holding a ceremony or putting up a monument
+ **commemoration** • NOUN•

commemorations a commemoration of a person or event is something that is done to remember and celebrate that person or event

commence • VERB• **commences, commencing, commenced** to commence is to begin: *The meeting will commence at 3 o'clock precisely.*
+ **commencement** • NOUN• the beginning of something

ⓘ This is a formal word.

commend • VERB• **commends, commending, commended** to praise

someone or something or to say that they deserve praise
+ **commendable** • ADJECTIVE• deserving praise
+ **commendation** • NOUN• **commendations** an honour or praise given to someone who has done something well

comment • NOUN• **comments** a remark or opinion about someone or something: *The school would welcome any comments from parents about the revised timetable.*
•VERB• **comments, commenting, commented** to comment, or comment on something, is to make a remark or give your opinion about it: *The teacher commented on what I've written so far.*
+ **commentary** • NOUN• **commentaries** a description or explanation of an event as it happens by someone who is there

Aa
Bb
Cc
Dd
Ee
Ff
Gg
Hh
Ii
Jj
Kk
Ll
Mm
Nn
Oo
Pp
Qq
Rr
Ss
Tt
Uu
Vv
Ww
Xx
Yy
Zz

♦ **commentator** •NOUN• **commentators** someone who gives a commentary: *a cricket commentator*

commerce •NOUN• commerce is the buying and selling of goods and services: *international commerce*

♦ **commercial** •ADJECTIVE• 1 to do with trade or making money by selling goods and services 2 paid for by selling advertising space or time: *commercial TV*
•NOUN• **commercials** an advertisement for a product on TV or radio

commiserate •VERB• **commiserates, commiserating, commiserated** to commiserate with someone is to sympathize with them about something that is making them unhappy

♦ **commiserations** •PLURAL NOUN• when you offer someone your commiserations you let them know you are sorry about a disappointment or upset they have suffered

commission •NOUN• **commissions** 1 an order to do or produce something for payment
2 a commission is a group of people who investigate something or have authority over something: *the Commission for Racial Equality*
3 someone who is paid commission is paid a fee for each thing they sell
•VERB• **commissions, commissioning, commissioned** to commission something, or to commission someone to do something, is to give an instruction or order that it should be done, or that they should do it: *He'd been commissioned to write a book.*

commit •VERB• **commits, committing, committed** 1 to commit a crime is to do something that breaks the law 2 to commit yourself to something is to say, promise or decide that you will do it

♦ **commitment** •NOUN• **commitments** a promise or duty: *made a definite commitment to be there*

♦ **committed** •ADJECTIVE• having strong beliefs: *a committed Christian*

committee •NOUN• **committees** a number of people chosen to deal with a task or special business: *the organizing committee for the school show*

commodity •NOUN• **commodities** anything that can be bought and sold

common •ADJECTIVE• **commoner, commonest** 1 seen or happening often and in many places: *Traffic jams are a common occurrence in cities.* • *one of the commonest childhood diseases*
2 ordinary: *the common people*
3 shared by many: *Their common goal was to make the Games a success.*
•NOUN• **commons** a common is a piece of land that belongs to and can be used by all the people in a town: *Wimbledon Common*
• **have something in common** if people or things have something in common they are similar in some way

Common Market •NOUN• the Common Market is another name for the European Economic Community or European Union

commonplace •ADJECTIVE• not at all unusual

common room •NOUN• **common rooms** a room in a school or college where a group of teachers or students can relax together between classes

common sense •NOUN• the ability to think and behave sensibly

commonwealth •NOUN• a group of countries or states that cooperate with each other, especially in trade

commotion •NOUN• a noisy disturbance

communal •ADJECTIVE• shared by several people: *a communal garden*

commune •NOUN• **communes** a group of people who live together and share work, possessions and expenses

communicable •ADJECTIVE• a communicable disease can be passed from one person to another

communicate •VERB• **communicates, communicating, communicated** 1 to communicate is to give information to others, for example by making sounds or by writing: *The monkeys communicate with loud barking calls.* 2 to communicate with someone is to get in touch with them: *We communicate mainly by telephone and e-mail.*

◆ communication •NOUN•
communciations 1 communication is
conveying information: *Text messaging is a
common form of communication.* **2** a
communication is a message: *We've
received an urgent communication from
head office.*
◆ communicative •ADJECTIVE• a
communicative person is willing to talk to
others and give them information

Communion •NOUN• in the Christian
Church, Communion is the ceremony
celebrating the Last Supper of Jesus and his
disciples

communism •NOUN• communism is the
belief that all the wealth created by industry
should be shared by everyone in society
◆ communist •NOUN• communists
someone who believes in communism
•ADJECTIVE• believing in communism or to
do with communists: *a communist country*

community •NOUN• communities 1 a group
living in a particular area or a group sharing
the same background: *a school serving the
local community* **2** the community is all of
society or all the people of the world

**commute •VERB• commutes, commuting,
commuted** to travel regularly between two
places, especially between home and the
place where you work
◆ commuter •NOUN• commuters someone
who commutes

compact •ADJECTIVE• with all its parts fitted
tightly or closely together so that they take
up very little space: *a compact little garden*

compact disc •NOUN• compact discs a
small metal disc on which sound and images
are recorded in digital form. The information
on a compact disc is read by a laser beam in a
compact disc player or computer

companion •NOUN• companions someone
who spends a lot of time with another
person
◆ companionship •NOUN• being with each
other and having a friendly relationship

company •NOUN• companies 1 a business
firm: *They've formed a company to design
video games.*
  2 companionship: *He's very good company.*

3 a group of people who spend time
together: *She got into bad company and
started going out late.*
• **keep someone company** if you keep
someone company you stay with them or go
somewhere with them
• **part company** to part company is to leave
each other

comparable •ADJECTIVE• similar: *The two
games are comparable in difficulty.*

comparative •ADJECTIVE• 1 judged by
comparing with something else: *He had not
lived here as long as the rest of us and was a
comparative stranger.* **2** in grammar, a
comparative form of an adjective or adverb
is the form that usually ends with *-er* or is
used with *more*. For example *better, worse,
luckier, braver* and *more dangerous* are
comparative forms. See the box called
Comparison of adjectives on the next page
•NOUN• comparatives a comparative form of
an adjective or adverb
◆ comparatively •ADVERB• compared
with something else: *The house was noisy,
and the garden was comparatively quiet.*

**compare •VERB• compares, comparing,
compared 1** to put two or more things
together to show how different they are or
which is better: *The weather today is lovely
compared to last week.* **2** to describe
someone or something as like another
person or thing: *She compared him to a mad
dog.*
◆ comparison •NOUN• comparisons
putting two or more things together to show
how they are similar or different

compartment •NOUN• compartments a
separate enclosed part within a larger thing:
a secret compartment at the back of the desk

compass •NOUN• compasses an instrument
that shows the direction of north with a
magnet and which you can use to find your
way

compasses •PLURAL NOUN• compasses, or a
pair of compasses, are an instrument with
two hinged prongs used to draw circles or
to measure out distances between two
points

compassion •NOUN• if you have or show

Comparison of adjectives

There are different forms of adjectives that you can use, called the **positive**, the **comparative**, and the **superlative**.

A **positive** adjective does not compare the person, thing or place you are describing with anything else.

> I am **old.**
>
> Coffee is **expensive.**
>
> Mount Everest is **high.**

A **comparative** adjective compares two people, things or places. The word *than* follows it.

> I am **older** *than* Leo.
>
> Coffee is **more expensive** *than* tea.
>
> Mount Everest is **higher** *than* Mont Blanc.

A **superlative** adjective compares three or more people, things or places, and tells you which one that stands out above the rest.

> I am **the oldest** in my family.
>
> Coffee is **the most expensive** hot drink.
>
> Mount Everest is **the highest mountain** in the world.

Making comparatives and superlatives

You make comparatives of most short adjectives by adding **-er** on the end.

> soft + -er = **softer**

You make superlatives by adding **-est** on the end of the adjective and putting *the* in front of it.

> *the* + soft + -est = **the softest**

To make comparatives and superlatives of longer words put **more** or **the most** in front of them.

Comparative	*Superlative*
more expensive	the most expensive
more important	the most important

A few comparatives and superlatives are very different. Beware of the exceptions!

Adjective	*Comparative*	*Superlative*
good	better	best
bad	worse	worst
little	less	least
many	more	most

compassion for people you feel pity for their suffering

compassionate . ADJECTIVE. showing pity or mercy for people who are suffering or in trouble

compatible . NOUN. able to exist or work well together: *The two computer programs weren't compatible.*

compatibility . ADJECTIVE. the quality that allows people or things to get on or work well together

compatriot . NOUN. **compatriots** your compatriots are people who come from the same country as you do

compel . VERB. **compels, compelling, compelled** to compel someone to do something is to force them to do it

compelling . ADJECTIVE. 1 so interesting or exciting that you are forced to go on reading, watching or listening 2 a compelling argument is so strong that you cannot disagree with it
⇒ **compulsion**

compendium . NOUN. **compendiums** or **compendia** 1 a book in which lots of different information about a particular subject is brought together 2 a box that contains several different board games

compensate . VERB. **compensates, compensating, compensated** 1 to compensate someone is to give them something, especially money, in exchange for loss or damage they have suffered 2 if one thing compensates for another it makes up for it: *His sunny personality compensates for his lack of learning.*

compensation . NOUN. compensation is something given to make up for loss or damage

compère . NOUN. **compères** someone who introduces the different acts in an entertainment show

compete . NOUN. **competes, competing, competed** to compete is to try to beat or be more successful than others: *athletes competing in the Olympics*
⇒ **competition**

competence . NOUN. the ability or skill to do something properly or well

competent . ADJECTIVE. capable, efficient or skilled: *a very competent pianist*

competently . ADVERB. efficiently or skilfully

competition . NOUN. **competitions** a contest between people who are each trying to win or be better than the others

competitive . ADJECTIVE. a competitive person likes to compete and win against other people

competitor . NOUN. **competitors** someone taking part in a competition

compilation . NOUN. **compilations** 1 compilation is the process of compiling something 2 a compilation is a collection of pieces of writing, music or information: *The album is a compilation of the band's greatest hits.*

compile . VERB. **compiles, compiling, compiled** to compile something, such as an encyclopedia, is to make it using information that has been collected together

compiler . NOUN. **compilers** a person or machine that compiles

complacency . NOUN. an attitude in which you become lazy because you think you have done all that you need to

complacent . ADJECTIVE. too satisfied with what you do

complain . VERB. **complains, complaining, complained** to say or write that you are not happy or satisfied: *He complained that it was too hot and that he hated the food.*

complaint . NOUN. **complaints** 1 a statement that lets people know that you are not happy or satisfied 2 an illness

complement . NOUN. **complements**
1 something that is added to make something complete
2 the number needed to make something complete
3 something that goes very well with another thing: *The sauce is a lovely complement to the meal.*
. VERB. **complements, complementing, complemented** if two things complement each other they go very well together

complementary . ADJECTIVE. 1 going well together 2 together making up a whole

Aa
Bb
Cc
Dd
Ee
Ff
Gg
Hh
Ii
Jj
Kk
Ll
Mm
Nn
Oo
Pp
Qq
Rr
Ss
Tt
Uu
Vv
Ww
Xx
Yy
Zz

Aa
Bb
Cc
Dd
Ee
Ff
Gg
Hh
Ii
Jj
Kk
Ll
Mm
Nn
Oo
Pp
Qq
Rr
Ss
Tt
Uu
Vv
Ww
Xx
Yy
Zz

ⓘ Try not to **complement** with **compliment**. Remember that the meaning of **complement** is related to **complete**, and so their first six letters are the same.

complementary angle •NOUN• **complementary angles** an angle that must be added to one that is less than 90 degrees to make a right angle

complete •VERB• **completes, completing, completed** to complete something is to finish it or make it whole: *He completed the test in time.*
•ADJECTIVE• **1** with nothing missing: *a complete set of golf clubs*
2 finished: *When the dam is complete it will be over 150 metres high.*
3 total: *I felt a complete fool.*
♦ **completely** •ADVERB• totally: *I agree completely.*
♦ **completeness** •NOUN• wholeness
♦ **completion** •NOUN• a finish: *The filming is nearing completion.*

complex •ADJECTIVE• **1** made up of many parts: *a complex network of streets* **2** difficult to understand or work out: *a complex problem*
•NOUN• **complexes 1** a group of buildings all with the same use: *a sports complex* **2** if someone has a complex there is something that they are very sensitive about
⇒ **complexity**

complexion •NOUN• **complexions** your complexion is the colouring of your skin: *a rosy complexion*

complexity •NOUN• **complexities** complexity is being complicated or difficult

compliance •NOUN• compliance is obeying someone else's wishes
♦ **compliant** •ADJECTIVE• a compliant person is someone who does what another person wants

complicate •VERB• **complicates, complicating, complicated** to complicate something is to make it more difficult
♦ **complicated** •ADJECTIVE• difficult to work out or understand: *a complicated sum*
♦ **complication** •NOUN• **complications** something that creates a problem or difficulty

compliment •NOUN• **compliments** something that you say that praises someone: *He paid me a compliment.*
•VERB• **compliments, complimenting, complimented** to compliment someone is to praise them: *He complimented her on her good taste.*
♦ **complimentary** •ADJECTIVE• **1** flattering or praising: *The article she wrote was very complimentary.* **2** given free: *a complimentary ticket for the show*
♦ **compliments** •PLURAL NOUN• to give your compliments to someone is to give them your good wishes

comply •VERB• **complies, complying, complied** to comply is to obey or agree to do something: *It is impossible to comply with such demands.*
⇒ **compliance**

component •NOUN• **components** one of the parts that are put together to make a whole, for example one of the different parts that make up a machine

compose •VERB• **composes, composing, composed 1** to compose something is to create it by putting together various things, such as the notes to make a piece of music **2** to compose yourself is to become calm
♦ **composed** •ADJECTIVE• in control of your feelings
♦ **composer** •NOUN• **composers** someone who writes music
♦ **composition** •NOUN• **compositions 1** composition is composing: *a lesson in spelling and composition* **2** a composition is something made up, such as a piece of writing or music
⇒ **composure**

compost •NOUN• compost is a mixture made up of decayed plants and manure that is spread on soil

composure •NOUN• being in control of your feelings so that you are calm

compound •NOUN• **compounds 1** something formed from two or more parts: *a chemical compound*
2 an area enclosed by a fence or wall, for example at a factory or prison
3 a word made up from two or more other

a computer

words. The words *airport*, *tape recorder* and *birdbath* are compounds
•VERB• **compounds, compounding, compounded** to compound a problem is to make it worse by adding to it

comprehend •VERB• **comprehends, comprehending, comprehended** to understand
♦ **comprehensible** • ADJECTIVE• if something is comprehensible it can be understood
♦ **comprehension** • NOUN• comprehension is understanding: *a test of reading and comprehension*
♦ **comprehensive** • ADJECTIVE• dealing with everything: *a comprehensive report*
•NOUN• **comprehensives** a comprehensive school

comprehensive school • NOUN•
comprehensive schools a secondary school run by the state where pupils of all abilities are educated in all subjects

compress •VERB• **compresses, compressing, compressed** to compress something is to make it fit into a smaller space, often by squeezing it or shortening it
•NOUN• **compresses** a compress is a thick pad of material pressed on a wound or painful area

comprise •VERB• **comprises, comprising, comprised** to contain or be made up of: *The test will comprise two parts.*

compromise •VERB• **compromises, compromising, compromised** to compromise is to give up some part of what you want so that an agreement can be made
• NOUN• **compromises** an agreement in which each person or side involved gives up something they originally asked for

compulsion • NOUN• **compulsions** 1 compulsion is being forced to do something
2 a compulsion is a feeling that you must do something: *a compulsion to eat chocolate*
♦ **compulsive** • ADJECTIVE• if you are compulsive you cannot help doing something: *a compulsive liar*
♦ **compulsory** • ADJECTIVE• something that is compulsory must be done

compute •VERB• **computes, computing, computed** to calculate

computer • NOUN• **computers** an electronic machine that can store and work with very large amounts of information
♦ **computerize** *or* **computerise** •VERB•
computerizes, computerizing, computerized to computerize a system or a set of information is to organize it so that it can be

Aa
Bb
Cc
Dd
Ee
Ff
Gg
Hh
Ii
Jj
Kk
Ll
Mm
Nn
Oo
Pp
Qq
Rr
Ss
Tt
Uu
Vv
Ww
Xx
Yy
Zz

held in a computer's memory

♦ **computerized** •ADJECTIVE• stored in or dealt with by a computer: *computerized records of fingerprints*

♦ **computing** •NOUN• the operation of computers or the skill of working with computers

comrade •NOUN• **comrades** a friend or close companion, for example soldiers who are in the same army in a war

con •VERB• **cons, conning, conned** to con someone is to trick them into doing something or thinking something is true •NOUN• **cons** a trick used to deceive someone

con- •PREFIX• look at the entry for **co-**

concave •ADJECTIVE• curving inwards or downwards. Look up and compare **convex**

conceal •VERB• **conceals, concealing, concealed** to hide carefully or keep secret: *She concealed herself behind a bush.*

♦ **concealment** •NOUN• concealment is the careful hiding of something: *concealment of his true feelings*

concede •VERB• **concedes, conceding, conceded** 1 to concede something is to admit that it is true: *'It may be possible,' he conceded.* 2 to concede defeat is to accept that you have lost
⇒ **concession**

conceit •NOUN• conceit is thinking very highly of yourself and what you can do: *Miss Evans was amazed at the child's lack of conceit.*

♦ **conceited** •ADJECTIVE• having a very high opinion of yourself and what you can do

conceivable •ADJECTIVE• something that is conceivable is possible to imagine or believe

♦ **conceivably** •ADVERB• possibly

conceive •VERB• **conceives, conceiving, conceived** 1 to conceive something is to form an idea of it in your mind 2 if a woman conceives she becomes pregnant
⇒ **concept**

concentrate •VERB• **concentrates, concentrating, concentrated** 1 if you concentrate, or concentrate on something,

you give all your attention to it: *Try to concentrate on one thing at a time.* 2 if things are concentrated in one place they are all together in that place

♦ **concentrated** •ADJECTIVE• a concentrated liquid is stronger and thicker because some of the water in it has been taken out

♦ **concentration** •NOUN• concentration is giving all your attention to something

concentration camp •NOUN• **concentration camps** a camp where certain types of people are kept prisoner

concentric •ADJECTIVE• concentric circles are inside each other and have the same centre

concept •NOUN• **concepts** an idea or picture in your mind: *He doesn't seem to have any concept of right and wrong.*

♦ **conception** •NOUN• **conceptions** 1 conception is the forming of ideas or pictures in your mind 2 conception happens when a woman becomes pregnant

concern •VERB• **conerns, concerning, concerned** 1 if something concerns you it worries you or is important to you: *His disappearance was beginning to concern us.* 2 if something concerns you it affects or involves you: *Don't interfere in things that don't concern you.*
•NOUN• **concerns** 1 concern is caring about something: *They showed no concern for the law.*
2 a concern is a worry or doubt: *If you have any concerns about the exam, you should speak to your class teacher.*
3 a concern is a business: *The garage has always been a family concern.*

♦ **concerned** •ADJECTIVE• worried or caring about someone or something: *concerned parents*

♦ **concerning** •PREPOSITION• about or involving someone or something: *a matter concerning the older pupils*

concert •NOUN• **concerts** a performance by musicians or singers

♦ **concerted** •ADJECTIVE• done together: *We must make a concerted effort to win this match.*

concertina •NOUN• **concertinas** a musical instrument that you hold in both hands and play by squeezing it inwards while pressing buttons to make the notes

concerto •NOUN• **concertos** a piece of music to be played by a solo instrument and an orchestra: *a piano concerto*

concession •NOUN• **concessions** something that you allow someone to have so that an argument or protest can be ended: *The company refused to make any concessions and the strike continued.*

concise •ADJECTIVE• short and containing all the information without unnecessary details

conclude •VERB• **concludes, concluding, concluded** 1 to end: *That concludes today's lesson.* 2 to decide: *He concluded she was lying.*
♦ **concluding** •ADJECTIVE• last: *the concluding chapter of the novel*
♦ **conclusion** •NOUN• **conclusions** a decision you make after thinking about something: *I've come to the conclusion that she just doesn't care.*
♦ **conclusive** •ADJECTIVE• conclusive proof or evidence shows that something is definitely true
♦ **conclusively** •ADVERB• without any doubt: *The video tape proved conclusively that he was the person who had broken in.*

concoct •VERB• **concocts, concocting, concocted** 1 to concoct something is to make it by mixing different things together 2 to concoct a story or plan is to make it up
♦ **concoction** •NOUN• **concoctions** something made by mixing different things together: *The drink is a concoction of fruit juices.*

concourse •NOUN• **concourses** a large hall where people can gather, for example at an airport or station building

concrete •NOUN• concrete is a strong hard building material made by mixing sand, cement, tiny stones and water
•ADJECTIVE• 1 made of concrete: *a concrete floor*
2 something that is concrete can be seen or touched

3 something that is concrete is definite: *Do you have any concrete proposals to make?*
•VERB• **concretes, concreting, concreted** to concrete something is to put concrete on it: *Dad's going to concrete the driveway this weekend.*

ⓘ The opposite of meaning 3 of **concrete** is **abstract**.

concussion •NOUN• injury to the brain that makes a person feel dizzy or become unconscious for a while, caused by a blow to the head

condemn •VERB• **condemns, condemning, condemned** 1 to condemn someone or something is to say that they are wrong or bad 2 someone condemned to a punishment is sentenced by a court to that punishment: *Mary Queen of Scots was condemned to death.*
♦ **condemnation** •NOUN• **condemnations** saying that something is wrong or bad

condensation •NOUN• condensation happens when moisture in the air cools and becomes liquid, for example when water in the air in a warm room cools and forms drops on the cooler surface of a window

condense •VERB• **condenses, condensing, condensed** 1 vapour condenses when it turns to liquid 2 to condense something is to make it shorter

condescending •ADJECTIVE• if you are condescending, you act like you are better than other people

condiment •NOUN• **condiments** condiments are things that you add to food to give it more flavour, such as salt, pepper and mustard

condition •NOUN• **conditions** 1 the state or circumstances a person or thing is in: *The building is in a dangerous condition.* 2 something that has to happen before something else does: *I'll go on the condition that you come too.*
♦ **conditional** •ADJECTIVE• depending on something else happening
♦ **conditionally** •ADVERB• only if something else happens
♦ **conditioner** •NOUN• **conditioners**

Aa
Bb
Cc
Dd
Ee
Ff
Gg
Hh
Ii
Jj
Kk
Ll
Mm
Nn
Oo
Pp
Qq
Rr
Ss
Tt
Uu
Vv
Ww
Xx
Yy
Zz

conditioner is a liquid that improves the texture and condition of your hair or of things washed in a machine

condolences • PLURAL NOUN • you give or send your condolences to someone to show your sympathy when someone close to them has died

condone • VERB • **condones, condoning, condoned** to condone bad behaviour is to allow it to happen without saying that it is wrong

conduct • VERB • **conducts, conducting, conducted** 1 to conduct someone or something is to guide, manage or control them: *The butler conducted us into the library.* • *Mrs Hobbs, the music teacher, conducted the school orchestra.*
2 if you conduct yourself in a certain way you behave in that way: *We expect you to conduct yourselves well on the school trip.*
3 if a material conducts electricity or heat it allows electricity or heat to flow through it or be transferred from one place to another by it
• NOUN • your conduct is the way you behave
✦ **conduction** • NOUN • conduction is the transfer of electricity or heat through something
✦ **conductor** • NOUN • **conductors** 1 someone who leads the musicians in an orchestra
2 an object that conducts electricity: *a lightning conductor*

cone • NOUN • **cones** 1 a solid shape with a round base and sides that slope up to a point at the top
2 a container of this shape made of wafer and used to hold ice cream
3 a fruit of a pine or fir tree containing its seeds
⇒ **conic**

confectioner • NOUN • **confectioners**
1 someone who makes cakes and sweets
2 a confectioner's is a shop selling cakes and sweets
✦ **confectionery** • NOUN • cakes and sweets

confederate • NOUN • **confederates** someone's confederates are the people who help them, especially to do something illegal
✦ **confederation** • NOUN • **confederations** several groups who have united so that they can work together

confer • VERB • **confers, conferring, conferred** people confer when they discuss something together
✦ **conference** • NOUN • **conferences** a meeting of people to discuss a particular subject

confess • VERB • **confesses, confessing, confessed** to confess is to admit to other people that you have done something, especially something wrong: *I don't mind confessing that I was terrified.*
✦ **confession** • NOUN • **confessions** confession is admitting you are guilty of a crime or some other bad thing: *He made a full confession to the police.*

confetti • NOUN • tiny pieces of coloured paper that are thrown over a married couple after the wedding ceremony

confide • VERB • **confides, confiding, confided** to confide in someone is to tell them your secrets

confidence • NOUN • **confidences**
1 confidence is being sure of yourself
2 a confidence is a secret
• in confidence if you tell someone something in confidence, you expect them not to tell it to anyone else
⇒ **confident**

confidence trick • NOUN • **confidence tricks** a trick that is meant to deceive people, especially in order to get their money

confident • ADJECTIVE • 1 sure of yourself or of your ability to do something: *She's a very confident swimmer.* 2 sure that something will happen the way you expect it to: *I'm confident we'll find the lost children safe and well.*

confidential • ADJECTIVE • confidential information should not be told to other people
✦ **confidentially** • ADVERB • in confidence

confine • VERB • **confines, confining, confined** to keep something or someone within limits or shut up inside a place: *The soldiers were confined to barracks.*
✦ **confined** • ADJECTIVE • a confined space is very small and restricted

- **confinement** •NOUN• being locked up or confined

confirm •VERB• **confirms, confirming, confirmed** to confirm something is to say or make sure that it is correct or true: *Please confirm that you will be able to come to the meeting.*
- **confirmation** •NOUN• something that confirms: *Have you had confirmation of your marks yet?*

confiscate •VERB• **confiscates, confiscating, confiscated** to confiscate something is to take it away from someone as a punishment
- **confiscation** •NOUN• taking something away as a punishment

conflagration •NOUN• **conflagrations** a fierce fire that spreads and destroys a lot of things

conflict •NOUN• **conflicts 1** conflict is argument or disagreement **2** a conflict is a battle or war: *the conflict in the Balkans* **3** if there is a conflict between two things they cannot work together: *a conflict of ideas*
- **conflicting** •ADJECTIVE• two conflicting things contradict each other or compete with each other

conform •VERB• **conforms, conforming, conformed** to conform is to behave in a way that obeys the rules or laws that most other people obey

confound •VERB• **confounds, confounding, confounded** if something confounds you it puzzles you

confront •VERB• **confronts, confronting, confronted 1** to confront something unpleasant is to deal with it in a determined way **2** to confront a person is to meet them as an enemy or to accuse them of something: *He turned and confronted his attackers.* • *You should confront her and ask her about the missing money.*
- **confrontation** •NOUN• **confrontations** a face-to-face argument or fight between two people or sides

confuse •VERB• **confuses, confusing, confused 1** to confuse things is to mix them up so that you think one thing is the other **2** if something confuses you, you aren't able to think clearly and don't know what to do or say next
- **confusing** •ADJECTIVE• difficult to follow or understand
- **confusion** •NOUN• being confused or mixed up

congeal •VERB• **congeals, congealing, congealed** if a liquid congeals it forms a thick jelly-like mass

congested •ADJECTIVE• a congested road or passageway is crowded or blocked up so people or things can't move through easily
- **congestion** •NOUN• crowding or blocking

congratulate •VERB• **congratulates, congratulating, congratulated** to congratulate someone is to tell them you are happy about something they have achieved: *I congratulated her on her exam results.*
- **congratulations** •PLURAL NOUN• you say 'congratulations' to someone when you want to show them that you are happy at their success

congregate •VERB• **congregates, congregating, congregated** to congregate is to gather together somewhere in a group or crowd
- **congregation** •NOUN• **congregations** a church congregation is all the people who have gathered to hear a church service

congress •NOUN• **congresses 1** a meeting of many different people: *an international congress to discuss refugees* **2** Congress is the parliament of the United States, made up of the Senate and the House of Representatives

congruent •ADJECTIVE• congruent things are the same shape or size: *congruent triangles*

conic •ADJECTIVE• to do with a cone or forming part of a cone
- **conical** •ADJECTIVE• shaped like a cone

conifer •NOUN• **conifers** a type of tree with long thin leaves shaped like needles and seeds inside cones
- **coniferous** •ADJECTIVE• coniferous trees grow cones

conjunction •NOUN• something that

Aa
Bb
Cc
Dd
Ee
Ff
Gg
Hh
Ii
Jj
Kk
Ll
Mm
Nn
Oo
Pp
Qq
Rr
Ss
Tt
Uu
Vv
Ww
Xx
Yy
Zz

Conjunctions

Conjunctions are words that link short sentences to make a longer one. Without them, writing would be dull and sound jerky. Compare these examples.

> Jane dashed down the road. She didn't look ahead. She bumped into the old man. She knocked him to the ground.

> Jane dashed down the road **but** didn't look ahead. She bumped into the old man **and** knocked him to the ground.

There are different kinds of conjunctions.

Coordinating conjunctions

A coordinating conjunction joins two sentences of equal importance. The most common ones are **and**, **but**, **or**, and **so**.

> Annie threw the ball **and** Billy caught it.

> We went to the theatre, **but** the play was sold out.

> I could draw a picture of the bridge **or** (I could) make a model of it.

Coordinating conjunctions can also join words or phrases.

> Jack **and** Jill ate fish **and** chips.

> The horse was small **but** sturdy.

> Are they friends **or** the worst of enemies?

Subordinating conjunctions

Certain conjunctions join two sentences so that one becomes a main statement (*main clause*) and the one after the conjunction becomes a less important statement (*subordinate clause*). These are called subordinating conjunctions.

> Bernard played outside **because** it was too hot to stay indoors.

> **Although** it was snowing, Bernard played outside.

> Bernard will not go outside **until** the rain stops.

happens or is done **in conjunction with** something else happens or is done at the same time
• PART OF SPEECH• **conjunctions** in grammar, a conjunction is a word that links other words or parts of a sentence. For example, the words *and*, *but*, and *or* are conjunctions. See the box called **Conjunctions**

conjure • VERB• **conjures, conjuring, conjured 1** to conjure is to do magic tricks that seem to make things appear or disappear **2** if something **conjures something**

up it makes it appear in your mind: *The smell of new hay conjured up a picture of the countryside.*
• **conjuror** • NOUN• **conjurors** someone who does tricks that make things seem to appear or disappear by magic

conker • NOUN• **conkers** a large brown seed of the horse chestnut tree
• **conkers** • NOUN• a game played with conkers tied to pieces of string. Each player takes a turn to hit the other player's conker until one conker breaks

conman •NOUN• **conmen** someone who tricks or deceives other people, usually to get money

connect •VERB• **connects, connecting, connected 1** to connect things is to join them: *How do you connect the PC to the Internet?* • *The detective hadn't connected the two events in his mind.*
  ✦ **connection** •NOUN• **connections 1** something that joins two things together **2** a train, bus or plane that you need to catch so that you can continue a journey: *We missed our connection to Dover because the train was late.*
  • **in connection with** to do with: *He is wanted by the police in connection with a theft.*

connotation •NOUN• **connotations** what is suggested by a word as well as its obvious meaning

conquer •VERB• **conquers, conquering, conquered** to conquer is to defeat: *Napoleon tried to conquer Egypt.* • *She struggled to conquer her shyness.*
  ✦ **conqueror** •NOUN• **conquerors** someone who conquers a country or people
  ✦ **conquest** •NOUN• **conquests** something that is won by great effort or force

conscience •NOUN• **consciences** your conscience is your sense of right and wrong
  ✦ **conscientious** •ADJECTIVE• a conscientious person works hard and carefully to get things right
  ✦ **conscientiously** •ADVERB• carefully and diligently

ⓘ Be careful how you spell this word. Remember it is spelt **con + science**.

conscious •ADJECTIVE• **1** you are conscious when you are awake and aware of your surroundings
  2 you are conscious of something happening when you are aware of it
  3 a conscious act or decision is one that you have thought about
  ✦ **consciously** •ADVERB• deliberately or being aware of what you are doing
  ✦ **consciousness** •NOUN• the state of being aware of yourself and what is going on around you: *She lost consciousness and woke up in hospital.*

conscript •VERB• **conscripts, conscipting, conscripted** to force someone by law to join the armed forces: *The government conscripted young men.*
  •NOUN• **conscripts** someone who is forced by law to join the armed forces
  ✦ **conscription** •NOUN• forcing people to join the armed forces

consecrate •VERB• **consecrates, consecrating, consecrated** to consecrate something is to put it aside for a religious or holy use
  ✦ **consecration** •NOUN• giving something a religious use

consecutive •ADJECTIVE• one after the other: *It snowed on three consecutive days.*

consensus •NOUN• **consensuses** consensus, or a consensus, is agreement or a feeling shared by most people

consent •VERB• **consents, consenting, consented** someone consents to something when they agree to it
  •NOUN• to give consent for something is to allow it

consequence •NOUN• **consequences**
  1 consequence is importance: *It was of no consequence.* **2** a consequence is something that follows as a result of something else: *He did no work and the consequence was that he failed all his exams.*
  • **take** or **suffer the consequences** if you take or suffer the consequences for something you have to accept anything unpleasant that results from it: *If you break the law you have to take the consequences.*
  ✦ **consequent** •ADJECTIVE• following as a result
  ✦ **consequently** •ADVERB• as a result

conservation •NOUN• **1** looking after things, such as old buildings, works of art, or the environment, and working to prevent them being damaged or destroyed **2** keeping the same amount
  ✦ **conservationist** •NOUN• **conservationists** a conservationist is someone who works to stop things being ruined

conservative •ADJECTIVE• **1** a conser-

Aa
Bb
Cc
Dd
Ee
Ff
Gg
Hh
Ii
Jj
Kk
Ll
Mm
Nn
Oo
Pp
Qq
Rr
Ss
Tt
Uu
Vv
Ww
Xx
Yy
Zz

Aa
Bb
Cc
Dd
Ee
Ff
Gg
Hh
Ii
Jj
Kk
Ll
Mm
Nn
Oo
Pp
Qq
Rr
Ss
Tt
Uu
Vv
Ww
Xx
Yy
Zz

vative person does not like changes or new fashions: *He's a very conservative dresser.* **2** a conservative estimate or guess is cautious and is usually less than the actual amount

conservatory •NOUN• **conservatories** a room or building which has walls and a roof made of glass

conserve •VERB• **conserves, conserving, conserved** to conserve things is to keep them from being wasted or lost: *Close the windows to conserve heat.*
⇒ **conservation, conservative**

consider •VERB• **considers, considering, considered 1** to consider something is think about it carefully: *I'll consider your idea.*
2 to consider someone or something as being something is to think of them like that: *I consider him to be a true friend.*
3 to consider other people is to think about what they want or need
⇒ **considerate, consideration, considering**

considerable • ADJECTIVE• quite big: *a considerable distance*
♦ **considerably** •ADVERB• quite a lot: *He earns considerably more than I do.*

considerate • ADJECTIVE• thinking of other people and what they want: *It was considerate of you to help me.*

consideration •NOUN• **1** consideration is thinking carefully about things **2** a consideration is something that you take into account when you are making a decision
• **take into consideration** to take something into consideration is to think about it while you are making a decision

considering •PREPOSITION• taking into account: *Considering how clever you are, I think you should have got a better mark.*

consignment •NOUN• **consignments** a load of goods sent from one place to another

consist •VERB• **consists, consisting, consisted** to be made up of: *a simple meal consisting of a small loaf and cheese*

consistency •NOUN• **consistencies 1** consistency is being always the same **2** something's consistency is its thickness or firmness: *a sauce with the consistency of cream*

♦ **consistent** • ADJECTIVE• staying the same all the way through: *Keep the style of your essay consistent.*
♦ **consistently** •ADVERB• without changing: *He consistently spells the word wrong.*

consolation •NOUN• **consolations** something that makes a disappointment seem less bad

consolation prize •NOUN• **consolation prizes** a prize given to someone who has come second in a competition

console[1] •VERB• **consoles, consoling, consoled** to console someone is to comfort them
⇒ **consolation**

console[2] •NOUN• **consoles** a console is a board or box with the controls for a machine arranged on it

consolidate •VERB• **consolidates, consolidating, consolidated** to consolidate something is to strengthen it or make it more solid

consonant •NOUN• **consonants** a consonant is any letter of the alphabet except *a, e, i, o,* or *u*

consort •VERB• **consorts, consorting, consorted** to consort with people is to be in their company
•NOUN• **consorts** a husband or wife

conspicuous • ADJECTIVE• very obvious or easily seen

conspiracy •NOUN• **conspiracies** a secret plot between several people to commit a crime together
♦ **conspirator** •NOUN• **conspirators** someone who plots with others to commit a crime

conspire •VERB• **conspires, conspiring, conspired 1** to conspire is to plot with other people to commit a crime **2** if things conspire against you, they come together to stop you doing something you want to do

constable •NOUN• **constables** an ordinary police officer
♦ **constabulary** •NOUN• the constabulary are the police

constant • ADJECTIVE• **1** never stopping:

constant sunshine **2** faithful: *His little dog was his constant companion.*
- **constancy** •NOUN• being faithful or never changing or stopping
- **constantly** •ADVERB• all the time: *It rained constantly for a week.*

constellation •NOUN• **constellations** a large group of stars that can be seen in the sky at night

constipated •ADJECTIVE• someone is constipated when their bowels don't work well and they can't get rid of the waste from their body
- **constipation** •NOUN• being constipated

constituency •NOUN• **constituencies** a district of the country that has a member of parliament
- **constituent** •NOUN• **constituents 1** something that is a part of a larger thing: *The main constituent of the human body is water.* **2** a voter in a constituency

constitute •VERB• **constitutes, constituting, constituted** to constitute is to be or to form something: *Global warming constitutes a risk to the environment.*
- **constitution** •NOUN• **constitutions 1** a constitution is a set of rules of laws by which a country or organization is governed **2** your constitution is the health and strength of your body, especially its ability to fight off illness or injury
- **constitutional** •ADJECTIVE• to do with a constitution

constrain •VERB• **constrains, constraining, constrained** to constrain someone or something is to stop them making progress or developing
- **constraint** •NOUN• **constraints** something that prevents progress or development

constrict •VERB• **constricts, constricting, constricted** to constrict something is to squeeze it tightly

construct •VERB• **constructs, constructing, constructed** to build up from several parts: *construct a model*
- **construction** •NOUN• **constructions 1** construction is building **2** a construction is something built up from several parts
- **constructive** •ADJECTIVE• helpful: *a constructive comment*

consul •NOUN• **consuls** a person who represents his or her country in a foreign country and helps people from his or her own country who are there
- **consulate** •NOUN• **consulates** the office of a consul

consult •VERB• **consults, consulting, consulted** to consult is to ask advice or get information from someone or something: *He consulted the road map to find out where he was.*
- **consultant** •NOUN• **consultants 1** someone whose job is to give advice on a subject that they know a lot about **2** a hospital doctor who is an expert in a particular type of illness
- **consultation** •NOUN• **consultations** a meeting with an expert who can give you advice and information

consume •VERB• **consumes, consuming, consumed 1** to consume something is to use it up
  2 to consume food is to eat it
  3 to consume something is to destroy it: *The fire consumed the forest.*
- **consumer** •NOUN• **consumers** someone who buys and uses things
- **consumption** •NOUN• consuming or the amount that is consumed: *the world's consumption of oil*

contact •VERB• **contacts, contacting, contacted 1** to contact someone is to get in touch with them **2** things contact each other when they touch or come together
•NOUN• **contacts 1** contact is being in touch or touching **2** your contacts are the people you keep in touch with

contact lens •NOUN• **contact lenses** a thin piece of plastic worn on the front of the eye to help you see better

contagious •ADJECTIVE• a contagious disease can be spread

contain •VERB• **contains, containing, contained 1** to contain is to hold or have inside: *How much does this bucket contain?* **2** to contain yourself is to hold back your feelings: *She couldn't contain her excitement.*

Aa
Bb
Cc
Dd
Ee
Ff
Gg
Hh
Ii
Jj
Kk
Ll
Mm
Nn
Oo
Pp
Qq
Rr
Ss
Tt
Uu
Vv
Ww
Xx
Yy
Zz

the continents

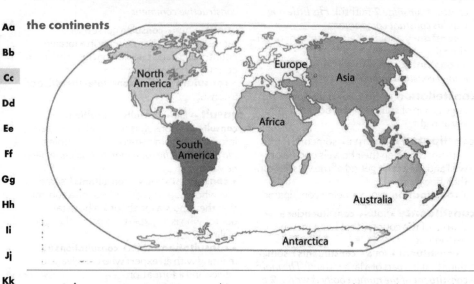

North America

Europe

Asia

Africa

South America

Australia

Antarctica

♦ **container** • NOUN• **containers** something for putting things in, such as a box or jar

contaminate •VERB• **contaminates, contaminating, contaminated** to contaminate something clean or pure is to make it dirty or poisonous by putting something in it
♦ **contaminated** • ADJECTIVE• not clean or pure because something dirty or dangerous has been added
♦ **contamination** • NOUN• making impure or poisonous

contemplate •VERB• **contemplates, contemplating, contemplated** to think about something: *The possibility is just too horrible to contemplate.*
♦ **contemplation** • NOUN• **contemplations** thinking in a quiet, serious way
♦ **contemplative** • ADJECTIVE• spending time thinking

contemporary • ADJECTIVE• **1** belonging to the time now: *contemporary art* **2** if one thing is contemporary with another they exist at the same time
•NOUN• **contemporaries** your contemporaries are people who are living at the same time as you

contempt • NOUN• if you have contempt for someone or something you have a very low opinion of them and don't think they deserve any respect

contend •VERB• **contends, contending, contended** to contend with something is to struggle with it: *He has enough to contend with, studying for all these exams.*
♦ **contender** • NOUN• **contenders** someone who has entered a competition
♦ **contention** • NOUN• **contentions** contention is disagreement or struggle between people

content[1] • ADJECTIVE• to be content is to be happy and satisfied
♦ **contented** • ADJECTIVE• a contented person is happy and satisfied
♦ **contentment** • NOUN• being content

content[2] • NOUN• **contents** the content or contents of something are the things that it contains

contest • NOUN• **contests** a competition: *a contest of strength*
♦ **contestant** • NOUN• **contestants** someone involved in a contest

context • NOUN• **contexts** the context of a word or sentence is what is said or written before and after it and which makes its meaning clear

continent • NOUN• **continents** one of the

large areas that the Earth's land is divided into. The continents are Africa, Antarctica, North America, South America, Asia, Australia and Europe
• **the Continent** the Continent is a British name for the European mainland: *They always go to the Continent on holiday.*
✦ **continental** • ADJECTIVE • to do with a continent, especially the European continent seen from the point of view of people living in Britain

continual • ADJECTIVE • 1 going on without stopping: *the continual noise of traffic* 2 happening again and again: *I'm tired of your continual bad behaviour.*
✦ **continually** • ADVERB • all the time or again and again: *Matt is continually late for work.*

continue • VERB • **continues, continuing, continued** 1 to continue is to go on in the same way or in the same direction as before 2 to continue with something is to go on with it
✦ **continuous** • ADJECTIVE • going on without a break or stop: *a continuous line from north to south*
✦ **continuity** • NOUN • being without breaks or stops

contorted • ADJECTIVE • twisted in an unnatural way
✦ **contortion** • NOUN • **contortions** a twist

contour • NOUN • **contours** 1 the contours of something is its shape seen in outline: *a car with sleek contours* 2 a line on a map which links points of the same height and shows the shape of a hill or mountain

contra- • PREFIX • if a word starts with **contra-** it adds the meaning 'against' or 'opposite to' to the rest of the word. For example, a *contraflow* is a flow in the opposite direction

contract • NOUN • **contracts** a contract is a written agreement
• VERB • **contracts, contracting, contracted**
1 to contract work out to someone is to make an agreement with them that they will do the work
2 to contract is to get smaller: *As the muscle contracts your arm is raised.*
3 to contract a disease is to catch it: *People*

who *contracted polio were often left crippled.*
✦ **contraction** • NOUN • contraction is getting smaller or shorter
✦ **contractor** • NOUN • **contractors** someone who is given a contract to do a particular job: *a building contractor*

contradict • VERB • **contradicts, contradicting, contradicted** to contradict someone is to say that what they have just said is not correct
✦ **contradiction** • NOUN • **contradictions** something that makes a statement or fact seem untrue because it shows the opposite
✦ **contradictory** • ADJECTIVE • a contradictory statement is one that states the opposite of what has just been said

contraflow • NOUN • **contraflows** a contraflow is a line of traffic that goes in the opposite direction to another line of traffic on the same side of a main road

contraption • NOUN • **contraptions** a contraption is an odd-looking machine or instrument

contrary • ADJECTIVE • opposite or opposed to each other: *They have contrary views on the subject*
• **on the contrary** you say 'on the contrary' when you want to say that the opposite is true

contrast • NOUN • **contrasts** if there is a contrast between things they are different in some way
• VERB • **contrasts, contrasting, contrasted** to contrast one thing with another is to show the differences between them

contravene • VERB • **contravenes, contravening, contravened** if something contravenes a rule it breaks it or goes against it
✦ **contravention** • NOUN • **contraventions** breaking or going against a rule, or something that does this

contribute • VERB • **contributes, contributing, contributed** 1 to contribute money or time is to give it: *We each had to contribute towards Gran's present.* 2 if one thing contributes to another it is one of its causes: *People driving too close to the car in*

Aa

front contributed to the accident.

Bb

✦ **contribution** •NOUN• **contributions**
something that is given towards something

✦ **contributor** •NOUN• **contributors**
someone who makes a contribution

Cc

contrite •ADJECTIVE• if someone is contrite

Dd

they feel or show that they are sorry for
something bad they have done

✦ **contrition** •NOUN• feeling or showing

Ee

that you are sorry

Ff

contrive •VERB• **contrives, contriving,**
contrived 1 to contrive something is to make

Gg

it, especially from things that are available:
He'd contrived a sort of ladder out of pieces

Hh

of wood. 2 to contrive to do something is to
try to do it: *She contrived to hide her*

Ii

disappointment.

✦ **contrived** •ADJECTIVE• something that is

Jj

contrived is false and unnatural: *a contrived*

Kk

story about things that would never happen

control •NOUN• **controls** 1 control is the

Ll

power someone has to rule or make
decisions 2 if you have control over

Mm

someone or something you are able to make
them behave in the way you want: *She keeps*

Nn

tight control over her class.
• **in control** to be in control is to be in charge

Oo

• **out of control** behaving or working in a way
that can't be controlled

Pp

•VERB• **controls, controlling, controlled** 1 to
control something is to have power over it or

Qq

to run it 2 to control yourself is to stay calm
and not show your feelings

Rr

✦ **controls** •PLURAL NOUN• the controls of a
vehicle or other machine are the buttons,

Ss

levers and pedals that make it go or work

✦ **controller** •NOUN• **controllers** a person or

Tt

thing that controls or directs something

Uu

control tower •NOUN• **control towers** a tall
building at an airport where air traffic

Vv

controllers direct the planes that are taking
off and landing

Ww

controversial •ADJECTIVE• if something is

Xx

controversial it causes arguments because
some people don't agree with it

Yy

✦ **controversy** •NOUN• **controversies**
something that causes arguments or

Zz

discussions because some people agree with
it and some people don't

conundrum •NOUN• **conundrums** a

puzzling question or riddle

conurbation •NOUN• **conurbations** two
towns or cities that have been joined by
building on the land between them

convalesce •VERB• **convalesces,**
convalescing, convalesced someone who
has been ill convalesces when they rest and
recover their health

✦ **convalescence** •NOUN• the time taken by
someone to recover their health and
strength after an illness

✦ **convalescent** •NOUN• **convalescents**
someone recovering from an illness

convection •NOUN• convection is the
spreading of heat through air or water

✦ **convector** •NOUN• **convectors** a heater
that works by convection

convene •VERB• to convene is to come
together or to call people to come together:
convene a meeting

✦ **convener** •NOUN• **conveners** 1 someone
who calls a meeting 2 someone who is the
chairperson of a committee

convenience •NOUN• **conveniences**
1 convenience is being easy to use, reach or
do, or being suitable: *I like the convenience*
of living so close to the shops. • *For*
everyone's convenience, we will meet after
work.
2 a convenience is something that makes
people's lives easy or comfortable: *The hotel*
has every modern convenience.
3 a convenience is a lavatory
• **at your convenience** to do something at
your convenience is to do it when it suits you

✦ **convenient** •ADJECTIVE• handy or
suitable: *If it isn't convenient just now, I can*
call round later.

✦ **conveniently** •ADVERB• in a convenient
way

convent •NOUN• **convents** a building where
a group of nuns lives

convention •NOUN• **conventions**
1 convention, or a convention, is a way of
behaving that has become normal because
people have been doing it for a long time 2 a
convention is a meeting of people, usually to
discuss a particular subject

✦ **conventional** •ADJECTIVE• if something

is conventional it is traditional and not at all unusual
* **conventionally** •ADVERB• by custom or tradition

converge •VERB• **converges, converging, converged** to converge is to come together at a certain point: *The two roads converge just beyond the bridge.*

conversation •NOUN• **conversations** talk or a talk between people: *He's not very good at making conversation.* • *We had a long conversation about music.*
* **conversational** •ADJECTIVE• to do with conversation: *written in a conversational tone*

converse [1] •VERB• **converses, conversing, conversed** when people converse they talk to each other

converse [2] •NOUN• the converse of something is its opposite
* **conversely** •ADVERB• in the opposite way or from the opposite point of view

conversion •NOUN• conversion is changing from one thing to another

convert •VERB• **converts, converting, converted** to convert something is to change it into something else: *Convert this sum of money from pounds into dollars.*
•NOUN• **converts** a convert is someone who has changed one set of opinions or beliefs for another set of opinions or beliefs
* **convertible** •ADJECTIVE• able to be changed from one thing to another

convex •ADJECTIVE• curving outwards or upwards. Look up and compare **concave**

convey •VERB• **conveys, conveying, conveyed** 1 to convey something or someone is to carry or transport them: *A bus conveyed us to school.* 2 to convey a meaning is to pass it on to other people: *What are you trying to convey in this poem?*

conveyor belt •NOUN• **conveyor belts** a moving surface used to carry things from one place to another, especially in a factory

convict •VERB• **convicts, convicting, convicted** to convict someone is to say in a court of law that they are guilty of a crime
•NOUN• **convicts** someone who has been found guilty of a crime and sent to prison
* **conviction** •NOUN• **convictions** 1 conviction is strong belief 2 a conviction is a sentence given to someone who has been found guilty of a crime: *He's had many convictions for theft.*

convince •VERB• **convinces, convincing, convinced** to convince someone of something is to make them believe that it is true or real: *Stephanie felt confident she would have no difficulty convincing her mother and father that she was ill and could not go to school.*
* **convinced** •ADJECTIVE• certain that something is true or real: *He's convinced that he saw a ghost.*

convoy •NOUN• **convoys** a number of ships, lorries or other vehicles travelling along together in a line

convulse •VERB• **convulses, convulsing, convulsed** to convulse is to twist or shake violently: *We were convulsed with laughter.*
* **convulsion** •NOUN• **convulsions** a sudden jerking, twisting or shaking, especially caused by muscle movements that you can't control

coo •NOUN• **coos** a soft gentle sound made by a dove or a pigeon
•VERB• **coos, cooing, cooed** to make this sound

cook •VERB• **cooks, cooking, cooked** 1 to cook food is to heat it by baking, frying, roasting or boiling 2 food cooks when it heats up and becomes ready to eat
•NOUN• **cooks** a cook is someone who prepares and cooks food
* **cooker** •NOUN• **cookers** a device found in kitchens and used to cook food
* **cookery** •NOUN• the skill or activity of cooking food

cookie •NOUN• **cookies** a biscuit

cool •ADJECTIVE• **cooler, coolest** 1 slightly cold: *a cool drink*
2 calm and controlled: *If you find yourself in a dangerous situation, try to stay cool.*
3 not friendly: *He gave a cool reply.*
4 an informal way of describing someone or something you think is great: *He has a really cool haircut.*

Aa
Bb
Cc
Dd
Ee
Ff
Gg
Hh
Ii
Jj
Kk
Ll
Mm
Nn
Oo
Pp
Qq
Rr
Ss
Tt
Uu
Vv
Ww
Xx
Yy
Zz

Aa

Bb

Cc

Dd

Ee

Ff

Gg

Hh

Ii

Jj

Kk

Ll

Mm

Nn

Oo

Pp

Qq

Rr

Ss

Tt

Uu

Vv

Ww

Xx

Yy

Zz

♦ **coolly** •ADVERB• 1 calmly 2 in an unfriendly way

♦ **coolness** •NOUN• being cool

coop •NOUN• **coops** a cage where chickens are kept
•VERB• **coops, cooping, cooped** if you are **cooped up** somewhere you are inside or in a small space that you would like to escape from

cooperate •VERB• **cooperates, cooperating, cooperated** 1 people co-operate when they work together to do or achieve something 2 to cooperate with someone is to do what they want you to do

♦ **cooperation** •NOUN• 1 working with others so that something can be done or achieved 2 doing what someone asks or tells you to do

♦ **cooperative** •ADJECTIVE• 1 willing to do something someone asks you or tells you to do 2 a cooperative business or organization is one that is managed or owned by everyone who works in it or uses it

coordinate •VERB• **coordinates, coordinating, coordinated** to coordinate movements or actions is to make them fit in with each other or work smoothly together

♦ **coordinates** •PLURAL NOUN• two sets of numbers or letters used to show a position on a graph or find a place on a map

♦ **coordination** •NOUN• 1 the organization of different people or things so that they work together smoothly or well 2 the ability to control your body so that different parts work well together: *hand and eye coordination*

cop[1] •VERB• **cops, copping, copped** to **cop out** of something that is your responsibility is to avoid doing it

cop[2] •NOUN• **cops** an informal word for a police officer: *a New York cop*

cope •VERB• **copes, coping, coped** to cope with something is to manage to deal with it: *She said she couldn't cope with any more work.*

copious •ADJECTIVE• in large quantities: *He made copious notes during the lecture.*

copper[1] •NOUN• 1 copper is a reddish brown metal

2 a reddish brown colour

3 a coin that is made of copper and which usually has a low value: *He gave the beggar a few coppers.*

copper[2] •NOUN• **coppers** an informal word for a police officer

copse *or* **coppice** •NOUN• **copses** *or* **coppices** a wood made up of small or low-growing trees

copy •VERB• **copies, copying, copied** 1 to copy something is to make another thing that looks exactly the same or nearly the same

2 to copy something down is to write it down

3 to copy someone is to do the same thing that they do: *He copies everything his big brother does.*
•NOUN• **copies** 1 a copy is something that has been copied from something else 2 a copy of a book, magazine or newspaper is one of several that have been printed

copyright •NOUN• copyright is the right a person or organization has to copy or publish a book, a piece of music, a film or a video game

coral •NOUN• a hard material made up of the skeletons of tiny sea creatures
•ADJECTIVE• made of coral: *a coral island*

coral reef •NOUN• **coral reefs** a hard rock-like mass of coral that builds up over many years on the seabed

cord •NOUN• **cords** 1 cord is thin rope or thick string: *His hands were tied with cord.*
2 a cord is a thin rope: *a window cord*
3 an electric cable or flex

ⓘ Do not confuse the spellings of **cord** and **chord**, which have different meanings.

cordial •ADJECTIVE• polite and friendly in a formal way: *Their discussions were perfectly cordial.*
•NOUN• **cordials** a fruit juice that you drink diluted with water: *lime cordial*

cordon •NOUN• **cordons** a line of police, soldiers or guards around an area to keep people back
•VERB• **cordons, cordoning, cordoned** to **cordon off** an area is to put a barrier of

some sort around it to stop people going there

corduroy . NOUN. a cotton cloth with rows of soft velvety ridges on the outer surface

core . NOUN. cores the inner part of something, such as a fruit or the earth **. VERB. cores, coring, cored** to core an apple is to take out the inner part that you don't normally eat

corgi . NOUN. corgis a breed of dog with short legs and upright ears

cork . NOUN. corks 1 a light substance that floats, which comes from the bark of a type of oak tree 2 a piece of this used as a stopper for a bottle

corkscrew . NOUN. corkscrews a device with a twisted metal spike used to pull corks from wine bottles

cormorant . NOUN. cormorants a type of large black sea bird with a long curved beak

corn 1 **. NOUN.** 1 wheat or a similar crop 2 maize

corn 2 **. NOUN. corns** a sore hard lump on your toe caused by your shoe rubbing the skin

cornea . NOUN. corneas the see-through covering at the front of your eyeball

corned beef . NOUN. beef that has been salted and packed into tins

corner . NOUN. corners 1 a point where two roads, walls, edges or lines meet: *I'll meet you at the corner of George Street and Alexander Road.* 2 a place away from the main part or far away: *a secluded corner in the garden* • *travelling to the far corners of the world* 3 in soccer and hockey, a kick or hit that you take from one of the corners at the opposing team's end of the pitch **. VERB. corners, cornering, cornered** to force a person or animal into a position from which they can't escape

cornerstone . NOUN. cornerstones 1 a stone at one corner of a building's foundations used as a support for other stones built on top 2 something on which everything else depends: *the cornerstone of his argument*

cornet . NOUN. cornets 1 a musical instrument that looks like a small trumpet 2 a cornet-shaped wafer which is used to contain ice cream

cornflour . NOUN. a white powder made from ground maize and used in cooking, for example to thicken sauces

cornflower . NOUN. cornflowers a plant with bright blue flowers that grows wild in fields

corny . ADJECTIVE. cornier, corniest 1 weak or silly, or heard many times before: *a corny joke* 2 sentimental: *a corny old film*

corona . NOUN. coronas the sun's corona is the spiky circle of light shaped rather like a crown that you see when the moon passes in front of the sun

coronation . NOUN. coronations the crowning of a king, queen or emperor

coronet . NOUN. coronets a small crown, especially one worn by a duke

corporal 1 **. NOUN. corporals** a soldier with a rank between private and sergeant

corporal 2 **. ADJECTIVE.** to do with the body

corporal punishment . NOUN. punishment in which the person being punished is hit or beaten

corporation . NOUN. corporations a corporation is a large business or a group of businesses

corps . NOUN. corps a division of the army, especially one that does a special job: *the Army Medical Corps*

ⓘ This word is pronounced **cor**.

corpse . NOUN. corpses a dead body

corral . NOUN. corrals an enclosure, usually surrounded by a wooden fence, where animals such as cattle and horses are kept

correct . ADJECTIVE. 1 right, not wrong: *The correct answer is 15.* 2 correct behaviour is the sort of behaviour that people find acceptable **. VERB. corrects, correcting, corrected** 1 to correct something is to mark or change any mistakes or faults in it: *The teacher corrects our homework books.* 2 to correct someone

Aa Bb Cc Dd Ee Ff Gg Hh Ii Jj Kk Ll Mm Nn Oo Pp Qq Rr Ss Tt Uu Vv Ww Xx Yy Zz

is to tell them that what they have said or done is wrong

♦ **correction** •NOUN• **corrections** 1 a correction is a mark or change made to correct a mistake 2 correction is checking and altering something to make it better or more accurate: *Hand in your exercise books for correction.*

correspond •VERB• **corresponds, corresponding, corresponded** 1 if two things correspond they are the same 2 people correspond when they write to each other

♦ **correspondence** •NOUN• 1 letters 2 likeness or similarity: *There was no correspondence between their two stories.*

♦ **correspondent** •NOUN• **correspondents** a journalist who writes news reports about a particular subject: *a war correspondent*

corridor •NOUN• **corridors** a corridor is a passageway in a building or train

corrie •NOUN• **corries** a large bowl-shaped hollow high on a mountain and sometimes filled with water

corrode •VERB• **corrodes, corroding, corroded** metal corrodes when it rusts or is eaten away by a chemical

♦ **corrosion** •NOUN• corroding

♦ **corrosive** •ADJECTIVE• able to destroy or wear away metal: *a corrosive acid*

corrugated •ADJECTIVE• folded or shaped into a series of ridges: *a corrugated iron roof*

corrupt •VERB• **corrupts, corrupting, corrupted** to corrupt someone is to make them dishonest or evil •ADJECTIVE• someone who is corrupt behaves dishonestly, usually by taking bribes

♦ **corruption** •NOUN• dishonesty by people in positions where they should be expected to behave honestly

corset •NOUN• **corsets** a stiff garment that fits tightly around the middle part of the body and is worn under other clothes to support your back or give your body a better shape

cosh •NOUN• **coshes** a short heavy stick used for hitting people

cosmetic •NOUN• **cosmetics** cosmetics are things like lipstick, powder and face cream that people use to improve their looks

cosmetic surgery •NOUN• surgery done to change a person's appearance rather than for any medical reason

cosmic •ADJECTIVE• to do with the universe and outer space

cosmonaut •NOUN• **cosmonauts** a Russian astronaut

cosmopolitan •ADJECTIVE• including people or ideas from many parts of the world: *cosmopolitan cities like London and New York*

cosmos •NOUN• the cosmos is the universe ⇒ **cosmic**

cost •VERB• **costs, costing, cost** 1 if something costs a certain amount of money, that is the amount you have to pay for it: *How much does a litre of milk cost?* 2 to cost someone something is to make them lose that thing: *His heroism cost him his life.*
•NOUN• **costs** 1 the cost of something is the amount of money that has to be spent to buy it or make it 2 the cost of something is what has to be suffered to do it or get it
• **at all costs** no matter what cost or suffering may be involved

♦ **costly** •ADVERB• costing a lot: *a costly item of jewellery*

costume •NOUN• **costumes** 1 a special set of clothes worn by an actor in a play or film 2 the clothes worn by the people of a particular country or in a particular period of history: *The children were dressed in national costume for the parade.* 3 fancy dress

cosy •ADJECTIVE• **cosier, cosiest** warm and comfortable: *a cosy little bedroom* • *I'm nice and cosy sitting here by the fire.*

cot •NOUN• **cots** a bed with high sides for a baby or young child to sleep in

ⓘ This word comes from the Hindi language of India. It comes from the word **khat**, which means *bedstead*.

cot death •NOUN• **cot deaths** the death of a baby while it is asleep in its cot

cottage •NOUN• **cottages** a small house in the country or in a village

cottage cheese • NOUN • a soft white lumpy type of cheese

cotton • NOUN • a type of cloth made from the fibres inside the seeds of a plant, that is grown in warm climates

cotton wool • NOUN • a mass of soft loose fibres of cotton used to clean wounds or take off make-up

couch • NOUN • **couches** a sofa

couch potato • NOUN • **couch potatoes** a person who is not active enough, especially someone who sits watching TV a lot

cougar • NOUN • **cougars** a large wild animal of the cat family that lives in America. Another name for the cougar is the **mountain lion**

cough • VERB • **coughs, coughing, coughed** you cough when you make a loud rough sound in your throat as you force air out of your lungs
• NOUN • **coughs 1** the noise you make when you cough **2** an illness that causes you to cough

could • VERB • **1** you use **could** with another verb to say that something is or might be possible, or to ask politely if something is possible: *He could do it if he tried hard enough. • Could I have a drink of water, please?* **2 could** is the past tense form of the verb **can**: *He could run fast when he was young.*

couldn't • SHORT FORM • a short way to say and write **could not**

council • NOUN • **councils** a group of people who are elected to discuss and manage the affairs of a town or city
• **councillor** • NOUN • **councillors** someone elected to a town or city council

---

(i) Be careful not to confuse the noun **council** with the noun and verb **counsel**.

---

counsel • VERB • **counsels, counselling, counselled** to counsel someone is to give them advice
• NOUN • **counsels 1** advice **2** a lawyer who presents evidence at a trial: *the counsel for the defence*
• **counsellor** • NOUN • **counsellors** someone

who gives advice

count¹ • VERB • **counts, counting, counted**
1 to count is to say numbers in order: *Can you count backwards from 10?*
2 to count something, or to **count things up**, is to work out the total: *He was busy counting his money.*
3 if something counts, it is important or has value: *They tried to make every day they were together count.*
4 if you can **count on** someone or something you can rely on them
• NOUN • **counts** a count is a number of things to be counted: *The teacher did a head count before we left.*
• **keep count** to keep count is to know how many there are or have been
• **lose count** to lose count is forget how many you have already counted
⇒ **countless**

count² • NOUN • **counts** a nobleman in certain countries

countdown • NOUN • a countdown is counting backwards to the exact time when a spacecraft or rocket will be launched

counter¹ • VERB • **counters, countering, countered** to counter something is to respond to it by fighting back or saying or doing the opposite
• ADVERB • against or in the opposite direction: *Counter to our advice, he wants to be a racing driver.*

counter² • NOUN • **counters 1** a table or surface across which customers are served, for example in a shop, a bank or a café **2** a small plastic or metal disc used in some board games

counter- • PREFIX • if **counter-** is put at the beginning of a word it adds the meaning 'opposite' to the rest of the word. For example, in American English, *counterclockwise* means going round in the opposite direction to clockwise

counteract • VERB • **counteracts, counteracting, counteracted** if one thing counteracts another thing it reduces or takes away the effect of that other thing by doing the opposite: *a face cream that is supposed to counteract wrinkles*

Aa
Bb
Cc
Dd
Ee
Ff
Gg
Hh
Ii
Jj
Kk
Ll
Mm
Nn
Oo
Pp
Qq
Rr
Ss
Tt
Uu
Vv
Ww
Xx
Yy
Zz

Countries and people

Country	People from the country	Country	People from the country
Afghanistan	Afghans	Iran	Iranians
Albania	Albanians	Iraq	Iraqis
America	Americans	Ireland, Republic of	Irish
Argentina	Argentinians		
Australia	Australians	Israel	Israelis
Austria	Austrians	Italy	Italians
Bangladesh	Bangladeshis	Jamaica	Jamaicans
Barbados	Barbadians	Japan	Japanese
Belgium	Belgians	Luxembourg	Luxembourgs
Bosnia and Herzegovina	Bosnians, Herzegovinians	Macedonia	Macedonians
		Malaysia	Malaysians
Brazil	Brazilians	Malta	Maltese
Britain	British	Mexico	Mexicans
Bulgaria	Bulgarians	Netherlands	Dutch
Canada	Canadians	New Zealand	New Zealanders
Chile	Chileans	Nigeria	Nigerians
China	Chinese	Norway	Norwegians
Colombia	Colombians	Pakistan	Pakistanis
Congo, Democratic Republic of the	Congolese	Poland	Poles
		Portugal	Portuguese
		Romania	Romanians
Croatia	Croats	Russia	Russians
Cyprus	Cypriots	Saudi Arabia	Saudi Arabians
Czech Republic	Czechs	Scotland	Scots
Denmark	Danes	Slovakia	Slovaks
Egypt	Egyptians	South Africa	South Africa
England	English	Spain	Spaniards
Ethiopia	Ethiopians	Sweden	Swedes
Finland	Finns	Switzerland	Swiss
France	French	Thailand	Thais
Germany	Germans	Trinidad and Tobago	Trinidadians and Tobagonians
Great Britain	British		
Greece	Greeks	Turkey	Turks
Guatemala	Guatemalans	United Kingdom	British
Holland	Dutch	United States of America (USA)	Americans
Hungary	Hungarians		
Iceland	Icelanders	Vietnam	Vietnamese
India	Indians	Wales	Welsh
Indonesia	Indonesians	West Indies	West Indians

counterattack •NOUN• **counterattacks** a counterattack is an attack made against an enemy who has attacked first

counterfeit •ADJECTIVE• not real or genuine: *a counterfeit stamp*
•NOUN• **counterfeits** a counterfeit is a copy made to look like the real thing

counterfoil •NOUN• **counterfoils** the counterfoil of a cheque or ticket is the part you tear off and keep as a record

counterpart •NOUN• **counterparts** someone's counterpart is a person who has a similar job in a different place: *The British Prime Minister will be meeting his European counterparts.*

countess • NOUN• **countesses** 1 a woman with the same rank as a count or earl 2 the wife of a count

countless • ADJECTIVE• too many to count: *I've done this countless times.*

country • NOUN• **countries** 1 a nation or one of the areas of the world controlled by its own government. See the box called **Countries and people**
2 the land where certain people or animals live: *This is grizzly bear country.*
3 an area: *the West Country*
4 the country is the parts of the land away from towns and cities: *They live in the country.*

countryman • NOUN• **countrymen** 1 a man who lives and works in the countryside 2 your countrymen are men who come from the same country as you do

countryside • NOUN• the countryside is land away from towns and cities

countrywoman • NOUN• **countrywomen** 1 a woman who lives and works in the countryside 2 your countrywomen are the women who come from the same country as you do

county • NOUN• **counties** a county is one of the areas that some countries or states are divided into, which each have their own local government

coup • NOUN• **coups** a coup is a sudden change of government in which new people take power without an election being held

ⓘ This word is pronounced **coo**.

couple • NOUN• **couples** 1 two or approximately two: *I hadn't seen him for a couple for months.* 2 a husband and wife or two people who have a similar close relationship: *an elderly couple*
• VERB• **couples, coupling, coupled** to couple things is to join one to the other

coupon • NOUN• **coupons** a coupon is a piece of paper that you can use to claim a free gift or get money off something

courage • NOUN• courage is the quality some people have that allows them to do dangerous or frightening things
• **pluck up** *or* **screw up your courage** to force yourself to be brave
♦ **courageous** • ADJECTIVE• brave

courgette • NOUN• **courgettes** a type of vegetable that looks like a small cucumber

courier • NOUN• **couriers** someone who carries messages or packages from one place to another
• VERB• **couriers, couriering, couriered** to courier something is to send it using a courier

course • NOUN• **courses** 1 a number of lessons on a particular subject: *a French course*
2 a course of treatment is medical treatment given in stages or over a period of time
3 a course is the ground that a race is run over or game is played on: *a racecourse* • *a golf course*
4 one of the parts of a meal: *We had soup for the first course.*
5 the route or direction that something moves or travels along: *following the river's course for several miles*
• **in due course** after a while or at its proper time
• **in the course of** during
• **of course** you say 'of course' when you want to agree to a request someone has made in polite way or when you want to show that something was expected: *'Can I borrow that book for a few days?' 'Of course you can.'* • *We went on holiday and of course it rained the whole time.*

ⓘ Do not confuse the spelling of the noun **course** with the adjective **coarse**.

court • NOUN• **courts** 1 a court is a building or room where judges or magistrates make decisions on legal subjects or where trials are held
2 a royal court is the place where a king or queen and the people who attend to them have their official home
3 a court is an area marked out with lines where a game, such as tennis, basketball or squash, is played

•VERB• **courts, courting, courted** to court someone is to try to win their love or friendship ⇒ **courtship**

courteous **•ADJECTIVE•** polite and respectful towards other people

♦ **courtesy** **•NOUN•** **courtesies** 1 courtesy is polite behaviour towards other people 2 a courtesy is a polite action

courtier **•NOUN•** **courtiers** someone who attends a king or queen at their official home

court-martial **•NOUN•** **court-martials** or **courts-martial** a military trial
•VERB• **court-martials, court-martialling, court-martialled** to court-martial someone in the armed forces is to put them on trial for breaking military law

courtship **•NOUN•** **courtships** courtship is the process of or time spent winning the love of someone you want to marry

courtyard **•NOUN•** **courtyards** an open area inside a building surrounded on all sides by walls

cousin **•NOUN•** **cousins** the son or daughter of your aunt or uncle

cove **•NOUN•** **coves** a small bay on the sea coast

coven **•NOUN•** **covens** a group of witches

covenant **•NOUN•** **covenants** a solemn agreement that people make to do or not to do something

cover **•VERB•** **covers, covering, covered** 1 to cover something is to put or spread something else on or over it so that it is hidden: *She'd covered the table with a clean cloth.*

2 to cover a distance or period of time is to travel over that distance or stretch over that period of time: *We covered ten miles in three hours.* • *The history book covers the whole of Queen Victoria's reign.*

3 to cover something is to deal with it: *The local newspaper covered the story.* • *We'll need some cash to cover our expenses.*

4 to cover or **cover something up** is to hide it completely: *His actions since then had been merely to cover up the crime.*

•NOUN• **covers** something that covers, hides or protects: *a bed cover*

♦ **coverage** **•NOUN•** coverage is the

amount of space or time given to an item of news in a newspaper or on a TV or radio programme

covert **•ADJECTIVE•** covert actions are done in secret

covet **•VERB•** **covets, coveting, coveted** to covet something is to want it for yourself

♦ **covetous** **•ADJECTIVE•** a covetous person wants very much to own or get things

cow **•NOUN•** **cows** 1 a large animal kept on farms for its milk: *a dairy cow* 2 a female animal of the ox family or a female elephant or whale

cowed **•ADJECTIVE•** behaving in a timid way

coward **•NOUN•** **cowards** someone who lacks courage

♦ **cowardly** **•ADJECTIVE•** behaving like a coward

♦ **cowardice** **•NOUN•** being cowardly

cowboy **•NOUN•** **cowboys** a man who herds cattle while on horseback, especially in the western United States

cower **•VERB•** **cowers, cowering, cowered** to cower is to shrink back in fear

cowgirl **•NOUN•** **cowgirls** a woman who herds cattle while on horseback

cowl **•NOUN•** **cowls** 1 a monk's hood 2 a cap for a chimney

cowslip **•NOUN•** **cowslips** a wild plant with yellow sweet-smelling flowers that grow on long stalks

cox **•NOUN•** **coxes** the cox of a rowing boat or a lifeboat is the person whose job it is to steer. Cox is a shortened form of **coxswain**
•VERB• **coxes, coxing, coxed** to cox a boat is to steer it

coxswain **•NOUN•** **coxswains** 1 someone who steers a boat 2 someone who is in charge of the crew on a ship

coy **•ADJECTIVE•** **coyer, coyest** pretending to be shy: *a coy smile*

coyote **•NOUN•** **coyotes** a type of wild dog that lives in North America

crab **•NOUN•** **crabs** a sea animal with a broad shell and five pairs of legs. A crab has claws on its front pair of legs

Aa
Bb
Cc
Dd
Ee
Ff
Gg
Hh
Ii
Jj
Kk
Ll
Mm
Nn
Oo
Pp
Qq
Rr
Ss
Tt
Uu
Vv
Ww
Xx
Yy
Zz

crab apple • NOUN• **crab apples** a type of small bitter apple that grows wild

crack • NOUN• **cracks** 1 a narrow break or split 2 a sudden sharp sound: *the crack of a whip*
• **have a crack at** to have a crack at something is to make an attempt to do it
•VERB• **cracks, cracking, cracked** 1 to crack is to split or break so that a small gap appears 2 to crack a joke is to make a joke
♦ **cracker** • NOUN• **crackers** a Christmas toy made up of a paper tube which two people pull and which makes a bang or crack when it comes apart

crackle •VERB• **crackles, crackling, crackled** to make a series of short cracking noises: *Thunder roared and lightning crackled.*
• NOUN• these noises: *the crackle of twigs underfoot*

cradle • NOUN• **cradles** a baby's bed, especially one that can be rocked from side to side
•VERB• **cradles, cradling, cradled** to cradle something is to hold it gently: *She cradled his head in her arms.*

craft • NOUN• **crafts** 1 a skill, like pottery or wood carving, in which you make something with your hands 2 a boat, ship, aeroplane or spaceship

craftsman • NOUN• **craftsmen** a man who is skilled at making things with his hands

craftswoman • NOUN• **craftswomen** a woman who is skilled at making things with her hands

crafty • ADJECTIVE• **craftier, craftiest** a crafty person is clever at getting things done in the way they want, often by tricking or deceiving people

crag • NOUN• **crags** a high steep rock or rough mass of rocks
♦ **craggy** • ADJECTIVE• **craggier, craggiest** 1 steep and rough: *a great craggy mountain* 2 someone with craggy features has lots of lines on their face

cram •VERB• **crams, cramming, crammed** 1 to cram things somewhere is to push or force them into a space that is too small: *Elizabeth tried to cram even more crisps into her mouth.*

2 if a place or container is crammed with things it is filled very full: *All the shelves were crammed with books of every size.*
3 to cram for an exam is to learn as much as possible in the short time before you have to sit the exam

cramp • NOUN• **cramps** 1 cramp is pain somewhere in your body caused when a muscle suddenly tightens 2 cramps are pains in a muscle or muscles, especially in your stomach
•VERB• **cramps, cramping, cramped** muscles cramp when they tighten up suddenly causing pain
♦ **cramped** • ADJECTIVE• a cramped space is uncomfortable because it is too small to move about in or because it is crowded with people or things

cranberry • NOUN• **cranberries** cranberries are small red fruits with a sour taste, used to make sauces and drinks

crane • NOUN• **cranes** 1 a tall machine used to lift heavy weights, such as pieces of cargo that have to be taken off a ship 2 a type of large bird with a long neck and long thin legs
•VERB• **cranes, craning, craned** if you crane your neck, you stretch your neck as far as possible so that you can get a better view of something

crane fly • NOUN• **crane flies** an insect with a thin body and very long legs. Another name for a crane fly is a **daddy-long-legs**

cranium • NOUN• **crania** or **craniums** your cranium is your skull

crank • NOUN• **cranks** 1 a crank is a lever that you turn to make an engine or a piece of machinery move or work 2 a crank is someone who has strange ideas or behaves in an odd way
•VERB• **cranks, cranking, cranked** to crank an engine or a piece of machinery, or to **crank it up**, is to turn a lever over and over again to make it move or work
♦ **cranky** • ADJECTIVE• **crankier, crankiest** 1 a cranky person has strange ideas or behaves in a peculiar way 2 if someone is cranky they are bad-tempered

cranny • NOUN• **crannies** a narrow opening or crack, especially in a room or rock

Aa
Bb
Cc
Dd
Ee
Ff
Gg
Hh
Ii
Jj
Kk
Ll
Mm
Nn
Oo
Pp
Qq
Rr
Ss
Tt
Uu
Vv
Ww
Xx
Yy
Zz

crash •NOUN• **crashes** 1 a loud noise, especially one made when something hard hits another hard thing causing damage 2 a car crash is an accidental collision between two cars while one or both are moving 3 a computer crash is the failure of the computer which happens if it can't process information properly or if the system has been damaged
•VERB• **crashes, crashing, crashed** 1 to crash is to make a loud noise 2 to crash is to be involved in a car crash 3 if a computer crashes it stops working because it can't process information or because it has been damaged

crash helmet •NOUN• **crash helmets** a hard helmet worn by motorcyclists or racing drivers to protect their head

crash-land •VERB• **crash-lands, crash-landing, crash-landed** if an aeroplane crash-lands it hits the ground hard, either because it is out of control or because the pilot has to land in an emergency
♦ **crash-landing** •NOUN• **crash-landings** an aeroplane makes a crash-landing when it hits the ground hard

crate •NOUN• **crates** a wooden or plastic box used for carrying things, especially breakable things like bottles

crater •NOUN• **craters** 1 a bowl-shaped hole in the ground where a bomb has exploded or a meteor has landed 2 a bowl-shaped hollow at the top of a volcano where it has erupted

cravat •NOUN• **cravats** a wide strip of thin cloth that is folded and tied around the neck. Men sometimes wear cravats instead of ties

crave •VERB• **craves, craving, craved** to crave something is to want it very much
♦ **craving** •NOUN• **cravings** if you have a craving for something you have a strong urge to have it

crawl •VERB• **crawls, crawling, crawled** 1 if a person crawls they move forwards on their hands and knees: *Pat had to crawl under the desk to get the pen she'd dropped.* 2 insects or reptiles crawl when they move about on their legs: *Look! There's a spider crawling up the wall behind you.*

3 to crawl is to move at a very slow pace: *The traffic was crawling along at about 2 miles an hour.*
•NOUN• 1 a very slow pace: *We were moving forward at a crawl.* 2 the crawl is a way of swimming where you kick your legs and swing first one arm and then the other into the water ahead of you
♦ **crawler** •NOUN• **crawlers** something that crawls

crayon •NOUN• **crayons** a stick of coloured wax or a coloured pencil for drawing with

craze •NOUN• **crazes** a fashion or pastime that is very popular for a short time

crazy •ADJECTIVE• **crazier, craziest** 1 mad: *a crazy idea* • *I think he's gone crazy.* 2 if you are crazy about someone or something you love them or like them very much

creak •VERB• **creaks, creaking, creaked** to creak is to make a squeaking or grating noise: *The floorboards creaked as he tried to tiptoe along the corridor.*
•NOUN• **creaks** a squeaking or grating noise
♦ **creaky** •ADJECTIVE• **creakier, creakiest** making squeaking or grating noises: *a creaky old bed*

cream •NOUN• **creams** 1 cream is a thick yellowish-white liquid that is separated from milk 2 a cream is a thickish liquid that you put on your skin or hair: *suntan cream*
♦ **creamy** •ADJECTIVE• **creamier, creamiest** containing cream or thick like cream: *creamy milk*

crease •NOUN• **creases** a wrinkle, line or fold made by bending or crushing fabric or paper: *Always fold your trousers along the creases before you hang them up.*
•VERB• **creases, creasing, creased** 1 material that creases will crush easily so that lines or wrinkles form in it 2 to crease material is to press it or bend it into lines or folds

create •VERB• **creates, creating, created** to create something is to make it or invent it, or to make it happen or exist: *They created a big fuss until they got what they wanted.*
♦ **creation** •NOUN• **creations** 1 the creation of something is making it: *the creation of the universe* 2 a creation is something new that

has been made: *one of the designer's latest creations*

♦ **creative** • ADJECTIVE• a creative person has the skill and imagination to make new things, especially works of art

♦ **creativity** • NOUN• creativity is the talent or imagination to make or invent things

♦ **creator** • NOUN• **creators** someone who makes something new

creature • NOUN• **creatures** a living thing that is able to move about. Animals are creatures, but plants are not

crèche • NOUN• **crèches** a place where young children are looked after together while their parents are elsewhere

credible • ADJECTIVE• something credible can be believed

credit • NOUN• **credits** 1 if people give you credit for something good they give you praise or approval because of it
2 credit is a system used in shops and businesses where customers can get things now and pay for them later
3 your bank account is in credit when you have money in it
• VERB• **credits, crediting, credited** 1 to credit someone with an achievement or a good quality is to say that they have done it or have it 2 to credit something is to believe it: *You wouldn't credit how many times we had to go back over the same thing.*

♦ **creditable** • ADJECTIVE• good enough to deserve praise or respect: *a very creditable performance*

credit card • NOUN• **credit cards** a small plastic card that allows you to buy things when you want them and to pay for them later

creed • NOUN• **creeds** something that you believe in, especially the religious beliefs that you have

creek • NOUN• **creeks** a short or narrow river, especially one that flows into the sea or a lake

creep • VERB• **creeps, creeping, crept** 1 to creep is to move forwards slowly and quietly: *He crept downstairs in the middle of the night.* 2 animals that creep move slowly with their bodies close to the ground
• NOUN• **creeps** someone who is unpleasant or weird

• **give someone the creeps** if someone or something gives you the creeps, they make you shiver with disgust or fear

♦ **creeper** • NOUN• **creepers** a plant that grows slowly over the ground or up a wall

♦ **creepy** • ADJECTIVE• **creepier, creepiest** a creepy place or person makes you shiver with fear or disgust

cremate • VERB• **cremates, cremating, cremated** to cremate a dead person is to burn their body rather than bury it

♦ **cremation** • NOUN• **cremations** the burning of a dead body or dead bodies

♦ **crematorium** • NOUN• **crematoriums** or **crematoria** a building where dead people's bodies are burned

creosote • NOUN• a type of thick dark brown paint made from wood tar and used to stop wood rotting

crêpe • NOUN• a thin fabric with a wrinkled surface: *a crêpe bandage*

crêpe paper • NOUN• a type of very thin wrinkled paper used for decoration or for wrapping things in

crept • VERB• a way of changing the verb **creep** to make a past tense. It can be used with or without a helping verb: *We had crept in unnoticed.* • *They crept up on him and said 'Boo!'.*

crescendo • NOUN• **crescendos** 1 if sounds reach a crescendo they grow louder and louder until they are at their loudest 2 in a piece of music, a crescendo is a place where the music gets louder

crescent • NOUN• **crescents** a curved shape which comes to a point at each end and is wider in the middle, like the shape of the moon at certain times of the month

ⓘ The word **crescent** comes from the French word **creissant**. The French word comes from the Latin word **crescere**, which means to *grow*. This is because the moon is in a crescent shape when it is growing into a full moon.

cress • NOUN• a small green plant with peppery-tasting leaves which are used in salads and sandwiches

crest • NOUN• **crests** 1 the crest of a wave or hill is its highest point

Aa

2 the feathers that stick up on the top of some birds' heads

3 a family's or organization's badge or emblem

Bb

Cc

crestfallen •ADJECTIVE• if someone is crestfallen they look sad and disappointed because something they had hoped for or had being trying to do has not turned out well

Dd

Ee

crevasse •NOUN• **crevasses** a deep crack in ice

Ff

Gg

crevice •NOUN• **crevices** a thin crack or opening in rock

Hh

crew[1] •NOUN• **crews** a group of people who work together, especially on a ship or aeroplane: *The lifeboat has a crew of five.* • *The film crew were busy setting up lights and cameras.*

Ii

Jj

•VERB• **crews, crewing, crewed** to crew a boat or ship is to work as a member of its crew

Kk

Ll

crew[2] •VERB• a way of changing the verb **crow** to make a past tense: *The cock crew.*

Mm

crewcut •NOUN• **crewcuts** a very short hairstyle for men and boys, first used in the army and navy

Nn

Oo

crib •NOUN• **cribs** a small cot for a baby

Pp

•VERB• **cribs, cribbing, cribbed** to crib is to copy someone else's work and pretend it is your own

Qq

crick •NOUN• **cricks** if you have a crick in your neck, your neck feels stiff and painful because the muscles have tightened up

Rr

Ss

cricket[1] •NOUN• a game played outdoors between two sides of eleven players with a wooden bat and ball

Tt

♦ **cricketer** •NOUN• **cricketers** someone who plays cricket

Uu

cricket[2] •NOUN• **crickets** a small insect that lives in grass. A cricket makes a high-pitched whirring sound by rubbing its wings together

Vv

Ww

cried •VERB• a way of changing the verb **cry** to make a past tense. It can be used with or without a helping verb: *The baby cried and cried.* • *He had cried all day.*

Xx

Yy

cries •NOUN• the plural of the noun **cry**: *No one heard their cries for help.*

Zz

•VERB• the form of the verb **cry** in the present tense that you use with **he, she,** or **it**: *She always cries when she watches romantic films.*

crime •NOUN• **crimes** 1 a crime is an illegal activity, such as robbery, murder, assault or dangerous driving. Someone who has committed a crime can be punished by law 2 crime is all these activities

♦ **criminal** •NOUN• **criminals** someone who has committed a crime

•ADJECTIVE• 1 to do with crime or criminals: *a criminal court* 2 against the law or very wrong: *a criminal act*

crimp •VERB• **crimps, crimping, crimped** 1 to crimp hair is to bend it into little waves or curls using a special heated rod 2 to crimp something, such as paper or pastry, is to press down on its edge to make lots of little folds

crimson •NOUN• a bright red colour

cringe •VERB• **cringes, cringing, cringed** 1 to cringe is to crouch or back away from something in fear: *The dog cringed and showed its teeth.* 2 if something you or someone else has done makes you cringe, it makes you feel very embarrassed

crinkle •NOUN• **crinkles** a small crease or wrinkle

•VERB• **crinkles, crinkling, crinkled** to crinkle something is to form small creases or wrinkles in it

♦ **crinkly** •ADJECTIVE• **crinklier, crinkliest** having lots of small creases or wrinkles

cripple •VERB• **cripples, crippling, crippled** 1 an injury or disease cripples someone if it causes damage to their body, or part of their body, which stops them moving about normally 2 to cripple something is to damage it so that it cannot function properly

♦ **crippled** •ADJECTIVE• 1 unable to move about normally: *a crippled bird with a broken wing* 2 so badly damaged it cannot work normally: *The crippled warship limped back into port.*

crisis •NOUN• **crises** a very difficult or dangerous time or event which causes suffering or worry

crisp •ADJECTIVE• **crisper, crispest** 1 stiff or hard and easily broken: *nice crisp salad*

leaves 2 crisp weather is frosty and dry
• NOUN• **crisps** a thin slice of potato that has been fried in oil until it is crisp: *a bag of crisps*
♦ **crispness** • NOUN• being crisp
♦ **crispy** • ADJECTIVE• **crispier, crispiest** hard or firm enough to break easily: *a crispy sugar topping*

criss-cross • VERB• **criss-crosses, criss-crossing, criss-crossed** things criss-cross when they cross each other again and again to form a pattern of crossed lines

critic • NOUN• **critics** 1 someone who finds faults in something: *a critic of the government* 2 someone who writes about new books, films, music or shows and says what is good or bad about them
♦ **critical** • ADJECTIVE• to be critical of something is to say what you think its faults are
♦ **criticism** • NOUN• **criticisms** 1 criticism is pointing out faults: *Try not to be hurt by criticism.* 2 a criticism is a statement about a fault you think someone or something has: *My only criticism is the story is too long.*
♦ **criticize** or **criticise** • VERB• **criticizes, criticizing, criticized** to criticize something is to say what you think its faults are: *It always hurts when you criticize me.*

croak • VERB• **croaks, croaking, croaked** 1 to croak is to speak in a hoarse voice because your throat is sore or dry 2 a frog croaks when it makes its deep harsh sound
• NOUN• **croaks** 1 the sound made by a frog or toad 2 a low hoarse voice
♦ **croaky** • ADJECTIVE• **croakier, croakiest** a croaky voice is deep and hoarse

crochet • NOUN• crochet is a type of knitting in which stitches are made by twisting thread or wool around a single needle
• VERB• **crochets, crocheting, crocheted** to crochet is to make something out of wool or thread using a single needle to make the stitches

ⓘ This word is pronounced **cro**-shay.

crock • NOUN• **crocks** 1 a pot or jar made out of clay 2 a crock is an old broken-down person or machine

crockery • NOUN• crockery is plates, bowls and cups used for eating food

crocodile • NOUN• **crocodiles** a large reptile with thick skin, a long tail and big jaws. Crocodiles are found mainly in Africa and Australia and live in rivers and lakes
• **cry** or **shed crocodile tears** to pretend that you are sorry about something when you are really quite pleased about it

crocus • NOUN• **crocuses** a small plant that grows from a bulb and has white, purple or yellow flowers that come out in the spring

croft • NOUN• **crofts** a small farm in the Scottish Highlands with a cottage and a small amount of land
♦ **crofter** • NOUN• **crofters** someone who lives and works on a croft

crook • NOUN• **crooks** 1 a stick carried by a shepherd, which has a curved top that the shepherd uses for catching sheep by their necks
2 the crook of your arm or leg is the part at the inside of your elbow or the back of your knee that curves inwards
3 a crook is a criminal or someone who behaves dishonestly
• VERB• **crooks, crooking, crooked** to crook something is to bend it or form it into a curve: *He crooked one eyebrow and looked at me.*
♦ **crooked** • ADJECTIVE• bent or forming a curve

ⓘ **Crooked** is pronounced **crook**-id.

croon • VERB• **croons, crooning, crooned** to croon is to sing in a low loving voice

crop • NOUN• **crops** 1 crops are plants that are gathered or harvested for food from fields, trees or bushes
2 a crop is a particular kind of plant or fruit that grows and is harvested at one time: *We'll get a good crop of apples this year.*
3 a riding crop is a short whip used by jockeys and horse riders
• VERB• **crops, cropping, cropped** 1 to crop something is to cut it short 2 when something **crops up**, it happens without being expected or planned

cropper • NOUN• if you are doing something dangerous or illegal and you **come a cropper**, you have an accident or you are caught out

croquet • NOUN• a game played on a lawn with wooden balls that the players hit

Aa Bb Cc Dd Ee Ff Gg Hh Ii Jj Kk Ll Mm Nn Oo Pp Qq Rr Ss Tt Uu Vv Ww Xx Yy Zz

through metal hoops using long wooden hammers called mallets

Aa

Bb

ⓘ This word is pronounced **kro**-kay.

Cc **cross** •NOUN• **crosses** 1 a shape made when two straight lines go over each other at a point in the middle, **✗** or **+**

Dd 2 a symbol used in the Christian religion to stand for the cross on which Christ was crucified

Ee 3 a mixture of two things, especially an animal or plant that has been bred from two

Ff different animals or plants: *A mule is a cross between a donkey and a horse.*

Gg •VERB• **crosses, crossing, crossed** 1 to cross something is to go over it from one side to

Hh the other: *cross a bridge*

Ii 2 if one thing crosses another they meet at a certain point and go on beyond it: *at the place where the road crosses the railway line*

Jj 3 to cross things is to put one across and on top of the other: *cross your fingers*

Kk 4 to **cross something out** is to draw a line or lines through it because you want to get rid of

Ll it or to replace it with something else: *He crossed out John's name and wrote in his own.*

Mm •ADJECTIVE• **crosser, crossest** annoyed or angry: *I got very cross when he didn't turn up.*

Nn ◆ **crossly** •ADVERB• angrily

Oo **crossbar** •NOUN• **crossbars** 1 the crossbar on a man's bike is the horizontal piece of metal

Pp between the saddle and the handlebars 2 the crossbar on a goal is the horizontal piece of

Qq wood between the uprights

Rr **crossbow** •NOUN• **crossbows** a weapon for shooting arrows with a bow string stretched

Ss horizontally on cross-shaped frame

Tt **cross-country** •ADJECTIVE• a cross-country race is one where the runners go

Uu across the countryside rather than along a road or track

Vv

Ww **cross-examine** •VERB• **cross-examines, cross-examining, cross-examined** to cross-

Xx examine someone is to ask them questions so that their answers can be compared with

Yy answers they had given earlier ◆ **cross-examination** •NOUN• **cross-**

Zz **examinations** a series of questions asked to check whether earlier answers are the same

cross-eyed •ADJECTIVE• a cross-eyed

person has eyes that look towards their nose instead of straight ahead

crossfire •NOUN• crossfire is gunfire coming from different directions

crossing •NOUN• **crossings** 1 a place where a road or river can be crossed 2 a journey made by a ship between two pieces of land: *a short ferry crossing from Mull to Iona*

cross-purposes •NOUN• if two people are at cross-purposes they are talking about different things though they think they mean the same thing

cross-reference •NOUN• **cross-references** a note in a dictionary or encyclopedia that tells you to look at another entry for more information

crossroads •NOUN• a place where two or more roads meet

cross-section •NOUN• **cross-sections** 1 a cut made through a solid object so that you can see the structure inside, or a picture of this 2 a cross-section of a group of people or things is a sample that includes all the different types of people or things: *a cross-section of the public*

crossword •NOUN• **crosswords** a word game where you fill in words or letters on a grid by solving clues

crotch •NOUN• **crotches** the area of your body between your legs where the tops of your legs join your body

crotchet •NOUN• **crotchets** a musical note equal to a quarter of a semibreve. The symbol for a crotchet is ♩

crouch •VERB• **crouches, crouching, crouched** you crouch when you bend your legs and back so that your body is close to the ground

crow [1] •NOUN• **crows** a large black bird that makes a loud harsh sound

crow [2] •VERB• **crows, crowing, crowed** or **crew** 1 when a cock crows it makes a loud sound, especially early in the morning 2 to crow is to talk in a boastful way: *He was crowing about his success.*

crowbar •NOUN• **crowbars** a heavy metal bar curved at one end that is used as a lever

crowd •NOUN• **crowds** a large number of

people or things gathered in one place: *a football crowd* • *crowds of shoppers*
•VERB• **crowds, crowding, crowded** if people or things crowd in or into a place they fill it up so that there is hardly any space left
♦ **crowded** •ADJECTIVE• full of people or things: *a crowded street*

crown •NOUN• **crowns 1** an ornament, often made of gold and studded with jewels, worn by a king or queen on their head during formal occasions **2** the top of something, such as your head or a hill
•VERB• **crowns, crowning, crowned 1** a king or queen is crowned when they are made the monarch of a country in a ceremony where a crown is put on their head **2** to crown something is to add something on top: *We had a very long tiring journey, and to crown it all, our luggage was lost at the airport.*
⇒ **coronation**

crow's-nest •NOUN• **crow's nests** the place at the top of a ship's mast where a sailor goes to get a view of things far away

crucial •ADJECTIVE• of great importance: *a crucial exam*

crucifix •NOUN• **crucifixes** a cross with a figure of Christ on it, used as a symbol of the Christian religion
♦ **crucifixion** •NOUN• **crucifixions** nailing someone's hands and feet to a large wooden cross and leaving them to die. Crucifixion was often used as a punishment by the ancient Romans and Christ was killed in this way
♦ **crucify** •VERB• **crucifies, crucifying, crucified** to crucify someone is to nail their hands and feet to a large wooden cross and leave them to die

crude •ADJECTIVE• **cruder, crudest 1** made or done in a rough or simple way: *a crude map drawn on the back of an envelope*
2 crude oil is as it is when it came out of the ground and has not been refined
3 rude or vulgar: *a crude joke*
♦ **crudely** •ADVERB• roughly or simply: *a crudely made table*

cruel •ADJECTIVE• **crueller, cruellest** someone who is cruel causes pain or suffering to other people without showing any pity

♦ **cruelly** •ADVERB• in a cruel way or with cruelty
♦ **cruelty** •NOUN• being cruel

cruet •NOUN• **cruets** a container for holding small jars of pepper, salt and mustard put on a table during meals

cruise •VERB• **cruises, cruising, cruised** to cruise is to travel by ship, plane or car at a steady speed
•NOUN• **cruises** a holiday spent on a ship, travelling from one port to another
♦ **cruiser** •NOUN• **cruisers** a kind of fast warship

crumb •NOUN• **crumbs 1** crumbs are small pieces of bread, cake or biscuit **2** a crumb of something is a tiny piece of it: *a crumb of comfort*

crumble •VERB• **crumbles, crumbling, crumbled** to crumble is to break down into small pieces: *The walls of the old house were crumbling.*
♦ **crumbly** •ADJECTIVE• **crumblier, crumbliest** breaking down easily into small pieces the size of crumbs: *dry crumbly soil*

crumpet •NOUN• **crumpets** a type of small thick pancake with holes in the top

crumple •VERB• **crumples, crumpling, crumpled** to crumple something is to crush it or squeeze it so that lots of wrinkles or folds are made in it: *He crumpled the piece of paper and threw it in the bin.*

crunch •VERB• **crunches, crunching, crunched 1** if you crunch food you make a crushing noise as you break it up with your teeth **2** to crunch is to make a crushing or grinding noise: *The snow crunched under our feet.*
•NOUN• **crunches** a crushing or grinding noise: *the crunch of feet on the gravel path*
• **come to the crunch** to come to the crunch is to reach the point when you must make a decision of some kind
♦ **crunchy** •ADJECTIVE• **crunchier, crunchiest** crunchy food is hard and brittle

crusade •NOUN• **crusades** a campaign, often over a long period of time, in which people try to achieve something that they feel strongly about
♦ **crusader** •NOUN• **crusaders** someone who goes on a crusade

Aa Bb Cc Dd Ee Ff Gg Hh Ii Jj Kk Ll Mm Nn Oo Pp Qq Rr Ss Tt Uu Vv Ww Xx Yy Zz

crush •VERB• **crushes, crushing, crushed** 1 to crush something is to press it or squash it so that it is broken or damaged: *His leg was crushed by a falling rock.* 2 to crush something is to grind it or press it into a pulp or powder: *crush two cloves of garlic*
•NOUN• **crushes** 1 a crush is a crowd of people squeezed tightly together 2 to have a crush on someone older is to feel love for them, usually only for a short time
♦ **crushed** •ADJECTIVE• 1 broken or squashed by a heavy weight: *crushed ice* 2 completely defeated and miserable: *He felt crushed by their criticism.*

crust •NOUN• **crusts** 1 a crisp top or surface that forms on something, for example on bread or pastry as it bakes in the oven 2 the Earth's crust is its outside
♦ **crusty** •ADJECTIVE• **crustier, crustiest** having a crisp baked crust: *a delicious crusty pie*

crustacean •NOUN• **crustaceans** a sea animal with a hard outer shell, such as a crab, lobster or shrimp

crutch •NOUN• **crutches** a stick held under the armpit or elbow used as a support by someone with an injured leg or foot

cry •VERB• **cries, crying, cried** 1 to cry is to shout: *He cried out in pain.* 2 you cry when tears fall from your eyes, and often make a sobbing or wailing sound at the same time
•NOUN• **cries** a shout
• **a far cry** if people say that one thing is a far cry from another they mean it comes nowhere near or is nothing like that other thing

crypt •NOUN• **crypts** an underground room built beneath a church

cryptic •ADJECTIVE• having a hidden meaning or answer that is difficult to work out: *a cryptic crossword clue*

crystal •NOUN• **crystals** 1 a small, shaped part of a solid material that is formed naturally, for example in salt or ice or a mineral 2 a kind of high-quality glass
♦ **crystalline** •ADJECTIVE• with regularly shaped parts, as in a mineral
♦ **crystallize** or **crystallise** •VERB• **crystallizes, crystallizing, crystallized** a substance crystallizes when it forms crystals

♦ **crystallization** •NOUN• the process of forming crystals

cub •NOUN• **cubs** 1 a baby lion, tiger, bear or wolf 2 a member of the Cub Scouts, the junior branch of the Scout Association

cube •NOUN• **cubes** 1 a solid shape with six equally sized square sides 2 the cube of a number is the number you get when you multiply the number by itself twice. For example, the cube of 2 is $2 \times 2 \times 2$, which is 8. Look up and compare **square**

cubic •ADJECTIVE• 1 shaped like a cube 2 a cubic measurement is one used to measure volume. For example, a cubic metre is a space one metre long, one metre wide and one metre high 3 a cubic number is a number that has been multiplied by itself twice, for example $2 \times 2 \times 2$. Look up and compare **square**

cubicle •NOUN• **cubicles** a small enclosed area that has enough space for one person to stand in, for example when they are changing their clothes

cuboid •NOUN• **cuboids** a solid shape with six faces that are all rectangular

cuckoo •NOUN• **cuckoos** a bird that gets its name from the call it makes. The female cuckoo lays her eggs in other birds' nests

cucumber •NOUN• **cucumbers** a long green vegetable that is usually sliced and eaten raw in salads

cud •NOUN• a cow, goat or deer chews the cud when it brings partly digested food back up from its stomach to chew again

cuddle •VERB• **cuddles, cuddling, cuddled** to cuddle someone is to hold them in your arms to show your love and affection for them
•NOUN• **cuddles** if you give someone a cuddle, you put your arms around them and hold them closely
♦ **cuddly** •ADJECTIVE• **cuddlier, cuddliest** a cuddly person or thing makes you want to cuddle them

cudgel •NOUN• **cudgels** a heavy stick

cue[1] •NOUN• **cues** a signal to a performer to start doing something
• **on cue** if something happens on cue, it happens at exactly the right moment

cue ² •NOUN• **cues** a long tapered stick used to play snooker and billiards

cuff •NOUN• **cuffs** a cuff is the end of a sleeve where it fits tightly around the wrist
•VERB• **cuffs, cuffing, cuffed** to cuff someone is to hit them with your hand

cufflinks •PLURAL NOUN• cufflinks are decorative fasteners for shirt cuffs

cuisine •NOUN• cooking or a particular style of cooking: *French cuisine*

cul-de-sac •NOUN• **cul-de-sacs** a street that is blocked at one end

cull •NOUN• **culls** a cull is the organized killing of a number of animals
•VERB• **culls, culling, culled** to cull animals is to kill them

culminate •VERB• **culminates, culminating, culminated** to end or to reach the most important point: *The celebrations culminated in a fireworks display.*
♦ **culmination** •NOUN• the end of something

culprit •NOUN• **culprits** someone who is responsible for doing something bad

cult •NOUN• **cults** 1 a religion, especially one with secret or strange beliefs and rituals 2 a person or thing that becomes a cult becomes very popular

cultivate •VERB• **cultivates, cultivating, cultivated** 1 to cultivate land is to prepare it so that you can grow things on it
2 to cultivate a crop is to grow it and look after it
3 to cultivate something is to work at it so that grows or develops: *cultivate a friendship*
♦ **cultivation** •NOUN• preparing land to grow crops, or growing and looking after crops

cultural •ADJECTIVE• to do with culture, especially art, music and literature

culture •NOUN• **cultures** 1 a culture is a society with its own customs and beliefs that set them apart from other people or societies 2 culture is things like music, literature and painting that you learn about to develop your mind
♦ **cultured** •ADJECTIVE• a cultured person is well educated in things like art, music and literature

cumbersome •ADJECTIVE• awkward to carry or awkward to deal with

cunning •NOUN• someone who has cunning has the ability to get what they want by secret and clever planning
•ADJECTIVE• sly and clever: *I have a cunning plan.*

cup •NOUN• **cups** 1 a small container with a handle that you drink out of: *cups and saucers* 2 a decorated metal object or container used as a prize in a competition: *the World Cup*
•VERB• **cups, cupping, cupped** to cup your hands is to put them together and bend them into a bowl shape

cupboard •NOUN• **cupboards** a box with shelves, either built into a wall or standing on the floor, used to store things in

cupful •NOUN• **cupfuls** the amount a cup will hold

curable •ADJECTIVE• a curable disease can be cured

curate •NOUN• **curates** a priest whose job is to help a parish priest

curator •NOUN• **curators** a person in charge of a museum or gallery

curb •VERB• **curbs, curbing, curbed** to curb something is to control it or hold it back: *He tried hard to curb his spending.*

curd •NOUN• **curds** 1 curd is milk that has been thickened by adding acid to it 2 curds are the slightly solid lumps separated out from milk and used to make cheese. The liquid left over is called whey

curdle •VERB• **curdles, curdling, curdled** 1 milk curdles when it thickens because it has gone bad 2 if something makes your blood curdle it terrifies you

cure •VERB• **cures, curing, cured** 1 to cure a disease or illness is to make it go away
2 to cure a problem is to solve it and make it go away
3 to cure meat is to put salt on it or dry it to make it last longer
•NOUN• **cures** something that makes a disease or illness go away: *a cure for cancer*
⇒ **curable**

curfew •NOUN• **curfews** an official order

that people must stay inside their houses after a certain time or between certain hours

curious • ADJECTIVE• **1** if you are curious about something you want to know about it **2** if something is curious it is strange or difficult to understand

♦ **curiosity** • NOUN• **curiosities 1** curiosity is being curious **2** a curiosity is something strange and interesting

curl • NOUN• **curls** a soft twist or ring of hair: *blonde curls*

• VERB• **curls, curling, curled 1** to curl hair is to form soft twists or rings in it **2** smoke curls when it moves upwards in twisted or curving shapes **3** to **curl up** is to tuck your legs and arms in close to your body and bend your back in a curve

♦ **curler** • NOUN• **curlers 1** a tube of plastic or sponge that hair is wound around to make it curly **2** someone who plays the game of curling

⇒ **curling, curly**

curlew • NOUN• **curlews** a type of wild bird with a very long curved bill and long legs

curling • NOUN• a game played by sliding heavy round stones over ice towards a target stone

curly • ADJECTIVE• **curlier, curliest** having a curl or curls: *a curly tail* • *curly hair*

currant • NOUN• **currants** a small dried grape

currency • NOUN• **currencies** the money used in a particular country: *The euro is the new European currency.*

current • ADJECTIVE• something is current if it exists or is happening now: *the current job market*

• NOUN• **currents 1** a current is a flow of water or air going in one direction **2** an electric current is a flow of electricity through a wire or circuit

ⓘ Be careful not to confuse the spellings of **current** and **currant**.

current account • NOUN• **current accounts** a bank account that allows you to take money out at any time

curriculum • NOUN• **curriculums** *or* **curricula**

a curriculum is a course of study or all the courses of study at a school or college

curriculum vitae • NOUN• someone's curriculum vitae is a document that gives details of their education and working career. Curriculum vitae is usually shortened to **CV**

curry • NOUN• **curries** a type of food cooked with spices

curse • NOUN• **curses 1** a swearword **2** if someone puts a curse on you they say a magic spell that will cause you to have bad luck **3** something you have to put up with even though it is hard

• VERB• **curses, cursing, cursed 1** to curse is to use swearwords **2** to curse someone or something is to complain angrily about them

cursor • NOUN• **cursors** a flashing mark on a computer screen that shows you where to start keying in information

curt • ADJECTIVE• short and sounding unfriendly: *a curt reply*

curtain • NOUN• **curtains** a long piece of material that can be drawn or dropped across a window, stage or cinema screen

curtsy *or* **curtsey** • VERB• **curtsies, curtsying** *or* **curtseying, curtsied** a woman or girl curtsies when she bends her knees with one leg behind the other: *All the girls curtsied to the princess.*

• NOUN• **curtsies** a curtsy is this movement made to show respect to someone important

curve • NOUN• **curves** a curve is a line that bends

• VERB• **curves, curving, curved** to curve is to bend

cushion • NOUN• **cushions 1** a soft plump pad of material that you sit on, rest against or kneel on **2** something that gives protection or keeps something off a hard surface

• VERB• **cushions, cushioning, cushioned** to cushion a blow is to make it less painful

cushy • ADJECTIVE• **cushier, cushiest** easy to do: *a cushy job*

custard • NOUN• a thick dessert made from eggs, milk or cream, and sugar

custody •NOUN• 1 someone who is in custody is being kept in a cell until they can be charged with a crime 2 to have custody of children is to have the right to keep them

custom •NOUN• **customs** 1 a custom is something that people usually or traditionally do: *Japanese customs* • *It is my custom to walk to the station each morning.* 2 you give a shop your custom when you buy things from it
♦ **customary** •ADJECTIVE• something that is customary is usual or is done by custom
⇒ **customer**

custom-built or **custom-made** •ADJECTIVE• something that is custom-built is built for a particular purpose

customer •NOUN• **customers** a person who buys things or services from a shop or business

customize or **customise** •VERB• **customizes, customizing, customized** to customize something is to make changes to it so that it suits an individual person

customs •NOUN• customs is the place where you have your luggage inspected when you travel to and from a foreign country

cut •VERB• **cuts, cutting, cut** 1 to cut something is to divide it, separate it, make a hole in it or shape it, using scissors, a knife or some other sharp instrument
2 to make something less: *My mother cut my pocket money.*
3 to **cut off** something such as gas or electricity is to stop it being supplied to a home
4 if someone tells you to **cut it out**, they are telling you to stop doing something
•NOUN• 1 a split or small wound made by something sharp 2 a share of something
⇒ **cutting**

cute •ADJECTIVE• **cuter, cutest** 1 attractive or pretty: *a cute little puppy* 2 smart or clever: *Don't try to be cute with me.*

cutlass •NOUN• **cutlasses** a curved sword that is sharp along only one edge

cutlery •NOUN• cutlery is knives, forks and spoons

cutlet •NOUN• **cutlets** a piece of food cut from a larger piece

cutting •NOUN• **cuttings** 1 an article cut out of a newpaper or magazine 2 a piece cut off a plant from which a new plant will grow

cyanide •NOUN• a kind of deadly poison

cyber- •PREFIX• if a word starts with **cyber-** it has something to do with communication by computers and other electronic devices, as happens on the Internet. For example, *cyberspace* is the space used in electronic communication rather than real space

cycle •VERB• **cycles, cycling, cycled** to cycle is to ride a bicycle
•NOUN• **cycles** 1 a bicycle 2 a series of things that happen one after the other and then start again: *the cycle of the seasons*
♦ **cyclist** •NOUN• **cyclists** someone riding a bicycle

cyclone •NOUN• **cyclones** a large storm that happens in tropical countries, with high winds circling round a calm centre called the eye of the storm

cygnet •NOUN• **cygnets** a baby swan

cylinder •NOUN• **cylinders** a solid shape with a round top and bottom and straight sides
♦ **cylindrical** •ADJECTIVE• shaped like a cylinder

cymbals •PLURAL NOUN• two circles of brass that are banged together to make a musical sound

cynic •NOUN• **cynics** someone who sees something bad in everyone and everything no matter how good they may be
♦ **cynical** •ADJECTIVE• a cynical person believes the worst about everyone and everything
♦ **cynicism** •NOUN• the belief that something bad can be found in everything, no matter how good it may seem

cypress •NOUN• **cypresses** a type of tall tree with dark green needles

cyst •NOUN• **cysts** a lump filled with liquid on or just under the skin

czar •NOUN• **czars** another spelling of **tsar**

czarina •NOUN• **czarinas** another spelling of **tsarina**

Aa
Bb
Cc
Dd
Ee
Ff
Gg
Hh
Ii
Jj
Kk
Ll
Mm
Nn
Oo
Pp
Qq
Rr
Ss
Tt
Uu
Vv
Ww
Xx
Yy
Zz

Dd

dab • VERB• **dabs, dabbing, dabbed** to touch lightly with your fingers or something soft: *Dab your eyes with a tissue.*
• NOUN• **dabs** a light touch of something: *a dab of blusher on each cheek*

dabble • VERB• **dabbles, dabbling, dabbled** to dabble in an activity is to do it for fun but not very seriously: *He was a rich man who dabbled in many hobbies that happened to take his fancy.*

dachshund • NOUN• **dachshunds** a type of dog with short legs and a long body

dad *or* **daddy** • NOUN• **dads** *or* **daddies** a word that people use for **father**, especially when speaking: *Thanks to all the mums and dads who have helped.*

daffodil • NOUN• **daffodils** a yellow flower that grows from a bulb and blooms in spring

daft • ADJECTIVE• **dafter, daftest** silly: *a daft thing to do*

dagger • NOUN• **daggers** a knife like a small sword

daily • ADJECTIVE• happening or done every day: *a daily newspaper*
• ADVERB• every day: *We met daily for a month.*
• NOUN• **dailies** a newspaper that is published every weekday

dainty • ADJECTIVE• **daintier, daintiest** small and neat

dairy • NOUN• **dairies** 1 a place where products like butter and cheese are made from milk 2 a shop where you can buy products made from milk
• ADJECTIVE• dairy farming is keeping cows to produce milk

daisy • NOUN• **daisies** a type of small white flower with a yellow centre. Daisies often grow wild in grass

(i) The word **daisy** has been changed from **day's eye**. It was called this because the flower opens during the day.

dale • NOUN• **dales** a valley

Dalmatian • NOUN• **Dalmatians** a type of large dog that has a white coat with dark spots

dam • NOUN• **dams** a wall across a river that holds a lot of the water back
• VERB• **dams, damming, dammed** to build a wall across a river to stop it from flowing naturally

damage • NOUN• any kind of harm that has been done: *No lasting damage has been found.*
♦ **damages** • PLURAL NOUN• an amount of money that someone gets to make up for a loss or injury
• VERB• **damages, damaging, damaged** to hurt, spoil or break something

dame • NOUN• **dames** 1 in Britain, a title that can be given to a woman who has done something remarkable 2 a woman's part in pantomime that is usually played by a man

damn • INTERJECTION• an impolite word that someone who is very irritated might use
• VERB• **damns, damning, damned** to blame someone or say that they are very bad

damp • ADJECTIVE• **damper, dampest** a bit wet: *Wipe with a damp cloth.*
• NOUN• slight wetness: *a patch of damp on the wall*
♦ **dampen** • VERB• **dampens, dampening, dampened** to make something a bit wet: *Dampen the brush before using it.*

damson • NOUN• **damsons** a small type of plum

dance • VERB• **dances, dancing, danced** to move your feet to a rhythm, usually in music
• NOUN• **dances** 1 a set of steps that you do to some kind of music 2 a party for dancing
♦ **dancer** • NOUN• **dancers** someone who dances

dandelion • NOUN• **dandelions** a yellow flower that is a common weed in people's gardens

(i) **Dandelion** comes from the French phrase **dent de lion**, which means *lion's tooth*. This describes what the long, thin petals look like.

dandruff •NOUN• tiny dry flakes of dead skin that can collect near the roots of hair: *an anti-dandruff shampoo*

danger •NOUN• **dangers** something that may harm or injure you: *the dangers of skiing*
♦ **dangerous** •ADJECTIVE• 1 likely to hurt someone: *a dangerous substance* 2 risky: *It's dangerous to play near the railway.*
♦ **dangerously** •ADVERB• in a way that could be harmful: *driving dangerously close to the edge*

dangle •VERB• **dangles, dangling, dangled** to hang down loosely: *Her hair dangled in her eyes.*

dank •ADJECTIVE• **danker, dankest** wet and cold

dappled •ADJECTIVE• covered with patches of light or colour: *a dappled horse*

dare •VERB• **dares, daring, dared** 1 to dare someone to do something is to challenge them to do it: *I dare you to do that again!* 2 to dare to do something is to be brave enough to do it: *I wouldn't dare to argue with the headmaster.*

daredevil •NOUN• **daredevils** a person who enjoys danger and taking risks
•ADJECTIVE• dangerous or risky: *a daredevil project*

dark •ADJECTIVE• **darker, darkest** 1 without light: *a dark room*
2 strong or deep in colour: *dark blue*
3 gloomy, sad or miserable
•NOUN• 1 where there is no light: *I'm not afraid of the dark.* 2 nightfall: *Don't go out after dark without a torch.*
• **in the dark** if you are in the dark about something, you know nothing about it
♦ **darken** •VERB• **darkens, darkening, darkened** to get or make darker: *The sky darkened as the rain moved nearer.*
♦ **darkness** •NOUN• where there is no light: *a tiny point of light in the darkness*

darling •ADJECTIVE• very dear
•NOUN• **darlings** 1 someone you care very much about: *My darling, what's the matter?*

2 someone's favourite: *The child had been her darling since his first day in the class.*

darn •VERB• **darns, darning, darned** to mend a hole by sewing it up

dart •VERB• **darts, darting, darted** to move fast in a straight line: *A child darted out of the door as I entered.*
•NOUN• **darts** a little arrow that can be fired as a weapon or thrown in a game
♦ **darts** •NOUN• a game where you throw small arrow-shaped objects at a round board called a dartboard that has scores on it

dash •VERB• **dashes, dashing, dashed** to hurry somewhere: *I've got to dash to the shops.*
•NOUN• **dashes** 1 a rush to get somewhere: *a mad dash to the airport*
2 a small amount of something that you add to food or drink: *Add a dash of vinegar.*
3 a short line (–) between words in a text: *You could use a dash instead of a colon there.*

dashboard •NOUN• **dashboards** the panel in front of the driver of a car, containing dials or gauges for things like speed, petrol and oil

data •NOUN• information or facts

(i) **Data** is the plural of **datum**. The singular, **datum**, is not often used. In fact, **data** is usually used with a singular verb, although it is a plural noun: *The data is clear.*

database •NOUN• **databases** information that is stored on a computer in lists or tables

date [1] •NOUN• **dates** 1 the number of a day of a month or a year: *The date today is 30 July.*
2 a particular day of a particular month and year: *It was on that date that I left home.*
3 an arrangement to go out with someone: *Polly's got another date with Chris tonight.*
•VERB• **dates, dating, dated** 1 to decide how old something is: *The ring's very old but I couldn't date it exactly.*
2 to belong to a certain time: *Our house dates from the nineteenth century.*
3 to look old-fashioned: *Shoes always date very quickly.*

date [2] •NOUN• **dates** a small, dark fruit with a stone that grows on some palm trees

daub •VERB• **daubs, daubing, daubed** to put something like paint on a surface untidily

Aa
Bb
Cc
Dd
Ee
Ff
Gg
Hh
Ii
Jj
Kk
Ll
Mm
Nn
Oo
Pp
Qq
Rr
Ss
Tt
Uu
Vv
Ww
Xx
Yy
Zz

daughter • NOUN• **daughters** someone's female child: *She was the daughter of a poet.*

daughter-in-law • NOUN• **daughters-in-law** your son's wife

daunt • VERB• **daunts, daunting, daunted** 1 something that is daunting is off-putting because it is big, dangerous or difficult: *the daunting height of the next jump* 2 you are daunted by something if it puts you off doing something: *somewhat daunted by the cost of the project*

dawdle • VERB• **dawdles, dawdling, dawdled** to walk or do something slowly

dawn • NOUN• **dawns** the beginning of the day, when it gets light
• VERB• **dawns, dawning, dawned** 1 to start: *A new age has dawned.* 2 to **dawn on** someone is suddenly to become clear: *It dawned on him that he could pay someone else to do this.*

day • NOUN• **days** 1 the time of light between sunrise and sunset
2 the twenty-four hours between one midnight and another: *There are 365 days in a year.*
3 a time or period: *in my grandfather's day*

daydream • VERB• **daydreams, daydreaming, daydreamed** to think about things you would like to happen instead of concentrating on what you are meant to be doing

daze • VERB• **dazes, dazing, dazed** to make someone feel confused and unable to see or think straight
• NOUN• **dazes** to be **in a daze** is to be confused or unable to think clearly: *I stood there not knowing what to do, staring after her in a daze.*

dazzle • VERB• **dazzles, dazzling, dazzled** a light dazzles you when it shines so brightly that you cannot see properly

dead • ADJECTIVE• 1 no longer living: *a dead poet* 2 no longer working or active: *The telephone line's dead.*
• ADVERB• 1 completely: *He just stopped dead in front of me.* 2 exactly: *standing dead in the centre of the circle*
• NOUN• 1 the dead are all the people who

have died 2 the dead of night is the stillest part of it

dead end • NOUN• **dead ends** a road or path that does not lead anywhere

dead heat • NOUN• **dead heats** a competition that two people finish at exactly the same time

deadline • NOUN• **deadlines** the time when something, such as a piece of work, must be finished

deadly • ADJECTIVE• **deadlier, deadliest** able to kill: *a deadly poison*

deaf • ADJECTIVE• **deafer, deafest** not able to hear properly: *Grandma grew deafer and deafer as she got older.*
♦ **deafen** • VERB• **deafens, deafening, deafened** to make a person deaf or feel deaf: *The explosion deafened us for a moment.*
♦ **deafening** • ADJECTIVE• unpleasantly loud: *The music was deafening and we had to leave.*
♦ **deafness** • NOUN• being deaf

deal • NOUN• **deals** 1 an agreement, especially in business: *I think that's a fair deal.*
2 an amount of something: *a great deal of money*
3 a handing out of something, especially playing cards: *It's your deal.*
• VERB• **deals, dealing, dealt** 1 to give small amounts of something to a lot of people: *You deal the cards this time.*
2 to buy and sell: *They deal in luxury fabrics.*
3 to **deal with** a person or situation, especially a problem, is to do something about it: *The manager deals with all complaints personally.*
4 a text or speech that **deals with** something is about that subject: *a book dealing with birds*
♦ **dealer** • NOUN• **dealers** someone who buys and sells things: *an antiques dealer*
♦ **dealings** • PLURAL NOUN• someone's dealings are the business arrangements they make

dear • ADJECTIVE• **dearer, dearest** 1 a thing or person that is dear to you is important because you love them: *my dear old teddy*

2 expensive: *too dear for me to buy*
3 the word you use with the name of a person at the beginning of a letter: *Dear Mary*
• NOUN• **dears** a person that is very lovable: *Nancy is such a dear.*
✦ **dearly** • ADVERB• very much: *Of course she loves him dearly.*

dearth • NOUN• a shortage of something: *a dearth of good maths teachers*

death • NOUN• **deaths** the time when a person or animal stops living: *written just before the poet's death*
✦ **deathly** • ADJECTIVE• like a thing or person that is dead: *a deathly hush*

debate • NOUN• **debates** a public discussion or argument, for example on television or in parliament
• VERB• **debates, debating, debated** to discuss a lot of different aspects of something

debris • NOUN• the bits of something that has broken up: *the debris of a wrecked ship*

debt • NOUN• **debts** 1 something, especially money, that a person owes someone 2 if you are **in debt**, you owe someone money

début • NOUN• **débuts** the first time a performer appears in public: *The pair made their début at the King's Theatre in 1999.*

dec- *or* **deca-** • PREFIX• if a word starts with **dec-** or **deca-** it often has something to do with the number ten. For example, a *decagon* is a shape with ten sides

decade • NOUN• **decades** a period of ten years: *the third decade of the twentieth century*

decagon • NOUN• **decagons** a flat shape with ten straight sides

decathlon • NOUN• **decathlons** an athletics competition that has ten different kinds of sporting contest

decay • VERB• **decays, decaying, decayed** to go rotten
• NOUN• going bad or rotting: *tooth decay*

deceased • ADJECTIVE• a formal word meaning **dead**
• NOUN• the deceased is the dead person that has already been mentioned: *It's clear that*

the deceased did not know his attacker.

deceit • NOUN• **deceits** lies and trickery
✦ **deceitful** • ADJECTIVE• not telling the truth

deceive • VERB• **deceives, deceiving, deceived** to fool or trick someone by telling lies or suggesting something is true: *The sun deceived me into thinking it was warm outside.*
✦ **deceiver** • NOUN• **deceivers** someone who deceives another person
⇒ **deception**

December • NOUN• the twelfth month of the year, after November and before January

ⓘ December was the tenth month of the Roman year and the name comes from the word **decem**, which means *ten* in Latin.

decency • NOUN• **decencies** respectable and reasonable behaviour
✦ **decent** • ADJECTIVE• 1 good, honest and respectable: *a decent family* 2 acceptable or good enough: *a decent salary*

deception • NOUN• **deceptions** 1 deception is not telling the truth 2 a deception is a trick or lie
✦ **deceptive** • ADJECTIVE• not showing the true situation: *The photo's deceptive – I'm actually much older than I look there.*

decibel • NOUN• **decibels** a unit that is used for measuring how loud a sound is

decide • VERB• **decides, deciding, decided** 1 to make up your mind to do something: *Greg's decided to turn over a new leaf.* 2 to choose: *I can't decide between the blue one and the green one.* 3 to bring about a result: *That mistake decided the match.*
✦ **decided** • ADJECTIVE• definite: *a decided improvement*
✦ **decidedly** • ADVERB• very much: *You will feel decidedly better after a rest.*
⇒ **decision**

deciduous • ADJECTIVE• a deciduous plant does not have leaves in the winter. Look up and compare **evergreen**

decimal • ADJECTIVE• based on a system of tens or tenths: *decimal fractions*

Aa Bb Cc Dd Ee Ff Gg Hh Ii Jj Kk Ll Mm Nn Oo Pp Qq Rr Ss Tt Uu Vv Ww Xx Yy Zz

Aa

Bb

Cc

Dd

Ee

Ff

Gg

Hh

Ii

Jj

Kk

Ll

Mm

Nn

Oo

Pp

Qq

Rr

Ss

Tt

Uu

Vv

Ww

Xx

Yy

Zz

•NOUN• **decimals** a fraction shown as a number of tenths and hundredths: *A half, written as a decimal, is 0.5.*

decimal point •NOUN• **decimal points** the dot after the whole units and before the tenths in a decimal: *To multiply by ten, just move the decimal point to the right.*

decipher •VERB• **deciphers, deciphering, deciphered** to make sense of something, such as a coded message: *Philip's handwriting has always been difficult to decipher.*

decision •NOUN• **decisions** something that you have decided: *It was a very difficult decision to make, and I had to think hard before making a choice.*

♦ **decisive** •ADJECTIVE• **1** a decisive person is good at making up their mind quickly and firmly **2** a decisive action is firm and makes a difference to a result: *a decisive attack by the team*

deck •NOUN• **decks 1** a deck of a boat is one of its levels or the part you can walk on outside

2 a pack of playing cards: *your turn to shuffle the deck*

3 the turning part of a record player or tape recorder: *a stereo with a double tape deck*

deckchair •NOUN• **deckchairs** a folding chair for sitting outside and relaxing in

declare •VERB• **declares, declaring, declared** to announce something firmly: *She suddenly declared that she was leaving.*

♦ **declaration** •NOUN• **declarations** a clear or official announcement: *a declaration of war*

decline •VERB• **declines, declining, declined 1** to refuse an offer **2** to get weaker, worse or less: *The president's popularity has sharply declined.*

decode •VERB• **decodes, decoding, decoded** to work out the meaning of a coded message

decompose •VERB• **decomposes, decomposing, decomposed** to rot

decorate •VERB• **decorates, decorating, decorated 1** to add something fancy to something plain to make it look nicer: *We'll* decorate the cake with roses made of sugar. **2** to paint or paper the inside of a room **3** to give someone a medal or an award for doing something special: *He was decorated for bravery in the war.*

♦ **decoration** •NOUN• **decorations 1** decoration is adding things to improve the look of something **2** an ornament that makes something look better: *Christmas decorations*

♦ **decorator** •NOUN• **decorators** a person whose job is to paint and paper rooms

decorum •NOUN• proper and dignified behaviour

decoy •NOUN• **decoys** a thing or person that leads someone into a trap

decrease •VERB• **decreases, decreasing, decreased** to make or become less: *Jordan's interest in football has decreased as he's got older.*

•NOUN• **decreases** the amount that something decreases

decree •VERB• **decrees, decreeing, decreed** to announce publicly that something should happen •NOUN• **decrees** an official order or statement that something should happen

decrepit •ADJECTIVE• old and in bad condition

dedicate •VERB• **dedicates, dedicating, dedicated 1** to dedicate time to something is to spend time doing only that: *She dedicated her whole life to music.* **2** to mention someone's name right at the beginning of a work you have written, because they are important to you: *The author dedicated his play to his daughter.*

deduce •VERB• **deduces, deducing, deduced** to work something out from a lot of bits of information
⇒ **deduction**

deduct •VERB• **deducts, deducting, deducted** to take an amount away from a larger figure: *My wages have already had tax deducted from them.*

deduction •NOUN• **deductions 1** an amount that you take away from a bigger figure **2** something that you work out from all the information you have

deed • NOUN• **deeds** 1 something that someone has done: *my good deed for the day* 2 an official document that shows who owns something

deep • ADJECTIVE• **deeper, deepest** 1 going a long way down: *Is the river very deep?* 2 very low in tone: *a deep voice* 3 reaching a long way back: *a deep border of roses* 4 very strong: *deep blue* • *deep dislike* • ADVERB• **deeper, deepest** 1 in a downward direction: *a hole a metre deep* 2 from front to back: *rows of soldiers standing four deep*
♦ **deepen** • VERB• **deepens, deepening, deepened** 1 to go further down or back: *The river deepens here to more than 2 metres.* 2 to get stronger: *a deepening gloom*
♦ **deeply** • ADVERB• very much: *deeply in love*
⇒ **depth**

deer • NOUN• **deer** an animal with four thin legs that runs very fast and gracefully. A male deer has antlers like branches that grow on its head

ⓘ The singular and plural forms of **deer** are the same: *a deer in the woods* • *two deer in the park*.

deface • VERB• **defaces, defacing, defaced** to spoil the way something looks

defeat • VERB• **defeats, defeating, defeated** to beat someone in a competition or war • NOUN• **defeats** 1 a defeat is a game or a battle that you have lost 2 defeat is being beaten at something

defect [1] • NOUN• **defects** a fault that stops something from working properly: *a heart defect*
♦ **defective** • ADJECTIVE• having something wrong with it: *a defective computer program*

defect [2] • VERB• **defects, defecting, defected** to go over to the other side, for example to a different political party or an enemy country: *The spy defected to the United States.*
♦ **defection** • NOUN• **defections** going over to the other side
♦ **defector** • NOUN• **defectors** someone who defects

ⓘ Remember that the noun **de**-fect is pronounced with the stress at the beginning, but the verb de-**fect** has the stress at the end.

defence • NOUN• **defences** 1 protection against attack: *The wall was the city's main defence.* 2 protecting yourself against attack or criticism: *In my defence, I was only doing what I was told.* 3 in a court case, the side that tries to help a person who is accused of doing something wrong

defenceless • ADJECTIVE• defenceless people, animals or places have no way of protecting themselves: *a defenceless baby seal*

defend • VERB• **defends, defending, defended** to protect someone or something from being attacked: *Kim always defends his little brother if people say he's too quiet.*
♦ **defendant** • NOUN• **defendants** a person that is accused of committing a crime in a court case
♦ **defensive** • ADJECTIVE• 1 designed to protect: *defensive weapons* 2 worried about being criticized: *a defensive look*

defer • VERB• **defers, deferring, deferred** to put something off until later: *The meeting has been deferred until more people can come.*

defiance • NOUN• openly going against someone or something they have said: *Pamela went out, in defiance of her parents' instructions.*
♦ **defiant** • ADJECTIVE• refusing to obey: *a defiant child*
♦ **defiantly** • ADVERB• purposely not obeying: *John defiantly refused to go.*

deficiency • NOUN• **deficiencies** an amount that is less than it should be: *a deficiency of B vitamins*
♦ **deficient** • ADJECTIVE• without enough of something: *The team is deficient in communication skills.*

deficit • NOUN• **deficits** how much less money you really have than you expected to have: *The accounts show a deficit of several pounds.*

Aa
Bb
Cc
Dd
Ee
Ff
Gg
Hh
Ii
Jj
Kk
Ll
Mm
Nn
Oo
Pp
Qq
Rr
Ss
Tt
Uu
Vv
Ww
Xx
Yy
Zz

define → delay

define •VERB• **defines, defining, defined**
1 to give the exact meaning of something like a word or phrase **2** to show the exact outline of something: *The edges of the car park are clearly defined by white lines.*
⇒ **definition**

definite •ADJECTIVE• certain: *It's not definite, but the wedding will probably be in August.*
♦ **definitely** •ADVERB• certainly, without a doubt: *We'll definitely be back by 10 o'clock.*

definite article •NOUN• **definite articles** the name used in grammar for the word **the**

ⓘ There are two kinds of article in English grammar: **the** is the *definite article* and **a** or **an** is the *indefinite article*.

definition •NOUN• **definitions** the meaning of a word or phrase

deflate •VERB• **deflates, deflating, deflated**
1 to let the air out of something that has been blown up, like a tyre or balloon **2** to make someone feel less confident or enthusiastic: *Feeling deflated, the team clapped the winners and tried to smile.*

deflect •VERB• **deflects, deflecting, deflected** to change the direction that something is supposed to be travelling in: *He deflected the blow with his arm.*
♦ **deflection** •NOUN• **deflections** a change of direction

deforestation •NOUN• cutting down large numbers of trees in an area

deform •VERB• **deforms, deforming, deformed** to spoil the shape of something
♦ **deformed** •ADJECTIVE• not shaped normally
♦ **deformity** •NOUN• **deformities** when something is badly shaped

defrost •VERB• **defrosts, defrosting, defrosted 1** to defrost frozen food is to make it ready to cook or eat: *Do not refreeze this product after defrosting it.* **2** to defrost a fridge or freezer is to remove the ice from it

deft •ADJECTIVE• **defter, deftest 1** a deft movement is quick and clever **2** a deft person moves neatly and skilfully
♦ **deftly** •ADVERB• quickly and skilfully

defy •VERB• **defies, defying, defied 1** to defy someone to do something is to challenge them to do it: *I defy you to do that again!*
2 to defy a person or something like a rule is to openly disobey them
3 to make something impossible: *a scene that defies description*
⇒ **defiance**

degenerate •VERB• **degenerates, degenerating, degenerated** to get worse: *Jonathan's work has degenerated since he moved schools.*

degrade •VERB• **degrades, degrading, degraded** to make someone feel that they are not important or not worth anything
♦ **degrading** •ADJECTIVE• making a person feel worthless

degree •NOUN• **degrees 1** a unit for measuring temperature, shown by the symbol °: *It's 30° (degrees) here today.*
2 a unit for measuring angles, shown by the symbol °: *An angle of 90° (degrees) is a right angle.*
3 a very small amount: *improving slowly by degrees*
4 a qualification that students can study for at a university or college

dehydrate •VERB• **dehydrates, dehydrating, dehydrated** to dry out
♦ **dehydrated** •ADJECTIVE• **1** dried because of having the water removed: *dehydrated food* **2** weak and ill because of not having enough water to drink
♦ **dehydration** •NOUN• being dried up because of not containing as much water as usual

déjà vu •NOUN• a strange feeling of having had the very same experience before

ⓘ This is pronounced day-ja voo.

dejected •ADJECTIVE• feeling very fed up
♦ **dejection** •NOUN• a very depressed feeling

delay •NOUN• **delays** the extra time you have to wait if something happens later than expected: *There was a delay of half an hour before take-off.*
•VERB• **delays, delaying, delayed 1** to put something off until later: *Don't delay –*

apply now! **2** to make someone or something late: *I was delayed by the arrival of an unexpected visitor.*

delegate • VERB• **delegates, delegating, delegated** to give someone a job to do, especially one that is your responsibility • NOUN• **delegates** a person who represents someone else at a meeting

♦ **delegation** • NOUN• **delegations** a group of representatives at a meeting or conference

delete • VERB• **deletes, deleting, deleted** to cross out or remove something from a text
♦ **deletion** • NOUN• **deletions** a deletion is a part of a text that has been removed

deliberate • ADJECTIVE• not accidental, but done on purpose: *a deliberate lie*
•VERB• **deliberates, deliberating, deliberated** to think seriously about something for a while: *We're still deliberating about what to do next.*

♦ **deliberately** • ADVERB• on purpose, not by accident: *They deliberately left the door open so that the mice could escape.*

♦ **deliberation** • NOUN• careful consideration of a matter: *After much deliberation, they reached a decision.*

delicacy • NOUN• **delicacies** something delicious and unusual to eat: *These eggs are regarded as a great delicacy in some countries.*

delicate • ADJECTIVE• **1** a delicate object can easily be broken
2 a delicate pattern is fine and dainty
3 a delicate person is often ill
4 a delicate situation needs careful attention to avoid a problem arising

delicatessen • NOUN• **delicatessens** a shop that sells cooked meat, cheese and other prepared foods

delicious • ADJECTIVE• very good to eat, drink or smell: *a delicious meal*

delight • NOUN• **delights** great pleasure: *Felicity squealed with delight when she saw us.*
•VERB• **delights, delighting, delighted** to please someone very much
♦ **delighted** • ADJECTIVE• very pleased: *We'd be delighted to come to the party.*

♦ **delightful** • ADJECTIVE• very pleasing

delinquent • NOUN• **delinquents** a person who behaves badly in the community, especially by breaking the law
♦ **delinquency** • NOUN• bad behaviour or law-breaking

delirious • ADJECTIVE• **1** being confused and unable to think normally because of being ill with a high temperature **2** extremely happy or excited: *Martha was delirious when she found she'd passed her exam.*
♦ **delirium** • NOUN• a confused state of mind that occurs when you have a very high temperature

deliver • VERB• **delivers, delivering, delivered 1** to deliver something is to take it to the door of someone's home or workplace: *We're delivering leaflets to all the houses in this area.*
2 to deliver a speech is to say it out loud
3 to deliver a baby is to help with its birth
♦ **delivery** • NOUN• **deliveries** when or how something is delivered

delta • NOUN• **deltas** the area like a triangle that is formed if a river splits into separate branches where it flows into the sea

delude • VERB• **deludes, deluding, deluded** to delude someone is to make them believe something that is not true
⇒ **delusion**

deluge • NOUN• **deluges 1** a downpour or flood **2** a large amount of anything
•VERB• **deluges, deluging, deluged** to be deluged with something is to receive lots and lots of it: *We have been deluged with entries for our latest competition.*

delusion • NOUN• **delusions** something that a person believes that is not true

delve • VERB• **delves, delving, delved** to look for something as if you are digging for it: *Nan was delving into her handbag for something.*

demand • VERB• **demands, demanding, demanded 1** to ask for something as if you are giving an order: *I demand to know where you've been!* **2** to need: *This work demanded all our skills.*
• NOUN• **demands 1** a request that is almost an order **2** a need: *There is not much demand for sun cream at this time of year.*

Aa Bb Cc Dd Ee Ff Gg Hh Ii Jj Kk Ll Mm Nn Oo Pp Qq Rr Ss Tt Uu Vv Ww Xx Yy Zz

Aa Bb Cc **Dd** Ee Ff Gg Hh Ii Jj Kk Ll Mm Nn Oo Pp Qq Rr Ss Tt Uu Vv Ww Xx Yy Zz

♦ **demanding** •ADJECTIVE• needing a lot of time or effort: *a very demanding job*

demeanour •NOUN• the way you behave: *Something in his demeanour made me suspicious.*

demented •ADJECTIVE• out of your mind: *demented with worry*

democracy •NOUN• **democracies** 1 a form of government where people elect representatives to lead them 2 a country that has an elected government
♦ **democrat** •NOUN• **democrats** a person who believes that people should be allowed to vote for their government
♦ **democratic** •ADJECTIVE• involving a system where people elect the government

demolish •VERB• **demolishes, demolishing, demolished** to knock down: *The flats will be demolished immediately.*
♦ **demolition** •NOUN• knocking a building down

demon •NOUN• **demons** an evil spirit

demonstrate •VERB• **demonstrates, demonstrating, demonstrated** 1 to show someone how to do something or how something works: *Can you demonstrate how to turn the machine on?* 2 to let people know how you feel about something, especially by marching or waving signs in public
♦ **demonstration** •NOUN• **demonstrations** 1 an explanation of how to do something or how something works: *a cookery demonstration* 2 an expression of how someone feels about something, especially by marching in public to protest about it: *a demonstration against nuclear weapons*
♦ **demonstrative** •ADJECTIVE• a demonstrative person often or easily shows how they are feeling
♦ **demonstrator** •NOUN• **demonstrators** 1 a person who takes part in a protest march or public show of feeling 2 a person who shows how something is done

demoralize or **demoralise** •VERB• **demoralizes, demoralizing, demoralized** to take away someone's confidence or courage

demure •ADJECTIVE• a word that is sometimes used to describe women or girls who are quiet, shy and modest

den •NOUN• **dens** 1 the home of a wild animal: *a lion's den* 2 a person's private place where they can get away from other people

denial •NOUN• **denials** saying that something is not true

denim •NOUN• a tough cotton fabric that jeans and other clothes are made out of

denominator •NOUN• **denominators** the number below the line in a fraction

denounce •VERB• **denounces, denouncing, denounced** to say publicly that something is bad or that someone has done something bad

dense •ADJECTIVE• **denser, densest** 1 thick or very closely packed together: *dense fog* • *a dense forest* 2 slow to understand something
♦ **density** •NOUN• **densities** 1 how thick or closely packed something is 2 how heavy something is for its size

dent •NOUN• **dents** a hollow in a surface caused by hitting: *a dent in the side of the car* •VERB• **dents, denting, dented** to hit something and make a hollow shape in it

dental •ADJECTIVE• to do with teeth: *dental hygiene*

dentist •NOUN• **dentists** a doctor for people's teeth
♦ **dentistry** •NOUN• the work of a dentist

dentures •PLURAL NOUN• a set of false teeth

deny •VERB• **denies, denying, denied** 1 to deny something is to say that it is not true: *Nina denied that she had stolen anything.* 2 to deny a request is to say 'no' to it 3 to deny yourself something is to do without something you want or need
⇒ **denial**

deodorant •NOUN• **deodorants** a product, such as a spray, that stops unpleasant smells

depart •VERB• **departs, departing, departed** to leave: *The train departs at 9.15.*
⇒ **departure**

department •NOUN• **departments** a section of a school, shop, business or government: *the new head of the English department*

departure • NOUN• **departures** a time when a thing or person leaves a place: *All departures are shown on the left of the timetable.*

depend • VERB• **depends, depending, depended** 1 to depend on someone or something is to rely on them: *Mother depends on us to do the shopping.* 2 to depend on something is to be the same until that thing changes: *The price of our fruit depends on the weather.*

◆ **dependable** • ADJECTIVE• if someone is dependable, you can rely on them

◆ **dependant** • NOUN• **dependants** someone who is looked after by someone else who pays for everything they need: *Fill in the names of all your dependants.*

◆ **dependent** • ADJECTIVE• relying on something or someone: *She became dependent on her aunt.*

◆ **dependence** • NOUN• not being able to do without something

depict • VERB• **depicts, depicting, depicted** to show or describe: *The sketch depicts a railway station.*

deplete • VERB• **depletes, depleting, depleted** to become depleted is to get smaller or less: *The food stores were being depleted.*

deplorable • ADJECTIVE• very bad

deplore • VERB• **deplores, deploring, deplored** to say or think that something is very bad

depopulate • VERB• **depopulates, depopulating, depopulated** to reduce the number of people who live in an area: *A war depopulated this region in the last century.*

◆ **depopulation** • NOUN• the process where fewer and fewer people live in an area

deport • VERB• **deports, deporting, deported** to be deported is to be sent out of a country

◆ **deportation** • NOUN• **deportations** sending someone out of a country

depose • VERB• **deposes, deposing, deposed** to be deposed is to be removed from an important position: *The president has been deposed.*

deposit • NOUN• **deposits** 1 part of the price of something that you pay in advance: *Pay a deposit now and we won't sell this to anyone else.*
2 an amount of money that you pay into a bank or building society account
3 a layer of something that is left behind or that forms over a long time: *A deposit of dust was everywhere when the builders left.*
• VERB• **deposits, depositing, deposited** 1 to put money in an account 2 to leave something behind: *Deposit your luggage here and pick it up later.*

◆ **deposition** • NOUN• deposition takes place when running water slows down and leaves mud and stones behind

deposit account • NOUN• **deposit accounts** a bank account that you use to save money in

depot • NOUN• **depots** 1 a place where vehicles like buses or trains are kept when they are not in use 2 a store: *a weapons depot*

ⓘ The final *t* of **depot** is silent.

depress • VERB• **depresses, depressing, depressed** to make someone gloomy or unhappy

◆ **depressed** • ADJECTIVE• gloomy or fed up

◆ **depressing** • ADJECTIVE• making a person feel gloomy: *depressing weather*

◆ **depression** • NOUN• **depressions** 1 feeling gloomy or fed up
2 a bad time when things are not going as well as usual
3 a hollow or dip in a surface: *a depression left where he'd been sitting in the sand*
4 a patch of low air pressure that often brings bad weather

deprive • VERB• **deprives, depriving, deprived** to deprive somebody of something is to take it away from them: *She's been deprived of sleep since the noisy neighbours moved in.*

◆ **deprived** • ADJECTIVE• not having all the things that are necessary for a basically good life: *a deprived area of the inner city*

◆ **deprivation** • NOUN• not having the basic things that people need

depth • NOUN• **depths** 1 how deep something is: *measure the depth of the water*

Aa
Bb
Cc
Dd
Ee
Ff
Gg
Hh
Ii
Jj
Kk
Ll
Mm
Nn
Oo
Pp
Qq
Rr
Ss
Tt
Uu
Vv
Ww
Xx
Yy
Zz

2 a deep place: *the depths of the ocean*
3 how strong something is: *the depth of the colour*
• **in depth** in great detail
• **out of your depth** involved in things too difficult for you to understand

deputy •NOUN• **deputies** 1 someone who takes over when the person in charge is not there: *the deputy head teacher* 2 someone's assistant: *the sheriff and all his deputies*

derail •VERB• **derails, derailing, derailed** to force a train to leave the track
♦ **derailment** •NOUN• **derailments** a derailment happens when a train comes off the track

deranged •ADJECTIVE• mad

derby •NOUN• **derbies** 1 a race, especially for horses 2 a sports match between two teams from the same area

derelict •ADJECTIVE• deserted and falling apart: *a derelict factory building*

deride •VERB• **derides, deriding, derided** to laugh at someone or something because you think they are ridiculous
♦ **derision** •NOUN• mocking laughter

derivation •NOUN• **derivations** where something, especially a word, comes from
♦ **derivative** •NOUN• **derivatives** a word that is formed from another word. For example, *derision* is a derivative of the verb *deride*

derogatory •ADJECTIVE• a derogatory remark is something rude or critical that someone says

derrick •NOUN• **derricks** 1 a crane, especially at docks 2 a tower over an oil well that supports the drilling machinery

descend •VERB• **descends, descending, descended** to go or climb downwards
♦ **descendant** •NOUN• **descendants** someone's descendants are the people who live at a later time in the same family
♦ **descended** •ADJECTIVE• to be descended from someone is to come after them in the same family
♦ **descent** •NOUN• **descents** 1 going or climbing downwards: *Our descent of the*

mountain was as hard as the upward climb.
2 a downward slope

describe •VERB• **describes, describing, described** to tell someone what something or someone is like: *Can you describe what you saw?*
♦ **description** •NOUN• **descriptions**
1 explaining what someone or something is like: *an author who's good at description*
2 the way someone describes a thing, person or event: *a very funny description of what happened*
3 a sort, type or kind: *people of all descriptions*
♦ **descriptive** •ADJECTIVE• describing someone or something: *a descriptive poem*

desert¹ •VERB• **deserts, deserting, deserted** to go away and leave someone or something, especially the army

desert² •NOUN• **deserts** an area of land where it does not rain much, so the earth is very dry and not many plants will grow

ⓘ The verb **desert**, meaning to leave something, is pronounced diz-**ert**, with the stress at the end.
The noun **desert**, meaning an area of dry land, is pronounced **des**-irt, with the stress at the beginning.

desert island •NOUN• **desert islands** a tropical island where nobody lives

deserve •VERB• **deserves, deserving, deserved** to deserve something is to have earned it because of the way you are or something you have done
♦ **deservedly** •ADVERB• rightly
♦ **deserving** •ADJECTIVE• a deserving person or cause is good and should be helped

desiccated •ADJECTIVE• dried: *dessicated coconut*

design •VERB• **designs, designing, designed**
1 to plan a building or product before it is built or made 2 to intend: *This dictionary is designed to be used by school pupils.*
•NOUN• **designs** 1 design is planning new shapes and ideas: *studying craft and design*
2 a design is a plan or diagram of something that could be made: *a design for a new racing car*

3 a pattern: *a geometric design*

designate •VERB• **designates, designating, designated** to choose someone or something to do a particular job
♦ **designation** •NOUN• **designations** a name or title

desirable •ADJECTIVE• worth having and wanted very much: *a desirable house by the sea*

desire •VERB• **desires, desiring, desired** to want very much: *all the riches you could desire*
•NOUN• **desires** a longing or something you want very much: *a secret desire*

desk •NOUN• **desks** a table for writing at

desolate •ADJECTIVE• 1 a desolate place is empty of people 2 a desolate person is lonely and very unhappy
♦ **desolation** •NOUN• a feeling of unhappiness and emptiness

despair •NOUN• no hope: *a feeling of despair*
•VERB• **despairs, despairing, despaired** to give up hope
♦ **despairing** •ADJECTIVE• feeling that there is no hope

despatch •VERB• another spelling of **dispatch**

desperate •ADJECTIVE• 1 extremely bad or serious: *a desperate situation* 2 needing something very much: *desperate for food*
♦ **desperately** •ADVERB• extremely or very much: *desperately in need*
♦ **desperation** •NOUN• a feeling that you will do anything to make things better

despicable •ADJECTIVE• hateful

despise •VERB• **despises, despising, despised** to hate very much

despite •PREPOSITION• despite someone or something means without taking any notice of them: *Despite the rain, we had a great picnic.*

despondency •NOUN• feeling fed up
♦ **despondent** •ADJECTIVE• fed up or depressed

dessert •NOUN• **desserts** a pudding or sweet at the end of a meal

ⓘ **Dessert** (with two **s**), meaning a part of a meal, is pronounced diz-**ert**, with the stress at the end.
Desert (with one **s**), meaning an area of dry land, is pronounced **dez**-irt, with the stress at the beginning.
The verb **desert**, meaning to leave something, is pronounced diz-**ert**.

destination •NOUN• **destinations** the place someone is on the way to

destined •ADJECTIVE• if something is destined, it will happen anyway: *destined to become a star*

destiny •NOUN• **destinies** what will happen in the future: *I believe you can change your own destiny.*

destitute •ADJECTIVE• without money, food or anywhere to live

destroy •VERB• **destroys, destroying, destroyed** 1 to wreck or ruin: *a city destroyed in the war* 2 to kill: *animals that had to be destroyed*
♦ **destroyer** •NOUN• **destroyers** 1 someone who destroys something 2 a fast warship
♦ **destruction** •NOUN• completely destroying something
♦ **destructive** •ADJECTIVE• doing a lot of damage: *the destructive effects of a bad diet*

detach •VERB• **detaches, detaching, detached** to separate things from each other: *You can detach the hood from the jacket.*
♦ **detached** •ADJECTIVE• 1 a detached house stands all by itself 2 not caring or interested in either side of an argument
♦ **detachment** •NOUN• **detachments** 1 not feeling involved in what other people have strong opinions about 2 a group of people, especially soldiers, chosen for a special job

detail •NOUN• **details** a small part, fact or item: *Draw the outline and then fill in the details.*
• **in detail** with nothing left out
♦ **detailed** •ADJECTIVE• including all the small facts or the smallest parts of something: *a detailed drawing*

detain •VERB• **detains, detaining, detained** 1 to make someone stay somewhere:

Aa
Bb
Cc
Dd
Ee
Ff
Gg
Hh
Ii
Jj
Kk
Ll
Mm
Nn
Oo
Pp
Qq
Rr
Ss
Tt
Uu
Vv
Ww
Xx
Yy
Zz

detained by the police for 24 hours **2** to delay someone: *I'm sorry to have detained you.*

detect • VERB• **detects, detecting, detected** to discover something that is not obvious to notice: *I detected a hint of annoyance in his voice.*

♦ **detection** • NOUN• finding out or noticing things: *Early detection of this illness is very important.*

♦ **detective** • NOUN• **detectives** someone who tries to find out information, especially to solve crimes

detention • NOUN• **detentions** making a person stay in a place, especially in prison or in school after everyone else has left, as a punishment

deter • VERB• **deters, deterring, deterred** to put someone off doing something
⇒ **deterrent**

detergent • NOUN• **detergents** a chemical for cleaning things: *washing-up detergent*

deteriorate • VERB• **deteriorates, deteriorating, deteriorated** to get worse: *deteriorating health*

♦ **deterioration** • NOUN• growing worse: *a deterioration in her condition*

determination • NOUN• a fixed idea that you will do something, however difficult it may be: *a determination to win*

♦ **determine** • VERB• **determines, determining, determined** **1** to control or influence what happens: *The weather will determine how long the event lasts.* **2** to decide to do something: *William determined to do something about this.*

♦ **determined** • ADJECTIVE• with a fixed idea that you are going to do something: *The team was determined to finish first if they possibly could.*

deterrent • NOUN• **deterrents** something that puts people off doing something

detest • VERB• **detests, detesting, detested** to hate very much

detonate • VERB• **detonates, detonating, detonated** to explode or make something explode: *The shell could detonate at any moment.*

♦ **detonator** • NOUN• **detonators** something that sets off an explosive like a bomb

detour • NOUN• **detours** a different and longer way of getting somewhere

detract • VERB• **detracts, detracting, detracted** to take something away or make something less: *The rain detracted from the fun of the picnic.*

deuce • NOUN• the tennis score of 40-40

devastate • VERB• **devastates, devastating, devastated** to ruin a place completely

♦ **devastated** • ADJECTIVE• **1** completely ruined **2** very shocked and upset

♦ **devastation** • NOUN• **1** ruin and destruction: *scenes of devastation after the explosion* **2** a feeling of being very badly shocked

develop • VERB• **develops, developing, developed** **1** to grow or make something grow bigger, better or more complicated: *The young animals develop very quickly.* • *The story soon developed into an interesting mystery.*
2 to make a photograph on a film into a picture
3 to put up new buildings: *plans to develop this land*

♦ **development** • NOUN• **developments**
1 there is development or a development when something grows bigger, better or more advanced or more complicated
2 a new event in a story
3 an area of land with new buildings on it

deviate • VERB• **deviates, deviating, deviated** to do something different or go in a different direction from what you might expect or predict

♦ **deviation** • NOUN• **deviations** something that is different from what is normal

device • NOUN• **devices** a tool, instrument or piece of equipment: *a device for cleaning keyboards*

devil • NOUN• **devils 1** an evil spirit **2** a wicked person

♦ **devilish** • ADJECTIVE• very wicked

devious • ADJECTIVE• clever in a sly way

devise • VERB• **devises, devising, devised** to think up a plan or way of doing something

devolution • NOUN• giving some government power to smaller areas

devote •VERB• **devotes, devoting, devoted**
1 to devote time to a thing or person is to
spend that time with them 2 to devote
yourself to a thing or person is to be
interested and involved only with them
♦ **devoted** •ADJECTIVE• extremely loving: *a
devoted daughter*
♦ **devotion** •NOUN• great love

devour •VERB• **devours, devouring,
devoured** to eat up or swallow very quickly

devout •ADJECTIVE• a devout person takes
the rules and beliefs of a religion very seriously

dew •NOUN• tiny drops of water that form,
especially on the ground, at night
♦ **dewy** •ADJECTIVE• wet, especially with
moisture from the cool night air

dhoti •NOUN• **dhotis** a long piece of cloth
that Hindu men wear wrapped around the
lower half of their bodies

di- •PREFIX• if a word starts with **di-** it usually
has something to do with two, twice or
double. For example, a *dioxide* has two
atoms of oxygen

diabolical •ADJECTIVE• devilish or very
wicked

diagnose •VERB• **diagnoses, diagnosing,
diagnosed** to decide what is wrong with a
thing or person
♦ **diagnosis** •NOUN• **diagnoses** a decision
about what is wrong: *The doctor made a
diagnosis from one look at the patient.*

diagonal •ADJECTIVE• going from one
corner and across the middle to the opposite
corner

diagram •NOUN• **diagrams** a drawing that
explains something

dial •NOUN• **dials** a circle of numbers that
often has a central pointer that moves
around it to show a measurement
•VERB• **dials, dialling, dialled** to dial a
telephone number is to call it

dialect •NOUN• **dialects** the language used
by people who live in a particular area

ⓘ People who speak different **dialects** use
different words from each other. People who
have different **accents** pronounce the same
words differently.

dialogue •NOUN• **dialogues** 1 talk between
people 2 a conversation

diameter •NOUN• **diameters** a straight line
from one side of a circle to the other that
passes through its centre

diamond •NOUN• **diamonds** 1 a very hard,
clear gemstone that is a form of carbon
2 a four-sided pointed shape (♦)
3 diamonds is one of the four suits of
playing cards, which have the symbol ♦
printed on them

diaper •NOUN• **diapers** the American
English word for a **nappy**

diaphragm •NOUN• **diaphragms** a layer of
muscle that separates the stomach from the
chest and that moves up and down when
you breathe

diarrhoea •NOUN• if you have diarrhoea,
you go to the toilet very often and the solid
waste from your body is too watery

diary •NOUN• **diaries** a book listing the dates
of the year and the arrangements you
make for the future or the things you did in
the past

dice •NOUN• a small cube with different
numbers of dots on each face. You throw a
dice and use the number of dots as a score
when it's your turn in a game

ⓘ **Dice** is the plural of **die**. The singular, **die**, is
not often used. In fact, **dice** is now used as a
singular or a plural noun: *Where are the
dice?* • *The dice is on the floor.*

dictate •VERB• **dictates, dictating, dictated**
1 to dictate something is to say words for
someone to write down: *I have to type the
letters that my boss dictates.* 2 to dictate to
someone is to order them to do things
♦ **dictation** •NOUN• **dictations** a piece of
text that someone speaks and another
person writes down
♦ **dictator** •NOUN• **dictators** a person who
has complete power over everyone else

dictionary •NOUN• **dictionaries** a book that
gives words in alphabetical order and their
meanings: *a French dictionary* • *a
dictionary of medical words*

did •VERB• a way of changing the verb **do** to

Aa

make a past tense: *I did the dishes yesterday, it's your turn today.*

Bb

didn't • SHORT FORM• a short way to say and write **did not**

Cc

die[1] • VERB• **dies, dying, died** 1 to stop living 2 to **die away** is to fade away

Dd

3 to **die down** is to get less: *wait for the fuss to die down*

Ee

4 to **die out** is to disappear gradually: *More and more species of animal are dying out.*

Ff

die[2] • NOUN• **dies** a type of mould, used to shape metals and plastics

Gg

diesel • NOUN• a heavy type of oil that is used as fuel for engines and boilers

Hh

diet • NOUN• **diets** 1 the food that a person eats: *Do you have a healthy diet?* 2 a special course of foods for a person who, for example, has an illness or wants to lose weight: *Maybe you need to go on a diet.*

Ii

Jj

• VERB• **diets, dieting, dieted** to eat only certain foods, especially when trying to lose weight

Kk

Ll

Mm

differ • VERB• **differs, differing, differed** 1 to differ from something is not to be the same as it 2 to differ is to disagree with someone: *They differ over just about everything.*

Nn

Oo

• **difference** • NOUN• **differences** 1 the way that something is not the same as something else 2 the amount between two numbers: *The difference between 6 and 10 is 4.*

Pp

Qq

• **different** • ADJECTIVE• a thing or person is different from another if they are not the same

Rr

Ss

ⓘ Many people think it is wrong if you say **different to**, so you should say **different from**: *This pencil is different from that one.* In American English, people use **different than**.

Tt

Uu

difficult • ADJECTIVE• 1 not easy 2 hard to please: *a difficult customer*

Vv

• **difficulty** • NOUN• **difficulties** 1 difficulty is not being easy: *You should be able to do this without difficulty.* 2 a difficulty is something that causes a problem: *We had a few difficulties at the beginning of the day.*

Ww

Xx

Yy

diffuse • VERB• **diffuses, diffusing, diffused** to spread something, especially light, widely and evenly

Zz

dig • VERB• **digs, digging, dug** 1 to lift up and

turn over earth with a spade
2 to make a hole, especially in the ground
3 to poke someone
• NOUN• **digs** 1 a poke: *a dig in the ribs*
2 a remark that you make to irritate someone deliberately: *I pretended not to hear her dig about dieting.*
3 a place where archaeologists remove earth to look for ancient remains
⇒ **digger**

digest • VERB• **digests, digesting, digested** to break down food in the stomach so that your body can use it properly
• **digestion** • NOUN• the way your body treats what you eat

digger • NOUN• **diggers** a machine that can move or break up large amounts of earth

digit • NOUN• **digits** 1 a number from 0 to 9
2 a finger or toe

digital • ADJECTIVE• 1 based on the use of numbers
2 a digital clock or watch shows the time as a row of numbers, rather than on a round face. Look up and compare **analogue**
3 digital recording stores sound as sets of numbers

digital television • NOUN• a method of broadcasting that uses digital technology

dignified • ADJECTIVE• calm and serious

dignitary • NOUN• **dignitaries** someone with an important job or position

dignity • NOUN• 1 a calm manner: *He told them to be quiet, to behave with some dignity.* 2 pride and self-respect: *It takes all the dignity out of a horse to make him do tricks.*

dike or **dyke** • NOUN• **dikes** or **dykes** 1 a wall that holds water back 2 a ditch that water runs along

dilapidated • ADJECTIVE• falling to pieces

dilate • VERB• **dilates, dilating, dilated** to make or get larger or wider: *The pupils of your eyes dilate in the dark.*

dilemma • NOUN• **dilemmas** a problem situation when you have to make a difficult choice between two options

diligence • NOUN• a serious and careful

attitude to work
+ **diligent** •ADJECTIVE• hard-working

dilute •VERB• **dilutes, diluting, diluted** to add water to a liquid so that it is not as strong: *Try diluting the juice with fizzy water.*
+ **diluted** •ADJECTIVE• a diluted liquid is weaker because water has been added to it
+ **dilution** •NOUN• adding water to a strong liquid to make it weaker

dim •ADJECTIVE• **dimmer, dimmest** 1 a dim light or colour is not bright or clear 2 a dim person is not very quick at understanding
•VERB• **dims, dimming, dimmed** to get or make darker or more difficult to see
+ **dimly** •ADVERB• not very brightly or clearly: *I can only see you very dimly through the lens.*
+ **dimness** •NOUN• 1 half-light that is difficult to see through 2 slowness in understanding

dime •NOUN• **dimes** one tenth of a US or Canadian dollar, which is ten cents

dimension •NOUN• **dimensions** a measurement such as the length, width or area of something: *Please give the dimensions of the doorway.*

diminish •VERB• **diminishes, diminishing, diminished** to get or make less or smaller

dimple •NOUN• **dimples** a small hollow like a dent in the skin of your chin or cheek: *He has dimples when he smiles.*

din •NOUN• a very loud noise

dine •VERB• **dines, dining, dined** to have dinner
+ **diner** •NOUN• **diners** 1 someone who is eating dinner, especially in a restaurant 2 in the US, a restaurant like a motorway service station

dinghy •NOUN• **dinghies** a small boat for rowing or sailing

dinner •NOUN• **dinners** a main meal in the evening or in the middle of the day

dinosaur •NOUN• **dinosaurs** an extinct prehistoric giant reptile

ⓘ **Dinosaur** comes from Greek words which mean 'terrible lizard'.

dip •VERB• **dips, dipping, dipped** 1 to put something in and out of a liquid quickly: *Dip the clothes in the dye.*
2 to slope downwards: *The field dips down towards the bottom of the valley.*
3 to dip a vehicle's headlights is to lower them so that they are not dazzling to other drivers
•NOUN• **dips** 1 a liquid that something can be put into for a short time
2 a slope downwards in the land
3 a quick swim
4 a soft food that you eat by dipping things in it

diploma •NOUN• **diplomas** a qualification that someone can study for in a particular subject

diplomacy •NOUN• 1 communication between countries 2 managing to deal with people without offending them
+ **diplomat** •NOUN• **diplomats** a person whose job is to keep good relationships and communications between countries
+ **diplomatic** •ADJECTIVE• 1 to do with the relationships between countries: *the diplomatic service* 2 tactful and able to keep people happy

dire •ADJECTIVE• **direr, direst** dreadful: *in dire need*

direct •ADJECTIVE• 1 straight, or as straight as possible: *a direct route to the airport* 2 frank and honest
•VERB• **directs, directing, directed** 1 to aim or make something go a particular way: *Their weapons were directed at us.*
2 to tell someone how to get somewhere: *Could you please direct me to the post office?*
3 to control or guide: *The police direct the traffic when it's busy.*
+ **direction** •NOUN• **directions** 1 direction is controlling or organizing
2 a direction is the place or point a thing or person goes towards or faces: *Which direction is the library?*
3 a direction is an order or instruction: *a list of directions on the side of the packet*
4 directions are instructions for getting somewhere: *Try to follow my directions to the hidden treasure.*
+ **directly** •ADVERB• 1 straight away: *The*

Aa

manager will see you directly. **2** straight: *looking directly at me*

♦ **directness** • NOUN• being straightforward with people: *Geraldine's directness sometimes seems like rudeness.*

Bb

Cc

♦ **director** • NOUN• **directors 1** the manager of a business **2** a person who makes a film or organizes a stage show

Dd

direct speech • NOUN• in a story or report, the exact words that a person said

Ee

Ff

dirt • NOUN• any substance that is not clean or makes something unclean, such as mud or dust

Gg

♦ **dirty** • ADJECTIVE• **dirtier, dirtiest 1** not clean: *dirty floors*

Hh

2 not polite: *dirty language*

Ii

3 unfair or dishonest: *a dirty trick*

Jj

dis- • PREFIX• **1** if a word starts with **dis-** it can have something to do with separation and moving apart. For example, *disjointed* means 'not connected properly' **2** if a word starts with **dis-** it may also mean 'not' something. For example, *dislike* means 'not to like'

Kk

Ll

Mm

Nn

disabled • ADJECTIVE• having a physical or mental problem that makes some aspects of life difficult

Oo

♦ **disability** • NOUN• **disabilities** a physical or mental problem that makes some aspects of life difficult

Pp

Qq

disadvantage • NOUN• **disadvantages** something that makes things difficult or not desirable: *It's a great idea – the only disadvantage is that it's expensive.*

Rr

Ss

disagree • VERB• **disagrees, disagreeing, disagreed 1** to have a different opinion about something: *I completely disagree with you about that.* **2** to make you feel ill: *The prawns in the curry disagreed with me.*

Tt

Uu

Vv

♦ **disagreeable** • ADJECTIVE• unpleasant

♦ **disagreement** • NOUN• **disagreements 1** disagreement is having different opinions **2** a disagreement is an argument: *We've had several disagreements on this subject.*

Ww

Xx

Yy

disallow • VERB• **disallows, disallowing, disallowed** to disallow a goal or point in sport is to say that it does not count: *Our next shot was disallowed by the referee.*

Zz

disappear • VERB• **disappears,**

disappearing, disappeared to vanish or go out of sight

♦ **disappearance** • NOUN• **disappearances** when something or someone vanishes: *The police are investigating the disappearance of the necklace.*

disappoint • VERB• **disappoints, disappointing, disappointed** to let someone down: *I'm sorry to disappoint you, but I can't come to your party.*

♦ **disappointed** • ADJECTIVE• feeling let down

♦ **disappointment** • NOUN• **disappointments** a feeling of being let down because something does not happen or turns out worse than expected: *It was a disappointment to find that all the tickets had already been sold.*

disapproval • NOUN• thinking something is not good

♦ **disapprove** • VERB• **disapproves, disapproving, disapproved** to disapprove of someone or something is to think that they are bad, wrong or unsuitable: *My parents definitely disapproved of my new friend.*

disarm • VERB• **disarms, disarming, disarmed 1** to take a weapon away from someone: *A security guard managed to disarm the man.* **2** to give up weapons that you have

♦ **disarmament** • NOUN• getting rid of war weapons

disarray • NOUN• untidiness: *a shelf in disarray*

disaster • NOUN• **disasters** a terrible happening, especially if there is great damage or injury

♦ **disastrous** • ADJECTIVE• causing great damage, injury or loss

disbelief • NOUN• not believing something: *an expression of complete disbelief*

♦ **disbelieve** • VERB• **disbelieves, disbelieving, disbelieved** to think someone is lying or something is untrue

disc • NOUN• **discs 1** something flat and round **2** a CD

discard • VERB• **discards, discarding, discarded** to throw something away: *a* *discarded wrapper on the pavement*

discern •VERB• **discerns, discerning, discerned** to see or understand something

discharge •VERB• **discharges, discharging, discharged** 1 to discharge a prisoner is to let them go 2 to discharge a substance like a polluting liquid or gas is to give it off or let it out: *a factory that discharges dangerous products into the environment* •NOUN• **discharges** 1 carrying out an order or duty: *injured in the discharge of his duty* 2 letting someone go: *an honourable discharge from the army* 3 a substance that comes or leaks out of something

disciple •NOUN• **disciples** 1 a person who follows and believes in someone else's ideas 2 one of the original followers of Jesus Christ

disciplinarian •NOUN• **disciplinarians** a person who is very strict

disciplinary •ADJECTIVE• to do with rules for how to behave and with punishment for breaking rules

discipline •NOUN• strict training or rules that are supposed to lead to ordered and controlled behaviour

disclose •VERB• **discloses, disclosing, disclosed** 1 to uncover something 2 to tell someone a secret or something private

disco •NOUN• **discos** a place or party where people dance to recorded music

discolour •VERB• **discolours, discolouring, discoloured** to go or make something a strange or unpleasant colour

discomfort •NOUN• being uncomfortable: *The doctor asked if I had felt any discomfort.*

disconnect •VERB• **disconnects, disconnecting, disconnected** to separate things that were joined together

discontent •NOUN• a feeling of not being happy or satisfied with a situation
♦ **discontented** •ADJECTIVE• not satisfied and wanting to change a situation

discontinue •VERB• **discontinues, discontinuing, discontinued** to stop something that was going on

♦ **discontinued** •ADJECTIVE• a discontinued product is one that is not made any more

discount •NOUN• **discounts** some money taken off a price to make it cheaper: *10% discount on all goods*

discourage •VERB• **discourages, discouraging, discouraged** to put someone off doing something: *I was discouraged by all the people I knew who had failed.*
♦ **discouragement** •NOUN• 1 a disappointment that puts you off doing something 2 an effort to put you off something that you want to do
♦ **discouraging** •ADJECTIVE• making you feel less hopeful or confident about something: *discouraging news.*

discover •VERB• **discovers, discovering, discovered** to find information, a place or an object, especially for the first time: *The settlers discovered gold in the mountains.* • *We discovered that the paint wouldn't mix with water.*
♦ **discoverer** •NOUN• **discoverers** a person who finds something for the first time
♦ **discovery** •NOUN• **discoveries** finding something, especially by accident: *the discovery of America*

discreet •ADJECTIVE• quiet and not attracting people's attention

discriminate •VERB• **discriminates, discriminating, discriminated** 1 to see differences between things and prefer one to another 2 to treat different people or groups differently in the same situation, often because of their colour, religion or sex
♦ **discrimination** •NOUN• 1 being able to see differences in things and decide if they are good or bad 2 treating people differently for no good reason

discus •NOUN• **discuses** a heavy disc that athletes throw as far as they can in a competition

discuss •VERB• **discusses, discussing, discussed** to talk about something: *You should try to discuss this with your parents.*
♦ **discussion** •NOUN• **discussions** talks or conversations between people:

Aa
Bb
Cc
Dd
Ee
Ff
Gg
Hh
Ii
Jj
Kk
Ll
Mm
Nn
Oo
Pp
Qq
Rr
Ss
Tt
Uu
Vv
Ww
Xx
Yy
Zz

discussions between world leaders

disdain • NOUN • not liking a thing or person because you do not think they are good or interesting enough

✦ **disdainful** • ADJECTIVE • looking down on a thing or person as not good or interesting enough

disease • NOUN • **diseases** an illness

✦ **diseased** • ADJECTIVE • not healthy, especially because of an illness: *diseased leaves on the roses*

ⓘ This word comes from the Old French word **desaise**, which is made up of **des**, which means *not*, and **aise**, which means *ease*. So disease means 'not at ease'.

disfavour • NOUN • not liking or approving of a thing or person: *They looked at our grubby anoraks and boots with disfavour.*

disfigure • VERB • **disfigures, disfiguring, disfigured** to spoil the look of something

disgrace • NOUN • 1 something that makes you feel ashamed: *It's no disgrace to come last if you tried hard.* 2 if you are in disgrace, other people do not approve of what you have done: *Debbie's in disgrace for telling us all Jane's secrets.*

✦ **disgraceful** • ADJECTIVE • shameful or very bad

disgust • NOUN • a strong feeling that you do not like or approve of something: *The sight of the worms filled Lottie with disgust.*

✦ **disgusted** • ADJECTIVE • sickened by something bad, wrong or unpleasant

✦ **disgusting** • ADJECTIVE • extremely unpleasant: *a disgusting drink*

dish • NOUN • **dishes** 1 a plate or bowl for food 2 food that has been prepared for eating: *a fish dish* 3 a large disc that is an aerial for receiving satellite signals, especially for television broadcasts
• VERB • **dishes, dishing, dished** to **dish out** something is to give it out

dishearten • VERB • **disheartens, disheartening, disheartened** to make someone feel less hopeful or confident

✦ **disheartened** • ADJECTIVE • feeling down and losing hope

dishevelled • ADJECTIVE • with messed-up hair and untidy clothes

dishonest • ADJECTIVE • not telling the truth and cheating people: *a dishonest way of doing business*

✦ **dishonesty** • NOUN • cheating or not being honest

disinfect • VERB • **disinfects, disinfecting, disinfected** to disinfect something is to destroy germs on it that might cause disease: *disinfect the bathroom once a week*

✦ **disinfectant** • NOUN • **disinfectants** a product that kills germs

disintegrate • VERB • **disintegrates, disintegrating, disintegrated** to fall to pieces

✦ **disintegration** • NOUN • falling apart

disinterested • ADJECTIVE • not having personal feelings for or against someone or something: *A disinterested judge will make a fair decision.*

disk • NOUN • **disks** a round flat object that computers use to store information on: *Save the file on a floppy disk.* • *The virus could infect your hard disk.*

disk drive • NOUN • **disk drives** the part of a computer that holds and operates the disks that store information

dislike • VERB • **dislikes, disliking, disliked** not to like someone or something: *I dislike having to get up early, but I have to do it.*

dislocate • VERB • **dislocates, dislocating, dislocated** to dislocate a joint is to put a bone out of its correct position: *Tom dislocated his shoulder in a rugby match.*

✦ **dislocation** • NOUN • when something, especially a bone, gets moved from its correct position

dislodge • VERB • **dislodges, dislodging, dislodged** to move something, especially when it is stuck, from its place

disloyal • ADJECTIVE • not loyal or faithful to your side

✦ **disloyalty** • NOUN • not being loyal or faithful to someone you should be supporting

dismal • ADJECTIVE • gloomy and not at all bright or attractive

dismantle • VERB • **dismantles, dismantling,**

dismantled to take something apart

dismay •NOUN• an unpleasant feeling of surprise and worry: *We watched in dismay as Tom fell into the water.*

dismiss •VERB• dismisses, dismissing, dismissed **1** to dismiss someone is to send them away: *The class were dismissed by the teacher early today.* **2** to dismiss a subject is to decide not to consider it any longer: *They dismissed my excuses and gave me a punishment anyway.*
♦ **dismissal** •NOUN• dismissals when someone gets sent away especially from their job: *an unfair dismissal*

dismount •VERB• dismounts, dismounting, dismounted to get off a bicycle or horse

disobedience •NOUN• when someone does not do as they are told
♦ **disobedient** •ADJECTIVE• not doing as you are told
♦ **disobey** •VERB• disobeys, disobeying, disobeyed not to do what you are told to do: *Do not disobey me!*

disorder •NOUN• **1** disorder is a state of confusion or a disturbance **2** a disorder is an illness
♦ **disorderly** •ADJECTIVE• behaving badly: *a disorderly crowd*

disown •VERB• disowns, disowning, disowned to claim that you do not have any connection with someone: *I'll disown you completely if you make a scene.*

dispatch or **despatch** •VERB• dispatches, dispatching, dispatched or despatches, despatching, despatched **1** to send off: *a parcel dispatched on the 29th* **2** to kill someone

dispel •VERB• dispels, dispelling, dispelled to drive away thoughts or feelings: *The commander dispelled any possible thoughts we had of escaping.*

dispense •VERB• dispenses, dispensing, dispensed **1** to give something out, especially medicine **2** to dispense with something is to decide to do without it
♦ **dispenser** •NOUN• dispensers a machine or container that you can get measured amounts of something from: *a cash dispenser*

disperse •VERB• disperses, dispersing, dispersed to scatter or send things or people off in different directions: *The crowd is now beginning to disperse.*
♦ **dispersal** •NOUN• things or people going in different directions

displace •VERB• displaces, displacing, displaced to put or take something or someone out of the place they seemed to be fixed in: *I think she's going to displace the champion.* • *Thousands of people were displaced during the war.*
♦ **displacement** •NOUN• movement out of the usual place

display •NOUN• displays **1** a show or exhibition: *a display of the children's work* • *an air display* **2** the way you see things on a computer screen: *You can change the display so that it's bigger.*
• **on display** something that is on display is arranged for people to see
•VERB• displays, displaying, displayed to set things out for an exhibition or to show something off for people to see: *The treasure will be displayed in the museum for two months.*

displease •VERB• displeases, displeasing, displeased to annoy someone
♦ **displeasure** •NOUN• annoyance

disposable •ADJECTIVE• a disposable product is meant to be used and then thrown away

disposal •NOUN• getting rid of something: *a waste-disposal unit in the kitchen*
• **at your disposal** a thing or person that is at your disposal is ready for you to use: *There will be a car at your disposal.*

dispose •VERB• disposes, disposing, disposed to dispose of something is to get rid of it: *People dispose of their rubbish in the yard.*
♦ **disposed** •ADJECTIVE• to be disposed to do something is to be willing to do it: *I don't like her and I'm not disposed to help her.*

disprove •VERB• disproves, disproving, disproved to prove that something is not true

dispute •NOUN• disputes an argument, especially about work or between countries

Aa
Bb
Cc
Dd
Ee
Ff
Gg
Hh
Ii
Jj
Kk
Ll
Mm
Nn
Oo
Pp
Qq
Rr
Ss
Tt
Uu
Vv
Ww
Xx
Yy
Zz

•VERB• **disputes, disputing, disputed** to argue about something: *They dispute that they have been treated fairly.*

disqualification • NOUN • stopping someone from taking part in a competition because they have done something wrong
•VERB• **disqualifies, disqualifying, disqualified** to prevent someone from taking part in a competition because they are unsuitable or have broken the rules: *Three contestants have been disqualified for wearing the wrong kind of shoes.*

disregard •VERB• **disregards, disregarding, disregarded** to take no notice of something: *They have completely disregarded my instructions.*

disrepair • NOUN • a bad state or condition: *a building that had fallen into disrepair*

disrespect • NOUN • being rude and behaving without respect towards someone
♦ **disrespectful** • ADJECTIVE • not polite towards someone: *disrespectful language*

disrupt •VERB• **disrupts, disrupting, disrupted** to disturb the normal way things run: *Power cuts have disrupted two schooldays.*
♦ **disruption** • NOUN • **disruptions** disturbance of the smooth running of something: *disruption in the town centre caused by a burst water pipe*
♦ **disruptive** • ADJECTIVE • causing disturbance and disorder: *Disruptive pupils will be sent out of the room.*

dissatisfaction • NOUN • irritation or not being pleased about something
♦ **dissatisfied** • ADJECTIVE • to be dissatisfied with something is not to be pleased about it

dissect •VERB• **dissects, dissecting, dissected** to cut something up so that you can examine it
♦ **dissection** • NOUN • cutting something up so that you can see all its parts in detail

dissimilar • ADJECTIVE • not the same

dissolve •VERB• **dissolves, dissolving, dissolved** to melt or be melted in liquid: *Keep stirring and the sugar will dissolve completely.*

dissuade •VERB• **dissuades, dissuading, dissuaded** to dissuade someone from doing something is to persuade them not to do it

distance • NOUN • **distances** the space between things: *Measure the distance between the lines accurately.*
• **in the distance** a long way off: *the sound of a train in the distance*
• **keep your distance** to keep back or right away from someone or something
♦ **distant** • ADJECTIVE • **1** far off, not close: *a distant shout* • *a distant cousin* **2** cold and unfriendly: *behaving in a distant manner*

distil •VERB• **distils, distilling, distilled** to make a liquid pure by boiling it and cooling the vapour that is produced
♦ **distillery** • NOUN • **distilleries** a factory that makes strong alcoholic drinks like whisky and brandy
♦ **distillation** • NOUN • the process of making a liquid pure by boiling it and cooling the vapour that is produced

distinct • ADJECTIVE • **1** clear: *a distinct improvement* **2** different: *two languages that are quite distinct*
♦ **distinction** • NOUN • **distinctions** **1** a difference: *We have to make a distinction between pupils who don't care and pupils who don't try.*
2 an honour: *She had the distinction of being the first woman airline pilot.*
3 a high mark in an examination: *Sandy always got distinctions in his piano exams.*
♦ **distinctive** • ADJECTIVE • different and easy to recognize: *a distinctive singing voice*

distinguish •VERB• **distinguishes, distinguishing, distinguished 1** to see a difference between things: *Jamie can't distinguish green from brown because he's colour blind.* **2** to make something out, either by seeing or hearing it
♦ **distinguished** • ADJECTIVE • famous and respected: *a distinguished novelist*

distort •VERB• **distorts, distorting, distorted 1** to twist something out of shape: *a face distorted with pain*
2 to express information so that it seems to mean something different: *a newspaper report that distorts the truth*
3 to make a sound strange and unclear: *A*

Aa
Bb
Cc
Dd
Ee
Ff
Gg
Hh
Ii
Jj
Kk
Ll
Mm
Nn
Oo
Pp
Qq
Rr
Ss
Tt
Uu
Vv
Ww
Xx
Yy
Zz

microphone can distort your voice.
* **distortion** •NOUN• changing something so that it is noticeably different

distract •VERB• distracts, distracting, distracted to take your attention away: *Gerry distracted the teacher while the others swopped answers.*
* **distraction** •NOUN• distractions something that takes your attention away from what you are doing: *I've had so many distractions today that I haven't finished.*

distraught •ADJECTIVE• extremely worried or upset

distress •NOUN• pain, sadness or worrying problems
•VERB• distresses, distressing, distressed to upset someone
* **distressed** •ADJECTIVE• upset
* **distressing** •ADJECTIVE• making someone feel very upset: *very distressing news*

distribute •VERB• distributes, distributing, distributed to give something out to lots of people: *Please distribute the books around the class.* • *a company that distributes products to shops*
* **distribution** •NOUN• when something goes or is taken out to different places

district •NOUN• districts one part of a country or town: *the district council*

distrust •VERB• distrusts, distrusting, distrusted not to trust someone or something
•NOUN• suspecting, or not trusting someone or something: *a look of distrust*
* **distrustful** •ADJECTIVE• full of suspicion

disturb •VERB• disturbs, disturbing, disturbed 1 to interrupt something that is going on, or someone who is doing something: *I'm sorry to disturb you, but I need to ask you a question.*
2 to disturb something is to change the way it has been arranged: *I knew that someone had been at my desk because the papers had been disturbed.*
3 something that disturbs you, upsets or worries you
* **disturbance** •NOUN• disturbances an outbreak of noise or noisy behaviour:

disturbances in the street during the night
* **disturbing** •ADJECTIVE• upsetting: *disturbing scenes of violence*

disused •ADJECTIVE• not used any more: *a disused railway station*

ditch •NOUN• ditches a long narrow hole in the ground, especially one that has water in it
•VERB• ditches, ditching, ditched to get rid of something

dither •VERB• dithers, dithering, dithered to hesitate and be unable to make a decision

ditto •NOUN• the same again
* **ditto mark** •NOUN• a symbol (") in a list that means that the word above it should be repeated

divan •NOUN• divans a bed that has no headboard at the top or or footboard at the bottom

dive •VERB• dives, diving, dived 1 to go into water headfirst 2 to go down steeply and quickly: *an eagle diving down into a field*
•NOUN• dives a downwards movement, especially headfirst into water

diverse •ADJECTIVE• different or varied: *a diverse selection of cheeses*
* **diversity** •NOUN• variety

diversion •NOUN• diversions 1 an alternative route to the usual one: *There was a diversion because the bridge was closed.* 2 something that takes your attention away, especially an amusement: *The little boys created a diversion while the big ones stole our bikes.* • *The puppet show was a welcome diversion.*

divert •VERB• diverts, diverting, diverted 1 to make something, especially traffic, go a different way 2 to amuse or entertain someone

divide •VERB• divides, dividing, divided 1 to separate into parts: *divide the class into small groups* • *a single cell that divides and becomes two cells* 2 in maths, to find how many times one number contains another: *If you divide 12 by 3 you get 4.* • *12 divided by 3 is 4.*
⇒ divisible, division, divisor

dividend •NOUN• dividends 1 in maths, an

amount to be divided **2** part of the profits that a company makes, which is paid to people who own shares in the company

divine •ADJECTIVE• **1** belonging to a god or like a god **2** wonderful •VERB• **divines, divining, divined** to search for underground water or minerals by holding a special Y-shaped stick that moves when it is near them

divisible •ADJECTIVE• able to be divided exactly: *12 is divisible by 2, 3, 4 and 6.*

division •NOUN• **divisions 1** dividing things, numbers or people: *We're learning a different way of doing division sums.* **2** something that divides **3** a section of something: *There are eight teams in our division.*

divisor •NOUN• **divisors** a number that you divide into another number

divorce •NOUN• **divorces** the official end of a marriage •VERB• **divorces, divorcing, divorced** to end a marriage with someone

divulge •VERB• **divulges, divulging, divulged** to let out some information, like a secret

Diwali •NOUN• the Hindu or Sikh religious festival of lights that takes place in October or November

dizzy •ADJECTIVE• **dizzier, dizziest** giddy: *Spinning round like that will make you dizzy.*

DJ •ABBREVIATION• short for **disc jockey**

DNA •ABBREVIATION• short for **deoxyribonucleic acid**, the substance in living things that carries information about your individual genes

do •VERB• **does, doing, did, done 1** to carry out an action or deal with a task: *always doing something • do your homework* **2** to get along: *How are you doing?* **3** to be enough: *Will a pound do?* **4** to swindle someone: *They'll do you if they can, so make sure you check your change.* **5** to **do away with** something or someone is to get rid of them or kill them **6** to **do something up** is to fasten it: *Do your jacket up – it's cold out there.*

7 to **do something up** is to decorate it: *We're doing up our hall.* •NOUN• **dos** a party: *The wedding's at 3 and there's an evening do afterwards.*

ⓘ The verb **do** is very important in making good English sentences.
Use it to avoid repeating a verb: *We rarely have a picnic, but when we do, it always rains.*
Use it with a more important verb:
(1) in questions: *Do you understand?*
(2) in sentences with **not**: *I don't know.*
(3) to stress something: *I do like your dress.*

docile •ADJECTIVE• tame and easy to manage: *a docile pet*

dock¹ •NOUN• **docks** part of a harbour where ships can load and unload their cargo •VERB• **docks, docking, docked 1** to go into, or put a ship into a dock: *When we've docked, a crane will unload the containers.* **2** a spacecraft docks when it joins another craft during a flight
✦ **docker** •NOUN• **dockers** someone who works at the docks, loading and unloading ships

dock² •VERB• **docks, docking, docked 1** to dock someone's pay is to make it less **2** to dock an animal's tail is to cut it short

doctor •NOUN• **doctors** someone who has been trained in medicine and treats people who are ill

ⓘ **Doctor** is the Latin word for *teacher*, but the meaning has changed in English.

document •NOUN• **documents** a paper with official information on it: *Keep this document for your records.*

dodge •VERB• **dodges, dodging, dodged** to avoid something by a quick or clever movement: *Graeme managed to dodge out of the way before the ball hit him.* •NOUN• **dodges** a trick to avoid something

dodo •NOUN• **dodoes** or **dodos** a type of large bird that is extinct

doe •NOUN• **does** the female of certain animals like deer, rabbits or hares

does •VERB• the form of the verb **do** that is used with **he**, **she** and **it**

doesn't •SHORT FORM• a short way to say and write **does not**

dog •NOUN• **dogs** a four-footed animal that barks and that people often keep as a pet •VERB• **dogs, dogging, dogged** to follow and trouble someone: *The group were dogged by technical problems on their latest tour.*

dog collar •NOUN• **dog collars** 1 a collar for a dog, which you can attach a lead to 2 a plain, straight white collar that a minister or priest wears

dog-eared •ADJECTIVE• a dog-eared page has a curled or bent corner

dogged •ADJECTIVE• determined or stubborn

ⓘ This word is pronounced **dog**-id.

dogsbody •NOUN• **dogsbodies** someone who gets all the small, uninteresting jobs to do

doily or **doyley** •NOUN• **doilies** or **doyleys** a piece of paper with a pattern of holes in it that is used under cakes or biscuits on a plate

doldrums •PLURAL NOUN• someone who is **in the doldrums** is fed up

dole •NOUN• someone who is **on the dole** has no job and is getting payments from the government •VERB• **doles, doling, doled** to **dole something out** is to give it out in small amounts

doll •NOUN• **dolls** a toy model of a person

dollar •NOUN• **dollars** the main unit of money in many countries including the United States, Canada, Australia and New Zealand

dolphin •NOUN• **dolphins** a very intelligent sea mammal of the whale family that has a long pointed mouth

domain •NOUN• **domains** the area that one person or government rules over

dome •NOUN• **domes** the roof of a building in the shape of the top half of a ball

domestic •ADJECTIVE• 1 to do with homes and houses: *domestic tasks like cleaning and cooking* 2 a domestic animal is not wild, but kept as a pet or on a farm
♦ **domesticated** •ADJECTIVE• 1 a domesticated animal is one that lives in contact with humans, either as a pet or on a farm 2 a domesticated person likes looking after their home and family

dominant •ADJECTIVE• stronger or more noticeable than others: *The dominant feature of this illness is a rash.*

dominate •VERB• **dominates, dominating, dominated** to control others by being strongest or most powerful: *He dominates every conversation.*
♦ **domination** •NOUN• when a powerful person controls everyone else

dominoes •NOUN• a game played with small rectangular blocks that have different numbers of dots on them

donate •VERB• **donates, donating, donated** to give something, especially money, as a gift: *Would you donate something to our charity?*
♦ **donation** •NOUN• **donations** something that someone gives without getting anything back
⇒ **donor**

done •VERB• a form of the verb **do** that is used with a helping verb to make a past tense: *I've done my homework and now I'm going out on my bike.*

donkey •NOUN• **donkeys** a type of animal that looks like a small horse with long ears. A donkey may also be called an **ass**

donor •NOUN• **donors** someone who gives something that someone else can use: *Blood donors are urgently needed.*

don't •SHORT FORM• a short way to say and write **do not**

doom •NOUN• an unpleasant end like ruin or death
♦ **doomed** •ADJECTIVE• bound to fail: *The project was doomed from the start.*

door •NOUN• **doors** a panel, often on a hinge, that you can open and close. It usually covers the entrance to a building, room or cupboard

doorstep •NOUN• **doorsteps** the step in front of the door of a house

Aa
Bb
Cc
Dd
Ee
Ff
Gg
Hh
Ii
Jj
Kk
Ll
Mm
Nn
Oo
Pp
Qq
Rr
Ss
Tt
Uu
Vv
Ww
Xx
Yy
Zz

Aa
Bb
Cc
Dd
Ee
Ff
Gg
Hh
Ii
Jj
Kk
Ll
Mm
Nn
Oo
Pp
Qq
Rr
Ss
Tt
Uu
Vv
Ww
Xx
Yy
Zz

dope • NOUN• **dopes** 1 a type of drug 2 an idiot
•VERB• **dopes, doping, doped** to drug someone

dormant • ADJECTIVE• not active at the moment: *a dormant volcano*

dormitory • NOUN• **dormitories** a bedroom for several people, especially in a school

ⓘ **Dormitory** comes from the Latin word **dormire**, which means *to sleep.*

dormouse • NOUN• **dormice** a small animal like a mouse that has a long furry tail, lives in forests and hibernates

dose • NOUN• **doses** an amount of medicine that you take at one time
♦ **dosage** • NOUN• **dosages** the amount of a medicine that you should take

dossier • NOUN• **dossiers** a set of papers with information about a certain person or subject

dot • NOUN• **dots** a small round mark
• **on the dot** exactly on time: *Belinda arrived at three o'clock on the dot, just as she'd promised.*
•VERB• **dots, dotting, dotted** to put dots on something

dote •VERB• **dotes, doting, doted** to **dote on** someone is to be extremely fond of them

double • ADJECTIVE• 1 containing twice as much: *a double dose of medicine*
2 made up of two of the same sort: *double doors*
3 suitable for two: *a double cabin*
• NOUN• **doubles** 1 twice as much: *Jan earns double what I get.* 2 a thing or person that looks exactly like another one: *I saw your double in the street yesterday.*
• **at the double** very quickly
•VERB• **doubles, doubling, doubled** 1 to multiply something by two 2 to **double up** is to bend over in laughter or pain
⇒ **doubly**

double bass • NOUN• **double basses** the largest instrument in the violin family, which plays very low notes

double-cross •VERB• **double-crosses, double-crossing, double-crossed** to cheat someone

double-decker • NOUN• **double-deckers** a bus with an upper floor

doubly • ADVERB• twice: *Make doubly sure that the door's locked.*

doubt • NOUN• **doubts** a feeling of not being sure about something: *I have doubts about this plan.* • *I have no doubt you are quite right.*
•VERB• **doubts, doubting, doubted** to be unsure about something: *I doubt that you will understand.*

doubtful • ADJECTIVE• 1 to be doubtful about something is to be unsure about it 2 something that is doubtful is not likely: *It was doubtful that they would ever be found now.*

dough • NOUN• a mixture of flour and water for making bread

ⓘ The word **dough** sounds the same as the word **doe** (a female deer), and rhymes with **slow.**

doughnut • NOUN• **doughnuts** a round cake that is deep-fried. It may have a hole in the middle or be filled with something like jam or chocolate

dour • ADJECTIVE• **dourer, dourest** stern and unhappy: *a dour expression*

dove • NOUN• **doves** a kind of pigeon that is usually white

dowdy • ADJECTIVE• **dowdier, dowdiest** looking dull, uninteresting and unfashionable

down¹ • ADVERB• 1 towards or in a lower position: *get down* • *sit down*
2 to a smaller size: *cut the picture down to fit the frame*
3 along: *go down to the post office*
• **go down with** to become ill with something: *She's gone down with flu.*
• PREPOSITION• 1 towards or in a lower part: *tears running down his face* 2 along: *walking down the road*

down² • NOUN• light, soft feathers

downcast • ADJECTIVE• feeling sad

downfall • NOUN• **downfalls** ruin or defeat: *the downfall of a powerful leader*

downpour • NOUN• **downpours** a heavy fall of rain

downs •PLURAL NOUN• low grassy hills

downstairs •ADVERB• to a lower floor of a building: *go downstairs*
•ADJECTIVE• on a lower floor: *the downstairs bathroom*

downstream •ADVERB• further down a river in the direction that it flows, usually towards the sea

downwards •ADVERB• moving or leading to a lower place or position: *The path winds downwards to the lakeside.*

dowry •NOUN• **dowries** money and property that a woman brings to a marriage from her family

doze •VERB• **dozes, dozing, dozed** 1 to doze is to sleep lightly 2 to **doze off** is to fall into a light sleep
•NOUN• **dozes** a light sleep: *I had a doze after lunch.*

dozen •NOUN• **dozens** twelve: *a dozen eggs*

drab •ADJECTIVE• **drabber, drabbest** uninteresting and without any bright colours

draft •NOUN• **drafts** a rough experimental outline of something: *This is just the first draft of my essay.*
•VERB• **drafts, drafting, drafted** to make a rough plan of something

draftsman *or* **draftswoman** •NOUN• **draftsmen** *or* **draftswomen** another spelling of **draughtsman** *or* **draughtswoman**

drag •VERB• **drags, dragging, dragged** 1 to pull along roughly: *Thomas came out dragging his schoolbag behind him.*
2 to move too slowly: *The play seemed to drag on for hours.*
3 to drag a river or lake is to search it with a net
•NOUN• a boring task or event: *Choir practice was always such a drag.*

dragon •NOUN• **dragons** an imaginary, fire-breathing reptile with wings

dragonfly •NOUN• **dragonflies** a long thin insect with double wings

drain •VERB• **drains, draining, drained** 1 to drain something is to let the water run out of it: *They must drain the reservoir to repair the*

dam. • *Drain the washed cabbage well before cutting it up.*
2 to drain is to flow away: *watching the liquid drain down the sink*
3 to drain a container of drink is to drink it all
4 to drain a person is to make them very tired
•NOUN• **drains** 1 a pipe or ditch for waste water to flow away in 2 something that uses up your energy or money: *Our holiday was a big drain on our income.*
♦ **drainage** •NOUN• removing waste water by systems of pipes and rivers
♦ **drained** •ADJECTIVE• with no strength left: *After being in court all day, I felt completely drained.*

drake •NOUN• **drakes** a male duck

drama •NOUN• **dramas** 1 drama is acting, directing and producing plays
2 a drama is a play for the theatre or television
3 drama is something exciting happening
♦ **dramatic** •ADJECTIVE• 1 to do with plays and the theatre: *a dramatic production*
2 exciting
3 sudden and unexpected: *a dramatic rise in exam passes*
♦ **dramatist** •NOUN• **dramatists** a person who writes plays
♦ **dramatize** *or* **dramatise** •VERB• **dramatizes, dramatizing, dramatized** 1 to turn something into a play for the theatre or television: *This story has been dramatized several times.* 2 to make a story or report more exciting than the actual event
♦ **dramatization** *or* **dramatisation** •NOUN• **dramatizations** a dramatization is a play based on an existing story or book

drank •VERB• a way of changing the verb **drink** to make a past tense: *We drank our tea and left as quickly as possible.*

drape •VERB• **drapes, draping, draped** to arrange cloth so that it hangs gracefully: *She draped the scarf over her head.*
♦ **drapes** •PLURAL NOUN• in American English, drapes are long heavy curtains

draper •NOUN• **drapers** a person who owns a shop that sells curtains and cloth
♦ **drapery** •NOUN• fabric and cloth that hangs, such as curtains

Aa
Bb
Cc
Dd
Ee
Ff
Gg
Hh
Ii
Jj
Kk
Ll
Mm
Nn
Oo
Pp
Qq
Rr
Ss
Tt
Uu
Vv
Ww
Xx
Yy
Zz

drastic •ADJECTIVE• a drastic action has an extreme effect: *We need to do something drastic here.*
✦ **drastically** •ADVERB• in a sudden and extreme way: *Nora has changed drastically in the last few months.*

draught •NOUN• **draughts** a current of air
✦ **draughty** •ADJECTIVE• **draughtier, draughtiest** a place that is cold and full of moving air currents

draughts •NOUN• a game for two people who move round black or white pieces on a squared board

draughtsman •NOUN• **draughtsmen** a man whose job is to draw plans

draughtswoman •NOUN• **draughtswomen** a woman whose job is to draw plans

draw •VERB• **draws, drawing, drew, drawn**
1 to make a picture with a pencil or pen
2 to pull along behind: *Horses drew the carriage.*
3 to attract: *The circus always draws huge audiences.*
4 to come near: *Draw your chair up to the table.*
5 to score equal points in a game: *This pair have drawn every match they've played so far.*
•NOUN• **draws** 1 an equal score: *The game ended in a draw.* 2 a lottery or raffle
⇒ **drawing**

drawback •NOUN• **drawbacks** a disadvantage: *The main drawback of the plan is that it's expensive.*

drawbridge •NOUN• **drawbridges** a bridge at the entrance of a castle that can be raised or lowered

drawer •NOUN• **drawers** a sliding box in a table, chest or cupboard

drawing •NOUN• **drawings** a picture drawn with a pencil or pen

drawing pin •NOUN• **drawing pins** a short pin with a large flat head that you use to fix paper to an upright surface like a board

drawl •VERB• **drawls, drawling, drawled** to speak slowly and lazily
•NOUN• **drawls** a slow, lazy way of speaking

drawn •VERB• a form of the verb **draw** that is used with a helping verb to make a past tense: *I've drawn several styles for you to choose from.*

dread •VERB• **dreads, dreading, dreaded** to be very afraid and worried about something: *We're all dreading the exams.*
•NOUN• a feeling of great fear: *The thought of flying fills me with dread.*

dreadful •ADJECTIVE• terrible: *dreadful news • a dreadful film*
✦ **dreadfully** •ADVERB• 1 very badly: *The children have been behaving dreadfully all day.* 2 very much: *I'm dreadfully sorry.*

dreadlocks •PLURAL NOUN• hair that is worn in long twisted strands

dream •NOUN• **dreams** 1 the things you think while you are asleep: *I had a very strange dream last night.*
2 if you are in a dream, you are concentrating on your thoughts and not on what is going on around you
3 a hope or ambition: *It was always her dream to go to Hollywood.*
•VERB• **dreams, dreaming, dreamt** or **dreamed** to imagine something: *Did you say that or did I dream it?*

dreary •ADJECTIVE• **drearier, dreariest** dull and boring

dredge •VERB• **dredges, dredging, dredged** to scrape mud or waste off the bottom of a lake or river
✦ **dredger** •NOUN• **dredgers** a ship that digs a channel in a river or seabed

drench •VERB• **drenches, drenching, drenched** to be drenched is to be completely wet

dress •NOUN• **dresses** 1 a dress is a piece of clothing for girls or women like a top and skirt joined together 2 dress is clothing: *dancers in traditional dress*
•VERB• **dresses, dressing, dressed** 1 to put clothes on: *The doorbell rang while I was dressing.* • *You dress the children and I'll get the breakfast.*
2 to prepare food for eating: *I just need to dress the salad.*
3 to put a bandage or plaster on a wound
4 to **dress up** is to put on special clothes:

Colin always loved to dress up as a pirate.

✦ **dresser** •NOUN• **dressers** a kitchen cupboard with open shelves at the top

✦ **dressing** •NOUN• **dressings** 1 a light sauce for food, especially salad 2 a bandage or plaster for a wound

dressmaker •NOUN• **dressmakers** a person who makes clothes for women

dress rehearsal •NOUN• **dress rehearsals** the final rehearsal for a stage show when the actors wear their costumes

drew •VERB• a way of changing the verb **draw** to make a past tense: *Who drew this face on the board?*

dribble •VERB• **dribbles, dribbling, dribbled** 1 to let liquid leak out of your mouth 2 in football, to kick the ball gently along in front of you as you run

dried •VERB• a way of changing the verb **dry** to make a past tense. It can be used with or without a helping verb: *Julia dried the glasses with a soft cloth.* ✦ *After the fruit has been dried, it will keep for ages.*

drift •VERB• **drifts, drifting, drifted** 1 to move with the tide or current of flowing water: *The boat drifted for days before being found.* 2 to wander about or live with no clear purpose
•NOUN• **drifts** 1 a pile of snow or sand that has been blown by the wind 2 the general meaning of what someone says: *I think I get your drift.*

driftwood •NOUN• wood that the sea washes up on to beaches

drill •VERB• **drills, drilling, drilled** 1 to make a hole in something hard 2 to do repeated exercises, especially in the army
•NOUN• **drills** 1 a tool for making holes in hard materials like wood or stone 2 an exercise that is repeated frequently: *a fire drill*

drink •VERB• **drinks, drinking, drank, drunk** 1 to swallow a liquid 2 to drink alcohol: *I refused the wine because I don't drink.*
•NOUN• **drinks** 1 a liquid that you swallow when you are thirsty 2 alcoholic liquids: *Please do not bring drink into the hostel.*

drip •NOUN• **drips** 1 a drop of liquid: *We're*

trying to catch the drips in a bucket. 2 a series of falling drops of liquid: *I could hear the drip of the bathroom tap all night.* 3 a piece of equipment for slowly giving a hospital patient a liquid that their body needs
•VERB• **drips, dripping, dripped** 1 to fall in drops: *water dripping from the trees* 2 to let a liquid fall in drops: *I can hear a tap dripping somewhere.*

dripping •NOUN• the fat that comes out of roasting meat

drive •VERB• **drives, driving, drove, driven**
1 to control a vehicle such as a car
2 to hit a ball very hard, especially in golf
3 to force someone into a certain state: *That tune's driving me crazy.*
•NOUN• **drives** 1 a journey in a car: *Let's go for a drive.*
2 a private road up to a house: *a car parked in the drive*
3 energy and enthusiasm: *someone with a lot of drive*
⇒ **driver**

drivel •NOUN• written or spoken nonsense

driven •VERB• a form of the verb **drive** that is used with a helping verb to make a past tense: *Have you ever driven a car like this before?*

driver •NOUN• **drivers** a person who drives a vehicle such as a car

drizzle •NOUN• light rain
•VERB• **drizzles, drizzling, drizzled** to rain gently
✦ **drizzly** •ADJECTIVE• drizzly weather is when it is dull and raining gently

droll •ADJECTIVE• **droller, drollest** funny or amusing: *a droll story that made us giggle*

drone •VERB• **drones, droning, droned** 1 to speak in a dull, boring voice: *The man seemed to drone on and on.* 2 to make a low humming sound
•NOUN• **drones** 1 a low humming sound 2 a male bee

drool •VERB• **drools, drooling, drooled** 1 to dribble 2 to **drool over** a thing or person is to be enthusiastic about them in a silly way: *We stood drooling over the dresses in the window.*

droop •VERB• **droops, drooping, drooped** to bend weakly or hang down: *The flowers are drooping.*

drop •NOUN• **drops 1** a small blob of liquid: *drops of water on the window* **2** a small quantity: *only a drop of milk left in the bottle* **3** a fall or decrease: *Kevin's new job will mean a drop in pay.* •VERB• **drops, dropping, dropped 1** to let something fall: *Drop the gun now!* **2** to fall suddenly: *The temperature drops a lot in the evening.*

droplet •NOUN• **droplets** a tiny drop of liquid

drought •NOUN• **droughts** a time when very little rain falls

ⓘ This word is pronounced **drowt**.

drove •VERB• a way of changing the verb **drive** to make a past tense: *We drove to London down the M1.*

drown •VERB• **drowns, drowning, drowned 1** to die because of not being able to breathe under water **2** to kill someone by keeping them under water so that they cannot breathe **3** to block out a sound with a louder one: *The music in the club drowned out our conversation.*

drowsy •ADJECTIVE• **drowsier, drowsiest** sleepy

drudgery •NOUN• boring, hard work

drug •NOUN• **drugs 1** a medicine: *a new drug for curing colds* **2** a chemical that people take to make them feel or think differently, or because they cannot stop using it •VERB• **drugs, drugging, drugged** to give someone a drug that will make them unconscious

drum •NOUN• **drums 1** an instrument that is round and has a skin stretched over it that you hit to make a rhythm **2** a container in the shape of a cylinder: *an oil drum* •VERB• **drums, drumming, drummed 1** to beat a drum **2** to tap your fingers repeatedly ♦ **drummer** •NOUN• **drummers** a person who plays the drums

drunk •VERB• a form of the verb **drink** that is used with a helping verb to make a past tense: *Haven't you drunk your cup of tea yet?* •ADJECTIVE• **drunker, drunkest** suffering from the effects of drinking too much alcohol: *He was so drunk he couldn't stand up straight.* •NOUN• **drunks** someone who is always drinking too much alcohol

dry •ADJECTIVE• **drier, driest 1** not wet or damp **2** not lively or interesting: *a dry book* **3** dry humour is funny in a way that is not obvious •VERB• **dries, drying, dried** to remove or lose all the liquid from something ♦ **dryly** or **drily** •ADVERB• **1** without any humour **2** in a sarcastic way ♦ **dryness** •NOUN• being dry

dry cleaning •NOUN• a way of cleaning clothes with special chemicals instead of water

dual •ADJECTIVE• made up of two of something: *Our plan has a dual purpose.*

dual carriageway •NOUN• **dual carriageways** a road where the traffic going in each direction is separated by some kind of barrier

dub •VERB• **dubs, dubbing, dubbed 1** to add new sound to a film: *We watched Robin Hood, dubbed into Italian.* **2** to give someone another name, especially a nickname: *He's been dubbed 'The Eye' by his students.*

dubious •ADJECTIVE• **1** feeling doubtful about something: *I'm a bit dubious about this new timetable.* **2** probably dishonest: *a dubious character*

duchess •NOUN• **duchesses 1** the title of a woman who has the same rank as a duke **2** the wife of a duke

duck •NOUN• **ducks** a water bird with webbed feet, short legs and a wide, flat beak •VERB• **ducks, ducking, ducked 1** to duck is to lower your head quickly, as if you were avoiding being hit **2** to duck someone is to push them under water

duckling •NOUN• **ducklings** a baby duck

duct •NOUN• **ducts** a tube or pipe

dud •NOUN• **duds** something that is faulty or does not work properly

due •ADJECTIVE• 1 expected to arrive: *Their plane is due in ten minutes.* 2 needing to be paid: *The rent is due at the beginning of the month.*
• **due to** because of: *The delay was due to roadworks on the motorway.*
•ADVERB• directly: *due south of here*
⇒ **duly**

duel •NOUN• **duels** a fight between two people that they arrange to settle an argument
•VERB• **duels, duelling, duelled** to fight another person to decide an argument

duet •NOUN• **duets** a piece of music for two singers or players

dug •VERB• a way of changing the verb **dig** to make a past tense. It can be used with or without a helping verb: *The children dug a hole under the apple tree.* • *A huge hole had been dug.*

dugout •NOUN• **dugouts** 1 a boat like a canoe, made by hollowing out a log or tree trunk 2 a hole that you dig in a bank or slope where you can shelter or hide

duke •NOUN• **dukes** a nobleman of high rank

dull •ADJECTIVE• **duller, dullest** 1 not bright: *a dull day* • *a dull blue colour*
2 not lively: *a dreadfully dull party*
3 not clear or ringing: *a dull thump on the door*
✦ **dully** •ADVERB• 1 in a boring and uninteresting way 2 not brightly: *lights shining dully in the distance*
✦ **dullness** •NOUN• being dull

duly •ADVERB• as expected: *We duly handed over our gifts to the birthday girl.*

dumb •ADJECTIVE• **dumber, dumbest** 1 not able to speak 2 stupid: *That's the dumbest idea you've ever had.*

dumbfounded •ADJECTIVE• to be dumbfounded is to be speechless with astonishment

dummy •NOUN• **dummies** 1 a model of a person, especially for displaying clothes in a shop: *The cars are crash-tested with dummies in them.*
2 an imitation teat that a baby sucks for comfort
3 an imitation of anything

dump •VERB• **dumps, dumping, dumped** 1 to unload and leave rubbish or something you do not want 2 to drop something heavily: *The kids dumped their schoolbags in the hall.*
•NOUN• **dumps** 1 a place for leaving rubbish 2 an informal word for a messy or dirty place

dumpling •NOUN• **dumplings** a cooked ball of dough that may be served with meat dishes

dumpy •ADJECTIVE• **dumpier, dumpiest** short and thick or fat

dun •NOUN• a greyish brown colour

dunce •NOUN• **dunces** a person who finds learning difficult

dune •NOUN• **dunes** a low hill of sand

dung •NOUN• the solid waste of animals

dungarees •PLURAL NOUN• a pair of trousers with a bib and braces attached

dungeon •NOUN• **dungeons** a dark underground prison

duo •NOUN• **duos** two people, especially a pair of musicians

dupe •VERB• **dupes, duping, duped** to trick or cheat someone: *The tourists were duped into handing over their money.*

duplicate •VERB• **duplicates, duplicating, duplicated** to make a copy or copies of something
•ADJECTIVE• exactly the same: *a duplicate key*
•NOUN• **duplicates** an exact copy
✦ **duplication** •NOUN• copying something exactly

durable •ADJECTIVE• lasting a long time: *a durable fabric for working clothes*
✦ **durability** •NOUN• how long-lasting something is: *We do tests on the products for durability.*

duration •NOUN• how long something lasts or continues: *a play of two hours' duration*

during •PREPOSITION• while something else

Aa
Bb
Cc
Dd
Ee
Ff
Gg
Hh
Ii
Jj
Kk
Ll
Mm
Nn
Oo
Pp
Qq
Rr
Ss
Tt
Uu
Vv
Ww
Xx
Yy
Zz

is happening: *We left during the interval.*

dusk •NOUN• twilight, when night is falling in the evening

dust •NOUN• a fine powder of something, especially household dirt
•VERB• **dusts, dusting, dusted** 1 to clean dry dirt from surfaces: *The books have to be dusted regularly.* 2 to cover something with a fine powder: *Dust the cake with icing sugar.*
⇒ **duster**

dustbin •NOUN• **dustbins** a large container for household rubbish

duster •NOUN• **dusters** a cloth for removing dust from surfaces

dustman •NOUN• **dustmen** a person whose job is to collect household rubbish

dutiful •ADJECTIVE• obedient: *He was always a dutiful son.*

duty •NOUN• **duties** 1 something a person should do, especially as part of their job: *It's your duty to check the doors are locked.* 2 a tax: *raising the duty on imports*

duty-free •ADJECTIVE• products that are duty-free are cheaper because the price does not include tax

duvet •NOUN• **duvets** a quilt stuffed with feathers or artificial fibres and used instead of blankets on a bed

ⓘ This word is pronounced **doo**-vay.

DVD •ABBREVIATION• short for **digital versatile disk** or **digital video disk**, a type of disk that pictures and sounds can be recorded on, and which can hold more information than a CD

dwarf •NOUN• **dwarfs** *or* **dwarves** a person or thing that is much smaller than normal
•VERB• **dwarfs, dwarfing, dwarfed** to make

something else look small: *The new hotel dwarfs the old shops that surround it.*

dwell •VERB• **dwells, dwelling, dwelt** 1 to live somewhere 2 to **dwell on** something is to think or speak about it for a long time: *There's no point on dwelling on your mistakes now.*

dwindle •VERB• **dwindles, dwindling, dwindled** to grow less and less: *our dwindling supplies*

dye •NOUN• **dyes** a powder or liquid that you use to change the colour of fabric
•VERB• **dyes, dyeing, dyed** to make something such as fabric a different colour: *I dyed my white shirt black.*

ⓘ When you add **-ing** to the verb **dye**, you keep the **e** to make **dyeing**. The word **dying**, without an **e**, comes from the verb **die**.

dying •VERB• a way of changing the verb **die** when it is combined with a helping verb or to make it into a noun: *I'm dying to see that film.* • *He says he isn't afraid of dying.*

dyke •NOUN• **dykes** another spelling of **dike**

dynamic •ADJECTIVE• full of energy and very active

dynamite •NOUN• a type of powerful explosive

dynamo •NOUN• **dynamos** a machine that converts the energy of movement into electricity

dynasty •NOUN• **dynasties** a series of rulers or leaders from the same family

dyslexia •NOUN• difficulty in learning to read and in spelling
♦ **dyslexic** •ADJECTIVE• a dyslexic person has difficulty in learning to recognize and form written words correctly

Ee

E ·ABBREVIATION· short for **east**

each ·ADJECTIVE· each person or thing in a group or pair is every one as an individual: *He had a heavy suitcase in each hand.*
·PRONOUN· every one individually: *Each of the girls had a different costume.*
· **each other** to, or for, the other: *The team hugged each other.* • *The cat and dog don't like each other much.*

eager ·ADJECTIVE· very keen to do or have something: *He seems eager to learn.*
✦ **eagerly** ·ADVERB· keenly, enthusiastically: *All her fans were eagerly waiting for the next book.*
✦ **eagerness** ·NOUN· being eager: *In his eagerness to be first, he kept on running.*

eagle ·NOUN· **eagles** a large bird with a hooked beak and sharp claws called talons

ear¹ ·NOUN· **ears** your ears are the two parts of your body at each side of your head that you hear with

ear² ·NOUN· **ears** an ear of corn or wheat is the part at the top of the plant's stem where the grains or seeds grow

earache ·NOUN· pain inside your ear

eardrum ·NOUN· **eardrums** the part inside your ear that vibrates when sound hits it

earl ·NOUN· **earls** a British nobleman

earlobe ·NOUN· **earlobes** the soft rounded part that hangs down at the bottom of your ear

early ·ADJECTIVE AND ADVERB· **earlier, earliest** 1 happening or arriving before others or before the expected or normal time: *He'd taken an earlier train.* • *I'm tired so I'm going to bed early tonight.* 2 near the beginning of something: *He likes getting up in the early morning.* • *She showed musical talent early in life.*

earmark ·VERB· **earmarks, earmarking, earmarked** to earmark something is to select it to be used for a special purpose or to be given special attention

earn ·VERB· **earns, earning, earned** 1 to earn is to get money in return for work: *She is trying to earn her living as an artist.* 2 to earn something good, such as praise, is to get it because you have done something well

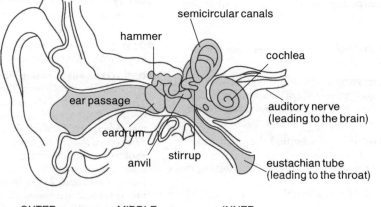

the ear

semicircular canals — hammer — cochlea — ear passage — eardrum — anvil — stirrup — auditory nerve (leading to the brain) — eustachian tube (leading to the throat)

OUTER EAR   MIDDLE EAR   INNER EAR

193

Aa
Bb
Cc
Dd
Ee
Ff
Gg
Hh
Ii
Jj
Kk
Ll
Mm
Nn
Oo
Pp
Qq
Rr
Ss
Tt
Uu
Vv
Ww
Xx
Yy
Zz

the Earth

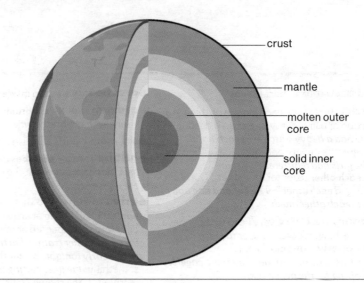

crust

mantle

molten outer core

solid inner core

earnest •ADJECTIVE• serious about, or really meaning, what you do or say
• **in earnest** if someone is in earnest they are serious or sincere about something

earnings •PLURAL NOUN• your earnings are all the money that you get from working or by investing money

earphones •PLURAL NOUN• two small speakers that you wear in or on your ears so that you can listen to music or other sounds

earplugs •PLURAL NOUN• two small plugs that you put in your ears to block out loud noises

earring •NOUN• **earrings** a piece of jewellery worn on the ear

earshot •NOUN• if a sound is in earshot it is within the range of your hearing: *I couldn't hear what they were saying because they were just out of earshot.*

earth •NOUN• **earths** 1 the Earth is the planet we live on
2 earth is the ground or soil: *digging in the earth*
3 a fox's earth is the burrow or hole it lives in
4 the earth is the wire in an electrical circuit or piece of equipment that channels the electric current into the ground and makes it safe to use
♦ **earthly** •ADJECTIVE• to do with the Earth, rather than the sky or heaven
⇒ **earthy**

earthquake •NOUN• **earthquakes** an event when the ground shakes because of pressure that has built up in the rocks of the Earth's crust

earthworm •NOUN• **earthworms** a common type of worm found in soil

earthy •ADJECTIVE• **earthier, earthiest** 1 like soil: *an earthy smell* 2 earthy humour is rather rude or vulgar

earwig •NOUN• **earwigs** a common garden insect with pincers at its tail

ease •VERB• **eases, easing, eased** 1 to ease is to make or become less difficult or painful: *The doctor gave him some painkillers to ease the pain.* 2 to ease something into or out of a place is to put it there or take it out gently: *They eased the last big block into position.*
•NOUN• 1 to do something with ease is to do it without any effort or difficulty: *He won the race with ease.* 2 ease is rest: *He was taking his ease in a hammock in the garden.*
• **at ease** if you are at ease with something you feel comfortable about it: *He sounded more at ease with her than he really was.*

easel • NOUN• **easels** a frame used by an artist to support the picture he or she is working on

(i) This word comes from the Dutch word **ezel**, which means a *donkey*, because of its shape and its job of carrying things.

easily • ADVERB• **1** without a lot of effort or difficulty: *He won easily.*
2 by a long way: *She's easily the most successful female pop singer today.*
3 very possibly: *It could easily be two weeks before you get a replacement.*

east • NOUN• **1** the direction where you see the sun rising in the morning, opposite to west **2** the East and the Far East are the countries in Asia
• ADJECTIVE• in, from, or towards the east: *an east wind* • *East London*
• ADVERB• to the east: *We headed east.*
⇒ **easterly, eastern, eastward**

Easter • NOUN• a Christian festival commemorating Christ's rising from the dead, celebrated in spring

easterly • ADJECTIVE• coming from, or going towards, the east: *an easterly breeze* • *They headed off in an easterly direction.*
• NOUN• **easterlies** a wind that comes from the east

eastern • ADJECTIVE• belonging to or coming from the east: *an eastern custom*

eastward or **eastwards** • ADVERB• to or towards the east: *sailing eastwards towards the rising sun*

easy • ADJECTIVE• **easier, easiest** not difficult or hard to do: *an easy sum*
• **take it easy** you take it easy when you relax or don't work too hard
⇒ **easily**

eat • VERB• **eats, eating, ate 1** to eat food is to chew and swallow it
2 to eat is to have a meal: *What time would you like to eat?*
3 to **eat something up** is to eat it all or to use it all up: *Eat up your greens.* • *The repairs had eaten up all their savings.*
4 to **eat something away** is to destroy it gradually: *The cliffs were being eaten away by the sea.*

eaves • PLURAL NOUN• the eaves of a building are the parts where the roof hangs over the walls

eavesdrop • VERB• **eavesdrops, eavesdropping, eavesdropped** to eavesdrop is to listen to other people's conversations without them knowing

ebb • VERB• **ebbs, ebbing, ebbed 1** the tide ebbs when the water in the sea goes back from the land. Look up and compare **flow**
2 something **ebbs away** when it gradually gets less and less until it disappears
• **at a low ebb** if something is at a low ebb it is at a low level: *Her confidence was at a low ebb.*

ebony • NOUN• a very hard black wood from an African tree

eccentric • ADJECTIVE• an eccentric person behaves very oddly
✦ **eccentricity** • NOUN• **eccentricities** odd behaviour

echo • NOUN• **echoes** an echo happens when a sound travelling away from you bounces off a surface and comes back towards you, so you hear it for a second time
• VERB• **echoes, echoing, echoed 1** a sound echoes when it is comes back and you hear it again **2** to echo what someone has said is to repeat it

(i) **Echo** comes from the Greek word for *sound*.

éclair • NOUN• **éclairs** a long thin cake made of special light pastry filled with cream and with chocolate on top

eclipse • NOUN• **eclipses 1** an eclipse of the sun happens when the sun disappears behind the moon and the sky goes dark for a few minutes **2** an eclipse of the moon happens when the Earth comes between the moon and the sun, and the Earth's shadow falls on the moon

eco- • PREFIX• if a word starts with **eco-** it has something to do with the environment. For example, *eco-friendly* means not damaging to the environment

ecology • NOUN• **1** ecology is the study of how plants and animals exist together in their environment and how they are affected

Aa
Bb
Cc
Dd
Ee
Ff
Gg
Hh
Ii
Jj
Kk
Ll
Mm
Nn
Oo
Pp
Qq
Rr
Ss
Tt
Uu
Vv
Ww
Xx
Yy
Zz

by their environment **2** the ecology of a particular area is all the plants and animals in that area and how they depend on each other and on the special conditions in that area to exist

✦ **ecological** •ADJECTIVE• to do with ecology or the ecology of a particular area

✦ **ecologist** •NOUN• **ecologists** someone who studies ecology

economic •ADJECTIVE• **1** to do with an economy: *an economic forecast* **2** making money or profit: *The business was no longer economic and closed down.*

✦ **economical** •ADJECTIVE• not wasting money: *an economical car that doesn't use a lot of fuel*

✦ **economics** •NOUN• economics is the study of how money is created and spent

✦ **economist** •NOUN• **economists** someone who studies economics

✦ **economize** or **economise** •VERB• **economizes, economizing, economized** to economize is to be careful about spending money

economy •NOUN• **economies 1** a country's economy is all the wealth it creates through producing and selling goods, and the way that wealth is used
2 economy is using something, especially money, carefully to avoid waste
3 to make economies is to make savings

ecosystem •NOUN• **ecosystems** a system in which plants and animals exist together, depending on each other and on the surrounding conditions for survival

ecstasy •NOUN• **ecstasies** ecstasy is a feeling of wild joy or pleasure

✦ **ecstatic** •ADJECTIVE• if someone is ecstatic they are as happy as it is possible to be: *If I get A's in my exams I'll be ecstatic.*

eczema •NOUN• a disease in which itchy red patches appear on the skin

edge •NOUN• **edges 1** the end of something: *the edge of the cliff* • *the edge of the table* **2** a side of something that is sharp enough to cut: *The knives have sharp edges.*
• **on edge** nervous and easily irritated: *He's a bit on edge because he's waiting for his exam results.*
•VERB• **edges, edging, edged 1** to edge

something is to border it: *pillowcases edged with lace* **2** to move slowly and carefully: *Harry edged along the narrow ledge.*

✦ **edging** •NOUN• **edgings** something that forms a border around something else

✦ **edgy** •ADJECTIVE• **edgier, edgiest** to be edgy is to feel nervous and a bit bad-tempered

edible •ADJECTIVE• if something is edible it can be eaten: *edible mushrooms*

edit •VERB• **edits, editing, edited 1** to edit a book, magazine or newspaper is to prepare it to be published or printed by correcting the text or putting all its parts together in order **2** to edit a film or tape recording is to cut it or alter it so that it is ready to be broadcast

✦ **edition** •NOUN• **editions** an edition of a book, magazine or newspaper is all the copies that are printed at the same time

✦ **editor** •NOUN• **editors 1** someone who corrects or brings together all the parts of a book, magazine, newspaper or film **2** someone in charge of what goes into a newspaper, or part of a newspaper

educate •VERB• **educates, educating, educated** to educate people is to teach them and to give them knowledge

✦ **educated** •ADJECTIVE• an educated person is someone who has knowledge as a result of having a good education

✦ **education** •NOUN• education is teaching, especially in schools or colleges

✦ **educational** •ADJECTIVE• to do with teaching and learning

eel •NOUN• **eels** a type of fish that has a long thin body like a snake

eerie •ADJECTIVE• if something is eerie, it is strange in a frightening way: *a dark and eerie old house*

✦ **eerily** •ADVERB• strangely or weirdly: *The forest suddenly became eerily silent.*

ⓘ **Eerie** comes from an old Scots word which means *afraid* or *cowardly.*

effect •NOUN• **effects 1** if one thing has an effect on another, it influences or causes something to happen to it: *His asthma has no effect on his brilliance as a footballer.*
2 the effect of something is the result it has:

He was suffering from the effects of a long plane journey.
♦ **effective** •ADJECTIVE• working well or giving the results you want: *an effective treatment for the common cold*

ⓘ You have to be careful not to confuse **effect**, which is a noun, with **affect**, which is a verb.
*One thing has an **effect** on another.*
*One thing **affects** another.*

---

effervescent •ADJECTIVE• 1 an effervescent liquid bubbles or fizzes because it is full of gas: *an effervescent drink* 2 someone with an effervescent personality seems to bubble with enthusiasm and energy

efficiency •NOUN• efficiency is working well

efficient •ADJECTIVE• an efficient process or system is one that works quickly and well

effort •NOUN• **efforts** 1 effort is hard work: *It needs a lot of effort to be an athlete.* 2 an effort is a try: *It was a really good effort.*
♦ **effortless** •ADJECTIVE• not needing, or seeming not to need, a lot of hard work or energy

eg or **e.g.** •ABBREVIATION• short for **exempli gratia**, which is Latin for 'for example': *animals found in Africa, eg the lion and the giraffe*

egg •NOUN• **eggs** 1 an egg is a shell or case with a developing baby bird, reptile or fish inside
2 an egg is one of these laid by a hen or other bird that we eat as food: *a hard-boiled egg*
3 an egg is a special cell stored inside the body of a female mammal which can grow into a baby
• **put all your eggs in one basket** if you put all your eggs in one basket you put all your money or effort into one thing, and if it fails you will lose everything
•VERB• **eggs, egging, egged** to **egg someone on** is to encourage them, usually to do something bad

ego •NOUN• **egos** your ego is the opinion you

have of your own importance: *All the attention and praise was good for her ego.*

Eid •NOUN• Eid is an Arabic word meaning *festival*. The **Eid-ul-Fitr** is a Muslim festival held each year to celebrate the end of **Ramadan**, when there is a feast and people give each other presents

eiderdown •NOUN• **eiderdowns** a warm top covering for a bed, filled with feathers or some other light material

eight •NOUN• **eights** the number 8

eighteen •NOUN• the number 18

eighteenth •ADJECTIVE AND ADVERB• after seventeenth and before nineteeth: *my cousin's eighteenth birthday party*

eighth •ADJECTIVE AND ADVERB• after seventh and before ninth: *the eighth book in the series • I came eighth in the sack race.*
•NOUN• **eighths** the fraction $\frac{1}{8}$, which means one of eight equal parts of something: *an eighth of a mile*

eighty •NOUN• **eighties** the number 80

either •ADJECTIVE• 1 the one or the other: *She can write with either hand.* 2 both: *goalposts at either end of the pitch*
•PRONOUN• the one or the other of two: *He can't afford either of them.*
•ADVERB• as well: *If you don't go, I won't go either.*
•CONJUNCTION• **either** is used with **or** to show a choice or alternative: *You can have either a video game or a CD.*

ⓘ Remember that the verb that follows **either** and **or** should be singular if a singular noun comes before it, and the verb should be plural if a plural noun comes before it.
*Either George or his brother **was** telling lies.*
*Either George or his brothers **were** telling lies.*

---

eject •VERB• **ejects, ejecting, ejected** 1 to eject something is to throw it out with sudden force: *The octopus ejected a cloud of black ink.* 2 if a pilot ejects from an aircraft in an emergency, he or she operates a special seat which is fired out of the cockpit

elaborate •ADJECTIVE• involving complicated detail or decoration: *an*

Aa
Bb
Cc
Dd
Ee
Ff
Gg
Hh
Ii
Jj
Kk
Ll
Mm
Nn
Oo
Pp
Qq
Rr
Ss
Tt
Uu
Vv
Ww
Xx
Yy
Zz

elaborate plan • *an elaborate costume*
•VERB• **elaborates, elaborating, elaborated**
to **elaborate on** something is to explain it
more fully or in more detail

elastic •ADJECTIVE• able to stretch and then
spring back
•NOUN• elastic is a strip of fabric with rubber
or some other stretchy material woven into
it to make it springy
♦ **elasticity** •NOUN• the quality of being
stretchy or springy

elated •ADJECTIVE• very pleased and
excited: *They were elated at the thought of
the holidays.*

elbow •NOUN• **elbows** the joint in the middle
of your arm that bends
•VERB• **elbows, elbowing, elbowed** to
elbow someone is to poke or push them with
your elbow

elder •ADJECTIVE• older: *elder brothers and
sisters*
•NOUN• **elders** your elders are people who
are older than you
♦ **elderly** •ADJECTIVE• an elderly person is
old
♦ **eldest** •ADJECTIVE• oldest: *his eldest child*

elect •VERB• **elects, electing, elected** to elect
someone is to choose them by voting: *elect a
president*
♦ **election** •NOUN• **elections** the choosing of
someone by voting: *standing for election* • *a
presidential election*
♦ **elector** •NOUN• **electors** someone who
votes in an election
♦ **electorate** •NOUN• **electorates** all the
people who can vote in an election

electric •ADJECTIVE• made or worked by
electricity: *an electric spark* • *an electric
light*
♦ **electrical** •ADJECTIVE• carrying or
producing electricity: *an electrical circuit*
• *an electrical storm*

electrician •NOUN• **electricians** someone
whose job is to fit or repair electric lights and
other electrical equipment

electricity •NOUN• a form of energy used to
make light and heat and to give power to
machinery

ⓘ This word comes from the Greek word
elektron, which means *amber*. This is
because amber makes electricity when it is
rubbed.

electrify •VERB• **electrifies, electrifying,
electrified 1** to electrify machinery or
equipment is to make it work on electric
power **2** if something electrifies you, it
excites, shocks or startles you

electro- •PREFIX• if a word starts with
electro- it has something to do with
electricity. For example, an *electromagnet* is
a magnet that is worked by an electric
current

electrocute •VERB• **electrocutes,
electrocuting, electrocuted** to be
electrocuted is to be killed by a strong
electric current which passes through the
body: *He was electrocuted while he was
trying to fix the lights.*
♦ **electrocution** •NOUN• electrocuting
someone or being electrocuted

electrode •NOUN• **electrodes** a small metal
device that allows electric current to pass
from a source of power, such as a battery, to
a piece of equipment

electromagnet •NOUN• **electromagnets** a
magnet that works when an electric current
passes through it

electron •NOUN• **electrons** a particle with an
electric charge that orbits the nucleus of an
atom

electronic •ADJECTIVE• **1** electronic
equipment uses very small electrical circuits
such as silicon chips and transistors **2** to do
with electronics: *an electronics lab*
♦ **electronics** •NOUN• electronics is a
branch of physics that studies electrons and
the way they can be used in machinery

electroplating •NOUN• using electricity to
coat one metal with another metal

elegance •NOUN• being graceful and
tastefully dressed
♦ **elegant** •ADJECTIVE• stylish and smart:
an elegant lady

element •NOUN• **elements 1** a chemical
element is a substance which cannot be split
into separate or simpler substances.

Hydrogen, oxygen, nitrogen and carbon are elements

2 the elements of something are the basic parts that make it up: *the elements of mathematics*

3 the elements are things like rain and wind that make the weather, especially bad weather: *They were stuck on a bare hillside, completely exposed to the elements.*

4 a small part or bit of something: *There is an element of truth in what he said.*

5 a bent or coiled piece of metal containing an electric wire that heats an electric kettle or oven

• **in your element** if you are in your element you are doing the thing that you are best at or that you enjoy the most

✦ **elementary** •ADJECTIVE• at the simplest or most basic level: *an elementary particle* • *an elementary school*

elephant •NOUN• **elephants** a very large animal with a long trunk, large flapping ears, thick grey skin and tusks made of ivory

elevate •VERB• **elevates, elevating, elevated** to elevate something is to raise it

✦ **elevator** •NOUN• **elevators** an elevator is a lift for carrying people between the floors in a building

eleven •NOUN• **elevens** the number 11

eleventh •ADJECTIVE• after tenth and before twelfth: *the eleventh day of the eleventh month*

elf •NOUN• **elves** in stories, a tiny fairy that gets up to mischief. An elf is often described as having a thin face with pointed ears

✦ **elfin** •ADJECTIVE• like an elf: *a small elfin face*

eligible •ADJECTIVE• an eligible person is suitable for or allowed to do something: *Am I eligible for a payment?*

✦ **eligibility** •NOUN• being suitable or qualifying for something

eliminate •VERB• **eliminates, eliminating, eliminated** to eliminate something is to get rid of it completely: *eliminate poverty*

✦ **elimination** •NOUN• getting rid of something completely

elite •NOUN• **elites** the elite in a society or

group are the best or most important people in it: *the sporting elite*

•ADJECTIVE• belonging to an elite

elk •NOUN• **elk** *or* **elks** a type of very large deer with large horns that is found in northern Europe and Asia

ellipse •NOUN• **ellipses** an oval shape

✦ **elliptical** •ADJECTIVE• shaped like an oval: *a planet with an elliptical orbit*

elm •NOUN• **elms** a type of tall tree with broad round leaves

elocution •NOUN• elocution is the art of speaking correctly and clearly

elongate •VERB• **elongates, elongating, elongated** to elongate is to get or make longer

eloquent •ADJECTIVE• able to talk and express yourself well

else •ADVERB• other than or besides the thing or person already talked about: *They didn't have anywhere else to go.*

• **or else** otherwise: *Put on a jumper or else you'll catch cold.*

elsewhere •ADVERB• in another place: *Luckily, he'd been elsewhere when his house was destroyed.*

elude •VERB• **eludes, eluding, eluded 1** to elude someone who is looking for you is to get away from them without being seen or caught **2** if something eludes you, you can't get hold of it or remember it: *The phrase he wanted eluded him.*

✦ **elusive** •ADJECTIVE• difficult to see or find

e-mail •NOUN• **e-mails** short for **electronic mail**, a message or messages that are sent between computers: *They keep in touch by e-mail.* • *He sends me an e-mail every day.*

•VERB• **e-mails, e-mailing, e-mailed** to e-mail someone is to send them an e-mail

embankment •NOUN• **embankments** a steep bank of earth or rock built up along the sides of a railway, canal or motorway

embark •VERB• **embarks, embarking, embarked 1** to embark is to get on a ship at the beginning of a journey **2** to **embark on** something is to begin it: *They'd embarked on an exciting new project.*

Aa Bb Cc Dd **Ee** Ff Gg Hh Ii Jj Kk Ll Mm Nn Oo Pp Qq Rr Ss Tt Uu Vv Ww Xx Yy Zz

Aa Bb Cc Dd Ee Ff Gg Hh Ii Jj Kk Ll Mm Nn Oo Pp Qq Rr Ss Tt Uu Vv Ww Xx Yy Zz

embarrass •VERB• **embarrasses, embarrassing, embarrassed** to embarrass someone is to make them feel uncomfortable or ashamed
♦ **embarrassed** •ADJECTIVE• looking or feeling ashamed or self-conscious
♦ **embarrassing** •ADJECTIVE• causing embarrassment
♦ **embarrassment** •NOUN• being embarrassed

embassy •NOUN• **embassies** a building where an ambassador lives and works

embellish •VERB• **embellishes, embellishing, embellished** to embellish something is to add details to it to make it more fancy or more interesting
♦ **embellishment** •NOUN• **embellishments** an embellishment is something added as decoration or to make something more interesting

embers •PLURAL NOUN• the small hot pieces left when coal or wood is burnt in a fire

emblem •NOUN• **emblems** an object or image that is used as a symbol for something else : *The thistle is the emblem of Scotland.*

embrace •VERB• **embraces, embracing, embraced 1** to embrace someone is to put your arms round them and hold them tight **2** to embrace something, such as an idea or belief, is to accept it or adopt it **3** to embrace something is to include it : *a subject that embraces both maths and science*
•NOUN• **embraces** a hug

embroider •VERB• **embroiders, embroidering, embroidered** to embroider is to stitch patterns with coloured threads
♦ **embroidery** •NOUN• decorative stitching

embryo •NOUN• **embryos** a baby animal or bird at the very earliest stages of its development when it starts growing inside its mother's womb or inside an egg

emend •VERB• **emends, emending, emended** to emend something is to take out any errors or faults in it

emerald •NOUN• **emeralds 1** a green precious stone **2** a bright green colour

emerge •VERB• **emerges, emerging, emerged** to emerge is to come out : *The baby crocodiles emerge from the eggs.*

emergency •NOUN• **emergencies** an emergency is a sudden, unexpected event, often one that puts people's lives or property in danger

emigrant •NOUN• **emigrants** someone who leaves one country to go and live in another

emigrate •VERB• **emigrates, emigrating, emigrated** to emigrate is to leave your country to go and live in another country

eminent •ADJECTIVE• an eminent person is famous and well-respected : *an eminent lawyer*

emission •NOUN• **emissions 1** emission is emitting something **2** an emission is something that is given out, such as the fumes from a car's exhaust or smoke from a factory chimney

emit •VERB• **emits, emitting, emitted** to emit something, such as light, heat, gas or a sound, is to give it out : *The machine emitted a high-pitched screech.*

emotion •NOUN• **emotions** emotions are strong feelings, such as love, hate, fear, jealousy or anger : *He showed no emotion as he was sentenced to jail.* • *She tried to control her emotions.*
♦ **emotional** •ADJECTIVE• showing or having strong feelings : *an emotional farewell*

empathize *or* **empathise** •VERB• **empathizes, empathizing, empathized** to empathize with someone is to feel close to them because you have experienced the same things they have
♦ **empathy** •NOUN• empathy is feeling close to someone because you know how they feel

emperor •NOUN• **emperors** the ruler of an empire

emphasis •NOUN• **emphases** emphasis is special importance given to something or extra stress put on something to make it stand out : *Say the line with a bit more emphasis.*
♦ **emphasize** *or* **emphasise** •VERB•

emphasizes, emphasizing, emphasized to emphasize something is to make it stand out: *I want to emphasize the importance of road safety.*
♦ **emphatic** •ADJECTIVE• an emphatic statement is made strongly or firmly

empire •NOUN• **empires** 1 an empire is a group of countries governed by a single ruler 2 a business empire is a group of companies or businesses controlled by one person or organization

employ •VERB• **employs, employing, employed** you employ someone who works for you, usually in return for pay: *The company employs skilled workers.*
♦ **employee** •NOUN• **employees** someone who works for a company or another person
♦ **employer** •NOUN• **employers** a company or person who employs people
♦ **employment** •NOUN• employment is work, especially for pay

empress •NOUN• **empresses** a female ruler of an empire

emptiness •NOUN• being empty

empty •ADJECTIVE• **emptier, emptiest** having nothing or no one inside: *an empty glass • an empty classroom*
•VERB• **empties, emptying, emptied** 1 to empty is to make or become empty: *Empty your pockets.* 2 to empty something is to tip or pour it out of a container: *The dustmen were emptying the rubbish out of the bins.*

emu •NOUN• **emus** a large Australian bird that cannot fly and looks similar to, but is smaller than, an ostrich

emulate •VERB• **emulates, emulating, emulated** to emulate someone is to copy them because you admire them

en- •PREFIX• look up **in-**

enable •VERB• **enables, enabling, enabled** if something enables you to do something, it makes it possible for you to do it: *Sponsorship would enable more young athletes to develop.*

enamel •NOUN• **enamels** 1 a hard shiny coating that is baked on to metal in a very hot oven to protect or decorate it

2 the hard white coating on teeth
•ADJECTIVE• made of or covered with enamel: *an enamel plate*

enchant •VERB• **enchants, enchanting, enchanted** 1 if something enchants you, it delights or charms you 2 fairies and witches in stories enchant people when they put a magic spell or charm on them
♦ **enchanted** •ADJECTIVE• magical or under a magic spell: *an enchanted forest*
♦ **enchanting** •ADJECTIVE• delightful or charming: *an enchanting smile*
♦ **enchantment** •NOUN• **enchantments** a feeling of delight or wonder

enclose •VERB• **encloses, enclosing, enclosed** 1 to enclose something is to surround it with a fence or wall 2 to enclose something in an envelope or package is to put it inside
♦ **enclosure** •NOUN• **enclosures** 1 an area of land with a wall or fence around it 2 something you put in an envelope or package with a letter

encore •NOUN• **encores** an extra song or dance performed at the end of a stage show because the audience has shown that they want more

ⓘ This word is pronounced **on**-cor.

encounter •VERB• **encounters, encountering, encountered** 1 to encounter something is to come up against it: *They encountered many difficulties on their journey.* 2 to encounter someone is to meet them by chance
•NOUN• **encounters** a meeting: *an encounter with enemy troops*

encourage •VERB• **encourages, encouraging, encouraged** 1 to encourage someone is to support them and make them feel confident about what they are doing or are planning to do 2 to encourage something is to do something that will make it more likely to happen
♦ **encouraging** •ADJECTIVE• giving confidence or hope: *an encouraging sign*
♦ **encouragement** •NOUN• supporting or giving confidence to someone or something: *The crowd roared, all shouting encouragement to the team they favoured.*

Aa
Bb
Cc
Dd
Ee
Ff
Gg
Hh
Ii
Jj
Kk
Ll
Mm
Nn
Oo
Pp
Qq
Rr
Ss
Tt
Uu
Vv
Ww
Xx
Yy
Zz

Aa
Bb
Cc
Dd
Ee
Ff
Gg
Hh
Ii
Jj
Kk
Ll
Mm
Nn
Oo
Pp
Qq
Rr
Ss
Tt
Uu
Vv
Ww
Xx
Yy
Zz

encyclopedia *or* **encyclopaedia**
• NOUN • **encyclopedias** *or* **encyclopaedias** a book with information about many subjects, or on a particular subject
♦ **encyclopedic** • ADJECTIVE • giving or having a lot of facts and information about many things

ⓘ The word **encyclopedia** comes from the Greek word **enkyklios**, which means *everyday*, and **paideia**, which means *education*. An encyclopedia is thought to give you a general education because it informs you about a wide variety of subjects.

end • NOUN • **ends** 1 the end of something is its last part or the place where it finishes: *the end of the day* • *I read the book from beginning to end.*
2 the ends of something are the parts farthest away from the middle: *He was running from one end of the pitch to the other.*
3 an end is a result that you aim for or a purpose that you have: *They used their power for their own private ends.*
• **make ends meet** to make ends meet is to have enough money to buy what you need
• **on end** without a stop: *The rain continued for days and weeks on end.*
• VERB • **ends, ending, ended** 1 to finish: *Our holiday ends tomorrow.* • *He ended his speech with a joke.* 2 to **end up** somewhere is to finish there or come to a stop there
⇒ **ending**

endanger • VERB • **endangers, endangering, endangered** to endanger something is to put it in danger or at risk

endangered species • NOUN •
endangered species an endangered species is a type of animal or plant that is in danger of dying out

endeavour • VERB • **endeavours, endeavouring, endeavoured** to endeavour to do something is to try to do it, especially in a serious or determined way
• NOUN • **endeavours** 1 endeavour is the effort or energy people put into doing things: *human endeavour* 2 an endeavour is an attempt to do something which needs effort or energy: *I wish you luck in all your endeavours.*

ending • NOUN • **endings** the last part: *The story had a happy ending.*

endorse • VERB • **endorses, endorsing, endorsed** to endorse something is to give it your support
♦ **endorsement** • NOUN • **endorsements** something that supports or confirms: *an endorsement of the new plan*

endure • VERB • **endures, enduring, endured** 1 to endure something is to put up with it over a long period of time: *He didn't know if he could endure the loneliness any more.* 2 to endure is to last: *These trees have endured for decades.*
♦ **endurance** • NOUN • the ability to last or to survive long periods of strain

enemy • NOUN • **enemies** 1 someone or something that is against you or wants to do you harm 2 in a war, the enemy is the people or country you are fighting against

energetic • ADJECTIVE • very active and lively: *an energetic dance*

energy • NOUN • **energies** 1 the strength or power to work or be active: *He's got bags of energy.* 2 a form of power, such as heat or electricity: *trying to save energy* • *nuclear energy*

enforce • VERB • **enforces, enforcing, enforced** to enforce a rule or law is to use it and make sure people obey it

engage • VERB • **engages, engaging, engaged** 1 to engage someone is to start to employ them 2 to engage in an activity is to do it or keep busy doing it
♦ **engaged** • ADJECTIVE • 1 if two people are engaged they have promised to marry each other 2 a telephone or toilet is engaged when it is being used
♦ **engagement** • NOUN • **engagements** 1 a promise of marriage 2 an appointment to meet someone or to do something for a certain period of time

engine • NOUN • **engines** 1 a machine that turns the energy made by burning fuel into movement 2 the vehicle at the front of a train that pulls the coaches

engineer • NOUN • **engineers** 1 someone who works with or designs engines and machines 2 someone who designs and

makes things like bridges and roads
•VERB• **engineers, engineering, engineered**
to engineer something is to make it happen
by clever planning: *He tried to engineer a
meeting between the two sides.*
♦ **engineering** •NOUN• engineering is the
science or work of designing and making
machinery, or of designing roads and bridges

engrave •VERB• **engraves, engraving,
engraved** to engrave a design or lettering is
to carve it into a hard surface, such as metal
or glass
♦ **engraving** •NOUN• **engravings** the
process or skill of carving designs or lettering
into metal or glass

engrossed •ADJECTIVE• if you are
engrossed in something it takes your whole
attention or interest

enhance •VERB• **enhances, enhancing,
enhanced** to enhance something is to make
it better or greater

enjoy •VERB• **enjoys, enjoying, enjoyed**
1 to enjoy something is to get a feeling of
pleasure from it: *They seemed to enjoy the
concert.* **2** to enjoy yourself is to have a good
time: *We enjoyed ourselves at the party.*
♦ **enjoyable** •ADJECTIVE• giving a feeling of
pleasure
♦ **enjoyment** •NOUN• pleasure

enlarge •VERB• **enlarges, enlarging,
enlarged** to enlarge something is to make it
bigger
♦ **enlargement** •NOUN• **enlargements**
1 increasing in size **2** a larger photograph
made from a smaller one

enlist •VERB• **enlists, enlisting, enlisted 1** to
enlist is to join the army, navy or air force **2** if
you enlist the help or support of someone
you get it

enormous •ADJECTIVE• very big: *an
enormous tree*
♦ **enormously** •ADVERB• **1** very greatly:
They all enjoyed themselves enormously.
2 extremely: *enormously grateful*

ⓘ This word comes from the Latin word
enormis, which means *unusual* or *not normal*.

enough •ADJECTIVE• as much or as many as
you need, want or can put up with: *I've got

enough problems without this!*
•PRONOUN• as much as you need, want or
can put up with: *Have you all had enough to
eat and drink?*
•ADVERB• as much as is needed or wanted:
You've gone far enough.

enquire •VERB• **enquires, enquiring,
enquired** another spelling of **inquire**
♦ **enquiry** •NOUN• **enquiries** another
spelling of **inquiry**

enrage •VERB• **enrages, enraging, enraged**
if something enrages you it makes you very
angry

enrich •VERB• **enriches, enriching, enriched**
to enrich something is to improve it by
adding something to it: *Art enriches people's
lives.*

enrol *or* **enroll** •VERB• **enrols, enrolling,
enrolled** to enrol is to put your name on a
register or list: *Jackie enrolled at a stage
school.*
♦ **enrolment** •NOUN• enrolling or the
number of people enrolled

ensue •VERB• **ensues, ensuing, ensued** to
ensue is to come after or as a result of
something else: *Hundreds of people came
into the shop and chaos ensued.*

ensure •VERB• **ensures, ensuring, ensured**
to ensure is to make certain: *Please ensure
you have all your belongings with you.*

entail •VERB• **entails, entailing, entailed**
1 one thing entails another when it makes
that other thing necessary: *Learning the
piano entails hours of practice.* **2** what
something entails is what is involved in doing
it: *Can you tell me what the job will entail?*

entangled •ADJECTIVE• if things are
entangled they are wound around each
other so that it is difficult to separate them

enter •VERB• **enters, entering, entered 1** to
enter, or enter a place, is to go in, or to go into
it
   2 to enter a competition is to take part in
it
   3 to enter something in a book, list or
computer is to write it in the book or list, or
key it into the computer

enterprise •NOUN• **enterprises 1** if

Aa Bb Cc Dd Ee Ff Gg Hh Ii Jj Kk Ll Mm Nn Oo Pp Qq Rr Ss Tt Uu Vv Ww Xx Yy Zz

Aa
Bb
Cc
Dd
Ee
Ff
Gg
Hh
Ii
Jj
Kk
Ll
Mm
Nn
Oo
Pp
Qq
Rr
Ss
Tt
Uu
Vv
Ww
Xx
Yy
Zz

someone shows enterprise they have the ability to think of and try out new ideas and find ways to carry them out **2** an enterprise is something that involves planning and risk, such as a business

♦ **enterprising** • ADJECTIVE • an enterprising person is adventurous and able to think of new ways of doing things

entertain • VERB • **entertains, entertaining, entertained 1** to entertain people is to amuse them: *Emily entertained us by telling jokes.* **2** to entertain people is to invite them as your guests for a meal or a drink

♦ **entertainer** • NOUN • **entertainers** someone who does an act on stage, radio or TV to entertain people

♦ **entertaining** • ADJECTIVE • amusing

♦ **entertainment** • NOUN • **entertainments** something that amuses people or gives them pleasure

enthral • VERB • **enthrals, enthralling, enthralled** if something enthrals you it fascinates you and holds your attention completely

enthusiasm • NOUN • if someone has enthusiasm they are very keen to do or try things or they show a great deal of interest in something

♦ **enthusiast** • NOUN • **enthusiasts** someone who is very interested or involved in a particular thing: *James is a great cycling enthusiast.*

♦ **enthusiastic** • ADJECTIVE • eager and showing keenness: *enthusiastic applause*

entire • ADJECTIVE • an entire thing is the whole of it: *He spent the entire day paddling in the sea.*

♦ **entirely** • ADVERB • totally or completely: *It was my fault entirely.*

entitle • VERB • **entitles, entitling, entitled** if something entitles you to something it gives you the right to have it or do it: *You are entitled to five weeks' holiday per year.*

♦ **entitlement** • NOUN • something you are entitled to: *holiday entitlement*

entrance • NOUN • **entrances 1** a place where you can go in or out: *He left by a side entrance.* **2** to make an entrance is to come into a room or come on to a stage

♦ **entrant** • NOUN • **entrants** someone who enters a competition or contest

entry • NOUN • **entries 1** going in or entering: *his entry into politics* • *There was a high iron gate barring our entry.* **2** an entry in a diary or book is one of the items written or printed in it

envelop • VERB • **envelops, enveloping, enveloped** if one thing envelops another it surrounds it and covers it completely: *A thick fog enveloped the hills.*

envelope • NOUN • **envelopes** a folded paper covering for a letter or other document, especially one that is to be sent by post

envious • ADJECTIVE • if you are envious of someone you want something that they have

environment • NOUN • **environments 1** a person's or animal's environment is their surroundings where they live **2** the environment is all the things, such as air, land, sea, animals and plants, that make up the natural world around us

♦ **environmental** • ADJECTIVE • to do with the environment

envy • NOUN • if you feel envy, you want what someone else has

• VERB • **envies, envying, envied** to envy someone is to want what they have: *We envied him, because he did not have to go to school.*

⇒ **envious**

enzyme • NOUN • **enzymes** one of a group of chemical substances made in both animals and plants, which cause certain chemical changes to begin or which control the speed of chemical changes

epic • NOUN • **epics** an epic is a long story, poem or film about great events or exciting and heroic adventures

epicentre • NOUN • **epicentres** the epicentre of an earthquake is the point on the ground just above where the earthquake starts and where it is strongest

epidemic • NOUN • **epidemics** an epidemic happens when an illness or disease spreads and many people get it: *a flu epidemic*

epilepsy • NOUN • epilepsy is an illness that

affects the brain and which causes short spells of unconsciousness and uncontrolled movements of the body called convulsions
✦ **epileptic** • ADJECTIVE • caused by epilepsy: *an epileptic fit*
• NOUN • **epileptics** someone who suffers from epilepsy

episode • NOUN • **episodes** 1 an episode is one of the parts of a story or one of the programmes in a radio or TV series 2 an episode is an event: *It was one of the most embarrassing episodes of his life.*

epitaph • NOUN • **epitaphs** a dead person's epitaph is what is written about them on their gravestone

epoch • NOUN • **epochs** a long period of time in history at the beginning and end of which there were great or important changes

equal • ADJECTIVE • 1 two or more things are equal when they are of the same size, value or amount 2 if you are equal to a task you are fit or able to do it
• VERB • **equals, equalling, equalled** one thing equals another when they are the same in size, value or amount
• NOUN • **equals** a person's equal is someone who is as good as they are
✦ **equality** • NOUN • being equal
✦ **equalize** *or* **equalise** • VERB • **equalizes, equalizing, equalized** to equalize things is to make them equal
✦ **equalizer** *or* **equaliser** • NOUN • **equalizers** *or* **equalisers** something that makes things equal, especially a goal that makes two teams' scores equal
✦ **equally** • ADVERB • evenly or in the same way: *The two drivers were equally to blame for the accident.*

equation • NOUN • **equations** in maths, a statement that two things are equal with the two parts written on either side of an equals sign, for example $15 + 4 = 25 - 6$

equator • NOUN • the equator is the line drawn on maps that goes around the Earth halfway between the North Pole and the South Pole

equestrian • ADJECTIVE • to do with horse riding

equilateral • ADJECTIVE • having equal sides: *an equilateral triangle*

equilibrium • NOUN • equal balance between two things

equinox • NOUN • **equinoxes** either of two times of year, in March and September, when day and night are equal in length

equip • VERB • **equips, equipping, equipped** to equip someone is to provide them with all the things that will be needed to do a particular job: *They equipped themselves with ropes, crampons, ice axes and oxygen for the ascent of Everest.*
✦ **equipment** • NOUN • equipment is a set of tools and special clothing needed to do a particular activity or job: *a shop selling camping and climbing equipment*

equivalent • ADJECTIVE • if two or more things are equivalent they have the same value, use, meaning or effect
• NOUN • **equivalents** something that is equivalent to something else: *Two sixes are the equivalent of three fours.*

era • NOUN • **eras** a particular period in history: *the era of the dinosaurs*

erase • VERB • **erases, erasing, erased** to erase something is to rub it out or make it disappear
✦ **eraser** • NOUN • **erasers** an eraser is a rubber used to remove writing or marks made in pencil or ink

erect • ADJECTIVE • upright: *an erect posture*
• VERB • **erects, erecting, erected** to erect something is to put it up: *They erected their tents.*
✦ **erection** • NOUN • **erections** something that stands up or is built

erode • VERB • **erodes, eroding, eroded** if something erodes or is eroded, it is slowly worn away
✦ **erosion** • NOUN • the gradual wearing away of something, such as stone or soil

errand • NOUN • **errands** if you go on an errand for someone you go somewhere to do something for them

error • NOUN • **errors** a mistake: *There's an error in this column of figures.*

erupt • VERB • **erupts, erupting, erupted** 1 if a volcano erupts, hot lava, ash and dust is

Aa
Bb
Cc
Dd
Ee
Ff
Gg
Hh
Ii
Jj
Kk
Ll
Mm
Nn
Oo
Pp
Qq
Rr
Ss
Tt
Uu
Vv
Ww
Xx
Yy
Zz

thrown out of it **2** something erupts when it suddenly bursts or breaks out: *Violence erupted at the demonstration.*

♦ **eruption** •NOUN• **eruptions** an eruption is the throwing out of lava, ash and dust by a volcano

escalate •VERB• **escalates, escalating, escalated** if something escalates it increases or gets more intense

♦ **escalator** •NOUN• **escalators** a moving stairway for carrying people between the floors of a building

escapade •NOUN• **escapades** an adventure, often one where rules or laws are broken

escape •VERB• **escapes, escaping, escaped**
1 to escape is to get out or away to safety or freedom: *The lion had escaped from its cage.*
2 to escape something is to avoid it: *You're lucky to have escaped punishment.*
3 if something escapes you, it slips from your memory
•NOUN• **escapes 1** escaping **2** a way to get free or get away to safety

escort •VERB• **escorts, escorting, escorted** to escort someone is to go somewhere with them: *We were escorted into the room by the butler.*
•NOUN• **escorts** someone who escorts another person

Eskimo •NOUN• **Eskimos** Eskimos are the Inuit people, who live in cold places such as Greenland, Canada and Alaska

---

ⓘ Nowadays, the Inuit prefer not to be called Eskimos.

---

especially •ADVERB• particularly: *It was especially cold that morning.*

ⓘ Remember the difference between **especially** and **specially**.
Especially means 'particularly': *I like all of the characters, especially Harry.*
Specially means 'for a special purpose': *I cooked this meal specially for you.*

---

espionage •NOUN• spying to find out another country's or company's secrets

esplanade •NOUN• **esplanades** a long level road, especially along the seafront in a town

essay •NOUN• **essays** a long piece of writing about a particular subject

essence •NOUN• **essences 1** the essence of something is its most important part or its true character **2** essence is a concentrated liquid, especially taken from a plant and containing its flavour or scent

essential •ADJECTIVE• if something is essential it is absolutely necessary and you must have it or do it
•NOUN• **essentials** an essential is something that you must have

establish •VERB• **establishes, establishing, established 1** to establish something is to set it up: *He established a small bakery business.*
2 to establish something is to find it out and prove it: *establishing the truth*

♦ **establishment** •NOUN• **establishments**
1 the establishment of something is setting it up or proving it **2** an establishment is a place where a business is set up and is operating

estate •NOUN• **estates 1** a large piece of land belonging to one person or one family
2 a large area with lots of houses or factories and businesses built on it: *a housing estate • an industrial estate*
3 a person's estate is all the things they have or own, such as property and money

estate agent •NOUN• **estate agents** someone who is employed to sell people's houses and who charges them a fee for doing so

estate car •NOUN• **estate cars** a large type of car with a lot of space behind the seats for carrying things

esteem •NOUN• esteem is thinking well of someone: *He was held in high esteem by his team mates.*
•VERB• **esteems, esteeming, esteemed** to esteem someone or something is to think highly of them

estimate •VERB• **estimates, estimating, estimated** to estimate something is to try to judge what its size, amount or value is without measuring it accurately
•NOUN• **estimates** a rough judgement of what something's size, amount or value is

♦ **estimation** •NOUN• estimating or rough

judgement made without accurate measurements or all the facts

estuary • NOUN• **estuaries** the wide part of a river where it meets the sea

etc *or* **etc.** • ABBREVIATION• short for **et cetera**, which is Latin for 'and the rest'. **Etc** is used after a list to show that there are other things that have not been named: *An art shop selling paints, canvases, brushes, etc.*

etch • VERB• **etches, etching, etched** to draw lines and patterns on metal and glass by letting acid eat away the places where you want the lines to be
   ✦ **etching** • NOUN• **etchings** an etching is a print made from a metal plate that has the picture etched on to it

eternal • ADJECTIVE• lasting for ever or seeming to last for ever: *the eternal cycle of the seasons*
   ✦ **eternally** • ADVERB• for ever
   ✦ **eternity** • NOUN• eternity is time that never ends

ethic • NOUN• **ethics 1** an ethic is a rule or principle by which someone lives: *the work ethic* **2** ethics are rules or principles about what is right and wrong
   ✦ **ethical** • ADJECTIVE• to do with ethics or what is morally right

ethnic • ADJECTIVE• ethnic is used to refer to the particular race or culture that someone belongs to: *an ethnic group*

etiquette • NOUN• a code of good manners

eucalyptus • NOUN• **eucalyptuses** *or* **eucalypti** a type of Australian tree that is evergreen and whose leaves contain a strong-smelling oil that is used as a flavouring

euphemism • NOUN• **euphemisms** a word or phrase that you use instead of one that might offend or shock people. For example, euphemisms such as *to pass on*, or *to slip away* are used when people want to avoid mentioning death or dying

European • ADJECTIVE• to do with or belonging to the continent of Europe
   • NOUN• **Europeans** someone who comes from Europe

euphoria • NOUN• euphoria is a feeling of excited happiness or joy
   ✦ **euphoric** • ADJECTIVE• feeling euphoria

euthanasia • NOUN• euthanasia is helping someone who is suffering from an incurable disease to die

evacuate • VERB• **evacuates, evacuating, evacuated 1** if people evacuate a place they leave it because it has become dangerous **2** to evacuate people from a place is to help or order them to leave because it has become dangerous
   ✦ **evacuation** • NOUN• **evacuations** leaving or emptying a place, especially because it has become dangerous
   ✦ **evacuee** • NOUN• **evacuees** someone who has been evacuated from a place, especially during a war

evade • VERB• **evades, evading, evaded** to evade something is to avoid it or avoid dealing with it directly
   ⇒ evasion

evaluate • VERB• **evaluates, evaluating, evaluated** to evaluate something is to decide how good or useful it is

evaporate • VERB• **evaporates, evaporating, evaporated** if liquid evaporates it turns into a gas or vapour and disappears
   ✦ **evaporation** • NOUN• turning into a vapour or gas

evasion • NOUN• **evasions** evasion is purposely avoiding something

eve • NOUN• **eves** the eve of a particular day is the day or evening before

even • ADJECTIVE• **1** an even surface is level and smooth
   2 things are even when they are equal: *The scores were even.*
   3 an even number is one that can be divided by 2 without a remainder, for example 12 104 and 6000. Look up and compare **odd**
   4 someone who has an even temper is calm and doesn't suddenly change their mood
   • **get even with** to get even with someone who has done something to harm you is to get your revenge on them
   • ADVERB• even is used to emphasize another word: *It was even colder the next morning.*

Aa
Bb
Cc
Dd
Ee
Ff
Gg
Hh
Ii
Jj
Kk
Ll
Mm
Nn
Oo
Pp
Qq
Rr
Ss
Tt
Uu
Vv
Ww
Xx
Yy
Zz

Aa

• **even so** though that may be true: *It looks like the right one, but even so, I'd like to check.*

Bb

•VERB• **evens, evening, evened 1** if something **evens out** it becomes level **2** if two or more things **even out** they become equal or balanced

Cc

Dd

evening •NOUN• **evenings** evening is the last part of the day and the early part of the night

Ee

Ff

evenly •ADVERB• **1** levelly or smoothly: *Spread the icing evenly over the top of the cake.* **2** equally: *evenly balanced*

Gg

Hh

event •NOUN• **events 1** a happening that stands out or is important for some reason: *events in history* **2** one of the items in a programme of sports or entertainment: *The next event is the sack race.*

Ii

◆ **eventful** •ADJECTIVE• full of action, excitement and important events: *She's led an eventful life.*

Jj

Kk

Ll

eventual •ADJECTIVE• happening at the end of a period of time or as a result of some process: *the eventual winner*

Mm

◆ **eventually** •ADVERB• finally

Nn

ever •ADVERB• **1** at any time or at all: *Have you ever been to France?*

Oo

2 always: *ever ready to help*
3 of all time or on record: *the biggest pizza ever*

Pp

• **ever after** from that time onwards and for always: *They got married and lived happily ever after.*

Qq

Rr

• **ever so** extremely: *It's ever so kind of you.*

Ss

evergreen •ADJECTIVE• evergreen plants do not lose their leaves in the winter. Look up and compare **deciduous**

Tt

•NOUN• **evergreens** an evergreen tree or shrub

Uu

Vv

everlasting •ADJECTIVE• going on or lasting for ever

Ww

every •ADJECTIVE• all the people or things of a particular kind without leaving any out: *Every runner will get a medal for taking part.*

Xx

• *Every day, he does 200 press-ups.*
• **every so often** something happens or is done every so often when it happens or is done occasionally but not regularly or all the time

Yy

Zz

everybody •PRONOUN• all people or every person: *I thought everybody liked ice cream.*

everyday •ADJECTIVE• not special or unusual: *an everyday occurrence*

everything •PRONOUN• all things: *Everything in the room was covered in dust.*

everywhere •ADVERB• in every place: *We looked for him everywhere.*

evict •VERB• **evicts, evicting, evicted** to evict someone from a house or land is to force them to leave it

◆ **eviction** •NOUN• **evictions** evicting someone from their home or land

evidence •NOUN• **1** evidence is anything that makes people believe that something is true or has happened **2** someone gives evidence in court when they tell the jury or judge what they know about the case

◆ **evident** •ADJECTIVE• obvious or easily understood: *It was evident that he was not going to speak.*

◆ **evidently** •ADVERB• seemingly: *Evidently, there was some sort of argument.*

evil •ADJECTIVE• an evil person or an evil act is wicked and causes great harm
•NOUN• **evils 1** wickedness **2** something that causes great harm or destruction

evolution •NOUN• evolution is the long slow process by which animals and plants change over hundreds and thousands of years to adapt better to their environment

evolve •VERB• **evolves, evolving, evolved** to evolve is to change very gradually

ewe •NOUN• **ewes** an adult female sheep

ex- •PREFIX• if **ex-** comes at the beginning of a word it adds the meaning 'outside' or 'former' to the rest of the word. For example, the *exterior* of something is its outside surface and an *ex-president* is someone who used to be president but isn't any longer

exact •ADJECTIVE• **1** an exact amount has nothing left out or nothing left over **2** to be exact is to be correct, accurate and precise

◆ **exactly** •ADVERB• correctly or in an exact way

exaggerate •VERB• **exaggerates, exaggerating, exaggerated** to exaggerate is to make something seem better, bigger or

more important than it really is
♦ **exaggeration** •NOUN• **exaggerations** exaggerating or a statement that exaggerates

exam •NOUN• **exams** an examination

examination •NOUN• **examinations** 1 an examination is a formal test of someone's knowledge or ability 2 examination is looking carefully at something

examine •VERB• **examines, examining, examined** 1 to examine something is to look at it carefully 2 to examine pupils or students is to test their knowledge by asking them questions

example •NOUN• **examples** 1 an example of something is a thing of that kind 2 if someone is or sets a good example they behave in a way that others should copy
⇒ **exemplary, exemplify**

exasperate •VERB• **exasperates, exasperating, exasperated** something exasperates you when it makes you feel very annoyed and frustrated
♦ **exasperated** •ADJECTIVE• extremely annoyed
♦ **exasperating** •ADJECTIVE• extremely annoying
♦ **exasperation** •NOUN• a feeling of frustrated anger

excavate •VERB• **excavates, excavating, excavated** to excavate is to dig in the ground or dig something out of the ground: *They'd excavated tons of rock to build the foundations.*
♦ **excavation** •NOUN• **excavations** a hole made by digging in the ground or something dug out of the ground
♦ **excavator** •NOUN• **excavators** a machine that is used for digging

exceed •VERB• **exceeds, exceeding, exceeded** to exceed something is to go beyond or above it: *This year's profit exceeded our expectations.*
♦ **exceedingly** •ADVERB• very: *an exceedingly boring journey*
⇒ **excess**

excel •VERB• **excels, excelling, excelled** to excel at something is to be extremely good at it and better than most other people

♦ **excellence** •NOUN• excellence is very high quality or great ability
♦ **excellent** •ADJECTIVE• extremely good or of a very high standard

except •PREPOSITION AND CONJUNCTION• other than, apart from, or not including: *He works every day except Sunday.*
♦ **exception** •NOUN• **exceptions** something that is not the same as the others in a group or something that a statement does not apply to: *an exception to the rule*
♦ **exceptional** •ADJECTIVE• unusual or outstanding: *Gail has an exceptional gift for writing.*
♦ **exceptionally** •ADVERB• very: *exceptionally fine weather*

excerpt •NOUN• **excerpts** a short piece of writing, music or film that has been taken from a larger complete work

excess •NOUN• **excesses** an excess of something is too much of it
♦ **excessive** •ADJECTIVE• too much or too great

exchange •VERB• **exchanges, exchanging, exchanged** to exchange things is to swop them or to give one and take the other instead
•NOUN• **exchanges** a swop

excite •VERB• **excites, exciting, excited** to excite someone is to make them feel very eager or to give them a pleasant feeling of danger
♦ **excited** •ADJECTIVE• not calm because you are looking forward very much to something
♦ **excitement** •NOUN• being excited
♦ **exciting** •ADJECTIVE• thrilling or full of lively action

exclaim •VERB• **exclaims, exclaiming, exclaimed** to exclaim is to say something suddenly or loudly: *'What a wonderful surprise!' she exclaimed, clapping her hands in delight.*
♦ **exclamation** •NOUN• **exclamations** an exclamation is a word, phrase or sentence spoken suddenly or loudly and expressing strong feelings and emotions, such as surprise, anger, pain, admiration, frustration or desperation

exclamation mark •NOUN• **exclamation marks** a punctuation mark (!) used instead of a full stop after an exclamation

exclude •VERB• **excludes, excluding, excluded** to exclude someone or something is to not include them or to prevent them from taking part: *He was excluded from school for a week as a punishment.*
✦ **exclusive** •ADJECTIVE• **1** an exclusive place is meant for or used by only a certain special group of people, such as the rich **2** if something is exclusive it is found in only one place, and you can't get it anywhere else: *an exclusive offer* **3** if one thing is exclusive of another it does not include that other thing: *It costs £20, exclusive of postage.*
✦ **exclusively** •ADVERB• only: *The stadium is used exclusively for big international events.*

excrement •NOUN• excrement is the solid waste that comes out of the bodies of humans and animals

excrete •VERB• **excretes, excreting, excreted** to excrete waste or some other substance is to send it out of the body or a body part
✦ **excretion** •NOUN• sending out waste from the body

excruciating •ADJECTIVE• excruciating pain is very very severe

excursion •NOUN• **excursions** a trip somewhere for pleasure

excuse •VERB• **excuses, excusing, excused 1** to forgive someone for doing something, especially if there is a good reason for it: *Such behaviour cannot be excused.* **2** to be excused from doing something is to be let off doing it
•NOUN• **excuses** something you say to explain something you have done wrong

execute •VERB• **executes, executing, executed 1** to execute someone is to kill them as an official punishment **2** to execute something is to carry it out
✦ **execution** •NOUN• **executions** killing someone by order of the law
✦ **executioner** •NOUN• **executioners** someone who executes people who have been condemned to death

executive •NOUN• **executives** a senior manager in a business or organization

exemplary •ADJECTIVE• exemplary behaviour is so good it should be followed as an example

exemplify •VERB• **exemplifies, exemplifying, exemplified** to exemplify something is to be an example of it or to show what it is by giving an example

exempt •ADJECTIVE• if you are exempt from something, such as a law, it does not apply to you
✦ **exemption** •NOUN• **exemptions** being exempt

exercise •NOUN• **exercises 1** exercise is movements or games done to keep your body fit and healthy **2** an exercise is something you do to practise something
•VERB• **exercises, exercising, exercised** to exercise is to move around and be active so that you use your muscles and keep fit and healthy

exert •VERB• **exerts, exerting, exerted** to exert yourself is to make an effort
✦ **exertion** •NOUN• **exertions** exertion is hard physical work or effort

exhale •VERB• **exhales, exhaling, exhaled** to breath air out of your lungs through your nose and mouth. Look up and compare **inhale**
✦ **exhalation** •NOUN• breathing out

exhaust •VERB• **exhausts, exhausting, exhausted 1** if something exhausts you, it uses up all your strength or energy **2** to exhaust a supply of something is to use it all up
•NOUN• **exhausts** a device which carries the fumes out of a vehicle's engine through a pipe
✦ **exhausted** •ADJECTIVE• very tired or worn out
✦ **exhaustion** •NOUN• a feeling of great tiredness

exhibit •NOUN• **exhibits** something that is put on display in a gallery or museum
•VERB• **exhibits, exhibiting, exhibited** to exhibit something is to show it: *She exhibits her paintings at a small local gallery.*
✦ **exhibition** •NOUN• **exhibitions** a public show or open display

♦ **exhibitor** •NOUN• **exhibitors** someone who exhibits their work or produce at a public gallery or show

exile •VERB• **exiles, exiling, exiled** to exile someone from their country is to drive them away and make them live in another country •NOUN• **exiles 1** someone who has been exiled **2** exile is a time spent living in a country that is not your own

exist •VERB• **exists, existing, existed 1** to exist is to be or to have life: *Do fairies really exist, do you think?* **2** to exist is to stay alive: *How do they exist on such a low wage?*
♦ **existence** •NOUN• **1** being or being alive **2** a way of living: *a solitary existence*

exit •VERB• **exits, exiting, exited** to exit is to go out: *They exited the stadium by the west gate.* •NOUN• **exits 1** a way out of somewhere: *Leave the motorway by the next exit.* **2** to make an exit is to leave: *He made a hasty exit.*

exorcism •NOUN• **exorcisms** a spell or ritual to drive out an evil spirit from a place or a person
♦ **exorcist** •NOUN• **exorcists** someone who performs exorcism
♦ **exorcize** or **exorcise** •VERB• **exorcizes, exorcizing, exorcizing** to exorcize a demon or other evil spirit is to drive it out

exotic •ADJECTIVE• something exotic is interesting, colourful or strange, usually because it comes from a foreign country that is very different from your own

expand •VERB• **expands, expanding, expanded** something expands when it grows bigger or wider or opens out to become bigger or wider

expanse •NOUN• **expanses** an area of land, sea or sky that stretches over a big distance: *a wide expanse of desert*

expansion •NOUN• getting bigger or wider: *the expansion of metal when it is heated*

expect •VERB• **expects, expecting, expected 1** to expect something is to believe that it will happen or it will be the case: *I expect it will be warm in Portugal.*
2 if you are expecting something you are waiting for it to happen or arrive: *I'm expecting a parcel.*

3 to expect something is to think that it ought to happen or that you have a right to it: *I expected a bit more gratitude.*
♦ **expectant** •ADJECTIVE• **1** to be expectant is to be hopeful that something good will happen **2** an expectant mother is a pregnant woman
♦ **expectation** •NOUN• **expectations** something you expect to happen at some time in the future

expedition •NOUN• **expeditions** a journey made for a purpose, especially one made by a group of people: *an expedition to the South Pole*

expel •VERB• **expels, expelling, expelled 1** to expel something is to drive or force it out **2** to expel a pupil from school is to make them leave the school in disgrace
⇒ **expulsion**

expense •NOUN• **expenses 1** expense is the cost of something in money **2** your expenses are the sums of money you have to spend in order to live or do your job
♦ **expensive** •ADJECTIVE• costing a lot of money

experience •NOUN• **experiences 1** experience is knowledge that a person gains by doing something or doing it for a long time **2** an experience is an event that you are involved in
♦ **experienced** •ADJECTIVE• having knowledge gained from practice

experiment •NOUN• **experiments 1** a scientific test to discover something unknown or to check that an idea is true **2** something done to find out what will happen or what its effect will be
•VERB• **experiments, experimenting, experimented** to experiment is to do scientific experiments or to try something to find out what the result will be
♦ **experimental** •ADJECTIVE• as a test or trial

expert •NOUN• **experts** someone who knows a lot about a particular subject •ADJECTIVE• very knowledgeable or skilled at something
♦ **expertise** •NOUN• skill or knowledge

expire •VERB• **expires, expiring, expired**

Aa

something expires when it runs out or becomes out of date: *Your passport expired last week.*

Bb

 expiry •NOUN• running out or becoming out of date

Cc

explain •VERB• **explains, explaining, explained** 1 to explain something is to give more or simpler information or instructions so that it is easier to understand or do 2 to explain yourself is to give someone reasons for your behaviour

Dd

Ee

Ff

 explanation •NOUN• **explanations** something that explains

 explanatory •ADJECTIVE• intended to explain

Gg

Hh

explicit •ADJECTIVE• shown or said very clearly and frankly

Ii

explode •VERB• **explodes, exploding, exploded** 1 to explode is to blow up like a bomb with a loud noise 2 if someone explodes they suddenly lose their temper ⇒ **explosion**

Jj

Kk

Ll

exploit •VERB• **exploits, exploiting, exploited** to exploit someone or a situation is to use them to get some benefit for yourself •NOUN• **exploits** a daring action or adventure

Mm

Nn

Oo

 exploitation •NOUN• exploiting someone or something

Pp

exploration •NOUN• **explorations** exploration is exploring a place or thing

Qq

explore •VERB• **explores, exploring, explored** 1 to explore a place is to look around it and find out what it is like 2 to explore something is to study it to discover things about it or find out how good it might be

Rr

Ss

Tt

 explorer •NOUN• **explorers** someone who travels to a remote or unknown place to find out what it is like

Uu

Vv

explosion •NOUN• **explosions** a very loud noise made, for example, when a bomb goes off or something is blown up

Ww

Xx

 explosive •ADJECTIVE• likely to explode: *a highly explosive gas* •NOUN• **explosives** explosives are substances, like gunpowder or gelignite, that are used to blow things up

Yy

Zz

export •VERB• **exports, exporting,**

exported to export goods is to send them out of your country to be sold abroad •NOUN• **exports** exports are goods that are sent and sold abroad

expose •VERB• **exposes, exposing, exposed** 1 to expose something is to uncover it so that it is seen 2 to expose someone is to show people what or who they really are 3 to expose someone to something is to let them experience it or suffer it

 exposure •NOUN• **exposures** 1 exposing 2 a piece of film that has been exposed to light and will become a photograph when it is developed

express •VERB• **expresses, expressing, expressed** to express a thought or feeling is to put it into words or show it by your actions •ADJECTIVE• travelling fast from one place to another: *an express train* • *an express package*

 expression •NOUN• **expressions** 1 expressing things by words or actions 2 a group of words that have a particular meaning

 expressive •ADJECTIVE• having the ability to express meaning or feelings clearly

expulsion •NOUN• **expulsions** being driven out or expelled

exquisite •ADJECTIVE• very beautiful

extend •VERB• **extends, extending, extended** 1 to extend a part of your body is to hold it out 2 to extend something is to make it longer or last longer

 extension •NOUN• **extensions** 1 extending 2 something that adds length or more time to something 3 a part added on to a building

 extensive •ADJECTIVE• covering a large space or wide area

 extent •NOUN• 1 the space something covers 2 an amount or degree: *It was, to a great extent, his own fault.*

exterior •ADJECTIVE• at, on or for the outside: *exterior walls* •NOUN• **exteriors** the exterior of something is its outside: *The exterior of the house was painted bright blue.*

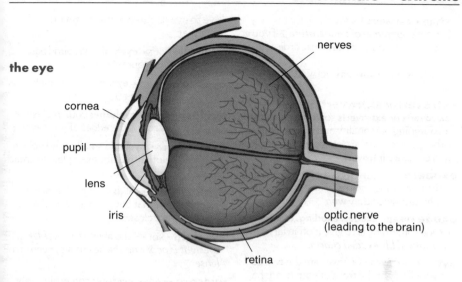

the eye

nerves

cornea

pupil

lens

iris

optic nerve
(leading to the brain)

retina

Aa
Bb
Cc
Dd
Ee
Ff
Gg
Hh
Ii
Jj
Kk
Ll
Mm
Nn
Oo
Pp
Qq
Rr
Ss
Tt
Uu
Vv
Ww
Xx
Yy
Zz

exterminate •VERB• **exterminates, exterminating, exterminated** to exterminate living things, especially pests, is to kill them all and get rid of them

external • ADJECTIVE• outside or on the outside: *an external wall*

extinct • ADJECTIVE• **1** extinct animals or plants have died out completely and no longer exist **2** an extinct volcano stopped erupting a long time ago
• **extinction** •NOUN• being destroyed completely or dying out completely

extinguish •VERB• **extinguishes, extinguishing, extinguished** to extinguish a light or flame is to put it out
• **extinguisher** •NOUN• **extinguishers** a device used to spray foam or chemicals on to a fire to put it out

extortionate • ADJECTIVE• far too expensive: *an extortionate price*

extra • ADJECTIVE• an extra thing or amount is more than usual or necessary
• ADVERB• very: *extra large*
• NOUN• **extras 1** something extra, especially a charge that is not included in the original price **2** an actor who appears for a short time in a film as one of a crowd in the background

extract •VERB• **extracts, extracting, extracted** to extract something is to take it out: *extract a tooth* • *extracting oil from the sea bed*
• NOUN• **extracts 1** a substance that has been extracted **2** a short piece from a book or film
• **extraction** •NOUN• **extractions 1** being extracted or something that is extracted, especially a tooth **2** where you come from: *of Italian extraction*

extraordinary • ADJECTIVE• very special or unusual: *an extraordinary child*
• **extraordinarily** • ADVERB• very unusually or surprisingly

extraterrestrial • ADJECTIVE• from a planet or place other than the Earth
• NOUN• **extraterrestrials** a being from another planet

extravagant • ADJECTIVE• spending too much money or using too much of something

extravaganza •NOUN• **extravaganzas** a spectacular public show

extreme • ADJECTIVE• **1** far from being ordinary or usual: *His reaction to the news was a bit extreme.*
   2 far away from the centre or middle: *The boy on the extreme right of the picture.*
   3 very great: *extreme cold*

Aa
Bb
Cc
Dd
Ee
Ff
Gg
Hh
Ii
Jj
Kk
Ll
Mm
Nn
Oo
Pp
Qq
Rr
Ss
Tt
Uu
Vv
Ww
Xx
Yy
Zz

•NOUN• **extremes 1** something that is extreme: *extremes of temperature* **2** if you go to extremes you do or say extraordinary things

♦ **extremely** •ADVERB• very: *extremely naughty*

extrovert or **extravert** •NOUN• **extroverts** or **extraverts** someone who has an outgoing personality and is interested in other people and the outside world. Look up and compare **introvert**

exuberant •ADJECTIVE• to be exuberant is to be in very high spirits: *The players were exuberant when they won.*

exude •VERB• **exudes, exuding, exuded** to exude something is to give it off in large quantities: *He exuded charm.*

eye •NOUN• **eyes** your eyes are the two parts of your body at the front of your head that you see with
•VERB• **eyes, eyeing, eyed** to eye someone or something is to look at them, especially because you are interested in them
• **not see eye to eye** people who don't see eye to eye disagree or do not get on well together

eyeball •NOUN• **eyeballs** the round part that makes up your whole eye

eyebrow •NOUN• **eyebrows** your eyebrows are the lines of hair above your eyes

eyelash •NOUN• **eyelashes** your eyelashes are the hairs round the edges of your eyes

eyelet •NOUN• **eyelets** a small round hole in leather or cloth, used, for example, to thread a lace through

eyelid •NOUN• **eyelids** your eyelids are the pieces of skin that cover your eyes when your eyes are closed

eyesight •NOUN• the ability to see: *Her eyesight is poor and she has to wear contact lenses.*

eyesore •NOUN• **eyesores** something ugly that spoils a view or scene

eyewitness •NOUN• **eyewitnesses** someone who has seen something happen, for example a crime being committed

Ff

F •ABBREVIATION• short for **Fahrenheit**

fable •NOUN• **fables** a story, usually about animals, that teaches a lesson

fabric •NOUN• **fabrics** cloth: *Wool is a natural fabric.*

fabulous •ADJECTIVE• extremely good: *The weather was fabulous.*

façade •NOUN• **façades** 1 the front of a building 2 a false impression that someone or something gives: *His happiness was just a façade.*

face •NOUN• **faces** 1 the front of your head where your eyes, nose, and mouth are 2 the part of a clock or watch where the numbers are 3 the steep side of a mountain or cliff 4 one of the flat outside surfaces of a shape •VERB• **faces, facing, faced** 1 to be opposite someone or something: *My house faces the park.* 2 to look or turn in the direction of someone or something: *They turned and faced each other.* 3 to have to deal with a difficult situation: *She faced many difficulties.* 4 to **face up to** a difficult problem is to accept and deal with it: *You must face up to your responsibilities.*

facelift •NOUN• **facelifts** a medical operation to remove the lines on someone's face and make them look younger

facial •ADJECTIVE• relating to your face: *a facial expression*

facility •NOUN• **facilities** 1 an ability: *He has a facility for solving problems* 2 a building or piece of equipment that you can use for doing something: *a mobile phone with an Internet facility* • *sports facilities*

fact •NOUN• **facts** something that you know is true • **in fact** you say **in fact** when you are going to give more exact information: *They know* each other well; in fact they went to school together.
⇒ **factual**

factor •NOUN• **factors** 1 something that causes or influences a situation: *The weather is often one of the main factors in choosing where to go for a holiday.* 2 a number that you can divide another by and not have a remainder. For example, 3 is a factor of 6

factory •NOUN• **factories** a building where something is made in large amounts: *a chocolate factory*

factual •ADJECTIVE• based on facts: *factual information*

faculty •NOUN• **faculties** a natural ability that people have: *the faculty of speech*

fad •NOUN• **fads** something that is popular or fashionable for a short time: *a passing fad for skateboarding*

fade •VERB• **fades, fading, faded** 1 to disappear gradually: *Hopes of finding him were starting to fade.* 2 to lose colour and brightness: *The jeans had faded.*

faeces •PLURAL NOUN• solid waste from people's or animal's bodies

Fahrenheit •NOUN• a system for measuring temperature in which water freezes at 32 degrees and boils at 212 degrees

ⓘ This word is pronounced **far**-ren-height.

fail •VERB• **fails, failing, failed** 1 to not pass an exam or test: *My brother failed his driving test.* 2 to be unsuccessful in what you are trying to do: *They failed in their attempt to sail round the world.* 3 to not do what is expected or needed: *The parcel failed to arrive.* • *The brakes failed.*
♦ **failing** •NOUN• **failings** a fault
♦ **failure** •NOUN• **failures** 1 someone or something that is not successful: *She felt*

Aa

like a failure. **2** the act of failing: *Their first attempt ended in failure.*

Bb

faint •ADJECTIVE• **fainter, faintest 1** difficult to see, hear or smell: *There's a faint mark on the carpet.* • *the faint sound of footsteps* **2** if you feel faint, you feel as though you might become unconscious

Cc

Dd

•VERB• **faints, fainting, fainted** to suddenly become unconscious and fall to the ground: *Richard fainted when he saw the blood.*

Ee

Ff

♦ **faintly** • ADVERB• **1** in a way that is difficult to see, hear or smell: *'Yes,' she said faintly.* **2** slightly: *He looked faintly ridiculous.*

Gg

fair[1] •ADJECTIVE• **fairer, fairest 1** treating everyone equally: *It's not fair that my brother can stay up later than me.*
2 fair skin or hair is very light in colour
3 fair weather is very pleasant, with no rain
4 quite good but not very good: *His work is only fair.*
5 quite large in size or amount: *He lives a fair distance away from here.*
♦ **fairly** • ADVERB• **1** quite: *I was fairly nervous about the test.* **2** in a way that is reasonable: *We were treated very fairly.*
♦ **fairness** •NOUN• being fair

Hh

Ii

Jj

Kk

Ll

Mm

Nn

fair[2] •NOUN• **fairs 1** an event with lots of stalls where you can buy things **2** a collection of rides that you can go on for entertainment, which moves from town to town

Oo

Pp

Qq

fairy •NOUN• **fairies** an imaginary creature which has magical powers and looks like a small person

Rr

Ss

fairy lights •PLURAL NOUN• coloured lights for decoration, especially on a Christmas tree

Tt

fairy story or **fairy tale** •NOUN• **fairy stories** or **fairy tales** a traditional story in which magic things happen

Uu

Vv

faith •NOUN• **faiths 1** great trust: *I have a lot of faith in him.* **2** religious belief: *people of different faiths*
♦ **faithful** • ADJECTIVE• loyal and keeping your promises: *a faithful friend*
♦ **faithfully** • ADVERB• trustfully and loyally

Ww

Xx

Yy

fake • ADJECTIVE• not real, but copying something else: *fake diamonds*
•NOUN• **fakes** a copy of something rather than the real thing

Zz

•VERB• **fakes, faking, faked 1** to pretend something: *John faked a cough so he could miss school.* **2** to make a copy of something and pretend it is real

falcon •NOUN• **falcons** a type of bird that kills other animals for food

fall •VERB• **falls, falling, fell, fallen 1** to drop down to the ground: *The apples fell from the tree.*
2 if you fall, you have an accident and hit the ground: *Ben fell downstairs.*
3 if an amount, price or temperature falls, it goes down
4 to **fall out** is to stop being friends with someone: *Jane and Anne have fallen out.*
•NOUN• **falls 1** an accident in which you hit the ground: *My grandmother had a fall last week.*
2 a drop in a price, amount or temperature: *a fall in prices*
3 the American English word for **autumn**

fallout •NOUN• radioactive dust from a nuclear explosion

fallow • ADJECTIVE• fallow land has been left without crops on it so the soil can improve

false • ADJECTIVE• **1** if something you say or believe is false, it is not true or correct: *He made a false statement to the police.* **2** an object that is false is not real or natural: *false teeth*
♦ **falsely** • ADVERB• incorrectly: *I was falsely accused of theft.*
♦ **falseness** •NOUN• being false

falter •VERB• **falters, faltering, faltered 1** to speak in an uncertain way and keep stopping **2** to move in an unsteady way

fame •NOUN• the quality of being famous: *young actors who look for fame*

familiar • ADJECTIVE• **1** if someone or something is familiar, you know them very well: *His voice sounded familiar.* **2** if you are familiar with something you have seen it or used it before: *I'm not familiar with this software.*
♦ **familiarize** or **familiarise** •VERB• **familiarizes, familiarizing, familiarized** to familiarize yourself is to make sure you know something: *Try to familiarize yourself with the rules.*

family •NOUN• **families 1** a group of people who are related to each other: *Most people in my family have brown hair.* **2** a group of animals, plants or languages that are related to each other

ⓘ **Family** can be used with a singular or plural verb in British English, for example: *The family next door has a dog.* *The family next door have a dog.*

famine •NOUN• **famines** a situation in which many people do not have enough food and may die

famished •ADJECTIVE• extremely hungry

famous •ADJECTIVE• known by many people: *a famous actor*

fan ¹ •NOUN• **fans** someone who likes a person or thing very much: *football fans*

fan ² •NOUN• **fans 1** a machine with thin blades that spin round and make the air cooler **2** something that you hold and wave in front of your face to make you feel cooler
•VERB• **fans, fanning, fanned** to fan yourself is to use a fan to cool yourself down

fanatic •NOUN• **fanatics** someone who likes someone or something in an extreme way: *a cycling fanatic*
♦ **fanatical** •ADJECTIVE• extremely enthusiastic about something

fanciful •ADJECTIVE• silly and unrealistic: *fanciful ideas*

fancy •VERB• **fancies, fancying, fancied 1** to like the idea of having or doing something: *Do you fancy going swimming?* **2** an informal word meaning to be attracted to someone: *My friend fancies you.*
•ADJECTIVE• **fancier, fanciest** decorated and not plain: *fancy cakes*

fancy dress •NOUN• clothes that you wear to a party to make you look like another person or thing

fanfare •NOUN• **fanfares** a short, loud piece of music played on a trumpet

fang •NOUN• **fangs** a long, sharp tooth of a fierce animal

ⓘ This word comes from an Old English word **fang**, which means 'something caught', because animals seize things in their teeth.

fantastic •ADJECTIVE• extremely good: *We had a fantastic time at the zoo.*

fantasy •NOUN• **fantasies** something good that you imagine will happen but that probably will not happen: *He has a fantasy about being rich and famous.*

FAQ •ABBREVIATION• short for **frequently asked question**

ⓘ This term is used in computing and on the Internet.

far •ADVERB• **farther** or **further, farthest** or **furthest 1** a long distance: *We have walked quite far.* • *I haven't got far with my homework.* **2** much: *She's a far better swimmer than I am.*
• **so far** until now: *I've only read ten pages so far.*
•ADJECTIVE• the far part of something is the part that is the greatest distance from you: *a house on the far side of the lake*

farce •NOUN• **farces 1** a situation that is funny or stupid **2** a play in which funny and stupid things happen

fare •NOUN• **fares** the price of a journey by bus, train or aeroplane: *The train fare to London is £33.*

farewell •INTERJECTION• an old-fashioned word for **goodbye**

far-fetched •ADJECTIVE• extremely unlikely to be true

farm •NOUN• **farms** an area of land where crops are grown and animals are kept
♦ **farmer** •NOUN• **farmers** someone who owns and works on a farm

farmhouse •NOUN• **farmhouses** a house on a farm where the farmer lives

farmyard •NOUN• **farmyards** an area surrounded by buildings on a farm

fascinate •VERB• **fascinates, fascinating, fascinated** to interest someone very much
♦ **fascinated** •ADJECTIVE• very interested in someone or something: *I was fascinated by the monkeys in the zoo.*

♦ **fascinating** •ADJECTIVE• extremely interesting: *a fascinating story*

♦ **fascination** •NOUN• a great interest in something: *I've always had a fascination for unusual animals.*

fashion •NOUN• **fashions** something that is very popular at a particular time: *a fashion for tight jeans*
• **in fashion** fashionable: *Short skirts were in fashion then.*
• **out of fashion** not fashionable
♦ **fashionable** •ADJECTIVE• liked by many people at a particular time

fast •ADJECTIVE• **faster, fastest 1** quick: *a fast car* **2** if a clock or watch is fast, it shows a time that is later than the correct time
•ADVERB• **faster, fastest** quickly: *She can run very fast.*

fasten •VERB• **fastens, fastening, fastened** to join or tie two things together
♦ **fastener** •NOUN• **fasteners** something that is used to join two things together

fat •ADJECTIVE• **fatter, fattest** a fat person has a wide round body
•NOUN• **fats 1** an oily substance that forms a layer under your skin which keeps you warm **2** an oily substance in food or used in cooking ⇒ **fatten**

fatal •ADJECTIVE• **1** causing someone to die: *a fatal accident* **2** causing serious problems: *a fatal mistake*
♦ **fatality** •NOUN• **fatalities** a death in an accident
♦ **fatally** •ADVERB• in a way which causes death: *He was fatally wounded.*

fate •NOUN• **1** a power that seems to control what happens **2** the things that will happen to someone, especially unpleasant things: *It was his fate to be captured again after his escape.*

father •NOUN• **fathers** your male parent
♦ **fatherhood** •NOUN• being a father

father-in-law •NOUN• **father-in-laws** or **fathers-in-law** the father of your wife or husband

fatherly •ADJECTIVE• kindly and protective: *a fatherly hug*

fathom •VERB• **fathoms, fathoming,**

fathomed to understand something after thinking about it: *I still can't fathom why he didn't tell me.*

fatigue •NOUN• extreme tiredness

fatten •VERB• **fattens, fattening, fattened** to make an animal fatter so it can be eaten
♦ **fattening** •ADJECTIVE• making you fat: *Chocolate is quite fattening.*

fatty •ADJECTIVE• **fattier, fattiest** fatty food contains a lot of fat

faucet •NOUN• **faucets** in American English, a faucet is a water tap

fault •NOUN• **faults 1** a mistake or something that is wrong: *There's a fault in the engine.*
2 if something bad is your fault, you are responsible for it: *Whose fault is it that we lost the keys?*
3 a long crack in the Earth's surface which causes an earthquake if it moves
♦ **faultless** •ADJECTIVE• perfect
♦ **faulty** •ADJECTIVE• something that is faulty has something wrong with it: *a faulty computer*

fauna •NOUN• animals: *the fauna and flora of the area*

ⓘ **Fauna** is a technical word.

favour •NOUN• **favours 1** something you do for someone to help them: *Could you do me a favour and check my homework?* **2** if you are in favour of something, you think that it is a good idea
♦ **favourable** •ADJECTIVE• good and suitable: *favourable weather conditions*
♦ **favourably** •ADVERB• in a way that makes something seem good: *This computer compares favourably with others.*

favourite •ADJECTIVE• your favourite person or thing is the one you like best: *My favourite colour is purple.* • *Who's your favourite teacher?*
♦ **favouritism** •NOUN• favouritism is treating one person or group better than others

fawn •NOUN• **fawns** a young deer

fax •NOUN• **faxes 1** a message that is sent and printed by a special machine attached to

a telephone line **2** a machine used for sending a message like this
•VERB• **faxes, faxing, faxed** to send someone a fax

fear •NOUN• **fears 1** a feeling of being very frightened: *She was shaking with fear.* **2** a frightened feeling that you have about something: *John has a fear of spiders.*
•VERB• **fears, fearing, feared** to be afraid of someone or something
♦ **fearful** •ADJECTIVE• feeling frightened about something
♦ **fearless** •ADJECTIVE• not frightened by anything

feast •NOUN• **feasts** a large meal for a special occasion

ⓘ This word comes from the Latin word **festum**, which means *holiday*. Nowadays, **feast** has come to mean the meal rather than the celebration.

feat •NOUN• **feats** something someone does that impresses you because it needs a lot of skill, strength or courage

feather •NOUN• **feathers** one of the long light things that cover a bird's body
♦ **feathery** •ADJECTIVE• soft and light like a feather

feature •NOUN• **features 1** a part or quality of something: *a house with many interesting features* **2** a part of your face, such as your eyes, nose or mouth

February •NOUN• the second month of the year, after January and before March

ⓘ **February** comes from the Latin word **Februarius**, which means 'the month of the feast of purification'. This was a Roman festival.

fed •VERB• a way of changing the verb **feed** to make a past tense. It can be used with or without a helping verb: *Anna fed the dog.* • *Have you fed the cat?*

federal •ADJECTIVE• relating to a group of states which have their own government
♦ **federation** •NOUN• **federations** a group of states or organizations which have joined together

fed up •ADJECTIVE• slightly annoyed or

bored: *I'm fed up with this work.*

fee •NOUN• **fees** an amount of money that you must pay for a service

feeble •ADJECTIVE• **feebler, feeblest** extremely weak
♦ **feebly** •ADVERB• in a weak way

feed •VERB• **feeds, feeding, fed 1** to give food to a person or animal: *Dad was feeding the baby.* **2** to feed on something is to eat it: *Rabbits feed on grass.*

feel •VERB• **feels, feeling, felt 1** to have a particular feeling: *I feel tired.* • *Do you feel better today?*
2 to touch something with your fingers to see what it is like
3 to experience something touching you or happening to you: *Suddenly, she felt a hand on her shoulder.* • *He could feel himself falling.*
4 if something feels hot, smooth, dry etc, that is how it seems when you touch it: *Your forehead feels hot.*
5 to think or believe something: *I feel he should have asked my opinion first.*
6 if you feel like something you want it or want to do it: *I feel like going for a swim.*
♦ **feeler** •NOUN• **feelers** one of the two long things on an insect's head
♦ **feeling** •NOUN• **feelings** something that you experience in your mind or body: *a feeling of excitement*
• **hurt someone's feelings** to make someone feel upset

feet •NOUN• the plural of **foot**

feline •ADJECTIVE• to do with cats

fell[1] •VERB• a way of changing the verb **fall** to make a past tense: *Suddenly, she fell off the chair.*

fell[2] •VERB• **fells, felling, felled** to cut a tree down

fellow •NOUN• **fellows** an informal word for a boy or man: *He's an unusual fellow.*
•ADJECTIVE• your fellow students or workers are the people who study or work with you
♦ **fellowship** •NOUN• **1** a feeling of friendliness between people who have similar interests **2** a club or organization

Aa

felt[1] •NOUN• a type of cloth made of rolled and pressed wool

felt[2] •VERB• a way of changing the verb **feel** to make a past tense. It can be used with or without a helping verb: *He felt very tired.* • *Have you felt how soft this fur is?*

Bb

Cc

Dd

female •ADJECTIVE• belonging to the sex which can give birth or lay eggs: *A female lion is called a lioness.*
•NOUN• **females** a female animal or person

Ee

Ff

feminine •ADJECTIVE• 1 to do with women, or having qualities that are typical of a woman 2 in English grammar, feminine forms of words refer to females. For example, *she* is a feminine pronoun
♦ **femininity** •NOUN• being like a woman

Gg

Hh

Ii

feminism •NOUN• the belief that women should have the same rights and opportunities as men
♦ **feminist** •NOUN• **feminists** someone who has this belief

Jj

Kk

Ll

fen •NOUN• **fens** an area of flat, wet land

Mm

fence •NOUN• **fences** a wooden or metal barrier

Nn

fencing •NOUN• a sport in which people fight with swords

Oo

fend •VERB• **fends, fending, fended** if you **fend for yourself**, you look after yourself

Pp

fender •NOUN• **fenders** the American English word for **bumper**

Qq

ferment •VERB• **ferments, fermented, fermenting** when beer or wine ferments, it is changed chemically because of the effect of yeast or bacteria

Rr

Ss

fern •NOUN• **ferns** a plant with long leaves like feathers

Tt

Uu

ferocious •ADJECTIVE• extremely fierce: *a ferocious dog*
♦ **ferociously** •ADVERB• in a fierce way
♦ **ferocity** •NOUN• being fierce

Vv

Ww

ferret •NOUN• **ferrets** a small animal with a long body, used to hunt rabbits

Xx

Yy

ferry •NOUN• **ferries** a boat that carries people and vehicles

Zz

fertile •ADJECTIVE• 1 fertile land is good for growing crops on 2 able to produce children or young animals

♦ **fertility** •NOUN• the state of being fertile
♦ **fertilization** *or* **fertilisation** •NOUN• the act of fertilizing something
♦ **fertilize** *or* **fertilise** •VERB• **fertilizes, fertilizing, fertilized** 1 to put male and female cells together so that a baby or a young plant or animal is produced 2 to add a substance to soil so that plants grow better
♦ **fertilizer** *or* **fertiliser** •NOUN• **fertilizers** a substance you put on soil to make plants grow better

fervent •ADJECTIVE• extremely enthusiastic: *a fervent belief* • *a fervent football fan*

festival •NOUN• **festivals** 1 a special time when people have a holiday to celebrate something: *a religious festival* 2 a time when there are a lot of special events of a particular type: *a film festival*
♦ **festive** •ADJECTIVE• relating to happy celebrations
♦ **festivities** •PLURAL NOUN• the things you do to celebrate a special event

festoon •VERB• **festoons, festooning, festooned** to decorate a place with lots of ribbons, balloons or flowers

fetch •VERB• **fetches, fetching, fetched** to go somewhere and bring something or someone back with you: *Could you fetch the newspaper for me, please?*

fete *or* **fête** •NOUN• **fetes** *or* **fêtes** a special event with stalls and games, to raise money for a school, church etc

fetlock •NOUN• **fetlocks** the part of a horse's leg above its hoof

feud •NOUN• **feuds** an argument between two people or groups that continues for a very long time
•VERB• **feuds, feuding, feuded** to have a feud with someone

ⓘ This word is pronounced **fyood**.

fever •NOUN• **fevers** if you have a fever, your body temperature is higher than normal because you are ill
♦ **feverish** •ADJECTIVE• feeling very hot because you are ill

few •ADJECTIVE• **fewer, fewest** not many: *She has few friends.*

•NOUN• a small number: *'Did you take any photos?' 'Only a few.'*

fez •NOUN• **fezzes** a round red hat with a tassel, worn by men in Egypt and some other countries

fiancé •NOUN• **fiancés** a woman's fiancé is the man she is engaged to

fiancée •NOUN• **fiancées** a man's fiancée is the woman he is engaged to

fiasco •NOUN• **fiascos** a situation that is a complete failure

fib •NOUN• **fibs** a lie that is not about anything important: *He's telling fibs again.* •VERB• **fibs, fibbing, fibbed** to tell a harmless lie
♦ **fibber** •NOUN• **fibbers** someone who tells unimportant lies

fibre •NOUN• **fibres** 1 a thin thread of something
2 a cloth made up of thin threads
3 a substance in food which humans cannot digest and which helps your bowels work properly

fibreglass •NOUN• a strong material made from tiny pieces of glass and plastic

fickle •ADJECTIVE• not staying loyal to one particular thing

fiction •NOUN• books that describe imaginary people and situations rather than real ones
♦ **fictional** •ADJECTIVE• relating to fiction
♦ **fictitious** •ADJECTIVE• imaginary and not true

fiddle •NOUN• **fiddles** a violin
•VERB• **fiddles, fiddling, fiddled** 1 to play or interfere with something in an annoying way: *Stop fiddling with your hair.* 2 to play the fiddle
♦ **fiddly** •ADJECTIVE• something that is fiddly is difficult to do or use because it is so small

fidget •VERB• **fidgets, fidgeting, fidgeted** to keep moving because you are nervous or bored

field •NOUN• **fields** 1 an area of ground used for growing crops or keeping animals on 2 an area of grass used for playing sport on
•VERB• **fields, fielding, fielded** in games like cricket and baseball, to be the person or team that throws the ball back after someone has hit it

fieldwork •NOUN• research that is done outside and not in a classroom or laboratory

fiend •NOUN• **fiends** 1 an evil spirit 2 someone who is very keen on something: *a computer games fiend*

fierce •ADJECTIVE• **fiercer, fiercest** violent and angry: *a fierce animal • a fierce storm*
♦ **fiercely** •ADVERB• in a fierce way

fiery •ADJECTIVE• 1 like fire 2 becoming angry very easily

fifteen •NOUN• the number 15

fifteenth •ADJECTIVE AND ADVERB• after fourteenth and before sixteenth: *the fifteenth of November*

fifth •ADJECTIVE AND ADVERB• after fourth and before sixth: *the fifth day of my holiday* •NOUN• **fifths** the fraction $\frac{1}{5}$, which means one of five equal parts of something: *A fifth of the money is mine.*

fiftieth •ADJECTIVE AND ADVERB• after forty-ninth and before fifty-first: *It's my grandfather's fiftieth birthday tomorrow.*

fifty •NOUN• **fifties** the number 50

fig •NOUN• **figs** a fruit with a lot of seeds in it, which can be dried

fight •VERB• **fights, fighting, fought** 1 to use your body or weapons to try to hurt someone who is doing the same to you 2 to argue with someone
•NOUN• **fights** the act of fighting with someone: *They had a fight in the playground.*
♦ **fighter** •NOUN• **fighters** 1 someone who is fighting 2 a fast military plane used for attacking

figment •NOUN• **figments** a figment of your imagination is something you have imagined that does not really exist

figurative •ADJECTIVE• figurative language is using a word or phrase in a different way from the usual way, to show a likeness or create a particular image. For example, if you say someone is a *mouse*, you mean that they are as timid as a mouse

Aa

figure •NOUN• **figures** 1 a number 2 the shape of a person: *There was a dark figure in the doorway.*

Bb

Cc

figure of speech •NOUN• **figures of speech** a word or phrase used in a different way from usual to create a particular image. For example, if you say someone is a *lion*, you do not mean that they are really a lion, but they are as brave or fierce as a lion

Dd

Ee

Ff

file [1] •NOUN• **files** 1 a folder for keeping papers in 2 a place for storing information together in a computer
• **in single file** if people walk in single file, they walk one behind another

Gg

Hh

file [2] •NOUN• **files** a tool with a rough edge, used for making things smooth: *a nail file*
•VERB• **files, filing, filed** to shape something and make it smooth using a file

Ii

Jj

Kk

fill •VERB• **fills, filling, filled** 1 to make a container full: *He filled our glasses with water.*
2 to become full: *The concert hall quickly filled with people.*
3 to **fill in** a form is to write information on it

Ll

Mm

Nn

fillet •NOUN• **fillets** a piece of meat or fish with no bones in it
•VERB• **fillets, filleting, filleted** to fillet a fish or a piece of meat is to remove bones from it

Oo

Pp

Qq

filling •NOUN• **fillings** 1 something used for filling a hole in your tooth: *Ben hasn't got any fillings.* 2 something used for filling something else: *pancakes with a chocolate filling*

Rr

Ss

filling station •NOUN• **filling stations** a place where you buy petrol

Tt

Uu

filly •NOUN• **fillies** a young female horse

Vv

film •NOUN• **films** 1 a story that you watch in a cinema or on television 2 something you put inside a camera so you can take photographs
•VERB• **films, filming, filmed** to make a film of something

Ww

Xx

Yy

filter •NOUN• **filters** something that traps solid material and lets liquid or gas pass through
•VERB• **filters, filtered, filtering** to put something through a filter

Zz

filth •NOUN• 1 dirt 2 rude words or behaviour
• **filthy** •ADJECTIVE• 1 very dirty 2 very rude: *filthy language*

fin •NOUN• **fins** one of the parts on a fish that help it to swim

final •ADJECTIVE• coming at the end: *the final chapter of a book*
•NOUN• **finals** the last game in a competition, which decides who will win

finale •NOUN• **finales** the last part of a show or piece of music

finalize *or* **finalise** •VERB• **finalizes, finalizing, finalized** to arrange the last details of something, such as a plan or trip

finally •ADVERB• 1 after a long time: *When he finally arrived, it was after midnight.* 2 used to introduce the last in a list of things: *Finally, I would like to thank everyone who has helped.*

finance •NOUN• **finances** 1 affairs to do with money: *John is an expert in finance.* 2 the money needed for something: *We do not have the finance for a holiday.*
•VERB• **finances, financing, financed** to give someone money to pay for a plan or business
• **financial** •ADJECTIVE• relating to money

finch •NOUN• **finches** a small bird with a short beak

find •VERB• **finds, finding, found** 1 to get or see something accidentally, or after you have been looking for it: *I can't find my pencil case.* • *I found a £10 note in the street.*
2 to discover something: *Have you found the answer yet?*
3 to have a particular opinion about someone or something: *I found him very rude.*
4 to **find something out** is to discover information about it: *I'll try and find out the train times.*

fine [1] •NOUN• **fines** money that someone must pay as a punishment
•VERB• **fines, fined, fining** to make someone pay a fine: *He was fined £100 for parking illegally.*

fine [2] •ADJECTIVE• **finer, finest** 1 if you are fine, you are healthy and well: *'How are you?' – 'Fine, thanks.'*

2 good or acceptable: *'Shall we meet at 4 o'clock?' 'Yes, that's fine.'* • *fine weather*
3 very thin or delicate: *fine lines*
✦ **finely** •ADVERB• **1** in very thin small pieces: *Chop the onion finely.* **2** in a beautiful or impressive way: *a finely decorated room*

finger •NOUN• **fingers** one of the long parts at the end of your hand

fingerprint •NOUN• **fingerprints** the mark that your finger makes when you touch something

finish •VERB• **finishes, finishing, finished**
1 to end: *What time did the film finish?*
2 to stop doing something or complete it: *Have you finished your homework?* • *I'll just finish my drink.*
3 to **finish with** something is to stop using it because you do not need it any more

fir •NOUN• **firs** a type of tree that keeps its leaves in winter

fire •NOUN• **fires 1** flames and heat that burn and destroy something: *The building was destroyed by fire.* • *There was a fire at the school last night.*
2 a pile of wood or coal that is burning to give heat
3 a device that heats a room using gas or electricity: *Put the fire on if you're cold.*
• **on fire** burning and producing flames: *The house was on fire.*
•VERB• **fires, firing, fired 1** to fire a gun is to shoot a bullet from it **2** to fire someone from their job is to dismiss them from it so they no longer have it

fire alarm •NOUN• **fire alarms** a bell that rings to warn you of a fire

firearm •NOUN• **firearms** a gun

fire brigade •NOUN• **fire brigades** the group of people whose job is to put out fires

fire engine •NOUN• **fire engines** a vehicle that carries firefighters and equipment to put out a fire

fire escape •NOUN• **fire escapes** stairs on the outside of a building that you use if there is a fire

firefighter •NOUN• **firefighters** someone whose job is to put out a fire

firefly •NOUN• **fireflies** a fly with a tail that shines in the dark

fireguard •NOUN• **fireguards** something you put round a fire to protect people from it

fireman •NOUN• **firemen** a man whose job is to put out a fire

fireplace •NOUN• **fireplaces** the space for a fire in the wall of a room

firewood •NOUN• wood for burning as fuel

fireworks •PLURAL NOUN• things that explode and make bright lights in the sky for entertainment

firm[1] •ADJECTIVE• **firmer, firmest 1** not soft: *a firm bed* **2** strict and not changing your mind: *She is a very firm leader.*

firm[2] •NOUN• **firms** a company: *She works for a firm in the City.*

first •ADJECTIVE• coming before everyone or everything else: *the first name on the list*
•ADVERB• **1** before anyone or anything else: *I finished the exam first.* • *Finish your dinner first.* **2** doing better than everyone else: *Philip came first in the cookery competition.*
•PRONOUN• the person or thing that comes before all others: *Who is first in the queue?*
• **at first** at the start of a period of time: *At first, I hated school, but I like it now.*
✦ **firstly** •ADVERB• used for introducing the first of several points or items: *Firstly, I'd like to welcome everybody.*

first aid •NOUN• simple treatment that you give to someone who is injured or ill

first-class •ADJECTIVE AND ADVERB• something that is first class is the best or most expensive type: *a first-class compartment on the train*

first-hand •ADJECTIVE• learned through personal experience or involvement and not from being told by other people

first name •NOUN• **first names** the name that is before your surname or before your middle name

first-rate •ADJECTIVE• excellent: *a first-rate doctor*

fish •NOUN• **fish** or **fishes** a creature that lives and swims in water, which people often eat as food. See the illustration on the next page

Aa Bb Cc Dd Ee **Ff** Gg Hh Ii Jj Kk Ll Mm Nn Oo Pp Qq Rr Ss Tt Uu Vv Ww Xx Yy Zz

Aa
Bb
Cc
Dd
Ee
Ff
Gg
Hh
Ii
Jj
Kk
Ll
Mm
Nn
Oo
Pp
Qq
Rr
Ss
Tt
Uu
Vv
Ww
Xx
Yy
Zz

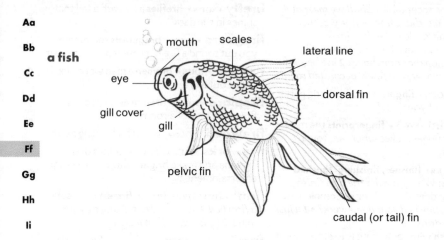

a fish

mouth
scales
lateral line
eye
dorsal fin
gill cover
gill
pelvic fin
caudal (or tail) fin

•VERB• **fishes, fishing, fished** to catch fish

fisherman •NOUN• **fishermen** someone who catches fish as a job or sport

fishing •NOUN• the sport of catching fish

fishmonger •NOUN• **fishmongers 1** someone who sells fish **2** a fishmonger's is a shop that sells fish

fission •NOUN• splitting up the nucleus of an atom so that energy is given out

fissure •NOUN• **fissures** a long, deep crack in something, especially in rock

fist •NOUN• **fists** your hand when it is closed tightly

fit [1] •ADJECTIVE• **fitter, fittest 1** healthy and active because you do exercise: *I'm trying to get fit.* **2** good enough: *This food isn't fit to eat.*

•VERB• **fits, fitting, fitted 1** to be the right size for someone or something: *The dress fits you perfectly.* • *The cupboard will fit in the corner.*

2 to fix something in a place: *We're having new kitchen units fitted next week.*

3 to have space to put people or things: *I can't fit any more into the suitcase.*

♦ **fitness** •NOUN• how healthy and well someone is: *exercises to improve fitness*

♦ **fitting** •ADJECTIVE• suitable: *a fitting end to the day*

fit [2] •NOUN• **fits** if someone has a fit they

suddenly become unconscious and may make uncontrolled movements

five •NOUN• **fives** the number 5

fix •VERB• **fixes, fixing, fixed 1** to attach something to something else: *She fixed the shelves to the wall.*

2 to mend something: *He's trying to fix my computer.*

3 to arrange something: *Have you fixed a date for the wedding?*

♦ **fixed** •ADJECTIVE• not changing or moving: *a fixed expression*

fizz •VERB• **fizzes, fizzing, fizzed** if liquid fizzes, it produces a lot of bubbles

♦ **fizzy** •ADJECTIVE• **fizzier, fizziest** a fizzy drink has bubbles in it

fjord •NOUN• **fjords** a narrow area of water surrounded by cliffs, especially in Norway

ⓘ This word is pronounced **fee**-ord.

flabbergasted •ADJECTIVE• extremely surprised or shocked

flabby •ADJECTIVE• **flabbier, flabbiest** fat, with too much flesh on the body

flag •NOUN• **flags** a piece of cloth with a pattern on it, used as the symbol of a country or organization: *The American flag has stars and stripes on it.*

flagpole •NOUN• **flagpoles** a tall pole that a flag is hung from

flagstone •NOUN• **flagstones** a flat piece of stone used for making a path or floor

flake •NOUN• **flakes** a small thin piece of something

flamboyant •ADJECTIVE• **1** confident and lively: *a flamboyant actor* **2** bright and colourful: *flamboyant clothes*

flame •NOUN• **flames** the bright burning gas that you see in a fire
• **in flames** burning: *The building was in flames.*

flamingo •NOUN• **flamingoes** *or* **flamingos** a large pink bird with long legs

flammable •ADJECTIVE• something that is flammable burns easily

---

ⓘ **Inflammable** means the same as **flammable**.

---

flan •NOUN• **flans** a pie that is not covered at the top: *a lemon flan*

flank •NOUN• **flanks** the side of an animal's body, especially a horse's
•VERB• **flanks, flanking, flanked** if you are flanked by two people, you have one person on each side of you: *She left the courtroom flanked by police officers.*

flannel •NOUN• **flannels 1** a soft, light cloth **2** a piece of cloth used for washing yourself

flap •VERB• **flaps, flapping, flapped** if a bird flaps its wings, it moves them up and down
•NOUN• **flaps 1** a movement up and down, like that of a bird's wings **2** a piece of something that hangs down over an opening

flapjack •NOUN• **flapjacks** a thick biscuit made from oats, butter and sugar

flare •VERB• **flares, flared, flaring 1** to burn with a sudden bright light: *If you poke a fire, it flares more fiercely.*
2 to **flare up** is to suddenly become angry
3 if an illness or injury **flares up**, it suddenly starts again or becomes worse

flash •VERB• **flashes, flashing, flashed** to shine quickly
•NOUN• **flashes** a sudden bright light: *a flash of lightning*

flashlight •NOUN• **flashlights** the American English word for **torch**

flashy •ADJECTIVE• **flashier, flashiest** expensive and meant to impress people: *a flashy car*

flask •NOUN• **flasks 1** a bottle or other container for liquid **2** a special container for keeping drinks hot or cold

flat •ADJECTIVE• **flatter, flattest 1** level and not sloping: *a flat roof*
2 a flat tyre does not have any air in it
3 a flat battery has no more power in it
• **flat out** as quickly as possible: *We worked flat out to get it finished.*
•NOUN• **flats 1** a set of rooms that someone lives in, which are part of a larger building **2** in written music, a sign (♭) that makes a note lower by half a tone
♦ **flatly** •ADVERB• in a definite way: *He flatly refused to do it.*
♦ **flatten** •VERB• **flattens, flattening, flattened** to make something become flat

flatter •VERB• **flatters, flattering, flattered** to say nice things about someone, often because you want them to do something for you
♦ **flattery** •NOUN• nice things you say to someone because you want to please them

flavour •NOUN• **flavours** the taste that something has: *Chocolate is my favourite ice-cream flavour.*
♦ **flavouring** •NOUN• **flavourings** something added to food to give it a particular taste

flaw •NOUN• **flaws** a fault in someone or something
♦ **flawed** •ADJECTIVE• not perfect
♦ **flawless** •ADJECTIVE• perfect, with no faults: *a flawless performance*

flea •NOUN• **fleas** a very small insect that jumps and bites people or animals

fleck •NOUN• **flecks** a very small mark or dot of colour
♦ **flecked** •ADJECTIVE• marked with flecks

fled •VERB• a way of changing the verb **flee** to make a past tense. It can be used with or without a helping verb: *The burglar fled through the front door.* • *She had fled when she heard us coming.*

fledgling •NOUN• **fledglings** a young bird that has just learned to fly

Aa
flee •VERB• **flees, fleeing, fled** to run away or escape: *She turned and fled.*

Bb
fleece •NOUN• **fleeces 1** the wool on a sheep **2** a soft, warm material

Cc
3 a jacket or top made from fleece
◆ **fleecy** •ADJECTIVE• soft and warm, like wool

Dd

Ee
fleet •NOUN• **fleets** a large number of ships or vehicles: *a fleet of boats*

Ff
fleeting •ADJECTIVE• lasting for only a short time: *a fleeting smile*

Gg
flesh •NOUN• **1** the soft part of your body that covers your bones **2** the soft inside part of fruit and vegetables

Hh
◆ **fleshy** •ADJECTIVE• having a lot of flesh

Ii
flew •VERB• a way of changing the verb **fly** to make a past tense: *The bird flew along the coast.*

Jj

Kk
flex •VERB• **flexes, flexing, flexed** to bend
•NOUN• a piece of wire covered in plastic, which carries electricity to a piece of equipment

Ll

Mm
◆ **flexible** •ADJECTIVE• **1** able to bend without breaking **2** able to change to suit different people or situations: *flexible arrangements*

Nn

Oo
◆ **flexibility** •NOUN• the quality of being flexible

Pp

Qq
flexitime •NOUN• a system in which you can choose what time you start and finish work each day

Rr
flick •VERB• **flicks, flicking, flicked** to hit something suddenly and quickly

Ss

Tt
flicker •VERB• **flickers, flickering, flickered** if a light or flame flickers, it does not burn steadily but seems to get darker then lighter

Uu

Vv
flight •NOUN• **flights 1** a journey on a helicopter or aeroplane **2** the action of flying: *a flock of geese in flight* **3** a flight of stairs is a set of stairs

Ww

Xx
flimsy •ADJECTIVE• **flimsier, flimsiest** likely to break or tear

Yy

Zz
flinch •VERB• **flinches, flinching, flinched** to move part of your body suddenly, for example because you are frightened or in pain

fling •VERB• **flings, flinging, flung** to throw something using a lot of force: *He flung the curtains open.*

flint •NOUN• **flints** a hard, grey stone that can produce a spark

flip •VERB• **flips, flipped, flipping** to flick or toss something over

flippant •ADJECTIVE• not serious enough: *a flippant answer*

flipper •NOUN• **flippers 1** one of the large flat feet that some animals such as seals and turtles have to help them swim **2** a wide, flat shoe that you wear to help you swim underwater

flirt •VERB• **flirts, flirting, flirted** to behave as though you think someone is attractive: *Emma was flirting with her sister's boyfriend.*
•NOUN• **flirts** someone who often flirts with people
◆ **flirtation** •NOUN• behaviour in which someone flirts
◆ **flirtatious** •ADJECTIVE• flirting a lot

flit •VERB• **flits, flitting, flitted** to move quickly and lightly from one place to another: *His eyes flitted round the room.*

float •VERB• **floats, floating, floated** to move along or stay on the surface of water and not sink
•NOUN• **floats 1** something that is designed to float, such as a raft or something you hold when you are learning to swim **2** an electric van used for delivering milk **3** a decorated platform that is pulled along by a vehicle in a parade

flock •NOUN• **flocks** a group of sheep, goats or birds

flog •VERB• **flogs, flogging, flogged 1** to hit someone several times, especially with a whip or cane **2** to sell something

ⓘ **Flog** meaning 'to sell something' is informal.

flood •NOUN• **floods** a lot of water in a place that is usually dry
•VERB• **floods, flooding, flooded** if water floods a place, it covers it in large amounts

floodlight •NOUN• **floodlights** a bright light

a flower

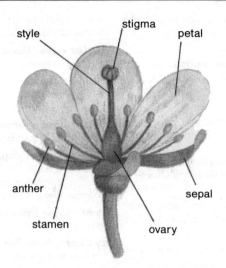

style
stigma
petal
anther
stamen
ovary
sepal

used at night for lighting a sports field or the outside of a building
♦ **floodlit** •ADJECTIVE• lit by a floodlight

floor •NOUN• **floors** 1 the surface that you stand on in a room: *There were lots of toys on the bedroom floor.* 2 one of the levels in a building: *Which floor is your apartment on?*

flop •VERB• **flops, flopping, flopped** 1 to fall or sit down suddenly and heavily: *He flopped into the nearest armchair.* 2 to hang in a loose and untidy way: *His hair flopped over his eyes.*
♦ **floppy** •ADJECTIVE• **floppier, floppiest** soft and able to bend easily

floppy disk •NOUN• **floppy disks** a piece of plastic that you put in a computer, which can store information

flora •NOUN• plants: *prehistoric flora and fauna*
♦ **floral** •ADJECTIVE• 1 made of flowers 2 decorated with pictures of flowers: *floral wallpaper*
♦ **florist** •NOUN• **florists** 1 someone who sells flowers 2 a florist's is a shop selling flowers

ⓘ **Flora** is a technical word.

floss •NOUN• 1 a mass of fine, silky threads: *candy floss* 2 floss or dental floss is thread you use for cleaning between your teeth

•VERB• **flosses, flossing, flossed** to clean your teeth using floss

flotsam •NOUN• objects from a ship or shipwreck that have been floating in the sea. Look up and compare **jetsam**

flounce •VERB• **flounces, flouncing, flounced** to walk away suddenly, for example because you are angry or upset: *He flounced out of the room and slammed the door.*

flounder •VERB• **flounders, floundering, floundered** to struggle or move in a clumsy way

flour •NOUN• powder made from wheat, used for making bread and cakes

ⓘ This word used to be the same as the word **flower**. Just as a flower is thought to be the prettiest part of a plant, flour was thought to be made from the best part of the wheat. Nowadays, these two words do not seem to be connected.

flourish •VERB• **flourishes, flourishing, flourished** to develop quickly and well

flout •VERB• **flouts, flouting, flouted** if you flout a law or rule, you do not obey it

flow •VERB• **flows, flowing, flowed** 1 if a liquid flows, it moves along: *The River Thames flows through London.* 2 the tide flows when the water in the sea moves

towards the land. Look up and compare **ebb**
•NOUN• **flows** a steady movement of
something

flow chart •NOUN• **flow charts** a chart
showing the different steps you have to take
to make something work, for example a
computer program

flower •NOUN• **flowers** the part of a plant
that has coloured petals: *Tulips are my
favourite flower.*
•VERB• **flowers, flowering, flowered** to
produce flowers: *Bluebells usually flower in
May.*

flu •NOUN• an illness like a very bad cold with
muscle pains and weakness. Flu is short for
influenza

flue •NOUN• **flues** a passage that takes air or
smoke away from a fire or heater

fluent •ADJECTIVE• speaking a language
clearly, easily and well: *She speaks fluent
German.* • *Ben is fluent in French.*

fluff •NOUN• small, soft pieces that come off
wool or other material
♦ **fluffy** •ADJECTIVE• **fluffier, fluffiest** soft
like fluff

fluid •NOUN• **fluids** a liquid
•ADJECTIVE• able to flow like a liquid: *Blood
is a fluid substance.*

fluke •NOUN• **flukes** a lucky or unusual thing
that happens by accident

flume •NOUN• **flumes** a channel carrying
water that you can slide down at a
swimming pool

flung •VERB• a way of changing the verb
fling to form a past tense. It can be used with
or without a helping verb: *He flung his bag
down on the floor.* • *She had flung herself on
the ground.*

fluorescent •ADJECTIVE• a fluorescent
light is a tube filled with a gas that gives off
rays when electricity is passed through it

fluoride •NOUN• a chemical added to
toothpaste or water to protect your teeth

flurry •NOUN• **flurries** a small amount of
something that happens quickly over a short
period of time: *a flurry of snow*

flush •VERB• **flushes, flushing, flushed 1** to

press or pull a handle to make water go down
a toilet **2** to become red in the face

fluster •VERB• **flusters, flustering, flustered**
to make someone feel nervous and confused

flute •NOUN• **flutes** an instrument you play by
holding it at one side of your mouth and
blowing into it

flutter •VERB• **flutters, fluttering, fluttered**
to move lightly and quickly through the air

fly •VERB• **flies, flying, flew, flown 1** to move
through the air: *The bird flew across the
garden.* **2** to move very quickly
•NOUN• **flies** a small insect that flies

flyer •NOUN• **flyers** a small piece of paper
that advertises something

flyover •NOUN• **flyovers** a road that goes up
and crosses another road

flywheel •NOUN• **flywheels** a heavy wheel
in a machine or engine

foal •NOUN• **foals** a young horse

foam •NOUN• **1** a mass of small bubbles on
top of a liquid **2** a soft material that is full of
small holes and used in mattresses and chairs

fob [1] •NOUN• **fobs** a decoration attached to a
bunch of keys

fob [2] •VERB• **fobs, fobbing, fobbed** to **fob
someone off** is to try to stop someone asking
questions or complaining, by telling them a
lie

focus •VERB• **focuses, focusing, focused 1** to
concentrate on one particular thing: *The
report focused on the need to improve
standards.* **2** to adjust the way you look at
something or a camera lens so you get a clear
picture

fodder •NOUN• food for horses or farm
animals

foe •NOUN• **foes** an enemy

ⓘ **Foe** is an old-fashioned or formal word.

foetus •NOUN• **foetuses** a baby before it is
born

ⓘ This word is pronounced **fee**-tus.

fog •NOUN• thick cloud that makes it difficult
to see
♦ **foggy** •ADJECTIVE• having a lot of fog: *a*

foggy day

foghorn •NOUN• **foghorns** something that makes a loud noise to warn of danger at sea when it is foggy

foil •NOUN• metal in very thin sheets, used for wrapping food

fold •VERB• **folds, folding, folded** to bend one part of something so that it covers another part: *Dan folded the letter and put it in the envelope.*
• **fold your arms** to cross your arms over your chest

folder •NOUN• **folders 1** a cardboard cover for holding papers **2** a place where you keep documents on a computer

foliage •NOUN• the leaves on a tree or plant

folk •NOUN• **1** people **2** belonging to the people of a country or area or their traditions: *folk music • folk tales*

(i) **Folk** always takes a plural verb, for example: *Folk **are** unhappy about these events.*

folk music •NOUN• traditional music from a particular country or area

follow •VERB• **follows, following, followed**
1 to go after someone or something: *He followed her down the street*
2 to happen after something: *The meal was followed by a dance.*
3 if you follow a road, you go in the same direction as it: *Follow the path to the end and turn right.*
4 to understand what someone is saying: *Do you follow me?*
5 to obey instructions or advice: *I followed his advice.*
• **follower** •NOUN• **followers** someone who supports or admires someone or something
• **following** •ADJECTIVE• the following day, week etc is the next one: *School finished on Friday and we went on holiday the following Wednesday.*

fond •ADJECTIVE• **fonder, fondest** if you are fond of someone or something, you like them very much
• **fondly** •ADVERB• in a way that shows you like someone or something
• **fondness** •NOUN• being fond of someone

or something

font •NOUN• **fonts** in a church, a large stone bowl for holding water during a baptism ceremony

food •NOUN• things that you eat to stay alive: *What's your favourite food?*

food chain •NOUN• a series of creatures where one type is eaten in turn by the next type in the series

fool •NOUN• **fools** a stupid person
• **make a fool of yourself** to do something that makes people think you are silly
•VERB• **fools, fooling, fooled 1** to fool someone is to trick them **2** to **fool about** or **fool around** is to behave in a silly way
• **foolish** •ADJECTIVE• silly or stupid

foot •NOUN• **feet 1** your feet are the parts of your body that you stand on
2 the bottom of something: *the foot of a mountain*
3 a unit of length equal to 12 inches or about 30 centimetres

football •NOUN• **footballs 1** a game played by two teams who try to kick a ball into a goal **2** a ball used for playing football

foothill •NOUN• **foothills** a hill at the bottom of a higher mountain

foothold •NOUN• **footholds** a place where you can put your foot when you are climbing

footing •NOUN• **1** your balance on your feet: *I lost my footing and fell.* **2** the relationship between two people or groups: *two groups on an equal footing*

footpath •NOUN• **footpaths** a path you can walk on, especially in the countryside

footprint •NOUN• **footprints** a mark that your foot leaves: *footprints in the snow*

footstep •NOUN• **footsteps** the sound of someone walking: *I could hear footsteps.*

footwear •NOUN• things such as shoes and boots that you wear on your feet

for •PREPOSITION• **1** intended to be received by someone: *There's a letter for you.*
2 intended to do something: *What's this switch for?*
3 used to show a certain amount: *I've lived here for eight years. • We walked for two*

Aa Bb Cc Dd Ee **Ff** Gg Hh Ii Jj Kk Ll Mm Nn Oo Pp Qq Rr Ss Tt Uu Vv Ww Xx Yy Zz

miles. • *I got these trainers for £30.*
4 showing who a feeling is about: *I felt very sorry for him.*
5 used to show a reason: *He was given detention for swearing.*
6 meaning: *What's the word for 'girl' in French?*
7 in favour of something: *Are you for or against the new plan?*

forbid •VERB• **forbids, forbidding, forbade, forbidden** to tell someone that they must not do something

♦ **forbidden** •ADJECTIVE• not allowed: *Smoking is forbidden throughout the hospital.*

force •VERB• **forces, forcing, forced 1** to make someone do something: *He forced me to give him money.* **2** to make something move by using your strength: *She forced the door open.*
•NOUN• **1** power or strength: *The force of the explosion damaged many buildings.* **2** a group of police, soldiers etc who are trained to work together

♦ **forceful** •ADJECTIVE• powerful: *a forceful argument*

♦ **forcefully** •ADVERB• in a powerful way

ford •NOUN• **fords** a shallow part of a river that you can drive across

fore- •PREFIX• if a word starts with **fore-**, it adds the meaning 'before' or 'at the front of'. For example, your *forehead* is at the front of your head

forearm •NOUN• **forearms** the part of your arm between your elbow and your wrist

foreboding •NOUN• if you have a sense of foreboding, you feel that something bad is going to happen

forecast •NOUN• **forecasts** a statement about what is going to happen, especially with the weather

forefather •NOUN• **forefathers** someone in your family who lived a long time ago

forefinger •NOUN• **forefingers** the finger that is next to your thumb

foregone •ADJECTIVE• a **foregone conclusion** is something that is certain to happen

foreground •NOUN• the part of a view or picture that is nearest to you

forehead •NOUN• **foreheads** the top front part of your head

foreign •ADJECTIVE• a foreign person comes from a country that is not your country: *foreign languages*

♦ **foreigner** •NOUN• **foreigners** someone who comes from a country that is not your country

foreleg •NOUN• **forelegs** one of the front legs of an animal that has four legs

foreman •NOUN• **foremen** the person who is in charge of a group of factory workers or builders

foremost •ADJECTIVE• the most famous or important

foresee •VERB• **foresees, foreseeing, foresaw, foreseen** to know about something before it happens

♦ **foresight** •NOUN• the ability to know what will happen in the future

forest •NOUN• **forests** a place where a lot of trees are growing together

♦ **forestry** •NOUN• planting and looking after trees and forests

forever •NOUN• always: *You can't stay in your room forever.*

foreword •NOUN• **forewords** a short introduction at the start of a book

forfeit •VERB• **forfeits, forfeiting, forfeited** to have something taken away from you because you have done something wrong

forge •VERB• **forges, forging, forged 1** to make an illegal copy of something: *He was sent to prison for forging passports.* **2** to forge hot metal is to hammer it into a shape
•NOUN• **forges** a place where metal is heated to be shaped, for example a blacksmith's

♦ **forgery** •NOUN• **forgeries 1** the crime of copying something and trying to make it look real **2** an illegal copy of something

forget •VERB• **forgets, forgetting, forgot, forgotten** not to remember something: *I forgot to send Dad a birthday card.*

♦ **forgetful** •ADJECTIVE• often forgetting things

forgive •VERB• **forgives, forgiving, forgave,**

Aa
Bb
Cc
Dd
Ee
Ff
Gg
Hh
Ii
Jj
Kk
Ll
Mm
Nn
Oo
Pp
Qq
Rr
Ss
Tt
Uu
Vv
Ww
Xx
Yy
Zz

forgiven to stop being angry with someone: *Have you forgiven him for breaking your skateboard?*
 ✦ **forgiveness** •NOUN• forgiving someone
 ✦ **forgiving** •ADJECTIVE• willing to forgive someone

forgot •VERB• a way of changing the verb **forget** to make a past tense: *I forgot to ask what time we were meeting.*
 ✦ **forgotten** •VERB• a form of the verb **forget** that is used with a helping verb to show that something happened in the past: *He has forgotten to lock the door.*
 •ADJECTIVE• not remembered by anyone: *forgotten heroes*

fork •NOUN• **forks** 1 something with a handle and points that you use for lifting food to your mouth 2 a point where a road or river divides and goes off in two different directions

fork-lift truck •NOUN• **fork-lift trucks** a vehicle with equipment on the front for lifting and moving heavy things

forlorn •ADJECTIVE• looking lonely and unhappy

form •NOUN• **forms** 1 a type of something: *a form of transport*
 2 a piece of paper with questions and spaces to write your answers: *You have to fill in a form to get a passport.*
 3 a class at school: *Which form are you in?*
 4 a shape something has or makes: *The chairs had been arranged in the form of a circle.*
 •VERB• **forms, forming, formed** 1 to start or make something start to appear or exist: *How was the Earth formed?*
 2 to make a particular shape: *The children held hands and formed a circle.*
 3 to start an organization or club

formal •ADJECTIVE• 1 suitable for an official or important situation: *a formal letter*
 2 formal language and words follow rules strictly and are suitable for writing
 ✦ **formality** •NOUN• **formalities** something that must be done but does not have much meaning

format •NOUN• **formats** the way something is designed or arranged: *The album is*
available in cassette or CD format.

formation •NOUN• **formations** 1 forming something: *the formation of a new government* 2 a formation is a shape made by the way people or things are arranged

former •ADJECTIVE• before but not now: *the former President* • *In former times, people did not travel so much.*
 •NOUN• the former is the first of two people or things you are mentioning. The second one is the **latter**: *We visited America and Canada but stayed longer in the former.*
 ✦ **formerly** •ADVERB• once, in the past: *Their house was formerly a shop.*

formidable •ADJECTIVE• difficult or frightening: *a formidable task*

formula •NOUN• **formulas** *or* **formulae** 1 in maths or chemistry, a set of letters, numbers or symbols that stand for an idea or chemical compound: *What's the formula for calculating the area of a circle?* 2 the way to make something and the substances used in it
 ✦ **formulate** •VERB• **formulates, formulating, formulated** to invent and develop a plan or idea

forsake •VERB• **forsakes, forsaking, forsook, forsaken** to leave someone or something for ever

---
ⓘ This is a formal word.

---

fort •NOUN• **forts** a building that has been strengthened to protect it against attack

forth •ADVERB• forwards or onwards: *They went forth into the desert.*
 • **back and forth** first in one direction then in the opposite direction

---
ⓘ This word is used mainly in literature.

---

forthcoming •ADJECTIVE• happening soon: *forthcoming events*

forthright •ADJECTIVE• very honest and direct: *a forthright chat* • *John spoke in a forthright fashion.*

fortieth •ADJECTIVE AND ADVERB• after thirty-ninth and before forty-first: *It's Mum's fortieth birthday tomorrow.*

fortification •NOUN• **fortifications**

Aa
Bb
Cc
Dd
Ee
Ff
Gg
Hh
Ii
Jj
Kk
Ll
Mm
Nn
Oo
Pp
Qq
Rr
Ss
Tt
Uu
Vv
Ww
Xx
Yy
Zz

something that is built to defend a place against attack

fortify •VERB• **fortifies, fortifying, fortified** to strengthen someone or something

fortnight •NOUN• a period of two weeks: *We're going to Greece for a fortnight.*
♦ **fortnightly** •ADVERB• happening every two weeks

fortress •NOUN• **fortresses** a place that has been protected against attack

fortunate •ADJECTIVE• lucky: *We were fortunate to catch our train, we were so late.*
♦ **fortunately** •ADVERB• luckily: *Fortunately, nobody was injured.*

fortune •NOUN• **fortunes** 1 a fortune is a lot of money: *His uncle died and left him a fortune.* 2 fortune is luck: *She had the good fortune to win first prize.*

forty •NOUN• **forties** the number 40

forward •ADJECTIVE• in the direction that is in front of you: *a forward movement*
•VERB• **forward, forwarding, forwarded** to send a letter or e-mail you have received to someone else
•NOUN• **forwards** in football and hockey, a forward is a player who mostly plays in the front line of a team and tries to score goals. In rugby a forward is one of the players that makes up a scrum. Look up and compare **back**
♦ **forwards** or **forward** •ADVERB• in the direction that is in front of you: *The car moved slowly forwards.*
• **look forward to something** to feel pleased about something that is going to happen: *I'm looking forward to seeing her.*

fossil •NOUN• **fossils** the remains of an animal or plant that have hardened into rock after a very long time
♦ **fossilize** or **fossilise** •VERB• **fossilizes, fossilizing, fossilized** to become a fossil

fossil fuel •NOUN• **fossil fuels** fuels that are made from the remains of animals and plants. Coal, crude oil and natural gas are fossil fuels

foster •VERB• **fosters, fostering, fostered** 1 to have a child that is not yours living with you for a period of time 2 to encourage

something to develop

foster child •NOUN• **foster children** a child who you look after for a period of time when its parents cannot look after it

foster parent •NOUN• **foster parents** someone who looks after children that are not their own

fought •VERB• a way of changing the verb **fight** to make a past tense. It can be used with or without a helping verb: *He fought with his brother.* • *They had fought for freedom and lost.*

foul •ADJECTIVE• **fouler, foulest** extremely unpleasant: *a foul smell*
•NOUN• **fouls** in sport, a foul is an action that is against the rules

found •VERB• **founds, founding, founded** to start an organization: *The college was founded in 1950.*

foundations •PLURAL NOUN• the foundations of a building are its solid base under the ground

founder •NOUN• **founders** the person who starts an organization

foundling •NOUN• **foundlings** an old-fashioned word for a baby who has been abandoned by its parents

foundry •NOUN• **foundries** a factory where metal or glass is melted and made into things

fountain •NOUN• **fountains** a jet of water used for decoration in a garden or park

fountain pen •NOUN• **fountain pens** a pen full of ink that flows out through a nib

four •NOUN• **fours** the number 4

fourteen •NOUN• the number 14

fourteenth •ADJECTIVE AND ADVERB• after thirteenth and before fifteenth: *It's my sister's fourteenth birthday tomorrow.*

fourth •ADJECTIVE AND ADVERB• after third and before fifth: *He finished fourth in the race.*

fowl •NOUN• **fowl** or **fowls** a bird that is kept for its meat and eggs, for example a chicken

ⓘ This word has developed from the Old English word for *bird*, which is **fugel**.

fox •NOUN• **foxes** a wild animal that looks like a dog, and that has red fur and a thick tail

foxglove •NOUN• **foxgloves** a tall flower with purple bell-shaped flowers

foyer •NOUN• **foyers** the entrance hall in a theatre, office building etc

fraction •NOUN• **fractions** an amount such as $\frac{1}{2}$ or $\frac{3}{8}$, that is part of a whole number

fracture •VERB• **fractures, fracturing, fractured** to crack or break something, especially a bone in your body: *Emma's fractured her arm.*
•NOUN• **fractures** a crack or break in something, especially a bone in your body

fragile •ADJECTIVE• not very strong and likely to break
♦ **fragility** •NOUN• the state of being fragile

fragment •NOUN• **fragments** a fragment of something is a small piece that has broken off

fragrance •NOUN• **fragrances** a pleasant smell
♦ **fragrant** •ADJECTIVE• something that is fragrant smells very pleasant

frail •ADJECTIVE• **frailer, frailest** weak
♦ **frailty** •NOUN• weakness

frame •NOUN• **frames** 1 a piece of wood or metal around the edge of a picture, mirror etc
2 the part that holds the lenses in a pair of glasses
3 the structure around which something is built or made: *the frame of a house*

framework •NOUN• **frameworks** the structure on which something is planned or built

franchise •NOUN• **franchises** a right to sell the goods of a particular company

frank •ADJECTIVE• **franker, frankest** honest and saying what you think
♦ **frankly** •ADVERB• as an honest opinion: *Frankly, I don't think he's good enough for the job.*

frankincense •NOUN• a sweet-smelling substance that is burned to give a pleasant smell

frantic •ADJECTIVE• done in a quick, excited or worried way: *a frantic search*
♦ **frantically** •ADVERB• in a frantic way

fraud •NOUN• **frauds** 1 the crime of deceiving people to get money 2 someone who deceives other people by pretending

fraught •ADJECTIVE• 1 if you are fraught, you are anxious and tense
2 if something such as a situation is fraught, it causes worry
3 if a situation is **fraught with** something such as danger, it is full of danger and problems

frayed •ADJECTIVE• frayed material is starting to come apart at the edges

freak •NOUN• **freaks** 1 a strange person 2 a keen fan of something: *a football freak*
•ADJECTIVE• extremely unusual: *a freak accident*

freckle •NOUN• **freckles** a small brown mark on your skin, especially your face
♦ **freckled** •ADJECTIVE• covered in freckles

free •ADJECTIVE• 1 not costing any money: *It's free to get into the museum.*
2 available: *Is this seat free?* • *Are you free this evening?*
3 if you are free to do something, you are allowed to do it: *You are free to go anywhere you like.*
♦ **freedom** •NOUN• the right to do what you want
♦ **freely** •ADVERB• without being limited or blocked: *You can speak freely to me.*

free-range •ADJECTIVE• 1 free-range animals are allowed to move freely around a farm 2 free-range eggs come from chickens that are allowed to move around freely

freeway •NOUN• **freeways** in America, a freeway is a fast road with many lanes

freewheel •VERB• **freewheels, freewheeling, freewheeled** to ride a bicycle without turning the pedals

freeze •VERB• **freezes, freezing, froze, frozen** 1 to become very cold and go hard or turn into ice
2 to store food at a very cold temperature so it keeps for a long time
3 to stop moving suddenly: *He froze when he saw the big dog.*

Aa
Bb
Cc
Dd
Ee
Ff
Gg
Hh
Ii
Jj
Kk
Ll
Mm
Nn
Oo
Pp
Qq
Rr
Ss
Tt
Uu
Vv
Ww
Xx
Yy
Zz

Aa
Bb
Cc
Dd
Ee
Ff
Gg
Hh
Ii
Jj
Kk
Ll
Mm
Nn
Oo
Pp
Qq
Rr
Ss
Tt
Uu
Vv
Ww
Xx
Yy
Zz

◆ **freezer** •NOUN• **freezers** a machine for keeping food very cold

freezing point •NOUN• the temperature at which a liquid becomes solid

freight •NOUN• goods that are being carried by a lorry, ship or plane

◆ **freighter** •NOUN• **freighters** a large ship or plane for carrying goods

French fries •PLURAL NOUN• a long thin piece of potato, that is fried in deep fat

French window •NOUN• **French windows** a long window that is used as a door

frenzy •NOUN• a state of great excitement, activity and emotion

frequency •NOUN• **frequencies** 1 the number of times that something happens 2 the frequency of sound or radio waves is the number that pass the same point over one second. Human beings cannot hear sounds that have extremely high frequencies

◆ **frequent** •ADJECTIVE• happening often: *Dan makes frequent visits to his grandmother.*

◆ **frequently** •ADVERB• often: *He is frequently late for school.*

fresh •ADJECTIVE• **fresher, freshest** 1 just made or collected: *fresh orange juice* 2 clean: *He put fresh sheets on the bed.*

◆ **freshen** •VERB• **freshens, freshening, freshened** to make something fresher

◆ **freshly** •ADVERB• only just made or done: *freshly made bread*

freshwater •ADJECTIVE• a freshwater fish lives in rivers and lakes, rather than in the sea

fret •VERB• **frets, fretting, fretted** to feel worried, unhappy and unable to relax

friar •NOUN• **friars** a Roman Catholic monk

◆ **friary** •NOUN• **friaries** a building where friars live

friction •NOUN• the rubbing of one surface against another surface

Friday •NOUN• **Fridays** the day of the week after Thursday and before Saturday: *It's my birthday on Friday.*

ⓘ **Friday** comes from the Old English word **Frigedaeg**, which means **Freya's Day**. Freya is the Norse goddess of love.

fridge •NOUN• **fridges** a machine for keeping food cool. Fridge is short for **refrigerator**

fried •VERB• a way of changing the verb **fry** to make a past tense. It can be used with or without a helping verb: *She fried the fish in butter.* • *Have you fried the chicken?* •ADJECTIVE• cooked in hot oil or fat: *a fried egg*

friend •NOUN• **friends** someone who you know and like: *Lindsay is my best friend.*

◆ **friendly** •ADJECTIVE• kind and welcoming: *She's very friendly to everyone.*

◆ **friendship** •NOUN• **friendships** the relationship you have with a friend

frieze •NOUN• **friezes** a long strip of decorated paper that you put on a wall

frigate •NOUN• **frigates** a small warship

fright •NOUN• a sudden feeling of fear: *You gave me a fright, jumping out like that!*

◆ **frighten** •VERB• **frightens, frightening, frightened** to frighten someone is to make them feel scared

◆ **frightened** •ADJECTIVE• scared: *He's frightened of snakes.*

◆ **frightening** •ADJECTIVE• something that is frightening makes you feel scared: *a frightening experience*

◆ **frightful** •ADJECTIVE• very bad

◆ **frightfully** •ADVERB• an old-fashioned word for **very**: *I'm frightfully sorry.*

frill •NOUN• **frills** folds of cloth used as a decoration around the edge of something

◆ **frilly** •ADJECTIVE• decorated with frills

fringe •NOUN• **fringes** hair that hangs down over your forehead

frisky •ADJECTIVE• **friskier, friskiest** lively and full of energy: *a frisky puppy*

fritter[1] •NOUN• **fritters** a piece of food that is covered in batter and fried

fritter[2] •VERB• **fritters, frittering, frittered** if you **fritter away** money or time, you waste it

frivolous •ADJECTIVE• a frivolous person is playful and not serious

frizzy •ADJECTIVE• **frizzier, frizziest** frizzy hair has very tight curls in it

frock •NOUN• **frocks** an old-fashioned word for a dress

frog •NOUN• **frogs** a small brown or green animal that can jump and lives near water

frogman •NOUN• **frogmen** someone whose job is to swim underwater wearing a rubber suit and using special breathing equipment

frolic •VERB• **frolics, frolicking, frolicked** to play in a lively and happy way

from •PREPOSITION• **1** showing where something started: *She's driving up from London.* • *Read the poem from the beginning.*
2 showing what has made something happen: *Yogurt is made from milk.* • *He was shivering from the cold.*
3 out of a place or away: *He took a notebook from the drawer.* • *Take those sweets from her before she eats them all!*

front •NOUN• **fronts 1** the front of something is the part of it that faces forwards: *The front of the house is painted red.*
2 a seashore or a road or walkway along it
3 an area where fighting takes place during a war
4 a weather front is the warm or cold edge of a mass of air
•ADJECTIVE• at the front of something: *the front door*
• **in front of** so that you are facing someone or something: *He stood in front of the class and started to speak.*

frontier •NOUN• **frontiers** a dividing line between two countries

frost •NOUN• a very thin layer of white ice crystals that forms on surfaces outside when the weather is cold
♦ **frosted** •ADJECTIVE• frosted glass has been specially treated so you cannot see through it
♦ **frosty** •ADJECTIVE• **frostier, frostiest**
1 when it is frosty, everything is covered in frost **2** not very friendly: *a frosty welcome*

froth •NOUN• foam on top of a liquid
♦ **frothy** •ADJECTIVE• a frothy liquid has foam on top

frown •VERB• **frowns, frowning, frowned** to wrinkle your forehead because you are thinking very hard or because you are worried or angry

•NOUN• **frowns** an expression in which your forehead is wrinkled

frozen •VERB• the form of the verb **freeze** that is used with a helping verb to show that something happened in the past: *It's so cold that the lake has frozen.*
•ADJECTIVE• frozen food is stored at a very cold temperature to make it keep for a long time: *a packet of frozen peas*

frugal •ADJECTIVE• if you are frugal, you are careful with your money and saving it rather than spending a lot

fruit •NOUN• the fleshy part of a plant, which you can sometimes eat, that holds seeds: *Grapes are my favourite fruit.*
♦ **fruitful** •ADJECTIVE• something that is fruitful has good results: *a fruitful meeting*
♦ **fruitless** •ADJECTIVE• not producing the result you wanted: *a fruitless search*

frustrate •VERB• **frustrates, frustrating, frustrated** if something frustrates you it makes you feel annoyed because you cannot do or achieve what you want
♦ **frustration** •NOUN• **frustrations** a feeling of being annoyed because you cannot do or achieve what you want

fry •VERB• **fries, frying, fried** to cook something in hot oil or fat

fudge •NOUN• a soft sweet made from butter and sugar

fuel •NOUN• **fuels** a substance such as gas, wood or coal that burns to give heat, light, or power

fugitive •NOUN• **fugitives** someone who has escaped from the police

-ful •SUFFIX• **1** if a word ends with **-ful**, it means 'full of a particular feeling or quality'. For example, *joyful* means 'full of joy' **2** if a word ends with **-ful**, it has something to do with the amount that something holds. For example, a *spoonful* is the amount of something that a spoon can hold

fulfil •VERB• **fulfils, fulfilling, fulfilled** to do what you wanted to do or what you are expected to do: *He fulfilled his promise to help.*
♦ **fulfilling** •ADJECTIVE• making you feel that you have achieved something good:

Being a doctor is a fulfilling job.
◆ **fulfilment** •NOUN• a feeling of having achieved something successfully

full •ADJECTIVE• **fuller, fullest** 1 containing as much as possible: *The train was full.* • *a full bottle of milk* • *The room was full of children.*
2 if you are full or **full up**, you cannot eat any more.
3 if something is full it is complete and has nothing missed out: *He told me the full story.*
• **full up** with no space for anyone or anything else: *I'm sorry, the hotel is full up.*
⇒ **fully**

full moon •NOUN• **full moons** the moon when it is a full circle

full stop •NOUN• **full stops** the mark (.) used for showing where a sentence ends and after an abbreviation

full-time •ADJECTIVE AND ADVERB• if you work full-time or have a full-time job, you work for all the hours of a normal job

fully •ADVERB• completely: *He hasn't fully recovered from the accident.*

fumble •VERB• **fumbles, fumbling, fumbled** to use your hands in an awkward way: *Raj fumbled in his pocket for the key.*

fume •VERB• **fumes, fuming, fumed** to be very angry
◆ **fumes** •PLURAL NOUN• smoke or gas that is unpleasant to breathe in

fun •NOUN• enjoyment and pleasure: *Skateboarding is good fun.* • *We had a lot of fun at the party.*
• **make fun of** if you make fun of someone, you tease them or make others laugh at them

function •NOUN• **functions** 1 the purpose of someone or something: *The function of an iron is to press the creases out of clothes.* 2 in mathematics, a function is what you do to change one set of numbers into another set
•VERB• **functions, functioning, functioned** to work in the correct way
◆ **functional** •ADJECTIVE• practical and useful

fund •NOUN• **funds** an amount of money for a particular purpose

•VERB• **funds, funding, funded** to provide money for a particular purpose

fundamental •ADJECTIVE• important and necessary: *the fundamental rules of football*

funeral •NOUN• **funerals** a ceremony that people have when someone dies

funfair •NOUN• **funfairs** a collection of rides that you can go on for entertainment

fungus •NOUN• **fungi** a plant with no leaves or flowers, for example a mushroom

funnel •NOUN• **funnels** 1 something that is wide at the top and narrow at the bottom, used for pouring liquids or powder into a narrow opening 2 a chimney through which smoke leaves a ship

funny •ADJECTIVE• **funnier, funniest** 1 a funny person or thing makes you laugh: *a funny story* 2 strange or unusual: *There was a funny noise coming from the engine.*
◆ **funnily** •ADVERB• in a way that is odd: *Funnily enough, we were born at the same time on the same day.*

funny bone •NOUN• **funny bones** a part of your elbow that tingles when you bang it

fur •NOUN• the soft hair on some animals
⇒ **furry**

furious •ADJECTIVE• extremely angry

furnace •NOUN• **furnaces** a large oven for melting metal or glass

furnish •VERB• **furnishes, furnishing, furnished** to put furniture in a house or room
◆ **furnishings** •PLURAL NOUN• the furniture, carpets and curtains that you put in a house or room

furniture •NOUN• objects such as beds, tables and chairs that you put in a room

furrow •NOUN• **furrows** a long narrow cut made in the ground by a plough

furry •ADJECTIVE• **furrier, furriest** covered in fur

further •ADJECTIVE• 1 a greater distance: *Which is further from here, London or Aberdeen?* 2 more: *If you need further information, please ask.*
•ADVERB• for a greater distance: *I walked further than I needed.*

furthermore •ADVERB• a word that is used when you are adding something to what you have just said: *I don't want to go, and furthermore, I won't go.*

(i) **Furthermore** is a formal word, used mainly in writing.

furthest •ADVERB• to the greatest distance or degree: *Who can throw the ball the furthest?*

furtive •ADJECTIVE• an action that is furtive is done secretly: *a furtive glance*
♦ **furtively** •ADVERB• in a secret way

fury •NOUN• extreme anger
⇒ **furious**

fuse •NOUN• **fuses** a wire inside a plug or piece of electrical equipment that melts if too much electricity passes through it, and stops the equipment from working
•VERB• **fuses, fusing, fused 1** to join together, or to join two things together **2** if a piece of electrical equipment fuses, it stops working because the fuse has melted

fuselage •NOUN• **fuselages** the main body of an aeroplane

fusion •NOUN• joining things together, such as the nuclei of atoms

fuss •NOUN• unnecessary worry or excitement about something: *I don't know what all the fuss is about.*
• **make a fuss of someone** to give someone a lot of attention
•VERB• **fusses, fussing, fussed** to worry too much about something or give it too much attention: *She fusses over her pet dog.*
♦ **fussy** •ADJECTIVE• **fussier, fussiest** someone who is fussy worries too much about small details that are not important

futile •ADJECTIVE• useless and having no effect
♦ **futility** •NOUN• being futile

futon •NOUN• **futons** a mattress on a wooden frame that you can use as a bed or a seat

future •NOUN• the future is the time that will come: *You can't know what will happen to you in the future.*
• **in future** from now: *In future, please be more careful.*

future tense •NOUN• the form of a verb that you use when you are talking about what will happen in the future

fuzz •NOUN• fine, light hair or feathers
♦ **fuzzy** •ADJECTIVE• **fuzzier, fuzziest 1** a fuzzy picture is unclear **2** fuzzy hair is soft and curly

Aa
Bb
Cc
Dd
Ee
Ff
Gg
Hh
Ii
Jj
Kk
Ll
Mm
Nn
Oo
Pp
Qq
Rr
Ss
Tt
Uu
Vv
Ww
Xx
Yy
Zz

Gg

Aa
Bb
Cc
Dd
Ee
Ff
Gg
Hh
Ii
Jj
Kk
Ll
Mm
Nn
Oo
Pp
Qq
Rr
Ss
Tt
Uu
Vv
Ww
Xx
Yy
Zz

g •ABBREVIATION• short for **gram** or **grams**

gabble •VERB• **gabbles, gabbling, gabbled** to gabble is to talk so quickly it is difficult for other people to understand what you are saying

gable •NOUN• **gables** an end of a house or building where the wall and the roof form a triangular shape

gadget •NOUN• **gadgets** a tool or small piece of equipment

Gaelic •NOUN• a language spoken in Ireland and parts of Scotland

gag •NOUN• **gags 1** something put round, in or over someone's mouth to stop them speaking **2** a joke or funny story told by a comedian
•VERB• **gags, gagging, gagged** to gag someone is to stop them speaking

gaggle •NOUN• **gaggles** a group of geese

gaiety •NOUN• being lively and having fun

gaily •ADJECTIVE• if you do something gaily you do it in a lively happy way

gain •VERB• **gains, gaining, gained 1** to gain something is to win it, get it or earn it: *You gain twenty extra points for that move.*
2 to **gain on** someone is to get closer to them
3 if a clock or watch gains, it goes faster than it should and shows a later time than the real time
•NOUN• **gains** gain, or a gain, is something that you get that is more than you had before

gait •NOUN• **gaits** your gait is the way you walk

gaiter •NOUN• **gaiters** gaiters are a pair of coverings for the bottom part of the legs, which go over the top of shoes or boots and are used to protect trousers from water or mud

gala •NOUN• **galas** a special public event or entertainment: *a swimming gala • a fund-raising gala*

galaxy •NOUN• **galaxies** a galaxy is a huge group of stars in the universe. Our galaxy is the Milky Way

gale •NOUN• **gales** a very strong wind

gall •VERB• **galls, galling, galled** if something galls you, it annoys you
•NOUN• cheek or courage: *He wouldn't have the gall to call me that to my face.*

gallant •ADJECTIVE• **1** gallant behaviour shows courage and honour: *a gallant effort* **2** very polite and considerate: *a gallant young man*
• **gallantry** •NOUN• **gallantries** gallant behaviour or a gallant act

galleon •NOUN• **galleons** a large Spanish sailing ship used in the sixteenth and seventeenth centuries for making long sea journeys

gallery •NOUN• **galleries 1** a large building or a shop where works of art are displayed to the public **2** a high open balcony at the back or side of a church, theatre or law court

galley •NOUN• **galleys 1** a type of ship used in ancient times that was moved through the water by lots of large oars **2** a room or area on a boat or aeroplane where cooking is done

gallon •NOUN• **gallons** a measurement of liquids equal to about 4.55 litres. There are 8 pints in a gallon

gallop •NOUN• **gallops** a fast running pace
•VERB• **gallops, galloping, galloped** a horse gallops when it runs at its fastest pace with all four feet off the ground at the same time

gallows •NOUN• a high wooden frame where criminals used to be hanged: *sent to the gallows*

galore •ADJECTIVE• a large number: *There were presents galore.*

ⓘ **Galore** is one of the adjectives that is always placed immediately after the noun it is describing.

ⓘ The word **galore** comes from an Irish Gaelic phrase **go leor**, which means *enough*.

galoshes •PLURAL NOUN• galoshes are waterproof shoes worn over other shoes in wet weather

galvanize *or* **galvanise** •VERB• **galvanizes, galvanizing, galvanized** to galvanize iron or steel is to coat it with zinc to stop it rusting

gamble •VERB• **gambles, gambling, gambled** 1 to bet money on the result of something, for example a card game or horse race 2 to take a risk or chance
•NOUN• **gambles** something you decide to do that may not turn out the way you want
✦ **gambler** •NOUN• **gamblers** someone who gambles money on the result of a race or game

ⓘ Be careful not to confuse the spellings and meanings of **gamble** and **gambol**.

gambol •NOUN• **gambols, gambolling, gambolled** if baby animals or children gambol they jump about in a playful way

game •NOUN• **games** 1 a game is any activity or contest with a set of rules in which players try to do better than others or try to get points: *a computer game • card games*
    2 games are all the sports children are taught in school
    3 in some sports, a game is one of the parts of a complete match: *He won the first set 7 games to 5.*
    4 game is wild animals and birds that are hunted for sport
• **give the game away** to give the game away is to let other people know about something you have been trying to hide or keep secret
•ADJECTIVE• 1 someone who is game is ready to do things, especially things that involve risk 2 someone with a game leg is lame

gamekeeper •NOUN• **gamekeepers** someone whose job is to look after wild animals and birds on private land in the countryside

gammon •NOUN• gammon is the salted and smoked meat from the leg of a pig

gander •NOUN• **ganders** a male goose

gang •NOUN• **gangs** 1 a group of friends who meet regularly or go around together 2 a group of criminals or other troublemakers
•VERB• **gangs, ganging, ganged** if several people **gang up on** another person they act together against that person

gangster •NOUN• **gangsters** a member of a gang of criminals

gangway •NOUN• **gangways** 1 a narrow passage, for example where people can walk between rows of seats 2 a narrow platform or bridge used to get on and off a ship, which can be moved away when the ship sails

gantry •NOUN• **gantries** a high metal frame that heavy machines like cranes are supported on

gaol •NOUN• **gaols** another spelling of **jail**
✦ **gaoler** •NOUN• **gaolers** another spelling of **jailer**

ⓘ **Gaol** and **gaoler** are pronounced the same way as **jail** and **jailer**.

gap •NOUN• **gaps** 1 an opening or space in the middle of something or between things: *a gap in the wall • a gap between his front teeth*
    2 something missing: *a gap in his memory*
    3 a difference between two things: *the gap between rich and poor*

gape •VERB• **gapes, gaping, gaped** 1 to gape is to stare with your mouth open, usually because you are very surprised or impressed 2 something that gapes is wide open

garage •NOUN• **garages** 1 a buiding, often a small one beside a house, for storing a car or other vehicle 2 a place where vehicles are repaired, or a shop selling petrol and often other items for vehicles or road journeys

ⓘ This word comes from the French word **garer**, which means *to shelter*.

garbage •NOUN• rubbish

garble •VERB• **garbles, garbling, garbled** to garble words or pieces of information is to mix them up

garden •NOUN• **gardens** an area of land

gargle → gather

where flowers, trees and vegetables are grown

✦ **gardener** •NOUN• **gardeners** someone who does gardening

✦ **gardening** •NOUN• working in and taking care of a garden

gargle •VERB• **gargles, gargling, gargled** to rinse your mouth and throat with a liquid by holding it in your mouth and letting air from your throat bubble through it

gargoyle •NOUN• **gargoyles** a stone carving of an ugly creature's head, with an open mouth forming a spout, used to carry rainwater that comes off the roof of a building

garish •ADJECTIVE• garish colours or patterns are too bright

garland •NOUN• **garlands** flowers or leaves woven together into a circle

garlic •NOUN• a plant related to the onion with bulbs that divide into sections called cloves, which are used in cooking to add flavour

garment •NOUN• **garments** a piece of clothing

garnet •NOUN• **garnets** a hard red precious stone

garnish •VERB• **garnishes, garnishing, garnished** to garnish food is to decorate it •NOUN• **garnishes** something used to decorate food, for example herbs or nuts

garret •NOUN• **garrets** a room in an attic

garrison •NOUN• **garrisons** a group of soldiers guarding a town or fortress, or the building they live in

garter •NOUN• **garters** a broad band of elastic used to keep a stocking or sock up

gas •NOUN• **gases** or **gasses 1** a substance that is not liquid or solid and that moves about like air: *Oxygen and carbon dioxide are two of the gases that make up air.* **2** any natural or manufactured gas that burns easily and is used as fuel: *natural gas* • coal gas **3** gas is short for gasoline, the name used in North America for petrol

✦ **gaseous** •ADJECTIVE• in the form of a gas

gash •NOUN• **gashes** a deep open cut •VERB• **gashes, gashing, gashed** to gash something is to cut deeply into it

gasket •NOUN• **gaskets** a ring or flat strip of padding or rubber used to seal joints in metal to stop gas or steam from escaping

gas mask •NOUN• **gas masks** a mask worn over the face so that poisonous gas is not inhaled

gasoline •NOUN• the American English word for petrol

gasometer •NOUN• **gasometers** a large tank used for storing gas

gasp •VERB• **gasps, gasping, gasped 1** to gasp is to take a short sudden breath in through your open mouth making a sound as you do so: *They all gasped in horror.* **2** to gasp for air is to take sudden short breaths because you need to get oxygen into your lungs quickly •NOUN• **gasps** the sound of a sudden short breath

gastric •ADJECTIVE• to do with the stomach: *a gastric ulcer*

gasworks •NOUN• a gasworks is a place where gas is made, especially from coal

gate •NOUN• **gates 1** a movable structure with hinges that is used to close an opening in a wall or fence **2** the barrier where passengers wait before getting on an aeroplane **3** all the people attending a sports match or the total amount of money they pay to get into the match

gateau •NOUN• **gateaus** or **gateaux** a light cake made in layers, usually with cream or chocolate filling

gatecrash •VERB• **gatecrashes, gatecrashing, gatecrashed** if someone gatecrashes an event, such as a party, they go to it though they haven't been invited

gateway •NOUN• **gateways 1** an opening with a gate across it **2** anything that is an entrance or like an entrance: *a gateway to the future*

gather •VERB• **gathers, gathering, gathered 1** to meet or come together in a group

2 to gather things is to collect them or bring them together
3 to gather speed is to get faster and faster
4 to gather something is to hear or read about it: *I gather he's lived here for more than fifty years.*
♦ **gathering** •NOUN• **gatherings** a meeting of people or animals

gaudy •ADJECTIVE• **gaudier, gaudiest** gaudy colours are very strong and bright
♦ **gaudily** •ADVERB• too brightly or strongly: *gaudily coloured posters*

gauge •NOUN• **gauges 1** a device for measuring things, such as temperature, depth or height **2** the distance between railway tracks
•VERB• **gauges, gauging, gauged 1** to gauge something is to measure it **2** to gauge something is to make a guess at it: *I can never gauge what his reaction will be.*

gaunt •ADJECTIVE• if someone is gaunt they are thin and bony, often because they are ill

gauntlet •NOUN• **gauntlets** a type of thick glove with a part that covers the wrist and lower part of the arm
• **throw down the gauntlet** to throw down the gauntlet is to challenge someone, especially to a fight

gauze •NOUN• a very thin material that you can see through. Gauze is sometimes used to cover cuts and scratches
♦ **gauzy** •ADJECTIVE• **gauzier, gauziest** transparent

gave •VERB• a way of changing the verb **give** to make a past tense: *Janey gave Robbie some of her sweets.*

gawky •ADJECTIVE• **gawkier, gawkiest** a gawky person is tall and awkward-looking

gay •ADJECTIVE• **gayer, gayest 1** lively and full of fun: *happy and gay* **2** brightly coloured: *gay banners*
⇒ **gaiety, gaily**

gaze •VERB• **gazes, gazing, gazed** to look at something steadily
•NOUN• **gazes** a long steady look

gazelle •NOUN• **gazelles** a type of African or Asian animal that looks like a small deer and that can move quickly and gracefully

gear •NOUN• **gears 1** gear is the clothes and equipment you need or use for a particular sport or job: *tennis gear* **2** a gear is a mechanism made up of connecting toothed wheels that transfers power to the moving parts of a machine, for example from a car's engine to its wheels
•VERB• **gears, gearing, geared 1** to gear things to a particular group of people is to adapt things for that group: *The course is geared to more advanced students.* **2** to **gear up** for something is to get ready for it

geese •NOUN• the plural of **goose**

gel •NOUN• **gels** gel is a thick substance that looks like jelly and is used to hold your hair in a certain style

gelatine •NOUN• a clear substance used in cooking that sets to form jelly

gem •NOUN• **gems** a valuable stone or mineral, for example a diamond or emerald, that can be cut and polished and used in jewellery

gender •NOUN• **genders 1** gender is being male or female **2** in grammar, the gender of a word tells you if it is masculine, feminine or neuter

gene •NOUN• **genes** a part of a living cell of an animal or plant which contains information inherited from its parents and which affects things like hair or skin colour

genealogy •NOUN• **genealogies** the history of how people in a family are linked from one generation to the next

genera •NOUN• the plural of **genus**

general •ADJECTIVE• **1** involving everyone or most things: *a general feeling of gloom* • *general knowledge* **2** broad and not detailed: *Can you give me a general idea of what it will cost?*
• **in general** to do with most people or things: *Schools in general are achieving better results.*
•NOUN• **generals** an important army officer
♦ **generalize** or **generalise** •VERB• **generalizes, generalizing, generalized** to make a statement that does not go into any detail
♦ **generally** •ADVERB• usually: *Children generally start school at about age five.*

Aa
Bb
Cc
Dd
Ee
Ff
Gg
Hh
Ii
Jj
Kk
Ll
Mm
Nn
Oo
Pp
Qq
Rr
Ss
Tt
Uu
Vv
Ww
Xx
Yy
Zz

general practitioner •NOUN• **general practitioners** a doctor who sees ill people from a particular area at a local clinic or surgery, or visits them at home

ⓘ **General practitioner** is often shortened to **GP**.

generate •VERB• **generates, generating, generated** to generate something is to create it: *His work generated a lot of interest.*
♦ **generation** •NOUN• **generations** 1 generation is creating something 2 a generation is a single step in a family tree. For example, your grandparents are from one generation and your parents are from the next generation
♦ **generator** •NOUN• **generators** a machine that makes power, especially electricity

generosity •NOUN• being kind and giving

generous •ADJECTIVE• 1 a generous person is kind and gives to others in an unselfish way 2 a generous gift is bigger or more than expected
♦ **generously** •ADJECTIVE• in a generous way: *Please give generously.*

genetic •ADJECTIVE• to do with genes, or inherited through the genes: *a genetic defect*

genetically modified •ADJECTIVE• genetically modified plants or animals have had one or more of their genes changed artificially so that their natural characteristics are changed or improved

ⓘ **Genetically modified** is often shortened to **GM**, as in *GM foods*.

genetics •NOUN• finding out about genes, and how they work

genial •ADJECTIVE• a genial person is good-natured
♦ **geniality** •NOUN• being good-natured
♦ **genially** •ADVERB• in a good-natured way

genie •NOUN• **genies** or **genii** in Arabian and Persian stories, a magical spirit who watches over and grants the wishes of the person who controls it

genitals •PLURAL NOUN• a person's genitals are their sexual organs

genius •NOUN• **geniuses** 1 a genius is someone who is unusually clever or skilful 2 genius is extraordinary cleverness or skill

genteel •ADJECTIVE• if someone is genteel they behave in a very polite, good-mannered way, often because they think this makes them seem more high-class

gentle •ADJECTIVE• **gentler, gentlest** 1 a gentle person is kind and calm: *a gentle giant* 2 soft and light: *a gentle breeze* • *a gentle tap on his shoulder*
♦ **gentleness** •NOUN• being gentle
♦ **gently** •ADJECTIVE• in a gentle way

ⓘ The word **gentle** comes from the French word **gentil**, which means well-bred and well-mannered.

gentleman •NOUN• **gentlemen** 1 a word used to refer politely to a man: *Good morning, gentlemen.* 2 a man who is very polite and good-mannered: *He's a real gentleman.*
♦ **gentlemanly** •ADJECTIVE• gentlemanly behaviour is polite and good-mannered

gentry •NOUN• an old-fashioned word for people from one of the higher classes of society

gents •NOUN• the gents is a public toilet for boys and men: *Where is the gents, please?*

genuine •ADJECTIVE• 1 real, not fake: *a genuine work of art* 2 honest and not pretending: *a genuine person*
♦ **genuinely** •ADVERB• really or honestly: *I was genuinely impressed.*
♦ **genuineness** •NOUN• being real or honest

genus •NOUN• **genera** a genus is a class of animals or plants which usually includes several different species

geo- •PREFIX• if a word starts with **geo-**, it has something to do with the Earth. For example, *geology* is the study of the Earth's rocks

geographer •NOUN• **geographers** someone who studies geography

geographic or **geographical** •ADJECTIVE• to do with geography and where things are placed on the Earth's surface

geography •NOUN• geography is the study of the Earth's surface and the people on it

geologist •NOUN• **geologists** someone who studies geology

geology •NOUN• the study of the Earth's rocks, minerals and soil, what they are made up of, and how they were created

geometric or **geometrical** •ADJECTIVE• a geometric shape is made up of straight lines and angles

geometry •NOUN• geometry is a type of mathematics which deals with the study of angles, lines, curves and shapes

geranium •NOUN• **geraniums** a kind of bushy garden plant that has red, pink, purple or white flowers

gerbil •NOUN• **gerbils** a small animal similar to a rat, but with long back legs

germ •NOUN• **germs** a tiny living thing that can cause disease

germinate •VERB• **germinates, germinating, germinated** a seed germinates when it begins to sprout or grow
   ✦ **germination** •NOUN• germinating

gesticulate •VERB• **gesticulates, gesticulating, gesticulated** to gesticulate is to wave your hands or arms to express something

gesture •NOUN• **gestures** a movement made with part of your body which expresses a meaning or feeling, such as pointing at something, nodding or winking
   •VERB• **gestures, gesturing, gestured** to make a gesture with part of your body, especially your hand, arm or head

get •VERB• **gets, getting, got** 1 you get something when someone gives it to you or you fetch it: *Isabel got lots of birthday presents.*
   2 you have got something when you have it or own it: *Have you got a rubber I could borrow?* • *They haven't got a TV.*
   3 you get someone to do something for you when you ask or persuade them to do it: *Get Raymond to help you lift that big box.*
   4 you get somewhere when you arrive there: *We got to New York at 5 o'clock in the morning.*
   5 you get a bus or some other form of transport when you travel on it: *Uncle George gets the train to work.*
   6 if you get a disease or illness you catch it: *They had an injection to stop them getting measles.*
   7 to **get by** is to manage, especially with the money you have
   8 to **get away with** something is to manage to do something wrong or illegal without being caught or punished
   9 to **get on** is to make progress or to do well in your career: *You have to study hard if you want to get on.* • *I've got to get on with my homework.*
   10 if people **get on** or **get on with** each other, they like each other and are friendly to each other: *Jake and Mikey seem to get on really well.*
   11 to **get out of** something is to avoid doing it
   12 to **get over** something is to recover from it: *It took her a long time to get over the shock.*

geyser •NOUN• **geysers** a spout of hot water that comes out of the ground

ghastly •ADJECTIVE• **ghastlier, ghastliest** horrible or very ugly: *a ghastly smell*

gherkin •NOUN• **gherkins** a kind of pickled vegetable that looks like a small cucumber

ghetto •NOUN• **ghettos** an area in a town or city where a certain group of people live, especially poor people

ghost •NOUN• **ghosts** a spirit of a dead person
   ✦ **ghostly** •ADJECTIVE• **ghostlier, ghostliest** 1 like a ghost 2 very pale

ghoul •NOUN• **ghouls** 1 in Muslim stories, an evil spirit that steals and eats dead bodies 2 someone who is very interested in death and disaster
   ✦ **ghoulish** •ADJECTIVE• unnaturally interested in death and disaster

giant •NOUN• **giants** 1 in stories, an imaginary being like a huge person that is often evil or frightening 2 a very large thing: *an industrial giant*
   •ADJECTIVE• huge or bigger than normal: *a giant crane* • *a giant tortoise*

gibbon •NOUN• **gibbons** a type of ape with long thin arms and legs

Aa
Bb
Cc
Dd
Ee
Ff
Gg
Hh
Ii
Jj
Kk
Ll
Mm
Nn
Oo
Pp
Qq
Rr
Ss
Tt
Uu
Vv
Ww
Xx
Yy
Zz

giblets •PLURAL NOUN• the parts of a chicken or turkey that are used in cooking to make stock for soup or gravy, especially the neck, heart and lungs

giddiness •NOUN• a feeling of dizziness

giddy •ADJECTIVE• **giddier, giddiest** if you feel giddy you feel dizzy

gift •NOUN• **gifts** a present
  ✦ **gifted** •ADJECTIVE• a gifted person is extremely good at something or extremely clever

gigantic •ADJECTIVE• huge, like a giant

giggle •VERB• **giggles, giggling, giggled** to giggle is to laugh in a silly or nervous way •NOUN• **giggles** a silly or nervous laugh

gild •VERB• **gilds, gilding, gilded** to gild something is to cover it with gold

gills •PLURAL NOUN• a fish's gills are the openings at each side of its body just behind its head, which allow it to breathe

gimmick •NOUN• **gimmicks** something that is meant to attract people's attention, but has no other value

gin •NOUN• an alcoholic drink made with grain and flavoured with juniper berries

ginger •NOUN• **1** the knobbly root of a tropical plant which has a spicy taste and is used in cooking **2** a reddish-orange colour

gingerbread •NOUN• a kind of cake flavoured with powdered ginger

gingerly •ADVERB• if you do something gingerly, you do it very slowly and carefully because you are nervous: *He stepped gingerly on the wobbly bridge.*

gipsy •NOUN• **gipsies** another spelling of gypsy

giraffe •NOUN• **giraffes** an African animal with a spotted coat, long legs and a very long neck

girder •NOUN• **girders** a beam made of iron, steel or wood, used as a support in bridges and buildings

girdle •NOUN• **girdles 1** something that goes around the waist like a belt **2** a tight piece of underwear that makes the waist look slimmer

girl •NOUN• **girls** a female child or young woman
  ⇒ **girlish**

girlfriend •NOUN• **girlfriends 1** a female friend **2** a girl or woman that a boy or man is having a special relationship with or is in love with

girlish •ADJECTIVE• like a girl, usually used to describe an older woman's behaviour or appearance: *a girlish laugh*

girth •NOUN• **girths** something's girth is the distance it measures around the middle

gist •NOUN• the gist of a story or argument is its basic meaning or its main point

give •VERB• **gives, giving, gave, given 1** to give something to someone is to let them have it or to pass it on to them: *My brother gave me his old bike.*
  2 if someone gives a party or performance, they hold a party or they perform in front of other people
  3 to give a cry, shout or laugh is to make that sound out loud: *He gave a whoop of joy.*
  4 if something gives, it bends, sags or collapses when too much weight is put on top of it: *The rotten floorboard gave under him and his foot went through.*
  5 to **give away** a secret is to tell it to someone without meaning to
  6 to **give in** is to admit defeat
  7 if a machine or a part of your body **gives out**, it stops working
  8 to **give up** is to stop trying to do something because it has become too difficult
  • **give way 1** something gives way when it breaks or collapses **2** drivers give way when they stop at a junction or roundabout and allow other traffic to pass in front of them
  ✦ **given** •ADJECTIVE• decided or selected: *On any given day, there are several dozen accidents.*
  ✦ **giver** •NOUN• **givers** someone who gives something

glacier •NOUN• **glaciers** a huge mass of ice moving slowly down a valley

glacial •ADJECTIVE• to do with ice or glaciers: *a glacial period*

glad •ADJECTIVE• **gladder, gladdest** pleased

or happy: *We're very glad you could make it to the party.*

✦ **gladden** • VERB• **gladdens, gladdening, gladdened** to make glad: *a sight to gladden your heart*

✦ **gladly** • ADVERB• happily or with pleasure: *I'll gladly do what you ask.*

✦ **gladness** • NOUN• a feeling of pleasure or happiness

glade • NOUN• **glades** an open space in a wood or forest

gladiator • NOUN• **gladiators** in ancient Rome, a man trained to fight with other men or with wild animals to amuse spectators

glamorous • ADJECTIVE• attractive, fashionable and exciting

glamour • NOUN• 1 extravagant beauty, especially if it is rather false 2 the excitement of being rich, fashionable or famous

glance • VERB• **glances, glancing, glanced** 1 to look quickly at something and then look away again 2 if something moving **glances off** another thing, it hits that thing then flies off sideways
• NOUN• **glances** a short quick look

gland • NOUN• **glands** a part of the body which stores substances from the body to be used later or to be got rid of

✦ **glandular** • ADJECTIVE• to do with a gland or glands

glare • VERB• **glares, glaring, glared** 1 to look at someone or something angrily 2 to shine with a very bright light that hurts your eyes
• NOUN• **glares** 1 a fierce or angry look 2 very strong bright light that dazzles you

✦ **glaring** • ADJECTIVE• standing out in a very obvious way: *a glaring mistake*

✦ **glaringly** • ADVERB• very clearly: *It was glaringly obvious that he was lying.*

glass • NOUN• **glasses** 1 glass is a hard breakable material that lets light through 2 a glass is a container for drinks made of this material, or the amount it will hold: *a tall glass* • *She drank three glasses of milk.*
• ADJECTIVE• made of glass: *a glass bowl*

✦ **glasses** • PLURAL NOUN• glasses are a pair of clear lenses inside a frame that you wear over your eyes to help you see more clearly

✦ **glassy** • ADJECTIVE• **glassier, glassiest** 1 shiny like glass, or transparent like glass 2 if someone's eyes are glassy, they have no expression in them

glaze • VERB• **glazes, glazing, glazed** 1 to glaze a window is to fit a sheet or sheets of glass into it
2 to glaze pots is to bake a hard shiny covering on their surface
3 if someone's eyes **glaze over**, they become expressionless
• NOUN• **glazes** a shiny covering

✦ **glazier** • NOUN• **glaziers** someone whose job is to put glass in windows

gleam • VERB• **gleams, gleaming, gleamed** to shine or glow brightly: *The lion's fangs gleamed.*
• NOUN• **gleams** 1 a beam or flash of light: *the gleam of headlights in the distance* 2 brightness or shininess: *the gleam of newly polished furniture*

glee • NOUN• joyful excitement or pleasure

✦ **gleeful** • ADJECTIVE• feeling or showing glee

✦ **gleefully** • ADVERB• happily or joyfully

glen • NOUN• **glens** a valley in Scotland

glide • VERB• **glides, gliding, glided** 1 to move smoothly, especially over a surface
2 to fly in a glider

✦ **glider** • NOUN• **gliders** a kind of aeroplane with no engine that is towed into the air by another aeroplane, where it flies on air currents

glimmer • VERB• **glimmers, glimmering, glimmered** to burn or shine weakly or faintly
• NOUN• **glimmers** 1 a faint light 2 a glimmer of something, such as hope, is a faint or slight sign of it

glimpse • NOUN• **glimpses** a brief look at something
• VERB• **glimpses, glimpsing, glimpsed** to glimpse something is to see it for a very short time

glint • VERB• **glints, glinting, glinted** to reflect flashes of light
• NOUN• **glints** a light reflected off a surface, especially a metal one

glisten • VERB• **glistens, glistening, glistened** if a surface glistens, light reflects off it, because it has a shiny surface or is wet

glitter •VERB• **glitters, glittering, glittered** to shine or sparkle with small flashes of light • NOUN• glitter is tiny pieces of shiny material used to decorate your skin, hair or clothes or for making pictures
♦ **glittery** •ADJECTIVE• shining with little sparks of light or tiny pieces of shiny material: *glittery makeup*

gloat •VERB• **gloats, gloating, gloated** to show too much pleasure at your own success or at someone else's failure

global •ADJECTIVE• **1** to do with or involving the whole world: *global businesses* **2** involving everyone or everything: *a global increase in pay*
♦ **globally** •ADVERB• world-wide or generally

global warming •NOUN• the gradual warming of the Earth's surface and atmosphere as a result of the greenhouse effect, causing rises in sea temperature and weather changes around the world

globe •NOUN• **globes 1** the globe is the Earth: *people from around the globe* **2** a large ball with a map of the Earth printed on it that can be turned on a stand **3** anything shaped like a ball or sphere

glockenspiel •NOUN• **glockenspiels** a musical instrument made up of a row of metal bars that you hit with sticks to make different notes

gloom •NOUN• **1** darkness or near-darkness: *A shape appeared out of the gloom.* **2** sadness or depression: *They were filled with gloom when their team lost the final.*
♦ **gloominess** •NOUN• **1** being dark, nearly dark or dull: *the gloominess of a winter's morning* **2** being sad or depressed: *Her gloominess made us all feel bad.*
♦ **gloomy** •ADJECTIVE• **gloomier, gloomiest 1** dark or nearly dark: *a gloomy passageway* **2** sad or depressing: *a gloomy picture of the future*

glorify •VERB• **glorifies, glorifying, glorified** to glorify someone or something is to praise them very highly, in a way that makes them seem impressive: *glorify God* • *The book glorifies war.*

glorious •ADJECTIVE• **1** splendidly beautiful: *glorious singing* **2** deserving or having glory: *a glorious victory*

glory •NOUN• **glories 1** honour and praise **2** a splendidly beautiful thing: *the glories of medieval architecture*
•VERB• **glories, glorying, gloried** to glory in something is to feel or show great delight or pride in it: *They gloried in their unexpected victory.*

gloss •NOUN• gloss is surface brightness
⇒ **glossy**

glossary •NOUN• **glossaries** a list of words, with explanations of their meanings

glossy •ADJECTIVE• **glossier, glossiest** smooth and shiny: *a glossy surface* • *glossy hair*

glove •NOUN• **gloves** gloves are two matching pieces of clothing that you wear on your hands

glow •VERB• **glows, glowing, glowed** to burn or shine with a warm or soft light • NOUN• warm or soft light: *the glow of the fire*
⇒ **glowing**

glower •VERB• **glowers, glowering, glowered** to stare at something or somebody with a frown

glowing •ADJECTIVE• **1** burning or shining with a warm or soft light: *glowing embers* **2** full of praise and admiration: *He got a glowing report from his teacher.*

glow-worm •NOUN• **glow-worms** a kind of beetle that glows in the dark

glucose •NOUN• a kind of sugar that is found in certain foods, like fruit, and which gives you energy

glue •NOUN• **glues** a substance used for sticking things together
•VERB• **glues, gluing** or **glueing, glued** to glue something is to stick it with glue
♦ **gluey** •ADJECTIVE• covered with glue or sticky like glue

glum •ADJECTIVE• **glummer, glummest** looking or feeling sad and depressed

gluten •NOUN• a sticky protein found in wheat and some other cereals

glutton •NOUN• **gluttons 1** someone who is very greedy and eats too much **2** someone who is very eager for something, especially something that does them no good: *a glutton for punishment*
♦ **gluttony** •NOUN• eating too much

gnarled •ADJECTIVE• twisted and knobbly

gnash •VERB• **gnashes, gnashing, gnashed** if someone gnashes their teeth, they grind them or snap them together, especially because they are angry

gnat •NOUN• **gnats** a small flying insect that bites and sucks blood

gnaw •VERB• **gnaws, gnawing, gnawed** to chew something hard or scrape at it with the teeth

gnome •NOUN• **gnomes 1** in stories, a small fairy creature that looks like a little old man wearing a soft pointed hat **2** a figure like this that some people put in their gardens as a decoration

gnu •NOUN• **gnu** or **gnus** a type of antelope found in Africa

ⓘ **Gnu** is pronounced **noo** or **nyoo**.

go •VERB• **goes, going, went, gone 1** to go somewhere is to travel or move there: *I'm going home now.*
2 to go somewhere is to lead to that place: *Does this road go to Inverness?*
3 to leave: *It's six o'clock. I'll have to go soon.*
4 the place where something goes is the place where it fits or is kept: *That piece of the jigsaw goes at the top.*
5 to become: *Her face went pale.* • *Your soup's gone cold.*
6 to **go in for** something is to take part in it
7 food **goes off** when it becomes bad
8 to **go on** is to continue: *Go on with your work* • *The baby went on crying.*
• **going to** about to: *What were you going to say?*
• NOUN• **goes** a go is a try or a shot
• **on the go** if someone is on the go, they are busy or active

goad •VERB• **goads, goading, goaded** to goad someone is to annoy them until they do something that you want them to do

go-ahead •NOUN• if something gets the go-ahead, it is allowed to begin
• ADJECTIVE• a go-ahead person is someone who is full of ideas and plans for the future

goal •NOUN• **goals 1** in games like football and hockey, the goal is the area where you have to put the ball to score a point
2 a goal is a point scored when a ball goes into this area
3 an aim that you want to achieve

goat •NOUN• **goats** an animal with horns and long rough hair. Goats are kept for their milk, meat and hair

gobble •VERB• **gobbles, gobbling, gobbled 1** if someone gobbles their food, they eat it very quickly **2** a turkey gobbles when it makes a series of loud sounds

goblet •NOUN• **goblets** a drinking cup with a stem and a rounded bowl

goblin •NOUN• **goblins** in stories, an evil ugly fairy creature

gobstopper •NOUN• **gobstoppers** a big round hard sweet that you suck

god •NOUN• **gods 1** a god is one of several beings that some people believe have the power to change or affect nature, or what happens to individuals **2** God is the being that Christians, Muslims, Jews and members of other religions worship

godchild •NOUN• **godchildren** a god-daughter or godson

god-daughter •NOUN• **god-daughters** someone's god-daughter is a girl that they are godmother or godfather to

goddess •NOUN• **goddesses** a female god

godfather •NOUN• **godfathers** a child's godfather is a man who has agreed to help make sure that the child is brought up as a Christian

godmother •NOUN• **godmothers** a child's godmother is a woman who has agreed to help make sure that the child is brought up as a Christian

godparent •NOUN• **godparents** a godfather or godmother

godsend •NOUN• **godsends** a piece of good luck that you are very grateful for

Aa
Bb
Cc
Dd
Ee
Ff
Gg
Hh
Ii
Jj
Kk
Ll
Mm
Nn
Oo
Pp
Qq
Rr
Ss
Tt
Uu
Vv
Ww
Xx
Yy
Zz

godson • NOUN • **godsons** someone's godson is a boy that they are godmother or godfather to

goggles • PLURAL NOUN • people wear goggles over their eyes to protect them, for example when they are swimming underwater or working with materials that might damage their eyes

go-kart • NOUN • **go-karts** a small low vehicle that is used for racing, but which has a much less powerful engine than a real racing car

gold • NOUN • 1 a pale yellow precious metal 2 a yellow colour
♦ **golden** • ADJECTIVE • gold-coloured or made of gold: *golden hair*

golden wedding • NOUN • **golden weddings** the 50th anniversary of a couple's marriage

goldfish • NOUN • **goldfish** a small fish with golden or orange scales that is kept as a pet

gold medal • NOUN • **gold medals** a medal made of gold awarded to the person who comes first in a sporting event

golf • NOUN • a game played on a large area of specially designed land. The players hit a small ball with long clubs into a series of small holes
♦ **golfer** • NOUN • **golfers** someone who plays golf

gondola • NOUN • **gondolas** a type of open boat used on the canals and waterways of Venice and rowed by a single oar at the back
♦ **gondolier** • NOUN • **gondoliers** someone who rows a gondola

gone • VERB • the form of the verb **go** that is used with a helping verb to show that something happened in the past: *I tried to catch him before he left, but he had gone.*

gong • NOUN • **gongs** a large round piece of metal that is hit with a stick, especially to let people know that a meal is about to be served

good • ADJECTIVE • **better, best** 1 something good is enjoyable or pleasant, or is of a high standard: *Did you have a good holiday?*
2 a good person is kind and thoughtful: *My grandparents are very good to me.*

3 good behaviour is correct or proper: *He has very good manners.*
4 to be good at something is to be able to do it well: *Janey's very good at drawing horses.*
5 satisfactory or substantial: *He earns a good salary.*
6 something is good for you when it benefits you in some way, especially by keeping you healthy
• NOUN • good is rightness: *the difference between good and evil*
• **for good** for ever: *He won't be coming back; he's gone for good.*
⇒ **better, best, goodness**

goodbye • INTERJECTION • you say 'goodbye' to people you are leaving or who are leaving you

goodness • NOUN • 1 being good and kind 2 the goodness in food is the things in it that will make you healthy when you eat it

goods • PLURAL NOUN • goods are things for sale: *goods from other countries*

goodwill • NOUN • goodwill is kind wishes: *The King and Queen sent him a message of goodwill.*

goose • NOUN • **geese** a bird with a long neck and webbed feet

gooseberry • NOUN • **gooseberries** a small round pale green fruit with a hairy skin that grows on a low bush

goosebumps *or* **goosepimples**
• PLURAL NOUN • if you get goosebumps or goosepimples, tiny lumps appear on your skin, usually because you are cold or have had a fright

gore • VERB • **gores, goring, gored** if a bull or other animal gores someone, it injures them with its horns or tusks
• NOUN • gore is lots of blood
⇒ **gory**

gorge • NOUN • **gorges** a deep narrow valley between hills

gorgeous • ADJECTIVE • beautiful: *The baby's absolutely gorgeous.* • *lots of gorgeous food*

gorilla • NOUN • **gorillas** a kind of West African ape with a large head, long arms and a strong heavy body

ⓘ Be careful not to confuse the spellings of **gorilla** and **guerilla**, a type of fighter.

gorse • NOUN• gorse is a type of wild shrub with yellow flowers and sharp spines on its stems

gory • ADJECTIVE• **gorier, goriest** with lots of blood: *a gory film*

gosling • NOUN• **goslings** a baby goose

gospel • NOUN• **gospels** 1 the gospel is the teachings of Christ
2 the Gospels are the parts of the Christian Bible describing the teachings of Christ
3 the truth: *He swore that what he had told me was gospel.*

gossip • VERB• **gossips, gossiping, gossiped** to gossip is to have a conversation with someone about what other people are doing • NOUN• **gossips** 1 gossip is informal talk, often about what other people are doing 2 a gossip is someone who gossips a lot

ⓘ This word comes from the Old English word **godsipp**, which means *godparent*. This is because your godparent is thought of as someone you can talk to.

got • VERB• a way of changing the verb **get** to make a past tense. It can be used with or without a helping verb: *Kathy got a bike for her birthday.* • *She had got a pony the previous year.*

ⓘ In North America and Australia another form, **gotten**, is also used with a helping verb: *She had gotten a pony the previous year.*

gouge • VERB• **gouges, gouging, gouged** to gouge something out is to dig it out using your fingernails or a sharp tool

govern • VERB• **governs, governing, governed** to govern something, such as a country, is to control it and decide its rules
♦ **governess** • NOUN• **governesses** especially in the past, a woman employed by parents to teach their children at home
♦ **government** • NOUN• **governments** a government is the group of people who put the laws of a country into effect
♦ **governor** • NOUN• **governors** 1 school governors are the group of people who manage a particular school's business
2 someone who is the head of government in a country or state

gown • NOUN• **gowns** a long formal dress that women wear at special occasions

GP • ABBREVIATION• **GPs** short for **general practitioner**, a doctor who sees patients at a local surgery

grab • VERB• **grabs, grabbing, grabbed** 1 to grab something is to grasp or take it suddenly or roughly: *He grabbed my bag and ran away.* 2 to grab something is to take it eagerly or in a hurry: *Let's stop and grab a bite to eat.*

grace • NOUN• **graces** 1 grace is beauty or elegance of movement
2 if someone behaves with grace they are gentle, pleasant and thoughtful
3 approval or favour: *with the grace of God*
• **with bad grace** unwillingly or in a grudging way
• **with good grace** willingly or without complaint

graceful • ADJECTIVE• graceful movements are elegant and attractive
♦ **gracefully** • ADVERB• with grace

gracious • ADJECTIVE• behaving in a polite and kind way: *a gracious lady* • *It was very gracious of you to apologize.*
♦ **graciously** • ADVERB• politely and kindly

grade • NOUN• **grades** a grade is a placing or stage on a scale of quality or rank
• **make the grade** to make the grade is to reach the standard necessary
• VERB• **grades, grading, graded** to grade things is to sort them according to their size or quality, or to mark them according to how good they are

gradient • NOUN• **gradients** a measure of how steep a slope is, which is shown as a percentage or a number out of ten

gradual • ADJECTIVE• going or changing slowly and steadily: *a gradual increase*
♦ **gradually** • ADVERB• slowly and steadily: *The weather gradually got colder.*

graduate • VERB• **graduates, graduating, graduated** to graduate from college or university is to successfully finish your course and get a degree or diploma

graffiti → graphic

•NOUN• **graduates** someone who has a degree from a university or college

♦ **graduation** •NOUN• **graduations** the ceremony held when students at a college or university graduate

graffiti •NOUN• words or pictures painted or drawn on a wall

ⓘ This is an Italian word that means 'little scribbles'.

graft •VERB• **grafts, grafting, grafted** to attach one thing on to another, for example a piece of skin that has been taken from one part of the body and sewn on to another damaged part
•NOUN• **grafts** something, such as the stem of a plant or a piece of skin, that has been attached to another plant or another part of the body so that it can begin to grow there

grain •NOUN• **grains** 1 a grain is a single seed from a cereal plant like wheat or maize
2 grain is the seeds of cereal plants
3 a tiny piece of something: *a grain of pollen*
4 the grain on wood is the pattern of lines that run along or across its surface

gram *or* **gramme** •NOUN• **grams** *or* **grammes** the basic measurement of weight in the metric system. This is often shortened to **g**

grammar •NOUN• 1 grammar is the correct use of words in speech and writing, and the rules about putting them together: *It's bad grammar to say 'I done'.* 2 the rules that apply to how words are formed and used in a particular language: *French grammar*
⇒ **grammatical**

grammar school •NOUN• **grammar schools** a type of secondary school

grammatical •ADJECTIVE• grammatical speech or writing is correct according to the rules of grammar

gramme •NOUN• **grammes** another spelling of **gram**

gramophone •NOUN• **gramophones** an old-fashioned word for a record-player

gran •NOUN• **grans** an informal word for grandmother

grand •ADJECTIVE• **grander, grandest** 1 great or fine: *a grand house* 2 noble: *She's a very grand old lady.*

grandchild •NOUN• **grandchildren** a child of your child

grand-daughter •NOUN• **grand-daughters** the daughter of your son or daughter

grandfather •NOUN• **grandfathers** your father or mother's father

grandmother •NOUN• **grandmothers** your father or mother's mother

grandparent •NOUN• **grandparents** a parent of your father or mother

grandson •NOUN• **grandsons** the son of your son or daughter

grandstand •NOUN• **grandstands** a place for spectators at a sports stadium or race ground with rows of seats built in tiers one above the other

granite •NOUN• a very hard greyish or reddish rock

granny •NOUN• **grannies** an informal word for **grandmother**

grant •VERB• **grants, granting, granted** 1 to grant something that someone has asked for is to allow it or give it: *grant permission* 2 to admit that something is true: *It's very difficult, I grant you.*
•NOUN• **grants** a sum of money that has been given or awarded for a special purpose: *a repair grant*

granule •NOUN• **granules** a very small grain or part: *sugar granules*

grape •NOUN• **grapes** a small green or blackish-red berry that grows in bunches and is used to make wine

grapefruit •NOUN• **grapefruit** *or* **grapefruits** a large citrus fruit with yellow skin and yellow or pink flesh

graph •NOUN• **graphs** a diagram with lines drawn between different points on squared paper, used to show how things compare to each other

graphic •ADJECTIVE• 1 to do with drawing, painting or writing: *the graphic arts* 2 showing or giving a lot of detail, often too much detail

Aa Bb Cc Dd Ee Ff Gg Hh Ii Jj Kk Ll Mm Nn Oo Pp Qq Rr Ss Tt Uu Vv Ww Xx Yy Zz

♦ **graphics** •PLURAL NOUN• pictures, drawings and decorative lettering, especially those done on a computer or used in computer games or Web pages

grapple •VERB• **grapples, grappling, grappled** 1 to grapple with someone is to wrestle or struggle with them 2 to grapple with a difficult problem is to try hard to deal with it

grasp •VERB• **grasps, grasping, grasped** 1 to grasp something is to take hold of it, or hold it tightly 2 to grasp something is to understand it: *I'm hearing the words more clearly now, but I still can't grasp their meaning.*

grass • NOUN• **grasses** a plant with long thin leaves called blades, which grows on lawns and in fields
♦ **grassy** •ADJECTIVE• covered with grass: *a grassy field*

grasshopper • NOUN• **grasshoppers** an insect with long back legs that can hop or jump long distances

grassland •NOUN• **grasslands** a large area covered with grass

grate ¹ •VERB• **grates, grating, grated** 1 to grate food is to cut it into fine strands or shreds using a grater 2 something grates when it makes an unpleasant squeaking or scratching noise as it rubs, or is rubbed, against something
⇒ **grater**

grate ² • NOUN• **grates** a framework of metal bars in a fireplace, where the fuel is burned

grateful •ADJECTIVE• feeling thankful or showing or giving thanks: *I'm very grateful for all your kindness.*
♦ **gratefully** •ADVERB• thankfully

grater •NOUN• **graters** a kitchen tool that has lots of small holes with sharp edges on its surface, used for grating things like cheese or vegetables

grating •NOUN• **gratings** a covering for an outside drain with holes in it so that water and air can pass through

gratitude •NOUN• if you feel gratitude towards someone, you want to repay them for something kind that they have done

grave ¹ • NOUN• **graves** a place where a dead body is buried

grave ² • ADJECTIVE• **graver, gravest** 1 very serious: *a grave mistake* 2 solemn-looking

gravel • NOUN• small stones used to cover roads, paths and driveways

gravestone • NOUN• **gravestones** a piece of stone with writing on it which says who is buried in a grave

graveyard • NOUN• **graveyards** a place where dead people or animals are buried

gravity • NOUN• 1 gravity is the force that pulls things towards the earth and causes them to fall to the ground 2 gravity is seriousness: *the gravity of the crime*

ⓘ This word comes from the Latin word **gravitas**, which means *heaviness*. The force of gravity makes things seem heavier by pulling them down.

gravy •NOUN• a sauce made from the juices that come out of meat while it is cooking

graze •VERB• **grazes, grazing, grazed** 1 animals graze when they move around eating grass and other plants
2 to graze your skin is to scratch it by dragging it against something hard
3 if something grazes you it touches you lightly as it goes past
• NOUN• **grazes** a graze is a scratch or scratches on your skin made by something hard and rough

grease • NOUN• thick fat or oil, or any oily substance
•VERB• **greases, greasing, greased** to grease something is to rub grease on it
♦ **greasy** • ADJECTIVE• **greasier, greasiest** oily or fatty

great • ADJECTIVE• **greater, greatest** 1 very important or special: *a great day for the school*
2 very talented or distinguished: *one of the greatest scientists of all time*
3 very large: *The elephant lifted one of its great feet.*
4 very enjoyable or very good: *It was a great film.*
• NOUN• **greats** an extremely famous, special

Aa
Bb
Cc
Dd
Ee
Ff
Gg
Hh
Ii
Jj
Kk
Ll
Mm
Nn
Oo
Pp
Qq
Rr
Ss
Tt
Uu
Vv
Ww
Xx
Yy
Zz

or important or thing: *one of Hollywood's greats*
⇒ **greatly, greatness**

great-grandchild •NOUN• **great-grandchildren** your grandson's or granddaughter's child

great-grand-daughter •NOUN• **great-grand-daughters** your grandson's or granddaughter's daughter

great-grandfather •NOUN• **great-grandfathers** your grandfather's father

great-grandmother •NOUN• **great-grandmothers** your grandmother's mother

great-grandparent •NOUN• **great-grandparents** a parent of your grandmother or grandfather

great-grandson •NOUN• **great-grandsons** your grandson's or granddaughter's son

greatly •ADVERB• very much: *She wasn't greatly pleased.*

greatness •NOUN• being very impressive, important or talented

greed •NOUN• great or selfish desire for more of something than you need, especially food or money
♦ **greedily** •ADVERB• in a greedy way
♦ **greediness** •NOUN• being greedy
♦ **greedy** •ADJECTIVE• **greedier, greediest** wanting more of something than you actually need

green •NOUN• the colour of grass and the leaves of most plants
♦ **greenery** •NOUN• green leaves
⇒ **greens**

green belt •NOUN• an area of green fields around a city where you are not allowed to put up buildings

green fingers •PLURAL NOUN• someone who has green fingers is good at gardening and making plants grow

greengrocer •NOUN• **greengrocers**
1 someone who sells fruit and vegetables to the public 2 a greengrocer's is a shop selling fruit and vegetables

greenhouse •NOUN• **greenhouses** a shed with glass walls and roof that gets warm when the sun shines and is used for growing plants in

greenhouse effect •NOUN• the greenhouse effect is the heating of the Earth's surface caused by pollution in the atmosphere which traps the heat from the sun

greens •PLURAL NOUN• green vegetables such as cabbage: *Be sure to eat all your greens.*

greet •VERB• **greets, greeting, greeted** 1 to greet someone is to say something to them when they arrive or when you meet them 2 if something is greeted in a certain way people react to it in that way: *The announcement was greeted with howls of protest.*
♦ **greeting** •NOUN• **greetings** something said when you meet someone, such as 'hello' or 'hi' or 'good morning'

grenade •NOUN• **grenades** a weapon that is timed to explode a few seconds after it is thrown

grew •VERB• a way of changing the verb **grow** to make a past tense: *Stephen grew three centimetres last summer.*

grey •NOUN• a colour between black and white

greyhound •NOUN• **greyhounds** a type of dog with a slim body and narrow head, which can run very fast over short distances and is used for racing

grid •NOUN• **grids** 1 a pattern of lines that cross each other horizontally and vertically and form squares in between
2 a map or chart with a set of numbered lines
3 a grating made up of bars that cross each other like a grid
4 a network of electricity lines over a wide area

grid reference •NOUN• **grid references** a set of two numbers or letters used to show a place on a grid

grief •NOUN• great sorrow, especially when someone has died
♦ **come to grief** if you come to grief you fail or have an accident

grievance •NOUN• **grievances** something

Aa Bb Cc Dd Ee Ff Gg Hh Ii Jj Kk Ll Mm Nn Oo Pp Qq Rr Ss Tt Uu Vv Ww Xx Yy Zz

that you think is wrong and that you complain about

grieve •VERB• **grieves, grieving, grieved** to grieve is to feel very sad for a while, especially because someone has died or because you miss something that you have lost

grievous •ADJECTIVE• **1** a grievous wound or injury is very serious **2** something grievous causes sorrow or sadness

grill •VERB• **grills, grilling, grilled 1** to grill food is to cook it by putting it close to something hot **2** to grill someone is to ask them lots of questions •NOUN• **grills** the part of a cooker where food can be grilled

grille •NOUN• **grilles** a metal grating covering a door, window or other space in a wall

grim •ADJECTIVE• **grimmer, grimmest 1** if someone looks grim they have a serious and slightly fierce expression on their face **2** something grim is dreadful, upsetting or shocking

grimace •VERB• **grimaces, grimacing, grimaced** to twist your face in an ugly way, because you are in pain or you are disgusted at something •NOUN• **grimaces** an ugly twisted expression

grime •NOUN• dirt that has been on a surface for a long time and is difficult to get off ✦ **grimy** •ADJECTIVE• **grimier, grimiest** covered with grime

grin •VERB• **grins, grinning, grinned** to grin is to smile broadly showing your teeth •NOUN• **grins** a wide smile

grind •VERB• **grinds, grinding, ground 1** to grind something solid is to crush it into a powder between two hard surfaces **2** to grind something is to sharpen or polish it against a hard or rough surface **3** to grind your teeth is to rub them together sideways •NOUN• something that is difficult and boring to do: *the daily grind of work* ✦ **grinder** •NOUN• **grinders** a machine that grinds things, such as coffee beans

grindstone •NOUN• **grindstones** a circular stone that turns on top of another stone and is used in mills to grind corn
• **have your nose to the grindstone** to be working very hard, usually for long periods of time

grip •VERB• **grips, gripping, gripped 1** if you grip something you hold it tightly **2** if something grips you, it holds your attention completely •NOUN• **grips 1** a hold or grasp: *a tight grip* • *in the grip of winter* **2** a small U-shaped wire used to keep hair in place ✦ **gripping** •ADJECTIVE• holding your attention completely: *the climax of a gripping film*

grisly •ADJECTIVE• frightful or ghastly: *a grisly story about a mad axeman*

gristle •NOUN• a kind of tough stretchy tissue that is sometimes found in meat ✦ **gristly** •ADJECTIVE• gristly meat is tough and chewy because it has pieces of gristle in it

grit •NOUN• **1** grit is tiny sharp pieces of stone or sand **2** if someone has grit they have courage and determination ✦ **gritty** •ADJECTIVE• **grittier, grittiest 1** having a rough texture like grit **2** courageous or plucky **3** showing the harsher side of life as it really is

grizzly •ADJECTIVE• grey •NOUN• **grizzlies** a grizzly bear

grizzly bear •NOUN• **grizzly bears** a type of large brown bear with greyish brown hair on its head and back. Grizzly bears are found in parts of the United States and Canada

groan •VERB• **groans, groaning, groaned 1** to make a long deep sound because you are in pain or you think something is bad **2** to make a sound like a groan: *The trees creaked and groaned.* •NOUN• **groans** a deep moan made in the back of your throat

grocer •NOUN• **grocers 1** someone who runs a shop or supermarket selling groceries **2** a grocer's is a shop selling groceries ✦ **groceries** •PLURAL NOUN• groceries are foods and other household goods that you buy in a shop or supermarket

Aa
Bb
Cc
Dd
Ee
Ff
Gg
Hh
Ii
Jj
Kk
Ll
Mm
Nn
Oo
Pp
Qq
Rr
Ss
Tt
Uu
Vv
Ww
Xx
Yy
Zz

groggy • ADJECTIVE • **groggier, groggiest** if you feel groggy you can't think clearly, for example because you are weak after an illness

groin • NOUN • **groins** your groin is the part of your body between your legs where they join your body

groom • VERB • **grooms, grooming, groomed 1** to groom an animal is to look after it, especially by brushing or combing its coat
2 animals groom each other when they clean each other's coats by licking or picking through the hair
3 to groom yourself is to make yourself look neat and smart
• NOUN • **grooms 1** someone who looks after horses **2** a bridegroom

groove • NOUN • **grooves** a long narrow channel cut into a surface

grope • VERB • **gropes, groping, groped 1** to grope for something you can't see is to feel about with your hand to try to find it **2** to grope for an answer, or for the right word, is to try to find it without being sure how to do so

gross • ADJECTIVE • **grosser, grossest**
1 coarse, vulgar and bad-mannered
2 very bad: *gross ignorance*
3 an informal word meaning disgusting
4 very fat
5 a gross amount is the total amount without anything being taken away: *The gross weight of the parcel includes all the packaging.*
• NOUN • **gross** or **grosses** a gross is 12 dozen or 144
◆ **grossly** • ADVERB • hugely: *grossly inflated prices*

grotesque • ADJECTIVE • very strange and ugly-looking: *grotesque masks*

grotty • ADJECTIVE • **grottier, grottiest** an informal word meaning dirty and run-down: *a grotty little apartment*

ground¹ • NOUN • **grounds 1** the ground is the Earth's surface: *fall to the ground* • *on higher ground*
2 ground is earth or soil: *stony ground*
3 a ground is a sports field, especially one belonging to a particular club: *What's the name of Tottenham Hotspur's ground?*
• **get something off the ground** to get something started
• **suit someone down to the ground** to suit someone very well indeed
◆ **grounded** • ADJECTIVE • **1** a child is grounded when they aren't allowed out, as a punishment **2** a pilot or plane is grounded when they aren't allowed to fly
◆ **grounds** • PLURAL NOUN • **1** the grounds of a large house or building are the areas of land that surround it and are part of the same property
2 to have grounds for doing something is to have reasons for doing it
3 grounds are tiny pieces or powder made by grinding: *coffee grounds*

ground² • VERB • a way of changing the verb **grind** to make a past tense. It can be used with or without a helping verb: *The miller ground the corn.* • *The coffee has been ground too finely.*

group • NOUN • **groups** a number of people or things that are together or that belong together
• VERB • **groups, grouping, grouped** to bring people or things together in a group or groups

grouse¹ • NOUN • **grouse** a type of plump speckled bird that lives on moorland and is hunted for sport

grouse² • NOUN • **grouses** a complaint
• VERB • **grouses, grousing, groused** to grouse about something is to complain about it

grove • NOUN • **groves** a small group of trees growing close together

grovel • VERB • **grovels, grovelling, grovelled 1** to grovel is to crawl or lie on the ground
2 to grovel to someone is to make yourself humble to them

grow • VERB • **grows, growing, grew, grown 1** to grow is to get bigger, taller, wider or stronger: *He's grown as tall as his father.*
2 to grow plants is to look after them while they grow: *We grow vegetables in our garden.*
3 to become: *It was growing dark.*

4 to **grow out of** something you used to do or wear when you were younger is to become too old or big for it

growl •VERB• **growls, growling, growled**
1 an animal, like a dog or lion, growls when it makes a deep threatening noise in its throat **2** a person growls when they talk in a deep voice, often because they are angry
•NOUN• **growls** a deep threatening sound: *The dog let out a low growl.*

growth •NOUN• **growths 1** growing or getting bigger: *the rapid growth of computer technology*
2 the process by which things grow: *Warmth and longer days stimulates growth in the garden.*
3 a lump that grows on the body: *A growth developed on his hand.*

grub •NOUN• **grubs 1** a grub is the soft-bodied form of an insect just after it has hatched from the egg **2** grub is an informal word for food

grubby •ADJECTIVE• **grubbier, grubbiest** dirty: *Go and wash those grubby hands at once!*

grudge •VERB• **grudges, grudging, grudged** if you grudge giving something to someone, you feel annoyed because you think they don't deserve it: *We did not grudge them their good fortune, because they had earned it.*
•NOUN• **grudges** if you have a grudge against someone, they have done something to you that you are angry about and haven't forgiven

gruel •NOUN• gruel is a kind of thin porridge made with oatmeal and water or milk

gruelling •ADJECTIVE• very difficult and tiring: *a gruelling climb to the summit of the mountain*

gruesome •ADJECTIVE• horrible or sickening

gruff •ADJECTIVE• **gruffer, gruffest** a gruff voice is deep and harsh-sounding

grumble •VERB• **grumbles, grumbling, grumbled** to grumble is to complain in a bad-tempered way

grumpy •ADJECTIVE• **grumpier, grumpiest** bad-tempered: *He's grumpy if he has to get up early.*

grunt •VERB• **grunts, grunting, grunted** to make a deep snorting noise like a pig
•NOUN• **grunts** a deep snorting noise

guarantee •NOUN• **guarantees** a promise that something will definitely be done or that something will be replaced free of charge if it goes wrong
•VERB• **guarantees, guaranteeing, guaranteed** to guarantee something is to make a promise that it will happen or be done

guard •NOUN• **guards 1** someone, or a group of people, whose job is to watch over or protect a person or place, or to make sure that prisoners don't escape
2 to **keep** or **stand guard** is to watch over someone or something
3 something that protects from damage or accidents: *a gum guard • a fire guard*
4 someone who is in charge of a railway train or coach
• **catch someone off guard** to catch someone off guard is to say or do something that they weren't prepared for
•VERB• **guards, guarding, guarded 1** to guard a person or place is to watch over them **2** to **guard against** something is to take care not to let it happen
♦ **guardian** •NOUN• **guardians 1** someone who watches over and protects **2** a child's or young person's guardian is someone with the legal right and duty to take care of them

guerrilla •NOUN• **guerrillas** a fighter who is a member of a small or unofficial army, which makes surprise attacks on larger armies but does not fight openly
•ADJECTIVE• involving guerrillas: *a guerrilla war*

guess •VERB• **guesses, guessing, guessed** to guess is to give an answer or opinion without knowing or being sure of all or any of the facts
•NOUN• **guesses** an answer or opinion made by guessing

guest •NOUN• **guests 1** someone you invite to your house or to a party **2** someone staying in a hotel

guffaw •VERB• **guffaws, guffawing,**

Aa
Bb
Cc
Dd
Ee
Ff
Gg
Hh
Ii
Jj
Kk
Ll
Mm
Nn
Oo
Pp
Qq
Rr
Ss
Tt
Uu
Vv
Ww
Xx
Yy
Zz

guffawed to guffaw is to laugh loudly and suddenly
• NOUN• **guffaws** a sudden loud laugh

guidance • NOUN• if someone gives you guidance they give you advice about how you should do something

guide • VERB• **guides, guiding, guided** 1 to guide someone is to show them the way or how to do something 2 to guide something is to make it go in a certain direction
• NOUN• **guides** 1 someone who shows tourists around or who leads travellers
2 a book that gives information about a place
3 a Guide is a young person who is a member of the Guide Association

guide dog • NOUN• **guide dogs** a specially trained dog used by a blind person to help them get around

guild • NOUN• **guilds** 1 a society of craftsmen or tradesmen 2 a society or social club

guile • NOUN• guile is cunning cleverness

guillotine • NOUN• **guillotines** 1 an instrument with a blade that falls very quickly from a height and which was used in the past, especially in France, to execute people by cutting off their heads 2 a machine with a very sharp blade used for cutting paper

guilt • NOUN• 1 an uneasy feeling you get when you know you have done something wrong: *She felt no guilt at what she had done.* 2 the fact that you have done something wrong: *He admitted his guilt and accepted the punishment.*
♦ **guilty** • ADJECTIVE• **guiltier, guiltiest** 1 you feel guilty when you feel that you have done something wrong
2 if someone is guilty of something, other people think that something they do is wrong: *He's guilty of neglecting his school work to play sport.*
3 someone is found guilty of a crime when a jury or judge decides that they did it

guinea • NOUN• **guineas** a British gold coin used in the past

guinea pig • NOUN• **guinea pigs** a small animal with a squarish face, small round ears and long soft hair that is kept as a pet

guise • NOUN• **guises** a disguise or appearance

guitar • NOUN• **guitars** an instrument with a rounded body shaped like a figure of eight, a long neck and strings that you play with your fingers

gulf • NOUN• **gulfs** 1 a large bay filled by the sea 2 if there is a gulf between people or things they are very far apart or very different from each other

gull • NOUN• **gulls** a common sea bird

gullet • NOUN• **gullets** your gullet is the tube that food goes down into your stomach

gullible • ADJECTIVE• a gullible person believes what they are told and is easily tricked

gully • NOUN• **gullies** a deep channel worn away by a river or stream

gulp • VERB• **gulps, gulping, gulped** to gulp is to swallow air or liquid quickly in large mouthfuls: *He gulped down his tea.*
• NOUN• **gulps** 1 the sound made when you gulp 2 a large mouthful

gum • NOUN• **gums** 1 a type of glue used to stick paper or card
2 chewing gum
3 a sticky jelly-like sweet: *fruit gums*
4 your gums are the parts inside your mouth just above your top teeth and below your bottom teeth
•VERB• **gums, gumming, gummed** to stick something with gum
♦ **gummy** • ADJECTIVE• **gummier, gummiest** 1 sticky like gum 2 toothless: *The baby gave a big gummy smile.*

gum tree • NOUN• **gum trees** a tree that produces gum, especially the eucalyptus tree
• **up a gum tree** to be up a gum tree is to be in a very difficult situation

gun • NOUN• **guns** a weapon that fires bullets or shells from a metal tube
• **jump the gun** to start before you should
• **stick to your guns** you stick to your guns when you refuse to change your mind

gunfire • NOUN• 1 the firing of guns 2 the sound of bullets being fired from a gun

gunpowder • NOUN• a powder that explodes when it is lit

gurgle •VERB• **gurgles, gurgling, gurgled**
1 water gurgles when it makes a pleasant
bubbling sound as it flows **2** to make small
bubbling sounds in your throat with saliva or
some other liquid
• NOUN• **gurgles** a bubbling sound

guru •NOUN• **gurus 1** a Hindu or Sikh
religious leader and teacher **2** any greatly
respected teacher or leader

gush •VERB• **gushes, gushing, gushed**
1 water or other liquid gushes when it flows
out suddenly and strongly **2** to gush is to talk
with exaggerated feeling or emotion

gust •NOUN• **gusts** a sudden strong rush of
wind
• **gusty** •ADJECTIVE• **gustier, gustiest** gusty
weather has sudden rushes of wind between
calmer periods

gut •NOUN• **guts** your gut is your stomach
and intestines
•VERB• **guts, gutting, gutted 1** to gut a dead
fish or animal is to remove the organs from
inside its body **2** to gut a place is to destroy or
remove everything inside it
• **guts** •PLURAL NOUN• **1** guts are intestines
2 someone who has guts has courage

gutter •NOUN• **gutters** a channel for carrying
water, especially one fixed to the edge of a
roof or by the side of the road for carrying
away rainwater into the underground drains

guy •NOUN• **guys 1** an informal word for a
man or boy **2** a figure made to represent Guy
Fawkes, which is burnt on a bonfire on 5
November, Guy Fawkes Night

guzzle •VERB• **guzzles, guzzling, guzzled** to
guzzle food or drink is to eat or drink it
quickly and greedily

gym •NOUN• **gyms 1** a gym is a gymnasium
2 gym is the exercises and games that you do
in a school gymnasium

gymkhana •NOUN• **gymkhanas** a horse-
riding event which includes races and
jumping competitions

gymnasium •NOUN• **gymnasiums** or
gymnasia a large room in a school or sports
centre with special equipment for doing
exercises on

gymnast •NOUN• **gymnasts** someone
trained to do gymnastics
• **gymnastic** •ADJECTIVE• to do with
gymnastics, or strong and graceful like the
exercises done by a gymnast
• **gymnastics** •NOUN• exercises done
indoors in a gym and using special equipment
like bars, ropes and beams

gypsy •NOUN• **gypsies** a member of a race of
people who travel from place to place and
have no fixed home

ⓘ **Gypsy** comes from the word **Egyptian**,
because people used to think gypsies came
from Egypt.

Aa Bb Cc Dd Ee Ff Gg Hh Ii Jj Kk Ll Mm Nn Oo Pp Qq Rr Ss Tt Uu Vv Ww Xx Yy Zz

257

Hh

habit • NOUN• **habits** a habit is something that you do regularly: *Tommy has a bad habit of grinding his teeth.*
⇒ **habitual**

habitat • NOUN• **habitats** an animal's or plant's habitat is the place where it lives or grows
• **habitation** • NOUN• **habitations** a place where someone lives

habitual • ADJECTIVE• **1** doing something again and again: *a habitual criminal* **2** done regularly, as a habit: *a habitual morning cup of coffee*

hack • VERB• **hacks, hacking, hacked 1** to chop, or to chop up, roughly: *They hacked their way through the thick jungle.* **2** to get access to the information in a computer without permission

hacker • NOUN• **hackers** someone who uses their computer skills to get access to information in other people's computers illegally or without permission

hacksaw • NOUN• **hacksaws** a saw with a thin blade used to cut metal

had • VERB• **1** a way of changing the verb **have** to make a past tense: *I had a cold last week.* **2 had** is also used as a helping verb along with a main verb: *I had enjoyed my stay in France.* • *He had had enough.*

haddock • NOUN• **haddock** *or* **haddocks** a type of sea fish with firm white flaky flesh

Hadith • NOUN• in Islam, the traditions based on what Mohammed and his followers did in their lives, which give Muslims guidance on how to live

hadn't • SHORT FORM• a short way to say and write **had not**: *He hadn't expected to win.*

haemorrhage • NOUN• **haemorrhages** very serious bleeding that is difficult to stop •VERB• **haemorrhages, haemorrhaging, haemorrhaged** to bleed very heavily and suddenly

hag • NOUN• **hags** an ugly old woman

haggard • ADJECTIVE• tired and ill-looking

haggis • NOUN• **haggises** a Scottish food made with minced sheep's heart mixed with oatmeal and spices

haggle • VERB• **haggles, haggling, haggled** to bargain over something you want to buy, trying to lower the price first asked by the seller

haiku • NOUN• **haiku** a type of Japanese poem

hail¹ •VERB• **hails, hailing, hailed 1** to hail someone is to shout or wave to get their attention: *He hailed a taxi on the main road.* **2** to **hail from** a place is to come from that place: *He hails from Manchester.*

hail² • HAIL• hailstones falling from the sky •VERB• **hails, hailing, hailed** it hails when hailstones fall

hailstones • PLURAL NOUN• small white balls of frozen water that fall in showers from the sky

hair • NOUN• **hairs 1** a hair is one of the thread-like things that grow on the surface of the skin of animals and humans **2** your hair is the mass of hairs that grow on your head • **split hairs** to split hairs is to give too much importance to small and unimportant details

hairdresser • NOUN• **hairdressers** someone who cuts, styles and colours people's hair
• **hairdressing** • NOUN• the art, skill or work of a hairdresser

hairgrip • NOUN• **hairgrips** a narrow piece of bent metal pushed into the hair to keep it in place

hairiness • NOUN• being hairy

hair-raising • ADJECTIVE• terrifying or dangerous: *a hair-raising ride on the Big Dipper*

hairstyle • NOUN• **hairstyles** a way of cutting or wearing your hair

hairy • ADJECTIVE• **hairier, hairiest** 1 covered with hair: *A hobbit is a small creature with hairy feet.* 2 terrifying or dangerous: *If it is stormy, the ferry crossing can get a bit hairy.*
⇒ **hairiness**

hajj or **hadj** • NOUN• the journey or pilgrimage to Mecca that all Muslims should try to make at least once in their lifetime
• **hajji** or **hadji** • NOUN• **hajjis** or **hadjis** a Muslim who has made a pilgrimage to Mecca

halal or **hallal** • ADJECTIVE• halal meat is from animals killed and prepared according to the laws of Islam

half • NOUN• **halves** 1 a half is one of two equal parts that together make up the whole of something: *He ate half and I ate the other half.* 2 the fraction $\frac{1}{2}$, equivalent to the decimal fraction 0.5 and equal to one divided by two
• ADJECTIVE• 1 being one of two equal parts: *a half brick* 2 not full or complete: *a half smile*
• ADVERB• 1 to the level or extent of a half: *This glass is only half full.*
2 partly or almost: *a half-open door*
3 nearly: *It wasn't half as scary as I expected it to be.*
• **by half** if you say that someone is too clever by half, you mean that their cleverness is annoying and will end up causing trouble for them
• **not half** people say 'not half' when they want to emphasize that they agree completely with what someone else has just said: *'That was a great goal, wasn't it?' 'Not half.'*
⇒ **halve**

half-baked • ADJECTIVE• a half-baked idea is one that has not been properly worked out

half-brother • NOUN• **half-brothers** your half-brother has either the same father or the same mother as you do

half day • NOUN• **half days** a holiday for half the working or school day, either for the morning or the afternoon

half-hearted • ADJECTIVE• without much enthusiasm

• **half-heartedly** • ADVERB• not very enthusiastically: *Thomas started his homework half-heartedly.*

half-mast • NOUN• if a flag is at half-mast it is flown from a position halfway up the flagpole, usually as a sign of mourning for someone who has died

half moon • NOUN• **half moons** the moon when it looks like a semicircle

half-sister • NOUN• **half-sisters** your half-sister has either the same father or the same mother as you do

half-term • NOUN• **half-terms** a short holiday from school about halfway through the school term

half-time • NOUN• in games like football, hockey and rugby, a break from play in the middle of the match, after which the teams usually change ends

halfway • ADVERB AND ADJECTIVE• in the middle between two points, or between the beginning and the end: *Halfway down the stairs is the stair where I sit.*

hall • NOUN• **halls** 1 an area just inside the entrance to a house from which you can get to other rooms or to the stairs 2 a large building or room where meetings, concerts and other events are held

hallelujah • INTERJECTION• a shout or exclamation of praise to God

hallmark • NOUN• **hallmarks** 1 a mark stamped on things made of gold or silver to show their quality 2 the hallmark of something is its main feature: *The hallmark of a good writer is the ability to hold your attention.*

hallo • INTERJECTION• another spelling of **hello**

Hallowe'en • NOUN• October 31, the time when ghosts and witches are traditionally supposed to wander about, and when people get dressed up in costumes and masks

ⓘ This word comes from the old word **All-Hallow-Even**, which means 'the eve of All Saints' Day'.

hallucinate • VERB• **hallucinates, hallucinating, hallucinated** to see things that aren't really there

♦ **hallucination** • NOUN• **hallucinations** a vision someone has of something that doesn't really exist

hallway • NOUN• **hallways** an entrance hall in a house or building

halo • NOUN• **haloes** a ring of light round the head of an angel or saint in pictures and paintings, showing that they are holy

halt • VERB• **halts, halting, halted** to stop moving and stand still • NOUN• **halts** a stop: *The train came to a halt and we got off.*

halter • NOUN• **halters** a rope or strap put over a horse's head, so that it can be held or led

halve • VERB• **halves, halving, halved** 1 to divide, split or cut something into two equal parts 2 if something is halved it is reduced to half its original size or amount

halves • NOUN• the plural of **half**

ham¹ • NOUN• **hams** ham is smoked and salted meat from the leg of a pig

ham² • NOUN• **hams** 1 an actor who overacts 2 a radio ham is someone who operates a radio transmitter and receiver as a hobby

hamburger • NOUN• **hamburgers** a round flat cake of minced meat that is fried and usually eaten in a bun

ⓘ Hamburgers were named after the city of **Hamburg** in Germany. The meat used to be called Hamburg steak.

hammer • NOUN• **hammers** a tool with a heavy metal or wooden head at the end of a handle, used for knocking nails in or for breaking up hard material like stones and concrete •VERB• **hammers, hammering, hammered** 1 to hit something with a hammer: *hammering the nails in one by one* 2 to hit something hard: *hammering on the door with his fists* 3 to beat someone severely or completely: *We hammered the other team 10-0.* 4 to **hammer something out** is to discuss it until everyone is satisfied: *hammer out an agreement*

hammock • NOUN• **hammocks** a kind of bed made up of a long piece of canvas or heavy fabric which is hung from ropes at either end so that it swings above the ground

hamper¹ • NOUN• **hampers** a large basket with a lid used for carrying food, plates and cutlery, especially for picnics

hamper² • VERB• **hampers, hampering, hampered** to hamper someone or something is to stop them making progress

hamster • NOUN• **hamsters** a small animal with soft fur and a short tail, often kept as a pet

hand • NOUN• **hands** 1 your hand is the part of your body at the end of your arm just below your wrist 2 a narrow pointer on a clock or watch that moves round and shows the time 3 if you give someone a hand you give them your help 4 a unit, equal to 4 inches or about 10 centimetres, used for measuring the height of horses: *a huge horse of almost 16 hands* 5 a number of playing cards dealt to a player in a card game: *Both my partner and I had good hands.* 6 a worker on a farm, in a factory or on a ship: *The captain gave the order 'All hands on deck!'* 7 to give a performer a big hand is to clap or applaud them loudly and enthusiastically • **at hand** something that is at hand is available quickly: *Help is at hand.* • **by hand** you do or make something by hand when you use your hands to do or make it • **in hand** something is in hand when it is being dealt with • **on hand** if someone or something is on hand they are ready and available to help or be used • **out of hand** if things get out of hand they get out of control • **to hand** if something is to hand, it is near you and you are able to reach it or use it easily •VERB• **hands, handing, handed** to hand something to someone is to pass it to them

handbag • NOUN• **handbags** a small bag for carrying personal belongings like your purse and keys

handbook • NOUN• **handbooks** a book of instructions on how to do something: *an illustrated handbook on first aid*

handcuffs • PLURAL NOUN• a pair of metal rings joined by a chain which are used by the police to lock around the wrists of someone they have arrested

handful • NOUN• **handfuls** 1 an amount that you can hold in your hand: *a handful of rice*
2 a small number: *Only a handful of people turned up.*
3 a person or animal whose behaviour makes them difficult to deal with

handicap • NOUN• **handicaps** a physical or mental injury or disability that prevents someone from living normally
•VERB• **handicaps, handicapping, handicapped** to handicap someone is to disable them or make them unable to do something properly
♦ **handicapped** • ADJECTIVE• disabled, either mentally or physically

handicraft • NOUN• **handicrafts** a craft done using the hands, such as sewing, knitting or pottery

handiwork • NOUN• someone's handiwork is something that they have made or done

handkerchief • NOUN• **handkerchiefs** a small piece of cloth or tissue paper used for wiping your nose

handle • NOUN• **handles** 1 a part of an object that you use to pick it up and hold it: *a brush with a long handle* 2 a lever or knob on a door that you hold when you open and close the door
• **fly off the handle** if someone flies off the handle they lose their temper
•VERB• **handles, handling, handled** 1 to touch something or hold it with your hands: *Try not to handle the fruit too much.* 2 to deal or cope with something: *Mr Peters is handling all the arrangements for the trip.*

handlebars • PLURAL NOUN• the curved part at the front of a bicycle that you rest your hands on and use to steer the bicycle

handler • NOUN• **handlers** 1 someone who trains or controls an animal: *police dogs and their handlers* 2 someone whose job is to

move or carry things: *a baggage handler at the airport*

hand-me-downs • PLURAL NOUN• clothes that older brothers or sisters have worn and grown out of and that have been passed on to younger brothers or sisters

handout • NOUN• **handouts** 1 a free leaflet or booklet containing information that is given out to people at a class or lecture 2 money, food or clothing that is given free to poor people

handrail • NOUN• **handrails** a narrow rail that people can hold on to for safety

handsome • ADJECTIVE• **handsomer, handsomest** 1 good looking: *a handsome young actor* 2 large or generous: *They made a handsome profit.*

hands-on • ADJECTIVE• done or experienced by yourself in a practical way, rather than watching others do it

handstand • NOUN• **handstands** a gymnastic movement in which you balance your body upside down carrying your weight on your hands and holding your legs straight up in the air

handwriting • NOUN• writing done with a pen or pencil
♦ **handwritten** • ADJECTIVE• written with a pen or pencil, not typed or printed

handy • ADJECTIVE• **handier, handiest** 1 useful and easy to use: *a handy size for carrying in your pocket* 2 nearby and easily reached: *The house is handy both for the station and the bus stop.*

handyman • NOUN• **handymen** someone who does small building and repair jobs

hang •VERB• **hangs, hanging, hung** or **hanged** 1 to hang something is to attach it or support it at the top so that most of it is held loosely above the ground: *Hang your jackets up on the pegs.*
2 something hangs when it is supported near the top and is held above the ground: *He was hanging upside down by his feet.*
3 to hang someone is to kill them by tying a rope around their neck and removing a support from under their feet
4 to **hang about** or **hang around** is to stay

in one place doing nothing: *Don't let's hang about any more. Let's get started.*
• NOUN• to **get the hang of** something is to understand it or learn how to do it after a bit of practice
⇒ hanger

ⓘ **Hung** is the usual form of the past tense of the verb **hang**. However, you use **hanged** instead of **hung** to refer to someone who dies by hanging.

hangar • NOUN• **hangars** a big shed that aeroplanes are kept in

hanger • NOUN• **hangers** a shaped piece of metal, wood or plastic with a hook, used to hang clothes

hangman • NOUN• **hangmen** someone whose job it is to hang people who are condemned to death

hangover • NOUN• **hangovers 1** a sick feeling, often with an aching head, that people sometimes get after they have drunk too much alcohol **2** something that remains after an event or period of time is over: *a hangover from the 1960's*

hangdog • ADJECTIVE• someone with a hangdog expression looks very guilty and ashamed

hang-glider • NOUN• **hang-gliders** a type of vehicle that flies using air currents with the pilot strapped in a harness that hangs beneath a large kite-like frame
♦ **hang-gliding** • NOUN• the sport or pastime of flying in hang-gliders

hank • NOUN• **hanks** a small loose bundle made up of strands of hair, wool or thread

hanker • VERB• **hankers, hankering, hankered** to hanker for or after something is to long to have it

hankie *or* **hanky** • NOUN• **hankies** an informal short form of the word **handkerchief**

Hanukkah *or* **Chanukkah** • NOUN• Hanukkah is a Jewish festival lasting for eight days in December. It is also called the Feast of Dedication or the Festival of Lights, because a candle is lit on each of the eight days

haphazard • ADJECTIVE• with no planning or system

hapless • ADJECTIVE• unlucky: *the hapless victims of the shipwreck*

happen • VERB• **happens, happening, happened 1** something happens when it takes place or occurs: *When did this happen?* • *I pressed the button but nothing happened.*
2 if something happens to a person or thing, an event or situation affects or involves them: *Do you know what's happened to the front door key?*
3 if you happen to do or see something, you do or see it by chance: *She just happened to be there and saw the whole thing.*
♦ **happening** • NOUN• **happenings** an event

happily • ADVERB• joyfully, contentedly or luckily: *smiling happily* • *Happily, it all turned out well.*

happiness • NOUN• being happy

happy • ADJECTIVE• **happier, happiest**
1 joyful: *the happiest day of her life*
2 pleased or contented: *I'd be happy to help.*
3 lucky: *a happy coincidence*

happy-go-lucky • ADJECTIVE• a happy-go-lucky person is cheerful, enjoying anything good that happens to come along and not worrying about the future

haram • ADJECTIVE• forbidden under the laws of Islam

harass • VERB• **harasses, harassing, harassed** to harass someone is to keep annoying them, pestering them or interfering with their life
♦ **harassed** • ADJECTIVE• feeling worried and anxious because you have too much to do
♦ **harassment** • NOUN• harassing someone or being harassed

harbour • NOUN• **harbours** a place protected from wind and rough seas where ships and boats can shelter and dock
• VERB• **harbours, harbouring, harboured**
1 to harbour a criminal is to protect them from being found or arrested by the police **2** to harbour a feeling is to keep it in your mind: *She'd harboured a grudge against them.*

(i) This word comes from the Old English words **here**, which means *army*, and **beorg**, which means *protection*. A harbour was thought to be a safe place for troops.

hard • ADJECTIVE• **harder, hardest** 1 feeling firm and solid when touched and not easily broken or bent out of shape: *hard as rock* • *a hard bed*
  2 difficult: *a very hard sum* • *He's had a hard life.*
  3 needing a lot of effort: *hard work*
  4 tough or not easy to deal with: *hard luck* • *They drive a hard bargain.*
  5 hard water doesn't form a good lather when you add soap to it and contains minerals that form deposits in equipment like kettles
  • ADVERB• **harder, hardest** 1 strongly or violently: *It was raining hard when we got there.* 2 with more effort: *You must work harder.*
  • **hard of hearing** someone who is hard of hearing is nearly deaf

hardback • NOUN• **hardbacks** a book that has a stiff hard cover. Look up and compare **paperback**

hardboard • NOUN• thin strong board made from wood pulp that has been softened and pressed together

hard disk • NOUN• **hard disks** a disk inside a computer where large amounts of information is stored

harden • VERB• **hardens, hardening, hardened** 1 to become firm or solid: *The molten lava hardens to form rock.* 2 to become tougher or less sympathetic: *His heart had been hardened by constant rejection.*

hard-hearted • ADJECTIVE• tough and unsympathetic to other people's feelings or problems

hardline • ADJECTIVE• people with hardline attitudes or opinions stick to what they believe and refuse to change or compromise

hardly • ADVERB• 1 only just or almost not: *I hardly know him.* • *She'd hardly put the key in the door when down came the rain.*
  2 **hardly** is used for emphasis to mean 'not at

all': *She's hardly likely to want him at the party after the way he insulted her.*

hardness • NOUN• **hardnesses** the state of being hard or how hard something is in comparison to other things

hardship • NOUN• **hardships** something that is very difficult to cope with: *financial hardship*

hard shoulder • NOUN• the hard shoulder is the strip of tarmac or concrete at either side of a motorway for use in an emergency, for example if your car has broken down

hard up • ADJECTIVE• poor: *He's too hard up to be able to afford the fees.*

hardware • NOUN• 1 hardware is tools and equipment used, for example, in the house and garden 2 computer hardware is electronic machinery like the processor and disk drives. Look up and compare **software**

hardy • ADJECTIVE• **hardier, hardiest** strong and tough and able to cope with difficult and uncomfortable conditions

hare • NOUN• **hares** an animal similar to a rabbit, but larger and with longer back legs and bigger ears

hare-brained • ADJECTIVE• mad or foolish: *a hare-brained scheme*

hare lip • NOUN• **hare lips** a deformity that some babies are born with in which the top lip is split

hark • VERB• **harks, harking, harked** 1 an old-fashioned word meaning listen: *Hark, the herald angels sing.* • *Hark at him!* 2 to **hark back** to some event in the past is to refer to it or return to it

harlequin • NOUN• **harlequins** a comic pantomime character who wears a costume that has many bright colours

harm • VERB• **harms, harming, harmed** to harm someone or something is to hurt or damage them: *You might harm your eyes if you sit too close to the TV.*
  • NOUN• damage or injury: *No harm will come to you.* • *It would do no harm to ask.*
  ◆ **harmful** • ADJECTIVE• causing damage or injury: *protecting your skin from the sun's harmful rays*
  ◆ **harmless** • ADJECTIVE• not dangerous or

not causing any damage or annoyance: *a harmless little insect*

harmonica •NOUN• **harmonicas** an instrument that you hold to your mouth and play by blowing and sucking air through it

harmonious •ADJECTIVE• 1 harmonious sound or music is pleasant to listen to
2 harmonious colours or designs go well together and don't clash
3 people who have a harmonious relationship cooperate with each other and don't have disagreements
♦ **harmoniously** •ADVERB• in a pleasant or peaceful way

harmonize or **harmonise** •VERB• **harmonizes, harmonizing, harmonized**
1 singers or musicians harmonize when they sing or play together using notes that combine pleasantly with the main tune
2 things harmonize when they fit or combine well together

harmony •NOUN• **harmonies** 1 harmony is combining notes or colours in a way that sounds or looks pleasant
2 a harmony is a musical part that combines pleasantly with the main melody
3 harmony is peaceful agreement and cooperation between people: *living in harmony with our neighbours*

harp •NOUN• **harps** an instrument with strings stretched across an open triangular frame. A harp stands upright and is played by plucking the strings with your fingers
•VERB• **harps, harping, harped** to **harp on** or **harp on about** something is to keep on talking about it in an annoying way
♦ **harpist** •NOUN• **harpists** someone who plays the harp

harpoon •NOUN• **harpoons** a spear with a rope attached at one end and used to kill fish and whales

harpsichord •NOUN• **harpsichords** an instrument with keys similar to a piano but with strings that are plucked when the keys are pressed

harrowing •ADJECTIVE• very upsetting or disturbing: *a harrowing experience*

harry •VERB• **harries, harrying, harried** to harry someone is to harass or worry them

harsh •ADJECTIVE• **harsher, harshest** 1 very uncomfortable: *a harsh climate*
2 unpleasantly strong or loud: *harsh light*
• *the harsh cry of a raven*
3 cruel and unkind: *a harsh punishment*
♦ **harshly** •ADVERB• roughly, severely or cruelly
♦ **harshness** •NOUN• being harsh

harvest •NOUN• **harvests** 1 harvest is the time of year when ripe crops are gathered
2 a harvest is the amount of a crop that is gathered: *This year's coffee harvest was very poor.*
•VERB• **harvests, harvesting, harvested** to gather a crop when it is ripe: *harvesting grapes*
♦ **harvester** •NOUN• **harvesters** 1 a piece of machinery that gathers in a crop of a particular type 2 a worker who helps to pick, cut or gather in a crop

has •VERB• 1 the form of the verb **have** that is used with *he, she* and *it* to make a present tense: *He has large and dreamy eyes.* 2 **has** is also used as a helping verb along with a main verb: *He has gone home.*

has-been •NOUN• **has-beens** someone who used to be famous or successful but who isn't any more

hash •NOUN• **hashes** 1 a dish made with cooked meat and vegetables that have been chopped up and recooked 2 to make a hash of something is to make a mess of it

hasn't •SHORT FORM• a short way to say and write **has not**: *Hasn't it been a lovely day?*

hassle •VERB• **hassles, hassling, hassled** to hassle someone is to put pressure on them or cause them problems
•NOUN• **hassles** hassle, or a hassle, is something that causes you problems or inconvenience

haste •NOUN• 1 haste is hurry or speed 2 to make haste is to hurry
♦ **hasten** •VERB• **hastens, hastening, hastened** to hasten is to hurry or push forward: *I met him hastening from his room in his dressing gown.*
♦ **hastily** •ADVERB• in a hurried way: *Hastily, he hid the sweets he had stolen.*
♦ **hasty** •ADJECTIVE• **hastier, hastiest** a

hasty action is one that is done too quickly without enough thought

hat • NOUN• **hats** a covering for your head

hatch[1] •VERB• **hatches, hatching, hatched** 1 baby birds and reptiles hatch when they break out of their eggs: *The eggs should hatch in six to eight days.* 2 to hatch a plot is to think of it and develop its details, especially in secret

hatch[2] • NOUN• **hatches** a door or covering over an opening in a floor, wall or ship's deck

hatchback • NOUN• **hatchbacks** a car with a sloping door at the back that opens upwards

hatchet • NOUN• **hatchets** a small axe • **bury the hatchet** people who have been fighting or quarrelling bury the hatchet when they make up

hate •VERB• **hates, hating, hated** to dislike very much: *He hates tidying his bedroom.* • NOUN• 1 hate is very strong dislike: *Her eyes were full of hate and disappointment.* 2 your hates are the things that you dislike very much: *It's one of his pet hates.* ✦ **hateful** • ADJECTIVE• very nasty or very bad: *a hateful thing to say* ✦ **hatred** • NOUN• hatred is a very strong feeling of dislike

hat-trick • NOUN• **hat-tricks** 1 in games like football and hockey, a hat-trick is three goals scored by one player in a single match 2 in cricket, a bowler gets a hat-trick when gets three batsmen out with three balls bowled one after the other

haughty • ADJECTIVE• **haughtier, haughtiest** a haughty person is proud and thinks they are better or more important than other people

haul •VERB• **hauls, hauling, hauled** to haul something heavy is to pull it or drag it using a lot of effort: *He managed to haul himself up on to a narrow ledge.* • NOUN• **hauls** 1 a quantity gathered or caught at one time: *a huge haul of cod and haddock* 2 a strong tug or pull: *Give the rope one more good haul.* • **a long haul** a long and difficult journey, job or process

haulage • NOUN• people or companies involved in haulage carry goods from one place to another for payment

haunch • NOUN• **haunches** 1 your haunches are your bottom and the upper part of your thighs: *He squatted down on his haunches in the dust.* 2 a haunch of meat comes from the upper part of the animal's leg

haunt •VERB• **haunts, haunting, haunted** 1 a ghost is believed to haunt a place when it is present there or appears there 2 someone haunts a place when they go there again and again: *He haunts the football ground, trying to get a glimpse of his heroes.* 3 a bad feeling or memory haunts you when you can't stop thinking about it • NOUN• **haunts** a place where you go again and again: *The deer had vanished, gone to their secret daytime haunts.* ✦ **haunted** • ADJECTIVE• a haunted place is somewhere where ghosts are believed to be

have •VERB• **has, having, had** 1 to have something is to own or possess it, or to include it: *I'll look at your essay as soon as I have a free moment.* • *He has a limp.* 2 to have an illness is to suffer from it: *Carol's had chickenpox.* • *Mum has a terrible headache.* 3 to have something is to get or receive it: *I had a phone call from him last week.* 4 to have a baby is to give birth to it: *The cat had kittens.* 5 to have food or drink is to eat it or drink it: *You'll have lunch with us, won't you?* 6 you have something done when you get it done: *He's having a tooth out.* 7 if you have to do something, you must do it: *You have to tell me what was said.* 8 **have** is also used as a helping verb along with a main verb: *I have left some money for you.* 9 to **have someone on** is to tell them something is true when it isn't 10 to **have it out** with someone is to talk to them to settle an argument or disagreement

haven • NOUN• **havens** a place that people go to for safety or peace

haven't • SHORT FORM• a short way to say and write **have not**: *I haven't seen the film.*

Aa
Bb
Cc
Dd
Ee
Ff
Gg
Hh
Ii
Jj
Kk
Ll
Mm
Nn
Oo
Pp
Qq
Rr
Ss
Tt
Uu
Vv
Ww
Xx
Yy
Zz

haversack •NOUN• **haversacks** a canvas bag with shoulder straps that you use to carry things on your back when you are walking or marching

havoc •NOUN• to cause havoc is to cause damage, destruction or confusion

hawk •NOUN• **hawks** a bird of prey with a short, strong hooked beak and very good eyesight

hawthorn •NOUN• **hawthorns** a small tree with thorny stems, white flowers and small red berries

hay •NOUN• grass that has been cut and dried and is used to feed animals

hay fever •NOUN• an allergy to pollen that some people have, which causes them to sneeze and have watery or itchy eyes and a runny nose

haystack •NOUN• **haystacks** a large pile of cut hay stacked up in layers and stored until it is needed

haywire •ADJECTIVE• if something goes haywire it goes out of control

hazard •NOUN• **hazards** a risk of harm or danger
•VERB• **hazards, hazarding, hazarded 1** to hazard something is to risk it **2** to hazard a guess is to make a guess that is quite likely to be wrong
✦ **hazardous** •ADJECTIVE• dangerous or risky

haze •NOUN• **hazes** thin mist: *a heat haze*
⇒ **hazy**

hazel •NOUN• **hazels 1** a small tree on which round reddish-brown nuts grow **2** a light greenish-brown colour

hazelnut •NOUN• **hazelnuts** an edible nut that grows on a hazel tree

hazy •ADJECTIVE• **hazier, haziest 1** with a thin mist: *hazy sunshine* **2** vague and unclear: *He only had hazy memories of his parents.*

he •PRONOUN• a word you use to talk about a man, boy, or male animal that has already been mentioned or pointed out: *I like Tommy. He is very friendly.*

head •NOUN• **heads 1** the part of a human's or animal's body that contains the brain, eyes and mouth
2 your mind or intelligence: *The idea just popped into my head.*
3 the head of a group or organization is the person in charge
4 the top of something: *the title at the head of the page*
• **go to someone's head** if praise or success goes to someone's head they become conceited
• **head over heels** to be head over heels is to be very much in love with someone
• **off your head** if you say someone is off their head, you mean they are mad
• **over your head 1** if someone goes over your head, they talk to the person who is your boss instead of you **2** if you are in over your head, you are involved in something that is too complicated or serious for you to cope with or control
•VERB• **heads, heading, headed 1** if you head a group of people, you lead them or are in charge of them
2 to head somewhere is to go towards that place
3 to head a ball is to hit it with your head
4 to **head someone or something off** is to get in front of them to stop them going any further
⇒ **heads**

headache •NOUN• **headaches** a pain in the head

headboard •NOUN• **headboards** the upright part at the top of a bed

headdress •NOUN• **headdresses** a decoration worn on the head, for example as part of a costume

header •NOUN• **headers** a header is when you hit the ball in football with your head

headfirst •ADVERB• you jump or fall headfirst when you jump or fall forwards with your head in front of the rest of your body

heading •NOUN• **headings** a title at the top or beginning of a page or a section of writing

headland •NOUN• **headlands** a piece of land that sticks out into the sea

headlight •NOUN• **headlights** one of a pair

of lights at the front of a car, van or lorry

headline • NOUN• **headlines** a line printed in large letters at the top of a newspaper page or article

headlong • ADVERB AND ADJECTIVE•
1 headfirst or in an uncontrolled way: *He dived headlong into the muddy stream.* • *a headlong dash towards the finish line* 2 without giving yourself enough time to think: *They were all rushing headlong into silly actions.*

headmaster • NOUN• **headmasters** a male teacher in charge of running a school

headmistress • NOUN• **headmistresses** a female teacher in charge of running a school

head-on • ADJECTIVE AND ADVERB• 1 with the head or front first: *The other car hit us head-on.* • *a head-on collision* 2 directly, without trying to avoid what may be unpleasant: *tackling their problems head-on*

headphones • PLURAL NOUN• a device for listening to music or radio broadcasts with two receivers that you wear over your ears

headquarters • PLURAL NOUN• 1 a place from which an army, navy, air force or police force is controlled 2 the central office from which a large business or organization is controlled

ⓘ **Headquarters** can be used with a singular or plural verb, for example:
*The company headquarters **is** in London.*
*The company headquarters **are** in London.*

heads • PLURAL NOUN• the side of a coin that has a person's head stamped on it: *Call heads or tails when I toss the coin.*

headstart • NOUN• if you get a headstart, you get an advantage by starting or beginning before other people

headstrong • ADJECTIVE• a headstrong person is determined to do what they want to do and won't take advice from other people

head teacher • NOUN• **head teachers** a teacher in charge of a school

headway • NOUN• to make headway is to make forward progress

heal • VERB• **heals, healing, healed** 1 a wound or injury heals when it gets better 2 if you are sick and someone heals you, they make you better or healthy again
♦ **healer** • NOUN• **healers** someone or something that heals people who are sick

health • NOUN• 1 your health is the condition of your body or mind, and how well you are: *His health is not good.* • *mental health* 2 the health of something is how good or bad its condition is: *the health of the economy*
⇒ **healthily, healthiness, healthy**

health centre • NOUN• **health centres** a place where doctors and nurses see people from a particular area and hold clinics

health food • NOUN• **health foods** a food that people believe is good for their health

healthily • ADVERB• in a way that is good for your health: *eat healthily*

healthiness • NOUN• being healthy

health visitor • NOUN• **health visitors** a nurse who visits ill or old people, or newly born babies, in their homes

healthy • ADJECTIVE• **healthier, healthiest**
1 fit and well: *a healthy baby*
2 good for you: *lots of healthy exercise*
3 in a good state or condition: *a healthy bank balance*

heap • NOUN• **heaps** 1 an untidy pile of things: *a heap of dirty clothes* 2 a lot or lots: *There's heaps of time before the match starts.*
• VERB• **heaps, heaping, heaped** to heap things is to pile them up: *His plate was heaped with food.*

hear • VERB• **hears, hearing, heard** 1 to hear sounds is to be aware of them through your ears: *Can you hear that clicking noise?*
2 to hear news is to be told it: *I heard that she had got into the next round of the competition.*
3 to have heard of someone or something is to know that they exist: *I'd never heard of him before.*
4 you hear from someone when they get in touch with you: *We haven't heard from him for over a month.*
♦ **hearer** • NOUN• **hearers** your hearers are the people who are listening to you when you are speaking

Aa
Bb
Cc
Dd
Ee
Ff
Gg
Hh
Ii
Jj
Kk
Ll
Mm
Nn
Oo
Pp
Qq
Rr
Ss
Tt
Uu
Vv
Ww
Xx
Yy
Zz

hearing • NOUN • **hearings** 1 your hearing is your ability to hear
2 if something is said in your hearing you can hear it
3 a court trial

hearing aid • NOUN • **hearing aids** a small device that is fitted into or at the back of the ear to help a deaf person hear

hearsay • NOUN • hearsay is things other people have told you, which may or may not be true: *Someone told me Jason had run away, but I think it's only hearsay.*

hearse • NOUN • **hearses** a specially designed car or carriage used to carry the coffin at a funeral

heart • NOUN • **hearts** 1 your heart is the hollow muscular organ inside your chest that pumps blood around your body
2 someone's heart is their feelings and emotions: *She captured the hearts of the audience.* • *He has a kind heart.*
3 a heart is a shape, ♥, that represents the human heart and human love
4 hearts is one of the four suits of playing cards, which have the symbol ♥ printed on them
5 the heart of something is its central or most important part: *getting to the heart of the problem*
• **by heart** if you learn something by heart, you learn it so that you can repeat it exactly
⇒ **hearten, hearty**

heart attack • NOUN • **heart attacks** if someone has a heart attack, their heart suddenly stops working properly and they feel very ill and may die

heartbeat • NOUN • **heartbeats** the regular sound that the heart makes as it pumps blood round the body

heartbreak • NOUN • great sadness
♦ **heartbreaking** • ADJECTIVE • causing deep sadness
♦ **heartbroken** • ADJECTIVE • feeling very sad: *One day the bird did not return, and I was heartbroken.*

hearten • VERB • **heartens, heartening, heartened** something heartens you when it makes you feel happier or more hopeful

heartfelt • ADJECTIVE • heartfelt feelings or words are completely sincere: *my heartfelt thanks*

hearth • NOUN • **hearths** the floor of a fireplace or the area surrounding it

heartily • ADVERB • 1 loudly and enthusiastically: *They laughed heartily at all his jokes.* 2 sincerely or completely: *I'm heartily sick of their constant complaints.*

heartless • ADJECTIVE • unkind and cruel

heart-rending • ADJECTIVE • something heart-rending fills you with pity and sadness

heart-throb • NOUN • **heart-throbs** a very attractive person with whom lots of people fall in love

heart-to-heart • NOUN • **heart-to-hearts** a talk with someone in which you discuss private or intimate things

hearty • ADJECTIVE • **heartier, heartiest**
1 strong and healthy
2 cheerful, loud and friendly: *a hearty welcome*
3 a hearty meal is a large and satisfying meal
⇒ **heartily**

heat • NOUN • **heats** 1 heat is high temperature or the warmth that something hot gives out: *the heat from the sun*
2 heat is anger or strong feelings: *She tried to calm them down and take the heat out of the situation.*
3 a heat is a round in a competition or race: *Ian won his heat and went through to the semi-final.*
• VERB • **heats, heating, heated** 1 to heat something, or heat it up, is to raise its temperature or make it warm or hot 2 if something heats up, it becomes warmer or hotter
♦ **heated** • ADJECTIVE • full of anger or strong feelings: *a heated discussion*
♦ **heater** • NOUN • **heaters** a device used to heat a space, such as a room or the inside of a car
♦ **heating** • NOUN • the system or machinery used to heat a building

heatwave • NOUN • **heatwaves** a spell of unusually hot weather, usually lasting for several days or weeks

heath •NOUN• **heaths** a high wild area of land covered with grass and low bushes

heathen •NOUN• **heathens** someone who doesn't believe in God and is not a member of one of the main world religions

heather •NOUN• **heathers** a small shrub that grows close to the ground on hills and moors and has tiny purple or white flowers

heave •VERB• **heaves, heaving, heaved**
1 to heave something heavy is to lift, pull, push or throw it using a lot of effort: *The men heaved the bags of coal on to their shoulders.* • *Both teams heaved at the rope.*
2 you heave a sigh when you sigh deeply making your shoulders and chest rise up

heaven •NOUN• **heavens** 1 the place where good people are supposed to go when they die and where God and the angels are believed to live
2 the sky is sometimes called the heavens: *The heavens opened and the rain came lashing down.*
3 a very pleasant place or thing: *This chocolate cake is just heaven.*
• **heavenly** •ADJECTIVE• 1 to do with heaven: *the heavenly choir of angels* 2 very pleasant: *It's heavenly being able to relax in the sunshine.*

heavy •ADJECTIVE• **heavier, heaviest**
1 something that is heavy weighs a lot
2 the amount that something weighs is how heavy it is
3 heavy rain or a heavy blow has a lot of force
4 a heavy smoker smokes a lot and a heavy drinker drinks a lot of alcohol
5 if your heart is heavy, you feel sad
• **heavily** •ADVERB• with a lot of force or weight
• **heaviness** •NOUN• the state of being heavy or the weight of something

heavy-duty •ADJECTIVE• heavy-duty material or machinery can stand up to a lot of very hard use

heavy industry •NOUN• **heavy industries** an industry or industries such as coal-mining, steel-making and ship-building

Hebrew •NOUN• Hebrew is the ancient language of the Jewish race, which was revived and is used in a modern form in Israel
•ADJECTIVE• in, or to do with, ancient or modern Hebrew

heckle •VERB• **heckles, heckling, heckled** to interrupt a speaker or performer with loud comments or questions
• **heckler** •NOUN• **hecklers** a member of an audience who heckles a speaker or performer

hectare •NOUN• **hectares** a unit of area equal to 10 000 square metres or approximately $2\frac{1}{2}$ acres

hectic •ADJECTIVE• very busy or having too much to do in too short a time: *Today has been absolutely hectic.*

he'd •SHORT FORM• a short way to say and write **he had** or **he would**: *He'd never been there before.* • *He'd never have guessed.*

hedge •NOUN• **hedges** a line of bushes, trees or shrubs planted close together and growing into each other to form a boundary
•VERB• **hedges, hedging, hedged** to avoid answering a question

hedgehog •NOUN• **hedgehogs** a small wild mammal with prickles all over its body

hedgerow •NOUN• **hedgerows** a line of shrubs and small trees growing close together along the side of a road or field

heed •VERB• **heeds, heeding, heeded** to heed something is to pay attention to it
•NOUN• if you pay heed to something, or take heed of it, you pay attention to it
• **heedless** •ADJECTIVE• if you are heedless of something you take no notice of it

heel •NOUN• **heels** 1 your heels are the back parts of your feet
2 the heel of a shoe or boot is the part under the back of your foot
3 the heel of a sock or stocking is the part that covers your heel
• **take to your heels** if you take to your heels, you start running

hefty •ADJECTIVE• **heftier, heftiest** 1 big and heavily or strongly built: *a hefty wrestler*
2 powerful: *a hefty blow*
3 large in amount: *a hefty sum of money*

Hegira •NOUN• the beginning of the Islamic era, which dates from the migration of the

Aa
Bb
Cc
Dd
Ee
Ff
Gg
Hh
Ii
Jj
Kk
Ll
Mm
Nn
Oo
Pp
Qq
Rr
Ss
Tt
Uu
Vv
Ww
Xx
Yy
Zz

Aa
Bb
Cc
Dd
Ee
Ff
Gg
Hh
Ii
Jj
Kk
Ll
Mm
Nn
Oo
Pp
Qq
Rr
Ss
Tt
Uu
Vv
Ww
Xx
Yy
Zz

prophet Mohammed from Mecca to Medina in 622AD

height • NOUN• **heights** 1 how tall or high someone or something is: *What height is Mount Everest?* 2 the highest, greatest or strongest point something reaches or can reach: *It is the height of stupidity to throw a lighted firework.* 3 a high place: *looking down from the heights*
✦ **heighten** • VERB• **heightens, heightening, heightened** 1 to make something higher: *We'll have to heighten the seat of the bike a little.* 2 something heightens, or is heightened, when it increases or is increased: *The music heightens the tension of the film.*

heir • NOUN• **heirs** someone who is entitled by law to get money, property or a title from someone when they die

heiress • NOUN• **heiresses** a girl or woman who receives property or money from someone who has died

heirloom • NOUN• **heirlooms** something valuable that has been handed down in a family from parents or grandparents to their children or grandchildren

held • VERB• a way of changing the verb **hold** to make a past tense. It can be used with or without a helping verb: *I held my breath and waited.* • *He had held the job for ten years.*

helicopter • NOUN• **helicopters** a flying machine without wings that is lifted into the air by large propellers on top which spin round very fast

helix • NOUN• **helixes** or **helices** a screw-shaped coil or spiral

hell • NOUN• 1 hell is the place where people who have sinned are supposed to go when they die and where the Devil and demons are believed to live 2 an evil or very unpleasant place

he'll • SHORT FORM• a short way to say and write **he will** or **he shall**: *He'll be here soon.*

hello • INTERJECTION• you say 'hello' as a greeting when you meet someone or begin talking to them

• NOUN• **hellos** or **helloes** a greeting: *We said our hellos.*

helm • NOUN• **helms** the wheel or handle used to steer a ship or boat

helmet • NOUN• **helmets** a hard covering worn to protect the head, for example by soldiers, cyclists and firemen

help • VERB• **helps, helping, helped** 1 to do something useful for someone: *I find a warm bath helps to relax me.* 2 if you **help yourself** you take something without waiting for someone to give it to you 3 if you cannot help something, you cannot stop yourself from doing it, or you cannot stop it happening
• NOUN• **helps** 1 you give someone help when you do something useful for them: *He gave some help with the gardening.* 2 a help is someone or something that helps: *Thanks for the tip. It was a great help.*
• INTERJECTION• people shout 'Help!' when they are in danger and want someone to come and help them
✦ **helper** • NOUN• **helpers** someone who helps another person: *one of Santa's helpers*

helpful • ADJECTIVE• willing to help, or giving help
✦ **helpfully** • ADVERB• in a helpful way

helping • NOUN• **helpings** a portion or serving of food: *He always has second helpings.*

helping verb • NOUN• **helping verbs** a short verb like *should, will* or *can* that you use with a main verb to make slight differences of meaning, for example a past tense in *Have you finished?* The helping verbs are also called **auxiliary verbs**. Look at the box called **Verbs**

helpless • ADJECTIVE• not able to do anything for yourself, or to help other people in trouble
✦ **helplessly** • ADVERB• in a helpless way: *I stared helplessly as the dog ran towards me.*

helter-skelter • NOUN• **helter-skelters** a tall spiral slide
• ADVERB• to go helter-skelter is to go very fast in an uncontrolled way

hem • NOUN• **hems** the edge of a piece of

material that has been folded over and sewn down
•VERB• **hems, hemming, hemmed 1** to hem a piece of cloth is to sew a hem on its edge **2** if people or things **hem you in** they surround you and stop you moving in any direction

hemline •NOUN• **hemlines** the point on your legs that a coat, dress or skirt reaches down to: *Short hemlines are fashionable again.*

hemisphere •NOUN• **hemispheres 1** a shape which is half a sphere or ball **2** half the Earth, either divided around the equator or from the north to the south pole: *the northern hemisphere*

hemp •NOUN• a plant grown for the fibres it produces, which are used to make ropes and rough cloth for sacks

hen •NOUN• **hens** a female chicken

hence •ADVERB• **1** from this time or from this place: *five years hence* **2** for this reason: *He's just got some bad news, hence his glum expression.*

henna •NOUN• a reddish-brown dye got from a plant and used to colour the hair and body

heptagon •NOUN• **heptagons** a flat shape with seven straight sides
♦ **heptagonal** •ADJECTIVE• having seven sides

her •PRONOUN• a word you use to talk about a woman, a girl, a female animal or a vehicle or ship that has already been mentioned or pointed out: *I'm looking for Mrs Peters. Have you seen her?*
•ADJECTIVE• belonging to her: *Her hair is blonde.*

herald •NOUN• **heralds 1** in the past, someone who made important announcements or carried important messages for a king or queen **2** something that is a sign of something that is going to happen or come soon: *snowdrops, the herald of spring*
•VERB• **heralds, heralding, heralded** to herald something is to announce it or show that it will come soon

heraldic •ADJECTIVE• to do with heraldry

heraldry •NOUN• heraldry is the study of coats of arms and family crests

herb •NOUN• **herbs** a plant, such as camomile, parsley, rosemary or thyme, that is used for making medicines or for flavouring food: *herbs and spices*
♦ **herbal** •ADJECTIVE• using herbs or to do with herbs: *herbal medicines • herbal tea*

herbivore •NOUN• **herbivores** an animal that eats only grass and plants. Look up and compare **carnivore** and **omnivore**
♦ **herbivorous** •ADJECTIVE• eating only grass and plants: *Deer are herbivorous.*

herd •NOUN• **herds** a large group of animals of one type: *a herd of buffalo*
•VERB• **herds, herding, herded** to herd animals or people is to gather them together and make them go somewhere in a group: *We were herded into a small room at the back.*

here •ADVERB• **1** at, in or to this place or time: *I like it here.*
•INTERJECTION• **1** people say 'Here!' to express surprise or anger at something someone is doing: *Here! You aren't supposed to do that!* **2** you say 'here' when you are offering something to someone: *Here, take this one. It's better than the one you have.*
• **here and there** things that are here and there are in several different places

hereafter •ADVERB• after this or from this time on
•NOUN• the hereafter is life after death

hereby •ADVERB• hereby is used in a statement to announce what you are going to do and how it will be done: *We hereby pledge our loyalty to the king.*

hereditary •ADJECTIVE• passed down from one generation to the next: *a hereditary disease*

heredity •NOUN• the passing on of qualities and characteristics from parents to children through the genes

heritage •NOUN• things that are passed down from previous generations, or things that have been, or should be, preserved because they provide a link with the past

hermit •NOUN• **hermits** someone who lives all alone and doesn't have contact with other people
♦ **hermitage** •NOUN• **hermitages** a place

Aa
Bb
Cc
Dd
Ee
Ff
Gg
Hh
Ii
Jj
Kk
Ll
Mm
Nn
Oo
Pp
Qq
Rr
Ss
Tt
Uu
Vv
Ww
Xx
Yy
Zz

where a hermit lives or a place where someone can go to get away from the world for a while

hero • NOUN• **heroes** 1 a man or boy who many people admire for his courage and bravery 2 the most important male character in a story or film

♦ **heroic** • ADJECTIVE• 1 very brave 2 to do with heroes or heroines

♦ **heroine** • NOUN• **heroines** 1 a woman or girl who many people admire for her courage and bravery 2 the most important female character in a story or film

♦ **heroism** • NOUN• great bravery and courage that many people admire

heron • NOUN• **herons** a bird with long legs and a long neck that lives near water and catches fish in its long sharp beak

herring • NOUN• **herring** or **herrings** an edible sea fish with silvery-grey scales that swims in large shoals

hers • PRONOUN• a word you use to talk about something belonging to a woman, girl, female animal or a vehicle or ship that has already been mentioned or pointed out: *I gave Sandra my phone number and she gave me hers.*

ⓘ Notice that there is no apostrophe between the *r* and the *s* in **hers**.

herself • PRONOUN• 1 you use **herself** after a verb or preposition when the woman or girl who performs the action is affected by it: *Did Barbara hurt herself when she fell down?*

2 **herself** is also used to show that a girl or woman does something without any help from other people: *She always answers every fan letter herself.*

3 you can use **herself** to show more clearly who you mean: *I wanted to ask Moira herself, but I couldn't get in touch with her.*

he's • SHORT FORM• a short way to say and write **he is** or **he has**: *He's my brother.* • *He's done all the work.*

hesitant • ADJECTIVE• if someone is hesitant, they aren't very willing to do something or they keep pausing while they are doing it: *He talked in a shy hesitant way.*

hesitate • VERB• **hesitates, hesitating, hesitated** 1 to pause for a short time while you are doing something 2 to hesitate to do something is to be slightly unwilling to do it

♦ **hesitation** • NOUN• **hesitations** 1 hesitating: *He did it without hesitation.* 2 a pause: *After a slight hesitation, he said he would do it.*

hew • VERB• **hews, hewing, hewed, hewn** to hew something is to cut it: *hewing wood to build a log cabin*

hexagon • NOUN• **hexagons** a flat shape with six straight sides

♦ **hexagonal** • ADJECTIVE• having six sides

hey • INTERJECTION• an exclamation used to get someone's attention: *Hey, stop that!*

hi • INTERJECTION• a word you use to greet someone: *Hi, how are you?*

hibernate • VERB• **hibernates, hibernating, hibernated** an animal that hibernates goes into a kind of sleep for long periods during the winter when food is difficult to find

♦ **hibernation** • NOUN• hibernating

hiccup • NOUN• **hiccups** 1 if you have hiccups, you make loud gasping noises in your throat 2 a hiccup is a small problem that causes a delay

• VERB• **hiccups, hiccupping, hiccupped** to hiccup is to make loud gasping noises that you can't control

hide¹ • VERB• **hides, hiding, hid, hidden** to put or keep someone or something in a place where they can't be seen or found easily: *You hide, and I'll come and look for you.* • *He hid behind a tree.*
⇒ **hiding**

hide² • NOUN• **hides** the skin of an animal

hide-and-seek • NOUN• a game in which one person hides and the other players look for him or her

hideous • ADJECTIVE• ugly or horrible to look at

hideout • NOUN• **hideouts** a hiding place: *The gang had a secret hideout in the mountains.*

hiding¹ • NOUN• if someone who is being hunted or searched for goes into hiding, they hide themselves in a secret place

hiding [2] • NOUN • **hidings** a beating or defeat: *The other team was far better and gave us a terrible hiding.*

hieroglyphics • PLURAL NOUN • a form of writing in which little pictures are used instead of letters and words. Hieroglyphics were used in ancient Egypt

hi-fi • NOUN • **hi-fis** a hi-fi is a piece of equipment for playing or recording high-quality sound
• ADJECTIVE • short for **high fidelity**, which means reproducing very high-quality sound

high • ADJECTIVE AND ADVERB • **higher, highest**
1 extending far upwards, or a long way off the ground: *a high building* • *diving from the highest board*
2 having a certain height: *10 metres high* • *How high is Snowdon?*
3 near the top of a scale of measurement or list: *high marks* • *a high temperature*
4 a high sound or musical note is near the top of the range of pitch or musical notes: *high voices of the children* • *the highest note you can sing*
5 great or large in amount or importance: *a high number*
• ADVERB • **higher, highest** 1 far above in the air or a long way off the ground: *satellites orbiting high above the Earth.* 2 far up a scale or ranking: *The temperature rose higher and higher.*
• NOUN • **highs** 1 a peak or maximum: *Confidence was at an all-time high.* 2 if someone is on a high, they are feeling very excited and elated
⇒ **highly**

high chair • NOUN • **high chairs** a chair with long legs for a baby or young child to sit in while they are eating

high jump • NOUN • the high jump is an athletic competition in which competitors try to jump over a horizontal pole supported on upright stands
• **for the high jump** if someone is for the high jump they are going to get into serious trouble

highland • ADJECTIVE • to do with the highlands: *a highland cottage*
• **highlands** • PLURAL NOUN • the highlands are areas of a country that are high and

mountainous: *the Scottish Highlands*

highlight • VERB • **highlights, highlighting, highlighted** to highlight something is to make it stand out or draw attention to it
• NOUN • **highlights** 1 the highlight is the best part of an event or period of time: *His singing was the highlight of the concert.*
2 highlights in your hair are streaks or parts that are a lighter colour than the rest of your hair
• **highlighter** • NOUN • **highlighters** a pen with a special type of brightly coloured ink which you use to mark writing or printing to make it stand out and which allows you to see what is written or printed underneath

highly • ADVERB • 1 very: *a highly infectious disease*
2 to or at a high level: *highly paid computer experts*
3 if you think highly of someone or something, you think they are excellent

highly strung • ADJECTIVE • very nervous and easily upset

Highness • NOUN • **Highnesses** a title you use when you are speaking about or to a prince or princess

high-rise • ADJECTIVE • high-rise buildings are modern buildings in the shape of tall narrow blocks
• NOUN • **high-rises** a very tall building, especially a tall block of flats

high school • NOUN • **high schools** a secondary school

highway • NOUN • **highways** 1 in Britain, the highway is the public road or the main road 2 in the United States and other countries, a highway is a road that links towns and cities

highwayman • NOUN • **highwaymen** in historical times, a robber who attacked people travelling on the public road

hijack • VERB • **hijacks, hijacking, hijacked** people hijack an aeroplane or other vehicle when they take control of it by force and make it go where they want it to go
• **hijacker** • NOUN • **hijackers** someone who hijacks an aeroplane or other vehicle

hike • VERB • **hikes, hiking, hiked** 1 to hike is

Aa

Bb

Cc

Dd

Ee

Ff

Gg

Hh

Ii

Jj

Kk

Ll

Mm

Nn

Oo

Pp

Qq

Rr

Ss

Tt

Uu

Vv

Ww

Xx

Yy

Zz

to go for long walks in the countryside **2** to hike something, or **hike it up**, is to raise it
• NOUN• **hikes** a long walk in the countryside
✦ **hiker** • NOUN• **hikers** someone who goes for long walks in the countryside
✦ **hiking** • NOUN• the pastime of taking long walks in the countryside

hilarious • ADJECTIVE• very funny
✦ **hilarity** • NOUN• loud laughter: *His antics caused much hilarity.*

hill • NOUN• **hills 1** a raised or high area of land, smaller than a mountain **2** a mound or heap: *a molehill*
• **over the hill** a person who is over the hill is old
✦ **hilly** • ADJECTIVE• **hillier, hilliest** a hilly area has lots of hills

hilt • NOUN• **hilts** the handle of a sword or dagger

him • PRONOUN• a word you use to talk about a man, boy or male animal that has already been mentioned or pointed out: *I'm looking for Mr Peters. Have you seen him anywhere?*

ⓘ Try not to confuse the spellings of the pronoun **him** and the noun **hymn**.

himself • PRONOUN• **1** you use **himself** after a verb or preposition when the man or boy who performs the action is affected by it: *He poked himself in the eye by mistake.*
2 himself is also used to show that a boy or man does something without any help from other people: *He can tie his shoelaces himself.*
3 you can use **himself** to show more clearly who you mean: *I was surprised when Mr Blair himself answered the telephone.*

hind • ADJECTIVE• an animal's hind parts are the back parts of its body

hinder • VERB• **hinders, hindering, hindered** to hinder someone or something is to delay them or stop them making progress
✦ **hindrance** • NOUN• **hindrances** something that keeps you back and stops you making progress

hindsight • NOUN• knowledge you have after some event, when you know how it has turned out and therefore how it could be done better

Hindu • NOUN• **Hindus** a person whose religion is Hinduism
• ADJECTIVE• to do with Hinduism: *The main Hindu gods are Brahma, Vishnu and Shiva.*
✦ **Hinduism** • NOUN• a religion of India and parts of South East Asia, which teaches that by a cycle of birth and rebirth, life continues forever or until the soul can be released from the cycle

hinge • NOUN• **hinges** a piece of metal or plastic attaching a door to its frame, so that it can be opened and closed
• VERB• **hinges, hinging, hinged** if one thing **hinges on** another, it depends on it

hint • NOUN• **hints 1** something that is said in a roundabout way without making the meaning absolutely clear: *She gave me a hint that something exciting was about to happen.*
2 a helpful piece of advice: *Can you give me any hints on how to grow roses?*
3 a small amount of something: *fizzy water with a hint of lemon*
• VERB• **hints, hinting, hinted** to hint is to give information in a way that is not clear or direct: *Laura hinted that she might be going to get engaged.*

hip • NOUN• **hips** your hips are the parts at each side of your body, between your waist and the tops of your legs

hippo • NOUN• **hippos** a hippopotamus

hippopotamus • NOUN• **hippopotamuses** or **hippopotami** a large African animal with a heavy body, a large squarish head, small rounded ears and thick legs. Hippopotamuses live near or in rivers

ⓘ This word comes from Greek words that mean *river horse*.

hire • VERB• **hires, hiring, hired 1** you hire something when you pay to use it for a certain period of time and then return it: *On holiday, we hired bikes and cycled for miles.*
2 to hire someone is to pay them to do work
• **for hire** something is for hire when you can hire it

his • PRONOUN• a word you use to talk about something belonging to a man, boy or male animal that has already been mentioned or

pointed out: *I didn't have an umbrella so Grandad lent me his.* • *The peacock spread his magnificent tail.*
• **ADJECTIVE•** belonging to him: *He has left his coat behind.*

hiss •VERB• **hisses, hissing, hissed** 1 to make a noise like a long 's' sound: *The snake hissed.* 2 if someone hisses they say something through their teeth without moving their lips: *'Quiet, everyone,' he hissed, crouching down.*
• NOUN• **hisses** a sound like that made by a snake

historian • NOUN• **historians** someone who studies history

historic • ADJECTIVE• important and likely to be remembered for a long time
♦ **historical** • ADJECTIVE• to do with history

history • NOUN• **histories** 1 history is all the things that happened in the past, or the study of things that happened in the past: *local history* • *My brother is doing history at university.* 2 the history of something is where it came from and what has happened to it before now: *What's the history of this old toy?* 3 a person's history is their past life

hit •VERB• **hits, hitting, hit** 1 to strike someone or something with a blow: *The lorry hit the car head-on.* 2 an idea or feeling hits you when you realize it or feel it: *It suddenly hit me that I was quite alone.* 3 to **hit on** something is to think of it or discover it: *By sheer accident, he'd hit on the perfect solution to the problem.* 4 if two people **hit it off** they get on well together
• NOUN• **hits** 1 a blow or stroke: *That was a great hit by the golfer.* 2 a shot that strikes a target 3 a success with the public: *The show was an instant hit.*
• ADJECTIVE• successful: *a hit song*

hit-and-miss *or* **hit-or-miss**
• ADJECTIVE• done without being sure what the result will be, sometimes successfully and sometimes not: *Their methods are pretty hit-and-miss.*

hit-and-run • ADJECTIVE• a hit-and-run driver knocks someone down and doesn't stop to help or doesn't report the accident
• NOUN• **hit-and-runs** an accident in which someone is knocked down in this way

hitch • NOUN• **hitches** a problem that holds you up
•VERB• **hitches, hitching, hitched** 1 to fasten or attach one thing to another: *He hitched the caravan to the back of the car.* 2 to hitch a lift in someone's car is to signal to the driver to stop and give you a lift to the place where you want to go 3 to **hitch up** a piece of your clothing is to pull it up: *She hitched up her skirt and climbed over the wall.*

hitchhike •VERB• **hitchhikes, hitchhiking, hitchhiked** to travel around by getting lifts in other people's cars
♦ **hitchhiker** • NOUN• **hitchhikers** someone who hitchhikes

hitherto • ADVERB• up to now: *Hitherto, she'd always taken the train, but today she took the bus.*

HIV • ABBREVIATION• short for **human immunodeficiency virus**, the virus that causes the disease AIDS

HMS • ABBREVIATION• short for **His** or **Her Majesty's Ship**, used in the names of British Royal Navy ships: *HMS Victory*

hoard •VERB• **hoards, hoarding, hoarded** to gather things and store them up in large quantities
• NOUN• **hoards** a large store of things that you have gathered and kept
♦ **hoarder** • NOUN• **hoarders** someone who likes saving and keeping lots of things

hoarding • NOUN• **hoardings** a large board in the street for displaying advertisements

hoarse • ADJECTIVE• **hoarser, hoarsest** 1 a hoarse sound is rough and harsh 2 if you are hoarse your voice sounds rough because your throat is sore

hoax • NOUN• **hoaxes** a kind of trick in which someone says that something has happened or warns that it will happen, but they are not telling the truth
•VERB• **hoaxes, hoaxing, hoaxed** to trick people into thinking something has happened or will happen

hob • NOUN • **hobs** a set of rings or plates for cooking on, either on top of a cooker or as a separate unit

hobble • VERB • **hobbles, hobbling, hobbled** to walk with short unsteady steps, because your feet or legs are injured or sore

hobby • NOUN • **hobbies** something you enjoy doing in your spare time

hobby-horse • NOUN • **hobby-horses** 1 a wooden toy with a horse's head attached to a long stick, which you pretend to ride 2 someone's hobby-horse is the subject that they most enjoy talking about

hobgoblin • NOUN • **hobgoblins** a type of wicked fairy

hockey • NOUN • 1 a game for two teams of eleven players, played with curved sticks and a ball on a field with a goal at either end 2 ice hockey

hoe • NOUN • **hoes** a garden tool with a metal blade at one end, used for digging out weeds • VERB • **hoes, hoeing, hoed** to use a hoe to dig out weeds from the soil

hog • VERB • **hogs, hogging, hogged** to hog something is to keep it for yourself and not share it with others • NOUN • **hogs** another word for a pig • **go the whole hog** to leave nothing out, especially to do something in the most expensive or luxurious way possible

Hogmanay • NOUN • the name used in Scotland for December 31, or New Year's Eve, and the celebrations held that night

hoist • VERB • **hoists, hoisting, hoisted** to hoist something is to lift it up • NOUN • **hoists** a machine for lifting things

hold • VERB • **holds, holding, held** 1 to have something in your hand or hands: *He was holding a lovely little puppy.* 2 to keep something in a certain position for a while: *Raise your legs up and hold them there for a count of three.* 3 to contain something: *This rack holds my CDs.* 4 a container that holds a certain amount can have that amount put into it: *It can hold 50 CDs.* 5 a place or vehicle that holds a certain

number of people has enough room or seats for that number: *The stadium holds about 70000 spectators.* 6 to hold an event or celebration, such as a party, is to organize it: *Where are the next Olympic Games going to be held?* 7 to **hold on** is to wait for a while: *Can you hold on while I get my coat?* 8 if one thing **holds up** another thing, it supports it: *The walls hold the roof up.* 9 to **hold someone or something up** is to delay them or it 10 a robber **holds up** a person or place when they threaten that person, or the people in that place, with a weapon • NOUN • **holds** 1 a ship's hold is the space inside it where its cargo is stored 2 a grip: *Take a hold of the railing.* • **no holds barred** using every method, no matter how rough or unpleasant, to beat your opponent

holdall • NOUN • **holdalls** a kind of large soft bag that you use to carry your clothes and belongings when you are travelling

holder • NOUN • **holders** 1 a container for putting or keeping something in 2 the holder of a job, title, qualification or ticket is the person who has it

hold-up • NOUN • **hold-ups** 1 a robbery in which guns or other weapons are used to threaten the people being robbed 2 a delay

hole • NOUN • **holes** 1 an opening, tear or gap in something: *a hole in my sock* 2 a pit or burrow in the ground: *They dug a deep hole to plant the tree in.* • *a rabbit hole* ◆ **holey** • ADJECTIVE • full of holes: *holey socks*

Holi • NOUN • a Hindu festival held near the end of February

holiday • NOUN • **holidays** 1 a day or period of time when you don't have to work or go to school 2 a period of time spent in a place other than where you live, in order to relax or enjoy yourself

---

① This word comes from the Old English words **halig**, which means *holy*, and **dæg**, which means *day*. A holiday used to be a day when you did not work because it was a religious festival.

holiness •NOUN• 1 being holy 2 a title used for the Pope: *His Holiness, Pope John Paul*

hollow •ADJECTIVE• **hollower, hollowest** something hollow has an empty space inside it

holly •NOUN• **hollies** an evergreen tree with sharp spiky leaves and red berries

holocaust •NOUN• **holocausts** 1 a huge fire or other disaster that causes death and destruction 2 the Holocaust was the murder of millions of Jewish people by the Nazis in the 1930's and 1940's

hologram •NOUN• **holograms** a photograph made using laser beams that seems to be three-dimensional when it is looked at from certain angles

holster •NOUN• **holsters** a leather holder for a gun, usually worn on a belt

holy •ADJECTIVE• **holier, holiest** 1 to do with God or religion 2 pure and good and having strong religious feelings
⇒ holiness

homage •NOUN• to pay homage to someone is to honour them and show or express your respect for them

home •NOUN• **homes** 1 your home is the place where you live or where you were born and brought up
2 the home of something is the place where it began or was invented: *Bombay, the home of the Indian film industry*
3 a home is a place where people or animals with no one to look after them live and are cared for
•VERB• **homes, homing, homed** to **home in on** something is to focus very closely on it or move directly towards it
⇒ homing

home economics •NOUN• a school subject that teaches the skills needed to run a home

home page •NOUN• **home pages** on the Internet, the home page of a website is the page that you start from and which gives you links to all the other parts of the site

homesick •ADJECTIVE• when people who are away from their home feel homesick, they feel unhappy and want to be back at home

♦ **homesickness** •NOUN• the feeling of being homesick

homestead •NOUN• **homesteads** a farmhouse, especially with land and smaller buildings around it

homewards •ADVERB• towards home: *trudging homewards after a hard day's work*

homework •NOUN• school work that you do while you are at home, especially in the evenings or at weekends

homing •ADJECTIVE• a homing pigeon can find its way back home from a very long way away

homonym •NOUN• **homonyms** a word spelt the same way as another word, but with a different meaning and sometimes a different sound. For example, *calf* meaning 'a young cow' and *calf* meaning 'the muscle at the back of your leg' are homonyms

ⓘ Homonyms in this dictionary are given separate entries with a small number following the word, for example **calf¹** and **calf²**.

homophone •NOUN• **homophones** a word that sounds the same as another word, but has a different meaning and sometimes a different spelling. For example, *bare* and *bear*, *sea* and *see*, and *hour* and *our* are homophones. See the box called **Homophones**

honest •ADJECTIVE• an honest person tells the truth and does not cheat or steal
♦ **honestly** •ADVERB• 1 truthfully: *He told me honestly what he thought.* • *Honestly, I didn't realize the door should have been kept locked.*
2 without cheating, stealing or breaking the law
3 you say 'honestly' to show that you are annoyed or angry: *Honestly, it just makes me sick!*
♦ **honesty** •NOUN• being honest, truthful or trustworthy

honey •NOUN• a sweet thick liquid that bees make from the nectar of flowers and which they store in their hives

honeycomb •NOUN• **honeycombs** a structure made by bees with special wax,

Homophones

Homophones are words that sound alike, but which are sometimes spelt differently and mean different things. Here are some examples:

The **brake** stops a car.	**Break** the chocolate in half.
She wore a **plain** jumper.	The **plane** flew overhead.
Have you **read** this book?	The Swiss flag is **red**.
A wound takes time to **heal**.	The **heel** is at the back of the foot.
I can **hear** the doorbell.	She ran **here** and there.
Peace and quiet.	Have a **piece** of fruit cake.
Buy some eggs, please.	They sat **by** the stream.
People **die** in accidents.	Shall I **dye** my hair pink?
Right is the opposite of left.	I must **write** a letter to my grandmother.
Do you **know** your times tables?	There were **no** tickets left.
The wind **blew**.	The sky is **blue**.
Two ladies went to town.	Their children went **too**.
Ben **threw** the ball to Bill.	The car sped **through** the tunnel.
The clock strikes every **hour**.	**Our** uncle is a deep-sea diver.
Three minus two is **one**.	Who **won** the World Cup?
Would you like **some** fruit?	What is the **sum** of 19 and 281?
The men dug a **hole**.	He ate a **whole** pizza.
I have **cereal** for breakfast.	What is your favourite **serial** on TV?
Which one is mine?	The **witch** made a vanishing spell.

with lots of compartments or cells in which honey is stored

honeymoon • NOUN • **honeymoons** a holiday that a husband and wife take together immediately after they get married

honeysuckle • NOUN • a climbing plant with sweet-smelling yellow or pinkish flowers

honk • NOUN • **honks** a loud short sound made by a goose or a car horn
• VERB • **honks, honking, honked** to honk is to make this sound

honorary • ADJECTIVE • someone who is given an honorary title, or honorary membership of a club or organization, is given it as a mark of respect or honour

honour • NOUN • **honours** 1 a person's honesty and ability to be trusted: *You are all on your honour to behave like young gentlemen.*
2 the respect or good reputation someone or something deserves: *You'll be doing it for the honour of the school.*
3 something that makes you proud: *the honour of meeting the king*
4 an award given to someone for good work or long service
5 to do something **in honour of** a person or event is to do it as a way of remembering that person or celebrating that event
• VERB • **honours, honouring, honoured** 1 to honour someone is to make them proud, pay them respect or give them an honour or

award for good work **2** to honour a promise or agreement is to keep it

honourable •ADJECTIVE• trustworthy or deserving respect
♦ **honourably** •ADVERB• in an honourable way

hood •NOUN• **hoods 1** a part attached to the back of a coat or jacket that you can pull up to cover the top and back of your head **2** a folding cover for something

-hood •SUFFIX• if **-hood** appears at the end of the word it means 'the state or time of being'. For example, *childhood* is the time in someone's life when they are a child, and *manhood* is the state of being or becoming a man

hoodwink •VERB• hoodwinks, hoodwinking, hoodwinked to hoodwink someone is to deceive them

hoof •NOUN• **hooves** the hard horny part of the foot of some animals, such as horses, cows or sheep

hook •NOUN• **hooks 1** a bent piece of metal or plastic that you hang things on **2** a bent piece of metal with a very sharp end used for catching fish
• **off the hook** if you are off the hook, you do not have to do something difficult or unpleasant that you thought you would have to do
•VERB• **hooks, hooking, hooked 1** to catch a fish using a hook **2** to attach something using a hook or hooks
♦ **hooked** •ADJECTIVE• a hooked nose curves like a hook

hooligan •NOUN• **hooligans** someone who behaves in a wild or violent way
♦ **hooliganism** •NOUN• the behaviour of hooligans

hoop •NOUN• **hoops** a thin ring of metal or wood

hooray •INTERJECTION• another spelling of **hurrah**

hoot •NOUN• **hoots 1** the sound made by an owl or a car horn **2** a loud, sudden burst of laughter, or something that you find very amusing
•VERB• **hoots, hooting, hooted 1** to hoot is

to make the sound of an owl or a car horn **2** to hoot with laughter is to laugh very loud in sudden bursts

hoover •NOUN• **hoovers** a machine for cleaning carpets and floors which sucks dirt into a bag or container inside. This word is a trademark
•VERB• **hoovers, hoovering, hoovered** to clean a carpet or floor using a hoover or vacuum cleaner

hooves •PLURAL NOUN• the plural of **hoof**

hop[1] •VERB• **hops, hopping, hopped 1** to jump on one leg **2** to jump: *Hop in and I'll give you a lift to the station.*
•NOUN• **hops** a jump
• **on the hop** very busy

hop[2] •NOUN• **hops** a climbing plant with fruits that are used to flavour beer

hope •VERB• **hopes, hoping, hoped** to hope for something is to think that it is possible or wish that it would happen
•NOUN• **hopes 1** hope is the feeling that what you want may happen: *We're not giving up hope, are we?* **2** your hopes are the things that you want to happen

hopeful •ADJECTIVE• having or feeling hope: *He's very hopeful that things will turn out well.*
♦ **hopefully** •ADVERB• in a hopeful way

hopeless •ADJECTIVE• **1** without any hope of succeeding: *a hopeless dream* **2** very bad: *He was hopeless in goal.*
♦ **hopelessly** •ADVERB• in a hopeless way

hopscotch •NOUN• a game played on a grid of squares marked on the ground. You throw a stone and hop from one square to another and back again avoiding the square with the stone in it

horde •NOUN• **hordes** a large moving crowd

horizon •NOUN• **horizons** the horizon is the line where the land and sky seem to meet
♦ **horizontal** •ADJECTIVE• lying level or flat and not upright

hormone •NOUN• **hormones** a chemical made in your body that controls things like your body's growth and development

horn •NOUN• **horns 1** horns are the hard pointed objects that grow out of some

Aa
Bb
Cc
Dd
Ee
Ff
Gg
Hh
Ii
Jj
Kk
Ll
Mm
Nn
Oo
Pp
Qq
Rr
Ss
Tt
Uu
Vv
Ww
Xx
Yy
Zz

animals' heads, such as sheep, goats and cows **2** a device in a vehicle that makes a loud noise as a warning to others **3** a musical instrument that you blow into ◆ **horned** ▪ ADJECTIVE▪ having horns

hornet ▪ NOUN▪ **hornets** a type of large wasp

horoscope ▪ NOUN▪ **horoscopes** your horoscope is information about what some people believe is going to happen to you in the future depending on your zodiac sign

horrendous ▪ ADJECTIVE▪ terrible and shocking: *a horrendous crime*

horrible ▪ ADJECTIVE▪ very nasty, ugly or unpleasant
◆ **horribly** ▪ ADVERB▪ in a horrible way

horrid ▪ ADJECTIVE▪ nasty: *a horrid cold* ▪ *a horrid man*

horrific ▪ ADJECTIVE▪ awful, terrifying or upsetting: *a horrific car crash*
◆ **horrifically** ▪ ADVERB▪ in a horrific way

horrify ▪ VERB▪ **horrifies, horrifying, horrified** to shock and terrify someone
◆ **horrifying** ▪ ADJECTIVE▪ shocking or terrifying

horror ▪ NOUN▪ **horrors 1** horror is a feeling of great shock or alarm: *She threw up her hands in horror.*
2 you have a horror of something if you are very afraid of it: *She has a horror of any creeping, slimy thing.*
3 horrors are very frightening, shocking or terrible experiences: *the horrors of war*
▪ ADJECTIVE▪ meant to frighten you: *horror movies*

horse ▪ NOUN▪ **horses** a large animal with long hair on its neck and tail. Horses are used by people to ride on and to pull carts or ploughs

horse-chestnut ▪ NOUN▪ **horse-chestnuts** a type of tree on which large reddish-brown nuts called conkers grow

horseplay ▪ NOUN▪ rough games

horsepower ▪ NOUN▪ a unit for measuring the power of engines, equal to about 746 watts

horseradish ▪ NOUN▪ a type of plant whose root is used to make a very hot-tasting sauce

horseshoe ▪ NOUN▪ **horseshoes** a curved piece of iron nailed on to a horse's hoof to stop the hoof from being worn down

horticulture ▪ NOUN▪ the science or study of growing fruit, vegetables and flowers in gardens and greenhouses

hose ▪ NOUN▪ **hoses** a tube made from bendy material used for carrying liquids and gases

hosiery ▪ NOUN▪ hosiery is socks and stockings

hospice ▪ NOUN▪ **hospices** a special type of hospital where sick people who can't be cured are cared for

hospitable ▪ ADJECTIVE▪ welcoming to guests and strangers

hospital ▪ NOUN▪ **hospitals** a building where people who are sick or have been injured can go to be treated

ⓘ This word comes from the Latin word **hospes**, which means *guest*. A hospital used to be a place where guests could stay.

hospitality ▪ NOUN▪ hospitality is being welcoming and friendly to people, giving them food, entertainment or accommodation

host¹ ▪ NOUN▪ **hosts 1** a person who welcomes guests, for example at a party, in a hotel or on a radio or TV show **2** a parasite's host is the plant or animal it lives or feeds on
▪ VERB▪ **hosts, hosting, hosted** to host an event is to be its host: *The city of Sydney, Australia, hosted the Olympics in the year 2000.*

host² ▪ NOUN▪ a host of things is a very large number of them

hostage ▪ NOUN▪ **hostages** someone who is held prisoner until their captors get what they want

hostel ▪ NOUN▪ **hostels** a building with rooms that students or travellers can stay in

hostess ▪ NOUN▪ **hostesses** a female host

hostile ▪ ADJECTIVE▪ **1** unfriendly or showing strong dislike **2** hostile forces in a war are enemy forces
◆ **hostility** ▪ NOUN▪ unfriendliness or strong dislike

hot •ADJECTIVE• **hotter, hottest** 1 feeling very warm: *Don't touch the oven. It's very hot.* 2 spicy: *hot curries*
⇒ **hotly**

hotdog •NOUN• **hotdogs** a hot sausage served in a long thin roll

hotel •NOUN• **hotels** a building with rooms that people pay to stay in when they are away from home

hotheaded •ADJECTIVE• someone who is hotheaded is quick to get angry, or is too quick to act

hothouse •NOUN• **hothouses** a heated greenhouse for growing plants that come from hot climates

hotline •NOUN• **hotlines** a direct telephone line by which people can get or give information quickly in an emergency

hotly •ADVERB• to discuss, argue or deny something hotly is to do it in an angry or lively way

hotpot •NOUN• **hotpots** a mixture of meat and vegetables cooked in the oven in a covered dish

hotseat •NOUN• if someone is **in the hotseat** they are in a situation in which they have to make difficult or important decisions

hound •NOUN• **hounds** a type of dog used for hunting
•VERB• **hounds, hounding, hounded** to hound someone is to go on for a long time bothering or annoying them

hour •NOUN• **hours** a period of time that lasts 60 minutes. There are 24 hours in one day
⇒ **hourly**

hour-glass •NOUN• **hour-glasses** an instrument used to measure time with two glass containers joined by a thin glass tube through which sand trickles slowly

hourly •ADJECTIVE• happening once every hour or calculated by the hour: *an hourly service • an hourly rate of pay*
•ADVERB• 1 happening once every hour: *Buses to London leave hourly.* 2 if you are paid hourly, you earn a certain amount of money for each hour that you work

house •NOUN• **houses** 1 a building in which people, especially one family, live
2 the part of a theatre or cinema where the audience sits
3 one of the groups into which the pupils of a school are sometimes divided so they, for instance, can compete against each other in sports
• **on the house** if something you are given in a restaurant, hotel or bar is on the house, you get it free of charge
•VERB• **houses, housing, housed** 1 to house people is to provide them with houses to live in 2 to house something somewhere is to put it in a place inside which it will be kept
⇒ **housing**

houseboat •NOUN• **houseboats** a boat on a river with cabins for living in

housebreaker •NOUN• **housebreakers** a thief who breaks into people's houses to steal things
✦ **housebreaking** •NOUN• the crime of breaking into people's houses

household •NOUN• **households** all the people who live in the same house
✦ **householder** •NOUN• **householders** someone who owns or rents a house

household name •NOUN• **household names** someone or something that is a household name is famous

housekeeper •NOUN• **housekeepers** someone who organizes all the work needed to run a house

house-proud •ADJECTIVE• keeping the house always clean and tidy

house-trained •ADJECTIVE• a house-trained pet has learnt to be clean inside the house

housewarming •NOUN• **housewarmings** a party held in someone's new home

housewife •NOUN• **housewives** a woman who stays at home to look after her family and do the housework, instead of going out to work

housework •NOUN• housework is all the work you need to do to keep a house clean and tidy

housing •NOUN• 1 housing is houses of various kinds for people to live in 2 the

Aa
Bb
Cc
Dd
Ee
Ff
Gg
Hh
Ii
Jj
Kk
Ll
Mm
Nn
Oo
Pp
Qq
Rr
Ss
Tt
Uu
Vv
Ww
Xx
Yy
Zz

housing for a machine is the box or structure that the machine fits into

hover •VERB• **hovers, hovering, hovered**
1 if something hovers it stays still in the air
2 if someone hovers they stand close to you, usually because they are watching you

hovercraft • NOUN• **hovercrafts** a vehicle that travels along supported on a cushion of air

how • ADVERB• 1 how something is done is the way it is done or the means used to do it : *I'll show you how to tie a reef knot.* • *How will we get there?*
2 how is used in questions about measurement, extent, distance, time and age : *I don't know how old Granny is exactly.* • *How much is that doggie in the window?*
3 how you are is how well or ill you feel : *Hello, how are you today?*
4 how you feel about someone or something is the feelings you have for them
5 you use how to show anger or for emphasis : *How dare you!* • *How sad is that?*

however • ADVERB• 1 no matter how : *Do it however you like.* 2 in spite of what has just been said : *He thinks it is a great movie. However, no one else thinks so.*

howl • NOUN• **howls** 1 a long, loud, sad sound made by a wolf or dog 2 a loud shout of pain or laughter
•VERB• **howls, howling, howled** 1 a dog or wolf howls when it makes a long, loud, sad-sounding noise 2 to shout or cry loudly : *He was howling with pain.*

howler • NOUN• **howlers** a very bad and obvious mistake

HQ • ABBREVIATION• short for **headquarters**

hub • NOUN• **hubs** 1 the centre part of a wheel where the axle passes through 2 the part of a place where most of the activity is : *the hub of the town*

hubbub • NOUN• **hubbubs** the noise made by many people talking at the same time

huddle •VERB• **huddles, huddling, huddled** people or animals huddle, or huddle together, when they move very close to each other and form a tightly packed group
• NOUN• **huddles** a group of people standing or sitting very close to each other

hue • NOUN• **hues** a colour or shade

hue and cry • NOUN• a hue and cry is a noisy fuss, often with people shouting or protesting loudly

huff • NOUN• **huffs** if someone is in **a huff**, they are sulking
♦ **huffy** • ADJECTIVE• **huffier, huffiest** sulky

hug •VERB• **hugs, hugging, hugged** two people hug when they put their arms around each other's bodies in an affectionate way
• NOUN• **hugs** the affectionate action of putting your arms around someone

huge • ADJECTIVE• very big

hula-hoop • NOUN• **hula-hoops** a large circle of plastic that you step inside and swing round and round your body by moving your hips

hulk • NOUN• **hulks** 1 a very large and clumsy person or thing 2 an old ship that is not being used
♦ **hulking** • ADJECTIVE• very large and clumsy

hull • NOUN• **hulls** the part of a ship or boat that sits in the water

hullabaloo • NOUN• **hullabaloos** a noisy fuss

hullo • INTERJECTION• another spelling of **hello**

hum •VERB• **hums, humming, hummed** you hum when you make musical noises in your throat with your mouth closed

human • NOUN• **humans** a human or a **human being** is a person
• ADJECTIVE• typical of human beings : *a very human emotion*

humane • ADJECTIVE• kind and causing as little suffering as possible
♦ **humanely** • ADVERB• in a way that causes the least pain possible : *The dog was destroyed humanely.*

humanity • NOUN• 1 humanity is all human beings 2 someone who shows humanity is kind and understanding towards other people

humble • ADJECTIVE• **humbler, humblest** a humble person believes they are no better than other people

Aa Bb Cc Dd Ee Ff Gg **Hh** Ii Jj Kk Ll Mm Nn Oo Pp Qq Rr Ss Tt Uu Vv Ww Xx Yy Zz

⇒ **humility**

• **eat humble pie** if someone eats humble pie, they show that they are very sorry for a mistake they have made by admitting it and being humble

humbug •NOUN• **humbugs 1** humbug is an old-fashioned word for nonsense **2** humbugs are hard sweets made from boiled sugar that you suck

humdrum •ADJECTIVE• a humdrum existence is boring because things always stay the same and nothing exciting ever happens

humid •ADJECTIVE• the air or atmosphere is humid when it has a lot of moisture in it
♦ **humidity** •NOUN• humidity is the amount of moisture that is in the air

humiliate •VERB• **humiliates, humiliating, humiliated** to humiliate someone is to make them feel silly or ashamed, especially in front of other people
♦ **humiliating** •ADJECTIVE• causing embarrassment or making you feel silly
♦ **humiliation** •NOUN• **humiliations 1** humiliation is being humiliated **2** a humiliation is something that makes you feel disgraced or embarrassed

humility •NOUN• being humble

humming-bird •NOUN• **humming-birds** a tiny bird with a long beak that feeds on nectar from flowers and beats its wings so fast they make a humming sound

humorous •ADJECTIVE• funny or amusing

humour •NOUN• **1** the ability someone has to be funny or amusing, or to find things funny or amusing **2** someone's humour is the mood they are in
•VERB• **humours, humouring, humoured** to humour someone is to agree with them just to please them

hump •NOUN• **humps 1** a rounded lump on an animal's back **2** a rounded raised part on a road or other surface

humpback bridge •NOUN• **humpback bridges** a bridge that is higher in the middle than at either end

hunch •NOUN• **hunches** an idea you have about someone or something, which you

believe but cannot prove
•VERB• **hunches, hunching, hunched** to hunch your shoulders or your back is to bring your shoulders up towards your ears so that your body is bent over at the top

hunchback •NOUN• **hunchbacks** someone whose spine is bent so that there is a lump on their back
♦ **hunchbacked** •ADJECTIVE• having a crooked back with a lump

hundred •NOUN• **hundreds** the number 100
♦ **hundredth** •ADJECTIVE AND ADVERB• coming last in a series of one hundred things: *This is my hundredth visit here.*
•NOUN• **hundredths** one of a hundred equal parts of something: *A centimetre is a hundredth of a metre.*

hung •VERB• a way of changing the verb **hang** to make a past tense. It can be used with or without a helping verb: *I hung the poster on my bedroom wall.* • *He had hung the washing out before it started raining.*

hunger •NOUN• the feeling you get when you need to eat
•VERB• **hungers, hungering, hungered** to hunger for something is to long for it
♦ **hungrily** •ADVERB• in a hungry way
♦ **hungry** •ADJECTIVE• **hungrier, hungriest** having an empty feeling in your stomach and wanting food

hunk •NOUN• **hunks** a big piece of something: *a hunk of rock*

hunt •VERB• **hunts, hunting, hunted 1** to chase and kill animals for food or sport **2** to hunt for something is to look hard for it everywhere
•NOUN• **hunts 1** a search for something or someone: *a police hunt for the criminal* **2** an event where people search for or chase animals in order to kill them **3** an animal is **on the hunt** when it is searching for prey
♦ **hunter** •NOUN• **hunters** a person or animal that hunts
♦ **hunting** •NOUN• chasing and killing animals

hurdle •NOUN• **hurdles 1** one of several jumps placed round a race track that athletes or horses have to jump over **2** a

Aa

Bb

Cc

Dd

Ee

Ff

Gg

Hh

Ii

Jj

Kk

Ll

Mm

Nn

Oo

Pp

Qq

Rr

Ss

Tt

Uu

Vv

Ww

Xx

Yy

Zz

problem that you have to overcome •VERB• **hurdles, hurdling, hurdled** to hurdle is to compete in hurdle races

✦ **hurdler** • NOUN• **hurdlers** a competitor in a race with hurdles

✦ **hurdling** • NOUN• jumping over hurdles in a race

hurl • VERB• **hurls, hurling, hurled** to hurl something is to throw it with a lot of force

hurrah or **hooray** • INTERJECTION• an exclamation of approval or joy: *Hurrah! No more school for three whole days!*

hurricane • NOUN• **hurricanes** a fierce storm with very high winds that cause damage

hurried • ADJECTIVE• something that is hurried is done quickly

✦ **hurriedly** • ADVERB• quickly

hurry • VERB• **hurries, hurrying, hurried** 1 to move or go quickly 2 to **hurry up** is to move faster

• NOUN• hurry is trying or needing to get somewhere or get something done quickly: *in a hurry to catch the bus* • *There's no hurry.*

hurt • VERB• **hurts, hurting, hurt** 1 to hurt someone or something is to injure or damage them: *She hurt her ankle playing hockey.* • *Try not to hurt anyone's feelings.* 2 if something hurts, or hurts you, it injures you or makes you feel pain

• ADJECTIVE• injured or showing pain

• NOUN• pain, injury or distress

hurtful • ADJECTIVE• causing pain or distress: *a hurtful remark*

hurtle • VERB• **hurtles, hurtling, hurtled** to move very fast, often in a dangerous or uncontrolled way: *The sledge came hurtling down the bank and crashed into a tree.*

husband • NOUN• **husbands** a woman's husband is the man she has married

hush • INTERJECTION• if someone says 'hush!' they want you to be quiet

• VERB• **hushes, hushing, hushed** to **hush something up** is to stop people getting to know about it

• NOUN• silence after there has been noise

husk • NOUN• **husks** the husk of a seed is its dry outer covering

husky¹ • ADJECTIVE• 1 deep and rough: *a*

low husky voice 2 big and strong: *broad husky shoulders*

husky² • NOUN• **huskies** a type of large dog with a thick warm coat that is used to pull sledges over snow in the Arctic and Antarctic

hustle • VERB• **hustles, hustling, hustled** to push someone somewhere or to hurry them along

• NOUN• hurried movements or actions

hut • NOUN• **huts** a small building or shed made of wood, mud or metal

hutch • NOUN• **hutches** a box, usually with an open front covered with wire, where pet rabbits are kept

hyacinth • NOUN• **hyacinths** a plant that grows from a large bulb and has lots of small sweet-smelling flowers growing on one stem

hyaena • NOUN• **hyaenas** another spelling of **hyena**

hybrid • NOUN• **hybrids** a hybrid animal or plant has been bred from two different types or species of animal or plant

hydrant • NOUN• **hydrants** a pipe connected to the main water supply to which a hose can be attached to get water to put out fires

hydraulic • ADJECTIVE• to do with, or powered by the movement of liquid: *hydraulic brakes*

hydro- • PREFIX• if **hydro-** comes at the beginning of a word it has something to do with water. For example, *hydrogen* is one of the elements that makes water

hydrocarbon • NOUN• **hydrocarbons** hydrocarbons are various chemical substances containing only carbon and hydrogen. They are found in coal and oil

hydroelectric • ADJECTIVE• using or to do with electricity made by water power

✦ **hydroelectricity** • NOUN• electricity made by using fast flowing water whose power is converted into electrical power

hydrofoil • NOUN• **hydrofoils** a fast type of boat or ship that can skim over the water on long structures shaped like an aeroplane's wings

hydrogen • NOUN• hydrogen is the lightest

gas, which combines with oxygen to make water

hyena or **hyaena** • NOUN• **hyenas** or **hyaenas** a wild animal that lives in Africa and parts of Asia. Hyenas belong to the same family as dogs and make a howling noise that sounds like mad laughter

hygiene • NOUN• keeping yourself and your surroundings clean, so that you stay healthy
♦ **hygienic** • ADJECTIVE• without any dirt or germs

hymn • NOUN• **hymns** a religious song praising God

hype • NOUN• hype is publicity or advertising, especially when it makes something seem better than it is

hyper- • PREFIX• if **hyper-** comes at the beginning of a word it adds the meaning 'much bigger', 'much more' or 'too much'. For example, a *hypermarket* is much bigger than a supermarket

hyperactive • ADJECTIVE• someone who is hyperactive is more active than normal

hypertext • NOUN• in computers, hypertext is a special electronic text with cross-reference links called hyperlinks which let you go to information elsewhere by clicking on a symbol or word

hyphen • NOUN• **hyphens** a punctuation mark (-) used to join words or parts of words together, or used at the end of a line of printed text to show that a word is split and part of it is on the next line
♦ **hyphenate** • VERB• **hyphenates, hyphenating, hyphenated** to put a hyphen in a word or to join words or parts of words with a hyphen

hypnosis • NOUN• if someone is under hypnosis they have been put into a state that is similar to a deep sleep but in which they can still obey someone's instructions
♦ **hypnotic** • ADJECTIVE• having a hypnotizing effect

♦ **hypnotism** • NOUN• using hypnosis to put someone into a sleep-like state
♦ **hypnotist** • NOUN• **hypnotists** someone who hypnotizes people, often as a public entertainment
♦ **hypnotize** or **hypnotise** • VERB• **hypnotizes, hypnotizing, hypnotized** to put someone into a sleep-like state

hypochondriac • NOUN• **hypochondriacs** someone who is very worried about their health and imagines they are suffering from illnesses and diseases

hypocrisy • NOUN• the behaviour of someone who is not as sincere or honest as they pretend to be
♦ **hypocrite** • NOUN• **hypocrites** someone who pretends to be sincere and concerned for other people
♦ **hypocritical** • ADJECTIVE• not having the feelings or beliefs that you pretend to have

hypotenuse • NOUN• **hypotenuses** the side of a right-angled triangle that is opposite the right angle

hypothermia • NOUN• a dangerous lowering of someone's body temperature caused by extreme cold

hypothesis • NOUN• **hypotheses** a theory or idea that has been worked out as a possible explanation for something, but which hasn't been proved to be correct
♦ **hypothetical** • ADJECTIVE• a hypothetical situation or example is one that is based on what might be possible, rather than fact

hysteria • NOUN• if someone is suffering from hysteria, they become very emotional and cry or scream in a wild way
♦ **hysterical** • ADJECTIVE• 1 suffering from hysteria 2 if you find something hysterical you think it is very funny
♦ **hysterically** • ADVERB• in a hysterical way
♦ **hysterics** • NOUN• if someone has hysterics, they cry, scream or laugh in a wild and uncontrolled way

Aa
Bb
Cc
Dd
Ee
Ff
Gg
Hh
Ii
Jj
Kk
Ll
Mm
Nn
Oo
Pp
Qq
Rr
Ss
Tt
Uu
Vv
Ww
Xx
Yy
Zz

Ii

I •PRONOUN• a word you use when talking about yourself: *I like ice cream.*

ice •NOUN• frozen water
⇒ **icy**

ice age •NOUN• the period of time when the Earth was mostly covered with ice

iceberg •NOUN• **icebergs** a large piece of ice floating in the sea

icebox •NOUN• **iceboxes** the American English word for **fridge**

ice-cap •NOUN• **ice-caps** a permanent covering of ice, for example at the North and South Poles

ice cream •NOUN• **ice creams** a sweet frozen food made from milk or cream: *strawberry ice cream* • *Would you like an ice cream?*

ice hockey •NOUN• a sport played on ice in which two teams try to hit an object called a puck into a net

ice lolly •NOUN• **ice lollies** a lump of frozen fruit-flavoured juice on a stick

ice-skate •NOUN• **ice-skates** ice-skates are boots with blades on the bottom, used for moving across ice
♦ **ice-skating** •NOUN• the sport or pastime of moving across ice wearing ice-skates

icicle •NOUN• **icicles** a long thin piece of ice that is hanging from something

icing •NOUN• a mixture of sugar and water, used for decorating cakes

icon •NOUN• **icons** **1** a small symbol on a computer screen that represents a program or file **2** a statue or painting of a holy person

icy •ADJECTIVE• **icier, iciest** **1** covered with ice: *icy roads* **2** extremely cold: *an icy wind*

ID •NOUN• **IDs** an official document that proves who you are: *We need some ID before we can give you a library card.*

I'd •SHORT FORM• **1** a short way to say and write **I would** or **I had**: *I'd like another drink,*

please. • *I'd just gone to bed when the phone rang.*

idea •NOUN• **ideas** a thought or plan that you have: *That's a good idea.*
• **have no idea** not to know something: *I've no idea where he is.*

ideal •ADJECTIVE• perfect, especially for a particular purpose: *It's an ideal house for a family.*
♦ **idealism** •NOUN• the belief that something perfect can be achieved, even though this is not likely
♦ **idealist** •NOUN• **idealists** someone who believes in idealism
♦ **idealize** or **idealise** •VERB• **idealizes, idealizing, idealized** to think that something is perfect when it really is not
♦ **ideally** •ADVERB• in a perfect situation: *Ideally, I'd like to finish this by tomorrow.*

identical •ADJECTIVE• if two things are identical, they are exactly the same

identification •NOUN• **1** an official document that proves who you are **2** the process of finding out who someone is or what something is

identify •VERB• **identifies, identifying, identified** **1** to say who someone is or what something is: *Can you identify this flower?* **2** if you **identify with** someone, you feel that you understand them and share their feelings

identity •NOUN• **identities** who someone is or what something is: *Police are trying to discover the identity of the thief.*

idiom •NOUN• **idioms** a phrase that has a special meaning. For example, 'let the cat out of the bag' is an idiom that means 'to tell someone a secret'

idiot •NOUN• **idiots** a stupid person
♦ **idiotic** •ADJECTIVE• extremely stupid

ⓘ This word comes from the Greek word **idiotes**, which means a person with no skill.

idle • ADJECTIVE • 1 someone who is idle is lazy or not doing anything useful 2 a machine or other piece of equipment that is idle is not being used
* **idly** • ADVERB • in a lazy way

ⓘ This word comes from the Old English word **idel**, which means *empty* or *worthless*.

ⓘ Be careful not to confuse the spellings and meanings of **idle** and **idol**.

idol • NOUN • **idols** 1 a famous person who is admired by a lot of people 2 something which people worship as a god
* **idolize** or **idolise** • VERB • **idolizes, idolizing, idolized** to admire someone or something very much *He idolizes his football heroes.*

ie or **i.e.** • ABBREVIATION • short for **id est**, which is Latin for 'that is'. You use **ie** when you are giving more information to show what you mean: *The whole trip, ie food, travel, and hotel, cost £500.*

if • CONJUNCTION • 1 whether: *I don't know if I can come on Thursday.*
2 used when talking about possibilities: *If we leave now, we should catch the train.*
• *He will have to go into hospital if his condition gets worse.*
3 whenever: *I always call in at his house if I'm passing.*

igloo • NOUN • **igloos** a hut made from blocks of snow

ignite • VERB • **ignites, igniting, ignited** 1 to catch fire: *The paper suddenly ignited.* 2 to set something on fire: *Flames had ignited the curtains.*
* **ignition** • NOUN • 1 the part of a car that ignites the petrol when you turn the key to start the engine 2 the igniting of something

ignorance • NOUN • being ignorant
* **ignorant** • ADJECTIVE • not knowing about something: *Many people are ignorant about the dangers.*

ignore • VERB • **ignores, ignoring, ignored** to pay no attention to someone or something: *He ignored all my advice.* • *I said hello, but she just ignored me.*

iguana • NOUN • **iguanas** a large lizard that lives in trees

ill • ADJECTIVE • not well: *I was ill yesterday and had the day off school.*
⇒ **illness**

I'll • SHORT FORM • a short way to say and write **I will**: *I'll see you tomorrow.*

illegal • ADJECTIVE • not allowed by the law: *It's illegal to park here.*
* **illegality** • NOUN • being illegal

illegible • ADJECTIVE • illegible writing is so bad you cannot read it
* **illegibility** • NOUN • being illegible
* **illegibly** • ADVERB • in a way that is impossible to read: *You write illegibly.*

ill-gotten • ADJECTIVE • got in a dishonest or unfair way: *thieves and their ill-gotten gains*

illiterate • ADJECTIVE • not able to read or write

illness • NOUN • **illnesses** 1 illness is bad health: *There is a lot of illness among the pupils.* 2 an illness is a disease: *childhood illnesses*

illogical • ADJECTIVE • not based on good reason or logic

illuminate • VERB • **illuminates, illuminating, illuminated** to make something brighter using lights: *We added lights to illuminate the garden.*
* **illuminated** • ADJECTIVE • lit by lights
* **illumination** • NOUN • lighting something with lights

illusion • NOUN • **illusions** 1 an idea or belief you have which is false: *He's under the illusion that it's easy to get a job.* 2 something that seems to exist but does not really exist

illustrate • VERB • **illustrates, illustrating, illustrated** to provide pictures and photographs for a book or magazine: *a book illustrated with colour photographs*
* **illustration** • NOUN • **illustrations** a picture or photograph in a book or magazine
* **illustrator** • NOUN • **illustrators** someone who draws pictures for a book or magazine

ill-will • NOUN • bad feelings towards someone

Aa
Bb
Cc
Dd
Ee
Ff
Gg
Hh
Ii
Jj
Kk
Ll
Mm
Nn
Oo
Pp
Qq
Rr
Ss
Tt
Uu
Vv
Ww
Xx
Yy
Zz

I'm •SHORT FORM• a short way to say and write **I am**: *I'm hungry*.

im- •PREFIX• if a word starts with **im-**, it means 'not'. For example, *impossible* means 'not possible'

image •NOUN• **images 1** a picture that you have in your mind **2** the impression that someone or something gives to other people: *He needs to improve his image*.
• **be the image of someone** to look exactly like someone: *She's the image of her mother*.
✦ **imagery** •NOUN• words that produce pictures in your mind when you are reading something or listening to something

imaginary •ADJECTIVE• existing in your mind but not real: *Dragons are imaginary creatures*.

imagination •NOUN• **imaginations** your ability to form pictures and ideas in your mind: *Most children have a good imagination*.
✦ **imaginative** •ADJECTIVE• using new and interesting ideas: *He's very imaginative*.
• *an imaginative design*

imagine •VERB• **imagines, imagining, imagined 1** to form a picture of someone or something in your mind: *I tried to imagine what he would look like*. **2** to think or believe something, especially something that is not true: *You must be imagining things*.

imam •NOUN• **imams** in the religion of Islam, a man who leads the prayers in a mosque

imitate •VERB• **imitates, imitating, imitated** to copy someone or something
✦ **imitation** •NOUN• **imitations 1** imitation is copying someone or something **2** an imitation is a copy of something
✦ **imitator** •NOUN• **imitators** someone who copies someone else

immaculate •ADJECTIVE• spotlessly clean: *The house looked immaculate*.

immature •ADJECTIVE• behaving in a silly and childish way
✦ **immaturity** •NOUN• silly and childish behaviour

immediate •ADJECTIVE• happening now without any delay: *I can't give you an immediate answer*.

✦ **immediately** •ADVERB• now and without any delay: *Come here immediately!*

immense •ADJECTIVE• very big: *Crime is becoming an immense problem*.
✦ **immensely** •ADVERB• extremely: *He's immensely popular*.

immerse •VERB• **immerses, immersing, immersed 1** to put something in a liquid so it is completely covered **2** if you immerse yourself in something, you give it all of your attention
✦ **immersion** •NOUN• putting something in liquid

immigrant •NOUN• **immigrants** someone from another country who has come to live in your country

immigrate •VERB• **immigrates, immigrating, immigrated** to come and live in a foreign country
✦ **immigration** •NOUN• coming to live in a foreign country

ⓘ Do not confuse this with the word **emigrate**. You **immigrate** if you come to a new country and live there but you **emigrate** if you leave your country.

imminent •ADJECTIVE• something that is imminent will happen very soon

immobile •ADJECTIVE• not moving or not able to move
✦ **immobilize** or **immobilise** •VERB• **immobilizes, immobilizing, immobilized** to prevent someone or something from moving normally

immoral •ADJECTIVE• wrong or bad: *immoral behaviour*
✦ **immorality** •NOUN• behaviour that is not good or honest

immortal •ADJECTIVE• living for ever
✦ **immortality** •NOUN• being immortal
✦ **immortalize** or **immortalise** •VERB• **immortalizes, immortalizing, immortalized** to make someone famous for ever

immune •ADJECTIVE• if you are immune to an illness, you cannot get it
✦ **immunity** •NOUN• your ability to avoid getting an illness
✦ **immunization** or **immunisation** •NOUN• putting a substance into someone's

Aa Bb Cc Dd Ee Ff Gg Hh Ii Jj Kk Ll Mm Nn Oo Pp Qq Rr Ss Tt Uu Vv Ww Xx Yy Zz

body, usually by an injection to prevent them from getting an illness

♦ immunize *or* **immunise** • VERB• **immunizes, immunizing, immunized** to put a substance into someone's body to prevent them from getting an illness

imp • NOUN• **imps** 1 an imaginary creature in stories that looks like a small man and behaves badly 2 a naughty child

impact • NOUN• **impacts** 1 the strong effect that something has: *The changes will have a big impact on schools.* 2 the force of one thing hitting another thing: *The impact of the meteor left a crater on the moon.*

impair • VERB• **impairs, impairing, impaired** to damage something or make it worse: *His hearing was impaired by the constant noise.*
♦ impairment • NOUN• **impairments** a condition that stops part of your body from working correctly

impale • VERB• **impales, impaling, impaled** to push a sharp object through something

impartial • ADJECTIVE• fair and not supporting one person more than another: *an impartial referee*
♦ impartiality • NOUN• being impartial

impatience • NOUN• the feeling that you want something to happen now and that you cannot wait
♦ impatient • ADJECTIVE• having or showing impatience
♦ impatiently • ADVERB• in a way that shows you are impatient: *'Hurry up!' she said impatiently.*

impede • VERB• **impedes, impeding, impeded** to delay the progress of someone or something
♦ impediment • NOUN• **impediments** 1 something that delays progress 2 a problem that makes it difficult for someone to speak properly

impending • ADJECTIVE• going to happen very soon: *an impending disaster*

imperative • ADJECTIVE• extremely important or necessary: *It is imperative that you wash your hands before dinner.*
• NOUN• **imperatives** a form of a verb which tells you to do something. For example, *go* in the phrase *Go away!* is imperative

imperfect • ADJECTIVE• not perfect
• NOUN• the imperfect is the form of the verb that expresses action in the past that is not complete. For example, *The sun was shining* is in the imperfect
♦ imperfection • NOUN• **imperfections** a fault
♦ imperfectly • ADVERB• in a way that is not perfect

imperial • ADJECTIVE• 1 relating to an empire: *an imperial ruler* 2 a system of measuring or weighing that uses units such as gallons and ounces

impersonal • ADJECTIVE• not very friendly or welcoming: *Big hotels can be a bit impersonal.*

impersonate • VERB• **impersonates, impersonating, impersonated** to copy the way someone talks and behaves, especially to entertain people
♦ impersonation • NOUN• **impersonations** an act in which you impersonate someone: *Ben can do a brilliant impersonation of our teacher.*
♦ impersonator • NOUN• **impersonators** someone who impersonates people

impertinence • NOUN• rude behaviour that shows you do not respect someone
♦ impertinent • ADJECTIVE• behaving in a rude way and not showing respect: *an impertinent child*
♦ impertinently • ADVERB• in an impertinent way: *Do not speak so impertinently!*

implement • NOUN• **implements** a tool
• VERB• **implements, implementing, implemented** to start using a new plan or system: *The new rules will be implemented next year.*
♦ implementation • NOUN• implementing something: *the implementation of new laws*

implication • NOUN• **implications** 1 a possible effect or result: *What are the implications of the President's announcement?* 2 something that is suggested and not said directly

implore • VERB• **implores, imploring, implored** to ask in a desperate way for someone to do something

Aa Bb Cc Dd Ee Ff Gg Hh **Ii** Jj Kk Ll Mm Nn Oo Pp Qq Rr Ss Tt Uu Vv Ww Xx Yy Zz

imply •VERB• implies, implying, implied to suggest that something is true without saying it directly: *Are you implying that he lied?*
⇒ implication

impolite •ADJECTIVE• bad mannered and rude to others: *an impolite boy* • *an impolite way to talk*
♦ **impolitely** •ADVERB• in a rude way: *She spoke impolitely to the teacher.*
♦ **impoliteness** •NOUN• rude behaviour and bad manners

import •VERB• imports, importing, imported to bring goods into a country from another country in order to sell them: *Many electrical goods are imported from Japan.* •NOUN• imports something that has been imported

importance •NOUN• being important: *He emphasized the importance of education.*
♦ **important** •ADJECTIVE• 1 something is important if it matters a lot: *an important meeting* 2 an important person has a lot of power
♦ **importantly** •ADVERB• seriously or crucially: *You must go to school and, more importantly, you must listen.*

impose •VERB• imposes, imposing, imposed 1 to bring in a new rule or law, especially one that is not wanted: *the government imposed a new tax* 2 if you impose on someone, you expect someone to do something for you that may not be convenient for them
♦ **imposing** •ADJECTIVE• looking very impressive: *an imposing building*

impossibility •NOUN• impossibilities something that is not possible

impossible •ADJECTIVE• not possible: *an impossible task*

impostor •NOUN• impostors someone who pretends to be someone else in order to deceive people

impractical •ADJECTIVE• not sensible or reasonable: *an impractical suggestion*

imprecise •ADJECTIVE• not exact or correct: *imprecise measurements*

impress •VERB• impresses, impressing, impressed to make someone feel admiration: *His drawings really impressed me.*
♦ **impression** •NOUN• impressions a feeling that you get about someone or something: *I got the impression that he wasn't happy.*
♦ **impressive** •ADJECTIVE• making you feel admiration: *an impressive performance*
♦ **impressively** •ADVERB• in a way that makes you feel admiration

imprison •VERB• imprisons, imprisoning, imprisoned to put someone in prison or a place they cannot escape from

improbable •ADJECTIVE• not likely to happen or be true: *an improbable story*

improper •ADJECTIVE• improper behaviour is not suitable or right

improve •VERB• improves, improving, improved 1 to improve is to get better: *I hope the weather improves soon.* 2 to improve something is to make it better: *I want to improve my French.*
♦ **improvement** •NOUN• improvements 1 improvement is making something better 2 an improvement is a change that makes something better: *improvements to the home*

improvise •VERB• improvises, improvising, improvised to use whatever is available because you do not have what you need: *They improvised a shelter from branches and blankets.*

impudence •NOUN• cheeky behaviour or remarks
♦ **impudent** •ADJECTIVE• rude and not showing respect

impulse •NOUN• impulses a sudden feeling you have that makes you do something
♦ **impulsive** •ADJECTIVE• doing something suddenly without thinking about the possible results

impure •ADJECTIVE• not pure
♦ **impurity** •NOUN• impurities something in a substance that makes it dirty or not pure: *impurities in water*

in •PREPOSITION• 1 inside something: *He keeps his keys in the drawer.* • *The books are in my bedroom.* 2 at a place: *They live in Nottingham.*

3 at a particular time: *It's my birthday in May.*

4 after a period of time: *I'll be back in a few minutes.*

5 using a particular thing: *They were speaking in Japanese.* • *The letter was written in purple ink.*

6 wearing particular clothes: *Who's the woman in the red dress?*

• ADVERB• **1** at your home or place of work: *I'm sorry, Dad's not in. Can I take a message?* **2** at or into a place: *What time does your train get in?* • *Come in!*

inability • NOUN• the fact of not being able to do something

inaccuracy • NOUN• **inaccuracies** something that is not exact or correct: *a newspaper full of inaccuracies*

inaccurate • ADJECTIVE• not exact or correct: *inaccurate information*

inaction • NOUN• not doing anything
 • **inactive** • ADJECTIVE• **1** not doing anything **2** not working or not being used
 • **inactivity** • NOUN• the state of not doing anything

inadequacy • NOUN• **inadequacies** not being good enough or not being enough: *his inadequacy as a golfer*
 • **inadequate** • ADJECTIVE• if something is inadequate there is not enough of it or it is not good enough: *inadequate water supplies*

inadvertent • ADJECTIVE• done by mistake or by accident
 • **inadvertently** • ADVERB• by accident: *I had inadvertently left the door unlocked.*

inanimate • ADJECTIVE• not alive: *inanimate objects like chairs and books*

inappropriate • ADJECTIVE• not suitable for a particular situation or occasion: *inappropriate behaviour*
 • **inappropriateness** • NOUN• being inappropriate

inattention • NOUN• lack of attention
 • **inattentive** • ADJECTIVE• not paying attention: *Try not to be inattentive in class.*

inaugural • ADJECTIVE• marking the beginning of something important: *an inaugural speech to open the new school*

inaugurate • VERB• **inaugurates, inaugurating, inaugurated** to mark the beginning of something important with a ceremony
 • **inauguration** • NOUN• **inaugurations** a ceremony to mark the beginning of something important

incapable • ADJECTIVE• not able to do something: *He seemed incapable of understanding me.*
 • **incapability** • NOUN• being unable to do something

incapacity • NOUN• **1** lack of skill or ability **2** being ill or disabled

incense • NOUN• a substance that smells sweet when you burn it, often used in religious ceremonies

incentive • NOUN• **incentives** something that encourages you to do something

inch • NOUN• **inches** a unit of measurement that is equal to about 2.5 centimetres

incident • NOUN• **incidents** something that happens: *The incidents of the night before were still in my mind.*
 • **incidental** • ADJECTIVE• happening in connection with something else, but not intended or important
 • **incidentally** • ADVERB• you say incidently when you are talking about a new subject or adding some more information: *Incidentally, did you know Jack was getting married?*

incinerate • VERB• **incinerates, incinerating, incinerated** to burn something until it becomes ashes
 • **incinerator** • NOUN• **incinerators** a container for burning waste

incisor • NOUN• **incisors** one of the teeth at the front of your mouth that you use to cut food

incite • VERB• **incites, inciting, incited** to encourage people to cause trouble or fight
 • **incitement** • NOUN• encouraging people to cause trouble or fight

inclination • NOUN• **inclinations** a desire or tendency to do something: *He had no inclination to laugh now.*

incline • NOUN• **inclines** a slope

Aa
Bb
Cc
Dd
Ee
Ff
Gg
Hh
Ii
Jj
Kk
Ll
Mm
Nn
Oo
Pp
Qq
Rr
Ss
Tt
Uu
Vv
Ww
Xx
Yy
Zz

•VERB• **inclines, inclining, inclined** 1 if you are inclined to do something you feel like doing it or have a tendency to do it: *I was inclined to tell him exactly what I thought.* 2 to slope or lean: *He inclined his head towards mine.*

include •VERB• **includes, including, included** a person or thing is included when they are part of a larger group or amount: *Did you remember to include Andy?* • *The price of the ticket includes dinner.*
 • **including** •PREPOSITION• a word used to show that a person or thing is part of a larger group: *We went to all the museums, including the new one.*
 • **inclusion** •NOUN• the act of including someone or something or the fact they are included
 • **inclusive** •ADJECTIVE• including everything: *From Tuesday to Thursday inclusive is three days.*

income •NOUN• **incomes** the amount of money you earn

incomparable •ADJECTIVE• so good, beautiful etc that no one or nothing is better

incompatible •ADJECTIVE• 1 if people are incompatible, they are so different that they cannot have a good relationship 2 too different to exist or be used together: *The software is incompatible with the operating system.*
 • **incompatibility** •NOUN• being incompatible

incompetence •NOUN• being incompetent
 • **incompetent** •ADJECTIVE• not having the skill to do something, especially your job, very well

incomplete •ADJECTIVE• not finished or not having all the parts it should: *an incomplete painting*

incomprehensible •ADJECTIVE• impossible to understand

inconsiderate •ADJECTIVE• not thinking about other people's feelings

inconsistency •NOUN• **inconsistencies** 1 inconsistency is behaving or doing something differently each time 2 an inconsistency is something that cannot be

true if other information is true
 • **inconsistent** •ADJECTIVE• doing something in a different way each time
 • **inconsistently** •ADVERB• in an inconsistent way

inconsolable •ADJECTIVE• so upset that no one can comfort you

inconspicuous •ADJECTIVE• not easy to see

inconvenience •NOUN• **inconveniences** 1 inconvenience is difficulty or problems: *We apologize for any inconvenience caused.* 2 an inconvenience is something that causes problems for you
 •VERB• **inconveniences, inconveniencing, inconvenienced** to cause problems for someone
 • **inconvenient** •ADJECTIVE• causing problems: *Have I called at an inconvenient time?*

incorporate •VERB• **incorporates, incorporating, incorporated** to include something: *a television that incorporates all the latest features*

incorrect •ADJECTIVE• wrong: *The answers to the sums are incorrect.*
 • **incorrectly** •ADVERB• in a way that is wrong

increase •VERB• **increases, increasing, increased** 1 to increase is to become larger in size or amount: *Sales have increased over the last year.* 2 to increase something is to make it larger in size or amount: *My parents have increased my pocket money.*
 •NOUN• **increases** increasing or the amount by which something gets bigger: *There's been a big increase in the number of students in the school.*
 • **increasing** •ADJECTIVE• becoming larger in size or amount: *An increasing number of people have a computer in their house.*
 • **increasingly** •ADVERB• happening more or more often: *I am becoming increasingly angry at him.*

incredible •ADJECTIVE• difficult to believe: *an incredible story*
 • **incredibly** •ADVERB• used for saying that something is difficult to believe: *Incredibly, no one was injured.*

incriminate •VERB• **incriminates, incriminating, incriminated** to show that someone has taken part in a crime: *All the evidence incriminated her.*

incubate •VERB• **incubates, incubating, incubated** to hatch eggs by sitting on them
♦ **incubation** •NOUN• incubating eggs
♦ **incubator** •NOUN• **incubators** 1 a piece of hospital equipment that keeps a very small baby alive 2 a piece of equipment that keeps eggs warm until they hatch

incurable •ADJECTIVE• an incurable illness cannot be cured

indecency •NOUN• behaviour that shocks and offends people
♦ **indecent** •ADJECTIVE• shocking and offensive
♦ **indecently** •ADVERB• in an indecent way: *indecently dressed*

indeed •ADVERB• **indeed** is used to emphasize what you have just said: *He was driving very fast indeed.*

indefinite •ADJECTIVE• 1 not certain: *The competition will take place on an indefinite date.* 2 not having a fixed limit: *an indefinite amount of time*
⇒ **indefinitely**

indefinite article •NOUN• **indefinite articles** the name used in grammar for the words *a* and *an*

ⓘ There are two kinds of article in English grammar: **a** or **an** is the *indefinite article* and **the** is the *definite article*.

indefinitely •ADVERB• for a period of time with no fixed limits: *The match was postponed indefinitely.*

indelible •ADJECTIVE• impossible to remove or forget: *indelible ink*
♦ **indelibly** •ADVERB• in an indelible way: *The photograph is indelibly marked in my memory.*

indent •VERB• **indents, indenting, indented** to start a line of writing further from the edge of the page than other lines
♦ **indentation** •NOUN• **indentations** a hollow or dent

independence •NOUN• being independent

independent •ADJECTIVE• 1 an independent country is not controlled by another country 2 not relying on other people for help and support

indestructible •ADJECTIVE• impossible to destroy

index •NOUN• **indexes** *or* **indices** a list in a book that tells you what page you can find information on

ⓘ This is a Latin word which means both *forefinger* and *informer*. An index *informs* you where you can find something in a book.

index finger •NOUN• **index fingers** the finger that is next to your thumb

Indian summer •NOUN• **Indian summers** a period of warm weather in the autumn

indicate •VERB• **indicates, indicating, indicated** to show: *an arrow indicating where to go*
♦ **indication** •NOUN• **indications** a sign: *Did he give you any indication when it would be finished?*
♦ **indicative** •ADJECTIVE• if something is indicative of something else, it shows that it is likely to be true: *The footprints are indicative of life on the planet.*
♦ **indicator** •NOUN• **indicators** 1 a flashing light on a car that shows which way the car is going to turn 2 something that is a sign of something else

indifference •NOUN• a lack of interest in something
♦ **indifferent** •ADJECTIVE• 1 not good but not bad either: *The restaurant was nice but the food was indifferent.* 2 if you are indifferent to something, you show no interest in it or do not have any opinions on it

indigestion •NOUN• an uncomfortable feeling in your stomach after you have eaten

indignant •ADJECTIVE• angry because you think you have been treated unfairly: *The policeman stopped his indignant protests and led him off.*
♦ **indignantly** •ADVERB• in an indignant way
♦ **indignation** •NOUN• being indignant

indigo •NOUN• a dark purplish-blue colour

Aa
Bb
Cc
Dd
Ee
Ff
Gg
Hh
Ii
Jj
Kk
Ll
Mm
Nn
Oo
Pp
Qq
Rr
Ss
Tt
Uu
Vv
Ww
Xx
Yy
Zz

indirect • ADJECTIVE• 1 not leading straight to a place: *an indirect route* 2 not directly caused by something or related to something
 ✦ **indirectly** • ADVERB• in an indirect way

indirect speech • NOUN• reporting what someone said without repeating their actual words. Look up and compare **direct speech**

indiscreet • ADJECTIVE• careless in what you say or do, especially talking about something that should be secret

indispensable • ADJECTIVE• someone or something that is indispensable is so useful that you cannot manage without them or it

indistinct • ADJECTIVE• not easy to see, hear or remember

individual • ADJECTIVE• 1 for one person only: *Each child had an individual peg to put their coat on.* 2 considered separately from other things: *Put a price ticket on each individual item.*
 • NOUN• **individuals** one person rather than a group
 ✦ **individuality** • NOUN• a quality that makes someone or something different from others
 ✦ **individually** • ADVERB• separately from other things: *Wrap each cake individually.*

indoor • ADJECTIVE• inside a building: *an indoor swimming pool*
 ✦ **indoors** • ADVERB• inside a building: *Come indoors if it starts to rain.*

indulge • VERB• **indulges, indulging, indulged** 1 to indulge someone is to let them have or do what they want, especially something that is bad for them 2 to **indulge in** something is to allow yourself to do or have it: *We've all indulged in too much food.*
 ✦ **indulgence** • NOUN• indulging yourself or someone else
 ✦ **indulgent** • ADJECTIVE• letting someone do what they want even if it is not good for them

industrial • ADJECTIVE• relating to industry and factories: *an industrial area of town*
 ✦ **industrialize** or **industrialise** • VERB• **industrializes, industrializing, industrialized** to develop a lot of industry in a place

industrious • ADJECTIVE• working very hard: *an industrious pupil*

industry • NOUN• **industries** 1 industry is the production of goods, especially in a factory 2 an industry is a particular type of trade or production: *the steel industry*

inedible • ADJECTIVE• not good enough to eat

ineffective • ADJECTIVE• not achieving anything useful

inefficient • ADJECTIVE• not working well and wasting time or money: *an inefficient use of school funds*
 ✦ **inefficiency** • NOUN• **inefficiencies** being inefficient, or something that is inefficient
 ✦ **inefficiently** • ADVERB• in an inefficient way

ineligible • ADJECTIVE• not allowed to have or do something because of a rule or law: *You are ineligible to vote until you are 18.*

inept • ADJECTIVE• having or showing no skill: *an inept performance by the actors*

inequality • NOUN• **inequalities** a lack of equality

inevitable • ADJECTIVE• certain to happen: *It is inevitable that it will rain on sports day.*

inexcusable • ADJECTIVE• too bad to be excused

inexpensive • ADJECTIVE• cheap in price

inexperience • NOUN• a lack of experience or knowledge
 ✦ **inexperienced** • ADJECTIVE• not having much experience or knowledge

inexplicable • ADJECTIVE• impossible to explain: *an inexplicable wish to go out in the rain*

infamous • ADJECTIVE• well-known for something bad
 ✦ **infamy** • NOUN• being well-known for something bad: *Dick Turpin was an infamous highwayman.*

infancy • NOUN• the time when someone is a baby or very young child
 ✦ **infant** • NOUN• **infants** a baby or very young child
 ✦ **infantile** • ADJECTIVE• 1 to do with babies or very young children 2 infantile behaviour is very silly

(i) **Infant** came into English from the French word **enfant**, which means *child*. This in turn came from the Latin word **infans**, which means 'not able to speak'.

infantry •NOUN• soldiers who fight on foot

infect •VERB• infects, infecting, infected to give someone or something an illness or germs: *The wound was newly infected.* • *I am afraid I may infect you with my cold.*
  ✦ **infection** •NOUN• infections 1 infection is taking in germs 2 an infection is an illness: *an ear infection*
  ✦ **infectious** •ADJECTIVE• 1 an infectious illness can be spread from person to person 2 an infectious feeling or action is one that other people cannot help doing: *infectious laughter*

infer •VERB• infers, inferring, inferred to form an opinion from information you already know

inferior •ADJECTIVE• not as good as someone or something else: *Amy often felt inferior to the other children in her class.*
  ✦ **inferiority** •NOUN• being inferior to someone or something else

inferno •NOUN• infernos a large and dangerous fire

infested •ADJECTIVE• full of insects or other pests: *The whole house was infested with mice.*

infidelity •NOUN• infidelities not being faithful to someone

infinite •ADJECTIVE• without any limits or end: *The universe is infinite.*
  ✦ **infinitely** •ADVERB• very much: *This computer is infinitely better than the last one.*
  ⇒ **infinity**

infinitive •NOUN• infinitives the basic form of a verb that can be used to make all the other forms, for example *to play* or *to eat*

infinity •NOUN• space or time without an end or limit

infirm •ADJECTIVE• weak, especially because of old age or illness
  ✦ **infirmary** •NOUN• infirmaries a hospital
  ✦ **infirmity** •NOUN• infirmities a weakness

inflamed •ADJECTIVE• red and swollen because of an infection
  ⇒ **inflammation**

inflammable •ADJECTIVE• easy to set on fire: *Paper is highly inflammable.*

inflammation •NOUN• swelling, pain and redness in part of your body

inflate •VERB• inflates, inflating, inflated to fill something with air: *The tyres need to be inflated.*
  ✦ **inflation** •NOUN• 1 filling something with air 2 when prices and wages increase

inflect •VERB• inflects, inflecting, inflected 1 when a word inflects, it changes its ending 2 to change the tone of your voice
  ✦ **inflection** •NOUN• inflections 1 a change in the form of a word to show its tense or number 2 a word that has been changed in this way. For example, *finds, finding* and *found* are inflections of the verb *find* 3 changing the tone of your voice

inflexible •ADJECTIVE• 1 stiff and unable to bend: *inflexible plastic* 2 impossible or unwilling to change

inflict •VERB• inflicts, inflicting, inflicted to make someone suffer something unpleasant or painful: *The home team inflicted a heavy defeat on the visitors.*

influence •NOUN• influences 1 influence is the power to affect other people or things: *a teacher who has a lot of influence on his pupils* 2 an influence is someone or something that has an effect on other people or things: *Ann is a good influence on you.*
  •VERB• influences, influencing, influenced to have an effect on someone or something: *His advice influenced my decision.*
  ✦ **influential** •ADJECTIVE• having a lot of influence

influenza •NOUN• a formal word for **flu**

influx •NOUN• influxes the arrival of a lot of people or things

info •NOUN• an informal short form of the word **information**

inform •VERB• informs, informing, informed to tell someone about something: *I'll inform you what my decision is.*
  ⇒ **information**

informal → initiate

informal • ADJECTIVE• **1** relaxed and friendly, or suitable for relaxed occasions **2** informal language and words might be used when you are speaking to your friends, but they are not as suitable for writing.

information • NOUN• knowledge, facts or details: *Have you got any information on things to do in the area?*
 ✦ **informative** • ADJECTIVE• giving you a lot of useful information: *an informative book*
 ✦ **informer** • NOUN• **informers** someone who gives information to the police in return for money

information technology • NOUN• the study or use of computers for dealing with information

ⓘ The abbreviation of information technology is **IT**.

infra-red • ADJECTIVE• infra-red light cannot be seen, but gives out heat

infrequent • ADJECTIVE• not happening very often
 ✦ **infrequently** • ADVERB• not often

infuriate • VERB• **infuriates, infuriating, infuriated** to make someone very angry
 ✦ **infuriated** • ADJECTIVE• extremely angry
 ✦ **infuriating** • ADJECTIVE• making you extremely angry

ingenious • ADJECTIVE• clever and having new ideas: *an ingenious idea* • *He's very ingenious.*
 ✦ **ingenuity** • NOUN• being ingenious

ingot • NOUN• **ingots** a block of metal, especially gold or silver

ingratitude • NOUN• being ungrateful

ingredient • NOUN• **ingredients** one of the things you use to make a particular food

ingrown or **ingrowing** • ADJECTIVE• an ingrown nail is growing into your skin

inhabit • VERB• **inhabits, inhabiting, inhabited** to live in a particular place: *the world around us and the creatures that inhabit it*
 ✦ **inhabitant** • NOUN• **inhabitants** someone who lives in a place: *There are differences between the inhabitants of the two islands.*
 ✦ **inhabited** • ADJECTIVE• with people living

there: *A light twinkled in one of the windows, so I knew the place was inhabited.*

inhale • VERB• **inhales, inhaling, inhaled** to breathe air into your lungs through your nose and mouth. Look up and compare **exhale**
 ✦ **inhaler** • NOUN• **inhalers** a piece of equipment for breathing in medicine or steam
 ✦ **inhalation** • NOUN• breathing in

inherit • VERB• **inherits, inheriting, inherited 1** to get money or other things from someone who has died **2** to get a particular characteristic from one of your parents: *I inherited my fair hair from my mother.*
 ✦ **inheritance** • NOUN• **inheritances** money or things that you get from someone who has died

inhibit • VERB• **inhibits, inhibiting, inhibited** to prevent someone or something from doing something: *My shyness inhibits me from speaking in public.*
 ✦ **inhibited** • ADJECTIVE• not feeling relaxed or confident enough to do or say what you want
 ✦ **inhibition** • NOUN• **inhibitions** a feeling of worry or shyness that stops you doing or saying what you want

inhuman • ADJECTIVE• extremely cruel
 ✦ **inhumanity** • NOUN• **inhumanities** cruel behaviour

initial • ADJECTIVE• at the beginning: *initial difficulties*
 • NOUN• **initials** the first letter of someone's name
 ✦ **initially** • ADVERB• at first: *Initially, things were very difficult.*

initiate • VERB• **initiates, initiating, initiated 1** to start something: *He initiated a scheme to help old people with their shopping.* **2** to accept someone into a group or organization with a secret or special ceremony
 ✦ **initiation** • NOUN• **initiations 1** initiating something or someone **2** an initiation is a special ceremony to make someone a member of a group
 ✦ **initiative** • NOUN• **initiatives 1** initiative is the ability to do something without waiting

Aa Bb Cc Dd Ee Ff Gg Hh Ii Jj Kk Ll Mm Nn Oo Pp Qq Rr Ss Tt Uu Vv Ww Xx Yy Zz

for someone else to tell you what to do **2** an initiative is a new plan or process

inject •VERB• **injects, injecting, injected**
1 to put a substance into someone's body using a needle **2** to improve something by adding a particular quality to it: *The teacher tried to inject some enthusiasm into her students.*
♦ **injection** •NOUN• **injections** putting a substance into someone's body using a needle

injure •VERB• **injures, injuring, injured** to hurt someone or something: *He injured his knee in a skiing accident.*
♦ **injured** •ADJECTIVE• hurt: *He was badly injured in a road accident.*
♦ **injury** •NOUN• **injuries** a wound or damage to part of your body: *head injuries*

injustice •NOUN• **injustices 1** injustice is when people are treated unfairly **2** an injustice is an action that is unfair

ink •NOUN• **inks** a black or coloured liquid used for writing or printing
♦ **inky** •ADJECTIVE• covered in ink

inland •ADJECTIVE• not by the sea •ADVERB• in a direction away from the sea

-in-law •SUFFIX• when **-in-law** is added to a word, it means that person is a relative of your husband or wife. For example, your *mother-in-law* is your husband's or wife's mother

in-laws •PLURAL NOUN• the relatives of your husband or wife

inlet •NOUN• **inlets** a small area of water that comes into the land

inmate •NOUN• **inmates** someone who is being kept in a prison

inn •NOUN• **inns** a small hotel in the country

innards •PLURAL NOUN• the parts inside a person, animal or machine

inner •ADJECTIVE• **1** on the inside or close to the centre of something: *She kept her purse in the inner pocket of her bag.* **2** inner feelings are ones that you keep secret

innermost •ADJECTIVE• your innermost thoughts and feelings are ones that you keep secret

innings •NOUN• one team's turn at batting in cricket

innocence •NOUN• **1** when someone is not guilty of a crime: *The witnesses' stories proved his innocence.* **2** when someone does not have much experience of life and how cruel people can be: *The bully took advantage of Billy's innocence.*
♦ **innocent** •ADJECTIVE• **1** not guilty of a crime **2** not having much experience of life and how cruel people can be
♦ **innocently** •ADVERB• in an innocent way: *I acted quite innocently in front of my mother.*

inoculate •VERB• **inoculates, inoculating, inoculated** to inject someone with a substance to stop them getting a disease
♦ **inoculation** •NOUN• **inoculations** inoculating someone

inoffensive •ADJECTIVE• not likely to offend or upset anyone

in-patient •NOUN• **in-patients** someone who is staying in a hospital for treatment

input •NOUN• **1** energy or ideas that you put into something: *I had very little input in the project.* **2** information that is put into a computer

inquest •NOUN• **inquests** a legal process to find out how someone died

inquire or **enquire** •VERB• **inquires, inquiring, inquired** or **enquires, enquiring, enquired** to ask: *He inquired how to get to the library.*
♦ **inquiry** or **enquiry** •NOUN• **inquiries** or **enquiries 1** a question you ask in order to get information **2** an official process to find out why something happened: *There was an inquiry into the children's deaths.*

inquisitive •ADJECTIVE• interested in a lot of things and wanting to know more: *an inquisitive child*
♦ **inquisitively** •ADVERB• in an inquisitive way

insane •ADJECTIVE• **1** if someone is insane, they are out of their mind or mad **2** if an action is insane it is extremely foolish: *It is insane to run across the road without looking.*
♦ **insanity** •NOUN• being mad

Aa
Bb
Cc
Dd
Ee
Ff
Gg
Hh
Ii
Jj
Kk
Ll
Mm
Nn
Oo
Pp
Qq
Rr
Ss
Tt
Uu
Vv
Ww
Xx
Yy
Zz

Aa
Bb
Cc
Dd
Ee
Ff
Gg
Hh
Ii
Jj
Kk
Ll
Mm
Nn
Oo
Pp
Qq
Rr
Ss
Tt
Uu
Vv
Ww
Xx
Yy
Zz

an insect

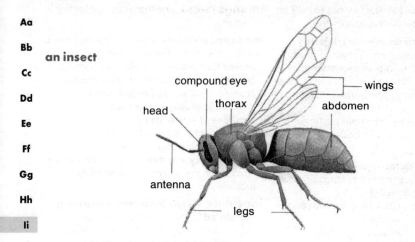

compound eye

head

thorax

wings

abdomen

antenna

legs

inscribe •VERB• **inscribes, inscribing, inscribed** to cut or write words on the surface of something
  ◆ **inscription** •NOUN• **inscriptions** writing on a piece of stone or in the front of a book: *There was an inscription on the gravestone.*

insect •NOUN• **insects** a very small creature with six legs, such as an ant or wasp.

insecure •ADJECTIVE• **1** not safe or firm: *The bridge is insecure.* **2** not feeling confident about your abilities or relationships
  ◆ **insecurity** •NOUN• being insecure

insensitive •ADJECTIVE• **1** not noticing other people's feelings **2** not affected by physical things such as pain or cold: *He seemed to be insensitive to the noise around him.*
  ◆ **insensitively** •ADVERB• in an insensitive way
  ◆ **insensitivity** •NOUN• being insensitive

inseparable •ADJECTIVE• not able to be separated or kept apart: *The two boys are inseparable.*

insert •VERB• **inserts, inserting, inserted** to put something into something else: *He inserted some coins in the meter.* • *You need to insert a few more examples.*

inside •PREPOSITION• in or into something: *She put the book inside her bag.*

• ADVERB• into something: *Come inside, it's raining.*
• ADJECTIVE• in or facing the middle of something rather than outside: *the inside walls of the house*
• NOUN• **insides** the inside of something is the part that is in the middle and not on the outside: *The inside of his jacket was torn.*

insight •NOUN• **insights** an ability to understand something clearly

insignificant •ADJECTIVE• not at all important

insincere •ADJECTIVE• pretending to have a feeling that you do not really have: *insincere laughter*
  ◆ **insincerely** •ADVERB• in an insincere way
  ◆ **insincerity** •NOUN• being insincere

insist •VERB• **insists, insisting, insisted** **1** to say that something must happen or be done: *He insisted on paying.* **2** to keep saying in a firm way that you think something is true: *Mark insists that he hasn't done anything wrong.*
  ◆ **insistent** •ADJECTIVE• saying that something must happen or be done: *She was insistent that we visit her.*

insolence •NOUN• speaking without politeness or respect
  ◆ **insolent** •ADJECTIVE• rude and impolite

insoluble •ADJECTIVE• **1** an insoluble

substance cannot dissolve **2** impossible to solve
◆ **insolubility** •NOUN• being insoluble

insomnia •NOUN• not being able to sleep

inspect •VERB• **inspects, inspecting, inspected 1** to look very carefully at someone or something **2** to officially visit somewhere to make sure that it is being run properly
◆ **inspection** •NOUN• **inspections 1** inspection is looking very carefully at someone or something **2** an inspection is an examination or a visit by an inspector to check something
◆ **inspector** •NOUN• **inspectors 1** someone whose job is to inspect a place such as a school or restaurant to make sure it is run properly **2** a rank of police officer above a sergeant

inspiration •NOUN• **inspirations** someone or something that encourages someone and gives them new ideas
◆ **inspirational** •ADJECTIVE• encouraging someone and giving them new ideas

inspire •VERB• **inspires, inspiring, inspired** to encourage someone by giving them confidence and new ideas: *My mother inspired me to write stories.*
◆ **inspired** •ADJECTIVE• having a lot of special qualities: *an inspired performance*

install or **instal** •VERB• **installs** or **instals, installing, installed 1** to put a piece of equipment in place and make it ready to use: *We're installing a new computer system.* **2** to put someone in an important job or position
◆ **installation** •NOUN• installing someone or something
◆ **instalment** •NOUN• **instalments 1** one of a number of payments that you make to pay for something **2** one part of a long story that is told in a magazine or on television

instance •NOUN• **instances** an example of a situation: *an instance of John's quick thinking*
• **for instance** for example: *Some birds, penguins for instance, cannot fly at all.*

instant •ADJECTIVE• **1** happening at once: *The film was an instant success.* **2** able to be prepared very quickly: *instant coffee*

◆ **instantaneous** •ADJECTIVE• done or happening immediately or very quickly
◆ **instantly** •ADVERB• immediately

instead •ADVERB• in place of someone or something else: *Ben was ill so John went instead.* • *You could use a pencil instead of a pen.*

instep •NOUN• **insteps** the bottom of your foot where it curves upwards

instinct •NOUN• **instincts** a natural feeling or knowledge that you have without being taught
◆ **instinctive** •ADJECTIVE• happening because of instinct: *Parents have an instinctive urge to protect their children.*
◆ **instinctively** •ADVERB• in an instinctive way: *I knew instinctively that something was wrong.*

institute •NOUN• **institutes** an organization of people who want to study something, or the building they use
◆ **institution** •NOUN• **institutions** a large organization: *banks and other financial institutions*

instruct •VERB• **instructs, instructing, instructed 1** to tell someone what to do **2** to teach someone
◆ **instruction** •NOUN• **instructions** a piece of information that tells you how to do something: *Read the instructions before you begin.*
◆ **instructive** •ADJECTIVE• providing a lot of useful information

instrument •NOUN• **instruments 1** something used for making music **2** a tool for doing something
◆ **instrumental** •ADJECTIVE• **1** instrumental music is written for musical instruments rather than singers **2** helpful in making something happen

insufficiency •NOUN• when there is not enough of something
◆ **insufficient** •ADJECTIVE• not enough: *insufficient food supplies*

insulate •VERB• **insulates, insulating, insulated** to cover something with a material that does not let electricity, heat or frost through
◆ **insulation** •NOUN• insulating something,

Aa
Bb
Cc
Dd
Ee
Ff
Gg
Hh
Ii
Jj
Kk
Ll
Mm
Nn
Oo
Pp
Qq
Rr
Ss
Tt
Uu
Vv
Ww
Xx
Yy
Zz

or the material used to do this

insult •VERB• **insults, insulting, insulted** to insult someone is to say something rude to them
•NOUN• **insults** a rude remark
♦ **insulting** •ADJECTIVE• very rude to someone

ⓘ The verb, in-**sult**, is said with the stress on *sult*.
The noun, **in**-sult, is said with the stress on *in*.

insurance •NOUN• an arrangement in which you pay a company money each year and they pay the costs if something you own is damaged or stolen: *car insurance*

insure •VERB• **insures, insuring, insured** to pay money to a company who will pay the costs if you are injured or if things you own are damaged or stolen

ⓘ Do not confuse **insure** with **ensure**, which means 'to make sure'.

intact •ADJECTIVE• not broken or damaged

intake •NOUN• **intakes** the amount of people or things taken in: *this year's intake of students at the school*

integer •NOUN• **integers** a whole number, not a fraction. An integer can also be 0 or a negative number such as *-1* or *-2*

integral •ADJECTIVE• forming an essential part of something: *Games are an integral part of life at school.*

integrate •VERB• **integrates, integrating, integrated** 1 to combine two or more things together to make a system 2 to mix with other groups of people
♦ **integration** •NOUN• integrating people or things

integrity •NOUN• being honest and having high moral standards

intellect •NOUN• **intellects** your ability to think about things and understand them
♦ **intellectual** •ADJECTIVE• relating to your intellect
•NOUN• **intellectuals** someone who is intelligent and likes thinking about serious issues

intelligence •NOUN• 1 your ability to learn and understand things 2 secret information about other countries
♦ **intelligent** •ADJECTIVE• clever and able to understand things quickly

intend •VERB• **intends, intending, intended** to plan to do something: *I intend to visit Will when I'm in Seattle.*
⇒ **intent**

intense •ADJECTIVE• very great: *intense heat*
♦ **intensify** •VERB• **intensifies, intensifying, intensified** 1 to intensify is to increase and become greater: *The darkness intensified.* 2 to intensify something is to make it increase and become greater: *I intensified my effort to finish on time.*
♦ **intensity** •NOUN• the strength of something, such as a feeling or colour
♦ **intensive** •ADJECTIVE• involving a lot of effort or activity
♦ **intensively** •ADVERB• in an intensive way: *I studied intensively for the test.*

intent •NOUN• purpose or intention: *It was her intent to become a doctor.*
•ADJECTIVE• 1 if you are intent on doing something, you are determined to do it 2 doing something with a lot of attention and concentration: *an intent stare*
♦ **intention** •NOUN• **intentions** the thing you plan to do: *It is my intention to finish before 5 o'clock.*
♦ **intentional** •ADJECTIVE• done deliberately
♦ **intentionally** •ADVERB• deliberately: *You tripped me up intentionally!*
♦ **intently** •ADVERB• with a lot of attention and concentration

inter- •PREFIX• if a word starts with **inter-** it means *between* or *among* a group of people or things. For example, *international* means 'among a number of nations'

interact •VERB• **interacts, interacting, interacted** 1 to talk to other people and do things with them 2 if two things interact, they have an effect on each other
♦ **interactive** •ADJECTIVE• involving communication between two people or things, for example a person and a computer

intercept •VERB• **intercepts, intercepting, intercepted** to stop something that is going from one place to another

intercom •NOUN• **intercoms** a system that allows you to talk to people who are in a different part of a building

interest •NOUN• **interests** 1 a feeling that makes you think something is good and want to find out more about it: *I have no interest in cricket.*
2 something that you enjoy doing: *My main interests are sport and reading.*
3 extra money that you have to pay back when you have borrowed money, or that a bank puts into your account regularly
•VERB• **interests, interesting, interested** if something interests you, you think it is good and want to find out more about it
♦ **interested** •ADJECTIVE• having or showing interest: *Dan is very interested in old cars.*
♦ **interesting** •ADJECTIVE• making you feel interested: *an interesting story*

interface •NOUN• **interfaces** something that helps a computer program work with another program

interfere •VERB• **interferes, interfering, interfered** 1 to get involved in a situation where you are not wanted 2 if something **interferes with** something, it prevents it from happening: *His visit interfered with my plans to go out.*
♦ **interference** •NOUN• interfering with something

interior •NOUN• **interiors** the interior of something is the inside of it: *the interior of a house*
•ADJECTIVE• on the inside of something

interjection •PART OF SPEECH• **interjections** a word or phrase used to express a strong feeling like surprise, shock or anger. For example, *Oh!* and *Hooray!* are interjections

interlude •NOUN• **interludes** a short pause or interval

intermediate •ADJECTIVE• if something is intermediate, it is or takes place between two other stages or levels

intermission •NOUN• **intermissions** a short break in the middle of a play or concert

intermittent •ADJECTIVE• starting and stopping again and again: *intermittent rain showers*

internal •ADJECTIVE• 1 on the inside of something, especially your body: *internal injuries* 2 within an organization or country

international •ADJECTIVE• for or involving several countries: *an international sports competition*

Internet •NOUN• the Internet is a computer network that allows people around the world to share information

interpret •VERB• **interprets, interpreting, interpreted** 1 to translate what somebody is saying from one language to another 2 to think that something has a particular meaning: *I interpreted his quietness as shyness.*
♦ **interpreter** •NOUN• **interpreters** someone whose job is to translate what someone says into another language
♦ **interpretation** •NOUN• **interpretations** interpreting or a way of interpreting something: *What is your interpretation of the poem?*

interrogate •VERB• **interrogates, interrogating, interrogated** to ask someone a lot of questions in order to get information
♦ **interrogation** •NOUN• interrogating someone
♦ **interrogator** •NOUN• **interrogators** someone who is interrogating another person

interrupt •VERB• **interrupts, interrupting, interrupted** 1 to stop someone in the middle of saying or doing something: *I'm sorry to interrupt, but what time do we have to leave?* 2 to stop a process or activity for a short time: *He interrupted the meeting to make a phone call.*
♦ **interruption** •NOUN• **interruptions** interrupting someone or something: *Interruptions when you're trying to study are annoying.*

intersect •VERB• **intersects, intersecting, intersected** if lines or roads intersect, they cross each other
♦ **intersection** •NOUN• **intersections** a place where lines or roads cross each other

Aa
Bb
Cc
Dd
Ee
Ff
Gg
Hh
Ii
Jj
Kk
Ll
Mm
Nn
Oo
Pp
Qq
Rr
Ss
Tt
Uu
Vv
Ww
Xx
Yy
Zz

Aa
Bb
Cc
Dd
Ee
Ff
Gg
Hh
Ii
Jj
Kk
Ll
Mm
Nn
Oo
Pp
Qq
Rr
Ss
Tt
Uu
Vv
Ww
Xx
Yy
Zz

interval •NOUN• **intervals** 1 a short break in the middle of a play, concert or lessons 2 a period of time between two things

intervene •VERB• **intervenes, intervening, intervened** to do something to try to stop an argument or fight between other people or countries
♦ **intervention** •NOUN• intervening in something

interview •NOUN• **interviews** 1 a meeting when someone asks you questions to see if you are suitable for a job 2 a meeting when someone asks a famous person questions
•VERB• **interviews, interviewing, interviewed** to ask someone questions at an interview
♦ **interviewer** •NOUN• **interviewers** the person who asks the questions at an interview

intestines •PLURAL NOUN• the long tubes that take food from your stomach out of your body

intimate •ADJECTIVE• 1 having a very close relationship with someone: *intimate friends* 2 relating to private and personal things: *intimate details* 3 an intimate knowledge of something is a very good and detailed knowledge

intimidate •VERB• **intimidates, intimidating, intimidated** to frighten someone, especially by threatening them
♦ **intimidating** •ADJECTIVE• making you feel worried and less confident: *The test paper was intimidating.*
♦ **intimidation** •NOUN• intimidating someone

into •PREPOSITION• 1 so as to be inside something: *We went into the house.* 2 used for saying how something changes: *She cut the cake into four pieces.* • *The caterpillar changed into a butterfly.* 3 used when talking about dividing one number by another: *2 into 4 goes twice.*

intolerable •ADJECTIVE• too difficult or bad for you to be able to deal with or put up with
♦ **intolerably** •ADVERB• in an intolerable way: *It is intolerably hot in here.*

intolerance •NOUN• being intolerant
♦ **intolerant** •ADJECTIVE• not willing to accept behaviour and ideas that are different from your own

intonation •NOUN• the way that your voice rises and falls when you speak

intricate •ADJECTIVE• containing a lot of small parts or details: *an intricate pattern*

intrigue •VERB• **intrigues, intriguing, intrigued** to make someone feel very interested or curious
•NOUN• **intrigues** a secret plan or the process of planning this
♦ **intriguing** •ADJECTIVE• very interesting and unusual

introduce •VERB• **introduces, introducing, introduced** 1 if you introduce two people who do not know each other, you tell each of them the other person's name 2 to make something start to happen or be used: *The new law was introduced in 1999.*
♦ **introduction** •NOUN• **introductions** 1 bringing in something new for the first time 2 an introduction is a piece of writing at the front of a book that tells you what the book is about
♦ **introductory** •ADJECTIVE• coming at the beginning

introvert *or* **intravert** •NOUN• **introverts** *or* **intraverts** someone who has a quiet and thoughtful personality. Look up and compare **extrovert**

intrude •VERB• **intrudes, intruding, intruded** 1 to become involved in a situation where you are not wanted 2 to enter a place where you should not be
♦ **intruder** •NOUN• **intruders** someone who enters a place where they should not be
♦ **intrusion** •NOUN• **intrusions** someone or something that is not wanted in a situation
♦ **intrusive** •ADJECTIVE• affecting or interrupting you in a way you do not want: *intrusive questions*

intuition •NOUN• **intuitions** 1 intuition is an ability to understand or know something without thinking or being told about it 2 an intuition is an idea that something is true based on your feelings rather than facts

invade •VERB• **invades, invading, invaded**

Inverted commas

Inverted commas are also called **speech marks** and **quotation marks**. They look like this **' '** or this **" "**. They are used in writing to show when someone is talking.

Inverted commas are put at the beginning and the end of the actual words someone speaks.

'I've been bitten by a snake,' said Joe.

If you do not need to say who has spoken the words, you can end the words with a full stop, a question mark or an exclamation mark. The inverted commas at the end go after the full stop, question mark or exclamation mark.

'Won't it get dark soon?'

If you are going to say who has spoken the words, end the spoken words with a comma (or a question mark or an exclamation mark if it was a question or exclamation). The inverted commas go after this.

'Oh, no! I've lost my door keys,' said Fred.
'What are we going to do?' Ann asked.
'Don't worry, I've found them!' Fred exclaimed.

---

to enter a country with an army to attack it or take it over

◆ **invader** • NOUN• **invaders** someone who invades another country

⇒ **invasion**

invalid [1] • ADJECTIVE• not able to be used: *an invalid bus pass* • *invalid reasons for being late*

invalid [2] • NOUN• **invalids** someone who is ill or unable to look after themselves

ⓘ The adjective **invalid** is pronounced in-**va**-lid, with the stress on *va*. The noun **invalid** is pronounced **in**-va-lid, with the stress on *in*.

invaluable • ADJECTIVE• extremely useful: *an invaluable piece of advice*

invariably • ADVERB• always: *Dean is invariably late for school.*

invasion • NOUN• **invasions** an attack on a country by an army entering it

invent • VERB• **invents, inventing, invented** 1 to design or make something that no one else has ever made: *Thomas Edison invented the electric light bulb.* 2 to think of a story or excuse that is not true

◆ **invention** • NOUN• **inventions** something someone has invented

◆ **inventive** • ADJECTIVE• good at thinking of new and interesting ideas

◆ **inventor** • NOUN• **inventors** someone who has invented something new

inverse • NOUN• **inverses** the inverse of something is its opposite
• ADJECTIVE• opposite

◆ **inversely** • ADVERB• in the opposite way

◆ **invert** • VERB• **inverts, inverting, inverted** to turn something upside down

◆ **inverted** • ADJECTIVE• turned upside down

invertebrate • NOUN• **invertebrates** an animal that does not have a backbone, for example an insect or worm

inverted commas • PLURAL NOUN• the symbols ' ' or " ", used in writing to show what someone says. They are sometimes called **quotation marks**. See the box called **Inverted commas**

invest • VERB• **invests, investing, invested** to put money in a bank or business in order to make more money: *I invested my money in a savings account.*

Aa Bb Cc Dd Ee Ff Gg Hh Ii Jj Kk Ll Mm Nn Oo Pp Qq Rr Ss Tt Uu Vv Ww Xx Yy Zz

♦ **investment** •NOUN• **investments**
1 investing money 2 an investment is something you buy because you think it will be useful or make a profit for you: *A warm coat is a good investment.*

♦ **investor** •NOUN• **investors** someone who invests money in something

investigate •VERB• **investigates, investigating, investigated** to try to find out the truth about something: *Police are investigating the crime.*

♦ **investigation** •NOUN• **investigations** a search for information about something: *a police investigation into the murder*

♦ **investigator** •NOUN• **investigators** someone who is investigating something

invigorating •ADJECTIVE• making you feel full of energy

invincible •ADJECTIVE• impossible to defeat

♦ **invincibility** •NOUN• being impossible to defeat

invisible •ADJECTIVE• impossible to see

♦ **invisibility** •NOUN• being impossible to see

invitation •NOUN• **invitations** an offer that asks if you would like to do something or go somewhere: *I've had an invitation to Helen's birthday party.*

invite •VERB• **invites, inviting, invited** to ask someone if they would like to do something or go somewhere: *Clare's invited me for tea at her house.*

♦ **inviting** •ADJECTIVE• very attractive and making you want to do something

invoice •NOUN• **invoices** a piece of paper sent with things you have bought, to tell you how much you must pay
•VERB• **invoices, invoicing, invoiced** to send someone an invoice

involuntary •ADJECTIVE• happening without your control: *Sneezing is an involuntary action.*

involve •VERB• **involves, involving, involved**
1 to have something as a necessary part: *The job will involve a lot of travelling.* 2 if you are involved in something, you take part in it: *I don't want to get involved in your argument.*

♦ **involvement** •NOUN• being involved in something

inward •ADJECTIVE• 1 inside or towards the inside of something 2 inward feelings are ones in your mind that you do not tell other people about

♦ **inwardly** •ADVERB• in your own mind but not told or shown to other people: *Inwardly, she felt very scared.*

♦ **inwards** •ADVERB• towards the inside of something

ion •NOUN• **ions** an atom with an electrical charge

IOU •ABBREVIATION• short for **I owe you**. An IOU is a note that you sign to say that you owe someone money

IQ •ABBREVIATION• short for **intelligence quotient**. Someone's IQ is a measure of how intelligent they are

ir- •PREFIX• if a word starts with **ir-**, it means 'not'. For example, *irregular* means 'not regular'

irate •ADJECTIVE• extremely angry

iris •NOUN• **irises** 1 the coloured part of your eye 2 a tall flower

iron •NOUN• **irons** 1 a hard metal used for making tools 2 a piece of electrical equipment that you use for pressing the creases out of clothes
•VERB• **irons, ironing, ironed** to make clothes smooth using an iron

ironic •ADJECTIVE• 1 an ironic situation is funny in a strange way: *It's ironic that we're moving to Edinburgh just as they're leaving it.* 2 saying the opposite of what you really mean: *I think he was being ironic when he said this was the happiest day of his life.*

♦ **ironically** •ADVERB• in a way that is ironic

ironmonger •NOUN• **ironmongers**
1 someone who sells items such as tools and garden equipment 2 an ironmonger's is a shop selling items such as tools and garden equipment

irony •NOUN• **ironies** 1 irony is using words that are the opposite of what you really mean in order to be funny 2 an irony is a situation that is strange or funny
⇒ **ironic**

irregular • ADJECTIVE• 1 having a shape that is not even or smooth: *a skirt with an irregular hem*
2 happening at different times so there is no pattern: *an irregular train service*
3 not obeying the usual rules: *irregular behaviour*
 • **irregularity** • NOUN• **irregularities** 1 being irregular 2 an irregularity is something that breaks a rule: *irregularities in John's behaviour*
 • **irregularly** • ADVERB• in an irregular way

irrelevance • NOUN• **irrelevances** 1 irrelevance is when something is not important in a situation 2 an irrelevance is someone or something that is not important in a situation: *His recent injury seemed an irrelevance when he won the race.*
 • **irrelevant** • ADJECTIVE• not important in a situation: *Your comments are irrelevant to this discussion.*

irreplaceable • ADJECTIVE• too special or valuable to be replaced

irresistible • ADJECTIVE• too strong or attractive to resist: *The chocolate cake looked irresistible.*

irresponsible • ADJECTIVE• behaving in a silly way without thinking about bad things that might happen
 • **irresponsibility** • NOUN• irresponsible behaviour
 • **irresponsibly** • ADVERB• in an irresponsible way

irrigate • VERB• **irrigates, irrigating, irrigated** to supply land or crops with water
 • **irrigation** • NOUN• supplying land or crops with water

irritable • ADJECTIVE• becoming annoyed very easily: *Jamal is irritable if he does not get enough sleep.*
 • **irritability** • NOUN• being irritable
 • **irritably** • ADVERB• in an irritable way

irritate • VERB• **irritates, irritating, irritated** 1 to make someone feel annoyed 2 to make something such as your skin or eyes sore or itchy: *Some sun creams can irritate your skin.*
 • **irritation** • NOUN• **irritations** 1 irritation is feeling annoyed about something

2 an irritation is something that annoys you: *His constant complaints are an irritation.*
3 a sore feeling on your skin or in your eyes

is • VERB• 1 the form of the verb **be** in the present tense that you use with **he**, **she** or **it**: *He is a fool.* • *It is raining.* 2 **is** is also used as a helping verb along with a main verb: *Lisa's mother is going away for a month.*

-ish • SUFFIX• if a word ends in **-ish**, it means 'slightly'. For example, *greenish* means 'slightly green'

Islam • NOUN• the Muslim religion that was started by Mohammed
 • **Islamic** • ADJECTIVE• relating to the religion of Islam

island • NOUN• **islands** an area of land surrounded by sea

isle • NOUN• **isles** an island. **Isle** is used in poems or in the names of islands: *the Scilly Isles*

-ism • SUFFIX• if a word ends with **-ism**, it has something to do with a belief, principle or quality. For example, *Buddhism* is the religion started by Buddha

isn't • SHORT FORM• a short way to say and write **is not**: *It isn't raining.*

isolate • VERB• **isolates, isolating, isolated** to separate or keep someone or something separate from others: *The infected animals were isolated in a field.*
 • **isolated** • ADJECTIVE• 1 feeling alone and unable to meet other people
2 a long way from anywhere else: *an isolated farmhouse*
3 happening only once and not related to other events: *This theft was an isolated incident.*
 • **isolation** • NOUN• being isolated

isosceles triangle • NOUN• **isosceles triangles** a triangle that has two sides of the same length

issue • NOUN• **issues** 1 a subject that people discuss: *a discussion on the issue of education* 2 a newspaper or magazine that is one of a number printed and sold at the same time: *Have you seen this week's issue of the magazine?*

Aa
Bb
Cc
Dd
Ee
Ff
Gg
Hh
Ii
Jj
Kk
Ll
Mm
Nn
Oo
Pp
Qq
Rr
Ss
Tt
Uu
Vv
Ww
Xx
Yy
Zz

Aa

Bb

Cc

Dd

Ee

Ff

Gg

Hh

Ii

Jj

Kk

Ll

Mm

Nn

Oo

Pp

Qq

Rr

Ss

Tt

Uu

Vv

Ww

Xx

Yy

Zz

•VERB• **issues, issuing, issued** to supply someone with something: *We were all issued with pens.*

-ist •SUFFIX• if a word ends in **-ist**, it has something to do with having a particular belief. For example, a *Buddhist* believes in the religion of Buddhism

IT •ABBREVIATION• short for **information technology**

it •PRONOUN• **1** a word you use to talk about a thing that has already been mentioned or pointed out: *I've lost the book. Have you seen it?*
2 used for talking about the weather, time and dates: *It rained yesterday.* • *It's 3 o'clock.*
3 used for talking about a fact or opinion: *It's expensive to travel by train.* • *It's very quiet here, isn't it?*

italic •ADJECTIVE• using a style of writing in which the letters slope to the right. The examples given in this book are in *italic*

itch •VERB• **itches, itching, itched** if part of your body itches, you want to scratch it
•NOUN• **itches** a feeling that you want to scratch part of your body: *I've got an itch on my back.*
• **itchy** •ADJECTIVE• an itchy part of your body makes you feel as though you want to scratch it

it'd •SHORT FORM• a short way to say and write **it would** or **it had**: *It'd work! I know it would!* • *If you have an excuse, it'd better be good.*

item •NOUN• **items** one of a number of things: *There were several items on the list.*

-itis •SUFFIX• if a word ends in **-itis** it has

something to do with an illness that causes swelling and pain in part of your body. For example, *tonsillitis* is an illness that causes the tonsils in your throat to swell and become painful

it'll •SHORT FORM• a short way to say and write **it will**: *It'll all end in tears.*

its •ADJECTIVE• belonging to it: *Keep the hat in its box.*

it's •SHORT FORM• a short way to say and write **it is** or **it has**: *It's raining.* • *It's been a long time since I saw you.*

ⓘ Try not to confuse the spellings of **its** and **it's**.
Its is the possessive form of **it**, and tells you something belongs to **it**: *The bird built its nest.*
It's is a short form of two words put together: *I think it's going to rain.*

itself •PRONOUN• **1** you use **itself** after a verb or preposition when the thing that performs the action is affected by it: *The baby looked at itself in the mirror.* **2** you use **itself** to show that **it** has done something without any help from others: *The dog managed to get free all by itself.* **3** you can use **itself** to show more clearly the thing you mean: *The garden is big but the house itself is quite small.*

I've •SHORT FORM• a short way to say and write **I have**: *I've finished my homework.*

ivory •NOUN• the hard white substance that forms the tusks of an elephant

ivy •NOUN• a plant that has leaves all year and can grow up walls

jab • VERB• **jabs, jabbing, jabbed** to poke or prod roughly or sharply : *Jack jabbed me with his finger.*
• NOUN• **jabs** 1 a quick prod or punch 2 an injection, especially one given to prevent an infectious disease : *a flu jab*

jabber • VERB• **jabbers, jabbering, jabbered** to talk nonsense, especially very fast

jack • NOUN• **jacks** 1 a tool used to raise something heavy off the ground, especially a car or other vehicle 2 a playing card with a picture of a young man, also called a knave. The jack or knave comes between the queen and the ten in value
• VERB• **jacks, jacking, jacked** to jack something, or to **jack it up**, is to lift it using a jack

jackal • NOUN• **jackals** a wild animal that looks like a dog or fox and is found in Africa and Asia

jackdaw • NOUN• **jackdaws** a type of small black crow with a greyish head

jacket • NOUN• **jackets** 1 a short coat, usually with long sleeves, that reaches down to your waist or hips 2 a loose paper covering wrapped around a hardback book

jacket potato • NOUN• **jacket potatoes** an unpeeled potato baked in the oven

jack-in-the-box • NOUN• **jack-in-the-boxes** a doll fixed on a spring inside a box which pops up out of the box suddenly when the lid is opened

jack-knife • VERB• **jack-knifes, jack-knifing, jack-knifed** if a lorry jack-knifes it skids out of control and the trailer swings round against the cab

jackpot • NOUN• **jackpots** the jackpot in a game or lottery is the top prize made up of the money everyone else has bet and which increases until someone wins it

jade • NOUN• a type of hard green stone used in jewellery and for making ornaments

jaded • ADJECTIVE• feeling tired and bored because you have been doing the same thing over and over again

jagged • ADJECTIVE• with sharp or uneven edges or angles : *jagged rocks* • *a jagged tear in the tent*

jaguar • NOUN• **jaguars** a large South American spotted cat, similar to a leopard, that lives in the jungle

jail • NOUN• **jails** a prison
• VERB• **jails, jailing, jailed** to jail someone is to put them in prison
• **jailer** • NOUN• **jailers** someone whose job is to watch over prisoners in a jail

Jain • NOUN• **Jains** a member of an Indian religious group, whose beliefs are similar to Buddhism

jam • NOUN• **jams** 1 jam is a thick sticky food made by boiling fruit with sugar 2 a jam happens when lots of vehicles or people are packed close together so that they become stuck and can't move
• VERB• **jams, jamming, jammed** 1 to push something into a space so that it fits very tightly or is difficult to get out again
2 something like a door or window jams when it becomes stuck and can't be moved
3 people or vehicles jam a place when they crowd it so that it is difficult for any of them to move
⇒ **jammy**

jamb • NOUN• **jambs** the jamb of a door or window is the upright piece of wood or metal at either side of the frame

jamboree • NOUN• **jamborees** a large organized event where people from many different places gather, especially a gathering of Scouts

jammy • ADJECTIVE• **jammier, jammiest** 1 filled or covered with jam 2 an informal word meaning 'lucky'

jangle • VERB• **jangles, jangling, jangled** 1 to jangle is to make a harsh ringing sound like metal hitting metal **2** if something jangles your nerves, it gives you an unpleasant and uncomfortable sensation

janitor •NOUN• **janitors** someone whose job is to look after a building, especially a school

January •NOUN• the first month of the year, after December and before February

(i) **January** comes from the name of the Roman god **Ianus**, who had two faces. One face was looking into the new year, the other looking back to the old year.

jape •NOUN• **japes** a slightly old-fashioned word for a trick or joke

jar •NOUN• **jars 1** a cylindrical container with a wide neck and no handles
2 the amount a jar will hold: *She made six big jars of marmalade from the oranges.*
3 a bump or blow that causes an unpleasant or painful vibration
•VERB• **jars, jarring, jarred 1** to shake or hurt with an unpleasant or painful vibration: *He fell awkwardly, jarring his spine.* **2** if something jars, or it **jars on** you, it has an unpleasant effect on you: *The bird's screeching jarred on my ears.*

jargon •NOUN• **jargons** the special words used by people working in a particular trade or profession, which are difficult for other people to understand: *legal jargon*

jasmine •NOUN• **jasmines** a shrub or climbing plant with sweetly scented white or yellow flowers

jaundice •NOUN• an illness that makes the skin and the whites of the eyes turn yellow, usually caused by the liver not working properly
◆ **jaundiced** •ADJECTIVE• **1** having jaundice **2** feeling unhappy and bitter about life in general

jaunt •NOUN• **jaunts** a trip made for pleasure: *Dad's on one of his fishing jaunts.*
◆ **jaunty** •ADJECTIVE• **jauntier, jauntiest** cheerful, confident and lively: *a jaunty manner*

javelin •NOUN• **javelins** a long light spear used in ancient times as a weapon and nowadays thrown in a sporting competition

jaw •NOUN• **jaws 1** your jaw is the lower part of your face around your mouth and chin, made up of two bones that your teeth grow in **2** an animal's jaws are its mouth and teeth: *The crocodile snapped its jaws shut.*

jay •NOUN• **jays** a bird with pink, grey, white and black feathers

jaywalker •NOUN• **jaywalkers** someone who walks across a traffic-filled street at a place where there is no crossing for pedestrians
◆ **jaywalking** •NOUN• walking across streets used by cars and other traffic at a place where there is no pedestrian crossing

(i) This word came from the United States. **Jaywalking** was so called because **jay** was a slang word meaning *fool*, and it is a dangerous thing to do.

jazz •NOUN• a type of music in which the musicians often change the notes or add to the music as they play
•VERB• **jazzes, jazzing, jazzed** to **jazz something up** is to make it brighter or more colourful
◆ **jazzy** •ADJECTIVE• **jazzier, jazziest** bright and colourful: *That's a very jazzy tie you have on.*

JCB •NOUN• **JCBs** a large machine used for digging and moving earth and stones

(i) The **JCB** gets its name from the initials of its manufacturer, *J C Bamford*.

jealous •ADJECTIVE• feeling jealousy: *He's jealous of his brother's success.* • *She made me jealous by going out with her other friends.*
◆ **jealousy** •NOUN• **jealousies** a feeling of dislike that people have because someone else has something that they want or because they are afraid that another person will take something away from them

jeans •PLURAL NOUN• jeans are casual trousers made of denim with pockets at the front and back

Jeep •NOUN• **Jeeps** a type of four-wheeled vehicle that can travel over rough ground. This word is a trademark

jeer •VERB• **jeers, jeering, jeered** to jeer at

Aa
Bb
Cc
Dd
Ee
Ff
Gg
Hh
Ii
Jj
Kk
Ll
Mm
Nn
Oo
Pp
Qq
Rr
Ss
Tt
Uu
Vv
Ww
Xx
Yy
Zz

someone is to shout insults at them and make fun of them
• NOUN• **jeers** a scornful shout or laugh

Jehovah • NOUN• Jehovah is the name given to the Hebrew God of the Old Testament

jelly • NOUN• **jellies** 1 a wobbly food made with gelatine and fruit juice 2 any wobbly substance

jellyfish • NOUN• **jellyfish** or **jellyfishes** a sea animal with a soft see-through body

jemmy • NOUN• **jemmies** a long iron tool used by burglars to break open locks
• VERB• **jemmies, jemmying, jemmied** to break a lock using a jemmy

jerk • VERB• **jerks, jerking, jerked** 1 to jerk something is to pull it with a sudden rough movement: *He jerked his hand away.* 2 to jerk is to make a short sudden movement: *The driver started the engine and the old bus jerked forward.*
• NOUN• **jerks** a short sudden movement
⇒ **jerky**

jerkin • NOUN• **jerkins** a type of short jacket or coat

jerky • ADJECTIVE• **jerkier, jerkiest** jerky movements are short and quick, and are often awkward-looking or uncomfortable

jersey • NOUN• **jerseys** 1 a jersey is a warm piece of clothing for the top part of your body 2 jersey is a fine knitted material

jest • VERB• **jests, jesting, jested** to joke
• NOUN• **jests** a joke
♦ **jester** • NOUN• **jesters** in the past, a man who was employed by a king or queen to tell jokes and amuse the court

jet[1] • NOUN• **jets** 1 a powerful stream of liquid or gas forced through a narrow opening 2 a fast aeroplane with powerful engines that drive the plane forward by sucking air in at the front and forcing it out behind
• VERB• **jets, jetting, jetted** to jet somewhere is to travel there on a jet plane: *jetting off to sunny holiday destinations*

jet[2] • NOUN• jet is a black mineral that is polished and used to make jewellery

jet lag • NOUN• a feeling of tiredness that people get who have made a long journey by aeroplane, because their body isn't able to

adjust to the time changes from one part of the world to another

jetsam • NOUN• objects thrown from a boat or ship and washed ashore. Look up and compare **flotsam**

jettison • VERB• **jettisons, jettisoning, jettisoned** 1 cargo on a ship or aeroplane is jettisoned when it is thrown overboard to lighten the load, especially in an emergency 2 to jettison something is to throw it away or abandon it

jetty • NOUN• **jetties** a platform built at the edge of a lake or the sea for small boats to tie up at

Jew • NOUN• **Jews** someone who belongs to the Hebrew race of people or who practises the religion of Judaism
⇒ **Jewish**

jewel • NOUN• **jewels** a precious stone, used for decoration or display
♦ **jeweller** • NOUN• **jewellers** someone who makes or sells jewellery
♦ **jewellery** • NOUN• things that you wear to decorate your body and clothing, such as rings, earrings, bracelets, necklaces and brooches

ⓘ In the United States and Canada, **jeweller** is usually spelt **jeweler**, and **jewellery** is spelt **jewelry**.

Jewish • ADJECTIVE• to do with the Hebrew people or Judaism

jib • NOUN• **jibs** 1 the arm that sticks out from the upright part of a crane 2 a triangular sail at the front of some sailing boats

jiffy • NOUN• **jiffies** a very short time: *I'll be down in a jiffy.*

jig • NOUN• **jigs** a lively dance in which people jump about

jigsaw • NOUN• **jigsaws** 1 a puzzle made up of lots of different-shaped pieces that fit together to make a picture 2 a type of electric saw with a very thin blade that can cut curved and rounded shapes

jilt • VERB• **jilts, jilting, jilted** to jilt someone you have promised to marry, or who you have been going out with, is to reject and abandon them

Aa
Bb
Cc
Dd
Ee
Ff
Gg
Hh
Ii
Jj
Kk
Ll
Mm
Nn
Oo
Pp
Qq
Rr
Ss
Tt
Uu
Vv
Ww
Xx
Yy
Zz

jingle •VERB• **jingles, jingling, jingled** pieces of metal jingle when they make a pleasant ringing sound as they hit each other: *coins jingling in his trouser pocket*
•NOUN• **jingles 1** a ringing sound made when small or light pieces of metal knock against each other **2** a short catchy song used in an advertisement

jinx •NOUN• **jinxes** an evil spell or a person or thing that brings bad luck
◆ **jinxed** •ADJECTIVE• to be jinxed is always to have bad luck

ⓘ This word comes from the name of a bird called a **jinx**, which was used in spells and charms.

jittery •ADJECTIVE• nervous

job •NOUN• **jobs 1** someone's job is the work they do regularly for pay **2** a job is a task or a piece of work: *There are plenty of jobs to do about the house.*

job centre •NOUN• **job centres** a government office where jobs are advertised

jockey •NOUN• **jockeys** someone who rides a horse, especially in races

jodhpurs •PLURAL NOUN• trousers that are tight around the bottom part of the leg and wider near the top, worn by jockeys and other horse riders

joey •NOUN• **joeys** a baby kangaroo, especially one that is still in its mother's pouch

jog •VERB• **jogs, jogging, jogged 1** to jog is to run at a slowish pace for exercise **2** to jog someone or something is to nudge them or knock against them gently: *You jogged my elbow and made me splash the paint everywhere!* **3** to jog someone's memory is to help them remember
◆ **jogger** •NOUN• **joggers** someone who jogs for exercise
◆ **jogging** •NOUN• running at a slowish pace for exercise

join •VERB• **joins, joining, joined 1** to join two or more things is to put them together or connect them **2** one thing joins another when they come together or meet: *The track joins the main*

road just around this corner. **3** you join a club or other organization when you become a member
•NOUN• **joins** a place where two things are joined

joiner •NOUN• **joiners** someone who works with wood, especially fitting together the wooden parts of houses

joint •NOUN• **joints 1** a place where two or more things join **2** your joints are the parts of your body where two or more bones meet **3** a joint of meat is a large piece of meat •ADJECTIVE• done together or shared: *a joint effort • joint responsibility*
◆ **jointly** •ADVERB• together

joke •NOUN• **jokes** something that is said or done to make people laugh
•VERB• **jokes, joking, joked** to make a joke
◆ **joker** •NOUN• **jokers 1** someone who likes telling jokes or doing things to make people laugh **2** one of two cards in a pack of playing cards that have a picture of a clown. The jokers are extra cards and are only used in certain card games

jolly •ADJECTIVE• **jollier, jolliest** cheerful and happy
•ADVERB• very: *That was jolly unfair of you!*

jolt •NOUN• **jolts 1** a sudden sharp uncomfortable movement: *The train stopped with a jolt.* **2** an unpleasant shock: *The news gave Liam a bit of a jolt.*
•VERB• **jolts, jolting, jolted** to make a sudden sharp movement

jostle •VERB• **jostles, jostling, jostled** to push roughly: *The prime minister was jostled by an angry crowd.*

jot •VERB• **jots, jotting, jotted** to jot something down is to write it down quickly
•NOUN• **jots** a small amount: *They don't care a jot what happens.*
◆ **jotter** •NOUN• **jotters** a book of blank pages used for taking down notes or for doing school exercises

joule •NOUN• **joules** a unit of energy

journal •NOUN• **journals 1** someone's journal is a book in which they write down what they have done each day **2** a magazine or newspaper

◆ **journalism** •NOUN• the work of journalists

◆ **journalist** •NOUN• **journalists** someone who writes for a newspaper or magazine or for radio or TV

journey •NOUN• **journeys 1** you go on a journey when you travel from one place to another **2** a journey is the distance you travel from one place to another: *a long and difficult journey*
•VERB• **journeys, journeying, journeyed** to journey somewhere is to travel there

joust •NOUN• **jousts** in medieval times, a joust was a fight between two knights on horseback who charged at each other with long lances
•VERB• **jousts, jousting, jousted** to fight, especially on horseback

jovial •ADJECTIVE• cheerful and jolly

joy •NOUN• **joys 1** joy is a feeling of great happiness **2** a joy is something that gives you this feeling: *full of the joys of spring*

joyful or **joyous** •ADJECTIVE• filled with or showing great happiness

joyride •NOUN• **joyrides** a fast or reckless ride in a stolen car for amusement
◆ **joyrider** •NOUN• **joyriders** someone who rides in a stolen car for amusement

joystick •NOUN• **joysticks** a lever used to control an aircraft or a computer game

Jr •ABBREVIATION• short for **Junior** and used after someone's name, as in *John Willis Jr*

jubilant •ADJECTIVE• full of triumph and happiness at a success
◆ **jubilation** •NOUN• rejoicing at success

jubilee •NOUN• **jubilees** a celebration of a special anniversary, for example of a wedding or a coronation

ⓘ This word comes from a Hebrew word meaning *ram's horn*. This is because a ram's horn used to be blown to mark the beginning of a Jewish year of celebration.

Judaism •NOUN• the Jewish religion which follows the teachings of the Old Testament of the Bible
◆ **Judaic** •ADJECTIVE• to do with the Jewish religion or way of life

judder •VERB• **judders, juddering, juddered** to vibrate or make uncomfortable shaky movements: *The old plane juddered to a halt.*
•NOUN• **judders** a strong vibration or shaky movement

judge •VERB• **judges, judging, judged 1** to judge something is to form an idea or opinion about it
2 to judge a competition is to decide which of the competitors is best
3 to judge a case in a court of law is to hear the evidence and decide on what is to be done or how someone should be punished
•NOUN• **judges 1** someone who hears cases in a law court and decides what is to be done
2 someone who judges a competition
3 someone who can decide whether something is good or bad: *a good judge of character*
◆ **judgement** or **judgment** •NOUN• **judgements** or **judgments 1** the ability to make decisions, especially good or sensible decisions
2 the decision made by a judge in a law court
3 an opinion about something: *In my judgement, it wouldn't be a very sensible thing to do.*

judicial •ADJECTIVE• to do with judges, judgement or a court of justice

judicious •ADJECTIVE• wise and showing good judgement

judo •NOUN• a form of wrestling that came originally from Japan

jug •NOUN• **jugs** a container for liquids with a handle and a shaped part at its top edge for pouring

juggernaut •NOUN• **juggernauts** a very long or large lorry

juggle •VERB• **juggles, juggling, juggled** to juggle is to keep several things in the air by continuously throwing them up and catching them
◆ **juggler** •NOUN• **jugglers** someone who juggles

juice •NOUN• **juices 1** juice is the liquid in fruits or vegetables **2** the juices from meat

Aa
Bb
Cc
Dd
Ee
Ff
Gg
Hh
Ii
Jj
Kk
Ll
Mm
Nn
Oo
Pp
Qq
Rr
Ss
Tt
Uu
Vv
Ww
Xx
Yy
Zz

Aa

are the liquids that flow out of it while it is being cooked

Bb

♦ **juicy** •ADJECTIVE• **juicier, juiciest** full of juice

Cc

jukebox •NOUN• **jukeboxes** a coin-operated machine that automatically plays records that you select by pressing buttons

Dd

July •NOUN• the seventh month of the year, after June and before August

Ee

Ff

ⓘ **July** comes from the Latin word for this month, **Iulius**, which was named after the Roman emperor *Julius Caesar*.

Gg

jumble •VERB• **jumbles, jumbling, jumbled** to jumble things up is to mix them up so that they are out of order or in an untidy mess •NOUN• a jumble is lots of things that have been mixed up in a confused or untidy mess

Hh

Ii

Jj

jumble sale •NOUN• **jumble sales** a sale where second-hand or unwanted things are sold to raise money

Kk

Ll

jumbo •ADJECTIVE• very big: *a jumbo crossword* •NOUN• **jumbos** 1 a jumbo jet 2 an informal name for an elephant

Mm

Nn

jumbo jet •NOUN• **jumbo jets** a very big jet aeroplane that can carry a lot of passengers

Oo

jump •VERB• **jumps, jumping, jumped** 1 to leap off the ground: *I jumped down from the bus, into the slush of the gutter.*
2 to jump something is to leap over it
3 to make a startled movement: *I jumped as something crawled out from under the stone.*
4 if you **jump to** do something or **jump at** something you move quickly to do it: *I thought you would jump at the chance.*
5 if you jump a queue you join it in front of other people already in the queue •NOUN• **jumps** 1 a leap
2 something to be jumped over, or a distance that has to be jumped
3 a startled movement
⇒ **jumpy**

Pp

Qq

Rr

Ss

Tt

Uu

Vv

Ww

jumper •NOUN• **jumpers** a warm piece of clothing with sleeves that you pull on over your head and wear on the top half of your body

Xx

Yy

Zz

jumpsuit •NOUN• **jumpsuits** an all-in-one

piece of clothing made up of trousers and top

jumpy •ADJECTIVE• **jumpier, jumpiest** nervous and anxious: *His face was pale and he looked jumpy.*

junction •NOUN• **junctions** a place where roads or railway lines meet and cross

June •NOUN• the sixth month of the year, after May and before July

ⓘ **June** comes from the name of the Roman queen of the gods, **Juno**.

jungle •NOUN• **jungles** trees and plants growing thickly together, especially in tropical areas of the world

junior •ADJECTIVE• 1 younger: *junior members of the tennis club*
2 meant for younger people: *junior classes*
3 lower in rank: *junior staff* •NOUN• **juniors** 1 a younger pupil in a school
2 someone who is your junior is younger than you are
3 someone who is lower in rank: *an office junior*

juniper •NOUN• **junipers** an evergreen bush with small purple berries used to flavour drinks and in cooking

junk •NOUN• useless or unwanted things: *What will we do with all this old junk?*

junk food •NOUN• food that is easy to make but is not good for your health

juror •NOUN• **jurors** one of the members of a jury

jury •NOUN• **juries** a group of people chosen to decide on the evidence presented in a court of law whether someone accused of a crime is guilty or not guilty

just •ADVERB• 1 exactly: *A cold drink was just what I needed.*
2 barely: *I could only just see him.*
3 a very short time ago: *The clock's just struck five.*
4 simply: *I just want to go home.*
• **just about** more or less: *I've just about finished here.*

justice •NOUN• **justices** 1 justice is fairness in dealing with people and their problems
2 justice is being treated properly and fairly by the law

3 a justice is a judge in a court of law

justifiable •ADJECTIVE• able to be justified
• **justifiably** •ADVERB• in a justifiable way

justification •NOUN• **justifications** a good reason or reasons given for doing something, showing that it is worthwhile or necessary

justify •VERB• **justifies, justifying, justified** to justify something is to give good reasons for it or to show that it is worthwhile or necessary: *She could justify her decision to leave.*

justly •ADVERB• fairly
•ADJECTIVE• **1** fair or showing justice: *a just decision* **2** deserved: *It was a just reward for all his efforts.*

jut •VERB• **juts, jutting, jutted** to jut, or to **jut out**, is to stick out

juvenile •ADJECTIVE• **1** to do with young people, especially when they are too young to be treated as adults: *a juvenile court* **2** childish: *a juvenile sense of humour*
•NOUN• **juveniles** a young person or animal

Aa
Bb
Cc
Dd
Ee
Ff
Gg
Hh
Ii
Jj
Kk
Ll
Mm
Nn
Oo
Pp
Qq
Rr
Ss
Tt
Uu
Vv
Ww
Xx
Yy
Zz

Kk

kaftan •NOUN• **kaftans** a long, loose piece of clothing that men in Arab countries wear

kaleidoscope •NOUN• **kaleidoscopes** a long tube that you look down, with mirrors and pieces of coloured glass at the bottom that form different patterns when you turn the tube

kangaroo •NOUN• **kangaroos** an Australian animal that jumps, and that carries its babies in a pouch at the front of its body

kaput •ADJECTIVE• broken or not working

ⓘ **Kaput** is a very informal word.

karaoke •NOUN• entertainment in which someone sings a pop song while a machine plays the music

karate •NOUN• a Japanese type of fighting in which you use your hands and feet

ⓘ **Karate** is a Japanese word which means *empty hand*, because you do not hold or use any weapons in this type of fighting.

karma •NOUN• in the religion of Buddhism or Hinduism, the good or bad things that happen to you which are believed to be decided by the things you did in a previous life

kayak •NOUN• **kayaks** a type of canoe for one person

KB •ABBREVIATION• short for **kilobyte**

kebab •NOUN• **kebabs** small pieces of meat and vegetables cooked on a wooden or metal stick

keel •NOUN• **keels** a long piece of wood or steel at the bottom of a ship
•VERB• **keels, keeling, keeled** to **keel over** is to fall over

keen •ADJECTIVE• **keener, keenest**
1 enthusiastic and wanting to do something or wanting something to happen: *Jim's a keen swimmer.* • *Everyone seemed very keen*

to help. 2 sharp: *The old lady's keen eyes stared at her.*
♦ **keenly** •ADVERB• in an enthusiastic or sharp way: *He spoke keenly about the new game.*
♦ **keenness** •NOUN• being keen

keep •VERB• **keeps, keeping, kept** 1 to continue to have something and not give it to anyone else: *You can keep the book. I don't want it back.*
2 to put something in a particular place when you are not using it: *I keep my toys under the bed.*
3 to make someone or something stay a particular way: *Keep the door closed.* • *Keep off the grass.*
4 if you keep or **keep on** doing something, you continue to do it: *I keep forgetting to bring my homework.*
5 if food keeps, it stays fresh: *Milk doesn't keep for very long.*
6 if you keep animals, you have them and look after them: *They keep chickens and goats.*
7 to **keep up** with someone or something is to move or do something as fast as they do: *He was running so fast that I couldn't keep up.*
♦ **keeper** •NOUN• **keepers** the person who looks after something, especially animals in a zoo
♦ **keeping** •NOUN• 1 if something is in your keeping, it is in your care 2 if something is in **keeping with** something else, it is suitable for a particular situation

keepsake •NOUN• **keepsakes** something that someone gives you so that you will remember them or an occasion

keg •NOUN• **kegs** a small barrel

kennel •NOUN• **kennels** a hut for a dog

kept •VERB• a way of changing the verb **keep** to make a past tense. It can be used with or without a helping verb: *He kept all her letters.* • *I have kept the receipt.*

kerb •NOUN• **kerbs** the edge of a pavement

kernel •NOUN• **kernels** a soft substance in the shell of a nut or inside the stone of a fruit

kestrel •NOUN• **kestrels** a small bird of the falcon family that kills other creatures for food

ketchup •NOUN• a sauce made from tomatoes

kettle •NOUN• **kettles** a container for boiling water in

kettledrum •NOUN• **kettledrums** a large drum made of a metal bowl covered with skin

key •NOUN• **keys 1** something you use for locking and unlocking something such as a door or window
   2 a button on a computer keyboard or typewriter
   3 one of the white or black parts you press on a piano to make a sound
   4 a set of musical notes: *in the key of D minor*
   5 something that makes you able to understand or achieve something: *Hard work is the key to success.* • *The key to the map is over the page.*
   •ADJECTIVE• most important: *Dean is one of the team's key players.*

keyboard •NOUN• **keyboards 1** the set of keys on a computer or typewriter
   2 the set of keys on a musical instrument such as a piano
   3 an electronic musical instrument that has keys like a piano

keyhole •NOUN• **keyholes** the part of a lock that you put a key into

keynote •NOUN• **1** the basic note of a musical key, for example *D in D minor* **2** the main idea of a book or speech

kg •ABBREVIATION• short for **kilogram** or **kilograms**

khaki •NOUN• a greenish-brown colour

ⓘ **Khaki** comes from a word in the Urdu language of Pakistan and India that means *dusty*, and this describes the dull colour.

kibbutz •NOUN• **kibbutzim** a type of farm in Israel in which a group of people live together and share all the work

kick •VERB• **kicks, kicking, kicked 1** to hit someone or something with your foot: *Jane kicked the ball over the fence.* **2** to move your legs strongly, for example when swimming
   •NOUN• **kicks 1** a strong movement of your leg or foot **2** a feeling of pleasure or excitement: *He gets a kick out of driving fast.*

kick-off •NOUN• the start of a football game

kid •NOUN• **kids 1** a child **2** a young goat
   • **with kid gloves** if you treat someone with kid gloves, you are very careful not to upset them
   •VERB• **kids, kidding, kidded** to kid someone is to trick them for fun

kidnap •VERB• **kidnaps, kidnapping, kidnapped** to take someone away using force, and ask for money to return them safely
   ◆ **kidnapper** •NOUN• **kidnappers** someone who kidnaps someone else
   ◆ **kidnapping** •NOUN• **kidnappings** taking someone away using force and asking for money to return them: *Kidnapping is a serious crime.* • *There have been several kidnappings recently.*

kidney •NOUN• **kidneys** one of the two organs in your body that remove waste from your blood and produce urine

kill •VERB• **kills, killing, killed** to make a person or animal die: *People were killed in the crash.*
   ◆ **killer** •NOUN• **killers** a person who kills someone

kiln •NOUN• **kilns** a large oven for baking pottery or bricks, or for drying grain

kilo- •PREFIX• if a word starts with **kilo-**, it adds the meaning *one thousand*. For example, a *kilogram* is equal to 1000 *grams*

kilobyte •NOUN• **kilobytes** a unit used to measure computer memory or data, equal to 1024 bytes. This is often shortened to **KB**

kilogram or **kilogramme** •NOUN• **kilograms** or **kilogrammes** a unit for measuring weight, equal to 1000 grams. This is often shortened to **kg**

Aa
Bb
Cc
Dd
Ee
Ff
Gg
Hh
Ii
Jj
Kk
Ll
Mm
Nn
Oo
Pp
Qq
Rr
Ss
Tt
Uu
Vv
Ww
Xx
Yy
Zz

Aa Bb Cc Dd Ee Ff Gg Hh Ii Jj **Kk** Ll Mm Nn Oo Pp Qq Rr Ss Tt Uu Vv Ww Xx Yy Zz

kilometre •NOUN• **kilometres** a unit for measuring distance, equal to 1000 metres. This is often shortened to **km**

kilowatt •NOUN• **kilowatts** a unit for measuring electrical power, equal to 1000 watts

kilt •NOUN• **kilts** a pleated tartan skirt that is part of a traditional Scottish way of dressing for both men and women

kimono •NOUN• **kimonos** a traditional Japanese piece of clothing that looks like a long dress, tied round the middle

kin •NOUN• your kin are your relatives
• **next of kin** your closest relative, who would be informed if you had an accident

kind¹ •NOUN• **kinds** a type of something: *What kind of dog have you got?*

kind² •ADJECTIVE• **kinder, kindest** nice, generous and wanting to make other people happy
⇒ **kindly, kindness**

kindergarten •NOUN• **kindergartens** a school for very young children

kindhearted •ADJECTIVE• kind and generous

kindle •VERB• **kindles, kindling, kindled** 1 to light a fire 2 to start burning
• **kindling** •NOUN• pieces of wood used to start a fire

kindly •ADVERB• 1 in a way that shows kindness: *The teacher spoke to us kindly.* 2 you can say 'kindly' to mean 'please' when you are rather angry: *Would you kindly be quiet!* 3 if you **do not take kindly** to something, you are annoyed about it: *I do not take kindly to being called a liar.*
•ADJECTIVE• kind and caring: *He was a kindly man who wished us well.*

kindness •NOUN• helpfulness and generosity: *an act of kindness*

kinetic •ADJECTIVE• relating to or produced by movement

king •NOUN• **kings** 1 a man who rules a country: *the King of Norway* 2 in the game of chess, a king is a piece that has a crown and has to be captured to win the game

• **kingdom** •NOUN• **kingdoms** 1 a country ruled by a king 2 one of the three divisions of the natural world, which are the animal, vegetable and mineral kingdoms

kingfisher •NOUN• **kingfishers** a brightly coloured bird that eats fish

king-size •ADJECTIVE• larger than the usual size: *a king-size bed*

kink •NOUN• **kinks** a bend or twist in something

kiosk •NOUN• **kiosks** a small stall selling items such as newspapers and sweets

kipper •NOUN• **kippers** a smoked fish

kirk •NOUN• **kirks** a Scottish word for a church

kiss •VERB• **kisses, kissing, kissed** to touch someone with your lips as a sign of love: *Ellie kissed her mother.*
•NOUN• **kisses** the act of kissing someone: *He gave her a kiss.*

kiss of life •NOUN• the kiss of life is a way of helping an ill or injured person to start breathing again by blowing air into their mouth

kit •NOUN• **kits** 1 the clothes or tools that you need for a particular activity or job: *I forgot to bring my football kit.* 2 a set of parts that you can put together to make something: *a model boat kit*

kitchen •NOUN• **kitchens** a room for preparing and cooking food

kite •NOUN• **kites** 1 a toy that you fly in the air when it is windy 2 a bird from the hawk family

kitten •NOUN• **kittens** a young cat

kitty¹ •NOUN• **kitties** a collection of money that a group of people regularly add money to, and use for a particular purpose

kitty² •NOUN• **kitties** an informal name for a cat or kitten

kiwi •NOUN• **kiwis** a bird from New Zealand that can run but not fly

kiwi fruit •NOUN• **kiwi fruit** a fruit with bright green flesh, black seeds and a hairy skin

km •ABBREVIATION• short for **kilometre** or **kilometres**

knack •NOUN• **knacks** a special talent: *You have a knack for baking perfect cakes.*

knapsack •NOUN• **knapsacks** a bag that you carry on your back

knave •NOUN• **knaves** the jack in a pack of playing cards

knead •VERB• **kneads, kneading, kneaded** to press dough or clay with your hands to make it ready to use

knee •NOUN• **knees** the joint in the middle of your leg where it bends

kneecap •NOUN• **kneecaps** the bone at the front of your knee

kneel •VERB• **kneels, kneeling, knelt** to move down so you are resting on your knees

knickerbockers •PLURAL NOUN• trousers that fit tightly just below the knee

knickers •PLURAL NOUN• a piece of underwear for women or girls, which covers their bottom

knick-knack •NOUN• **knick-knacks** a small decorative object

knife •NOUN• **knives** a tool used for cutting something, which has a handle and a blade •VERB• **knifes, knifing, knifed** to stab someone with a knife

knight •NOUN• **knights 1** in history, a man of a high social rank who was trained to fight **2** a man who has been given an honour by a king or queen that lets him use the title *Sir* **3** in the game of chess, a knight is a piece which is shaped like a horse

knighthood •NOUN• **knighthoods** the rank or title of a knight

knit •VERB• **knits, knitting, knitted** to make something using two long needles and wool: *Sandy was knitting a scarf.* • *Do you know how to knit?* ✦ **knitting** •NOUN• **1** the activity of making things by knitting **2** something that has been or is being knitted

knitting needle •NOUN• **knitting needles** one of the two long needles used for knitting

knives •NOUN• the plural of **knife**

knob •NOUN• **knobs 1** a round handle on a door or drawer

2 a round button used for controlling a machine
3 a lump: *a knob of butter*

knock •VERB• **knocks, knocking, knocked**
1 to hit something so that it moves or falls: *The cat knocked the vase off the table.*
2 to hit a door or window several times with your knuckles or a knocker in order to attract attention: *Knock before you come in.*
3 to bump into something: *I knocked my elbow on the edge of the door.*
4 to **knock someone out** is to make someone become unconscious, especially by hitting them
•NOUN• **knocks 1** the sound of someone knocking on a door or window: *There was a knock at the door.* **2** a blow or injury caused by hitting something: *He's had a nasty knock on the head.*
✦ **knocker** •NOUN• **knockers** a metal object on a door, which you knock with

knockout •NOUN• **knockouts** a hit that makes someone unconscious

knoll •NOUN• **knolls** a small hill

knot •NOUN• **knots 1** a join made by tying two ends of string or rope together
2 a hard lump in a piece of wood where there used to be a branch
3 a unit for measuring how fast a ship is travelling
•VERB• **knots, knotting, knotted** to tie something with a knot
✦ **knotty** •ADJECTIVE• **1** having a lot of knots **2** difficult or complicated: *a knotty problem*

know •VERB• **knows, knowing, knew, known 1** to have information about something: *Do you know where he lives?*
2 to have learnt about something: *I don't know much German.*
3 to be familiar with a person or place: *I didn't know anyone at the party.*
✦ **knowing** •ADJECTIVE• showing that you know something that is supposed to be secret: *He gave me a knowing look.*
✦ **knowledge** •NOUN• the information and understanding that you have about something: *She has a good knowledge of sport.*

Aa
Bb
Cc
Dd
Ee
Ff
Gg
Hh
Ii
Jj

Kk

Ll
Mm
Nn
Oo
Pp
Qq
Rr
Ss
Tt
Uu
Vv
Ww
Xx
Yy
Zz

knowledgeable •ADJECTIVE• knowing a lot about something
♦ **knowledgeably** •ADVERB• in a way that shows you know a lot about something: *Joe spoke knowledgeably about history.*

knuckle •NOUN• **knuckles** one of the parts on your hands where your fingers bend

koala •NOUN• **koalas** an Australian animal that looks like a small bear, climbs trees and eats eucalyptus leaves

Koran •NOUN• the holy book of the Islamic religion

kosher •ADJECTIVE• kosher food is prepared according to Jewish law

kung-fu •NOUN• a Chinese type of fighting using your hands and feet

kW •ABBREVIATION• short for **kilowatt** or **kilowatts**

l •ABBREVIATION• short for **litre** or **litres**

label •NOUN• **labels** a small note that is fixed on to something and gives information about it: *The washing instructions are on the label.* •VERB• **labels, labelling, labelled** to fix a small note to something: *All the boxes have been carefully labelled.*

laboratory •NOUN• **laboratories** a scientist's workroom

labour •NOUN• **1** hard work **2** the process of giving birth to a baby **3** people who work: *the rising cost of labour* •VERB• **labours, labouring, laboured** to work hard: *workers labouring in the fields* ✦ **labourer** •NOUN• **labourers** a person who does hard physical work

labrador •NOUN• **labradors** a large black or fawn-coloured dog

labyrinth •NOUN• **labyrinths** a maze that is difficult to find your way through

lace •NOUN• **laces 1** a cord for doing up shoes or other clothing: *learn to tie your shoe laces* **2** fabric that is made in open patterns in fine thread: *a collar trimmed with lace* •VERB• **laces, lacing, laced 1** to lace your shoes is to put laces in them or tie the laces in a knot or bow **2** to lace a drink is to add alcohol to it

lack •VERB• **lacks, lacking, lacked** to be completely without something or not to have enough of it: *Audrey lacks a sense of humour.* •NOUN• something that you do not have: *Lack of sleep was making us grumpy.*

lacquer •NOUN• **lacquers** a kind of varnish •VERB• **lacquers, lacquering, lacquered** to cover something with varnish to protect or decorate it

lacrosse •NOUN• a game for two teams of twelve players who throw and catch the ball with a stick that has a shallow net on the end

lad •NOUN• **lads** a boy or young man

ladder •NOUN• **ladders 1** a set of steps that you can move around to climb up to places that you cannot normally reach **2** a long tear that has started from a hole or broken stitch in a stocking or tights

laden •ADJECTIVE• loaded: *laden with shopping*

ladies •NOUN• the ladies is a public toilet for women and girls: *Where is the ladies, please?*

ladle •NOUN• **ladles** a large spoon for liquids, especially soup •VERB• **ladles, ladling, ladled** to lift or serve liquid with a large spoon: *Mrs Moore was busy ladling soup into bowls.*

lady •NOUN• **ladies 1** a polite word for a woman: *Ask that lady if the seat by her is free.* **2** a woman with good manners: *Mrs Kingsley was a real lady.* **3** the title for the wife of a lord or knight or for a woman with a high social rank

ladybird •NOUN• **ladybirds** a small beetle that is usually red with black spots

lag •VERB• **lags, lagging, lagged 1** to move slowly and fall behind other people **2** to cover something such as pipes with a warm covering ⇒ **lagging**

lager •NOUN• **lagers** a light-coloured beer

lagging •NOUN• material for covering pipes and floors to stop heat or cold passing through them: *Lagging stops the pipes from freezing in the winter.*

lagoon •NOUN• **lagoons** a shallow stretch of water within sandbanks by the sea

laid •VERB• the form of the verb **lay** that is used with a helping verb to show that something happened in the past: *Have you laid the table yet?*

laid-back •ADJECTIVE• relaxed and easy-going: *a very laid-back kind of chap*

Aa
Bb
Cc
Dd
Ee
Ff
Gg
Hh
Ii
Jj
Kk
Ll
Mm
Nn
Oo
Pp
Qq
Rr
Ss
Tt
Uu
Vv
Ww
Xx
Yy
Zz

lain •VERB• the form of the verb **lie** that is used with a helping verb to show that something happened in the past: *I had lain down for a moment and fallen fast asleep.*

lair •NOUN• **lairs** the den of a wild animal

lake •NOUN• **lakes** a large stretch of water that has land all around it

lama •NOUN• **lamas** a Buddhist priest in Tibet

lamb •NOUN• **lambs** 1 a young sheep 2 meat from a young sheep

lame •NOUN• **lamer, lamest** 1 not able to walk properly: *Mr Harris has been lame since his accident.* 2 a lame excuse is weak and not very convincing
♦ **lamely** •ADVERB• weakly: *'I'm not coming because I just can't,'* she said lamely.

lament •NOUN• **laments** a sad song or poem, especially about someone's death
•VERB• **laments, lamenting, lamented** to feel or show how sad you are about something: *Grandfather was lamenting the loss of the old days.*

laminated •ADJECTIVE• 1 covered with thin, see-through plastic 2 made by sticking layers together: *laminated glass windows*

lamp •NOUN• **lamps** a piece of equipment that has a light in it: *a table lamp*

lamppost •NOUN• **lampposts** a tall pillar or pole in the street with a light at the top

lance •NOUN• **lances** a weapon like a long spear

lance-corporal •NOUN• **lance-corporals** a soldier ranking above a private and below a corporal

landform •NOUN• **landforms** a natural feature of the surface of the Earth: *valleys and other landforms*

landing •NOUN• **landings** 1 an aircraft or boat returning to land: *an emergency landing* 2 the level floor between flights of steps on a staircase

landlady •NOUN• **landladies** 1 a woman who owns a house that someone else pays to live in 2 a woman who runs a pub

landlocked •ADJECTIVE• almost or completely surrounded by land

landlord •NOUN• **landlords** 1 a man who owns a house that someone else pays to live in 2 a man who runs a pub

landmark •NOUN• **landmarks** a place, especially a building, that helps you know where you are because you can see it from all around

landscape •NOUN• **landscapes** a view of a large area of land, especially a painting or photograph: *a rocky landscape • a landscape artist*

landslide •NOUN• **landslides** a large amount of the ground slipping down the side of a hill

lane •NOUN• **lanes** 1 a narrow road 2 a strip of a road, the air or the sea that certain vehicles should travel in: *Cyclists are allowed in the bus lanes.*

language •NOUN• **languages**
1 communication in speaking and writing
2 the words that one particular group uses, such as the people that live in one country: *learn a foreign language*
3 a system of symbols or signs that give information, for example in computers

lanky •ADJECTIVE• **lankier, lankiest** tall and thin

lantern •NOUN• **lanterns** a case holding a light

lap •NOUN• **laps** 1 the top part of a person's legs when they are sitting down 2 one round of a racecourse
•VERB• **laps, lapping, lapped** 1 to lap something is to lick it up: *a cat lapping milk from a saucer*
2 water laps when it splashes gently against rocks or on a beach
3 to lap someone is to pass them more than once as you go round a racecourse
4 to **lap something up** is to enjoy it very much: *She lapped up the compliments in her new dress.*

lapdog •NOUN• **lapdogs** a small pet dog

lapel •NOUN• **lapels** the front part of a coat or jacket collar: *a flower pinned to his lapel*

lapse •NOUN• **lapses** 1 a space of time: *After a lapse of ten years, Jones started to play football again.* 2 a failure to work properly for a short time: *a memory lapse*

•VERB• **lapses, lapsing, lapsed 1** to lapse into a certain condition is to gradually pass into it: *The patient has lapsed into unconsciousness.* **2** an agreement or contract lapses when it stops being valid

laptop •NOUN• **laptops** a small, portable computer that you can use, for example, when you are travelling

lard •NOUN• fat that can be used in cooking and that comes from a pig

larder •NOUN• **larders** the place where food is kept in a house: *a well-stocked larder*

large •ADJECTIVE• **larger, largest** big or bigger than normal: *a large man • a large house*
• **at large 1** free, not in captivity: *There is a wild cat at large in the area.* **2** in general: *The public at large do not like the idea.*
♦ **largely** •ADVERB• mainly: *The church has been largely rebuilt.*
♦ **largeness** •NOUN• the big size of something

lark •NOUN• **larks 1** a singing bird that flies high in the sky **2** a bit of fun
•VERB• **larks, larking, larked** to **lark about** is to fool about or play tricks

larva •NOUN• **larvae** an insect in its first stage after coming out of the egg

lasagne •NOUN• **lasagnes 1** flat sheets of pasta **2** an Italian dish made up of layers of pasta, meat sauce and cheese

laser •NOUN• **lasers** a very narrow, powerful beam of light

lash •NOUN• **lashes 1** a sudden whipping movement: *ten lashes of the whip* **2** an eyelash
•VERB• **lashes, lashing, lashed 1** to hit with a whipping movement: *rain that lashed against the windows* **2** to tie up with rope or string: *The banners were lashed to the walls of the buildings.*

lass •NOUN• **lasses** a girl

lasso •NOUN• **lassoes** or **lassos** a long rope with a loop that tightens when the rope is pulled, used especially for catching wild horses
•VERB• **lassoes, lassoing, lassoed** to throw a rope around something to catch it

last •ADJECTIVE• **1** coming after all the others: *the last bus of the day*
2 the final one remaining: *my last toffee*
3 most recent: *on my last birthday*
•ADVERB• **1** after all the others: *Who came last in the relay?*
2 after everything else: *I'll do my maths homework last.*
3 most recently: *When did you see Anna last?*
•VERB• **lasts, lasting, lasted 1** to continue or go on: *The lesson seemed to last for ever.* **2** to remain in good condition: *These boots should last for ever.*
•NOUN• the final person or thing: *You are always the last to finish.*
• **at last** in the end: *At last we saw the sea.*
♦ **lastly** •ADVERB• finally: *Lastly, I just want to thank my wife.*

latch •NOUN• **latches** a piece of wood or metal that rises and falls to open or fasten a door

latchkey •NOUN• **latchkeys** a key to unlock an outer door

late •ADJECTIVE• **later, latest 1** coming after the expected time: *a late arrival*
2 far on in time: *a late movie*
3 recently dead: *our late uncle*
•ADVERB• **later, latest 1** coming after the expected time: *The train arrives later every day.* **2** far on in time: *It's getting late.*
♦ **lately** •ADVERB• recently: *I haven't been to any parties lately.*
♦ **lateness** •NOUN• being late

lathe •NOUN• **lathes** a machine that turns and cuts wood or metal

lather •NOUN• foam that you get when you mix soap in water
•VERB• **lathers, lathering, lathered** to form a froth: *The soap won't lather in dirty water.*

Latin •NOUN• the language of the ancient Romans

latitude •NOUN• the position of a place along an imaginary line north and south of the equator. Look up and compare **longitude**

latter •ADJECTIVE• the latter is the second one of two people or things you are mentioning. The first one is the **former**: *If I*

Aa
Bb
Cc
Dd
Ee
Ff
Gg
Hh
Ii
Jj
Kk
Ll
Mm
Nn
Oo
Pp
Qq
Rr
Ss
Tt
Uu
Vv
Ww
Xx
Yy
Zz

am offered coffee or chocolate, I'll always take the latter.

+ **latterly** •ADVERB• recently

lattice •NOUN• **lattices** a pattern of strips that cross over one another

laugh •VERB• **laughs, laughing, laughed** to make a sound of enjoyment when you think something is funny

•NOUN• **laughs** the sound a person makes when they think something is funny

laughing stock •NOUN• **laughing stocks** a person who people laugh at in an unkind way because they seem ridiculous

laughter •NOUN• laughing: *the sound of laughter • roaring with laughter*

launch •VERB• **launches, launching, launched 1** to put a boat or ship in the water for the first time

2 to fire a rocket off

3 to start something like a project or start to sell a new product: *The company are launching a new chocolate bar.*

•NOUN• **launches 1** the act of launching something: *We'll be able to watch the shuttle launch on the TV.* **2** a large motorboat

launch pad •NOUN• **launch pads** a platform that a spacecraft is launched from

launder •VERB• **launders, laundering, laundered** to launder clothes is to wash or clean them so that they are ready to wear again

+ **launderette** •NOUN• **launderettes** a shop full of washing machines that you can pay to use

+ **laundry** •NOUN• **laundries 1** clothes that are going to be washed, or have just been washed **2** a business where you can send washing to be done

lava •NOUN• the hot liquid rock that comes out of an erupting volcano and becomes solid as it cools down

lavatory •NOUN• **lavatories** a toilet

lavender •NOUN• a plant with purple flowers that smell strong and sweet

lavish •VERB• **lavishes, lavishing, lavished** to **lavish something on** someone is to give them a lot, or too much of it: *Her parents had always lavished gifts on her.*

•ADJECTIVE• very generous, with more than enough of everything: *a lavish dinner*
• *lavish praise*

law •NOUN• **laws 1** a rule or set of rules for everyone in a country or state: *Driving at the age of 13 is against the law.* • *You could study law at university.* **2** a scientific rule that explains what always happens in certain circumstances: *The law of gravity means that the apple will fall downwards.*

lawful •ADJECTIVE• allowed by the law
+ **lawfully** •ADVERB• according to the law: *Were they lawfully married?*

lawn •NOUN• **lawns** an area of smooth grass in a garden

lawnmower •NOUN• **lawnmowers** a machine for cutting large areas of grass

lawyer •NOUN• **lawyers** someone whose job is to advise people about the law

lax •ADJECTIVE• **laxer, laxest** not strict: *Discipline has been too lax recently.*

lay •VERB• **lays, laying, laid 1** to put something down: *lay the book on the table* **2** to arrange something: *lay the table • lay a trap* **3** to lay an egg is to produce it **4** to **lay off** is to stop doing something or using something: *Tom's trying to lay off sweets.* **5** to **lay someone off** is to stop them working for you: *The local factories have been laying off workers.*

ⓘ Try not to confuse **lay** with **lie**. You **lay** something somewhere, whereas you **lie** somewhere:
Lay your pencils on your desks.
I am going to lie in bed for a while.
The past tenses can be confusing too. **Lay** is also a past tense of **lie**:
The cat lay on the mat.

---

layabout •NOUN• **layabouts** a lazy person

lay-by •NOUN• **lay-bys** an area at the side of a road for drivers to stop for a while out of the way of moving traffic

layer •NOUN• **layers** a covering that lies flat over something or a thickness under something: *grass covered with a layer of*

layout → leap year

snow • *a layer of jam in the middle of the cake*

layout •NOUN• **layouts** the way things are set out or arranged: *The layout of the rooms is different.*

laze •VERB• **lazes, lazing, lazed** to be lazy and do very little: *I just like to laze around in the holidays.*

lazily •ADVERB• in a slow, unhurried way

lazy •ADJECTIVE• **lazier, laziest** not wanting to do anything much, especially work: *You must be the laziest pupil in this school.*

lb •ABBREVIATION• short for **pound** or **pounds** in weight: *2lbs of sugar*

lead¹ •VERB• **leads, leading, led** 1 to show someone the way by going first: *You lead and I'll follow on my bike.*
2 to direct or control a group of people: *Kim was leading a discussion about homework.*
3 if you lead a busy life, you are always busy
4 a road that leads somewhere goes to that place
•NOUN• **leads** 1 the first or front place: *Jenkins has been in the lead for most of the race.*
2 help or guidance: *Follow my lead and just do what I do.* • *The police are following up several new leads.*
3 an electrical wire or cable: *Someone had cut the lead to the alarm.*
4 a strap or chain attached to a dog's collar that you can hold when you walk with it: *Please keep your dog on its lead.*
⇒ **leader**

ⓘ The verb **lead**, and the nouns connected with it, are pronounced *leed*. The noun **lead**, a kind of metal, is pronounced *led*.

lead² •NOUN• **leads** 1 a soft, dark grey metal
2 the inside part of a pencil that writes, made of graphite

leader •NOUN• **leaders** a person who leads: *the leader of the expedition*
♦ **leadership** •NOUN• 1 being a leader: *The club's done well under Will's leadership.*
2 the ability to lead: *He's a good worker but he lacks leadership.*

leaf •NOUN• **leaves** 1 a part of a plant that grows out from the side of the stem and is usually green 2 a page of a book
• **turn over a new leaf** to make a new start and do better

leaflet •NOUN• **leaflets** a small printed sheet of paper

leafy •ADJECTIVE• **leafier, leafiest** 1 a leafy plant or tree has a lot of leaves 2 a leafy place has a lot of plants or trees

league •NOUN• **leagues** 1 a group of people or nations who agree to work together
2 a group of teams that play sports matches against each other
3 an old measure of distance that was about 3 miles
• **in league with** working together with someone: *The man and the woman were in league with each other.*

leak •NOUN• **leaks** 1 a hole that liquid or gas can escape or enter through
2 an escape of gas or liquid
3 there is a leak when someone lets out secret information
•VERB• **leaks, leaking, leaked** 1 to escape: *Gas was leaking from somewhere under the floor.*
2 to let liquid or gas in or out through a hole: *My boots leak.*
3 to give secret information away: *This news was leaked to a newspaper yesterday.*
♦ **leakage** •NOUN• **leakages** an escape of gas, a liquid or information: *We lost a lot of oil through leakage.*

lean •VERB• **leans, leaning, leant** 1 to rest against something: *a boy leaning on the wall*
2 to slope over to one side: *Lean over and get the salt for me would you?*
3 to rely on someone: *You know you can always lean on me.*
•ADJECTIVE• **leaner, leanest** without any or much fat: *Models have to look lean these days.* • *I'll only buy lean meat.*

leap •VERB• **leaps, leaping, leapt** to jump high or long: *dolphins leaping out of the water*
•NOUN• **leaps** a big jump: *a leap over the river*

leap year •NOUN• **leap years** a year that

Aa Bb Cc Dd Ee Ff Gg Hh Ii Jj Kk Ll Mm Nn Oo Pp Qq Rr Ss Tt Uu Vv Ww Xx Yy Zz

occurs every four years and has 366 days. The extra day is February 29

learn •VERB• **learns, learning, learnt** or **learned** to get to know something or how to do something: *learn your lines for the play* • *learning how to swim*

♦ **learner** •NOUN• **learners** a person who is being taught something

♦ **learning** •NOUN• knowledge: *a man of great learning*

lease •NOUN• **leases** an agreement to rent something like a flat or house to someone
•VERB• **leases, leasing, leased** to rent something to someone

leash •NOUN• **leashes** a lead for taking a dog for a walk

least •ADJECTIVE• the smallest amount of anything: *The person who had the least difficulty was the tallest.*
•ADVERB• the lowest amount: *Which trousers cost least?*
• **at least** 1 not less than: *She must be at least forty years old.* 2 at any rate: *John has finished, at least he should have.*

leather •NOUN• **leathers** a material for making shoes, bags and clothes that is made from the skin of an animal

leave •VERB• **leaves, leaving, left** 1 to go away from someone, something or somewhere: *I left school early.*
2 to not take something with you when you go away: *Mum always leaves her umbrella on the bus.*
3 to give something to someone in your will: *Granny left Joy all her jewellery.*
•NOUN• 1 holiday time from work: *a week's leave* 2 permission to do something

lecture •NOUN• **lectures** 1 a talk by someone to an audience or a group of students 2 a long telling-off
•VERB• **lectures, lecturing, lectured** 1 to give a talk on a particular subject to a class or audience 2 to give someone a good telling-off: *'This is not good for your children,' he lectured. 'You are letting them get away with too much.'*

led •VERB• a way of changing the verb **lead** to make a past tense. It can be used with or without a helping verb: *Connor led a wild*

life for many years. • *Where have you led us?*

ledge •NOUN• **ledges** a shelf or something that sticks out like a shelf: *a ledge of rock* • *a window ledge*

leek •NOUN• **leeks** a long green and white vegetable of the onion family

lee •NOUN• the sheltered side of something, away from the wind: *sitting in the lee of the wall*

left¹ •ADJECTIVE• on the other side from the right side, for example, on the side of a page you usually start reading: *Do you write with your right or left hand?*
•ADVERB• on or towards the other side from the right: *Now turn left.*
•NOUN• the left is the other side from the right side: *Can we stop just here on the left?*

left² •VERB• a way of changing the verb **leave** to make a past tense. It can be used with or without a helping verb: *I have left my book at home.* • *We all thanked them when they left.*

left-handed •ADJECTIVE• 1 preferring to use your left hand to do things, rather than your right 2 meant to be used by the left hand rather than the right: *a left-handed pair of scissors*

leftovers •PLURAL NOUN• food that has not been eaten up at a meal: *Shall I put the leftovers in the fridge?*

leg •NOUN• **legs** 1 one of the parts of the body that animals and humans stand and walk on
2 one half of a pair of trousers
3 one of the upright supports of a piece of furniture like a table or chair
4 one stage in a journey or a contest: *This is the second leg of the race across Europe.*

legacy •NOUN• **legacies** something that someone leaves in their will

legal •ADJECTIVE• 1 allowed by the law: *Is it legal to ride your bike on the pavement?* 2 to do with the law: *legal studies*
♦ **legalize** or **legalise** •VERB• **legalizes, legalizing, legalized** to legalize something is to make it allowed by law: *Most states have legalized gambling.*

Aa
Bb
Cc
Dd
Ee
Ff
Gg
Hh
Ii
Jj
Kk
Ll
Mm
Nn
Oo
Pp
Qq
Rr
Ss
Tt
Uu
Vv
Ww
Xx
Yy
Zz

legend •NOUN• **legends** a traditional story that is handed down through generations
  ♦ **legendary** •ADJECTIVE• **1** belonging to legends: *legendary knights* **2** very famous: *His goal-scoring exploits were legendary.*

legible •ADJECTIVE• easy to read: *The letter became less legible towards the end.*
  ♦ **legibility** •NOUN• how easy something is to read
  ♦ **legibly** •ADVERB• in a way that is easy to read: *Could you write your name more legibly please?*

legion •NOUN• **legions 1** a group of several thousand Roman soldiers **2** a very great number

legislation •NOUN• a law or set of laws

legitimate •ADJECTIVE• **1** lawful: *the legitimate government* **2** logical and reasonable: *a legitimate complaint*
  ♦ **legitimately** •ADVERB• according to the law: *not legitimately married*

leisure •NOUN• your leisure is your spare time
  ♦ **leisurely** •ADJECTIVE• not rushed or hurried: *walking at a leisurely pace*

lemon •NOUN• **lemons 1** an oval fruit with a hard, yellow skin and very sour juice **2** a pale yellow colour

lemonade •NOUN• a soft drink that has a lemon flavour

lend •VERB• **lends, lending, lent** to let someone borrow something for a time
  • **lend a hand** to help someone

length •NOUN• **lengths 1** how long something is in time or in space: *twice the length of a normal lesson* • *measure the table's length* **2** a piece of something that can be measured in length: *a length of plastic piping*
  • **at length 1** in detail: *The doctor explained the different treatments at length.* **2** at last: *At length everyone had arrived.*
  ♦ **lengthen** •VERB• **lengthens, lengthening, lengthened 1** to lengthen something is to make it longer: *I think you should lengthen that skirt.* **2** to lengthen is to grow longer: *a lengthening queue*
  ♦ **lengthy** •ADJECTIVE• **lengthier, lengthiest** taking a long time: *a lengthy delay*

lenient •ADJECTIVE• not very strict in giving punishments

lens •NOUN• **lenses 1** a piece of glass that is curved on one or both sides and is used in equipment like glasses, cameras and telescopes **2** a part of your eye behind your pupil

ⓘ **Lens** comes from the Latin word for *lentil.* This is because it was believed that the lens in your eye is shaped like a lentil.

Lent •NOUN• in the Christian church, the forty days before Easter when, for religious reasons, people give up something they enjoy

lent •VERB• a way of changing the verb **lend** to make a past tense. It can be used with or without a helping verb: *Here's the book you lent me yesterday.* • *You haven't lent him money, have you?*

lentil •NOUN• **lentils** a small seed that is often cooked in soups and other dishes

leopard •NOUN• **leopards** an animal of the cat family with a spotted skin

ⓘ This word is pronounced **lep**-ird.

leotard •NOUN• **leotards** a tight-fitting, stretchy piece of clothing that you wear for doing exercises or dancing

leper •NOUN• **lepers** someone who suffers from leprosy

leprechaun •NOUN• **leprechauns** a small, magical creature in Irish folk tales that likes to cause mischief

leprosy •NOUN• a serious infectious skin disease that can cause damage to parts of the body
  ⇒ **leper**

less •ADJECTIVE AND ADVERB• not as much: *We'll have to spend less money.*
  •NOUN• a smaller amount: *I've got less than he has.*
  •PREPOSITION• minus: *I save all my money, less my money for sweets.*
  ♦ **lessen** •VERB• **lessens, lessening, lessened** to make or become smaller: *My sadness lessened as the days passed.*
  ♦ **lesser** •ADJECTIVE• smaller

Aa
Bb
Cc
Dd
Ee
Ff
Gg
Hh
Ii
Jj
Kk
Ll
Mm
Nn
Oo
Pp
Qq
Rr
Ss
Tt
Uu
Vv
Ww
Xx
Yy
Zz

lesson •NOUN• **lessons 1** a period of teaching: *When's our next lesson?* **2** something that you learn or that someone teaches you: *one of the most important lessons about history* **3** a reading from the Bible in a church service

let •VERB• **lets, letting, let 1** to let someone do something is to allow them to do it: *Please let me go!* **2** to let a property is to rent it out **3** to **let someone down** is to disappoint them: *If she promises me something, she won't let me down.* **4** to **let someone off** is to not punish them even though they have done something wrong **5** if something **lets up**, it becomes less: *It seemed as if the rain would never let up.*

lethal •ADJECTIVE• able to kill: *a lethal weapon*

let's •VERB• another way of saying 'shall we?': *Let's have a game of cards.*

letter •NOUN• **letters 1** a message that you write and send to another person **2** one of the written shapes that you combine to write words, like *a*, *b* or *c* ✦ **lettering** •NOUN• writing, especially when it is for decoration: *The title is on the picture frame in gold lettering.*

lettuce •NOUN• **lettuces** a green vegetable whose leaves are used in salads

leukaemia •NOUN• a kind of cancer that affects the body's white blood cells

level •ADJECTIVE• **1** flat or horizontal: *a piece of level ground* **2** being as high as something else: *The picture needs to be level with the mirror next to it.* •NOUN• **levels 1** a particular position: *pictures at eye level all around the room* **2** a particular standard or grade: *It's best to start at beginners' level.* **3** a tool that shows if a surface is horizontal or vertical •VERB• **levels, levelling, levelled 1** to level something is to make it flat, smooth or horizontal: *The ground will have to be levelled before they can build on it.* **2** to level things is to make them equal:

Grey scored again to level the scores. **3** to level a gun at someone or something is to aim it at them **4** to **level off** or **level out** is to become horizontal: *The plane levelled out at 2000 feet.*

level crossing •NOUN• **level crossings** a place where a road crosses a railway track

lever •NOUN• **levers 1** a strong bar for pushing against or pulling on in order to move something heavy **2** a handle that operates a machine: *Push the lever up to start the engine.* •VERB• **levers, levering, levered** to move something by forcing a bar under or behind it: *It should be possible to lever the door open.*

lexical •ADJECTIVE• to do with words

lexicon •NOUN• **lexicons** a dictionary or a list of words for a certain subject

liability •NOUN• **liabilities 1** responsibility for something **2** a person or thing that is likely to cause a problem for you

liable •ADJECTIVE• **1** very likely to: *She's liable to lose her temper very suddenly.* **2** responsible for something: *You are liable to pay for any damage.*

liar •NOUN• **liars** someone who tells lies

liberal •ADJECTIVE• **1** broad-minded and seeing many different points of view **2** a liberal amount of something is a lot of it: *a very liberal helping of chocolate pudding* ✦ **liberally** •ADVERB• generously: *pour the sauce liberally over the dish*

liberate •VERB• **liberates, liberating, liberated** to set someone free ✦ **liberation** •NOUN• being set free from someone else's control

liberty •NOUN• **liberties** freedom, especially to do or say what you want: *You are at liberty to walk around the grounds.*

librarian •NOUN• **librarians** a person whose job is to look after a library

library •NOUN• **libraries** a building or room that has a collection of books or recordings

lice •NOUN• the plural form of the word **louse**

licence •NOUN• **licences** an official document that gives someone permission to

Aa Bb Cc Dd Ee Ff Gg Hh Ii Jj Kk Ll Mm Nn Oo Pp Qq Rr Ss Tt Uu Vv Ww Xx Yy Zz

do or have something: *a driving licence • a licence to fish*

ⓘ Remember that **licence** with a **c** is a noun: *a driving licence*
License with an **s** is a verb: *You are not licensed to fish here.*

license •VERB• **licenses, licensing, licensed** to allow or permit someone to do something

lichen • NOUN• **lichens** a kind of mossy plant that grows on surfaces like rocks and tree trunks

ⓘ This word is pronounced the same as the verb **liken**.

lick •VERB• **licks, licking, licked** to move your tongue over something: *licking your lips* •NOUN• **licks 1** a movement of your tongue over something: *Give the spoon one last lick.* **2** a small amount of something: *This room needs a lick of paint.*

licorice • NOUN• another spelling of **liquorice**

lid •NOUN• **lids 1** a cover that fits a container like a box or a pot **2** an eyelid

lie [1] •VERB• **lies, lying, lied** to say something that is not true: *We know Auntie May lies about her age.* •NOUN• **lies** a statement that is not true: *The boy's story is a pack of lies.*
⇒ **liar, lying**

lie [2] •VERB• **lies, lying, lay, laid 1** to rest in a flat position: *Lie flat on your back.* **2** to be or remain a certain way: *The buildings lay in ruins.*

ⓘ The past tense of **lie** when it means 'to tell an untruth' is **lied**.
The past tense of **lie** when it means 'to rest flat' is **lay**.

lieutenant • NOUN• **lieutenants** an officer in the army or navy

ⓘ This word is pronounced lef-**ten**-int.

life • NOUN• **lives 1** a life is the time between being born and dying
  2 life is the state of being alive: *feeling her pulse for any sign of life*
  3 life is energy and liveliness: *Try to put a bit more life into your singing.*

4 your life is the way you live: *Life on a boat is great fun.*
  5 life is all living things: *a book about pond life*

lifebelt • NOUN• **lifebelts** a large ring that will float and that someone can hold to stop them sinking under water

lifeboat • NOUN• **lifeboats** a boat for rescuing people at sea

life-cycle • NOUN• **life-cycles** the different stages that a living thing goes through from its birth to its death

lifeguard • NOUN• **lifeguards** someone who works at a swimming pool or on a beach to rescue people who are in danger of drowning

life-jacket • NOUN• **life-jackets** a jacket filled with air or other light material that will float and stop someone from sinking

lifeless • ADJECTIVE• **1** dead
  2 unconscious or without any signs of life
  3 dull and boring: *a lifeless performance*

lifelike • ADJECTIVE• very like a real living thing or person

lifeline • NOUN• **lifelines 1** a way of communicating or getting help if you need it: *The telephone is our lifeline.* **2** a rope used to rescue a person who has fallen in water

life-size • ADJECTIVE• a life-size picture or statue is the same size as the real person

lifespan • NOUN• **lifespans** the length of a life: *This creature has a lifespan of only one day.*

lifestyle • NOUN• **lifestyles** the way that someone lives: *We try to have a healthy lifestyle.*

lifetime • NOUN• **lifetimes** the time that a certain person is alive: *They've changed that law twice in my lifetime.*

lift •VERB• **lifts, lifting, lifted 1** to lift something is to pick it up or raise it: *She lifted her hand to her forehead.* **2** to lift is to move upwards: *The fog seems to be lifting.* •NOUN• **lifts 1** a movement upwards: *ten lifts with each leg*
  2 a moving platform that can take things or people between the floors of a building

3 a ride in someone's car: *Do you want a lift home?*

lift-off •NOUN• **lift-offs** the time when a spacecraft leaves the ground

light [1] •NOUN• **lights 1** light is what allows you to see things. Otherwise it would be dark: *The light in this room is good for painting.* **2** a light is something that gives light, such as a lamp or a candle: *Don't forget to switch off the light.*
• **come to light** if information comes to light, it is discovered or it turns up
•ADJECTIVE• **lighter, lightest 1** not dark: *It's still light enough to read.* • *Mike got up as soon as it began to get light.* **2** pale in colour: *light blue* • *You can make colours lighter by adding white to them.*
•VERB• **lights, lighting, lit 1** to light something is to make it burn with a flame: *Let's light the fire.*
2 to light is to start burning: *Why won't the cooker light?*
3 to light a place is to make it brighter: *The stage was lit with candles.*
⇒ **lighter, lighting**

light [2] •ADJECTIVE• **lighter, lightest 1** not heavy: *a light suitcase*
2 easy and not too serious: *light work* • *light music*
3 not large or strong: *a light shower*
⇒ **lightly**

lighten [1] •VERB• **lightens, lightening, lightened** to make something less heavy

lighten [2] •VERB• **lightens, lightening, lightened** to make something brighter

lighter •NOUN• **lighters** a device with a flame or spark that can make something burn, especially a cigarette

light-hearted •ADJECTIVE• **1** a light-hearted person is cheerful **2** something that is light-hearted is not very serious: *a light-hearted quiz*

lighthouse •NOUN• **lighthouses** a building like a tower that has a flashing light at the top to warn or guide ships

lighting •NOUN• equipment for giving light

lightly •ADVERB• **1** gently: *Mum touched me lightly on the arm and smiled.* **2** not in a very serious way: *They treated the problem too lightly.*

lightning •NOUN• an electric flash in the sky that often happens just before a clap of thunder

lightweight •ADJECTIVE• **1** not very heavy: *a lightweight raincoat* **2** not very important or serious

light-year •NOUN• **light-years** the distance that light travels in a year, which is 6 billion miles

like [1] •PREPOSITION• **1** similar to: *Geraldine looks just like her mother.*
2 in a similar way to: *She dances like a professional.*
3 typical of: *It's not like you to be late.*
•CONJUNCTION• as if: *You look like you've seen a ghost.*
⇒ **liken, likeness**

like [2] •VERB• **likes, liking, liked** to think that something or someone is nice or good: *I like pizza.*

likeable or **likable** •ADJECTIVE• a likeable person is attractive and pleasant

likelihood •NOUN• if there is a likelihood of something happening, it might or will probably happen

likely •ADJECTIVE• probable or expected: *It's very likely that nobody will come.*

liken •VERB• **likens, likening, likened** to say that two things are like each other: *Her writing has been likened to Enid Blyton's.*

likeness •NOUN• **likenesses 1** something similar: *I do see a likeness between the girls.* **2** a good likeness is something that looks very similar to the real thing or person: *The portrait is an excellent likeness of Katy.*

likewise •ADVERB• in the same way: *Keep the trimmings and likewise any fabric left over.*

lilac •NOUN• **lilacs** a bush or tree with hanging clusters of sweet-smelling white or purple flowers
•ADJECTIVE• pale purple

lilt •NOUN• **lilts** a light, swinging rhythm: *speaking with a lilt*

lily •NOUN• **lilies** a tall plant with large white

or coloured flowers that smell very sweet

limb •NOUN• **limbs 1** a leg or arm **2** a branch of a tree

limber •VERB• **limbers, limbering, limbered** to **limber up** is to stretch and warm your muscles up before doing harder exercise

lime •NOUN• **limes 1** a small fruit like a green lemon
2 a large tree with yellow blossom
3 a white substance that is used for making cement and fertilizers
4 a bright yellowish-green colour

limelight •NOUN• to be **in the limelight** is to be getting a lot of attention, especially from the public

limerick •NOUN• **limericks** a funny five-line poem

ⓘ This word comes from the place-name **Limerick** in Ireland. This name was repeated in a nonsense song in a game played in Victorian times.

limestone •NOUN• a type of rock that is used in building and making cement

limit •NOUN• **limits 1** a place or point that should not, or cannot, be passed: *There's a time limit for this test.* **2** a boundary: *within the city limits*
•VERB• **limits, limiting, limited** to keep someone or something within certain amounts: *I shall have to limit you to one cake each.*
♦ **limited** •ADJECTIVE• not great: *a limited choice*
♦ **limitation** •NOUN• **limitations** a weakness, or something that makes another thing imperfect: *Living in a city has its limitations.*

limousine •NOUN• **limousines** a large and luxurious car, especially one with a chauffeur

limp •VERB• **limps, limping, limped** to walk unevenly because of a problem with one leg or foot
•NOUN• **limps** an uneven walk: *walking with a limp*
•ADJECTIVE• **limper, limpest** not stiff or firm: *a limp lettuce • a limp handshake*

limpet •NOUN• **limpets** a small cone-shaped shellfish that clings to rocks

line[1] •NOUN• **lines 1** a long thin mark or stripe: *a white line in the middle of the road • walk in a straight line*
2 a row of things or people: *lines of marching soldiers • the third line down on the next page*
3 a length of rope, wire or string: *hanging the washing on the line*
4 a wrinkle, especially on someone's face
5 a railway: *the east coast line*
6 a telephone connection: *There's a strange noise on this line.*
7 a short letter: *I'll drop you a line to let you know how we get on.*
8 a subject or activity that you are interested or involved in: *What line are you in?*
•VERB• **lines, lining, lined 1** to line something like a street is to be along both sides of it: *Police officers will line the route of the procession.*
2 to **line up** is to stand or place in a row: *Line up for your dinner.*
3 to **line something up** is to arrange it: *Have we got anything lined up for this evening?*

line[2] •VERB• **lines, lining, lined** to cover something with a layer on the inside: *a jacket lined with silk*
⇒ **liner, lining**

line graph •NOUN• **line graphs** a chart that shows different amounts or quantities by using lines of different lengths next to each other

linen •NOUN• **1** a kind of cloth that is made from flax **2** things such as sheets or table cloths that used to be made from linen but are now often made from other fabrics

liner[1] •NOUN• **liners** a large passenger ship

liner[2] •NOUN• **liners** something that forms a layer inside a container and can be taken out: *a bin liner*

linesman or **lineswoman** •NOUN• **linesmen** or **lineswomen** someone who judges whether a ball has crossed a line during a game such as tennis

linger •VERB• **lingers, lingering, lingered**

Aa Bb Cc Dd Ee Ff Gg Hh Ii Jj Kk **Ll** Mm Nn Oo Pp Qq Rr Ss Tt Uu Vv Ww Xx Yy Zz

linguist → litre

to be slow to leave: *members of the audience lingering in the hall*

linguist •NOUN• **linguists** someone who knows a lot about languages

liniment •NOUN• **liniments** an oil or ointment that you rub into your skin to stop your muscles or joints hurting

lining •NOUN• **linings** a layer on the inside of something: *a silver box with a velvet lining*

link •NOUN• **links 1** one of the rings of a chain **2** someone or something that connects two things: *a rail link between the airport and the station*
•VERB• **links, linking, linked** to connect: *A footpath links the two buildings of the school.*

linoleum *or* **lino** •NOUN• a smooth, tough covering for floors

lint •NOUN• a soft material for putting on wounds

lion •NOUN• **lions** a powerful animal of the cat family. A male lion has a big shaggy mane

(i) This word comes from the Latin word for a lion, which is **leo**.

lioness •NOUN• **lionesses** a female lion

lip •NOUN• **lips 1** either the upper or the lower outside edge of your mouth **2** the shaped part of the outside edge of a container such as a jug: *a saucepan with a lip for pouring*

lip-read •VERB• **lip-reads, lip-reading, lip-read** to understand what someone is saying by watching the way their lips are moving, rather than by listening to them
• **lip-reader** •NOUN• **lip-readers** a person who understands what someone is saying by watching their lips

lipstick •NOUN• **lipsticks** a stick of creamy colour that you can put on your lips

liquid •NOUN• **liquids** a substance that can flow, such as oil or water

liquidize *or* **liquidise** •VERB• **liquidizes, liquidizing, liquidized** to make something into a liquid, especially a thick liquid: *Add some cream and liquidize the soup.*
• **liquidizer** *or* **liquidiser** *or* **liquidisers** •NOUN• **liquidizers** *or* **liquidisers** a machine

for making solid or lumpy foods into smooth liquid or paste

liquor •NOUN• **liquors** alcoholic drink

liquorice *or* **licorice** •NOUN• a black, sticky sweet that is flavoured with the root of the liquorice plant

lisp •VERB• **lisps, lisping, lisped** to say *th* for *s* or *z* because you cannot say these letters properly
•NOUN• a speech problem that makes a person say *s* and *z* like *th*

list •NOUN• **lists** a series of things like names, numbers or prices, one after another: *a shopping list*
•VERB• **lists, listing, listed** to say or write a lot of words, such as names, one after another: *Shall I list my crimes one by one?*

listen •VERB• **listens, listening, listened** to pay attention to something that you can hear: *Listen to me.*

listless •ADJECTIVE• without energy or interest: *feeling listless all day*

lit •VERB• a way of changing the verb **light** to make a past tense. It can be used with or without a helping verb: *Her face lit up at the idea.* • *I haven't lit the candles yet.*

literacy •NOUN• being able to read and write

literal •ADJECTIVE• meaning exactly what it says
♦ **literally** •ADVERB• in a literal way: *When she told you to jump in the lake, she didn't mean it literally.*

literary •ADJECTIVE• to do with books, authors and literature

literate •ADJECTIVE• able to read and write ⇒ **literacy**

literature •NOUN• **1** novels, poetry and plays: *19th-century literature* **2** all the written information about a subject

lithe •ADJECTIVE• **lither, lithest** a lithe person is able to bend and move very easily

litmus paper •NOUN• special paper that changes colour when it is dipped into an acid or alkaline

litre •NOUN• **litres** the basic measurement of volume in the metric system. This is often shortened to **l**

330

little •ADJECTIVE• **littler, littlest** small: *a little child* • *in a little while*
•ADVERB• **less, least** 1 a bit: *Jump up and down a little to keep warm.* 2 not very much: *We little understood how important this was.*
•PRONOUN• a small amount: *Would you like a little more milk?* • *We were a little worried by then.*

live¹ •VERB• **lives, living, lived** 1 to be alive
2 to have your home in a certain place: *How long have you lived in Bradford?*
3 to pass your life in a certain way: *She's used to living alone.*
⇒ **living**

live² •ADJECTIVE• 1 not dead
2 connected to an electricity supply: *a live socket*
3 a live broadcast or concert actually happens as you watch or listen to it

livelihood •NOUN• **livelihoods** the way you earn enough money to live properly

lively •ADJECTIVE• **livelier, liveliest** cheerful and full of energy: *a lively evening with lively people*

liver •NOUN• **livers** a large organ in the body that is very important for cleaning the blood

livestock •NOUN• farm animals: *All the livestock is kept indoors here.*

livid •ADJECTIVE• extremely angry *He was livid when she broke his camera.*

living •NOUN• **livings** a way of earning money: *What do you do for a living?*

living room •NOUN• **living rooms** a room for sitting and relaxing in

lizard •NOUN• **lizards** a four-footed reptile with a long body and tail and a scaly skin

llama •NOUN• **llamas** a South American animal like a shaggy camel without a hump, that is kept for its wool and to carry loads

load •VERB• **loads, loading, loaded** 1 to fill a vehicle like a car or ship with what it is going to carry
2 to load a gun is to put bullets in it
3 to load a machine is to put something in it: *load the camera with film*
4 to weight dice so that they always fall the same way

•NOUN• **loads** 1 a cargo that a vehicle carries
2 as much as a thing or person can carry at one time: *take another load upstairs*
3 a large amount: *a load of rubbish*

loaf •NOUN• **loaves** a loaf of bread has been shaped and baked in one piece
•VERB• **loafs, loafing, loafed** to **loaf about** is to spend your time being lazy

loan •VERB• **loans, loaning, loaned** to lend something to someone: *Mum loaned me the money for my new jacket.*
•NOUN• **loans** money that you borrow

loathe •VERB• **loathes, loathing, loathed** to hate: *Harold loathes shopping.*

lob •VERB• **lobs, lobbing, lobbed** to throw or hit a ball high into the air
•NOUN• **lobs** a hit or throw that curves high up into the air

lobby •NOUN• **lobbies** an entrance hall

lobe •NOUN• **lobes** 1 the soft round part at the bottom of your ear 2 one part of a body organ that has divisions, like the brain

lobster •NOUN• **lobsters** a large sea animal with a hard shell, two large claws and eight legs

local •ADJECTIVE• belonging to and around a certain area: *our local library*
•NOUN• **locals** 1 a person who lives within a certain area: *If you want to know the way, you'd better ask a local.* 2 someone's local is the pub nearest their home

locality •NOUN• **localities** a certain place and the area round about

locate •VERB• **locates, locating, located** 1 to find an exact position: *trying to locate the school on the map* 2 to be located in a place is to be situated there: *a cottage located in the Highlands*
♦ **location** •NOUN• **locations** a position or situation: *the exact location of the buried treasure*
♦ **on location** a film is shot on location when it is not filmed in a studio, but in the real world

loch •NOUN• **lochs** a lake in Scotland

lock¹ •NOUN• **locks** 1 a device that you work with a key to fasten things such as doors and drawers 2 a small section of a canal or river

Aa
Bb
Cc
Dd
Ee
Ff
Gg
Hh
Ii
Jj
Kk
Ll
Mm
Nn
Oo
Pp
Qq
Rr
Ss
Tt
Uu
Vv
Ww
Xx
Yy
Zz

with gates at each end. The level of the water in the lock can be changed so that boats can pass to higher or lower sections of the canal or river

•VERB• **locks, locking, locked** 1 to lock something like a door is to fasten it with a key 2 something like a door locks if it is possible to fasten it with a key: *Don't leave valuables in this room because the door doesn't lock.* 3 to **lock something up** or **away** is to put it somewhere that can be locked with a key: *I locked all my jewellery away in a box.*

lock² •NOUN• **locks** a lock of hair is a piece of it

locker •NOUN• **lockers** a small cupboard, especially one that can be locked

locket •NOUN• **lockets** a little case, usually of silver or gold, on a necklace chain

locomotion •NOUN• the power of moving from place to place
   ♦ **locomotive** •NOUN• **locomotives** a railway engine that pulls trains

locust •NOUN• **locusts** a large insect like a grasshopper that flies in large groups that eat and destroy growing plants

lodge •VERB• **lodges, lodging, lodged** 1 to get stuck somewhere: *A piece of apple had lodged between his front teeth.* 2 to live in a room in someone else's house and pay them rent 3 to lodge a complaint is to make it officially
   •NOUN• **lodges** 1 a small house, often at the gate of a larger property 2 a house in the country used by hunters and sportspeople: *a hunting lodge*
   ♦ **lodger** •NOUN• **lodgers** a person who lives in rooms that they rent in someone else's house
   ♦ **lodging** •NOUN• **lodgings** 1 a place to stay, especially for a short time 2 lodgings are where you stay when you rent rooms in someone else's house

loft •NOUN• **lofts** the space between the roof of a house and the rooms: *suitcases stored in the loft*

lofty •ADJECTIVE• **loftier, loftiest** high or tall: *lofty ceilings*

log •NOUN• **logs** 1 a section of a branch or tree trunk that has been cut up 2 an official record of what happens on a journey,

especially of a ship or aeroplane

logic •NOUN• a way of thinking that involves correct reasoning
   ♦ **logical** •ADJECTIVE• following reasonably and sensibly from facts or events: *the logical thing to do next*

logo •NOUN• **logos** a small design that is the symbol of a company or product

loiter •VERB• **loiters, loitering, loitered** to stand around doing nothing: *Her friends loitered at the door.*

loll •VERB• **lolls, lolling, lolled** 1 to lie or sit about lazily: *Pete's been lolling about, watching football all afternoon.* 2 your head or tongue lolls when it hangs loosely

lollipop •NOUN• **lollipops** a hard sticky sweet on a stick

lollipop man *or* **lollipop woman** •NOUN• **lollipop men** *or* **lollipop women** a person whose job is to hold up a tall stick with a round sign on it to stop the traffic so that schoolchildren can cross the road

lolly •NOUN• **lollies** 1 a lollipop 2 an ice lolly

ⓘ In some dialects in Britain the word **lolly** means *tongue*, and the words lollipop and lolly may have come from this.

lone •ADJECTIVE• a lone person or thing is all alone

loneliness •NOUN• 1 being unhappy because you are alone 2 being a long way from anything or anyone else

lonely •ADJECTIVE• **lonelier, loneliest** 1 a lonely person feels sad because they are alone, with no friends around them 2 a lonely place has very few people living in it or visiting it: *a lonely cottage on the hillside*

long¹ •ADJECTIVE• **longer, longest** 1 big from one end to the other: *a long supermarket queue* • *a long way home* 2 lasting or taking a lot of time: *a long delay* • *the long summer holidays*
   •ADVERB• **longer, longest** 1 for a long time: *Have you been waiting long?* • *It won't be long till she starts school.* 2 through the whole time: *I've been looking forward to this all day long.*
   ⇒ **length**

long[2] •VERB• **longs, longing, longed** to want something very much: *longing to sit down* • *longing for a rest*
♦ **longing** •NOUN• **longings** a very strong wish for something: *looking at the food with longing*

long division •NOUN• a dividing sum where you write all the working out in full

longitude •NOUN• the position of a place east or west of an imaginary line that passes from north to south through Greenwich, London. This line is shown on maps as 0°. Look up and compare **latitude**

long jump •NOUN• the long jump is an athletics contest where you run and then jump as far as possible along the ground

long-range •ADJECTIVE• 1 able to reach a great distance: *long-range missiles* 2 looking a long way into the future: *a long-range weather forecast*

long-sighted •ADJECTIVE• a long-sighted person sees objects that are far away more clearly than they see things closer to them

long-term •ADJECTIVE• lasting or taking place for a long time: *the long-term effects of this medicine* • *long-term plans*

loo •NOUN• **loos** a toilet

look •VERB• **looks, looking, looked** 1 to turn your eyes to see something
2 to appear or seem: *You look tired.*
3 to face a certain direction: *The window looks south.*
4 to **look after** something or someone is to take care of them: *Her husband looks after the baby during the day.*
5 to **look down on** someone is to think they are not as good or important as you: *Don't look down on me just because I'm not as rich as you.*
6 to **look forward to** something is to feel happy because you know you're going to enjoy it: *looking forward to the holidays*
•NOUN• **looks** 1 a glance at something or an examination of it: *Take a look at this.*
2 a certain expression on your face: *She gave me a warning look.*
3 the appearance of a thing or person: *I don't like the look of those black clouds.*

look-alike •NOUN• **look-alikes** a person who looks very like someone else: *a Prince Charles look-alike*

looking-glass •NOUN• **looking-glasses** a mirror

lookout •NOUN• **lookouts** 1 a person who watches for danger: *The lookout spotted a boat on the horizon.*
2 a place where someone can keep watch
3 to **keep a lookout** is to watch carefully for something
4 something that is **your lookout** is your problem or concern and nobody else's: *If you do not study for the exam, that's your own lookout.*

loom[1] •NOUN• **looms** a weaving machine for making cloth

loom[2] •VERB• **looms, looming, loomed** 1 to appear over or in front of you, especially in a frightening way: *A shadowy figure loomed towards us.* 2 to wait in the future, especially in a worrying way: *A big decision is looming before us.*

loop •NOUN• **loops** the shape of something like a thread or piece of string when it curves around and crosses over itself: *Make a loop and pull one end through it.*
•VERB• **loops, looping, looped** to twist something around loosely: *a scarf looped around her neck*

loose •ADJECTIVE• **looser, loosest** 1 not tight or firmly fixed: *a loose knot* 2 not tied up or shut in: *hair hanging loose* • *Let the dogs run around loose.*
• **on the loose** free, especially after escaping: *a dangerous criminal on the loose*
♦ **loosen** •VERB• **loosens, loosening, loosened** to make something less firm, fixed or tight: *I had to loosen my belt.*

loot •NOUN• stolen goods or money
•VERB• **loots, looting, looted** to steal things quickly from shops, businesses or homes, especially during times of violence, like a war: *Shops were looted during the riot.*

lopsided •ADJECTIVE• uneven, with one side higher or lower than the other: *a lopsided smile*

lord •NOUN• **lords** 1 a man who has the title *Lord* in front of his name

Aa Bb Cc Dd Ee Ff Gg Hh Ii Jj Kk Ll Mm Nn Oo Pp Qq Rr Ss Tt Uu Vv Ww Xx Yy Zz

Aa

2 the title of men with high social rank, of judges and of bishops: *Lord Asquith* • *the Lord Mayor of London*

Bb

3 a master or ruler: *He was lord of all he could see.*

Cc

lore •NOUN• all the knowledge, stories and beliefs that get handed down through the generations

Dd

Ee

lorry •NOUN• **lorries** a large motor vehicle for taking heavy loads by road

Ff

lose •VERB• **loses, losing, lost 1** to forget where you put something: *I've lost my keys.*

Gg

2 to have something taken away from you: *Fifty people have lost their jobs.*

Hh

3 to have less of something than you had before: *I'm losing patience with you all.*

Ii

4 to be beaten in a contest: *I lost by 4 games to 6.*

Jj

5 a clock or watch loses time when it goes too slowly: *My watch is losing about a minute a day.*

Kk

Ll

♦ **loser** •NOUN• **losers 1** the person who does not win an argument, contest or battle: *Even the loser will win a huge amount of money.* **2** someone who never seems to succeed at anything

Mm

Nn

loss •NOUN• **losses 1** when you cannot find something or have had something taken away: *the loss of his home in a fire*

Oo

2 having less of something than you had before: *a loss of nearly a million pounds*

Pp

3 a disadvantage: *It'll be your loss if you do not buy this wonderful car.*

Qq

Rr

lost •ADJECTIVE• **1** something that is lost is missing: *The painting has been lost for centuries.*

Ss

2 someone who is lost does not know where they are: *How did you get lost when you had a map?*

Tt

Uu

3 you are lost when you are confused: *I'm lost – can you explain that last bit again?*

Vv

4 a person is lost if they are killed: *soldiers lost in battle*

Ww

lot •NOUN• **lots 1** a large number or amount: *a lot of people* • *lots of money*

Xx

2 a group of things or people: *Another lot of visitors will arrive tomorrow.*

Yy

3 an area of land: *a parking lot*

Zz

• **draw lots** to draw lots is to decide who should do something by drawing a different

card, stick or piece of paper from several that look the same

• **the lot** everything: *Alice only wanted one but decided to take the lot.*

lotion •NOUN• **lotions** a liquid for putting on your skin or hair: *a moisturizing lotion*

lottery •NOUN• **lotteries** an event where people win money or prizes when their number or ticket is chosen by chance from many others

loud •ADJECTIVE• **louder, loudest 1** making a lot of sound: *a loud noise* **2** a loud colour is very bright

•ADVERB• **louder, loudest** making a lot of sound: *Could you speak a little louder please?*

♦ **loudly** •ADVERB• making a lot of sound or noise: *crying loudly*

loudhailer •NOUN• **loudhailers** an electronic device that you can put over your mouth to make your voice much louder so that you do not have to shout

loudspeaker •NOUN• **loudspeakers** the part of a sound system that the sound actually comes out of

lounge •NOUN• **lounges** a sitting room
•VERB• **lounges, lounging, lounged** to sit or lie around lazily: *students lounging around the common room*

louse •NOUN• **lice** a small insect that lives on a person or animal

lout •NOUN• **louts** a young man who behaves in a rough and unpleasant way

lovable •ADJECTIVE• easy to love or like a lot: *a lovable child*

love •NOUN• **loves 1** a deep feeling of liking something or someone very much: *I have great love for my grandparents.*

2 something or someone that you like very much: *Her great love was music.*

3 in a game such as tennis, a score of nothing: *The score was now forty-love.*
•VERB• **loves, loving, loved** to like someone or something very much: *Greg had always loved cricket.*

♦ **lover** •NOUN• **lovers 1** a person who loves someone else, especially someone who is having a love affair **2** someone who is very enthusiastic about something: *an art lover*

loveliness •NOUN• how lovely a thing or person is: *gazing at her loveliness*

lovely •ADJECTIVE• **lovelier, loveliest**
1 beautiful or attractive: *lovely eyes*
2 enjoyable or pleasing: *It was lovely to see you again.*

loving •ADJECTIVE• full of love: *a loving look*

low[1] •ADJECTIVE AND ADVERB• **lower, lowest**
1 near to the ground: *a low hedge* • *clouds getting lower and lower*
2 near the bottom of something such as a list or a scale of measurement: *Your name's quite low on the list.*
3 a low sound or musical note is near the bottom of the range of pitch or musical notes: *She spoke in a low voice.* • *the lowest note you can sing*
4 less than usual in amount or importance: *low prices* • *Soon their supplies began to run low.*
5 sad or fed up: *Are you feeling a bit low?*

low[2] •VERB• **lows, lowing, lowed** to make the noise that a cow makes

lower •VERB• **lowers, lowering, lowered** to move something to a position nearer the bottom of something or nearer the gound: *If we lower the hem, you'll trip over it.*

lowland •ADJECTIVE• to do with land that is quite flat and near sea level: *lowland farms*
• **lowlands** •PLURAL NOUN• areas of land without mountains

lowly •ADJECTIVE• **lowlier, lowliest** having a low, unimportant position

loyal •ADJECTIVE• supporting and faithful: *a loyal fan*
• **loyally** •ADVERB• in a faithful way: *I loyally voted for him every time.*
• **loyalty** •NOUN• faithful support for your friends

lozenge •NOUN• **lozenges** 1 a sweet that you suck, especially to help a sore throat 2 a diamond shape

LP •NOUN• **LPs** a record that plays for about 30 minutes on each side

Ltd •ABBREVIATION• short for the word

Limited in the names of companies: *Joe Bloggs Shoes Ltd*

lubricate •VERB• **lubricates, lubricating, lubricated** to put oil or grease on something like an engine or machine, to make it run smoothly
• **lubrication** •NOUN• 1 making something move more easily by adding oil or grease 2 a substance like oil or grease that will help moving parts to work more smoothly

luck •NOUN• 1 the way things happen by chance: *What bad luck that it rained all that day!* 2 something good that happens by chance: *It was a piece of luck that I found the money.*
• **luckily** •ADVERB• by a good chance: *The car hit us, but luckily, nobody was badly hurt.*
• **lucky** •ADJECTIVE• **luckier, luckiest** a lucky person has good things happen to them by chance: *You're lucky to live so near the school.*

ludicrous •ADJECTIVE• completely ridiculous or silly: *a ludicrous idea*

ludo •NOUN• a board game with counters that the players move according to the numbers they throw on the dice

lug •VERB• **lugs, lugging, lugged** to pull or drag something with difficulty: *lugging the suitcases up the stairs*

luggage •NOUN• a traveller's suitcases and bags: *Make sure all your luggage is labelled.*

lukewarm •ADJECTIVE• 1 slightly warm: *The water in the shower was only lukewarm.*
2 not very interested or enthusiastic: *We got a lukewarm welcome when we arrived.*

lull •VERB• **lulls, lulling, lulled** to make someone feel calm and relaxed: *lulling the baby to sleep*
•NOUN• **lulls** a time when something noisy or busy stops for a while: *a lull in the fighting*

lullaby •NOUN• **lullabies** a gentle song to lull a child to sleep

lumber •VERB• **lumbers, lumbering, lumbered** 1 to move heavily, slowly and clumsily: *We saw a bear lumbering through the forest.* 2 to **be lumbered with** something is to be given something that you do not want: *I got lumbered with the washing up.*

Aa Bb Cc Dd Ee Ff Gg Hh Ii Jj Kk Ll Mm Nn Oo Pp Qq Rr Ss Tt Uu Vv Ww Xx Yy Zz

lumberjack •NOUN• **lumberjacks** a person whose job is to cut down and chop up trees

luminous •ADJECTIVE• glowing in the dark: *luminous stars that you can stick on your ceiling*

lump •NOUN• **lumps 1** a small, shapeless piece of something: *a lump of coal* • *I can't make custard without lumps in it.* **2** a hard swelling on your body
•VERB• **lumps, lumping, lumped** to **lump someone** or **something together** is to treat them all in the same way

lunacy •NOUN• madness

lunar •ADJECTIVE• to do with the moon

lunatic •NOUN• **lunatics** someone who is mad: *driving like a lunatic*
⇒ **lunacy**

ⓘ This word comes from the Latin word **luna**, which means *moon*. In Latin, **lunaticus** meant 'made mad by the moon'.

lunch •NOUN• **lunches** the meal that you eat in the middle of the day between breakfast and dinner

lung •NOUN• **lungs** the two bag-like organs inside your chest that you use for breathing

lunge •VERB• **lunges, lunging, lunged** to make a sudden strong or violent move forwards
•NOUN• **lunges** a sudden violent move forwards: *An angry customer made a lunge at the manager.*

lurch •VERB• **lurches, lurching, lurched** to move along unevenly, especially suddenly rolling to one side: *The boat lurched and we fell over.*

•NOUN• **lurches** a sudden roll to one side

lure •VERB• **lures, luring, lured** to tempt a person or animal with some kind of reward: *Scraps of food are used to lure the animals out of their burrows.*
•NOUN• **lures** something that tempts an animal or person to do something: *The lure of going out was too strong to resist.*

lurk •VERB• **lurks, lurking, lurked** to wait secretly where you cannot be seen: *Was there someone lurking over there in the shadows?*

luscious •ADJECTIVE• sweet, delicious and juicy

lush •ADJECTIVE• **lusher, lushest** lush plants are healthy and growing well: *cows grazing on lush farmland*

lustre •NOUN• a shiny appearance
✦ **lustrous** •ADJECTIVE• shining or glossy

luxuriant •ADJECTIVE• growing richly and thickly: *luxuriant forest*

luxurious •ADJECTIVE• very comfortable and expensive

luxury •NOUN• **luxuries 1** extremely comfortable, expensive surroundings and possessions: *living in luxury* **2** something very pleasant, but not necessary: *We can't afford many luxuries.*

lying •NOUN• telling lies: *Are you accusing me of lying?*

lyric •NOUN• **lyrics 1** a lyric is a short poem about feelings and emotions **2** the lyrics of a song are its words
✦ **lyrical** •ADJECTIVE• sounding like poetry or music: *a lyrical description of the scenery*

Mm

m •ABBREVIATION• short for **metre** or **metres**, or **million**

mac •ABBREVIATION• **macs** short for **mackintosh**, a type of raincoat: *a plastic mac*

macabre •ADJECTIVE• something that is macabre is strange and horrible, because it involves evil or death: *a macabre painting of skulls and bones*

macaroni •NOUN• tubes of pasta cut into short lengths

macaroon •NOUN• **macaroons** a biscuit or cake made with ground almonds and sugar

machine •NOUN• **machines** a device with moving parts and operated by some form of power, designed to do a particular job or work: *a washing machine*
•VERB• **machines, machining, machined** to machine something is to sew it, shape it, or cut it using a machine or a machine tool

machine-gun •NOUN• **machine-guns** a type of automatic gun that fires bullets quickly one after the other

machinery •NOUN• machines: *combine harvesters and other farming machinery*

machine tool •NOUN• **machine tools** a piece of equipment used to cut and shape metals

macho •ADJECTIVE• a macho man behaves in a tough and aggressive way

mackerel •NOUN• **mackerels** or **mackerel** a small edible sea fish with a narrow striped body

mackintosh •NOUN• **mackintoshes** a waterproof coat, usually reaching down to the knees or below

mad •ADJECTIVE• **madder, maddest**
1 mentally ill: *The poor woman went mad with grief.*
2 foolish or reckless: *Swimming in shark-infested waters is a mad thing to do.*
3 very angry: *Mum will be mad when she sees the state of your clothes.*

4 to be mad about someone or something is to like them or it very much: *mad about football*
• **like mad** desperately or using a lot of energy: *She was pedalling like mad to keep up with the rest.*
⇒ **madden, madly, madness**

madam •NOUN• **madams** a formal and polite way of addressing a woman, especially at the beginning of a letter or when serving her in a shop

madcap •ADJECTIVE• foolish and reckless

mad cow disease •NOUN• the common name for **BSE**, a disease that affects the brains and nervous systems of cattle

madden •VERB• **maddens, maddening, maddened** if something maddens you it annoys you a lot or makes you very angry
♦ **maddening** •ADJECTIVE• very annoying

made •VERB• a way of changing the verb **make** to form a past tense. It can be used with or without a helping verb: *When he was on the beach, he made a sandcastle.* • *I think you have made a mistake.*
• **made for** suiting or fitting a particular person very well: *The role was just made for someone with his talents.*

madly •ADVERB• desperately, or in a great hurry: *We were rushing about madly trying to get ready in time.*

madness •NOUN• mental illness, or great foolishness

magazine •NOUN• **magazines** 1 a paper published regularly, for example, once a week or once a month, and which has articles and features by various writers and usually lots of photographs or pictures: *a football magazine* • *women's magazines* 2 a place where military equipment is stored

ⓘ The meaning of magazine as 'a paper' came from the meaning of magazine as 'a military storehouse'. The idea is that a

Aa

magazine is a storehouse of useful items and information.

Bb **maggot** •NOUN• **maggots** a fly in the worm-like stage after it has hatched out of its egg and before it develops wings

Cc

Dd **magic** •NOUN• **1** a strange power that causes things to happen that cannot be explained

Ee **2** tricks, such as making things disappear, which seem to people watching to be impossible

Ff **3** something beautiful or wonderful: *the island's special magic*

Gg

Hh ✦ **magical** •ADJECTIVE• wonderful or charming: *a magical atmosphere*

Ii ✦ **magically** •ADVERB• using magic or as if by magic

Jj ✦ **magician** •NOUN• **magicians 1** a man or boy who has magic powers, especially in stories: *Harry Potter and Gandalf are magicians.* **2** someone who does magic tricks to entertain people

Kk

Ll

Mm **magistrate** •NOUN• **magistrates** a person who judges cases of minor crime where there is no jury

Nn

Oo **magma** •NOUN• **magmas** *or* **magmata** hot melted rock beneath the Earth's crust which is sometimes forced up to the surface, for example, when a volcano erupts

Pp

Qq **magnet** •NOUN• **magnets** a piece of iron or other metal which has the power to attract other pieces of metal to it and which points north to south when it hangs free

Rr

Ss ✦ **magnetic** •ADJECTIVE• **1** something that is magnetic has the power to attract iron and some other metals towards it **2** someone with a magnetic personality is very popular with other people

Tt

Uu

Vv ✦ **magnetically** •ADVERB• using magnetism

Ww ✦ **magnetism** •NOUN• **1** the power that a magnet has to attract metals **2** the power some people have to attract or influence other people

Xx

Yy ✦ **magnetize** *or* **magnetise** •VERB• **magnetizes, magnetizing, magnetized** to magnetize a metal is to make it magnetic

Zz

magnification •NOUN• **magnifications 1** making things seem larger or closer, or

making things more important than they are **2** the amount by which an instrument like a microscope or telescope makes things seem larger, for example, a magnification of 20 makes something look 20 times larger than it really is

magnificence •NOUN• being magnificent: *People climb the hill for the magnificence of the view from the top.*

magnificent •ADJECTIVE• very impressive or splendid: *a magnificent lion* • *a magnificent achievement*

✦ **magnificently** •ADVERB• in an impressive way: *He coped magnificently with the crisis.*

magnified •ADJECTIVE• made to seem larger or closer by using a lens, microscope or telescope: *a magnified image of a hair*

magnifier •NOUN• **magnifiers** an instrument or lens that makes things look bigger than they really are

magnify •VERB• **magnifies, magnifying, magnified 1** to make something seem bigger or closer than it really is **2** to make something seem more important or serious than it really is
⇒ **magnification**

magnifying glass •NOUN• **magnifying glasses** a hand-held lens that you use to look at a small object or very small writing so that you can see it more clearly

magnitude •NOUN• **magnitudes** a situation's or problem's magnitude is its great size, extent or importance

magnolia •NOUN• **magnolias** a tree or shrub with large white, pink or purplish bowl-shaped or star-shaped flowers that have a sweet scent

magpie •NOUN• **magpies** a black and white bird of the crow family that likes to collect shiny objects

mahogany •NOUN• a hard reddish wood used to make furniture, which comes from a tree that grows in tropical parts of Central and South America

maid •NOUN• **maids** a girl or woman whose job is to keep the rooms clean and tidy in a hotel or house

maiden •NOUN• **maidens** an old-fashioned word for a young unmarried woman

•ADJECTIVE• 1 first: *a ship's maiden voyage*
2 in cricket, a maiden over is when no runs are scored by the batting side after six balls

maiden name •NOUN• **maiden names** the surname or last name that a woman had before she was married

mail¹ •NOUN• letters or parcels carried by post
•VERB• **mails, mailing, mailed** to send a letter or parcel using the postal service

mail² •NOUN• mail, or chain mail, is armour worn on the body, which is made up of lots of small connected steel rings or plates

mail order •NOUN• **mail order** a system for buying and selling things in which the customer chooses what they want from a catalogue and the goods are delivered by post

maim •VERB• **maims, maiming, maimed** to injure a person or animal very seriously so that one or more of their limbs is crippled

main •ADJECTIVE• most important or principal: *a main road* • *The main thing is to stay calm.*
•NOUN• **mains** a pipe that carries water or gas into houses or buildings: *a burst gas main*
♦ **mains** •PLURAL NOUN• the mains are the pipes or cables that carry water or electricity to houses and buildings: *plug this into the mains*

mainland •NOUN• the mainland of a country is its biggest single area of land rather than any island or islands that form part of the same country

mainly •ADVERB• mostly or in most cases: *This week we've mainly been revising for exams.*

maintain •VERB• **maintains, maintaining, maintained** 1 to keep something at the same amount, or to keep it going: *The rally drivers have to maintain high speeds on dangerous and twisty roads.*
2 to keep a house or piece of equipment in good condition or working well
3 to maintain someone is to give them the money they need to live on
♦ **maintenance** •NOUN• 1 regular cleaning or repair done to keep something in good condition or good working order 2 money paid to someone for them to live on

maisonette •NOUN• **maisonettes** a flat or apartment on two floors within a building

maize •NOUN• a tall cereal plant that has large seedheads called cobs. The yellow seeds, called sweetcorn, are packed tightly together on the cob

majestic •ADJECTIVE• very impressive, or behaving in a very dignified or impressive way, as a king or queen might do
♦ **majestically** •ADVERB• impressively or regally

majesty •NOUN• **majesties** 1 majesty is greatness: *the majesty of the mountains* 2 a title used when speaking to or about a king or queen: *Their Majesties will be attending a thanksgiving service next week.*

major •ADJECTIVE• 1 something major is very big, very serious or very important: *a major catastrophe* • *a major route into the city* 2 in music, a major scale has a semitone between the first and the third notes and between the seventh and eighth notes. A major key or chord is based on this scale
•NOUN• **majors** an army officer above the rank of captain

majority •NOUN• **majorities** 1 the largest number of people or things in a group 2 the number of votes by which the winner of an election beats the person who comes second

make •VERB• **makes, making, made** 1 to create, produce or prepare something: *She makes all her own clothes.* • *I'm making a cup of coffee.* • *Let's make the bedclothes into a tent.*
2 something makes something else happen when it causes or forces that other thing to happen: *The explosion made the house shake.* • *He made the dog sit and stay.* • *Hay always makes me sneeze.*
3 to make a point, suggestion or promise is to give it
4 you make the answer to a sum a particular amount when that is the amount you calculate it to be: *I make that £1.20 you owe me.* • *What time do you make it?*
5 two or more quantities make a certain amount when they add up to that amount: *Six and six makes twelve.*

6 to make a particular place or point is to reach that place or point: *We climbed part of the way, but we didn't make the summit.* • *If we hurry, we might just make the earlier train.*
7 to make money is to earn it
8 to **make for** a place is to go in that direction
9 to **make off** is to run away or escape
10 to **make something out** is to be able to see it or see what it is
11 to **make something out** is to understand it
12 to **make out** a cheque or application is to complete it by writing in the details needed
13 people who have been quarrelling **make up** when they agree to become friends again
14 to **make something up** is to invent it
15 to **make up for** something that you have done wrong is to balance it by doing something good
• **make do** to try to manage on what you have
• **make it** to reach the point that you have been aiming at
• **make up your mind** to decide

make-believe • NOUN • pretending or fantasy
• **make believe** if you make believe, you pretend something is real when it isn't: *Let's make believe it's winter and we have to hibernate until the snow goes away.*

maker • NOUN • **makers** a person, business or machine that makes a particular type of thing: *a film maker* • *a coffee maker*

makeshift • ADJECTIVE • made from whatever is available and used instead of the real thing or something better: *a makeshift bed of leaves and moss*

make-up • NOUN • **1** cosmetics that are put on the face or body **2** a person's or thing's make-up is their character or what they or it consists of

makings • PLURAL NOUN • if someone or something has the makings of a particular thing they have all the qualities needed to become that thing: *Olivia has the makings of a successful singer.*

malaria • NOUN • a serious disease passed to humans by the bite of a type of mosquito, which causes spells of very high fever

male • ADJECTIVE • **1** a male animal is of the sex that fathers children but does not give birth: *A male swan is called a cob.* **2** to do with men or boys or the things that involve them: *It's mostly a male hobby.*
• NOUN • **males** a male animal

malevolent • ADJECTIVE • evil and wanting to do harm to other people: *It's obvious that girl is malevolent by nature.*

malfunction • VERB • **malfunctions, malfunctioning, malfunctioned** a machine malfunctions when it stops working properly or breaks down
• NOUN • **malfunctions** a fault that causes a machine to stop working properly

malice • NOUN • malice is a feeling of spite and wanting to harm someone else
◆ **malicious** • ADJECTIVE • spiteful
◆ **maliciously** • ADVERB • deliberately causing harm or hurt to someone else

mall • NOUN • **malls** a shopping centre

mallet • NOUN • **mallets** a heavy wooden hammer

malnutrition • NOUN • someone suffering from malnutrition is ill because they have not had enough to eat for a long time

malt • NOUN • a substance in barley and other grains that is used to flavour beer

maltreat • VERB • **maltreats, maltreating, maltreated** to treat a person or animal badly or cruelly
◆ **maltreatment** • NOUN • bad or cruel treatment

mama or **mamma** • NOUN • **mamas** or **mammas** a name some people use for their mother

mammal • NOUN • **mammals** a warm-blooded animal that is not a reptile, fish or bird. Female mammals give birth to their babies, instead of laying eggs, and feed them on milk made in their own bodies

mammoth • NOUN • **mammoths** a huge hairy type of elephant that lived in prehistoric times
• ADJECTIVE • huge: *a mammoth task*

man • NOUN • **men 1** an adult male human being **2** man is a word sometimes used for human beings generally: *Man is closely related to the apes.*
• VERB • **mans, manning, manned** to man

something is to be the person that runs it or operates it

manage • VERB• **manages, managing, managed** 1 to manage to do something is to succeed in doing it 2 to manage something like a shop or business is to be in charge of running it 3 to survive on very little money: *I don't know how he manages on his student grant.*

manageable • ADJECTIVE• something is manageable if it can be controlled or dealt with fairly easily

management • NOUN• 1 controlling a business or other activity: *He always wanted to go into football management.* 2 the management of a company are the people who work as its managers

manager • NOUN• **managers** someone who is responsible for managing a shop or other business, or an organization

manageress • NOUN• **manageresses** a woman who runs a shop, restaurant or other business

mandarin • NOUN• **mandarins** 1 a high-ranking official in China when it was ruled by an emperor 2 a mandarin, or mandarin orange, is a small fruit rather like an orange but easier to peel because it has a looser skin

mandolin • NOUN• **mandolins** an instrument shaped like a guitar but with a rounded instead of a flat back

mane • NOUN• **manes** a horse's or lion's mane is the long hair that grows on its neck

manger • NOUN• **mangers** a box for holding hay or other food for animals in a stable

mangle • VERB• **mangles, mangling, mangled** to crush or twist something out of shape • NOUN• **mangles** an old-fashioned machine with two heavy rollers, used for squeezing water out of washed clothes

mango • NOUN• **mangos** or **mangoes** a large pear-shaped fruit with orange sweet-smelling flesh and a large stone in the middle

mangy • ADJECTIVE• **mangier, mangiest** 1 suffering from mange, a skin disease of dogs and other hairy animals, which causes scabs on the skin and makes the hair fall out

in patches 2 dirty and worn thin: *a mangy old rug*

manhandle • VERB• **manhandles, manhandling, manhandled** to push, pull or drag a person or thing using your hands

manhole • NOUN• **manholes** a covered hole in a road big enough for a person to go down to inspect or repair underground drains

manhood • NOUN• being a man: *the age when a boy reaches manhood*

mania • NOUN• **manias** 1 a person suffering from mania has a type of madness in which they become very excited and often violent 2 a mania is a very strong enthusiasm for something
• **maniac** • NOUN• **maniacs** a mad or dangerous person
• **manic** • ADJECTIVE• 1 suffering from mania 2 manic actions are done at a very fast and wild pace: *a manic dash round the shops*

manicure • VERB• **manicures, manicuring, manicured** to manicure your fingernails is to cut and polish them so that they are neat and well-shaped • NOUN• **manicures** you have a manicure when someone cuts and polishes your fingernails

manifest • VERB• **manifests, manifesting, manifested** to be revealed or displayed: *The codes manifest as symbols when you print out the file.*
• **manifestation** • NOUN• **manifestations** something that displays or reveals a characteristic: *a manifestation of evil*

manifesto • NOUN• **manifestos** or **manifestoes** a written statement of a political party's policies

manipulate • VERB• **manipulates, manipulating, manipulated** 1 to handle something in a skilful way 2 to influence someone cleverly and make them behave in a way that suits you without them realising
• **manipulation** • NOUN• manipulating something or someone

mankind • NOUN• all human beings

manly • ADJECTIVE• **manlier, manliest** having the qualities many people expect a man to have, such as strength and courage
• **manliness** • NOUN• being manly

Aa Bb Cc Dd Ee Ff Gg Hh Ii Jj Kk Ll **Mm** Nn Oo Pp Qq Rr Ss Tt Uu Vv Ww Xx Yy Zz

Aa
Bb
Cc
Dd
Ee
Ff
Gg
Hh
Ii
Jj
Kk
Ll
Mm
Nn
Oo
Pp
Qq
Rr
Ss
Tt
Uu
Vv
Ww
Xx
Yy
Zz

mannequin •NOUN• **mannequins**1 a lifesize model of a human body used to display clothes in a shop or store **2** an old-fashioned word for a model who shows off clothes for a fashion designer or shop

manner •NOUN• **manners**1 a way in which something is done: *They had been scattered around in a haphazard manner.* **2** the way in which a person behaves towards other people: *I thought his manner was a bit offhand.*
• **all manner of** all kinds of: *all manner of exciting opportunities*
✦ **manners** •PLURAL NOUN• to have good manners is to behave politely towards other people, and to have bad manners, or no manners, is to behave rudely towards others
✦ **mannerism** •NOUN• **mannerisms** a person's mannerisms are their special ways of speaking or behaving that are different from other people

manoeuvre •NOUN• **manoeuvres**1 a difficult movement that needs skill and planning
2 something that you do in a clever or skilful way that affects how a situation will develop
3 military manoeuvres are planned movements of large numbers of troops and equipment
•VERB• **manoeuvres, manoeuvring, manoeuvred 1** to manoeuvre is to move skilfully **2** to manoeuvre something somewhere is to move it there carefully and accurately: *The prams were impossible to manoeuvre round the corner.*

manor •NOUN• **manors** a name given to some large old houses, originally built for noblemen

mansion •NOUN• **mansions** a large grand house

manslaughter •NOUN• the crime of killing someone without intending to kill them

mantelpiece •NOUN• **mantelpieces** a frame around a fireplace, especially the top part that forms a shelf

mantle •NOUN• **mantles** a protective covering: *The garden looked magical under its mantle of crisp white snow.*

manual •NOUN• **manuals** a book containing information about something, for example, the parts of a machine and how to operate it
•ADJECTIVE• **1** working or operated by a person rather than being automatic: *an old manual loom* **2** involving the hands or physical strength and skills: *manual labour*
✦ **manually** •ADVERB• by hand: *manually operated machines*

manufacture •VERB• **manufactures, manufacturing, manufactured 1** to make things on a large scale, often in a factory **2** to invent an excuse or evidence
✦ **manufacturer** •NOUN• **manufacturers** a person or business making things for sale on a large scale
✦ **manufacturing** •NOUN• the part of industry involved in making products for sale

ⓘ **Manufacture** comes from the Latin words **manu**, which means *by hand*, and **facere**, which means *to make*, so together it means 'to make by hand'.

manure •NOUN• a mixture containing animal dung, spread on soil to grow better flowers and crops

manuscript •NOUN• **manuscripts**1 a book or document written by hand **2** an author's manuscript is his or her handwritten or typed version of a book before it is edited and printed

Manx •ADJECTIVE• coming from the Isle of Man, an island between England and Ireland: *A Manx cat has no tail.*

many •PRONOUN• **1** a lot or a large number: *I've got lots of CD's. Do you have many?*
2 how many means 'what quantity or number': *If you take three chairs away how many will be left?*
•ADJECTIVE• **more, most** a lot or a large number: *He has many friends.* • *Many people in the world don't have enough to eat.*

Maori •NOUN• **Maoris** a member of the race of people who lived in New Zealand before anyone arrived from other countries

map •NOUN• **maps** a diagram of an area of land showing the position of things like hills, rivers and roads as if you are looking at them from above
•VERB• **maps, mapping, mapped 1** to map

an area is to make a map of it **2** to make a detailed diagram or chart of something to show the position of each of its parts: *mapping DNA*

maple • NOUN• **maples** a tree with broad leaves that turn red, brown, orange and yellow in the autumn

mar • VERB• **mars, marring, marred** to mar something is to spoil it in some way

maracas • PLURAL NOUN• a musical instrument made up of two hollow containers filled with small stones, which are shaken so that the stones rattle

marathon • NOUN• **marathons 1** a race in which runners cover a distance of 26 miles or 42 kilometres **2** a long and difficult task or activity
• ADJECTIVE• very long and difficult: *a marathon session at the dentist*

ⓘ This word comes from the place name **Marathon** in Greece. There is a story that in 490 BC a messenger ran from Marathon to Athens after the Greeks won a war against the Persians. The distance he ran is about the same as that in the marathon race.

marauder • NOUN• **marauders** someone who roams about robbing, plundering and killing people

marble • NOUN• **marbles 1** marble is a type of rock, which can be black, dark green, pink or white, and usually has veins of other colours through it. It is used for sculpture and for making fireplaces and work tops **2** marbles are small coloured glass balls used for playing a children's game
• ADJECTIVE• made of marble: *a marble table top*

March • NOUN• the third month of the year, after February and before April

ⓘ **March** comes from the name of the Roman god **Mars**. He was god of war and was also connected with the growing of new crops in Spring.

march • VERB• **marches, marching, marched 1** soldiers march when they walk together at the same regular pace **2** people march when they walk in a large group through the streets, usually because they are protesting about something **3** to march someone somewhere is to force them to go there by holding them or walking beside them so that they do not escape
• NOUN• **marches 1** a steady walking pace or a distance covered by marching: *a slow march* • *a long march* **2** music for marching to

mare • NOUN• **mares** a female horse or zebra

margarine • NOUN• a substance made from vegetable oils or animal fats used for cooking or for spreading on bread like butter

margin • NOUN• **margins 1** a blank area at the top, bottom or either side of a written or printed page **2** an edge or border: *reeds growing on the margins of the lake* **3** an extra amount of something: *We allowed ourselves a margin of several hours, in case we got held up anywhere.*
♦ **marginal** • ADJECTIVE• if something is of marginal importance it is not very important, because it is not the central or main part of something
♦ **marginally** • ADVERB• slightly

marigold • NOUN• **marigolds** a yellow or orange flower

marina • NOUN• **marinas** a harbour for private boats

marine • ADJECTIVE• to do with the sea or belonging to the sea: *marine life*

mariner • NOUN• **mariners** someone who sails boats or ships on the sea

marital • ADJECTIVE• to do with marriage: *marital status*

mark • NOUN• **marks 1** a spot or stain: *There's a dirty mark on the sofa.* **2** a written or printed sign or symbol that stands for something: *a punctuation mark* **3** a point or grade given as a reward for good or accurate work: *He could get much higher marks if he made a bit more effort.*
• VERB• **marks, marking, marked 1** to put a mark, scratch or stain on something **2** to look at someone's work and give it points or a grade to show how good or accurate it is
♦ **marked** • ADJECTIVE• noticeable or obvious: *There has been a marked improvement in her work.*

Aa Bb Cc Dd Ee Ff Gg Hh Ii Jj Kk Ll **Mm** Nn Oo Pp Qq Rr Ss Tt Uu Vv Ww Xx Yy Zz

Aa
Bb
Cc
Dd
Ee
Ff
Gg
Hh
Ii
Jj
Kk
Ll
Mm
Nn
Oo
Pp
Qq
Rr
Ss
Tt
Uu
Vv
Ww
Xx
Yy
Zz

◆ marker •NOUN• **markers 1** something used to mark the position of something **2** a pen with a thick point and often containing special ink that is used to write on various surfaces

market •NOUN• **markets 1** a place where people gather to buy and sell things: *a street market* • *a fruit market* **2** there is a market for something when people will buy it • **on the market** for sale •VERB• **markets, marketing, marketed** to offer something for sale to the public, often using advertising to encourage people to buy it

market garden •NOUN• **market gardens** a large garden where fruit and vegetables are grown to be sold

marksman •NOUN• **marksmen** someone who can shoot very accurately

marmalade •NOUN• jam made from oranges or other citrus fruit and usually eaten on toast at breakfast time

maroon¹ •VERB• **maroons, marooning, marooned** to leave someone in a helpless or uncomfortable position, especially on a lonely island from which they cannot escape

maroon² •NOUN• a dark bluish red colour

marquee •NOUN• **marquees** a very large tent used for circuses, weddings or parties

marriage •NOUN• **marriages 1** the ceremony in which a man and woman become husband and wife **2** the period of time when two people are married to each other: *a long and happy marriage*

marrow •NOUN• **marrows 1** marrow is the spongy tissue inside long bones such as the ones in your leg **2** a marrow is a large rounded vegetable that grows on the ground

marry •VERB• **marries, marrying, married** to make someone your husband or wife in a special ceremony, or to perform the ceremony making two people into husband and wife

marsh •NOUN• **marshes** an area of land that is soft and wet all the time

◆ marshy •ADJECTIVE• marshy ground is very wet and soft

marshal •NOUN• **marshals 1** an official who controls the crowds at big public events like pop concerts

2 a high-ranking officer in the army, air force or navy
3 in the United States, the chief police officer or fire officer in a city or area
•VERB• **marshals, marshalling, marshalled** to marshal people or things is to gather them together in an organized way

marshmallow •NOUN• **marshmallows** a very soft, spongy pink or white sweet

marsupial •NOUN• **marsupials** an animal, such as the kangaroo, that gives birth to partly developed babies, which then crawl into a pouch on their mother's belly where they are fed and protected until they grow bigger

martial art •NOUN• **martial arts** martial arts are fighting sports or techniques of self-defence, such as karate and judo

Martian •NOUN• **Martians** in science fiction stories, a creature from the planet Mars

martyr •NOUN• **martyrs** someone who is killed or tortured because they refuse to give up their beliefs
•VERB• **martyrs, martyring, martyred** to kill or torture someone for their beliefs
◆ martyrdom •NOUN• **martyrdoms** being martyred

marvel •NOUN• **marvels** an astonishing or wonderful person or thing
•VERB• **marvels, marvelling, marvelled** you marvel at something when it fills you with wonder
◆ marvellous •ADJECTIVE• wonderful or astonishing: *She was always telling marvellous stories about dragons and sorcerers.*

marzipan •NOUN• a thick paste made with sugar and crushed almonds and used to make sweets and to decorate cakes

mascara •NOUN• make-up that is brushed on to the eyelashes to make them thicker and darker

mascot •NOUN• **mascots** a person, animal or object that a group of people keep to bring them luck

masculine •ADJECTIVE• **1** to do with men, typical of men, or suitable for men **2** in English grammar, masculine forms of words

refer to males. For example, *he* is a masculine pronoun
+ **masculinity** • NOUN• being like a man

mash • VERB• **mashes, mashing, mashed** to crush something into a soft mass: *Mash the potatoes.*
• NOUN• mashed potatoes: *bangers and mash*

mask • NOUN• **masks** a covering that you wear over your face to protect it or as a disguise
• VERB• **masks, masking, masked** to cover, hide or disguise something: *She sprayed air freshener to mask the cooking smells.*

mason • NOUN• **masons** a craftsman who cuts and carves stone
+ **masonry** • NOUN• the parts of a building that are made of stone

mass • NOUN• **masses** 1 a large lump or heap of something or a large quantity gathered together: *a mass of tangled metal* • *a mass of blonde curls*
2 a big quantity or number: *He's got masses of toys.*
3 in science, mass is a measure of the quantity of matter in an object: *A solid rubber ball has greater mass than a hollow one of the same size.*
• ADJECTIVE• made up of large quantities or numbers: *a mass meeting*
• VERB• **masses, massing, massed** people or things mass, or mass together, when they gather in large numbers: *soldiers massing on the border*
+ **Mass** • NOUN• one of several kinds of service held in the Roman Catholic Church and some other Christian churches

massacre • NOUN• **massacres** the killing of large numbers of people or animals
• VERB• **massacres, massacring, massacred** to kill large numbers of people or animals in a cruel and violent way

massage • VERB• **massages, massaging, massaged** to rub parts of the body gently but firmly to relax the muscles or treat pain and stiffness
• NOUN• **massages** treatment by massaging

massive • ADJECTIVE• 1 very big: *a massive amount* 2 large and heavy: *Hyenas have massive jaws for tearing flesh and crunching bones.*

+ **massively** • ADVERB• hugely

mass production • NOUN• making goods in very large quantities, usually in a factory using machines

mast • NOUN• **masts** a wooden or metal pole for holding up the sails of a boat or ship, or a radio or television aerial

master • NOUN• **masters** 1 a man who owns or is in charge of something: *a dog and its master* • *the master of the house*
2 a male teacher: *Mr Green, the science master*
3 if someone is a master of some activity, they are very good at it: *a master of disguise*
• ADJECTIVE• fully qualified and experienced: *a master craftsman*
• VERB• **masters, mastering, mastered** 1 to learn enough about a subject or a skill to be able to use it or do it successfully: *Juggling needs quite a lot of practice before you master it.* 2 to master a feeling, such as fear, is to overcome it
+ **Master** • NOUN• in the past, a title used for a boy: *young Master Copperfield*
+ **masterly** • ADJECTIVE• very clever or skilful: *a masterly performance*

mastermind • NOUN• **masterminds** the mastermind of a clever scheme or crime is the person who thinks of it and organizes the people who carry it out
• VERB• **masterminds, masterminding, masterminded** to mastermind a scheme or crime is to think of it and do the planning or organization needed to carry it out

masterpiece • NOUN• **masterpieces** 1 a book, painting, piece of music or other work of art that is one of the greatest of its kind 2 someone's masterpiece is the greatest piece of work they have done

mastery • NOUN• 1 great skill at something: *We were amazed at his mastery of chess at such a young age.* 2 control of something: *mastery of the seas*

mat • NOUN• **mats** 1 a flat piece of material for covering or protecting part of a floor 2 a small piece of material for protecting a table's surface or for resting something on: *a table mat* • *a mouse mat*

matador • NOUN• **matadors** the man who kills the bull in a bullfight

Aa
Bb
Cc
Dd
Ee
Ff
Gg
Hh
Ii
Jj
Kk
Ll
Mm
Nn
Oo
Pp
Qq
Rr
Ss
Tt
Uu
Vv
Ww
Xx
Yy
Zz

match[1] •NOUN• **matches** a short piece of wood or other material tipped with a substance that catches fire when it is rubbed against a rough surface

match[2] •NOUN• **matches 1** a contest or game between two players or two teams **2** something that is similar to, or the same as, another thing, especially in its colour or pattern: *This isn't the same make of paint but it's a very good match.* **3** a person or animal who is able to equal another: *I could beat him over a mile, but I was no match for him when it came to the 100 metres.* •VERB• **matches, matching, matched 1** two things match when they are similar to or the same as each other **2** to match, or match up to, another person or thing is to be as good as them

matchbox •NOUN• **matchboxes** a small cardboard box for holding matches

mate •NOUN• **mates 1** a friend or companion **2** an officer on a ship **3** an animal's mate is the male or female it mates with •VERB• **mates, mating, mated** animals mate when a male and a female come together so that they can produce young

material •NOUN• **materials 1** cloth or fabric: *I need ten metres of material to make the curtains.* **2** anything used for making something else: *a shop selling artist's materials*

maternal •ADJECTIVE• **1** to do with, or typical of, a mother: *strong maternal feelings* **2** from your mother's side of your family: *your maternal grandmother*

maternity •ADJECTIVE• to do with pregnancy and giving birth: *a maternity dress • a maternity hospital*

math •NOUN• a short form of the word **mathematics** that is used mainly in the United States and Canada

mathematical •ADJECTIVE• to do with or using mathematics: *a mathematical genius • a mathematical calculation*

mathematician •NOUN• **mathematicians** someone who studies mathematics or is an expert in mathematics

mathematics •NOUN• the study of measurements, numbers, quantities and shapes

maths •NOUN• a short form of the word **mathematics**

matinée •NOUN• **matinées** a performance at a theatre or cinema in the afternoon or morning

matrimony •NOUN• the state of being married

matrix •NOUN• **matrices** a rectangular table of numbers in rows and columns

matron •NOUN• **matrons 1** a senior nurse in charge of a hospital **2** a woman in charge of housekeeping or nursing at a hostel or boarding school

matt *or* **mat** •ADJECTIVE• a matt surface or matt finish is dull, without any shine or gloss

matted •ADJECTIVE• tangled and stuck together in a thick mass: *matted hair*

matter •NOUN• **matters 1** matter is any substance that takes up space and is part of the physical universe **2** a subject, situation or issue: *He wants to see you to discuss a personal matter.* **3** if something is the matter, something is wrong or someone is ill or has a problem: *What's the matter with Rachel? She's very quiet.*
• **as a matter of fact** in fact
• **for that matter** you use 'for that matter' when you are adding to something you have just said about something: *My sister was furious, and, for that matter, so was I.*
•VERB• **matters, mattering, mattered** to matter is to be important: *Winning matters to him more than it should.*
◆ **matters** •PLURAL NOUN• the situation being discussed or dealt with now: *It won't help matters if you start to cry.*
◆ **matter-of-fact** •ADJECTIVE• a matter-of-fact person deals with or talks about an unusual or upsetting situation in a calm way, as if it was something that happened every day: *She tried hard to be matter-of-fact about it all.*

matting •NOUN• stiff material used to make mats

Aa Bb Cc Dd Ee Ff Gg Hh Ii Jj Kk Ll Mm Nn Oo Pp Qq Rr Ss Tt Uu Vv Ww Xx Yy Zz

mattress • NOUN• **mattresses** a thick firm layer of padding for lying on, usually as part of a bed

mature • ADJECTIVE• **1** fully grown or developed: *A mature male elephant can weigh several tons.* **2** grown-up: *He's not very mature for his age.*
• VERB• **matures, maturing, matured** to become mature
♦ **maturity** • NOUN• being mature or adult

maul • VERB• **mauls, mauling, mauled** to maul a person or animal is to hurt them badly in a rough and savage attack: *The zookeeper was mauled by one of the lions.*

mauve • NOUN• a pale purple colour

maximum • NOUN AND ADJECTIVE• the greatest number or quantity, or the highest point: *The maximum I'm prepared to pay is £20.*

May • NOUN• the fifth month of the year, after April and before June

(i) **May** comes from the name of the Roman earth goddess **Maia**.

may • VERB• **might 1** you may do something if there is a possibility you will do it: *I may go to college to study art.* **2** you may do something when you have someone's permission to do it: *You may leave the table now.* • *May I ask what you're doing in my room?*

maybe • ADVERB• perhaps or possibly: *Maybe you'd like to come to lunch one day?*

mayday • NOUN• **maydays** a word used as an international signal of distress, especially by ships or aeroplanes in trouble

mayhem • NOUN• great confusion and noise

mayonnaise • NOUN• a smooth creamy sauce made by blending oil, egg yolks and vinegar

mayor • NOUN• **mayors** a man or woman elected as the official leader of a town or city

mayoress • NOUN• **mayoresses** a mayor's wife

maypole • NOUN• **maypoles** a tall decorated pole with long ribbons attached at the top. People hold the ribbons as they dance round the pole in a traditional celebration of the first day of May

maze • NOUN• **mazes** a confusing network of paths each with a high wall or hedge on either side, designed as a puzzle to see how well you can find your way

MB • ABBREVIATION• short for **megabyte**

me • PRONOUN• a word you use to talk about yourself: *Would you make me a cup of tea, please.* • *Lots of cakes for tea, all for you and me.*

(i) In a sentence in which you are doing the action, you use **I** before the verb. You use **me** after the verb or a preposition.
Be careful to use **me**, not **I**, in sentences like this: *The teacher gave the best mark to Emily, Rory and me.*
An easy way to check if you have chosen the correct word is to take away the other names, like this:
✓ *The teacher gave the best mark to me.*
✗ *The teacher gave the best mark to I.*

mead • NOUN• an alcoholic drink made from honey

meadow • NOUN• **meadows** a field of grass

meagre • ADJECTIVE• a meagre amount is a very small amount: *They can't possibly survive the winter on such meagre supplies.*

meal • NOUN• **meals** a meal is food that you eat at one time, for example, breakfast, lunch or dinner

mean¹ • VERB• **means, meaning, meant 1** a word or action means something when it shows something or you understand something from it: *The definitions in this dictionary tell you what the words mean.* • *Dark clouds usually mean rain.* **2** you mean to do something when you intend to do it: *I'm sorry. I didn't mean to stand on your foot.* **3** you mean what you say when you aren't joking or telling lies **4** something that means something to you is important to you: *That puppy means an awful lot to her.*

mean² • ADJECTIVE• **meaner, meanest 1** a mean person won't spend money or share what they have with others **2** if someone is mean to you, they are nasty and unkind

Aa

mean [3] •ADJECTIVE• 1 a mean point or quantity is halfway between two other points or quantities 2 average: *The mean*

Bb
rainfall is worked out by taking a measurement every day, adding all the

Cc
measurements together and dividing by the number of days.

Dd

meander •VERB• **meanders, meandering,**

Ee
meandered if a river meanders, it forms a series of bends as it flows slowly across a flat

Ff
area of land

Gg
ⓘ This word comes from a river in Turkey called **Maeander**, which winds in this way.

Hh
meaning •NOUN• **meanings** what a word or

Ii
action means

Jj
meaningful •ADJECTIVE• 1 a meaningful expression or gesture is intended to show

Kk
something: *a meaningful look* 2 something meaningful is useful or important:

Ll
meaningful discussions

Mm
meaningless •ADJECTIVE• 1 having no meaning: *It's just all meaningless waffle.*
2 having no purpose or importance: *He felt*

Nn
as if his life was meaningless.

Oo
meanness •NOUN• 1 selfishness or lack of generosity 2 nastiness

Pp
means •NOUN• 1 a means of doing something is a way or method of doing it:

Qq
Traffic jams are so frequent, many people are looking for a different means of

Rr
transport. 2 a person's means is the money they have or earn: *Living beyond your means*

Ss
is spending more than you have or can earn.
• **by all means** yes, of course: *'Can I have a*

Tt
look at your magazine?' 'By all means.'
• **by no means** in no way: *It is by no means*

Uu
the best film I've ever seen.

meant •VERB• a way of changing the verb
mean to form a past tense. It can be used

Vv
with or without a helping verb: *I meant every*

Ww
word I said. • *She had meant to tell him the news, but had forgotten.*

Xx
meantime •ADVERB• meantime is used to

Yy
refer to the time between now and some event in the future

Zz
• **in the meantime** means for now: *If you have lost your pencil you can use mine in the meantime.*

meanwhile •ADVERB• meanwhile is used to refer to something that is happening during this time or at the same time as something else is happening

measles •NOUN• an infectious disease, which mostly affects children, with red spots appearing on the skin and a high fever

measly •ADJECTIVE• **measlier, measliest** small in value or amount: *All I had to eat was one measly little biscuit.*

measure •VERB• **measures, measuring, measured** 1 to measure something is to find its width, height, length, weight or amount: *Stand straight against the wall so that I can measure your height.* 2 if something measures a certain number of units, its size or amount is given in that number of units: *The room measures 3.5 metres from the door to the window.*
•NOUN• **measures** a unit used in measuring: *A kilogram is a measure of weight, while a kilometre is a measure of distance or length.*
♦ **measures** •PLURAL NOUN• actions taken to achieve a particular aim: *strict measures to reduce crime*
♦ **measurement** •NOUN• **measurements** a size or amount found by measuring

meat •NOUN• **meats** the flesh of animals used as food, such as pork, lamb or beef
♦ **meaty** •ADJECTIVE• **meatier, meatiest** full of meat or tasting of meat: *a nice meaty pie with a crisp crust*

mechanic •NOUN• **mechanics** someone whose job is to keep machinery working and repair it when it breaks down

mechanical •ADJECTIVE• 1 to do with machines, or worked by machinery: *mechanical engineering* • *a mechanical toy* 2 mechanical behaviour or actions are done without thinking or concentrating

mechanics •NOUN• 1 mechanics is the study and art of building machinery: *car mechanics* 2 the mechanics of something are the details or processes involved in making it work: *the mechanics of their campaign*

mechanism •NOUN• **mechanisms** a working part of a machine, or its system of working parts: *the cogs and springs that are part of the clock's mechanism*

medal •NOUN• **medals** a metal disc, usually with a design or writing stamped on it, given as a prize in a competition

medallion •NOUN• **medallions** a piece of jewellery with a disc like a medal hanging on a long chain that is worn around the neck

medallist •NOUN• **medallists** someone who has won a medal in a competition

meddle •VERB• **meddles, meddling, meddled** to meddle is to interfere in someone else's business or to tamper with something

meddlesome •ADJECTIVE• interfering

media •PLURAL NOUN• the media are newspapers, television and radio or any other means of communicating information to the public

ⓘ Some people use a singular verb with **media**, as in: *The media **was** waiting when the movie star came out of the hotel.* However, if you want to be strictly correct you should use a plural verb, as in: *The media **were** waiting when the movie star came out of the hotel.*

mediaeval •ADJECTIVE• another spelling of **medieval**

median •NOUN• **medians** 1 the middle number or point in a series. For example, the median of *2, 4, 6, 8, 10* is *6* 2 a straight line from an angle of a triangle to the opposite side of the triangle

medical •ADJECTIVE• to do with healing and medicine or doctors and their work •NOUN• **medicals** a general examination done by a doctor to find out the state of a person's health
✦ **medically** •ADVERB• by or using medicine

medicinal •ADJECTIVE• to do with medicine or having an effect like medicine

medicine •NOUN• **medicines** 1 the science of the treatment of illness and disease: *studying medicine* 2 any substance used to treat or prevent diseases and illnesses: *cough medicine*

medieval *or* **mediaeval** •ADJECTIVE• to do with or in the Middle Ages, the period of history from about the beginning of the 12th century to the end of the 15th century

mediocre •ADJECTIVE• dull and ordinary, with no special or exciting qualities
✦ **mediocrity** •NOUN• being dull and ordinary

meditate •VERB• **meditates, meditating, meditated** 1 to spend time being quiet, still and relaxed, especially for spiritual or religious reasons: *He was sitting cross-legged, meditating.* 2 to think about something deeply and carefully: *She was meditating about the future.*
✦ **meditation** •NOUN• **meditations** meditating or deep thought

medium •ADJECTIVE• at the middle point between two ends in a range, for example, between small and large, low and high, or light and dark: *a man of medium height with medium brown hair*
•NOUN• **mediums** *or* **media** 1 a means or substance by which something is expressed, communicated or produced: *The World Wide Web is a new medium for advertising.* 2 someone who is supposed to be able to communicate with the dead

ⓘ Either plural, **mediums** or **media**, can be used for the first sense of the noun, but only **mediums** is used for the second sense.

medley •NOUN• **medleys** 1 a mixture: *a medley of exotic fruits* 2 a piece of music combining several other pieces of music: *He played a medley of Scottish tunes.*

meek •ADJECTIVE• **meeker, meekest** a meek person is gentle and not likely to complain or argue with other people
✦ **meekly** •ADJECTIVE• without complaining or arguing: *'Sorry', said Lily meekly.*
✦ **meekness** •NOUN• being meek

meet •VERB• **meets, meeting, met** 1 to come face to face with someone by chance: *I met a puppy as I was walking. We got talking, puppy and I.*
2 to come together with one other person, or a group of other people, at the same time and in the same place: *Let's meet for a coffee next week sometime.*
3 to be introduced to someone and get to know them for the first time: *Have you met my big sister, Jane?*

Aa
Bb
Cc
Dd
Ee
Ff
Gg
Hh
Ii
Jj
Kk
Ll
Mm
Nn
Oo
Pp
Qq
Rr
Ss
Tt
Uu
Vv
Ww
Xx
Yy
Zz

Aa
Bb
Cc
Dd
Ee
Ff
Gg
Hh
Ii
Jj
Kk
Ll
Mm
Nn
Oo
Pp
Qq
Rr
Ss
Tt
Uu
Vv
Ww
Xx
Yy
Zz

4 two things meet when they come together or touch: *I've got so fat, my waistband doesn't meet round my middle.*
5 to meet a challenge, or a certain attitude or response, is to face it, or be faced with it
6 to meet the cost of something is to pay for it
7 to meet a need is to provide what is needed
♦ **meeting** • NOUN• **meetings** a gathering of people, usually to discuss something

mega- • PREFIX• **1** when **mega-** comes at the beginning of some words it means *a million*. For example, a *megabyte* is a million bytes of computer memory, and a *megaton* is a million tons **2** when **mega-** comes at the beginning of other words it means *huge* or *great*. For example, if someone is called a *megastar*, they are a very big star

megabyte • NOUN• **megabytes** a unit used to measure computer memory or data, equal to approximately a million bytes. This is often shortened to **MB**

megaphone • NOUN• **megaphones** a device shaped like an open-ended cone that someone speaks through to make their voice sound louder

melancholy • NOUN• sadness
• ADJECTIVE• sad and lonely, or making you feel sad: *The dog gave a melancholy howl.*

mellow • ADJECTIVE• **mellower, mellowest** soft, not strong or unpleasant: *the mellow sound of the clarinet*
• VERB• **mellows, mellowing, mellowed**
1 fruit or wine mellows when it becomes ripe or mature, and soft **2** a person mellows with age when they become more tolerant and pleasant as they get older

melodic • ADJECTIVE• having a melody

melodious • ADJECTIVE• a melodious sound or voice is tuneful and pleasant to listen to

melodrama • NOUN• **melodramas** a style of drama with lots of exciting action that is more extreme than in real life, or a play or film in this style
♦ **melodramatic** • ADJECTIVE• someone behaves in a melodramatic way when they exaggerate to make things seem more sensational or exciting than they really are

melody • NOUN• **melodies** a tune, especially a pleasant-sounding one
⇒ **melodic, melodious**

melon • NOUN• **melons** a large rounded fruit with a green or yellow skin, yellow or orange sweet-tasting flesh, and lots of seeds in the middle

melt • VERB• **melts, melting, melted** something melts when it becomes soft and runny as it is heated

melting point • NOUN• **melting points** the temperature at which a particular substance melts when it is heated

member • NOUN• **members** a person who belongs to a group, club or society
♦ **membership** • NOUN• **memberships**
1 being a member: *He has membership of many clubs.* **2** the membership of a group, club or society is all the people who are its members

membrane • NOUN• **membranes 1** a thin layer of skin that covers or connects the organs inside the body **2** any thin layer or covering

memento • NOUN• **mementos** a memento is something that you buy or keep to remind you of something you have done or a place you have visited

memo • NOUN• **memos** a short note or written instruction that you send to someone who works in the same company or organization as you do

ⓘ The full form of this word is **memorandum**, which has two plural forms, **memorandums** or **memoranda**.

memoirs • PLURAL NOUN• someone's memoirs are a book that they write about their life's experiences

memorable • ADJECTIVE• a memorable event is one that you can, or will, remember because it is special or important
♦ **memorably** • ADVERB• in a way that will not be forgotten

memorial • NOUN• **memorials** a statue or monument put up as a way of remembering and honouring a person or event: *the Prince Albert Memorial* • *a war memorial*

•ADJECTIVE• acting as a memorial: *the John Andrews memorial trophy*

memorize *or* **memorise** •VERB•
memorizes, memorizing, memorized to learn something thoroughly so that you are able to remember it in every detail later on

memory •NOUN• **memories 1** memory is the power of your mind to remember things **2** a memory is something you remember: *happy memories of his school days*
• **in living memory** from a time that people who are alive now can still remember
• **in memory of** as a way of remembering a dead person: *a minute's silence in memory of the accident victims*

men •NOUN• the plural of **man**

menace •NOUN• **menaces 1** something that causes trouble or danger: *These biting flies are a real menace.* **2** threatening trouble, harm or violence: *His voice was full of menace.*
•VERB• **menaces, menacing, menaced** to threaten someone or something with trouble, harm or violence
♦ **menacing** •ADJECTIVE• threatening or evil-looking

mend •VERB• **mends, mending, mended** to repair or fix something
• **on the mend** if someone who has been ill or injured is on the mend, they are starting to get better or to heal

menstruation •NOUN• menstruation is the regular flow of blood that a woman or girl has from her womb each month

mental •ADJECTIVE• **1** to do with or using the brain or intelligence: *mental ability • mental arithmetic* **2** an informal word for mad or suffering from an illness of the mind
♦ **mentality** •NOUN• **mentalities** someone's mentality is the attitudes and opinions they have
♦ **mentally** •ADVERB• in or with the mind: *You must commit yourself mentally and physically when you practice yoga.*

mention •VERB• **mentions, mentioning, mentioned** to mention something is to say it to someone

menu •NOUN• **menus 1** a list of the food available in a restaurant **2** on a computer, a list of options that you can choose from by clicking with the mouse or scrolling down the list

mercenary •NOUN• **mercenaries** a soldier who hires himself out to any army or country that will pay him to fight

merchandise •NOUN• goods that are bought and sold

merchant •NOUN• **merchants** someone who carries on a business buying and selling goods

merchant navy •NOUN• **merchant navies** a country's merchant navy is its fleet of ships that are used to transport goods and passengers, not its fighting ships

merciful •ADJECTIVE• kind and forgiving
♦ **mercifully** •ADVERB• people say 'mercifully' to show that they are glad or grateful for something: *After the heat outside, the room was mercifully cool.*

merciless •ADJECTIVE• cruel and without showing any mercy: *The heat was merciless.*

mercury •NOUN• a silvery chemical element mostly used in liquid form in things like thermometers and barometers

mercy •NOUN• **mercies** someone who has or shows mercy is kind and willing to forgive someone they could punish if they wanted to
• **at the mercy of** if you are at the mercy of someone or something, you are in their power: *The defeated Armada was at the mercy of the winds.*

mere •ADJECTIVE• **merest** nothing more than or only: *The flight from London to Madrid cost a mere £25.*
♦ **merely** •ADVERB• only or simply: *I asked him again but he merely shrugged his shoulders.*

merge •VERB• **merges, merging, merged** two or more things merge when they combine with each other or they become mixed together: *The highway merged with several others to form a new road.*
♦ **merger** •NOUN• **mergers** the joining of two businesses to form a single large company

meridian •NOUN• **meridians** an imaginary line around the Earth passing through the north and south pole

Aa
Bb
Cc
Dd
Ee
Ff
Gg
Hh
Ii
Jj
Kk
Ll
Mm
Nn
Oo
Pp
Qq
Rr
Ss
Tt
Uu
Vv
Ww
Xx
Yy
Zz

Aa
Bb
Cc
Dd
Ee
Ff
Gg
Hh
Ii
Jj
Kk
Ll
Mm
Nn
Oo
Pp
Qq
Rr
Ss
Tt
Uu
Vv
Ww
Xx
Yy
Zz

meringue • NOUN• **meringues** a mixture of whipped eggs whites and sugar cooked slowly in the oven until it is dry and crisp

merit • NOUN• **merits** 1 merit is value or importance 2 the merits of something are the things that make it good or valuable • VERB• **merits, meriting, merited** to merit something is to deserve it

mermaid • NOUN• **mermaids** in stories, a beautiful creature who lives in the sea and is half woman, half fish

merrily • ADVERB• happily and cheerfully

merry • ADJECTIVE• **merrier, merriest** happy and cheerful

merry-go-round • NOUN• **merry-go-rounds** a ride at a funfair with wooden animals and vehicles that you sit on as the ride goes round and round

mesh • NOUN• **meshes** mesh is lengths of wire or thread formed into a net

mess • NOUN• **messes** 1 an untidy or dirty state or sight 2 something that is in a confused state or that involves lots of problems • VERB• **messes, messing, messed** 1 to mess **about** or mess **around** is to do silly or annoying things 2 to mess something up is to spoil it or damage it

message • NOUN• **messages** a piece of news or information sent from one person to another • VERB• **messages, messaging, messaged** to message someone is to send them a message using a mobile phone or computer • **messaging** • NOUN• sending and receiving messages using mobile phones or computers

messenger • NOUN• **messengers** someone who carries messages or letters from one person to another

messiah • NOUN• **messiahs** someone who comes to save or deliver people from misery or evil

messily • ADVERB• sloppily or untidily

messy • ADJECTIVE• **messier, messiest** untidy or dirty

met • VERB• a way of changing the verb **meet** to form a past tense. It can be used with or without a helping verb: *We met yesterday.* • *I thought you two had met before.*

metal • NOUN• **metals** a hard shiny material that melts when it is heated, for example iron, steel, gold, silver and tin ✦ **metallic** • ADJECTIVE• hard and shiny like metal or sounding like metal when it is hit

metallurgy • NOUN• the study of metals

metamorphose • VERB• **metamorphoses, metamorphosing, metamorphosed** something metamorphoses when it changes its appearance or form completely and becomes something else ✦ **metamorphosis** • NOUN• **metamorphoses** a complete change made in something's appearance or form, such as happens with some living creatures, like frogs and butterflies, as they grow and develop

metaphor • NOUN• **metaphors** a way of describing something in a powerful and expressive way by comparing it to something else. For example, it is a metaphor to say that someone who is very eager to do something is *straining at the leash* suggesting they are like a dog that wants to be let off the lead so that it can run free. See the box called **Similes and metaphors** ✦ **metaphorical** • ADJECTIVE• using a metaphor or metaphors

meteor • NOUN• **meteors** a mass of rock travelling through space very fast, sometimes seen in the night sky as a shooting star

meteoric • ADJECTIVE• very fast, like a meteor travelling through space

meteorite • NOUN• **meteorites** a meteor that has fallen to Earth

meteorologist • NOUN• **meteorologists** someone who studies the weather and makes weather forecasts

meteorology • NOUN• the study of weather

meter • NOUN• **meters** an instrument that measures and records something, such as the amount of gas or electricity used in a house

ⓘ Try not to confuse **meter** with **metre**, which is a measure of length.

methane •NOUN• a gas found in coal mines and marshes and produced when plant material rots

method •NOUN• **methods 1** a way of doing something: *What's the best method of cleaning silver?* **2** if something you do has method, you do it in a well-planned or organized way
♦ **methodical** •ADJECTIVE• well-ordered and efficient: *Let us be methodical and take one thing at a time.*
♦ **methodically** •ADVERB• orderly and efficiently

meths •PLURAL NOUN• a short form of **methylated spirits**

methylated spirits •PLURAL NOUN• a type of alcohol used as a fuel in lamps and heaters and to remove oily substances

meticulous •ADJECTIVE• paying careful attention to every detail
♦ **meticulously** •ADVERB• very carefully

metre •NOUN• **metres 1** the basic measurement of length in the metric system. This is often shortened to **m 2** the regular rhythm of poetry or music

metric •ADJECTIVE• a system of measuring and weighing that uses units such as litres and grams. It is based on tens and multiples of ten
♦ **metrical** •ADJECTIVE• having the regular rhythm of poetry or music

metronome •NOUN• **metronomes** an instrument that keeps a regular beat, used for musical practice

mettle •NOUN• **1** if something tests your mettle, it tests your courage or ability **2** if you are on your mettle, you are ready and prepared to do your best

mew •VERB• **mews, mewing, mewed** to make a sound like a cat
•NOUN• **mews** the sound a cat makes
♦ **mews** •PLURAL NOUN• buildings built around a yard or lane. Mews were originally stables

mg •ABBREVIATION• short for **milligram** or **milligrams**

miaow •NOUN• **miaows** the call or sound that a cat makes
•VERB• **miaows, miaowing, miaowed** a cat miaows when it makes this sound

mice •NOUN• the plural of **mouse**

micro- •PREFIX• if **micro-** comes at the beginning of a word it adds the meaning *very small*. For example, a *microchip* is a very small silicon chip used to make computer circuits

microbe •NOUN• **microbes** a tiny living creature that can only be seen under a microscope

microchip •NOUN• **microchips** a very small part used in computers that has several tiny electrical circuits on it

microcomputer •NOUN• **microcomputers** a small computer containing microchips or a microprocessor

microfilm •NOUN• photographic film on which documents, newspapers or books are recorded in a size that is very much smaller than their actual size

microorganism •NOUN• **microorganisms** a tiny living thing, such as a virus or bacterium, that can only be seen under a microscope

microphone •NOUN• **microphones** an electronic instrument for picking up sound waves to be recorded or made louder

microprocessor •NOUN• **microprocessors** a set of microchips that make up a computer's central processor

microscope •NOUN• **microscopes** an instrument with lenses that make very tiny objects look much larger so that you can study them closely
♦ **microscopic** •ADJECTIVE• microscopic objects are so small they can only be seen using a microscope

microwave •NOUN• **microwaves 1** a very short radio wave **2** a microwave oven

microwave oven •NOUN• **microwave ovens** an oven that cooks food very quickly using electrical and magnetic waves rather than heat

mid- •PREFIX• if **mid-** comes at the beginning of a word it has something to do with the middle of something. For example, *midwinter* is the middle of the winter

Aa

midday • NOUN• noon, or the middle of the day

Bb

midden • NOUN• **middens** a rubbish heap or dung heap

Cc

middle • NOUN• **middles** 1 the point, position or part furthest from the sides or edges: *an island in the middle of the ocean* • *Let me sit in the middle.*
2 the point in a period of time that is halfway through that period of time: *Autumn half-term comes in the middle of October.* • *The teacher fainted in the middle of our history lesson.*
3 your middle is your waist
• ADJECTIVE• between two things or at the halfway point: *He's the middle child of a family of five boys.* • *the middle section of the book*

Dd

Ee

Ff

Gg

Hh

Ii

Jj

middle-aged • ADJECTIVE• between the ages of 40 and 60

Kk

middle class • NOUN• **middle classes** the middle class is the social class between the working class and the upper class, and consists of educated, professional or skilled people
• ADJECTIVE• coming from, or to do with the middle class

Ll

Mm

Nn

Oo

middle school • NOUN• **middle schools** a school for children between the ages of 8 or 9 and 12 or 13

Pp

Qq

midge • NOUN• **midges** a type of tiny biting insect

Rr

midget • NOUN• **midgets** a person who is fully developed but has not grown to normal size
• ADJECTIVE• very small: *a midget submarine*

Ss

Tt

midland • ADJECTIVE• coming from or in the midlands

Uu

✦ **midlander** • NOUN• **midlanders** someone who is born in or lives in the midlands

Vv

✦ **midlands** • PLURAL NOUN• the midlands of a country are the areas in the middle of the country

Ww

Xx

midnight • NOUN• twelve o'clock at night

Yy

midriff • NOUN• **midriffs** the area around the middle of your body just under your ribs

Zz

midst • NOUN• 1 to be in the midst of several people or things is to be surrounded by them
2 if you are in the midst of something you are in the middle of doing it

midsummer • NOUN• the middle of the summer

midway • ADVERB• at the middle point between two places

midwife • NOUN• **midwives** a nurse who is specially trained to help women when they are having their babies

ⓘ This word comes from the Old English words **mid**, which means *with*, and **wif**, which means *woman*, because a **midwife** is *with a woman* who is having a baby.

might[1] • VERB• 1 **might** is used as a past tense of **may**: *John asked if he might come with us.*
2 **might** is also used if there is a possibility of something: *He might stay.* • *It might rain.*

might[2] • NOUN• power or strength: *He pulled with all his might.*

mightily • ADVERB• 1 extremely: *He was mightily grateful for his warm snowsuit when the blizzard came.* 2 with great strength or power: *The wind blew mightily and shook the windows and doors.*

mightiness • NOUN• great power or strength

mighty • ADJECTIVE• **mightier, mightiest**
1 powerful: *Atlas took the weight of the sky on his mighty shoulders.* 2 very great: *a mighty effort*

migraine • NOUN• **migraines** a very severe headache

migrant • NOUN• **migrants** migrants are people who move from place to place, usually looking for work
• ADJECTIVE• moving from place to place
✦ **migration** • NOUN• **migrations** a movement from place to place: *the migration of millions of animals across the African plains*

migrate • VERB• **migrates, migrating, migrated** birds, and sometimes animals, migrate when they travel from one region or country to another at certain times of the year

mike • NOUN• **mikes** an informal short form of the word **microphone**

mild •ADJECTIVE• **milder, mildest** 1 mild weather is quite warm
  2 mild things don't have a strong or powerful effect: *Use a mild soap on baby's skin.*
  3 a mild person is gentle and quiet
⇒ **mildly**

mildew •NOUN• a disease of plants in which a spongy white fungus covers their leaves and stems

mildly •ADVERB• 1 in a calm and gentle way
  2 slightly: *I was mildly amused at his antics.*
  • **to put it mildly** used to show that you are not expressing yourself as strongly as you could in the circumstances: *It was a bit of a shock, to put it mildly.*

mile •NOUN• **miles** a unit of distance equal to 1760 yards or 1.6 kilometres
  ♦ **mileage** •NOUN• the number of miles travelled, or the number of miles a vehicle will travel on a certain amount of fuel

mileometer or **milometer** •NOUN• **mileometers** or **milometers** an instrument for measuring distance travelled in miles

milestone •NOUN• **milestones** 1 an upright stone or post beside a road that marks the number of miles from a place 2 an important point, especially in your life or career

militant •ADJECTIVE• taking strong, sometimes violent action
  •NOUN• **militants** someone who takes strong, sometimes violent action to change the political or social system

military •ADJECTIVE• to do with the army, navy or air force
  •NOUN• the military is a country's armed forces, especially its officers

milk •NOUN• 1 a white liquid that female mammals make in their bodies to feed their young 2 this liquid that we get from cows, goats and sheep and use to drink or to make butter and cheese
  •VERB• **milks, milking, milked** 1 to milk an animal is to take milk from it 2 to milk a person or a situation is to get as much as possible from them or it, in a clever or selfish way

milk float •NOUN• **milk floats** a vehicle used for delivering milk to people's houses, often run on electric power

milkman •NOUN• **milkmen** someone whose job is to deliver milk to people's houses

milkshake •NOUN• **milkshakes** a drink made by blending milk, ice cream and a flavouring

milk tooth •NOUN• **milk teeth** the first set of teeth that grows in a child's mouth. They fall out and are replaced by larger adult teeth at about the age of 7 or 8

milky •ADJECTIVE• **milkier, milkiest** 1 pale and cloudy, like milk: *a milky liquid* 2 containing a lot of milk: *a hot milky drink*

Milky Way •NOUN• the light band that can be seen in the night sky made up of thousands of millions of stars. The Milky Way is the galaxy to which our sun belongs

mill •NOUN• **mills** 1 a building with machinery for grinding corn and other grain
  2 a factory where goods of a particular type are made, by crushing, grinding or rolling a natural material: *a paper mill* • *a steel mill*
  3 a machine for grinding things like coffee or pepper by crushing it between hard surfaces
  •VERB• **mills, milling, milled** to mill something is to crush it or roll it between hard or heavy surfaces
⇒ **miller**

millennium •NOUN• **millennia** a period of a thousand years

ⓘ This word comes from the Latin words **mille**, which means *a thousand*, and **annus**, which means *year*.

miller •NOUN• **millers** someone who grinds corn and other grain in a mill

millet •NOUN• a type of grain grown especially in dry areas of Africa and Asia and often used as animal food

milligram or **milligramme** •NOUN• **milligrams** or **milligrammes** a unit for measuring weight, equal to one thousandth of a gram. This is often shortened to **mg**

millilitre •NOUN• **millilitres** a unit for measuring the amount of a liquid, equal to one thousandth of a litre. This is often shortened to **ml**

millimetre •NOUN• **millimetres** a unit for

measuring length, equal to one thousandth of a metre. This is often shortened to **mm**

milliner • NOUN• **milliners** someone who makes and sells women's hats
• **millinery** • NOUN• hats and other goods sold by a milliner

million • NOUN• **millions** the number 1 000 000, a thousand thousand

millionaire • NOUN• **millionaires** someone who has, or has wealth to the value of, a million pounds or a million dollars

millipede • NOUN• **millipedes** a small crawling insect with lots of pairs of legs on its long body

millstone • NOUN• **millstones** a heavy round stone used to grind grain
• **a millstone round your neck** a problem or duty that prevents you from doing what you want

mime • NOUN• **mimes** mime is acting using movements and gestures, but no words
• VERB• **mimes, miming, mimed** 1 to mime is to express something by making movements or gestures rather than using words 2 a singer mimes when they move their mouth as if they were singing, but without making a sound

mimic • VERB• **mimics, mimicking, mimicked** to mimic someone or something is to copy their actions, the way they talk, or their appearance
• NOUN• **mimics** a mimic is someone who copies the way other people speak or behave, usually for fun
• **mimicry** • NOUN• mimicking

min • ABBREVIATION• **mins** a short form of the word **minute** used in writing: *Fry for 10-15 mins until golden brown.*

mince • NOUN• meat that has been cut up into very small pieces
• VERB• **minces, mincing, minced** to mince meat or some other food is to cut it into very small pieces
• **mince your words** you don't mince your words when you say exactly what you think of something

mincemeat • NOUN• a mixture of chopped dried fruits and nuts, with suet and spices, used to fill pies
• **make mincemeat of** to make mincemeat of

someone is to beat or defeat them in a very thorough way

mince pie • NOUN• **mince pies** a pie filled with mincemeat, usually eaten at Christmas time

mind • NOUN• **minds** your mind is your brain, or your ability to think, understand or remember
• **in two minds** to be in two minds is not to be able to decide between two alternatives
• **make up your mind** to decide
• **speak your mind** to say what you really think
• VERB• **minds, minding, minded** 1 you mind something when it upsets or annoys you
2 you ask someone if they would mind doing something, or if they would mind if you did something, when you are asking them politely to do it, or if they object to you doing it: *Would you mind opening the window?*
3 to mind someone or something is to look after them
4 you tell someone to mind something when you are telling them to watch out for some hazard or danger: *Mind your head on that branch.*
• **minder** • NOUN• **minders** someone who looks after another person and protects them from harm

mindless • ADJECTIVE• 1 a mindless task is boring and does not need any thought or imagination 2 mindless violence or destruction is stupid and done for no purpose

mine[1] • PRONOUN• a word you use to talk about something belonging to **me**: *Is this book yours or mine?* • *a friend of mine*

mine[2] • NOUN• **mines** 1 a place where things are dug out of the ground, for example, coal, metals and minerals, or precious stones 2 a type of bomb that is hidden in the ground or in the sea and which explodes when someone stands on it, or a ship hits it
• VERB• **mines, mining, mined** 1 to mine something like coal or gold is to dig it out of the ground 2 to mine an area of land or sea is to place explosive mines in it

minefield • NOUN• **minefields** 1 an area of land with explosive mines in it 2 a situation that is full of hidden dangers or problems

miner • NOUN• **miners** someone who works in a mine

mineral • NOUN• **minerals** any of various substances found in the ground, such as coal, or dissolved in water, such as salt

mineral water • NOUN• water containing dissolved minerals thought to be good for your health

mingle • VERB• **mingles, mingling, mingled** people or things mingle when they are mixed together or move about amongst each other

mini- • PREFIX• if **mini-** comes at the beginning of a word, it means it is a small or short type of something. For example, a *minibus* is a small bus

miniature • ADJECTIVE• very small
• NOUN• **miniatures** a very small copy or model of a larger thing, or a very small portrait of someone

minibus • NOUN• **minibuses** a small bus for around 12 to 15 passengers

minim • NOUN• **minims** a musical note equal in length to two crotchets, or half a semibreve or whole note. The symbol for a minim is ♩

minimal • ADJECTIVE• something minimal is very small or the least amount possible: *Having this machine means that there is minimal effort involved in washing up.*

minimize *or* **minimise** • VERB• **minimizes, minimizing, minimized** to minimize something is to reduce it to the smallest size or extent possible

minimum • NOUN AND ADJECTIVE• the smallest number or quantity, or the lowest point: *The minimum contribution is £5.*

minister • NOUN• **ministers** 1 the name given to a priest in some branches of the Christian church 2 a government minister is a politician in charge of a government department: *the Minister for Rural Affairs*
• VERB• **ministers, ministering, ministered** to minister to someone is to provide them with some sort of help, usually because they are sick
• **ministry** • NOUN• **ministries** 1 the profession of a priest or minister 2 a government department

mink • NOUN• **mink** 1 a small slim animal with a pointed face, short legs and very soft fur 2 the dark-brown fur of the mink
• ADJECTIVE• made from the fur of the mink: *a mink coat*

minnow • NOUN• **minnows** a type of small fish that lives in fresh water

minor • ADJECTIVE• 1 something minor is not very big, not very serious or not very important: *a minor problem • a minor road* 2 in music, a minor scale has a semitone between the second and third notes. A minor key or chord is based on this scale
• NOUN• **minors** someone who is under the age when people legally become adults

minority • NOUN• **minorities** 1 a small group of people which is part of a much larger group 2 a group of people in a society that are a different race or have a different religion than most other people in the society

minstrel • NOUN• **minstrels** a singer who travelled from place to place in medieval times

mint¹ • NOUN• **mints** 1 a plant with strong-smelling leaves used as a flavouring in cooking 2 a sweet flavoured with mint

mint² • NOUN• 1 a place, controlled by the government, where new coins are made 2 a very large sum of money: *That fancy house must have cost a mint.*
• **in mint condition** something is in mint condition when it looks as if it has just been newly made

minus • PREPOSITION• 1 taking away or subtracting: *8 minus 2 is 6* 2 without: *He came back home covered in mud and minus one shoe.*
• ADJECTIVE• 1 less than zero: *minus ten degrees* 2 minus is used after a letter to show that a mark or grade is slightly less than by the letter alone: *I got an A minus for my essay.*
• NOUN• **minuses** a minus, or minus sign (−), is a mathematical symbol showing that a number is to be taken away from another, or that a number is less than zero

minuscule • ADJECTIVE• tiny: *a minuscule spot on her blouse*

Aa
Bb
Cc
Dd
Ee
Ff
Gg
Hh
Ii
Jj
Kk
Ll
Mm
Nn
Oo
Pp
Qq
Rr
Ss
Tt
Uu
Vv
Ww
Xx
Yy
Zz

minute[1] •NOUN• **minutes** 1 sixty seconds or a sixtieth part of an hour
2 in measuring an angle, the sixtieth part of a degree
3 a moment or very short time: *Wait a minute while I go back for my schoolbag.*
4 the minutes of a meeting are notes taken while the meeting is going on describing what has been discussed or agreed
•ADJECTIVE• showing the number of minutes: *the minute hand of your watch*

minute[2] •ADJECTIVE• tiny: *You only need to use a minute amount of the ointment.*

ⓘ This word is pronounced my-**nyoot**.

miracle •NOUN• **miracles** 1 a wonderful act or event that cannot be explained 2 a piece of great good luck: *It's a miracle that you weren't killed running across that busy road.*
♦ **miraculous** •ADJECTIVE• wonderful and amazing, like a miracle
♦ **miraculously** •ADVERB• amazingly: *Miraculously, he got out of the wrecked car without a scratch.*

mirage •NOUN• **mirages** in deserts and hot countries, you see a mirage when you see something that is not really there, usually a false image of a large area of water in the distance caused by currents of hot air rising

mire •NOUN• deep mud or dirt

mirror •NOUN• **mirrors** a piece of glass with a reflective backing that you can look at yourself in
•VERB• **mirrors, mirroring, mirrored** one thing mirrors another when it looks or behaves exactly like that other thing or like a reflection of it

mirth •NOUN• mirth is laughter

mis- •PREFIX• if **mis-** comes at the beginning of a word it adds the meaning *bad* or *badly*, or *wrong* or *wrongly*. For example, to *mistreat* something is to treat it badly

misbehave •VERB• **misbehaves, misbehaving, misbehaved** to behave badly

miscarriage •NOUN• **miscarriages** 1 if a pregnant woman has a miscarriage, the baby comes out of her womb too early and does not survive 2 a miscarriage of justice happens when someone is wrongly punished for a crime they did not commit

miscellaneous •ADJECTIVE• a miscellaneous collection or group is one that contains many different kinds of things

mischief •NOUN• naughty behaviour that does not cause any serious harm: *I hope you children haven't been getting up to mischief.*
♦ **mischievous** •ADJECTIVE• full of mischief

miser •NOUN• **misers** someone who hates spending money, and saves as much as they can
♦ **miserly** •ADJECTIVE• very unwilling to spend money

miserable •ADJECTIVE• 1 very unhappy: *She's miserable because all her friends are away.*
2 making you feel unhappy or depressed: *What a miserable wet day it's been!*
3 sad and grumpy: *Smile! Don't be such a miserable old so-and-so!*
4 mean: *I got a miserable £2.50 for three hours work!*

misery •NOUN• **miseries** 1 great unhappiness, or something that causes great unhappiness 2 a depressing person, who spoils other people's fun

misfit •NOUN• **misfits** someone whose behaviour or attitudes is very different from most other people, and who does not fit in with any group well

misfortune •NOUN• **misfortunes** bad luck

misgivings •PLURAL NOUN• if you have misgivings about something, you have doubts about it because you think it might not work

misguided •ADJECTIVE• a misguided person is lead astray by mistaken ideas, or shows bad judgement

mishap •NOUN• **mishaps** an unlucky accident

mislay •VERB• **mislays, mislaying, mislaid** to mislay something is to lose it, usually because you can't remember where you put it

mislead •VERB• **misleads, misleading, misled** to give someone wrong information, so that they believe something is the case when it is not

♦ **misleading** • ADJECTIVE• giving the wrong impression or information

misprint • NOUN• **misprints** a mistake in printing: *That's definitely a misprint. It should be 10, not 1000.*

Miss • NOUN• **Misses** 1 a title used for girls and unmarried women 2 a word used by schoolchildren when they are talking to a female teacher, whether she is married or not

miss • VERB• **misses, missing, missed** 1 to fail to hit or catch something you are aiming at: *The arrow missed the target.*
2 to miss an event is to be unable to attend it or watch it: *Granny never misses this programme.*
3 to miss a train, bus or plane is to not arrive in time to catch it
4 to miss a person or place is to be sad because they are not with you, or you are not at that place
5 to miss something is to realize that you do not have it or that it is lost: *When did you first miss your purse?*
6 to **miss something out** is to not include it, either by mistake or on purpose
7 if you **miss out on** something good, you do not get any of it, or you do not take part in it: *He arrived late and missed out on all the games.*
• NOUN• **misses** 1 a failure to hit a target: *He scored two hits and a miss.* 2 to give something a miss is to not do it
⇒ **missing**

missile • NOUN• **missiles** a weapon or other object that is thrown or fired

missing • ADJECTIVE• lost: *two missing front teeth*

mission • NOUN• **missions** 1 a task or purpose: *astronauts on a mission to Mars* 2 a group of people representing a country or religion who are sent to another country: *a diplomatic mission*
♦ **missionary** • NOUN• **missionaries** a person who goes to another country to convert the people there to a particular religion

misspell • VERB• **misspells, misspelling, misspelt** *or* **misspelled** to spell something in the wrong way

♦ **misspelling** • NOUN• **misspellings** a word that is spelt the wrong way

mist • NOUN• **mists** a thin fog, made up of tiny water droplets in the air
• VERB• **mists, misting, misted** something mists up, or mists over, when it becomes covered with tiny droplets of water or mist
⇒ **misty**

mistiness • NOUN• being misty

mistake • NOUN• **mistakes** something wrong that you do or say and which you did not mean to do or say
• VERB• **mistakes, mistaking, mistook, mistaken** to mistake one person or thing for another person or thing is to think wrongly they are that other person or thing
♦ **mistaken** • ADJECTIVE• you are mistaken if you are wrong about something
♦ **mistakenly** • ADVERB• wrongly

Mister • NOUN• **Misters** a title used for men and boys. It is usually shortened to **Mr**

mistletoe • NOUN• a plant with green leaves and small white berries that grows on the branches of trees. Traditionally, at Christmas time, people kiss each other under a piece of mistletoe hung up somewhere in a room

mistook • VERB• a way of changing the verb **mistake** to make a past tense: *I mistook him for someone else.*

mistreat • VERB• **mistreats, mistreating, mistreated** to treat someone or something badly or cruelly
♦ **mistreatment** • NOUN• bad or cruel treatment

mistress • NOUN• **mistresses** 1 a woman who owns or is in charge of something: *Are you the mistress of the house?* • *a dog and his mistress* 2 a female teacher: *a games mistress*

mistrust • VERB• **mistrusts, mistrusting, mistrusted** to mistrust a person or thing is to be suspicious of them or it
• NOUN• mistrust is a feeling of doubt or suspicion that people who do not trust each other have

misty • ADJECTIVE• **mistier, mistiest** 1 the weather is misty when there is mist in the air
2 your eyes are misty when you cannot see

Aa
Bb
Cc
Dd
Ee
Ff
Gg
Hh
Ii
Jj
Kk
Ll
Mm
Nn
Oo
Pp
Qq
Rr
Ss
Tt
Uu
Vv
Ww
Xx
Yy
Zz

very clearly, usually because your eyes are filled with tears

misunderstand •VERB• **misunderstands, misunderstanding, misunderstood** to think you have understood what someone has said or done, when in fact you have not understood it correctly: *I misunderstood the directions he gave and ended up in south London.*
◆ **misunderstanding** •NOUN• **misunderstandings 1** a mistake you make about what someone else means **2** a slight disagreement or argument

misuse •VERB• **misuses, misusing, misused** to misuse something is to use it in the wrong way or to treat it badly
•NOUN• misuse of something is using it in the wrong way

mite •NOUN• **mites** a tiny creature belonging to the same family as spiders

mitt or **mitten** •NOUN• **mitts** or **mittens** a type of glove without separate parts for the four fingers

mix •VERB• **mixes, mixing, mixed 1** to put two or more things together so that they combine or form a mass: *Mixing a little black paint into the white will give you a light grey.* • *We each took a turn to mix the Christmas cake.*
2 things mix when they combine: *Oil and water don't mix.*
3 you mix with other people when you talk to them or get to know them socially
4 if you mix things up, you confuse them and think one is the other: *He said he might have got me mixed up with our Jim.*
•NOUN• **mixes** a mixture: *an odd mix of comedy and horror*
◆ **mixed** •ADJECTIVE• containing several different things or types of people: *a mixed grill*
◆ **mixer** •NOUN• **mixers** any machine used for mixing things: *a cement mixer*
◆ **mixture** •NOUN• **mixtures** a combination of several things: *cough mixture* • *a mixture of joy and sadness*

ml •ABBREVIATION• short for **millilitre** or **millilitres**

mm •ABBREVIATION• short for **millimetre** or **millimetres**

mnemonic •NOUN• **mnemonics** a word, phrase, or poem that helps you remember something. For example, the phrase *i before e, except after c* is a mnemonic that many people use to remind them if *e* or *i* comes first in words like *relief* and *receive*

moan •VERB• **moans, moaning, moaned 1** to make a deep noise in your throat because you are in pain or distress **2** to complain
•NOUN• **moans 1** a deep noise of pain or distress that someone makes in their throat **2** something you say that shows your dissatisfaction with something

moat •NOUN• **moats** a deep ditch dug round a castle and filled with water to stop attackers being able to get to the castle walls easily

mob •NOUN• **mobs** a mob is an angry crowd of people
•VERB• **mobs, mobbing, mobbed** people mob someone they want to see or meet when they crowd round that person
◆ **mobbed** •ADJECTIVE• if a place is mobbed it is very crowded

mobile •ADJECTIVE• something is mobile when it moves or can move around
•NOUN• **mobiles 1** a mobile phone, a telephone that you can carry around with you **2** a hanging decoration that moves in air currents
◆ **mobility** •NOUN• being able to move around

mobilize or **mobilise** •VERB• **mobilizes, mobilizing, mobilized** to mobilize people is to make them move or take action

moccasin •NOUN• **moccasins** moccasins are shoes made from pieces of soft leather stitched together with thin strips of leather, worn originally by Native American people

mock •VERB• **mocks, mocking, mocked** to mock someone is to make fun of them in a cruel way, by making jokes about them or copying what they say or do
•ADJECTIVE• not real or genuine: *a mock leather sofa*
◆ **mockery** •NOUN• mocking

mode •NOUN• **modes 1** a way or method of doing something: *a mode of transport* **2** in a range of numbers, the mode is the number that occurs most frequently. For example, the mode of *2, 4, 5, 2, 7* is *2*

model • NOUN• **models** 1 a copy of something made on a much smaller scale: *a model of the Crystal Palace*
2 a particular type or design of something that is made in large numbers: *This is our latest model of washing machine.*
3 a person who wears new clothes or fashions to show them off to possible buyers • VERB• **models, modelling, modelled** 1 to model something in clay is to form the clay into the shape of that thing
2 to model for an artist is to sit or stand while the artist draws or paints you
3 to model a piece of clothing or jewellery is to wear it to show it off to possible buyers

modem • NOUN• **modems** a device used to send information from a computer to other computers on a network down a telephone line

moderate • ADJECTIVE• 1 not going to extremes: *The doctor told him to take a moderate amount of exercise every day.* 2 of medium or average quality or ability : *People of moderate intelligence find the quiz quite easy.*
• VERB• **moderates, moderating, moderated** to moderate something is to make it less extreme or less strong
♦ **moderately** • ADVERB• slightly, quite or fairly: *moderately cheap accommodation*
♦ **moderation** • NOUN• behaviour that is not too extreme

ⓘ The adjective is pronounced mod-i-rit. The verb is pronounced mod-i-rate.

modern • ADJECTIVE• modern things belong to the present or recent times rather than the past
♦ **modernity** • NOUN• being modern

modernization *or* **modernisation**
• NOUN• **modernizations** the modernization of something is adding new parts or equipment to it to make it more modern

modernize *or* **modernise** • VERB•
modernizes, modernizing, modernized to modernize something is to make it more up-to-date

modest • ADJECTIVE• 1 a modest person does not like boasting or talking about their achievements 2 a modest amount is a small amount

modification • NOUN• **modifications** a change made in something to make it work better or more efficiently

modify • VERB• **modifies, modifying, modified** 1 to modify something is to make a small change or changes in it to improve it
2 to modify your views or opinions is to change them so that they are less extreme

module • NOUN• **modules** 1 a separate unit that is part of a larger unit or structure: *the space station's escape module* 2 a unit of work that forms one part of an educational course

mohair • NOUN• long soft hair from the angora goat, which is mixed with other types of wool to make jumpers or material for suits and jackets

moist • ADJECTIVE• **moister, moistest** slightly wet
♦ **moisten** • VERB• **moistens, moistening, moistened** to make something moist: *He licked his lips to moisten them.*
♦ **moisture** • NOUN• wetness, especially tiny drops of water in the air or condensed on a surface

moisturize *or* **moisturise** • VERB•
moisturizes, moisturizing, moisturized you moisturize your skin when you put cream on it to make it feel softer
♦ **moisturizer** • NOUN• **moisturizers** a cosmetic cream put on the skin to make it feel softer

molar • NOUN• **molars** one of the large square teeth at the back of your mouth that you use for chewing and grinding food

molasses • NOUN• molasses is a thick dark syrup left after raw sugar is refined

mole[1] • NOUN• **moles** a small black or dark brown furry animal that lives underground in tunnels that it digs with its strong claws. Moles have poor eyesight but very good hearing

mole[2] • NOUN• **moles** a small dark-coloured permanent mark or lump on someone's skin

Aa
Bb
Cc
Dd
Ee
Ff
Gg
Hh
Ii
Jj
Kk
Ll
Mm
Nn
Oo
Pp
Qq
Rr
Ss
Tt
Uu
Vv
Ww
Xx
Yy
Zz

molecular •ADJECTIVE• to do with molecules: *molecular structure*

molecule •NOUN• **molecules** the smallest unit that a chemical element or compound can be divided into and still remain what it is. Molecules are made up of two or more atoms

molehill •NOUN• **molehills** a pile of earth that a mole pushes up on to the surface while it is digging its tunnels underground

molest •VERB• **molests, molesting, molested** to molest someone is to attack or annoy them

mollusc •NOUN• **molluscs** any of a large group of animals with no bones inside their bodies, but protected by an outer shell. Shellfish and snails are molluscs

mollycoddle •VERB• **mollycoddles, mollycoddling, mollycoddled** to mollycoddle someone is to treat them in a fussy and over-protective way, never letting them do anything risky

molten •ADJECTIVE• molten rock or metal is in a liquid state, having been melted

moment •NOUN• **moments** 1 a short period of time: *Stop what you're doing for a moment.* 2 a particular point in time: *Just at that moment, she heard a door slam.*
• **momentarily** •ADVERB• for a short period of time: *He was momentarily suspended in the air.*
• **momentary** •ADJECTIVE• lasting for only a moment: *There was a momentary pause, and then everyone started talking.*

momentous •ADJECTIVE• very important or significant: *a momentous occasion*

momentum •NOUN• 1 the force that makes a moving object continue moving 2 something gains momentum when it begins to move or develop faster and faster

monarch •NOUN• **monarchs** a royal ruler of a country, especially a king or queen
• **monarchy** •NOUN• **monarchies** a system of government in which the official head of state is a monarch, or a country with this system

monastery •NOUN• **monasteries** a building or other place where a community of monks lives
• **monastic** •ADJECTIVE• to do with monks or monasteries

Monday •NOUN• **Mondays** the day of the week after Sunday and before Tuesday

ⓘ **Monday** is from the Old English word **Monandæg**, which means *day of the moon.*

money •NOUN• 1 money is coins or banknotes used to buy things: *I don't have enough money to buy the jacket I want.* 2 money is wealth: *Only people with money can afford yachts and personal jets.*

mongoose •NOUN• **mongooses** a small animal related to the weasel, found in South East Asia and Africa, which kills and eats snakes

mongrel •NOUN• **mongrels** a dog whose parents are of different breeds

monitor •VERB• **monitors, monitoring, monitored** to monitor something is to keep a careful check on it
•NOUN• **monitors** 1 an instrument used to keep a constant check on something: *a heart monitor*
2 a screen attached to a computer which displays or shows the file or program being worked on
3 a school pupil who helps to see that school rules are kept

monk •NOUN• **monks** a member of a community of men who spend their lives in religious worship in a monastery

monkey •NOUN• **monkeys** an animal with a long tail that walks on four legs and lives in trees
• **make a monkey out of someone** to make someone look foolish
•VERB• **monkeys, monkeying, monkeyed** to **monkey about** or **monkey around** is to behave in a silly or mischievous way

monkey nut •NOUN• **monkey nuts** monkey nuts are peanuts in their shells

mono- •PREFIX• if **mono-** comes at the beginning of a word it adds the meaning *one* or *single*. For example, a *monologue* is a long speech made by one person

monocle •NOUN• **monocles** a lens worn in front of one eye and held in place between the top and bottom of the eye socket

monopolize *or* **monopolise** •VERB•

monopolizes, monopolizing, monopolized to monopolize something is to keep it all for yourself, and to exclude others: *He monopolized the conversation and no one had the chance to speak.*

monopoly • NOUN• **monopolies** a business company or organization has a monopoly when it is the only company selling a particular product or providing a particular service

monorail • NOUN• **monorails** a railway on which the trains run on a single rail, rather than two rails

monotone • NOUN• **monotones** 1 if you say something in a monotone, you do not vary the tone of your voice while you are speaking 2 a single tone

monotonous • ADJECTIVE• something is monotonous when it is boring because it never varies
♦ **monotony** • NOUN• dullness and lack of variety

monsoon • NOUN• **monsoons** the monsoon is a season in some hot countries when heavy rain falls

monster • NOUN• **monsters** 1 in stories, a huge or frightening creature 2 a cruel or evil person
• ADJECTIVE• enormous: *a monster truck*

monstrosity • NOUN• **monstrosities** a very large and very ugly thing

monstrous • ADJECTIVE• 1 extremely large: *a monstrous crocodile* 2 monstrous behaviour is very unfair and cruel

month • NOUN• **months** 1 one of twelve periods that a year is divided into: *In Britain, the winter months are December, January and February.* 2 any period of approximately four weeks or 30 days: *We had to wait for months for an appointment.*
♦ **monthly** • ADJECTIVE AND ADVERB• happening once a month or each month: *a monthly salary* • *He is paid monthly.*

monument • NOUN• **monuments** 1 something that has been built in memory of a person or event: *a monument to Sir Walter Scott* 2 any building or structure that is historically important: *The Parthenon is one of Greece's ancient monuments.*

♦ **monumental** • ADJECTIVE• 1 like a monument, or used on a monument: *monumental sculpture* 2 enormous: *I felt like a monumental idiot when I realized what I had done.*

moo • VERB• **moos, mooing, mooed** a cow moos when it makes a long low sound
• NOUN• **moos** the long low sound a cow makes

mood • NOUN• **moods** your mood is your feelings or temper at a particular time: *I woke up in a bad mood this morning.*
♦ **moodily** • ADVERB• in a bad-tempered way
♦ **moodiness** • NOUN• being moody
♦ **moody** • ADJECTIVE• **moodier, moodiest** a moody person changes their mood often or suddenly, from cheerful to grumpy and impatient

moon • NOUN• **moons** 1 the large sphere that orbits the Earth once a month and which you can see in the night sky as a full circle or a partial circle depending on the time of month 2 a similar body going round certain other planets, such as Saturn

moonbeam • NOUN• **moonbeams** a shaft of moonlight

moonlight • NOUN• the light that seems to come from the moon, but which is really light from the sun reflected off the surface of the moon
♦ **moonlit** • ADJECTIVE• lit by the moon: *a clear moonlit night*

moor[1] • NOUN• **moors** a large stretch of open land with poor soil and very few, or no, trees

moor[2] • VERB• **moors, mooring, moored** to moor a boat is to tie it up using a rope, cable or anchor

mooring • NOUN• **moorings** a place where a boat or ship can be tied up

moorland • NOUN• **moorlands** a stretch of moor

moose • NOUN• **moose** a type of large deer with large, flat, rounded horns

mop • NOUN• **mops** 1 a tool for washing floors made up of a pad or mass of thick threads attached to a long handle 2 a mop of hair is a thick, often untidy, mass of hair

Aa
Bb
Cc
Dd
Ee
Ff
Gg
Hh
Ii
Jj
Kk
Ll
Mm
Nn
Oo
Pp
Qq
Rr
Ss
Tt
Uu
Vv
Ww
Xx
Yy
Zz

Aa
Bb
Cc
Dd
Ee
Ff
Gg
Hh
Ii
Jj
Kk
Ll
Mm
Nn
Oo
Pp
Qq
Rr
Ss
Tt
Uu
Vv
Ww
Xx
Yy
Zz

•VERB• **mops, mopping, mopped** 1 to mop a floor is to rub or wipe it with a mop 2 to mop up is to clean or wipe liquid off a surface

mope •VERB• **mopes, moping, moped** someone mopes when they are in a bored and depressed mood and do not want to do anything

moped •NOUN• **mopeds** a light motorcycle with a small engine that you can also pedal like a bicycle

moral •NOUN• **morals** a story or event has a moral if a lesson about how to behave is learned from it
•ADJECTIVE• 1 having to do with character or principles, especially right and wrong, or good and evil 2 a moral person behaves in a way that is right, good or proper

morale •NOUN• the morale of a person or group of people is how confident they are, or how successful they think they will be

morality •NOUN• 1 the morality of something is whether it is right or wrong according to standards of good or bad behaviour 2 a person's morality is their standard of behaviour and the beliefs they have about what is right and wrong

morally •ADVERB• to behave morally is to behave in a good or proper way

morals •PLURAL NOUN• someone's morals are the beliefs they have about what is right and wrong

morbid •ADJECTIVE• having or showing an unhealthy interest in death or sad and unpleasant things
♦ **morbidity** •NOUN• being morbid
♦ **morbidly** •ADVERB• in a morbid way

more •ADJECTIVE• a greater quantity or amount: *He has more toys than anyone else I know.* • *Could you get me three more mugs from the cupboard?*
•PRONOUN• 1 a greater quantity or amount: *More than forty people turned up.* 2 an additional quantity or amount: *Is there any more jelly?*
•ADVERB• 1 **more** is used to make comparative forms of adjectives and adverbs: *He's more patient than I am.* 2 **more** is the comparative form of **much** and means 'to a greater degree': *At first I didn't*

like her much, but I'm beginning to like her more and more.
♦ **moreish** •ADJECTIVE• something is moreish if it makes you want more

moreover •ADVERB• you use **moreover** to mean 'besides', when you are adding information to a statement you have just made: *We came home early because it started to rain. Moreover, the children were getting tired.*

morning •NOUN• **mornings** the part of the day from midnight to midday

morning star •NOUN• the planet Venus is called the morning star when it rises before the sun

moron •NOUN• **morons** a very stupid person
♦ **moronic** •ADJECTIVE• very stupid

ⓘ It is very rude to call someone this.

morose •ADJECTIVE• silent and bad-tempered

morphine •NOUN• a drug used to make someone sleep or to relieve pain

morse code •NOUN• a code used in signalling and telegraphy, made up of long and short signals called dots and dashes

morsel •NOUN• **morsels** a small piece of food: *a tasty morsel*

mortal •ADJECTIVE• 1 being mortal is being certain to die at some time and unable to live forever 2 a mortal wound causes death 3 people who are mortal enemies hate each other so much they want to kill each other
•NOUN• **mortals** a human being
♦ **mortality** •NOUN• being mortal
♦ **mortally** •ADVERB• causing, or resulting in, death: *The soldier was mortally wounded.*

mortar •NOUN• 1 a mixture of cement, sand and water used in building to hold bricks in place 2 a type of heavy gun that fires shells

mortarboard •NOUN• **mortarboards** a cap with a square flat top worn by university graduates

mortgage •NOUN• **mortgages** a type of loan made by a bank or building society to people who want to buy a house or land

mortified •ADJECTIVE• extremely embarrassed

mortuary •NOUN• **mortuaries** a place where dead bodies are kept before they are buried or cremated

mosaic •NOUN• **mosaics** a design formed by fitting together small pieces of coloured marble or glass

Moslem •NOUN AND ADJECTIVE• another spelling of **Muslim**

mosque •NOUN• **mosques** a place of worship for Muslims

mosquito •NOUN• **mosquitoes** an insect found in many parts of the world, which feeds by biting and sucking blood

moss •NOUN• **mosses** a small plant found in damp places and forming a soft green mat over the ground
♦ **mossy** •ADJECTIVE• **mossier, mossiest** covered with moss

most •ADJECTIVE• **most** is the superlative form of **many** and **much** and means 'more than other people or things': *Who scored most goals last season?*
•PRONOUN• **1** nearly all, or the majority: *Most of my friends are allowed to walk to school.* **2** the largest amount: *They both had a lot, but who had the most?*
•ADVERB• **most** is the superlative form of **much** and means 'to a greatest degree': *What kind of music do you like most?*
♦ **mostly** •ADVERB• in most cases or in most parts: *They mostly play indoors.*

MOT •NOUN• **MOTs** a test done in the United Kingdom by qualified mechanics on cars over a certain age to find out if they are safe to be driven

motel •NOUN• **motels** a type of cheap hotel near a motorway or highway, where travellers can get rooms for the night

moth •NOUN• **moths** a creature similar to a butterfly, but usually active at night, rather than during the day

mothball •NOUN• **mothballs** a small ball of a strong-smelling substance that is put amongst clothes to stop moths eating them

mother •NOUN• **mothers** your female parent

•VERB• **mothers, mothering, mothered** to mother someone is to treat them with protective kindness, like a mother does
♦ **motherhood** •NOUN• being a mother

mother-in-law •NOUN• **mothers-in-law** the mother of your husband or wife

motherly •ADJECTIVE• kind and protective

motif •NOUN• **motifs** a shape or design that may be repeated to form a pattern

motion •NOUN• **motions 1** motion is moving or movement: *The motion of the waves made him sleepy.* **2** a motion is a single movement or gesture: *He flicked the fly away with a quick motion of his wrist.*
• **go through the motions** to pretend to do something or to do it without any enthusiasm
•VERB• **motions, motioning, motioned** you motion to someone when you signal to them using your hand or some other part of your body
♦ **motionless** •ADJECTIVE• not moving at all

motivate •NOUN• **motivates, motivating, motivated 1** you are motivated by particular feelings or desires when they cause you to act in a certain way **2** to motivate someone is to make them feel interested and enthusiastic enough to do something
♦ **motivation** •NOUN• something that motivates a person

motive •NOUN• **motives** the reason someone has for doing something

motor •NOUN• **motors** a machine, usually a petrol engine or electrical device, that provides power
•ADJECTIVE• driven by an engine: *a motor mower*

motorbike •NOUN• **motorbikes** a two-wheeled vehicle with a powerful engine that you sit astride like a bicycle

motor car •NOUN• **motor cars** a car

motorcycle •NOUN• **motorcycles** a motorbike, motor scooter or moped
♦ **motorcyclist** •NOUN• **motorcyclists** someone who rides a motorbike, motor scooter or moped

motorist •NOUN• **motorists** someone who drives a car

Aa

motorway • NOUN• **motorways** a wide road with several lanes going in both directions

Bb

mottled • ADJECTIVE• covered with patches of different colours or shades

Cc

motto • NOUN• **mottoes** a short sentence or phrase used by a person or organization as a principle to guide their behaviour: *The motto of the Scouts is 'Be prepared'*.

Dd

Ee

mould[1] • NOUN• **moulds** a hollow shaped container into which a substance in liquid form is poured so that it may take on that shape when it cools and hardens: *a jelly mould*

Ff

Gg

• VERB• **moulds, moulding, moulded** 1 to form something in a mould: *The gold is moulded into ingots.* 2 to shape something using your hands: *Mum moulded the icing into pretty flower shapes.*

Hh

Ii

Jj

mould[2] • NOUN• **moulds** mould is a fungus that forms green or black patches on stale food or on damp walls and ceilings

Kk

Ll

✦ **mouldy** • ADJECTIVE• **mouldier, mouldiest** covered with mould: *a mouldy old loaf*

Mm

moult • VERB• **moults, moulting, moulted** birds and animals moult when they shed their feathers or hair, or their skin

Nn

Oo

mound • NOUN• **mounds** a small hill or heap of earth or some other material

Pp

mount • VERB• **mounts, mounting, mounted**
1 to mount stairs is to go up them
2 to mount a horse is to get up on its back
3 the level of something mounts when it rises: *Fear and panic were mounting as the seconds ticked away.*
4 to put a picture or object in a frame or to stick it on card to display it
• NOUN• **mounts** 1 a mountain: *Mount Everest* 2 an animal you ride on, such as a horse or a camel

Qq

Rr

Ss

Tt

Uu

Vv

mountain • NOUN• **mountains** a very high hill

Ww

✦ **mountaineer** • NOUN• **mountaineers** someone who climbs mountains using ropes and other special equipment

Xx

✦ **mountaineering** • NOUN• the sport or pastime of climbing mountains

Yy

✦ **mountainous** • ADJECTIVE• a mountainous area has a lot of mountains

Zz

mounted • ADJECTIVE• on horseback: *a mounted policeman*

Mounties • PLURAL NOUN• the Canadian Mounties are the police force of Canada, who ride on horses and wear bright red jackets and wide-brimmed hats

mourn • VERB• **mourns, mourning, mourned** to mourn is to be very sad because someone has died
✦ **mournful** • ADJECTIVE• full of sadness
✦ **mourning** • NOUN• someone who is in mourning is grieving for someone who has died

mouse • NOUN• **mice** 1 a small animal with a long tail, bright eyes and grey or brown fur 2 a device that you move with your hand to point to places on a computer screen. It has a button or buttons that you press to instruct the computer to do something

mousse • NOUN• **mousses** 1 a light fluffy dessert made with whipped cream and eggs: *chocolate mousse* 2 a white fluffy substance used for styling hair

moustache • NOUN• **moustaches** a line of hair that some men grow above their top lip

mousy • ADJECTIVE• **mousier, mousiest** 1 a mousy person is shy and timid 2 mousy hair is a light brown colour

mouth • NOUN• **mouths** your mouth is the part of your face that you use to speak and eat and which contains your tongue and teeth
• **down in the mouth** someone who is down in the mouth looks unhappy
• VERB• **mouths, mouthing, mouthed** to mouth words is to make the shapes of the words with your mouth without making the sounds
✦ **mouthful** • NOUN• **mouthfuls** an amount you put or hold in your mouth at one time: *He took a mouthful of water and spat it out again.*

mouth-organ • NOUN• **mouth-organs** an instrument that you hold to your mouth and play by blowing and sucking through the rows of reeds inside it

mouthpiece • NOUN• **mouthpieces** the part of a musical instrument or telephone that you put in or close to your mouth

movable • ADJECTIVE• able to be moved

move •VERB• **moves, moving, moved** 1 you move something when you take it from one place and put it in another: *Please move your toys off the kitchen table.*
  2 if something moves, it changes its position: *I'm sure I saw that curtain move.*
  3 to move is to change from one house or place of work to another
  4 if something moves you, it makes you feel deep emotion
•NOUN• **moves** 1 a change of position: *They made no move to help.*
  2 the moving of a piece in a boardgame, such as ludo or chess: *Come on, it's your move.*
  3 a change to another home or another place of work
♦ **movement** •NOUN• **movements**
  1 changing position or a change of position
  2 a division in a long piece of classical music
  3 an organization or association with a common purpose or aim: *the Scout movement*

movie •NOUN• **movies** a film

moving •ADJECTIVE• having a strong effect on your feelings and emotions: *She made a moving speech.*
♦ **movingly** •ADVERB• in a moving way

mow •VERB• **mows, mowing, mowed** to mow grass is to cut it with a mower
♦ **mower** •NOUN• **mowers** a machine for cutting grass

MP •ABBREVIATION• **MPs** short for **Member of Parliament**, someone who has been elected to the British parliament

Mr •ABBREVIATION• short for **Mister**, a title used before a man's name, for example, when writing his name on an envelope or at the beginning of a letter

Mrs •ABBREVIATION• short for **Mistress**, a title used before a married woman's name, for example, when writing her name on an envelope or at the beginning of a letter

Ms •NOUN• a title sometimes used before a woman's name, whether she is married or unmarried

much •ADJECTIVE• 1 a lot or a large amount: *There was much laughter coming from the girls' room.* 2 **much** is used in questions about quantities or amounts: *How much fruit do you eat each day?*
•PRONOUN• a lot or a large amount: *I usually don't have much to eat at lunchtime.*
•ADVERB• 1 about: *Both books are much the same.* 2 greatly or a lot: *Do you miss your old school much?*

muck •NOUN• 1 dirt or filth: *The floor is covered in muck from your muddy boots.* 2 manure: *The farmer was spreading muck on the fields.*
•VERB• **mucks, mucking, mucked** 1 to **muck about** or **muck around** is to behave in a silly way
  2 to **muck out** horses or other farm animals is to clean their stalls or pens
  3 to **muck something up** is to spoil or ruin it
♦ **mucky** •ADJECTIVE• **muckier, muckiest** dirty: *Don't leave those mucky boots in the hall, please.*

mucus •NOUN• a thick slimy liquid that protects the delicate tissues that line certain parts of your body, for example, inside your nose

mud •NOUN• soft wet soil that sticks to your clothes and shoes

muddle •NOUN• **muddles** a muddle is a confused or disorganized state
•VERB• **muddles, muddling, muddled** 1 to **muddle things up** is to mix them up so that you do not know which is which, or where they are 2 if something muddles you, it confuses you

muddy •ADJECTIVE• **muddier, muddiest** covered or filled with mud

mudguard •NOUN• **mudguards** a flap over the back wheel of a car, lorry or bicycle, which stops mud from the road being splashed upwards

muesli •NOUN• a food eaten at breakfast time consisting of a mixture of grains, nuts and dried fruit

muff •NOUN• **muffs** a tube of warm material that you put your hands in to keep them warm
•VERB• **muffs, muffing, muffed** to muff something is to do it wrong: *He muffed his lines again.*

muffin •NOUN• **muffins** a round flat cake eaten toasted or hot with butter

Aa
Bb
Cc
Dd
Ee
Ff
Gg
Hh
Ii
Jj
Kk
Ll
Mm
Nn
Oo
Pp
Qq
Rr
Ss
Tt
Uu
Vv
Ww
Xx
Yy
Zz

Aa
Bb
Cc
Dd
Ee
Ff
Gg
Hh
Ii
Jj
Kk
Ll
Mm
Nn
Oo
Pp
Qq
Rr
Ss
Tt
Uu
Vv
Ww
Xx
Yy
Zz

muffle • VERB• **muffles, muffling, muffled** to muffle a sound is to make it quieter by putting a cover over the source of the sound
 ✦ **muffled** • ADJECTIVE• muffled sounds or voices are low and indistinct because they are heard through something that blocks out most of the sound
 ✦ **muffler** • NOUN• **mufflers** a type of long scarf worn wrapped around the neck and the bottom of the face

mug¹ • NOUN• **mugs** a cup with straight sides and a handle

mug² • VERB• **mugs, mugging, mugged** to attack and rob someone in the street
 ✦ **mugger** • NOUN• **muggers** a criminal who attacks and robs people in the street

muggy • ADJECTIVE• **muggier, muggiest** muggy weather is hot and humid

mule¹ • NOUN• **mules** an animal bred from a male donkey and a female horse

mule² • NOUN• **mules** mules are slippers with no backs

multi- • PREFIX• if **multi-** comes at the beginning of a word it adds the meaning *many* to the word. For example, *multicultural* means 'involving many cultures'

multimedia • ADJECTIVE• a multimedia computer can run sound and images as well as ordinary programs

multiple • ADJECTIVE• involving many things of the same sort: *multiple injuries*
 • NOUN• **multiples** a number or quantity that contains another an exact number of times: *9 and 12 are multiples of 3*

multiplication • NOUN• **multiplications** multiplying

multiplier • NOUN• **multipliers** the number by which a number is multiplied. For example, 10 is the multiplier in 150 × 10

multiply • VERB• **multiplies, multiplying, multiplied 1** to multiply is to increase a number by adding it to itself a certain number of times: *13 multiplied by 3 is 39.* **2** things multiply when they increase in number

multi-racial • ADJECTIVE• involving or including people from many races

multitude • NOUN• **multitudes** a huge number: *I've got a multitude of things to do before I go.*

mum¹ • NOUN• **mums** an informal word for **mother**

mum² • ADJECTIVE• to keep mum is to keep quiet and not speak to anyone about something that should remain a secret

mumble • VERB• **mumbles, mumbling, mumbled** to mumble is to speak without opening your mouth wide enough to make words sound separate and clear

mummify • VERB• **mummifies, mummifying, mummified** to mummify a dead body is to make it into a mummy

mummy¹ • NOUN• **mummies** a child's word for **mother**

mummy² • NOUN• **mummies** a mummy is a dead body that has been preserved and wrapped in bandages

mumps • NOUN• an infectious disease, mainly affecting children, in which glands in the neck become very swollen and sore

munch • VERB• **munches, munching, munched** to munch something is to chew it with regular movements of your jaws and your mouth closed

mundane • ADJECTIVE• something that is mundane is dull because it is so ordinary or familiar

municipal • ADJECTIVE• to do with a city or town, especially the local government of that city or town: *municipal elections*

munitions • PLURAL NOUN• weapons and ammunition used in a war

mural • NOUN• **murals** a picture that is painted directly on to a wall

murder • NOUN• **murders** murder is the crime of killing someone deliberately
 • VERB• **murders, murdering, murdered** to murder someone is to kill them deliberately
 ✦ **murderer** • NOUN• **murderers** someone who has murdered another person
 ✦ **murderous** • ADJECTIVE• **1** meaning to commit murder: *a murderous look* **2** likely to kill you: *We had to escape from the murderous heat.*

murky •ADJECTIVE• murkier, murkiest
1 dark and difficult to see through: *murky water* 2 dark and sinister: *A man with a murky past.*

murmur •VERB• murmurs, murmuring, murmured to murmur is to speak so softly that people can hardly hear you
•NOUN• murmurs 1 a low weak voice 2 a low continuous humming noise made by voices or sounds in the distance

muscle •NOUN• muscles the parts of your body that move your limbs and organs, which you can make bigger and stronger by exercising
•VERB• muscles, muscling, muscled someone muscles in when they involve themselves in something that is not their business
♦ **muscular** •ADJECTIVE• to do with the muscles

museum •NOUN• museums a place where collections of interesting things are displayed for people to see

mush •NOUN• mush is a soft wet mass of something: *The fruit turns into a mush as it boils.*

mushroom •NOUN• mushrooms a type of fungus that you can eat, with a round top
•VERB• mushrooms, mushrooming, mushroomed something mushrooms when it increases its size very quickly

mushy •ADJECTIVE• mushier, mushiest 1 in a soft wet mass: *mushy peas* 2 sentimental: *The film got all mushy and I stopped watching.*

music •NOUN• sounds arranged or combined in patterns, sung or played by instruments
• **face the music** to face someone who is angry with you and will tell you off or punish you
♦ **musical** •ADJECTIVE• 1 to do with music: *musical training* 2 a musical sound is pleasant to listen to
•NOUN• musicals a play or film in which there is lots of singing and dancing
♦ **musician** •NOUN• musicians someone who plays music on an instrument

musk •NOUN• musk is a strong perfume

musket •NOUN• muskets a type of old fashioned gun with a long barrel

♦ **musketeer** •NOUN• musketeers a soldier who carried a musket

Muslim *or* **Moslem** •NOUN• Muslims *or* Moslems a person who is a follower of Islam •ADJECTIVE• to do with Islam: *Friday is the Muslim holy day.*

muslin •NOUN• a thin loosely-woven cotton cloth

mussel •NOUN• mussels a type of shellfish with two hinged black oval shells

must •VERB• must is used with another verb to show that you have to do something or that something is certain or very likely: *You must finish your homework before you go out.* • *I saw it on the telly so it must be true.*

mustard •NOUN• crushed seeds of the mustard plant made into a paste and used to give food a hot taste

muster •VERB• musters, mustering, mustered 1 to muster troops is to gather them together in a group for inspection 2 to muster something like courage is to try to find as much of it as possible
• **pass muster** if something passes muster, it is found to be acceptable by the person examining it or inspecting it

mustn't •SHORT FORM• a short way to say and write **must not**: *You mustn't tease the cat.*

musty •ADJECTIVE• mustier, mustiest having a damp unpleasant smell

mute •ADJECTIVE• not speaking or not able to speak
♦ **muted** •ADJECTIVE• 1 muted colours are soft and not harsh or bright 2 muted voices or sounds are low or made quieter

mutilate •VERB• mutilates, mutilating, mutilated to mutilate something is to damage it by breaking a part off or cutting pieces off it
♦ **mutilation** •NOUN• being damaged

mutinous •ADJECTIVE• likely to rebel, or wanting to rebel against someone in authority

mutiny •NOUN• mutinies rebelling against someone in authority, especially sailors on a ship rebelling against their captain and officers

mutter • VERB• **mutters, muttering, muttered** to speak quietly under your breath: *Katy sighed and muttered but did as she was told.*

mutton • NOUN• meat from a sheep

mutual • ADJECTIVE• **1** given or done by people to one another: *mutual admiration* **2** shared by two people: *Peter and Ahmed have a mutual friend who works at the library.*
 ♦ **mutually** • ADVERB• in a mutual way: *mutually involved*

muzzle • NOUN• **muzzles 1** a dog's muzzle is the part, including its nose and mouth, that sticks out from its face
 2 a muzzle is a set of straps put over a dog's nose and mouth to stop it biting people
 3 the muzzle of a gun is the open end of its barrel, where the bullet or shell comes out
 • VERB• **muzzles, muzzling, muzzled 1** to muzzle a dog is to put a muzzle on it **2** to muzzle someone is to do something to stop them talking

my • ADJECTIVE• belonging to me: *There's my Mum and Dad.* • *Have you seen my boots anywhere?*

myriad • NOUN• a very great number or range of things: *a myriad of stars in the night sky*
 • ADJECTIVE• countless: *flowers in myriad colours and shapes*

myrrh • NOUN• a brown strong-smelling resin that comes from an African or Asian tree and is used in medicines and perfumes

myrtle • NOUN• a type of evergreen shrub with scented leaves

myself • PRONOUN• **1** you use **myself** after a verb or preposition when *I* is the subject of the action and is also affected by it: *I've washed myself all over, even behind my ears.* • *I felt rather proud of myself.*

2 you also use **myself** to show that you do something without any help from anyone else: *I suppose I'll have to do it myself if no one else can be bothered.*

3 you can use the word **myself** to show more clearly who you mean: *I have not seen the film myself.*

mysterious • ADJECTIVE• **1** difficult to understand or explain **2** if someone is being mysterious about something, they avoid talking about it, making you even more curious to know about it
 ♦ **mysteriously** • ADVERB• in a mysterious way: *It disappeared mysteriously in a little puff of smoke.*

mystery • NOUN• **mysteries** something that you do not understand and which cannot be, or has not been, explained

mystic • NOUN• **mystics** someone who tries to gain knowledge about sacred or spiritual things, usually by meditating or going into a trance
 ♦ **mystical** • ADJECTIVE• to do with the spiritual world, or beyond ordinary human understanding

mystify • VERB• **mystifies, mystifying, mystified** if you are mystified by something you are very puzzled by it

myth • NOUN• **myths 1** a story about ancient gods, heroes and monsters: *Greek and Roman myths* **2** something that many people believe is a fact, but which is not true or real
 ♦ **mythical** • ADJECTIVE• existing only in myths: *mythical creatures like dragons and unicorns*
 ♦ **mythological** • ADJECTIVE• to do with myth or mythology
 ♦ **mythology** • NOUN• stories about ancient gods and heroes

Nn

N •ABBREVIATION• short for **north**

nab •VERB• **nabs, nabbing, nabbed** 1 to grab or take something: *Someone's nabbed all the best sandwiches already.* 2 to catch or arrest someone: *The police nabbed a man climbing out of the back window.*

nag •VERB• **nags, nagging, nagged** to remind someone again and again about something they have not done: *Mum has to nag me every night to do my homework.*
•NOUN• **nags** an informal word for a horse

nail •NOUN• **nails** 1 a thin pointed piece of metal that you hit into a surface with a hammer 2 the hard covering on top of the ends of your fingers and toes
•VERB• **nails, nailing, nailed** to attach or join something by hammering it with nails: *Nail the number on the door.*

naïve •ADJECTIVE• believing things are simple and people are good when in fact life is more difficult: *She had a naïve belief that he never lied to her.*

naked •ADJECTIVE• 1 without clothes: *naked children playing in the water* 2 not covered or protected: *a naked flame*

ⓘ **Naked** is pronounced with two syllables: **nay-kid**.

name •NOUN• **names** 1 the word or words that you always call a certain person, place or thing: *What's your name?* • *I can't remember the name of the street.* 2 someone's **good** or **bad name** is their reputation: *This is how football fans get a bad name.*
•VERB• **names, naming, named** to decide on a certain word to call a person, place or thing: *They've named their son Samuel.*

nameless •ADJECTIVE• without a name or with a name that is not known: *The writer of the letter wants to remain nameless.*

namely •ADVERB• that is to say: *Two of our members, namely the Grimes brothers, have won medals this term.*

namesake •NOUN• **namesakes** your namesake is someone who has the same name as you: *Hi John, I've just been talking to your namesake in the supermarket.*

nanny •NOUN• **nannies** 1 a person whose job is to look after a child in its own home 2 a word that some children use for their grandmother

nanny-goat •NOUN• **nanny-goats** a female goat

nap •NOUN• **naps** a short sleep during the day: *Dad sometimes has a nap in the afternoon.*
•VERB• **naps, napping, napped** to have a short sleep

nape •NOUN• the nape of your neck is the back of your neck

napkin •NOUN• **napkins** a piece of cloth or paper that you can use during a meal to wipe your mouth or fingers

nappy •NOUN• **nappies** a pad for fastening around a baby's bottom to soak up any liquid or solid waste it produces: *a packet of disposable nappies* • *Mum's changing the baby's nappy.*

nark •VERB• **narks, narking, narked** to annoy someone: *Her voice really narks me.*
• **narky** •ADJECTIVE• bad-tempered and irritable: *Miss Graham was a bit narky this morning.*

narrate •VERB• **narrates, narrating, narrated** to tell a story: *Freddie narrated the events that led up to the explosion.*
• **narration** •NOUN• **narrations** the telling of a story: *a documentary about the war with a narration by some of the soldiers*
• **narrator** •NOUN• **narrators** the narrator of a story is the person who tells it: *We never find out the name of the narrator.*

narrow •ADJECTIVE• **narrower, narrowest** 1 not very wide: *a narrow gateway* • *The road was too narrow for overtaking.* 2 only just happening, with hardly any room or time

Aa
Bb
Cc
Dd
Ee
Ff
Gg
Hh
Ii
Jj
Kk
Ll
Mm
Nn
Oo
Pp
Qq
Rr
Ss
Tt
Uu
Vv
Ww
Xx
Yy
Zz

to spare: *a narrow escape*

♦ narrowly . ADVERB. closely: *We were narrowly defeated by 6 goals to 5.*

narrow-minded . ADJECTIVE. not willing to consider anybody else's beliefs or ideas

nasal . ADJECTIVE. to do with the nose: *a nasal voice*

ⓘ This word comes from the Latin word **nasus**, which means *nose*.

nasty . ADJECTIVE. nastier, nastiest 1 very unpleasant or unkind: *a nasty taste in my mouth* • *saying nasty things about her family* 2 serious: *a nasty injury*

nation . NOUN. nations 1 a country with its own government 2 the people of a country: *Today the nation is voting for a new government.*

♦ national . ADJECTIVE. to do with a whole country: *the local, national and international news*

national anthem . NOUN. national anthems the official song of a country

nationalism . NOUN. 1 the belief that the people of a country should have their own government 2 a great love for your own country

♦ nationalist . NOUN. nationalists 1 someone who wants their country to have its own government 2 someone with a great love for their own country

• ADJECTIVE. wanting your country to have its own government: *nationalist beliefs*

nationality . NOUN. nationalities your nationality is your membership of a nation: *Louis has dual nationality because his mother is French and his father is American.*

nationalize *or* **nationalise . VERB. nationalizes, nationalizing, nationalized** to nationalize an industry is to bring it under the control of the government: *The railways in many countries have been nationalized for years.*

national park . NOUN. national parks an area of countryside that the government controls in order to protect it

nationwide . ADJECTIVE. in every area

throughout a country: *a nationwide search for the robbers*

native . ADJECTIVE. 1 your native country is the one you were born in 2 your native language is the first one you learnt

• NOUN. natives a native of a country is someone who was born there

Native American . NOUN. Native Americans a person from the race of people who lived in North or South America before the Europeans arrived there

Nativity . NOUN. the birth of Jesus Christ

natural . ADJECTIVE. 1 to do with or made by nature, not by people or machines: *the natural world* • *An earthquake is an example of a natural disaster.* 2 natural behaviour is what you do normally without thinking: *It's only natural to be a little nervous before a test.*

natural gas . NOUN. gas that comes from under the sea or underground and can be used as fuel

natural history . NOUN. studying plants, animals and rocks

naturalist . NOUN. naturalists a person who studies plants or animals

naturalize *or* **naturalise . VERB. naturalizes, naturalizing, naturalized** a person is naturalized when they become a legal citizen of a country they were not born in

naturally . ADVERB. 1 you say 'naturally' to mean 'of course': *'Will you take me with you?' 'Naturally.'*
2 in a way that is normal: *Joe began to relax and behave a bit more naturally.*
3 without help from anything artificial: *Let the skin heal naturally.*

natural resources . NOUN. things that people use and that exist naturally, like forests, coal and water

nature . NOUN. natures 1 everything in the world that was not made or changed by people: *I love those nature programmes about animals.*
2 what something is basically like: *questions of a difficult nature*
3 the kind of person someone is: *It's not in her nature to be unkind.*

Aa Bb Cc Dd Ee Ff Gg Hh Ii Jj Kk Ll Mm **Nn** Oo Pp Qq Rr Ss Tt Uu Vv Ww Xx Yy Zz

nature reserve • NOUN • **nature reserves** an area of land that is kept separate to protect the plants and animals that live there

nature trail • NOUN • **nature trails** a path through the countryside where you can see particularly interesting plants and wildlife

naughtiness • NOUN • bad behaviour or disobedience

naughty • ADJECTIVE • **naughtier, naughtiest** a naughty child does things they should not do

nausea • NOUN • the feeling that you are about to be sick
♦ **nauseate** • VERB • **nauseates, nauseating, nauseated** something nauseating makes you feel sick: *a nauseating smell*

nautical • ADJECTIVE • to do with ships and the sea

naval • ADJECTIVE • to do with the navy

ⓘ This word comes from the Latin word **navis**, which means *ship*.

navel • NOUN • **navels** the small hollow in the centre of your stomach where the cord connected you to your mother before you were born

navigate • VERB • **navigates, navigating, navigated** to decide where to steer a vehicle such as a car, aeroplane or ship: *Mother always drove and father had to navigate.*
♦ **navigation** • NOUN • deciding which way to go in a vehicle such as a car, plane or boat
♦ **navigator** • NOUN • **navigators** a person who decides which direction a vehicle should go in

navy • NOUN • **navies** the part of a country's armed forces that works at sea

navy blue • NOUN • a dark blue colour

NB • ABBREVIATION • short for the Latin phrase **nota bene**, which means *note well*. You can write this to make someone pay particular attention to something in a piece of writing

near • PREPOSITION • not far away: *the shop near our house*
• ADVERB • **nearer, nearest** close by a thing or person: *Stand a little nearer and you'll be able to see better.*
• ADJECTIVE • **nearer, nearest** not far away: *the near future* • *a near neighbour*
• VERB • **nears, nearing, neared** to approach or get close: *As we neared the building, the faces at the window became clearer.*

nearby • ADJECTIVE AND ADVERB • quite close to where you are or the place you are talking about: *We went to a nearby restaurant for dinner.* • *Do you live nearby?*

nearly • ADVERB • almost but not completely: *We're nearly there.* • *Nearly everyone had a good time.*

neat • ADJECTIVE • **neater, neatest** 1 clean and tidy: *a neat bedroom* 2 done skilfully: *a neat shot into the corner of the goal* 3 a liquid, especially a drink, is neat when it is not mixed with anything

nebula • NOUN • **nebulae** a cloud of dust or gas that shines in the night sky

necessarily • ADVERB • for certain: *Men aren't necessarily stronger than women.*

necessary • ADJECTIVE • needed in order to get a result: *Is it necessary for everyone to fill in their own form?* • *We can stay a bit longer if necessary.*

necessity • NOUN • **necessities** something that is needed or that must happen: *A warm coat is a necessity in this weather.*

neck • NOUN • **necks** 1 the part of the body between the head and the shoulders 2 the opening in a piece of clothing that you put your head through 3 the narrow part of a bottle near its opening
• **neck and neck** almost level with each other in a race or competition

necklace • NOUN • **necklaces** a piece of jewellery for wearing around your neck, such as a string of beads or jewels or a chain

nectar • NOUN • the sweet liquid that bees collect from flowers to make honey

nectarine • NOUN • **nectarines** a fruit very similar to a peach but with a smooth skin

need • VERB • **needs, needing, needed** 1 to have to do something: *We all need to eat and drink.* 2 to be without something that would be helpful or useful: *What I need here is a sharp knife.*

Aa
Bb
Cc
Dd
Ee
Ff
Gg
Hh
Ii
Jj
Kk
Ll
Mm
Nn
Oo
Pp
Qq
Rr
Ss
Tt
Uu
Vv
Ww
Xx
Yy
Zz

• NOUN• **needs** 1 you have a need for something when you want it but do not have it: *If you feel the need of some company, just give me a call.* 2 if there is no need to do something, it is not necessary: *There's no need to shout.* 3 your needs are the things that it is necessary for you to have

needle • NOUN• **needles** 1 a small pointed piece of metal for sewing 2 a long thin piece of wood, metal or plastic that is used for knitting 3 an instrument for giving injections of medicine 4 a moving pointer, especially on a dial, for example on a compass 5 the pointed piece of diamond in a record-player that transfers the sound from a record

needless • ADJECTIVE• not necessary: *a needless waste of money*

needy • ADJECTIVE• **needier, neediest** poor: *help for needy families who have lost their homes*

negative • ADJECTIVE• 1 a negative answer or response says or means *no*: *We got a very negative reaction.* 2 to have a negative attitude is to feel uncertain and not very hopeful 3 a negative number is one that is less than zero, for example −5 4 a negative electric charge carries electrons
• NOUN• **negatives** a film before it is printed, where light objects appear dark and dark objects appear light

neglect • VERB• **neglects, neglecting, neglected** 1 to not give a thing or person proper care and attention: *I've been neglecting the housework because I've been so busy.* 2 to forget to do something: *I neglected to lock the door and found it wide open when I got home.*
• NOUN• lack of proper care: *All the houseplants had died from neglect.*

negligence • NOUN• not doing the things you should do, or not doing them carefully enough
♦ **negligent** • ADJECTIVE• careless about the things you should do carefully

negligible • ADJECTIVE• so small that you can ignore it: *negligible differences between the two stories*

negotiate • VERB• **negotiates, negotiating, negotiated** 1 to try to reach an agreement with someone by having discussions with them: *I've negotiated with dad to stay out till 11 o'clock.* 2 to go along a path or way successfully: *We just managed to negotiate the last corner and came in third.*
♦ **negotiation** • NOUN• **negotiations** discussion of a subject in order to reach an agreement on it
♦ **negotiator** • NOUN• **negotiators** a person who tries to make people come to an agreement by having discussions

neigh • VERB• **neighs, neighing, neighed** to make the noise that a horse makes
• NOUN• **neighs** the noise that a horse makes

neighbour • NOUN• **neighbours** the people who live near you
♦ **neighbourhood** • NOUN• **neighbourhoods** an area of a town or city: *This is a pretty neighbourhood with a lot of trees and parks.*
♦ **neighbouring** • ADJECTIVE• next or nearby: *the mayors of all the neighbouring towns*

ⓘ **Neighbour** comes from the Old English word **neachgebur**, which means 'someone living nearby'. **Neach** meant *near*, and *gebure* meant 'a person living in (a place)'.

neither • ADJECTIVE AND PRONOUN• not either: *Neither woman seemed to understand English.* • *Neither of us can go.*
• CONJUNCTION• neither is often used with **nor** to show negative possibilities: *I neither know, nor care, where he is.*

ⓘ You can say *Neither of us **is*** or ***are** able to be there.*

neon • NOUN• a kind of gas that shines very brightly when electricity passes through it: *your name in neon lights*

nephew • NOUN• **nephews** your nephew is the son of your brother or sister

nerve • NOUN• **nerves** 1 a nerve is one of the tiny thread-like connections that carry

messages about feelings and movements between your brain and other parts of your body **2** nerve is a kind of boldness or courage: *I didn't have the nerve to jump.*
• **get on someone's nerves** to irritate someone

nerve-racking • ADJECTIVE• making you feel extremely anxious or worried

nerves • PLURAL NOUN• a nervous feeling: *Breathe deeply before the performance to try to calm your nerves.*

nervous • ADJECTIVE• **1** worried or frightened: *I get terribly nervous just before I go on stage.* **2** to do with the body's nerves: *an infection that affects the nervous system*
• **nervously** • ADVERB• in a worried, rather scared way: *She answered, nervously wondering why they were asking her.*
• **nervousness** • ADJECTIVE• a worried, rather scared feeling

nervous system • NOUN• **nervous systems** the body's nervous system is its network of nerves and the way they link to the brain to send messages about feeling and movement

nest • NOUN• **nests** a place where birds or some kinds of insects and animals live and bring up their young
• VERB• **nests, nesting, nested** to build a place to live, especially from twigs and leaves, in a tree

nestle • VERB• **nestles, nestling, nestled 1** to settle yourself in a warm and comfortable place or position **2** to be in a partly hidden, sheltered place: *a cottage nestling at the edge of the wood*

net[1] • NOUN• **nets 1** net is a material made by crossing and knotting threads and making a pattern of holes **2** a net is made from crossed and knotted threads and is used for catching things like fish or in sports like tennis, football or basketball
• **the Net** • NOUN• the Internet

net[2] • ADJECTIVE• **1** a net profit is the money you have made after you have paid all your expenses **2** the net weight of something is its weight without its packaging

netball • NOUN• a game where teams of players throw a ball to each other and try to score goals by putting the ball through a high loop surrounded by a net at the end of a court. It is similar to basketball but players may not run with the ball

nettle • NOUN• **nettles** a wild plant that stings if you touch its leaves

network • NOUN• **networks 1** an arrangement of lines that cross and connect with one another: *a railway network* **2** a system of something like computers or radio stations that are all connected together

neuter • ADJECTIVE• in grammar, neuter words are neither masculine nor feminine. For example, the word *it* is not masculine or feminine, but neuter
• VERB• **neuters, neutering, neutered** to carry out an operation on an animal so that it cannot breed

neutral • ADJECTIVE• **1** a person who is neutral in an argument does not support either side
2 a neutral colour is not strong or noticeable
3 an engine's neutral gear is not connected to its forward or backward driving parts
• **neutralize** or **neutralise** • VERB• **neutralizes, neutralizing, neutralized** to make something useless or harmless

neutron • NOUN• **neutrons** a particle that joins with **protons** to make up the **nucleus** of an atom

never • ADVERB• not ever, or not at any time: *I've never been abroad.* • *It's never too late to learn.*

nevertheless • ADVERB• however or anyway: *I couldn't swim; nevertheless I jumped in to try to save him.*

new • ADJECTIVE• **newer, newest 1** not existing or known about before: *a new discovery*
2 just bought, made or received: *a new jacket*
3 different: *Take this book back and get a new one from the library.*

newcomer • NOUN• **newcomers** a person who has recently arrived

newfangled • ADJECTIVE• new and irritatingly complicated: *a newfangled washing machine*

Aa

newly • ADVERB• only recently: *a newly-painted room*

Bb

new moon • NOUN• the moon when it is shaped like a thin curve or crescent

Cc

news • PLURAL NOUN• **1** information about something that has just happened **2** a radio or television report about recent events: *listening to the news at 9 o'clock*

Dd

Ee

newsagent • NOUN• **newsagents** **1** someone who sells newspapers and magazines **2** a newsagent's is a shop that sells newspapers and magazines and usually other things like sweets and stationery: *She bought some envelopes at the newsagent's.*

Ff

Gg

Hh

newspaper • NOUN• **newspapers** a collection of reports and pictures about recent events that is published daily or weekly on a set of folded sheets of paper

Ii

Jj

newt • NOUN• **newts** a small animal like a lizard that lives both in water and on land

Kk

Ll

newton • NOUN• **newtons** a unit for measuring how strong a force is

Mm

new town • NOUN• **new towns** a town that was planned by the government and built quickly, rather than growing and developing slowly out of a village

Nn

Oo

next • ADJECTIVE• the one that follows immediately after: *What's the next name on the list?* • *Let's meet next week.*
• ADVERB• after the present thing, person or time: *Who's next?* • *What will happen next?*

Pp

Qq

Rr

nib • NOUN• **nibs** the point of a pen

Ss

nibble • VERB• **nibbles, nibbling, nibbled** to take little bites of something: *A mouse had nibbled right through the wires.*
• NOUN• **nibbles** a small bite or several small bites out of something

Tt

Uu

Vv

nice • ADJECTIVE• **nicer, nicest** **1** pleasant, good or attractive: *We'll find somewhere nice to sit, out in the fresh air.* **2** kind or friendly: *James is quite nice really, once you get used to him.*
✦ **nicely** • ADVERB• **1** in a pleasant way: *Ask the lady nicely, dear.* **2** well: *A cheque will do nicely, thank you.*
✦ **niceness** • NOUN• being pleasant or attractive

Ww

Xx

Yy

Zz

niche • NOUN• **niches** **1** a hollow space in a wall for a statue **2** a situation that you fit into very comfortably: *She seems to have found her niche in life.*

nick • NOUN• **nicks** **1** a small cut **2** an informal word for a police station
• VERB• **nicks, nicking, nicked** **1** to make a very small cut in something
2 an informal word that means to steal something: *Who's nicked my pen?*
3 an informal word that means to arrest someone

nickel • NOUN• **1** a greyish-white metal that is often mixed with other metals **2** an American or Canadian coin worth 5 cents

nickname • NOUN• **nicknames** a name that you use for someone that is not their real name
• VERB• **nicknames, nicknaming, nicknamed** to call someone a name that is not their real one: *They nicknamed him 'Scottie'.*

nicotine • NOUN• the poisonous substance that is the drug contained in tobacco

niece • NOUN• **nieces** your niece is the daughter of your brother or sister

nifty • ADJECTIVE• **niftier, niftiest** neat and clever: *You should have seen his nifty footwork when he got near the goal.*

niggle • VERB• **niggles, niggling, niggled** to worry or irritate you slightly, but continually
✦ **niggling** • ADJECTIVE• a niggling doubt or worry is a small one that will not go away

night • NOUN• **nights** the time of darkness between the sun going down in the evening and rising again in the morning

nightdress or **nightgown** • NOUN• **nightdresses** a loose dress for sleeping in

nightfall • NOUN• the time when it gets dark in the evening: *We arranged to meet at nightfall.*

nightingale • NOUN• **nightingales** a small bird that sings beautifully

nightly • ADJECTIVE AND ADVERB• every night: *nightly visits to the cinema* • *adverts that you see at least twice nightly*

nightmare • NOUN• **nightmares** **1** a frightening dream **2** a very unpleasant experience: *The journey turned out to be a complete nightmare.*

(i) The ending of this word comes from the Old English word **mare**, which means *evil spirit*. It used to be believed that bad dreams at night were caused by evil spirits.

nightshirt •NOUN• **nightshirts** a long loose shirt for sleeping in

nil •NOUN• nothing: *The score was eight-nil.*

nimble •ADJECTIVE• **nimbler, nimblest** 1 a nimble movement is quick, quiet and easy 2 a nimble person moves quickly and neatly
♦ **nimbly** •ADVERB• in a quick neat way: *He jumped nimbly aside and let the bike pass.*

nimbus •NOUN• dark grey cloud that usually brings rain or snow

nine •NOUN• **nines** the number 9

nineteen •NOUN• the number 19

nineteenth •ADJECTIVE AND ADVERB• after eighteenth and before twentieth: *the nineteenth day of the month*

ninetieth •ADJECTIVE AND ADVERB• after eighty-ninth and before ninety-first: *It's my great-grandfather's ninetieth birthday tomorrow.*

ninety •NOUN• **nineties** the number 90

ninth •ADJECTIVE AND ADVERB• after eighth and before tenth: *I came ninth out of ten – it could have been worse!*
•NOUN• **ninths** the fraction $\frac{1}{9}$, which means one of nine equal parts of something: *There are nine of us, so divide the cake into ninths.*

nip •VERB• **nips, nipping, nipped** 1 to pinch, squeeze sharply, or bite 2 to go somewhere quickly or for a short time: *I must just nip to the shops.*
•NOUN• **nips** 1 a small bite or pinch 2 a cold feeling: *a nip in the air that feels like winter*
♦ **nipper** •NOUN• **nippers** an informal word for a child

nipple •NOUN• **nipples** the pointed part of a breast that a baby sucks milk from

nippy •ADJECTIVE• **nippier, nippiest** 1 cold or frosty: *It's a bit nippy out today.* 2 a nippy car is easy to turn and move quickly

nit •NOUN• **nits** 1 the egg of a louse or other small insect 2 an idiot

nitrogen •NOUN• a colourless gas that makes up about four-fifths of the air we breathe

no •INTERJECTION• a word that you use to express things like refusing, denying or disagreeing: *'Are you alright?' 'No.'*
•ADJECTIVE• not any: *They have no money.*
•ADVERB• not at all: *She's no better.*

nobility •NOUN• 1 people in the highest classes of society, for example royalty 2 being noble

noble •ADJECTIVE• **nobler, noblest** 1 brave, fine and good: *making a noble effort to be nice* 2 belonging to a high social class or royalty: *coming from a noble family*
•NOUN• **nobles** a member of the upper classes of a society

nobleman •NOUN• **noblemen** a man of high rank in society

noblewoman •NOUN• **noblewomen** a woman of high rank in society

nobody •PRONOUN• not any person: *Nobody tells me what to do!* • *There was nobody at home.*
•NOUN• **nobodies** a person who is not at all important: *He's just a nobody who thinks he's somebody.*

nocturnal •ADJECTIVE• to do with the night-time: *Nocturnal animals do not usually hunt during the day.*

nod •VERB• **nods, nodding, nodded** to move your head up and down as if you were agreeing or saying 'yes'
•NOUN• **nods** an up-and-down movement of your head

Noël •NOUN• another name for **Christmas**

noise •NOUN• **noises** 1 a noise is a sound: *Did you hear a noise outside?* 2 noise is sound that you do not like: *Could you please make a little less noise?*

(i) This word comes from the Old French word **noise**, which means an *uproar*.

♦ **noisy** •ADJECTIVE• **noisier, noisiest** making a lot of sound that you do not like: *a noisy party* • *The fridge seems very noisy – is there something wrong with it?*

nomad •NOUN• **nomads** a person who wanders from place to place, rather than living in the same place all the time

nominate • VERB• **nominates, nominating, nominated** to nominate someone to do something is to suggest that they should do it: *Charles nominated Peter as leader of the group.*

✦ **nomination** • NOUN• **nominations** a suggestion that a certain thing or person should be chosen for something: *We've had several nominations, so we'll have to have a vote.* • *There are five nominations for Best Picture.*

✦ **nominee** • NOUN• **nominees** a person who has been suggested for a certain job or prize

non- • PREFIX• you can add **non-** to the beginning of many words to make them mean the opposite, or *not*, for example, *non-smokers* are people who do not smoke

nonagon • NOUN• **nonagons** a flat shape that has nine straight sides

none • PRONOUN• not one: *None of them are going to admit to being wrong.* • *We looked for more biscuits but there were none left.* • ADVERB• not at all: *I heard the answer but I'm none the wiser.*

non-existent • ADJECTIVE• not existing: *Many types of butterfly are almost non-existent in this area.*

nonplussed • ADJECTIVE• puzzled and confused

nonsense • NOUN• **1** something that does not make sense: *His theory is a load of nonsense.* **2** silly behaviour: *Stop your nonsense now please.*

non-stop • ADJECTIVE AND ADVERB• without a break or a pause: *There was non-stop hammering from the room above.* • *It's rained non-stop for three days.*

noodle • NOUN• **noodles** long thin pieces of pasta

nook • NOUN• **nooks** a corner or a space, especially where someone or something can be hidden

noon • NOUN• twelve o'clock in the daytime: *We'll have our lunch at noon.*

no one *or* **no-one** • PRONOUN• not any person: *No one's in at the moment.*

noose • NOUN• **nooses** a loop of rope that tightens when the end is pulled

nor • CONJUNCTION• a word that is used with **neither**, before a second negative possibility: *Neither Jack nor Jenny is at home.*

ⓘ You use **or** when you start with **either**: *Either he goes or I do.*
You use **nor** when you start with **neither**: *Neither you nor I will ever understand this.*

norm • NOUN• **norms** the norm is what people usually do or what usually happens: *It has become the norm to send young children to nursery school.*

normal • ADJECTIVE• usual and expected: *It's normal to feel hungry at lunchtime.*
✦ **normality** • NOUN• the state of things as they usually are: *After all the excitement it was good to return to normality.*
✦ **normally** • ADVERB• **1** usually: *We normally go to bed pretty early.* **2** in the usual way: *This plant has developed normally, but this one is diseased.*

north • NOUN• **1** the direction a compass needle points, opposite to south **2** the part of a country or the world that is in the north • ADJECTIVE• in, from, or towards the north: *the cold North wind* • *the north wall of the building* • ADVERB• to the north: *travelling north on the motorway*

north-east • NOUN• the area midway between north and east: *the north-east of Scotland*

northerly • ADJECTIVE• coming from, or going towards, the north: *a northerly breeze* • *going in a northerly direction* • *the island's most northerly point* • NOUN• **northerlies** a wind that comes from the north

northern • ADJECTIVE• belonging to or coming from the north: *the cold northern climate* • *Northern districts will have some rain.*

northward *or* **northwards** • ADJECTIVE• to or towards the north: *going in a northward direction* • ADVERB• to or towards the north: *We cycled northwards for several miles.*

north-west •NOUN• the area midway between north and west: *the north-west of England*

nose •NOUN• **noses 1** the part of your face that you breathe and smell through **2** the front part of something that sticks out, for example, the front of an aircraft

nosedive •NOUN• **nosedives** a dive straight downwards
•VERB• **nosedives, nosediving, nosedived** to dive down headfirst: *The rocket flew straight up and then nosedived straight down again.*

nostalgia •NOUN• a feeling of sadness when you remember happy times in the past
♦ **nostalgic** •ADJECTIVE• thinking of, or reminding you of happy times in the past: *a nostalgic evening of black and white movies*

nostril •NOUN• **nostrils** your nostrils are the two openings in your nose that you breathe and smell through

ⓘ This word comes from the Latin words **nosu**, which means *nose*, and **thyrel**, which means *hole*, so together they mean 'a hole in the nose'.

nosy *or* **nosey** •ADJECTIVE• **nosier, nosiest** always wanting to find out about other people and what they are doing

not •ADVERB• a word that is used to express negatives and opposites. It often becomes **n't** when it is added to verbs: *I'm not going.* • *It isn't fair.* • *I can't hear you.*

notable •ADJECTIVE• important and worth remembering: *The most notable part of the evening was the music.*
♦ **notably** •ADVERB• particularly: *I loved the old buildings, notably the palace.*

notch •NOUN• **notches** a small, V-shaped cut: *We cut notches in a stick as the days passed.*
•VERB• **notches, notching, notched** to make a V-shaped cut in something

note •NOUN• **notes 1** a word or sentence to tell or remind someone of something: *They've left a note to say that dinner's in the oven.*
2 a short letter: *This is just a quick note to let you know we're well.*

3 a written comment: *a note at the bottom of the page*
4 a piece of paper money: *a five pound note*
5 a single musical sound or the sign that stands for it
6 a piano key
•VERB• **notes, noting, noted** to pay attention to something so that you remember it: *I noted that she always wore red, and wondered why.*

notebook •NOUN• **notebooks 1** a small book that you use to write things down in **2** a laptop computer

notepaper •NOUN• plain paper that you use for writing letters on

nothing •PRONOUN• not anything: *There was nothing in the cupboard.* • *Nothing's the matter with me.*
♦ **nothingness** •NOUN• complete emptiness

notice •VERB• **notices, noticing, noticed** to realize something because you see, hear, feel, smell or taste it: *I noticed a funny smell in the hall.* • *Did you notice the way George was looking at Emily?*
•NOUN• **notices 1** an announcement: *a notice pinned on the board*
2 something **comes to your notice** when you realize it: *It's come to our notice that you are always late.*
3 you **give someone notice** of something happening when you warn them about it: *Please give me notice if you plan to visit.*

noticeable •ADJECTIVE• obvious or easy to see: *a noticeable difference in his appearance*
♦ **noticeably** •ADVERB• that you can easily see: *We were all noticeably more relaxed after dinner.*

notify •VERB• **notifies, notifying, notified** to tell someone about something in an official way: *Please notify the headteacher if you are not able to attend this meeting.*

notion •NOUN• **notions** an idea, a belief or an understanding: *I had a notion that this wouldn't really matter to you.*

notorious •ADJECTIVE• famous for something bad
♦ **notoriously** •ADVERB• well known to be

Aa
Bb
Cc
Dd
Ee
Ff
Gg
Hh
Ii
Jj
Kk
Ll
Mm
Nn
Oo
Pp
Qq
Rr
Ss
Tt
Uu
Vv
Ww
Xx
Yy
Zz

Aa

(something bad): *That model is notoriously unreliable.*

Bb

nougat • NOUN• a sticky kind of sweet that contains nuts

Cc

nought • NOUN• **noughts** 1 nothing 2 the figure 0: *Write twenty as a two and a nought.*

Dd

noun • PART OF SPEECH• **nouns** a word that refers to a person or a thing. For example, *tree*, *Sue*, and *idea* are nouns. See the box called **Nouns**

Ee

Ff

nourish • VERB• **nourishes, nourishing, nourished** to provide people, animals or plants with what they need to keep them healthy

Gg

Hh

✦ **nourishment** • NOUN• healthy food and drink

Ii

Jj

novel • NOUN• **novels** a book that tells a story that is not true: *a romantic novel*
• ADJECTIVE• completely new and original: *What a novel idea!*

Kk

Ll

November • NOUN• the eleventh month of the year, after October and before December

Mm

Nn

ⓘ **November** was the ninth month of the Roman year and the name comes from the word **novem**, which means *nine* in Latin.

Oo

Pp

novice • NOUN• **novices** a beginner, who is only just learning how to do something: *Don't ask me for advice – I'm just a novice at this.*

Qq

now • ADVERB• 1 at the present time: *It is now five o'clock.* 2 immediately: *I'll do it now.*
• **just now** 1 a moment ago: *I saw Mabel outside just now.* 2 right now: *I can't come out, I'm doing my homework just now.*
• **now and again** or **now and then** from time to time

Rr

Ss

Tt

Uu

nowadays • ADVERB• these days: *Nowadays, women usually have their babies in hospital.*

Vv

Ww

nowhere • ADVERB• not anywhere: *We've got nowhere to go.*

Xx

noxious • ADJECTIVE• harmful or poisonous: *noxious gases leaking from factories*

Yy

Zz

nozzle • NOUN• **nozzles** a part at the end of a pipe that controls how fast a liquid comes out of it

nuclear • ADJECTIVE• 1 to do with the reaction that occurs when atoms are split apart or forced together: *A nuclear submarine is powered by nuclear energy.* 2 to do with the nucleus of an atom

nuclear energy • NOUN• the energy that is created when atoms are split apart or forced together

nucleus • NOUN• **nuclei** the central part of an atom, made up of **protons** and **neutrons**

nude • ADJECTIVE• naked
• NOUN• **nudes** a nude is a picture or statue of someone without clothes on

nudge • VERB• **nudges, nudging, nudged** to give someone a gentle push, especially with your elbow: *I nudged him and he began to speak.*
• NOUN• **nudges** a gentle push, especially with your elbow: *Give him a nudge or he'll fall asleep.*

nudity • NOUN• not having any clothes on

nugget • NOUN• **nuggets** a small lump of something, especially gold or chicken

nuisance • NOUN• a thing or person that annoys you: *That cat is a dreadful nuisance, scratching at the door to get in.*

numb • ADJECTIVE• **number, numbest** a part of your body is numb when you cannot feel it properly: *I was so cold my hands had gone completely numb.*
✦ **numbness** • NOUN• when you lose the feeling in a part of your body

ⓘ Remember there is a *b* in **numb** that you do not pronounce.

number • NOUN• **numbers** 1 a word or figure showing how many or a position in a series: *the number four* • *Please write down any three figure number.*
2 a group or collection of people or things: *a large number of animals*
3 a popular song or piece of music: *a catchy number*
• VERB• **numbers, numbering, numbered**
1 to give a thing or person a number as part of a series: *The boxes are all clearly numbered.* 2 a group that numbers a certain quantity is made up of that many: *The crowd*

Nouns

A **noun** is a word that names a person, a thing or a place in a sentence. For example, in the sentence below, *children*, *ball* and *playground* are all nouns:

The **children** play **ball** in the **playground**.

Count nouns

Count nouns, which are also called **countable nouns**, name things that we can count one by one:

one **teacher**

two **bells**

three **flowers**

five hundred **apples**

Noncount nouns

Noncount nouns, which are also called **mass nouns**, name things that come in a mass and that you are not thinking about as separate pieces, for example:

gases: air, oxygen
liquids: water, milk, blood, petrol
powders: salt, sand, sugar, flour
substances: coal, concrete, iron, rice, steel, cotton, grass
things: luggage, furniture, machinery, clothing, equipment

Proper nouns

Proper nouns are the names of particular people, groups, places, events and occasions. They begin with a capital letter:

people: John, Superman, Mr Green
groups and organizations: Manchester United, Greenpeace
places: The Louvre, Paris, France, Europe, Atlantic Ocean, Earth
geographical places: Mount Everest, Hoover Dam, Lake Geneva, Sherwood Forest
days, months, special occasions and events: Tuesday, April, Christmas, Eid

Collective nouns

Collective nouns refer to a group of people or things that make up a larger whole:

a **flock** (of sheep)

an **army** (of soldiers)

a **bunch** (of flowers)

a **crowd** (of people)

a **swarm** (of insects)

a **team** (of players)

a **herd** (of cows)

a **pile** (of clothes or papers)

a **gang** (of children)

Aa

Bb

Cc

Dd

Ee

Ff

Gg

Hh

Ii

Jj

Kk

Ll

Mm

Nn

Oo

Pp

Qq

Rr

Ss

Tt

Uu

Vv

Ww

Xx

Yy

Zz

numbered many thousands.

numeral • NOUN • **numerals** a symbol that stands for a number: *a Roman numeral*

numerate • ADJECTIVE • a numerate person knows how to use numbers to do calculations

numerator • NOUN • **numerators** the number above the line in a fraction, for example 3 in $\frac{3}{4}$

numerical • ADJECTIVE • to do with numbers: *Put the cards into numerical order.*

numerous • ADJECTIVE • many: *Numerous people have had the same experience.*

nun • NOUN • **nuns** a member of a religious group of women who live in a convent

nurse • NOUN • **nurses** a person whose job is to look after people when they are ill or injured, especially in a hospital
• VERB • **nurses, nursing, nursed** to look after someone when they are ill or injured: *He had nursed her back to health over several weeks.*
⇒ **nursing**

nursery • NOUN • **nurseries 1** a place where parents can take their children to be looked after while they are at work
2 a room for young children
3 a place where lots of young plants are grown and sold

nursery school • NOUN • **nursery schools** a school for children between three and five years old

nursing • NOUN • the job of looking after people who are ill or injured

nursing home • NOUN • **nursing homes** a small private hospital or home, especially for old people

nurture • VERB • **nurtures, nurturing, nurtured** to look after a person, animal or plant so that it grows healthily

nut • NOUN • **nuts 1** a fruit from certain trees that has a hard shell and a firm inside that you can eat **2** a small piece of metal with a hole in the middle of it for screwing onto the end of a bolt

nutmeg • NOUN • **nutmegs** a hard seed that is grated or used as a brown powder to flavour food

nutrient • NOUN • **nutrients 1** a substance in food that gives you energy and makes you healthy **2** a substance in the soil that helps plants to grow healthily

nutrition • NOUN • eating healthy food: *Good nutrition is necessary for a quick recovery.*
✦ **nutritious** • ADJECTIVE • good for you to eat or drink

nutshell • NOUN • to **put something in a nutshell** is to say it using as few words as possible: *To put it in a nutshell, we must stop spending so much money.*

nutty • ADJECTIVE • **nuttier, nuttiest 1** containing nuts or tasting of nuts **2** silly or crazy

nuzzle • VERB • **nuzzles, nuzzling, nuzzled** an animal nuzzles you when it rubs its nose gently against you

nylon • NOUN • **nylons 1** nylon is a strong fabric made from chemicals **2 nylons** are nylon stockings

Oo

oaf • NOUN• **oafs** a stupid or clumsy person: *That big oaf is always knocking things over.*

oak • NOUN• **oaks** a large tree with hard wood and seeds called acorns

OAP • ABBREVIATION• short for **old age pensioner**

oar • NOUN• **oars** a long piece of wood with a flat end, used to row a boat: *Jane let go of the oar and it fell in the water.*

oasis • NOUN• **oases** a place in a desert where there is water and where trees grow: *The travellers stopped at an oasis.*

oath • NOUN• **oaths** 1 a solemn promise: *He swore an oath to support the king.* 2 a swear word: *curses and oaths*

oatmeal • NOUN• oats that have been ground to a powder

oats • PLURAL NOUN• a type of grassy plant or its grain, used as food: *Horses eat oats.*

obedience • NOUN• being willing to do what you are told: *Teachers expect obedience from their pupils.*
♦ **obedient** • ADJECTIVE• ready to do what you are told: *an obedient child*

obese • ADJECTIVE• very fat

obey • VERB• **obeys, obeying, obeyed** to do what you are told to do: *I obeyed the order.* ⇒ **obedience, obedient**

obituary • NOUN• **obituaries** an announcement in a newspaper that someone has died, often with a short account of their life

object • NOUN• **objects** 1 something that can be seen or felt: *There were various objects on the table.*
2 an aim or purpose: *His main object in life was to become rich.*
3 the word or words in a sentence that stand for the person or thing that the verb affects, for example *me* in *He hit me.* See the box called **Subjects and objects**
• VERB• **objects, objecting, objected** to

object to someone or something is to say that you do not like them or do not agree with them: *I object to her rudeness.* • *Jack objected to going to bed so early.*
♦ **objection** • NOUN• **objections** 1 objecting to something: *His view is open to objection.* 2 a reason for objecting: *My objection is that he is too young.*

ⓘ The noun is pronounced **ob**-jict, with the stress on *ob*. The verb is pronounced ob-**ject**, with the stress put on *ject*.

objective • NOUN• **objectives** an aim or purpose: *His objective was to score more than one goal.*
• ADJECTIVE• if you are objective, you are fair and try to look at things from different points of view

obligation • NOUN• **obligations** a promise or duty: *You are under no obligation to buy this.*

obligatory • ADJECTIVE• something that is obligatory must be done: *It is obligatory to pay tax.*

oblige • VERB• **obliges, obliging, obliged** 1 to oblige someone is to do something to help them: *Could you oblige me by carrying this, please?* 2 to oblige someone to do something is to force them to do it: *I was obliged to invite him to my party.*
♦ **obliged** • ADJECTIVE• grateful: *I am obliged to you for all your help.*
♦ **obliging** • ADJECTIVE• ready to help others: *a most obliging gentleman*

oblique • ADJECTIVE• 1 sloping: *an oblique line* 2 not direct or saying exactly what is meant: *an oblique reply*

oblivious • ADJECTIVE• not aware of what is happening: *I was oblivious to her exhaustion.*

oblong • NOUN• **oblongs** a rectangle that is longer than it is wide
• ADJECTIVE• shaped like an oblong: *an oblong table*

Aa Bb Cc Dd Ee Ff Gg Hh Ii Jj Kk Ll Mm Nn Oo Pp Qq Rr Ss Tt Uu Vv Ww Xx Yy Zz

383

oboe •NOUN• **oboes** a woodwind musical instrument

obscene •ADJECTIVE• disgusting: *obscene photographs*

✦ **obscenity** •NOUN• **obscenities** 1 obscenity is being obscene: *the obscenity of war* 2 an obscenity is a word or act that is obscene: *The youths shouted obscenities at the police.*

obscure •ADJECTIVE• 1 not easy to see or understand: *an obscure outline* • *obscure references to Shakespeare* 2 not famous or well-known: *an obscure poet*
•VERB• **obscures, obscuring, obscured** to hide something: *Thick clouds obscured the sun.*
✦ **obscurity** •NOUN• being obscure: *the obscurity of his poems* • *actors who slip into obscurity*

observant •ADJECTIVE• good at noticing things

observation •NOUN• **observations** 1 observation is noticing or watching: *He has been kept in hospital for observation.* 2 an observation is a remark or comment: *She made a couple of observations about the weather.*

observatory •NOUN• **observatories** a place with large telescopes for studying the stars or weather

observe •VERB• **observes, observing, observed** 1 to observe something is to notice it: *I observed her smiling face.*
2 to observe something is to watch it carefully: *She continued to observe his actions with interest.*
3 to observe something is to obey or keep it: *observe the rules* • *observe a tradition*
4 to observe is to remark: *'It's a lovely day,' he observed.*
✦ **observer** •NOUN• **observers** someone who observes

obsess •VERB• **obsesses, obsessing, obsessed** if something obsesses you, it fills your mind completely
✦ **obsessed** •ADJECTIVE• always thinking about something: *obsessed by football* • *obsessed with his work*
✦ **obsession** •NOUN• **obsessions** 1 an obsession is a feeling or idea that you cannot stop thinking about: *his obsession with motorbikes* 2 obsession is being obsessed: *David's tidiness borders on obsession.*

obsolete •ADJECTIVE• out of date or no longer in use: *The steam locomotive has become obsolete.*

obstacle •NOUN• **obstacles** something that stands in your way and stops you from doing something

obstacle race •NOUN• **obstacle races** a race in which various obstacles such as fences and nets have to be jumped, climbed or crawled through

obstinacy •NOUN• being obstinate

obstinate •ADJECTIVE• refusing to give in to someone or something: *She won't change her mind – she's very obstinate.*
✦ **obstinately** •ADVERB• in an obstinate way: *Anil obstinately refused to speak to me.*

obstruct •VERB• **obstructs, obstructing, obstructed** 1 to obstruct something is to block it: *The road was obstructed by a fallen tree.* 2 to obstruct someone or something is to stop them from getting past or to hold them back: *The crashed lorry obstructed the traffic.*
✦ **obstruction** •NOUN• **obstructions** blocking or preventing something: *an obstruction in the pipe* • *the obstruction of justice*

obtain •VERB• **obtains, obtaining, obtained** to get: *He obtained a large sum of money by selling houses.*

obtuse •ADJECTIVE• stupid and slow to understand: *Are you being deliberately obtuse?*

obtuse angle •NOUN• **obtuse angles** an angle that is more than 90 degrees and less than 180 degrees

obvious •ADJECTIVE• easily seen or understood: *It was obvious that she was ill.* • *an obvious reason*
✦ **obviously** •ADVERB• clearly: *Obviously, I'll need some help.*

occasion •NOUN• **occasions** 1 a particular time when something happens: *I've met him on several occasions.* 2 a special event: *The Queen's birthday was a great occasion.*

♦ **occasional** • ADJECTIVE• happening now and then: *occasional outings to the seaside*
♦ **occasionally** • ADVERB• now and then: *I occasionally go to the theatre.*

occupant • NOUN• **occupants** someone who lives or works in a place: *the occupants of the flat*

occupation • NOUN• **occupations** 1 a person's occupation is their job
2 an occupation is something that you do in your free time: *Reading is his favourite occupation.*
3 occupation is the occupying of territory: *the Roman occupation of Britain*

occupier • NOUN• **occupiers** the person who lives in a particular house or flat

occupy • VERB• **occupies, occupying, occupied** 1 to occupy a space is to fill it: *A table occupied the centre of the room.*
2 to occupy a house or building is to live or work there: *The family used to occupy a small flat.*
3 to occupy yourself or your time is to keep busy: *He occupied himself with the garden.*
4 to occupy territory is to capture it: *Soldiers were occupying the town.*

occur • VERB• **occurs, occurring, occurred**
1 to happen: *The accident must have occurred last night.*
2 to exist or be found: *Giants occur in fairy tales.*
3 if something occurs to you, it comes into your mind: *That never occurred to me.*
♦ **occurrence** • NOUN• **occurrences** something that happens

ocean • NOUN• **oceans** 1 the ocean is the salt water that covers most of the Earth's surface 2 an ocean is one of the five large areas of sea in the world, for example the Atlantic Ocean

octagon • NOUN• **octagons** a flat shape with eight sides
♦ **octagonal** • ADJECTIVE• having eight sides: *an octagonal coin*

octave • NOUN• **octaves** a range of eight musical notes, for example from one C to the C next above or below it

October • NOUN• the tenth month of the year, after September and before November

ⓘ **October** was the eighth month of the Roman year and the name comes from the word **octo**, which means *eight* in Latin.

octopus • NOUN• **octopuses** a sea creature with eight arms which are called tentacles

ⓘ This word comes from the Greek words **octo**, which means *eight*, and **pous**, which means *feet*.

odd • ADJECTIVE• **odder, oddest** 1 unusual or strange: *He's wearing very odd clothes.*
2 an odd number is one that cannot be divided exactly by 2: *5 and 7 are odd numbers.*
3 not one of a matching pair or group: *an odd shoe*
4 left over: *Have you got any odd bits of wood I could use?*
5 not regular: *She makes the odd mistake when she speaks English.*
♦ **oddity** • NOUN• **oddities** a strange or unusual person or thing: *He's always been a bit of an oddity.*
♦ **oddly** • ADVERB• strangely: *You're behaving very oddly.*
♦ **oddness** • NOUN• being odd: *the oddness of the situation*
⇒ **odds**

oddments • PLURAL NOUN• scraps or pieces left over from something else: *She made the jacket from oddments of material.*

odds • PLURAL NOUN• 1 the chances of something happening: *The odds are that he will win.* 2 difference: *It makes no odds.*
• **odds and ends** small objects of different kinds

ode • NOUN• **odes** a type of poem, often written to someone or something: *ode to autumn*

odour • NOUN• **odours** a smell, especially an unpleasant one: *the odour of cigarette smoke*

of • PREPOSITION• 1 belonging to: *a friend of mine* • *Where is the lid of this box?*
2 away from: *within two miles of his home*
3 from among: *one of my friends*
4 made from or out of: *a house of bricks*
5 used to show an amount or measurement of something: *a gallon of petrol*
6 about: *the story of his adventures*
7 containing: *a box of chocolates*

Aa
Bb
Cc
Dd
Ee
Ff
Gg
Hh
Ii
Jj
Kk
Ll
Mm
Nn
Oo
Pp
Qq
Rr
Ss
Tt
Uu
Vv
Ww
Xx
Yy
Zz

Aa
Bb
Cc
Dd
Ee
Ff
Gg
Hh
Ii
Jj
Kk
Ll
Mm
Nn
Oo
Pp
Qq
Rr
Ss
Tt
Uu
Vv
Ww
Xx
Yy
Zz

8 used to show the cause of something: *She died of hunger.*

9 used to show a removal or taking away: *robbed of her jewels*

off • ADVERB• 1 away from a place or position: *He marched off down the road.* • *Take your shoes off.*

2 not working or in use: *Switch off the light.*

3 completely: *Finish off your work.*

• ADJECTIVE• 1 cancelled: *The holiday is off.*

2 gone sour or rotten: *This milk is off.*

3 not being used: *The radio was off.*

• PREPOSITION• 1 away from or down from: *a mile off the coast* • *It fell off the table.*

2 out of a vehicle: *We got off the bus.*

3 taken away from: *There is £10 off the usual price.*

4 not wanting something: *Jane is not well and is off her food.*

• **badly off** if you are badly off, you are poor

• **well off** if you are well off, you are rich

offence • NOUN• **offences** 1 a crime: *The police charged him with several offences.* 2 a feeling of hurt, anger or annoyance: *His rudeness caused offence.*

• **take offence at** to feel hurt or angry at something

offend • VERB• **offends, offending, offended** 1 to offend someone is to make them feel upset or angry: *She will be offended if you don't go to her party.* 2 to offend is to do wrong or break a law: *young people who offend again and again*

✦ **offender** • NOUN• **offenders** a person who has committed a crime

✦ **offensive** • ADJECTIVE• 1 insulting: *even more offensive remarks*

2 disgusting: *an offensive smell*

3 used for attacking: *offensive weapons*

• NOUN• **offensives** an attack: *a military offensive*

offer • VERB• **offers, offering, offered** 1 to offer someone something is to ask if they would like it: *She offered me more tea.*

2 to offer to do something is to say that you will do it: *No one offered to help me carry the bags.*

3 to offer an amount of money is to say how much you are willing to pay for something: *I'll offer you £50 for the picture.*

• NOUN• **offers** 1 an act of offering: *an offer of help* 2 an amount of money offered: *They made an offer of £100,000 for the house.*

✦ **offering** • NOUN• **offerings** 1 a gift: *a birthday offering* 2 money given during a church service: *The offering will now be collected.*

offhand • ADJECTIVE• rude or impolite: *You were a bit offhand with her this morning.*

• ADVERB• without having or taking time to think carefully: *Can you tell me offhand how much it might cost?*

office • NOUN• **offices** 1 a building or set of rooms in which the business of a company is done: *Our head offices are in London.*

2 the room in which a particular person works: *the bank manager's office*

3 a room or building used for a particular purpose: *lost property office*

4 an important job or position: *the office of President*

officer • NOUN• **officers** 1 a person in the army, navy or air force who is in charge of ordinary soldiers 2 a policeman or policewoman

official • ADJECTIVE• 1 done or given out by people in power: *official announcement*

2 making up part of the tasks of a job or office: *official engagements*

• NOUN• **officials** a person who holds a job with authority: *government officials*

✦ **officially** • ADVERB• 1 as an official: *He attended the ceremony officially.* 2 formally: *The new library is now officially open.*

offpeak • ADJECTIVE• when there is lowest demand for something: *The train fare is less if you travel during offpeak periods.*

off-putting • ADJECTIVE• unpleasant: *His description of the hotel was a bit off-putting.*

offset • VERB• **offsets, offsetting, offset** one thing offsets another when it balances it out or makes up for it: *The price rises will be offset by tax cuts.*

offshore • ADJECTIVE• 1 in or on the sea, not far from the coast: *offshore oilrigs* 2 blowing away from the coast, out to sea: *offshore breezes*

offside • ADJECTIVE• in a position not allowed by the rules of a game such as football: *The goal was disallowed because the player was offside.*

offspring • NOUN• **offspring** a child or baby animal: *How many offspring does a cat usually have at one time?*

often • ADVERB• many times: *I often go to the cinema.*

ogre • NOUN• **ogres** 1 a frightening cruel giant in fairy tales 2 a frightening person

oh • INTERJECTION• a cry of surprise, admiration, pain or annoyance: *Oh, what a lovely present! • Oh no, I've forgotten my keys.*

oil • NOUN• **oils** 1 a greasy liquid that will not mix with water: *olive oil • vegetable oil* 2 a substance, also called **crude oil** or **petroleum**, made from the remains of dead animals and plants. It can be taken out of the ground and used as fuel
•VERB• **oils, oiling, oiled** to put oil on or into something: *The machine will work better if it's oiled.*
⇒ **oily**

oilfield • NOUN• **oilfields** a place where oil is found in the ground or under the sea: *the oilfields of the North Sea*

oil paint • NOUN• **oil paints** paint made with oil
♦ **oil painting** • NOUN• **oil paintings** a picture painted with oil paints

oil rig • NOUN• **oil rigs** a structure set up for drilling an oil well

oilskin • NOUN• **oilskins** 1 cloth made waterproof with oil 2 a piece of clothing made of this

oil well • NOUN• **oil wells** a hole that is drilled into the ground or seabed in order to get oil

oily • ADJECTIVE• **oilier, oiliest** 1 like, or covered with, oil: *an oily liquid • an oily rag* 2 too friendly or flattering: *his oily manner*

oink • NOUN• **oinks** the sound made by a pig
•VERB• **oinks, oinking, oinked** to make the sound of a pig: *pigs oinking noisily in the farmyard*

ointment • NOUN• **ointments** a greasy substance that is rubbed on the skin to soothe or heal it

OK *or* **okay** • INTERJECTION, ADJECTIVE AND

ADVERB• an informal way of saying 'all right': *OK! I'll do it! • an okay song • Do I look OK?*

ⓘ **OK** probably comes from an American advertisement from the past, in which 'all correct' was spelt *oll korrect* as a joke.

old • ADJECTIVE• **older, oldest** 1 having lived or existed a long time: *an old man • an old building*
2 having a particular age: *nine years old*
3 belonging to times long ago: *the good old days*
4 worn-out or no longer used: *She threw away her old clothes.*
5 former or previous: *I preferred my old school to this one.*

old age • NOUN• the later part of a person's life: *He wrote poems in his old age.*

old age pensioner • NOUN• **old age pensioners** an old person, especially one who has retired from work and gets money to live on from the government

Old English • NOUN• the English language before about 1150

old-fashioned • ADJECTIVE• of a kind that was usual some time ago: *old-fashioned clothes*

olive • NOUN• **olives** 1 a small oval fruit with a hard stone, which is used to make cooking oil 2 the tree on which it grows 3 a yellowish-green colour

Olympic games *or* **Olympics** • PLURAL NOUN• a sports competition held once every four years for sportsmen and sportswomen from all over the world

omelette *or* **omelet** • NOUN• **omelettes** a dish made of eggs beaten and fried, sometimes with a filling: *a cheese omelette*

omen • NOUN• **omens** a sign of future events: *The storm was a bad omen.*
♦ **ominous** • ADJECTIVE• giving a warning about something bad that is going to happen: *ominous clouds*

omission • NOUN• **omissions** 1 omission is the leaving out of something: *the omission of his name from the list* 2 an omission is something that has been left out: *There are omissions in his report.*

Aa
Bb
Cc
Dd
Ee
Ff
Gg
Hh
Ii
Jj
Kk
Ll
Mm
Nn
Oo
Pp
Qq
Rr
Ss
Tt
Uu
Vv
Ww
Xx
Yy
Zz

omit • VERB • **omits, omitting, omitted 1** to omit something is to leave it out: *You can omit the last chapter of the book.* **2** to omit to do something is to fail to do it: *I omitted to tell him about the meeting.*

omni- • PREFIX • if **omni-** appears at the start of a word it means *all, every* or *everywhere*. For example, *omniscient* means knowing everything, and *omnipresent* means present everywhere

omnivore • NOUN • **carnivores** an animal that eats all kinds of food, plants as well as meat. Look up and compare **carnivore** and **herbivore**
✦ **omnivorous** • ADJECTIVE • eating all kinds of food: *Human beings are omnivorous.*

on • PREPOSITION • **1** touching, fixed to or covering the upper or outer side of something: *on the table*
2 supported by: *standing on one leg*
3 during a certain day: *on Friday*
4 about: *a book on Scottish history*
5 with: *Do you have a pen on you?*
6 near or beside: *a shop on the main road*
7 taking part in: *He is on the committee.*
• ADVERB • **1** so as to be touching, fixed to or covering the upper or outer side of something: *Put your coat on.*
2 forwards or onwards: *They moved on.*
3 working or being used: *Switch the light on.*
• ADJECTIVE • **1** working or being used: *The television is on.*
2 planned: *Do you have anything on this evening?*
3 not cancelled: *Is the party still on?*
• **you're on!** I agree or I accept your challenge

once • ADVERB • **1** a single time: *He did it once.* **2** at a time in the past: *People once lived in caves.*
• CONJUNCTION • when or as soon as: *Once you've finished, you can go.*

oncoming • ADJECTIVE • moving towards you: *oncoming traffic*

one • NOUN • **ones** the number 1: *One and one is two.*
• PRONOUN • **1** a single person or thing: *One of my friends called round.* **2** a rather formal word for **anyone** or **you**: *One can see the sea from here.*
• ADJECTIVE • a single: *We had only one reply.*
• **one another** used when an action takes place between two or more people: *They looked at one another.*

oneself • PRONOUN • **1** you use **oneself** after a verb or preposition when the subject is **one**: *One should wash oneself every day.* **2** you also use the word **oneself** for emphasis: *One always has to do these things oneself.*

one-sided • ADJECTIVE • **1** with one person or side having a big advantage over the other: *a one-sided contest* **2** showing only one view of a subject: *a one-sided discussion*

one-way • ADJECTIVE • a one-way street is one in which traffic can move in one direction only

ongoing • ADJECTIVE • continuing: *ongoing talks*

onion • NOUN • **onions** a round vegetable that has a strong taste and smell

onlooker • NOUN • **onlookers** someone who watches something happening: *A crowd of onlookers had gathered.*

only • ADVERB • **1** not more than: *There are only two weeks left.*
2 alone: *Only you can do it.*
3 not longer ago than: *I saw her only yesterday.*
• ADJECTIVE • without any others of the same type: *the only book of its kind*
• CONJUNCTION • but or however: *I'd like to come, only I have to work.*

onset • NOUN • **onsets** the onset of something is the beginning of it: *the onset of a cold*

onward • ADJECTIVE • going forward in place or time: *their onward journey* • *the onward march of science*
✦ **onwards** or **onward** • ADVERB • forward: *He led them onward through the night.*
• *from nine o'clock onwards*

ooze • VERB • **oozes, oozing, oozed** to flow slowly: *The glue oozed out of the tube.*

ⓘ **Ooze** comes from an Old English word, **wos**, which means *juice* or *sap*.

opal • NOUN • **opals** a precious stone that is milky in colour, with traces or streaks of other colours

opaque •ADJECTIVE• not able to be seen through: *an opaque liquid*

open •ADJECTIVE• 1 not shut: *The door is wide open.*
2 allowing the inside to be seen: *an open book*
3 not enclosed: *open countryside*
4 honest: *He was very open with me about his work.*
5 not yet decided: *The matter is still open for discussion.*
•VERB• **opens, opening, opened** 1 to open something is to make it open: *He opened the door.*
2 to open is to become open: *The door opened.*
3 to open something is to begin it: *He opened the meeting with a speech of welcome.*
• **open to** likely or willing to receive something: *open to attack* • *open to suggestions*
♦ **opener** •NOUN• **openers** something that opens something else: *a tin opener*
♦ **opening** •NOUN• **openings** 1 a hole or space: *an opening in the fence*
2 a beginning: *the opening of the film*
3 a chance, especially for a job: *There are few openings for ex-footballers.*
♦ **openly** •ADVERB• without trying to hide anything: *She talked openly about her illness.*

open-minded •ADJECTIVE• ready to take up new ideas

opera •NOUN• **operas** a musical play in which the words are sung: *an opera by Verdi*

operate •VERB• **operates, operating, operated** 1 to operate is to work: *The printer doesn't seem to be operating properly.*
2 to operate a machine is to make it work: *How do you operate this computer?*
3 to operate on someone is to perform a surgical operation on them: *The surgeon operated on the man's heart.*
♦ **operation** •NOUN• **operations** 1 a carefully planned action: *a rescue operation*
2 the process of working: *Our plan is now in operation.*
3 something done to a person's body, usually by a surgeon, in order to remove part

of it or to treat a disease: *an operation for appendicitis*
♦ **operator** •NOUN• **operators** 1 someone who works a machine: *a lift operator* 2 someone who connects telephone calls: *Ask the operator to put you through to that number.*

opinion •NOUN• **opinions** what you think or believe: *My opinions about education have changed.*

opinion poll •NOUN• **opinion polls** a survey of what people think, made by questioning a certain number of them

opponent •NOUN• **opponents** someone who is against you, for example in a war or competition: *He beat his opponent by four points.*

opportunity •NOUN• **opportunities** a chance to do something: *I'd like to have an opportunity to go to Paris.*

oppose •VERB• **opposing, opposes, opposed** to oppose someone or something is to be against them: *We opposed the government on this question.* • *Who is opposing him in the election?*
⇒ **opponent, opposition**

opposite •ADJECTIVE• 1 on the other side of something: *on the opposite side of town*
2 completely different: *They walked off in opposite directions.*
•PREPOSITION AND ADVERB• facing: *the house opposite mine* • *Who lives in the house opposite?*
•NOUN• **opposites** one thing is the opposite of another if it is completely different from it: *Hot is the opposite of cold.* See the box called **Opposites** on the next page

opposition •NOUN• 1 opposition is resisting or fighting against someone or something: *There is a lot of opposition to his new ideas.*
2 opposition can also be the people you are fighting or competing against: *a strong opposition*
3 the Opposition is the main political party that opposes the party in government

oppress •VERB• **oppresses, oppressing, oppressed** 1 to oppress someone is to govern or treat them cruelly: *The king*

Opposites

Words that mean the **opposite** of each other are called **antonyms**. They may be nouns, adjectives, verbs, adverbs or prepositions, for example:

nouns		adjectives	
sunrise	sunset	white	black
stranger	friend	hot	cold
knowledge	ignorance	right	left

verbs		adverbs	
arrive	leave	generously	meanly
lose	find	kindly	cruelly
offend	please	strongly	weakly
raise	lower		

prepositions	
to	from
with	without
before	after

A word can have more than one antonym or opposite, for example:

hard (1) soft, pliable. (2) easy, comfortable. (3) simple, uncomplicated. (4) easy-going.
old (1) young, youthful. (2) fresh, brand-new.
open (1) closed, shut. (2) private, secretive. (3) filled, taken.
poor (1) rich, wealthy. (2) good, excellent. (3) lucky, fortunate.

Some **thesauruses**, which are reference books full of **synonyms** (words that mean the same thing), also give you lists of **antonyms** (opposites of the words).

oppressed his people. **2** if something oppresses you, it worries or distresses you: *The heat oppressed her.*

◆ **oppression** • NOUN• **1** cruel treatment **2** worry or distress

◆ **oppressive** • ADJECTIVE• **1** cruel and harsh: *oppressive government*
  2 causing worry: *an oppressive situation*
  3 unpleasantly hot: *the oppressive heat of the desert*

opt • VERB• **opts, opting, opted 1** to **opt for** something is to choose it: *I opted for the strawberry gateau.*
  2 to **opt to** do something is to decide to do it: *She opted to stay on at school.*

3 to **opt out** is to decide not to do something: *I opted out of the exam.*

optic or **optical** • ADJECTIVE• to do with the eyes or sight: *optic nerve* • *an optical aid*

optical illusion • NOUN• **optical illusions** something which deceives the eye, often making you think you can see something that is not actually there: *The water he thought he could see was actually an optical illusion caused by the light.*

optician • NOUN• **opticians** someone who tests your eyesight and makes and sells spectacles

optics • NOUN• the science of light

optimism • NOUN• the habit of expecting things to turn out well: *full of optimism*
♦ **optimist** • NOUN• **optimists** someone who usually expects or hopes that something good will happen
♦ **optimistic** • ADJECTIVE• hoping or believing that something good will happen: *an optimistic person*
♦ **optimistically** • ADVERB• in an optimistic way: *'She might still come,' he said optimistically.*

option • NOUN• **options** 1 choice: *You have no option.* 2 a thing that you choose or that may be chosen: *There are several options open to me.*
♦ **optional** • ADJECTIVE• a matter of choice, not compulsory: *Music is optional at my school.*

opulent • ADJECTIVE• 1 very rich: *There are a lot of opulent people in America.* 2 showing wealth: *She lived in opulent surroundings.*

or • CONJUNCTION• 1 used to show choices or alternatives: *Would you prefer tea or coffee?* 2 because if not: *You'd better go or you'll miss your bus.*

oral • ADJECTIVE• 1 spoken, not written: *an oral examination* 2 to do with the mouth: *oral hygiene*
♦ **orally** • ADVERB• 1 by speaking: *I prefer to communicate orally rather than by email.* 2 by mouth: *medicine to be taken orally*

orange • NOUN• **oranges** 1 an orange is a juicy citrus fruit with a thick skin of a colour between red and yellow 2 orange is the colour of this fruit

orang-utan • NOUN• **orang-utans** a large man-like ape

ⓘ **Orang-utan** comes from the Malay language. It means *wild man* or *forest man*.

oration • NOUN• **orations** a formal speech: *a funeral oration*
♦ **orator** • NOUN• **orators** someone who makes formal speeches

orb • NOUN• **orbs** anything in the shape of a ball, a sphere

orbit • NOUN• **orbits** the path along which something moves around a planet or other body in space: *The spaceship is in orbit round the moon.*
• VERB• **orbits, orbiting, orbited** to go round something in space: *The spacecraft is orbiting Earth.*

orchard • NOUN• **orchards** an area where fruit trees are grown: *a cherry orchard*

orchestra • NOUN• **orchestras** a large group of musicians playing together: *Jo plays violin in the school orchestra.*

orchid • NOUN• **orchids** a plant with brightly-coloured flowers

ordain • VERB• **ordains, ordaining, ordained** to ordain someone is to make them a priest or minister: *Some Christian churches have decided to ordain women.*

ordeal • NOUN• **ordeals** a difficult or painful experience: *The exam was a great ordeal.*

order • NOUN• **orders** 1 an instruction to do something: *The soldier was given the order to shoot.*
2 an instruction to supply something: *The waiter came to take our order.*
3 the way things are arranged: *alphabetical order*
4 peaceful conditions and behaviour: *law and order*
5 an organized state when things are in their proper places: *It was time to bring some order into my life.*
• VERB• **orders, ordering, ordered** 1 to order someone to do something is to tell them to do it: *The doctor ordered her to rest for a few days.* 2 to order something is to ask for it to be supplied: *I ordered some magazines from the newsagent.*
♦ **orderly** • ADJECTIVE• 1 well-behaved, quiet: *Please form an orderly queue.* 2 in proper order: *an orderly arrangement of objects*

ordinal number • NOUN• **ordinal numbers** an ordinal number is any number which shows where something comes in a series, for example *first, second, third*

ordinary • ADJECTIVE• normal and not very special: *an ordinary Monday morning*

ore • NOUN• **ores** solid material, for example rock, from which a metal is obtained: *iron ore*

Aa
Bb
Cc
Dd
Ee
Ff
Gg
Hh
Ii
Jj
Kk
Ll
Mm
Nn
Oo
Pp
Qq
Rr
Ss
Tt
Uu
Vv
Ww
Xx
Yy
Zz

organ • NOUN• **organs** 1 a part of your body that has a special purpose: *Eyes are the organs that we use to see.* 2 a musical instrument with keys like a piano ⇒ **organist**

organic • ADJECTIVE• 1 to do with the organs of the body 2 found in or made by living things: *organic fertilizers* 3 organic food is produced without using chemicals: *I only buy organic vegetables.* ✦ **organically** • ADVERB• in an organic way: *vegetables that are organically grown*

organism • NOUN• **organisms** any living thing

organist • NOUN• **organists** someone who plays the organ

organization or **organisation** • NOUN• **organizations** 1 an organization is a group of people who work together for a purpose: *a business organization* 2 organization is the organizing of something: *The success of the project depends on good organization.*

organize or **organise** • VERB• **organizes, organizing, organized** 1 to arrange and prepare something: *We've organized a surprise party for his birthday.* 2 to put something in order: *He organized all the papers on his desk.* ✦ **organizer** or **organiser** • NOUN• **organizers** or **organisers** someone who organizes something

oriental • ADJECTIVE• in or from the east: *oriental art*

orienteering • NOUN• a sport in which you run across country, finding your way with a map and a compass

origami • NOUN• the Japanese art of paper-folding

ⓘ **Origami** comes from the Japanese words **ori**, which means *fold*, and **kami**, which means *paper*.

origin • NOUN• **origins** 1 the place from which someone or something comes: *the origins of the English language* 2 the cause: *the origin of his fear of flying* ✦ **original** • ADJECTIVE• 1 existing from the start, first: *The original story had been* changed down through the centuries. 2 not copied, new: *an original design* • *original ideas* 3 done by the artist himself: *The original painting is in the museum, but there are hundreds of copies.* • NOUN• **originals** the earliest version: *This is the original – all the others are copies.* ✦ **originally** • ADVERB• 1 in or from the beginning: *His family comes from Scotland originally.* 2 in a new and different way: *She dresses very originally.*

originate • VERB• **originates, originating, originated** 1 to originate is to start or come into being: *This style of painting originated in China.* 2 to originate something is to create it: *She is responsible for originating the word.*

ornament • NOUN• **ornaments** an object used to decorate something: *china ornaments on the mantelpiece* • VERB• **ornaments, ornamenting, ornamented** to decorate: *The ceiling was richly ornamented.* ✦ **ornamental** • ADJECTIVE• for decoration: *an ornamental pond* ✦ **ornamentation** • NOUN• things added to something to decorate it

ornate • ADJECTIVE• decorated with a complicated design: *an ornate doorway*

ornithologist • NOUN• **ornithologists** someone who studies or is an expert on birds ✦ **ornithology** • NOUN• the study of birds

orphan • NOUN• **orphans** a child whose parents are both dead ✦ **orphanage** • NOUN• **orphanages** a home for orphans

orthodox • ADJECTIVE• having beliefs that are thought correct by most people, generally accepted: *orthodox Jews* • *orthodox medical treatment*

osprey • NOUN• **ospreys** a type of eagle that feeds on fish

ostrich • NOUN• **ostriches** a large bird which cannot fly but runs very fast

other • ADJECTIVE• 1 the second of two: *Where is the other glove?* 2 the rest: *Jack is here and the other children are at school.*

Aa
Bb
Cc
Dd
Ee
Ff
Gg
Hh
Ii
Jj
Kk
Ll
Mm
Nn
Oo
Pp
Qq
Rr
Ss
Tt
Uu
Vv
Ww
Xx
Yy
Zz

3 different or extra: *There must be some other reason.*

4 recently past: *just the other day*

• **PRONOUN** • **1** the second of two: *Here's one sock, but where is the other?* **2** the rest: *Joe is here, but where are the others?*

• **other than** except: *There was no one there other than an old woman.*

otherwise • ADVERB • **1** or else: *You can't leave now, otherwise you'll always wonder what it would've been like.*

2 in any other way: *The new boy raised his hand. Otherwise, no one stirred.*

3 in a different way: *He must have asked somebody because he couldn't possibly know otherwise.*

otter • NOUN • **otters** a small furry river animal that feeds on fish

ottoman • NOUN • **ottomans** a low cushioned seat without a back

ought • VERB • **1 ought** is used to show what you should do: *You ought to help them.*
2 ought is also used to show what is likely to happen: *The weather ought to be fine.*

ounce • NOUN • **ounces** a unit of measurement of weight, equal to $\frac{1}{16}$ of a pound or 28.35 grams: *You need five ounces of flour to make this cake.*

our • ADJECTIVE • belonging to us: *That is our car.*

ours • PRONOUN • a word you use to talk about something belonging to us: *That car is ours.* • *These books are ours.*

ourselves • PRONOUN • **1** you use **ourselves** after a verb or preposition when **we** is the subject of the action and is also affected by it: *We saw ourselves in the mirror.*

2 ourselves is also used to show that you have done something without any help from other people: *We painted the room ourselves.*

3 you can use **ourselves** to show more clearly who you mean: *We ourselves played no part in this.*

out • ADVERB • **1** into or towards the open air: *go out for a walk*

2 from inside something: *She opened her bag and took out an umbrella.*

3 away from a place, such as home or from

the office: *I'm afraid he's out at the moment.*

4 loudly: *shout out the answer*

5 completely: *tired out*

6 no longer hidden or secret: *The secret is out.*

7 dismissed from a game: *The batsman is out.*

• **out of** to be out of something is to have no more of it left: *We're out of biscuits.*

• **out of date** old or old-fashioned: *This telephone directory is out of date.*

out-and-out • ADJECTIVE • complete: *an out-and-out liar*

outback • NOUN • the remote parts in the middle of Australia where few people live

outbreak • NOUN • **outbreaks** a sudden beginning, usually of something unpleasant: *the outbreak of war*

outburst • NOUN • **outbursts** an explosion, especially of angry feelings: *a sudden outburst of rage*

outcast • NOUN • **outcasts** someone who has been driven away by their friends, family or society

outcome • NOUN • **outcomes** a result: *What was the outcome of your discussion?*

outcry • NOUN • **outcries** a strong reaction or protest by a large number of people: *The decision caused a public outcry.*

outdo • VERB • **outdoes, outdoing, outdid, outdone** to outdo someone is to do better than them: *The girls tried to outdo each other in their kindness.*

outdoor • ADJECTIVE • outside or for use outside: *an outdoor swimming pool*
• *outdoor shoes*

◆ **outdoors** • ADVERB • outside: *She sat outdoors in the sun.* • *Don't go outdoors if it's raining.*

outer • ADJECTIVE • nearer the outside: *outer space* • *outer layers*

outfit • NOUN • **outfits** a set of clothes worn together: *a wedding outfit*

outgrow • VERB • **outgrows, outgrowing, outgrew, outgrown** to outgrow something is to grow too big or too old for it: *She has outgrown all her clothes.* • *Babies quickly outgrow their toys.*

out-house • NOUN• **out-houses** a small building such as a shed which is attached to or close to a larger building

outing • NOUN• **outings** a short trip, made for pleasure: *an outing to the seaside*

outlaw • NOUN• **outlaws** someone who is given no protection by the law in their country because they are a criminal •VERB• **outlaws, outlawing, outlawed** to outlaw something is to make it illegal: *The sale of alcohol was outlawed.*

outlay • NOUN• money that is spent, especially in order to start a business or a project

outlet • NOUN• **outlets** 1 a way of letting something out: *an outlet from the main tank* • *an outlet for his energy* 2 a place to sell goods: *We must find new outlets for this product.*

outline • NOUN• **outlines** 1 the line forming the outside of something: *First he drew the outline of the face, then added the features.* 2 a short description of something: *Don't tell me the whole story – just give me the outline.* •VERB• **outlines, outlining, outlined** 1 to outline something is to draw the line forming the outside of it 2 to outline a plan or story is to give a short description of it

outlook • NOUN• **outlooks** 1 a view: *Their house has a wonderful outlook.* 2 the way that a person thinks about things: *He has a strange outlook on life.* 3 what seems likely to happen: *the weather outlook*

outlying • ADJECTIVE• far from a town or city: *a small outlying village*

outnumber •VERB• **outnumbers, outnumbering, outnumbered** to outnumber something is to be more in number than it: *The boys in the class outnumber the girls.*

out-patient • NOUN• **out-patients** someone who comes to hospital for treatment but does not stay overnight

outpost • NOUN• **outposts** 1 a small military camp far away from the main army, especially to protect it from a surprise attack 2 a settlement far from where most people live

output • NOUN• **outputs** 1 a quantity of goods produced or an amount of work done: *The output of this factory increased last year.* 2 the information produced by a computer •VERB• **outputs, outputting, output** to output data in computing is to cause it to be produced

outrage • NOUN• **outrages** a shocking or cruel action: *The decision to close the hospital is an outrage.* •VERB• **outrages, outraging, outraged** to outrage someone is to hurt, shock or insult them: *Fay was outraged by his remarks.* • **outrageous** • ADJECTIVE• shocking, terrible: *outrageous behaviour*

outright • ADVERB• 1 immediately: *He was killed outright.* 2 completely: *We won outright.* • ADJECTIVE• 1 complete: *an outright fool* 2 without any doubt: *She is the outright winner.*

outset • NOUN• the beginning: *Joe hated school from the outset.*

outside • NOUN• **outsides** the outer surface of something: *The outside of the house was painted white.* • ADJECTIVE• 1 of, on or near the outer part of anything: *the outside edge* 2 slight: *an outside chance of winning* • ADVERB• on or to the outside, outdoors: *Let's eat outside.* • PREPOSITION• on the outer side of, not inside: *He was standing outside the gate.* • **outsider** • NOUN• **outsiders** 1 someone not included in a particular group: *The new boy in the class felt like an outsider.* 2 a horse or person not expected to win a race or contest

outskirts • PLURAL NOUN• the outer parts, especially of a town or city: *He lives on the outskirts of Edinburgh.*

outspoken • ADJECTIVE• saying exactly what you mean, even if it upsets people: *She makes enemies because she is so outspoken.*

outstanding • ADJECTIVE• 1 excellent: *an outstanding student* 2 not yet paid or done: *You must pay all outstanding bills.*

outward • ADJECTIVE• 1 on or towards the outside: *She shows no outward sign of*

unhappiness. **2** away from a place: *the outward voyage*
♦ **outwardly** •ADVERB• on the outside so you can see: *Outwardly they were cheerful.*
♦ **outwards** •ADVERB• towards the outside: *a window that opens outwards*

outweigh •VERB• **outweighs, outweighing, outweighed** to outweigh something is to be more important than it: *The advantages outweigh the disadvantages.*

outwit •VERB• **outwits, outwitting, outwitted** to outwit someone is to defeat them by being cleverer than they are: *She outwitted the police and managed to escape.*

oval •ADJECTIVE• shaped like an egg but flat: *an oval table*
•NOUN• **ovals** an oval shape: *He drew an oval.*

ⓘ This word comes from the Latin word **ovalis**, which means *like an egg.*

ovary •NOUN• **ovaries 1** part of a woman's body where eggs are formed **2** the part of a flower where seeds are formed

oven •NOUN• **ovens** an enclosed space, usually part of a cooker, for cooking and heating food

over •PREPOSITION• **1** higher than, above: *Hang that picture over the fireplace.*
2 more than: *He's over 90 years old.*
3 across: *We ran over the bridge.*
4 about: *They quarrelled over the children.*
5 by means of: *We often talk over the telephone.*
•ADVERB• **1** across: *He walked over to speak to them.*
2 downwards: *The baby's fallen over.*
3 above in number: *children aged seven and over*
4 left or remaining: *two cakes each, and two over*
5 through: *read the passage over*
•ADJECTIVE• finished: *The match is already over.*
•NOUN• **overs** in cricket, a series of six balls bowled by the same bowler from the same end of the pitch
⇒ **overly**

over- •PREFIX• **over-** at the start of a word means *too* or *too much.* For example, to *overeat* is to eat too much, and *overcareful* means too careful

overall •NOUN• **overalls** a piece of clothing worn over ordinary clothes to protect them: *She wears an overall when cleaning the house.*
•ADJECTIVE• including everything: *the overall cost*

overalls •PLURAL NOUN• trousers or a suit made of hardwearing material worn by workmen to protect their clothes

overarm •ADJECTIVE AND ADVERB• with the hand and arm raised above the level of the shoulder and coming down in front of the body: *an overarm throw* • *Try throwing it overarm.*

overbearing •ADJECTIVE• bossy and over-confident: *I can't stand his overbearing manner.*

overboard •ADVERB• over the side of a ship or boat into the water: *He jumped overboard.*

overcast •ADJECTIVE• dark with clouds: *It became overcast but it didn't rain.*

overcoat •NOUN• **overcoats** a heavy coat worn over all other clothes

overcome •VERB• **overcomes, overcoming, overcame, overcome 1** to overcome someone or something is to defeat them eventually: *She overcame her fear of the dark.* **2** to be overcome by something is to become helpless because of it: *overcome with grief* • *overcome by fumes*

overdo •VERB• **overdoes, overdoing, overdid, overdone 1** to overdo something is to do it too much: *It's good to work hard, but don't overdo it.* **2** to overdo food is to cook it for too long: *The meat was rather overdone.*

overdose •NOUN• **overdoses** more of a drug or medicine than is safe: *Her daughter took an overdose.*
•VERB• **overdoses, overdosing, overdosed** to overdose is to take too much of a drug or medicine

overdue •ADJECTIVE• **1** not yet paid, done or delivered although the time for doing this

Aa Bb Cc Dd Ee Ff Gg Hh Ii Jj Kk Ll Mm Nn **Oo** Pp Qq Rr Ss Tt Uu Vv Ww Xx Yy Zz

Aa

has passed: *overdue library books* **2** late: *The train is overdue.*

Bb

overflow • VERB• **overflows, overflowing, overflowed 1** liquid overflows when it reaches the top of a container and starts to spill over the sides: *The river overflowed its banks.* **2** a container overflows when it is so full that its contents spill out: *boxes overflowing with toys*

Cc

Dd

Ee

overgrown • ADJECTIVE• full of plants that have grown too large and thick: *The back garden is completely overgrown with weeds.*

Ff

Gg

overhang • VERB• **overhangs, overhanging, overhung** to overhang something is to stick out or hang over it: *The stream was overhung by the branches of a tree.*

Hh

Ii

Jj

overhaul • VERB• **overhauls, overhauling, overhauled** to overhaul something is to examine it carefully and repair any faults: *He had his car overhauled at the garage.*
• NOUN• **overhauls** a thorough examination and repair: *The mechanic gave the car a complete overhaul.*

Kk

Ll

Mm

overhead • ADVERB• above your head: *A plane was flying overhead.*
• ADJECTIVE• placed high above the ground: *overhead cables*

Nn

Oo

Pp

overheads • PLURAL NOUN• the money that a business has to spend regularly on things like rent and electricity

Qq

overhear • VERB• **overhears, overhearing, overheard** to hear something when you were not meant to: *I overheard them talking about me.*

Rr

Ss

Tt

overjoyed • ADJECTIVE• very happy: *We were overjoyed to hear that he was safe.*

Uu

overland • ADVERB AND ADJECTIVE• across land, rather than by sea or air: *travelling overland across America* • *an overland safari*

Vv

Ww

overlap • VERB• **overlaps, overlapping, overlapped 1** to overlap something is to cover a part of it: *Each roof-tile overlaps the one below it.* **2** if things overlap, they lie partly over each other: *The curtains should be wide enough to overlap.*
• NOUN• **overlaps** the amount by which

Xx

Yy

Zz

something overlaps: *an overlap of half an hour between the two programmes*

overleaf • ADVERB• on the other side of the page: *See the table overleaf.*

overlook • VERB• **overlooks, overlooking, overlooked 1** to overlook something such as a place is to look down on it: *The house overlooks the river.*
2 to overlook something is to fail to see or notice it: *You have overlooked one important detail.*
3 to overlook something such as a fault is to take no notice of it: *I shall overlook your lateness this time.*

overly • ADVERB• too much: *an overly possessive mother*

overnight • ADJECTIVE AND ADVERB• **1** for the night: *an overnight bag* • *We stayed in London overnight.* **2** sudden or suddenly: *an overnight success* • *He became a hero overnight.*

overpower • VERB• **overpowers, overpowering, overpowered** to overpower someone is to defeat them through being stronger: *He was overpowered by two policemen.*
✦ **overpowering** • ADJECTIVE• very strong: *an overpowering smell* • *overpowering sadness*

overrated • ADJECTIVE• something that is overrated is thought to be better than it really is: *His new film is overrated.*

overrun • VERB• **overruns, overrunning, overran, overrun 1** to overrun a place is to spread quickly all over it: *The house is overrun with mice.* **2** if something overruns, it goes on for longer than it should: *The programme overran by half an hour.*

overseas • ADJECTIVE AND ADVERB• abroad: *an overseas job* • *They went overseas.*

oversee • VERB• **oversees, overseeing, oversaw, overseen** to oversee something is to watch over or supervise it: *His job is to oversee the factory workers.*

overshadow • VERB• **overshadows, overshadowing, overshadowed** to overshadow someone or something is to seem much more successful or important than them or it: *Clare was always overshadowed by her brilliant sister.*

oversight • NOUN• **oversights** a mistake, especially one that you make because you have not noticed something: *It was a serious oversight on his part.*

overtake • VERB• **overtakes, overtaking, overtook, overtaken** to overtake a vehicle is to catch up with and pass it: *He overtook a police car.*

overthrow • VERB• **overthrows, overthrowing, overthrew, overthrown** to overthrow someone is to force them out of power: *The government has been overthrown.*

overtime • NOUN• time spent working outside your normal hours

overture • NOUN• **overtures** 1 a piece of music played at the start of an opera or ballet 2 a friendly attempt to start a discussion or relationship: *overtures of peace*

overweight • ADJECTIVE• too heavy: *I'm about half a stone overweight.*

overwhelm • VERB• **overwhelms, overwhelming, overwhelmed** 1 to overwhelm someone is to defeat them completely: *Our soldiers were overwhelmed by the enemy.* 2 to overwhelm someone is to load them with too great an amount of something: *overwhelmed with work* 3 to overwhelm someone is to have a strong and sudden effect on them: *overwhelmed with joy*
♦ **overwhelming** • ADJECTIVE• very great or strong: *an overwhelming victory* • *overwhelming relief*

overwork • VERB• **overworks, overworking, overworked** 1 to overwork is to work too hard 2 to overwork someone is to make them work too hard • NOUN• the act of working too hard: *Overwork made him ill.*
♦ **overworked** • ADJECTIVE• made to work too hard: *The staff are overworked.*

ovum • NOUN• **ova** an egg from which a young animal or person develops

owe • VERB• **owes, owing, owed** 1 to owe someone something is to be in debt to them: *I owe Val £10.* 2 to owe something to someone is to have them to thank for it: *He owes his success to his family.*
• **owing to** because of: *Owing to the rain, the football has been cancelled.*

owl • NOUN• **owls** a bird that hunts at night and feeds on small birds and animals

own • VERB• **owns, owning, owned** 1 you own something if it belongs to you: *I own a car.* 2 to **own up** is to admit that you did something: *No one owned up to breaking the window.*
• ADJECTIVE• belonging to the person mentioned: *all his own work*
• PRONOUN• own is used for something belonging to another person: *I lent him a pencil, because he forgot to bring his own.*
• **get your own back** to have revenge
• **on your own** 1 without help: *Did he do it all on his own?* 2 alone: *Please don't leave me on my own.*
♦ **owner** • NOUN• **owners** a person who owns something

own goal • NOUN• **own goals** a goal someone scores by mistake against their own side in a game

ox • NOUN• **oxen** a bull used for pulling loads

oxide • NOUN• **oxides** a compound of oxygen and another element

oxidize or **oxidise** • VERB• **oxidizes, oxidizing, oxidized** 1 to oxidize something is to cause it to combine with oxygen 2 to oxidize is to be combined with oxygen

oxygen • NOUN• a gas that has no taste, colour or smell, and forms part of the air

oyster • NOUN• **oysters** a type of shellfish that can be eaten

oz • ABBREVIATION• short for **ounce** or **ounces**

ozone • NOUN• a form of oxygen with a strong smell

ozone layer • NOUN• the layer of ozone that is part of the Earth's atmosphere and that protects the planet from the radiation of the sun

Pp

p •ABBREVIATION• short for **page** or **pence**

pace •VERB• **paces, pacing, paced 1** to pace is to walk, especially with steps of about the same length and at a steady speed **2** to walk backwards and forwards: *She was pacing the floor, waiting for the phone to ring.*
•NOUN• **paces 1** a step, or a speed of walking or running: *Take four paces forward.* • *a slow pace* **2** a rate at which something happens or moves forward: *the pace of change*

pacemaker •NOUN• **pacemakers** a small device, fitted by a surgeon, that keeps someone's heart beating at the correct rhythm

pacifist •NOUN• **pacifists** someone who believes war is wrong and should be avoided

pacify •VERB• **pacifies, pacifying, pacified** to pacify someone is to calm them down

pack •NOUN• **packs 1** things that are tied together or put in a bag, so that you can carry them
2 a packet: *two packs of playing cards*
3 a set of 52 playing cards
4 a group of certain animals, especially animals of the dog family: *a pack of hyenas*
•VERB• **packs, packing, packed 1** to put your belongings into a bag or suitcase for a journey: *She packed hurriedly and caught the next train.*
2 if people pack a place, they fill it so that there is very little, or no, space left
3 if someone is **packed off** somewhere, they are sent there, often without having any choice about it
4 to **pack something in** is to stop doing it

package •NOUN• **packages 1** a parcel that has been wrapped up for sending by post **2** a number of things that are sold or used together: *a software package*
•VERB• **packages, packaging, packaged** to package something, or **package it up**, is to put it in a parcel, wrapping or bundle

package holiday •NOUN• **package holidays** a holiday in which all the travel and accommodation is arranged for you by a travel agent

packaging •NOUN• the wrapping or container that something comes in

packet •NOUN• **packets** a container made of paper or cardboard, or the container with its contents: *a packet of biscuits*

pact •NOUN• **pacts** an agreement or treaty between two people, groups or countries: *They made a pact always to look out for each other.*

pad •NOUN• **pads 1** a cushion-like object made of a soft material
2 a soft cushion-like part on the paw of some animals, such as dogs
3 a book of several sheets of paper fixed together at one edge and used for writing on
4 a platform for launching rockets
•VERB• **pads, padding, padded 1** to pad something is to stuff or protect it with soft material
2 to **pad out** an essay or speech is to add extra and unnecessary material to it to make it longer
3 to pad is to walk softly making little or no sound
• **padding** •NOUN• **1** material used for stuffing chairs or cushions **2** extra and unnecessary material added to an essay or speech

paddle •VERB• **paddles, paddling, paddled 1** you paddle when you walk about in shallow water **2** to paddle a boat or canoe is to move it through the water using a paddle
•NOUN• **paddles** a short oar, often with a wide part at one or both ends, used for paddling a small boat or canoe

paddock •NOUN• **paddocks** a grassy field with a fence around it where horses and other animals are kept

paddy field •NOUN• **paddy fields** a field

used to grow rice. Paddy fields are usually flooded with a few centimetres of water because rice needs wet and muddy conditions to grow

padlock • NOUN• **padlocks** a lock with a U-shaped bar which hinges to one side and can be passed through a ring or chain and locked in position

pagan • NOUN• **pagans** someone who is not a member of any of the world's main religions, but who does practise some sort of religion
• ADJECTIVE• to do with pagans or paganism: *a pagan festival celebrating the coming of Spring*
♦ **paganism** • NOUN• pagan beliefs and practices

page [1] • NOUN• **pages** one side of a sheet of paper in a book, newspaper or magazine, or one of the sheets of paper that make up a book, newspaper or magazine: *Turn to page 135 in your history books.*

page [2] • NOUN• **pages** 1 a small boy who attends a bride at her wedding 2 in historical times, a boy who worked as an attendant to a knight
• VERB• **pages, paging, paged** to page someone is to call them by sending a message to their electronic pager

pageant • NOUN• **pageants** 1 a type of outdoor entertainment or parade with people dressed up in colourful costumes and often acting out scenes from history 2 any splendid and colourful show or display
♦ **pageantry** • NOUN• splendid and colourful display that forms part of a grand ceremony or parade

pager • NOUN• **pagers** an electronic device used to call someone, for example a doctor in a hospital, through a small radio receiver that they carry with them and that beeps to get their attention

pagoda • NOUN• **pagodas** a Chinese temple, with several storeys or levels and overhanging roofs

pail • NOUN• **pails** a bucket, or its contents: *a milk pail* • *a pail of water*

pain • NOUN• **pains** an unpleasant uncomfortable feeling in your body or mind, because you have been hurt: *He's broken his leg in three places and is in great pain.* • *the pain of leaving loved ones behind*
♦ **pained** • ADJECTIVE• if someone has a pained expression, their face shows that they are upset or offended

painful • ADJECTIVE• 1 sore, or causing pain or distress: *Is your knee still painful?* • *Will the treatment be painful?* 2 involving a lot of hard work or effort: *Their progress up the steep mountain was slow and painful.*
♦ **painfully** • ADVERB• in a painful or distressing way: *The poor little dog was painfully thin.*

painkiller • NOUN• **painkillers** a drug that takes away pain

painless • ADJECTIVE• causing no pain

painstaking • ADJECTIVE• paying careful attention to every detail, or needing a lot of careful attention to detail: *It's painstaking work building a model out of matchsticks.*
♦ **painstakingly** • ADVERB• very carefully or thoroughly

paint • NOUN• **paints** a colouring substance to be put on surfaces, in the form of liquid or paste
• VERB• **paints, painting, painted** 1 to put paint on walls and other parts of a building 2 to make a picture, or pictures, using paint
♦ **painter** • NOUN• **painters** 1 a person whose job is to put paint on walls and other parts of buildings 2 an artist who makes pictures using paint
♦ **painting** • NOUN• **paintings** 1 painting is the activity of painting walls or pictures 2 a painting is a picture made using paints

pair • NOUN• **pairs** 1 two things of the same kind used or kept together: *a pair of socks* • *a pair of china dogs* 2 a single thing made up of two parts: *a pair of shears*
• VERB• **pairs, pairing, paired** 1 to pair things is to form them into pairs or sets of two 2 people **pair off** when they form pairs or couples

ⓘ Try not to confuse the spelling of **pair** with **pear**, which is a fruit.

pal • NOUN• **pals** your pals are your friends

palace • NOUN• **palaces** a large and

Aa
Bb
Cc
Dd
Ee
Ff
Gg
Hh
Ii
Jj
Kk
Ll
Mm
Nn
Oo
Pp
Qq
Rr
Ss
Tt
Uu
Vv
Ww
Xx
Yy
Zz

magnificent house, especially one for a king, queen or emperor

palate •NOUN• **palates** 1 your palate is the top part of the inside of your mouth. The front part feels hard and bony and the part further back is soft 2 a person's palate is their particular taste or liking, especially for certain kinds of food: *dishes to suit every palate*

pale •ADJECTIVE• **paler, palest** 1 light in colour: *pale blue • the pale light of dawn* 2 someone who is pale has less colour in their skin than normal, often because they are ill or have had a shock: *What's the matter? You've gone pale all of a sudden.*

palette •NOUN• **palettes** a small flat piece of wood on which artists mix their colours

pall •NOUN• **palls** a pall of smoke is a cloud of smoke that hangs over something
•VERB• **palls, palling, palled** if something palls, it begins to bore you, usually because you have done or seen it too often

pallet •NOUN• **pallets** a wooden tray or platform on which things are stacked so that they can be lifted or moved by a fork-lift truck

pallid •ADJECTIVE• unnaturally or unhealthily pale in colour: *There were tears running down his pallid cheeks.*

pallor •NOUN• unnatural or unhealthy paleness of the skin

palm •NOUN• **palms** 1 the inner surface of your hand between your wrist and fingers 2 a tree with very large leaves which spread out from the top of the trunk
•VERB• **palms, palming, palmed** 1 to palm an object is to hide it in the palm of your hand 2 to **palm off** an unwanted thing on someone is to get rid of it by giving it to them

palmistry •NOUN• palmistry is telling fortunes by looking at the pattern of lines or markings on a person's hand

paltry •ADJECTIVE• very small or unimportant, or not enough to be useful: *a paltry sum of money*

pampas grass •NOUN• a very tall type of grass with feathery tips

pamper •VERB• **pampers, pampering,** **pampered** to pamper someone is to spoil them by doing too much for them

pamphlet •NOUN• **pamphlets** a thin book with a paper cover

pan •NOUN• **pans** 1 a metal container with a handle or handles, used for cooking food 2 a toilet bowl
•VERB• **pans, panning, panned** 1 to pan is to move a film, television or video camera to the left or right to give a wider view of a scene 2 the way something **pans out** is the way it turns out

pancake •NOUN• **pancakes** a thin cake made by frying a mixture of milk, flour and eggs in a pan

pancreas •NOUN• **pancreases** a gland just behind the stomach that produces substances which help in digestion

panda •NOUN• **pandas** a large and rare black and white bear-like animal that lives in the mountains of China and eats bamboo

panda car •NOUN• **panda cars** a police car

(i) Panda cars were originally painted black and white, the colours of a panda.

pandemonium •NOUN• wild and noisy confusion

pander •VERB• **panders, pandering,** **pandered** to **pander to** someone is to do things their way, or to always try to please them

pane •NOUN• **panes** a flat piece of glass used in a window

panel •NOUN• **panels** 1 a flat rectangular piece of wood or other material, often set into a door or wall
2 a group of people chosen to judge a contest or take part in a quiz or other game
3 a separate section on the page of a book
• **panelling** •NOUN• wood or other material used for panels in walls and doors
• **panellist** •NOUN• **panellists** one of the members of a panel in a contest or game

pang •NOUN• **pangs** a sudden sharp or painful feeling: *pangs of hunger*

panic •NOUN• panic is sudden great fear, especially the kind that spreads through a crowd and causes people to scream or rush about not knowing what to do

•VERB• **panics, panicking, panicked** to panic is to become so frightened that you lose the power to think clearly

♦ **panic-stricken •ADJECTIVE•** filled with terror and anxiety

♦ **panicky •ADJECTIVE•** tending to panic

ⓘ This word comes from the Greek word **panikon**, which means *fear of Pan*. Pan was a Greek god who was said to scare people and animals.

panorama •NOUN• panoramas a wide view in all directions, usually of a large area of land, or of a city and the surrounding landscape

pansy •NOUN• pansies a small garden flower with large flat rounded petals, usually white, yellow or shades of purple

pant •VERB• pants, panting, panted 1 to gasp for breath 2 to say something while gasping for breath: *'I've just sprinted two miles to catch this train,' he panted.*

panther •NOUN• panthers a leopard, especially one that is black rather than having a spotted coat

pantomime •NOUN• pantomimes a show put on at Christmas time, often based on a popular fairy tale, and including singing, dancing and comedy acts

pantry •NOUN• pantries a small room near a kitchen, used for storing food

pants •PLURAL NOUN• 1 a piece of underwear that covers your bottom 2 the American English word for trousers

papa •NOUN• papas a name some people use for their father

papal •ADJECTIVE• to do with the pope: *a papal visit*

papaya •NOUN• papayas a large yellow fruit with sweet orange flesh, which grows on a tropical tree. Another name for the papaya is the **pawpaw**

paper •NOUN• papers 1 paper is a material made from wood pulp or rags and used for writing, printing and wrapping things in 2 a newspaper: *Have you read today's paper?*

3 paper is wallpaper: *She chose a floral paper with little rosebuds.*
4 a piece of paper with things written or printed on it: *a briefcase full of legal papers* • *an examination paper* • *identity papers*
•VERB• papers, papering, papered to paper a wall or room is to put wallpaper on it

paperback •NOUN• paperbacks a book with a cover that can bend easily, made of very thin card. Look up and compare **hardback**

papier-mâché •NOUN• a mixture of shredded paper and glue, which is used to make models, bowls and boxes and which hardens as it dries

papyrus •NOUN• papyri or **papyruses**
1 papyrus is a type of paper made from the reed-like stems of a tall water plant that grows in North Africa. Papyrus was used by the ancient Egyptians, Romans and Greeks 2 a papyrus is an ancient manuscript written on this paper

par •NOUN• in golf, par is the number of strokes that a good golfer should take to complete a hole, or all the holes on the golf course
• **below par** something that is below par does not reach a certain standard required
• **on a par** equal in size or importance

parable •NOUN• parables a story, especially in the Bible, that is told to teach people something, especially a moral or religious lesson

parabola •NOUN• parabolas a type of curve

parachute •NOUN• parachutes an umbrella-shaped piece of light material attached to a person or object so that, when they are dropped from a plane, they fall slowly to the ground
•VERB• parachutes, parachuting, parachuted to parachute is to jump from a plane and fall slowly to the ground supported by a parachute
♦ **parachutist •NOUN• parachutists** someone who parachutes

parade •NOUN• parades 1 a line of people or vehicles moving forward in a procession, often as a celebration of some event

Paragraphs

A **paragraph** is a section of a piece of writing. It does not have to be a particular length. It can be as short as a single sentence or can be ten sentences or more.

Using paragraphs helps readers to follow what is written and give them time to pause.

Writing in paragraphs

• Each paragraph should be about one main point or idea.

• A **topic sentence** tells the reader what the main idea of the paragraph is. This usually comes at the beginning of the paragraph, but it can go elsewhere.

• All the sentences in a paragraph should be about the main topic and give a little more information about it.

• A new idea should be given in a new paragraph.

• A new paragraph starts on a new line.

• A new paragraph begins in a little bit from the margin. This is called the **indent**.

2 soldiers are on parade when they are gathered together in formal rows or ranks for marching or to be inspected •VERB• **parades, parading, paraded** to parade is to march in line or move forward in a procession

paradise • NOUN • **1** paradise is heaven: *eternal paradise* **2** any place that has everything you want can be called a paradise: *The island is a paradise for bird watchers.*

paradox • NOUN • **paradoxes** a statement or situation in which two things that seem to contradict each other are combined, but which is true or real despite this
• **paradoxical** • ADJECTIVE • combining two things that seem to contradict each other

paraffin • NOUN • a type of oil that is made from coal or petroleum and is used as a fuel in heaters and camping stoves

paragraph • NOUN • **paragraphs** a section of a piece of writing, which has its first sentence starting on a new line. See the box called **Paragraphs**

parallel • ADJECTIVE • parallel lines go in the same direction and are always the same distance apart along their length

parallelogram • NOUN • **parallelograms** a flat shape with four sides, and opposite sides that are parallel to each other

paralyse •VERB• **paralyses, paralysing, paralysed 1** something paralyses a person or animal when it stops the normal movement in their body, or part of their body: *The scorpion paralyses its prey with its sting.* **2** to make something come to a complete stop where no movement is possible: *Heavy snow falls paralysed the road and rail network.*
• **paralysis** • NOUN • paralysis is loss of the power of movement in a part of the body, or loss of the ability to move or work

paramedic • NOUN • **paramedics** a person who is not a doctor, but who is trained to give emergency medical treatment

paramilitary • ADJECTIVE • paramilitary organizations operate like an army, but are not part of a country's official army

paramount • ADJECTIVE • more important than anything else: *The children's safety is paramount.*

paranoia • NOUN • **1** paranoia is a form of mental illness in which someone imagines they are very important or that they have been badly treated by others **2** paranoia is a tendency some people have to be sensitive and suspicious because they imagine other people want to harm them or are making fun of them

♦ **paranoid** •ADJECTIVE• suffering from paranoia: *He was paranoid about getting caught.*

parapet •NOUN• **parapets** a low wall along the edge of a bridge, balcony or roof

paraphernalia •NOUN• paraphernalia is a large number of different objects and pieces of equipment: *Kevin packed all his fishing paraphernalia into the back of the car.*

paraphrase •NOUN• **paraphrases** a paraphrase of something is a different way of saying or writing it
•VERB• **paraphrases, paraphrasing, paraphrased** to paraphrase something is to express it in a different way

parasite •NOUN• **parasites** an animal or plant that lives on, and gets its food from, another animal or plant

parasol •NOUN• **parasols** a light umbrella used to give shade from the sun

paratrooper •NOUN• **paratroopers** a soldier trained to drop by parachute into enemy country
♦ **paratroops** •PLURAL NOUN• a group of these soldiers

parcel •NOUN• **parcel** something wrapped in paper or cardboard and tied with string or sticky tape

parched •ADJECTIVE• 1 if you are parched, you are very thirsty 2 parched land has been dried by the sun so that there is no moisture for plants to grow

parchment •NOUN• **parchments** 1 parchment is a material made from animal skin, used long ago for writing on 2 a parchment is a piece of this with writing on

pardon •VERB• **pardons, pardoning, pardoned** 1 to forgive or excuse someone for a fault they have or a crime they have committed 2 some people say 'pardon' or 'pardon me', either because they haven't heard what has been said, or they want to apologize for something they have done
•NOUN• **pardons** someone who has been sentenced to be punished for a crime

receives a pardon when their punishment is cancelled

pare •VERB• **pares, paring, pared** to pare something is to cut or trim it, layer by layer

parent •NOUN• **parents** your parents are your mother and father
♦ **parentage** •NOUN• a person or animal's parentage is who or what each of their parents are
♦ **parental** •ADJECTIVE• to do with a parent or parents

parenthesis •NOUN• **parentheses** parentheses are curved brackets put round information that adds to the main point but is not an essential part of a sentence

parenthood •NOUN• the condition of being or becoming a parent: *the responsibilities of parenthood*

parish •NOUN• **parishes** a district or area with its own church and priest or minister
♦ **parishioner** •NOUN• **parishioners** someone who lives in a parish, especially someone who goes to services in the parish church

park •NOUN• **parks** a piece of land in a town or city that has grass and trees and where people can go for fresh air or leisure
•VERB• **parks, parking, parked** to park a vehicle is to stop it somewhere, for example, by the side of the road or in a driveway or car park

parka •NOUN• **parkas** a type of long warm jacket with a hood

parking lot •NOUN• **parking lots** the American term for a **car park**

parking meter •NOUN• **parking meters** a metal box on a pole that has a slot where you can put coins to pay for parking your car in the space next to the meter

parliament •NOUN• **parliaments** a group of people, usually politicians, who meet to discuss and make a particular country's laws: *the new parliament of Scotland*
♦ **parliamentary** •ADJECTIVE• to do with a parliament: *a parliamentary debate*

parlour •NOUN• **parlours** 1 a room in a house used for sitting in, and for receiving guests 2 a shop selling a particular product

Aa

or service: *an ice-cream parlour* • *a beauty parlour*

Bb

parody • NOUN • **parodies** a parody is an imitation of an author's, artist's or musician's work or style, done to make fun of them • VERB • **parodies, parodying, parodied** to parody someone or their work is to imitate them or their style in an amusing way

Cc

Dd

Ee

parole • NOUN • a criminal on parole has been allowed out of prison before their sentence is finished on condition that they behave well

Ff

Gg

Hh

ⓘ **Parole** is French for *word*. A prisoner gives his *word* of honour he will not break the law when he is released.

Ii

Jj

parrot • NOUN • **parrot** a bird with a strong curved beak, beady eyes, and brightly-coloured or grey feathers, that can be taught to imitate human speech and is often kept as a pet
• **parrot fashion** to learn something parrot fashion is to learn it and be able to repeat it exactly

Kk

Ll

Mm

Nn

parsley • NOUN • a type of herb with curly or flat green leaves, used to add flavour in cooking

Oo

Pp

parsnip • NOUN • **parsnips** a vegetable, similar in shape to a carrot, and which is a pale creamish colour and grows underground

Qq

Rr

parson • NOUN • **parsons** any Christian priest, especially one belonging to the Church of England
✦ **parsonage** • NOUN • **parsonages** a parson's house

Ss

Tt

Uu

part • NOUN • **parts** 1 a division or piece of something: *The pizza is cut into six equal parts.* • *a part for the engine* • *part of the day* 2 a character in a play or film, or the words or actions that a character has to say or do in a play or film: *a leading part in the musical* • *He's learned his part well.*
• **take part** to take part in some activity is to do it or become involved in it
• VERB • **parts, parting, parted** 1 people or things part when they separate and move away from each other or out of each other's company 2 to **part with** something is to give

Vv

Ww

Xx

Yy

Zz

it away, sell it, or let it be taken away from you
⇒ **parting, partly**

partial • ADJECTIVE • 1 not complete: *a partial success*
2 to be **partial to** something is to be fond of it: *Wallace is partial to a little piece of cheese.*
3 to be partial is to prefer or favour one person or side over another in an unfair way: *She's too partial to be a good judge.*
✦ **partiality** • NOUN • preferring one side over another, for example in a competition or trial
✦ **partially** • ADVERB • partly: *a partially eaten biscuit*

participant • NOUN • **participants** someone who takes part in something with other people

participate • VERB • **participates, participating, participated** to participate in something is to take part in it: *I was among two or three girls asked to participate in the school sports day.*
✦ **participation** • NOUN • taking part

participle • NOUN • **participles** a participle is a word formed from a verb and used as an adjective, or to form different tenses of the verb. For example, *spending*, *looking* and *passing* are called **present participles** and *canned*, *stolen* and *dealt* are called **past participles**

particle • NOUN • **particles** a very small piece that you can hardly see: *a particle of dust*

particular • ADJECTIVE • a particular person or thing is a special or separate one that is not to be confused with any other
• **in particular** especially
• NOUN • **particulars** your particulars, or the particulars of a situation, are your personal details, or the details of that situation

parting • NOUN • **partings** 1 leaving someone or saying goodbye to them 2 you have a parting in your hair when it has been brushed or combed in opposite directions on either side of a line across your head

partition • NOUN • **partitions** 1 a kind of thin wall, used to divide up a room, but not usually reaching up as far as the ceiling 2 dividing something in parts

partly • ADVERB • in some ways or to a

certain extent: *I was partly to blame for the mix-up.*

part of speech •NOUN• **parts of speech** in grammar, the parts of speech are the various groups that words belong to depending on the job they do. The parts of speech you will find in this dictionary are noun, pronoun, verb, adjective, adverb, preposition, conjunction and interjection

partner •NOUN• **partners 1** one of two people who do something together, like dance or play in a game
2 people who are business partners share the ownership of a business
3 someone's partner is the person they are married to or live with
♦ **partnership** •NOUN• **partnerships** being a partner

partridge •NOUN• **partridges** a small plump grey and brown wild bird that nests on the ground and is hunted for sport and food

part-time •ADJECTIVE AND ADVERB• if you work part-time or have a part-time job, you work for only part of a full working day or week

party •NOUN• **parties 1** a party is an event where people gather to celebrate something or to enjoy each other's company
2 a political party is an organized group of people who share the same political beliefs
3 a party of people is a group of people travelling or doing something together

pass •VERB• **passes, passing, passed 1** to pass is to move towards and then go beyond something: *The procession passed in front of the town hall.* • *The lorry passed us on a bend.*
2 to pass something to someone is to hand it to them or give it to them: *Pass me the butter, please.*
3 to pass a test or exam is to be successful in it
4 something passes when it ends or goes away: *The storm passed and the sun came out again.*
5 to pass a law is to make it a law
6 if someone **passes away**, they die
7 to **pass out** is to faint or become unconscious

8 to **pass something up** is to decide not to take it or use it
•NOUN• **passes 1** a ticket or card that allows you to get into a place or to travel somewhere
2 in games like football, hockey and rugby, a pass is a kick, hit or throw that sends the ball from one player to another in the same team
3 a successful result in an exam
4 a narrow gap between mountains

passable •ADJECTIVE• **1** if something is passable, it is of quite a good standard but is not the best **2** a road is passable if it is not completely blocked

passage •NOUN• **passages 1** a narrow corridor
2 a tube from an opening in the body: *Your nasal passages are connected to your nose.*
3 a part or section in a piece of writing or music: *Read the next passage aloud.*
4 a journey in a ship
5 passing: *the passage of time*

passageway •NOUN• **passageways** a way through between walls or other barriers

passenger •NOUN• **passengers** someone travelling in a car, bus, ship or plane who is not the driver or one of the crew

passer-by •NOUN• **passers-by** someone who is passing in the street when something happens

ⓘ Remember that you make this word plural by adding the *s* to *passer*, not to *by*.

passion •NOUN• **passions** very strong feeling or emotion, especially anger or love
♦ **passionate** •ADJECTIVE• showing strong emotions

passive •ADJECTIVE• **1** someone who is passive stays or lies still and does not react to anything **2** in grammar, a passive verb is the form of a verb used when the person or thing that is the subject of the verb has something done to them, rather than doing it, for example in the sentence *The leaves **are being eaten** by caterpillars.* See the box called **Active and passive**
♦ **passively** •ADVERB• in a passive way

Passover •NOUN• a Jewish festival held in March or April celebrating the freeing of the Jews from slavery in Egypt

passport • NOUN• **passports** a document with your photograph and personal details that you must carry when you are travelling abroad

password • NOUN• **passwords** a secret word or phrase that you have to know before you are allowed into a place, or which you must type into a computer before you can see the information in it

past • NOUN• 1 the past is the time before the present 2 someone's past is what they have done in their life before the present time • ADJECTIVE• over or ended: *in the past year* • *Summer is nearly past and autumn is on the way.* • PREPOSITION• 1 up to and beyond: *She dashed past me, gasping as she ran.* 2 later than: *Are the children in their beds? It's past eight o'clock.*

pasta • NOUN• a food made from a special type of flour, water and eggs and formed into lots of different shapes, all of which have special names, such as spaghetti, macaroni or lasagne

paste • NOUN• **pastes** 1 a soft moist mixture 2 a type of glue for sticking paper together or to fix wallpaper to walls • VERB• **pastes, pasting, pasted** to paste something is to stick it with glue

pastel • ADJECTIVE• pastel colours are pale and contain a lot of white: *pastel blue* • NOUN• **pastels** pastels are chalky crayons used to draw and colour with

pasteurization *or* **pasteurisation** • NOUN• a process which involves heating milk to kill all the bacteria in it ✦ **pasteurize** *or* **pasteurise** • VERB• **pasteurizes, pasteurizing, pasteurized** to pasteurize milk is to heat it so that all the bacteria in it are killed

ⓘ This is named after Louis **Pasteur**, a French chemist who invented the process in the 19th century.

pastille • NOUN• **pastilles** a small sugary sweet, often sucked as a medicine for sore throats or coughs

pastime • NOUN• **pastimes** something you enjoy spending your time doing

pastor • NOUN• **pastors** a religious minister or priest

pastoral • ADJECTIVE• 1 to do with the countryside or country life: *a pastoral scene* 2 concerned with people's general needs rather than their religion or education

past participle • NOUN• **past participles** the form of a verb used after a helping verb such as *has* or *was* to show that something happened in the past. For example, *fought* in *I have fought with my brother* is a past participle

pastry • NOUN• **pastries** 1 pastry is a mixture of flour and fat used to make pies and cakes 2 a pastry is a cake made with pastry

past tense • NOUN• the past tense of a verb is used to refer to things that happened or existed before the present. For example, *The race **was** over so I **relaxed** and **put** my feet up.*

pasture • NOUN• **pastures** a field with grass for cattle and other animals to eat

pasty[1] • ADJECTIVE• **pastier, pastiest** having unhealthily pale skin, especially on the face

pasty[2] • NOUN• **pasties** a small pie made with pastry filled with chopped meat and vegetables

ⓘ **Pasty**[1] is pronounced **paste**-y. **Pasty**[2] is pronounced **pass**-ty.

pat • VERB• **pats, patting, patted** to pat someone or something is to hit them or it gently with your hand, usually as a sign of affection • NOUN• **pats** a light, gentle blow or touch, usually with the palm of your hand

patch • NOUN• **patches** 1 a piece of material sewn on to a piece of clothing to cover a hole or tear 2 a piece of material worn over a damaged or blind eye 3 a small area of something: *a patch of grass* • **not a patch on** not nearly as good: *He's a good player, but not a patch on David Beckham.* • VERB• **patches, patching, patched** 1 to

patch something is to repair a tear or hole in it by sewing a piece of material over it
2 to **patch something up** is to mend it, and to **patch someone up** is to treat their injuries
3 to **patch up** a quarrel is to end it and be friendly again
⇒ **patchy**

patchwork •NOUN• small pieces of fabric sewn together in a decorative pattern

patchy •ADJECTIVE• **patchier, patchiest** not evenly spread, or good only in parts: *patchy fog • The standard of cooking can be a bit patchy.*

pâté •NOUN• **pâtés** a smooth or lumpy paste made by chopping and blending meat, fish or vegetables with flavourings

patent •NOUN• **patents** a licence from the government that gives one person or company the right to make and sell a product and to stop others from copying it
•VERB• **patents, patenting, patented** to patent something you have invented or developed is to get a licence for it from the government
•ADJECTIVE• obvious: *his patent lack of enthusiasm*
♦ **patently** •ADVERB• very clear: *It's patently obvious he had no intention of doing it.*

ⓘ The adjective is pronounced **pay**-tent. The noun and verb can be pronounced **pay**-tent or **pa**-tent.

---

paternal •ADJECTIVE• **1** to do with, or behaving like, a father: *He showed off his daughter's trophy with paternal pride.* **2** from your father's side of the family: *my paternal grandparents*

path •NOUN• **paths 1** a track across a piece of land made or used by people or animals walking
2 the line along which something travels
3 a particular course of action or way of doing something

pathetic •ADJECTIVE• **1** something pathetic causes you to feel pity or sadness: *the pathetic cries of a lost kitten* **2** if you say a person or thing is pathetic you think they are useless or hopeless: *This knife is pathetic. It won't even cut butter!*

pathway •NOUN• **pathways** a route from one place to another that people or things travel along

patience •NOUN• **1** the ability or willingness to stay calm: *Mr Green lost patience with him, which he seldom did with any of the pupils.* **2** a card game played by one person
♦ **patient** •ADJECTIVE• a patient person is able to stay calm and self-controlled, especially when they have to wait a long time for something
•NOUN• **patients** someone being seen or treated by a doctor, or being treated for a particular illness: *The nurse called, 'Next patient, please.' • kidney patients*
♦ **patiently** •ADVERB• in a patient way: *waiting patiently for a bus*

patio •NOUN• **patios** a paved area beside or at the back of a house, used for sitting outdoors in good weather

patriot •NOUN• **patriots** someone who loves and is loyal to his or her country
♦ **patriotic** •ADJECTIVE• loving, and loyal to, your country
♦ **patriotism** •NOUN• being patriotic

patrol •VERB• **patrols, patrolling, patrolled** to patrol an area is to go around it looking out for trouble or making sure no one is there who should not be
•NOUN• **patrols 1** a police or army patrol is the group of soldiers or policemen who patrol an area **2** someone on patrol is walking around a building or area making sure there is no trouble or no one is trying to get in without permission

patron •NOUN• **patrons 1** if an artist or musician has a patron, they have someone who supports them and buys their work
2 a patron of a charity is someone, usually someone well-known, who gives it their public support
3 a shop's or business's patrons are its customers
♦ **patronage** •NOUN• support or money given by a patron to the arts or a charity

patron saint •NOUN• **patron saints** a saint who is believed to protect a place, activity or trade: *the patron saint of Scotland*

patter¹ •VERB• **patters, pattering, pattered**

Aa
Bb
Cc
Dd
Ee
Ff
Gg
Hh
Ii
Jj
Kk
Ll
Mm
Nn
Oo
Pp
Qq
Rr
Ss
Tt
Uu
Vv
Ww
Xx
Yy
Zz

to make quick, light, tapping sounds: *rain pattering on the windows*
• NOUN• a series of quick, light, tapping sounds : *the patter of mice as they scurried around in the attic*

patter² • NOUN• patter is fast talk, such as when someone is trying to sell you something

pattern • NOUN• **patterns 1** a guide used for making something: *a sewing pattern*
2 a design that is repeated over and over again, for example on a piece of fabric or on wallpaper
3 the way in which something happens or is organized: *the pattern of the seasons*
♦ **patterned** • ADJECTIVE• having a pattern

patty • NOUN• **patties** a small flat cake made with chopped meat or vegetables and usually fried

pause • VERB• **pauses, pausing, paused** to pause is to stop what you are doing for a short time
• NOUN• **pauses** a short stop

pave • VERB• **paves, paving, paved** to pave an area is to lay paving stones or some other hard material on it

pavement • NOUN• **pavements** a raised path beside a road used by pedestrians to walk along

pavilion • NOUN• **pavilions 1** a building at a sports ground where players change their clothes and keep their equipment **2** a large building or tent

paw • NOUN• **paws** an animal's foot
• VERB• **paws, pawing, pawed** an animal paws something when it feels or touches it with its paw

pawn • VERB• **pawns, pawning, pawned** to pawn something valuable is to give it to someone in exchange for a loan. If the loan is repaid, the article is given back to the person who has pawned it
• NOUN• **pawns** in the game of chess, a pawn is one of the small, least important pieces
♦ **pawnbroker** • NOUN• **pawnbrokers** someone who runs a shop where articles of value can be pawned

pay • VERB• **pays, paying, payed 1** to pay for

something is to give money in exchange for it
2 to pay someone is to give them money for something or for doing something for you
3 it pays to do something if it brings you a benefit of some sort: *Crime does not pay.*
4 to pay for something you have done is to suffer because of it: *I paid for my laziness when I failed the test.*
5 to pay attention or a compliment is to give it
6 if someone has done something bad to you and you **pay them back**, you do something bad to them in return
7 something you do **pays off** if it brings a good result, or a profit: *I hope your hard work pays off and you do well at school.*
8 if a company or employer **pays off** workers, the workers lose their jobs
• NOUN• someone's pay is the amount of money they are paid by their employer
♦ **payment** • NOUN• **payments 1** a sum of money paid for something **2** paying money or being paid

PC • ABBREVIATION• **PCs 1** short for **personal computer 2** short for **police constable**, used before a police officer's name: *PC Evans*

PE • ABBREVIATION• short for **physical education**

pea • NOUN• **peas** a small round green vegetable that grows in pods on a climbing plant

peace • NOUN• there is peace when there is no war, or everything is quiet and calm: *The two countries have been at peace for 50 years.* • *I want a little peace to get on with my homework.*
♦ **peaceful** • ADJECTIVE• **1** a peaceful place is quiet and calm **2** a peaceful nation does not try to go to war with other countries
♦ **peacefully** • ADVERB• quietly and calmly

peach • NOUN• **peaches** a soft round fruit with a velvety skin, pale orange flesh and a large stone inside

peacock • NOUN• **peacocks** a large bird belonging to the same family as pheasants. The male bird's tail, which he can raise and spread out like a fan, has long blue and green feathers with round black markings at the ends

peak •NOUN• **peaks 1** a peak is the pointed top of a mountain or hill, or anything that looks like this: *snow-covered peaks* • *Beat the egg whites until they form soft peaks.*
2 the peak of something is its highest, greatest or busiest point or time: *the peak of perfection*
3 the peak of a cap is the front part that sticks out and shades the eyes
•VERB• **peaks, peaking, peaked** something peaks when it reaches its highest, greatest or busiest point or time: *Traffic usually peaks about 5 or 6 o'clock.*

peal •NOUN• **peals 1** a sound made by one or more large bells ringing together **2** a loud rolling noise, such as thunder makes
•VERB• **peals, pealing, pealed 1** bells peal when they ring loudly together **2** thunder peals when it makes a loud continuous noise

peanut •NOUN• **peanuts** a kind of nut that grows underground in a shell similar to a pea pod.

peanut butter •NOUN• a thick paste made with crushed peanuts and used to spread on bread

pear •NOUN• **pears** a fruit which is round at the bottom and narrows towards the stem at the top

pearl •NOUN• **pearls 1** a valuable, white, rounded stone formed by oysters and some other shellfish inside their shells **2** something valuable: *pearls of wisdom*

peasant •NOUN• **peasants** someone who lives and works on the land, especially a farmer who owns a small piece of land that he works on himself

peat •NOUN• **peats** material formed in the ground over many years as layers of dead plants rot down, and used for gardening and as a fuel for burning

pebble •NOUN• **pebbles** a small stone that has been worn smooth by water

pebble dash •NOUN• a covering layer for the outside of houses made of cement with lots of tiny stone chips or pebbles stuck in it

peck •VERB• **pecks, pecking, pecked** a bird pecks when it taps or hits something, or picks something up, with its beak
•NOUN• **pecks 1** a tap or bite with the beak **2** a quick light kiss: *a peck on the cheek*

peckish •ADJECTIVE• if you feel peckish, you feel a little bit hungry

peculiar •ADJECTIVE• **1** strange or odd: *a very peculiar smell* **2** something that is peculiar to a person, place or thing, belongs to, or is found in, that particular person, place or thing, and no other
♦ **peculiarly** •ADVERB• **1** strangely: *behaving very peculiarly* **2** in a distinctive way: *a peculiarly British habit*
♦ **peculiarity** •NOUN• **peculiarities 1** an odd or strange thing, or the quality of being odd or strange **2** a distinctive feature or characteristic

pedal •NOUN• **pedals** a lever worked by the foot, such as on a bicycle, piano or organ
•VERB• **pedals, pedalling, pedalled** to pedal a bike or toy car is to make it move forward by pressing down on the pedals

peddle •VERB• **peddles, peddling, peddled** to peddle goods or wares is to go from place to place or house to house selling them
⇒ **pedlar**

pedestal •NOUN• **pedestals** the base that something stands on, for example a statue or wash hand basin
• **put someone on a pedestal** to worship someone as if they were a god or goddess and can do no wrong

pedestrian •NOUN• **pedestrians** someone who walks on pavements or roads

pedigree •NOUN• **pedigrees 1** if an animal has a pedigree there is a record showing that its parents and other ancestors were all of the same breed **2** your pedigree is your background or the people you are descended from
•ADJECTIVE• having a pedigree: *a pedigree cow*

pedlar •NOUN• **pedlars** a person who travels round selling small objects, usually from door to door

peek •VERB• **peeks, peeking, peeked** to peek is to look, especially when you should not be looking
•NOUN• **peeks** a quick look

Aa

ⓘ Try not to confuse the spelling of **peak**, which is the top of something, with **peek**.

Bb

peel • VERB• peels, peeling, peeled 1 to peel a fruit or vegetable is to take off its skin or outer covering 2 paint or skin peels when it comes off in small pieces

Cc

• NOUN• peel is the skin of certain fruits and vegetables

Dd

Ee

peep • VERB• peeps, peeping, peeped to peep is to look through a narrow opening or from behind something

Ff

• NOUN• peeps a quick look at something

Gg

peer • VERB• peers, peering, peered to peer at something is to look at it with your eyes narrowed because you cannot see very clearly

Hh

Ii

• NOUN• peers 1 your peers are the people who are the same age, class or status as you 2 in Britain, peers are members of the nobility or people who have been awarded a title

Jj

Kk

Ll

peg • NOUN• pegs 1 a wooden, plastic or metal clip used for hanging clothes on a washing line

Mm

2 a hook for hanging coats, hats or jackets on

Nn

3 a piece of wood or metal driven into the ground to secure a tent, or as a marker

Oo

Pekinese or **Pekingese** • NOUN•

Pp

Pekineses or **Pekingeses** a type of small dog with long silky hair, large eyes, and a small wrinkled nose

Qq

Rr

pelican • NOUN• pelicans a large white bird found in tropical parts of the world, which dives for fish and stores the ones it catches in a pouch under its beak

Ss

Tt

pelican crossing • NOUN• pelican crossings a road crossing for pedestrians with lights that are operated by the people waiting to cross

Uu

Vv

Ww

ⓘ This word comes from the first letters of the words **pe**destrian **li**ght **con**trolled crossing. The spelling was changed to **pelican**.

Xx

Yy

pellet • NOUN• pellets a small hard round object formed by pressing and rolling material into a tightly-packed ball

Zz

pelmet • NOUN• pelmets a long narrow piece of cloth or wood fitted along the top of a window to hide the curtain rail

pelt • VERB• pelts, pelting, pelted 1 to pelt someone with things is to throw things at them one after the other

2 rain pelts down when it falls fast and heavily

3 to pelt is to run or move very fast: *He came pelting down the road on his bike.*

• NOUN• pelts the skin from an animal: *beaver pelts*

pelvis • NOUN• pelvises your pelvis is the bowl-shaped bone at your hips

pen [1] • NOUN• pens an instrument for writing or drawing in ink

pen [2] • NOUN• pens a small area of land surrounded by a fence and used for keeping animals in

• VERB• pens, penning, penned 1 to pen an animal is to put it in a pen 2 to **pen someone in** is to surround them or shut them in so that they cannot move or escape

pen [3] • NOUN• pens a female swan

penalize or **penalise** • VERB• penalizes, penalizing, penalized to penalize someone is to punish them for doing something that is against the rules

penalty • NOUN• penalties 1 a punishment for doing wrong 2 in games like football, rugby and hockey, a penalty is a free shot at goal given because a player in the other team has broken a rule of the game

penance • NOUN• if someone does penance they suffer a punishment willingly to make up for doing something wrong

pence • NOUN• the plural of **penny**

pencil • NOUN• pencils an instrument made up of a hollow shaft containing a stick of lead or graphite, or coloured chalk, and used for writing or drawing

pendant • NOUN• pendants an ornament that hangs from a chain or necklace

pendulum • NOUN• pendulums a weight that swings from side to side and operates the mechanism of a clock

penetrate • VERB• penetrates, penetrating, penetrated 1 to get into or through something: *Rain could not penetrate those thick trees.* **2** if something you have been told penetrates, you understand it: *In a second the detective had penetrated the whole mystery.*

◆ **penetrating** •ADJECTIVE• **1** a penetrating voice or sound seems to carry for a long distance **2** if someone gives you a penetrating look, they look at you hard as if they are searching your mind

◆ **penetration** •NOUN• going into or through something

pen-friend •NOUN• **pen-friends** a friend you exchange letters with, but do not meet

penguin •NOUN• **penguins** a bird that cannot fly but which uses its wings like flippers to swim underwater. Penguins are found in the Antarctic

penicillin •NOUN• a drug used to treat diseases and illnesses caused by bacteria

peninsula •NOUN• **peninsulas** a piece of land surrounded by water on every side except the end where it joins a larger land mass

◆ **peninsular** •ADJECTIVE• to do with, or formed like, a peninsula

penis •NOUN• **penises** the organ male animals use to urinate and reproduce

penknife •NOUN• **penknives** a small knife with blades that fold into the handle and which you can carry in your pocket

pennant •NOUN• **pennants** a small narrow flag that tapers to a point at one end

penniless •ADJECTIVE• if someone is penniless, they have no money

penny •NOUN• **pennies** a small bronze British coin worth one hundredth of £1

pension •NOUN• **pensions** a sum of money paid regularly to a person who has retired from work

◆ **pensioner** •NOUN• **pensioners** a retired person who is receiving a pension

pentagon •NOUN• **pentagons** a flat shape with five straight sides and five angles

◆ **pentagonal** •ADJECTIVE• having five sides: *a pentagonal dish*

pentathlon •NOUN• **pentathlons** an athletics competition that has five different kinds of sporting contest: swimming, cross-country riding, running, fencing and pistol-shooting

penultimate •ADJECTIVE• the penultimate thing is the last but one in a series

people •NOUN• **peoples 1** people are men, women and children **2** a people is one of the races of human beings: *all the peoples of the world* **3** the plural of **person**: *one person or many people*
•VERB• **peoples, peopling, peopled** a place is peopled by a certain group if they are the people who live there

ⓘ **People** always takes a plural verb, for example: *People **are** always happy to go on holiday.*

pepper •NOUN• **peppers 1** pepper is a hot-tasting powder made by grinding dried seeds called peppercorns **2** a pepper is a red, yellow, orange or green hollow fruit used as a vegetable

◆ **peppery** •ADJECTIVE• hot-tasting, like pepper

peppermint •NOUN• **peppermints 1** peppermint is a strong flavouring obtained from a type of mint plant, used in sweets and toothpaste **2** a sweet flavoured with peppermint
•ADJECTIVE• flavoured with peppermint: *peppermint toothpaste*

per •PREPOSITION• **1** for every or for each: *The meal will cost £15 per person.* **2** in every or in each: *sixty kilometres per hour*

perceive •VERB• **perceives, perceiving, perceived** to perceive something is to notice it with one of your senses: *I perceived the object to be a painted chalice.*
⇒ **perception, perceptive**

percent •ADVERB• in or for every 100: *forty per cent*

◆ **percentage** •NOUN• **percentages 1** a number or amount in each hundred, written as a fraction with that number over a hundred, for example $\frac{35}{100}$. It can also be written with a percentage sign, for example 35% **2** a part or proportion of something: *A high percentage of pupils get top grades.*

perception •NOUN• **perceptions 1** the

perceptive → period

ability to see, hear or understand 2 your perception of something is the way you see or understand it

perceptive · ADJECTIVE · a perceptive person is good at noticing or understanding things

perch · VERB · perches, perching, perched
1 a bird perches when it sits or stands on a branch or some other place above the ground 2 to perch somewhere high or narrow is to sit there
· NOUN · perches a branch or other place above the ground that a bird sits or stands on

percolator · NOUN · percolators a pot for making coffee with ground coffee beans in a small container at the top that boiling water bubbles through

percussion · NOUN AND ADJECTIVE · musical instruments that you play by hitting them with your hands or with sticks, or by shaking them. Drums, cymbals, tambourines and triangles are percussion instruments

perfect · ADJECTIVE · 1 without any mistakes or faults: *a perfect score*
2 exact: *a perfect circle*
3 complete: *a perfect stranger*
· VERB · perfects, perfecting, perfected to perfect something is to make it perfect, without any faults
· **perfection** · NOUN · making perfect or being perfect
· **perfectly** · ADVERB · 1 without any mistakes or faults: *She did the pirouette perfectly.*
2 exactly: *perfectly square*
3 completely: *perfectly ridiculous*

ⓘ The adjective is pronounced **per**-fict, with the stress on *per*. The verb is pronounced pir-**fect**, with the stress on *fect*.

perfect number · NOUN · perfect numbers a number that is the sum of all the numbers (including 1 but excluding the number itself) that can be multiplied to give that number as a result. For example, 6 is a perfect number because 1 + 2 + 3 = 6, and 28 is also a perfect number because 1 + 2 + 4 + 7 + 14 = 28

perforate · VERB · perforates, perforating, perforated to perforate something is to

pierce it and make a small hole in it
· **perforated** · ADJECTIVE · pierced with a hole or a series of holes
· **perforation** · NOUN · perforations a small hole made in something, especially the series of small holes made around the edges of stamps so that they can be torn from the sheet

perform · VERB · performs, performing, performed 1 to perform something, such as a play, piece of music or a dance is to do it in front of an audience 2 to perform something is to do it or carry it out: *Surgeons perform operations.*
· **performance** · NOUN · performances 1 something performed in front of an audience 2 a level of success achieved in doing something: *a brilliant performance*
· **performer** · NOUN · performers someone who does an act in front of an audience

perfume · NOUN · perfumes 1 a perfume is a smell, especially a pleasant one 2 perfume is a pleasant smelling liquid or cream that you put on your body to make it smell nice
· VERB · perfumes, perfuming, perfumed to perfume something is to put perfume on it or fill it with a pleasant smell

perhaps · ADVERB · possibly or maybe: *The bus is late – perhaps it has broken down again.*

peril · NOUN · perils danger: *The perils of sailing round the world alone.* · *The business's future was in peril.*
· **perilous** · ADJECTIVE · very dangerous or full of danger: *a perilous journey on foot across miles of desert*

perimeter · NOUN · perimeters 1 the perimeter of area is its outer edge or boundary 2 the perimeter of a flat shape is the length around its outside edge

period · NOUN · periods 1 a period of time is a length of time: *a period of several weeks*
2 a stage or phase in history: *the Regency period* · *one of the earliest geological periods*
3 a girl's or woman's period is the time each month when she menstruates
· ADJECTIVE · from or in the style of a period in history: *period costumes*
· **periodic** · ADJECTIVE · for a certain length

412

of time and at regular intervals: *He gets periodic bouts of asthma.*

♦ **periodical** • NOUN• **periodicals** a magazine that is published regularly, for example once a week or once a month

periscope • NOUN• **periscopes** an instrument consisting of a special arrangement of angled mirrors in a tube, which makes it possible for you to look at things over the top of a barrier in front of you. Periscopes are used in submarines

perish • VERB• **perishes, perishing, perished** to perish is to die, especially in a war or from extreme cold

periwinkle • NOUN• **periwinkles** a shellfish that looks like a small snail and clings to rocks

perk • VERB• **perks, perking, perked** if you **perk up**, you feel more lively and cheerful
• NOUN• **perks** a perk is an extra benefit or advantage that someone gets from their job

perm • NOUN• **perms** a chemical treatment for hair that gives a long-lasting curly hairstyle
•VERB• **perms, perming, permed** to perm hair is to treat it with chemicals so that it stays in a curly style for a long time

permafrost • NOUN• permafrost is permanently frozen ground just below the surface in cold areas of the world

permanent • ADJECTIVE• **1** lasting for ever, or for a long time: *Will the scar be permanent?*
2 a permanent job is one that is expected to last for a long time, rather than being temporary
3 never changing: *a permanent state of chaos*
♦ **permanently** • ADVERB• for ever

permissible • ADJECTIVE• something that is permissible is allowed

permission • NOUN• you get or are given permission to do something when someone says you are allowed to do it

permit •VERB• **permits, permitting, permitted** to permit something is to allow it to happen
• NOUN• **permits** an official document

allowing a person to do something: *a fishing permit*

perpendicular • ADJECTIVE• **1** standing straight upwards: *a perpendicular line* **2** touching another line to make a right angle. For example, the touching lines in a rectangle are perpendicular to each other

perpetual • ADJECTIVE• never ending or continuous: *perpetual darkness* • *a perpetual noise*

perplex • VERB• **perplexes, perplexing, perplexed** if something perplexes you, it puzzles or baffles you
♦ **perplexed** • ADJECTIVE• puzzled: *a perplexed expression*
♦ **perplexity** • NOUN• being perplexed: *'Hum!' said he, scratching his chin in some perplexity.*

persecute • VERB• **persecutes, persecuting, persecuted** to persecute someone is to make them suffer, especially because of their opinions or beliefs
♦ **persecution** • NOUN• being persecuted

perseverance • NOUN• persevering

persevere •VERB• **perseveres, persevering, persevered** to persevere is to continue with something even though it is difficult

persist •VERB• **persists, persisting, persisted**
1 if something persists, it continues for a long time
2 you persist with something when you keep on doing it and refuse to give up
3 to keep talking about something: *'It was you,' I persisted.*
♦ **persistence** • NOUN• continuing with something in spite of people saying you should not
♦ **persistent** • ADJECTIVE• **1** refusing to give up: *Even though I said I wasn't interested, the salesman was very persistent.* **2** continuing without a break: *persistent rain*

person • NOUN• **people** or **persons** a human being
• **in person** someone does something in person when they do it themselves, instead of someone else doing it for them

personal • ADJECTIVE• **1** belonging to, or done by, one particular person and no one

Aa
Bb
Cc
Dd
Ee
Ff
Gg
Hh
Ii
Jj
Kk
Ll
Mm
Nn
Oo
Pp
Qq
Rr
Ss
Tt
Uu
Vv
Ww
Xx
Yy
Zz

else: *a personal opinion • a personal appearance* **2** private: *It's personal and none of your business.*
♦ **personality** •NOUN• **personalities 1** your personality is your character and the qualities you have
2 someone with personality behaves in a way that makes a strong impression on you
3 a personality is a famous person
♦ **personally** •ADVERB• **1** you say 'personally' when you are giving your own opinion about something: *'Personally, I would have ignored it.'* **2** done by you and not by anyone else: *He wrote to everyone personally.*

personnel •NOUN• the personnel in a business or organization are the people employed in it or who are part of it

perspective •NOUN• **perspectives 1** the technique of drawing solid objects on a flat surface, so that they appear to have the correct shape and distance from each other **2** if you get a situation into perspective, you do not make it more important than it is **3** a point of view

perspiration •NOUN• sweat

perspire •VERB• perspires, perspiring, perspired to sweat

persuade •VERB• persuades, persuading, persuaded to persuade someone is to give them good reasons why they should, or should not, do something
♦ **persuasion** •NOUN• persuading
♦ **persuasive** •ADJECTIVE• a persuasive person or argument can change your mind or make you decide to do something

perturb •VERB• perturbs, perturbing, perturbed something perturbs you when it makes you feel uncomfortable and worried
♦ **perturbed** •ADJECTIVE• worried

pessimism •NOUN• the habit of expecting things to turn out badly. Look up and compare **optimism**
♦ **pessimist** •NOUN• pessimists someone who usually expects bad things to happen
♦ **pessimistic** •ADJECTIVE• expecting that things will turn out badly: *a pessimistic outlook*

pest •NOUN• **pests 1** a pest is an insect that

eats crops and garden plants, or an animal that destroys things **2** someone who is a pest is a nuisance

pester •VERB• pesters, pestering, pestered to pester someone is to annoy them continually

pesticide •NOUN• pesticides a substance used to kill insects that eat or destroy plants and crops

pet •NOUN• **pets 1** a tame animal that you keep in your home **2** a favourite: *He's teacher's pet.*
•VERB• **pets, petting, petted** to pet an animal is to pat it and stroke it

petal •NOUN• petals one of the coloured parts of a flower

peter •VERB• peters, petering, petered if something **peters out**, it gradually comes to an end or stop

petite •ADJECTIVE• a girl or woman who is petite is attractively small or slim

petition •NOUN• petitions a request for something, especially one signed by many people and sent to a government or someone in authority

petrify •VERB• petrifies, petrifying, petrified if something petrifies you, it terrifies you so much that you cannot move

petrochemical •NOUN• petrochemicals a chemical made from petroleum or natural gas

petrol •NOUN• a fuel for engines, made from oil

petroleum •NOUN• an oil found underground or under the seabed and used to make petrol

petticoat •NOUN• petticoats a piece of clothing that a girl or woman wears under her skirt

petty •ADJECTIVE• **pettier, pettiest 1** having very little importance: *petty details* **2** if someone is being petty, they concentrate on or criticize small unimportant details

petty cash •NOUN• small sums of money spent or received by a company or business

petulance •NOUN• being petulant
♦ **petulant** •ADJECTIVE• someone who is

petulant is bad-tempered, impatient and huffy, like a spoilt child

pew • NOUN• **pews** a long wooden bench in a church

pewter • NOUN• a dull grey metal made from a mixture of lead and tin

PG • ABBREVIATION• short for **parental guidance**, a film classification used in Britain, which means that a child can only be allowed to see the film if an adult is with them

pH • NOUN• a scale used to measure the acidity or alkalinity of a solution. Acids have a pH value between 0 and 7, and alkalis have a pH value between 7 and 14

phantom • NOUN• **phantoms** a ghost

pharaoh • NOUN• **pharaohs** one of the powerful rulers of ancient Egypt

pharmacist • NOUN• **pharmacists** someone who prepares and sells medicines
  • **pharmacy** • NOUN• **pharmacies** a shop where medicines are prepared and sold

phase • NOUN• **phases** a stage in something's development or progress
  •VERB• **phases, phasing, phased** to **phase something in**, or to **phase it out**, is to introduce it, or get rid of it, gradually or in stages

pheasant • NOUN• **pheasants** a large bird with a long tail, that is hunted for sport and eaten

phenomenal • ADJECTIVE• extraordinary or amazing
  • **phenomenally** • ADVERB• in a phenomenal way

phenomenon • NOUN• **phenomena** something that is seen to happen or exist, especially something that is interesting or unusual

philatelist • NOUN• **philatelists** someone who collects postage stamps
  • **philately** • NOUN• stamp collecting

philosopher • NOUN• **philosophers** someone who studies philosophy

philosophical • ADJECTIVE• **1** to do with philosophy **2** if you are philosophical about something, such as a disappointment, you stay calm and are not upset by it

philosophy • NOUN• **philosophies**
  1 philosophy is the search for knowledge and truth about the universe and human beings and their behaviour **2** a philosophy is a set of beliefs

phobia • NOUN• **phobias** an unreasonable fear or hatred of something

phoenix • NOUN• **phoenixes** in stories and myths, a bird that burns itself on a fire and is born again from its own ashes

phone • NOUN• **phones** a telephone
  •VERB• **phones, phoning, phoned** to phone someone is to call them on the telephone

phonecard • NOUN• **phonecards** a card that you use instead of money in a public phone box

phoney or **phony** • ADJECTIVE• **phonier, phoniest** fake or false: *a phoney French accent*

photo • NOUN• **photos** a photograph

photo- • PREFIX• a word beginning with **photo-** has something to do with light, or photography. For example, *photosensitive* means sensitive to light, and *photojournalism* is using pictures or photographs to report stories that are in the news

photocopier • NOUN• **photocopiers** a machine that copies a document by taking a photograph of it

photograph • NOUN• **photographs** a picture taken by a camera
  •VERB• **photographs, photographing, photographed** to photograph something is to take a picture of it using a camera
  • **photographer** • NOUN• **photographers** someone who takes photographs, either as a hobby or as a profession
  • **photography** • NOUN• the art of taking photographs

ⓘ **Photograph** comes from the Greek words **photo**, which means *light*, and **graphein**, which means *to draw*, so together they mean 'to draw with light'.

photosynthesis • NOUN• photosynthesis is the process by which a plant converts energy from sunlight into compounds that the plant uses as food

Aa
Bb
Cc
Dd
Ee
Ff
Gg
Hh
Ii
Jj
Kk
Ll
Mm
Nn
Oo
Pp
Qq
Rr
Ss
Tt
Uu
Vv
Ww
Xx
Yy
Zz

phrase •NOUN• **phrases** a group of words expressing a single meaning or idea and that is used on its own or as part of a sentence

physical •ADJECTIVE• **1** to do with the body: *physical pain* **2** to do with things that you can see or touch, rather than things that exist only in your mind

physical education •NOUN• a school subject in which you learn sports, games and exercises and how to keep your body fit

physicist •NOUN• **physicists** someone who studies physics

physics •NOUN• the scientific study of things that occur naturally, such as heat, light, sound, electricity and magnetism

physiotherapist •NOUN• **physiotherapists** someone trained in physiotherapy
♦ **physiotherapy** •NOUN• the treatment of injuries and diseases by physical exercise and massage, rather than drugs

pianist •NOUN• **pianists** a musician who plays the piano

piano •NOUN• **pianos** a stringed instrument that you sit at and play by pressing the black and white keys on a long keyboard

piccolo •NOUN• **piccolos** a type of small flute with a high-pitched sound

pick •VERB• **picks, picking, picked 1** to pick a person or thing is to choose them
2 to pick something, or pick it off, is to lift it off, using your finger and thumb
3 to pick fruit or flowers is to break or pull them off the plant or tree they are growing on
4 to pick a lock is to use a piece of wire to open it
5 to pick a fight or quarrel is to deliberately get someone to fight or quarrel with you
6 to **pick on someone** is to bully them or treat them unkindly
7 to **pick something up** is to lift it using your fingers or hands
8 to **pick something up** is to learn it by watching or listening rather than being taught in a lesson
9 to **pick someone up** is to go and fetch them from the place where they are waiting to be collected
•NOUN• **picks 1** if you have, or take, your pick

of things, you choose whichever you like
2 the pick of a group of people or things are the best in that group
⇒ **picky**

picket •VERB• **pickets, picketing, picketed** to stand outside a factory or other place of work in order to protest about something and to persuade other workers not to go in

pickpocket •NOUN• **pickpockets** a criminal who steals things from people's pockets

picky •ADJECTIVE• **pickier, pickiest** fussy

picnic •NOUN• **picnics** a meal that you have outdoors at a place that you walk or travel to
•VERB• **picnics, picnicking, picnicked** to have a picnic
♦ **picnicker** •NOUN• **picnickers** people who are having a picnic

pictogram •NOUN• **pictograms** a picture or symbol which represents a letter, word or idea, used instead of letters of the alphabet in some writing systems, for example in Chinese

pictorial •ADJECTIVE• having lots of pictures or using pictures to show something

picture •NOUN• **pictures 1** a painting, drawing or photograph **2** an image: *He had a picture in his mind of what he wanted to do.* • *television pictures*
•VERB• **pictures, picturing, pictured** to picture something is to form an image of it in your mind
•ADJECTIVE• with a picture or pictures: *a picture postcard* • *a picture book*

picturesque •ADJECTIVE• attractive or interesting to look at: *a picturesque old castle*

pie •NOUN• **pies** food baked in a covering of pastry

piebald •ADJECTIVE• having patches of two different colours, especially black and white: *a piebald horse*

piece •NOUN• **pieces 1** a part or bit of something: *a jigsaw with 300 pieces* • *a piece of cake*
2 something that has been written or composed: *There's a a short piece in the paper about our school.* • *He played one of*

the more romantic pieces.

3 one of the objects you move about the board in games like chess

4 a coin of a particular value : *a 50p piece*

• *'Pieces of eight, pieces of eight,' squawked the parrot.*

•**VERB**• **pieces, piecing, pieced** to **piece things together** is to fit them together to try to make something that is complete

ⓘ Try not to confuse the spelling of **piece** with **peace**, which is quietness and calmness.

piecemeal • **ADJECTIVE**• to do things piecemeal is to do a little bit at a time and in no particular order

pied • **ADJECTIVE**• having two colours, like the red and yellow costume of the Pied Piper or the black and white plumage of a magpie

pier • **NOUN**• **piers** a platform of stone or wood by a lake or the sea, where boats and ships can tie up

pierce • **VERB**• **pierces, piercing, pierced** a sharp object pierces something when it goes in or through it

♦ **piercing** • **ADJECTIVE**• a piercing sound is very sharp and seems to travel through solid objects

pig • **NOUN**• **pigs** an animal with a broad heavy body, small eyes and a snout

pigeon • **NOUN**• **pigeons** a bird with a plump body and a small head, often seen in towns and cities or kept for racing

pigeon-hole • **NOUN**• **pigeon-holes** one of a series of boxes or compartments, each for a different person, used to put their letters or messages in

•**VERB**• **pigeon-holes, pigeon-holing, pigeon-holed** to pigeon-hole someone is to decide what type of person they are or what they are suitable for

piggy-back • **NOUN**• **piggy-backs** someone gives you a piggy-back when they carry you on their back with their arms supporting your legs

pig-headed • **ADJECTIVE**• stubborn

piglet • **NOUN**• **piglets** a baby pig

pigment • **NOUN**• **pigments 1** any substance used for colouring or making paint or dye **2**

the substance in your skin that gives it its colour

pigmy • **NOUN**• **pigmies** another spelling of pygmy

pigsty • **NOUN**• **pigsties 1** a pen where pigs are kept **2** a dirty or very untidy place

pigtail • **NOUN**• **pigtails** hair that has been plaited and hangs down at the side or back of the head

pike • **NOUN**• **pike** *or* **pikes** a large fish that lives in freshwater lakes

pilchard • **NOUN**• **pilchards** a small sea fish rather like a herring, that you eat fresh or buy packed in tins

pile • **NOUN**• **piles 1** a heap or stack of things one on top of the other **2** piles of something means a lot of it : *My little brother has piles of toys.*

•**VERB**• **piles, piling, piled** to put things one on top of the other in a heap or stack

pilfer • **VERB**• **pilfers, pilfering, pilfered** someone pilfers when they steal small amounts or small items

pilgrim • **NOUN**• **pilgrims** a person who is travelling to a holy place

♦ **pilgrimage** • **NOUN**• **pilgrimages** a journey that someone makes to a holy place

pill • **NOUN**• **pills** a small tablet of medicine

pillage • **VERB**• **pillages, pillaging, pillaged** when invaders or enemies pillage they steal things from the place they have invaded or conquered

• **NOUN**• pillage is taking things from people or places during an invasion or war

pillar • **NOUN**• **pillars** an upright post used in building as a support or decoration

pillarbox • **NOUN**• **pillarboxes** a metal container in the street for posting letters in

pillion • **NOUN**• **pillions** a seat for a passenger behind the rider or driver of a bicycle or motorbike

pillow • **NOUN**• **pillows** a large soft cushion that you lay your head on when you are in bed

pillowcase *or* **pillowslip** • **NOUN**• **pillowcases** *or* **pillowslips** a cloth covering for a pillow

Aa
Bb
Cc
Dd
Ee
Ff
Gg
Hh
Ii
Jj
Kk
Ll
Mm
Nn
Oo
Pp
Qq
Rr
Ss
Tt
Uu
Vv
Ww
Xx
Yy
Zz

pilot •NOUN• **pilots** someone who flies a plane, or who guides a ship into and out of a harbour
•VERB• **pilots, piloting, piloted** to pilot a plane is to operate its controls

pilot light •NOUN• **pilot lights** a flame that burns inside a gas boiler or water heater and which ignites gas burners when the boiler or heater is in use

pimple •NOUN• **pimples** a raised spot on the skin

PIN •ABBREVIATION• short for **personal identification number**, which is a secret number that every person with a card for an automatic cash machine is given so that they can get into their bank account

pin •NOUN• **pins** a short thin pointed piece of metal for pushing through fabric or paper to hold it in place
•VERB• **pins, pinning, pinned** 1 to pin something is to fasten it with a pin 2 to pin something or someone is to keep it or them stuck in a place: *They pinned me to the ground.*

pinafore •NOUN• **pinafores** a sleeveless dress, worn over a blouse or jumper

pinball •NOUN• a game played on a slot machine in which a ball is struck by little paddles and runs down a sloping board between obstacles into holes

pincers •PLURAL NOUN• 1 a tool for gripping things tightly 2 a lobster's or crab's claws

pinch •VERB• **pinches, pinching, pinched** 1 to pinch someone is to squeeze their skin or flesh tightly between your thumb and forefinger
2 if a shoe or piece of clothing pinches it hurts you because it is too small or tight
3 to pinch something is to steal it
•NOUN• **pinches** 1 a small amount that you can pick up between your finger and thumb: *add a pinch of salt* 2 a nip with the thumb and forefinger
• **feel the pinch** someone who is feeling the pinch is having problems because of lack of money
♦ **pinched** •ADJECTIVE• if someone's face is pinched, it looks thin and pale because of cold or illness

pine [1] •NOUN• **pines** a tall evergreen tree with cones and needlelike leaves

pine [2] •VERB• **pines, pining, pined** 1 to pine for something is to long for it 2 to **pine away** is to become weaker and weaker because of grief for a person or thing you have lost

pineapple •NOUN• **pineapples** a large fruit with sweet firm yellow flesh and a tough brown skin divided into small diamond shapes

ping •VERB• **pings, pinging, pinged** 1 to make a noise like a small hard object bouncing off metal 2 to ping something, like a wire or piece of elastic, is to pull it so that it bends or stretches, and then let it go suddenly so that it makes a sharp noise
•NOUN• **pings** a pinging noise: *electronic pings and bleeps*

ping-pong •NOUN• another name for the game of table-tennis

pink •NOUN• a pale red colour with a lot of white in it

pinkie •NOUN• **pinkies** your little finger

pinnacle •NOUN• **pinnacles** 1 a high pointed rock or mountain, or a tall thin spire built on the roof of a church or castle 2 the highest point of something: *the pinnacle of his acting career*

pint •NOUN• **pints** a measurement of liquid equal to 0.57 of a litre. There are 8 pints in a gallon

pioneer •VERB• **pioneers, pioneering, pioneered** to pioneer something is to be the first to do or make it
•NOUN• **pioneers** 1 someone who is one of the first people to go to a new country to live and work there 2 a person who is the first to develop a new skill or method

pious •ADJECTIVE• a pious person takes religious rules and morals very seriously and always thinks and acts in a good and religious way

pip •NOUN• **pips** a small seed from fruits like apples and oranges

pipe •NOUN• **pipes** 1 a metal or plastic tube through which water or gas can flow
2 a tube with a hollow bowl at one end used for smoking tobacco

3 an instrument that you play by blowing air into one end of a hollow tube
• VERB• **pipes, piping, piped** 1 to pipe liquid or gas is to carry it from one place to another through pipes
2 to play a pipe or bagpipes
3 to **pipe down** is to be quiet
4 someone **pipes up** when they suddenly say something after they have been quiet for a while

pipeline • NOUN• **pipelines** a long pipe that crosses the land or sea and carries oil or gas
• **in the pipeline** if something is in the pipeline it is being dealt with or is going to happen

piper • NOUN• **pipers** someone who plays a pipe or bagpipes

piping • NOUN• piping is playing the bagpipes
• **piping hot** boiling or nearly boiling

piracy • NOUN• robbery on the high seas

piranha • NOUN• **piranhas** a small fierce fish that lives in rivers in South America

pirate • NOUN• **pirates** someone who robs ships and boats at sea
⇒ **piracy**

pirouette • NOUN• **pirouettes** a dance movement in which you spin round very fast while standing on one leg
• VERB• **pirouettes, pirouetting, pirouetted** to pirouette is to spin your body in a full circle once or several times

piston • NOUN• **pistons** a round piece of metal that fits inside a cylinder in an engine and moves up and down or backwards and forwards inside it

pit • NOUN• **pits** 1 a large hole in the ground
2 a deep mine, especially a coal mine
• **the pits** the place on a motor-racing track where the cars can stop to get fuel or have their tyres changed by the mechanics in their team
• VERB• **pits, pitting, pitted** to **pit someone against** another person is to make them fight or compete with each other

pitch¹ • NOUN• **pitches** 1 an area of ground, often with special lines marked on it, used to play games like football, rugby or cricket
2 a sound's pitch is how high or low it is
3 the level or intensity that something reaches: *The excitement reached fever pitch*

when *Zidane headed the ball into the net.*
• VERB• **pitches, pitching, pitched** 1 to pitch a tent is to erect it and set up camp
2 to pitch something at a particular level is to set it or direct it at that level: *She pitched her voice low.* • *The programme is pitched at children under 2.*
3 to pitch forward, is to fall forward suddenly
4 if a ship pitches, it goes up and down from front to back as it moves forward
5 in baseball, you pitch when you are the player who throws the ball at the batting team
6 to **pitch in** is to join in or make a contribution to something

pitch² • NOUN• pitch is a black sticky substance made from tar
• ADJECTIVE• it is pitch dark when it is very dark and you can see nothing

pitched battle • NOUN• **pitched battles** a pitched battle is a fierce fight or argument with two people or groups drawn up against each other like armies

pitcher • NOUN• **pitchers** a large jug

pitchfork • NOUN• **pitchforks** a tool with two prongs and a long handle, used to lift hay and straw

pitfall • NOUN• **pitfalls** a possible danger or difficulty, or a mistake that can be made easily

pith • NOUN• pith is the white layer between the skin and the flesh of an orange or other citrus fruit

pitiful • ADJECTIVE• 1 sad and pathetic: *a pitiful sight* 2 of such poor or bad quality that it makes you feel contempt: *a pitiful excuse*

pittance • NOUN• a very small sum of money

pitted • ADJECTIVE• covered with small dents

pity • NOUN• 1 pity is sorrow you feel for other people's troubles or difficulties
2 you say that something is a pity if you are sorry about it
3 to take pity on someone is to feel so sorry for them that you help them or give them something
• VERB• **pities, pitying, pitied** to pity someone is to feel sorry for them

pivot •NOUN• **pivots** a pin or centre on which something balances and turns
•VERB• **pivots, pivoting, pivoted** to pivot is to turn or revolve while balancing on a central point

pixel •NOUN• **pixels** one of the tiny elements that pictures on a computer or TV screen are made up of, with each pixel occupying a unit of computer memory

pixie •NOUN• **pixies** in stories, a small good fairy or elf

pizza •NOUN• **pizzas** a flat round piece of dough topped with cheese, tomatoes and herbs and baked in an oven

placard •NOUN• **placards** a board with a notice or message on it that is carried by someone in public

place •NOUN• **places 1** a particular area or position: *a place by the sea • Put the books back in their proper place on the shelf. • I imagine Beijing is a very interesting place.*
2 a seat, or a space at a table for someone to sit and eat: *Please go back to your places and sit down.*
3 a position in an order, series or queue: *She was in first place after the second round.*
• *Work out this sum to two decimal places.*
• **in place of** instead of: *Kelly's here in place of John, who is ill.*
• **out of place 1** something is out of place when it is not in its usual position **2** you feel out of place when you feel that you do not fit in with the people or things around you
•VERB• **places, placing, placed 1** to place something somewhere is to put it there
2 to place someone in a certain position is to put them there: *He had placed me in a very awkward spot by promising that I would go to the party.*
3 to place a bet or an order is to make a bet or an order

placid •ADJECTIVE• gentle and calm

plague •NOUN• **plagues 1** a large number of insects or other pests that suddenly appear and cause damage or a nuisance **2** the plague is a disease that spreads rapidly and kills many people
•VERB• **plagues, plaguing, plagued** something plagues you when it causes you a lot of discomfort or annoyance

plaice •NOUN• **plaice** a type of flat fish found in the sea

plaid •NOUN• **plaids** a long piece of cloth, especially with a tartan pattern, that people in Scottish Highland costume wear over their shoulders

plain •ADJECTIVE• **plainer, plainest**
1 without any decoration or without a pattern: *a plain white room*
2 simple or ordinary: *good plain cooking*
3 easy to see or understand: *as plain as the nose on your face • He made it quite plain that he didn't like me.*
4 straightforward: *That's just plain nonsense.*
•NOUN• **plains** a large flat area of land

plait •NOUN• **plaits** lengths of something such as hair or straw that are twisted over each other in turn
•VERB• **plaits, plaiting, plaited** to twist strands of hair or straw in this way

plan •VERB• **plans, planning, planned 1** to plan something is to work out how it may be done or make the arrangements to do it
2 to plan something, such as a building, is to design it
3 to plan to do something is to decide to do it at some time before you actually do it
•NOUN• **plans 1** an idea of how to do something or a method worked out for doing it **2** a drawing showing the layout of a building or town as if you are looking at it from above

plane[1] •NOUN• **planes** an aeroplane

plane[2] •NOUN• **planes 1** a carpenter's tool with a cutting blade set in a frame and used for making a level or smooth surface **2** a flat or level surface: *A cube has six planes.*
•VERB• **planes, planing, planed** to plane wood is to make it smooth and level using a plane

① Be careful not to confuse the spelling of **plane** with **plain**, which means ordinary.

planet •NOUN• **planets** any of the large objects in space that orbit round a sun. The planets that orbit round our sun are Mercury, Venus, Earth, Mars, Jupiter,

Saturn, Uranus, Neptune and Pluto
+ **planetary** •ADJECTIVE• to do with the planets, especially those in our own solar system

plank •NOUN• **planks** a long flat piece of wood

plankton •NOUN• tiny animals and plants that float in the sea just below the surface and are eaten by many larger sea creatures

plant •NOUN• **plants 1** any living thing that grows from the ground and has a stem, roots and leaves **2** a factory or industrial building •VERB• **plants, planting, planted 1** to plant seed or plants is to put them in the ground so that they grow **2** to plant something is to place or fix it firmly: *He planted his feet on either side of the rope and pulled as hard as he could.*
+ **plantation** •NOUN• **plantations** a piece of land where a certain crop is grown or where trees are planted

plaque •NOUN• **plaques 1** a metal plate with writing on it fixed to a wall and usually put up to remember a famous person or event **2** a substance that forms on teeth and which helps bacteria to grow

plasma •NOUN• the clear liquid part of blood

plaster •NOUN• **plasters 1** plaster is a thin paste put on walls that dries to form a hard smooth surface **2** a plaster is a sticky dressing that you put over a scratch or wound to protect it from germs •VERB• **plasters, plastering, plastered 1** to apply plaster to walls **2** to plaster a surface is to cover it with thick liquid: *paper plastered with paint*
+ **plasterer** •NOUN• **plasterers** someone whose job is to plaster walls

plaster cast •NOUN• **plaster casts** a hard casing put around a broken limb to support it while the bone heals

plaster of Paris •NOUN• a type of white plaster that dries out quickly and is used to make models or plaster casts for broken bones

plastic •NOUN• **plastics** a substance made from chemicals that can be moulded while it is still soft and stretched to make objects

Plasticine •NOUN• a soft substance rather like clay that can be moulded to make models. This word is a trademark

plastic surgery •NOUN• an operation to improve a patient's appearance or to repair scars

plate •NOUN• **plates 1** a shallow dish for holding food **2** a thin flat sheet of metal or some other hard substance **3** a large picture or photograph in a book **4** one of the large areas of rock that make up the Earth's surface and that move very slowly under or over each other •VERB• **plates, plating, plated** to plate an object is to cover it with a thin layer of metal, such as silver or tin

plateau •NOUN• **plateaus** or **plateaux** a broad, fairly flat area of land that is higher than the land around it on at least one side

plate-glass •NOUN• glass made in thick sheets and used for shop windows and mirrors

platform •NOUN• **platforms 1** a raised floor from which performers or speakers can be seen by an audience **2** a raised area beside the tracks at a railway station, where passengers can get on and off trains **3** a floating structure used as a base for drilling for oil

platinum •NOUN• a silvery-white precious metal

platoon •NOUN• **platoons** a group of soldiers

platter •NOUN• **platters** a large flat dish used for serving food

platypus •NOUN• **platypuses** a small animal found in Australia. It has a broad flat beak like a duck, webbed feet and a hairy body

play •VERB• **plays, playing, played 1** to play is to spend time amusing yourself with games or toys: *Are you coming out to play?* **2** you play a team game when you take part in it: *He plays cricket on Saturdays.* **3** to play a musical instrument is to make music with it **4** to play a DVD, CD or tape is to put it into the player and listen to it or watch it **5** an actor plays a particular part when he or

Aa

she acts that part

6 to play a part in something is to be one of the people involved in it

Bb

7 to **play down** a success or a problem is to make it seem less impressive or serious

Cc

8 a person or animal **plays up** when they behave badly

Dd

• **play safe** to play safe is to take no risks

• NOUN• **plays 1** play is having fun with games and toys, or the action that goes on in a team game: *learning through play* • *Rain stopped play.* **2** a play is a story acted out in the theatre or on TV or radio

Ee

Ff

Gg

♦ **player** • NOUN• **players 1** someone who plays a game **2** a machine for playing DVDs, CDs, tapes or records

Hh

♦ **playful** • ADJECTIVE• full of fun or wanting to play

Ii

Jj

playground • NOUN• **playgrounds** an area, for example beside a school or in a public park, where children can play

Kk

playgroup • NOUN• **playgroups** an organized group where very young children can play and learn together

Ll

Mm

playing-card • NOUN• **playing-cards** a card from a set of 52, made up of four suits of 13 cards: hearts, clubs, diamonds and spades

Nn

Oo

playmate • NOUN• **playmates** someone you play with

Pp

play-off • NOUN• **play-offs** a match or game played to decide the winner from two players or teams with equal points in a competition

Qq

Rr

playschool • NOUN• **playschools** a nursery school or playgroup

Ss

playwright • NOUN• **playwrights** someone who writes plays

Tt

Uu

plea • NOUN• **pleas 1** an urgent and emotional request for something **2** someone charged with a crime makes a plea when they state to a court whether they are guilty or not guilty

Vv

Ww

plead • VERB• **pleads, pleading, pleaded** *or* **pled 1** to plead is to try to persuade someone in an urgent and emotional way, because you want something very much **2** to plead in a court is to answer a charge, saying 'guilty' or 'not guilty'

Xx

Yy

Zz

pleasant • ADJECTIVE• **1** something

pleasant gives you a feeling of enjoyment and happiness **2** a pleasant person has a friendly and likeable manner

♦ **pleasantly** • ADVERB• in a pleasant way: *His laugh was pleasantly like a chuckle.*

please • VERB• **pleases, pleasing, pleased 1** to please someone is to do what they want or to give them pleasure or satisfaction **2** to do as you please is to do exactly as you want, not thinking what other people may want

• ADVERB AND INTERJECTION• a polite word you use when you are asking for something or accepting an offer: *Please don't park in front of the driveway.* • *'Would you like another biscuit?' 'Yes, please.'*

♦ **pleasing** • ADJECTIVE• giving pleasure or satisfaction: *a pleasing result*

pleasurable • ADJECTIVE• giving pleasure or enjoyment

pleasure • NOUN• **pleasures 1** a feeling of enjoyment or satisfaction, or something that gives you this feeling **2** pleasure is time spent enjoying yourself rather than working: *Is your trip business or pleasure?*

pleat • NOUN• **pleats** a fold sewn or pressed into a piece of cloth

♦ **pleated** • ADJECTIVE• having folds or folded lines: *a pleated skirt*

plectrum • NOUN• **plectrums** a small hard piece of plastic or metal used to pick the strings of a guitar

pledge • NOUN• **pledges** a solemn promise

• VERB• **pledges, pledging, pledged** to pledge to do something is to promise solemnly to do it

plentiful • ADJECTIVE• something is plentiful when there is a good supply of it or it exists in large amounts

plenty • NOUN• **1** as much as you need: *You have plenty of time to complete the test.* **2** a large amount or number: *There's plenty more bread in the freezer if we run out.*

ⓘ If the noun with **plenty** is singular, you use a singular verb: *Plenty of money **is** being made available to spend on computer equipment.* If the noun is plural, you use a plural verb: *There **are** plenty of people who don't have access to a computer.*

pliable •ADJECTIVE• easy to bend or shape without breaking

pliant •ADJECTIVE• easy to bend, or easy to influence

pliers •PLURAL NOUN• pliers are a tool with two flat surfaces that come together to grip things

plight •NOUN• **plights** a bad condition or situation

plimsolls •PLURAL NOUN• light rubber-soled canvas shoes worn for games

plod •VERB• **plods, plodding, plodded** 1 to walk slowly as if your feet and legs are heavy 2 to work slowly but steadily, especially on a job that you find boring

plonk •NOUN• **plonks** a sound made by something dropping heavily
•VERB• **plonks, plonking, plonked** to plonk something somewhere is to put it down heavily: *He plonked himself down on the sofa and turned on the telly.*

plop •NOUN• **plops** the sound of a small or light object dropping into water: *The frog jumped back into the pond with a plop.*
•VERB• **plops, plopping, plopped** to plop is to fall or drop making this sound

plot •NOUN• **plots** 1 a secret plan, especially for doing something illegal or evil 2 the story of a play, novel or film 3 a small piece of land to be used as a gardening area or for building a house on: *a vegetable plot*
•VERB• **plots, plotting, plotted** 1 to plan to do something illegal or evil 2 to plot things on a graph is to mark them as points on the graph and then make a connecting line between the points

plough •NOUN• **ploughs** a farm tool with a heavy blade which is pulled through the top layer of the soil to turn it over or break it up
•VERB• **ploughs, ploughing, ploughed** 1 to plough is to turn over soil with a plough 2 to **plough through** work is to do your work slowly and with difficulty until you reach the end

plover •NOUN• **plovers** a wading bird that nests on open ground

ploy •NOUN• **ploys** a carefully thought-out plan or method of achieving something

pluck •VERB• **plucks, plucking, plucked** 1 to pluck something is to take hold of it and pull it sharply so that it comes out or off 2 to pluck a chicken or turkey is to pull its feathers off before cooking it
•NOUN• a rather old-fashioned word for courage
♦ **plucky** •ADJECTIVE• **pluckier, pluckiest** having courage

plug •NOUN• **plugs** 1 an object attached to an electrical appliance by a wire and which you fit into a socket in the wall so that electric current can reach the appliance 2 an object that you use for blocking a hole, especially in a bath or sink to stop the water from running away
•VERB• **plugs, plugging, plugged** 1 to plug a hole or gap is to push something into it to block it 2 to plug something new is to mention it so that people know about it: *The author plugged his new book during the interview.*

plum •NOUN• **plums** a soft red or yellow fruit with a smooth skin and a stone in the centre

plumage •NOUN• a bird's plumage is its covering of feathers

plumb •NOUN• **plumbs** a small weight that is hung on a string and used to test if a wall or other upright structure is straight
•VERB• **plumbs, plumbing, plumbed** 1 to plumb the depths of something is to reach its deepest or lowest point 2 to plumb in something like a washing machine is to connect it to the water supply
•ADJECTIVE• perfectly straight or vertical

plumber •NOUN• **plumbers** someone whose job is to fit and repair water, gas and sewage pipes
♦ **plumbing** •NOUN• 1 the work of a plumber 2 the plumbing in a building is the system of pipes that carry water and gas

plume •NOUN• **plumes** a long broad feather, or something that has the shape of a long broad feather: *ostrich plumes • a plume of smoke*
⇒ **plumage**

plummet •VERB• **plummets, plummeting, plummeted** to plummet is to fall very fast

Aa
Bb
Cc
Dd
Ee
Ff
Gg
Hh
Ii
Jj
Kk
Ll
Mm
Nn
Oo
Pp
Qq
Rr
Ss
Tt
Uu
Vv
Ww
Xx
Yy
Zz

Aa Bb Cc Dd Ee Ff Gg Hh Ii Jj Kk Ll Mm Nn Oo Pp Qq Rr Ss Tt Uu Vv Ww Xx Yy Zz

plump • ADJECTIVE• **plumper, plumpest** fat or rounded, in a pleasant way: *plump rosy cheeks*
• VERB• **plumps, plumping, plumped 1** to plump up cushions or pillows is to squash and shake them so that they become rounded **2** to **plump for** something is to choose it

plunder • VERB• **plunders, plundering, plundered** to plunder is to rob or steal from a place, especially taking everything valuable that is there
• NOUN• plundering, or the things got by plundering

plunge • VERB• **plunge, plunging, plunged 1** to plunge is to dive: *He plunged off the high board.* • *She plunged into the crowd, pushing her way through.*
2 to plunge something into water is to push it quickly into the water so that it is covered **3** to plunge something into something else is to push it violently or suddenly into that thing: *The pirate plunged his dagger into the sack, spilling the contents all over the deck.*
• NOUN• **plunges** a dive, or a pool for diving into

plural • NOUN• **plurals** a plural is the form of a noun, pronoun, adjective or verb that you use when there is more than one of something. For example, *feet* is the plural of *foot* and *toes* is the plural of *toe*. See the box called **Plurals**
• ADJECTIVE• in the plural form

plus • PREPOSITION• **1** adding: *8 plus 2 is 10* **2** as well as: *There are six children, plus two adults.*
• ADJECTIVE• **1** more than zero: *plus ten degrees* **2** plus is used after a letter or number to show that a mark or number is more than the mark or number indicated by the letter or number alone: *He got a B plus for his project.* • *You have to be 60 plus to join the club.*
• NOUN• **pluses** a plus, or plus sign (+), is a mathematical symbol showing that a number is to be added to another

plush • ADJECTIVE• **plusher, plushest** plush places are very smart, elegant and expensive

ply • NOUN• **plies 1** a thickness, layer or

strand: *two-ply wool* **2** plywood

plywood • NOUN• a material made up of thin layers of wood glued together

PM • ABBREVIATION• short for **prime minister**

pm *or* **p.m.** • ABBREVIATION• short for **post meridiem** which is Latin for 'after midday'. **pm** is added after the time to show that the time is the afternoon or evening rather than the morning, for example *2pm*. Look up and compare **am**

pneumatic • ADJECTIVE• **1** filled with air: *pneumatic tyres* **2** worked by air pressure or compressed air: *a pneumatic drill*

pneumonia • NOUN• a serious illness of the lungs caused by infection, which makes breathing difficult and can be fatal

poach • VERB• **poaches, poaching, poached 1** to hunt and kill fish, birds or animals without permission on someone else's land **2** to poach food is to cook it by heating it gently in water or some other liquid
• **poacher** • NOUN• **poachers** someone who hunts and kills fish or game illegally

pocket • NOUN• **pockets 1** an extra piece of cloth sewn into a piece of clothing and used for keeping small items in, like money or keys **2** any pouch-like container, such as in a suitcase or car door, or at the sides of a billiard or snooker table **3** the amount of money you have or can afford: *presents to suit every pocket* **4** a small isolated area or group: *pockets of mist*
• **out of pocket** you are out of pocket when you have spent money, usually without getting any benefit
• VERB• **pockets, pocketing, pocketed** to pocket something is to put it in your pocket, or to take it and keep it for yourself, especially dishonestly

pocket-book • NOUN• **pocket-books** a wallet

pocket money • NOUN• an allowance of money that you get or use for buying small personal items or things like sweets and magazines

pockmark • NOUN• **pockmarks** a scar or dent left in the skin by a disease or spots

Plurals

The **plural** of a noun is used when there is more than one.

- You can turn most nouns into plurals by adding **-s**:
  books, cats, hands, lions, nails, shoes, stars, tables

- You add **-es** to nouns ending in **-ch**, **-s**, **-sh**, or **-x**:

watch	→	watches	clash	→	clashes
bus	→	buses	fox	→	foxes

- You add **-s** to some words ending with **-o** and **-es** to others. Be sure to check in the dictionary which is which:

-s			**-es**		
video	→	videos	hero	→	heroes
zoo	→	zoos	potato	→	potatoes

- You change some words ending in **-f** or **-fe** to **-ves**:

half	→	halves	knife	→	knives
leaf	→	leaves	life	→	lives

There are a few words that do not become plurals this way, for example **beliefs** and **roofs**. If you are not sure, look up the word in the dictionary.

- If nouns end with a vowel (a, e, o, u) followed by **-y**, you add **-s**:

day	→	days	toy	→	toys
key	→	keys	guy	→	guys

- However, if nouns end with a consonant followed by **-y**, you change the **-y** to **-ies**:

baby	→	babies
country	→	countries

- Some common nouns have plurals that are formed in unusual ways, and you have to learn these separately:

child	→	children	mouse	→	mice
foot	→	feet	woman	→	women

- A few nouns are the same when they are singular and plural:

aircraft	→	aircraft	deer	→	deer
crossroads	→	crossroads	sheep	→	sheep

- Some nouns are usually or always plural. They are often a single tool or item of clothing that has two joined parts, for example:

binoculars	pliers	pyjamas	tights
glasses	scissors	shorts	trousers

Aa

Bb

Cc

Dd

Ee

Ff

Gg

Hh

Ii

Jj

Kk

Ll

Mm

Nn

Oo

Pp

Qq

Rr

Ss

Tt

Uu

Vv

Ww

Xx

Yy

Zz

pod • NOUN• **pods** a long narrow seed case that grows on plants like peas and beans

podgy • ADJECTIVE• **podgier, podgiest** slightly fat

podium • NOUN• **podiums** a small platform that someone stands on, for example an orchestra's conductor or a speaker at a public meeting

poem • NOUN• **poems** a piece of writing in imaginative language arranged in patterns of lines and sounds, often, but not always, rhyming

♦ **poet** • NOUN• **poets** someone who writes poetry

♦ **poetic** • ADJECTIVE• written in verse, or having qualities of beauty and imagination like poetry

♦ **poetry** • NOUN• poems as a group or as a form of literature. Look up and compare **prose**

poignant • ADJECTIVE• something poignant makes you feel great sadness or pity

point • NOUN• **points 1** a sharp end: *the point of a needle*
2 a small dot (.) used in decimal fractions
3 a particular place or a particular moment: *the highest point on the British mainland* • *At that point, we all burst out laughing.*
4 a mark used to score a competition, game or test: *Who got the highest number of points?*
5 your good points and bad points are your personal qualities or characteristics
6 a fact, idea or opinion that is a part of an argument or discussion, or the most important part of what is being said: *What's your point?*
7 the point of doing something is its purpose: *What's the point of going home if you just have to go straight back out again?*
• VERB• **points, pointing, pointed 1** to point is to stretch your finger in the direction of something to show other people what or where you mean
2 to point something is to aim it in a particular direction: *He pointed the toy gun at me.*
3 to **point to** something is to show that it is true or to explain it: *All the evidence points to an inside job.*

point-blank • ADJECTIVE AND ADVERB• **1** in an abrupt or rude way: *She refused point-blank to come.* **2** very close: *The gun was fired at point-blank range.*

pointed • ADJECTIVE• with a sharp end: *a pointed stick*

pointer • NOUN• **pointers 1** a long instrument used to point at things, for example on a wall map or blackboard **2** the needle on a dial

pointless • ADJECTIVE• having no purpose or meaning: *a pointless argument*

point of view • NOUN• **points of view** your point of view is the way you look at things

poise • NOUN• **1** to have poise is to have dignity and self-confidence **2** poise is balance
• VERB• **poises, poising, poised** to be poised somewhere is to balance there ready to move or take off: *He was poised on the edge of the diving board.*
♦ **poised** • ADJECTIVE• someone who is poised is dignified and self-confident

poison • NOUN• **poisons** any substance that causes death or illness when taken into your body
• VERB• **poisons, poisoning, poisoned 1** to poison is to kill or harm with poison **2** to poison something is to add poison to it
♦ **poisonous** • ADJECTIVE• **1** a poisonous substance causes illness or death when taken into your body: *This cleaning liquid is poisonous.* **2** producing poison: *a poisonous snake*

poke • VERB• **pokes, poking, poked 1** to poke is to push something sharp into something: *He poked me in the ribs.* **2** to poke something through a gap or hole is to stick it through: *She poked her head through the hatch.*
• NOUN• **pokes** a sharp prod
♦ **poker** • NOUN• **1** a heavy metal rod used for moving wood or coal about in a fire **2** poker is a card game played for money

poky • ADJECTIVE• **pokier, pokiest** a poky place is small and uncomfortable

polar • ADJECTIVE• at or to do with the north or south pole

polar bear • NOUN• **polar bears** a large

white bear that lives in the Arctic

polaroid •NOUN• **polaroids** a type of photograph that is developed inside the camera. This word is a trademark

pole[1] •NOUN• **poles** a long thin rounded piece of wood or metal

pole[2] •NOUN• **poles 1** the north and south pole are the two points on the Earth at the north and south end of its axis **2** either of the opposite ends of a magnet

pole cat •NOUN• **pole cats** an animal like a large weasel

pole star •NOUN• the star that is directly above the north pole

pole vault •NOUN• **pole vaults** an athletic event in which competitors try to jump over a high bar by pushing themselves up and over it with a long flexible pole

police •NOUN• the police are the people whose job is to prevent crime, keep order and see that laws are obeyed

policeman •NOUN• **policemen** a male police officer

police officer •NOUN• **police officers** a member of the police, both the uniformed officers and detectives in plain clothes

police station •NOUN• **police stations** a building where the police have their offices and where people are taken when they are arrested

policewoman •NOUN• **policewomen** a female police officer

policy •NOUN• **policies** a planned or agreed course of action: *It is not the school's policy to have a uniform.*

polio •NOUN• polio is a serious disease that affects the nerves and muscles and can cause paralysis. Nowadays, polio is very rare because most children are vaccinated against it

polish •VERB• **polishes, polishing, polished 1** to polish something is to rub it until it shines **2** to **polish something off** is to finish it completely
•NOUN• **polishes** a substance used to polish wood or metal

polite •ADJECTIVE• **politer, politest** a polite

person has good manners
♦ **politely** •ADVERB• in a well-mannered way: *'Would you like a seat?' he asked her politely.*
♦ **politeness** •NOUN• being polite

political •ADJECTIVE• to do with politics, politicians or government

politician •NOUN• **politicians** someone involved in politics, especially someone who tries to get elected to a parliament or local council

politics •NOUN• politics is the study of the ways in which countries are governed, or the work of governing a country

polka •NOUN• **polkas** a kind of fast lively dance, or music for this dance

poll •NOUN• **polls 1** a political election in which people vote, or the number of votes cast in an election **2** a poll is a survey of people picked at random to find out what the general public opinion of something is

pollen •NOUN• the powder, often yellow, that a flower releases and which fertilizes the female part of the plant

pollinate •VERB• **pollinates, pollinating, pollinated** a plant is pollinated when pollen fertilizes it and its fruit and seeds begin to form
♦ **pollination** •NOUN• when pollen from a male flower lands on the female part of a plant and fruit and seeds begin to form

pollute •VERB• **pollutes, polluting, polluted** to pollute the air, the soil or a river is to release harmful substances into it
♦ **pollution** •NOUN• the release of harmful chemicals and other substances into the air, water or soil

polo •NOUN• a game played on horseback by two teams of players who hit a ball along the ground using long-handled hammers called mallets

polo neck •NOUN• **polo necks** a jumper with a high round neck

poltergeist •NOUN• **poltergeists** a type of ghost that is believed to move or throw solid objects around, or cause strange things to happen in a house

poly- •PREFIX• if **poly-** comes at the

Aa

beginning of a word it adds the meaning *many* to the word. For example, a *polygon* is a figure with many sides and angles

Bb

polyester • NOUN• polyester is a man-made fabric used for making clothes

Cc

polygon • NOUN• **polygons** a figure or shape with three or more sides and angles

Dd

♦ **polygonal** • ADJECTIVE• having many sides and many angles

Ee

Ff

polyhedron • NOUN• **polyhedrons** a solid shape with many sides

Gg

polymer • NOUN• **polymers** a chemical compound, such as nylon, with large molecules made up of identical smaller molecules bonded together

Hh

Ii

polystyrene • NOUN• a very light plastic substance like stiff foam, used for packaging and insulation

Jj

Kk

polythene • NOUN• a very thin plastic material used for making bags, light containers and protective coverings

Ll

Mm

pomp • NOUN• pomp is solemn and splendid display or ceremony

Nn

pompous • ADJECTIVE• a pompous person is too full of their own importance

Oo

poncho • NOUN• **ponchos** a loose piece of clothing covering the shoulders and top half of the body which has a hole for your head to go through

Pp

Qq

pond • NOUN• **ponds** a small area of water, smaller than a lake and larger than a pool

Rr

Ss

ponder • VERB• **ponders, pondering, pondered** to think about something carefully and for a long time

Tt

pontoon • NOUN• a card game where you try to gather cards that add up to 21

Uu

pony • NOUN• **ponies** a type of small horse

Vv

pony-tail • NOUN• **pony-tails** a hairstyle in which the hair is gathered up at the back of the head and tied so that it hangs down like a tail

Ww

Xx

Yy

pony-trekking • NOUN• travelling across the countryside, often for quite long distances, on ponies

Zz

poodle • NOUN• **poodles** a breed of dog with curly hair, often clipped in a fancy way

pool¹ • NOUN• **pools** 1 a pond or puddle, or any other small area of still water 2 a swimming pool

pool² • NOUN• **pools** 1 a group of people or things shared by several people: *a typing pool* • *a car pool* 2 the money played for in a gambling game
• VERB• **pools, pooling, pooled** to pool things is to put them all together into one large fund or group that everyone can use or benefit from

poor • ADJECTIVE• **poorer, poorest** 1 a poor person has very little money or property 2 of a low standard: *a poor imitation* 3 you call a person or animal 'poor' when you think they deserve pity or sympathy: *The poor little thing is all wet.*
♦ **poorly** • ADVERB• 1 badly: *a poorly lit passage* 2 ill: *Gran's feeling a bit poorly.*

pop¹ • NOUN• **pops** 1 a sudden sound like a small explosion 2 fizzy drink
• VERB• **pops, popping, popped** 1 to pop is to make a sudden sound like a small explosion 2 something pops out when it comes out suddenly

pop² • NOUN• popular music

popadom or **popadum** or **poppadom** • NOUN• **popadoms** in Indian cookery, a very thin circle of dough fried in oil until it is crisp

popcorn • NOUN• the seeds of maize that burst open into crisp fluffy balls when they are heated

pope • NOUN• **popes** the head of the Catholic Church
⇒ **papal**

poppy • NOUN• **poppies** a tall flower that grows wild in fields and has broad, flat, red petals

popular • ADJECTIVE• something that is popular is liked by a lot of people
♦ **popularity** • NOUN• the popularity of something is how many people like it
♦ **popularize** or **popularise** • VERB• **popularizes, popularizing, popularized** to popularize something is to make it popular

populate • VERB• **populates, populating, populated** people or animals populate an area when they live there

428

✦ **populated** •ADJECTIVE• a populated area has a lot of people living in it

✦ **population** •NOUN• **populations** the population of an area is the number or type of people living in it

porcelain • NOUN AND ADJECTIVE• a type of fine china, used to make crockery and ornaments: *a porcelain doll*

porch •NOUN• **porches** a small roofed entrance to a building

porcupine •NOUN• **porcupines** an animal that has lots of long sharp spines called quills growing on its back

pore[1] •NOUN• **pores** one of the tiny openings in your skin that sweat comes out of

pore[2] •VERB• **pores, poring, pored** to **pore over** books or documents is to read them very closely and carefully giving them your full attention
⇒ **porous**

pork •NOUN• meat from a pig

porous •ADJECTIVE• a porous material lets liquids and gases pass through it

porpoise •NOUN• **porpoises** a large sea mammal, similar to a dolphin but with a shorter and rounder nose

porridge •NOUN• a food made by boiling oats in water and often eaten for breakfast

port •NOUN• **ports** 1 a place where ships can load and unload, or shelter during stormy weather 2 a town or city which has harbours
•ADJECTIVE• the port side of a ship or aircraft is the left side when you are facing the front. Look up and compare **starboard**

portable •ADJECTIVE• something portable can be carried around

portcullis •NOUN• **portcullises** a kind of spiked gate, found in some old castles, that slides downwards from above

porter •NOUN• **porters** 1 someone whose job is to carry baggage for people at railway stations or on long treks 2 a doorman or caretaker at a college, office or factory

portfolio •NOUN• **portfolios** 1 a flat case for carrying papers or drawings 2 an artist's portfolio is a collection of drawings, paintings or sketches that represent their work

porthole •NOUN• **portholes** a round window in a ship's or boat's side

portion •NOUN• **portions** a portion of something is one of several pieces or parts it can be or is divided into: *a portion of land*

portly •ADJECTIVE• **portlier, portliest** a portly person is rather fat, especially round their middle

portrait •NOUN• **portraits** 1 a painting, drawing or photograph of a person 2 a description in words of a person, place or thing

portray •VERB• **portrays, portraying, portrayed** 1 to portray a person or thing is to make a picture or written description of them or it 2 an actor portrays a person or an emotion when they act the part of that person or act out that emotion

✦ **portrayal** •NOUN• **portrayals** a description or representation of something, especially in words

pose •VERB• **poses, posing, posed** 1 to pose for a photo or portrait is to stay in a particular position so that the photographer or artist can take or paint your picture

2 to pose as something is to pretend to be that person or thing: *a thief posing as a gas repair man*

3 to pose a question or problem is to ask a question or put a problem to someone
•NOUN• **poses** 1 a particular position into which you put your body 2 pretence or exaggerated behaviour intended to impress people: *He's not tough at all. It's all just a pose.*

✦ **poser** •NOUN• **posers** 1 a poser is a question or problem that is difficult to answer or solve 2 someone who pretends to be something they are not, just to impress other people

posh •ADJECTIVE• **posher, poshest** 1 a posh place is very smart and expensive 2 a posh person is from a high social class

position •NOUN• **positions** 1 a place or situation: *The sentry had an all-round view from his position high in the tower.* • *This puts me in a very difficult position.*

Aa
Bb
Cc
Dd
Ee
Ff
Gg
Hh
Ii
Jj
Kk
Ll
Mm
Nn
Oo
Pp
Qq
Rr
Ss
Tt
Uu
Vv
Ww
Xx
Yy
Zz

2 a way of standing, sitting or lying: *sleeping in an awkward position*

3 a job or post: *He applied for a position as a butler.*

•VERB• **positions, positioning, positioned** if you position an object, or yourself, somewhere, you place or put it, or yourself, there

positive •ADJECTIVE• **1** you are positive about something when you are very sure about it

2 a positive answer or response means or says 'yes'

3 to have a positive attitude is to feel hopeful and confident

4 a positive number is one that is greater than zero

5 a positive electric charge does not carry electrons

• **positively** •ADVERB• completely or absolutely: *He was positively seething with rage.*

posse •NOUN• **posses** a group of people, usually including an officer of the law, who chase a criminal who is on the run

possess •VERB• **possesses, possessing, possessed** to possess something is to have it or own it

• **possessed** •ADJECTIVE• someone who is possessed is being controlled by an emotion or an evil spirit

• **possession** •NOUN• **possessions 1** possession is having or owning something **2** your possessions are the things you have or own

• **possessive** •ADJECTIVE• **1** a possessive person is not willing to share the things they have with other people **2** in grammar, a possessive is a word that shows who or what a person or thing belongs to. For example, *my*, *yours* and *theirs*, and nouns with *'s* added at the end, are possessives. See the box called **Possessives**

possibility •NOUN• **possibilities** something that is possible

possible •ADJECTIVE• **1** something that is possible can happen, or may happen: *It isn't possible for human beings to travel to the planets yet.* **2** something that is possible may be true: *It's possible I made a mistake.*

• **possibly** •ADVERB• perhaps: *Possibly I was wrong.*

post¹ •NOUN• **posts** a long piece of wood or metal fixed upright in the ground

post² •NOUN• the postal service, which collects and delivers letters and parcels, or the letters and parcels sent or delivered by this service: *I sent it by post, not by fax.* • *Has the morning post arrived yet?* •VERB• **posts, posting, posted** to post a letter or parcel is to send it by the postal service, for example by taking it to the post office or putting it in a postbox
⇒ **postage, postal**

post³ •NOUN• **posts 1** a job: *He was dismissed from his post.* **2** a place where someone, such as a soldier or security guard, is on duty
•VERB• **posts, posting, posted** if someone is posted somewhere they are sent there for a while to work

post- •PREFIX• if **post-** comes at the beginning of a word it adds the meaning *after* to the word. For example, *postwar* means 'after a war'

postage •NOUN• the amount of money you have to pay to send a letter or parcel through the post

postage stamp •NOUN• **postage stamps** a small printed label stuck on letters and parcels to show that the postage has been paid

postal •ADJECTIVE• to do with the service that collects and delivers letters and parcels

postal order •NOUN• **postal orders** a piece of paper that you buy at the post office which represents a certain sum of money, and which is a safe way of sending money through the post

postbox •NOUN• **postboxes** a box in a public place where letters can be posted

postcard •NOUN• **postcards** a card for writing messages on that you can send through the post without an envelope

post code •NOUN• **post codes** a special series of letters and numbers at the end of an address that helps the postal service to sort letters and parcels

---

Possessives

An apostrophe plus **s** added to a noun shows ownership. It makes the noun **possessive**.

my **mother's** purse = the purse *belonging to* my mother

Where the apostrophe goes depends upon whether the noun is singular or plural.

Singular possessives

Add **'s** when only one person or thing has something:

Joe's hat   the **girl's** coat   a **week's** holiday

Even if the singular noun ends with an **s**, add **'s**:

James's jacket   the **boss's** jacket

Plural possessives

When more than one person or thing has something, add **'** (an apostrophe alone) to plural words ending with **s**:

the **boys'** boots   her **parents'** car   the **Frasers'** house

Add **'s** to plural words that do not end with **s**:

the **children's** room   **women's** clothes   **sheep's** wool

---

poster •NOUN• **posters** a large notice in a public place advertising something or giving information

posterior •ADJECTIVE• at the back or rear: *in a posterior position*
•NOUN• **posteriors** 1 the back of something 2 your posterior is your bottom

postman •NOUN• **postmen** someone who delivers letters and parcels to people's houses or businesses

postmark •NOUN• **postmarks** the postmark on a letter or parcel is a stamp put on it by the post office showing the date when it was posted and the place it was posted

postmaster •NOUN• **postmasters** a man who is in charge of running a post office

postmistress •NOUN• **postmistresses** a woman who is in charge of running a post office

post mortem •NOUN• **post mortems** a medical examination of a dead body to find out the cause of death

post office •NOUN• **post offices** a place where you can post letters and parcels, buy stamps and use various other postal services

postpone •VERB• **postpones, postponing, postponed** to postpone something is to put it off until a later time
• **postponement** •NOUN• **postponements** putting something off until a later time

postscript •NOUN• **postscripts** if a letter has a postscript, it has an extra message under the writer's signature, usually with the abbreviation **PS** before it

posture •NOUN• **postures** your posture is the way you usually stand, sit or walk

posy •NOUN• **posies** a small bunch of flowers

pot •NOUN• **pots** a deep container, often with a lid, used for cooking, holding liquids, for storing things like jam, or for growing plants in

potassium •NOUN• potassium is a soft, silvery-white metallic element

potato •NOUN• **potatoes** a round white or yellowish vegetable that grows underground

Aa
Bb
Cc
Dd
Ee
Ff
Gg
Hh
Ii
Jj
Kk
Ll
Mm
Nn
Oo
Pp
Qq
Rr
Ss
Tt
Uu
Vv
Ww
Xx
Yy
Zz

potency •NOUN• power or strength

potent •ADJECTIVE• powerful or strong: *a potent drug*

potential •ADJECTIVE• capable of developing into a particular thing: *He's a potential prime minister.*
•NOUN• your potential is the qualities you have that can be developed successfully

pothole •NOUN• **potholes** a hole in the road

potion •NOUN• **potions** a drink containing medicine or poison, or having a magic effect

pot-luck •NOUN• if you take pot-luck, you choose something from what is available or being offered without knowing exactly what you will get

potter[1] •VERB• **potters, pottering, pottered** to wander about doing small jobs or nothing very important

potter[2] •NOUN• **potters** someone who makes pottery and articles out of clay
✦ **pottery** •NOUN• **potteries** 1 pottery is things, such as jugs, bowls and ornaments, made out of baked clay 2 a pottery is a workshop or factory where things are made out of baked clay

potty[1] •NOUN• **potties** a deep container that a small child can sit on to go to the toilet

potty[2] •ADJECTIVE• **pottier, pottiest** someone who is potty is mad

pouch •NOUN• **pouches** 1 a small bag 2 the fold of skin that a female kangaroo carries her baby in

pouffe •NOUN• **pouffes** a low soft seat with no back or arms

poultry •NOUN• birds, such as chickens and turkeys, that are raised for us to eat

pounce •VERB• **pounces, pouncing, pounced** to jump forward suddenly to attack or catch hold of something: *The cat pounced on the mouse.*

pound •NOUN• **pounds** 1 the main unit of money in Britain, made up of 100 pence and usually written £ 2 a measure of weight, equal to 0.454 kilograms
•VERB• **pounds, pounding, pounded** to pound something is to hit it hard: *Someone was pounding at the door trying to get in.*

pour •VERB• **pours, pouring, poured** 1 to pour a liquid is to make it flow out of a container in a stream
2 to pour is to flow out fast and in large quantities
3 people or things pour in when they arrive in large numbers
4 if it is pouring it is raining heavily

pout •VERB• **pouts, pouting, pouted** if someone pouts, they push out their lips, or only their lower lip, because they are annoyed

poverty •NOUN• being poor

powder •NOUN• **powders** 1 a substance in the form of a fine dry dust 2 powder is a cosmetic that some women pat on their skin to make it look smooth
✦ **powdered** •ADJECTIVE• dried and made into a powder: *powdered milk*
✦ **powdery** •ADJECTIVE• made up of very small pieces or particles, like powder: *powdery snow*

power •NOUN• **powers** 1 power is strength or force
2 to have power is to have the ability or authority to control people or things: *political power*
3 to have the power to do something is to have the ability to do it: *He's lost the power of speech.*
4 power is any form of energy used to drive machines: *wind power* • *The power was cut off in the storm.*
5 in maths, the power of a number is the result you get by multiplying the number by itself a certain number of times, for example $2 \times 2 \times 2$ or 2^3 is the third power of 2, or 2 to the power of 3
•VERB• **powers, powering, powered** to power something is to provide it with the energy to work: *a machine powered by steam*
✦ **powerful** •ADJECTIVE• strong or having the ability to control other people
✦ **powerless** •ADJECTIVE• unable to control or affect things

power station •NOUN• **power stations** a building where electricity is made from coal, oil, gas or nuclear power

practical •ADJECTIVE• 1 something that is practical is useful or efficient: *a very practical solution to the problem* 2 a practical person is good at doing things rather than thinking about them
• NOUN• **practicals** an examination that tests practical ability and skill rather than theory

practical joke •NOUN• **practical jokes** a trick played on someone by doing something rather than using words

practically •ADVERB• almost: *It was practically full.*

practice •NOUN• **practices** 1 practice is doing something often so that you get better at it: *He'll soon get the hang of the violin with a bit more practice.*
2 to put a theory, plan or idea into practice is to do it
3 a doctor's or lawyer's practice is the place where they work

practise •VERB• **practises, practising, practised** 1 to practise something is to do it again and again so that you get better at it
2 to practise something is to make it a habit or to do it: *He practises yoga.*
3 a doctor or lawyer practises when they do their professional work

ⓘ Remember that **practice** with a **c** is a noun: *I need some **practice**.*
Practise with an **s** is a verb: *You must **practise** often.*

prairie •NOUN• **prairies** a large area of flat grassy land in North America

praise •VERB• **praises, praising, praised** to praise someone or something is to say how well they have done
• NOUN• **praises** praise is saying how good someone is or how well they have done

praiseworthy •ADJECTIVE• something is praiseworthy if it deserves praise

pram •NOUN• **prams** a small wheeled vehicle that a baby sits or lies in and which is pushed about by someone walking

prance •VERB• **prances, prancing, pranced** to prance is to dance or jump about

prank •NOUN• **pranks** a trick or practical joke

prattle •VERB• **prattles, prattling, prattled** to talk or chatter in a silly or meaningless way

prawn •NOUN• **prawns** a shellfish that looks like a large shrimp

pray •VERB• **prays, praying, prayed** 1 to speak to God 2 to pray for something is to hope and beg for it: *We were praying for a nice sunny day.*
◆ **prayer** •NOUN• **prayers** 1 prayer is praying: *They knelt in prayer.* 2 a prayer is the words that you use when you pray

ⓘ Try not to confuse the spelling of **pray** with **prey**, which is the creatures an animal hunts.

pre- •PREFIX• if **pre-** is added at the beginning of a word it adds the meaning *before* to the word. For example, *prehistoric* times are the times before history was written down

preach •VERB• **preaches, preaching, preached** 1 to talk about right and wrong, often as part of a religious service 2 to preach a particular thing is to speak in favour of it: *He preached patience and understanding.*
◆ **preacher** •NOUN• **preachers** someone who preaches or gives sermons

precarious •ADJECTIVE• in a risky or dangerous state or position: *Abruptly the path became steep and the footing became more precarious.*

precaution •NOUN• **precautions** something you do to avoid an accident or problem happening

precede •VERB• **precedes, preceding, preceded** one thing precedes another when it comes before that other thing
◆ **precedence** •NOUN• one person or thing takes precedence over another when they come before, or have the right to come before, the other
◆ **precedent** •NOUN• something that has happened in the past that guides or provides a rule for what should happen now or in the future
◆ **preceding** •ADJECTIVE• coming before

precinct •NOUN• **precincts** 1 an area of shops in the centre of a town or city where

Aa
Bb
Cc
Dd
Ee
Ff
Gg
Hh
Ii
Jj
Kk
Ll
Mm
Nn
Oo
Pp
Qq
Rr
Ss
Tt
Uu
Vv
Ww
Xx
Yy
Zz

Aa
Bb
Cc
Dd
Ee
Ff
Gg
Hh
Ii
Jj
Kk
Ll
Mm
Nn
Oo
Pp
Qq
Rr
Ss
Tt
Uu
Vv
Ww
Xx
Yy
Zz

no cars or motor vehicles are allowed **2** the precincts of a building are the areas within its boundaries or inside its walls: *the cathedral precincts*

precious •ADJECTIVE• **1** valuable or highly valued by someone: *precious stones* • *His books are very precious to him.* **2** precious little or precious few means very little or very few

precipice •NOUN• **precipices** a very steep cliff

precise •ADJECTIVE• **1** exact: *At that precise moment, the bell rang.* **2** careful and accurate: *Her work is very precise.*
♦ **precisely** •ADVERB• exactly: *Precisely when did he give you the letter?*
♦ **precision** •NOUN• being exact and accurate: *He hit the target again and again with precision.*

precocious •ADJECTIVE• a precocious child is more advanced than is usual for his or her age

predator •NOUN• **predators** an animal that hunts and eats other animals
♦ **predatory** •ADJECTIVE• hunting, killing and eating other animals

predecessor •NOUN• **predecessors** someone's predecessor in a job is the person who had the job before them

predicament •NOUN• **predicaments** if someone is in a predicament they are in a difficult situation

predict •VERB• **predicts, predicting, predicted** to predict something is to say that it will happen before it actually does happen
♦ **predictable** •ADJECTIVE• something that is predictable can be predicted
♦ **prediction** •NOUN• **predictions** predicting, or something that is predicted

predominant •ADJECTIVE• the predominant person or thing in a group is the one that stands out most: *The predominant colour in his paintings is blue.*
♦ **predominantly** •ADJECTIVE• mostly or mainly: *The trains are predominantly old, out-of-date, models.*

preen •VERB• **preens, preening, preened 1** a bird preens when it smoothes and cleans its

feathers **2** you preen yourself when you stroke your hair or adjust your appearance

preface •NOUN• **prefaces** the preface to a book is a short section at the beginning that introduces the rest of the book or the story

prefect •NOUN• **prefects** a senior pupil in a school who has been given some powers to help in the running of the school

prefer •VERB• **prefers, preferring, preferred** to prefer one thing to another is to like the first one better
♦ **preferable** •ADJECTIVE• if one thing is preferable to another you like it, or would like it, better than the other thing
♦ **preference** •NOUN• **preferences** your preferences are the things you like or prefer

prefix •NOUN• **prefixes** a letter or a group of letters that is added to the beginning of a word to make another word. See the box called **Prefixes**

pregnancy •NOUN• **pregnancies** being pregnant, or the time when a woman or female animal is pregnant
♦ **pregnant** •ADJECTIVE• a woman or female animal is pregnant when she is carrying an unborn baby in her womb

prehistoric •ADJECTIVE• belonging to the time before history was written down: *prehistoric cave paintings*

prejudice •NOUN• **prejudices** an unfair opinion or dislike of a person or thing without trying to understand that person or thing
•VERB• **prejudices, prejudicing, prejudiced** one thing prejudices another when it harms it or puts it in danger
♦ **prejudiced** •ADJECTIVE• having a prejudice or prejudices against a person or thing

preliminary •ADJECTIVE• preliminary things are said or done to prepare for a main event or what is to come next
•NOUN• **preliminaries** preliminaries are things said or done to prepare for a main event

premature •ADJECTIVE• **1** a premature baby is born before the time it should have been born **2** an action is premature when it is done too early

Prefixes

Prefixes are word parts that can be attached to the beginning of a word to create a completely new word with a different meaning.

Every prefix means something particular, for example:

re (again) + **visit** = **revisit**

un (not) + **dressed** = **undressed**

A list of prefixes

Prefix	Meaning	Examples
al-	all	almighty, always
arch-	chief	archbishop, archduke
ambi-	both	ambidextrous, ambiguous
auto-	self	autograph, autopilot
bi-	two	bicycle, bilingual
contra-, counter-	against	contrary, counterbalance
de-	take back or away	decode, deforest
dis-	the opposite of	dishonest, disagree
ex-	out of, outside	export, exclude
extra-	outside, more	extraordinary, extravagant
fore-	before, earlier	forecast, foretell, forefather
il-, im-, in-, ir-	not	illegal, impossible, invisible, irresponsible
inter-	between	international, interval
mis-	wrong	misbehave, misspell
multi-	many	multicoloured, multipurpose
non-	not	nonsense, nonstop
over-	too much	overweight, overwork, overheat
poly-	many	polygon, polyhedron
post-	after	post-war, postdate
pre-	before	prefix, prehistoric, premature
re-	again, repeated	rearrange, replace
semi-	half	semicircle
sub-	under	submarine, subway
super-	above, beyond	supernatural, supersonic
tele-	far, distant	telephone, television
trans-	across, beyond	transatlantic, transport, transfer
tri-	three	triangle, tricycle
un-	not	unable, undo
uni-	one	unicycle, uniform

Aa
Bb
Cc
Dd
Ee
Ff
Gg
Hh
Ii
Jj
Kk
Ll
Mm
Nn
Oo
Pp
Qq
Rr
Ss
Tt
Uu
Vv
Ww
Xx
Yy
Zz

premier •ADJECTIVE• leading or most important: *France's premier resort* •NOUN• **premiers** a prime minister

première •NOUN• **premières** the première of a film or play is its first public showing or performance

premises •PLURAL NOUN• the premises of a company or business are the buildings and land it uses

premium •NOUN• **premiums** a premium is a regular amount paid to an insurance company for insurance cover
• **at a premium** if something is at a premium it is difficult to get and so is more expensive

premonition •NOUN• **premonitions** a strange feeling that something is going to happen before it actually does happen

preoccupation •NOUN• **preoccupations** something you think about all or most of the time
• **preoccupied** •ADJECTIVE• thinking so much about one thing that you do not pay enough attention to other things
• **preoccupy** •VERB• **preoccupies, preoccupying, preoccupied** something preoccupies you when you think about it a lot

prep •NOUN• homework
•ADJECTIVE• short for **preparatory**, as in *prep school*

preparation •NOUN• **preparations** 1 preparing for something 2 something done to prepare for something: *preparations for the wedding*

preparatory •ADJECTIVE• preparing for something that comes later

prepare •VERB• **prepares, preparing, prepared** 1 to prepare is to get ready for something or get into a fit state to deal with it or do it 2 to prepare food is to do whatever is needed to make it ready for eating
• **prepared** •ADJECTIVE• 1 made ready in advance 2 you are prepared for something, or prepared to do something, when you are ready for it, or are willing to do it

preposition •PART OF SPEECH• **prepositions** a word put before a noun or pronoun to show how it is related or connected to another word or phrase in the same clause or sentence. For example, in the sentence *I put my schoolbooks in my bag*, the word *in* is a preposition. See the box called **Prepositions**

prepossessing •ADJECTIVE• attractive: *It's not a very prepossessing building.*

preposterous •ADJECTIVE• ridiculous: *What a preposterous suggestion!*

prep school •NOUN• **prep schools** a prep school is a private school for children, especially boys, between the ages of 7 and 13

prescribe •VERB• **prescribes, prescribing, prescribed** a doctor prescribes a drug for a patient when he or she tells the patient which drug to take
• **prescription** •NOUN• **prescriptions** an instruction from a doctor to a pharmacist stating what medicine should be prepared for a particular patient

presence •NOUN• 1 your presence somewhere is your being there 2 to do something in someone's presence is to do it while they are there

present[1] •NOUN• **presents** something given as a gift
•VERB• **presents, presenting, presented** 1 to present someone with something is to give it to them, usually as an award for good work or high achievement
2 you present one person to another when you introduce them
3 someone presents a radio or TV show when they introduce it
4 you present information when you communicate it to other people
5 something presents a problem when it becomes difficult to deal with
6 you present yourself somewhere when you go there and let someone know you have arrived

present[2] •NOUN• the present is the time now
•ADJECTIVE• 1 someone is present somewhere when they are there 2 to do with the time now: *the present day* • *pupils past and present*

presentation •NOUN• **presentations** the presenting of something such as a gift or a talk

Prepositions

Prepositions are words that link nouns or pronouns, often showing either where things are or when things happen.

Some prepositions show *direction* or *movement*:

The cat ran **out of** the house, **across** the road, **down** the hill, **into** the park, **past** the pond, **between** the flowerbeds, **along** the wall, **around** the flowerpots, **through** the tunnel and **toward** the shop.

Others show the *position* of things:

Pat lives **at** 66 Richmond Grove **in** London. Today, she is **at** home **in** her bedroom, asleep **in** bed **under** the bedclothes. Her shoes are **on** the floor, her clothes are **beside** the bed and her coat is hanging **behind** the door.

Some prepositions show *when* something happens:

He is arriving **at** 6 p.m.

It is cold **in** winter.

My birthday is **on** Tuesday.

I have been waiting **for** ten minutes.

I have known her **since** 1999.

No-one spoke **during** the performance.

The castle is open **from** April **until** October.

Aa
Bb
Cc
Dd
Ee
Ff
Gg
Hh
Ii
Jj
Kk
Ll
Mm
Nn
Oo
Pp
Qq
Rr
Ss
Tt
Uu
Vv
Ww
Xx
Yy
Zz

presently • ADVERB• **1** soon: *The bus should be here presently.* **2** just now: *Are you employed presently?*

present participle • NOUN• the form of a verb used after a helping verb such as *is* or *was* to show that something is or was taking place at that time. For example, *going* in *I am going to the shops* is a present participle

present tense • NOUN• the present tense of a verb is the form used to show that the action of the verb is happening here and now. For example, *throw* and *throws* in *I throw the ball and he throws it back* are present tense forms of the verb to *throw*

preservation • NOUN• preserving: *preservation of the rainforest*

preservative • NOUN• **preservatives** a substance that is put in food or on wood to stop it rotting

preserve •VERB• **preserves, preserving, preserved** to preserve something is to keep it as it is and stop it being lost or destroyed • NOUN• **preserves** a food, such as jam or bottled fruit, that has been boiled with sugar to stop it going bad

preside •VERB• **presides, presiding, presided** to preside over a meeting or formal event is to be in overall charge of it

presidency • NOUN• **presidencies** the position of being a president or the time when someone is a president

president • NOUN• **presidents 1** a president is the elected head of state in a republic **2** the president of a company or organization is the person with the top job in that company or organization

press •VERB• **presses, pressing, pressed 1** to press something is to push it or squeeze it

Aa
Bb
Cc
Dd
Ee
Ff
Gg
Hh
Ii
Jj
Kk
Ll
Mm
Nn
Oo
Pp
Qq
Rr
Ss
Tt
Uu
Vv
Ww
Xx
Yy
Zz

2 you press clothes when you iron them
3 to press for something is to be forceful in trying to get someone to agree to it
•NOUN• **presses 1** a pressing action
2 a press is a printing machine
3 newspapers and journalists are the press
⇒ **pressing**

pressgang •NOUN• **pressgangs** in historical times, a pressgang was a group of tough men who went around ports and seaside towns forcing men to join the navy

pressing •ADJECTIVE• a pressing problem is one that needs to be dealt with now or very soon

press-up •NOUN• **press-ups** a floor exercise in which you push the top half of your body up off the floor by pressing down with your hands and arms

pressure •NOUN• **pressures 1** the force on or against a surface by something pressing on it: *air pressure*
2 pressure is strong persuasion: *He put me under pressure to agree.*
3 pressures are the stresses and strains of life
♦ **pressurize** or **pressurise** •VERB• **pressurizes, pressurizing, pressurized 1** to pressurize an aeroplane or a diving bell is to keep the air pressure the same as that on the ground or at sea level **2** to pressurize someone into doing something is to force them to do it

prestige •NOUN• someone has prestige when they are highly thought of or have influence because of their rank or success

presumably •ADVERB• you say 'presumably' when you suppose something is true: *Presumably someone will be arranging the chairs before the concert.*

presume •VERB• **presumes, presuming, presumed** to presume something is to believe that it is true without having any proof
♦ **presumption** •NOUN• **presumptions** presuming, or something presumed
♦ **presumptuous** •ADJECTIVE• a presumptuous person takes too much for granted and behaves in a bold way

pretence •NOUN• pretending something

pretend •VERB• **pretends, pretending, pretended 1** to make believe that something is true as part of play: *Let's pretend we're submarine captains.* **2** someone pretends to be or to do something when they try to make people believe they are that person or have done that thing: *He pretends to be a major, but he was really only a sergeant.*
♦ **pretender** •NOUN• **pretenders**
1 someone who pretends **2** someone who claims the right to be king or queen of a country

pretext •NOUN• **pretexts** to do something on a pretext is to give a false reason for doing it

prettiness •NOUN• being pretty

pretty •ADJECTIVE• **prettier, prettiest** attractive to look at: *pretty flowers* • *a pretty little girl*
•ADVERB• quite: *a pretty good mark*
• **pretty much, pretty well, pretty nearly** almost: *My homework is pretty much finished.*

prevail •VERB• **prevails, prevailing, prevailed** to prevail is to win a contest or battle
♦ **prevailing** •ADJECTIVE• the prevailing winds are winds that blow most frequently in a part of the world

prevalence •NOUN• how prevalent something is
♦ **prevalent** •ADJECTIVE• common and widespread

prevent •VERB• **prevents, preventing, prevented** to prevent something happening is to stop it happening
♦ **prevention** •NOUN• preventing something
♦ **preventive** •ADJECTIVE• a preventive medicine stops you getting a disease or illness

preview •NOUN• **previews** a viewing of something before it is released or shown to the general public

previous •ADJECTIVE• happening earlier or at some time in the past
♦ **previously** •ADVERB• before or earlier

prey •NOUN• the creatures a predator hunts, kills and eats are its prey: *Small birds are the* usual prey of the sparrow hawk.

•VERB• **preys, preying, preyed** 1 to prey on something is to hunt it and kill it: *Lions prey on the vast herds of wildebeest and antelope in the Serengeti.* 2 if something preys on your mind, you cannot stop thinking or worrying about it

price •NOUN• **prices** the price of something is the amount of money it costs: *What price are your apples today?* • *Prices in the shops were rising.*

•VERB• **prices, pricing, priced** to price things is to find out how much they cost or to mark a price on them

♦ **pricey** •ADJECTIVE• **pricier, priciest** expensive: *Petrol is getting very pricey.*

♦ **priceless** •ADJECTIVE• 1 a priceless item is so valuable that it is not possible to put a price on it 2 very funny: *The surprised expression on his face was priceless.*

prick •VERB• **pricks, pricking, pricked** if something sharp pricks you, it sticks into your skin, hurting you

prickle •NOUN• **prickles** a short sharp spine, as on a hedgehog's back or on a bramble's stems

•VERB• **prickles, prickling, prickled** if something prickles, it pricks or makes your skin feel as if it is being pricked by lots of sharp little points

♦ **prickly** •ADJECTIVE• **pricklier, prickliest** covered in prickles or feeling like lots of sharp little spines

pride •NOUN• **prides** 1 pride is the feeling you get when you know you have, or someone you are connected with has, done something well: *His heart swelled with pride.*

2 pride is self-respect: *taking pride in her appearance*

3 a pride of lions is a family group of lions ⇒ **proud**

priest •NOUN• **priests** 1 a person who is qualified to conduct services in one of the Christian churches 2 a person with official duties of various kinds in other religions

♦ **priestess** •NOUN• **priestesses** a female priest in certain ancient or non-Christian religions

♦ **priesthood** •NOUN• the position of being

a priest, or priests as a group

prig •NOUN• **prigs** a rather old-fashioned word for someone who always behaves correctly and tends to find fault with other people's behaviour

♦ **priggish** •ADJECTIVE• behaving like a prig

prim •ADJECTIVE• **primmer, primmest** very formal and correct and easily shocked by rudeness

primary •ADJECTIVE• first or most important: *the primary route into the city*

primary colour •NOUN• **primary colours** the primary colours are the colours red, blue and yellow. Most other colours can be made by mixing two or more of the primary colours

primary school •NOUN• **primary schools** a school for children between the ages of 4 and 12

primate •NOUN• **primates** 1 primates are animals that belong to the group that includes monkeys, apes and humans 2 an archbishop

prime •ADJECTIVE• greatest or of the best quality: *a matter of prime importance* • *a prime cut of beef*
• NOUN• someone is in their prime when they are at the time of their life when they are at their best because they are experienced and wise and are still physically fit
•VERB• **primes, priming, primed** to prime something is to make it ready for the next stage: *Prime the wood before painting.*

prime minister •NOUN• **prime ministers** the leader of the government in Britain, and many other countries of the world

prime number •NOUN• **prime numbers** a number that cannot be divided equally by any number except itself and 1. For example, 3, 5, 7 and 11 are prime numbers, but 9 is not a prime number because it can be divided equally by 3

primitive •ADJECTIVE• 1 belonging to the earliest stages of development: *primitive man* • *a primitive kind of computer* 2 rough and unsophisticated: *The accommodation was pretty primitive.*

primrose •NOUN• **primroses** a wild plant

with groups of small pale yellow flowers growing from the centre of a cluster of long rounded leaves

prince •NOUN• **princes** the son or grandson of a king or queen, or the ruler of a principality

princess •NOUN• **princesses** the daughter or granddaughter of a king or queen, or the wife of a prince

principal •ADJECTIVE• most important: *Steel-making was the principal industry in the area.*
•NOUN• **principals** the head of a school, college or university

✦ **principally** •ADVERB• mainly or mostly: *She collects old toys, principally dolls.*

principle •NOUN• **principles** 1 a principle is a general rule that something is based on: *We follow the principle of first come, first served.* 2 your principles are the rules of behaviour that you live by: *It was against his principles to borrow money.*
• **in principle** to agree to something in principle is to agree with it in a general way, though you may not agree with all its details
• **on principle** if you do something on principle, you do it because you believe it is right

print •VERB• **prints, printing, printed** 1 to print a book or newspaper is to publish it
2 you print when you write words with each letter separate from the one next to it, not joined up: *Print your name at the top of the form.*
3 to print something, or to **print it out** from a computer, is to make a copy of it using a printing machine or a computer printer
•NOUN• **prints** 1 print is the words in a book or newspaper that have been made by a printing machine 2 a print is a mark, picture or design made by something pressing down on a surface

✦ **printer** •NOUN• **printers** 1 a machine that prints words and pictures 2 a person or company whose business is printing documents, books and newspapers

prior •ADJECTIVE• earlier or previous: *I couldn't go because I had a prior engagement.*

priority •NOUN• **priorities** something that has to be dealt with before other things

priory •NOUN• **priories** a building where a group of monks or nuns lives

prise •VERB• **prises, prising, prised** to prise something is to force it open, off or out, often using a flat tool as a lever: *He prised open the lid with a knife.*

prism •NOUN• **prisms** 1 a piece of glass with many different planes and angles that split light into its rainbow colours 2 a solid shape with parallel sides and two ends that are the same shape and size

prison •NOUN• **prisons** a building where criminals are kept

✦ **prisoner** •NOUN• **prisoners** 1 someone who is kept in prison as a punishment 2 someone who is locked up or kept from moving about freely, against their will

pristine •ADJECTIVE• something pristine is in perfect condition, shiny and new-looking

privacy •NOUN• being private: *A higher fence will give us a bit more privacy.*

private •ADJECTIVE• 1 belonging to and used by only one person, or a small group of people: *a private beach*
2 kept secret or away from people in general: *Our discussions must be strictly private.*
3 owned and run by individual people or companies, not the government: *private industry*
•NOUN• **privates** an ordinary soldier in the army

✦ **privately** •ADVERB• 1 secretly: *Privately, he thought they were all fools.* 2 away from other people: *Can we talk privately?*

privatization *or* **privatisation** •NOUN• the process by which a business owned and controlled by the government is sold to private individuals and companies

privatize *or* **privatise** •VERB• **privatizes, privatizing, privatized** to privatize a government-owned business is to sell it to private individuals and companies

privet •NOUN• a plant used in hedges

privilege •NOUN• **privileges** a special right or advantage given to only one person, or to only a few people

◆ **privileged** •ADJECTIVE• having advantages or privileges that other people do not have

prize •NOUN• **prizes** something won in a competition or given as a reward for good work
•VERB• **prizes, prizing, prized** to prize something is to value it very much

pro •NOUN• **pros** short for **professional**: *a golf pro*

pro- •PREFIX• 1 if **pro-** comes at the beginning of a word it adds the meaning *at the beginning* or *forward*. For example, a *prologue* is the part at the beginning of a play, and to *proceed* is to go forward 2 if **pro-** comes at the beginning of a word it adds the meaning *in favour of* or *supporting*. For example, to be *pro-Europe* is to support the European Union

probability •NOUN• **probabilities** the probability of something happening is how likely it is to happen: *What's the probability of seeing the eclipse clearly?*

probable •ADJECTIVE• likely: *A lit cigarette was the probable cause of the fire.*
◆ **probably** •ADVERB• likely to be the case, or likely to happen: *It's probably just a cold, rather than flu.* • *The weather forecast said we'd probably get rain in the afternoon.*

probation •NOUN• if someone is on probation, they are being watched to see if they behave or do a job well

probe •NOUN• **probes** 1 an investigation 2 a spacecraft with no people aboard that is sent into space to investigate things
•VERB• **probes, probing, probed** to investigate a matter thoroughly by asking questions and examining evidence

problem •NOUN• **problems** 1 a situation, matter or person that causes difficulties, or is difficult to deal with: *There's a problem with the car. It won't start.* 2 a puzzle or question that has to be solved: *The teacher set us the problem of calculating how much water the tank would hold.*
◆ **problematic** •ADJECTIVE• causing problems

procedure •NOUN• **procedures** a way of doing something or the order in which things

are done: *What's the procedure for logging on to the Internet?*

proceed •VERB• **proceed, proceeding, proceeded** to proceed is to go on or go forward: *Let's proceed to the next chapter.*
◆ **proceedings** •PLURAL NOUN• things done or said: *A power cut interrupted proceedings.*
◆ **proceeds** •PLURAL NOUN• the proceeds from a sale or fund-raising event are all the money made from it

process •NOUN• **processes** 1 the series of stages or events that have to be gone through to achieve or do something 2 to be in the process of doing something is to be in the middle of doing it
•VERB• **processes, processing, processed** to process something is to deal with it in a number of stages
◆ **procession** •NOUN• **processions** a line of people or vehicles moving along one behind the other

proclaim •VERB• **proclaims, proclaiming, proclaimed** to proclaim something is to announce it publicly
◆ **proclamation** •NOUN• **proclamations** a public announcement of something important

prod •VERB• **prods, prodding, prodded** to prod something is to poke at it roughly

prodigal •ADJECTIVE• to be prodigal is to spend or waste money

prodigy •NOUN• **prodigies** a wonderfully clever or talented person, especially a young person

produce •VERB• **produces, producing, produced** 1 to produce something is to make, grow or create it: *factories producing goods for export* • *Will the tree produce fruit this year?* • *The sun produces both light and heat.*
2 to produce something is to bring it out or bring it forward so that people can see it: *The conjuror produced a rabbit from a hat.*
3 to produce a film or play is to arrange for it to be made and shown to the public
•NOUN• produce is things grown or produced on farms
◆ **producer** •NOUN• **producers** 1 someone

Aa
Bb
Cc
Dd
Ee
Ff
Gg
Hh
Ii
Jj
Kk
Ll
Mm
Nn
Oo
Pp
Qq
Rr
Ss
Tt
Uu
Vv
Ww
Xx
Yy
Zz

Aa
Bb
Cc
Dd
Ee
Ff
Gg
Hh
Ii
Jj
Kk
Ll
Mm
Nn
Oo
Pp
Qq
Rr
Ss
Tt
Uu
Vv
Ww
Xx
Yy
Zz

who arranges for a film, television programme or play to be made, by organizing all the equipment, sets and actors, and the money to pay for them **2** someone who makes products or grows produce to be sold: *meat producers*

ⓘ The verb **produce** is pronounced pro-**duce**, with the stress on *duce*. The noun is pronounced **pro**-duce, with the stress on *pro*.

product • NOUN• **products** **1** something that is produced, either by manufacturing it or growing it on a farm
  2 one thing is the product of another when it is the result of that other thing
  3 in maths, the product is the result you get when you multiply two numbers: *144 is the product of 12 multiplied by 12, or 4 multiplied by 36.*
  • **production** • NOUN• **productions** **1** making, growing or producing something, or the amount that is produced **2** a version of a play, opera or ballet
  • **productive** • ADJECTIVE• **1** producing a lot: *a productive piece of land* **2** giving good or useful results: *a productive meeting*
  • **productivity** • NOUN• the rate at which goods are made or produced, or the rate at which one person works to produce something

profession • NOUN• **professions** a profession is a job or occupation that needs special qualifications and training, such as medicine, law, teaching and engineering
  • **professional** • ADJECTIVE• **1** to do with a profession: *professional training*
  2 doing something for money rather than as a hobby or as an amateur: *a professional footballer*
  3 someone who is professional does their job with skill and care: *She is always very calm and professional.*
  • **professionally** • ADVERB• in a professional way, or for money rather than as an amateur: *a professionally qualified accountant* • *He used to play football professionally.*

professor • NOUN• **professors** **1** the head of a university department **2** in the United States, a professor is a teacher in a university or college

proficiency • NOUN• the level of skill you have reached in doing something
  • **proficient** • ADJECTIVE• good at something that needs skill or practice: *He's proficient in several languages.*

profile • NOUN• **profiles** **1** a person's profile is the shape of their face seen from the side **2** a profile of someone is a short description of their life

profit • NOUN• **profits** to make a profit is to make money by selling something for more than you paid for it
  • VERB• **profits, profiting, profited** to profit from something is to benefit from it
  • **profitable** • ADJECTIVE• making a good profit

profound • ADJECTIVE• **1** very deep: *a profound silence* **2** something said or written is profound if it shows great knowledge and deep thought
  • **profoundly** • ADVERB• deeply: *I was profoundly shocked by what she said.*

program • NOUN• **programs** a set of coded instructions put into a computer that allows the computer to perform a task
  • VERB• **programs, programming, programmed** to program a computer is to put a program into it which will control how it works or what it does with data

programme • NOUN• **programmes** **1** a show on TV or radio
  2 a leaflet or thin book that gives information and details about an event
  3 a list of planned events or actions: *a programme of exercise*

progress • NOUN• **1** progress is forward movement: *The bus made very slow progress on the wet and winding roads.* **2** progress is improvement: *Freya has made a lot of progress in the last year.*
  • VERB• **progresses, progressing, progressed** **1** to go forward: *They progressed slowly up the icy ridge.* **2** to develop or improve: *Things are progressing nicely.*
  • **progression** • NOUN• going forward, or forward movement
  • **progressive** • ADJECTIVE• progressive

ideas look forward to the future

prohibit •VERB• **prohibits, prohibiting, prohibited** to prohibit something is to forbid it

♦ **prohibition** •NOUN• **prohibitions** a law or order forbidding something

♦ **prohibitive** •ADJECTIVE• the cost of something is prohibitive if it is so expensive you cannot buy it

project •NOUN• **projects** 1 a piece of work done by a pupil or student, often involving study and research 2 a plan: *What's his next project going to be?*
•VERB• **projects, projecting, projected** 1 to stick or jut out
2 to project a film is to show it by running it through a projector
3 to project your voice is to make it carry over a long distance, especially to the back of a theatre

♦ **projection** •NOUN• **projections** 1 a projection is something that sticks or juts out 2 projection is projecting something, especially films

projectionist •NOUN• **projectionists** someone who operates a film projector, especially in a cinema

projector •NOUN• **projectors** a machine used to project films on to a screen by focussing a beam of light behind the film through a lens

prologue •NOUN• **prologues** a short introductory part at the beginning of a play, story or poem

prolong •VERB• **prolongs, prolonging, prolonged** to prolong something is to make it go on for longer

prom • NOUN• **proms** a promenade

promenade •NOUN• **promenades** a broad path or pavement for people to walk along, especially on the sea front in a town by the sea
•VERB• **promenades, promenading, promenaded** to walk, especially in a relaxed way for pleasure

prominence •NOUN• being prominent, or something that is prominent

♦ **prominent** •ADJECTIVE• 1 standing out or easily seen: *prominent teeth* • *a prominent*

landmark 2 a prominent person is famous: *a prominent writer*

promise •VERB• **promises, promising, promised** 1 you promise when you say that you will, or will not, do something: *I promise to be good.*
2 you promise something to someone when you say that you will give them something or help them in some way: *Sorry, you can't have this game. I promised it to Vishal.*
3 something promises something good when it shows signs of being good or successful: *It promises to be another lovely day tomorrow.*
• NOUN• **promises** 1 something promised: *Make me a promise that you won't be late.*
2 if someone or something shows promise they show signs of future success

♦ **promising** •ADJECTIVE• showing promise

promote •VERB• **promotes, promoting, promoted** 1 to promote someone is to move them to a higher ranking job 2 to promote something is to work to spread and encourage it, or to make it popular: *His aim was to promote peace amongst nations.*
• *This month, we're promoting a new range of make-up.*

♦ **promotion** •NOUN• **promotions** 1 if someone gets a promotion they are given a higher ranking job 2 special advertising, designed to make a product popular

prompt • ADJECTIVE• someone is prompt when they do something without delay
•VERB• **prompts, prompting, prompted** 1 to prompt someone to do something is to cause or encourage them to do it 2 to prompt an actor is to tell them the line that they have to say next

♦ **promptly** • ADVERB• without delay
♦ **promptness** •NOUN• being prompt

prone • ADJECTIVE• 1 you are prone to something if you are likely to suffer from it: *He's prone to headaches.* 2 someone who is prone is lying flat, especially face down

prong •NOUN• **prongs** a spike of a fork
♦ **pronged** • ADJECTIVE• having prongs

pronoun • PART OF SPEECH• **pronouns** a word that can be used in place of a noun or a noun phrase. For example, in the sentence *Gary ate the ice cream cone*, *Gary* and *the ice cream cone* could be changed to pronouns and the sentence would be *He ate it*. See the box called **Pronouns**

pronounce • VERB • **pronounces, pronouncing, pronounced** 1 to pronounce words or letters is to say them: *The two 'z's in pizza are pronounced 'tz'*. 2 to pronounce something is to declare it formally and publicly

♦ **pronounced** • ADJECTIVE • noticeable: *He had a pronounced limp.*
⇒ **pronunciation**

pronto • ADVERB • to do something pronto is to do it as fast as possible

pronunciation • NOUN • **pronunciations** pronouncing words, or the way a word is pronounced

proof • NOUN • **proofs** evidence that shows definitely that something is true

-proof • SUFFIX • when **-proof** comes at the end of a word it means 'protected against'. For example, a *waterproof* or *showerproof* coat does not let in water or rain

prop • NOUN • **props** 1 a heavy piece of wood or metal used to hold a building or other structure up 2 props are the pieces of furniture and other objects used on a stage or on a film set to help make a scene look real • VERB • **props, propping, propped** 1 to prop something against an upright surface is to lean it there

2 you **prop yourself up** when you support yourself, for example, with your elbows or with a pillow

3 to **prop something up** is to use a prop or props to stop it falling down

propaganda • NOUN • propaganda is ideas, news or opinions that are spread by a political group or by one side in a war, in order to influence people

propel • VERB • **propels, propelling, propelled** to propel something is to drive it forward, often using an engine or some other source of power

♦ **propeller** • NOUN • **propellers** a shaft with revolving blades that drives a ship or aeroplane forward

proper • ADJECTIVE • 1 right or correct: *Is this the proper way to fold a shirt?*
2 complete or thorough: *She gave the house a proper spring-clean.*
3 well-mannered and well-behaved: *a very proper young man*

♦ **properly** • ADVERB • correctly: *Sit up properly in your chair.*

proper noun • NOUN • **proper nouns** a noun that names a particular person, place or thing. Proper nouns usually begin with a capital letter, for example *Marianne*, *Mauritius*, *Mississippi* and *March*

property • NOUN • **properties** your property is something that belongs to you

prophecy • NOUN • **prophecies** if someone makes a prophecy they say that something will happen at some time in the future

prophesy • VERB • **prophesies, prophesying, prophesied** to say what will happen in the future

prophet • NOUN • **prophets** 1 someone who claims to be able to predict what will happen in the future 2 prophets are believed by some to be people chosen by God to communicate God's will to the people on Earth

proportion • NOUN • **proportions** 1 a proportion of an amount or total is part of it
2 the proportion of one thing to another is how much there is of one compared with the other
3 something's proportions are its size and measurements

♦ **proportional** • ADJECTIVE • one thing is proportional to another when it matches or corresponds with it by the same amount

proposal • NOUN • **proposals** 1 a plan or suggestion 2 when someone asks another person to marry them

propose • VERB • **proposes, proposing, proposed** 1 to propose something is to suggest it: *Dad proposed that we spend a long weekend in the country.*
2 if you propose to do something you intend to do it: *I don't propose to spend any time in Birmingham. I'll just be passing through.*
3 to propose to someone is to ask them to marry you

Aa Bb Cc Dd Ee Ff Gg Hh Ii Jj Kk Ll Mm Nn Oo Pp Qq Rr Ss Tt Uu Vv Ww Xx Yy Zz

Pronouns

Pronouns take the place of nouns. You can use them so that you do not repeat the same noun over and over again.

> **The boy** bought **an ice-cream.**   **He** *(the boy)* **ate it** *(an ice-cream).*

Singular pronouns replace singular nouns.

> **The man** found **a dog.**   **He** found **it.**

Plural pronouns replace plural nouns.

> **The men** cooked **sausages.**   **They** cooked **them.**

Masculine or feminine pronouns replace masculine or feminine nouns.

> **The boy** phoned **the girl.**   **He** phoned **her.**

There are different types of pronouns.

Personal pronouns
Use these to refer to places or things.

> **We** know **her.**   **They** never use **it.**

Possessive pronouns
Use these to show ownership.

> The boots are **his,** the slippers are **yours** and the shoes are **mine.**

Indefinite pronouns
Use these to talk about people or things that do not have exact details.

> **Nobody** knows **something** about **everything.**

Interrogative pronouns
Who, whom, which, whose and **what** are interrogative pronouns. Use them to begin questions.

> **Whose** is this? **Who** did that? **What** is that noise? **Which** shall I choose?

Demonstrative pronouns
This, that, these and **those** are demonstrative pronouns. Use them to point to the nouns they replace.

> **This** is a good book.   **Those** are horrible shoes.

proprietor • NOUN • **proprietors** the proprietor of a shop or business is its owner

prose • NOUN • writing that is not in verse

prosecute • VERB • **prosecutes, prosecuting, prosecuted** to prosecute someone is to accuse them of a crime and take them to court

♦ **prosecution** • NOUN • **prosecutions** 1 the process of taking someone to court 2 the lawyer or team of lawyers who try to prove that someone is guilty in a court of law

prospect • NOUN • **prospects** 1 a view of something into the future 2 your prospects are what you are likely to do in the future
• VERB • **prospects, prospecting, prospected** to prospect for gold and other precious metals is to search for it in the earth

prosper • VERB • **prospers, prospering, prospered** to do well, especially by making money

♦ **prosperity** • NOUN • success, especially having plenty of money

♦ **prosperous** • ADJECTIVE • a prosperous person has done well, especially by making a lot of money in business

prostrate • ADJECTIVE • lying flat

protect • VERB • **protects, protecting, protected** to protect someone or something is to guard them from harm and keep them safe: *Protect the young plants from frost.*

♦ **protection** • NOUN • 1 protecting 2 safety or shelter: *The boats were heading for the protection of the harbour.*

♦ **protective** • ADJECTIVE • providing protection

♦ **protector** • NOUN • **protectors** someone who protects another person

protein • NOUN • **proteins** a substance found in foods like eggs, meat and milk that is necessary for strength and growth

protest • VERB • **protests, protesting, protested** to protest about something is to say publicly that you think it is wrong
• NOUN • **protests** a strong statement saying that something is wrong or an organized demonstration against something

Protestant • NOUN • **Protestants** a member of one of the Christian churches that broke away from the Catholic Church at the time of the Reformation
• ADJECTIVE • to do with the Protestant church, or Protestants

proton • NOUN • **protons** a particle with a positive electric charge that along with **neutrons** makes up the **nucleus** of an atom

prototype • NOUN • **prototypes** the first built version of a new design, for example, for a new model of car, used to test how well it works before it is manufactured in large numbers

protractor • NOUN • **protractors** an instrument, shaped like a half circle, used to draw and measure angles on paper

protrude • VERB • **protrudes, protruding, protruded** to protrude is to stick out from something

♦ **protrusion** • NOUN • **protrusions** something that sticks or is pushed out

proud • ADJECTIVE • **prouder, proudest** 1 feeling pride 2 behaving in a haughty way towards other people

prove • VERB • **proves, proving, proved** to prove something is to show that it is true by providing evidence
⇒ **proof**

proverb • NOUN • **proverbs** a wise saying that gives advice or makes a statement about something that is true

♦ **proverbial** • ADJECTIVE • well-known, like a proverb

provide • VERB • **provides, providing, provided** 1 to provide something is to give or supply it 2 to provide for someone is to supply the money and other things they need to live
⇒ **provision**

province • NOUN • **provinces** 1 a division of a country, usually with its own local government 2 the provinces are the parts of a country away from the capital

♦ **provincial** • ADJECTIVE • belonging to the provinces or typical of the provinces

provision • NOUN • **provisions** 1 providing something 2 to make provision for something is to prepare for it

♦ **provisions** • PLURAL NOUN • food and

other items you need, for example, if you go on a long journey

provocation • NOUN• **provocations** provoking someone or something that provokes them

provoke •VERB• **provokes, provoking, provoked** to provoke someone is to make them angry

prow • NOUN• **prows** the prow of a boat is the raised part at the front or bows

prowl •VERB• **prowls, prowling, prowled** to wander about, especially in a secretive way
✦ **prowler** • NOUN• **prowlers** someone who wanders about an area, keeping themselves hidden and watching people or their houses

proximity • NOUN• nearness: *People living in such proximity can get on each other's nerves.*

prudence • NOUN• being prudent
✦ **prudent** • ADJECTIVE• careful and wise, and not taking any risks, especially with money

prune [1] •VERB• **prunes, pruning, pruned** to prune a plant or tree is to cut bits off it to make it smaller

prune [2] • NOUN• **prunes** a dried plum

pry •VERB• **pries, prying, pried** to try to find out things that people would rather you didn't know

PS • ABBREVIATION• short for **postscript**. PS is written before an extra bit that you add to the end of a letter, after your signature

psalm • NOUN• **psalms** a holy song, especially one from the Bible

pseudonym • NOUN• **pseudonyms** a name that someone, especially a writer, uses instead of their real name

psychiatric • ADJECTIVE• to do with psychiatry or mental illness
✦ **psychiatrist** • NOUN• **psychiatrists** a doctor who treats mentally ill people
✦ **psychiatry** • NOUN• the branch of medicine that studies and treats mental illness

psychological • ADJECTIVE• to do with the mind
✦ **psychologist** • NOUN• **psychologists**

someone who has studied psychology and human behaviour
✦ **psychology** • NOUN• the study of the mind and how it affects the way humans and animals act

pub • NOUN• **pubs** a place where alcoholic drinks can be bought and consumed

puberty • NOUN• the time when a child's body begins to change into an adult's

public • NOUN• 1 the public are people generally 2 to do something in public is to do it where anyone can see it or take part • ADJECTIVE• 1 to do with, or for, all the people of a country or community, or all people: *public opinion* • *a public park* 2 known by everyone: *It's public now that they're getting engaged.* 3 a public figure is someone who is well known and appears in newspaper or news reports a lot

publication • NOUN• **publications** something, such as a magazine or newspaper, that is printed and sold

publicity • NOUN• 1 advertising or anything done to make the public aware of something 2 public interest or attention

publicize *or* **publicise** •VERB• **publicizes, publicizing, publicized** to publicize something is to advertise it or make it known publicly

publish •VERB• **publishes, publishing, published** to publish something is to print it in a book, newspaper or magazine
✦ **publisher** • NOUN• **publishers** a person or company that publishes books, newspapers or magazines
✦ **publishing** • NOUN• the work or business of printing books, newspapers and magazines

puck • NOUN• **pucks** the hard disc hit by the players in ice hockey

pucker •VERB• **puckers, puckering, puckered** to form into, or create, folds or wrinkles

pudding • NOUN• **puddings** a sweet dish that you eat as the last course at dinner

puddle • NOUN• **puddles** water filling a shallow hole in the ground

Aa
Bb
Cc
Dd
Ee
Ff
Gg
Hh
Ii
Jj
Kk
Ll
Mm
Nn
Oo
Pp
Qq
Rr
Ss
Tt
Uu
Vv
Ww
Xx
Yy
Zz

Aa
Bb
Cc
Dd
Ee
Ff
Gg
Hh
Ii
Jj
Kk
Ll
Mm
Nn
Oo
Pp
Qq
Rr
Ss
Tt
Uu
Vv
Ww
Xx
Yy
Zz

puff •VERB• **puffs, puffing, puffed 1** to puff smoke or steam is to blow it out **2** you puff when you breath quickly because you have been exercising **3** to puff something out, or puff it up, is to make it swell or become larger •NOUN• **puffs** a small amount of breath, wind, air or smoke

puffin •NOUN• **puffins** a sea bird rather like a parrot that has a black and white body, and white, red and blue markings on its beak and face

puffy •ADJECTIVE• **puffier, puffiest** swollen: *puffy eyes*

pull •VERB• **pulls, pulling, pulled 1** to pull something is to take hold of it and bring it towards you **2** if you pull a muscle you stretch it or strain it so that it is painful **3** a driver **pulls in** when they move to the side of the road and stop **4** to **pull something off** is to manage to do it successfully **5** a driver **pulls out** when they move out of a side road on to a main road, or they move to an outer lane to overtake another vehicle **6** to **pull out** of an arrangement is to stop taking part in it **7** someone who has been dangerously ill **pulls through** when they recover **8** a driver **pulls up** when they slow down and stop • **pull a face** to twist your face into an ugly or funny shape • **pull yourself together** to get control of your emotions •NOUN• **pulls** a pulling movement

pulley •NOUN• **pulleys** a device for lifting or lowering loads or weights, with a grooved wheel through which the rope attached to the load runs

pullover •NOUN• **pullovers** a knitted piece of clothing for the top half of your body that you pull on over your head

pulpit •NOUN• **pulpits** a high platform that a minister stands at to give his or her sermon in a church

pulsate •VERB• **pulsates, pulsating, pulsated** to vibrate or move in and out with a regular beat or rhythm

pulse[1] •NOUN• **pulses** your pulse is the regular beat that you feel on your wrist or neck caused by the heart pumping blood through your arteries •VERB• **pulses, pulsing, pulsed** something that pulses vibrates or moves with a regular rhythm

pulse[2] •NOUN• **pulses** pulses are seeds you can eat, such as peas, beans and lentils

pulverize or **pulverise** •VERB• **pulverizes, pulverizing, pulverized** to pulverize something is to crush it to dust or powder

puma •NOUN• **pumas** a large, wild, cat-like animal found in North America

pumice •NOUN• a grainy kind of rock formed from lava that has gone solid and used to smooth hard skin

pummel •VERB• **pummels, pummelling, pummelled** to pummel someone or something is to beat them or it hard and repeatedly with your fists

pump •NOUN• **pumps** a device or machine used to force or drive liquids or gases in, through or out of something: *a bicycle pump* •VERB• **pumps, pumping, pumped** to pump liquid or gas is to force it up, through or out of something using a pump

pumpkin •NOUN• **pumpkins** a large rounded vegetable with thick yellow skin and soft orange flesh

pun •NOUN• **puns** a joke using words that have more than one meaning, or words that sound the same but have different meanings. For example: *Two pears make a pair.*

punch •VERB• **punches, punching, punched** to hit with the fist or fists •NOUN• **punches 1** a blow with the fist **2** a machine for making holes

punchline •NOUN• **punchlines** the punch-line of a joke or funny story is the part containing the point that makes you laugh

punchy •ADJECTIVE• **punchier, punchiest** having a forceful or striking effect: *a punchy performance*

punctual •ADJECTIVE• a person or thing is

punctual when they or it arrives exactly on time, not early or late

+ **punctuality** •NOUN• being punctual
+ **punctually** •ADVERB• arriving on time

punctuate •VERB• **punctuates, punctuating, punctuated** 1 to punctuate written work is to put commas, full stops and other punctuation marks in it 2 if something is punctuated with things, these things happen or are done all through it or during it: *Her story was punctuated by little squeaks and giggles.*

+ **punctuation** •NOUN• the process of putting commas, full stops and other punctuation marks in writing. See the box called **Punctuation**

punctuation mark •NOUN• **punctuation marks** any of the special marks such as full stops and commas used in writing to mark off pauses or breaks in what has been written. See the box called **Punctuation**

puncture •NOUN• **punctures** a hole made right through the outer surface of something •VERB• **punctures, puncturing, punctured** to puncture something is to make a hole in its outer skin or covering

pungent •ADJECTIVE• a pungent smell is very strong and noticeable

punish •VERB• **punishes, punishing, punished** to punish someone is to make them suffer for something they have done wrong

+ **punishable** •ADJECTIVE• having a particular punishment: *The crime of murder is punishable by death in many countries.*
+ **punishment** •NOUN• **punishments** 1 punishing someone, or being punished 2 a particular method of making someone suffer for something they have done wrong

punk •NOUN• **punks** 1 rock music played in a very loud and aggressive way 2 a young person with a style of dressing and behaving meant to shock people, such as wearing black or ripped clothes with chains and a spiky hairstyle

punnet •NOUN• **punnets** a small light box made of cardboard or plastic and used to hold soft fruits like strawberries or raspberries

punt •NOUN• **punts** a boat with a flat bottom

that is moved along on rivers by someone standing upright and pushing with a long pole
•VERB• **punts, punting, punted** to punt is to travel on a river in a punt

puny •ADJECTIVE• **punier, puniest** weak and small

pup •NOUN• **pups** a young dog or a young seal

pupa •NOUN• **pupae** the form that an insect takes when it is changing from a larva to its adult form, for example the form a caterpillar takes inside a chrysalis before it changes into a butterfly or moth

pupil •NOUN• **pupils** 1 a child or adult who is being taught 2 the pupil of your eye is the round opening in the middle of your eye through which light passes

puppet •NOUN• **puppets** a doll that can be moved by wires or strings, or fitted over your hand and moved by your fingers

+ **puppeteer** •NOUN• **puppeteers** someone who operates puppets

puppy •NOUN• **puppies** a baby dog

purchase •VERB• **purchases, purchasing, purchased** to purchase something is to buy it •NOUN• **purchases** something you have bought

+ **purchaser** •NOUN• **purchasers** a buyer

purdah •NOUN• purdah is the Muslim or Hindu tradition of keeping women hidden from men or strangers. Women in purdah cover their heads, bodies and faces when they are in public

pure •ADJECTIVE• **purer, purest** 1 not mixed with anything else: *pure gold* • *pure greed* 2 clean: *pure water* 3 a pure person is innocent and does not do any wrong things

+ **purely** •ADVERB• only or simply: *Our meeting was purely accidental.*
⇒ **purify, purity**

purge •VERB• **purges, purging, purged** to purge people or things is to get rid of them because they are not wanted •NOUN• **purges** the act of getting rid of people or things that are not wanted

purify •VERB• **purifies, purifying, purified** to purify something is to make it clean or pure

Aa
Bb
Cc
Dd
Ee
Ff
Gg
Hh
Ii
Jj
Kk
Ll
Mm
Nn
Oo
Pp
Qq
Rr
Ss
Tt
Uu
Vv
Ww
Xx
Yy
Zz

Aa
Bb
Cc
Dd
Ee
Ff
Gg
Hh
Ii
Jj
Kk
Ll
Mm
Nn
Oo
Pp
Qq
Rr
Ss
Tt
Uu
Vv
Ww
Xx
Yy
Zz

Punctuation

The **punctuation marks** that end different types of sentences are a **full stop**, a **question mark** and an **exclamation mark**.

Full stop (.)

Use a full stop at the end of a sentence that makes a statement:

> The children crossed the road.

Question mark (?)

Use a question mark at the end of a sentence that asks a **direct** question, such as:

> Have the children crossed the road?

Be careful *not* to use a question mark at the end of an **indirect** question. This means you are not actually asking anyone a question, but talking about one that was asked:

> I asked the teacher if the children had crossed the road.

Exclamation mark (!)

Use an exclamation mark at the end of a sentence that expresses a strong feeling (such as anger, fear or surprise), or that gives a command or a warning:

> I don't believe it!   Don't cross the road!
> Come back!   Watch out!

Using punctuation marks

A new sentence begins after a full stop, a question mark or an exclamation mark. The first letter of the new sentence always starts with a capital letter.

purity • NOUN • being pure

purl • NOUN • **purls** a stitch used in knitting

purple • NOUN • of a dark reddish blue colour

purpose • NOUN • **purposes 1** you have a purpose when you have an aim or goal **2** something's purpose is the job or role it is intended for
• **on purpose** to do something on purpose is to do it intentionally
♦ **purposeful** • ADJECTIVE • determined and having an aim : *a purposeful walk to the shops*
♦ **purposefully** • ADVERB • in a determined way : *Sarah began to walk purposefully towards the house.*
♦ **purposely** • ADVERB • on purpose

purr • VERB • **purrs, purring, purred** a cat purrs when it makes a low vibrating noise because it is contented
• NOUN • **purrs** the noise a cat makes when it is contented

purse • NOUN • **purses** a small container for money, for carrying in a handbag or pocket
• VERB • **purses, pursing, pursed** you purse your lips when you draw them together into a round shape with your mouth tightly shut

purser • NOUN • **pursers** an officer on a ship responsible for looking after money and valuables

pursue • VERB • **pursues, pursuing, pursued 1** to pursue someone is to follow or chase them, usually in order to catch them **2** to pursue an activity or aim is to be involved in it or work hard at it

♦ **pursuer** •NOUN• **pursuers** someone who tries to catch the person or thing in front

♦ **pursuit** •NOUN• **pursuits** 1 pursuing someone or something: *a pack of dogs in pursuit of a hare*

2 trying to achieve an aim or goal

3 an activity that interests you or that you do as a hobby: *My favourite pursuits are football and reading.*

pus •NOUN• a thick yellowish liquid that forms in infected wounds

push •VERB• **pushes, pushing, pushed** 1 to push something is to press against it with your hands or body, so that it moves

2 to push someone is to try hard to make them do something: *He wouldn't do any work if he wasn't pushed.*

3 to **push someone around** is to bully them

4 **push off** is a slang term for 'go away'

•NOUN• **pushes** a pushing movement

⇒ **pushy**

push-chair •NOUN• **push-chairs** a small folding chair on wheels used for pushing a young child around

pushy •ADJECTIVE• **pushier, pushiest** a pushy person behaves in a forceful way, determined to get their own way or to get attention

puss or **pussy** •NOUN• **pusses** or **pussies** a name people often call their pet cat

put •VERB• **puts, putting, put** 1 to put something somewhere is to move it or place it there: *Put the shopping over there.* • *He put his hand over his eyes.*

2 to put something is to say or to write it: *I wouldn't put it like that.* • *I had to write a message in the card but I didn't know what to put.*

3 something that causes you to feel a certain way puts you in that mood

4 to **put someone down** is to criticize them or make them feel small

5 to **put something off** is to delay it until a later time

6 if something **puts you off** doing something, it makes you not want to do it

7 if someone or something **puts you out**, they cause you inconvenience or trouble

8 to **put up with** someone or something is to tolerate them or it

putrid •ADJECTIVE• rotten and smelling bad

putt •NOUN• **putts** in golf, a gentle hit of the ball that you make so that it will go into the hole

•VERB• **putts, putting, putted** in golf to hit a ball gently so that it rolls forward on the green towards the hole

♦ **putter** •NOUN• **putters** a golf club used for putting

putty •NOUN• an oily grey or white paste used for fixing glass in window frames

puzzle •NOUN• **puzzles** 1 a game or toy that gives you a problem to solve 2 something that is a puzzle is hard to understand

•VERB• **puzzles, puzzling, puzzled** something puzzles you if you do not understand it or you cannot decide what it means

PVC •ABBREVIATION• short for **polyvinyl chloride**, which is a type of plastic

pygmy or **pigmy** •NOUN• **pygmies** a member of an African tribe of very small people

•ADJECTIVE• small: *a pygmy hippopotamus*

pyjamas •PLURAL NOUN• a suit with a top and matching trousers that you wear in bed

ⓘ **Pyjamas** comes from the Persian and Hindi word **payjamah**, which means 'clothing for the leg', because pyjamas have trousers.

pylon •NOUN• **pylons** a tall metal tower that supports electric power cables

pyramid •NOUN• **pyramids** 1 a solid shape, with flat triangular sides, that comes to a point at the top 2 a tomb with this shape built for one of the ancient Egyptian pharaohs

pyre •NOUN• **pyres** a fire in which a dead body is burned

python •NOUN• **pythons** a large snake that kills its prey by winding itself around it and crushing it in its powerful coils

Qq

Aa
Bb
Cc
Dd
Ee
Ff
Gg
Hh
Ii
Jj
Kk
Ll
Mm
Nn
Oo
Pp
Qq
Rr
Ss
Tt
Uu
Vv
Ww
Xx
Yy
Zz

quack •NOUN• **quacks** the sound made by a duck
•VERB• **quacks, quacking, quacked** to make the sound of a duck: *The ducks quacked noisily as they swam across the pond.*

quad •NOUN• **quads** short for **quadruplet** or **quadrangle**

quadrangle •NOUN• **quadrangles** 1 a square, rectangle or other figure with four sides 2 a four-sided courtyard surrounded by buildings, usually in a school or college

quadrant •NOUN• **quadrants** a quarter of a circle

quadrilateral •NOUN• **quadrilaterals** a shape with four straight sides
•ADJECTIVE• having four sides

quadruped •NOUN• **quadrupeds** an animal that has four feet: *Cows, goats and sheep are all quadrupeds.*

quadruple •ADJECTIVE• 1 four times as much or as many 2 made up of four parts
•VERB• **quadruples, quadrupling, quadrupled** 1 to quadruple something is to make it four times greater: *The shopkeeper had quadrupled the price.* 2 to quadruple is to become four times greater: *The river quadrupled in size during the rainy season.*

quadruplet •NOUN• **quadruplets** one of four children born at one time to the same mother

quagmire •NOUN• **quagmires** wet boggy ground: *Heavy rain had turned the garden into a quagmire.*

quail •NOUN• **quails** a type of small bird like a partridge

quaint •ADJECTIVE• **quainter, quaintest** pleasant, especially in an old-fashioned way: *quaint customs*

quake •VERB• **quakes, quaking, quaked** to quake is to tremble or shake: *The ground quaked under their feet.*

•NOUN• **quakes** an informal word for an earthquake

Quaker •NOUN• **Quakers** a member of a religious group founded in the 17th century which disagrees with violence and war

qualification •NOUN• **qualifications** an exam you have passed or a skill that you have that makes you suitable for a job or type of work: *What qualifications do you need for this job?*

qualify •VERB• **qualifies, qualifying, qualified** 1 to qualify for something such as a job is to be suitable for it: *He is too young to qualify for a place in the team.*
2 to qualify as something such as a doctor or a lawyer is to pass all the exams that are needed to do the job
3 to qualify something such as a statement or a remark is to make it less strong by adding or changing words

quality •NOUN• **qualities** 1 how good or bad something is: *cloth of poor quality* 2 a part of someone's character that makes them behave in a certain way: *Her best qualities are her kindness and honesty.*

quantity •NOUN• **quantities** amount or number: *a small quantity of paper* • *large quantities of tinned food*

quarantine •NOUN• if a person or animal is in quarantine they are kept away from other people or animals because they have or might have a disease that they could pass on

quarrel •VERB• **quarrels, quarrelling, quarrelled** to quarrel with someone is to argue angrily with them: *I've quarrelled with my brother.* • *We often hear them quarrelling next door.*
•NOUN• **quarrels** an angry argument: *I've had a quarrel with my brother.*
♦ **quarrelsome** •ADJECTIVE• quarrelling a lot: *quarrelsome children*

quarry •NOUN• **quarries** 1 a place where stone is dug out of the ground 2 an animal that is being hunted

452

quart •NOUN• **quarts** a measure of liquids, the same as 1.136 litres or 2 pints

quarter •NOUN• **quarters** 1 a quarter is one of four equal parts that together make up the whole of something: *We cut the cake into quarters.*
2 the fraction $\frac{1}{4}$, equivalent to the decimal fraction 0.25, and equal to one divided by four
3 one fourth of a year, three months: *In the first quarter of the year the company made a profit.*
•VERB• **quarters, quartering, quartered** to divide into four equal parts: *She quartered the melon.*

quarter-final •NOUN• **quarter-finals** the third-last round in a competition, immediately before the semi-final

quarterly •ADJECTIVE• happening every three months (quarter of a year): *quarterly payments*
•ADVERB• every three months: *We pay our gas bill quarterly.*
•NOUN• **quarterlies** a magazine that is published every three months

quarters •PLURAL NOUN• a place to stay, especially for soldiers

quartet •NOUN• **quartets** 1 a group of four musicians or singers 2 a piece of music written for four musicians or singers

quartz •NOUN• a hard substance found in rocks in the form of crystals that can be used in electronic clocks and watches

quash •VERB• **quashes, quashing, quashed** 1 to quash something such as a rebellion is to crush it or put an end to it 2 to quash a judge's decision is to wipe it out as though it never existed

quaver •VERB• **quavers, quavering, quavered** to shake or tremble: *Her voice quavered with fright as she spoke.*
•NOUN• **quavers** 1 a trembling: *He tried to sound brave but there was a quaver in his voice.* 2 a musical note equal to half a crotchet. The symbol for a quaver is ♪

quay •NOUN• **quays** the edge of a harbour where ships are loaded or unloaded

ⓘ This word is pronounced **key**.

queasy •ADJECTIVE• **queasier, queasiest** feeling sick: *The motion of the boat made her queasy.*

queen •NOUN• **queens** 1 a woman who rules a country: *Queen Elizabeth II*
2 the wife of a king: *the king and his queen*
3 in the game of chess, the queen is a piece that has a crown and can move in any direction
4 a playing card with a picture of a queen: *the queen of hearts*
5 a female bee, ant or wasp that lays eggs

queen mother •NOUN• the mother of the present king or queen who was once queen herself

queer •ADJECTIVE• **queerer, queerest** odd or strange: *queer behaviour*

quench •VERB• **quenches, quenching, quenched** 1 to quench your thirst is to drink until you no longer feel thirsty 2 to quench a fire is to put it out

query •NOUN• **queries** 1 a question: *Please phone me if you have any queries.* 2 a question mark
•VERB• **queries, querying, queried** to query something is to question whether it is correct or true: *I rang the gas company to query my bill.*

quest •NOUN• **quests** a search, especially a long one: *his quest for the truth*

question •NOUN• **questions** 1 what you ask when you want to know something: *After the talk, some people asked questions.*
2 a problem in an exam: *I didn't have time to answer all the questions*
3 a subject for discussion: *There is the question of how much to pay him.*
4 a suggestion or possibility: *There's no question of him leaving.*
• **out of the question** impossible: *It is quite out of the question for you to go out tonight.*

questionable •ADJECTIVE• that may not be good or proper: *Her reasons seem questionable.*

question mark •NOUN• **question marks** the mark (?) that you write after a sentence which is a question

questionnaire •NOUN• **questionnaires** a list of questions to be answered by several people to get information for a survey

queue •NOUN• **queues** a line of people waiting for something: *There was a long queue outside the cinema.*
•VERB• **queues, queueing, queued** to stand in a line waiting for something: *We had to queue for three hours to get the tickets.*

quibble •VERB• **quibbles, quibbling, quibbled** to quibble is to argue over or complain about details that are not important
•NOUN• **quibbles** an argument over or complaint about small or unimportant details

quiche •NOUN• **quiches** an open tart filled with beaten eggs, cheese and other savoury fillings

quick •ADJECTIVE• **quicker, quickest** 1 fast: *a quick walker*
2 done in a short time: *a quick trip into town*
3 doing something without delay: *She's always quick to help.*
•ADVERB• quickly: *Come quick!*
•NOUN• a tender area of skin under the nails
♦ **quickly** •ADVERB• if someone does something quickly, they do it rapidly or at great speed: *Come quickly! Someone's fallen in the river!*
♦ **quickness** •NOUN• being quick: *the quickness of his reply*

quicksand •NOUN• **quicksands** loose wet sand that sucks in anything that lands on it

quicksilver •NOUN• an old-fashioned word for the metal **mercury**

quick-tempered •ADJECTIVE• if someone is quick-tempered, they are easily made angry

quid •NOUN• **quid** a pound (£1): *He paid fifty quid for the jacket.*

ⓘ This is a slang word.

quiet •ADJECTIVE• **quieter, quietest** 1 not loud: *a quiet voice* 2 calm and peaceful: *a quiet life*
•NOUN• a quiet state or time: *in the quiet of the night*
•VERB• **quiets, quieted, quieting** 1 to quiet something or someone is to make them quiet

or calm: *quiet the baby* 2 to quiet is to become quiet or calm: *The teacher told the class to quiet down.*
♦ **quieten** •VERB• **quietens, quietening, quietened** 1 to quieten something or someone is to make them quiet: *He mother was trying to quieten her.* 2 to quieten or **quieten down** is to become quiet: *Things seem to have quietened down.*
♦ **quietly** •ADVERB• with little or no sound: *She slipped quietly from the room.*
♦ **quietness** •NOUN• being quiet: *the quietness of early morning*

quiff •NOUN• **quiffs** a tuft of hair at the front of the head, especially one brushed up above the forehead

quill •NOUN• **quills** a large feather of a goose or other bird made into a pen

quilt •NOUN• **quilts** a warm cover for a bed, filled with feathers or some other material
♦ **quilted** •ADJECTIVE• made of two layers of material with padding between them: *a quilted jacket*

quin •NOUN• **quins** short for **quintuplet**

quintet •NOUN• **quintets** 1 a group of five musicians or singers 2 a piece of music written for five musicians or singers

quintuplet •NOUN• **quintuplets** one of five children born at one time to the same mother

quip •NOUN• **quips** a witty remark or reply
•VERB• **quips, quipping, quipped** to make a witty remark: *'Flattery will get you nowhere,' she quipped.*

quirk •NOUN• **quirks** 1 something strange or unusual in a person's behaviour: *Wearing odd socks is just one of his little quirks.* 2 a strange happening: *By a quirk of fate, they met again years later.*
♦ **quirky** •ADJECTIVE• **quirkier, quirkiest** full of sudden and unexpected twists: *a quirky sense of humour*

quit •VERB• **quits, quitting, quit** or **quitted**
1 to quit doing something is to stop it: *I'm going to quit smoking.* 2 to quit something is to leave it: *He's quit his job.*
• **be quits** to be even with each other: *I've paid for the damage to your car – now we're quits.*

Aa Bb Cc Dd Ee Ff Gg Hh Ii Jj Kk Ll Mm Nn Oo Pp **Qq** Rr Ss Tt Uu Vv Ww Xx Yy Zz

◆ **quitter** •NOUN• **quitters** someone who gives up too easily

quite •ADVERB• **1** rather: *I'm quite hungry but I don't mind waiting.* **2** completely: *I'm afraid I'm not quite ready.*

quiver[1] •VERB• **quivers, quivering, quivered** to tremble or shake: *Her lip quivered and her eyes filled with tears.*
•NOUN• **quivers** a quivering sound or movement

quiver[2] •NOUN• **quivers** a carrying case for arrows

quiz •NOUN• **quizzes** a competition in which you have to answer questions on different subjects: *a TV quiz show*
•VERB• **quizzes, quizzing, quizzed** to quiz someone is to ask them lots of questions

quoits •NOUN• a game in which heavy flat rings called quoits are thrown onto small pegs

quota •NOUN• **quotas** the part or share given to each member of a group: *Each school has received its quota of funds.*

quotation •NOUN• **quotations 1** quotation is the act of repeating something said or written by someone else
2 a quotation is a set of words taken from a speech or piece of writing: *a quotation from Shakespeare*
3 a quotation can also be the price mentioned for doing a job: *I'd like a quotation for replacing these missing roof tiles.*

quotation marks •PLURAL NOUN• the symbols ' ' or " " which are used in writing to show that someone's words are being repeated exactly. They are sometimes called **inverted commas**

quote •VERB• **quotes, quoting, quoted 1** to quote someone is to repeat their words exactly as they said or wrote them
2 to quote words is to use them in a quotation
3 to quote a price is to state it: *He quoted a price for repairing the bicycle.*

quotient •NOUN• **quotients** the result you get when you divide one number by another. For example, 4 is the quotient when 12 is divided by 3

Qur'an •NOUN• another spelling of **Koran**

Rr

Aa Bb Cc Dd Ee Ff Gg Hh Ii Jj Kk Ll Mm Nn Oo Pp Qq Rr Ss Tt Uu Vv Ww Xx Yy Zz

rabbi • NOUN• **rabbis** a Jewish religious minister

ⓘ This is a Hebrew word that means *my master*.

rabbit • NOUN• **rabbits** a long-eared furry animal that lives in holes in the ground that are called burrows

rabble • NOUN• a noisy, uncontrolled crowd of people

rabid • ADJECTIVE• affected with rabies

rabies • NOUN• a disease that causes madness and then death. Humans catch rabies if they are bitten by an animal that has it

raccoon or **racoon** • NOUN• **raccoons** a small furry animal from North America that has a bushy striped tail

race¹ • NOUN• **races** a competition to be first at something: *a two-mile horse race • the race to put the first man on the moon* •VERB• **races, racing, raced** 1 to try to do something first, before anyone else: *I'll race you to the postbox.* 2 to go very fast: *The car raced along the narrow lanes. • I could feel my heart racing with excitement.*

race² • NOUN• **races** a large group of people who have the same ancestors and look the same in some ways, for example in the colour of their skin or their hair

racecourse • NOUN• **racecourses** the track that racehorses run on

racial • ADJECTIVE• to do with a person's race or different races of people: *efforts to stop racial prejudice*

racism • NOUN• disliking people, or treating them badly or unfairly, simply because they belong to a different race

rack • NOUN• **racks** 1 a framework with rails, shelves or hooks, for holding or storing things: *a mug rack* 2 a device for torturing people by stretching them •VERB• **racks, racking, racked** to rack your

brains is to try as hard as you can to think of something

racket¹ • NOUN• **rackets** an oval frame with strings stretched across it that you use for hitting the ball in games like tennis and squash

racket² • NOUN• **rackets** 1 a loud and disturbing noise: *Will you turn that racket down?* 2 an illegal scheme for making money

radar • NOUN• a system that uses radio waves that bounce off solid objects to find the position of aeroplanes or ships

radiance • NOUN• happiness that shows on your face
✦ **radiant** • ADJECTIVE• showing a lot of happiness: *a picture of the radiant bride*

radiate • VERB• **radiates, radiating, radiated** 1 to radiate heat or light is to send it out 2 things radiate from a central point when they form a pattern of lines like spokes in a wheel
✦ **radiation** • NOUN• radioactive energy that can harm or kill people if they are exposed to it
✦ **radiator** • NOUN• **radiators** 1 part of a central heating system that releases heat into a room 2 part of an engine that keeps it cool

radical • ADJECTIVE• a radical idea is one that involves big, important changes

radio • NOUN• **radios** 1 a system of broadcasting that uses sound waves instead of wires to send messages 2 an electrical device that receives or sends messages as sound waves •VERB• **radios, radioing, radioed** to communicate with someone by radio: *Tell them to radio for help.*

radioactive • ADJECTIVE• giving off rays that can be dangerous, even in very small amounts
✦ **radioactivity** • NOUN• the energy, that may be harmful, that is produced by the atoms of some substances, such as uranium

456

radish •NOUN• **radishes** a small round vegetable with a red skin that is eaten raw in salads

radius •NOUN• **radii** the distance from the centre of a circle to its outside edge

ⓘ A **radius** is so called because it is the Latin word for 'the spoke of a wheel', which goes from the centre to the outside edge.

raffia •NOUN• strips of palm tree leaf that are used in weaving things like hats and mats

raffle •NOUN• **raffles** a lottery to win a prize: *a book of raffle tickets*
•VERB• **raffles, raffling, raffled** to offer something as a prize in a lottery: *Flo only bought one ticket and won the car they were raffling.*

raft •NOUN• **rafts** a simple boat made from pieces of wood tied together to form a platform to sit on

rafter •NOUN• **rafters** one of the sloping pieces of wood that form the framework inside a roof

rag •NOUN• **rags** an old piece of cloth: *dressed in rags • Polish the wood with a soft rag.*

rage •NOUN• violent anger: *I've never seen him fly into a rage like that before.*
• **all the rage** very fashionable: *Flares were all the rage again.*

ragged •ADJECTIVE• torn and untidy: *ragged clothes*

ⓘ **Ragged** is pronounced with two syllables: **rag**-id.

raid •NOUN• **raids 1** a sudden unexpected attack: *a bombing raid* **2** a sudden unexpected visit from the police, who force their way into a building and search it
•VERB• **raids, raiding, raided 1** to attack a place suddenly, without warning **2** to visit a place unexpectedly and search it
• **raider** •NOUN• **raiders** a person who attacks, searches for something and removes it

rail •NOUN• **rails 1** a bar for hanging things on: *a towel rail*
2 a long steel bar that is one of the tracks that a train runs on

3 rail travel or travel by rail is travelling by train
• **railing** •NOUN• **railings** one of the vertical bars that make up a fence: *He was leaning on the railings.*

railroad •NOUN• **railroads** a railway

railway •NOUN• **railways** a track for trains to travel on: *a house by the railway • a short railway journey*

rain •NOUN• drops of water falling from the clouds: *a heavy shower of rain*
•VERB• **rains, raining, rained 1** it is raining when drops of water fall from the clouds
2 an event such as a sports match is **rained off** if rain stops it from happening
⇒ **rainy**

rainbow •NOUN• **rainbows** an arch of different colours that can often be seen in the sky when it is raining and the sun is shining at the same time

raincoat •NOUN• **raincoats** a light water-proof coat

rainfall •NOUN• the amount of rain that falls in a certain place over a certain period of time

rainforest •NOUN• **rainforests** an area of thick tropical forest with very tall trees and a high rainfall

rain gauge •NOUN• **rain gauges** an instrument for measuring how much rain has fallen

rainy •ADJECTIVE• **rainier, rainiest** a rainy day is one when it rains a lot

raise •VERB• **raises, raising, raised 1** to lift something up: *Raise your hand if you know the answer. • The wreck was slowly raised from the seabed.*
2 to increase an amount or number: *They've raised the rent again.*
3 to mention a new subject in a discussion: *I want to raise a matter that we all care very much about.*
4 to raise money is to get money together for a certain reason: *We're raising money for school funds.*
5 to raise children is to look after them until they are grown up
6 to raise crops is to grow them

Aa
Bb
Cc
Dd
Ee
Ff
Gg
Hh
Ii
Jj
Kk
Ll
Mm
Nn
Oo
Pp
Qq
Rr
Ss
Tt
Uu
Vv
Ww
Xx
Yy
Zz

• NOUN• **raises** a pay increase

raisin • NOUN• **raisins** a dried grape

rake • NOUN• **rakes** a gardening tool like a large comb with a long handle
•VERB• **rakes, raking, raked** 1 to use a rake, usually to collect leaves or smooth the soil
2 to **rake in** money is to get a lot of it easily: *We were raking the money in from everyone at the sale.*

(i) **Rake in** is a very informal phrase.

rally • NOUN• **rallies** 1 a large meeting of people, especially for an outdoor meeting
2 a car race on a course that includes ordinary roads and forest tracks
3 in sports like tennis, a rally is series of strokes and returns that make up one point
•VERB• **rallies, rallying, rallied** 1 to feel better and improve after being ill or suffering a setback: *The team have rallied now and will probably win.* 2 to rally or **rally round** is to come together to support someone: *We're hoping to rally all our members to vote.*

RAM • NOUN• short for **Random Access Memory**, which is a type of computer memory

ram • NOUN• **rams** a male sheep
•VERB• **rams, ramming, rammed** to push one thing very hard into another: *The boat was clearly going to ram the pier.*

Ramadan • NOUN• the ninth month of the Islamic calendar, when Muslims fast during the day

(i) This word is Arabic and means 'the hot month'. This is because the Ramadan fast used to take place at a hot time of year.

ramble •VERB• **rambles, rambling, rambled** 1 to walk about the countryside for pleasure
2 to ramble or **ramble on** is to speak or to write a lot without keeping to the subject
• NOUN• **rambles** a long walk in the countryside
♦ **rambler** • NOUN• **ramblers** a person who enjoys walking in the countryside

ramp • NOUN• **ramps** a sloping surface: *We should be able to get the wheelchair up the ramp quite easily.*

rampage •VERB• **rampages, rampaging,**

rampaged people or animals rampage when they rush about wildly or violently
• **on the rampage** to go on the rampage is to seem to go mad, causing damage and trouble

rampart • NOUN• **ramparts** a mound or wall that is built as part of a defence: *Bowmen were waiting patiently on the ramparts for the enemy to attack.*

ramshackle • ADJECTIVE• a ramshackle building is in very bad condition and falling apart

ran •VERB• a way of changing the verb **run** to make a past tense: *I ran all the way here.*

ranch • NOUN• **ranches** a large farm, especially one in North America, where they keep cattle and horses

rancid • ADJECTIVE• tasting or smelling sour: *When we came home we found the rancid butter in the fridge.*

random • ADJECTIVE• done without a plan or a system: *a random selection* • *Choose five of these cards at random – just take any five.*

range • NOUN• **ranges** 1 a number of different things that are of the same type: *a huge range of evening wear*
2 the distance that something can travel: *Spectators have to stand well out of range of the arrows.*
3 the distance between the top and bottom notes of a voice or musical instrument
4 an area where you can practise hitting golf balls or shooting: *a firing-range*
5 a group of hills or mountains: *a mountain range in the distance*
6 an old-fashioned kitchen stove
•VERB• **ranges, ranging, ranged** 1 to range between two things is to stretch or extend all the way between them: *holidays ranging from hostels to luxury hotels* 2 to wander around or over a place: *We ranged over the hills for days.*
♦ **ranger** • NOUN• **rangers** a person whose job is to look after a forest or park

rank • NOUN• **ranks** someone's position, grade or level in an organization or in society: *A private is the lowest rank in the British army.* • *A duchess has a very high social rank.*

•VERB• **ranks, ranking, ranked** to have a certain position amongst other things: *He ranks as one of the world's best actors.*

ransack •VERB• **ransacks, ransacking, ransacked** to search a place violently, without caring about damaging or destroying things in it: *The Inspector came home to find his flat had been ransacked.*

ransom •NOUN• **ransoms** a ransom is the money that kidnappers demand before they will give back someone they have taken hostage

rant •VERB• **rants, ranting, ranted** to speak in a loud, angry, uncontrolled way

rap •VERB• **raps, rapping, rapped** 1 to hit something quickly and sharply: *Mother's piano teacher used to rap her over the knuckles when she played a wrong note.* 2 to perform a song by speaking the words in rhythm
• NOUN• **raps** 1 a quick sharp tap or hit: *a rap at the door* 2 a pop song with very rhythmic words

rapid •ADJECTIVE• moving, acting or happening very quickly: *a rapid response to the emergency situation*
♦ **rapidly** •ADVERB• very quickly: *moving rapidly on to the next question*
♦ **rapids** •PLURAL NOUN• parts of a river where the water flows very quickly, usually over dangerous rocks

rare •ADJECTIVE• **rarer, rarest** 1 not often done or found, or not occurring often: *a rare example of a blue diamond* • *It's rare to find a vase like this in perfect condition.* 2 not cooked all the way through: *Dad always orders a rare steak.*
♦ **rarely** •ADVERB• not very often: *I rarely go out.*
♦ **rarity** •NOUN• **rarities** 1 something that is not found very often: *This vase is truly a rarity.* 2 unusualness: *very expensive because of its rarity*

rascal •NOUN• **rascals** 1 a cheeky or naughty child 2 a dishonest person

rash[1] •ADJECTIVE• **rasher, rashest** a rash person does foolish things quickly without thinking first

rash[2] •NOUN• **rashes** an area of redness or red spots on your skin, caused by an illness of some kind: *We took her to the doctor as soon as we noticed the rash.*

rasher •NOUN• **rashers** a rasher of bacon is a thin slice of it

rasp •VERB• **rasps, rasping, rasped** to make a rough grating noise
• NOUN• **rasps** a rough grating sound: *the loud rasp of the old hinges moving*

raspberry •NOUN• **raspberries** a red berry that you can eat and that grows on bushes.

rat •NOUN• **rats** a small furry animal like a large mouse with a long tail

rate •NOUN• **rates** how fast or often something happens: *The rate of progress has been very slow.* • *The disease is spreading at a tremendous rate.*
• **at any rate** anyway: *He's gone to see his cousin or something – a relative at any rate.*
•VERB• **rates, rating, rated** to decide how good or bad something is: *How do you rate him as a player?*

rather •ADVERB• 1 a bit or somewhat: *It's rather cold in here, isn't it?*
2 you **would rather** do something if you would prefer to do it: *I'd rather talk about this later if you don't mind.*
3 more correctly: *I've already agreed; or rather, I haven't said 'no'.*
4 an agreeing answer: *'Did you enjoy that?' 'Rather!'*

ratio •NOUN• **ratios** the relationship between two numbers or amounts. For example, if you say *The child to teacher ratio is five to one* then you mean there are five children to every teacher

ration •NOUN• **rations** your ration of something is how much of it you are allowed to have: *I ate my ration of biscuits for the day before lunchtime.*
•VERB• **rations, rationing, rationed** to limit the amount of something that people are allowed because there is not a lot available: *My granny is always telling me about when sugar was rationed.*

rational •ADJECTIVE• reasonable and sensible
♦ **rationally** •ADVERB• thinking reasonably and sensibly: *After the accident, Gill wasn't behaving rationally.*

rattle •VERB• **rattles, rattling, rattled 1** to rattle is to make lots of short, sharp, hard sounds: *a closed door rattling in the wind* **2** to rattle something is to shake it so that it makes a noise: *a person rattling a box and asking for money* **3** to rattle a person is to worry them or make them nervous: *A police warning had rattled the gang.* •NOUN• **rattles 1** a baby's toy that makes a noise when it is shaken **2** the noise something hard and loose makes when it is shaken: *There's a bad rattle coming from the engine.*

rattlesnake •NOUN• **rattlesnakes** a poisonous snake that lives in America. Its tail makes a rattling sound when it gets angry

raucous •ADJECTIVE• a raucous sound is rough and loud: *raucous laughter*

ravage •VERB• **ravages, ravaging, ravaged** to damage something until it is almost destroyed •NOUN• the ravages of something, such as time, are its damaging effects

rave •NOUN• **raves** a large party held in a large building where people dance to very loud music •VERB• **raves, raving, raved 1** to talk about something very enthusiastically: *The newspapers have been raving about this programme.* **2** someone is raving when they talk in an uncontrolled way, as if they were mad

raven •NOUN• **ravens** a large black bird like a crow

ravenous •ADJECTIVE• very hungry

ravine •NOUN• **ravines** a deep narrow valley with steep sides

raw •ADJECTIVE• **rawer, rawest 1** raw food is not cooked: *a salad of raw vegetables* **2** a raw substance is in its natural state before it is used for anything or put through any processes: *raw cotton* **3** a raw recruit is someone who has no training or experience **4** a raw wound is sore where the skin has been damaged **5** cold and wet and windy: *raw weather conditions*

raw material •NOUN• **raw materials** a natural substance that other things are made from

ray •NOUN• **rays** a beam of light: *a few rays of sunshine*

razor •NOUN• **razors** an instrument with a sharp blade that can be used to shave hair

re- •PREFIX• **1** if **re-** is put at the beginning of a word it can add the meaning *again*. For example, to *reappear* is to appear again **2 re-** can also add the meaning *back*. For example, to *refund* money is to give it back

reach •VERB• **reaches, reaching, reached 1** to reach a place is to arrive there: *We didn't reach the cottage till long after dark.* **2** to be able to reach something is to be able to touch or get hold of it: *I can't reach the top shelf.* • *I've been trying to reach you all day.* **3** to reach to somewhere is to extend as far as that: *Charlotte's hair reaches right down her back.* •NOUN• something is **within** or **out of reach** if you can or cannot touch it or get to it

react •VERB• **reacts, reacting, reacted** to do something as a result of something else happening: *How did Helen react when she heard the news?* ♦ **reaction** •NOUN• **reactions** behaviour that is a direct result of something else: *Did you see his reaction when he found out?*

read •VERB• **reads, reading, read 1** to look at something such as writing and understand it: *Read a book.* • *I'd like to learn to read music.* **2** to say aloud what is written or printed: *Read me a story please, Mummy.* **3** an instrument reads something when that is what it shows: *The thermometer reads 31 degrees.* •NOUN• **reads** is something that is **a good read** is enjoyable to read ♦ **readable** •ADJECTIVE• easy or enjoyable to read ♦ **reader** •NOUN• **readers** a person who reads, especially a particular book or newspaper: *Regular readers will recognize this name.*

readily •ADVERB• **1** something is readily available if it is easy to get **2** you do something readily if you do it willingly: *The whole family readily agreed to help.*

readiness •NOUN• being ready and prepared for something: *The car had been filled with petrol in readiness for the journey.*

reading •NOUN• **readings** 1 reading is looking at and understanding written words 2 a reading is a part of a book that someone reads to an audience 3 a reading is a measurement on a gauge

ready •ADJECTIVE• 1 prepared for something: *Are the children ready for bed?* • *Dinner's ready.* 2 willing: *Are you sure you're ready to give up chocolate for a whole week?*
⇒ **readily, readiness**

real •ADJECTIVE• 1 actually existing, not invented or imaginary: *real people with real problems* 2 genuine, not a copy: *The seats are made of real leather.*
⇒ **really**

realism •NOUN• the style that tries to show things as they really are, especially in art, books and films
◆ **realist** •NOUN• **realists** a person who deals with situations as they really are, rather than pretending that they are different
◆ **realistic** •ADJECTIVE• 1 very like real life: *The fight scenes were very realistic.* 2 dealing with the real situation in a sensible way: *a realistic outlook on life*
◆ **realistically** •ADVERB• 1 in a way that is very like real life: *The grapes were realistically painted.* 2 seeing things as they really are: *Realistically, there was no chance that he could win.*

realization *or* **realisation** •NOUN• **realizations** *or* **realisations** when you suddenly realize something: *The realization that they were sinking caused instant panic.*

realize *or* **realise** •VERB• **realizes, realizing, realized** to know and understand something: *I suddenly realized that he wasn't joking.*

really •ADVERB• 1 actually, in fact: *We're in the same class but we're not really friends.*
2 very: *a really lovely day*
3 certainly: *We'll really have to work hard to finish on time.*

realm •NOUN• **realms** 1 an area of activity, study or interest: *the realm of general science* 2 a country that is ruled by a king or queen

reap •VERB• **reaps, reaping, reaped** to cut and gather a crop such as corn
• **reap the benefit** to gain from something you did earlier: *Glyn has passed all his exams so now he's reaping the benefits of all that hard work.*
◆ **reaper** •NOUN• **reapers** a person or machine that brings in the harvest

rear •NOUN• 1 the back part of something: *seats towards the rear of the plane* 2 your rear is the part of your body that you sit on
•VERB• **rears, rearing, reared** 1 to rear children or animals is to look after them as they grow 2 a horse or other animal rears or **rears up** when it rises up on its back legs

reason •NOUN• **reasons** 1 the reason for something is why it happened or exists: *The reason I'm worried is that I've run out of money.* 2 your reason is your ability to think clearly and form opinions: *Will you please listen to reason?*
◆ **reasonable** •ADJECTIVE• 1 sensible and not foolish: *I suppose it's a reasonable decision from your point of view.* • *Any reasonable person would agree with that.* 2 a reasonable amount of something is quite a lot of it

reassurance •NOUN• **reassurances** something that stops someone from feeling worried

reassure •VERB• **reassures, reassuring, reassured** to say something to stop someone from feeling worried and to give them hope: *We would like to reassure parents that we will not leave the children alone.*
◆ **reassuring** •ADJECTIVE• helping to make a person feel confident and happy or safe: *a reassuring look*

rebate •NOUN• **rebates** part of a payment, especially a tax, that someone gets back because they paid, or were charged, too much

rebel •VERB• **rebels, rebelling, rebelled** to refuse to obey someone: *Teenagers often rebel against their parents.*

Aa
Bb
Cc
Dd
Ee
Ff
Gg
Hh
Ii
Jj
Kk
Ll
Mm
Nn
Oo
Pp
Qq
Rr
Ss
Tt
Uu
Vv
Ww
Xx
Yy
Zz

Aa

Bb

Cc

Dd

Ee

Ff

Gg

Hh

Ii

Jj

Kk

Ll

Mm

Nn

Oo

Pp

Qq

Rr

Ss

Tt

Uu

Vv

Ww

Xx

Yy

Zz

• NOUN• **rebels** a person who fights against, or simply does not obey, people in authority, especially their government

♦ **rebellion** • NOUN• **rebellions** 1 rebellion is when people refuse to do what they are told 2 a rebellion is a fight against an authority such as a government

♦ **rebellious** • ADJECTIVE• difficult to control and not wanting to obey: *a rebellious child*

ⓘ The verb **rebel** is pronounced ri-**bel**, with the stress at the end.
The noun **rebel** is pronounced **reb**-il, with the stress at the beginning.

reboot •VERB• **reboots, rebooting, rebooted** to start a computer up again: *You'll have to reboot to save these changes.*

rebound •VERB• **rebounds, rebounding, rebounded** to bounce back again: *The ball hammered against the crossbar, and rebounded into the net.*

rebuke •VERB• **rebukes, rebuking, rebuked** to tell someone off for doing something wrong: *Teachers are always rebuking her for being rude.*
• NOUN• **rebukes** a telling-off

recall •VERB• **recalls, recalling, recalled** 1 to remember: *Do you recall how we used to play here as children?* 2 to get someone or something to come back: *The manufacturer has recalled all the cars because of a fault.*

recap •VERB• **recaps, recapping, recapped** to go back over something that you have already said or heard: *To recap, this button switches it on, and this one controls volume.*

recapture •VERB• **recaptures, recapturing, recaptured** to catch again what has escaped or been lost: *The film perfectly recaptures the atmosphere of Hollywood.*

recede •VERB• **recedes, receding, receded** to move backwards or into the distance
♦ **receding** • ADJECTIVE• someone's hairline is receding if they are going bald at the front

receipt •NOUN• **receipts** 1 a receipt is a piece of paper you get when you pay money or hand something over to someone 2 receipt is the fact that you have received something: *On receipt of the card, you must sign it.*

receive •VERB• **receives, receiving, received** 1 to get something that someone gives or sends to you: *Did you receive my last letter?* 2 to receive guests is to greet and welcome them: *The mayor stood near the door and received his guests personally.*

♦ **receiver** • NOUN• **receivers** 1 the part of a telephone that you hear through 2 equipment that picks up radio or television signals
⇒ **receipt, reception, recipient**

recent • ADJECTIVE• happening only a short time ago: *a recent rise in prices* • *These changes are all quite recent.*

♦ **recently** • ADVERB• a short time ago: *I saw Ann quite recently.*

reception • NOUN• **receptions** 1 a formal party, for example for a wedding 2 the place where visitors arrive and are welcomed in hotels, office buildings or hospitals: *The people at reception will tell you which room to go to.* 3 how someone reacts to something: *I got a pretty cool reception when I asked the boss for more money.* 4 how clear the sound or picture is that you get on your radio or television: *Our reception up here in the hills is not always very good.*

♦ **receptionist** • NOUN• **receptionists** a person whose job is to welcome people who arrive in a building and answer enquiries

recess • NOUN• **recesses** 1 a place where a wall is set back a bit to make a small space: *The post office has a recess with a small shelf where you can write a note.* 2 a time when parliament or law courts do not work
♦ **recession** • NOUN• **recessions** a country is in recession when its businesses are not doing well and unemployment is increasing

recipe • NOUN• **recipes** a set of instructions on how to prepare or cook a particular dish and a list of its ingredients: *a recipe for chocolate-chip cookies*

recipient • NOUN• **recipients** a person who receives something

recital • NOUN• **recitals** a public performance of music, songs or poetry, usually by one person

recite •VERB• **recites, reciting, recited** to say something, such as a poem, aloud from memory

reckless •ADJECTIVE• doing things without caring or thinking about the results of your actions: *reckless driving*
  ◆ **recklessly** •ADVERB• carelessly and possibly dangerously
  ◆ **recklessness** •NOUN• behaving carelessly and possibly causing harm or damage

reckon •VERB• **reckons, reckoning, reckoned** 1 to suppose or believe: *I reckon they're in love.* 2 to calculate: *Do you reckon we'll be finished on time?*

reclaim •VERB• **reclaims, reclaiming, reclaimed** to reclaim land is to make it suitable for using, especially if it was too wet before: *The new factories by the river are built on reclaimed land.*

recline •VERB• **reclines, reclining, reclined** to lie or sit leaning back or sideways

recluse •NOUN• **recluses** a person who lives alone and prefers not to mix with other people

recognition •NOUN• recognizing someone or something: *a smile of recognition*

recognizable *or* **recognisable**
•ADJECTIVE• 1 easy to identify because you have seen it before: *He is barely recognizable since he shaved off his beard.* 2 easy to see or notice: *a recognizable difference*

recognize *or* **recognise** •VERB•
recognizes, recognizing, recognized 1 to know who or what you are seeing or hearing because you have seen or heard them before: *I recognized you from your photo.* 2 to accept that something is true: *The teacher recognized that I was not to blame.*

recoil •VERB• **recoils, recoiling, recoiled** to move back suddenly from a thing or person because you are afraid or disgusted: *Billy recoiled from the hand that tried to catch hold of him.*

recollect •VERB• **recollects, recollecting, recollected** to remember: *I recollect that it was a cold Tuesday morning.*
  ◆ **recollection** •NOUN• **recollections** something that you remember: *I have*

absolutely no recollection of what happened.*

recommend •VERB• **recommends, recommending, recommmended** 1 to advise someone to do something: *The doctor has recommended that the whole family takes a holiday.* 2 to suggest to someone that something would be good or suitable for them: *My friend recommended this book to me.*
  ◆ **recommendation** •NOUN• **recommendations** something that a person suggests would be good or suitable for someone else: *a list of recommendations from the tourist board*

reconcile •VERB• **reconciles, reconciling, reconciled** 1 to accept that you will have to do or deal with something unpleasant: *He isn't reconciled to the idea of spending six weeks in hospital.* 2 you are reconciled with someone when you are friendly with them again after an argument
  ◆ **reconciliation** •NOUN• being friendly with someone again after an argument or disagreement

reconstruction •NOUN• **reconstructions** a reconstruction of something like a crime, is when people try to act out how it happened

record •VERB• **records, recording, recorded** 1 to record something, such as music or a television programme, is to copy it on to a tape so that it can be played again later: *The band recorded their first album in 1982.* 2 to record a piece of information is to write it down
•NOUN• **records** 1 a piece of information that has been written down and stored: *We have a record of all the names of the past members.*
  2 a round flat piece of plastic that music and speech can be stored on: *a pile of old jazz records*
  3 the highest, lowest, best or worst level or performance: *Denise is determined to beat her own record on this jump.*
  ◆ **recorder** •NOUN• **recorders** 1 a machine that copies sounds or pictures, such as a tape recorder or video recorder 2 a simple wind instrument with holes that you cover with your fingers as you blow

Aa

♦ recording •NOUN• **recordings** a tape or video of sounds or pictures

Bb

ⓘ The verb **record** is pronounced ri-**kord**, with the stress at the end.
The noun **record** is pronounced **rek**-ird, with the stress at the beginning.

Cc

Dd

record player •NOUN• **record players** a machine that can play records

Ee

recover •VERB• **recovers, recovering, recovered** 1 to get better after being ill, injured or upset: *My aunt is recovering from a short illness.* • *The patient has not yet recovered consciousness.* 2 to get something back that has been lost, stolen or used up: *The wreck has been recovered from the seabed.*

Ff

Gg

Hh

Ii

♦ recovery •NOUN• **recoveries** 1 when someone gets better: *We expect all our patients to make a full recovery.* 2 getting something back: *the recovery of stolen goods*

Jj

Kk

Ll

recreation •NOUN• enjoyable things that you do in your spare time: *Shopping is my favourite form of recreation.*

Mm

recruit •VERB• **recruits, recruiting, recruited** to get someone to join your organization: *The company recruits a few school-leavers each year.*
•NOUN• **recruits** a person who joins an organization: *a line of new recruits*

Nn

Oo

Pp

Qq

♦ recruitment •NOUN• getting people to join organizations like clubs, military forces or businesses

Rr

rectangle •NOUN• **rectangles** a four-sided shape with opposite sides that are of equal length and four right angles
♦ rectangular •ADJECTIVE• with two pairs of straight sides and four right angles: *a rectangular table*

Ss

Tt

Uu

recuperate •VERB• **recuperates, recuperating, recuperated** to get better after being ill
♦ recuperation •NOUN• getting better after being ill

Vv

Ww

Xx

recur •VERB• **recurs, recurring, recurred** to happen again, either once or several times: *There is a possibility that this situation will recur.*
♦ recurrence •NOUN• **recurrences** when

Yy

Zz

something happens again: *a recurrence of the same problem*
♦ recurring •ADJECTIVE• happening again, and possibly again: *a recurring illness*

recycle •VERB• **recycles, recycling, recycled** to save something so that it can be used again: *I keep the bags in this drawer and recycle them.*
♦ recycled •ADJECTIVE• not made from new materials, but from something that has been saved and used again: *cardboard made from recycled paper*
♦ recycling •NOUN• saving things so that they can be used again, either as they are, or in another production process

red •NOUN• 1 the colour of blood, or any similar shade 2 an orangey-brown hair colour
• **see red** to suddenly get very angry: *The way she looked at me just made me see red.*

redeem •VERB• **redeems, redeeming, redeemed** 1 to redeem something is to get it back by paying some money: *You can redeem your coat from the cloakroom with this ticket.* 2 to redeem a person is to save them
♦ redeemer •NOUN• another name for Jesus Christ
♦ redemption •NOUN• 1 when a thing is paid for and returned to its owner 2 when a person is saved

red-handed •ADJECTIVE• to **catch someone red-handed** is to catch them as they are doing something wrong or illegal

red herring •NOUN• **red herrings** something designed to make someone believe the wrong thing or to give them the wrong idea about something

red-letter •ADJECTIVE• a **red-letter day** is a day that is especially happy or important

reduce •VERB• **reduces, reducing, reduced** to make something smaller or less: *We have reduced the number of classes to four.*
♦ reduction •NOUN• **reductions** when something is made smaller or less: *We're offering massive price reductions.*

redundancy •NOUN• **redundancies** when a person is not needed to do their job any more: *A company losing money often means redundancy for many workers.*

♦ **redundant** •ADJECTIVE• to be **made redundant** is to be told that your job is no longer needed

reed • NOUN• **reeds** 1 a tall stiff grass that grows in or near water. Reeds are used to make baskets 2 a part of the mouthpiece of some wind instruments

reef • NOUN• **reefs** a chain of rocks or a bank of sand just above or below the surface of the sea

reek •VERB• **reeks, reeking, reeked** to smell terrible: *His clothes reeked of fish.*

reel • NOUN• **reels** 1 a cylinder that turns to wind up anything long and untidy, such as thread or film 2 a lively Scottish or Irish dance
•VERB• **reels, reeling, reeled** 1 to walk unsteadily 2 to **reel something off** is to say a long list of things quickly, without having to think

ref • ABBREVIATION• 1 short for **reference** 2 short for **referee**

refer •VERB• **refers, referring, referred** 1 to mention something: *They referred to the letter I had written them last week.* 2 to refer a person to someone else or to a place is to direct them there to get more help: *My doctor referred us to the hospital to get an X-ray.*

referee • NOUN• **referees** in some sports, the person who makes sure the players obey the rules
•VERB• **referees, refereeing, refereed** to carefully watch the players and make decisions about whether a game is being played correctly

reference • NOUN• **references** 1 a mention of something: *She made no reference to what had happened the day before.* 2 a direction that tells you where else to look for something: *a reference in the dictionary to another entry.* 3 a written report on someone's character: *You'll need a reference from your previous employer.*

reference book • NOUN• **reference books** a book that you look in for information

referendum • NOUN• **referenda** or

referendums a chance for the people of a country to vote on whether they agree with something their government is suggesting

refill •VERB• **refills, refilling, refilled** to fill something again: *We'll need to refill the tank before we go much further.*
•NOUN• **refills** a full container to replace one that is empty of something that has been used up: *Can you buy refills for that kind of pen?*

refine •VERB• **refines, refining, refined** to make a substance pure
♦ **refined** •ADJECTIVE• a refined substance such as oil has been through a process that removes all dirt or other waste material from it
♦ **refining** •NOUN• the process of purifying substances like oil or food
♦ **refinery** •NOUN• **refineries** a factory where raw materials such as oil or foods are purified

refit •VERB• **refits, refitting, refitted** to repair and improve the condition of a vehicle such as a ship
•NOUN• **refits** a time when a ship is repaired and put back into good condition

reflect •VERB• **reflects, reflecting, reflected** 1 something is reflected when you can see an image of it in a surface like a mirror 2 to be a sign of something happening or existing: *Her face reflected how she felt inside.* 3 to think about something calmly
♦ **reflection** •NOUN• **reflections** 1 an image that you can see in a surface like a mirror 2 a sign of something being responsible: *Your bad manners are a reflection on your parents.* 3 thoughts: *I wrote my reflections in my diary.*
♦ **reflective** •ADJECTIVE• a reflective person thinks deeply about things
♦ **reflector** •NOUN• **reflectors** a piece of shiny metal, especially on a vehicle or bicycle, that throws back light from other vehicles

reflex • NOUN• **reflexes** 1 an automatic uncontrollable movement that you make in a certain situation: *The doctor will check your reflexes by tapping your knee with a small*

Aa
Bb
Cc
Dd
Ee
Ff
Gg
Hh
Ii
Jj
Kk
Ll
Mm
Nn
Oo
Pp
Qq
Rr
Ss
Tt
Uu
Vv
Ww
Xx
Yy
Zz

Aa

hammer. **2** you have good reflexes if you can react quickly and well when something unexpected and sudden happens

Bb

reflex angle •NOUN• **reflex angles** an angle that is more than 180 degrees and less than 360 degrees

Cc

Dd

reflexive •ADJECTIVE• to do with words that show that the subject of a verb is the same as its object. For example, in the sentence *He washed himself*, *wash* is a **reflexive verb** and *himself* is a **reflexive pronoun**

Ee

Ff

Gg

reform •VERB• **reforms, reforming, reformed** **1** to reform something is to make big changes to improve it **2** to reform is to stop doing bad things: *David decided to reform and not smoke any more.*
•NOUN• **reforms** big changes that improve something: *reforms in the health service*
♦ **reformation** •NOUN• **1** change in order to make an improvement **2** the Reformation was change in the Christian Church in the 16th century when the Protestant churches were formed
♦ **reformer** •NOUN• **reformers** a person who makes changes to improve things

Hh

Ii

Jj

Kk

Ll

Mm

Nn

refrain •VERB• **refrains, refraining, refrained** to stop yourself doing something: *Please refrain from talking in the library.*
•NOUN• **refrains** the chorus of a song

Oo

Pp

Qq

refresh •VERB• **refreshes, refreshing, refreshed** **1** to make you feel like you have new energy: *a rest to refresh you*
2 to make you feel cooler: *a drink that refreshes*
3 to refresh your memory is to remind yourself of something
♦ **refreshing** •ADJECTIVE• making you feel more energetic again: *a refreshing cup of tea*
♦ **refreshment** •NOUN• **refreshments** food and drink

Rr

Ss

Tt

Uu

Vv

Ww

refrigerate •VERB• **refrigerates, refrigerating, refrigerated** to make and keep food or drink cold to stop it going off
♦ **refrigeration** •NOUN• keeping things at a low temperature
♦ **refrigerator** •NOUN• **refrigerators** a machine that you can store food or drink in to keep it cold and fresh

Xx

Yy

Zz

refuel •VERB• **refuels, refuelling, refuelled**

to fill up with fuel again: *stopping on the motorway to refuel*

refuge •NOUN• **refuges** a place where someone can feel safe from danger
♦ **refugee** •NOUN• **refugees** a person who looks for protection in another country because they are not safe in their own country any more

refund •VERB• **refunds, refunding, refunded** to give someone back some money that they have paid: *We'll refund your money if you're not completely satisfied.*
•NOUN• **refunds** money that you have paid and then get back

refusal •NOUN• **refusals** **1** a decision not to accept something: *three refusals and twenty acceptances for our party invitations* **2** a decision not to do something that you are asked to do: *a refusal to shake hands*

refuse¹ •VERB• **refuses, refusing, refused** **1** to decide not to take something that you are offered: *Gerry refused a cup of tea but took a glass of water.* **2** to decide not to do something that you are asked to do: *I simply refuse to go shopping with you again.*

refuse² •NOUN• rubbish that people throw away

ⓘ **Refuse** meaning 'not to take' is pronounced ri-**fuse**, with the stress on *fuse*. **Refuse** meaning rubbish is pronounced **ref**-yoos, with the stress on *ref.*

regain •VERB• **regains, regaining, regained** to get something back: *Can the team regain the cup?*

regal •ADJECTIVE• royal, like a king or queen

regard •VERB• **regards, regarding, regarded** **1** to regard a person or thing as something is to think about them like that: *My mother still regards me as a child.* **2** to regard a thing or person is to study the way they look: *He regarded me for a moment, smiled, and patted me on the head.*
•NOUN• regard is consideration: *They went ahead without regard for our opinion.* • *The professor's work is held in high regard.*
♦ **regarding** •PREPOSITION• about: *I'd like to talk to you regarding next weekend.*
♦ **regardless** •ADVERB• without paying any

attention to something: *Regardless of the cost, Dad's determined to take this holiday.*
- **regards** •PLURAL NOUN• your regards are your best wishes: *Give my regards to Fiona when you see her.*

regatta •NOUN• **regattas** a series of yacht races

regenerate •VERB• **regenerates, regenerating, regenerated** to make or become new again: *The council is regenerating old housing.*
- **regeneration** •NOUN• making or growing again in good condition: *the regeneration of damaged skin*

reggae •NOUN• a West Indian style of music that has strong bouncy rhythms

regime •NOUN• **regimes** 1 a system of government: *a communist regime* 2 a routine: *a strict regime of diet and exercise*

regiment •NOUN• **regiments** a part of an army commanded by a colonel
- **regimental** •ADJECTIVE• to do with an army regiment

region •NOUN• **regions** a large area of land such as a part of a country: *the wine-making regions of Spain*
- **in the region of** approximately: *crowds in the region of ten or twelve thousand*
- **regional** •ADJECTIVE• to do with or coming from a particular region of a country: *a regional accent*

register •VERB• **registers, registering, registered** 1 to put your name down for something: *We registered for the new term's swimming class.*
2 to have a name added to an official list of records: *You must register your son's birth in the next week.*
3 information registers with someone if they understand it and take it in: *She certainly heard the news but I don't know if it really registered.*
4 an instrument registers a measurement when it shows it: *Earthquakes are measured by what they register on the Richter scale.*
•NOUN• **registers** a list of names: *the attendance register • a register of births and deaths*
- **registrar** •NOUN• **registrars** a person whose job is to keep a record of births, marriages and deaths
- **registration** •NOUN• **registrations** putting your name down for something: *a registration form*
- **registry** •NOUN• **registries** an office or building where official records are kept

regret •NOUN• **regrets, regretting, regretted** to regret something is to wish it had not happened: *Yes I'm sorry, I regret saying that.*
•NOUN• **regrets** a sad feeling: *Marion had no regrets about leaving home.*
- **regretful** •ADJECTIVE• feeling sad about something that has happened
- **regrettable** •ADJECTIVE• something is regrettable if you wish it had not happened: *a regrettable accident*

regular •ADJECTIVE• 1 happening after intervals of the same length of time: *a regular heartbeat • eating regular meals* 2 usual or normal: *our regular teatime* 3 of a standard size: *a regular portion of fries*
- **regularity** •NOUN• when something happens repeatedly after gaps of similar length: *check the regularity of his pulse*
- **regularly** •ADVERB• repeatedly: *We regularly have to call the police on a Saturday night.*

regulate •VERB• **regulates, regulating, regulated** to adjust a machine so that it works just as you want it to: *regulate the temperature of the central heating*
- **regulation** •NOUN• **regulations** a rule or law: *We can't allow that – it's against the regulations.*

rehearsal •NOUN• **rehearsals** 1 a rehearsal is a practice of a performance: *the dress rehearsal* 2 rehearsal is practising: *Regular rehearsal will help you to get it right.*

rehearse •VERB• **rehearses, rehearsing, rehearsed** to practise performing something: *Can we rehearse that last bit again?*

reign •VERB• **reigns, reigning, reigned** to rule over a country as a king or queen: *Queen Victoria reigned for over sixty years.*
•NOUN• **reigns** the time when someone is the king or queen of a country

reimburse •VERB• **reimburses, reimbursing, reimbursed** to give someone back the money they have paid out: *The theatre will reimburse everyone who had tickets for the cancelled performance.*

reins •PLURAL NOUN• straps attached to a horse's head that the rider uses to control it

reindeer •NOUN• **reindeer** a large deer with large horns that lives in Arctic regions

reinforce •VERB• **reinforces, reinforcing, reinforced** to make something stronger: *reinforced glass*
◆ **reinforcement** •NOUN• **reinforcements** 1 anything that makes something stronger 2 reinforcements are extra military troops

reject •VERB• **rejects, rejecting, rejected** 1 to refuse to accept something: *The machine rejected my coin.* 2 you are rejected if you apply for a job and do not get it
•NOUN• **rejects** a product that is not good enough to sell
◆ **rejection** •NOUN• **rejections** when a thing or person is not accepted: *I didn't apply because I was afraid of rejection.*

rejoice •VERB• **rejoices, rejoicing, rejoiced** to feel or show great happiness

relate •VERB• **relates, relating, related** 1 to relate to something is be connected or linked with it: *Is violent crime related to violence on TV?*
2 to relate a story is to tell it: *They related their strange experience to their friends.*
3 to relate to someone is to understand how they feel
◆ **related** •ADJECTIVE• 1 to be related to someone is to belong to the same family: *We have the same surname, but we're not related.* 2 to be related is to be linked or connected in some way
◆ **relation** •NOUN• **relations** 1 a relation between things is some kind of connection: *Your essay bears no relation to the title you were given.* 2 a relation is someone in your family: *all our friends and relations*
◆ **relationship** •NOUN• **relationships** 1 the way people feel about each other is their relationship: *Anne felt she had a good relationship with her brother.* 2 the way things are when you consider them together: *What's the relationship between these numbers?*

relative •NOUN• **relatives** a member of your family
•ADJECTIVE• compared with normal: *She lives in relative luxury.*
◆ **relatively** •ADVERB• fairly or quite: *That suit's relatively cheap.*

relax •VERB• **relaxes, relaxing, relaxed** 1 to become less tense, worried or stressed: *A short holiday will help you relax.*
2 to rest completely: *The family spent the afternoon relaxing in the garden.*
3 to relax something like a rule is to make it less strict
◆ **relaxation** •NOUN• rest from work or worrying things

relay •VERB• **relays, relaying, relayed** to pass on to someone else what has been passed to you
•NOUN• **relays** a relay race

relay race •NOUN• **relay races** a race for teams where a runner or swimmer takes over when the previous team member stops running or swimming

release •VERB• **releases, releasing, released** 1 to let someone or something go: *Release the handbrake slowly.* • *Three more prisoners have been released.* 2 a film or book is released when the public are allowed to see it
•NOUN• **releases** 1 when someone or something is set free: *the release of the hostages* 2 something like a film or book that has been made available to the public: *the band's latest release*

relegate •VERB• **relegates, relegating, relegated** to move someone down to a lower grade or level: *My team has been relegated to the Third Division.*
◆ **relegation** •NOUN• being moved down to a lower position

relent •VERB• **relents, relenting, relented** to give in a bit when you have been very strict
◆ **relentless** •ADJECTIVE• never letting up: *the relentless heat of the desert sun*

relevance •NOUN• how much something has to do with anything or anyone else: *What possible relevance can this have to me?*

relevant •ADJECTIVE• something is relevant if it has something to do with what is happening or being discussed: *Is this answer relevant to the question?*

reliable •ADJECTIVE• 1 a reliable person is someone you can depend on
2 reliable information is probably true or correct
3 a reliable machine does not often break down
◆ **reliability** •NOUN• how much you can depend on or trust a thing or person: *the reliability of the witness*

reliance •NOUN• the way you rely on a thing or person: *Our reliance on cars these days is frightening.*
◆ **reliant** •ADJECTIVE• you are reliant on a thing or person when you depend on them and cannot manage without them: *a charity totally reliant on donations from the public*

relic •NOUN• **relics** an object from the past

relief •NOUN• 1 a good feeling caused by a bad thing stopping or not happening: *It was a relief to be outside in the fresh air again.*
2 help for a large group of people in need, especially in the form of food and medicine: *relief workers in flood areas*

relief map •NOUN• **relief maps** a relief map shows where the land is higher or lower

relieve •VERB• **relieves, relieving, relieved**
1 to relieve pain or suffering is to make it less or stop it completely: *pills to relieve a headache* 2 to relieve someone of something is to take it away from them: *Let me relieve you of that heavy suitcase.*
◆ **relieved** •ADJECTIVE• feeling good because something bad that you were expecting has not happened: *I'm so relieved that you're home safely.*

religion •NOUN• **religions** belief in, or the worship of, a god or gods
◆ **religious** •ADJECTIVE• 1 to do with belief in a god or gods: *a religious service* 2 a religious person has strong beliefs about a god or gods

relish •VERB• **relishes, relishing, relished** to enjoy something very much: *Ben relishes singing in public.*
•NOUN• **relishes** 1 a relish is a spicy kind of food that you eat together with other food for extra flavour 2 relish is enjoyment: *watching the film with obvious relish*

reluctance •NOUN• being unwilling to do something: *disappointed by their reluctance to help*
◆ **reluctant** •ADJECTIVE• unwilling to do something: *I'm reluctant to do any more.*
• *three reluctant helpers*

rely •VERB• **relies, relying, relied** 1 to rely on someone is to need them or depend on them: *We rely on the help of parents and friends.*
2 if you can rely on someone, you can trust them to do what they say they will do
⇒ **reliable, reliance**

remain •VERB• **remain, remaining, remained** 1 to be left when everything else or everyone else has gone: *All that remains in the fireplace is a pile of ash.* 2 to stay in the same place or the same way, without changing: *The building remains in ruins to this day.*
◆ **remainder** •NOUN• 1 the remainder of something is what is left of it after some of it has gone 2 in maths, the remainder is the number that is left after a subtraction or division sum has been done

remake •NOUN• **remakes** a new version of an old film, that usually has the same title

remark •VERB• **remarks, remarking, remarked** to say something: *Tim remarked that he liked Di's hat.*
•NOUN• **remarks** something someone says, such as an opinion or a thought: *He made a nasty remark about my writing.*
◆ **remarkable** •ADJECTIVE• surprising, interesting or impressive: *It's remarkable how often you can see the same film and not get bored.*

remedy •NOUN• **remedies** something that gets rid of a problem: *a remedy for spots*
•VERB• **remedies, remedying, remedied** to put a situation right

remember •VERB• **remembers, remembering, remembered** 1 to have something in your mind from the past: *How much of what you saw can you remember?*
• *Can you remember the colour of his jacket?*
2 not to forget to do something: *Remember to take your key with you.*

Aa
Bb
Cc
Dd
Ee
Ff
Gg
Hh
Ii
Jj
Kk
Ll
Mm
Nn
Oo
Pp
Qq
Rr
Ss
Tt
Uu
Vv
Ww
Xx
Yy
Zz

✦ **remembrance** •NOUN• if you do something **in remembrance** of a person who is dead, you do it to show that they have not been forgotten

remind •VERB• **reminds, reminding, reminded** to make someone remember something: *Remind me to close the window before I go out.* • *That picture reminds me of our holiday last year.*
✦ **reminder** •NOUN• **reminders** a note that helps someone remember to do something

remnant •NOUN• **remnants** a small piece of something that is left after the rest has been used, lost or destroyed: *We can used the remnants of the curtains to make cushion covers.*

remorse •NOUN• a deep feeling of guilt about something bad or wrong that you have done: *a confession full of remorse*

remorseful •ADJECTIVE• feeling very guilty and sorry
✦ **remorsefully** •ADVERB• in a way that shows that you feel very guilty about having done something bad or wrong

remorseless •ADJECTIVE• 1 a remorseless person does not feel sorry or guilty at all 2 not ending

remote •ADJECTIVE• **remoter, remotest** 1 a remote place is very far away from other places: *a remote Highland village* 2 a remote chance is very slight: *There's not even a remote possibility that we'll win.*
✦ **remotely** •ADVERB• at all: *I'm not even remotely interested.*

remote control •NOUN• **remote controls** 1 remote control is controlling something from a distance by using an electronic device 2 a remote control is a device for controlling something, for example a television set, from a distance

removal •NOUN• **removals** taking something away: *the removal of a bad stain*

remove •VERB• **removes, removing, removed** 1 to take something away or get rid of it: *The police have removed the car that was dumped here.* 2 to remove clothes is to take them off: *Please remove your shoes at the door.*

render •VERB• **renders, rendering, rendered** to put a thing or person into a certain state or condition: *His cheek rendered me speechless.*

rendezvous •NOUN• **rendezvous** an arranged meeting, especially a secret one

renew •VERB• **renews, renewing, renewed** 1 to renew something like a licence is to pay for it to be valid again after it runs out: *You can renew your bus pass at the office.* 2 to start something or doing something again: *We'll renew our attempt to get the rules changed.*

renounce •VERB• **renounces, renouncing, renounced** to give up something or a belief in something: *trying to persuade the rebels to renounce violence*

renovate •VERB• **renovates, renovating, renovated** to do up a building so that it can be used again
✦ **renovation** •NOUN• **renovations** repairs to a building that restore it to good condition

renown •NOUN• fame: *a man of great renown*
✦ **renowned** •ADJECTIVE• famous: *a woman renowned for her stirring political speeches*

rent •VERB• **rents, renting, rented** 1 to pay someone money so that you can use their property, especially a house or flat: *a rented flat* 2 to rent something or **rent something out** is to let other people use it if they pay you: *We'll rent the house to students while we're away.*
•NOUN• **rents** money you pay to the owner of a house or other building so that you can live in it or use it
✦ **rental** •NOUN• **rentals** 1 renting things out to people: *a car rental business* 2 the amount of rent you pay

repair •VERB• **repairs, repairing, repaired** to fix something that is damaged or not working: *Can the washing-machine be repaired?*
•NOUN• **repairs** 1 something you do to fix something 2 **good** or **bad repair** is good or bad condition: *The car is in remarkably good repair for its age.*

repay •VERB• **repays, repaying, repaid** 1 to

give back money that you have borrowed **2** to do something for somebody in return for something they did for you: *How can we ever repay this kindness?*

✦ **repayment** •NOUN• **repayments** amounts of money that you pay back until you have paid back all the money you borrowed

repeat •VERB• **repeats, repeating, repeated 1** to say something again: *Could you repeat your name please?* • *Don't you dare repeat this to your friends.* **2** to do something again: *I hope this mistake will never be repeated.*
•NOUN• **repeats** something that happens again, especially a broadcast: *watching repeats of old comedy shows*
✦ **repeatedly** •ADVERB• again and again ⇒ repetition

repel •VERB• **repels, repelling, repelled 1** to force a thing or person away: *This material repels water and is used for rainwear.* **2** to be repelled by something is to be disgusted by it
✦ **repellent** •NOUN• **repellents** a chemical that you use to keep something away: *an insect repellent*
•ADJECTIVE• disgusting or very unpleasant: *a repellent sight*

repent •VERB• **repents, repenting, repented** to be sorry for something that you have done
✦ **repentance** •NOUN• being sorry for what you have done
✦ **repentant** •ADJECTIVE• sorry

repetition •NOUN• **repetitions 1** repetition is saying or doing things again: *learning by repetition* **2** a repetition of something is when it is said or done again: *We don't want a repetition of yesterday's argument.*
✦ **repetitive** •ADJECTIVE• boring because the same thing is repeated many times

replace •VERB• **replaces, replacing, replaced 1** to put something back in its previous or proper position: *Make sure you replace the books in exactly the right order.* **2** to take the place of another thing or person: *The company is about to replace all the old computers.*
✦ **replacement** •NOUN• **replacements** a person or thing that is in the place of a previous one: *This is broken so I'd like a replacement please.*

replay •VERB• **replays, replying, replayed** a sports match is replayed when it is played again, usually because there was no clear winner the first time.
•NOUN• **replays 1** a sports match that is played a second time: *He scored in the second-round replay.* **2** an incident in a sports match that is shown again during a broadcast: *an instant action replay*

replica •NOUN• **replicas** a model of something, usually much smaller than the original

reply •VERB• **replies, replying, replied** to answer: *You haven't replied to my question yet.*
•NOUN• **replies** an answer: *We've had a number of replies to our advertisement.* • *In reply, Phoebe gave a nod.*

report •NOUN• **reports 1** an account of something that has happened: *Reports of an accident are just coming in.* **2** a description of someone's progress: *a school report*
•VERB• **reports, reporting, reported 1** to tell people about what has happened: *Did you report the incident to the police?* • *The whole story was reported in the papers.*
2 to make a complaint about something that someone has done: *I reported the bus driver for not stopping for me.*
3 to go to a place and tell them that you have arrived: *Please report to reception when you enter the building.*

reported speech •NOUN• another name for **indirect speech**, where you report what someone has said without using their exact words

reporter •NOUN• **reporters** a person who writes articles and reports for newspapers or television or radio news programmes

repossess •VERB• **repossesses, repossessing, repossessed** to take back something, especially a car or a house, that someone has bought, but that they cannot finish paying for

represent •VERB• **represents, representing, represented 1** to represent people is to speak or act on their behalf: *Our MPs represent us in our government.*
2 to represent a thing is to be a symbol of it: *The crown represents the king or queen.*

Aa
Bb
Cc
Dd
Ee
Ff
Gg
Hh
Ii
Jj
Kk
Ll
Mm
Nn
Oo
Pp
Qq
Rr
Ss
Tt
Uu
Vv
Ww
Xx
Yy
Zz

Aa

Bb

Cc

Dd

3 to represent something in a certain way is to describe it that way: *The children in the picture were all represented as angels.*

♦ **representative** •NOUN• **representatives** **1** a person who acts or speaks on behalf of other people **2** a person whose job is to sell the products of the company they work for: *a sales representative*

Ee

Ff

Gg

Hh

Ii

repress •VERB• **represses, repressing, repressed** to keep people down or under control, by force

♦ **repression** •NOUN• very strict controlling of people, not allowing them to do things such as vote in elections

♦ **repressive** •ADJECTIVE• a repressive government controls the people of a country very strictly

Jj

Kk

Ll

Mm

reprieve •NOUN• **reprieves** an order to cancel or delay a punishment or other unpleasant event

•VERB• **reprieves, reprieving, reprieved** when someone is reprieved, something upleasant that was due to happen to them is cancelled or delayed

Nn

Oo

reprimand •NOUN• **reprimands** a telling-off: *We were given a severe reprimand by the teacher.*

reprint •NOUN• **reprints** a new copy of something like a photograph or a book

•VERB• **reprints, reprinting, reprinted** to print more copies of a book

Pp

Qq

Rr

Ss

Tt

reprisal •NOUN• **reprisals** something that is done against a person or group of people because of what they had done previously: *The country will suffer reprisals for their attacks.*

Uu

Vv

Ww

Xx

reproach •VERB• **reproaches, reproaching, reproached** to tell someone that you think they have behaved or are behaving badly: *The teacher reproached the pupils for their noisiness.*

•NOUN• criticism: *a look of reproach*

♦ **reproachful** •ADJECTIVE• criticizing someone's behaviour: *reproachful words*

Yy

Zz

reproduce •VERB• **reproduces, reproducing, reproduced** **1** to make or produce something again or copy it: *The child had reproduced his father's signature.* **2** to have babies

♦ **reproduction** •NOUN• **reproductions** **1** copying things, especially works of art: *reproduction furniture* **2** the process in which people, animals and plants produce others like themselves

reptile •NOUN• **reptiles** a cold-blooded animal such as a snake or lizard

republic •NOUN• **republics** a country with no king or queen, that is ruled by an elected government and usually has a president

♦ **republican** •ADJECTIVE• belonging to a republic or wanting to see your own country as a republic

repulsive •ADJECTIVE• disgusting

reputation •NOUN• **reputations** the opinion that most people have of a thing or person: *a restaurant with a very good reputation* • *He has a reputation for being a very tough player.*

request •VERB• **requests, requesting, requested** to ask for something: *Can I request a taxi for eight o'clock?*

•NOUN• **requests 1** something that someone asks: *I've got a request to make.* • *hundreds of requests for information* **2** something that someone asks for, especially a piece of music on the radio: *Tell me the title of your request.*

requiem •NOUN• **requiems** a religious piece of music that is played or sung at a Christian service for a person who has died

require •VERB• **requires, requiring, required 1** to need something: *Do you require any further information?* **2** to be required to do something is to have to do it: *All pupils are required to study at least one modern language.*

♦ **requirement** •NOUN• **requirements** something that is needed: *Write a list of your requirements and we'll design the kitchen for you.*

rerun •NOUN• **reruns** a repeated television programme

rescue •VERB• **rescues, rescuing, rescued** to save someone from danger: *Firefighters rescued the people from the burning house.*

•NOUN• **rescues** when someone is saved from danger: *stranded on an island with no hope of rescue*

♦ **rescuer** •NOUN• **rescuers** a person who saves someone from a dangerous situation

research •NOUN• **researches** to **do** or **carry out** research is to investigate a subject and study what you find out: *money for research into causes of cancer* •VERB• **researches, researching, researched** to carry out an investigation into a certain subject
♦ **researcher** •NOUN• **researchers** a person who finds out and studies background information about a subject: *a television documentary researcher*

resemblance •NOUN• **resemblances** something similar about things or people, especially in the way they look: *Can you see the resemblance between the brothers?*

resemble •VERB• **resembles, resembling, resembled** to be similar in some way, especially in looks: *Tom resembles his father in his laid-back attitude to life.*

resent •VERB• **resents, resenting, resented** to be irritated, angry or bitter about something: *I resent the way nobody asked me how I felt.*
♦ **resentful** •ADJECTIVE• feeling irritated, angry or bitter: *a resentful look*
♦ **resentment** •NOUN• a feeling of bitterness about something: *There was resentment amongst the other pupils when Julia was made class captain.*

reservation •NOUN• **reservations** 1 a reservation is a booking for something like a table in a restaurant, a hotel room, a theatre ticket or a ticket to travel somewhere: *I'd like to make reservations for two double rooms please.*
2 to **have reservations** about something is to be unsure about how good or sensible it is: *Peter had reservations about moving abroad.* • *We supported his ideas without reservation.*
3 a reservation is an area of land that is set aside for a particular purpose

reserve •VERB• **reserves, reserving, reserved** to keep something to use later: *Mix in half the sugar, reserving the rest for the icing.* • *I'd like to reserve a table for dinner tonight please.*
♦ **reserved** •ADJECTIVE• something like a table in a restaurant is reserved when it is being kept for someone in particular

reservoir •NOUN• **reservoirs** a large lake, often man-made, where water is collected and stored

reshuffle •NOUN• **reshuffles** a rearrangement of people doing different jobs within a group: *another cabinet reshuffle by the Prime Minister*

reside •VERB• **resides, residing, resided** to live in a place
♦ **residence** •NOUN• **residences** a residence, or a place of residence, is where someone lives: *one of the queen's official residences* • *What is your country of residence?*
♦ **resident** •NOUN• **residents** a resident of a place is someone who lives there: *a letter to all the residents in the street*
♦ **residential** •ADJECTIVE• 1 a residential area is mostly made up of housing, not offices or factories 2 a residential activity is one where you live and work in the same place: *a residential course for teachers*

residue •NOUN• **residues** an amount left after the rest has gone or been used up

resign •VERB• **resigns, resigning, resigned** to give up your job: *Harry resigned after a row with the manager.*
• **resigned to** be to be resigned to an unpleasant fact is to accept it and decide to put up with it: *I'm resigned to not being a musical genius but I can still enjoy playing.*
♦ **resignation** •NOUN• **resignations** 1 to hand in your resignation is to give up your job 2 resignation is accepting something unpleasant and putting up with it: *a look of resignation*

resilience •NOUN• resilience is a quality that things or people can have that means they are not easily damaged or hurt
♦ **resilient** •ADJECTIVE• resilient things or people are able to survive hard treatment without being badly affected

resin •NOUN• a sticky substance produced by certain trees

resist •VERB• 1 to resist something like change is to try to stop it happening 2 to resist someone is to try to stop them doing something 3 you resist a temptation when you do not give in to it

◆ resistance •NOUN• **1** an attempt to stop someone or something: *the body's resistance to disease* **2** the ability of a substance to slow down the way that electricity flows through it

◆ resistant •ADJECTIVE• not willing or likely to be changed by something: *a water-resistant watch*

resit •VERB• **resits, resitting, resat** to take an exam again

•NOUN• **resits** a chance to take an exam again

resolute •ADJECTIVE• very determined not to give up or change your mind

◆ resolutely •ADVERB• very firmly: *We have resolutely refused to do extra work.*

◆ resolution •NOUN• **resolutions 1** a firm decision to do something: *a New Year's resolution* **2** the solving of a problem

resolve •VERB• **resolves, resolving, resolved 1** to resolve to do something is to make a firm decision to do it: *We have resolved to try harder next time.* **2** to resolve a problem is to solve it or deal successfully with it

•NOUN• great determination: *I have always admired his resolve.*

resort •VERB• **resorts, resorting, resorted** you resort to doing something when everything else you have tried has failed: *The worst thing would be to resort to violence.*

•NOUN• **resorts** a place where people go for their holidays: *a popular seaside resort*
• a last resort something you would prefer not to do, but you do because everything else has failed: *As a last resort I suppose we could try asking someone to give us some money.*

resound •VERB• **resounds, resounding, resounded** to echo around

◆ resounding •ADJECTIVE• **a resounding success** is completely successful

resource •NOUN• **resources** resources are substances or qualities that you have and are able to use: *natural mineral resources like coal* • *We'll need all our resources of patience to put up with this.*

◆ resourceful •ADJECTIVE• good at finding ways of doing things, especially of solving problems

respect •NOUN• **respects 1** a feeling that a thing or person deserves your attention, admiration or consideration **2** a way of looking at things: *The plan was good in every respect.*

•VERB• **respects, respecting, respected** to treat someone with kindness and attention

respectable •ADJECTIVE• **1** decent and honest: *Simon comes from a perfectly respectable family.* **2** fairly good or, at least, not bad: *Now he's beginning to earn a respectable amount of money.*

◆ respectability •NOUN• being good, honest and decent

◆ respectably •ADVERB• quite well

respectful •ADJECTIVE• showing respect: *a respectful attitude*

◆ respectfully •ADVERB• in a way that shows respect: *Everyone respectfully bowed their heads as the coffin went past.*

respective •ADJECTIVE• to do with each thing that has been mentioned: *David and Diane are each good at their respective jobs.*

◆ respectively •ADVERB• according to the order of things already mentioned: *Colin, Jane and Ian were given £5, £3 and £1 respectively.*

respiration •NOUN• breathing

◆ respirator •NOUN• **respirators** a machine that helps a person to breathe when they are too ill to do it naturally

resplendent •ADJECTIVE• very bright and splendid-looking

respond •VERB• **responds, responding, responded** to answer or react: *If someone hits you, you tend to respond by hitting back.*

◆ response •NOUN• **responses** an answer or reaction: *His response was a shake of his head.*

responsibility •NOUN• **responsibilities**
1 responsibility for something is a duty that you must do or deal with properly: *The manager has responsibility for all the business.*
2 a responsibility is a job or duty that you are trusted to do: *It's my responsibilty to make sure all the doors are locked.*
3 responsibility is being able to sensibly do things that you are trusted with: *I am not*

ready for the reponsibility of having children.

responsible •ADJECTIVE• **1** to be responsible for something is to be the person whose job or duty that thing is: *Who is responsible for keeping the money?*
2 to be responsible for something like a mistake is to be the person whose fault it is
3 a responsible job is one that includes important duties and decisions
4 a responsible person is someone you can trust

rest •VERB• **rests, resting, rested 1** to spend time doing very little, or nothing, in order to relax: *You should rest every few minutes when you're lifting such heavy weights.*
2 to rest against something is to lean against it: *a spade resting against a wall*
3 to rest one thing on something else is to put it there gently: *Mo rested her hands on the piano keys for a moment.*
•NOUN• **rests 1** a time when you relax or sleep: *I need a rest before I can work any more.*
2 something that is used as a support: *an adjustable headrest*
3 the rest of something is what is left or remaining: *I don't want to spend the rest of my life here.* • *The rest of the country will have showers.*

restaurant •NOUN• **restaurants** a place where you can buy and eat a meal

ⓘ This is a French word that comes from the word **restaurer**, which means *to restore*, because the food was thought to refresh you and make you feel better.

restful •ADJECTIVE• making you feel calm and relaxed: *restful music* • *a restful afternoon*

restless •ADJECTIVE• not able to stay still or quiet because you are nervous and worried or bored: *The audience began to get restless after about an hour.*
• **restlessly** •ADVERB• in an uncomfortable, fidgety way: *standing and waiting restlessly by the door*
• **restlessness** •NOUN• an uncomfortable feeling that makes you want to move about or do something active

restoration •NOUN• putting something back the way it was before: *After the fire, the restoration of the church took three years.*

restore •VERB• **restores, restoring, restored** to put something back the way it was before: *In just a few minutes, Mr Cox had restored order in the classroom.*

restrain •VERB• **restrains, restraining, restrained** to hold tightly or control a thing or person: *One of the children got very excited and had to be restrained by a parent.* • *We had to restrain ourselves from laughing.*
• **restraint** •NOUN• **restraints 1** a restraint is something that prevents you from doing something: *A lack of money is a restraint on our holiday plans.* **2** restraint is self-control: *She behaved with amazing restraint considering how insulting Vera was being.*

restrict •VERB• **restricts, restricting, restricted** to limit or control something: *We are restricting people to one ticket each.*
• **restriction** •NOUN• **restrictions** a limit or control: *Are there any parking restrictions on this road?*
• **restrictive** •ADJECTIVE• preventing normal behaviour: *restrictive laws*

result •NOUN• **results 1** the result of something is what happens because of it: *Stuart failed all his exams, as a result of never doing any work.*
2 the result of a contest is the number of points each team or contestant won
3 a student's exam results are the marks or grades they got
•VERB• **results, resulting, resulted** to happen because of something else: *The fire apparently resulted from a cigarette not being put out properly.*

resume •VERB• **resumes, resuming, resumed** to start again: *Normal services will resume next week.*
• **resumption** •NOUN• when something starts again: *the resumption of peace talks*

resurrect •VERB• **resurrects, resurrecting, resurrected** to bring back to life or back into use: *We've resurrected the old custom of gathering the family together for dinner.*
• **resurrection** •NOUN• **1** bringing back to

Aa
Bb
Cc
Dd
Ee
Ff
Gg
Hh
Ii
Jj
Kk
Ll
Mm
Nn
Oo
Pp
Qq
Rr
Ss
Tt
Uu
Vv
Ww
Xx
Yy
Zz

Aa

Bb

Cc

Dd

Ee

Ff

Gg

Hh

Ii

Jj

Kk

Ll

Mm

Nn

Oo

Pp

Qq

Rr

Ss

Tt

Uu

Vv

Ww

Xx

Yy

Zz

life or use **2** the Resurrection is the Christian belief that Jesus Christ rose again three days after his death

resuscitate •VERB• **resuscitates, resuscitating, resuscitated** to revive someone who is unconscious

♦ **resuscitation** •NOUN• helping someone recover if they have passed out

retail •NOUN• selling goods to members of the public

♦ **retailer** •NOUN• **retailers** a person who sells goods to the public, usually in a shop

retain •VERB• **retains, retaining, retained** to keep something: *A smaller house would retain heat better in the winter.*

♦ **retention** •NOUN• keeping something and not letting it go

retina •NOUN• **retinas** or **retinae** the back of the eyeball, where images that you see are picked up by the brain

retinue •NOUN• **retinues** a group of people who travel along with an important or famous person: *The princess and her retinue are staying at the Victoria Hotel.*

retire •VERB• **retires, retiring, retired** to stop working because you are old enough to receive a pension: *Our third contestant is a retired teacher.*

♦ **retirement** •NOUN• the time when you stop working and receive a pension instead of earning a living: *I hope you enjoy your retirement.*

♦ **retiring** •ADJECTIVE• quiet and shy

retort •VERB• **retorts, retorting, retorted** to make a quick reply

•NOUN• **retorts** a sharp answer: *an angry retort*

retrace •VERB• **retraces, retracing, retraced** to **retrace your steps** is to go over the same route that you took earlier

retreat •NOUN• **retreats** a movement backwards

•VERB• **retreats, retreating, retreated** to move back or move away because you do not want to fight

retrieve •VERB• **retrieves, retrieving, retrieved** to get something back after leaving it somewhere: *Can you help me retrieve my pen from the back of the sofa?*

♦ **retriever** •NOUN• **retriever** a kind of large light brown or black dog that hunters use to fetch birds or animals that have been shot

return •VERB• **returns, returning, returned**
1 to return is to go back to a place: *We fly out on Friday and return the following Wednesday.* • *The search will continue as soon as daylight returns.*
2 to return something is to give it, put it, or send it back: *Please return your books by Friday.*
3 to return something like a look or a smile is to do it to someone who does it to you: *I hope I can return the favour one day.*
•NOUN• **returns 1** a time when you come or go back again: *On my return to the house, I found the door wide open.*
2 a **return ticket**: *Do you want a single or a return?*
3 something that is given or sent back
4 a shot that someone hits back in tennis or a similar game: *a wonderful return of service*

return match •NOUN• **return matches** a second match between the same teams

return ticket •NOUN• **return tickets** a ticket that allows you to travel to a place and back again

reunion •NOUN• **reunions** a meeting of people such as friends or family members who have not seen each other for a long time: *a reunion of the class of 1982*

♦ **reunite** •VERB• **reunites, reuniting, reunited** people are reunited when they meet again after not seeing each other for a long time

Rev •ABBREVIATION• short for **Reverend** when it is written down: *the vicar, Rev Green*

rev •NOUN• **revs** a revolution of an engine, which is one turn of its pistons
•VERB• **revs, revving, revved** to press the accelerator of a car to make the engine go faster. If you do this when the car is not moving, the engine makes a louder noise

reveal •VERB• **reveals, revealing, revealed**
1 to reveal something is to allow it to be seen
2 to reveal information is to tell it to someone: *The newspaper is claiming that it can reveal all the details.*

revel •VERB• **revels, revelling, revelled** 1 to celebrate in a jolly way: *friends revelling the night away* 2 to revel in something is to enjoy it very much: *Maxine revelled in all the attention she got at her birthday party.* ⇒ **reveller**

revelation •NOUN• **revelations** something unexpected that becomes known: *an article full of revelations about his private life*

reveller •NOUN• **revellers** somebody having a good time at a party

revenge •NOUN• to get revenge on someone who has harmed you is to harm them in return

revenue •NOUN• money that is given as payment to a business or organization: *Most of the government's revenue comes from taxes.*

reverberate •VERB• **reverberates, reverberating, reverberated** to produce several loud echoes: *the sounds of gunfire reverberating along the valley*
♦ **reverberation** •NOUN• **reverberations** a repeated echo

revere •VERB• **reveres, revering, revered** to respect and admire someone very much
♦ **reverence** •NOUN• great respect
♦ **Reverend** •NOUN• the title that comes before the name of a Christian minister: *Have you met Reverend Cook before?*

reversal •NOUN• **reversals** a reversal is when a change or decision that has been made is undone

reverse •VERB• **reverses, reversing, reversed** 1 to reverse is to move backwards 2 to reverse a vehicle is to drive it backwards 3 to reverse a decision is to cancel it
♦ **reversible** •ADJECTIVE• 1 a decision or process that is reversible can be cancelled 2 a reversible garment can be worn with either side in or out

revert •VERB• **reverts, reverting, reverted** to go back to the way something was before: *Many ex-prisoners revert to a life of crime.*

review •VERB• **reviews, reviewing, reviewed** 1 to check the way something works, to see if any changes need to be made

2 to say what you thought of something like a book or a performance
•NOUN• **reviews** 1 a check on the way something such as a process works, to see if it needs changing: *a review of the education system • All our contracts are under review.* 2 a critic's opinion of something such as a book or a performance: *The play received some wonderful reviews.*
♦ **reviewer** •NOUN• **reviewers** a person who gives their opinion about a book, a play, a piece of music or a performance

revise •VERB• **revises, revising, revised** 1 to make changes to improve a written work: *The revised dictionary has hundreds of new words in it.* 2 to study for an exam by looking again at the work you have done
♦ **revision** •NOUN• **revisions** 1 a new version of an old text, with improvements made 2 work that you do to learn your work before an exam

revival •NOUN• **revivals** when something becomes active or popular again: *a revival of an old children's TV programme*

revive •VERB• **revives, reviving, revived** 1 to revive someone is to bring them back to consciousness again 2 to revive something is to become interested in it again or make it popular again: *reviving some of the traditional customs of the countryside*

revolt •NOUN• **revolts** an attempt by the people to take power in a country by violence and force
•VERB• **revolts, revolting, revolted** 1 to rise up and try to seize power in a country 2 to disgust someone: *The very idea revolted me.*
♦ **revolting** •ADJECTIVE• disgusting

revolution •NOUN• **revolutions** 1 when people use force and violence to overturn a government and take power 2 a complete change in anything: *the industrial revolution of the nineteenth century* 3 a complete turn of something such as a wheel
♦ **revolutionary** •ADJECTIVE• completely new and different, and so bringing about a complete change: *revolutionary computerized machines in our factories*
•NOUN• **revolutionaries** a person who is

Aa
Bb
Cc
Dd
Ee
Ff
Gg
Hh
Ii
Jj
Kk
Ll
Mm
Nn
Oo
Pp
Qq
Rr
Ss
Tt
Uu
Vv
Ww
Xx
Yy
Zz

Aa

involved in or who is in favour of overturning a government

◆ revolutionize or **revolutionise** •VERB• revolutionizes, revolutionizing, revolutionized to introduce a lot of new and different methods or ideas so that something changes completely: *The silicon chip has revolutionized computers.*

Bb

Cc

Dd

Ee

revolve •VERB• revolves, revolving, revolved to turn round and round a central point: *a revolving door* • *The Earth revolves around the Sun.*

Ff

Gg

◆ revolver •NOUN• revolvers a pistol that has a cylinder of bullets in it that turns after each shot

Hh

Ii

reward •NOUN• rewards something you get for doing something good or useful: *a £300 reward for any information that helps catch the criminal*

Jj

Kk

•VERB• rewards, rewarding, rewarded to give someone something for being good or useful: *The class was rewarded for its good behaviour.*

Ll

Mm

rewind •VERB• rewinds, rewinding, rewound to wind a tape or cassette backwards to the beginning or an earlier place

Nn

Oo

rewrite •VERB• rewrites, rewriting, rewrote, rewritten to write something again: *You'll have to rewrite this because it is full of mistakes.*

Pp

Qq

•NOUN• rewrites a second version of something that has been written before

Rr

rhapsody •NOUN• rhapsodies a poem or a piece of music that expresses strong feelings or enthusiasm

Ss

Tt

rheumatism •NOUN• a disease that causes painful swelling in a person's joints and muscles

Uu

Vv

rhino •NOUN• rhinos a short form of the word **rhinoceros**

Ww

rhinoceros •NOUN• rhinoceroses a large animal from Africa and Asia that has thick grey skin and one or two horns on its nose

Xx

Yy

Zz

ⓘ A **rhinoceros** is so called because of the horn on its snout. The word comes from the Greek word **rhinokeros**, which is made up of **rhinos**, which means *nose*, and **keras**, which means *horn*.

rhododendron •NOUN• rhododendrons a large bush that has evergreen leaves and large flowers

rhombus •NOUN• rhombuses or rhombi a flat shape with four straight sides and four angles that are not right angles

rhubarb •NOUN• a plant that has red stems that are cooked and eaten as a fruit

rhyme •VERB• rhymes, rhyming, rhymed to sound like another word, especially at the end. For example, *ghost* rhymes with *toast*. •NOUN• rhymes 1 a rhyme is a word that sounds like another, or a pair of words that have a similar sound: *I don't think there is a rhyme for 'orange'.* 2 rhyme is poetry that uses similar-sounding words at the end of the lines

rhythm •NOUN• rhythms a repeated pattern of sounds or movements

rib •NOUN• ribs one of the curved bones in your chest, around your heart and lungs

ribbon •NOUN• ribbons a long narrow strip of fabric that you can use as a decoration for clothes, hair or parcels

rice •NOUN• brown or white grains that are cooked and used as food: *a bowl of boiled rice*

rice paper •NOUN• thin edible paper that can be put under something like a cake that is baked, to prevent it from sticking to the tin

rich •ADJECTIVE• richer, richest 1 a rich person has a lot of money or possessions 2 rich food contains a lot of sugar or fat 3 rich soil contains a lot of things that make plants grow well 4 rich colours are strong and bright 5 anything rich is full of a lot of good things: *fruit juices rich in vitamins* • *the city's rich history*

Richter scale •NOUN• a way of measuring how strong earthquakes are: *Earthquakes can measure anything between 0 and 8 on the Richter scale.*

rickshaw •NOUN• rickshaws a kind of two-wheeled cart for passengers that is pulled by one or more people and used in East Asia

ricochet •VERB• ricochets, ricocheting, ricocheted to bounce or rebound off a surface

ⓘ **Ricochet** is pronounced **rick**-oh-shay.

rid •VERB• **rids, ridding, rid** to clear or empty a place of something: *Scientists are working to rid the world of this virus.*
• **get rid of** to make something or someone go away: *We got rid of that old sofa and bought a new one.*
♦ **riddance** •NOUN• **good riddance** is a phrase you can use when you are glad that someone or something has gone

riddle¹ •NOUN• **riddles** 1 a word puzzle 2 a mystery that is difficult to solve: *How the burglar got into the house is a bit if a riddle.*

riddle² •VERB• **riddles, riddling, riddled** something is riddled with holes if it has holes all over it

ride •VERB• **rides, riding, rode, ridden** 1 to travel on a horse or bicycle: *I never learnt to ride a bike.* 2 to travel in or on a vehicle
•NOUN• a journey in or on a vehicle: *a bus ride into town*
♦ **rider** •NOUN• **riders** someone sitting on and controlling a bike or horse

ridge •NOUN• **ridges** 1 a narrow strip of land that is higher than the ground on either side of it, for example along the top of a mountain 2 the top edge of something where two sloping surfaces meet: *the ridge of the roof*

ridicule •VERB• **ridicules, ridiculing, ridiculed** to make fun of a thing or person
♦ **ridiculous** •ADJECTIVE• very silly: *Dad looked totally ridiculous in Mum's gardening boots.*

rife •ADJECTIVE• something is rife when it is all over the place: *Rumours about the row were rife.*

rifle •NOUN• **rifles** a powerful gun with a long barrel that you hold against your shoulder to fire
•VERB• **rifles, rifling, rifled** to **rifle through** something is to search through it quickly: *I caught him rifling through the papers on my desk.*

rift •NOUN• **rifts** 1 a break in a friendship between people because of a disagreement: *a rift between the two families that lasted for years* 2 a large long crack in the land

rig •VERB• **rigs, rigging, rigged** 1 to fix something dishonestly so that you get the results that you want: *Everyone agreed that the election must have been rigged.* 2 to **rig something up** is to make, fix or build something in a hurry: *We rigged up a new aerial using a wire coat hanger.*
•NOUN• **rigs** a large platform that supports the equipment that can get oil or gas from under the ground or the sea
♦ **rigging** •NOUN• the system of ropes that support and control the sails of a ship

right •ADJECTIVE• 1 correct: *I got most of the answers wrong, but a couple were right.*
2 good and proper: *It doesn't seem right that so many people in the world are hungry.*
3 on the other side from the left side: *I write with my right hand.*
•ADVERB• 1 on or towards the other side from the left: *Now turn right.*
2 exactly: *Don't move; stay right there.*
3 immediately: *I'll be right there.*
4 all the way: *This road goes right round the outside of the park.*
5 correctly: *Can't you do anything right?*
•NOUN• 1 the right is the opposite side to the left side: *There's a chemist over there on the right.* 2 a right is something that you should be allowed: *Everyone has a right to a decent education.*
• **in your own right** not because of anyone else: *His father is very well-known but Michael is also a famous actor in his own right.*

right angle •NOUN• **right angles** an angle of 90 degrees, like the corner of a square

right-angled triangle •NOUN• **right-angled triangles** a triangle that has one corner that is 90 degrees

righteous •ADJECTIVE• a righteous person is a very good person
♦ **righteousness** •NOUN• being very good and doing the right thing

rightful •ADJECTIVE• proper and as it should be: *return the stolen goods to their rightful owners*
♦ **rightfully** •ADVERB• properly and fairly: *She lives in the house which rightfully belongs to her.*

right-handed •ADJECTIVE• preferring to use your right hand to do things, rather than

Aa
Bb
Cc
Dd
Ee
Ff
Gg
Hh
Ii
Jj
Kk
Ll
Mm
Nn
Oo
Pp
Qq
Rr
Ss
Tt
Uu
Vv
Ww
Xx
Yy
Zz

Aa

your left: *It's not fair that most of these gadgets are designed for right-handed people.*

Bb

rightly •ADVERB• correctly or fairly: *Phil has rightly pointed out that we should include Robert.*

Cc

Dd

rigid •ADJECTIVE• 1 stiff and impossible to bend: *The girl stood in the doorway, rigid with fear.* 2 rigid rules are very strict and cannot be changed

Ee

Ff

✦ **rigidity** •NOUN• being very stiff or strict
✦ **rigidly** •ADVERB• stiffly or strictly

Gg

rigorous •ADJECTIVE• very careful, strict and thorough: *ready for the rigorous training that you get in the army* • *rigorous checks on all the equipment*

Hh

Ii

rim •NOUN• **rims** 1 the top edge of a container such as a cup or bowl 2 the outside edge of something like a wheel

Jj

Kk

rind •NOUN• 1 the hard outside edge of cheese or bacon 2 the skin or peel of fruit such as lemons

Ll

Mm

ring¹ •NOUN• **rings** 1 anything in the shape of a circle: *The children sit in a ring around the story-teller.* • *The curtains are attached to rings on a pole.*

Nn

Oo

2 a small circle, usually of some kind of metal, that you wear on your finger: *a wedding ring*

Pp

3 the area where a perfomance takes place: *a boxing ring* • *a circus ring*

Qq

Rr

ring² •NOUN• **rings** 1 the sound a bell makes: *Did I hear a ring at the door?* 2 a telephone call: *I'll give you a ring tomorrow.*

Ss

•VERB• **rings, ringing, rang, rung** 1 to make a sound like a bell: *I think I heard the doorbell ring.* 2 to telephone someone: *Can I ring you back later?*

Tt

Uu

Vv

ringleader •NOUN• **ringleaders** the leader of a gang of criminals or troublemakers

Ww

ringlet •NOUN• **ringlets** a long curl of hair

ringmaster •NOUN• **ringmaster** the person in charge at a circus, who introduces the performers

Xx

Yy

ring road •NOUN• **ring roads** a road that goes right around a town or city

Zz

rink •NOUN• **rinks** a large area of ice for skating on

rinse •VERB• **rinses, rinsing, rinsed** to wash something with clean water
•NOUN• **rinses** 1 a wash with clean water 2 a liquid hair dye

riot •NOUN• **riots** a crowd of people behaving noisily and violently in the streets
•VERB• **riots, rioting, rioted** to behave noisily and violently with a lot of other people in the street
✦ **rioter** •NOUN• **rioters** a person who is part of a violent crowd in the street
✦ **riotous** •ADJECTIVE• noisy and uncontrolled

RIP •ABBREVIATION• short for **rest in peace**, a phrase that is often written on gravestones

rip •VERB• **rips, ripping, ripped** 1 to tear something roughly: *ripping sheets into strips for bandages* • *Steve had ripped his trousers on the barbed wire.*
2 to snatch something from someone: *A reporter ripped the notebook right out of my hand.*
3 to **rip someone off** is to cheat them out of some money, especially by charging too much for something. This phrase is slang: *You're bound to get ripped off if you shop there.*
•NOUN• **rips** a rough tear: *There was a rip in my sleeve where the handlebars had caught it.*

ripe •ADJECTIVE• **riper, ripest** ready to be picked or eaten: *Slightly green bananas will soon be completely ripe.*
✦ **ripen** •VERB• **ripens, ripening, ripened** to ripen is to become ready to pick or eat: *The apples are ripening quickly this year.*
✦ **ripeness** •NOUN• how completely ready a growing food is to pick or eat: *Check the ripeness of the fruit by squeezing it very gently.*

ripple •NOUN• **ripples** a tiny wave on the surface of water

rise •VERB• **rises, rising, rose, risen** 1 to go upwards: *a column of smoke rising through the air* • *Ahead, the ground rose steeply.* • *The sun rises in the east.*
2 to get up: *We all rose when the judge entered.* • *His habit was to rise early for breakfast.*

3 to **rise up** is to rebel in protest
•NOUN• **rises** an increase: *a pay rise*
• **give rise to** to cause: *The accident has given rise to worries about safety.*

risk •NOUN• **risks** a possibility that something bad will happen: *There's a risk that the whole project might be called off.* • *Do we want to take this risk?*
•VERB• **risks, risking, risked** to take a chance of damaging or losing something: *Soldiers are risking their lives every day.*
♦ **risky** •ADJECTIVE• **riskier, riskiest** dangerous: *a risky route to the top of the mountain*

rite •NOUN• **rites** a ceremony, especially one to do with a religion

ritual •NOUN• **rituals** a set of actions that are part of a ceremony for certain occasions

rival •NOUN• **rivals** a person or organization that competes with another: *a match between fierce rivals*
•VERB• **rivals, rivalling, rivalled** to be as good, or nearly as good as something or someone else: *Shop-bought vegetables can't rival the ones you grow yourself.*
♦ **rivalry** •NOUN• when people or organizations compete against each other: *There's a lot of rivalry between the twins.*

river •NOUN• **rivers** a large stream of water that flows across land: *the River Thames*

rivet •NOUN• **rivets** a short kind of nail that holds pieces of metal together
•VERB• **rivets, riveting, riveted** to **be riveted by** something is to be very interested in it
♦ **riveting** •ADJECTIVE• holding all your attention: *The last half hour of the film was simply riveting.*

rivulet •NOUN• **rivulet** a small stream of liquid

road •NOUN• **roads** a hard, level surface for vehicles to travel along: *The British drive on the left-hand side of the road.*

road rage •NOUN• angry or violent behaviour by drivers on the road

roam •VERB• **roams, roaming, roamed** to travel or wander around: *There wasn't anything else to do but roam the streets.*

roar •VERB• **roars, roaring, roared** to make a loud, angry sound like a lion: *traffic roaring past in the street below*
•NOUN• **roars** a loud noise like the sound a lion makes

roast •VERB• **roasts, roasting, roasted** to cook or be cooked in an oven or over a fire: *Roast the potatoes at the same time as the turkey.*
•NOUN• **roasts** a piece of meat that has been cooked in the oven
•ADJECTIVE• cooked in the oven: *roast potatoes* • *roast beef*

rob •VERB• **robs, robbing, robbed** to rob someone is to steal something from them: *I've been robbed!* • *They stole thousands of pounds when they robbed the bank.*
♦ **robber** •NOUN• **robbers** a person who steals
♦ **robbery** •NOUN• **robberies** when something is stolen: *a bank robbery*

robe •NOUN• **robes** a long loose piece of clothing: *The mayor wears a chain and a robe on special occasions.*

robin •NOUN• **robins** a small brown bird with a red breast

robot •NOUN• **robots** a machine that can do things like a person

rock¹ •NOUN• **rocks 1** rock is the hard stone substance that the Earth is made of
2 a rock is a large stone
3 rock is a sweet that is sold at tourist attractions. It is usually in the form of a long stick

rock² •VERB• **rocks, rocking, rocked 1** to rock is to move or swing gently backwards and forwards or from side to side **2** to rock something is to make it move backwards and forwards or from side to side: *She was rocking the baby in her arms.*
•NOUN• a type of loud music with a deep beat
♦ **rocker** •NOUN• **rockers** the curved part of a chair or cradle that it can move backwards and forwards on
⇒ **rocky**

rockery •NOUN• **rockeries** a place where people grow small plants among rocks and stones

rocket •NOUN• **rockets 1** a spacecraft for travelling from Earth into space

Aa
Bb
Cc
Dd
Ee
Ff
Gg
Hh
Ii
Jj
Kk
Ll
Mm
Nn
Oo
Pp
Qq
Rr
Ss
Tt
Uu
Vv
Ww
Xx
Yy
Zz

2 a large missile

3 a kind of firework that explodes high in the sky

•VERB• **rockets, rocketing, rocketed** to go upwards very very quickly: *rocketing prices*

rocking horse •NOUN• **rocking horses** a child's toy horse that they can sit on and rock backwards and forwards

rocky¹ •ADJECTIVE• **rockier, rockiest** full of, or covered with rocks

rocky² •ADJECTIVE• shaky, unsteady or uncertain: *Their relationship got off to a rocky start when she didn't even recognize him.*

rod •NOUN• **rods** a long thin pole or bar, especially made of wood or metal: *a curtain pole*

rode •VERB• a way of changing the verb **ride** to make the past tense: *I rode my bike for hours at a time in those days.*

rodent •NOUN• **rodents** any kind of small furry animal with sharp teeth, such as a mouse, rat or rabbit

rodeo •NOUN• **rodeos** a show of riding and other skills by cowboys

roe •NOUN• **roes 1** roe is the eggs of a fish **2** a roe or a roe deer is small deer

rogue •NOUN• **rogues** a cheating and dishonest person, especially one that likes to play tricks

✦ **roguish** •ADJECTIVE• mischievous: *a roguish twinkle in his eye*

role •NOUN• **roles 1** the part that someone plays in a play or film: *a starring role in a new British film* **2** the purpose or reason for what something or someone does: *A parent's role is to provide a safe background to a child's life.*

roll •VERB• **rolls, rolling, rolled 1** to move along, turning over and over: *a ball rolling down a slope* **2** to move along on wheels: *Take the brake off and let the car roll forwards.* **3** to form something into the shape of a ball or cylinder: *Roll the sleeping bag up tightly and tie the string around it.* **4** to roll something is to make it flat by crushing it under a rolling cylinder: *I am*

going to roll the lawn. • *rolled metal* **5** to rock from side to side: *In rough weather, the ship rolls a bit.* **6** to **roll up** is to arrive: *Some guests were only just rolling up when the first ones started to leave.*

•NOUN• **rolls 1** a very small loaf of bread: *a cheese roll for lunch* **2** a cylinder shape made from a large flat piece of something like carpet or paper: *We'll need 12 rolls of wallpaper for this room.* **3** a list of names **4** a long rumbling sound: *a drum roll* • *a roll of thunder*

rollcall •NOUN• **rollcalls** when someone calls out the names from a list

roller •NOUN• **rollers 1** something in the shape of a cylinder that turns like a wheel, and is often used to flatten things **2** an object like a cylinder that you can wind hair around when it is wet, to make it curl **3** a long heavy wave on the sea

rollerblades •PLURAL NOUN• boots that have a single row of wheels on the bottom

rollerskates •PLURAL NOUN• boots with pairs of wheels on the bottom

rolling pin •NOUN• **rolling pins** a thick round stick or rod that you roll over pastry to flatten it

ROM •ABBREVIATION• short for **Read Only Memory**, a type of memory in a computer that allows you to see information, but not change it

romance •NOUN• **romances 1** the exciting emotions people feel when they are falling in love **2** a love affair: *his first romance* **3** a love story: *Betty used to read mainly romances.*

✦ **romantic** •ADJECTIVE• to do with love: *a romantic relationship* • *a romantic dinner for two*

✦ **romantically** •ADVERB• in a way that suggests love or a love affair: *She's not romantically involved with anyone just now.*

romp •VERB• **romps, romping, romped** to play in a lively way

•NOUN• **romps** a fast-moving, lively game

roof •NOUN• **roofs 1** the part that covers the

top of a building or vehicle: *The house has a red tiled roof.* 2 the top inside surface of your mouth

rook •NOUN• **rooks** 1 a large black bird like a crow 2 in the game of chess, a rook is a piece which is shaped like a castle

room •NOUN• **rooms** 1 one of the areas a building is divided into inside: *We have three rooms downstairs and four upstairs.* 2 enough space for something: *Is there room for a grand piano on the stage?*
♦ **roomy** •ADJECTIVE• **roomier, roomiest** having a lot of space

roost •NOUN• **roosts** the place where a bird rests at night
•VERB• **roosts, roosting, roosted** to sit or sleep at night
♦ **rooster** •NOUN• **roosters** a cockerel

root •NOUN• **roots** 1 the underground part of a plant
2 the part of a tooth or hair that attaches it to the body
3 the basic cause of a problem: *The root of all our troubles is that we don't have enough money.*
4 your roots are your family connections and where you come from
•VERB• **roots, rooting, rooted** 1 to grow roots: *The seedlings rooted nicely when I planted them in the compost.*
2 to **be rooted to the spot** is not to be able to move, for example because you are surprised or afraid
3 to **root around** is to search roughly and untidily for something: *Who's been rooting around in my desk?*
4 to **root something out** is to find something and get rid of it

rope •NOUN• **ropes** a very thick twisted cord: *an anchor tied on the end of a long piece of rope*

rose¹ •NOUN• **roses** 1 a garden plant with prickly stems and sweet-smelling flowers 2 a pink colour
⇒ **rosy**

rose² •VERB• a way of changing the verb **rise** to make a past tense: *The temperature in the room rose steadily as the day wore on.*

rosehip •NOUN• **rosehips** the fruit of a rose

rosemary •NOUN• an evergreen plant that has sweet-smelling leaves that can be used to flavour food in cooking

rosette •NOUN• **rosettes** a round decoration or a badge made of gathered ribbon. Rosettes may be given as prizes or worn to show that you support a particular group or party

rostrum •NOUN• **rostrums** a platform that someone stands on to make a speech

rosy •ADJECTIVE• **rosier, rosiest** 1 a pink colour: *rosy cheeks* 2 hopeful or cheerful: *The future certainly looks rosy for Hugh.*

rot •VERB• **rots, rotting, rotted** to go rotten and decay: *The leaves fall on the forest floor and gradually rot into the soil.*
•NOUN• 1 decay where something is going rotten: *They've discovered some rot in the roof timbers.* 2 nonsense: *You do talk such rot!*
⇒ **rotten, rotter**

rota •NOUN• **rotas** a list of people who take turns to do a job

rotary •ADJECTIVE• going round and round like a wheel

rotate •VERB• **rotates, rotating, rotated** 1 to turn or spin like a wheel: *Each wheel rotates on its own axle.* 2 to go through a series of changes and then start again at the beginning: *Rotating the different kinds of vegetables we grow keeps the soil healthy.*
♦ **rotation** •NOUN• **rotations** 1 going around like a wheel: *The rotation of the blades keeps the air moving.* 2 working through a series of changes and then beginning again

rotor •NOUN• **rotors** a part of a machine that turns round, especially a helicopter blade

rotten •ADJECTIVE• 1 going bad or decaying: *John stepped on a rotten floorboard and it gave way beneath him.*
2 bad quality: *a rotten meal*
3 unfair or unkind: *That was a rotten thing to say.*

rotter •NOUN• **rotters** a person who behaves badly towards someone else

rough •ADJECTIVE• **rougher, roughest** 1 not smooth: *a rough track along the side of the*

Aa
Bb
Cc
Dd
Ee
Ff
Gg
Hh
Ii
Jj
Kk
Ll
Mm
Nn
Oo
Pp
Qq
Rr
Ss
Tt
Uu
Vv
Ww
Xx
Yy
Zz

field • *rough skin on the bottom of your feet*
2 violent: *Rugby is such a rough game, some schools refuse to play it.*
3 not exact: *a rough sketch of the building*
♦ **roughen** •VERB• **roughens, roughening, roughened** to remove the smoothness of something: *Roughen the edges before you apply the glue to them.*
♦ **roughly** •ADVERB• 1 in a quick way, without being careful or gentle: *If you handle the flowers roughly, you'll damage them.* 2 approximately: *There were roughly a thousand people in the stadium.*
♦ **roughness** •NOUN• 1 not being gentle 2 not being smooth

roughage •NOUN• another name for the **fibre** in fruit, vegetables and whole grains, that you should eat to help your body deal with your food well

roulette •NOUN• a gambling game in which a ball is dropped on to a spinning wheel that has sections with different numbers on them

round •ADJECTIVE• **rounder, roundest** 1 the same shape as a circle: *a round table*
2 the same shape as part of a circle: *a round archway*
3 the same shape as a ball: *The Earth is round.*
•ADVERB AND PREPOSITION• 1 around or on all sides: *I glanced round at the pictures on the walls.* • *The Moon goes round the Earth.*
2 from one person or place to another: *The news got round pretty quickly.* • *Please pass the wine round all the guests.*
•NOUN• **rounds** 1 a burst of something like laughing, cheering, clapping or firing: *Let's give him a round of applause.*
2 a route of calls that someone makes: *We're always last on the postman's round.*
3 a level in a contest: *a second-round match*
4 a single bullet or shell for a gun
5 a song in which each singer begins the tune a little after the previous one
•VERB• **rounds, rounding, rounded** 1 to go around a corner: *As I rounded the corner, I came face to face with Sharon.*
2 to **round a number up** or **down** is to make it a whole number: *Round the fractions up to the nearest whole number.*

3 to **round on** someone is to attack them suddenly: *She rounded on me as if I'd hit her.*
4 to **round up** people or animals is to collect them together: *Farmers are rounding the animals up for the winter.*

roundabout •NOUN• **roundabouts** 1 a circular platform in a playground or a funfair that turns while you ride on it 2 a road junction where several roads meet and the traffic must travel around a central island before continuing

rounders •NOUN• a team game similar to baseball

roundly •ADVERB• plainly and thoroughly: *We were roundly criticized for failing to finish.*

rouse •VERB• **rouses, rousing, roused** to wake someone up
♦ **rousing** •ADJECTIVE• exciting and making people feel enthusiastic: *a rousing march from the brass band*

rout •NOUN• **routs** a complete defeat

route •NOUN• **routes** a way of getting somewhere: *Terry's route to school takes him past the swimming pool.*

routine •NOUN• **routines** 1 a fixed order of doing things: *Our daily routine includes three good meals and plenty of exercise.* 2 a dance routine is a fixed set of dance steps
•ADJECTIVE• a routine job or task is an ordinary one that is done regularly: *a routine inspection*

rove •VERB• **roves, roving, roved** to wander around: *Harry has been roving about the world.*
♦ **rover** •NOUN• **rovers** a wanderer or unsettled person

row[1] •NOUN• **rows** a number of things arranged beside each other in a line: *the front row of seats* • *Sow the seeds in a straight row.* • *a row of figures*
• **in a row** happening one after another: *They've lost five matches in a row.*

row[2] •VERB• **rows, rowing, rowed** to pull a boat through water using oars

row[3] •NOUN• **rows** 1 a noisy argument or a fight 2 a loud unpleasant noise: *Why are the children making such a row?*

•VERB• **rows, rowing, rowed** to argue noisily: *They were always rowing and falling out.*

ⓘ **row**¹ and **row**² rhyme with **low**. **row**³ rhymes with **how**.

rowdy •ADJECTIVE• **rowdier, rowdiest** noisy and rough: *a rowdy party*

rowing boat •NOUN• **rowing boats** a small boat that you row with oars

royal •ADJECTIVE• to do with a king or queen or their family: *a royal wedding*
♦ **royalty** •NOUN• all the members of the king or queen's family

rub •VERB• **rubs, rubbing, rubbed** 1 to move your hand backwards and forwards over a surface, usually pressing down at the same time: *He lowered his head and rubbed his eyes.* 2 to press against something and move backwards and forwards: *My shoes are rubbing and giving me blisters.*
•NOUN• **rubs** a backwards and forwards movement of your hand while pressing down: *Let me give your neck a rub where it's aching.*

rubber •NOUN• **rubbers** 1 rubber is a strong substance that stretches and can be man-made or made from tree juices: *rubber-soled shoes* 2 a rubber is a small block that you can use to rub on pencil marks to erase them

rubber stamp •NOUN• **rubber stamps** a small tool for printing numbers or short words on paper

rubbish •NOUN• 1 things that have been thrown away or should be thrown away: *a rubbish bin* 2 complete nonsense: *Her new chat show is utter rubbish.*

rubble •NOUN• the broken pieces that are left when a building falls down

ruby •NOUN• **rubies** a dark red stone that is used as a jewel

rucksack •NOUN• **rucksacks** a bag that you carry on your back, especially when you are walking or climbing

ⓘ This is a German word which comes from **Ruck**, which means *back*, and **Sack**, which means *bag*.

rudder •NOUN• **rudders** the flat piece of wood or metal at the back of a boat, under the water, that moves to steer it in a different direction. An aeroplane also has a rudder on its tail

ruddy •ADJECTIVE• **ruddier, ruddiest** pink and healthy looking: *a ruddy complexion*

rude •ADJECTIVE• **ruder, rudest** 1 not polite: *a rude answer* 2 embarrassing and not proper in a polite situation: *rude jokes* 3 rough and basic: *a rude stable*
♦ **rudely** •ADVERB• in a bad-mannered way, without being polite: 'Not likely!' he said rudely.
♦ **rudeness** •NOUN• bad manners or not being polite: *I apologize for my friend's rudeness.*

rueful •ADJECTIVE• feeling sorry about something and wishing it had not happened: *a rueful smile*

ruff •NOUN• **ruffs** a pleated frill that was worn round the neck in the past

ruffian •NOUN• **ruffians** a person who behaves in a rough violent way

ruffle •VERB• **ruffles, ruffling, ruffled** 1 to disturb something such as a hairstyle by making it untidy: *A small bird sat on the fence, ruffling its feathers.* 2 to annoy or upset someone: *She never seems to get ruffled.*

rug •NOUN• **rugs** a large mat on the floor

rugby •NOUN• a game played by two teams on a large field with an oval ball that the players must try to take over a line at the end of the pitch

ⓘ **Rugby** is named after *Rugby* School in Warwickshire, England. The game is supposed to have been invented there.

rugged •ADJECTIVE• rough or unevenly shaped: *rugged countryside* • *The man had a really rugged face.*

ruin •VERB• **ruins, ruining, ruined** to destroy something: *The rain ruined my hairstyle.*
•NOUN• **ruins** 1 a ruin is something such as a building that has fallen to pieces: *a Roman ruin*

Aa
Bb
Cc
Dd
Ee
Ff
Gg
Hh
Ii
Jj
Kk
Ll
Mm
Nn
Oo
Pp
Qq
Rr
Ss
Tt
Uu
Vv
Ww
Xx
Yy
Zz

2 to be **in ruins** is to be destroyed: *a city in ruins after the earthquake* • *All our plans were in ruins now that Bob had walked out.*

3 ruin is when someone has lost all the money they had: *If this plan did not work, he would be facing certain ruin.*

♦ **ruined** •ADJECTIVE• destroyed: *a ruined castle*

rule •NOUN• **rules 1** an instruction about what is or what is not allowed: *It's against the rules to move your feet when you're holding the ball.*

2 government or control by politicians or a king or queen: *a country under the rule of the military*

3 the way things usually happen: *As a rule, more people go to work by car when it's raining.*

•VERB• **rules, ruling, ruled 1** to rule something such as a country is to control it

2 to make an official decision: *The judge has ruled that the prisoner can go free.*

3 to rule a line is to draw a straight line: *a pad of ruled paper*

4 to **rule something out** is to decide that it is not a possibility: *The police have ruled out the suggestion that his death was an accident.*

♦ **ruler** •NOUN• **ruler 1** a person who controls or governs a country **2** a strip of wood, plastic or metal that can be used to help you to draw a straight line or for measuring short lengths

♦ **ruling** •NOUN• **rulings** a decision by someone like a judge: *The committee's ruling is that the race was a draw.*

rum •NOUN• a strong alcoholic drink made from sugar cane
•ADJECTIVE• strange or peculiar

rumble •VERB• **rumbles, rumbling, rumbled** to make a low continuous sound: *tanks rumbling along the road*
•NOUN• **rumbles** a long low sound like thunder

rummage •VERB• **rummages, rummaging, rummaged** to search for something by untidily moving things out of the way: *rummaging in her handbag for a pen*

rummy •NOUN• a card game where each player has seven cards and tries to collect sets of three or more by changing them for different ones

rumour •NOUN• **rumours** information that people pass to each other, although it may not be true: *There's a rumour going round that Steve and Julie are actually married.*
•VERB• **rumours, rumouring, rumoured** something is rumoured if people say it is true, although it may not be

rump •NOUN• **rumps** the area around an animal's tail or above its back legs

rumpus •NOUN• a disturbance when people are arguing noisily: *There was a bit of a rumpus in the street last night.*

run •VERB• **runs, running, ran, run 1** to move with very fast steps: *We had to run for the bus.*

2 to follow a certain route: *The number 5 bus runs every 10 minutes.* • *This road runs over the hill to the next village.*

3 to run someone somewhere is to give them a lift: *I run the children to school if it's raining.*

4 a liquid runs when it flows easily: *tears running down my face* • *Your nose is running.*

5 an engine or other machinery runs, or you run it, when it works or operates: *The engine runs on diesel oil.*

6 a scheme or system runs, or you run it, when it happens or works: *We're running a new course in the spring.*

7 to continue: *The film runs for 2 hours without a break.*

8 to run your hand over something is to pass your hand across its surface: *Grace ran her finger down the list until she came to her name.*

9 to compete: *Mr Bush was running for president*

10 to **run away** is to leave somewhere in secret

11 to **run out of something** is to use it all up: *We've run out of vinegar but we could use lemon juice instead.*

• **run a risk** to take a chance that something bad might happen: *If we don't leave now, we'll run the risk of having to return in the dark.*
•NOUN• **runs 1** a fast movement, quicker than a walk: *break into a run and get there faster*

2 a race or period of exercise: *a cross-country run*

3 a trip or journey in a vehicle: *a quick run*

into town to do the shopping
4 a point that a player wins in a game like cricket by running a certain distance after hitting the ball
5 a period of time during which something is repeated: *a run of bad luck*
6 a long fenced area where animals are kept: *a chicken run*
⇒ **runner, running, runny**

runaway •NOUN• someone who has run away from home
•ADJECTIVE• a runaway vehicle is out of control and moving very fast

run-down •ADJECTIVE• **1** continually feeling tired and not very healthy: *Mother's feeling run-down after having the flu.* **2** a run-down building is not kept in good condition

rung[1] •NOUN• **rungs** a step on a ladder

rung[2] •VERB• the form of the verb **ring** that is used with a helping verb to show that something hapened in the past: *I've rung all my friends and can't get anyone to go with me.*

runner •NOUN• **runners 1** a person or animal that runs: *a fast runner* **2** the blade of a skate or sledge

runner-up •NOUN• **runners-up** the person that finishes in second place in a competition

running •NOUN• **1** organization and management: *You'll be responsible for the running of the shop.* **2** to **be in** or **out of the running** for something is to have, or not have, the chance of winning it: *Henman is still in the running for the championship.*
•ADJECTIVE• continuing without a break: *a running commentary on the events*
•ADVERB• one after the other: *for three days running*

runny •ADJECTIVE• **runnier, runniest 1** like a liquid: *Heat the jam until it is runny.* **2** if you have a runny nose, you need to blow it frequently

runway •NOUN• **runways** the long road-like surface at an airport that aircraft take off from and land on

rupture •VERB• **ruptures, rupturing, ruptured** to break: *a patient with an appendix that has ruptured*

•NOUN• **ruptures** a break or tear, especially in a muscle or joint

rural •ADJECTIVE• to do with the countryside

rush •NOUN• **rushes 1** a hurry: *We were just in time but it had been a dreadful rush.* **2** a large number of people trying to get to the same place at the same time: *a rush for the door*
•VERB• **rushes, rushing, rushed 1** to go somewhere in a hurry: *I rushed downstairs as soon as I heard the thump.* • *Fletcher was rushed to the hospital in an ambulance.*
2 to do something too quickly or in a hurry: *Don't rush it or you'll just make a mistake.*
3 to attack someone suddenly, hoping to surprise them

rusk •NOUN• **rusks** a hard dry biscuit

russet •NOUN• a reddish-brown colour

rust •NOUN• a reddish-brown substance that forms on iron and other metals if they are exposed to air and wetness
•VERB• **rusts, rusting, rusted** to become rusty
⇒ **rusty**

rustle •VERB• **rustles, rustling, rustled** to make a soft sound like dry leaves rubbing together: *people rustling sweet papers at the cinema*
•NOUN• **rustles** a soft sound like dry leaves: *the rustle of a silk dress*

rusty •ADJECTIVE• **rustier, rustiest 1** rusty metal has a reddish-brown substance on it that makes it weak and brittle **2** a person's knowledge of something is rusty if it is not as good as it used to be: *My French is a bit rusty, but it'll come back to me with practice.*

rut •NOUN• **ruts 1** a deep track made by a wheel **2** a boring routine: *I'm in a rut and the only way out is to change my job.*

ruthless •ADJECTIVE• a ruthless person does what they think they must do without caring how cruel or kind they are being
♦ **ruthlessly** •ADVERB• without taking into account how kind or cruel you are being
♦ **ruthlessness** •NOUN• doing things without thinking about how kind or cruel you are being

rye •NOUN• a kind of grain that is used for making flour and whisky

Ss

S •ABBREVIATION• short for **south**

Sabbath •NOUN• the day of the week set aside for rest and worship in certain religions. The Jewish Sabbath is Saturday, for Muslims it is Friday and for most Christians, it is Sunday

sabotage •NOUN• **1** deliberate damage that someone does to buildings or equipment in secret **2** secret action that is intended to wreck someone's plan or system
•VERB• **sabotages, sabotaging, sabotaged** to deliberately damage an enemy's equipment or plans

sabre •NOUN• **sabres** a curved sword that was used in the past by soldiers on horses

sac •NOUN• **sacs** any part of a plant or animal that is like a bag, especially one that contains liquid

saccharin •NOUN• a very sweet chemical that can be used instead of sugar
♦ **saccharine** •ADJECTIVE• very sweet or sickly

sachet •NOUN• **sachets** a small plastic or paper packet containing a small amount of a liquid or powder: *a handy sachet of shampoo for your suitcase*

sack •NOUN• **sacks 1** a sack is a very large bag used for carrying or storing things **2 the sack** is when you are dismissed from your job: *That new boy got the sack for stealing coins from the till.*
•VERB• **sacks, sacking, sacked** to dismiss someone from their job, usually because they are not good at it: *I'll have to sack you if you can't keep the place tidy.*

sacrament •NOUN• **sacraments** any of several important Christian ceremonies such as baptism and communion

sacred •ADJECTIVE• **1** holy, or to do with a god **2** to do with religion or worship: *a CD of sacred music*

sacrifice •NOUN• **sacrifices 1** something that

is killed and offered to a god in the hope that something good will then happen: *Ancient peoples killed small and large animals in this place as sacrifices to their gods.* **2** giving up something for the sake of someone or something else: *We didn't earn much and we had to make a lot of sacrifices to afford a house.*
•VERB• **sacrifices, sacrificing, sacrificed 1** to kill something and offer it to a god **2** to give something up for the sake of someone or something else: *The boy bravely sacrificed his life for another.*

sad •ADJECTIVE• **sadder, saddest 1** feeling unhappy: *a sad look* **2** making you feel unhappy: *a sad film*
♦ **sadden** •VERB• **saddens, saddening, saddened** you are saddened if something makes you feel unhappy: *We were greatly saddened by the news.*
♦ **sadly** •ADVERB• **1** unfortunately: *Sadly, we must say goodbye to Mrs Green today.* **2** unhappily: *She looked up sadly and tried to smile.*
♦ **sadness** •NOUN• a feeling of unhappiness or pity

saddle •NOUN• **saddles** a seat for a rider of a horse or a bicycle
•VERB• **saddles, saddling, saddled 1** to put a seat on a horse so that you can ride it **2** to **saddle someone with something** is to give them a job that nobody wants to do: *They've saddled me with organizing the cleaning rota.*

sadism •NOUN• enjoying being cruel or hurting other people
♦ **sadist** •NOUN• **sadists** a person who enjoys hurting other people
♦ **sadistic** •ADJECTIVE• a sadistic person enjoys hurting other people

sae •ABBREVIATION• short for **stamped addressed envelope**

safari •NOUN• **safaris** an expedition or tour when people hunt or watch wild animals, especially in Africa

(i) This word comes from the African language Swahili and means *journey*.

safari park •NOUN• **safari parks** a large area of land where wild animals are kept for visitors to see

safe •ADJECTIVE• **safer, safest** 1 not harmed: *Thank goodness you're safe!* 2 not involving danger or risk: *the safest way to travel long distances* • *That ladder doesn't look very safe to me.*
•NOUN• **safes** a strongly built metal box for keeping valuables in: *The safe had been blown open with dynamite.*

safeguard •NOUN• **safeguards** protection against danger or harm: *The double lock is a safeguard against theft.*
•VERB• **safeguards, safeguarding, safeguarded** to protect something from danger: *Vaccinations should safeguard our children from these deadly diseases.*

safely •ADVERB• without risk or danger: *getting everyone home safely* • *safely tucked up in bed*

safety •NOUN• being safe: *Everyone dived for safety.* • *We must put the safety of our passengers first.*

safety belt •NOUN• **safety belts** a strap in a car or plane that stops you being thrown out of your seat if there is a crash

safety pin •NOUN• **safety pins** a pin with a guard that covers the sharp point when it is closed

sag •VERB• **sags, sagging, sagged** to sag is to droop or not to be firm: *a mattress that has begun to sag in the middle*

saga •NOUN• **sagas** a long story, especially one about several generations of a family

sage •NOUN• **sages** 1 a wise man 2 a herb that is used in cooking to add flavour

said •VERB• a way of changing the verb **say** to make a past tense. It can be used with or without a helping verb: *They've said I can come back any time.* • *I've told you everything he said.*

sail •VERB• **sails, sailing, sailed** 1 to travel in a ship or a boat: *My ambition is to sail across the Atlantic on an ocean liner.* 2 to start a journey in a ship: *The ferry sails at noon.* 3 to **sail through something** is to do it quickly and easily: *Amy sailed through her exams with no bother.*
•NOUN• **sails** 1 a sheet of canvas attached to a mast on a boat that catches the wind and carries the boat along 2 a broad flat blade that turns on a windmill
♦ **sailor** •NOUN• **sailors** someone who works on a ship

saint •NOUN• **saints** 1 someone that the Christian church believes was especially holy 2 a particularly good and kind person
♦ **saintly** •ADJECTIVE• very good or very holy

sake •NOUN• **sakes** 1 **for someone's sake** is for them or for their benefit: *For his mother's sake, he didn't want to make a fuss.* • *Please don't go to any trouble just for my sake.* 2 to do something **for the sake of it** is to do it simply because you want to: *I'm sure she argues with me just for the sake of it.* 3 to do something **for the sake of something** is to do it because you want to achieve that thing: *I gave in for the sake of peace.*

salaam •INTERJECTION• a greeting that is used especially by Muslims

salad •NOUN• **salads** a mixture of mostly raw vegetables that sometimes includes other foods like ham or cheese

salami •NOUN• a type of spicy sausage that is usually served cold in thin slices

salary •NOUN• **salaries** an amount of money that a person is paid for doing their job for a year. It is usually broken down into twelve monthly payments

salat •NOUN• the prayers that Muslims say five times each day

sale •NOUN• **sales** 1 when something is sold for money: *a sale of hand-made carpets* • *a house for sale* • *This week's edition is on sale now.* 2 an occasion when goods in a shop are sold at cheaper prices than usual: *the January sales*

salesman •NOUN• **salesmen** a man whose job is to sell goods to customers

saleswoman •NOUN• **saleswomen** a

Aa Bb Cc Dd Ee Ff Gg Hh Ii Jj Kk Ll Mm Nn Oo Pp Qq Rr Ss Tt Uu Vv Ww Xx Yy Zz

woman whose job is to sell goods to customers

saline •ADJECTIVE• containing salt

saliva •NOUN• the watery liquid produced in your mouth

sallow •ADJECTIVE• **sallower, sallowest** a person with a sallow complexion has pale, yellowish-brown, unhealthy-looking skin

sally •VERB• **sallies, sallying, sallied** to rush out suddenly
•NOUN• **sallies** 1 a sudden rush or attack 2 a witty remark

salmon •NOUN• **salmon** 1 a salmon is a large sea fish with a silvery skin, that swims up rivers to lay its eggs 2 salmon is an orange-pink colour

salmonella •NOUN• a type of bacteria that can cause food-poisoning

salon •NOUN• **salons** a shop where services such as hairdressing or beauty treatments take place

saloon •NOUN• **saloons** 1 a bar where alcoholic drinks are served
2 a car with a hard roof, several seats and a separate space for luggage
3 a dining-room for passengers on a ship

salt •NOUN• **salts** 1 salt is small white crystals that come from the ground (**rock salt**) or the sea (**sea salt**) and are used for flavouring food 2 a salt is a substance formed from a metal and an acid
•VERB• **salts, salting, salted** to put salt on something, usually on food for flavour, or on roads to stop ice forming
♦ **salty** •ADJECTIVE• **saltier, saltiest** containing salt or tasting very strongly of salt: *I thought the soup was awfully salty.*

salute •VERB• **salutes, saluting, saluted** 1 to greet someone with a formal gesture. Soldiers salute their officers by standing still and raising one hand to their forehead 2 to praise someone or what they have done: *Today we salute the brave people of this town.*
•NOUN• **salutes** a movement that shows respect to someone you meet, especially a military officer

salvage •VERB• **salvages, salvaging, salvaged** to rescue what you can after a

disaster of some kind, especially the sinking of a ship: *some furniture that was salvaged from the building after the fire*

salvation •NOUN• being saved or saving someone or something

same •ADJECTIVE• exactly alike or very similar: *I was wearing the same jacket as Barbara.* • *The two cases are exactly the same.*
•PRONOUN• something that is alike or similar: *You know I'd do the same for you.*
• **all the same** anyway, nevertheless, or in spite of something: *The flight might be delayed but you have to check in now all the same.*

sample •NOUN• **samples** a small part of something that shows what the rest is like
•VERB• **samples, sampling, sampled** to take or test a small part of something: *Would you like to sample our new product?*

sanatorium •NOUN• **sanatoriums** or **sanatoria** a hospital that cares for people who need treatment or rest for a long time

sanctuary •NOUN• **sanctuaries** 1 a holy place, for example in a church, mosque or temple 2 a safe place: *refugees seeking sanctuary* • *a bird sanctuary*

sand •NOUN• **sands** tiny grains of rock that are found on beaches, on river-beds and in deserts
•VERB• **sands, sanding, sanded** to make a rough surface smooth by rubbing it with sandpaper: *The wood looked very different after it had been sanded down and varnished.*
⇒ **sandy**

sandal •NOUN• **sandals** sandals are light open shoes with straps for wearing in warm weather

sandbag •NOUN• **sandbags** a small sack filled with sand. Sandbags are used to build walls to keep out flooding water or bullets

sand dune •NOUN• **sand dunes** a hill of sand on or near a beach

sandpaper •NOUN• strong paper with a layer of sand glued to one side, used for smoothing wood or rough metal surfaces

sandshoe •NOUN• **sandshoes** a light shoe made of fabric with a rubber sole

sandstone •NOUN• a type of soft rock that is often used in building

sandwich •NOUN• **sandwiches** two slices of bread with a filling between them: *What's so special about cucumber sandwiches?* •VERB• **sandwiches, sandwiching, sandwiched** to be sandwiched between things or people is to be squashed between them: *I was sandwiched between the backs of two huge people.*

ⓘ This word comes from the name of the Earl of **Sandwich**. It is said that in the 18th century he invented sandwiches so that he would not have to stop playing gambling games to be served meals.

sandy •ADJECTIVE• **sandier, sandiest 1** containing or covered with sand: *sandy soil* **2** light reddish-brown: *a sandy-haired child*

sane •ADJECTIVE• **saner, sanest 1** not mad or mentally ill: *The judge was told that Foster was sane at the time of the murder.* **2** sensible: *She seems like a sane enough person.* ⇒ **sanity**

sang •VERB• a way of changing the verb **sing** to make a past tense: *We sang folk songs all evening to Gerry's guitar.*

sanitary •ADJECTIVE• to do with keeping clean and healthy: *Diseases spread quickly where sanitary conditions are poor.*

sanitation •ADJECTIVE• ways of protecting people's health by providing clean water and getting dirty water and waste away from buildings

sanity •NOUN• not being mad or mentally ill

sank •VERB• a way of changing the verb **sink** to make a past tense: *Many ships sank without trace in those days.*

sap •NOUN• the juice inside plants and trees •VERB• **saps, sapping, sapped** to sap your strength or energy is to gradually make you feel more and more tired: *The terrible heat sapped our energy by lunchtime.*

sapling •NOUN• **saplings** a young tree

sapphire •NOUN• **sapphires** a dark blue precious stone that is used in jewellery

sarcasm •NOUN• saying one thing when you actually mean the opposite. People often use sarcasm when they are trying to be funny
♦ **sarcastic** •ADJECTIVE• meaning the exact opposite in order to hurt or amuse someone: *When we told Marge we liked her hat, she didn't know if we were being sarcastic or not.*

sardine •NOUN• **sardines** a type of small sea fish that is either eaten fresh or packed tightly in small tins

sari •NOUN• **saris** a long piece of fabric that is worn like a dress by Hindu women. It is wound round the waist and the end is draped over one shoulder or over the head

sarong •NOUN• **sarongs** a wide piece of fabric that covers the lower part of the body. It is wound round the waist or under the arms

sash •NOUN• **sashes** a strip of cloth worn around the waist or over one shoulder, usually as part of a uniform

sat •VERB• a way of changing the verb **sit** to make a past tense. It can be used with or without a helping verb: *Class 3 sat quietly, waiting for their teacher.* • *I've sat here for an hour waiting for you!*

satchel •NOUN• **satchels** a small bag with a shoulder strap that is used to carry schoolbooks

satellite •NOUN• **satellites** an object in space that moves around a planet or star

satellite television •NOUN• broadcasts that are sent and received using satellites that are designed for that purpose

satin •NOUN• a fabric with a shiny surface

satisfaction •NOUN• a contented feeling after getting or doing what you wanted: *I get a lot of satisfaction out of baking my own bread.*

satisfactory •ADJECTIVE• **1** good enough, but not outstanding: *Gareth's progress in maths has been satisfactory.* **2** right or wanted: *a very satisfactory result*

satisfy •VERB• **satisfies, satisfying, satisfied 1** to be satisfied is to be happy or contented: *I'm afraid I'm not satisfied with the way we've been treated.* **2** to satisfy someone is to give them what they want or need: *I don't think a biscuit will satisfy a boy who's been playing football all afternoon.*

satsuma •NOUN• **satsumas** a fruit like a small orange with no pips

saturate •VERB• **saturates, saturating,**

saturated to be saturated is to be soaking wet

Saturday • NOUN • **Saturdays** the day of the week after Friday and before Sunday

ⓘ **Saturday** comes from the Old English word **Sæterdæg**, which means *Saturn's day*. Saturn is the Roman god of harvest.

sauce • NOUN • **sauces** 1 a liquid that food is cooked in or served with: *I like plenty of tomato sauce with my chips.* 2 cheeky remarks: *That's enough of your sauce!*

saucepan • NOUN • **saucepans** a deep round cooking pot that usually has a long handle and a lid

saucer • NOUN • **saucers** a small shallow dish that is used for resting a cup on

saucy • ADJECTIVE • **saucier, sauciest** cheeky

sauna • NOUN • **saunas** a steam bath where you sit in a room filled with the steam produced by throwing cold water on hot coals

saunter • VERB • **saunters, sauntering, sauntered** to walk slowly in a relaxed way: *people sauntering round the park on a warm evening*
• NOUN • **saunters** a gentle stroll: *a saunter along the seafront*

sausage • NOUN • **sausages** meat that is minced and stuffed into a skin to make long tube shapes

savage • ADJECTIVE • fierce and cruel: *a savage attack by a stray dog*
• VERB • **savages, savaging, savaged** to be savaged by an animal is to be attacked and badly injured by it
• NOUN • **savages** an uncivilized person
♦ **savagely** • ADVERB • fiercely and cruelly

savanna or **savannah** • NOUN • **savannas** or **savannahs** a grassy plain without trees, especially in Africa

save • VERB • **saves, saving, saved** 1 to save someone or something is to rescue them from something unpleasant: *The firefighters saved everyone in the building.* • *We saved our photographs, but everything else in the loft was wrecked by the leaking water.* 2 to save someone's life is to prevent them from dying: *There's no doubt that the safety belts saved our lives.*

3 to save something is to store it for later: *Jamie saves half his pocket money every week.* • *Save the data on your files on a backup disk if you can.*
4 to save time or money is to use less time or money than you would normally do: *Save 20% on all our products this week.* • *You can save 40 minutes by going along the motorway.*
• NOUN • **saves** when a goalkeeper prevents the other team from scoring a goal: *a brilliant save, just in front of the goalpost*
♦ **savings** • PLURAL NOUN • money that you collect and keep to use at some time in the future: *Colin's going to spend all his savings on a drum kit.*
♦ **saviour** • NOUN • **saviours** 1 a person who rescues someone or something from danger 2 the Saviour, in Christian religions, is Jesus Christ

savour • VERB • **savours, savouring, savoured** to eat or drink something slowly in order to enjoy it for longer: *We ate the cakes slowly, savouring every mouthful.*
♦ **savoury** • ADJECTIVE • not sweet or containing sugar

saw[1] • NOUN • **saws** a tool with a thin notched blade that can cut through wood or metal

saw[2] • VERB • a way of changing the verb **see** to make a past tense: *I know you were there because I saw you with my own eyes.*

sawdust • NOUN • the thick dust that is created when wood is cut with a saw

sawmill • NOUN • **sawmills** a place where timber is taken to be cut before being used, for example, in building

saxophone • NOUN • **saxophones** a wind instrument with a long curved metal body. You play it by blowing it and pressing different keys

say • VERB • **says, saying, said** 1 to speak words out loud: *I was just going to say 'hello'.* 2 to express in written words: *What does the notice say?*
• NOUN • to **have a say** or to **have your say** is to be able to give your opinion: *The others all decided to go and I didn't even have a say in the matter.*
♦ **saying** • NOUN • **sayings** a phrase or

Aa
Bb
Cc
Dd
Ee
Ff
Gg
Hh
Ii
Jj
Kk
Ll
Mm
Nn
Oo
Pp
Qq
Rr
Ss
Tt
Uu
Vv
Ww
Xx
Yy
Zz

sentence that people often use and sometimes gives wise advice: *Gran's favourite saying is 'an apple a day keeps the doctor away'.*

scab •NOUN• **scabs** a crust of dried blood that forms over a wound as it heals
♦ **scabby** •ADJECTIVE• **scabbier, scabbiest** **1** covered in scabs: *a scabby knee* **2** not in good condition or nice-looking: *a scabby old hairbrush*

scaffold •NOUN• **scaffolds** a platform used in the past to execute criminals on

scaffolding •NOUN• a framework of poles and planks for workmen to stand on when they are working on the outside of a tall building

scald •VERB• **scalds, scalding, scalded** to be scalded is to be burnt by very hot liquid or steam
•NOUN• **scalds** a burn caused by hot liquid or steam

scale •NOUN• **scales 1** a series of marks or divisions used for measuring something: *an earthquake that measured 3.2 on the Richter scale* **2** the size of something such as a model or a map, compared to the actual size of the thing it represents: *A scale of 10:1 means the model is ten times bigger than the real thing.* **3** the general size of something: *steel production on a huge scale* **4** a sequence of musical notes, especially between notes that are octaves apart: *the scale of G major*
•VERB• **scales, scaling, scaled** to climb up something
♦ **scales** •NOUN• **1** the small overlapping plates that cover the skin of fish and reptiles **2** an instrument for weighing: *a set of kitchen scales*
⇒ **scaly**

scallop •NOUN• **scallops** a shellfish that you can eat and that lives inside two hinged fan-shaped shells

scalp •NOUN• **scalps** the skin on top of your head where your hair grows
•VERB• **scalps, scalping, scalped** to cut off someone's hair and the skin it grows from

scalpel •NOUN• **scalpels** a small knife, used especially by surgeons, with a very sharp thin blade

scaly •ADJECTIVE• **scalier, scaliest** covered with small, dry particles and flaky

scamp •NOUN• **scamps** a mischievous child

scamper •VERB• **scampers, scampering, scampered** to run quickly, taking short steps

scampi •PLURAL NOUN• large prawns that are usually deep fried in batter or breadcrumbs

scan •VERB• **scans, scanning, scanned 1** to scan something such as a page of writing is to read it very quickly: *Lou scanned the jobs section of the paper, looking for anything suitable.* **2** to scan an area is to look all around it from one position **3** to scan something with a scanner is to examine it with a device that uses the information from beams of light or sound to make a picture of it: *You can scan the picture, and then send it to me in an email.* **4** a poem scans when it has a rhythmic pattern
•NOUN• **scans 1** a quick look through a piece of writing or around an area **2** a process that produces an image on a screen by directing beams of light or sound at an object: *The doctor sent Amy for a brain scan.*

scandal •NOUN• **scandals 1** a scandal is a disgraceful or shocking situation **2** scandal is information about other people that is considered shocking: *Heard any juicy scandal recently?*
♦ **scandalous** •ADJECTIVE• disgraceful or outrageous: *It's scandalous that we can't do more to help these people.*

scanner •NOUN• **scanners** a machine that gets information about an object by directing beams of light or sound at it. It uses the information to make an image of the object that can be seen on a screen

scant •ADJECTIVE• **scanter, scantest** very little or hardly enough: *She had paid scant attention so I wasn't surprised when she looked at me blankly.*
♦ **scanty** •ADJECTIVE• **scantier, scantiest** very small or hardly big enough: *a scanty nightshirt*

scapegoat •NOUN• **scapegoats** a person who takes the blame for something that was not all their fault

Aa Bb Cc Dd Ee Ff Gg Hh Ii Jj Kk Ll Mm Nn Oo Pp Qq Rr Ss Tt Uu Vv Ww Xx Yy Zz

scar •NOUN• **scars** a mark that is left on skin after a wound has healed

•VERB• **scars, scarring, scarred** to be scarred is to have permanent marks where you were injured: *That small mistake will leave Ian scarred for life.*

scarce •ADJECTIVE• **scarcer, scarcest** difficult to get: *Food was scarce, as it always is in wartime.*

♦ **scarcely** •ADVERB• hardly, or almost not at all: *Carmen's throat was so sore she could scarcely speak.*

♦ **scarcity** •NOUN• a shortage of something

scare •VERB• **scares, scaring, scared** to be scared is to be frightened by something: *Some of the younger children were scared by the screeching fireworks.*

•NOUN• **scares 1** a scare is a fright: *It gave us all a bit of a scare when Mother fainted.* **2** a scare is a sudden worry that lots of people have about something: *a bomb scare*

⇒ **scary**

scarecrow •NOUN• **scarecrows** a simple model of a person in a field, set up to frighten birds and stop them from eating crops

scarf •NOUN• **scarves** a long strip or square of cloth that you wear around your neck, shoulders or head to keep warm or for decoration

scarlet •NOUN• a bright red colour

scarper •VERB• **scarpers, scarpering, scarpered** to run away

scary •ADJECTIVE• **scarier, scariest** making you feel frightened: *It was scary when the doors suddenly blew open.*

scatter •VERB• **scatters, scattering, scattered 1** to scatter a thing or things is to spread them in lots of places over a wide area: *Scatter the seeds evenly over the prepared soil.* **2** a group of people scatter when they run away in different directions

scavenge •VERB• **scavenges, scavenging, scavenged** to search amongst rubbish for things that can be used or eaten: *stray dogs scavenging food from the dustbins*

♦ **scavenger** •NOUN• **scavengers** a wild bird or animal that feeds mainly on the flesh of dead animals and on other waste material

scenario •NOUN• **scenarios** a situation that might happen, or one in a play, film or book: *The worst scenario would be if the two countries declare war.* • *I'm thinking about a couple of scenarios for a new story.*

scene •NOUN• **scenes 1** the setting that an event takes place in: *the scene of the crime* **2** a small section of a play, a book or a film: *We'll have to film the ball scene next.* **3** a place or situation as someone sees it: *Before me was a scene of celebration.* • *The scene in the town square is just the same as yesterday.* **4** to **make a scene** is to make an embarrassing fuss

♦ **scenery** •NOUN• the countryside around about you: *You get to see some wonderful scenery from the train.*

♦ **scenic** •ADJECTIVE• with pleasant things to look at: *The ringroad is a more scenic route to the other side of town.*

scent •NOUN• **scents 1** a perfume: *The scent of lilies can fill a whole room.* **2** the smell of an animal that other animals can follow

•VERB• **scents, scenting, scented** to discover by smell: *A hungry animal will scent food long before it sees it.*

sceptic •NOUN• **sceptics** a person who has doubts about things that other people are sure about: *Of course the sceptics said the photographs of the aliens were fakes.*

♦ **sceptical** •ADJECTIVE• doubting that something is true: *Ken thinks it'll work, but I'm still sceptical.*

sceptre •NOUN• **sceptres** a rod that a king or queen carries at official ceremonies

schedule •NOUN• **schedules** a plan or timetable that shows when certain things should happen or be done: *a flight schedule* • **on schedule** on time: *To my surprise, the coach left right on schedule.*

scheme •NOUN• **schemes** a plan of action: *a new scheme to build a carpark on the old playing field*

•VERB• **schemes, scheming, schemed** to make secret plans, especially to cause harm or damage

♦ **scheming** •ADJECTIVE• crafty or cunning

scholar •NOUN• **scholars** a person who

studies and knows a lot about a particular subject: *a scholar of Greek*
♦ **scholarly** •ADJECTIVE• showing a deep knowledge of a subject: *a scholarly work about Victorian art*
♦ **scholarship** •NOUN• **scholarships** 1 a scholarship is money for a student to study at a school or university: *There are several scholarships available for very bright students.* 2 scholarship is serious study of a subject

school •NOUN• **schools** 1 a place where children and teenagers go to be educated: *You'll go to school when you're five years old.* 2 all the pupils and teachers in a school: *The whole school was in the playground, watching the fire.* 3 a large number of fish or dolphins that swim together in a group
•VERB• **schools, schooling, schooled** to school someone to do something is to train them to do it: *The boys have been schooled to be polite to visitors.*
♦ **schooling** •NOUN• your schooling is the education you receive, especially at school

schoolchildren •PLURAL NOUN• children who go to school

schoolteacher •NOUN• **schoolteachers** a teacher in a school

schooner •NOUN• **schooners** a sailing ship with two masts

science •NOUN• **sciences** 1 studying the natural world and the things that happen in it 2 a particular study about the natural world, especially chemistry, physics or biology

---

ⓘ The word **science** comes from the Latin word **scientia**, which means *knowledge*.

---

science fiction •NOUN• stories and films that are set in the future or other parts of the universe

scientific •ADJECTIVE• 1 to do with science: *scientific research* 2 based on expert knowledge or a system of rules and tests, like the study of a science: *Jeremy's explanation of why my seeds didn't come up wasn't very scientific – he said it was because they were mine!*
♦ **scientifically** •ADVERB• according to the rules of science: *a scientifically proven law*

scientist •NOUN• **scientists** a person who studies science or whose work involves science: *a laboratory where scientists test bacteria found in food*

scissors •PLURAL NOUN• a cutting tool that has two blades joined in the middle. You use scissors by opening and closing the blades with the fingers and thumb of one hand

scoff •VERB• **scoffs, scoffing, scoffed** 1 to scoff at a thing or person is to think that they do not deserve your serious attention: *The president scoffed at the idea of a revolution in his country.* 2 to scoff something is to eat it very fast

scold •VERB• **scolds, scolding, scolded** to tell someone off for doing something wrong
♦ **scolding** •NOUN• **scoldings** a telling-off

scone •NOUN• **scones** a small, round, plain cake that is often eaten with butter and jam

scoop •VERB• **scoops, scooping, scooped** to lift something with your hands cupped like a spoon
•NOUN• **scoops** 1 a hollow instrument like a bowl or shovel for lifting liquid or loose substances like sand or sugar 2 a piece of news that nobody else has heard yet: *This story was a wonderful scoop for the Evening Mail.*

scooter •NOUN• **scooters** a vehicle with two wheels at either end of a board and a tall handle. You ride it by standing on the board with one foot and pushing the ground with the other

scope •NOUN• 1 the whole range of things that a subject deals with: *I'm afraid your question goes outside the scope of this meeting.* 2 freedom or opportunity to do something: *There's plenty of scope for improving these plans.*

scorch •VERB• **scorches, scorching, scorched** to burn the surface of something by touching it with something hot and leaving a brown mark
♦ **scorching** •ADJECTIVE• very hot: *It is a scorching day.*

score •VERB• **scores, scoring, scored** 1 to get a point in a game, test or competition: *Hamilton has scored again for the Rovers.* • *Jenny was first in the maths test because she scored 19 out of 20.*

Aa
Bb
Cc
Dd
Ee
Ff
Gg
Hh
Ii
Jj
Kk
Ll
Mm
Nn
Oo
Pp
Qq
Rr
Ss
Tt
Uu
Vv
Ww
Xx
Yy
Zz

2 to keep a record of the points that are won in a game or competition: *Who's scoring?*

3 to scratch a surface with something sharp: *Score a straight line across the card and fold it carefully.*

•NOUN• **scores 1** the number of points that you get in a game, test or competition: *What's the final score?* • *On this test, a score of more than 15 is good.* **2** an old word for twenty

scorn •VERB• **scorns, scorning, scorned** to look down on someone or something because you think they are bad or worthless: *The family scorned everyone's attempts to help them.*

•NOUN• a feeling of contempt

♦ **scornful** •ADJECTIVE• full of contempt and without any respect: *scornful remarks*

♦ **scornfully** •ADVERB• in a superior, mocking way: *He laughed scornfully.*

scorpion •NOUN• **scorpions** a small creature like an insect with four pairs of legs and a long tail with a sting on the end

scot-free •ADVERB• without being punished: *The girls got off scot-free because nobody had seen them.*

scoundrel •NOUN• **scoundrels** a man who cheats and behaves dishonestly

scour •VERB• **scours, scouring, scoured 1** to clean a surface by scraping and rubbing hard: *The saucepans needed hours of scouring.*
2 to search a large area thoroughly: *Teams of villagers scoured the hillside for the missing climber.*

scout •NOUN• **scouts 1** a scout is a person who is sent out to gather information, especially one who is sent ahead of a group on an expedition **2** a Scout is a young person who is a member of the Scout Association

•VERB• **scouts, scouting, scouted** to **scout around** for something is to go looking for it: *I'll scout around for a chair that matches the others.*

scowl •VERB• **scowls, scowling, scowled** to lower your eyebrows in an angry or puzzled way: *What are you scowling at?*

•NOUN• **scowls** an angry or puzzled look: *Mr Lee greeted the class with a scowl.*

scramble •VERB• **scrambles, scrambling, scrambled 1** to climb using your hands and

feet: *scrambling up the hillside*

2 to push and shove with other people to get to something: *people scrambling to get to the bargains before anyone else*

3 to scramble eggs is to mix them together and cook them

4 to scramble a broadcast or message is to code it so that it cannot be understood easily

•NOUN• **scrambles 1** a difficult climb over rough gound

2 a struggle to get to something before other people

3 a motorbike race over rough ground

scrap •NOUN• **scraps 1** a scrap is a small piece of something bigger: *a scrap of paper to write your address on* • *There isn't a scrap of evidence against us.*

2 scrap is rubbish, especially waste metal that could be used again

3 a scrap is a fight: *a bit of a scrap going on in the playground*

•VERB• **scraps, scrapping, scrapped** to throw something away because it is useless: *Let's just scrap the whole idea now.*

⇒ **scrappy**

scrapbook •NOUN• **scrapbooks** a book with blank pages that you can fill up with cuttings or pictures that you want to keep together

scrape •VERB• **scrapes, scraping, scraped**

1 to rub with or against something hard or rough: *I'll have to scrape the mud off this window before I clean it.* • *Lydia had scraped her elbow when she fell off her bike.*

2 to **scrape together** money is to just manage to collect enough money from different people or places

3 to **scrape through** an exam is to pass it, but only just

•NOUN• **scrapes 1** when something hard or rough is rubbed or scratched against a surface **2** a difficult or embarrassing situation: *You expect boys to get into scrapes when they're young.*

scrappy •ADJECTIVE• **scrappier, scrappiest** not well put together or organized: *a scrappy essay*

scratch •VERB• **scratches, scratching, scratched 1** to make a mark on a surface with something sharp or pointed: *Mick scratched*

the car when he brushed the wall.
• *Generations of students had scratched their names on these desks.* 2 to rub your nails on your skin, usually because you feel itchy: *Try not to scratch the spots or they will get spread.*
•NOUN• **scratches** a mark left on a surface by something sharp
• **from scratch** from the very beginning, often for the second time: *Let's just start again from scratch.*
• **up to scratch** good enough: *David's work has not been up to scratch this term.*

scrawl •VERB• **scrawls, scrawling, scrawled** to write in a very untidy way
•NOUN• very untidy handwriting

scrawny •ADJECTIVE• **scrawnier, scrawniest** very thin and bony

scream •VERB• **screams, screaming, screamed** to make a long high-pitched cry because you are frightened, angry or in pain: *Everyone screamed on the roller coaster.*
•NOUN• **screams** a loud and high-pitched cry: *The neighbours came running when they heard the screams.*

screech •NOUN• **screeches** a sudden, harsh, high-pitched sound: *the screech of an owl in the night* • *a screech of tyres as the car sped away*
•VERB• **screeches, screeching, screeched** to make a sudden, harsh, high-pitched sound

screen •NOUN• **screens** 1 the part of a computer, television or cinema that you look at to see images: *You should be sitting at least two metres away from the screen.* 2 an upright frame or panel that protects people from something or makes a more private area in a room: *You have to go behind the screen to be examined.*
•VERB• **screens, screening, screened** 1 to show a television programme or film: *They are screening the whole series for the third time.*
2 to hide something from view or shelter it: *This part of the garden is screened by a high fence.*
3 to test lots of people for a particular illness: *All the workers here should be screened for the virus.*

screw •NOUN• **screws** an object like a nail with a slot in its head and a spiral ridge all the way down it

•VERB• **screws, screwing, screwed** 1 to fix a screw into something: *Screw the bits of wood together.* 2 to fit something with a turning movement: *Screw the lid on tightly.*

screwdriver •NOUN• **screwdrivers** a tool with a metal stick that fits into the head of a screw so that when you turn it, the screw also turns

scribble •VERB• **scribbles, scribbling, scribbled** 1 to write very quickly and untidily: *I scribbled his name down before I forgot it.*
2 to draw meaningless lines in an untidy way: *The baby had a pen and was scribbling on the wall.*
•NOUN• **scribbles** 1 handwriting that is very untidy 2 meaningless untidy lines that someone has drawn

scribe •NOUN• **scribes** a person in the past whose job was to copy out manuscripts

scrimp •VERB• **scrimps, scrimping, scrimped** to spend as little money as possible by living cheaply: *After scrimping and saving for a year, we had enough money for a short holiday.*

script •NOUN• **scripts** 1 the words of a film or play: *The actors were reading from their scripts at rehearsal.* 2 a way of writing down language: *The Russian language is written in Cyrillic script.*

scripture •NOUN• **scriptures** the holy writings of a religion, for example the Bible

scroll •NOUN• **scrolls** a long roll of paper with writing on it
•VERB• **scrolls, scrolling, scrolled** to move text up or down on a computer screen so that you can see other parts of a file

scrounge •VERB• **scrounges, scrounging, scrounged** an informal word meaning to get the things you want by asking for them from other people: *You should buy your own sweets instead of scrounging off me all the time.*
• **scrounger** •NOUN• **scroungers** a person who gets what they want by asking other people instead of buying their own things

scrub •VERB• **scrubs, scrubbing, scrubbed** to rub something hard to get it clean: *We'll need to scrub these stains off the floor.*

scruff •NOUN• **scruffs** a scruff is a person who looks very untidy
• **by the scruff of the neck** by the collar or the back of a person's or animal's neck: *The mother cat lifts her kittens in her mouth by the scruff of the neck.*
✦ **scruffy** •ADJECTIVE• **scruffier, scruffiest** untidy and dirty

scrum •NOUN• **scrums** the part of a rugby game where groups of players from both teams form a circle by joining arms with their heads down and try to win the ball by pushing against the players of the other team

scrumptious •ADJECTIVE• delicious

scrunch •VERB• **scrunches, scrunching, scrunched 1** to crush or crumple something **2** to make the noise of something hard being crushed: *The gravel scrunched under our feet.*
•NOUN• **scrunches** the noise of something hard being crushed: *a horrible scrunch as the car hit the wall*
✦ **scrunchie** •NOUN• **scrunchies** a piece of elastic covered in cloth that you can use to hold long hair back from your face

scuba diving •NOUN• swimming underwater while breathing air through a pipe and mouthpiece connected to tanks fixed on the swimmer's back

scuffle •NOUN• **scuffles** a fight involving a small number of people

scull •VERB• **sculls, sculling, sculled 1** to row a boat using small paddles **2** to move in water paddling with your hands, but with your arms by your sides

scullery •NOUN• **sculleries** a small room by a kitchen, especially in a big old house, where the washing-up is done and food is cleaned before being used

sculpt •VERB• **sculpts, sculpting, sculpted** to carve or make models of objects or figures using materials such as clay or stone
✦ **sculptor** •NOUN• **sculptors** an artist who makes models of objects or figures
✦ **sculpture** •NOUN• **sculptures 1** a sculpture is a model of an object or figure that an artist carves or makes out of a material like stone, wood or clay **2** sculpture is the work of an artist who creates models: *go to art college to study sculpture*

scum •NOUN• **1** a layer of dirt or dust floating on the surface of a liquid **2** a very informal and impolite word for a person or people that you find disgusting

scurry •VERB• **scurries, scrurrying, scurried** to move in a hurry with a lot of short steps

scurvy •NOUN• a disease caused by not eating enough fresh fruit and vegetables

scuttle •VERB• **scuttles, scuttling, scuttled 1** to move along with lots of short fast steps: *a beetle scuttling away* **2** to scuttle a boat is to purposely make a hole in it to sink it

scythe •NOUN• **scythes** a tool with a handle and a long curved blade that is used for cutting long grass or harvesting crops

sea •NOUN• **seas 1** the salt water that covers most of the Earth's surface: *Australia is completely surrounded by sea.* **2** a large lake of salt water: *the Dead Sea*

seabed •NOUN• the floor of the sea: *a wreck on the seabed*

seafarer •NOUN• **seafarers** a sailor or a person who travels by sea
✦ **seafaring** •ADJECTIVE• used to travelling by or working at sea: *a seafaring nation*

seagull •NOUN• **seagulls** a sea bird with webbed feet, short legs and long wings with grey, black or white feathers

sea-horse •NOUN• **sea-horses** a type of small fish that swims upright and has a horse-like head and neck

seal¹ •VERB• **seals, sealing, sealed** to close something firmly: *Don't seal the envelope yet.*
•NOUN• **seals 1** anything that keeps something firmly closed: *Break the seal with scissors before opening the box.* • *We need a new seal on the washing-machine door.* **2** an official mark stamped on a piece of wax and attached to a document to show that it is genuine

seal² •NOUN• **seals** an animal with a small head and a shiny coat that lives mainly in the sea.

sea level •NOUN• the average level of the surface of the sea, when it is between high and low tide

sea lion •NOUN• **sea lions** a type of large seal

seam •NOUN• **seams 1** a join between two

Aa Bb Cc Dd Ee Ff Gg Hh Ii Jj Kk Ll Mm Nn Oo Pp Qq Rr Ss Tt Uu Vv Ww Xx Yy Zz

edges: *the trousers have split down the back seam* **2** a seam of coal is a band or layer of it in the ground

seaman •NOUN• **seamen** a sailor who is not an officer

seamstress •NOUN• **seamstresses** a woman who sews for a living, especially making dresses

seaplane •NOUN• **seaplanes** an aircraft that is designed to take off from, and land on water

sear •VERB• **sears, searing, seared** to hurt or burn

search •VERB• **searches, searching, searched** to search is to look carefully for a thing or person: *I've searched everywhere for my keys.*
•NOUN• **searches** an attempt to find something: *They made a thorough search of the countryside.*

searchlight •NOUN• **searchlights** a strong beam of light that can pick out distant objects at night: *A figure running across the field was caught in the searchlight.*

seashore •NOUN• the land next to the sea, especially the rocky or sandy parts that the sea covers when the tide is high

seasick •ADJECTIVE• feeling ill or being sick when you are on a boat or ship, because of its movement on the sea: *Some lucky people have never been seasick.*

seaside •NOUN• a place beside the sea where people go on holiday

season •NOUN• **seasons** **1** one of the four main periods that the year is divided into: *Spring is my favourite season.* **2** the particular period of the year that a certain activity takes place: *the football season*
•VERB• **seasons, seasoning, seasoned** to flavour food by putting salt, pepper or other herbs and spices into it
♦ **seasonal** •ADJECTIVE• happening only at certain times of the year
♦ **seasoning** •NOUN• **seasonings** salt, pepper and other herbs and spices that you can use to flavour food

season ticket •NOUN• **season tickets** a ticket that you can use as often as you want for a certain period of time

seat •NOUN• **seats** **1** a piece of furniture for sitting on: *a garden seat* • *a theatre seat* **2** the part of your body that you sit on: *There's a rip in the seat of my skirt.* **3** a position in parliament or on a committee: *The party lost three seats in the election.*
•VERB• **seats, seating, seated** **1** to seat a person is to give them somewhere to sit: *The host and hostess were seated at opposite ends of the table.* **2** to seat a certain number of people is to have enough room for them all to sit down: *The new theatre seats twice as many people as the old one did.*

seat belt •NOUN• **seat belts** a strap attached to a seat in a vehicle that prevents a passenger from being thrown forward in a crash: *Please fasten your seat belts now.*

seaweed •NOUN• a type of plant that grows in the sea

seaworthy •ADJECTIVE• in good enough condition to be sailed on the sea: *This yacht is not seaworthy with a crack in its mast.*

secluded •ADJECTIVE• quiet, private and hidden from view: *a secluded corner of the garden*
♦ **seclusion** •NOUN• peacefulness and privacy

second •ADJECTIVE AND ADVERB• next after the first: *Julia is their second daughter.* • *Craig came second in the final exam.*
•NOUN• **seconds** **1** a thing or person that is number two in a series: *This programme is the second in a series of three.* **2** one sixtieth of a minute or a very short time: *one minute and thirty seconds* • *Just wait a second.* **3** a product that has been made with a fault and so is not perfect: *The factory shop sells seconds at very cheap prices.*
•VERB• **seconds, seconding, seconded** **1** to second a fighter is to be an attendant and support them **2** to second an idea or plan is to support it and agree when someone suggests it
♦ **secondary** •ADJECTIVE• a development from something that came first or before: *Freddie had measles and then developed a secondary infection.*
⇒ **secondly**

secondary school •NOUN• **secondary schools** a school for pupils between the ages of 11 and 18, that children go to after primary school

second-hand •ADJECTIVE AND ADVERB• not new because of being owned before by someone else: *Our car was second-hand when we bought it.* • *Kathryn buys all her clothes second-hand.*

secondly •ADVERB• a word that you use to introduce the second thing in a list: *And secondly, I'd like to thank Mrs Ambrose for all her help.*

second nature •NOUN• a firmly fixed habit that you do not think about: *I took a long time to learn to drive but it's second nature to me now.*

secrecy •NOUN• being secret: *The mission must be carried out in total secrecy.*

secret •NOUN• **secrets** 1 a piece of information that must not be told to anyone else: *The birthday party was a well-kept secret.* 2 something that nobody knows or understands: *looking for the secret of eternal youth*
•ADJECTIVE• not to be told or shown to other people: *a secret passage* • *secret government files*

secretary •NOUN• **secretaries** 1 a person whose job is to type letters, keep files and take notes at business meetings for another person or a group of people: *Please leave a message with my secretary if I'm out.* 2 a person who is in charge of a government department
♦ **secretarial** •ADJECTIVE• to do with the job of a secretary

secrete •VERB• **secretes, secreting, secreted** to make and release a substance: *The plant secretes a sticky liquid that attracts flies.*
♦ **secretion** •NOUN• **secretions** a substance that a part of a plant or animal makes and releases

secretive •ADJECTIVE• liking to keep secrets from people: *Logan was very secretive about his past.*
♦ **secretively** •ADVERB• so that nobody else knows or finds out

secret service •NOUN• **secret services** a government department that deals with spying: *a secret service agent*

sect •NOUN• **sects** a small group of people within a larger group, who have certain different opinions about things, especially about their religion

sectarian •ADJECTIVE• to do with there being different small groups within a larger one, each with different opinions and beliefs, especially about religion

section •NOUN• **sections** 1 a part or a division of something: *The table has three sections that fit together.* • *The novels will be in the fiction section of the library.* 2 the side view of something when it is cut right through or across: *a section showing the inside of a plant stem*

sector •NOUN• **sectors** 1 a part of any kind of area: *the American sector of the city* • *the business sector of the community* 2 a part of a circle formed by two radii and the part of the circumference between them

secure •ADJECTIVE• **securer, securest** 1 safe, happy and not worried about any danger: *a secure family background*
2 safe against attack or harm: *Locks that keep your house secure against burglars.*
3 firmly fixed or fastened: *Check that the ropes are secure.*
•VERB• **secures, securing, secured** 1 to fix or fasten something firmly: *The tent was secured with ropes and pegs.* 2 to get something for sure: *Sheila has secured a place at the best college in the country.*
♦ **security** •NOUN• being protected from harm or any danger: *matters of national security* • *the security of a loving family*

sedate •VERB• **sedates, sedating, sedated** to give someone a drug to make them feel calmer and less nervous or excited
•ADJECTIVE• quiet, calm and dignified
♦ **sedation** •NOUN• giving someone a drug to make them feel calmer
♦ **sedative** •NOUN• **sedatives** a medicine that helps you feel calm

sediment •NOUN• the solid grains that settle at the bottom of a liquid

see •VERB• **sees, seeing, saw, seen** 1 to look at something and notice it: *The dog goes*

Aa Bb Cc Dd Ee Ff Gg Hh Ii Jj Kk Ll Mm Nn Oo Pp Qq Rr **Ss** Tt Uu Vv Ww Xx Yy Zz

mad whenever he sees a cat. • *We're going to London to see the sights.*

2 to meet someone or spend time with them: *Have you seen Peter much lately?*

3 to understand something: *Now I see what you mean.*

4 to see someone as something is to imagine them like it: *Can you see me as an astronaut?*

5 to see someone somewhere is to go there with them: *I'll see you to the door.*

6 to see that something happens is to make sure that it happens

7 to **see through** a thing or person is to know what they are up to when they are trying to trick you

8 to **see to something** is to deal with it: *Don't you worry about the travel arrangements – I'll see to them.*

seed •NOUN• **seeds** a thing that a plant produces and that new plants grow from: *Sow the seeds about two inches deep in the soil.*
♦ **seedling** •NOUN• **seedlings** a very young plant

seek •VERB• **seeks, seeking, sought 1** to search for something: *We sought him high and low but never found him.*
2 to try to get or achieve something: *She's seeking fame and fortune.*
3 to ask for something: *You should seek the teacher's advice.*

seem •VERB• **seems, seeming, seemed** to appear to be something or to give the impression of being something: *You didn't seem to be interested.* • *Things seem calm at the moment.*
♦ **seemingly** •ADVERB• apparently: *The queue to get in was seemingly endless.*
♦ **seemly** •ADJECTIVE• decent or suitable: *That's not very seemly behaviour for a little girl.*

seen •VERB• a form of the verb **see** that is used with a helping verb to show that something happened in the past: *I haven't seen you for ages.* • *I wouldn't have seen that if you hadn't pointed it out.*

seep •VERB• **seeps, seeping, seeped** to leak or flow slowly through something: *Water was seeping through the ceiling.*

seesaw •NOUN• **seesaws** a playground toy

that children sit on either end of, pushing off the ground with their feet and alternately swinging up and down

seethe •VERB• **seethes, seething, seethed** to be extremely angry

see-through •ADJECTIVE• so thin that you can see what is on the other side: *a blouse with see-through sleeves*

segment •NOUN• **segments** a section or a division of something: *Divide the orange into segments.*

segregate •VERB• **segregates, segregating, segregated** to keep one kind of person or animal separate from another kind: *The young bulls are segregated from the cows.*
♦ **segregation** •NOUN• separating different kinds of animals or people from each other

seismic •ADJECTIVE• to do with earthquakes

seize •VERB• **seizes, seizing, seized 1** to grab something: *Joel seized my hand and shook it.* **2** to **seize up** is to stop moving easily: *I knelt on the floor so long that my knees seized up.*
♦ **seizure** •NOUN• **seizures** a sudden attack of an illness, for example, a heart attack

seldom •ADVERB• rarely or not often: *Gran seldom goes out in the evenings any more.*

select •VERB• **selects, selecting, selected** to choose from several things that are available: *Gail has been selected for the school hockey team.*
♦ **selection** •NOUN• **selections 1** a range of things that you can chose from: *a wide selection of boots and shoes* **2** something that has been chosen from amongst others: *Bring your selection to the cash desk at the door.*

self •NOUN• **selves** the real you: *Actors try to forget their true selves.*
⇒ **selfish, selfless**

self-assurance •NOUN• being confident about your own talents and abilities
♦ **self-assured** •ADJECTIVE• confident

self-centred •ADJECTIVE• thinking only about yourself and not other people

self-confident •ADJECTIVE• believing in your own power and sure that you will succeed

Aa
Bb
Cc
Dd
Ee
Ff
Gg
Hh
Ii
Jj
Kk
Ll
Mm
Nn
Oo
Pp
Qq
Rr
Ss
Tt
Uu
Vv
Ww
Xx
Yy
Zz

self-conscious •ADJECTIVE• feeling nervous and uncomfortable when you are with other people because you feel they are looking at you and criticizing you

self-defence •NOUN• trying to defend yourself from someone who is attacking you: *classes in self-defence • He said he fired the gun in self-defence.*

self-esteem •NOUN• thinking well of yourself: *Robert lacks self-esteem.*

self-importance •NOUN• thinking too well of yourself and that you are more important than other people

self-indulgent •ADJECTIVE• always ready to allow yourself things that you like or want

selfish •ADJECTIVE• thinking only about yourself and not what other people might want or need: *It would be selfish not to offer one of your sweets to your friend.*
♦ **selfishly** •ADVERB• thinking only about yourself: *He selfishly finished the food before we'd taken any.*
♦ **selfishness** •NOUN• thinking only about yourself

selfless •ADJECTIVE• thinking about other people's wants or needs before your own
♦ **selflessly** •ADVERB• thinking about other people before yourself: *George selflessly looked after his parents at home.*

self-portrait •NOUN• **self-portraits** a drawing or painting that an artist makes of himself or herself

self-raising flour •NOUN• flour that is used in baking and that includes an ingredient that makes the mixture rise when it is cooked

self-reliance •NOUN• the ability to manage alone, without asking for help from other people
♦ **self-reliant** •ADJECTIVE• not needing the help of other people because you can manage by yourself

self-respect •NOUN• your respect for yourself and care that you behave correctly

self-righteous •ADJECTIVE• thinking that you are a very good person because you do not do bad things

self-satisfied •ADJECTIVE• irritatingly pleased with yourself and your achievements: *a self-satisfied grin*

self-service •NOUN• a system in a shop or restaurant where customers serve themselves and, usually, pay at a checkout

self-sufficient •ADJECTIVE• able to provide everything you need for yourself: *If we were a self-sufficient country, we would never need to import any food at all.*

sell •VERB• **sells, selling, sold** to give somebody something in exchange for money: *Nigel sold his car and bought a motorbike.*
♦ **seller** •NOUN• **sellers** a person who has something for sale

Sellotape •NOUN• a type of see-through sticky tape that is used especially for sticking pieces of paper together. This word is a trademark

semaphore •NOUN• a way of signalling using your arms in different positions to signal different letters

semi- •PREFIX• if a word starts with **semi-** it adds the meaning *half* or *partly*. For example, *semi-conscious* means not fully conscious

semibreve •NOUN• **semibreves** a musical note that is the same length as four crotchets. The symbol for a semibreve is ○

semicircle •NOUN• **semicircles** half a circle: *The class sits around the teacher in a semicircle.*

semicolon •NOUN• **semicolons** a punctuation mark (;) that separates items in a list or different parts of a sentence: *Several things need to be done: the menu; a seating plan; tickets.*

semi-detached •ADJECTIVE• joined to another house on one side: *Houses that are semi-detached may share a driveway.*

semi-final •NOUN• **semi-finals** one of the two matches in a competition just before the final, which is a match for the winners of the two semi-finals: *Sweden reached the semi-final of the 1994 World Cup.*

seminar •NOUN• **seminars** a class in a university or college where a small number of students discuss a subject with a tutor or teacher

semitone • NOUN• **semitones** the difference between two notes that are next to each other on the piano: *E to F is a semitone and so is F to F♯.*

semolina • NOUN• grains of wheat that are used for making pasta and milky puddings

senate • NOUN• **senates** the highest-ranking part of parliament in some countries, for example, the United States and France
♦ **senator** • NOUN• **senators** a member of a senate

send • VERB• **sends, sending, sent** 1 to post something somewhere
2 to arrange for something to be taken somewhere: *Our luggage was sent on the next flight.*
3 to tell someone to go somewhere: *Graham was feeling sick so the school sent him home.*
♦ **sender** • NOUN• **senders** the person that a letter or parcel comes from: *If this letter is undelivered, please return it to the sender.*

senile • ADJECTIVE• weak and confused because of old age

senior • ADJECTIVE• 1 higher in rank or more powerful: *You must salute when you meet a more senior officer.* 2 older: *We expect senior pupils to protect the younger children.*
♦ **seniority** • NOUN• how old or powerful a person is: *We sat along the table in order of seniority.*

senior citizen • NOUN• **senior citizens** a person who has passed the usual retiring age: *Senior citizens can travel free if they have applied for a pass.*

sensation • NOUN• **sensations** 1 a feeling, especially one coming from your sense of touch: *a burning sensation in his chest* 2 a state of excitement or shock: *The announcement caused quite a sensation.*
♦ **sensational** • ADJECTIVE• 1 wonderful and impressive: *Kate looked sensational in her new dress.* 2 causing a lot of excitement, shock or horror: *sensational news*

sense • NOUN• **senses** 1 one of the five powers of sight, touch, taste, hearing and smell: *Janet lost her sense of smell after an illness.*
2 an ability to understand or appreciate something: *I don't think he has much of a sense of humour.*
3 a feeling: *People need work that gives them a sense of achievement.*
4 sense is the ability to make sensible decisions: *Someone had the sense to call an ambulance.*
5 a meaning: *A single English word can have lots of different senses.* • *You only have to understand the general sense of the passage.*
• VERB• **senses, sensing, sensed** to become aware of something although it is not very obvious: *I sensed that not many people agreed with what I was saying.*
♦ **senseless** • ADJECTIVE• 1 unconscious or stunned: *A fireman was knocked senseless by a falling lamp post.* 2 foolish and with no purpose: *a senseless battle over a piece of useless ground*
♦ **senselessness** • NOUN• not having any good or sensible purpose: *the senselessness of war*

sensible • ADJECTIVE• not foolish, but showing common sense: *the most sensible thing to do* • *It would be sensible to get that promise in writing.*
♦ **sensibly** • ADVERB• using your common sense: *Jeff very sensibly pulled the curtains before putting the light on.*

sensitive • ADJECTIVE• 1 very quickly and easily affected by anything: *skin that is very sensitive to the sun* • *The alarm is very sensitive and is sometimes set off by birds or cats.* 2 very easily hurt or upset: *Brian's very sensitive about being bald.*
♦ **sensitively** • ADJECTIVE• in a way that carefully considers how people are feeling: *The matter has been dealt with very sensitively.*
♦ **sensitivity** • NOUN• how easily something or someone is affected by something

sensor • NOUN• **sensors** a device that notices things such as heat, light or movement: *A sensor on the front of the camera measures how much light is available.*

sent • VERB• a way of changing the verb **send** to make a past tense. It can be used with or without a helping verb: *I've sent ten email messages this morning.* • *Jenkins was sent to prison for ten years.*

Aa
Bb
Cc
Dd
Ee
Ff
Gg
Hh
Ii
Jj
Kk
Ll
Mm
Nn
Oo
Pp
Qq
Rr
Ss
Tt
Uu
Vv
Ww
Xx
Yy
Zz

Aa
Bb
Cc
Dd
Ee
Ff
Gg
Hh
Ii
Jj
Kk
Ll
Mm
Nn
Oo
Pp
Qq
Rr
Ss
Tt
Uu
Vv
Ww
Xx
Yy
Zz

sentence •NOUN• **sentences** 1 a sequence of words that usually includes a verb and expresses a statement, a question or a command. See the box called **Sentences** 2 the punishment that a judge gives a person who has been found guilty of a crime: *Floyd received a five year prison sentence.*
•VERB• **sentences, sentencing, sentenced** to tell a person who has been found guilty of a crime what their punishment will be: *The whole gang was sentenced to life imprisonment.*

sentiment •NOUN• **sentiments** a view or feeling about a subject: *Several other people share these sentiments.*
♦ **sentimental** •ADJECTIVE• 1 feeling or making you feel too much emotion: *a sentimental love story* 2 to do with emotions: *I know the ring is not valuable but I love it for sentimental reasons.*

sentry •NOUN• **sentries** a soldier who guards an entrance

sepal •NOUN• **sepals** one of the green leaves under the petals of a flower

separable •ADJECTIVE• able to be separated from each other or from the main part of something: *a coat with a separable hood*

separate •ADJECTIVE• different and not joined or connected: *This is a completely separate matter.* • *The farm is separate from the rest of the estate.*
•VERB• **separates, separating, separated** 1 to split up the people in a group or the parts of something that can be divided: *Could we please separate the boys from the girls for this exercise?* • *The north and the south are separated by a range of high mountains.* 2 to decide to live apart: *They are not divorced but they separated some time ago.*
♦ **separately** •ADVERB• not together: *Each of the suspects was interviewed separately by the police.*
♦ **separation** •NOUN• **separations** 1 when people are apart from each other: *Lily found the separation from her family very difficult while she was working abroad.* 2 keeping things apart: *I firmly believe in the separation of work from family life.*

ⓘ The adjective and the verb **separate** are pronounced differently. The adjective is pronounced sep-er-it. The verb is pronounced sep-a-rate.

September •NOUN• the ninth month of the year, after August and before October

ⓘ **September** was the seventh month of the Roman year and the name comes from the word **septem**, which means *seven* in Latin.

septic •ADJECTIVE• full of poisonous germs: *If the cut goes septic, you will have to take a course of antibiotics.*

sequel •NOUN• **sequels** a book, play or film that continues an earlier story

sequence •NOUN• **sequences** 1 a series of things that follow each other: *a remarkable sequence of events*
2 a short section of something like a dance or a film: *an opening sequence that involves the whole cast*
3 a series of things that follow each other in a particular order: *Can you fill in the next three figures in the sequence that starts 1,4,9?*

sequin •NOUN• **sequins** a small shiny disc that can be sewn on clothes to catch the light

ⓘ A **sequin** was the name of an old Turkish and Italian gold coin. The name was used for the discs on clothes because they look like shiny coins.

serenade •NOUN• **serenades** a song or other piece of music that, according to tradition, is performed at night, beneath a woman's window
•VERB• **serenades, serenading, serenaded** to sing or play music for someone

serene •ADJECTIVE• calm and peaceful: *a serene smile*

sergeant •NOUN• **sergeants** 1 a soldier who has a higher rank than a private or a corporal 2 a police officer who has the rank between constable and inspector

sergeant-major •NOUN• **sergeant-majors** an army rank above sergeant

serial •NOUN• **serials** a story in parts that you read, see or listen to at different times

Sentences

A **sentence** tells you about an event or a situation. It usually has an actor (a **subject**) and an action (a **verb**), and makes sense.

> **The tall man runs along the road.**
>
> **The tall man is my uncle.**

These are sentences. They have a **subject** (*the tall man*) and a **verb** (*runs, is*). They make sense.

> **the tall man**

This is *not* a sentence. It has no verb. It does not say what the man does or is.

Types of sentences

There are different types of sentences.

A statement:	The cockerel crows at daybreak.
A question:	Has anyone seen my keys?
A request:	Could you show me the way?
An exclamation:	What a shame!
A command:	Come here!

Simple sentences

A **simple sentence** has one clause, with a subject and one verb. It is complete on its own.

> **The lion growled.**

You can add more information about the subject (*the lion*) and the verb (*growled*).

> **The *fierce* lion *with a magnificent mane* growled *angrily*.**

Compound sentences

You can join one sentence to another with a connecting word, such as *and, but, or, so*. This is called a **compound sentence**. Both sentences (clauses) are of equal importance.

> **It was raining *and* the lion growled.**

Complex sentences

You can add a string of words that contains a verb but which would not make sense on its own to a sentence, for example

> **when the zookeeper arrived with a pail of fish**

This does not make sense on its own. It makes sense if it is joined to another main sentence.

> **The lion growled angrily *when the zookeeper arrived with a pail of fish*.**

Sentences made like this are called **complex sentences.**

series •NOUN• **series** 1 a number of similar things that are arranged or produced one after the other: *a series of accidents* 2 a set of television or radio programmes with the same subject and characters: *a nature series* • *an old series of 'Cheers'*

serious •ADJECTIVE• 1 important and needing proper attention: *a more serious matter* 2 very bad: *a serious accident* 3 not joking: *I can never tell when he's joking and when he's being serious.*

sermon •NOUN• **sermons** a talk such as the ones preachers give in church

serpent •NOUN• **serpents** an old word for a snake

servant •NOUN• **servants** a person whose job is to do things for someone else

serve •VERB• **serves, serving, served** 1 to work for someone: *Brown had served the family for fifty years.* • *Johnson served his country in two world wars.* 2 to hand people things they want to buy in a shop or what they want to eat: *Are you being served?* • *I'll serve the soup and you can give out the spoons.* 3 to have a certain purpose or use: *The cave served as a shelter for the night.* 4 to serve time or a prison sentence is to stay in prison as a punishment for committing a crime 5 to serve in tennis or some other games is to start play by throwing the ball up and hitting it 6 to **serve someone right** is to be right for them because they deserve it: *If you're sick, it serves you right for eating too much chocolate.*
•NOUN• **serves** throwing the ball up and hitting it to start playing a point in tennis: *a very fast serve*
♦ **server** •NOUN• **servers** 1 a central computer that gives out and stores information from lots of smaller computers 2 the person who starts playing a point in tennis

service •NOUN• **services** 1 working for someone or something: *resigning after 25 years' service to the company* • *He received an award for his services to the community.* 2 an industry that does things for people rather than producing goods: *the health service* • *Postal services are more frequent now.* 3 when someone does something for you: *I loved the things they sell but the service in that shop is awful.* • *Your car should have a regular service.* • *These aircraft have now been taken out of service.* 4 **the services** are a country's army, navy and air force 5 a religious ceremony, especially in a church: *a service of remembrance* 6 a set of matching plates and bowls or cups and saucers: *a dinner service* • *a china tea service* 7 throwing the ball up and hitting it to start playing a point in tennis: *a terrible first service*
•VERB• **services, servicing, serviced** to service a vehicle or machine is to check it to make sure it is working properly and to make any necessary small repairs

service station •NOUN• **service stations** a place where you can buy petrol

serviette •NOUN• **serviettes** a table napkin

sesame •NOUN• a plant that produces seeds that are eaten and also used for making an edible oil

session •NOUN• **sessions** 1 a period of time that you do something for: *Next session we'll be able to decorate the work you've done today.* 2 a meeting or a series of meetings: *the next session of Parliament* 3 a term of a school or college

set •VERB• **sets, setting, set** 1 to place something somewhere: *Set the tray down on the table.* • *a house that was set back from the road* • *Ask Rose to set the table.* 2 to adjust a clock or control so that it is ready to work: *Don't forget to set the video to record.* 3 to become hard or firm: *Wait an hour or so for the jelly to set.* 4 the sun sets when it goes down: *watching the setting sun* 5 to set words to music is to compose music to go with them 6 to set someone doing something is to start them doing it: *His comment set me thinking.*

7 to set someone something to do is to give it to them to do: *The teacher didn't set us any homework.*

8 to **set about** doing something is to start to do it: *It's time we set about learning our lines for the play.*

9 to **set in** is to begin: *It looks like winter has set in.*

• ADJECTIVE• **1** fixed: *a set menu*

2 compulsory, not something you can choose: *a set piece for this year's music exam*

3 ready or prepared: *Are we all set to go?*

• NOUN• **sets 1** a number of things or people that have something in common or are used together: *a set of chairs • a chess set • the set of odd numbers • I'm in the top set for maths.*

2 a radio or television: *We have a technical problem; please do not adjust your set.*

3 the scenery and furniture where actors perform in a play or film, on a stage or in a studio

4 a series of games that form part of a tennis match

⇒ **setting**

setback • NOUN• **setbacks** a problem that stops you making progress for a while

set-square • NOUN• **set-squares** a hard flat triangle with one right angle that you can use to help you draw angles and straight lines

settee • NOUN• **settees** a sofa

setting • NOUN• **settings 1** the position of the controls of a machine or instrument: *What setting did you have the oven on?*

2 the background for something such as a building or some sort of action, either in real life or in a story: *a beautiful setting for a hotel • The setting of the play is important because it's really possible.*

3 a place setting or a table setting is the cutlery and crockery for one person at a meal

settle • VERB• **settles, settling, settled 1** to decide or agree on something: *Can you settle this argument for us? • Have you settled a date for the wedding yet?*

2 to become relaxed and comfortable in a certain situation or position: *We settled into army life very easily. • Harry settled into his armchair and fell asleep.*

3 to go somewhere and make your home there: *The family settled in New South Wales.*

4 to land and rest somewhere: *A fly settled on the picture frame for a moment. • Shake the bottle, then wait while the flakes inside settle.*

5 to pay a bill or debt: *The bill can be settled in cash or with a cheque.*

✦ **settlement** • NOUN• **settlements 1** an agreement: *a new peace settlement* **2** a place where people arrived and set up their homes: *an ancient riverside settlement*

✦ **settler** • NOUN• **settlers** a person who goes to live in a new country or an area that has few or no people living in it

seven • NOUN• **sevens** the number 7

seventeen • NOUN• the number 17

seventeenth • ADJECTIVE AND ADVERB• after sixteenth and before eighteenth: *my sister's seventeenth birthday*

seventh • ADJECTIVE AND ADVERB• after sixth and before eighth: *the seventh day of the week*

• NOUN• **sevenths** the fraction $\frac{1}{7}$ which means one of seven equal parts of something: *There are seven of us, so divide the pie into sevenths.*

seventieth • ADJECTIVE AND ADVERB• after the sixty-ninth and before the seventy-first

seventy • NOUN• **seventies** the number 70

sever • VERB• **severs, severing, severed** to cut through something or cut something off: *The phone cables were severed in the high winds.*

several • ADJECTIVE• more than two but not very many: *Several people stopped to look in the window. • I've asked him several times but he hasn't repaid the money.*

severe • ADJECTIVE• **1** extremely bad: *severe weather conditions • a severe punishment* **2** stern and not gentle or kind: *a severe expression as she concentrated*

✦ **severity** • NOUN• extreme seriousness: *I don't think you understand the severity of the situation.*

sew • VERB• **sews, sewing, sewed, sewn** to use a needle and thread or a sewing machine to join fabric with stitches: *Could you teach me to sew? • I'll need some red thread to sew that button back on.*

Aa Bb Cc Dd Ee Ff Gg Hh Ii Jj Kk Ll Mm Nn Oo Pp Qq Rr **Ss** Tt Uu Vv Ww Xx Yy Zz

sewage •NOUN• waste matter that is carried away from toilets in buildings
♦ **sewer** •NOUN• **sewers** a large pipe or underground channel for carrying away waste matter from drains in and near buildings

sex •NOUN• **sexes** 1 either of two groups that humans are divided into: males and females 2 sex is an act that a man and a woman perform to make a baby or for enjoyment
♦ **sexual** •ADJECTIVE• to do with sex: *the body's sexual organs*

sexism •NOUN• the belief that one sex, particularly your own, is better than the other, and therefore the unfair treatment of the other sex
♦ **sexist** •NOUN• **sexists** a person who believes that their own sex is better than the other

shabby •ADJECTIVE• **shabbier, shabbiest** old and worn: *a shabby house full of shabby furniture*

shack •NOUN• **shacks** a roughly-built hut or shed

shackle •NOUN• **shackles** shackles are a pair of metal rings, joined by a chain, that are locked around a prisoner's wrists or ankles •VERB• **shackles, shackling, shackled** to shackle someone is to to lock them in chains to stop them from moving freely

shade •NOUN• **shades** 1 an area of slight darkness caused by blocking sunlight: *sitting in the shade of a tree* • *plants that grow in shade* 2 an object that prevents a light being too bright: *a lampshade* 3 a colour that is a bit lighter or darker than a similar colour: *a darker shade of lipstick* 4 a very small amount or difference: *Can you make it a shade looser?* •VERB• **shades, shading, shaded** 1 to block bright light from an area: *a row of trees shading the path* 2 to draw or paint an area of a picture to make it look darker
⇒ **shady**

shadow •NOUN• **shadows** 1 a shadow is a dark shape on a surface caused when an object is between the surface and a bright light: *children trying to jump on each other's*

shadow 2 shadow is an area darkened by the blocking out of light: *I couldn't see his face because it was in shadow.*
♦ **shadowy** •ADJECTIVE• like a shadow, not easy to see clearly: *The shadowy figures moved in and out of the trees.*

shady •ADJECTIVE• **shadier, shadiest** 1 a shady place is out of bright sunlight 2 a shady business does not seem to be open and honest

shaft •NOUN• **shafts** 1 the long straight part of a tool or weapon 2 a bar or rod in a machine that turns round to make other parts of the machine move: *The engine's drive shaft is twisted.* 3 a long narrow passage in the ground or in a building: *a lift shaft* • *a mine shaft* 4 a shaft of light is a ray or beam of light

shaggy •ADJECTIVE• **shaggier, shaggiest** shaggy hair is thick and untidy

shake •VERB• **shakes, shaking, shook, shaken** 1 to move quickly or unsteadily with very small movements: *The earth shook when the bomb landed.* • *Mina was shaking with fear.* 2 to move something quickly from side to side or backwards and forwards: *The wind shook the trees and rattled the windows.* 3 to shock or upset someone: *We were terribly shaken by the news of his death.* •NOUN• **shakes** 1 a quick movement from side to side or backwards and forwards: *Give the bottle a quick shake.* 2 a very quick moment: *I'll be there in two shakes.* 3 a drink of milk and some sort of flavouring
♦ **shakily** •ADVERB• in an unsteady way: *a new lamb walking shakily round its mother*
♦ **shaky** •ADJECTIVE• **shakier, shakiest** trembling: *Her voice was shaky as she tried to explain how she fell.*

shale •NOUN• a soft grey type of rock that breaks easily into flaky layers

shall •VERB• **should** a helping verb that is used along with a main verb to make future tenses when the subject of the verb is **I** or **we**: *I shall never forget this moment.*

shallow •ADJECTIVE• **shallower, shallowest** not deep: *a shallow lake*

sham •NOUN• a person or thing is a sham if they are not what they pretend to be or seem to be: *Her niceness was just a sham; she was really cruel.*

shamble •VERB• **shambles, shambling, shambled** if someone shambles, or shambles along, they walk slowly and awkwardly without lifting their feet properly: *The old man shambled along, leaning on his stick.*

shambles •NOUN• if something is a shambles it is completely disorganized or in a terrible mess: *The attic was a shambles, full of broken furniture.*

shame •NOUN• 1 an embarrassing feeling of guilt or foolishness, especially because you have done something wrong
2 if something **brings shame on** or **to** people it brings them disgrace or dishonour because it is bad or morally wrong
3 if you say something is a shame you mean it is a pity: *What a shame it is that you can't come to the party.*
• **put someone to shame** to put someone to shame is to do something much better than they do, so that they look foolish or a failure
•VERB• **shames, shaming, shamed** to shame someone is to make them feel ashamed or embarrassed
♦ **shameful** •ADJECTIVE• disgraceful: *shameful behaviour*
♦ **shamefully** •ADVERB• disgracefully
♦ **shameless** •ADJECTIVE• someone who is shameless feels no shame, although they have done something that other people think is wrong or immoral
♦ **shamelessly** •ADVERB• without feeling shame: *He lied shamelessly.*

shampoo •NOUN• **shampoos** a soapy liquid for washing your hair, or for cleaning carpets
•VERB• **shampoos, shampooing, shampooed** to shampoo your hair, or a carpet, is to wash it using shampoo

ⓘ This word comes from the Indian language Hindi, from the word **champu**, which means *squeeze*. You use a squeezing action to wash with it.

shamrock •NOUN• **shamrocks** a plant like clover with rounded leaves in three parts

shank •NOUN• **shanks** 1 the long straight part of a nail, screw or tool 2 the part of the leg, especially an animal's leg for eating, between the knee joint and the foot

shan't •SHORT FORM• a short way to say and write **shall not**: *I shan't be late.*

shanty •NOUN• **shanties** a roughly-built hut or shack

shantytown •NOUN• **shantytowns** an area where shanties have been put up, usually on the edge of a larger town or city

shape •NOUN• **shapes** 1 something's shape is its outline or form: *a mountain in the shape of a crown*
2 shapes are things like squares, circles, rectangles, diamonds and triangles. See the illustration on the next page
3 the shape that a person or thing is in is their condition: *The team is in good shape for Saturday's match.*
• **out of shape** 1 if a piece of clothing is out of shape, it has been stretched so that it is no longer the shape it should be 2 if a person is out of shape, they are not as fit as they once were
• **take shape** things take shape when they start to develop a form that you can recognize or start to become organized
•VERB• **shapes, shaping, shaped** 1 to shape something is to form it or model it into a certain shape: *He shapes the clay pots on the potter's wheel.* 2 to **shape up**, is to develop in a satisfactory way
♦ **shapeless** •ADJECTIVE• having no particular shape: *a shapeless old cardigan*
♦ **shapely** •ADJECTIVE• having an attractive shape or figure

share •VERB• **shares, sharing, shared** 1 to share something is to divide it among a number of people so that each person gets some: *Are you going to eat that whole pizza yourself, or are you going to share it?*
2 to share something with other people is to give some of it to them or allow them to use it too: *There aren't enough books to go round so some of you will have to share.*
3 to share experiences or interests with other people is to have the same experiences or interests as they have: *They shared an obsession with golf.*
•NOUN• **shares** 1 a share is one of the parts of

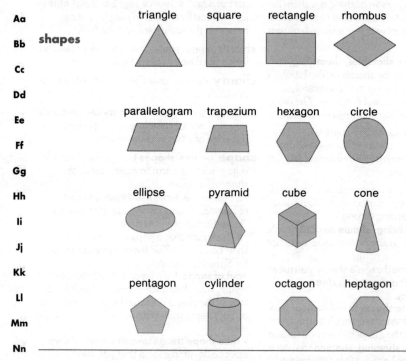

shapes

triangle square rectangle rhombus

parallelogram trapezium hexagon circle

ellipse pyramid cube cone

pentagon cylinder octagon heptagon

something that has been, or is to be, divided among several people **2** someone's share in an activity or project which involves several people, is the part they play in it

shark • NOUN• **sharks** a large fish whose mouth is full of rows of very sharp teeth.

sharp • ADJECTIVE• **sharper, sharpest 1** a sharp object has a thin edge that can cut, or a point that can pierce: *a sharp knife*
2 a sharp fall or increase is sudden and steep: *a sharp rise in crime*
3 sharp images are clear and distinct with no blurred edges
4 a sharp pain is sudden and stabbing
5 a person or animal with sharp hearing or eyesight is good at hearing or seeing
6 something that tastes sharp tastes bitter, like lemon juice
7 someone who is sharp is very quick to understand or react
• ADVERB• **1** punctually: *He was to be there at 5 o'clock sharp.* **2** with a sudden or abrupt change of direction: *Turn sharp left at the next set of traffic lights.*

• NOUN• **sharps** in written music, a sign (♯) that makes a note higher by another half tone

♦ **sharpen** • VERB• **sharpens, sharpening, sharpened** to sharpen something is to make it sharp or sharper: *The leopard was sharpening its claws on a tree.*

♦ **sharpener** • NOUN• **sharpeners** a device that you use to sharpen pencils or knives

shatter • VERB• **shatters, shattering, shattered 1** to break into lots of tiny pieces **2** if something shatters you, it upsets you a lot or makes you very tired

shave • VERB• **shaves, shaving, shaved 1** people shave when they cut away hair growing on their faces or bodies with a razor **2** to shave something is to cut or scrape thin layers off it with a sharp blade

♦ **shaver** • NOUN• **shavers** an electrical tool for shaving hair

♦ **shavings** • PLURAL NOUN• very thin strips of wood or metal that have been cut off a surface with a plane or other sharp tool

shawl •NOUN• **shawls** a large rectangular piece of cloth for covering your shoulders

she •PRONOUN• a word you use to talk about a woman, girl, female animal, or boat that has already been mentioned or pointed out for the first time: *Madeleine is funny. She tells jokes and imitates people.* • *This boat is great for racing and she can turn on a sixpence.*

sheaf •NOUN• **sheaves** a bundle, especially a bundle of ripe corn that has been cut and tied together

shear •VERB• **shears, shearing, sheared, sheared** or **shorn** 1 to clip or cut wool from a sheep using shears 2 if a piece of metal, such as a bolt, **shears off**, it breaks off
♦ **shears** •PLURAL NOUN• a tool with two large sharp-edged blades which move over each other, used for cutting sheep's wool or hair, or for trimming hedges

sheath •NOUN• **sheathes** a long narrow case for holding or carrying a sword or dagger
♦ **sheathe** •VERB• **sheathes, sheathing, sheathed** to sheathe a sword is to put it into a sheath

shed •NOUN• **sheds** a simple wooden or metal building used for working in or for storing things
•VERB• **sheds, shedding, shed** 1 people shed their clothes, reptiles shed their skins, and birds shed their feathers when they take or cast them off and get rid of them
2 a tree sheds its leaves when they drop off in the autumn
3 to shed tears or blood is to have tears flowing from your eyes or blood flowing from a wound

she'd •SHORT FORM• a short way to say and write **she had** or **she would**: *She'd forgotten her umbrella.* • *She'd rather not say.*

sheen •NOUN• a soft shine or glossiness on a surface

sheep •NOUN• **sheep** a medium-sized farm animal with a thick wool fleece

sheep-dip •NOUN• **sheep-dips** a chemical solution into which sheep are put so that any bacteria on their wool are killed

sheepdog •NOUN• **sheepdogs** a dog bred or trained to round up and drive sheep

sheepish •ADJECTIVE• if someone looks sheepish, they look embarrassed

sheer •ADJECTIVE• 1 a sheer cliff or rock face is vertical
2 a sheer fabric is so thin you can see through it
3 pure or complete: *He ate four bags of crisps. It was just sheer greed.*

sheet •NOUN• **sheets** 1 a large broad thin piece of fabric, metal or glass: *I'll just change the sheets on your bed.*
2 a single piece of paper used for writing or printing on
3 a continuous layer of ice

sheikh •NOUN• **sheikhs** an Arab chief or ruler

shelf •NOUN• **shelves** 1 a board fixed horizontally to a wall or as part of a cupboard, used for putting things on 2 a part of the landscape or seabed that is formed like a shelf, with a flat top
⇒ **shelve**

shell •NOUN• **shells** 1 a hard covering on an egg or a nut, or protecting the soft bodies of creatures like snails, crabs, shellfish and tortoises
2 an explosive missile or cartridge fired from a large gun
3 the framework of a building or other structure

she'll •SHORT FORM• a short way to say and write **she will** or **she shall**

shellfish •NOUN• **shellfish** shellfish are creatures with a hard outer shell that live in fresh water or the sea

shelter •NOUN• **shelters** 1 a shelter is a building or other structure that provides protection from harm or bad weather 2 to take shelter is to go somewhere that gives protection from danger or bad weather
•VERB• **shelters, sheltering, sheltered** 1 to shelter somewhere is to stay in a place where you are protected from harm or bad weather 2 to shelter someone or something is to protect them

shelve •VERB• **shelves, shelving, shelved** 1 to shelve a cupboard is to put up shelves in it 2 to shelve a plan is to postpone it or put it aside without carrying it out

Aa
Bb
Cc
Dd
Ee
Ff
Gg
Hh
Ii
Jj
Kk
Ll
Mm
Nn
Oo
Pp
Qq
Rr
Ss
Tt
Uu
Vv
Ww
Xx
Yy
Zz

Aa
Bb
Cc
Dd
Ee
Ff
Gg
Hh
Ii
Jj
Kk
Ll
Mm
Nn
Oo
Pp
Qq
Rr
Ss
Tt
Uu
Vv
Ww
Xx
Yy
Zz

shepherd •NOUN• **shepherds** someone who looks after sheep
•VERB• **shepherds, shepherding, shepherded** to shepherd people somewhere is to keep them in a group and direct them in or into a place

sherbet •NOUN• **sherbets** sherbet is a sharp-tasting powder with a fruit flavour

sheriff •NOUN• **sheriffs** **1** in the United States, a sheriff is the head of police in a particular county
2 in England and Wales, a sheriff is the representative of the king or queen in a particular county, who has mostly ceremonial duties
3 in Scotland, a sheriff is a county judge who tries cases in local courts

sherry •NOUN• sherry is a type of strong wine that has had brandy added to it

she's •SHORT FORM• a short way to say and write **she is** or **she has**: *She's my friend.*
• *She's always been my friend.*

shield •NOUN• **shields, shielding, shielded** **1** a piece of armour that is used to block an attack by a sword or other weapon
2 a competition trophy in the shape of this piece of armour
3 a protection from harm or danger: *The spacecraft has a heat shield for when it re-enters the Earth's atmosphere.*
•VERB• **shields, shielding, shielded** to shield someone or something is to protect them from harm or danger: *He had his hand over his eyes, shielding them from the strong sun.*

shift •VERB• **shifts, shifting, shifted** if you shift something, or it shifts, you move it, or it changes its position
• NOUN• **shifts** **1** a move or change to another position: *a slight shift in speed*
2 the period of time a worker does his or her job: *on the early shift*
3 a loose dress

shifty •ADJECTIVE• **shiftier, shiftiest** a shifty person looks or behaves in a way that makes you distrust them and think they are dishonest

shilling •NOUN• **shillings** an old British coin worth five pence

shimmer •VERB• **shimmers, shimmers, shimmering, shimmered** to shine with a quivering light

shin •NOUN• **shins** the front of your leg below the knee

shine •VERB• **shines, shining, shone**
1 something shines when it gives off or reflects light
2 you shine a light on something when you point the light in its direction
3 you shine something when you polish it
4 if you shine at something, you are so good at it you stand out from everyone else
⇒ **shining, shiny**

shingle •NOUN• shingle is a mass of small pebbles on a seashore or river bank

shining •ADJECTIVE• **1** having a shine **2** a shining example of something is one that stands out because it is so good

shiny •ADJECTIVE• **shinier, shiniest** reflecting light or polished so as to reflect light

ship •NOUN• **ships** a large boat that carries passengers or cargo, or both, on long sea journeys
•VERB• **ships, shipping, shipped** to ship something somewhere is to have it carried on a ship

-ship •SUFFIX• **1** if **-ship** comes at the end of a word, the word refers to a particular state or condition. For example, *friendship* is the condition of being friends **2** when **-ship** comes at the end of other words, the word refers to a particular skill. For example, *craftsmanship* is having the skill of a craftsman

shipment •NOUN• **shipments** a load of goods sent by ship

shipping •NOUN• the business of carrying goods, especially by ship, or ships travelling from place to place

shipshape •ADJECTIVE• tidy and in good order

shipwreck •NOUN• **shipwrecks** a ship that has been destroyed or sunk, especially by hitting rocks

shipyard •NOUN• **shipyards** a place where ships are built

shirk •VERB• **shirks, shirking, shirked** to shirk

something is to avoid doing something that you should be doing

◆ **shirker** •NOUN• **shirkers** someone who avoids work, a responsibility or a duty

shirt •NOUN• **shirts** a piece of clothing for the top half of your body, with long or short sleeves, a collar, and buttons down the front

shiver •VERB• **shivers, shivering, shivered** to tremble or quiver because you are cold or frightened
•NOUN• **shivers** a quivery or trembling feeling that goes through your body when you get cold or get a fright
◆ **shivery** •ADJECTIVE• having shivers

shoal •NOUN• **shoals** a shoal of fish is a large group of them swimming together

shock •NOUN• **shocks** 1 shock, or a shock, is a strong and unpleasant reaction you get when you have had a fright or a bad injury
2 a sudden bump or jolt that comes with great force: *The shock of the impact threw us all forward.*
3 if you get an electric shock, a current of electricity passes through your body
•VERB• **shocks, shocking, shocked** if something shocks you, it upsets or horrifies you
◆ **shocking** •ADJECTIVE• upsetting or horrifying

shoddy •ADJECTIVE• **shoddier, shoddiest** not very well made or made with poor quality materials

shoe •NOUN• **shoes** shoes are outer coverings for your feet, usually covering them from the toes to just below the ankles

shoehorn •NOUN• **shoehorns** a long hard curved object that you use to get shoes on, by slipping it between your heel and the back of the shoe

shoelace •NOUN• **shoelaces** a thin piece of cord or leather threaded through the holes of a lace-up shoe to fasten it

shoestring •NOUN• to do something **on a shoestring** is to do it for very little money

shone •VERB• a way of changing the verb **shine** to make a past tense. It can be used with or without a helping verb: *The sun shone all day.* • *It had shone all week.*

shoo •INTERJECTION• you say 'shoo!' when you want to chase a person or animal away

shook •VERB• a way of changing the verb **shake** to make a past tense: *He shook his head sadly.*

shoot •VERB• **shoots, shooting, shot** 1 to shoot a gun or other weapon is to fire it: *I shot an arrow in the air.*
2 to shoot someone or something with a gun or other weapon is to kill or wound them with it
3 a person or thing shoots somewhere when they travel there very fast: *He shot past me in his new red sports car.* • *Pain shot through his body.* • *Prices shot up overnight.*
4 in games like football and hockey, a player shoots when they kick or hit the ball at the goal
5 to shoot a scene for a film is to record it on film

ⓘ Be careful not to confuse the spelling of **shoot** with **chute**, which is a sloped channel.

shooting star •NOUN• **shooting star** a meteor that burns up in the Earth's atmosphere, making a trail of bright light in the night sky

shop •NOUN• **shops** 1 a place where goods are sold 2 a place where work of a particular kind is done
•VERB• **shops, shopping, shopped** to shop is to buy things in shops
⇒ **shopper, shopping**

shopkeeper •NOUN• **shopkeepers** someone who owns a shop

shoplifter •NOUN• **shoplifters** someone who steals things from shops
◆ **shoplifting** •NOUN• the crime of stealing things from shops

shopper •NOUN• **shoppers** someone who shops or is shopping: *crowds of Saturday shoppers*

shopping •NOUN• 1 the activity of going round shops to buy things: *Let's go shopping for new clothes.* 2 the things you buy at the shops: *She carried all the shopping in to the kitchen.*

shore •NOUN• **shores** the area of land beside the sea or beside a lake

Aa
Bb
Cc
Dd
Ee
Ff
Gg
Hh
Ii
Jj
Kk
Ll
Mm
Nn
Oo
Pp
Qq
Rr
Ss
Tt
Uu
Vv
Ww
Xx
Yy
Zz

Aa
Bb
Cc
Dd
Ee
Ff
Gg
Hh
Ii
Jj
Kk
Ll
Mm
Nn
Oo
Pp
Qq
Rr
Ss
Tt
Uu
Vv
Ww
Xx
Yy
Zz

shorn • VERB• a way of changing the verb **shear** to make a past tense. It is used with a helping verb: *The farmer had shorn the sheep.*

short • ADJECTIVE• **shorter, shortest 1** not very long: *a short skirt • a short speech* **2** small, not tall: *a short man* **3** if something is short, or in short supply, there is less than there should be, or there is not enough of it to go round: *We are two players short.* **4** if someone is short with you, they are rude and abrupt in the way they talk to you • **short of** to be short of something is to not have enough of it • **for short** as a shortened form: *I'm Alisdair, you can call me Al for short.* •ADVERB• **1** to **stop short** is to stop suddenly just before reaching a particular point: *My ball stopped slightly short of the last hole.* **2** if something **falls short**, it is not as good or as big as it should be ♦ **shortage** • NOUN• **shortages** a lack of something: *food shortages* ⇒ **shorten, shortly**

shortbread • NOUN• a rich sweet biscuit made from flour, sugar and butter

short-circuit • VERB• **short-circuits, short-circuiting, short-circuited** a piece of electrical equipment short-circuits when the electric current is carried away from its normal path by something breaking the normal electrical circuit

shortcoming • NOUN• **shortcomings** a fault or weakness a person has

shortcut • NOUN• **shortcuts** a quicker route between two places, or a quicker way of doing something

shorten • VERB• **shortens, shortening, shortened** to shorten something is to make it shorter: *I couldn't bring myself to shorten such a lovely name.*

short form • NOUN• **short forms** a word made from two words that have been joined together and some letters missed out. An apostrophe replaces the missing letters. See the box called **Short forms**

shorthand • NOUN• shorthand is a fast way of writing what someone is saying

short list • NOUN• **short lists** a list of the best people for a job

short-lived • ADJECTIVE• lasting only for a short time: *Mandy's quarrels with Jenny, though frequent and explosive, were usually short-lived.*

shortly • ADVERB• **1** soon: *We'll be arriving at Waverley Station shortly.* **2** not long: *Shortly before midday, the headmaster asked everyone to go to the assembly hall.*

shorts • PLURAL NOUN• shorts are a piece of clothing for the bottom half of your body, with short legs that reach down to the tops of your thighs or as far down as your knees

short-sighted • ADJECTIVE• **1** a short-sighted person cannot see things clearly unless the object is very close **2** an idea that is short-sighted does not take into account what is likely to happen in the future

short-tempered • ADJECTIVE• a short-tempered person loses their temper easily

short-term • ADJECTIVE• lasting or taking place for only a short time

shot • VERB• a way of changing the verb **shoot** to make a past tense. It can be used with or without a helping verb: *The ships shot at each other using large cannons.* • *Nelson's battleships had shot the rigging from most of the enemy ships.*

shotgun • NOUN• **shotguns** a type of long gun with one or two barrels, which fires little metal pellets

should • VERB• **1 should** is used as a past tense of the verb **shall**: *He said that we should all go home.* **2** ought to: *I wonder whether or not I should go.* **3** used to say what is likely to happen: *The train should be arriving in a couple of minutes.* **4** sometimes used with *I* or *we* to express a wish: *I should love to come to your party.* **5 should** is also used to refer to an event that is rather surprising: *There was a little tap on the door, and who should pop his head round but Uncle George.*

shouldn't • SHORT FORM• a short way to say and write **should not**: *You shouldn't have*

Short forms

Short forms are where two words have been joined together and an apostrophe has replaced the missing letters.

I'm	I am	I'll	I will
you're	you are	you'll	you will
he's	he is	he'll	he will
she's	she is	she'll	she will
it's	it is	it'll	it will
we're	we are	we'll	we will
they're	they are	they'll	they will
I've	I have	aren't	are not
you've	you have	can't	cannot
he's	he has	couldn't	could not
she's	she has	didn't	did not
it's	it has	doesn't	does not
we've	we have	don't	do not
they've	they have	hadn't	had not
		hasn't	has not
I'd	I had *or* I would	haven't	have not
you'd	you had *or* you would	isn't	is not
he'd	he had *or* he would	won't	will not
she'd	she had *or* she would	wouldn't	would not
it'd	it had *or* it would		
we'd	we had *or* we would		
they'd	they had *or* they would		

waited out in the rain.

shoulder •NOUN• **shoulders** one of the top parts of your body between your neck and the tops of your arms
•VERB• **shoulders, shouldering, shouldered** 1 to shoulder something is to carry it on your shoulder or shoulders 2 to shoulder a responsibility is to accept it as something you must do

shoulderblade •NOUN• **shoulderblades** one of the two flat bones at the top of your back on either side of your spine

shout •VERB• **shouts, shouting, shouted** to say something very loudly
•NOUN• **shouts** a loud cry or call

shove •VERB• **shoves, shoving, shoved** 1 to shove something is to push it hard or roughly 2 if someone tells another person to **shove off** they are telling that person rudely to go away

•NOUN• **shoves** a hard or rough push

shovel •NOUN• **shovels** a tool like a spade that can be small with a short handle or large with a long handle
•VERB• **shovels, shovelling, shovelled** to shovel things is to scoop them up and move them using a shovel

show •VERB• **shows, showing, showed, shown** 1 to show something is to allow it or cause it to be seen: *Show me your new bike.* • *There's a cartoon showing at the local cinema.*
2 something shows if it can be seen: *The scar hardly shows.*
3 to show someone something is to point it out to them or demonstrate it to them: *Can you show me how to tie a reef knot?*
4 to show someone somewhere is to guide them in that direction: *The steward showed us to our seats.*
5 something shows something, such as a

particular quality, when it makes it clear or proves that it is true: *His actions showed great courage.* • *The evidence shows that he couldn't have committed the crime.*

6 to **show off** is to behave in a way that attracts attention

7 to **show up** is to arrive

8 if someone **shows you up**, they embarrass you in front of other people

•NOUN• **shows 1** an entertainment in the theatre or on radio or TV

2 an event where people or businesses can exhibit their goods or produce to the public

3 a show of something is a sign of it or a demonstration of it: *There was no show of support for Tom's idea.*

4 if people do things for show, they do them to impress other people

⇒ **showy**

show business •NOUN• show business is the entertainment industry, including films, theatre, radio and television

ⓘ **Show business** is often shortened to showbiz.

shower •NOUN• **showers 1** a short fall of rain, snow or sleet: *sunshine and showers*

2 a sudden burst or fall of things: *a shower of sparks*

3 a device that sends out water in a stream or spray and that you stand under to wash your body

•VERB• **showers, showering, showered 1** to wash your body under a shower **2** someone is showered with gifts or compliments when they are given lots of them at the same time

♦ **showery** •ADJECTIVE• showery weather is when showers of rain fall between periods when it is dry

shown •VERB• a form of the verb **show** that is used with a helping verb to show that something happened in the past: *Niall had shown us how well he could act.*

showroom •NOUN• **showrooms** a place where goods are displayed for people to see: *a car showroom*

showy •ADJECTIVE• **showier, showiest** showy things attract attention because they are big and bright, although they may not be beautiful or in good taste

shrank •VERB• a way of changing the verb **shrink** to make a past tense: *The hot wash shrank my jersey.*

shrapnel •NOUN• shrapnel is pieces of metal from the case of an exploding bomb or shell that fly out in all directions

shred •NOUN• **shreds 1** a long thin strip: *His shirt was torn to shreds.* **2** a shred of something is a very small amount of it: *They didn't have a shred of evidence to link him to the crime.*

•VERB• **shreds, shredding, shredded** to tear into shreds

shrew •NOUN• **shrews** a tiny animal, similar to a mouse, but with a long pointed nose

shrewd •ADJECTIVE• **shrewder, shrewdest** wise and showing good judgement: *a shrewd politician* • *a shrewd guess*

shriek •VERB• **shrieks, shrieking, shrieked** to give a piercing scream or to speak in a loud shrill voice

•NOUN• **shrieks** a piercing scream

shrill •ADJECTIVE• high-pitched, clear and piercing

♦ **shrilly** •ADVERB• with a shrill sound or voice: *A child was calling shrilly for its mother.*

shrimp •NOUN• **shrimps** *or* **shrimp** a small shellfish with a long tail that turns pink when it is cooked and is similar to, but smaller than, a prawn

shrine •NOUN• **shrines** a sacred place where people go to worship, often because it has something to do with a holy person

shrink •VERB• **shrinks, shrinking, shrank, shrunk 1** to get smaller **2** you **shrink from** something when you move away from it in horror or disgust, or when you want to avoid it

shrivel •VERB• **shrivels, shrivelling, shrivelled** to become smaller and wrinkled

shroud •NOUN• **shrouds** a cloth wrapped around a dead body

•VERB• **shrouds, shrouding, shrouded** to shroud something is to cover it completely: *hills shrouded in mist*

shrub •NOUN• **shrubs** a small bush

♦ **shrubbery** •NOUN• **shrubberies** an area in a garden where shrubs are grown

shrug •VERB• **shrugs, shrugging, shrugged**
1 to raise and lower your shoulders in a movement that shows you do not know something or that you do not care about it **2** to **shrug something off** is to get rid of it easily: *He's fit enough to shrug off colds.*
•NOUN• **shrugs** a quick raising and lowering movement of the shoulders

shrunk •VERB• a way of changing the verb **shrink** to make a past tense. It is used with a helping verb: *The hot water had shrunk my jersey.*

shrunken •ADJECTIVE• having been shrunk: *a small, shrunken old man*

shudder •VERB• **shudders, shuddering, shuddered** you shudder when your whole body shakes for a moment because you have seen or heard something shocking or disgusting: *She shuddered when she heard the bad news.*
•NOUN• **shudders** a sudden shaking movement of your body

shuffle •VERB• **shuffles, shuffling, shuffled**
1 to slide your feet along the ground without lifting them **2** to shuffle things, such as playing-cards, is to mix them up so that they are in random order

shun •VERB• **shuns, shunning, shunned** to deliberately ignore someone because they have done something wrong

shunt •VERB• **shunts, shunting, shunted 1** to shunt railway engines or carriages is to move them from one track to another **2** to shunt people or things about or around is to move them from place to place

shut •VERB• **shuts, shutting, shut 1** to shut something is to close it or move it to a position where it covers an opening, or where its opening is covered
2 a shop or other business shuts when it stops being open or the staff stop working and go home
3 to **shut down** a machine or factory is to stop it working
4 to **shut a machine off** is to stop it working, and to **shut off** power or water is to stop it flowing
5 to **shut up** is to be quiet or stop talking
•ADJECTIVE• closed: *All the shops are shut after 6 o'clock.*

shutter •NOUN• **shutters 1** a wooden cover for a window that hinges from the side **2** the moving cover over the lens of a camera, which opens when a photograph is taken

shuttle •NOUN• **shuttles 1** in weaving, the shuttle is the part that carries the thread backwards and forwards across the loom **2** a shuttle is an air, train or other transport service that operates backwards and forwards between two places
•VERB• **shuttles, shuttling, shuttled** to shuttle between places is to travel to and fro between them

shuttlecock •NOUN• **shuttlecocks** an object made up of a cone of cork or plastic with feathers stuck around its rim, used in the game of badminton

shy •ADJECTIVE• **shyer, shyest** a shy person feels very uncomfortable when they have to speak or do something in front of other people, or when they meet new people
•VERB• **shies, shying, shied 1** if a horse shies, it turns to the side suddenly because it has been frightened **2** to **shy away** from something is to avoid it or move away from it quickly

Siamese cat •NOUN• **Siamese cats** a breed of cat with a slim body, blue eyes and greyish brown fur

Siamese twins •PLURAL NOUN• twins that are joined together at some part of their body when they are born. Another name for them is **conjoined twins**

sibling •NOUN• **siblings** a person's siblings are their brothers and sisters

sick •ADJECTIVE• **sicker, sickest 1** if you feel sick you feel like vomiting or you need to vomit
2 you are sick when you vomit
3 sick people or animals are ill
4 if you are sick of something, you are very tired of it
♦ **sicken** •VERB• **sickens, sickening, sickened 1** if someone sickens, they become ill **2** if something sickens you, it disgusts you or makes you feel like vomiting
♦ **sickening** •ADJECTIVE• disgusting
♦ **sickly** •ADJECTIVE• **sicklier, sickliest**

Aa

1 someone who is sickly is often ill or gets ill easily: *a sickly child* **2** something sickly is unhealthy looking or makes you want to vomit: *a sickly green colour* • *a sickly smell*
♦ **sickness** •NOUN• **sicknesses** an illness or disease

Bb

Cc

side •NOUN• **sides 1** the side of something is the part at or near its edge: *a house by the side of the river* • *at the side of the garden*
2 one of two or more surfaces of a figure, shape or structure, especially one of the surfaces that is not the top, bottom, front or back: *A cube has six sides.* • *Put the label on the side of the box.*
3 your sides are the left and right parts of your body: *I've got a pain in my left side.*
4 one of the two teams playing in a match, or one of the two groups of people involved in an argument or battle
• **on all sides** all around
• **side by side** next to each other
• **take sides** to agree with or support one person, or group of people, who is arguing or fighting with another person or group of people
•VERB• **sides, siding, sided** to **side with** someone is to support them against another person or group in an argument

Dd

Ee

Ff

Gg

Hh

Ii

Jj

Kk

Ll

Mm

Nn

Oo

sideboard •NOUN• **sideboards** a piece of furniture with cupboards and drawers

Pp

sidecar •NOUN• **sidecars** a small vehicle that is attached to the side of a motorbike for a passenger

Qq

Rr

side effect •NOUN• **side effects** if something has side effects, it has effects that are additional to the effect it is supposed to have

Ss

Tt

sideline •NOUN• **sidelines 1** an extra job apart from your normal work **2** on a sports pitch, the sidelines are the lines along both sides of the pitch marking the outer edges of the playing area

Uu

Vv

Ww

sidelong •ADJECTIVE• a sidelong look is made sideways

Xx

sideshow •NOUN• **sideshows** a small show that is part of a larger more important show

Yy

Zz

sidetrack •VERB• **sidetracks, sidetracking, sidetracked** if you are sidetracked by something, it makes you turn away from what you are doing or saying

sidewalk •NOUN• **sidewalks** the American English word for a pavement

sideways •ADVERB• something that goes sideways goes towards the side, or with its side facing the direction it is moving

siding •NOUN• **sidings** a short stretch of track where trains and coaches are shunted off the main track when they are not being used

sidle •VERB• **sidles, sidling, sidled** to move sideways, especially in a stealthy way, so that you are not noticed

siege •NOUN• **sieges** a situation in which a town or fort is completely surrounded by an enemy army that prevents supplies from getting in

siesta •NOUN• **siestas** a short sleep or nap, especially in hot countries when the sun gets very hot in the afternoon

sieve •NOUN• **sieves** a bowl with a bottom made of fine mesh, used to separate liquids from solids, or small fine pieces from larger ones

sift •VERB• **sifts, sifting, sifted 1** to sift a substance is to pass it through a sieve to separate out lumps or larger pieces **2** to sift things is to go through them, examining each one carefully

sigh •VERB• **sighs, sighing, sighed** to take a long, deep breath and breathe out noisily, because you feel tired, relieved or unhappy
•NOUN• **sighs** to breathe out loudly

sight •NOUN• **sights 1** sight is the power of seeing things: *A very young kitten's sight is not very good.*
2 a sight is something that you see or something that is worth seeing: *It was a sight I'll never forget.* • *We are going out today to look at the sights of London.*
3 something that is **in sight** can be seen, and something that is **out of sight** cannot be seen
4 a person or thing that looks ridiculous, unusual or shocking: *What a sight she is with that bright blue hair!*
• **a sight for sore eyes** a person or thing that you are very glad to see
• **set your sights on** to set your sights on something is to decide that you want it

ⓘ Be careful not to confuse the spelling of **sight** with **site**, which is a place where something is.

sight-read •VERB• **sight-reads, sight-reading, sight-read** if someone can sight-read music, they can play it or sing it by reading the notes printed on a sheet of music, even if they have never heard the music before

sightseeing •NOUN• sightseeing is travelling around looking at interesting things and places
♦ **sightseer** •NOUN• **sightseers** someone who travels round looking at interesting things

sign •NOUN• **signs** 1 a mark or gesture with a special meaning: *He gave the sign to join him.*
    2 a notice that gives information to the public: *The sign said 'No parking'.*
    3 one thing is **a sign of** another when it shows what is happening or what will happen: *Leaves falling are a sign of autumn.*
•VERB• **signs, signing, signed** 1 you sign something or sign your name on something when you write your signature on it
    2 to sign someone, especially a professional player in certain sports, is to sign a contract with them making them part of your team
    3 to sign to someone is to make a sign or gesture to them: *He signed to me to come in.*
    4 to **sign up** for something is to join in with that thing

signal •NOUN• **signals** 1 a sign, a gesture, a light or a sound giving a command, warning or other message 2 a radio or TV signal is the wave of sound or light received by a radio or TV: *a strong clear signal*
•VERB• **signals, signalling, signalled** 1 to send information by signals 2 to signal to someone is to make a signal or signals to them

signalman •NOUN• **signalmen** someone whose job is to control railway signals

signature •NOUN• **signatures** your name, written by you in a way that you and other people can recognize

signature tune •NOUN• **signature tunes** a tune that is used to identify a TV or radio

series, usually played at the beginning and end of the programme

significance •NOUN• meaning or importance: *a matter of great significance*
♦ **significant** •ADJECTIVE• important or meaning something: *a very significant remark*
♦ **significantly** •ADVERB• in a significant way

signify •VERB• **signifies, signifying, signified** to have a certain meaning: *A symbol of a skull and crossbones signifies a poison.*

sign language •NOUN• a system of gestures made with the hands and fingers used to communicate with deaf people

signpost •NOUN• **signposts** a post by a road showing which direction to go to get to a particular place

Sikh •NOUN• **Sikhs** someone whose religion is Sikhism
•ADJECTIVE• to do with Sikhs or Sikhism: *the Sikh temple at Amritsar*
♦ **Sikhism** •NOUN• a religion believing in one God, founded by Guru Nanak in Punjab in North India

silence •NOUN• **silences** 1 silence is complete quietness when no sound can be heard 2 a silence is a time when there is no sound or no one speaks
•VERB• **silences, silencing, silenced** 1 to silence someone is to stop them speaking 2 to silence something is to stop it making a noise
♦ **silencer** •NOUN• **silencers** 1 a device on a car exhaust that reduces noise 2 a device used on a gun to lessen the sound made when it is fired
♦ **silent** •ADJECTIVE• completely quiet
♦ **silently** •ADVERB• without making any sound

silhouette •NOUN• **silhouettes** the shape of a person or thing seen against a light background with just an outline filled with shadow

silicon •NOUN• a substance in the form of grey crystals or brown powder, used in electronic devices

silicon chip •NOUN• **silicon chips** a tiny piece

Aa
Bb
Cc
Dd
Ee
Ff
Gg
Hh
Ii
Jj
Kk
Ll
Mm
Nn
Oo
Pp
Qq
Rr
Ss
Tt
Uu
Vv
Ww
Xx
Yy
Zz

Aa

Bb

Cc

Dd

Ee

Ff

Gg

Hh

Ii

Jj

Kk

Ll

Mm

Nn

Oo

Pp

Qq

Rr

Ss

Tt

Uu

Vv

Ww

Xx

Yy

Zz

of silicon with very small electrical circuits printed on it, used in computers and other electronic devices

silk •NOUN• **silks** very soft fine fibres made by silkworms, or a soft smooth fabric with a slight sheen that is made from these
•ADJECTIVE• made of silk: *a silk kimono*
♦ **silken** •ADJECTIVE• soft, fine and slightly shiny
⇒ **silky**

silkworm •NOUN• **silkworms** a type of moth whose caterpillar spins fine silk threads which are used to make silk

silky •ADJECTIVE• **silkier, silkiest** soft and smooth, like silk: *silky hair*

silliness •NOUN• silly behaviour

sill •NOUN• **sills** a horizontal piece of wood or stone at the bottom part of the opening of a window or door

silly •ADJECTIVE• **sillier, silliest** foolish or stupid
⇒ **silliness**

silt •NOUN• fine sand and mud that is carried along and left behind by flowing water

silver •NOUN• **1** a shiny grey precious metal **2** a whitish grey colour **3** things made of silver or a silvery grey metal, such as cutlery and coins
•ADJECTIVE• silver-coloured or made of silver: *a silver cup • silver hair*
⇒ **silvery**

silver medal •NOUN• **silver medals** a medal made of silver awarded to the person who comes second in sporting events

silver wedding •NOUN• **silver weddings** a couple who celebrate their silver wedding have been married for 25 years

silvery •ADJECTIVE• like silver in colour: *Birch trees have silvery bark.*

similar •ADJECTIVE• two things are similar when they are quite like each other but not exactly the same: *An alligator is similar to a crocodile, but smaller.*
♦ **similarity** •NOUN• **similarities** the way one thing is like another thing
♦ **similarly** •ADVERB• in the same or a similar way

simile •NOUN• **similes** a sentence or phrase in which one thing is described by being compared with another, usually with *as* or *like*. For example, *Its fleece was white as snow* and *He ran like a hare* are similes. See the box called **Similes and metaphors**

simmer •VERB• **simmers, simmering, simmered 1** to simmer food is to cook it slowly over a low heat or to boil it very gently **2** someone who has been angry **simmers down** when they become calm again

simper •VERB• **simpers, simpering, simpered** to smile or speak in a silly unnatural way

simple •ADJECTIVE• **simpler, simplest 1** straightforward or very easy to do: *simple instructions • a simple sum* **2** plain or basic: *a simple design*
♦ **simplicity** •NOUN• being simple and uncomplicated

simplification •NOUN• making something less complicated and therefore easier to do or understand

simplify •VERB• **simplifies, simplifying, simplified** to simplify something is to make it simpler and therefore easier to do or understand

simply •ADVERB• **1** in a straightforward, uncomplicated way: *I'll explain it simply so that you all understand.*
2 only: *Now, it's simply a question of waiting until something happens.*
3 completely or absolutely: *The concert was simply fantastic.*

simulate •VERB• **simulates, simulating, simulated** to simulate a real thing is to create another thing that looks or seems like the real one
♦ **simulation** •NOUN• **simulations** simulating something, or something that simulates the real one
♦ **simulator** •NOUN• **simulators** a machine that creates the conditions of a real situation, especially the flight of an aeroplane

simultaneous •ADJECTIVE• happening or done at exactly the same time: *a simultaneous broadcast on radio and TV*
♦ **simultaneously** •ADVERB• at exactly the same time

Similes and metaphors

Similes

Similes compare one thing with another, and point out the likeness between them.

This loaf of bread is as hard as a brick.

Words which are often used before a simile are:

as	as good as gold
like	He looked like a ghost.
as if	The sky looked as if it was painted blue.
as though	He looked as though he had seen a ghost.

Metaphors

Metaphors compare one thing with another by saying one thing is another thing, or describing it as if it were something quite different.

My little sister is a cheeky monkey.
(my sister is not really a monkey, but she is cheeky)

The bus flew along the motorway.
(the bus did not really fly, but it travelled fast)

Writers use both similes and metaphors to make interesting images of people, places and things for their readers.

---

sin • NOUN• **sins** a wicked act, especially one that breaks a religious law
⇒ **sinful, sinner**

since • CONJUNCTION• **1 since** is used when you are giving a reason for something and has more or less the same meaning as **because**: *I decided to go shopping, since it was Saturday and I'd just got my pocket money.* **2** after a particular event or time: *He's getting on very well since he moved to the new school.* • *He's grown a lot since you saw him last.*
• PREPOSITION• from the time of something in the past until the present time: *Theresa has been dancing since she was three.* • *I've grown three inches since last year.*
• ADVERB• **1** from the time that has already been mentioned onwards: *She joined the choir last month and has been going to practice regularly since.* **2** at a later time than the time first mentioned: *They were enemies for years, but they have since become friends.*

sincere • ADJECTIVE• **1** a sincere person is honest and means what they say **2** sincere

feeling is real and not faked
♦ **sincerely** • ADVERB• honestly and truly
♦ **sincerity** • NOUN• being sincere

sinew • NOUN• **sinews** a type of strong body tissue like cord that joins your muscles to your bones

sinful • ADJECTIVE• **1** sinful behaviour is bad or wicked, especially because it breaks a religious law **2** a sinful person has committed a sin or sins
♦ **sinfulness** • NOUN• being sinful

sing • VERB• **sings, singing, sang, sung**
1 people sing when they make musical sounds with their voices **2** birds and some other animals sing when they make musical calls

singe • VERB• **singes, singeing, singed** to singe something is to burn its surface or edge slightly by touching it with something hot: *The cat singed its whiskers on the electric fire.*

ⓘ Be careful not to confuse the spelling of **singeing** with **singing**.

Aa
Bb
Cc
Dd
Ee
Ff
Gg
Hh
Ii
Jj
Kk
Ll
Mm
Nn
Oo
Pp
Qq
Rr
Ss
Tt
Uu
Vv
Ww
Xx
Yy
Zz

singer •NOUN• **singers** a person who sings

singing •NOUN• singing is making musical sounds with your voice

single •ADJECTIVE• 1 a single thing is only one and no more 2 someone who is single is not married 3 for use by one person: *a single room* •NOUN• **singles** 1 a ticket for a journey you make in one direction but not back again 2 a recording of a song that is released on its own, and not as part of an album 3 in games like tennis and badminton, you play singles when you play against only one other person •VERB• **singles, singling, singled** to single a person or thing out is to pick them in particular from a group of people or things ⇒ **singly, singular**

single-handed •ADJECTIVE• without anyone else's help

single-minded •ADJECTIVE• a single-minded person sticks in a determined way to one aim or purpose

singly •ADVERB• one at a time or one by one: *You usually see tigers singly, but sometimes you will see a small family group.*

sing-song •ADJECTIVE• a sing-song voice goes up and down like someone singing

singular •ADJECTIVE• 1 in grammar, a singular form of a word is the form used to refer to one person, thing or group, rather than two or more 2 very noticeable or out of the ordinary: *a poem of singular beauty* •NOUN• the form of a noun, pronoun, adjective or verb that you use when it expresses the idea of one person, thing or group, rather than two or more: *The singular is 'sheep' and the plural is also 'sheep'.*
♦ **singularly** •ADVERB• remarkably: *He was singularly unprepared for life in the outback.*

sinister •ADJECTIVE• threatening evil or harm: *a sinister black figure with a large hood covering the face*

ⓘ This is a Latin word which means *left*. The ancient Romans believed that the left side was unlucky.

sink •VERB• **sinks, sinking, sank, sunk** 1 to drop below the surface of water and go on moving downwards to the bottom: *The boat sank in a storm.* 2 to go down or get lower: *The sun was sinking towards the horizon.* • *He sank to his knees.* 3 to sink into something is to push or go deeply into it or pass through its surface: *The rainwater sank into the soil.* • *The dog sank its teeth into the postman's leg.* 4 if information you are given **sinks in**, you understand it properly •NOUN• **sinks** in a kitchen or bathroom, a large fixed container with taps and a drain, used for washing

sinner •NOUN• **sinners** someone who has committed a sin

sinuous •ADJECTIVE• with lots of curves or bends: *the sinuous movement of a snake*

sinus •NOUN• **sinuses** an air-filled hollow in the bones of your skull that connects with your nose

sip •VERB• **sips, sipping, sipped** to sip a drink is to drink it slowly taking only a little mouthful at a time

siphon *or* **syphon** •NOUN• **siphons** *or* **syphons** a bent pipe or tube through which a liquid is drawn from one container into a second container placed at a lower level

sir •NOUN• **sirs** 1 a polite way of addressing a man, for example at the beginning of a letter or when serving him in a shop 2 a title used before the name of a knight: *Sir Galahad*

sire •NOUN• **sires** 1 the father of an animal, especially an animal bred on a farm 2 a title that was sometimes used in the past when talking to a king

siren •NOUN• **sirens** a device that makes a very loud hooting or wailing noise to warn people of something: *The ambulance came hurtling along the road with its siren on.*

sirloin •NOUN• **sirloins** a cut of beef from the top of the back leg, or loin

sister •NOUN• **sisters** your sister is a girl or woman who has the same parents as you do
♦ **sisterhood** •NOUN• **sisterhoods** 1 sisterhood is a feeling of friendship among women and girls 2 a sisterhood is a group of women, especially nuns

sister-in-law •NOUN• **sister-in-laws** your brother's wife, or your husband or wife's sister

sit •VERB• **sits, sitting, sat** 1 you sit or **sit down** when you have your weight supported on your bottom rather than your feet
  2 you sit or **sit down** when you lower yourself into this position so that your bottom is resting on a surface
  3 something sits in the place where it is resting or lying: *There was a big parcel sitting on the kitchen table.*
  4 you sit an exam when you do the exam

sitcom •NOUN• **sitcoms** short for **situation comedy**, a television comedy series that is set in the same place and includes the same characters in each episode

site •NOUN• **sites** a place where something was, is, or is to be situated or located, or a place used for a certain purpose: *the site of a battle* • *a good site to build a house*

sitting-room •NOUN• **sitting-rooms** a room where people can sit down and relax

situate •VERB• **situates, situating, situated** something is situated in a certain place or position when it is put or placed there
  ♦ **situation** •NOUN• **situations** 1 a place where anything stands or is located: *Plant the sunflowers in a sunny situation.* **2** a set of circumstances or a state of affairs: *The situation in the areas affected by the drought is getting more and more difficult every day.*

six •NOUN• **sixes** the number 6

sixteen •NOUN• the number 16

sixteenth •ADJECTIVE AND ADVERB• after fifteenth and before seventeenth

sixth •ADJECTIVE AND ADVERB• after fifth and before seventh
  •NOUN• **sixths** the fraction $\frac{1}{6}$, which means one of six equal parts of something

sixtieth •ADJECTIVE AND ADVERB• after fifty-ninth and before sixty-first: *Grandmother's sixtieth birthday*

sixty •NOUN• **sixties** the number 60

size •NOUN• **sizes** 1 how big or small something is, or how long, wide, high, and deep it is **2** a shoe or clothes size is one that is made to fit a certain size of feet or body

•VERB• **sizes, sizing, sized** to **size up** a person or thing is to study them to find out what they are like
  ♦ **sizeable** *or* **sizable** •ADJECTIVE• fairly big

sizzle •VERB• **sizzles, sizzling, sizzled** to make a hissing noise like the sound of food frying

skate •NOUN• **skates** 1 a boot with a blade fitted to the bottom, used for gliding smoothly over ice **2** a **rollerskate**
•VERB• **skates, skating, skated** to move over ice wearing skates on your feet, or to move over the ground with rollerskates on your feet
⇒ **skater, skating**

skateboard •NOUN• **skateboards** a long narrow board with wheels fitted to the bottom, for riding on in a standing or crouching position
  ♦ **skateboarding** •NOUN• riding on skateboards

skater •NOUN• **skaters** someone who skates on ice

skating •NOUN• the sport or pastime of moving over the surface of ice wearing skates

skeleton •NOUN• **skeletons** the frame of bones inside your body that supports all your muscles and organs. See the illustration on the next page

skeleton key •NOUN• **skeleton keys** a key that will open several different locks

sketch •NOUN• **sketches** 1 a drawing that is done quickly, often as a guide for a more detailed picture or plan **2** a very short funny play
•VERB• **sketches, sketching, sketched** to sketch something is to draw it quickly

skew •VERB• **skews, skewing, skewed** something is skewed when it lies at an angle

skewer •NOUN• **skewers** a long thin pointed piece of metal or wood that is pushed through small pieces of food so that they can be cooked under a grill or on a barbecue

ski •NOUN• **skis** skis are two long narrow strips of wood or metal used for gliding over snow and which you attach to special boots
•VERB• **skis, skiing, skied** *or* **ski'd** to move

Aa
Bb
Cc
Dd
Ee
Ff
Gg
Hh
Ii
Jj
Kk
Ll
Mm
Nn
Oo
Pp
Qq
Rr
Ss
Tt
Uu
Vv
Ww
Xx
Yy
Zz

Aa
Bb
Cc
Dd
Ee
Ff
Gg
Hh
Ii
Jj
Kk
Ll
Mm
Nn
Oo
Pp
Qq
Rr
Ss
Tt
Uu
Vv
Ww
Xx
Yy
Zz

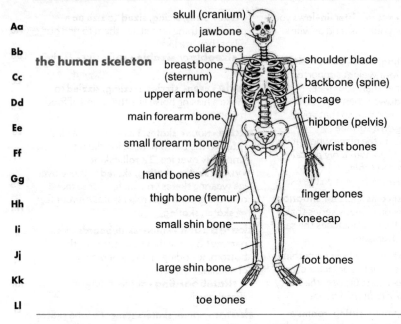

the human skeleton

skull (cranium)
jawbone
collar bone
breast bone (sternum)
shoulder blade
upper arm bone
backbone (spine)
ribcage
main forearm bone
hipbone (pelvis)
small forearm bone
wrist bones
hand bones
thigh bone (femur)
finger bones
kneecap
small shin bone
large shin bone
foot bones
toe bones

over snow with a pair of long narrow strips of wood or metal attached to your boots

skid •VERB• **skids, skidding, skidded** to slide over a surface in an uncontrolled way

skiing •NOUN• the sport of gliding over snow on skis

skilful •ADJECTIVE• having a lot of skill
✦ **skilfully** •ADVERB• with skill
✦ **skilfulness** •NOUN• being skilful

skill •NOUN• **skills** 1 to have skill is to be clever or expert at doing something 2 a skill is a talent that you develop through training and practice : *football skills*
✦ **skilled** •ADJECTIVE• 1 a skilled person is expert at what they do : *a skilled pianist* 2 a skilled job needs training and practice

skim •VERB• **skims, skimming, skimmed** 1 something skims a surface when it travels along just above the surface 2 to skim something floating on the top of a liquid is to remove it
✦ **skimmed** •ADJECTIVE• skimmed milk has had some of the cream removed

skimpy •ADJECTIVE• **skimpier, skimpiest** skimpy clothes do not cover much of your body

skin •NOUN• **skins** 1 the tissue that covers the outer surface of the bodies of humans and animals
2 the thin outer covering on fruit and some vegetables
3 a layer that forms on the top of some liquids
• **by the skin of your teeth** if you manage to do something by the skin of your teeth, you only just manage to do it
•VERB• **skins, skinning, skinned** to skin something is to remove its skin

skinflint •NOUN• **skinflints** a person who is very mean with money

skinny •ADJECTIVE• **skinnier, skinniest** thin

skint •ADJECTIVE• an informal way of saying you have no money : *I can't afford the ticket. I'm totally skint.*

skip •VERB• **skips, skipping, skipped** 1 to move forward springing or hopping from one foot to the other as you go
2 to jump over a skipping-rope
3 to skip something is to leave it out and go on to the next thing
4 to skip school or lessons is to not attend them

•NOUN• **skips** a skipping movement: *Off the rabbit went, with a hop, skip and a jump.*

skipper •NOUN• **skippers** the captain of a boat or ship, or of an aircraft or spacecraft

skipping rope •NOUN• **skipping ropes** a rope that you jump over and which is swung round repeatedly by two people holding it at either end, or which you hold and swing over and under your own body

skirmish •NOUN• **skirmishes** a short battle or fight

skirt •NOUN• **skirts** a piece of clothing that hangs from the waist
•VERB• **skirts, skirting, skirted 1** to go around the border or edge of something: *a dense wood that skirted the grounds* **2** you skirt around something when you avoid it by going around it

skirting or **skirting board** •NOUN• **skirtings** or **skirting boards** a length of wood fixed to the bottom of an inside wall where it meets the floor

skittle •NOUN• **skittles** one of several bottle-shaped objects that you try to knock down with a ball in the game of skittles

skive •VERB• **skives, skiving, skived** to avoid doing the work you should be doing
♦ **skiver** •NOUN• **skivers** someone who avoids work

skulk •VERB• **skulks, skulking, skulked** to wait somewhere, hidden from view

skull •NOUN• **skulls** the bony part of your head that contains your brain and forms a framework for your face

skull and crossbones •PLURAL NOUN• a flag flown on pirate ships that had a black skull with two crossed thighbones on a white background

skullcap •NOUN• **skullcaps** a small round hat that fits tightly round the top part of the head

skunk •NOUN• **skunks** a small North American animal with black-and-white fur and a long bushy tail, that defends itself by spraying a stinking liquid at its attacker

sky •NOUN• **skies** the area of space above the Earth where you can see the sun, moon, stars and clouds

ⓘ This is a word from the Old Norse language which was used long ago in Scandanavia.

sky-diving •NOUN• a sport in which people jump out of aeroplanes and let themselves fall for quite a while before they open their parachutes to land

skylark •NOUN• **skylarks** a small brown bird that flies upwards and hovers in the sky singing a sweet song

skylight •NOUN• **skylights** a window set into a roof

skyline •NOUN• the line where the sky seems to meet the land or sea at the horizon

skyscraper •NOUN• **skyscrapers** a tall building with lots of storeys

slab •NOUN• **slabs** a thick flat slice of something: *an enormous slab of chocolate cake*

slack •ADJECTIVE• **slacker, slackest 1** not firmly fixed in position: *My front tooth is slack.*
2 not stretched tight or fitting snugly: *These trousers are too slack around the waist.*
3 careless or lazy: *slack discipline* • *She's slack about her work and doesn't show much interest.*
•VERB• **slacks, slacking, slacked** to do less work than you should
♦ **slacken** •VERB• **slackens, slackening, slackened 1** to slacken something is to loosen it **2** the pace or strength of something slackens when it gets slower or weaker
♦ **slackness** •NOUN• being lazy
♦ **slacks** •PLURAL NOUN• slacks are smart but loose casual trousers

slalom •NOUN• **slaloms** a type of course in which skiers or canoeists move in a zigzag pattern around upright posts

slam •VERB• **slams, slamming, slammed 1** to slam something, such as a door, is to shut it with a bang **2** to slam something is to hit it or put it down hard

slang •NOUN• very informal words or expressions that you use in everyday speech or to people of your own age, but not in writing or when you are being polite

Aa
Bb
Cc
Dd
Ee
Ff
Gg
Hh
Ii
Jj
Kk
Ll
Mm
Nn
Oo
Pp
Qq
Rr
Ss
Tt
Uu
Vv
Ww
Xx
Yy
Zz

slant •VERB• **slants, slanting, slanted** to slope or move diagonally •NOUN• **slants 1** a slope or diagonal direction **2** someone's slant on something is their particular point of view

slap •NOUN• **slaps 1** a blow made with the palm of the hand or anything flat **2** a sound made by something hitting a flat surface •VERB• **slaps, slapping, slapped** to hit with the palm of the hand or something flat

slapdash •ADJECTIVE• careless: *slapdash work*

slapstick •NOUN• a type of comedy in which actors or comedians get laughs by behaving in a silly way, for example by falling over

slash •VERB• **slashes, slashing, slashed 1** to slash something is to cut it with a sharp blade swung in a quick swinging movement **2** to slash things like prices is to cut them by a large amount •NOUN• **slashes 1** a long cut made by a sharp blade **2** one of two punctuation marks (/) or (\), used especially in computing and in web site addresses

slat •NOUN• **slats** a long strip of plastic or wood put together with others to form something such as a window blind or bench

slate •NOUN• **slates 1** slate is a type of stone that can be split into thin pieces along natural lines in the stone **2** a slate is a rectangular piece of this rock used for roofing, or in the past, for schoolchildren to write on with chalk

slaughter •VERB• **slaughters, slaughtering, slaughtered** to slaughter people or animals is to kill them in large numbers •NOUN• the killing of large numbers of people or animals

slaughterhouse •NOUN• **slaughterhouses** a place where animals are killed for food

slave •NOUN• **slaves** a person who is owned by another person and who is usually made to work hard for little or no pay •VERB• **slaves, slaving, slaved** to work very hard
♦ **slavery** •NOUN• **1** buying, selling, and using slaves **2** very hard work for very little reward

slay •VERB• **slays, slaying, slew, slain** to slay a person or animal is to kill them: *The dragon was slain by Saint George.*

sled or **sledge** •NOUN• **sleds** or **sledges 1** a small vehicle with metal runners underneath or with a flat underside that you sit on to slide over snow **2** a vehicle with ski-like runners underneath that is pulled over snow by dogs or horses

sledgehammer •NOUN• **sledgehammers** a large heavy hammer that you swing with both arms

sleek •ADJECTIVE• **sleeker, sleekest** smooth, soft and glossy: *A mink has sleek dark-brown fur.*
♦ **sleekness** •NOUN• being sleek

sleep •NOUN• **sleeps 1** sleep is rest that you have with your eyes closed and in a natural state of unconsciousness **2** a sleep is a period of time when you rest in this way
• **go to sleep 1** to fall asleep **2** if part of your body goes to sleep you lose all the feeling in it •VERB• **sleeps, sleeping, slept 1** to rest with your eyes closed and in a state of unconsciousness **2** if you **sleep in**, you sleep for too long so that you are late for something
♦ **sleeper** •NOUN• **sleepers 1** someone who sleeps **2** a carriage on a train where you can sleep **3** one of the heavy wooden or metal beams that a railway track is laid on
⇒ **sleepless, sleepy**

sleepily •ADVERB• in a tired or sleepy way
♦ **sleepiness** •NOUN• being sleepy

sleeping bag •NOUN• **sleeping bags** a large sack made of layers of warm fabric and used for sleeping in, especially by someone who is camping

sleepless •ADJECTIVE• if you have a sleepless night you are unable to go to sleep at all
♦ **sleeplessness** •NOUN• being unable to sleep

sleepwalker •NOUN• **sleepwalkers** someone who walks about while they are sleeping
♦ **sleepwalking** •NOUN• walking about in an unconscious state, as if sleeping

sleepy •ADJECTIVE• **sleepier, sleepiest**
feeling tired and wanting to sleep
⇒ **sleepily, sleepiness**

sleet •NOUN• a mixture of rain and snow

sleeve •NOUN• **sleeves** the part of a piece of clothing that covers your arm or part of your arm
✦ **sleeved** •ADJECTIVE• having sleeves
✦ **sleeveless** •ADJECTIVE• having no sleeves

sleigh •NOUN• **sleighs** a large sledge pulled by a horse or horses

sleight-of-hand •NOUN• moving your hands quickly and skilfully so that people cannot see what you are doing, as a conjuror does when he performs magic tricks

slender •ADJECTIVE• **1** slim or thin, especially in an attractive way: *a tall slender tree* **2** small or slight: *His chances of winning are extremely slender.*

slept •VERB• a way of changing the verb **sleep** to make a past tense. It can be used with or without a helping verb: *He slept for ten hours.* • *He had slept all morning and afternoon.*

sleuth •NOUN• **sleuths** an old-fashioned word for a detective

slice •NOUN• **slices** a thin or smaller piece cut from a larger piece of food
•VERB• **slices, slicing, sliced 1** to slice something, or **slice it up**, is to cut it into slices **2** to slice something is to cut it with a sharp blade or knife: *The knife slipped and sliced my finger.*

slick •ADJECTIVE• **slicker, slickest 1** a slick performance is done well without seeming to involve much effort **2** a slick talker is clever at persuading people
•NOUN• **slicks** a layer of oil that has been spilt on the surface of the sea
✦ **slickly** •ADVERB• efficiently and effortlessly

slide •VERB• **slides, sliding, slid 1** to slip or move over a surface quickly and smoothly **2** to move downwards or get worse: *She's let standards slide since we were last here.*
•NOUN• **slides 1** an apparatus with a smooth sloping surface, for children to slide down **2** a small clear glass or plastic plate on

which specimens are put so that they can be looked at under a microscope **3** a small transparent photograph that you put in a projector to be viewed on a screen

slide-rule •NOUN• **slide-rules** an instrument used for calculating, made up of one ruler that slides along beside another

slight •ADJECTIVE• **slighter, slightest 1** small or not great: *a slight increase in temperature* • *a slight problem* • *Lewis has a slight cold.* **2** slim and light: *He has a slight build.*
• **not in the slightest** not at all
✦ **slightly** •ADVERB• by only a small amount

slim •ADJECTIVE• **slimmer, slimmest 1** thin or slender: *slim fingers* **2** small or slight: *The chances of winning the lottery are very slim.*
✦ **slimness** •NOUN• being thin or slender

slime •NOUN• a soft, sticky, half-liquid substance that looks a bit like thin jelly
✦ **slimy** •ADJECTIVE• **slimier, slimiest** covered with, or feeling like, slime

sling •VERB• **slings, slinging, slung 1** to sling something is to throw it hard **2** to sling something over your shoulder is to throw it over your shoulder so that it hangs down
•NOUN• **slings 1** a bandage that is hung from someone's neck or shoulder to support an injured arm **2** a strong band of material that is used to support something that is being lifted or to throw stones

slink •VERB• **slinks, slinking, slunk** to move quietly, trying not to be noticed

slip •VERB• **slips, slipping, slipped 1** to slide accidentally and lose your balance **2** to **slip in** or **out** of a place, or to **slip away**, is to go in or out, or go away, quietly and without anyone noticing you **3** to slip something somewhere is to slide it there or put it there quickly **4** to **slip up** is to make a mistake or do something wrong
•NOUN• **slips 1** an accidental slide **2** a small mistake **3** a small piece of paper: *Fill in the green slip and give it back to me.* **4** a piece of thin underclothing that a girl or woman wears under their dress or skirt
• **give someone the slip** to escape from someone without their noticing

slipper • NOUN • **slippers** a soft shoe for wearing indoors

slippery • ADJECTIVE • smooth, wet or shiny and not easy to balance on or hold

slip road • NOUN • **slip roads** a narrower or less important road used by traffic going on to or leaving a motorway

slipshod • ADJECTIVE • careless and untidy

slit • NOUN • **slits** a long cut or narrow opening • VERB • **slits, slitting, slit** to slit something is to make a long narrow cut in it

slither • VERB • **slithers, slithering, slithered** to slide or slip: *The ice-cubes slithered off the table.*

slitherly • ADJECTIVE • smooth and slippery: *a slithery path to the water's edge*

sliver • NOUN • **slivers** a long thin piece cut or broken from something

slobber • VERB • **slobbers, slobbering, slobbered** a person or animal slobbers when saliva dribbles out of their mouth

slog • VERB • **slogs, slogging, slogged** to work very hard

slogan • NOUN • **slogans** a phrase that is easy to remember and is often repeated, used especially in advertising

slop • VERB • **slops, slopping, slopped** liquid slops when it moves around or splashes or spills

slope • VERB • **slopes, sloping, sloped** to go in a direction that is not level or straight but at an upward or downward slant • NOUN • **slopes** 1 an upward or downward slant 2 the side of a hill

sloppy • ADJECTIVE • **sloppier, sloppiest** 1 careless 2 showing love in a way that is silly and embarrassing

slot • NOUN • **slots** a small narrow opening, especially one that you put coins into • VERB • **slots, slotting, slotted** to **slot someone** or **something in** is to fit them into a small space or gap

sloth • NOUN • **sloths** 1 a South American animal that lives mostly in trees and moves very slowly 2 sloth is laziness

slothful • ADJECTIVE • lazy and slow-moving

slot machine • NOUN • **slot machines** a machine that you work by putting in a coin or a token

slouch • VERB • **slouches, slouching, slouched** to move, stand or sit with your shoulders rounded and your head hanging forward

slovenly • ADJECTIVE • dirty or untidy: *slovenly work*

slow • ADJECTIVE • **slower, slowest** 1 not fast or not moving quickly: *a slow march* • *Our progress was slow.* 2 if a clock or watch is slow, it shows a time earlier than the correct time • VERB • **slows, slowing, slowed** to slow, or to **slow down**, is to become slower, or make something slower

slowly • ADVERB • in a slow way: *He walks very slowly.*

slowcoach • NOUN • **slowcoaches** someone who takes a long time to move or do something

slow-motion • ADJECTIVE • a slow-motion scene in a film has the action slowed down to slower than its real speed

sludge • NOUN • thick soft slimy mud or any substance that is like this

slug • NOUN • **slugs** a creature with a long soft body like a snail, but with no shell

slum • NOUN • **slums** a building or part of a town or city where the conditions are dirty and overcrowded

slumber • VERB • **slumbers, slumbering, slumbered** to sleep • NOUN • **slumbers** sleep

slump • VERB • **slumps, slumping, slumped** 1 to fall or sink: *Business has slumped in the last few months.* 2 you slump, or **slump down**, when your body sinks so that you are lying heavily against something: *He was slumped over his desk, fast asleep.* • NOUN • **slumps** a period when businesses are not selling many goods

slung • VERB • a way of changing the verb **sling** to form a past tense. It can be used with or without a helping verb: *He slung his backpack over his shoulder.* • *They had slung all their coats into a corner without hanging them up.*

slunk •VERB• a way of changing the verb **slink** to form a past tense. It can be used with or without a helping verb: *The fox slunk away into the bushes.* • *He had slunk up behind me and shouted 'Boo!'.*

slur •VERB• **slurs, slurring, slurred** to pronounce words unclearly •NOUN• **slurs** an insult that is likely to damage someone's reputation

slurp •VERB• **slurps, slurping, slurped** to drink very noisily

slush •NOUN• partly melted snow on the ground
♦ **slushy** •ADJECTIVE• **slushier, slushiest** 1 soft and almost liquid, like partly melted snow 2 romantic in a silly way: *a slushy novel*

sly •ADJECTIVE• **slyer** or **slier, slyest** or **sliest** cunning and good at deceiving others
♦ **slyly** •ADJECTIVE• in a sly way
♦ **slyness** •NOUN• being sly

smack •VERB• **smacks, smacking, smacked** 1 to smack someone is to slap them 2 to smack your lips is to make a loud sucking noise by bringing your lips together tightly and then opening your mouth again quickly •NOUN• **smacks** a slap, or the sound made by a slap

small •ADJECTIVE• **smaller, smallest** 1 little: *a small country* • *This coat is too small for you.* • *a small problem* 2 if something makes you feel small, it makes you feel silly and unimportant 3 a small voice is soft and difficult to hear

smallholding •NOUN• **smallholdings** an area of land used for farming on a small scale

small-minded •ADJECTIVE• someone who is small-minded has a limited view of the world and does not want to learn about different ways of doing things

smallness •NOUN• how small something is compared to other things

smart •ADJECTIVE• **smarter, smartest** 1 neat: *my smartest clothes* 2 clever and quick 3 fast: *a smart pace* •VERB• **smarts, smarting, smarted** to feel a sharp stinging pain

♦ **smarten** •VERB• **smartens, smartening, smartened** to smarten, or **smarten up**, is to become or to make something smarter: *Smarten up a bit before you go to school.*
♦ **smartly** •ADVERB• 1 neatly and fashionably: *smartly dressed businessmen* 2 quickly or briskly: *You'll have to walk pretty smartly if you want to catch the train.*
♦ **smartness** •NOUN• being smart

smash •VERB• **smashes, smashing, smashed** 1 to break, or break something into pieces 2 to smash something, or smash into it, is to hit or crash into it with great force •NOUN• **smashes** 1 the sound of something breaking 2 a road accident in which two vehicles hit each other and are damaged
♦ **smashing** •ADJECTIVE• great or splendid: *That was a smashing film.*

smear •VERB• **smears, smearing, smeared** to spread a surface with something sticky or oily

smell •NOUN• **smells** 1 smell is the power or sense of being aware of things through your nose 2 a smell is something you notice using this sense: *a strong smell of garlic* 3 a sniff at something: *Have a smell at this milk and tell me if you think it's off.* •VERB• **smells, smelling, smelled** or **smelt** 1 to smell something is to notice it through your nose 2 something that smells gives off a smell of some kind
♦ **smelly** •ADJECTIVE• giving off a strong or bad smell

smelt[1] •VERB• **smelts, smelting, smelted** to melt rock or other material that contains metal to separate the metal from the rest of the material

smelt[2] •VERB• a way of changing the verb **smell** to make a past tense. It can be used with or without a helping verb: *He smelt the rose.* • *He had never smelt one so sweet.*

smile •VERB• **smiles, smiling, smiled** to show pleasure or amusement by turning up the corners of your mouth •NOUN• **smiles** an expression of pleasure or amusement in which you turn up the corners of your mouth

smirk •VERB• **smirks, smirking, smirked** to smile in a self-satisfied, cheeky or silly way

Aa Bb Cc Dd Ee Ff Gg Hh Ii Jj Kk Ll Mm Nn Oo Pp Qq Rr Ss Tt Uu Vv Ww Xx Yy Zz

Aa

•NOUN• **smirks** a self-satisfied, cheeky or silly smile

Bb

smith •NOUN• **smiths** someone who works with metals: *a silversmith • a blacksmith*

Cc

smithereens •PLURAL NOUN• something that is smashed to smithereens is broken into lots of tiny pieces

Dd

smitten •ADJECTIVE• to be smitten by someone is to be strongly attracted to them

Ee

smock •NOUN• **smocks** a loose piece of clothing worn over other clothes to protect them

Ff

Gg

smog •NOUN• smoke from car exhausts and chimneys mixed with fog which hangs over some cities and towns

Hh

Ii

smoke •NOUN• the cloudlike gases and bits of soot given off by something that is burning •VERB• **smokes, smoking, smoked** 1 something smokes when it gives off smoke 2 someone who smokes puts a lit cigarette, cigar or pipe in their mouth and breathes in the smoke

Jj

Kk

Ll

Mm

♦ **smoker** •NOUN• **smokers** someone who smokes cigarettes, cigars or a pipe

Nn

♦ **smoking** •NOUN• the habit of smoking cigarettes, cigars or a pipe

Oo

♦ **smoky** •ADJECTIVE• **smokier, smokiest** 1 filled with smoke 2 like smoke: *a smoky grey colour*

Pp

Qq

smooth •ADJECTIVE• **smoother, smoothest** 1 something smooth has an even surface that is not rough or bumpy 2 a smooth substance has no lumps 3 a smooth ride or smooth progress has no jerks, stops or problems •VERB• **smoothes, smoothing, smoothed** to smooth something is to make it smooth or flat: *She smoothed the bed covers and tidied her bedroom.*

Rr

Ss

Tt

Uu

♦ **smoothly** •ADVERB• in a smooth way

Vv

♦ **smoothness** •NOUN• being smooth

Ww

smother •VERB• **smothers, smothering, smothered** 1 if someone is smothered they die because something is over their nose and mouth and they cannot breathe 2 to smother flames is to cover them so that no oxygen gets to the fire and it goes out

Xx

Yy

Zz

smoulder •VERB• **smoulders, smouldering, smouldered** to burn slowly, without a flame

smudge •NOUN• **smudges** a mark made by rubbing something across a surface or pressing something greasy against it •VERB• **smudges, smudging, smudged** to smudge something is to rub something across it so that it smears

smug •ADJECTIVE• **smugger, smuggest** someone who is smug shows by their behaviour that they are very pleased with themselves

♦ **smugly** •ADVERB• in a self-satisfied way

♦ **smugness** •NOUN• being smug

smuggle •VERB• **smuggles, smuggling, smuggled** 1 to bring things into a country secretly and illegally 2 to smuggle something somewhere is to take it there secretly: *He smuggled the puppy into his room without his parents knowing.*

♦ **smuggler** •NOUN• **smugglers** someone who smuggles goods into a country

snack •NOUN• **snacks** a small meal, or something like a biscuit or piece of fruit eaten between meals

snag •NOUN• **snags** a small problem •VERB• **snags, snagging, snagged** to snag your clothing is to catch or tear it on something sharp or rough

snail •NOUN• **snails** a small creature with a soft body and a shell on its back that it can draw its body into for protection

snake •NOUN• **snakes** a type of reptile with a long thin body and no legs, which moves along the ground with twisting movements

snap •VERB• **snaps, snapping, snapped** 1 to break with a sudden sharp noise 2 something snaps shut when it closes with a sudden sharp noise 3 you snap your fingers when you rub your thumb and finger together in a quick movement, making a cracking noise 4 if someone snaps at you, they speak to you in a sharp angry way 5 an animal snaps when it makes a biting movement with its jaws •NOUN• **snaps** 1 the sound of something breaking or of an animal bringing its teeth together quickly 2 a photograph

♦ **snappily** •ADVERB• 1 quickly 2 in a bad-tempered way

✦ snappy •ADJECTIVE• **snappier, snappiest** if someone is snappy, they speak to people in a bad-tempered way
• **make it snappy** if someone tells you to make it snappy, they mean you should be quick

snapshot •NOUN• **snapshots** a photograph taken quickly

snare •NOUN• **snares** a kind of trap for catching animals
•VERB• **snares, snaring, snared** to trap an animal

snarl •VERB• **snarls, snarling, snarled** an animal, such as a dog or wolf, snarls when it growls in a threatening way
•NOUN• **snarls** an angry-sounding growl

snatch •VERB• **snatches, snatching, snatched 1** to snatch something is to grab suddenly **2** to snatch something, like a sleep or a meal, is to take it quickly when you have time or the chance
•NOUN• **snatches** a short piece of music or conversation

sneak •NOUN• **sneaks** someone who tells tales or is deceitful
•VERB• **sneaks, sneaking, sneaked 1** to go somewhere quietly and secretly
2 to tell someone in authority something behind a person's back
3 to **sneak up on** someone is to creep up behind them, to surprise them or give them a fright
✦ sneakily •ADVERB• in a sneaky way
✦ sneaky •ADJECTIVE• **sneakier, sneakiest** deceitful or secretive

sneer •VERB• **sneers, sneering, sneered 1** to raise your top lip at one side in a kind of smile that shows scorn **2** to **sneer at** something is to be scornful about it: *John sneered at my attempt to write a story.*
•NOUN• **sneers** a sneering expression or remark

sneeze •VERB• **sneezes, sneezing, sneezed** to suddenly and uncontrollably blow out air from your nose and mouth
•NOUN• **sneezes** this action and sound

snide •ADJECTIVE• spiteful in an almost hidden way: *I made snide little remarks whenever he spoke.*

sniff •VERB• **sniffs, sniffing, sniffed** to breathe in air through your nose with a small noise, or to draw air into your nose so that you can smell something
•NOUN• **sniffs** a quick loud breath taken in through your nose

sniffle •VERB• **sniffles, sniffling, sniffled** to sniff over and over again, especially because you have a cold or are crying

snigger •VERB• **sniggers, sniggering, sniggered** to laugh quietly in an unpleasant and cruel way
•NOUN• **sniggers** a quiet unpleasant laugh

snip •VERB• **snips, snipping, snipped** to snip something is to cut small pieces off it using scissors
•NOUN• **snips** a quick cutting action made with a pair of scissors

sniper •NOUN• **snipers** a person armed with a gun who shoots at people from a hiding place

snippet •NOUN• **snippets** a small piece: *a snippet of information*

snivel •VERB• **snivels, snivelling, snivelled** to cry and sniff weakly and in a way that does not make other people feel sympathy for you

snob •NOUN• **snobs** a snob is someone who admires people of high social class, or things that are of high quality, and despises people who are of a lower class than they are, or does not like the things that ordinary people like
✦ snobbery •NOUN• the behaviour of snobs
✦ snobbish •ADJECTIVE• being a snob

snooker •NOUN• a game for two players played on a large table with several coloured balls which have to be hit into a pocket at the side of the table using a long stick called a cue

snoop •VERB• **snoops, snooping, snooped** try to find out things in a secretive way: *Jane was snooping around to try to find my diary.*
✦ snooper •NOUN• **snoopers** someone who snoops

snooty •ADJECTIVE• **snootier, snootiest** a snooty person behaves in a haughty way to people they think are not as good as they are

snooze •NOUN• **snoozes** a short light sleep
•VERB• **snoozes, snoozing, snoozed** to sleep, especially not very deeply or for a short time

snore •VERB• **snores, snoring, snored** to make a noise like a snort while you are sleeping, when you breathe in

snorkel •NOUN• **snorkels** a tube that allows an underwater swimmer to breathe, with one end sticking out above the water to let in air
•VERB• **snorkels, snorkelling, snorkelled** to swim underwater using a snorkel to breathe

snort •VERB• **snorts, snorting, snorted** 1 to make a noise by pushing air out through your nostrils: *The horses snorted, stamping their hooves.* 2 to make this noise because you are angry, disagree, or think something is funny: *'Don't be stupid!' she snorted.*
•NOUN• **snorts** a loud noise made by breathing out through your nose: *a snort of laughter*

snout •NOUN• **snouts** the mouth and nose of a pig or animal like that

snow •NOUN• water that has frozen into soft white pieces called flakes that fall from the sky: *The children loved playing in the snow.* • *Thick snow had blocked the road across the mountain.*
•VERB• **snows, snowing, snowed** to fall down like snow: *It's been snowing all night.*
⇒ **snowy**

snowball •NOUN• **snowballs** a ball of snow that children make and throw at each other: *a snowball fight*
•VERB• **snowballs, snowballing, snowballed** if a situation or a problem snowballs, it grows quickly and becomes more difficult to deal with: *The strike snowballed and soon all the post offices were closed.*

snowboarding •NOUN• a sport in which you move quickly down hills over snow on a flat plastic board called a snowboard

snowdrift •NOUN• **snowdrifts** a lot of snow that the wind has blown into a pile

snowdrop •NOUN• **snowdrops** a small white flower that grows from a bulb in the early spring

snowman •NOUN• **snowmen** a figure of a person, made of snow

snowplough •NOUN• **snowploughs** a large vehicle that clears snow from the roads

snowy •ADJECTIVE• **snowier, snowiest** 1 covered with snow 2 perfectly white: *a fat gentleman with a snowy beard*

snub •VERB• **snubs, snubbing, snubbed** to treat someone in a rude or insulting way: *I tried to speak to him but he just snubbed me and turned away.*
•ADJECTIVE• a snub nose is small and turns up at the end

snuff or **snuff out** •VERB• **snuffs, snuffing, snuffed** to put out a candle flame, often with your fingers
•NOUN• a type of tobacco in the form of a powder

snuffle •VERB• **snuffles, snuffling, snuffled** to make sniffing noises, especially because you have a cold

snug •ADJECTIVE• **snugger, snuggest** warm and cosy: *We were all quite snug in our sleeping bags.*

snuggle or **snuggle up** •VERB• **snuggles, snuggling, snuggled** to curl up and get warm: *Sam snuggled closer to his mother and soon fell asleep.*

so •ADVERB• 1 to such an extent or to a great extent: *I was so relieved to hear her voice.*
• *The box was so heavy he could not lift it.*
• *Thank you so much for all your help.*
2 you can use **so** when you are talking about something mentioned or shown by a gesture: *a little boy about so high* • *'I feel sick after all those sweets.'* *'I told you so, didn't I?'* • *'Are you coming to the party?'* *'I hope so.'*
3 also: *Jane's ten and so am I.*
4 in this way or that way: *Stretch your leg out so.*
• **so as to** in order to: *We got there early so as to get good seats.*
• **so far** up to now: *Well, I've enjoyed his lessons so far.*
• **so forth** more things that are similar: *pens, pencils, and so forth*
• **so that** in order that: *Could you wash my jeans so that I can wear them tomorrow?*
• **so what?** used for saying that something does not matter
•CONJUNCTION• therefore: *He asked me to come, so I did.* • *So they got married and lived happily ever after.*

soak •VERB• **soaks, soaking, soaked** 1 to soak something is to cover it in liquid and leave it there: *If you soak your blouse, the stain might come out.*
2 to soak someone is to make them very wet
3 if a piece of cloth or paper **soaks up** a liquid, it sucks it up or absorbs it: *Mum used a towel to soak up the spilt milk.*
♦ **soaking** or **soaking wet** •ADJECTIVE• very wet: *Take your clothes off – they're soaking.*

so-and-so •NOUN• 1 someone whose name you cannot remember: *She's always gossiping; so-and-so is getting married, so-and-so's got a new job...* **2** a word you use instead of saying something rude: *She can be a real so-and-so!*

soap •NOUN• **soaps** 1 a substance that you use to wash yourself and other things: *a bar of soap* **2** another word for **soap opera**: *Gran likes to watch all the soaps on TV.*
•VERB• **soaps, soaping, soaped** to rub something with soap

soap opera •NOUN• **soap operas** a television series about a group of families and their daily lives

① These shows were given their name because when they first started they were sponsored by soap companies, and so advertisements for soap would have been seen with the show.

soapy •ADJECTIVE• **soapier, soapiest** covered in or full of soap bubbles: *soapy water*

soar •VERB• **soars, soaring, soared** 1 to fly high up into the air: *An eagle soared high above their heads.* **2** if prices soar, things become much more expensive very quickly: *The price of petrol has soared over the last ten years.*

sob •VERB• **sobs, sobbing, sobbed** to cry noisily: *Lisa lay on her bed, sobbing.*
•NOUN• **sobs** the sound of someone sobbing

sober •ADJECTIVE• 1 not drunk
2 serious: *a sober man*
3 not bright or with a lot of decoration: *sober colours*

♦ **soberly** •ADVERB• in a sober way: *soberly dressed* • *a soberly worded message*
♦ **soberness** •NOUN• being sober: *the soberness of the mood*

sob story •NOUN• **sob stories** a story that you tell someone to make them feel sorry for you: *He gave me some sob story about his mother being ill.*

so-called •ADJECTIVE• called by this name, often mistakenly: *your so-called friend, Mr Williams*

soccer •NOUN• another word for association **football**

sociable •ADJECTIVE• friendly and enjoying being with other people

social •ADJECTIVE• 1 to do with society or a community: *social problems such as bad housing*
2 social animals live in groups
3 to do with meeting and being friendly with other people: *a social club*

socialism •NOUN• the belief that a country's main industries and land should be owned by the government and not by individual people
♦ **socialist** •NOUN• **socialists** someone who believes in socialism
•ADJECTIVE• believing in or to do with socialism: *a socialist state*

social security •NOUN• money that the government pays to people who are old, ill, or unemployed

social work •NOUN• work that the government pays for to help people who are poor, ill, or have problems
♦ **social worker** •NOUN• **social workers** someone who is paid by the government, whose job is to help people who are poor, ill, or have problems

society •NOUN• **societies** 1 all the people in the world in general: *Drugs are a huge danger to society.*
2 a particular group of people, especially fashionable and wealthy people: *high society*
3 a social club with a particular interest: *the debating society*
4 being with other people: *I've always enjoyed the society of people older than myself.*

Aa Bb Cc Dd Ee Ff Gg Hh Ii Jj Kk Ll Mm Nn Oo Pp Qq Rr **Ss** Tt Uu Vv Ww Xx Yy Zz

sociologist •NOUN• **sociologists** someone who studies how human societies are organized and how people behave
• **sociology** •NOUN• the study of human behaviour and societies

sock •NOUN• **socks** a covering for your foot that you wear inside your shoe: *a pair of socks*
• **pull your socks up** to try harder to do something better than before: *You'll have to pull your socks up if you want to pass this exam.*

socket •NOUN• **sockets** a shaped hole or hollow that something fits into: *an electric socket*

sod •NOUN• **sods** a piece of earth with grass growing on it

soda •NOUN• **sodas** 1 a word for a substance that contains **sodium** 2 another word for **soda-water**

soda-water •NOUN• **soda-waters** fizzy water that contains carbon dioxide gas

sodden •ADJECTIVE• very wet: *The ground's sodden after all that rain.*

sodium •NOUN• a silvery white element that is part of many substances, for example sodium chloride or salt

sofa •NOUN• **sofas** a long comfortable chair for two or three people

sofa bed •NOUN• **sofa beds** a sofa that you can make into a bed

soft •ADJECTIVE• **softer, softest** 1 not hard or firm: *a nice soft cushion* • *soft silky hair* 2 not strict or tough: *He's far too soft with his children.* • *Ben's too soft to get into a fight.* 3 not loud: *a soft voice* 4 not too bright: *Her bedroom is decorated in soft pastel colours.*

soft drink •NOUN• **soft drinks** a drink that does not contain alcohol: *The club serves cola and other soft drinks.*

soften •VERB• **softens, softening, softened** 1 to soften something is to make it become soft: *Soften the plasticine by working it with your hands.* 2 to soften is to become soft: *Her voice softened as she looked at the baby.*

softly •ADVERB• gently or quietly: *Snow*

was falling softly in the moonlight. • *She stroked the cat softly.*

softness •NOUN• being soft, gentle, or quiet: *the softness of the pillows*

software •NOUN• computer programs. Look up and compare **hardware**

soggy •ADJECTIVE• **soggier, soggiest** wet and soft: *soggy ground*

soil •NOUN• the top layer of the ground, that you can grow plants in: *sandy soil*
•VERB• **soils, soiling, soiled** to soil something is to make it dirty: *soiled linen*

solar •ADJECTIVE• relating to or powered by energy from the sun: *solar panels*

ⓘ **Solar** comes from the Latin word **sol**, which means *sun*.

solar power •NOUN• electricity that is made using the sun's light and heat

solar system •NOUN• the Sun and the planets that move around it

sold •VERB• a way of changing the verb **sell** to make a past tense. It can be used with or without a helping verb: *Tom sold me his old bike.* • *Have your parents sold their house yet?*

solder •VERB• **solders, soldering, soldered** to join two pieces of metal with metal that has been melted
•NOUN• melted metal used to join pieces of metal together

soldier •NOUN• **soldiers** someone who is in the army

sole¹ •ADJECTIVE• 1 only: *Her sole ambition was to be famous.* 2 belonging to one person alone: *He has sole ownership of the company.*

sole² •NOUN• **soles** 1 the underside of your foot 2 the underside of your shoe: *The sole came off my shoe as I was running.*

sole³ •NOUN• **soles** or **sole** a flat fish that people can eat

solely •ADVERB• only or alone: *You are solely responsible for your own actions.*

solemn •ADJECTIVE• 1 serious: *a solemn expression* • *a rather solemn little boy* 2 a solemn occasion is celebrated in a dignified

the solar system

Jupiter

sun

Mercury Earth

Venus Mars

Uranus

Pluto

Neptune

Saturn

way with a lot of ceremony
* **solemnity** • NOUN• when someone or something is solemn
* **solemnly** • ADVERB• in a solemn way

solicitor • NOUN• **solicitors** someone whose job is giving advice about the law system to people, for example when they buy a house or a business, or if the police arrest them

solid • ADJECTIVE• 1 with a fixed shape, not in the form of a liquid or a gas
2 not hollow: *a solid chocolate teddy*
3 firm and strong: *a solid piece of furniture*
4 a solid shape has length, width, and height: *A cube is a solid figure.*
5 with no pauses in between: *I've been working for six solid hours.*
• NOUN• **solids** 1 something that is not a liquid or a gas 2 a shape that has length, width, and height
* **solidify** • VERB• **solidifies, solidifying, solidified** 1 to solidify is to become solid 2 to solidify something is to make it become solid
* **solidly** • ADVERB• 1 strongly or firmly: *a solidly built structure* 2 continuously: *We've been working solidly since nine o'clock this morning.*

solitary • ADJECTIVE• lonely or alone: *a solitary figure*

solitude • NOUN• when you are alone

solo • NOUN• **solos** a piece of music or a song for one person to play or sing: *Emma sang a solo in the Christmas concert.*
• ADJECTIVE• alone: *a solo flight*
• ADVERB• alone: *It's the first time he's flown solo.*
* **soloist** • NOUN• **soloists** someone who sings or plays a musical instrument solo

solstice • NOUN• **solstices** the **summer solstice** is the day of the year when there are most hours of daylight and the **winter solstice** is the day when there are most hours of darkness

soluble • ADJECTIVE• 1 a soluble substance will dissolve in water: *soluble aspirin* 2 a soluble problem can be solved

solute • NOUN• **solutes** a substance dissolved in a liquid

solution • NOUN• **solutions** 1 an answer to a problem, question, or puzzle
2 the act of solving a problem or puzzle
3 a liquid with a substance dissolved in it: *a salt-water solution*

solve • VERB• **solves, solving, solved** 1 to work out the answer to a problem or puzzle: *Solve the riddle to win a prize.* 2 to understand and explain how a mystery happened or a crime took place

solvent • NOUN• **solvents** something that dissolves another substance

sombre • ADJECTIVE• 1 dark and gloomy: *sombre colours* 2 serious and sad: *a sombre mood*

sombrero • NOUN• **sombreros** a Mexican hat with a broad brim

some • ADJECTIVE• 1 quite a large number or amount: *It's all right; I've got some money.*
2 a small number or amount: *There's some soup left but not enough for everyone.*
• *Some people agreed but others didn't.*
3 certain: *You're just like your father in some ways.*
• PRONOUN• part of a number or amount: *I've made a cake – would you like some?*

somebody *or* **someone** •PRONOUN• 1 a person that you do not know or name: *Somebody knocked at the door.* 2 an important person: *He really thinks he's somebody in that big car.*

somehow •ADVERB• in some way: *Don't worry, we'll manage somehow.*

somersault •NOUN• **somersaults** a jump in which you turn over forwards or backwards in the air
•VERB• **somersaults, somersaulting, somersaulted** to do a somersault: *She somersaulted neatly into the water.*

something •PRONOUN• 1 a thing that is not known or stated: *Let's have something to eat before we go.* 2 a slight amount or degree: *There is something in what he says.*
• **or something** used when you are not sure about what you have just said: *He was an actor or something.*

sometimes •ADVERB• at times: *I still see him sometimes.*

somewhat •ADVERB• rather: *a somewhat lonely man*

somewhere •ADVERB• 1 in or to some place: *They live somewhere near Oxford.* 2 used when you are not sure of an amount, time, or number: *She must be somewhere between 35 and 40.*

son •NOUN• **sons** someone's male child

sonar •NOUN• special equipment that uses sound waves to find out where things are under water

song •NOUN• **songs** 1 a piece of music with words that you can sing: *a pop song* 2 the activity of singing: *A blackbird suddenly burst into song.*

songbird •NOUN• **songbirds** a bird that sings

sonic •ADJECTIVE• relating to sound: *a sonic boom*

son-in-law •NOUN• **sons-in-law** your daughter's husband

sonnet •NOUN• **sonnets** a type of poem that has fourteen lines

soon •ADVERB• **sooner, soonest** 1 in a short time from now: *It will soon be Christmas.*

2 early: *It's too soon to tell whether she'll recover.*
• **as soon** if you would as soon do one thing as another, you are equally willing to do them both: *I'll do the ironing, but I'd just as soon do the washing-up.*
• **as soon as** when: *We ate as soon as they arrived.*
♦ **sooner** •ADVERB• rather or more willingly: *I'd sooner do it myself than ask her to help.*
• **sooner or later** at some time in the future: *You're bound to bump into him sooner or later.*

soot •NOUN• the black powder that collects in chimneys

soothe •VERB• **soothes, soothing, soothed** 1 to make someone feel calmer or happier: *The little boy was so upset that it took his mother nearly an hour to soothe him.* 2 to make pain less strong: *I bathed to soothe my sore muscles.*
♦ **soothing** •ADJECTIVE• 1 making you feel calmer or happier 2 making pain less strong

sooty •ADJECTIVE• **sootier, sootiest** covered in soot or like soot

sophisticated •ADJECTIVE• 1 a sophisticated person knows a lot about the world and about what is fashionable 2 sophisticated ideas, machines and processes are complicated and well-developed
♦ **sophistication** •NOUN• when someone or something is sophisticated

sopping •ADJECTIVE• very wet

soppy •ADJECTIVE• **soppier, soppiest** too sentimental in a way that seems silly: *a soppy love song*

soprano •NOUN• **sopranos** 1 a very high singing voice 2 a woman or young boy with a high singing voice

sorcerer •NOUN• **sorcerers** a man who can make magic spells work

sorceress •NOUN• **sorceresses** a woman who can make magic spells work

sorcery •NOUN• magic or the ability to make magic spells work

sore •ADJECTIVE• **sorer, sorest** red and painful: *a sore finger*

• NOUN• **sores** a red, painful spot on your skin: *The horse had a nasty sore on its leg.*
✦ **sorely** • ADVERB• very much or a lot: *Mr. Watson will be sorely missed by the school.*
✦ **soreness** • NOUN• being sore

sorrow • NOUN• **sorrows** grief or sadness because you are disappointed or someone has died: *I couldn't find the words to comfort her in her sorrow.*
✦ **sorrowful** • ADJECTIVE• feeling or showing sorrow: *a long, sorrowful face*

sorry • ADJECTIVE• **sorrier, sorriest 1 sorry** is a word you use when you are apologizing or saying you regret something: *I'm sure Tim is sorry he upset you.* • *Sorry, I didn't mean to hurt you.*
2 if you are **sorry for** someone, you feel pity for them: *I felt so sorry for Lizzie when she failed her exam.*
3 bad or unfortunate: *the sorry plight of the refugees*

sort • NOUN• **sorts** a type or kind of person or thing: *What sort of books do you read?* • *You meet all sorts of people at school.*
• **out of sorts** if you feel out of sorts, you do not feel well
• **sort of** slightly: *It was sort of strange, seeing dad at school.*
• VERB• **sorts, sorting, sorted 1** to separate people or things into different groups according to their type: *Can you sort the washing into whites and coloureds?*
2 if you **sort out** one type of thing from a group of things, you separate it from them: *Sort out the books that have to go back to the library.*
3 if you **sort out** a problem or difficult situation, you solve it or deal with it: *There are a lot of things to sort out before we go on holiday.*

SOS • NOUN• a signal that you send to ask for help: *The ship sent an SOS to the coastguard after it hit the rocks.*

so-so • ADJECTIVE• not particularly good: *Jo's work this term has only been so-so.*

sought • VERB• a way of changing the verb **seek** to make a past tense. It can be used with or without a helping verb: *He sought his parents' permission.* • *I have sought to solve this problem.*

soul • NOUN• **souls 1** the part of a person that is not their body but is their spirit, which some people believe lives on after they die **2** a person: *The poor old soul got an awful shock.*

sound • NOUN• **sounds 1** something that you can hear: *There isn't a sound coming from the children's bedroom.* • *the sound of breaking glass* **2** the way that something such as a description or piece of news seems from what you have heard: *I don't much like the sound of your new boss.*
• VERB• **sounds, sounding, sounded 1** if something sounds good or bad, it seems that way from what you have heard about it: *Tom's holiday sounds wonderful.*
2 if something **sounds like** something else, the two sounds are very similar: *That sounds like Zoe's voice in the kitchen.*
3 to sound something is to make a noise with it: *Sound your horn before you turn the corner.*
4 if you **sound someone out**, you talk to them to find out their opinion: *Could you sound John out about my suggestion?*
• ADJECTIVE• **sounder, soundest 1** strong, firm, or healthy: *The walls of the old church were still sound.* • *a sound heart*
2 a sound sleep is deep and difficult to wake up from
3 thorough and complete: *a sound knowledge of French*
• **sound asleep** sleeping very deeply: *At ten o'clock I was still sound asleep.*

sound barrier • NOUN• if a plane breaks the sound barrier, there is a loud noise as it begins to go faster than the speed that sound travels at

soundproof • ADJECTIVE• a soundproof material, structure, or room is made so that sound cannot pass through it

soundtrack • NOUN• **soundtracks** a recording of the music from a film or television programme

soup • NOUN• **soups** a liquid food made from meat, fish, or vegetables

sour • ADJECTIVE• **sourer, sourest 1** sour food has a bitter taste like a lemon, sometimes because it is going bad: *sour plums* • *The milk had gone sour in the sun.* **2** a sour

Aa Bb Cc Dd Ee Ff Gg Hh Ii Jj Kk Ll Mm Nn Oo Pp Qq Rr Ss Tt Uu Vv Ww Xx Yy Zz

person is bad-tempered and unpleasant: *a sour face*

source •NOUN• **sources** 1 the place where something begins or is naturally present: *a rich source of gas* 2 a spring that is the start of a river

south •NOUN• 1 the direction on your right when you are facing towards the rising sun 2 the part of a country or the world that is in the south
•ADJECTIVE• in, from, or towards the south: *the south coast* • *the south wind*
•ADVERB• to the south: *The river flows south into the sea.*

south-east •NOUN• the area midway between south and east: *It should be another sunny day in the south-east.*

southerly •ADJECTIVE• coming from, or going towards, the south
•NOUN• **southerlies** a wind that comes from the south

southern •ADJECTIVE• belonging to or coming from the south: *the southern states of the USA*

southward or **southwards** •ADVERB• to or towards the south: *We were soon heading southward down the motorway.*

south-west •NOUN• the area midway between south and west

souvenir •NOUN• **souvenirs** something that you buy to remind you of a particular place or occasion: *We brought back some shells as souvenirs of our holiday.*

sou'wester •NOUN• **sou'westers** a waterproof hat that people sometimes wear in very heavy rain

sovereign •NOUN• **sovereigns** 1 a king or queen 2 an old gold coin
•ADJECTIVE• a sovereign state has its own government

sow[1] •VERB• **sows, sowing, sowed, sown** to scatter seeds on or in the ground so that they will grow

ⓘ This meaning of **sow** is pronounced **so**.

sow[2] •NOUN• **sows** a female pig

ⓘ This meaning of **sow** rhymes with **how**.

soya bean or **soy bean** •NOUN• **soya beans** or **soy beans** a type of bean that contains a lot of protein

spa •NOUN• **spas** a place where people go to drink or bathe in water that comes out of the ground at a natural spring

space •NOUN• **spaces** 1 a gap or empty place: *a parking space* • *Fill in the spaces on your answer sheet.*
2 the area available to use or do something: *There isn't enough space to hold a party here.* • *Can you make space for one more person?*
3 the empty area beyond the Earth's atmosphere, where the planets and stars are: *Another rocket was launched into space yesterday.*
•VERB• **spaces, spacing, spaced** if you space things or **space them out**, you leave gaps between them: *Try to space your work out neatly.*
⇒ **spacious**

spacecraft •NOUN• **spacecrafts** a vehicle that can travel into space

spaceman •NOUN• **spacemen** a man who travels into space

spaceship •NOUN• **spaceships** a vehicle that can travel into space

space shuttle •NOUN• **space shuttles** a vehicle like a plane that can travel into space and come back to Earth to be used again

spacesuit •NOUN• **spacesuits** a set of clothes worn by someone in a spaceship

spacious •ADJECTIVE• with a lot of room: *a spacious apartment*

spade •NOUN• **spades** 1 a tool with a broad blade that you use for digging 2 spades is one of the four suits of playing cards, which have the symbol ♠ printed on them: *the ace of spades*
• **call a spade a spade** to say clearly and honestly what you mean

spaghetti •NOUN• a type of pasta that is like long thin string: *a plate of spaghetti with tomato sauce*

span •NOUN• **spans** the length of time that something lasts: *The country had changed completely within the span of twenty years.*
•VERB• **spans, spanning, spanned** to span

something is to stretch across it: *An old wooden bridge spans the river.*

spangle • NOUN• **spangles** a small sparkling piece of metal used as a decoration on clothes: *The acrobat's costume was covered in spangles.*

♦ **spangly** • ADJECTIVE• covered with spangles: *a spangly scarf*

spaniel • NOUN• **spaniels** a type of dog with long ears that hang down

spank • VERB• **spanks, spanking, spanked** to hit someone on the bottom with your hand flat, especially as a punishment

• NOUN• **spanks** a hit on someone's bottom with your hand flat

spanner • NOUN• **spanners** a tool used for tightening or loosening nuts or screws

spar • VERB• **spars, sparring, sparred** to fight or argue with someone

spare • ADJECTIVE• **1** a spare room or thing is extra and is not being used at the moment: *a spare tyre* • *I've got a spare ticket for Saturday's concert, if you'd like it.* **2** spare time is time when you are free to do what you want

• VERB• **spares, sparing, spared** **1** if you can spare something or someone, you can manage without them: *We can't spare anyone to help out today.*

2 if you can spare the time to do something, you have enough time to do it: *I'm sorry, but I can't spare the time to go out tonight.*

3 to avoid hurting someone or making things difficult for them: *Break the news gently to spare her as much pain as possible.*

• **to spare** if you have time or money to spare, you have more than you need

• NOUN• **spares** a spare part for a car or piece of equipment

♦ **sparing** • ADJECTIVE• careful or using very little of something

spark • NOUN• **sparks** **1** a very small burning piece thrown out of a fire or when two hard surfaces are rubbed together: *Sparks were shooting out of the bonfire.* **2** a small amount of something such as enthusiasm or interest: *There seemed to be no spark of life in the old woman.*

• VERB• **sparks, sparking, sparked** **1** to make

a spark **2** to spark something is to start or cause it: *Her remark sparked off a huge row about football.*

spark-plug sparking-plug • NOUN• **spark-plugs** *or* **sparking-plugs** a small part in a car engine that produces a spark to light the gases that make it start

sparkle • VERB• **sparkles, sparkling, sparkled** to glitter or shine: *Her jewels sparkled in the firelight.*

♦ **sparkling** • ADJECTIVE• **1** shining or glittering: *sparkling lights* **2** a sparkling drink has bubbles of gas in it: *a sparkling mineral water*

sparrow • NOUN• **sparrows** a small brown bird

sparse • ADJECTIVE• **sparser, sparsest** if something is sparse, there is not much or not enough of it: *sparse hair*

spasm • NOUN• **spasm** a sudden movement of your muscles that you cannot control: *The muscles of his leg had gone into spasm.*

spastic • ADJECTIVE• suffering from brain damage that makes it difficult to control your movements

spate • NOUN• a sudden large number or amount: *a spate of burglaries*

spatter • VERB• **spatters, spattering, spattered** if you spatter something, you splash it with small drops of liquid: *His hair was spattered with paint.*

spatula • NOUN• **spatulas** a kitchen tool with a broad, flat blade, used for spreading or lifting things

spawn • NOUN• the eggs of frogs, toads or fish: *frog spawn*

• VERB• **spawns, spawning, spawned** **1** if fish or frogs spawn, they lay eggs **2** to spawn something is to cause or produce it: *the small businesses spawned by this new development*

speak • VERB• **speaks, speaking, spoke, spoken** **1** to say something: *Could I speak to you for a moment?* • *She was so tired she could hardly speak.*

2 to be able to talk in a particular language: *Do you speak Greek?*

3 to make a speech: *The headmaster spoke*

Aa
Bb
Cc
Dd
Ee
Ff
Gg
Hh
Ii
Jj
Kk
Ll
Mm
Nn
Oo
Pp
Qq
Rr
Ss
Tt
Uu
Vv
Ww
Xx
Yy
Zz

Aa
for almost an hour about the school's problems.

4 if you **speak up**, you speak more loudly: *Speak up, we can't hear you at the back.*

Bb

Cc
♦ **speaker** •NOUN• **speakers** 1 someone who is speaking 2 a piece of equipment that increases the sound coming out of a radio, CD-player, or cassette player

Dd

Ee
spear •NOUN• **spears** a long thin weapon with a metal point

Ff
•VERB• **spears, spearing, speared** to push a long thin point into something: *He speared a piece of meat with his fork.*

Gg

Hh
special •ADJECTIVE• 1 unusual and different from others: *We've been saving this wine for a special occasion.* • *Andrea's always been my special friend.* 2 meant for or having a specific purpose: *Special trains will take fans to the match.* • *a special tool for making rugs*

Ii

Jj

Kk
♦ **specialist** •NOUN• **specialists** someone who knows a lot about a particular subject: *a skin specialist*

Ll
♦ **speciality** •NOUN• **specialities** something that someone does particularly well: *Birthday cakes are my speciality.*

Mm

Nn
specialization or **specialisation** •NOUN• study of a particular subject or work at a particular job

Oo

Pp
♦ **specialize** or **specialise** •VERB• **specializes, specializing, specialized** to give all of your attention to studying one particular subject or working in one particular area: *Jessica's decided to specialize in Paediatrics.*

Qq

Rr

Ss
specially •ADVERB• with one particular purpose: *Jo's had her costume specially made for the party.*

Tt

Uu
ⓘ Remember the difference between **specially** and **especially**:

Vv
specially means 'for a special purpose': *I cooked this meal specially for you.*

Ww
especially means 'particularly': *I like all of the characters but especially Harry.*

Xx

Yy
species •NOUN• **species** a group of animals or plants whose members share most features

Zz
specific •ADJECTIVE• 1 giving all the details about something in a clear way: *Sarah's directions weren't very specific.* 2 exactly as

someone stated or described: *We each have our own specific jobs to do.*

♦ **specifically** •ADVERB• 1 for one particular purpose and no other: *flats designed specifically for the elderly* 2 clearly and exactly: *I specifically told you not to go out tonight.*

specification •NOUN• **specifications** a clear description of the details of something such as a plan, contract, or machine: *The car was built to his own specifications.*

specify •VERB• **specifies, specifying, specified** to specify what you want is to state it clearly: *Please specify the colour and size your require on the order form.*

specimen •NOUN• **specimens** something that is a sample of a particular group or kind of thing: *The specimens were arranged in cases, clearly labelled.*

speck •NOUN• **specks** 1 a very small piece of something: *a speck of dust* 2 a small spot: *a speck of paint*

speckle •NOUN• **speckles** a small coloured spot: *The egg was covered with speckles.*

♦ **speckled** •ADJECTIVE• covered in speckles: *a speckled hen*

spectacle •NOUN• **spectacles** a wonderful or impressive sight: *The royal wedding was a great spectacle.*

♦ **spectacles** •PLURAL NOUN• glasses that you wear to help you see properly: *a pair of spectacles*

spectacular •ADJECTIVE• very impressive: *a spectacular firework display* • *The scenery was absolutely spectacular.*

♦ **spectacularly** •ADVERB• impressively or by a very large amount: *a spectacularly successful film*

spectator •NOUN• **spectators** someone who is watching an event

spectre •NOUN• **spectres** a ghost

spectrum •NOUN• **spectra** or **spectrums** 1 all the different colours produced when light passes through glass or water 2 all the different types or forms of something: *a broad spectrum of opinions*

speculate •VERB• **speculates, speculating, speculated** to guess: *I wouldn't like to* speculate about what might have happened to him.

♦ **speculation** •NOUN• **speculations** 1 speculation is guessing something 2 a speculation is a guess

sped •VERB• a way of changing the verb **speed** to make a past tense. It can be used with or without a helping verb: *The holidays have just sped by.* • *A bullet sped past his ear.*

speech •NOUN• **speeches** 1 the ability to speak: *He seemed to have lost the power of speech.*
2 the way that you speak: *She was so tired that her speech was slurred.*
3 a talk that you give in front of a lot of people: *The bride's father usually makes a speech.*

♦ **speechless** •ADJECTIVE• if you are speechless, you cannot talk because you are so surprised or shocked: *His remarks left her speechless.*

speed •NOUN• **speeds** 1 the rate at which someone or something is moving: *He was driving at a speed of about 30 miles per hour.*
2 quickness: *Speed is important in this job.*
•VERB• **speeds, speeding, sped** or **speeded**
1 to move quickly or hurry: *I'm going to speed through my homework, then watch TV.* 2 to drive faster than the law says you can: *I really didn't think I was speeding until I saw the police car.*

♦ **speeding** •NOUN• the offence of driving faster than the law says you can: *He's been fined for speeding three times.*

speedometer •NOUN• **speedometers** a piece of equipment in a car that measures how fast you are travelling

speedway •NOUN• **speedways** the sport of motor-cycle racing

speedy •ADJECTIVE• **speedier, speediest** quick: *Thanks for the speedy reply to my letter.*

spell[1] •VERB• **spells, spelling, spelt** or **spelled** 1 to say or write the letters of a word in the correct order: *Could you spell your name for me?* 2 to make up a word: *L-i-g-h-t spells 'light'.*

spell[2] •NOUN• **spells** a short period of time: *The weather will be dull, with sunny spells.*

spell[3] •NOUN• **spells** a set of words that are supposed to make something magic happen: *The wicked witch cast a spell on Snow White.*

spelling •NOUN• 1 the way that a word is spelt: *What's the correct spelling of 'weird'?*
2 the ability to spell well: *Your spelling is terrible.*

spend •VERB• **spends, spending, spent** 1 to use money to buy things: *Adam spends all his pocket money on sweets.* 2 to pass time: *I used to spend hours reading in my room.*

spent •VERB• a way of changing the verb **spend** to make a past tense. It can be used with or without a helping verb: *Mum spent weeks making that sweater.* • *Have you spent your birthday money yet?*

sphere •NOUN• **spheres** a solid object that is the shape of a ball

♦ **spherical** •ADJECTIVE• shaped like a ball

spheroid •NOUN• **spheroids** a solid shape that is like a ball but is not a perfect sphere

spice •NOUN• **spices** any substance that adds flavour to food: *herbs and spices* • *Ginger is a spice.*

♦ **spiciness** •NOUN• being spicy: *the spiciness of the sauce*

♦ **spicy** •ADJECTIVE• **spicier, spiciest** tasting hot on your tongue: *spicy chilli tortillas*

spider •NOUN• **spiders** a small creature with eight legs that spins a web made of very fine threads

♦ **spidery** •ADJECTIVE• spidery handwriting is untidy with long, thin strokes

spike •NOUN• **spikes** a hard, thin point: *There were sharp spikes on top of the wall.*

♦ **spiky** •ADJECTIVE• **spikier, spikiest** with sharp points: *a spiky hairstyle*

spill •VERB• **spills, spilling, spilt** or **spilled** 1 to spill a liquid is to let it run out accidentally: *Careful! You're going to spill your tea.* 2 to spill is to run out accidentally: *The milk spilled all over the floor.*

spin •VERB• **spins, spinning, spun** 1 to turn round and round very quickly: *The ballerina spun round and round on her toes.* 2 to make long, thin threads out of cotton, wool, or another material by pulling it and twisting it

Aa
Bb
Cc
Dd
Ee
Ff
Gg
Hh
Ii
Jj
Kk
Ll
Mm
Nn
Oo
Pp
Qq
Rr
Ss
Tt
Uu
Vv
Ww
Xx
Yy
Zz

spinach • NOUN• a vegetable with large flat green leaves

spinal • ADJECTIVE• relating to your spine: *a spinal injury*

spinal cord • NOUN• **spinal cords** the nerve cells inside your spine

spindle • NOUN• **spindles** the pin that something turns on, for example a knob on a radio or a bobbin of thread
♦ **spindly** • ADJECTIVE• **splindlier, spindliest** long and thin: *a creature with long, spindly arms*

spindrier • NOUN• **spindriers** a machine that you put wet clothes into to dry them

spine • NOUN• **spines 1** the line of bones down the back of a person or animal **2** a stiff spike that grows on animals such as the hedgehog or on plants: *the spines of a cactus* ⇒ **spinal**

spinning wheel • NOUN• **spinning wheels** a piece of equipment for spinning thread, with a large wheel that turns and makes spindles move

spinster • NOUN• **spinsters** a woman who is not married

spiral • ADJECTIVE• coiled or winding round and round: *a spiral staircase*
• NOUN• **spirals** something with a spiral shape: *The shell formed a perfect spiral.*
• VERB• **spirals, spiralling, spiralled 1** to move in a spiral **2** to increase very quickly: *House prices have spiralled recently.*

spire • NOUN• **spires** a tall pointed roof on a church tower

spirit • NOUN• **spirits 1** your soul, which some people believe lives on after you die: *Some villagers thought the graveyard was haunted by evil spirits.*
2 bravery or liveliness: *a horse with spirit*
3 a strong alcoholic drink: *whisky, vodka, and other spirits*
4 a general feeling or attitude: *team spirit* • *a town with a strong community spirit*
♦ **spirited** • ADJECTIVE• lively and with a lot of personality: *a spirited performance*
♦ **spiritual** • ADJECTIVE• connected with someone's soul or to ghosts: *a spiritual experience*

spit • NOUN• **spits 1** the watery liquid inside your mouth **2** a metal bar that you put meat on to roast
• VERB• **spits, spitting, spat** if you spit, you push liquid or food out of your mouth: *She took one mouthful and then spat it out on to her plate.*

spite • NOUN• **1** a feeling of wanting to offend or upset someone: *He threw my picture away out of spite.* **2** if you do something or something happens **in spite of** something else, the first thing does not prevent the other: *We decided to go to the seaside in spite of the rain.*
♦ **spiteful** • ADJECTIVE• doing or saying something nasty just to hurt someone: *It isn't like Maddy to be spiteful.* • *a spiteful remark*
♦ **spitefully** • ADVERB• in a way that aims to hurt people
♦ **spitefulness** • NOUN• being spiteful

spitting image • NOUN• someone who looks exactly like someone else: *Tara's the spitting image of her mother.*

spittle • NOUN• saliva

splash • VERB• **splashes, splashing, splashed**
1 if you splash someone with a liquid, or splash a liquid over someone, you throw drops of it over them: *Kate quickly splashed her face with water.* • *The car drove off, splashing mud all over my new coat.*
2 if a liquid splashes somewhere, it flies there in drops: *The water splashed over the edge of the pan.*
3 if you splash or splash a part of your body in water, you move the water around in a noisy way: *The baby was splashing happily in his bath.*
• NOUN• **splashes 1** the water sent up when something moves through it, or the noise this makes: *He fell into the pool with a loud splash.*
2 a mark made on something where liquid has fallen on it: *jeans covered in splashes of paint*
3 a splash of colour is a bright patch of it

splay • VERB• **splays, splaying, splayed** to spread your legs, arms, or fingers out wide

spleen • NOUN• **spleens** an organ inside your body near your stomach

splendid •ADJECTIVE• 1 magnificent, rich, or grand: *The king was a splendid sight in his robes.* 2 very good: *What a splendid meal!*
• **splendour** •NOUN• when something looks very grand or magnificent: *the splendour of the royal palaces*

splint •NOUN• **splints** a piece of wood used to keep a broken arm or leg in the right position

splinter •NOUN• **splinters** a small piece of wood or glass that breaks off a large piece: *She got a splinter in her hand from the broken fence.*
•VERB• **splinters, splintering, splintered** if a piece of wood splinters, small thin pieces of it break off

split •VERB• **splits, splitting, split** 1 if something splits, it breaks or tears apart: *Your trousers have split down the back.*
2 if you split something, you break it or tear it apart: *The lightning had split the tree in two.*
3 to divide a group of people into smaller groups: *The teacher split us up into groups of six to do the experiment.*
4 if two people who have a relationship **split up**, they stop going out together: *Did you know Katy's split up with her boyfriend?*
•NOUN• **splits** a crack, tear, or break in something: *There's a long split in your sleeve.*
• **do the splits** to sit on the floor with one leg stretched straight out in front of you and one behind
• **split second** a very short time, less than a second

splutter •VERB• **splutters, spluttering, spluttered** to make spitting noises when you talk because you are excited, angry, or shocked: *'I don't know what you're talking about!' he spluttered.*

spoil •VERB• **spoils, spoiling, spoilt** or **spoiled** 1 to spoil something is to damage or ruin it: *Tommy scribbled on my picture and spoilt it.*
2 if food spoils, it starts to go bad: *If you don't put it in the fridge it will spoil.*
3 to spoil someone is to give them too much of what they want so that they do not appreciate it

spoil-sport •NOUN• **spoil-sports** someone who refuses to join in other people's fun: *Come on, Barry, don't be such a spoil-sport!*

spoke[1] •NOUN• **spokes** one of the thin pieces that come out from the centre of the wheel to the edge

spoke[2] •VERB• a way of changing the verb **speak** to make a past tense: *He spoke so fast that I couldn't understand him.*
• **spoken** •VERB• a form of the verb **speak** that is used with a helping verb to show that something happened in the past: *I've spoken to your teacher, and everything's fine.*

spokesman •NOUN• **spokesmen** someone who speaks on behalf of other people

spokeswoman •NOUN• **spokeswomen** a woman who speaks on behalf of other people

sponge •NOUN• **sponges** 1 a soft object, made from natural or artificial material, that you use to wash your body 2 a light cake or pudding: *a sponge pudding*
•VERB• **sponges, sponging, sponged** 1 to wash something with a sponge 2 to try to get money from people
• **spongy** •ADJECTIVE• feeling soft like a sponge: *a spongy texture*

sponsor •VERB• **sponsors, sponsoring, sponsored** 1 to pay some or all of the cost of an event or project: *A local company sponsors my son's football team.* 2 to promise to pay someone a sum of money, that they will give to charity, if they do a particular thing: *a sponsored swim*
•NOUN• **sponsors** a person or company that sponsors someone or something: *official sponsors of the 2002 World Cup*
• **sponsorship** •NOUN• the money someone pays to sponsor an event or a person

spontaneous •ADJECTIVE• 1 natural: *a spontaneous laugh* 2 not planned: *a spontaneous offer of help*
• **spontaneity** •NOUN• the quality of being spontaneous

spoof •NOUN• **spoofs** a trick or joke

spook •NOUN• **spooks** a ghost
• **spooky** •ADJECTIVE• **spookier, spookiest** frightening because it makes you think of ghosts: *a spooky ghost story* • *spooky music*

spool • NOUN • **spools** a cylindrical object that film or thread is wound around: *a spool of cotton*

spoon • NOUN • **spoons** an object with a thin handle and a shallow bowl at one end that you use for eating food

• VERB • **spoons, spooning, spooned** to lift up food on a spoon: *She was slowly spooning the cereal into the baby's mouth.*

♦ **spoonful** • NOUN • **spoonfuls** the amount a spoon will hold

spore • NOUN • **spores** a tiny cell like a seed that mushrooms and some other plants produce

sporran • NOUN • **sporrans** a type of bag that men wear hanging from their waists when they wear a kilt

sport • NOUN • **sports** 1 sport is games and physical activities like football, tennis, and swimming: *Adam loves all kinds of sport.* 2 a sport is a particular game or activity: *Alex particularly enjoys winter sports.* 3 a kind and helpful person: *Max'll give us a hand – he's a good sport.*

♦ **sporting** • ADJECTIVE • playing fair: *a very sporting player*

sports car • NOUN • **sports cars** a fast car that has only two seats and no roof

sportsman • NOUN • **sportsmen** a man who takes part in sport

sportswoman • NOUN • **sportswomen** a girl or woman who takes part in sport

spot • NOUN • **spots** 1 a small mark or stain on something 2 a round shape that is part of a pattern: *a pink dress with white spots* 3 a red raised mark on your skin: *Teenagers often suffer from spots.* 4 a place: *a lovely spot for a picnic* • *X marks the spot where the treasure is buried.*

• VERB • **spots, spotting, spotted** to notice something or someone: *I suddenly spotted Ian over by the window.*

⇒ **spotty**

spotless • ADJECTIVE • totally clean: *a spotless white handkerchief*

♦ **spotlessly** • ADVERB • something that is spotlessly clean is very clean

♦ **spotlessness** • NOUN • being very clean

spotlight • NOUN • **spotlights** a small bright light, for example on a stage

spotty • ADJECTIVE • **spottier, spottiest** 1 someone who is spotty has a lot of spots: *a spotty face* 2 covered in round shapes of a different colour: *a spotty scarf*

spouse • NOUN • **spouses** a husband or wife

spout • NOUN • **spouts** 1 the long thin part of a teapot or kettle that you pour the water out of 2 a jet of water

• VERB • **spouts, spouting, spouted** to come out in a fountain: *The oil came spouting up out of the ground.*

sprain • VERB • **sprains, spraining, sprained** to twist one of the joints in your body and hurt yourself: *a sprained ankle*

• NOUN • **sprains** a painful injury when you twist a joint such as your ankle or wrist: *Her wrist isn't broken; it's just a bad strain.*

sprang • VERB • a way of changing the verb **spring** to make a past tense: *The cat sprang on to the mouse.*

sprawl • VERB • **sprawls, sprawling, sprawled** 1 to sit, lie, or fall with your legs and arms spread out: *Tony lay sprawled at full length on the sofa.* 2 if a town, building, or group of buildings sprawls, it covers a large area in an untidy way: *a large, sprawling old house*

spray • NOUN • **sprays** 1 a fine mist of liquid: *The spray from the waterfall wet their hair.* 2 a device with a lot of little holes that produces a mist of liquid: *a perfume spray* 3 a liquid that you spray on to something: *a hairspray*

• VERB • **sprays, spraying, sprayed** to cover something with a mist of fine drops of liquid: *A sprinkler was spraying water on to the lawn.*

spread • VERB • **spread, spreading, spread** 1 to put a layer of something onto a surface: *She spread her toast thickly with butter.* • *Tom was carefully spreading cream onto the top of the cake.* 2 to open something out flat or to cover a surface: *Spread the map out so that we can look at it.* • *Ann spread all her shopping out on her bed.* 3 if news spreads, it becomes known by a

Aa
Bb
Cc
Dd
Ee
Ff
Gg
Hh
Ii
Jj
Kk
Ll
Mm
Nn
Oo
Pp
Qq
Rr
Ss
Tt
Uu
Vv
Ww
Xx
Yy
Zz

lot of different people: *Rumours spread very quickly in this little village.*
   4 to be spaced out over a period of time: *Luckily, the exams were spread out over two whole weeks.*
   •NOUN• **spreads 1** the area, time, or range that something covers: *the spread of a disease* **2** a type of paste that you spread on bread: *chicken spread*

spread-eagled •ADJECTIVE• if someone is spread-eagled, their arms and legs are spread out wide

spree •NOUN• **sprees** a burst of doing something: *a shopping spree*

sprig •NOUN• **sprigs** a small branch of a plant: *a sprig of holly*

sprightly •ADJECTIVE• a sprightly person is lively and moves quickly: *She's very sprightly for 85.*

spring •VERB• **springs, springing, sprang, sprung 1** to jump quickly, usually up: *He's the type who just springs out of bed in the morning.* **2** to develop from something else: *His confidence springs from his loving family background.*
   •NOUN• **springs 1** a coil of wire: *a chair with a broken spring*
   2 the season of the year between winter and summer when plants start to grow: *the first day of spring*
   3 a jump or quick movement
   4 a small stream that flows up out of the ground: *a mountain spring*
   •ADJECTIVE• happening after winter and before summer: *spring flowers*

springboard •NOUN• **springboards** a type of board that divers can jump from into the water

spring-cleaning •NOUN• thorough cleaning of your house, especially in the spring

springy •ADJECTIVE• **springier, springiest** a springy surface or substance easily springs back into its original shape: *a springy mattress* • *springy floorboards*

sprinkle •VERB• **sprinkles, sprinkling, sprinkled** to scatter small drops or pieces of something over a surface: *Mum sprinkled chocolate chips onto the trifle.*

♦ **sprinkler** •NOUN• **sprinklers** a device that you use to sprinkle something, especially water on to a garden

sprint •VERB• **sprints, sprinting, sprinted** to run fast for a short distance: *He sprinted down the street after her.*
   •NOUN• **sprints** a short running race: *the 100 metre sprint*
   ♦ **sprinter** •NOUN• **sprinters** an athlete who is good at running fast for short distances

sprite •NOUN• **sprites** a fairy

sprout •VERB• **sprouts, sprouting, sprouted 1** to produce new leaves and shoots: *Buds were sprouting on the sycamore tree.* **2** to grow: *His hair sprouted out of his head in clumps.*
   •NOUN• **sprouts 1** a new shoot: *bean sprouts* **2** a **Brussels sprout**

spruce [1] •NOUN• **spruces** a type of fir tree

spruce [2] •ADJECTIVE• **sprucer, sprucest** neat and smart: *You're looking very spruce in your new suit.*

sprung •VERB• a form of the verb **spring** that is used with a helping verb to show that something happened in the past: *James had sprung to his feet when she came in.*

spud •NOUN• **spuds** an informal word for a potato

spur •NOUN• **spurs 1** a small pointed object that a rider wears on his heel to stick into his horse to make it go faster **2** anything that makes someone try harder
   • **on the spur of the moment** suddenly, without thinking or planning first: *On the spur of the moment, he decided to take a day off work.*
   •VERB• **spurs, spurring, spurred** if something **spurs someone on**, it encourages them to do something: *Winning the prize spurred her on to try even harder.*

spurn •VERB• **spurns, spurning, spurned** to reject someone or something unkindly: *He spurned all her efforts to be friendly.*

spurt •VERB• **spurts, spurting, spurted** to pour out in a heavy flow: *Blood was spurting from a wound on his head.*
   •NOUN• **spurts 1** a sudden burst of a liquid: *a spurt of blood* **2** a sudden increase of effort,

Aa
Bb
Cc
Dd
Ee
Ff
Gg
Hh
Ii
Jj
Kk
Ll
Mm
Nn
Oo
Pp
Qq
Rr
Ss
Tt
Uu
Vv
Ww
Xx
Yy
Zz

Aa

energy, or feeling: *We'll have to put a spurt on if we want to catch that train.*

Bb

spy •NOUN• **spies** someone who is employed by the government of their country to secretly find out information about another country

Cc

•VERB• **spies, spying, spied** 1 to work as a spy 2 to see or notice someone or something: *I spy, with my little eye, something beginning with S.*

Dd

Ee

Ff

squabble •VERB• **squabbles, squabbling, squabbled** to quarrel: *Stop squabbling and eat your tea.*
•NOUN• **squabbles** a quarrel

Gg

Hh

squad •NOUN• **squads** a small group of people who are doing a job together: *a squad of bricklayers*

Ii

Jj

squadron •NOUN• **squadrons** a group of people in the army, navy, or air force

Kk

Ll

① **Squad** and **squadron** both come from the Latin word **exquadra**, which means a *square*. This is because soldiers used to stand in a square formation when they were being attacked.

Mm

Nn

squalid •ADJECTIVE• dirty and poor: *a squalid room in a hostel*

Oo

Pp

squall •NOUN• **squalls** a sudden bad storm
♦ **squally** •ADJECTIVE• stormy: *a squally night at sea*

Qq

squalor •NOUN• very dirty living conditions: *The old man had been living alone in squalor.*

Rr

Ss

squander •VERB• **squanders, squandering, squandered** to waste time or money: *He squandered all his pocket money on chocolate.*

Tt

Uu

square •NOUN• **squares** 1 a flat shape with four equal sides and four right angles
2 an open space with buildings on all four sides: *a tree-lined square* • *Trafalgar Square*
3 the square of a number is the number you get when you multiply the number by itself, for example the square of 3 is 3 x 3, which is 9. Look up and compare **cube**
•ADJECTIVE• 1 shaped like a square: *a square cushion*
2 measuring a particular amount on each side: *The room was about 3 metres square.*

Vv

Ww

Xx

Yy

Zz

3 a square measurement is one used to measure area. For example, a square metre is a space one metre long and one metre wide.

4 a square number is a number that has been multiplied by itself, for example 3 x 3, which is written as 3^2

5 with equal scores or amounts: *The two teams were all square at half-time, at 3-3.*
• *If you pay for the coffee, we'll be square.*

6 straight or level: *Keep the paper square with the edge of the table.*
•VERB• **squares, squaring, squared** 1 to make something have a square shape: *Square off the end of the piece of wood.* 2 to square a number is to multiply it by itself: *Four squared is sixteen.*

square root •NOUN• **square roots** the square root of a number is the number that gives the first number when it is multiplied by itself: *Three is the square root of nine.*

squash •VERB• **squashes, squashing, squashed** to press, squeeze, or crush someone or something: *We were all squashed together in the back of the car.*
•NOUN• **squashes** 1 a situation when people or things are squashed: *It was a bit of squash fitting everything in his suitcase.*
2 a drink with a fruit flavour: *an orange squash*
3 a game in which you hit a small rubber ball against the walls of a court with a racket

squat •VERB• **squats, squatting, squatted** 1 to crouch down on your heels: *He squatted on the ground to eat his lunch.* 2 to live in a building without having permission to be there
•ADJECTIVE• **squatter, squattest** short and fat: *a rather squat little man*
♦ **squatter** •NOUN• **squatters** someone who squats in a building: *The empty house had been taken over by squatters.*

squaw •NOUN• **squaws** a Native American woman

squawk •VERB• **squawks, squawking, squawked** to make a loud, high-pitched cry
•NOUN• **squawks** a loud, high-pitched cry: *The hen gave a squawk.*

squeak •VERB• **squeaks, squeaking,**

squeaked to make a small, high-pitched sound: *That door squeaks when you open it.* •NOUN• **squeaks** a small, high-pitched sound ✦ **squeaky** •ADJECTIVE• **squeakier, squeakiest** making a noise like a squeak: *a squeaky floorboard*

squeal •VERB• **squeals, squealing, squealed** to give a loud, shrill cry: *The baby squealed with delight when he saw his mother.* •NOUN• **squeals** a loud, shrill cry: *a squeal of pain*

squeamish •ADJECTIVE• easily shocked or made to feel sick: *I've always been squeamish about injections.*

squeeze •VERB• **squeezes, squeezing, squeezed** 1 to press something tightly: *She squeezed my hand encouragingly.* 2 to force something into or out of a small space or container: *The cat tried to squeeze itself under the sofa.* • *He was trying to squeeze the last of the toothpaste out of the tube.* •NOUN• **squeezes** 1 the action of squeezing or pressing something 2 a tight fit: *We all got into the car, but it was a tight squeeze.*

squelch •NOUN• **squelches** the noise you make when you move through something thick and sticky like mud

squid •NOUN• **squids** a sea creature with tentacles

squiggle •NOUN• **squiggles** a short, wavy line

squint •VERB• **squints** 1 to half-close your eyes when you are looking at something: *She looked up at him, squinting in the sunlight.* 2 to have eyes that look in different directions •NOUN• **squints** a problem with your eyes that makes them look in different directions: *He'd been treated for a squint when he was a child.*

squire •NOUN• **squires** a man who used to own land in the country in the past

squirm •VERB• **squirms, squirming, squirmed** to wriggle or twist your body because you are embarrassed or in pain: *She squirmed when she remembered how rude she had been.*

squirrel •NOUN• **squirrels** a small reddish-brown or grey animal with a bushy tail that lives in trees and eats nuts

squirt •VERB• **squirts, squirting, squirted** to shoot out a jet of liquid: *The kids were squirting each other with water.*

St •ABBREVIATION• short for **Saint** or **Street**

stab •VERB• **stabs, stabbing, stabbed** to push something sharp into someone or something with a lot of force: *The woman was stabbed with a knife.* • *She stabbed the pin into the cushion angrily.* •NOUN• **stabs** a sharp feeling: *a stab of pain* • **have a stab at something** to try to do something: *I'd love to have a stab at roller-blading.*

stability •NOUN• being steady and balanced

stabilize or **stabilise** •VERB• **stabilizes, stabilizing, stabilized** 1 to stabilize is to become balanced or steady: *She's been very ill but her condition has stabilized.* 2 to stabilize someone or something is to make them balanced or steady: *Put a book under the table leg to stabilize it.*

stable •ADJECTIVE• **stabler, stablest** 1 firm and steady: *This bracket will help to keep the shelf stable.* 2 a stable relationship is one that has lasted for some time and will probably continue 3 a stable person is sensible and calm •NOUN• **stables** 1 a building to keep a horse in 2 a place where you can learn to ride a horse: *a riding stables*

stack •NOUN• **stacks** a large pile of things: *a stack of books* •VERB• **stacks, stacking, stacked** to pile things up neatly: *Stack the dishes in the sink and I'll wash them later.*

stadium •NOUN• **stadiums** or **stadia** a large sports ground with seats for people to watch: *a football stadium*

staff •NOUN• **staffs** 1 the people who work in a particular place: *The company has a staff of 150.* • *Six new members of staff are joining the school this term.* 2 a stick 3 a set of spaced lines for writing music on

stag •NOUN• **stags** a male deer

Aa
Bb
Cc
Dd
Ee
Ff
Gg
Hh
Ii
Jj
Kk
Ll
Mm
Nn
Oo
Pp
Qq
Rr
Ss
Tt
Uu
Vv
Ww
Xx
Yy
Zz

stage • NOUN • **stages** 1 the raised platform in a theatre where the actors perform 2 a step in a process or series of developments: *The work is still in its early stages.* • *It's hard to predict what will happen at this stage.*
• VERB • **stages, staging, staged** to put a play or other performance on in a theatre: *an opera staged in Verona*

stagecoach • NOUN • **stagecoaches** a coach pulled by horses that people used in the past to travel around the country

stagger • VERB • **staggers, staggering, staggered** 1 to walk unsteadily, swaying from side to side: *He staggered across the room and fell into a chair.*
2 to amaze someone: *I was staggered when they got married.*
3 to arrange events so that they do not all happen at the same time: *We have to stagger our lunchbreaks to cover the phones.*
✦ **staggering** • ADJECTIVE • very surprising: *The amount of money collected was absolutely staggering.*

stagnant • ADJECTIVE • stagnant water is dirty and unhealthy because it does not flow: *a stagnant pond*

staid • ADJECTIVE • serious and not keen to try new things

stain • VERB • **stains, staining, stained** 1 to leave a permanent coloured mark on something: *The coffee you spilt has stained the carpet.* 2 to dye wood a different colour
• NOUN • **stains** a dirty mark that is hard to remove from something: *overalls covered in oil stains*

stained glass • NOUN • a glass panel made up of pieces of differently coloured glass that form a picture: *a stained glass window*

stainless steel • NOUN • steel mixed with chromium so that it does not rust: *stainless steel cutlery*

stair *or* **stairs** • NOUN • **stairs** 1 a set of steps that lead to another level in a building: *A flight of stairs led down to the cellar.* 2 one of these steps

staircase • NOUN • **staircases** a set of stairs: *a marble staircase*

stake • NOUN • **stakes** 1 a strong pointed stick, for example to support a fence 2 an amount of money that you bet on something: *a £5 stake*
• **at stake** if something is at stake, you risk losing it: *She felt that her whole future was at stake in the competition.*
• VERB • **stakes, staking, staked** to bet an amount of money on something: *I'll stake £10 on Paul winning.*

stalactite • NOUN • **stalactites** a spike of limestone that hangs from the roof of a cave

stalagmite • NOUN • **stalagmites** a spike of limestone that rises up from the floor of a cave

stale • ADJECTIVE • **staler, stalest** not fresh but dry and tasteless: *stale bread* • *The air smelt stale inside the room.*

stalemate • NOUN • a position in a game of chess or an argument when neither side can make a move or win

stalk • NOUN • **stalks** the stem of a flower, leaf, or fruit: *an apple stalk*
• VERB • **stalks, stalking, stalked** 1 to walk proudly and stiffly: *He was stalking angrily up and down.* 2 to hunt an animal quietly, trying to keep hidden: *a tigress stalking her prey*

stall • NOUN • **stalls** 1 a compartment for one animal in a cowshed or barn
2 a table or open-fronted shop where things are laid out to be sold: *a market stall*
3 **the stalls** are the lower floor of a theatre, where the audience sit
• VERB • **stalls, stalling, stalled** 1 if a vehicle stalls or someone stalls it, its engine suddenly stops while you are driving 2 to delay doing something: *I wish he'd stop stalling and give me an answer.*

stallion • NOUN • **stallions** a male horse

stamen • NOUN • **stamens** a spike inside a flower that produces pollen

stamina • NOUN • the strength to keep doing something for a long time: *exercises to increase your stamina*

stammer • VERB • **stammers, stammering, stammered** 1 to have a speech problem that makes it difficult for you to pronounce the first letters of some words 2 to speak like this because you are frightened or nervous: *'I'm s-s-sorry,'* he stammered.

• NOUN• **stammers** a speech problem that makes it difficult for you to pronounce the first letters of some words: *He had a bad stammer when he was a child.*

stamp •VERB• **stamps, stamping, stamped** 1 to bring your foot down firmly on the ground: *She stamped her feet to keep them warm.*

2 to stick a stamp on a letter

3 to print letters, numbers, or a design on something: *Each letter is stamped with the date we receive it.* • *a file stamped 'Urgent'*

4 if you **stamp something out**, you try to stop it happening: *a plan to stamp out crime*

• NOUN• **stamps** 1 a postage stamp: *first-class stamps*

2 the movement or sound of a foot being brought down hard on the ground

3 an object that you put into ink and press onto a surface to print words, numbers, or a design: *a date stamp*

4 a design or mark that you make with this object: *a manufacturer's stamp*

stampede • NOUN• **stampedes** a sudden wild rush of animals or people: *a buffalo stampede* • *The bell went and there was a stampede for the door.*

•VERB• **stampedes, stampeding, stampeded** to rush in a stampede: *The noise of the gun made the elephants stampede.*

stance • NOUN• **stances** 1 the way someone stands 2 an attitude or set of opinions: *What is the school's stance on homework?*

stand •VERB• **stands, standing, stood** 1 to be upright on your feet, not sitting or lying: *The horse was standing on three legs.* • *I was so tired I could barely stand.*

2 to get up onto your feet: *The whole class used to stand when a teacher came into the room.* • *Stand up and let me look at you.*

3 to be or stay in a particular position or way: *The train stood outside Waterloo for nearly an hour.* • *The judge ordered that the sentence should stand.* • *Durham stands on the River Wear.*

4 to bear: *I can't stand her brother, Mark.* • *Marie couldn't stand hearing her parents arguing any more.*

5 if particular letters **stand for** particular words, they are short for them: *UN stands for United Nations.*

6 if you **stand in for someone**, you take their place for a short time: *Emma will stand in for Mrs. Harris while she is on holiday.*

7 if you **stand up for someone**, you defend or support them: *My big sister, Fran, always stood up for me.*

8 if you **stand up to someone**, you fight back when they attack you: *You've got to learn to stand up to bullies.*

• NOUN• **stands** 1 something that an object stands on: *a television stand* • *a large mirror on a stand*

2 rows of seats where people sit to watch a game or event: *Spectators were cheering from the stands.*

3 someone's opinion about something: *a tough stand on crime*

standard • NOUN• **standards** 1 a level that you can judge things against: *a school with high standards of behaviour* 2 an official rule for measuring things: *The kilogram is the international standard of weight.*

• ADJECTIVE• normal or usual: *the standard charge for postage*

♦ **standardize** *or* **standardise** •VERB• **standardizes, standardizing, standardized** to make or keep things all the same shape or size as it is more convenient: *We're trying to standardize the filing system.*

standard lamp • NOUN• **standard lamps** a lamp on a tall base that stands on the floor

standby • NOUN• 1 something or someone that is available to be used when they are needed: *I always keep some long-life milk as a standby.* 2 if someone or something is **on standby**, they are ready to travel if needed or ready to do something

standstill • NOUN• a complete stop: *Icy roads brought traffic to a standstill.*

stank •VERB• a way of changing the verb **stink** to make a past tense: *The dirty fish tank really stank.*

stanza • NOUN• **stanzas** a verse of a poem

ⓘ This is an Italian word which means *stopping place*, because there is a break at the end of each verse where you stop.

Aa Bb Cc Dd Ee Ff Gg Hh Ii Jj Kk Ll Mm Nn Oo Pp Qq Rr **Ss** Tt Uu Vv Ww Xx Yy Zz

Aa Bb Cc Dd Ee Ff Gg Hh Ii Jj Kk Ll Mm Nn Oo Pp Qq Rr Ss Tt Uu Vv Ww Xx Yy Zz

staple¹ •STAPLE• **staples** a type of food or product that you use a lot of: *There's a village shop for staples such as milk and butter.*
•ADJECTIVE• main: *Their staple diet is rice.*

staple² •NOUN• **staples** a piece of wire that you force through papers to fasten them together: *a box of staples*
•VERB• **staples, stapling, stapled** to fasten papers together with a staple
◆ **stapler** •NOUN• **staplers** a small tool for stapling papers together

star •NOUN• **stars 1** a mass of burning gas in the sky that you can see at night as a point of light
2 a shape with five or six points
3 a famous actor, singer, or performer: *a film star* • *a pop star*
•ADJECTIVE• relating to a star: *a star performance*
•VERB• **stars, starring, starred 1** if an actor stars in something, he plays one of the main parts in it: *Tom Cruise is to star in the sequel.*
2 if a film or play stars someone, they have one of the main parts in it: *the new film starring Kate Winslet*
⇒ **stardom, starry**

starboard •ADJECTIVE• the starboard side of a ship or aircraft is the right side when you are facing the front. Look up and compare **port**

starch •NOUN• **starches 1** a white carbohydrate found in foods such as potatoes, pasta and bread **2** a powder used to make clothes stiff
◆ **starchy** •ADJECTIVE• containing a lot of starch

stardom •NOUN• being a famous performer: *She shot to stardom after appearing on a TV talent show.*

stare •VERB• **stares, staring, stared** to look at someone or something for a long time: *Gemma spends her days staring out of the window.* • *What are you staring at?*
•NOUN• **stares** a fixed look

starfish •NOUN• **starfishes** a sea creature with five points or arms

stark •ADJECTIVE• **starker, starkest 1** plain and bare: *a stark, barren landscape* **2**

complete: *The cool indoors was in stark contrast to the heat outside.*
• **stark naked** completely naked
◆ **starkly** •ADVERB• in a stark way: *a starkly furnished room*

starling •NOUN• **starlings** a common bird with dark, shiny feathers

starry •ADJECTIVE• **starrier, starriest** full of stars or shining like stars: *a starry sky* • *starry eyes*

start •VERB• **starts, starting, started 1** to begin: *Suddenly, a bird started to sing.* • *What time did you start working this morning?* • *Children may start school when they are four.*
2 to make a machine start to work: *Start the car and drive off.*
3 to jump because you are surprised: *The thunder made me start.*
•NOUN• **starts 1** the beginning: *Right from the start, I knew I'd be happy here.* • *The runners lined up for the start of the race.*
2 a sudden movement or shock: *Her news gave me quite a start.*
3 in a race or chase, the advantage of starting earlier or further forward than others: *We gave Amy a bit of a start as she's the youngest.*

startle •VERB• **startles, startling, startled** to give someone a shock or surprise: *Oh, you startled me!*
◆ **startling** •ADJECTIVE• shocking because unusual or unexpected

starvation •NOUN• when you are very hungry and have not got enough to eat: *Thousands are dying of starvation every year.*

starve •VERB• **starves, starving, starved**
1 to die or suffer because you have not got enough to eat: *If we don't get food aid into the country, these people are going to starve to death.*
2 to starve someone is to not give them enough to eat: *They were accused of starving their prisoners.*
3 an informal way of saying you are very hungry: *What's for supper? I'm starving.*

state •NOUN• **states 1** the condition that someone or something is in: *Look at the* state of your bedroom! • She's always complaining about the state of our public transport.

2 a government or a country: The state should provide for the sick and elderly.

3 a part of a country that has its own government: The law differs from state to state in America.

4 if someone is in a state, they are upset and worried: There's no point getting in a state about things.

• **VERB**• **states, stating, stated** to say or write something: The letter clearly states that you must bring some identification with you.

stately • ADJECTIVE• dignified and impressive: a stately procession of lords

stately home • NOUN• **stately homes** a large country house where a noble family lived

statement • NOUN• **statements 1** something that you say or write: The police asked me to make a written statement of what I saw. **2** a piece of paper that the bank sends you that shows how much money you have in your account and what you have spent

statesman • NOUN• **statesmen** an important political leader

static • ADJECTIVE• not moving or changing: Temperatures should stay static for the next few days.

• NOUN• tiny sparks of electricity caused by rubbing two surfaces together: You get static when you comb your hair with a plastic comb.

station • NOUN• **stations 1** a building where trains, buses, or coaches stop to let people get on or off

2 a place where police officers, fire officers, or ambulance drivers work: The police station is at the top of the High Street.

3 a radio or television station is a company which makes or broadcasts programmes

• VERB• **stations, stationing, stationed** to put someone in a particular position: They stationed a guard at each door.

♦ **stationary** • ADJECTIVE• not moving: a stationary vehicle

stationery • NOUN• paper, pens, crayons, and other things you use to write or draw with

statistics • PLURAL NOUN• figures and facts about a particular subject: Statistics show that more babies were born this year than last year.

♦ **statistical** • ADJECTIVE• to do with statistics: All the statistical evidence supports our case.

♦ **statistically** • ADVERB• using statistics

statue • NOUN• **statues** a figure of a person or animal carved out of stone, metal or wood: a statue of Napoleon

stature • NOUN• **1** size or height: He was small in stature but had a strong personality. **2** importance: a politician of great stature

status • NOUN• **statuses** someone's position or rank in a society: She achieved high status in her work.

staunch • ADJECTIVE• **stauncher, staunchest** loyal and faithful: a staunch supporter of the team

stave • NOUN• **staves** the set of spaced lines that musical notes are written on

• VERB• **staves, staving, staved** if you **stave something off**, you delay it happening: We had a packet of crisps to stave off our hunger.

stay • VERB• **stays, staying, stayed 1** to remain in a place: I stayed in Padua for three years. • Would you like to stay for dinner? **2** to continue to be in a particular condition: She tried to stay calm as they waited.

• NOUN• **stays** time spent in a place: The trip includes an overnight stay in Bangkok.

steadfast • ADJECTIVE• firm and never changing: a steadfast friend

steady • ADJECTIVE• firm and not moving: This table isn't very steady.

• VERB• **steadies, steadying, steadied 1** to steady something is to make it firm: I took a deep breath to steady my nerves. **2** to steady is stop moving or changing: House prices have begun to steady.

♦ **steadily** • ADVERB• at a gradual, steady pace: Your work is improving steadily.

steak • NOUN• **steaks** a thick slice of meat or fish: a fillet steak • two tuna steaks

steal • VERB• **steals, stealing, stole, stolen 1** to take something without the owner's permission: The thieves stole money and jewellery. • *It's wrong to steal.* 2 to move quietly: *She stole out to the garden.*

stealth •NOUN• action or movement that is secret or quiet: *the stealth of a hungry lion*
• **stealthy** •ADJECTIVE• **stealthier, stealthiest** done secretly or quietly: *stealthy footsteps*

steam •NOUN• 1 the clouds of tiny drops of liquid that rise from boiling water 2 power produced by steam: *Diesel fuel has replaced steam on the railways.*
•VERB• **steams, steaming, steamed** 1 to give off steam: *A kettle was steaming on the stove.*
2 to move by means of steam: *The ship steamed across the bay.*
3 to steam food is to cook it by steam: *steamed vegetables*
4 to **steam up** is to become covered with steam: *My glasses steamed up and I couldn't see a thing.*

steam engine •NOUN• **steam engines** an engine, especially a railway engine, that is driven by steam

steamer •NOUN• **steamers** a ship that is driven by steam

steamroller •NOUN• **steamrollers** a type of vehicle which has large, heavy wheels and is used to flatten the surface of newly-made roads. Steamrollers used to be, and sometimes still are, driven by steam

steed •NOUN• **steeds** an old word for a horse: *The knight mounted his trusty steed.*

steel •NOUN• a very hard metal that is a mixture of iron and carbon. Steel is used to make tools, vehicles and many other things
•ADJECTIVE• made of steel: *steel knives*
•VERB• **steels, steeling, steeled** if you **steel yourself**, you prepare yourself for something unpleasant: *She steeled herself for the test results.* • *He steeled himself to face his father.*
• **steely** •ADJECTIVE• **steelier, steeliest** hard or cold or strong like steel: *a steely gaze*

steep •ADJECTIVE• **steeper, steepest** a steep hill or slope rises sharply: *It was a steep climb.* • *The path was too steep for me to cycle up.*

steeple •NOUN• **steeples** a tall tower that comes to a point, sometimes part of a church

steeplechase •NOUN• **steeplechases** a race for horses or people in which obstacles must be jumped

ⓘ It is called a **steeplechase** because in the past these races were run across the country from one village to the next, and the church steeple in the next village marked the end of the race.

steer •VERB• **steers, steering, steered** to steer a vehicle is to control the direction it is going in: *He steered the car through the narrow streets.* • *The captain steered out of the harbour.*

steering wheel •NOUN• **steering wheels** the wheel inside a vehicle that the driver uses to control the direction it is moving in

stem •NOUN• **stems** 1 the part of a plant from which the leaves and flowers grow 2 the narrow part of various objects, for example of a wine glass
•VERB• **stems, stemming, stemmed** 1 to stem something is to stop it: *He used his scarf to stem the flow of blood.* 2 to stem from something is to come from it or be caused by it: *Her problems with her schoolwork stem from laziness.*

stench •NOUN• **stenches** a strong bad smell: *the stench of stale cigarette smoke*

stencil •NOUN• **stencils** 1 a piece of paper, metal or plastic with pieces cut out of it, which is coloured or painted over to produce a design on a surface 2 a design produced in this way
•VERB• **stencils, stencilling, stencilled** to use a stencil or stencils to decorate a surface: *We decided to paint the walls white then stencil them.* • *Why don't you stencil some flowers round the doorway?*

step •NOUN• **steps** 1 the action of lifting your foot off the ground and putting in down again in walking, running or dancing: *He took a step forward.*
2 the sound made by someone's foot coming down on the ground when they walk etc: *I'm sure I heard steps outside.*
3 a particular movement of the feet, for example in dancing: *Try to learn these simple steps.*
4 the flat part of a stair that you put your

foot on when going up or down: *The postman left the parcel on the front step.*
   5 one of a series of actions involved in doing or achieving something: *the first step to becoming an actor* • *I shall take steps to prevent this happening again.*
• VERB• **steps, stepping, stepped** 1 to step is to take a step: *He opened the door and stepped out.*
   2 to step is also to walk: *Please step this way.*
   3 to **step something up** is to increase it: *Brian stepped up his speed and won the race.*

step- • PREFIX• if a word starts with **step-** it shows that people are related not by blood but by another marriage. For example, your *stepfather* is a man who is married to your mother but is not your own father

stepfather • NOUN• **stepfathers** your stepfather is a man who is married to your mother but is not your own father

stepladder • NOUN• **stepladders** a small ladder that can be folded in and out, with flat steps

stepmother • NOUN• **stepmothers** your stepmother is a woman who is married to your father but is not your own mother

steppe • NOUN• **steppes** a dry grassy area of flat land, usually without trees, especially one found in central Europe and Asia

stepping-stone • NOUN• **stepping-stones** 1 a stone that rises above the surface of water and can be used for crossing over to the other side of a stream or river 2 anything that helps you get on: *Think of your Saturday job as a stepping-stone to better things.*

stereo • ADJECTIVE• short for **stereophonic**: *stereo sound*
• NOUN• **stereos** a CD, cassette or record player which plays the sound through two speakers

stereophonic • ADJECTIVE• a stereophonic system uses two speakers so that the listener feels surrounded by sound

sterile • ADJECTIVE• 1 not able to produce babies, seeds or crops: *sterile land* 2 completely clean and free from germs: *A surgeon's instruments must be sterile.*

• **sterility** • NOUN• being sterile: *the sterility of the soil*

sterilization • NOUN• 1 the treatment of food or surgical instruments in order to destroy germs 2 an operation that is carried out on people or animals so that they cannot have babies
• **sterilize** or **sterilise** • VERB• **sterilizes, sterilizing, sterilized** 1 to make something completely free from germs, for example by boiling it in water 2 to make a person or animal sterile by means of an operation

sterling • NOUN• the money used in Great Britain: *She changed her euros into sterling.*
• ADJECTIVE• of good quality: *He has done some sterling work.*

stern [1] • NOUN• **sterns** the back part of a ship

stern [2] • ADJECTIVE• **sterner, sternest** 1 looking or sounding angry, serious or unfriendly: *The teacher looked rather stern.* • *a stern voice* 2 harsh or severe: *a stern prison sentence*
• **sternly** • ADVERB• in a stern way: *The teacher spoke sternly to the class.*

stethoscope • NOUN• **stethoscopes** an instrument used by a doctor to listen to your heartbeat or breathing

stew • VERB• **stews, stewing, stewed** to stew something is to cook it by boiling it slowly: *First she stewed the apples to make the tart.*
• NOUN• **stews** a mixture of vegetables, or meat and vegetables, cooked slowly together in liquid in a pan: *beef stew and dumplings*

steward • NOUN• **stewards** 1 a man whose job is to look after passengers on an aircraft or a ship 2 a person who is an official at events such as races and concerts

stewardess • NOUN• **stewardesses** an old-fashioned word for a woman whose job is to look after passengers on an aircraft or a ship

stick [1] • NOUN• **sticks** 1 a branch or twig from a tree: *We searched for sticks to make a fire.* 2 a long thin piece of wood shaped for a special purpose: *a walking-stick* • *a hockey-stick* • *a drumstick* 3 a long piece of something: *a stick of rhubarb* • *a stick of rock*

Aa Bb Cc Dd Ee Ff Gg Hh Ii Jj Kk Ll Mm Nn Oo Pp Qq Rr Ss Tt Uu Vv Ww Xx Yy Zz

stick [2] •VERB• **sticks, sticking, stuck** 1 to stick something in or into something is to push it in: *Stop sticking your elbows into me!* • *Stick the knife in your belt.*

2 to stick something is to fix it with something like glue: *Never mind, we can always stick the pieces back together.*

3 to stick is to become fixed and unable to move: *The car stuck in the mud.*

4 to stick to something is to become attached firmly to it: *These seeds stick to your clothes.*

5 to stick to something such as a decision is to keep it: *We've decided to stick to our original plan.*

6 if something **sticks out** it pushes out and stays there: *A nail stuck out from the plank.*

7 if someone or something **sticks out** you notice them immediately: *Her bright red hair makes her stick out in a crowd.*

8 to **stick up for someone** is to defend them: *Maya sticks up for her best friend even when she is wrong.*
⇒ sticky

sticker •NOUN• **stickers** a label or sign with a design or message, for sticking on something

stick insect •NOUN• **stick insects** an insect with a long thin body and legs, that look like twigs

sticky •ADJECTIVE• **stickier, stickiest** 1 designed or likely to stick to another surface: *Mend the book with some sticky tape.* • *sticky fingers* 2 difficult: *They found themselves in a sticky situation.*

stiff •ADJECTIVE• **stiffer, stiffest** 1 difficult to bend or move: *stiff cardboard* • *a stiff neck* • *I can't turn the tap on – it's too stiff.*

2 difficult to do: *a stiff test*
3 strong: *a stiff breeze*
4 not relaxed or friendly: *She replied with stiff politeness.*

♦ **stiffen** •VERB• **stiffens, stiffening, stiffened** 1 to stiffen something is to make it stiff: *stiffen cotton with starch* 2 to stiffen is to become stiff: *She suddenly stiffened in fright.*

♦ **stiffly** •ADVERB• in a stiff way: *Grandad got up stiffly from his chair.* • *'No thank you,' she replied stiffly.*

♦ **stiffness** •NOUN• being stiff

stifle •VERB• **stifles, stifling, stifled** 1 to be stifled is to be prevented from breathing: *stifled by the fumes*

2 to stifle something is to keep it back: *She stifled a giggle.*

♦ **stifling** •ADJECTIVE• very hot and stuffy: *stifling heat*

stigma •NOUN• **stigmas** 1 shame or disgrace: *the stigma of being unemployed* 2 the sticky surface in a flower that receives pollen during pollination

stile •NOUN• **stiles** a step or a set of steps for climbing over a wall or fence

still •ADJECTIVE• **stiller, stillest** 1 without movement or noise: *Keep still while I brush your hair!* • *The city seems very still in the early morning.* 2 not fizzy: *still lemonade*
•ADVERB• 1 up to the present time or the time mentioned: *Are you still working for the same company?* • *By Sunday she still hadn't replied to the invitation.*

2 even so, nevertheless: *It's difficult but we must still try.*

3 even: *Still more people were arriving.*
•VERB• **stills, stilling, stilled** 1 to still something is to make it calm or quiet: *It was time to still the rumours.* 2 to still is to become calm or quiet: *Darkness fell and the forest stilled.*

♦ **stillness** •NOUN• being still: *the stillness of early morning*

stilts •PLURAL NOUN• 1 a pair of poles with supports for the feet, on which you can stand and walk about 2 tall poles to support a house built over water

stimulant •NOUN• **stimulants** something, such as a drug or medicine, that makes you feel more active: *Caffeine and nicotine are stimulants.*

stimulate •VERB• **stimulates, stimulated, stimulating** 1 to stimulate someone is to encourage or excite them: *After seeing the concert, he was stimulated to take up the violin again.* 2 to stimulate something is to make it more active: *changes designed to stimulate growth*

♦ **stimulation** •NOUN• being stimulated: *stimulation of the senses*

♦ **stimulus** •NOUN• **stimuli** something that

makes a living thing do something: *Light is the stimulus that causes a flower to open.*

sting • NOUN• **stings** 1 the part of some animals and plants, such as the wasp or nettle, which can prick the skin and cause pain or irritation: *Bees usually leave their stings in the wound.* 2 the wound, swelling or pain caused by a sting: *Use vinegar to soothe a wasp sting.*
•VERB• **stings, stinging, stung** 1 if an insect or plant stings you they prick your skin and put poison into the wound: *The child was badly stung by nettles.* • *Do these insects sting?* 2 if something stings it is painful: *The salt water made his eyes sting.*

stingy • ADJECTIVE• **stingier, stingiest** mean, not generous: *A very stingy person is sometimes called a Scrooge.*

stink • NOUN• **stinks** a bad smell: *the stink of rotting fish*
•VERB• **stinks, stinking, stank** or **stunk, stunk** to have a bad smell: *The house stinks of cats.*

stir • VERB• **stirs, stirring, stirred** 1 to stir something is to mix it with a circular movement: *He put sugar in his tea and stirred it.*
2 to stir is to move: *The baby stirred in its sleep.* • *The breeze stirred her hair.*
3 to **stir something up** is to cause it: *You're always trying to stir up trouble.*
• NOUN• **stirs** 1 an act of stirring: *Now give the paint a stir.* 2 a fuss: *Their arrival caused quite a stir.*
♦ **stirring** • ADJECTIVE• exciting: *stirring tales of knights and their heroic deeds*

stirrup • NOUN• **stirrups** a metal loop hanging from a horse's saddle, that you put your foot in when riding

stitch • NOUN• **stitches** 1 the loop you make in thread or wool, using a needle, when you are sewing or knitting: *She sewed the hem with small neat stitches.* 2 a sharp pain in your side, especially when you are running: *He was out of breath and had a stitch.*
•VERB• **stitches, stitching, stitched** to sew: *I stitched the button on to my coat.*

stoat • NOUN• **stoats** a small fierce animal similar to a weasel.

stock • NOUN• **stocks** 1 a store of goods, for example in a shop or warehouse: *Buy now while stocks last!*
2 the animals of a farm: *The farmer goes to market to buy more stock.*
3 stocks are shares in companies that people can buy through a stock exchange
4 liquid in which meat or vegetables have been cooked, used for example for making soup: *chicken stock*
5 a type of sweet-smelling garden flower
6 a person's stock is their family origins: *of peasant stock*
• VERB• **stocks, stocking, stocked** 1 to stock something is to keep a supply of it for sale: *Most supermarkets now stock organic products.* 2 to stock a place with something is to fill it or supply it with something: *Dad likes to stock the drinks cabinet with his favourite whiskies.*

stockade • NOUN• **stockades** a fence of strong posts put up round an area or building to protect or defend it

stock car • NOUN• **stock cars** a car that has been strengthened to take part in a type of racing where cars deliberately collide with each other

stock exchange • NOUN• **stock exchanges** a place where stocks and shares in companies are bought and sold

stocking • NOUN• **stockings** a close-fitting covering for the leg and foot, worn by women

stockpile • NOUN• **stockpiles** a large store of something: *She keeps a stockpile of flour in her cupboard.*
• VERB• **stockpiles, stockpiling, stockpiled** to stockpile something is to build up a store of it: *There are reports that weapons are being stockpiled.*

stocktaking • NOUN• the process of counting all the goods in a shop or factory at a particular time: *The shop is closed for stocktaking.*

stocky • ADJECTIVE• **stockier, stockiest** a stocky person is short and strongly built

stodgy • ADJECTIVE• **stodgier, stodgiest** 1 stodgy food is heavy and filling: *The rice pudding was stodgy and tasteless.* 2 a stodgy book or person is dull and boring

Aa Bb Cc Dd Ee Ff Gg Hh Ii Jj Kk Ll Mm Nn Oo Pp Qq Rr **Ss** Tt Uu Vv Ww Xx Yy Zz

Aa
Bb
Cc
Dd
Ee
Ff
Gg
Hh
Ii
Jj
Kk
Ll
Mm
Nn
Oo
Pp
Qq
Rr
Ss
Tt
Uu
Vv
Ww
Xx
Yy
Zz

stoke •VERB• **stokes, stoking, stoked** to stoke a fire is to put coal, wood or other fuel on it

stole •NOUN• **stoles** a length of material, such as fur or silk, worn by women around their shoulders

stole •VERB• a way of changing the verb **steal** to make a past tense: *How can you be sure that she stole the money?*

stomach •NOUN• **stomachs** 1 the bag-like part inside the body where food goes when it is swallowed, and where it is digested 2 courage: *I don't have the stomach for dangerous sports.*
•VERB• **stomachs, stomaching, stomached** to bear or put up with: *I can't stomach TV programmes that show real operations.*

stomp •VERB• **stomps, stomping, stomped** to walk heavily and noisily: *He stomped off to his room in a temper.*

stone •NOUN• **stones** *or* **stone** 1 stone is the hard material that rocks are made of: *a house built of stone* 2 a stone is a piece of this: *The boys were throwing stones into the water.* 3 a piece of this shaped for a special purpose, for example a tombstone or paving stones 4 a gem or jewel: *diamonds, rubies and other stones* 5 the hard shell around the seed in some fruits, for example peaches and cherries 6 a measure of weight equal to 14 pounds or 6.35 kilograms: *My dad weighs twelve stone.*
•VERB• **stones, stoning, stoned** 1 to stone someone is to throw stones at them 2 to stone fruit is to take the stones out of it
•ADJECTIVE• made of stone: *stone tools*

♦ **stony** •ADJECTIVE• **stonier, stoniest** 1 hard like stone 2 full of, or covered with, stones: *a stony beach* 3 hard and cold in manner: *He gave me a stony stare.*

ⓘ The plural of the noun is **stones**, except when it means a measure of weight. Then the plural **stone** is used.

stood •VERB• a way of changing the verb

stand to make a past tense. It can be used with or without a helping verb: *She stood quietly in the corner.* • *He had stood there all day.*

stool •NOUN• **stools** a seat without a back

stoop •VERB• **stoops, stooping, stooped** 1 to bend your body forward and downward: *The doorway was so low that she had to stoop to get through it.* 2 to **stoop to** doing something is to be wicked or bad enough to do it: *Surely he wouldn't stoop to stealing.*
•NOUN• **stoops** a forward bend of the body: *The old man walked with a stoop.*

stop •VERB• **stops, stopping, stopped** 1 to stop is to come to a halt or come to an end: *The car stopped in front of our house.* • *The rain stopped.*
2 to stop something is to bring it to a halt or bring it to an end: *Stop the car now!* • *Please stop this nonsense.*
3 to stop doing something is to finish doing it or not do it any longer: *We stopped talking and listened.*
4 to stop someone doing something is to prevent them from doing it: *Can't you stop her working so hard?*
5 to stop something or **stop something up** is to block it or close it up: *He stopped his ears with his hands.* • *Stop up the hole with newspaper.*
•NOUN• **stops** 1 the act of stopping: *We made two stops on our journey.*
2 a place where something, such as a bus, stops 3 a full stop: *All sentences should end with a stop.*

♦ **stoppage** •NOUN• **stoppages** 1 a stopping by workers, a strike: *The company lost millions because of the month-long stoppage.* 2 a blockage in a narrow part of something

♦ **stopper** •NOUN• **stoppers** something, such as a cork, that is put into the neck of a bottle or jar to close it

stop press •NOUN• the most recent news, put into a newspaper after printing has started

stopwatch •NOUN• **stopwatches** a watch that can be stopped and started, used for timing races

storage •NOUN• the storing of something: *Our furniture has gone into storage.*

store •NOUN• **stores** 1 a supply of goods from which things are taken as they are needed: *Squirrels keep a store of food.*
2 a place where things are kept: *a store for books*
3 a shop: *the village store • a department store*
•VERB• **stores, storing, stored** to store something is to keep it somewhere for use in the future: *Store the wine in a cool dry place.*

storey •NOUN• **storeys** one of the floors or levels in a building: *a house with two storeys*

stork •NOUN• **storks** a wading bird with a long bill, neck and legs

storm •NOUN• **storms** 1 a sudden burst of bad weather with strong winds, rain or snow, and sometimes thunder and lightning
2 a violent outburst: *a storm of protests • a storm of applause*
•VERB• **storms, storming, stormed** 1 to storm is to shout or move in an angry way: *She stormed out of the room. • 'How dare you!' he stormed.* 2 to storm a place is to attack it suddenly and violently in order to capture it: *Troops stormed the embassy.*
◆ **stormy** •ADJECTIVE• **stormier, stormiest**
1 stormy weather is weather with strong winds, rain or snow, and sometimes thunder and lightning 2 full of anger: *a stormy meeting • a stormy relationship*

story •NOUN• **stories** a description of an event or events, which can be real or invented: *The book is the story of his life. • She loves to write adventure stories.*

stout •ADJECTIVE• **stouter, stoutest** 1 fat: *a rather stout middle-aged man*
2 brave: *stout resistance*
3 thick and strong: *stout walking-boots*
◆ **stoutly** •ADVERB• in a stout way
◆ **stoutness** •NOUN• being stout

stove •NOUN• **stoves** a device for cooking or for heating a room: *a gas stove*

stow •VERB• **stows, stowing, stowed** 1 to stow something is to pack it or put it away: *The sailor stowed his belongings in his locker.*
2 to **stow away** is to hide yourself on a vehicle such as a ship or aeroplane before its departure so that you can travel without paying: *He stowed away on a cargo ship for New York.*

stowaway •NOUN• **stowaways** a person who hides on a ship or aircraft so that they can travel without paying the fare

straddle •VERB• **straddles, straddling, straddled** to straddle something is to stand or sit with one leg on each side of it: *Dad turned the chair round and straddled it.*

straggle •VERB• **straggles, straggling, straggled** to walk too slowly to keep up with others: *Some of the younger children were straggling behind.*
◆ **straggler** •NOUN• **stragglers** a person who walks too slowly and gets left behind the main group: *Let's stop for a minute and let the stragglers catch up.*
◆ **straggly** •ADJECTIVE• **stragglier, straggliest** growing untidily: *straggly hair*

straight •ADJECTIVE• **straighter, straightest**
1 not bent, curved or curly: *a straight line • straight hair*
2 honest: *Give me a straight answer!*
3 in the proper position, not crooked: *That picture isn't straight.*
4 tidy, sorted out: *I'll never get this room straight • Now let's get the facts straight!*
5 not smiling or laughing: *You should keep a straight face when you tell a joke.*
•ADVERB• 1 in a straight line, without changing direction: *Turn right, then go straight on.*
2 at once, without any delay: *I came straight here.*
3 honestly: *You're not playing straight.*
◆ **straight away** immediately: *Could you sign this for me straight away?*
◆ **straighten** •VERB• **straightens, straightening, straightened** to become or make something straight: *The road curved then straightened. • He straightened his tie.*

straightforward •ADJECTIVE• 1 simple: *a straightforward task* 2 honest: *a nice straightforward boy*

strain •VERB• **strains, straining, strained**
1 to strain a muscle or other part of the body is to injure through too much use: *You'll strain your eyes reading in the dark.*
2 to strain to do something is to make a

great effort to do it: *He strained to reach the rope.*

3 to strain something is to stretch it or pull it or push it too far: *Your constant demands are straining my patience.*

4 to strain a mixture is to separate the liquid from it by passing it through a sieve: *Now strain the water off the vegetables.*

• NOUN• **strains 1** an injury to a muscle or other part of the body caused by straining it: *eye-strain*

2 the bad effects on the mind and body of too much work and worry: *suffering from strain*

3 too great a demand on something: *You children are a strain on my patience!*

✦ **strainer** • NOUN• **strainers** a sieve for separating liquids from solids: *a tea-strainer*

strait • NOUN• **straits** a narrow strip of sea between two pieces of land: *the Straits of Gibraltar*

• **in dire straits** in a desperately difficult situation: *Losing my money left me in dire straits.*

strand • NOUN• **strands** a length of something soft and fine, for example hair or thread

stranded • ADJECTIVE• **1** a ship is stranded if it is stuck on sand or rocks: *The ships were stranded in shallow water.* **2** a person is stranded if they are left helpless: *She was left stranded without money or passport.*

strange • ADJECTIVE• **stranger, strangest**
1 unusual or odd: *a strange noise coming from the engine* **2** not familiar, not known or seen before: *a strange land*

✦ **strangely** • ADVERB• in a strange way: *Mum looked at me strangely.*

✦ **strangeness** • NOUN• being strange: *the strangeness of the situation*

✦ **stranger** • NOUN• **strangers 1** a person you do not know: *Children should never talk to strangers.* **2** a person who is in a place they do not know: *I'm afraid I don't know where the station is. I'm a stranger here myself.*

strangle • VERB• **strangles, strangling, strangled** to strangle someone is to kill them by squeezing their throat tightly: *The victim had been strangled with a scarf.*

strap • NOUN• **straps** a long narrow piece of leather or cloth used to hold things, fasten

things or hang things on: *a watch-strap* • *a bag with a shoulder strap*

• VERB• **straps, strapping, strapped** to strap something is to fasten it with a strap: *I usually strap my bag to my bike.*

strategy • NOUN• **strategies** planning that is designed to achieve something

stratosphere • NOUN• one of the layers of the Earth's atmosphere, between 12 and 50 kilometres above the Earth

stratum • NOUN• **strata** a layer of rock in the Earth's crust: *This stratum of rock was formed thousands of years ago.*

straw • NOUN• **straws 1** straw is dried stalks of grain: *The cows need fresh straw.* **2** a straw is a thin tube, usually made of plastic, for sucking up a drink: *She was drinking orange juice through a straw.*

• ADJECTIVE• made of straw: *a straw hat*

strawberry • NOUN• **strawberries** a soft red fruit with many tiny seeds on its skin

stray • VERB• **strays, straying, strayed** to wander or get lost: *Be careful not to stray from the path.* • *The farmer was searching for some sheep that had strayed.*

• ADJECTIVE• **1** wandering or lost: *stray dogs* **2** happening here and there, scattered: *The sky was clear except for a few stray clouds.*

• NOUN• **strays** a cat or dog that has no home

streak • NOUN• **streaks 1** a long thin line or mark: *hair with blonde streaks* • *dirty streaks on the window* • *a streak of lightning* **2** a trace of something that can be seen in a person: *He has a cowardly streak.*

• VERB• **streaks, streaking, streaked 1** to streak something is to mark it with streaks: *tears streaking her face* **2** to streak is to move very fast: *The runner streaked round the racetrack.*

✦ **streaked** • ADJECTIVE• having streaks: *a beard streaked with grey*

✦ **streaky** • ADJECTIVE• **streakier, streakiest** marked with streaks: *Her face was all streaky with crying.*

stream • NOUN• **streams 1** a small river: *He managed to jump across the stream.* **2** a flow of something: *streams of people* • *a stream of traffic*

• VERB• **streams, streaming, streamed** to

flow: *Tears streamed down her face* • *The workers streamed out of the factory gates.*
♦ **streamer** •NOUN• **streamers** a long narrow strip of paper or ribbon, used as a decoration

streamline •VERB• **streamlines, streamlining, streamlined** 1 to streamline something such as a vehicle is to shape it in such a way that it will cut through air or water as easily as possible 2 to streamline something is also to make it more efficient, especially by making it simpler: *The company streamlined its production methods.*

street •NOUN• **streets** a road with buildings such as houses and shops on one or both sides: *I live at 32 Montgomery Street.* • *the main shopping street*

strength •NOUN• **strengths** 1 strength is being strong: *He didn't have the strength to lift the box.* 2 a person's strengths are the good things about them: *Her greatest strength is her sense of humour.*
♦ **strengthen** •VERB• **strengthens, strengthening, strengthened** 1 to strengthen something is to make it strong or stronger: *He did exercises to strengthen his muscles.* 2 to strengthen is to become strong or stronger: *The wind strengthened.*

strenuous •ADJECTIVE• needing or using a lot of effort or energy: *Squash is a strenuous game.* • *The plans met strenuous resistance.*

stress •NOUN• **stresses** 1 a physical force that may bend or break something: *metal that bends under stress* 2 the effect on the mind or body of working or worrying too much: *headaches caused by stress* 3 special importance that is attached to something: *The General laid particular stress on the need for secrecy.* 4 extra weight that is put on a part of a word: *In the word 'bedroom' the stress is on 'bed'.*
•VERB• **stresses, stressing, stressed** 1 to stress someone is to make them suffer stress: *Many of the pressures of everyday life can stress us.* 2 to stress something is to place special importance on it: *Her speech stressed the need for change.*

3 to stress part of a word is to place extra weight on it: *When 'object' is a noun you stress the 'ob'.*

stressful •ADJECTIVE• causing you to feel nervous, worried and anxious: *Doing examinations can be stressful.*

stretch •VERB• **stretches, stretching, stretched** 1 to stretch something is to make it longer or wider, especially by pulling: *Stretch this rope between the two posts.* 2 to stretch is to become longer or wider: *This material stretches.* 3 to stretch from one place to another is to cover the distance between them: *The mountains stretch from the north to the south of the country.*
•NOUN• **stretches** 1 the action of stretching: *I always have a good stretch when I get out of bed.* 2 a length in distance or time: *a dangerous stretch of road* • *a three-year stretch*
♦ **stretcher** •NOUN• **stretchers** a light folding bed with handles for carrying a sick or wounded person

strew •VERB• **strews, strewing, strewed, strewn** to scatter untidily: *She has strewn paper all over the floor.* • *The ground was strewn with rubbish.*

strict •ADJECTIVE• **stricter, strictest** 1 someone who is strict expects other people to obey rules: *This class needs a strict teacher.* 2 something that is strict is meant to be obeyed: *strict school rules* • *under strict orders* 3 exact: *the strict sense of the word*

stride •VERB• **strides, striding, strode, stridden** to walk with long steps: *He strode up the path.*
•NOUN• **strides** a long step: *He crossed the road in three strides.*
• **get into your stride** to get the hang of something
• **take something in your stride** to manage to do it easily: *Her parents were worried about her changing school but she took it all in her stride.*

strife •NOUN• fighting or quarrelling: *There was a lot of strife within the political party.*

Aa Bb Cc Dd Ee Ff Gg Hh Ii Jj Kk Ll Mm Nn Oo Pp Qq Rr Ss Tt Uu Vv Ww Xx Yy Zz

Aa
Bb
Cc
Dd
Ee
Ff
Gg
Hh
Ii
Jj
Kk
Ll
Mm
Nn
Oo
Pp
Qq
Rr
Ss
Tt
Uu
Vv
Ww
Xx
Yy
Zz

strike • VERB • **strikes, striking, struck** 1 to strike someone or something is to hit them or it: *He struck me in the face with his fist.* • *My head struck the table.*
2 to strike is to attack: *The enemy troops struck at dawn.*
3 to strike a match is to light it
4 to strike is to produce a strong clear sound: *The clock struck three.*
5 something strikes you when it suddenly comes into your mind or when it impresses you: *It suddenly struck me that I was completely wrong.* • *He was struck by her beauty.*
6 workers strike when they stop work as a protest against something or in an attempt to get something: *The men were striking for higher wages.*
7 to strike oil or gold is to discover it
• NOUN • **strikes** 1 the stopping of work as a protest or in an attempt to get something: *The strike lasted for ten days.*
2 a sudden attack, especially a military one: *repeated air strikes*
3 a discovery of oil or gold
♦ **striker** • NOUN • **strikers** 1 a worker who strikes 2 in football, a player whose job is to try to score goals
♦ **striking** • ADJECTIVE • if you find something striking, you notice it or are impressed by it: *a striking resemblance* • *striking beauty*

string • NOUN • **strings** 1 thick thread used for tying things: *a ball of string*
2 the strings of a musical instrument, such as a guitar, are the pieces of wire or other material that are stretched across it
3 a string of things is a number of things coming one after the other: *a string of disasters*
• VERB • **strings, stringing, strung** 1 to string something is to tie it and hang it with string: *Coloured lights were strung across the ceiling.*
2 to string something such as beads is to put them on a string: *She took the pearls to a jeweller to be strung.*
3 to string a musical instrument is to put strings on it
♦ **stringy** • ADJECTIVE • **stringier, stringiest** 1 something that is stringy is long and thin

and looks like string: *stringy hair* 2 meat that is stringy is full of tough chewy bits

strip [1] • NOUN • **strips** 1 a long narrow piece: *a strip of paper* 2 an outfit worn by a sports team: *a red football strip*

strip [2] • VERB • **strips, stripping, stripped** 1 to strip something is to take the covering off it: *My mum always strips the beds on Mondays.*
2 to strip is to undress: *He stripped and dived into the water.* • *She stripped the baby for its bath.*
3 to strip someone of something is to take it away from them: *The officer was stripped of his rank.*

stripe • NOUN • **stripes** a band of colour: *a blue suit with thin white stripes*
♦ **striped** • ADJECTIVE • having stripes: *striped wallpaper*
♦ **stripy** • ADJECTIVE • **stripier, stripiest** having stripes: *a stripy T-shirt*

strive • VERB • **strives, striving, strove, striven** to try very hard: *He strives to please his teacher.*

strobe • NOUN • **strobes** a light that flashes rapidly

strode • VERB • a way of changing the verb **stride** to make a past tense: *He strode up the hill.*

stroke • NOUN • **strokes** 1 a stoke is a movement or hit made by swinging your arm or arms while holding an oar, a golf club, a tennis racket, or a long-handled weapon: *He felled the tree with one stroke of the axe.*
2 a stroke in swimming is one of the ways that you can move your arms and legs to travel through the water: *breast stroke*
3 a stroke is also the sound made by a clock when it strikes the hour: *We arrived on the stroke of midnight.*
4 a stroke is also a sudden illness in the brain that can leave a person unable to move or speak
• VERB • **strokes, stroking, stroked** to rub gently: *She was stroking the cat.*

strong • ADJECTIVE • **stronger, strongest** 1 powerful, not weak: *a strong young man* • *a strong wind* • *a strong smell*
2 not easily worn away or broken: *strong cloth* • *fastened with a strong chain*

3 in number: *a workforce 500 strong*
⇒ **strongly**

stronghold •NOUN• **strongholds** a fortress or castle built to survive attacks

strongly •ADVERB• **1** in a strong way: *The boxer fought back strongly.* **2** very much: *I strongly recommend that you follow the instructions.*

struck •VERB• a way of changing the verb **strike** to make a past tense. It can be used with or without a helping verb: *Her head struck the wall.* • *Lightning has struck the building.*

structure •NOUN• **structures 1** the way that the parts of something are arranged: *the structure of the story* **2** something that is built or constructed: *The bridge was a massive steel structure.*
♦ **structural** •ADJECTIVE• to do with the structure of something else: *The bomb caused major structural damage to the building.*

struggle •VERB• **struggles, struggling, struggled 1** to turn and twist your body and try to escape: *The child struggled in his arms.*
2 to struggle to do something is to try hard to do it: *She is struggling to finish her homework.*
3 to fight against difficulty: *All his life he has struggled against poverty.* • *struggling through the mud*
•NOUN• **struggles** a fight: *They got their money back after a long struggle.*

strum •VERB• **strums, strumming, strummed** to play a musical instrument such as the guitar by sweeping movements of the fingers: *He strummed a tune.* • *She was strumming away happily.*

strut •VERB• **struts, strutting, strutted** to walk in a stiff, proud way: *The cock strutted round the farmyard.*
•NOUN• **struts 1** a proud way of walking **2** a bar made of wood or metal which supports something

stub •NOUN• **stubs** a short piece of something such as a cigarette or pencil which is left over when the rest has been used up: *The ashtray was overflowing with cigarette stubs.*
•VERB• **stubs, stubbing, stubbed 1** to stub

your toe is to knock it painfully against something hard **2** to **stub out** a cigarette is to put it out by pressing it against something: *He stubbed out his cigarette in the ashtray.*

stubble •NOUN• **1** the short stalks of corn left standing in the fields after the crop has been harvested **2** short coarse hairs growing on a man's face when he has not shaved

stubborn •ADJECTIVE• a stubborn person refuses to do what other people tell them to do, or to follow advice: *a silly, stubborn child*
♦ **stubbornly** •ADVERB• in a stubborn way: *She stubbornly refused to listen to my advice.*
♦ **stubbornness** •NOUN• being stubborn: *Her stubbornness will get her into trouble one day.*

stuck •VERB• a way of changing the verb **stick** to make a past tense. It can be used with or without a helping verb: *He stuck the stamp on the envelope.* • *I've stuck the broken vase together again.*

stud •NOUN• **studs** a piece of metal with a large head, used as a fastener or decoration on clothes or on the soles of boots or shoes: *jeans with copper studs* • *I need new studs for my football boots.*

student •NOUN• **students** someone who is studying, especially at a college or university

studio •NOUN• **studios 1** the room that an artist or photographer works in
2 a place where films are made
3 a room from which radio or television programmes are broadcast

studious •ADJECTIVE• a studious person spends a lot of time studying: *Sue is a very studious girl.*

study •VERB• **studies, studying, studied 1** to study is to spend time learning about a subject: *I'm studying French language.* • *She's studying to be a teacher.* **2** to study something is to look at it carefully: *He studied the railway timetable.* • *We must study the problem in detail.*
•NOUN• **studies 1** study is reading and learning about something: *the study of history* **2** a study is a room used for studying or quiet work: *The headmaster wants to speak to you in his study.*
⇒ **student, studious**

Aa
Bb
Cc
Dd
Ee
Ff
Gg
Hh
Ii
Jj
Kk
Ll
Mm
Nn
Oo
Pp
Qq
Rr
Ss
Tt
Uu
Vv
Ww
Xx
Yy
Zz

stuff •NOUN• 1 a substance or material of any kind: *What's that black oily stuff on the beach?* 2 things or objects: *There's far too much stuff in this cupboard.*

•VERB• **stuffs, stuffing, stuffed** 1 to stuff something is to pack it or fill it tightly: *She used feathers to stuff the cushions.* • *We need to stuff the turkey before we cook it.* 2 to stuff something into a place is to push it in carelessly: *He stuffed the papers into his pocket.*

♦ **stuffed** • ADJECTIVE• a stuffed animal or bird has had its skin filled after it has died so that it looks like it did when it was alive

♦ **stuffing** •NOUN• **stuffings** 1 material used for stuffing things such as cushions or soft toys 2 a savoury mixture used to stuff meat such as turkeys and chickens before cooking: *sage and onion stuffing*

stuffy • ADJECTIVE• **stuffier, stuffiest** 1 a place that is stuffy lacks fresh air: *How can you sit in this stuffy office all day?* 2 a person who is stuffy is dull and old-fashioned: *Our new teacher is rather stuffy.*

stumble •VERB• **stumbles, stumbling, stumbled** 1 to trip and nearly fall: *Granny stumbled over the edge of the carpet.* 2 to walk with difficulty, nearly falling over: *He stumbled along the track in the dark.* 3 to make mistakes or hesitate: *She stumbled over the difficult words when reading to the class.* 4 to **stumble on** or **stumble across** something is to find it by chance: *I stumbled across this book today.*

stump •NOUN• **stumps** 1 the part of something such as a tree, limb or tooth left after the main part has been taken away 2 in cricket, one of the three wooden sticks which make up a wicket

•VERB• **stumps, stumping, stumped** 1 to stump the person batting in cricket is to put them out by touching the stumps with the ball 2 if something stumps you it is too hard for you: *Those exam questions stumped us all.*

♦ **stumpy** • ADJECTIVE• **stumpier, stumpiest** short and thick: *The dog had a stumpy tail.*

stun •VERB• **stuns, stunning, stunned** 1 to stun someone is to make them unconscious, usually by a blow on the head: *The punch stunned him.* 2 to stun someone is also to surprise or shock them greatly: *We were all stunned by the news of the accident.*

stung •VERB• a way of changing the verb **sting** to make a past tense. It can be used with or without a helping verb: *The wasp stung him on the finger.* • *Ouch! It's stung me.*

stunk •VERB• 1 a way of changing the verb **stink** to make a past tense. It can be used with or without a helping verb: *The room stunk of cigar smoke.* • *If the dead mouse hadn't stunk so much, I'd never have found it.*

stunt[1] • NOUN• **stunts** something daring or unusual that is done to attract attention: *He's always doing stunts on his motorbike.* • *The whole event was a big publicity stunt.*

stunt[2] •VERB• **stunts, stunting, stunted** to stunt something is to stop its growth or development: *Lack of water stunted the plants.*

♦ **stunted** • ADJECTIVE• small and badly shaped: *trees with stunted branches*

stupendous • ADJECTIVE• wonderful, amazing: *It was a stupendous concert.*

stupid • ADJECTIVE• **stupider, stupidest** not clever, slow at understanding: *a stupid mistake* • *You stupid boy!*

♦ **stupidity** •NOUN• being stupid: *His stupidity cost us first prize.*

♦ **stupidly** • ADVERB• in a stupid way: *Stupidly, I agreed to do it.*

sturdy • ADJECTIVE• **sturdier, sturdiest** strong, well built: *a sturdy body* • *sturdy furniture*

stutter •VERB• **stutters, stuttering, stuttered** to keep repeating parts of words, especially the first part

• NOUN• **stutters** a speech problem that makes you repeat parts of words: *That child has a bad stutter.*

sty[1] • NOUN• **sties** a place where pigs are kept

sty[2] or **stye** • NOUN• **sties** or **styes** a painful swelling on the eyelid

style • NOUN• **styles** 1 a way of doing something such as writing, acting or speaking: *I like the style of her writing.*

Subjects and objects

There is a verb in every sentence. A sentence cannot make sense without a verb.
Most verbs have a **subject**. The subject is the person or thing doing the action of the verb.

The sun shone.
The sun is the **subject**. *Shone* is the verb.

The lion roared.
The lion is the **subject**. *Roared* is the verb.

Some sentences have an **object** as well as a subject. The object tells you whom or what the verb affects.

The sun warmed the earth.
The sun is the **subject**. *Warmed* is the verb. *The earth* is the **object**.

The lion chased a zebra.
The lion is the **subject**. *Chased* is the verb. *A zebra* is the **object**.

2 a style is a fashion: *a new style of shoe*
3 style is being elegant: *She's got style.*
•VERB• **styles, styling, styled** to style something such as hair or clothes is to give them a certain style: *I'm having my hair cut and styled.* • *clothes styled for comfort*
♦ **stylish** •ADJECTIVE• smart, elegant, fashionable: *stylish clothes*

stylus •NOUN• **styluses** a needle for a record-player

sub- •PREFIX• if a word starts with **sub-** it has the meaning of *below* or *under*. For example, a *submarine* is a type of ship that is able to travel under water

subconscious •NOUN• the part of your mind of which you yourself are not aware but which makes you feel certain things and act in certain ways
•ADJECTIVE• which exist in the subconscious: *subconscious fears*
♦ **subconsciously** •ADVERB• in a subconscious way: *Subconsciously she wanted to be famous.*

subdivide •VERB• **subdivides, subdividing, subdivided** to subdivide something is to divide the parts it has already been divided into, making even smaller parts: *Each class is subdivided into groups according to reading ability.*

♦ **subdivision** •NOUN• **subdivisions** a part made by subdividing

subdue •VERB• **subdues, subduing, subdued** to subdue someone is to overpower them or bring them under control: *After months of fighting the rebels were subdued.*
♦ **subdued** •ADJECTIVE• quiet, in low spirits: *subdued voices* • *You seem very subdued today.*

subheading •NOUN• **subheadings** a heading that is less important than the main heading in a piece of writing

subject •NOUN• **subjects 1** something that you learn about, for example science or mathematics: *My favourite subject at school was French.*
2 the subject of something such as a story or conversation is the person or thing that it is about: *Can we change the subject, please?*
3 the subject of a sentence is the word or words that stand for the person or thing doing the action of the verb, for example *He* in *He hit me*. See the box called **Subjects and objects**
4 a person who is under the power of someone or something else: *the king's subjects*
•VERB• **subjects, subjecting, subjected** to

subject someone to something is to make them suffer it: *He was subjected to cruel treatment.*

ⓘ The noun is pronounced **sub**-jict, with the stress on *sub*. The verb is pronounced sib-**ject**, with the stress on *ject*.

subjective • ADJECTIVE • resulting from your own thoughts and feelings: *a subjective opinion*

sublime • ADJECTIVE • very great or beautiful: *It was a sublime moment in my life.*

submarine • NOUN • **submarines** a ship that can travel under water

submerge • VERB • **submerges, submerging, submerged** 1 to submerge something is to cover it with water: *Entire villages had been submerged.* 2 to submerge is to go under water: *I watched the whale submerge.*
  ♦ **submergence** or **submersion** • NOUN • submerging or being submerged

submission • NOUN • **submissions** 1 submission is the action of submitting: *forced into submission* 2 a submission is something such as an idea or plan that is offered to someone to be considered by them

submissive • ADJECTIVE • willing to obey: *a submissive servant*

submit • VERB • **submits, submitting, submitted** 1 to submit is to give in: *The rebels were ordered to submit.* • *I refuse to submit to his control.* 2 to submit something such as a plan or idea is to offer it to someone to be considered by them: *All competition entries must be submitted by Friday.*

subordinate • ADJECTIVE • lower in rank or less important: *his subordinate officers* • NOUN • **subordinates** someone who is lower in rank or less important than someone else: *She always tries to help her subordinates.*

subordinate clause • NOUN • **subordinate clauses** a clause which cannot stand on its own as a sentence, for example *that I got for my birthday* in the sentence *The book that I got for my birthday was boring.*

subscribe • VERB • **subscribes, subscribing, subscribed** 1 to subscribe to a charity or other cause is to give money to it: *We each subscribed £5 towards the cost of the clock.* 2 to subscribe to something such as a magazine is to promise to take and pay for a certain number of issues
  ♦ **subscriber** • NOUN • **subscribers** someone who subscribes to something
  ♦ **subscription** • NOUN • **subscriptions** money paid to subscribe to something

subsequent • ADJECTIVE • following or coming after something else: *The story tells of the soldier's capture and subsequent escape.*
  ♦ **subsequently** • ADVERB • later: *She ate the shellfish and subsequently became ill.*

subside • VERB • **subsides, subsiding, subsided** 1 to sink lower: *When building subside, cracks usually appear in the walls.* 2 to become less or quieter: *Let's stay here until the wind subsides.*
  ♦ **subsidence** • NOUN • sinking down, especially into the ground

subsidize or **subsidise** • VERB • **subsidizes, subsidizing, subsidized** 1 to subsidize someone or something is to give them money as a help: *The government subsidizes the mining industry.* 2 to subsidize something is to pay part of the cost so that the customer pays less: *The company subsidizes meals in its canteen.*

subsidy • NOUN • **subsidies** money given to help someone or something or to keep prices low

substance • NOUN • **substances** 1 a substance is a material that you can touch and see: *Glue is a sticky substance.* 2 the substance of something is its general meaning: *The substance of her argument was that women are more intelligent than men.*

substantial • ADJECTIVE • 1 solid and strong: *a substantial table* 2 large: *a substantial sum of money*
  ♦ **substantially** • ADVERB • 1 a lot: *Profits have increased substantially.* 2 mostly: *These two items are substantially the same.*

substitute • VERB • **substitutes, substituting,**

subtitle → suck

substituted to substitute something for something else is to use it instead of something else: *I substituted your name for mine on the list.*
• NOUN• **substitutes** a person or thing used instead of another: *Use lemons as a substitute for limes.* • *Our goalkeeper is injured. We need to find a substitute.*
♦ **substitution** • NOUN• **substitutions** substituting something or someone else, or being substituted

subtitle • NOUN• **subtitles** 1 a second title of something such as a book or film 2 a translation of a film that is in a foreign language, appearing at the bottom of the screen: *a French film with English subtitles*

subtle • ADJECTIVE• **subtler, subtlest** 1 slight, difficult to describe or explain: *There is a subtle difference between these two shades of blue.* 2 clever or cunning: *He has a subtle mind.*
♦ **subtlety** • NOUN• **subtleties** being delicate: *the subtlety of the colours in the painting*

subtotal • NOUN• **subtotals** the total of one set of figures within a larger group

subtract • VERB• **subtracts, subtracting, subtracted** to take one number away from another: *If you subtract 4 from 6, you get 2.* • *Most children learn to add and subtract in their first year at school.*
♦ **subtraction** • NOUN• **subtractions** the act of taking one number away from another: *First we learned addition, then we learned subtraction.*

suburb • NOUN• **suburbs** an area of houses at the edge of a town or city: *They decided to move out to the suburbs.*
♦ **suburban** • ADJECTIVE• of suburbs: *suburban housing*

succeed • VERB• **succeeds, succeeding, succeeded** 1 to succeed is to manage to do what you have been trying to do: *If you try hard, I'm sure you'll succeed.* • *She succeeded in getting the job.* 2 to succeed someone is to take their place: *He succeeded his father as manager of the company.*

success • NOUN• **successes** 1 success is managing to do something you have been

trying to do: *Have you had any success in finding a job?* 2 a success is someone who does well or something that turns out well: *She's a great success as a teacher.* • *The party was a great success.*
♦ **successful** • ADJECTIVE• 1 a successful person has managed to do something, or has done very well in a particular way: *Were you successful in passing the test?* • *a successful artist* 2 a successful event is one that goes well: *We had a successful meeting with the headmaster.*
♦ **successfully** • ADVERB• in a successful way: *I have successfully learned to drive.*

succession • NOUN• **successions** 1 the right to succeed to a throne or title: *He is third in succession to the throne.* 2 a number of things coming one after the other: *a succession of failures*
• **in succession** one after another: *five wet days in succession*
♦ **successive** • ADJECTIVE• following one after the other: *The team won three successive matches.*
♦ **successively** • ADVERB• one after the other

successor • NOUN• **successor** a person that follows, and takes the place of, another: *Who will be appointed as the headteacher's successor?*

succulent • ADJECTIVE• juicy and delicious: *succulent peaches*

succumb • VERB• **succumbs, succumbing, succumbed** to succumb to something is to give in to it: *She succumbed to temptation.*

such • ADJECTIVE• 1 of a kind already mentioned: *Such things are difficult to find.* 2 of the same kind: *doctors, nurses and such people* 3 so great or so much: *His excitement was such that he shouted out loud.* • *It's such a disappointment!*

such-and-such • ADJECTIVE• any: *Let's suppose that you go into such-and-such a shop.*
• NOUN• any person or thing: *Then you ask for such-and-such.*

suck • VERB• **sucks, sucking, sucked** 1 to take something into your mouth by drawing in

565

Suffixes

A **suffix** is a group of letters added to the end of a word. These word endings change words from one type of word to another, for example:

from a verb to a noun	work + **-er** = worker
from a noun to an adjective	hope + **-less** = hopeless
from an adjective to an adverb	quick + **-ly** = quickly
from an adjective to a verb	bright + **-en** = brighten
from an adjective to a noun	rough + **-ness** = roughness

Particular word endings can be added to make nouns, adjectives, verbs and adverbs. These endings can help you recognize which is which.

Suffixes that end nouns

-age	postage
-al	arrival
-ance	appearance
-ant	attendant
-dom	freedom
-ence	preference
-er	farmer
-ess	lioness
-ette	cigarette
-hood	childhood
-ian	musician
-ism	realism
-ist	artist
-ity	humanity
-let	booklet
-ling	duckling
-ment	punishment
-ness	kindness
-or	sailor
-tion	imagination
-y	honesty

Suffixes that end verbs

-ate	activate
-en	brighten
-ify, -fy	simplify
-ize or -ise	publicize

Suffixes that end adjectives

-able	lovable
-al	magical
-an	Italian
-ed	crooked
-ese	Chinese
-ful	helpful
-ible	edible
-ic	poetic
-ish	boyish
-less	homeless
-ous	dangerous
-uble	soluble
-y	spicy

Suffixes that end adverbs

-ly	happily
-ward	backward
-ways	sideways
-wise	clockwise

Aa Bb Cc Dd Ee Ff Gg Hh Ii Jj Kk Ll Mm Nn Oo Pp Qq Rr Ss Tt Uu Vv Ww Xx Yy Zz

air: *The baby was sucking milk from its bottle.* • *She was sucking lemonade through a straw.*

2 to hold something in your mouth while making pulling movements with your lips and tongue: *My friend still sucks his thumb.* • *If your throat's sore, try sucking this sweet.*

3 to **suck something up** or **suck something in** is to draw it in: *The vacuum cleaner sucked up the crumbs.* • *She sucked in her cheeks.*

• NOUN• **sucks** the action of sucking: *She took a suck of her lollipop.*

♦ **sucker** •NOUN• **suckers 1** a part of an animal's body which it uses to stick to objects **2** a rubber or plastic pad that can be pressed on to a surface and sticks there

♦ **suckle** •VERB• **suckles, suckling, suckled** to feed a baby or young animal from the breast or udder: *The cow suckled her calf.*

♦ **suction** •NOUN• reducing the air in a place, and so producing a vacuum which draws in other air or things to fill the space

sudden •ADJECTIVE• happening quickly without being expected: *a sudden attack*

♦ **suddenly** •ADVERB• quickly and unexpectedly: *He suddenly woke up.*

♦ **suddenness** •NOUN• being sudden: *We were shocked by the suddenness of his death.*

suds •PLURAL NOUN• soap bubbles: *You get a lot of suds from a small quantity of washing powder.*

sue •VERB• **sues, suing, sued** to sue a person or organization is to start a law case against them, usually to try to get money from them

suede •NOUN• a kind of leather with a soft, dull surface which feels like velvet
•ADJECTIVE• made of suede: *a suede jacket*

suet •NOUN• a kind of hard animal fat used to make pastry and puddings

suffer •VERB• **suffers, suffering, suffered**
1 to feel pain or misery: *She suffered a lot of pain after the accident.* **2** to suffer from an illness or condition is to have it: *She suffers from headaches.*

♦ **suffering** •NOUN• pain and misery

sufficiency •NOUN• enough of something: *a sufficiency of food*

♦ **sufficient** •ADJECTIVE• enough: *We*

haven't sufficient food for all these people.

♦ **sufficiently** •ADVERB• to a sufficient degree: *I have not learned the song sufficiently to sing it in the concert.*

suffix •NOUN• **suffixes** a letter or group of letters that is added to the end of a word to make another word. For example, the suffixes *-ly* and *-ness* can be added to the word *kind* to make *kindly* and *kindness*. See the box called **Suffixes**

suffocate •VERB• **suffocates, suffocating, suffocated 1** to suffocate someone is to kill them through lack of oxygen: *The thick black smoke was suffocating him.* **2** to suffocate is to die through lack of oxygen: *Babies can suffocate if they sleep with a pillow.*

♦ **suffocation** •NOUN• suffocating or being suffocated: *The cause of death was suffocation.*

sugar •NOUN• white or brown grains that you add to food and drink to make them taste sweeter: *Do you take sugar in your coffee?*

♦ **sugary** •ADJECTIVE• very sweet: *a cup of hot, sugary tea*

suggest •VERB• **suggests, suggesting, suggested 1** to suggest something is to put it forward as an idea or a possibility: *He suggested a picnic.* • *I suggest that we have lunch now.* **2** to suggest something is to hint at it: *Are you suggesting that I'm too old for the job?*

♦ **suggestion** •NOUN• **suggestions 1** an idea put forward: *What a clever suggestion!* **2** a suggestion of something is a hint or trace of it: *There was a suggestion of anger in her voice.*

suicide •NOUN• **suicides** killing yourself: *to commit suicide*

suit •NOUN• **suits 1** a set of clothes, for example a jacket and trousers, made to be worn together: *Our teacher always wears a suit and tie.*

2 a piece of clothing worn for a particular activity: *a bathing-suit*

3 one of the four sets (spades, hearts, diamonds, clubs) of playing-cards

4 a case in a law court: *He won his suit.*

•VERB• **suits, suiting, suited** 1 something such as a colour, hairstyle or piece of clothing suits you when it makes you look nice: *Blue really suits her.* 2 something suits you when you are happy to agree to it: *Would it suit you if I called round this evening?*

♦ **suitable** •ADJECTIVE• something is suitable when it is right for a purpose or occasion: *High-heeled shoes aren't suitable for walking in the country.* • *What would be a suitable time for our meeting?*

♦ **suitability** •NOUN• being suitable: *I am not sure of his suitability for the job.*

suitcase •NOUN• **suitcases** a container with flat sides and a handle, to put your clothes in when you are travelling

suite •NOUN• **suites** 1 a set of rooms: *a hotel suite*

2 a set of furniture: *a three-piece suite*

3 a set of short pieces of music to be played one after the other: *He has composed a suite of music for the film.*

suitor •NOUN• **suitors** a man who wants to marry a woman: *The princess had many suitors.*

sulk •VERB• **sulks, sulking, sulked** to show that you are angry by being silent: *He's sulking because he's not allowed an ice-cream.*

♦ **sulky** •ADJECTIVE• **sulkier, sulkiest** 1 sulking: *She's in a sulky mood.* 2 tending to sulk: *a sulky girl*

sullen •ADJECTIVE• angry and silent: *a sullen young man*

sulphur •NOUN• a solid yellow substance found in the ground, which burns with a blue flame and an unpleasant smell and is used to make matches and gunpowder

sulphuric acid •NOUN• a strong acid containing sulphur

sultan •NOUN• **sultans** a ruler in certain Muslim countries: *the Sultan of Brunei*

sultana •NOUN• **sultanas** 1 a light-coloured seedless raisin 2 a sultan's wife

sum •NOUN• **sums** 1 the total made by two or more things or numbers added together: *The sum of 2, 3 and 4 is 9.*

2 a problem in arithmetic: *I'm better at sums than my mum.*

3 an amount of money: *It will cost an enormous sum to repair the roof.*

•VERB• **sums, summing, summed** to **sum up** is to give the main points of something such as a discussion or evidence given in court: *So, to sum up, my main points were as follows ..*

summarize or **summarise** •VERB• **summarizes, summarizing, summarized** to give a shortened version of something: *He summarized the arguments.*

summary •NOUN• **summaries** a shortened form of something, giving only the main points: *A summary of his speech was printed in the newspaper.*

summer •NOUN• **summers** the warmest season of the year, between spring and autumn

•ADJECTIVE• happening or used after spring and before autumn: *summer clothes* • *summer holidays*

summit •NOUN• **summits** 1 the top of a hill or mountain 2 a meeting between heads of governments

summon •VERB• **summons, summoning, summoned** 1 to summon someone is to order them to come: *The headmaster summoned her to his room.* 2 to **summon up** something such as strength or courage is to gather it: *At last I summoned up the courage to tell him.*

♦ **summons** •NOUN• **summonses** an order to appear in court

sun •NOUN• **suns** 1 the star in the sky that you see as a huge white disc, and which gives light and heat to the Earth: *The Earth goes round the sun.* 2 sunshine: *We sat in the sun.*

sunbathe •VERB• **sunbathes, sunbathing, sunbathed** to lie or sit in the sun in order to get a suntan

sunbeam •NOUN• **sunbeams** a ray of light from the sun

sunburn •NOUN• redness and soreness of the skin caused by being out in the sun for too long

sundae •NOUN• **sundaes** a portion of ice-cream served with fruit, syrup or cream: *I think I'll have the toffee nut sundae.*

Aa Bb Cc Dd Ee Ff Gg Hh Ii Jj Kk Ll Mm Nn Oo Pp Qq Rr Ss Tt Uu Vv Ww Xx Yy Zz

Sunday •NOUN• **Sundays** the day of the week after Saturday and before Monday: *My parents always go to church on Sundays.*

ⓘ **Sunday** comes from the Old English word **Sunnandæg**, which means *day of the sun*.

sundial •NOUN• **sundials** an instrument that uses sunlight to cast a shadow and show the time

sunflower •NOUN• **sunflowers** a tall yellow flower whose seeds provide oil

sung •VERB• the form of the verb **sing** that is used with a helping verb to tell you that something happened in the past: *I've sung that song all day.*

sunglasses •PLURAL NOUN• dark glasses which protect your eyes from bright sunlight

sunk •VERB• the form of the verb **sink** that is used with a helping verb to tell you that something happened in the past: *The ship had sunk in minutes.*
♦ **sunken** •ADJECTIVE• **1** under water: *sunken treasure* **2** lower than the surrounding area: *a sunken bath*

sunlight •NOUN• the light of the sun: *Bright sunlight shone in through the window.*
♦ **sunlit** •ADJECTIVE• lit up by the sun: *a sunlit room*

sunny •ADJECTIVE• **sunnier, sunniest 1** full of sunshine: *It's a lovely sunny day.* **2** cheerful: *her sunny nature*

sunrise •NOUN• **sunrises** the rising of the sun in the morning, or the time of this: *a spectacular sunrise* • *I was up at sunrise.*

sunset •NOUN• **sunsets** the setting of the sun in the evening, or the time of this: *a beautiful golden sunset* • *The younger children were in bed by sunset.*

sunshine •NOUN• the light and heat of the sun: *The cat was enjoying the warm sunshine.*

sunstroke •NOUN• an illness caused by staying out in hot sun for too long

suntan •NOUN• **suntans** a brown colour of the skin, caused by the sun: *She thinks a suntan makes her look healthy.*

super •ADJECTIVE• extremely good or excellent: *We had a super time at the funfair.*

super- •PREFIX• if a word starts with **super-** it has the meaning of *above* or *beyond*. For example, someone who is *superhuman* has abilities which are beyond those of a normal person

superb •ADJECTIVE• magnificent or excellent: *The view from our balcony was superb.*

superficial •ADJECTIVE• **1** affecting the surface only: *The wound is only superficial.* • *The building suffered superficial damage.* **2** not deep or detailed: *a superficial knowledge of history*

superintendent •NOUN• **superintendents 1** a senior police officer **2** someone who is in charge of something such as a building or department

superior •ADJECTIVE• **1** higher in rank, better or greater: *Is a captain superior to a commander in the navy?* • *With his superior strength he defeated his opponent.* **2** thinking yourself better than others: *I can't stand her superior attitude.*
•NOUN• **superiors** a person who is better than, or has a higher rank than, others: *You should always respect your superiors.*
♦ **superiority** •NOUN• being superior: *his superiority over others*

superlative •NOUN• **superlatives** in grammar, the superlative form of an adjective or adverb is the form that usually ends with *-est* or is used with *most*. For example, *hardest, worst* and *most difficult* are superlative forms. See the box called **Comparison of adjectives**

supermarket •NOUN• **supermarkets** a large self-service shop that sells food and other goods

supernatural •ADJECTIVE• not natural or normal and impossible to explain: *supernatural happenings*

supernova •NOUN• **supernovae** or **supernovas** an exploding star surrounded by a bright cloud of gas

supersonic •ADJECTIVE• faster than the speed of sound: *a supersonic aeroplane*

superstition •NOUN• **superstitions 1** belief

Aa Bb Cc Dd Ee Ff Gg Hh Ii Jj Kk Ll Mm Nn Oo Pp Qq Rr Ss Tt Uu Vv Ww Xx Yy Zz

Aa
Bb
Cc
Dd
Ee
Ff
Gg
Hh
Ii
Jj
Kk
Ll
Mm
Nn
Oo
Pp
Qq
Rr
Ss
Tt
Uu
Vv
Ww
Xx
Yy
Zz

in magic and other strange powers **2** an example of this kind of belief: *There is an old superstition that walking under a ladder will bring you bad luck.*

• **superstitious** •ADJECTIVE• a superstitious person believes in superstitions

supervise •VERB• **supervises, supervising, supervised** to supervise something is to be in charge of it: *Who supervises this department?* • *His job is to supervise the factory workers.*

• **supervision** •NOUN• the act of supervising: *The prisoner was kept under close supervision.*

• **supervisor** •NOUN• **supervisors** a person whose job is to make sure that other people's work is done properly

supper •NOUN• **supper** a meal that you eat in the evening: *She has invited us to supper.*

supple •ADJECTIVE• **suppler, supplest** a supple person is able to bend and stretch easily: *Take exercise if you want to stay supple.*

• **suppleness** •NOUN• being suppleness

supplement •NOUN• **supplements 1** something extra that is added to something: *The supplement to the dictionary contains hundreds of new words.* **2** an extra part of a newspaper or magazine that comes with the main part: *Mum likes to read the Sunday supplement.*

•VERB• **supplements, supplementing, supplemented** to supplement something is to make it bigger by adding something else: *He supplements his wages by working in the evening.*

• **supplementary** •ADJECTIVE• extra or additional: *a few supplementary questions*

supply •VERB• **supplies, supplying, supplied** to supply something is to give or provide it: *The shop was unable to supply what she wanted.* • *The teacher will supply you with more paper.*

•NOUN• **supplies 1** supply is supplying something. *The company is involved in the supply of weapons to the Middle East.* **2** a supply is a stock or store: *a supply of food* •ADJECTIVE• a supply teacher takes another teacher's place for a time

support •VERB• **supports, supporting, supported 1** to support something is to carry its weight: *That chair won't support him.*

2 to support someone is to provide the money that they need to live: *He has a wife and two children to support.*

3 to support someone or something is to help and encourage them: *His family supported his decision.*
•NOUN• **supports 1** support is the action of supporting **2** a support is something such as a column or pillar which takes the weight of something else: *One of the supports of the bridge collapsed.*

• **supporter** •NOUN• **supporters** someone who supports something, especially a sports team: *a Liverpool supporter*

suppose •VERB• **supposes, supposing, supposed 1** to believe that something is probably so: *I suppose you'll be going to the concert.* **2** to consider something as a possibility: *Suppose you had £100 – what would you buy?*

• **supposed** •ADJECTIVE• **1** believed to be so even if it is not true: *her supposed generosity* **2** you are **supposed to** do something when people expect you to do it: *You were supposed to come straight home after school.*

• **supposedly** •ADVERB• so it is believed: *He is supposedly one of the best doctors in the country.*

suppress •VERB• **suppresses, suppressing, suppressed 1** to keep something back: *She suppressed a laugh.* **2** to defeat something such as a rebellion

• **suppression** •NOUN• the act of suppressing something: *the suppression of information*

supremacy •NOUN• being the most powerful: *the supremacy of the president*

supreme •ADJECTIVE• **1** most powerful: *the supreme ruler* **2** greatest: *supreme courage*

sure •ADJECTIVE• **1** you are sure of something when you have no doubts about it: *I'm sure I gave him the book.*

2 certain to do or get something: *He's sure to win.*

3 able to be trusted: *a sure way to cure hiccups*

•ADVERB• an informal way of saying 'of course' or 'certainly': *Sure I'll help you!*

◆ **surely** •ADVERB• **1** certainly, without doubt: *If you go near the pond you will surely fall in.* **2** surely is sometimes used to express a little doubt: *Surely you won't tell him.*

surf •NOUN• the foam made when waves break on rocks or on the shore
•VERB• **surfs, surfing, surfed 1** to ride on waves towards the shore, standing or lying on a surfboard **2** to surf the Internet is to browse through it looking at different websites
⇒ **surfer, surfing**

surface •NOUN• **surfaces** the outside or top part of something: *This road has a very bumpy surface.*
•VERB• **surfaces, surfacing, surfaced 1** to surface is to come up to the surface of water: *The submarine surfaced close to the ship.* **2** to surface something such as a road or path is to put a hard top layer on it: *They are surfacing this road with tarmac.*
•ADJECTIVE• travelling on the surface of land or water: *surface mail*

surfboard •NOUN• **surfboards** a long narrow board used in surfing

surfer •NOUN• **surfers** a person who surfs

surfing •NOUN• the sport of balancing on a surfboard and riding on waves towards the shore

surge •VERB• **surges, surging, surged** to suddenly move forward or upward: *The crowd surged towards the fire exit.*
•NOUN• a sudden rush: *He felt a surge of pain.*

surgeon •NOUN• **surgeons** a doctor who carries out operations

surgery •NOUN• **surgeries 1** the work of a surgeon, carrying out operations: *to specialize in surgery* **2** the room where a doctor or dentist examines their patients

surgical •ADJECTIVE• to do with a surgeon or his work: *surgical techniques*
◆ **surgically** •ADVERB• by means of an operation: *The lump will have to be surgically removed.*

surly •ADJECTIVE• **surlier, surliest** bad-tempered and rude: *He spoke in a surly voice.*

surname •NOUN• **surnames** your last name or family name: *Smith is a common British surname.*

surpass •VERB• **surpasses, surpassing, surpassed** to be or do better than: *His work surpassed my expectations.*

surplus •NOUN• **surpluses** an amount left over after what is needed has been taken away: *This country produces a surplus of grain.*
•ADJECTIVE• extra, left over: *We have surplus food.*

surprise •NOUN• **surprises 1** something sudden or unexpected: *Your letter was a nice surprise.* **2** the feeling caused by something sudden or unexpected: *He stared at her in surprise.*
•VERB• **surprises, surprising, surprised 1** to surprise someone is to cause them to feel surprise: *The news surprised me.* **2** to surprise someone is also to come upon them suddenly and without warning: *They surprised the enemy from the rear.*

surrender •VERB• **surrenders, surrendering, surrendered 1** to surrender is to give up: *They surrendered to the enemy.* **2** to surrender something is to give it up or hand it over: *She surrendered the note to the teacher.*
•NOUN• an act of surrendering: *the surrender of the fort to the enemy*

surround •VERB• **surrounds, surrounding, surrounded 1** to surround someone or something is to be or come all round them: *Enemy troops surrounded the town.* **2** to surround something is to enclose it or put something round it: *He surrounded the castle with a high wall.*
◆ **surroundings** •PLURAL NOUN• the area around a person or place: *The hotel is set in beautiful surroundings.* • *He was glad to be back in his own surroundings.*

survey •VERB• **surveys, surveying, surveyed** to survey something is to look at it or inspect it: *She surveyed her garden from the window.*
•NOUN• **surveys 1** an investigation into what

people think: *Would you mind answering some questions? I'm doing a survey.* 2 an inspection or examination

survival • NOUN • staying alive: *His survival depended on finding fresh water.*

survive • VERB • **survives, surviving, survived** to stay alive: *He didn't survive long after the accident.*

◆ **survivor** • NOUN • **survivors** someone who stays alive: *the only survivor of the crash*

suspect • VERB • **suspects, suspecting, suspected** 1 to suspect someone is to think that they have done something wrong: *I suspect her of the crime.* 2 to suspect something is to think that it is likely: *I suspect that she is hiding her true feelings.*
• NOUN • **suspects** someone who is thought to have done something wrong: *There are three suspects in this murder case.*

(i) The verb is pronounced sus-**pect**, with the stress on *pect*.
The noun is pronounced **sus**-pect, with the stress on *sus*.

---

suspend • VERB • **suspends, suspending, suspended** 1 to suspend something is to hang it: *The meat was suspended from a hook.*
2 to suspend something is to stop it for a while: *All business will be suspended until after New Year.*
3 to suspend someone is to stop them doing their job or taking part in an activity for a time: *suspended from the team for bad behaviour*

suspense • NOUN • a state of feeling uncertain and anxious: *We waited in suspense for the result.*

suspension • NOUN • 1 suspending something or someone: *a two-week suspension from school* 2 the system of springs that supports a motor vehicle, making it more comfortable to ride in

suspension bridge • NOUN • **suspension bridges** a type of bridge that is suspended from cables hanging from towers

suspicion • NOUN • **suspicions** 1 a thought or feeling that something is likely: *I have a suspicion she is not telling the truth.* 2 a

feeling of doubting on not trusting: *They looked at each other with suspicion.*
◆ **suspicious** • ADJECTIVE • 1 feeling or showing suspicion: *She gave him a suspicious glance.* 2 causing suspicion: *He died in suspicious circumstances.*
◆ **suspiciously** • ADVERB • in a suspicious way: *She looked at him suspiciously.* • *acting suspiciously*

sustain • VERB • **sustains, sustaining, sustained** 1 to sustain someone is to give help and strength to them: *a few sandwiches to sustain you during the journey*
2 to sustain an injury is to suffer it: *He sustained head injuries in the crash.*
3 to sustain something is to keep it up or keep it going: *It would be difficult to sustain such a fast pace.*
◆ **sustenance** • NOUN • food and drink: *We need sustenance if we are to carry on.*

swab • NOUN • **swabs** 1 a piece of cotton wool used for example to clean wounds or soak up blood 2 a sample of fluid taken from the body for examination: *The doctor took a swab from her throat to check for infection.*

swaddling clothes • PLURAL NOUN • in olden times, strips of cloth used to wrap up a small baby

swag • NOUN • in Australia, a bundle containing a traveller's belongings

swagger • VERB • **swaggers, swaggering, swaggered** to walk as though pleased with yourself, swinging the arms and body: *He swaggered along the street in his new suit.*
• NOUN • **swaggers** a proud and confident way of walking

swallow[1] • VERB • **swallows, swallowing, swallowed** 1 to swallow food or drink is to make it pass down your throat to your stomach: *Try to swallow the pill.*
2 to swallow something such as a lie or an insult is to accept it without question: *She'll never swallow that story!*
3 to **swallow something up** is to make it disappear: *She was swallowed up in the crowd.*
• NOUN • **swallows** an act of swallowing: *He took all the medicine in one swallow.*

swallow² •NOUN• a small bird with long pointed wings and a forked tail

swamp •NOUN• **swamps** a piece of wet, marshy ground: *These plants grow best in swamps.*
•VERB• **swamps, swamping, swamped** 1 to swamp something is to flood it: *A great wave swamped the deck.* 2 to swamp someone is to overload them with something: *I'm swamped with work.*

swan •NOUN• **swans** a large, usually white, water bird with a long neck

swap •VERB• **swaps, swapping, swapped** to exchange one thing for another: *They swapped books with each other.* • *She swapped her bike with another girl for a scooter.*

swarm •NOUN• **swarms** a large number of insects flying or moving together: *a swarm of bees*
•VERB• **swarms, swarming, swarmed** 1 to move in great numbers: *The children swarmed out of the school.* 2 to be swarming with something is to be crowded with it: *streets swarming with tourists*

swarthy •ADJECTIVE• **swarthier, swarthiest** dark-skinned

swashbuckling •ADJECTIVE• full of adventure and excitement: *a swashbuckling story of buccaneers*

swastika •NOUN• **swastikas** a cross with its arms bent at right angles, used as the sign of the German Nazi party

swat •VERB• **swats, swatting, swatted** to swat a fly is to crush it
•NOUN• **swats** a device for crushing flies, usually with a long handle and a flat end

sway •VERB• **sways, swaying, swayed** 1 to sway is to move from side to side with a swinging action: *She swayed in time to the music.* 2 to sway someone is to guide or influence them: *She's too easily swayed by her friends' opinions.*

swear •VERB• **swears, swearing, swore, sworn** 1 to promise: *I swear to tell the truth.* 2 to use words that are offensive: *He swore under his breath.* 3 to swear someone to something is to

make them give a promise about it: *The children were sworn to secrecy.*
4 to **swear by** something is to believe in it completely: *He swears by plenty of sleep.*

sweat •NOUN• the salty liquid that comes out of your skin when you are hot: *He was dripping with sweat after his run.*
•VERB• **sweats, sweating, sweated** to give out sweat: *Exercise makes you sweat.*
♦ **sweater** •NOUN• **sweaters** a jersey or pullover
⇒ **sweaty**

sweatshirt •NOUN• **sweatshirts** a type of thick jersey

sweaty •ADJECTIVE• **sweatier, sweatiest** wet with sweat: *I feel all sweaty.* • *Put those sweaty socks in the wash basket.*

swede •NOUN• **swedes** a kind of large round yellow vegetable like a turnip

sweep •VERB• **sweeps, sweeping, swept**
1 to sweep something is to clean it using a brush or broom: *He swept the floor.*
2 to sweep is to move quickly or forcefully: *The disease is sweeping through the country.* • *She swept into my room without knocking.*
3 to sweep someone or something is to move them with a sweeping movement: *The wind nearly swept me off my feet.* • *Whole villages were swept away by the flood.*
•NOUN• **sweeps** 1 the action of sweeping: *She gave the room a sweep.*
2 a sweeping movement: *He indicated the damage with a sweep of his hand.*
3 a person who cleans chimneys
♦ **sweeper** •NOUN• **sweepers** in football, a defensive player who stays behind the other defenders

sweepstake •NOUN• a system of gambling in which the prize money is the sum of the money gambled by all those taking part

sweet •ADJECTIVE• **sweeter, sweetest**
1 tasting like sugar: *strong sweet tea*
2 pleasant: *the sweet smell of flowers* • *the sweet song of the nightingale*
3 attractive or nice: *My baby brother is very sweet.*
•NOUN• **sweets** 1 a small piece of sweet food, for example chocolate or toffee: *a packet of sweets* 2 something sweet served

Aa
at the end of a meal: *Would you like to see the sweet menu?*
⇒ **sweeten, sweetly, sweetness**

Bb

sweetcorn •NOUN• sweetcorn is the yellow grains of a cereal crop called maize, that are eaten as a vegetable

Cc

Dd
sweeten •VERB• **sweetens, sweetening, sweetened 1** to sweeten something is to make it sweet: *Sweeten the raspberries with sugar.* **2** to sweeten is to become sweet: *Her smile sweetened.*

Ee

Ff

Gg
sweetheart •NOUN• **sweethearts** a boyfriend or girlfriend: *They were childhood sweethearts.*

Hh

li
sweetly •ADVERB• in a sweet way: *She smiled sweetly.*

Jj
sweetness •NOUN• being sweet

Kk
sweet pea •NOUN• **sweet peas** a climbing flower with a sweet smell, grown in gardens

Ll
sweet tooth •NOUN• a liking for things that taste sweet: *She never refuses chocolate – she has a very sweet tooth.*

Mm

Nn
swell •VERB• **swells, swelling, swelled, swollen 1** to swell is to get bigger: *The wasp sting made her finger swell.* **2** to swell something is to make it bigger: *Heavy rain had swollen the river.*

Oo
•NOUN• swell is the up and down movement of the sea when there are no breaking waves

Pp

Qq
•ADJECTIVE• an informal way of saying 'very good' that is used in American English: *What a swell idea!*

Rr

Ss
♦ **swelling** •NOUN• **swellings** a swollen part of the body: *She had a swelling on her arm where she had been stung.*

Tt
swelter •VERB• **swelters, sweltering, sweltered** to be too hot: *I'm sweltering in this heat!*

Uu

Vv
♦ **sweltering** •ADJECTIVE• very hot: *It's sweltering today.*

Ww
swept •VERB• a way of changing the verb **sweep** to make a past tense. It can be used with or without a helping verb: *He swept up the crumbs.* • *She has swept the floor.*

Xx

Yy
swerve •VERB• **swerves, swerving, swerved** to turn quickly to one side: *The driver had to swerve to miss the dog.*

Zz
•NOUN• **swerves** a quick turn to one side: *The*

bus gave a sudden swerve and I fell off my seat.

swift •ADJECTIVE• **swifter, swiftest** fast or quick: *a swift recovery*
•NOUN• **swifts** a small bird rather like a swallow
♦ **swiftly** •ADVERB• quickly: *'No way,' she answered swiftly.*
♦ **swiftness** •NOUN• being swift

swill •VERB• **swills, swilling, swilled** to swill something is to wash it out: *He swilled out the cups.*
•NOUN• leftover food mixed with water, given to pigs to eat

swim •VERB• **swims, swimming, swam, swum**
1 to swim is to move through water: *I learned to swim when I was five.*
2 to swim something is to cross it by swimming: *Her ambition is to swim the Channel.*
3 to be swimming in a liquid is to be covered with it: *meat swimming in grease*
4 if your head swims you feel dizzy
•NOUN• **swims** an act of swimming: *I think I'll go for a swim.*
♦ **swimmer** •NOUN• **swimmers** someone or something that swims: *Penguins are excellent swimmers.*

swimming baths •PLURAL NOUN• a place with a pool or pools of water, where people can go and swim

swimming costume •NOUN• **swimming costumes** a piece of clothing worn for swimming, usually by women and girls

swimming pool •NOUN• **swimming pools** an indoor or outdoor pool for swimming in

swimsuit •NOUN• **swimsuits** a piece of clothing worn for swimming, usually by women and girls

swindle •VERB• **swindles, swindling, swindled** to swindle someone is to cheat them, especially out of money: *That shopkeeper has swindled me out of £2!*
•NOUN• **swindles** an act of swindling: *I paid £20 for this watch and it doesn't work. What a swindle!*
♦ **swindler** •NOUN• **swindlers** a person who swindles others

ⓘ This word comes from the German word **Schwindler**, which means a *cheat*.

swine •NOUN• **swine 1** an old word for a pig **2** a rude word for someone who treats others badly: *He left me to pay the bill, the swine!*

swineherd •NOUN• **swineherds** in olden times, someone who looked after pigs

swing •VERB• **swings, swinging, swung 1** to move from side to side, or forwards and backwards from a fixed point: *You swing your arms when you walk.* • *The children were swinging on a rope hanging from a tree.* **2** to turn suddenly: *He swung round and stared at us.*
•NOUN• **swings 1** a seat for swinging, hung on ropes or chains from a support: *After we've fed the ducks, we'll go to the swings.* **2** a swinging movement: *the swing of a pendulum*
• **in full swing** going on busily: *The party was in full swing.*

swipe •VERB• **swipes, swiping, swiped** to swipe someone or something is to hit them with a heavy sweeping blow: *She swiped me across the face.*
•NOUN• **swipes** a heavy sweeping blow: *He took a swipe at the ball.*

swirl •VERB• **swirls, swirling, swirled** to move quickly round in circles: *Leaves swirled along the ground.*
•NOUN• **swirls** a swirling movement: *The dancers came on stage in a swirl of colour.*

swish •VERB• **swishes, swishing, swished** to move with a rustling sound: *Her long skirt swished as she danced.*
•NOUN• **swishes** a swishing sound: *He opened the curtains with a swish.*

switch •NOUN• **switches 1** a device for turning power on and off: *I can't find the light-switch.* **2** a change: *After several switches of direction they were at last on the right road.*
•VERB• **switches, switching, switched 1** to switch something on or off is to turn it on or off using a switch **2** to switch something is to change it: *Jane switched her job to become a driver.*

switchboard •NOUN• **switchboards** a board with lots of switches for making connections by telephone

swivel •VERB• **swivels, swivelling, swivelled** to turn round: *She swivelled her chair round to face the desk.* • *I swivelled round to look at him.*

swollen •ADJECTIVE• bigger than usual because of swelling: *He had a swollen ankle after falling downstairs.*
•VERB• the form of the verb **swell** that is used with a helping verb to show that something happened in the past: *Her face had swollen up with crying.*

swoon •VERB• **swoons, swooning, swooned** an old-fashioned word that means to faint: *She nearly swooned when the group appeared on stage.*
•NOUN• **swoons** an old word for a faint: *She fell into a swoon.*

swoop •VERB• **swoops, swooping, swooped** to rush or fly downwards: *The owl swooped down on its prey.*
•NOUN• **swoops** a sudden downward rush

swop •VERB• **swops, swopping, swopped** another spelling of **swap**

sword •NOUN• **swords** a weapon with a long blade

swordfish •NOUN• **swordfish** *or* **swordfishes** a type of large fish with a long pointed upper jaw like a sword

swore •VERB• a way of changing the verb **swear** to make a past tense: *She swore to tell the truth.*

sworn •VERB• the form of the verb **swear** that is used with a helping verb to show that something happened in the past: *He has sworn he will never tell anyone.*
•ADJECTIVE• promised always to be something: *They are sworn enemies.*

swot •VERB• **swots, swotting, swotted** to study hard: *She has been swotting for her exams.*
•NOUN• **swots** a person who studies hard or too hard: *His friends think he's a swot because he spent two days preparing for the test.*

sycamore •NOUN• **sycamores** a type of large tree with winged seeds

syllable •NOUN• **syllables** a word or part of a word that is a single sound. For example, *pen* has one syllable, *pen-cil* has two and *com-pu-ter* has three

Aa
Bb
Cc
Dd
Ee
Ff
Gg
Hh
Ii
Jj
Kk
Ll
Mm
Nn
Oo
Pp
Qq
Rr
Ss
Tt
Uu
Vv
Ww
Xx
Yy
Zz

Synonyms

Bb

Cc

Dd

Ee

Ff

Gg

Hh

Ii

Jj

Kk

Ll

Mm

Nn

Oo

Pp

Qq

Rr

Ss

Tt

Uu

Vv

Ww

Xx

Yy

Zz

Synonyms are words that have a meaning similar to another word. For example, **miserable**, **upset** and **unhappy** are synonyms of **sad**.

Using different synonyms rather than repeating the same word over and over again makes your writing more interesting. For example, see how using synonyms for **nice** makes the following passage more lively:

Last summer, we had a ~~nice~~ *wonderful* holiday in a ~~nice~~ *beautiful* resort. We stayed in a ~~nice~~ *charming* hotel which had a ~~nice~~ *spectacular* view of the sea. We had ~~nice~~ *gorgeous* weather and met a ~~nice~~ *friendly* family, who took us to a ~~nice~~ *fantastic* funfair with ~~nice~~ *thrilling* rides.

Here are some synonyms for common words:

afraid	frightened, scared, terrified
angry	annoyed, furious, raging
bad	*a bad person:* evil, naughty, wicked
	bad food: mouldy, rotten, sour
	a bad experience: awful, dreadful, unpleasant
big	enormous, huge, large
good	*a good person:* honest, kind, thoughtful
	a good event: enjoyable, exciting, excellent
	good at something: capable, skilful, talented
happy	cheerful, delighted, glad
little	short, small, tiny
nice	*a nice experience:* delightful, enjoyable, lovely
	a nice place: beautiful, charming, spectacular
	a nice person: friendly, pleasant, warm
	nice weather: fine, sunny, warm
answer	agree, respond, reply
ask	beg, inquire, plead
say	claim, exclaim, remark
tell	announce, explain, inform

Use a **thesaurus**, which is a reference book full of synonyms, to find different words for something. Try out different ones in a sentence and see which one sounds the best.

syllabus •NOUN• **syllabuses** or **syllabi** a list of things to be studied by a class

symbol •NOUN• **symbols** 1 a mark or sign that is used as a short form of something, for example + meaning *plus* and O meaning *oxygen* 2 something that stands for something else: *The dove is a symbol of peace.*
♦ **symbolic** •ADJECTIVE• used as a sign or symbol of something: *The gift was a symbolic gesture of friendship.*
♦ **symbolize** or **symbolise** •VERB• **symbolizes, symbolizing, symbolized** to symbolize something is to be a symbol of it: *A ring symbolizes everlasting love.*

symmetrical •ADJECTIVE• having symmetry: *The two sides of a person's face are never completely symmetrical.*
♦ **symmetry** •NOUN• the state of two parts or halves being exactly the same but the opposite way round, as if one were a mirror image of the other

sympathetic •ADJECTIVE• feeling or showing sympathy: *a sympathetic smile*
♦ **sympathetically** •ADVERB• in a sympathetic way: *She patted his hand sympathetically.*

sympathize or **sympathise** •VERB• **sympathizes, sympathizing, sympathized** to sympathize with someone is to feel or show sympathy for them: *I sympathize with your trouble.* • *I'm afraid I cannot help, I can only sympathize.*

sympathy •NOUN• **sympathies** 1 the feeling of being sorry for someone in trouble: *She received many letters of sympathy when her husband died.* 2 the sharing of the thoughts and opinions of others: *Are you in sympathy with the strikers?*

symphony •NOUN• **symphonies** a long piece of music to be played by an orchestra

symptom •NOUN• **symptoms** a symptom of an illness is a sign that someone has that illness: *A cold, fever and headache are the usual symptoms of flu.*

synagogue •NOUN• **synagogues** a Jewish place of worship

syndrome •NOUN• **syndromes** a group of symptoms which are the sign of a particular illness

synonym •NOUN• **synonyms** a word that means the same, or nearly the same, as another word. For example, *angry* and *cross* are synonyms. See the box called **Synonyms**

syntax •NOUN• the grammar rules to do with the position words may have in a sentence and how they relate to each other: *He finds English syntax difficult to understand.*

synthesis •NOUN• **syntheses** 1 the making of a product by combining different chemical substances: *Plastic is produced by synthesis.* 2 a mixture: *His latest plan is a synthesis of old and new ideas.*
♦ **synthesizer** or **synthesiser** •NOUN• **synthesizers** or **synthesisers** an electronic musical instrument that makes the sounds of various other musical instruments
♦ **synthetic** •ADJECTIVE• not real: *synthetic leather*

syringe •NOUN• **syringes** a small instrument shaped like a cylinder with a needle attached to it, used for injecting liquids into the body or for taking blood out of the body

syrup •NOUN• **syrups** a thick sticky liquid made by boiling water or fruit juice with sugar: *hot pancakes covered with syrup*

system •NOUN• **systems** 1 an arrangement of many parts that work together: *the railway system* 2 a way of organizing something: *a system of education*
♦ **systematic** •ADJECTIVE• well planned and following a system: *a systematic search of the area*

Aa
Bb
Cc
Dd
Ee
Ff
Gg
Hh
Ii
Jj
Kk
Ll
Mm
Nn
Oo
Pp
Qq
Rr
Ss
Tt
Uu
Vv
Ww
Xx
Yy
Zz

Tt

tab • NOUN• **tabs** a small piece of fabric, metal or paper attached to something and used to hang it up, identify it, open it, or hold it by

tabard • NOUN• **tabards** a tunic with no sleeves that hangs loosely from the shoulders

tabby • NOUN• **tabbies** 1 a cat with grey or brown fur marked with darker stripes 2 a female cat

table • NOUN• **tables** 1 a piece of furniture with a flat top that is supported on legs
2 figures or words laid out in rows and columns
3 a list of sums and the answers, which you learn by heart: *Do you know the five times table?*
• **turn the tables on someone** to turn the tables on someone is to change the situation around completely so that they are in the position, usually a bad or uncomfortable one, that they had put you in before

tablecloth • NOUN• **tablecloths** a cloth for covering a table

tablespoon • NOUN• **tablespoons** a large size of spoon, often used for measuring cooking ingredients
♦ **tablespoonful** • NOUN• **tablespoonfuls** the amount that a tablespoon will hold

tablet • NOUN• **tablets** 1 a pill
2 a flat solid piece of something, such as soap or chocolate
3 a flat surface, usually made of stone or wood, with words carved on it

table tennis • NOUN• an indoor game for two or four players in which a light hollow ball is hit with small rounded bats across a net on a table

tabloid • NOUN• **tabloids** a newspaper printed on pages that are almost square rather than rectangular, and often having lots of pictures

taboo • NOUN• **taboos** a taboo is anything people are not allowed to do, especially for religious or social reasons
• ADJECTIVE• forbidden: *a taboo subject*

tack • NOUN• **tacks** 1 a short nail with a broad flat head and a sharp point 2 a course of action or way of approaching something: *We aren't getting anywhere, so we need to try a different tack.*
• VERB• **tacks, tacking, tacked** 1 to tack something is to fasten it with tacks 2 to tack pieces of fabric is to sew them together with large loose temporary stitches

tackle • VERB• **tackles, tackling, tackled**
1 you tackle a job or problem when you try to deal with it
2 you tackle someone when you ask them directly about something they have done wrong or that they should have done
3 in games like football and rugby, you tackle a player in the other team when you try to get the ball from them
• NOUN• **tackles** 1 tackle is equipment: *fishing tackle* • *lifting tackle* 2 a tackle is the movement a rugby, football or hockey player makes to try to get the ball from a player in the other team

tacky • ADJECTIVE• **tackier, tackiest** 1 if glue is tacky, it is still rather sticky because it hasn't dried completely 2 cheap and badly made or in bad taste

tact • NOUN• the ability to avoid hurting people's feelings or offending them
♦ **tactful** • ADJECTIVE• with tact
♦ **tactfully** • ADVERB• in a tactful way
⇒ **tactless**

tactic • NOUN• **tactics** someone's tactics are the things they do or the methods they use to get what they want or to help them win
♦ **tactical** • ADJECTIVE• a tactical action or move is cleverly worked out to achieve the best result

tactless • ADJECTIVE• thoughtless and not considering other people's feelings

tadpole • NOUN• **tadpoles** a young frog or

toad with a rounded head and long tail, which eventually disappears as it develops legs

taffeta •NOUN• a stiff shiny silk fabric or a silky fabric with raised ridges on its surface

tag¹ •NOUN• **tags** a label with information such as someone's name printed on it •VERB• **tags, tagging, tagged 1** to tag something is to put a tag or label on it **2** if someone **tags along** with another person they go with that person somewhere, often without being invited

tag² •NOUN• a children's game in which one player chases the other players and if he or she manages to catch and touch someone, the player who has been touched then has to chase the others

tail •NOUN• **tails 1** an animal's, bird's or fish's tail is the part of its body that sticks out from the end of its spine or at the end of its body **2** any part that sticks out, or hangs down, at the back of an object : *The aeroplane had a red and black symbol painted on its tail.* • *His shirt tail was hanging out.* •VERB• **tails, tailing, tailed 1** to tail someone is to follow them, usually to watch what they do or where they go **2** if something **tails off**, it gets less and less, or smaller and smaller, until it eventually disappears

tailor •NOUN• **tailors** someone whose job is making suits, coats or other pieces of clothing •VERB• **tailors, tailoring, tailored 1** to tailor clothes is to make them so that they fit well **2** to tailor something for a particular purpose is to design it specially for that purpose

tails •PLURAL NOUN• the side of a coin opposite the side that has the head on it: *Call heads or tails.*

taint •VERB• **taints, tainting, tainted** to taint something is to add something bad or unpleasant to it so that it is spoiled

take •VERB• **takes, taking, took, taken 1** you take something when you reach out and get it or get it for yourself: *Take my hand.* • *I'm taking piano lessons.* • *Someone's taken my ruler.*
   2 to take someone or something to a place is to bring them or it with you when you go there: *Take me to your leader.* • *I took the parcel to the post office.*

3 you take one number from another when you subtract the first one from the second one: *If you take 5 from 16, you are left with 11.*
   4 you take something when you eat it, drink it or swallow it: *You must take your medicine if you want to get better quickly.*
   5 to take something is to accept it: *Take my advice. Wear a warm jumper when you go out.* • *He cannot take criticism.*
   6 to take something such as a form of transport or a route is to use it: *We usually take the bus rather than the train.* • *Take the next left after the town hall.*
   7 you take an exam or test when you do it
   8 to take a photograph is to use a camera to record an image
   9 something takes a certain length of time if it lasts for that length of time or you need that amounts of time to do it: *The journey took hours and hours.*
   10 if a space or container takes a certain amount it has enough room for it: *This jug takes nearly two pints.*
   11 take is used with nouns to refer to actions: *Let's take a look at that sore leg of yours.* • *He took a leap.*
   12 to **take someone in** is to deceive them
   13 a plane **takes off** when it leaves the ground at the beginning of a flight
   14 to **take over** from someone is to replace them and do what they had been doing
   15 to **take up** a hobby or other activity is to start doing it

take-away •NOUN• **take-aways** a cooked meal that you buy at a shop or restaurant and take away with you to eat somewhere else

take-off •NOUN• **take-offs** the moment when an aeroplane leaves the ground at the beginning of a flight

takings •PLURAL NOUN• the amount of money that is taken in a shop, or at a concert or other event that people pay to see or take part in

talc •NOUN• talcum powder

talcum powder •NOUN• a fine powder, usually with a pleasant scent, that people put on their bodies

tale •NOUN• **tales** a story: *tales of great adventures*

Aa
Bb
Cc
Dd
Ee
Ff
Gg
Hh
Ii
Jj
Kk
Ll
Mm
Nn
Oo
Pp
Qq
Rr
Ss
Tt
Uu
Vv
Ww
Xx
Yy
Zz

Aa
Bb
Cc
Dd
Ee
Ff
Gg
Hh
Ii
Jj
Kk
Ll
Mm
Nn
Oo
Pp
Qq
Rr
Ss
Tt
Uu
Vv
Ww
Xx
Yy
Zz

talent •NOUN• **talents** you have talent, or a talent, when you have special skill or natural ability to do something well
♦ **talented** •ADJECTIVE• having the skill or ability to do something well

talk •VERB• **talks, talking, talked** 1 to say words out loud
2 to talk to someone is to have a conversation with them
3 to **talk something over** with someone is to discuss it with them
•NOUN• **talks** 1 talk is speech or conversation 2 if someone gives a talk, they talk about some subject to an audience
♦ **talkative** •ADJECTIVE• a talkative person talks a lot

tall •ADJECTIVE• **taller, tallest** 1 big, or bigger than average, in height: *He's tall for his age.*
• *a tall building* 2 how big someone or something is in height: *He's only three feet tall.*
• *a tall story* a story that is difficult to believe

tally •NOUN• **tallies** a tally of things is a record you keep so that you can work out the total, for example, of points scored or money spent
•VERB• **tallies, tallying, tallied** two or more things tally when they match or are the same: *His answer tallied with mine.*

Talmud •NOUN• a book of religious laws written by rabbis, used by members of the Jewish faith

talon •NOUN• **talons** a long hooked claw on an eagle's or other large bird of prey's foot

tambourine •NOUN• **tambourines** an instrument made up of a circular frame with skin stretched tightly across it and small round pieces of metal set into the frame in pairs

tame •ADJECTIVE• **tamer, tamest** a tame animal is used to being with humans and is not dangerous
•VERB• **tames, taming, tamed** to tame a wild animal is to train it so that it is used to living or working with humans

tamper •VERB• **tampers, tampering, tampered** to tamper with something is to interfere with it, especially in a way that causes it not to work properly

tan •NOUN• **tans** 1 you get a tan when your skin is turned brown or browner by the sun 2 tan is a yellowish-brown colour
•VERB• **tans, tanning, tanned** 1 your skin tans when it is turned a darker colour by the sun 2 animal hides are tanned when they are treated with chemicals to make them into leather

tandem •NOUN• **tandems** a type of long bicycle for two riders that has two seats and two sets of pedals
• **in tandem** people or things work or go in tandem when they work or go along together

tang •NOUN• **tangs** a strong or sharp taste or flavour

tangent •NOUN• **tangents** a straight line that touches a curve or circle but does not go through it

tangerine •NOUN• **tangerines** a type of small orange with skin that is loose and easy to peel

tangle •NOUN• **tangles** 1 a tangle is an untidy twisted mass of something, such as rope, wire or hair 2 if you get in a tangle, you get into a confused or disorganized state
•VERB• **tangles, tangling, tangled** 1 to tangle is to become entwined 2 to tangle something is to twist it or disorganize it

tank •NOUN• **tanks** 1 a large container for holding liquids 2 a large heavy army vehicle covered with metal plates and with a long gun on the top

tankard •NOUN• **tankards** a large metal mug, usually with a handle and sometimes a hinged lid, used for drinking beer

tanker •NOUN• **tankers** a ship or lorry used to carry oil or other liquids

tanner •NOUN• **tanners** a person whose job or business is to tan leather
♦ **tannery** •NOUN• **tanneries** a place where animal skins are made into leather

tantalize or **tantalise** •VERB• **tantalizes, tantalizing, tantalized** if something tantalizes you, it makes you feel frustrated because you want it but cannot have it
♦ **tantalizing** or **tantalising** •ADJECTIVE• something that is tantalizing torments you

because you are tempted by it, but can't have it

tantrum •NOUN• **tantrums** if someone has or **throws a tantrum**, they suddenly start to shout, scream or kick in a furious and uncontrolled way

tap[1] •NOUN• **taps** a device fitted to a water or gas pipe used to turn the water or gas on and off and control the flow
• **on tap** if something is on tap, there is a supply of it available when you need it
•VERB• **taps, tapping, tapped** 1 to tap a source or supply of something is to use it
2 to tap someone's phone is secretly to put a device in their phone that lets you hear their telephone conversations

tap[2] •NOUN• **taps** a light quick knock
•VERB• **taps, tapping, tapped** to tap is to knock lightly: *He tapped on the window to get my attention.*

tapdance •VERB• **tapdances, tapdancing, tapdanced** to dance in special shoes with metal pieces in the toes and heels that make tapping noises as your feet hit the ground

tape •NOUN• **tapes** 1 tape is a long narrow ribbon or strip of material, used for tying or sticking things
2 the strip of material across a finishing line on a racetrack: *She was the first through the tape at the finish.*
3 a tape is a length of magnetic tape wound on a cassette, for recording sounds or pictures
•VERB• **tapes, taping, taped** 1 to tape sounds or images is to record them on tape
2 to **tape something up** is to fasten it with sticky tape

tape-measure •NOUN• **tape-measures** a long thin piece of plastic or fabric marked with units of measurement that you use to find out the length of things

taper •VERB• **tapers, tapering, tapered** 1 to get gradually thinner or narrower at one end
2 something **tapers off** when it decreases gradually
•NOUN• **tapers** a long thin candle used for lighting other candles and fires

tape-recorder •NOUN• **tape-recorders** a machine that records sounds on magnetic

tape and plays recordings back

tapestry •NOUN• **tapestries** a piece of cloth with a design or picture sewn on it in wool or thick thread

tapeworm •NOUN• **tapeworms** a long flat worm that lives in the guts of animals, including humans, as a parasite

tapioca •NOUN• a starchy food in the form of white grains that are cooked in milk and eaten as a pudding

tar •NOUN• a thick dark sticky liquid made from coal or wood, which goes hard when it gets cold and is used in making roads

tarantula •NOUN• **tarantulas** a large hairy spider that has a poisonous bite

target •NOUN• **targets** 1 a mark or object that people aim at when they are shooting
2 something or someone being aimed at: *My savings target is £100.* • *He was the target of all the other boys' jokes.*
•VERB• **targets, targeting, targeted** to target someone or something is to aim at them

tariff •NOUN• **tariffs** a list of prices or charges

tarmac •NOUN• a short form of the word **tarmacadam**

tarmacadam •NOUN• a mixture of small stones and tar used to make road surfaces

tarn •NOUN• **tarns** a small mountain lake, especially one that has been formed by a glacier

tarnish •VERB• **tarnishes, tarnishing, tarnished** 1 if metal tarnishes, it becomes dull and stained 2 something tarnishes a person's reputation when it spoils or damages it

tarot •NOUN• **tarots** tarot is a way of telling people's fortunes using cards with pictures that are supposed to predict what is going to happen in the future

tarpaulin •NOUN• **tarpaulins** a tarpaulin is a piece of strong waterproof canvas

tarry •VERB• **tarries, tarrying, tarried** an old-fashioned word which means to linger or wait: *O let us be married! Too long we have tarried: but what shall we do for a ring?*

tart[1] •NOUN• **tarts** a pastry case with a sweet filling of custard, jam or fruit

Aa
Bb
Cc
Dd
Ee
Ff
Gg
Hh
Ii
Jj
Kk
Ll
Mm
Nn
Oo
Pp
Qq
Rr
Ss
Tt
Uu
Vv
Ww
Xx
Yy
Zz

Aa
Bb
Cc
Dd
Ee
Ff
Gg
Hh
Ii
Jj
Kk
Ll
Mm
Nn
Oo
Pp
Qq
Rr
Ss
Tt
Uu
Vv
Ww
Xx
Yy
Zz

tart [2] •ADJECTIVE• **tarter, tartest** sour-tasting

tartan •NOUN• **tartans** woollen cloth with a check pattern made up of horizontal and vertical stripes of different colours

task •NOUN• **tasks** a job or duty that you have to do
• **take someone to task** to take someone to task is to challenge them and find fault with something they have done

task force •NOUN• **task forces** a group of people or soldiers with a special task to do

tassel •NOUN• **tassels** a bunch of threads tied firmly together at one end and used as decoration

taste •NOUN• **tastes** 1 taste is the sense by which you recognize different flavours or foods when you touch them with your tongue
2 something's taste is the particular flavour it has when it touches your tongue
3 to have a taste of something is to put a little bit of it in your mouth to find out what its flavour is like
4 your taste or tastes are the kinds of things you like
•VERB• **tastes, tasting, tasted** 1 you taste something when you put it in your mouth so that you can find out what sort of flavour it has: *Have you tasted this cheese?*
2 food tastes a certain way if it has that flavour: *This sauce tastes salty.*
3 if you taste something, you experience it briefly: *They'd tasted victory for the first time and wanted more.*
♦ **tasteful** •ADJECTIVE• showing good taste and judgement
♦ **tastefully** •ADVERB• in a tasteful way
♦ **tasteless** •ADJECTIVE• 1 having no flavour 2 vulgar or showing lack of taste
♦ **tasty** •ADJECTIVE• **tastier, tastiest** having a good flavour

tattered •ADJECTIVE• tattered clothing is torn and ragged

tatters •PLURAL NOUN• 1 clothes that are **in tatters** are badly torn 2 something that is **in tatters** is ruined: *Their holiday plans were in tatters.*

tattoo [1] •NOUN• **tattoos** a pattern or picture marked on someone's skin by making little holes in the surface of the skin and filling the holes with ink
•VERB• **tattoos, tattooing, tattooed** to tattoo someone is to put a tattoo on their skin

tattoo [2] •NOUN• **tattoos** an outdoor military display with music

tatty •ADJECTIVE• **tattier, tattiest** scruffy, old and worn

taught •VERB• a way of changing the verb **teach** to make a past tense. It can be used with or without a helping verb: *Who taught you how to do magic tricks?* • *Miss Kennedy had taught all my older brothers and sisters.*

taunt •VERB• **taunts, taunting, taunted** to taunt someone is to say cruel and hurtful things to them
•NOUN• **taunts** a cruel or hurtful remark or comment

taut •ADJECTIVE• **tauter, tautest** pulled or stretched tight

tavern •NOUN• **taverns** an old-fashioned word for an inn or pub

tawdry •ADJECTIVE• **tawdrier, tawdriest** cheap or cheap-looking

tawny •ADJECTIVE• something that is tawny has a yellowish-brown colour: *a tawny owl*

tax •NOUN• **taxes** a charge made by the government on a person's income or on the price of goods to help pay for the running of the country
•VERB• **taxes, taxing, taxed** 1 to tax income or goods is to charge tax on them 2 if something taxes you, you find it hard work or a strain
♦ **taxation** •NOUN• the system of taxing income or goods, or the amount of money the government gets by charging taxes

taxi •NOUN• **taxis** a car with a driver that you can hire to take you from one place to another
•VERB• **taxis, taxiing, taxied** an aeroplane taxis when it moves slowly forward along the ground, after it has landed or when it is getting into position to take off

TB •ABBREVIATION• short for **tuberculosis**

tea •NOUN• **teas** 1 a drink made by pouring

boiling water on dried leaves that come from a small tree or shrub that grows in Asia **2** a cup of tea: *Two teas and a coffee, please.* **3** a light meal, with tea and sandwiches, that some people have between lunch and dinner **4** the name some people give to the meal that they have in the early evening

teabag • NOUN• **teabags** a small bag of thin paper containing tea leaves that you put in a pot or cup and pour boiling water over to make tea

teach •VERB• **teaches, teaching, taught 1** to teach is to pass the knowledge and experience you have on to other people to help them learn new things: *Will you teach me how to sail a dinghy?* • *He taught in the local school.* **2** to teach a particular subject is to give people lessons in that subject: *He teaches violin.*
 ◆ **teacher** •NOUN• **teachers** someone who teaches, usually as their job
 ◆ **teaching** •NOUN• the work of a teacher

teacup •NOUN• **teacups** a cup used for drinking tea

teak •NOUN• a type of hard yellowish-brown wood

team •NOUN• **teams 1** a side in a game: *the England cricket team* • *Which football team do you support?* **2** a group of people working together: *a team of engineers*
 •VERB• **teams, teaming, teamed** to **team up** with other people is to join them so that you can do something together

ⓘ Be careful not to confuse **team** and **teem**.

teapot •NOUN• **teapots** a pot with a spout and a handle, used for making and pouring tea

tear[1] •VERB• **tears, tearing, torn 1** to tear something is to make a hole or split in it: *You've torn your sleeve on that barbed wire.* **2** to tear something is to pull it using force: *The old buildings were torn down and new ones built in their place.* **3** to tear somewhere is to rush there
 •NOUN• **tears** a hole or split made in something

tear[2] • NOUN• **tears 1** a drop of liquid that forms in, and drops from, your eyes when you cry **2** if someone is **in tears**, they are crying or weeping
 ◆ **tearful** • ADJECTIVE• crying or in tears

tear gas • NOUN• a gas which stings people's eyes and makes them stream with tears

tease •VERB• **teases, teasing, teased 1** to tease a person or animal is to annoy them or it on purpose: *Stop teasing the dog!* **2** to tease someone is to make fun of them or joke with them: *I didn't mean what I said. I was only teasing.*
 ◆ **teaser** •NOUN• **teasers** a problem or puzzle

teaspoon •NOUN• **teaspoons** a small spoon used for stirring tea or for measuring small amounts of ingredients when you are cooking
 ◆ **teaspoonful** •NOUN• **teaspoonfuls** the amount a teaspoon will hold

teat •NOUN• **teats 1** the part of a female animal that its babies suck at to get milk **2** a small rubber device that is fitted to the end of a baby's feeding bottle

technical • ADJECTIVE• to do with technology or practical skills: *Does he have any technical training?*
 ◆ **technicality** • NOUN• **technicalities** a technicality is a detail of the law or any other set of rules
 ◆ **technically** • ADVERB• according to the rules, or according to technical or scientific methods

technician • NOUN• **technicians** someone whose job is to do practical work in a laboratory or deal with technical equipment

technique • NOUN• **techniques** a particular method of doing something

technology • NOUN• **technologies** the study of the way things are made and work
 ◆ **technological** • ADJECTIVE• involving technology

teddy *or* **teddy bear** • NOUN• **teddies** *or* **teddy bears** a toy bear with soft fur

tedious • ADJECTIVE• long and boring
 ◆ **tedium** • NOUN• boredom

tee • NOUN• **tees 1** an area of level ground

Aa
Bb
Cc
Dd
Ee
Ff
Gg
Hh
Ii
Jj
Kk
Ll
Mm
Nn
Oo
Pp
Qq
Rr
Ss
Tt
Uu
Vv
Ww
Xx
Yy
Zz

Aa
Bb
Cc
Dd
Ee
Ff
Gg
Hh
Ii
Jj
Kk
Ll
Mm
Nn
Oo
Pp
Qq
Rr
Ss
Tt
Uu
Vv
Ww
Xx
Yy
Zz

from which a golf ball is hit at the beginning of a hole **2** a small plastic peg pushed into the ground and used to rest a golf ball on before it is hit from this flat area of ground
•VERB• **tees, teeing, teed** a golfer **tees off** when he or she hits the ball from the tee at the start of a hole

teem •VERB• **teems, teeming, teemed** **1** if a place teems with people or animals there are crowds or large numbers of them moving around there **2** it is teeming with rain when rain is falling very fast and heavily

teenage •ADJECTIVE• suitable for or to do with teenagers
♦ **teenager** •NOUN• **teenagers** someone who is aged between 13 and 19
♦ **teens** •PLURAL NOUN• your teens are the years of your life between the ages of 13 and 19

teeny •ADJECTIVE• **teenier, teeniest** very small

tee-shirt or **T-shirt** •NOUN• **tee-shirts** or **T-shirts** a loose shirt with short sleeves that you pull on over your head

teeter •VERB• **teeters, teetering, teetered** to move about unsteadily and be just about to fall over: *The vase was teetering on the edge of the shelf.*

teeth •NOUN• the plural of **tooth**: *He got fillings in one front tooth and two back teeth.*

teethe •VERB• **teethes, teething, teethed** a baby teethes when its first teeth start to come through its gums

teetotal •ADJECTIVE• someone who is teetotal does not drink any alcohol
♦ **teetotaller** •NOUN• **teetotallers** someone who does not drink alcohol

tele- •PREFIX• if **tele-** comes at the beginning of a word it adds the meaning *at* or *over a distance* to the rest of the word. For example, *television* is pictures sent over a long distance between a transmitter and the sets that receive the pictures

telecommunications •PLURAL NOUN• sending information over long distances by telephone, radio or television

telegram •NOUN• **telegrams** a message sent by telegraph

telegraph •NOUN• **telegraphs** a system of sending messages over long distances using

radio signals or electrical signals sent along wires
♦ **telegraphic** •ADJECTIVE• using telegraph
♦ **telegraphy** •NOUN• the system used for sending messages by telegraph

telepathic •ADJECTIVE• someone who is telepathic can communicate with another person's mind without speaking, writing or using gestures
♦ **telepathy** •NOUN• communicating by thought alone

telephone •NOUN• **telephones** a device which allows you to speak to someone at a distance, using electrical wires or radio
•VERB• **telephones, telephoning, telephoned** to telephone someone is to contact them using the telephone
♦ **telephonist** •NOUN• **telephonists** someone who operates a telephone switchboard

telescope •NOUN• **telescopes** an instrument with lenses and mirrors inside that make distant objects seem closer or larger
♦ **telescopic** •ADJECTIVE• **1** to do with telescopes **2** having sliding parts that can be pushed inside each other

teletext •NOUN• a service that provides news and information that is regularly updated and which can be viewed in written form on a TV screen

televise •VERB• **televises, televising, televised** to televise something is to film it and show it on television

television •NOUN• **televisions** **1** television is a system for sending images and sounds in the form of radio waves from a transmitter to a receiver, which changes the radio signal back into pictures and sounds **2** a television or television set, is the equipment which receives these pictures and sounds

tell •VERB• **tells, telling, told** **1** to tell someone something is to give them information by speaking to them: *Why won't you tell me your name?*
2 to tell someone to do something is to order them to do it: *I won't tell you again to be quiet.*
3 you can tell what something is, or what is happening, if you know what it is, or

understand what is happening: *I couldn't tell if it was a boat or a whale.*

4 to tell the truth or a lie is to give true or untrue information to someone

5 someone who tells gives away a secret

6 if someone **tells you off**, they give you a row

◆ **teller** •NOUN• **tellers** a person who works in a bank and whose job is to pay out and take in money from the bank's customers

tell-tale •NOUN• **tell-tales** a person who tells untrue stories about others

•ADJECTIVE• a tell-tale sign is a sign that shows where or what something that was secret or hidden is

telly •NOUN• **tellies** an informal word for **television**

temper •NOUN• **tempers** **1** a person's mood: *Don't ask him until he's in a better temper.* **2** if you **lose your temper**, you get angry

temperament •NOUN• **temperaments** your temperament is your nature, which affects the way you think and behave

◆ **temperamental** •ADJECTIVE• a temperamental person changes their mood suddenly and gets upset or excited easily

temperate •ADJECTIVE• a temperate climate never gets very cold or very hot

temperature •NOUN• **temperatures** **1** something's temperature is how hot or cold it is **2** if someone has a temperature, their body is hotter than it should be, usually because they are ill

tempest •NOUN• **tempests** a very violent storm, with strong winds

◆ **tempestuous** •ADJECTIVE• stormy

template •NOUN• **templates** a pattern that you can use to make the same shape many times

temple [1] •NOUN• **temples** a building in which the members of some religions worship

temple [2] •NOUN• **temples** your temples are the areas on either side of your forehead between your hairline and the sides of your eyes

tempo •NOUN• **tempos** *or* **tempi** the tempo of a piece of music is its speed and rhythm

temporarily •ADVERB• for a short or

limited time only: *He'd repaired the roof temporarily with a piece of plastic.*

temporary •ADJECTIVE• lasting or used only for a short or limited time: *The repair was temporary, but at least it stopped the rain getting in.*

tempt •VERB• **tempts, tempting, tempted** to tempt someone is to make them want to do something or have something, especially something that they should not do or have

◆ **temptation** •NOUN• **temptations** a feeling that you want to do something that you know is wrong or that might harm you

◆ **tempting** •ADJECTIVE• something tempting is attractive and makes you want to do it or have it

ten •NOUN• **tens** the number 10
⇒ **tenth**

tenancy •NOUN• **tenancies** the time when someone is a tenant or the agreement that makes someone a tenant

tenant •NOUN• **tenants** someone who pays rent to the owner of a house, building or land in return for being able to use the house, building or land

tend [1] •VERB• **tends, tending, tended** to tend someone or something is to look after them: *doctors and nurses tending the sick and injured*

tend [2] •VERB• **tends, tending, tended** something tends to happen when it is likely to happen, or often happens: *She tends to be a bit moody.*

◆ **tendency** •NOUN• **tendencies** if someone or something has a tendency to do something, they are likely to act in that way

tender •ADJECTIVE• **1** meat that is tender is easy to chew

2 showing gentle love: *a tender smile*

3 sensitive and delicate: *These plants are too tender to be grown outside.*

◆ **tenderly** •ADJECTIVE• gently and lovingly: *He smiled at her tenderly.*

◆ **tenderness** •NOUN• being tender

tendon •NOUN• **tendons** a type of strong body tissue that attaches your muscles to your bones

tendril •NOUN• **tendrils** **1** a long, thin,

curling stem with which a climbing plant fastens itself to something **2** a long curling section of hair

tenement •NOUN• **tenements** a building with several floors that contain flats or apartments

tenner •NOUN• **tenners** an informal word for ten pounds or a ten pound note

tennis •NOUN• a game played on a court that has a net stretched across the middle. Tennis is played by two or four players who use rackets to hit a ball to and fro across the net

tenor •NOUN• **tenors 1** a high male singing voice **2** a man who has this singing voice
•ADJECTIVE• a tenor instrument plays notes at the lower end of the range: *a tenor saxophone*

tenpin bowling •NOUN• an indoor game in which a large heavy ball is rolled along a polished wooden track towards ten skittles or tenpins at the end of the track with the aim of knocking them down

tense¹ •NOUN• **tenses** a verb's tense is the form of the verb that shows whether the action of the verb happens here and now (the **present tense**), in the past (the **past tense**), or in the future (the **future tense**). See the box called **Tense**

tense² •ADJECTIVE• **tenser, tensest 1** if you feel tense, you feel nervous and unable to relax
2 a tense situation makes people feel nervous and worried
3 your muscles are tense when they are stretched so that they feel tight
♦ **tension** •NOUN• **tensions 1** tension is nervousness or worry about something unpleasant that might happen **2** the tension of a piece of wire, rope or wool is how tightly it is stretched or twisted

tent •NOUN• **tents** a temporary shelter made of canvas or nylon supported by a frame

tentacle •NOUN• **tentacles** tentacles are the long, thin, flexible parts on the body of an octopus and some other sea animals

tenth •ADJECTIVE AND ADVERB• after ninth and before eleventh: *the tenth month of the year* • *He came tenth out of twenty in the*

singing competition.
•NOUN• **tenths** the fraction $\frac{1}{10}$, which means one of ten equal parts of something: *a tenth of a litre*

tepee •NOUN• **tepees** a sort of tent used by Native American people in the past, made by tying poles together in a cone shape and covering them with animal skins

tepid •ADJECTIVE• tepid liquid is slightly warm

term •NOUN• **terms 1** one of the periods of time that the school or college year is divided into: *the autumn term*
2 any limited period of time: *the president's term of office*
3 a word or expression with a particular meaning or used in a particular subject area: *What is the term for someone who collects old coins?* • *complicated medical terms*
4 the terms of a contract or other agreement are the individual points or conditions it contains
5 people who are on goods terms, or who are on bad terms, have a good, or bad, relationship with each other
•VERB• **terms, terming, termed** what something is termed is what it is named or called: *Dogs that are used for hunting are often termed 'hounds'.*

terminal •NOUN• **terminals 1** a building at an airport where passengers arrive or depart
2 a bus or rail terminus
3 a place or point where a connection is made to an electrical circuit
4 a computer terminal is one of several visual display units or monitors connected to one large central computer
•ADJECTIVE• **1** a terminal illness is one that cannot be cured and that causes death **2** or at the end

terminate •VERB• **terminates, terminating, terminated** to end or come to a stop
♦ **termination** •NOUN• the ending of something

terminus •NOUN• **termini** or **terminuses** a place or building at the end of a railway or bus route

termite •NOUN• **termites** a small pale-coloured insect that eats wood

Tense

All verbs have **tense**. The **tense** of a verb tells you the time when an action happens – either in the present, the past or the future.

The present tense

The present tense describes actions or situations that are happening now.

> I **work.**
> I **am working.**

The form of the verb agrees with the subject.

> You **work.**
> He **works.**
> It **works.**
> We **work.**
> They **work.**

The past tense

The past tense describes actions that have already happened.

> I **worked.**
> I **was working.**

You can turn many verbs into the past tense by adding **-ed**:

act	→	**acted**
collect	→	**collected**
talk	→	**talked**

Other common verbs have past tenses that are formed very differently:

buy	→	**bought**	go	→	**went**
catch	→	**caught**	sit	→	**sat**
eat	→	**ate**	take	→	**took**
find	→	**found**	win	→	**won**

The future tense

Actions that will happen in future time can be shown in different ways:

> I **shall work** next week.
> I **shall be working** next week.
> I **am going to work** next week.
> I **am working** next week.

terrace • NOUN • **terraces** 1 a row of houses that are connected to each other
2 a raised level area, usually with paving, beside a house
3 a raised bank of earth with a level top
4 the terraces at a football or rugby ground are the sloping banks or tiers of seats where spectators stand or sit

terrain • NOUN • terrain is land, especially a particular type of land: *This is wooded terrain.*

terrapin • NOUN • **terrapins** a type of small turtle that lives in freshwater ponds and rivers

terrestrial • ADJECTIVE • from the Earth, rather than from space or another planet

terrible •ADJECTIVE• very bad: *a terrible smell* • *a terrible shock* • *Your writing is really terrible.*

 • **terribly** •ADVERB• extremely: *I'm terribly sorry I broke your vase.* • *I feel terribly guilty about it.*

terrier •NOUN• **terriers** any of various breeds of small dog

terrific •ADJECTIVE• **1** excellent: *The party was terrific.* **2** very great or powerful: *a terrific wind*

 • **terrifically** •ADVERB• extremely or very greatly: *We were terrifically pleased to get the award.*

terrify •VERB• **terrifies, terrifying, terrified** if something terrifies you, it frightens you very much

territorial •ADJECTIVE• to do with territory: *a territorial dispute*

territory •NOUN• **territories** **1** the land that a country or ruler owns or controls: *on British territory* **2** an area or region: *They were travelling on foot across mountainous territory.*

terror •NOUN• **terrors** **1** terror is great fear **2** a terror is something that makes you very frightened
 ⇒ **terrify**

terrorism •NOUN• the use of violence by small or illegal political organizations with the aim of forcing a government or society to accept their demands

 • **terrorist** •NOUN• **terrorists** someone who uses terrorism

 • **terrorize** or **terrorise** •VERB• **terrorizes, terrorizing, terrorized** to terrorize people is to frighten them by using, or threatening to use, violence

tessellated •ADJECTIVE• tessellated geometric shapes fit together without any spaces in between them

 • **tessellation** •NOUN• **tessellation** being tessellated

test •NOUN• **tests** **1** a set of questions or a short examination to find out your ability or knowledge: *a spelling test* **2** something done to find out whether something is in good condition or is working well: *medical tests* •VERB• **tests, testing, tested** to test someone or something is to give them a short examination or to carry out tests on them

testament •NOUN• **testaments** **1** a written statement: *It was a testament of her friendship.* **2** the **Old Testament** and the **New Testament** are the two parts of the **Bible**

testicle •NOUN• **testicles** one of two glands in a male animal's body where sperm is made

testify •VERB• **testifies, testifying, testified** to give information or evidence, especially in a law court

testimonial •NOUN• **testimonials** **1** a written statement about someone's character, skills and abilities **2** a gift given to someone as a way of thanking them for service they have given in the past

testimony •NOUN• **testimonies** a witness's testimony is the statement they make in a law court

test match •NOUN• **test matches** one of a series of matches played between two international teams, especially cricket teams

test tube •NOUN• **test tubes** a thin glass tube, closed at one end and open at the other, used in chemical experiments

testy •ADJECTIVE• **testier, testiest** easily irritated or made angry

tetanus •NOUN• a disease caused by infection by bacteria

tether •VERB• **tethers, tethering, tethered** to tether an animal is to tie it with a rope to a post or bar

tetrahedron •NOUN• **tetrahedrons** a solid shape with four sides or faces

text •NOUN• **texts** the written or printed words in a book

textbook •NOUN• **textbooks** a book containing information on a particular subject, used by pupils in schools or students in colleges

textile •NOUN• **textiles** a cloth or fabric made by weaving

texture •NOUN• **textures** something's texture is the way it feels when you touch it

than •CONJUNCTION• **than** is used when you

Aa
Bb
Cc
Dd
Ee
Ff
Gg
Hh
Ii
Jj
Kk
Ll
Mm
Nn
Oo
Pp
Qq
Rr
Ss
Tt
Uu
Vv
Ww
Xx
Yy
Zz

are making comparisons: *The test was easier than I thought it would be.* • *He can run faster than his big brother.*

thank •VERB• **thanks, thanking, thanked** you thank someone when you let them know you are grateful for something they have done for you or have given you
• **thankful** •ADJECTIVE• happy, relieved and grateful
• **thankfully** •ADVERB• happily or gratefully
• **thankless** •ADJECTIVE• a thankless job or task is one for which you get no thanks or appreciation
• **thanks** •PLURAL NOUN• you say 'thanks' to someone, or express your thanks to them, when you express your gratitude or appreciation
• **thanks to 1** with the help of: *We didn't miss any of the film, thanks to Dad.* **2** owing to: *We were stuck in the airport all day, thanks to the strike.*
• **thank you** you say 'thank you' to someone to tell them you are grateful for something they have done

thanksgiving •NOUN• a church service giving thanks to God
• **Thanksgiving** •NOUN• a public holiday held on the fourth Thursday in November in the United States and the second Monday in October in Canada

that •ADJECTIVE• **those** the word **that** is used before a noun to refer to a person or thing that is some distance away from you, or that has already been mentioned : *Who is that girl over there?* • *Pass me that towel, please.*
• PRONOUN• **those** the word **that** is used instead of a noun to refer to a person or thing that is some distance away from you, or that has already been mentioned : *I don't want to know that.* • *Who is that at the door?* • *That's my friend, Gerry.*
• ADVERB• to the extent or degree mentioned: *I didn't think I'd run that far.* • *The film wasn't that bad.*
• CONJUNCTION• **that** is used after verbs that have to do with saying, thinking or feeling, and to connect clauses: *He said that he hated sports.* • *I'm afraid that I can't offer you much help.*

thatch •NOUN• thatch is reeds, rushes or straw used as a roofing material for houses
• VERB• **thatches, thatching, thatched** to thatch a roof is to cover it with reeds, rushes or straw

that'd •SHORT FORM• a short way to say and write **that had** or **that would**: *That'd better be the pizza delivery. I'm starving!* • *That'd be nice.*

that'll •SHORT FORM• a short way to say and write **that will**: *That'll be the day!*

that's •SHORT FORM• a short way to say and write **that is**: *That's not what I meant.*
• **that's that** if someone says 'That's that', they mean that there is no more to be done or said about something

thaw •VERB• **thaws, thawing, thawed** something that has been frozen thaws when it starts to melt or the ice in it melts

the •ADJECTIVE• **the** is used before nouns to refer to a particular person, thing or group: *The bus arrived late, as usual.* • *Is it on the right or the left side of the road?* • *The men rode on horses and the women rode in carriages.*

theatre •NOUN• **theatres 1** a building where plays, operas or musicals are performed **2** the acting profession or the dramatic arts **3** a special room in a hospital where operations are done
• **theatrical** •ADJECTIVE• to do with plays or acting

thee •PRONOUN• an old-fashioned word for **you**: *I tell thee again, eye of my eye, this hunting is ended.*

theft •NOUN• **thefts** stealing: *car thefts*

their •ADJECTIVE• belonging to them: *They're all going back to their games out there in the sunshine, and I'm being left by myself.*
• **theirs** •PRONOUN• a word you use to talk about something belonging to a group of people or things that have already been mentioned: *They say it belongs to them, but I know it's not theirs.*

ⓘ Be careful not to confuse the spellings of **their, they're**, and **there**.
Their is the possessive form of **they**, and shows you someone owns something: *They have*

brought **their** exercise books.

They're is short for **they are**: *They're late.*
There points something out: *Put this box over there.* • *There is nothing to do here.*

them • PRONOUN • a word you use to talk about two or more people or things that have already been mentioned: *The girls waved to me and I waved back to them.*
• *'Do you like your new boots?' 'Yes, I like them a lot.'*

theme • NOUN • **themes** the main idea, subject, or melody in a piece of writing, a talk, or a piece of music

theme park • NOUN • **theme parks** an amusement park with activities connected to a special subject or theme

themselves • PRONOUN • **1** you use **themselves** after a verb or preposition when the people who perform the action are affected by it: *They'd made themselves a cosy little shelter.*
2 themselves is also used to show that a group of people do something without any help from other people: *They'll have to work it out for themselves.*
3 you can use **themselves** to show more clearly who you mean: *They themselves are innocent.*

then • ADVERB • **1** at that time, in the past or future: *I didn't know you then.* • *The rest of the kids should be here by then.* **2** after that time, or next: *I went for a swim, and then I went home.*
• CONJUNCTION • as a result, or in that case: *If you have been eating sweets, then you must brush your teeth.*

theology • NOUN • the study of God and religion

theorem • NOUN • **theorems** in mathematics, a statement that has to be proved

theoretical • ADJECTIVE • something that is theoretical is based on theory and ideas rather than practical knowledge or experience
• **theoretically** • ADVERB • possibly but not absolutely certain

theory • NOUN • **theories 1** a theory is an idea or suggested explanation that has not yet

been proved **2** theory is the ideas and principle of an art or science rather than its practice

therapist • NOUN • **therapists** someone who is an expert in therapy of a particular sort: *a speech therapist*

therapy • NOUN • **therapies** the treatment o diseases or disorders, usually without surgery or drugs

there • ADVERB • at, in, or to that place: *Don' stop there. I was just beginning to enjoy the story.* • *My granny lives there.* • *I'm going there tomorrow.*
• PRONOUN • you use **there** with *is* or *are* to draw attention to what is going to follow: *There is a mouse somewhere in this house.*

thereabouts • ADVERB • approximately: *It will cost £50 or thereabouts.*

thereby • ADVERB • in that way: *We cut dowr all the trees, thereby letting more light into the house and providing wood for the fire.*

therefore • ADVERB • for that reason or because of that: *She had been awake all that night and therefore was very tired the next day.*

therm • NOUN • **therms** a unit of heat used for measuring gas
• **thermal** • ADJECTIVE • using heat or to do with heat

thermometer • NOUN • **thermometers** an instrument for measuring how hot or cold something is

Thermos • NOUN • **Thermoses** a container made with a special double layer of glass and metal, used for keeping hot things hot and cold things cold. This word is a trademark

thermostat • NOUN • **thermostats** a device that controls the temperature in a room or of a heating system
• **thermostatically** • ADVERB • using a thermostat

thesaurus • NOUN • **thesauri** or **thesauruses** a book that lists groups of words that have similar meanings and can be used instead of each other

these • ADJECTIVE • **these** is used before a noun to refer to people or things nearby or which are being mentioned: *Both these cups are dirty.* • *On these cold winter days, you* have to wrap up warmly. • *Can you make me a pair of these gloves?*

•PRONOUN• **these** is used instead of a noun to refer to people or things nearby or which are being mentioned: *Are these the same as the ones you had yesterday?* • *These are difficult times for everyone.*

hey •PRONOUN• you use **they** to talk about two or more people or things that have already been mentioned or pointed out for the first time: *Apes are not monkeys. They don't have tails.* • *What did they think of your idea?*

hey'd •SHORT FORM• a short way to say and write **they had**: *They'd all had their lunch.*

hey'll •SHORT FORM• a short way to say and write **they will** or **they shall**: *They'll not be hungry again until supper time.*

hey're •SHORT FORM• a short way to say and write **they are**: *They're going skating after school.*

hey've •SHORT FORM• a short way to say and write **they have**: *They've never been skating before.*

hick •ADJECTIVE• **thicker, thickest** 1 quite wide from one side to the other: *a thick piece of rope*
  2 something is a certain measurement thick when it measures that distance between one side and the other: *The ice was two feet thick.*
  3 made up of parts that are very close together or densely packed: *thick wool*
  4 not having a lot of liquid in it or not flowing easily: *thick gravy*
  5 thick smoke or fog is dense and difficult to see through
  • **in the thick of something** in the middle of something or in the place where all the action is happening
  • **through thick and thin** no matter what happens
  ✦ **thicken** •VERB• **thickens, thickening, thickened** to make thick or thicker

hicket •NOUN• **thickets** a mass of bushes growing together

hickness •NOUN• **thicknesses** how thick something is, especially compared with other things

hick-skinned •ADJECTIVE• a thick-skinned person does not get upset when they are insulted or criticized

thief •NOUN• **thieves** someone who steals
  ✦ **thieve** •VERB• **thieves, thieving, thieved** to steal
  ✦ **thieving** •NOUN• stealing
  ⇒ **theft**

thigh •NOUN• **thighs** your thighs are the parts of your legs between the tops of your legs and your knees

thimble •NOUN• **thimbles** a metal cover for your finger used when you are sewing to help push the needle through the fabric

thin •ADJECTIVE• **thinner, thinnest** 1 not wide from one side to the other
  2 a thin person doesn't have much fat on their body
  3 not dense or thick: *His hair is getting a bit thin.* • *a thin porridge*
  •VERB• **thins, thinning, thinned** to make something thin or thinner, for example by adding water or liquid to it

thing •NOUN• **things** 1 an object, or something that is not alive: *I bought a few things for the party when I was in town.* • *Where's the thing for opening bottles?* 2 a fact, item, action or event: *We've got lots of things to discuss.* • *I hope I haven't done the wrong thing.*

think •VERB• **thinks, thinking, thought** 1 to think is to have or form ideas in your mind: *Don't disturb him. He's thinking.*
  2 what you think about something is the opinion you have of it: *I don't think much of their new album.*
  3 if you are thinking of doing something, you are planning to do it

third •ADJECTIVE AND ADVERB• after second and before fourth: *That's the third time he's fallen off his bike.*
  •NOUN• **thirds** the fraction $\frac{1}{3}$, which means one of three equal parts of something: *The bottle holds a third of a litre.*

Third World •NOUN• the Third World is the name given to nations of the world that have not reached an advanced state of development and are fairly poor

thirst •NOUN• thirst is the feeling that you must have something to drink

Aa
Bb
Cc
Dd
Ee
Ff
Gg
Hh
Ii
Jj
Kk
Ll
Mm
Nn
Oo
Pp
Qq
Rr
Ss
Tt
Uu
Vv
Ww
Xx
Yy
Zz

♦ **thirsty** •ADJECTIVE• **thirstier, thirstiest** feeling you must have something to drink

thirteen •NOUN• the number 13
♦ **thirteenth** •ADJECTIVE AND ADVERB• after twelfth and before fourteenth: *You become a teenager on your thirteenth birthday.*

thirtieth •ADJECTIVE AND ADVERB• after twenty-ninth and before thirty-first: *February does not have a thirtieth day.*

thirty •NOUN• **thirties** the number 30

this •ADJECTIVE• **these** the word **this** is used before a noun to refer to a person or thing nearby or which is being mentioned: *This apple is sour.* • *We have got PE this afternoon.*
• •PRONOUN• the word **this** is used instead of a noun to refer to a person or thing nearby or which is being mentioned: *I can't eat this.* • *Where are you going after this?*
• •ADVERB• to the extent or degree mentioned: *It was this long and this wide.* • *We've come this far. Don't let's give up now.*

thistle •NOUN• **thistles** a plant with prickly leaves and purple flowers

thorn •NOUN• **thorns** a hard sharp point that sticks out from the stems of some plants
♦ **thorny** •ADJECTIVE• **thornier, thorniest** 1 covered with thorns 2 a thorny problem or question is difficult to solve or deal with

thorough •ADJECTIVE• 1 you are thorough when you do something carefully, paying attention to every detail: *He made a thorough search.* 2 complete: *It was a thorough nuisance.*
⇒ **thoroughly**

thoroughbred •NOUN• **thoroughbreds** a horse bred from parents that both have pedigrees

thoroughfare •NOUN• **thoroughfares** a public road or street that anyone can travel along

thoroughly •ADVERB• 1 with great care and attention to every detail: *Clean all the kitchen surfaces thoroughly.* 2 completely: *She was feeling thoroughly fed-up with the whole thing.*

those •ADJECTIVE• **those** is used before a noun to refer to people or things at a distance from you or which are being mentioned: *Who are those two boys?* • *In those days, people didn't have cars.*
• •PRONOUN• **those** is used instead of a noun to refer to people or things at a distance from you, or which are being mentioned: *What are those?* • *Those are just some of the coins in his collection.*

thou •PRONOUN• an old-fashioned word for **you**

though •CONJUNCTION• in spite of the fact that: *We only waited for half an hour, though it seemed like hours.* • *He went out though I told him not to.*
• •ADVERB• however: *It's a pity we didn't win. It was an exciting match, though.*
• **as though** as if: *He looks as though he needs a good meal.*

thought •VERB• a way of changing the verb **think** to make a past tense. It can be used with or without a helping verb: *I thought I heard a noise.* • *He had thought about the problem all day.*
• •NOUN• **thoughts** 1 thought is thinking 2 a thought is an idea or something you think
♦ **thoughtful** •ADJECTIVE• 1 if someone looks thoughtful, they look as if they are thinking 2 a thoughtful person is kind and thinks of other people
♦ **thoughtfully** •ADVERB• in a thoughtful way: *'I just can't work this out,' he said, scratching his head thoughtfully.* • *She'd very thoughtfully left drinks and sandwiches on the kitchen table for us.*
♦ **thoughtless** •ADJECTIVE• a thoughtless person does things without first thinking about how they or other people will be affected by their actions

thousand •NOUN• **thousands** the number 1000
♦ **thousandth** •ADJECTIVE AND ADVERB• coming last in a series of one thousand things: *the thousandth customer in the shop today*
• •NOUN• **thousandths** one of a thousand equal parts of something

thrash •VERB• **thrashes, thrashing, thrashed** 1 to thrash someone is to beat them 2 to thrash or **thrash about** is to make wild violent movements

thread •NOUN• **threads** a thin strand of

cotton, wool or silk used for sewing
•VERB• **threads, threading, threaded** to thread a needle is to push a strand of thread through the hole in the top of a sewing needle

threadbare •ADJECTIVE• a threadbare carpet or other piece of fabric has been worn thin by use

threat •NOUN• a warning that someone is going to hurt you or harm you, especially if you don't do what they say
♦ **threaten** •VERB• **threatens, threatening, threatened** to threaten someone is to say that they will be harmed or hurt if they do not do something

three •NOUN• **threes** the number 3

three-dimensional •ADJECTIVE• a three-dimensional shape is solid and has length, breadth and height that you can measure

thresh •VERB• **threshes, threshing, threshed** to thresh corn is to beat it so that the grain is separated from the straw

threshold •NOUN• **thresholds 1** a piece of wood or stone on the floor at a door **2** to be **on the threshold** of something is to be just about to begin it or enter it

threw •VERB• a way of changing the verb **throw** to make a past tense: *He threw the ball hard.*

thrift •NOUN• being careful about money, saving as much as you can, and not wasting any
♦ **thrifty** •ADJECTIVE• **thriftier, thriftiest** using money and other things carefully, without wasting any

thrill •VERB• **thrills, thrilling, thrilled** something thrills you when it makes you feel excited and very pleased
•NOUN• **thrills** something that gives you a glowing feeling of excitement and pleasure
♦ **thriller** •NOUN• **thrillers** a book, film or play with an exciting plot, full of danger and frightening events
♦ **thrilling** •ADJECTIVE• very exciting

thrive •VERB• **thrives, thriving, thrived** or **throve, thrived** or **thriven** if a person or thing thrives, they grow strong and healthy, or become successful

throat •NOUN• **throats 1** your throat is the top part of the tube that goes from your mouth down to your stomach **2** your throat is also the front part of your neck

throb •VERB• **throbs, throbbing, throbbed 1** something throbs when it beats regularly, as your heart or pulse does **2** an injured part of your body throbs when you feel pains in it that come and go like the regular beat of your pulse

throne •NOUN• **thrones 1** a special chair that a king or queen, or a bishop, sits on **2** the throne is the position or power of a monarch

throng •NOUN• **throngs** a large crowd or gathering

throttle •NOUN• **throttles** the throttle in a car or machine is the part of the engine through which petrol or steam can be turned on or off
•VERB• **throttles, throttling, throttled** to throttle someone is to grip them by the throat and strangle them

through •PREPOSITION• **1** entering at one side and coming out at the other: *He walked through the door.*
2 from end to end: *She was flicking through a magazine.*
3 because of, or by means of: *He ended up in hospital through his own stupidity.* • *I heard about it through a friend.*
•ADVERB• **1** entering at one side and coming out at the other: *He opened the hatch and stuck his head through.* **2** from end to end: *You're wet through.* • *Take this booklet away and read it through.*
•ADJECTIVE• **1** a through route is one that gets you from one place to another and is not blocked anywhere along the way **2** a through train does not stop between the place it leaves from and the end of the line

ⓘ Try not to confuse this spelling with **threw**, the past tense of **throw**.

throughout •PREPOSITION• all the way through or in every part: *It rained throughout June and July.* • *There will be regular news bulletins throughout the day.*
•ADVERB• all the way through or in every part: *The show was a great success, and the children behaved themselves throughout.*

Aa
Bb
Cc
Dd
Ee
Ff
Gg
Hh
Ii
Jj
Kk
Ll
Mm
Nn
Oo
Pp
Qq
Rr
Ss
Tt
Uu
Vv
Ww
Xx
Yy
Zz

throw •VERB• **throws, throwing, threw, thrown 1** to throw something is to send it through the air with force: *He threw the ball into the scrum.* • *She threw her schoolbag down and rushed to switch on the TV.* **2** a horse throws its rider when it makes the rider fall off its back **3** if something throws you, it confuses you •NOUN• **throws** a throwing movement: *That was a great throw!*

thrush •NOUN• **thrushes** a wild bird with brown feathers and lighter speckled breast

thrust •VERB• **thrusts, thrusting, thrust** to thrust something is to push it quickly and violently: *He thrust his hands into his coat pockets.* •NOUN• **thrusts** a quick and violent push forward: *With a thrust of his sword, he scored the winning point.*

thud •NOUN• **thuds** a dull sound made by something heavy hitting the ground •VERB• **thuds, thudding, thudded** to thud is to make this sound

thug •NOUN• **thugs** a violent and brutal man

thumb •NOUN• **thumbs** the short thick finger that is at a different angle from the other four fingers on your hand
• **be under someone's thumb** to be completely under someone's control

thump •VERB• **thumps, thumping, thumped 1** to fall with a loud heavy noise **2** to thump someone is to hit them hard

ⓘ This word came into being by imitating the sound it describes.

thunder •NOUN• the loud and deep rumbling sound that you hear after a flash of lightning •VERB• **thunders, thundering, thundered** to make a loud rumbling sound, or to talk in a very loud, angry voice
• **thunderbolt** •NOUN• **thunderbolts 1** a flash of lightning that is followed immediately by thunder **2** if something hits you like a thunderbolt, it has a sudden violent and disturbing effect on you
• **thunderclap** •NOUN• **thunderclaps** a sudden loud noise made by thunder
• **thunderous** •ADJECTIVE• very loud, like thunder

• **thunderstorm** •NOUN• **thunderstorms** a storm with thunder and lightning
• **thundery** •ADJECTIVE• the weather is thundery when there are dark clouds and thunder

Thursday •NOUN• **Thursdays** the day of the week after Wednesday and before Friday

ⓘ **Thursday** comes from the Old English word **Thursdæg**, which means *Thor's day*. Thor is the Norse god of thunder.

thus •ADVERB• **1** as a result of that: *The heating has broken down; thus everyone is being sent home early.* **2** in this or that way: *The poem begins thus: 'I must go down to the sea again.'*

thwart •VERB• **thwarts, thwarting, thwarted** to thwart someone is to stop them from doing what they want to do

thy •ADJECTIVE• an old-fashioned word for **your**: *Thy will be done*

thyme •NOUN• a herb with lots of tiny leaves growing on woody stalks

ⓘ This word is pronounced **time**.

tiara •NOUN• **tiaras** a piece of jewellery like a small crown

tick¹ •NOUN• **ticks 1** a small mark (✓) used to show that something is correct or to mark off the things on a list that you have dealt with **2** the soft regular tapping or clicking noise that a clock makes **3** a very short time: *Can you wait a tick while I get my coat?* •VERB• **ticks, ticking, ticked 1** to tick something is to mark it with a tick **2** a clock ticks when it makes regular tapping or clicking noises

tick² •NOUN• **ticks** a small insect that burrows into an animal's skin and sucks its blood

ticket •NOUN• **tickets** a small piece of printed paper or card that shows you have paid a fare on a bus, train or aeroplane, or that allows you to get into a concert or other event

ⓘ This word comes from the French word **estiquier**, which means *to attach* or *to stick*, because a ticket was originally a label attached to something.

tickle •VERB• **tickles, tickling, tickled 1** to tickle someone is to touch part of their body lightly so that they get a tingling or prickly feeling that makes them laugh **2** something tickles when it causes this tingling or prickly feeling on your skin
•NOUN• **tickles** a tickling movement
✦ **ticklish** •ADJECTIVE• if you are ticklish, you are sensitive to tickling
✦ **tickly** •ADJECTIVE• **ticklier, tickliest** causing a tingling or prickly feeling

tidal •ADJECTIVE• affected by tides or to do with tides

tidal wave •NOUN• **tidal waves** a huge wave, often caused by a volcano erupting under the sea or by unusually high tides

tiddler •NOUN• **tiddlers** a very small fish

tiddlywinks •NOUN• a game played with small round coloured discs, in which you press one disc down on another making it flip upwards and fall into a cup

tide •NOUN• the regular rise and fall of the level of the sea
•VERB• **tides, tiding, tided** if you have or get something to **tide you over**, it helps you get through a difficult time, especially one when you don't have enough money
⇒ **tidal**

tidily •ADVERB• neatly

tidiness •NOUN• being tidy or neat

tidings •PLURAL NOUN• a slightly old-fashioned word for **news**: glad tidings

tidy •ADJECTIVE• **tidier, tidiest 1** a place is tidy when it is neat and everything is in its proper place **2** a tidy person likes to keep things neat and in their proper place
•VERB• **tidies, tidying, tidied** to put things back in their proper places and make everything neat
⇒ **tidily, tidiness**

tie •VERB• **ties, tying, tied 1** to tie one thing to another is to join them or fasten them together, using string, rope or wire
2 to tie a knot or bow is to make loops that you twist round each other to form a knot or bow
3 two teams or competitors tie when they each have the same number of points: They tied for second place.

•NOUN• **ties 1** a narrow strip of material that goes round your neck under your shirt collar and is tied in a knot just under your chin
2 a situation in which two teams or competitors each have the same number of points
3 a match between two teams in a competition

tie-breaker •NOUN• **tie-breakers** an extra question or test that will decide the winner in a contest where two people or teams have the same score

tier •NOUN• **tiers** a row or layer, with another row or layer above or below it

tiff •NOUN• **tiffs** an argument, especially one that is not very serious

tiger •NOUN• **tigers** a large striped animal related to the cat

tight •ADJECTIVE• **tighter, tightest 1** fitting very closely or too closely: a tight shirt • The top on this jar is very tight.
2 very firm: Have you got a tight grip on that rope?
3 not leaving much room or space for movement: a tight bend
✦ **tighten** •VERB• **tightens, tightening, tightened** to make or become tight or tighter
✦ **tightly** or **tight** •ADVERB• **1** closely: She held her doll tight.
2 firmly: Hold tight. It's going to be a bumpy ride.
3 fully stretched: Make sure that rope is pulled tight.

tightrope •NOUN• **tightropes** a long piece of rope stretched tightly between supports, which an acrobat walks along

tights •PLURAL NOUN• tights are a one-piece covering for your feet, legs and bottom made of thin stretchy material

tigress •NOUN• **tigresses** a female tiger

tile •NOUN• **tiles** a piece of baked clay of various sizes, used for putting on roofs, walls or floors
•VERB• **tiles, tiling, tiled** to tile a roof, wall or floor is to put tiles on it

till¹ •NOUN• **tills** a machine in a shop used for counting up what customers have bought and which has a drawer or box for the money

Aa
Bb
Cc
Dd
Ee
Ff
Gg
Hh
Ii
Jj
Kk
Ll
Mm
Nn
Oo
Pp
Qq
Rr
Ss
Tt
Uu
Vv
Ww
Xx
Yy
Zz

till² •VERB• **tills, tilling, tilled** to till soil is to prepare it for crops or other plants by ploughing it or turning the soil over

till³ •PREPOSITION AND CONJUNCTION• until

tiller •NOUN• **tillers** a long piece of wood attached to the rudder at the back of a boat and which you use to steer the boat

tilt •VERB• **tilts, tilting, tilted** to lean over to one side

timber •NOUN• **1** wood that is used for building things such as houses **2** trees that can be used to provide wood for building

timbre •NOUN• **timbres** the timbre of someone's voice or of a musical instrument is the quality of sound it makes

ⓘ This word is pronounced tam-bir.

time •NOUN• **times 1** time is the passing of days, weeks, months and years
2 the time is the hour of the day: *What's the time?*
3 the time of something is when it happens or is done: *Do you know the times of the trains to Edinburgh?*
4 the number of minutes, hours, days or years that something takes to do or happen: *It takes a long time for water to wear down rocks.*
5 one of several occasions: *They've won the cup four times.*
6 a particular period: *in olden times*
7 a suitable or right moment: *Now is not a good time to ask for more money.*
•VERB• **times, timing, timed 1** to time something is to use a clock or watch to find out how long it takes or when it will be ready
2 to time something well is to choose a good time to do it
• **from time to time** things happen or are done from time to time if they happen or are done occasionally, but not all the time
• **in** or **on time** to be in time, or on time, is to arrive or happen at the right time and not be late, or too late
♦ **timely** •ADJECTIVE• something that is timely happens at just the right time
♦ **timer** •NOUN• **timers** a device for timing something
⇒ **timing**

times •PLURAL NOUN• **times** is used in multiplication between the numbers you are multiplying: *Two times four is eight.*

time scale •NOUN• **time scales** the time during which an event or process happens: *Evolution happens over a time scale of thousands of years.*

timetable •NOUN• **timetables** a table listing the times when things should or will happen

timid •ADJECTIVE• nervous, shy and easily frightened: *Pip's a rather timid child.* • *a timid smile*
♦ **timidity** •NOUN• being nervous and shy
♦ **timidly** •ADVERB• in a shy, nervous way: *Lou smiled a little less timidly when Sam spoke to her again.*

timing •NOUN• choosing just the right moment to do or say something: *All comedians need to learn good timing.* • *The timing of the party is very important.*

timpani •PLURAL NOUN• the large metal drums that are usually part of a symphony orchestra

tin •NOUN• **tins 1** tin is a soft, silvery metal **2** a tin is a metal container for food, either with a lid you can replace or seal to keep the food inside fresh until you want to use it: *Let's just open a tin of soup for lunch.*

tinder •NOUN• dry material, especially small bits of wood, that can be used to light a fire

tinfoil •NOUN• wrapping for food that is made from very thin metal

tinge •NOUN• **tinges** a slight amount of something, especially a colour or feeling: *white with a tinge of pink* • *a tinge of sadness in her voice*

tingle •VERB• **tingles, tingling, tingled** to prickle, tickle or sting slightly: *My face was tingling in the cold night air.*
•NOUN• **tingles** a prickling, tickling feeling: *I felt a tingle of excitement as the curtain went up.*
♦ **tingly** •ADJECTIVE• feeling excited about something that is about to happen

tinker •VERB• **tinkers, tinkering, tinkered** to try to repair or improve a machine by making small changes: *Phil loves spending hours tinkering with his motorbike.*

•NOUN• **tinkers** a person who used to travel around mending pots and pans for people

tinkle •VERB• **tinkles, tinkling, tinkled** to make a sound like small bells ringing
•NOUN• **tinkles** a small, repeated ringing sound: *the tinkle of the bell on the cat's collar*

tinny •ADJECTIVE• **tinnier, tinniest** 1 a tinny sound is thin, hard and high: *Keith pressed the buzzer and heard a tinny voice telling him to open the door and go upstairs.* 2 a tinny object is made of thin or bad quality metal

tinsel •NOUN• strands of shiny, glittery material that is used as a Christmas decoration

tint •NOUN• **tints** a small amount of colour: *a bluish tint in her green eyes*
•VERB• **tints, tinting, tinted** to colour something slightly

tiny •ADJECTIVE• **tinier, tiniest** very, very small: *a baby's tiny hands and feet* • *the tiniest handwriting you ever saw*

tip¹ •NOUN• **tips** the point at the end or the top of something: *arrows with poison tips* • *Point to it with the tip of your finger.*

tip² •VERB• **tips, tipping, tipped** 1 to tilt: *Tip the chairs forward against the tables.* 2 to spill the contents of a container: *They just tip the rubbish over the side of the ship.* • *Kitty tipped all her toys on to the floor.*
•NOUN• **tips** 1 a rubbish dump: *taking the old carpet to the tip* 2 a very untidy place: *Your bedroom's a tip.*

tip³ •NOUN• **tips** 1 a small extra amount of money for someone who has done a job for you: *They left almost ten dollars tip.* 2 a small piece of helpful advice: *useful tips on cutting your own hair*
•VERB• **tips, tipping, tipped** to give someone a small gift of money when they have done a good job for you: *How much did you tip the taxi-driver?*

tiptoe •VERB• **tiptoes, tiptoeing, tiptoed** to walk somewhere very quietly or carefully on your toes: *tiptoeing along the corridor, trying not to wake the other guests*
•NOUN• if you are **on tiptoe**, you are standing or walking balanced on your toes: *I can just see the sea if I stand on tiptoe.*

tire •VERB• **tires, tiring, tired** 1 to run out of energy and need a rest: *Auntie tires easily nowadays and has a rest every afternoon.* 2 to get bored with something: *I'm beginning to tire of Nigel's stories.*

♦ **tired** •ADJECTIVE• 1 needing a rest: *You must be tired after your journey.* 2 bored: *I'm tired of wearing the same clothes every day.*

♦ **tireless** •ADJECTIVE• having a lot of energy and never needing a rest: *her tireless efforts to raise money for charity*

♦ **tiresome** •ADJECTIVE• annoying or boring: *Mona has a tiresome habit of finishing my sentences for me.*

♦ **tiring** •ADJECTIVE• making you feel that you need a rest or sleep: *a tiring climb up the hill*

ⓘ Be careful not to confuse the spellings of **tire** and **tyre**, which is the covering of a wheel. However, in North America these words are both spelt **tire**.

tissue •NOUN• **tissues** 1 a paper handkerchief 2 very thin paper that is used for protecting delicate objects 3 the substance that animals and plants are made of: *muscle tissue* • *plant tissue*

tit •NOUN• **tits** a type of small bird

titbit •NOUN• **titbits** 1 a small tasty bit of food 2 a small but interesting bit of gossip

title •NOUN• **titles** 1 the name of something like a book, song or film: *What's the title of your poem?* 2 a word that you can use before your name: *Her title is 'Doctor', not 'Mrs'.*

titter •VERB• **titters, tittering, tittered** to laugh in a silly, nervous or embarrassed way
•NOUN• **titters** a silly, nervous laugh

to •PREPOSITION• 1 towards: *walking to the shops* 2 as far as: *a mile from the house to the station* 3 compared with: *win by two goals to one*
•ADVERB• 1 almost closed: *Would you pull the door to?* 2 awake: *He came to in a few moments.*
• **to and fro** backwards and forwards

toad •NOUN• **toads** an animal like a large frog

toadstool •NOUN• **toadstools** a fungus like a large mushroom that is often poisonous

toast •NOUN• **toasts** 1 toast is bread that has been made crisp by being sliced and heated: *toast and marmalade for breakfast* 2 a toast is when people drink together to express a good wish for someone: *I'd like to propose a toast to the bride and groom.*
•VERB• **toasts, toasting, toasted** 1 to toast food is to cook it under a grill or at a fire 2 to toast a person is to have a drink and wish them well
• **toaster** •NOUN• **toasters** a machine for heating slices of bread to make them crisp to eat

tobacco •NOUN• a type of plant whose leaves are dried and used for smoking or chewing
• **tobacconist** •NOUN• **tobacconists** someone who sells cigarettes, cigars and pipes and sometimes sweets and newspapers

toboggan •NOUN• **toboggans** a sledge

today •NOUN• this day: *Today is Tuesday.*
•ADVERB• 1 on this day: *I can't come today.* 2 nowadays, at the present time: *People are taller today than they were a hundred years ago.*

toddler •NOUN• **toddlers** a very young child who has just learned to walk

toe •NOUN• **toes** 1 one of the five jointed parts at the end of your foot: *reach up high, standing on your toes* 2 the closed end of a shoe or sock: *a hole in the toe of my sock*

toffee •NOUN• **toffees** a sticky sweet that may be chewy or hard: *a piece of toffee* • *a bag of toffees*

toga •NOUN• **togas** a long loose piece of clothing worn by men in ancient Rome

together •ADVERB• with each other: *The two friends always walk to school together.* • *Mix the sugar and eggs together in a bowl.*

toggle •NOUN• **toggles** a small bar of wood or plastic that passes through a loop to fasten a coat or jacket

toil •VERB• **toils, toiling, toiled** to work hard for a long time
•NOUN• hard work that takes a long time

toilet •NOUN• **toilets** 1 a large bowl-shaped piece of furniture where human waste can be washed away 2 a room with a toilet in it
• **toiletries** •PLURAL NOUN• products that people use to keep clean and to look and smell nice: *Perfume, toothpaste, shaving cream and hairspray are all toiletries.*

token •NOUN• **tokens** 1 a plastic or metal disc or a coupon or voucher that can be used instead of money: *a book token worth £10* • *You need to buy special tokens to make the machine work.* 2 a sign of something: *I've got a bracelet as a token of our friendship.*

told •VERB• the way of changing the verb **tell** to make a past tense. It can be used with or without a helping verb: *Every day the teacher told us a story.* • *Has Sarah told you her news yet?*

tolerable •ADJECTIVE• something is tolerable if you can put up with it

tolerance •NOUN• patience and willingness to accept other people's ideas and behaviour

tolerant •ADJECTIVE• willing to accept that other people have different opinions from yours

tolerate •VERB• **tolerates, tolerating, tolerated** to put up with something: *I can't tolerate this noise for much longer.*

toll[1] •NOUN• **tolls** 1 a fee you must pay to cross a bridge or use certain roads: *You only have to pay the toll if you're travelling north.* 2 the loss or damage caused in a disaster: *The death toll was highest in the city centre.*

toll[2] •VERB• **tolls, tolling, tolled** to ring a bell slowly

tomahawk •NOUN• **tomahawks** a small axe used by Native Americans as a weapon and a tool

tomato •NOUN• **tomatoes** a juicy red-skinned fruit that is used like a vegetable in salads, sauces and sandwiches

tomb •NOUN• **tombs** a place like a room where a dead body is buried

tombola •NOUN• **tombolas** a kind of lottery where certain numbered tickets win prizes

tomboy •NOUN• **tomboys** a girl who likes rough, energetic activities

tombstone •NOUN• **tombstones** a piece of stone with a dead person's name written on

Aa Bb Cc Dd Ee Ff Gg Hh Ii Jj Kk Ll Mm Nn Oo Pp Qq Rr Ss Tt Uu Vv Ww Xx Yy Zz

it that stands at the end of that person's grave

tomcat • NOUN• **tomcats** a male cat

tomorrow • NOUN• the day after today: *Tomorrow is Wednesday.*
• ADVERB• on the day after today: *Let's have our meeting tomorrow.*

tomtom • NOUN• **tomtoms** a drum that you beat with your hands

ton • NOUN• **tons** 1 a measure of weight that is about 1016 kilograms or 2240 pounds in Britain or about 907 kilograms or 2000 pounds in America 2 tons of things or people are a very many of them: *She's got tons of clothes to choose from.*

tone • NOUN• **tones** 1 the sound of something: *I could tell she was angry from the tone of her voice.* • *a cello with a soft gentle tone*
2 a brighter or darker version of a certain colour: *several tones of blue*
3 a musical interval that equals two **semitones**
• VERB• **tones, toning, toned** 1 to tone or **tone in** with something is to match it or look good with it: *The red scarf tones in with the plum-coloured coat.* 2 to tone or **tone up** your body or muscles is to do exercises to become fitter

tongs • PLURAL NOUN• a tool with two arms that are joined at one end and are squeezed together to pick something up

tongue • NOUN• **tongues** 1 the fleshy part of your mouth that you can move and that you use to lick, speak, eat and taste
2 a language: *speaking in a foreign tongue*
3 the leather flap underneath the opening of a shoe or boot

tongue-tied • ADJECTIVE• too nervous, shy or embarrassed to speak

tongue-twister • NOUN• **tongue-twisters** a phrase or sentence that is difficult to say quickly

tonic • NOUN• **tonics** 1 something that makes you feel stronger or gives you energy 2 tonic, or tonic water, is a clear, fizzy, bitter-tasting drink

tonight • NOUN• the night or evening of today: *I'll have to miss tonight's class, I'm afraid.*

• ADVERB• on the night or evening of today: *I'm going to bed early tonight.*

tonne • NOUN• **tonnes** a metric unit of weight of 1000 kilograms or about 2205 pounds

tonsil • NOUN• **tonsils** either of the soft lumps on either side of the back of your throat
✦ **tonsillitis** • NOUN• an infection that causes the tonsils to swell and hurt

too • ADVERB• 1 also: *Can I come too?* 2 more than necessary or more than is sensible: *If the water is too hot, add some cold.* • *You're driving much too fast!*

took • VERB• a way of changing the verb **take** to make a past tense: *Fran took me to a concert on my birthday.* • *The shopping took all morning.*

tool • NOUN• **tools** a piece of equipment that you hold to do a certain job: *Dad's plumbing tools are in the boot of the car.*

toot • VERB• **toots, tooting, tooted** to toot a horn is to make it sound
• NOUN• **toots** the noise a horn makes: *Mum gave us a toot on the car horn when she arrived.*

tooth • NOUN• **teeth** 1 the hard, white, bony parts of the jaw that are used for biting and chewing. Look at the illustration on the next page 2 one of the sharp points of something like a saw or a comb

toothache • NOUN• a pain in or near a tooth

toothpaste • NOUN• a cream that you use to clean your teeth

top¹ • NOUN• **tops** 1 the highest point or part of something: *climbing to the top of the tower* • *waiting at the top of the steps* • *distant mountain tops* • *Start reading at the top of the page.*
2 the upper surface of something: *a vase on the top of the television*
3 the lid or cap of a container: *Screw the top back on tightly.*
4 a piece of clothing for the upper half of your body: *green trousers and a black top*
• ADJECTIVE• highest or most important: *My office is on the top floor.* • *a top fashion designer*
• ADVERB• with the highest marks or score: *Elaine comes top in maths every term.*
• VERB• **tops, topping, topped** 1 to cover the

Aa
Bb
Cc
Dd
Ee
Ff
Gg
Hh
Ii
Jj
Kk
Ll
Mm
Nn
Oo
Pp
Qq
Rr
Ss
Tt
Uu
Vv
Ww
Xx
Yy
Zz

a tooth

blood vessels and nerves
enamel
gum
dentine
root

upper surface of something: *Top the cake with fruit and whipped cream.*
2 to come first in a list: *This album is expected to top the charts next week.*
3 to **top something up** is to fill it up again: *Can I top up your drink for you?*

top² •NOUN• **tops** a toy that spins around on a point

topaz •NOUN• a type of precious stone that is often yellow

top hat •NOUN• **top hats** a tall hat with a flat top that men often wore in the past

topic •NOUN• **topics** a subject or theme to study, write or talk about: *Choose one of the topics below as the title of your essay.*

topic sentence •NOUN• **topic sentences** a sentence that tells you what the topic or theme of a paragraph is

topless •ADJECTIVE• without any clothes on the top half of your body

topmost •ADJECTIVE• right at the top: *in the topmost branches of the tree*

topple •VERB• **topples. toppling, toppled** to wobble and fall over

top-secret •ADJECTIVE• very secret: *a spy passing on information that should have been top-secret*

topsyturvy •ADJECTIVE AND ADVERB• turned upside down

Torah •NOUN• the holy book of the Jewish people

torch •NOUN• **torches 1** a small electric light with batteries in it that you can hold in one hand **2** a big stick with something burning on the end that is carried as a light in a procession

tore •VERB• a way of changing the verb **tear** to make a past tense: *Heidi tore the parcel open to see what was inside.*

torment •VERB• **torments, tormenting, tormented 1** to treat someone cruelly or annoy them in a spiteful way **2** to be tormented by something is to suffer for a long time because of it: *still tormented by bad dreams*
•NOUN• **torments** very great pain or worry that goes on for a long time
♦ **tormentor** •NOUN• **tormentors** a person who makes a person or animal suffer on purpose

ⓘ The noun is pronounced **tor**-ment, with the stress on *tor*. The verb is pronounced tor-**ment**, with the stress on *ment*.

torn •VERB• the form of the verb **tear** that is used with a helping verb to show that something happened in the past: *The photograph had been torn right down the middle.*

tornado •NOUN• **tornadoes** a violent storm with a whirling wind that causes a lot of damage

torpedo •NOUN• **torpedos or torpedoes** a long thin bomb that moves quickly under

water and explodes when it hits its target, which is usually a ship or submarine
• VERB• **torpedoes, torpedoing, torpedoed** to fire a torpedo at something

torrent • NOUN• **torrents** a lot of water rushing or falling down quickly
♦ **torrential** • ADJECTIVE• torrential rain is very heavy rain

torso • NOUN• **torsos** the main part of your body, not including your arms, legs or head

tortoise • NOUN• **tortoise** a slow-moving animal with a hard shell that covers its body

tortoiseshell • NOUN• the brown and yellow shell of a sea turtle that has been used to make things like combs or jewellery

torture • VERB• **tortures, torturing, tortured** to hurt someone on purpose, usually either as a punishment or to get some information out of them
• NOUN• **tortures** hurting someone as a punishment or to get information from them: *an instrument of torture*
♦ **torturer** • NOUN• **torturers** a person who hurts another person on purpose for some reason

toss • VERB• **tosses, tossing, tossed** 1 to throw something lightly into the air: *Toss the keys over here, would you?*
2 to move from side to side again and again when you are lying down: *tossing and turning in her bed all night*
3 to throw a coin up in the air to see which side it lands on: *We decided to toss for the front seat.*

total • NOUN• **totals** the number you get when you add everything together: *We've got a total of fifteen cats.* • *thirty people in total*
• VERB• **totals, totalling, totalled** to come to a certain amount when added together: *Our collection totalled £320.*
• ADJECTIVE• complete or absolute: *a total eclipse of the sun* • *The job must be done in total secrecy.*
♦ **totally** • ADVERB• completely: *Is she totally deaf?* • *I agree with you totally.*

totem pole • NOUN• **totem poles** a tall wooden pole with carvings and paintings made by Native Americans

totter • VERB• **totters, tottering, tottered** to walk unsteadily and with small steps as if you are about to fall over

touch • VERB• **touches, touching, touched**
1 to put your hand or fingers on something: *Please do not touch the items on the shelf.* • *Can you touch the ceiling?*
2 to make contact with a thing or person: *We stood in a long line with our shoulders touching.* • *The car came close, but fortunately didn't actually touch us.*
3 to interfere with something: *Don't let anyone touch my desk while I'm away.*
4 to be touched by something is to be affected emotionally by it: *I was touched by your kind letter.*
5 to **touch something up** is to make small changes to something to improve it: *We decided to touch up the paintwork before we sold the house.*
• NOUN• **touches** 1 touch is the sense that tells you what things feel like: *The fur was smooth to the touch.*
2 putting a hand or finger on something: *You can start the engine at the touch of a button.*
3 a small thing that you add to improve something: *Fiona, of course, was able to add the finishing touch to the display.*
4 communication with someone: *Get in touch with me.* • *I have lost touch with Sally.*
⇒ **touching**

touch-and-go • ADJECTIVE• very uncertain or risky

touching • ADJECTIVE• making you feel sympathy: *a touching story about a lost puppy*

touchy • ADJECTIVE• **touchier, touchiest**
1 easily annoyed: *What's she so touchy about today?* 2 needing to be handled carefully: *Pocket money is a touchy subject in this family.*

tough • ADJECTIVE• **tougher, toughest**
1 strong and not easily worn out: *You'll need a tough pair of shoes for climbing.*
2 strong, fit and not easily beaten: *a tough businesswoman*
3 difficult to deal with: *a tough customer* • *a tough decision*
4 hard to chew: *tough meat*

Aa
Bb
Cc
Dd
Ee
Ff
Gg
Hh
Ii
Jj
Kk
Ll
Mm
Nn
Oo
Pp
Qq
Rr
Ss
Tt
Uu
Vv
Ww
Xx
Yy
Zz

Aa Bb Cc Dd Ee Ff Gg Hh Ii Jj Kk Ll Mm Nn Oo Pp Qq Rr Ss **Tt** Uu Vv Ww Xx Yy Zz

5 firm or strict: *It's time to get tough with football hooligans.*
◆ **toughen** •VERB• **toughens, toughening, toughened** to toughen or **toughen up** a thing *or* person is to make them stronger
◆ **toughness** •NOUN• being strong and not easily beaten or worn out

tour •NOUN• **tours** a visit somewhere, stopping several times at points of interest: *a coach tour of the Lake District* • *a tour of the cathedral*
•VERB• **tours, touring, toured** to go round a place, stopping at points of interest on the way: *We're going to tour the wine-making regions of France.* • *We've hired a car to tour the city.*
◆ **tourism** •NOUN• travelling to and visiting places for enjoyment
◆ **tourist** •NOUN• **tourists** a person who is travelling for enjoyment or on holiday

tournament •NOUN• **tournaments** a series of matches that make up a big competition

tousled •ADJECTIVE• tousled hair is untidy and looks tangled

tout •NOUN• **touts** a person who tries to sell something, especially very expensive tickets for popular events

tow •VERB• **tows, towing, towed** to pull something behind you with a rope or chain: *The car broke down and we had to get Dad to tow us home.*
•NOUN• **tows** pulling something behind you with a rope or chain: *Will you give us a tow home?*

towards *or* **toward** •PREPOSITION• 1 in a certain direction: *walking towards the gate* • *leaning over towards Bill*
2 in connection with: *Nothing has been done towards organizing the prize-giving.*
3 helping to pay for something: *a donation towards the new roof*

towel •NOUN• **towels** a piece of thick cloth for drying yourself: *a bath towel*
•VERB• **towels, towelling, towelled** to dry a thing or person with a towel: *Towel your hair dry before applying the cream.*
◆ **towelling** •NOUN• thick cotton material that absorbs water well and so is good for drying things: *a bath robe made of towelling*

tower •NOUN• **towers** a tall narrow building or part of a building: *the clocktower of the church* • *the Eiffel Tower*
•VERB• **towers, towering, towered** to be much taller than other things or people: *William towers over all his classmates.*
◆ **towering** •ADJECTIVE• very tall: *towering office blocks in the city centre*

town •NOUN• **towns** a place where people live and work, that has streets, buildings and a name

ⓘ This word comes from the Old English word **tun**, which means 'an enclosed area'.

town hall •NOUN• **town halls** a building that has council offices in it and, usually, a hall for public events

towpath •NOUN• **towpaths** a path beside a canal or river

toxic •ADJECTIVE• poisonous: *polluting the rivers with toxic waste*

toy •NOUN• **toys** an object made for a child to play with
•VERB• **toys, toying, toyed** 1 to **toy with** something is to push it around for no real reason: *toying with her food but not eating it* 2 to **toy with** an idea is to consider it, but not very seriously

trace •VERB• **traces, tracing, traced** 1 to find someone or something by following information about where they have been: *The man has been traced to a village in the south of the country.* 2 to make a copy of a picture by covering it with a sheet of thin paper and drawing over the lines you can see through it
•NOUN• **traces** 1 a mark or sign that someone or something leaves behind: *traces of footsteps in the sand* • *He vanished without trace.* 2 a very small amount of something: *traces of gunpowder on his shoes*

tracing paper •NOUN• very thin paper that you can see the lines of a picture through

track •NOUN• **tracks** 1 a mark on the ground left by a person, animal or thing that has passed: *following the bear's tracks through the forest*
2 a rough path or road: *a narrow track around the edge of the field*

3 a racecourse: *a running track*
4 a set of rails that a train or tram runs on
5 one of the songs or pieces of music on a CD, tape or record
6 a heavy strip linking the wheels of a vehicle such as a tank
• **keep track of** to keep track of someone or something is to make sure you know where they are and what is happening to them
•VERB• **tracks, tracking, tracked** 1 to follow the marks that an animal, person or thing leaves as they pass: *It was impossible to track anyone over such stony ground.* 2 to **track someone** or **something down** is to find them after a long search: *I'm trying to track down an old schoolfriend.* • *The shop has tracked down the book you ordered.*

tracksuit • NOUN• **tracksuits** a warm suit with a loose top and trousers that you can wear when exercising or to keep your body warm before or after exercise

tract[1] • NOUN• **tracts** 1 a large area of land 2 a system of tubes and organs in the body: *the digestive tract*

tract[2] • NOUN• **tracts** a leaflet or a short essay

traction • NOUN• pulling or dragging

tractor • NOUN• **tractors** a slow vehicle with two large rear wheels that is used for pulling heavy loads, for example, on a farm

trade • NOUN• **trades** 1 buying, selling or exchanging things or services: *foreign trade* 2 a job or occupation, especially when it involves skill and training: *a young joiner who is still learning his trade*
•VERB• **trades, trading, traded** 1 to buy, sell or exchange things or services: *The government wants companies to trade outside Europe.* 2 to **trade something in** is to give it as part of the price of a new one: *We traded in our old car for the latest model.*

ⓘ The word **trade** comes from the Old English word **trada**, which means a *track* or a *path*, because trade is carried out between two places or groups. The word **tread** is also connected to this word.

---

trademark • NOUN• **trademarks** a name, word or symbol that a company uses to identify its products

trader • NOUN• **traders** a person or company that buys and sells things

tradesman • NOUN• **tradesmen** 1 a person who has been trained in a particular skill as their job 2 a shopkeeper

trade union • NOUN• **trade unions** an organization of workers who are involved in similar work

tradition • NOUN• **traditions** 1 a tradition is a custom that has been passed down from one generation to the next: *Having special birthday meals is a family tradition.* 2 tradition is passing down beliefs and customs from one generation to the next
♦ **traditional** • ADJECTIVE• existing for a long time and being done by many generations: *traditional Christmas carols*

traffic • NOUN• 1 travelling vehicles: *air traffic controllers* • *road traffic reports* 2 trade that is illegal
•VERB• **traffics, trafficking, trafficked** to buy and sell things illegally: *drug trafficking*

traffic lights • PLURAL NOUN• a set of red, amber and green lights that controls traffic at road junctions

tragedy • NOUN• **tragedies** 1 a very sad event: *The driver avoided a tragedy by his quick reaction.* 2 a story that has a sad ending, especially when the main character dies: *Shakespeare wrote comedies, histories and tragedies.*
♦ **tragic** • ADJECTIVE• very sad or to do with suffering: *a tragic mistake*
♦ **tragically** • ADVERB• very sadly: *The poet died tragically young.*

trail • NOUN• **trails** 1 a series of signs that you follow to find a thing or person: *The children in the story left a trail of paper when they got lost.* 2 a path or track through rough or wild country
•VERB• **trails, trailing, trailed** 1 to drag or be dragged loosely behind someone: *Her long coat trailed on the floor.* • *Children trailed their boats through the water.*
2 to walk slowly because you are tired: *children trailing along behind their parents*
3 to be behind the winner of a competition: *The English team are trailing by 5 points.*
4 to grow across and down, rather than

upwards: *roses trailing over the wall*

trailer •NOUN• **trailers** 1 a container on wheels that is pulled behind another vehicle: *a tent in a trailer* 2 a short part of a film or programme that is used as an advertisement for it: *We saw some trailers for new films.*

train [1] •NOUN• **trains** 1 a series of railway carriages or trucks that are pulled by an engine 2 the back part of a long dress that trails on the floor: *The bride's gown had a long train made of lace.*

train [2] •VERB• **trains, training, trained** 1 to teach a person or animal to do something: *Veronica has trained her dog to carry her handbag.*

2 to train as something is to learn to do that job: *Andrew trained as a nurse as soon as he left school.*

3 to prepare for a sporting event: *The team trains for three hours every day.*

4 to point a camera or gun in a certain direction: *The enemy's guns are trained on the airport.*

trainer •NOUN• **trainers** 1 a person who teaches people or animals to improve their skills 2 trainers are soft shoes that are designed for sports use

training •NOUN• 1 practice and instruction in doing a certain job: *training in computing* 2 preparation for a sports event: *The team will be in training for the next year.*

traitor •NOUN• **traitors** a person who is not loyal to their friends or country

tram •NOUN• **trams** a type of electric bus that runs on rails in the street

tramp •NOUN• **tramps** a person without a fixed home or job who walks from place to place
•VERB• **tramps, tramping, tramped** to walk with slow, firm, heavy footsteps

trample •VERB• **tramples, trampling, trampled** to tread on something heavily and roughly: *The sheep have trampled all over the wheat.* • *If you stand there you'll get trampled on.*

trampoline •NOUN• **trampolines** a piece of canvas that is stretched across a frame for acrobats, gymnasts and children to jump on

trance •NOUN• **trances** a state like sleep when you are awake, but not aware of what is going on around you

tranquil •ADJECTIVE• quiet, calm and peaceful

tranquillity •NOUN• calm and peacefulness

tranquillize •VERB• **tranquillizes, tranquillizing, tranquillized** to give a person or animal a drug to make them calmer and more relaxed or to help them to sleep

tranquillizer •NOUN• **tranquillizers** a drug that makes people feel calmer and more relaxed

trans- •PREFIX• if a word starts with **trans-** it has something to do with moving across, through or over to the other side. For example, *transport* means 'to carry over' to another place

transaction •NOUN• **transactions** a business deal or one that involves money

transatlantic •ADJECTIVE• involving crossing the Atlantic Ocean: *a transatlantic flight*

transfer •VERB• **transfers, transferring, transferred** 1 to transfer a person or thing is to move it from one place to another: *transferring computer files to a floppy disk* • *George has been transferred to our London office.* 2 to change to a different vehicle or transport system: *At Kings Cross, transfer to the Central Line.*
•NOUN• **transfers** 1 moving a thing or person from one place to another: *The sergeant has asked for a transfer.* 2 a piece of paper with a design on one side that can be ironed or rubbed on to another surface

transferable •ADJECTIVE• a transferable ticket can be used by someone else or can also be used on a different transport system

transfix •VERB• **transfixes, transfixing, transfixed** to frighten or shock someone so much that they cannot move from the spot

transform •VERB• **transforms, transforming, transformed** to change something completely: *We could transform this room with a few tins of paint.*

transformation •NOUN• **transformations** a complete change in the way a thing or person looks

Aa Bb Cc Dd Ee Ff Gg Hh Ii Jj Kk Ll Mm Nn Oo Pp Qq Rr Ss Tt Uu Vv Ww Xx Yy Zz

• **transformer** •NOUN• **transformers** a device that changes an electric current from one voltage to another

transfusion •NOUN• **transfusions** a blood transfusion is blood that has been taken from one person and is given to another

transistor •NOUN• **transistors 1** a small piece of electronic equipment used in radios and televisions to make the sound louder **2** a transistor or a transistor radio is a small radio that you can carry around easily

transit •NOUN• to be **in transit** is to be travelling between one place and another: *The luggage has been lost in transit.*

transition •NOUN• a change from one state or place to another: *the transition from primary to secondary school*
• **transitional** •ADJECTIVE• to do with changing or developing from one state to another: *a transitional period of a few weeks when the old computer system is replaced*

translate •VERB• **translates, translating, translated** to put something into a different language: *Can you translate this into French?*
• **translation** •NOUN• **translations 1** writing or speech that has been put into a different language: *a new translation of an old book* **2** changing speech or writing into a different language: *I'm no good at translation although I can understand what's going on.*
• **translator** •NOUN• **translators** a person who puts speech or writing into a different language

translucent •ADJECTIVE• not transparent, but shiny because light is reflected or can get through

transmission •NOUN• **transmissions 1** a television or radio broadcast: *a transmission that will be heard by millions all over the world* **2** broadcasting television and radio signals: *a transmission breakdown*

transmit •VERB• **transmits, transmitting, transmitted** to send out the signals for television or radio programmes
• **tramsmitter** •NOUN• **transmitters** a piece of equipment that sends and receives signals for television and radio programmes

transparent •ADJECTIVE• see-through: *The box is made of transparent plastic so that you can see all the wires inside.*

transplant •VERB• **transplants, transplanting, transplanted 1** to remove a part from one person's body and put it in someone else's **2** to move a plant that is growing in one place to somewhere else: *The seedlings can be transplanted when they have four leaves.*
•NOUN• **transplants** an operation to put an organ from one person's body into someone else: *a heart transplant*

transport •NOUN• **1** the vehicles that you travel in, such as cars, trains, aircraft and boats: *travel by public transport* **2** moving people or things from one place to another: *This includes the cost of transport.*
•VERB• **transports, transporting, transported** to move something from one place to another
• **transportation** •NOUN• moving people or things

transporter •NOUN• **transporters** a long vehicle that is usually used for taking a number of large objects, such as cars, to another place

trap •NOUN• **traps 1** a piece of equipment for catching animals **2** a plan to trick someone into doing or saying something or to catch them doing something wrong: *a speed trap to catch people driving too fast* **3** a small, two-wheeled carriage pulled by a horse
•VERB• **traps, trapping, trapped 1** to catch an animal in a trap **2** to trick someone into doing or saying something: *The suspect was trapped into admitting that he had been there.* **3** to put someone in a situation that they cannot escape from: *One passenger was trapped in the crashed car until the fire brigade could cut him free.*

trapdoor •NOUN• **trapdoors** a door in a floor or a ceiling

trapeze •NOUN• **trapezes** a short bar hanging between two ropes high up from the ground, that gymnasts or acrobats swing on

Aa Bb Cc Dd Ee Ff Gg Hh Ii Jj Kk Ll Mm Nn Oo Pp Qq Rr Ss Tt Uu Vv Ww Xx Yy Zz

Aa

trapezium •NOUN• **trapeziums** a flat shape with four sides, but only two parallel sides which are different lengths

Bb

ⓘ **Trapezium** is a Latin word, which itself came from the Greek word **trapeza**, which means *table*.

Cc

Dd

trapezoid •NOUN• **trapezoids** a flat shape with four sides, but no parallel sides

Ee

trash •NOUN• rubbish: *a lot of trash in the newspapers*

Ff

♦ **trashy** •ADJECTIVE• **trashier, trashiest** of very bad quality: *trashy novels*

Gg

trauma •NOUN• **traumas** a very upsetting, unpleasant experience that has a lasting effect: *suffering the trauma of going to war*

Hh

♦ **traumatic** •ADJECTIVE• very upsetting, unpleasant or frightening: *a traumatic event*

Ii

Jj

travel •VERB• **travels, travelling, travelled** to go from one place to another, especially abroad or far from home: *Holly spent the summer travelling in the United States.* • *How fast does sound travel?*
•NOUN• **travels** 1 travel is going from one place to another, especially far from home 2 your travels are the journeys you make: *Did you have good weather on your travels?*

Kk

Ll

Mm

Nn

♦ **traveller** •NOUN• **travellers** 1 a person who is on a journey: *a hostel for travellers* 2 a person who lives in a vehicle and does not stay in one place

Oo

Pp

Qq

trawl •VERB• **trawls, trawling, trawled** to fish by dragging a net along behind a boat

Rr

♦ **trawler** •NOUN• **trawlers** a fishing boat that drags a large net deep in the sea behind it

Ss

tray •NOUN• **trays** a flat piece of something like wood or plastic with raised edges, for carrying food and drink

Tt

treacherous •ADJECTIVE• 1 a treacherous person is someone who betrays people they should be loyal to 2 treacherous things or places are very dangerous: *The rain made the road treacherous.*

Uu

Vv

Ww

♦ **treachery** •NOUN• doing something that might harm your country or someone who trusts you

Xx

Yy

treacle •NOUN• a sweet, thick, sticky liquid made from sugar

Zz

tread •VERB• **treads, treading, trod, trodden**

1 to tread on something is to walk or step on it: *I accidentally trod on the dog's tail.* • *Don't tread on the flowers.* 2 to walk in a certain way: *We trod carefully around the broken glass.*
•NOUN• **treads** 1 the sound you make when you walk: *the heavy tread of their boots on the bridge* 2 the tread of a tyre is the raised pattern on its surface that grips the road: *The tread on this tyre is completely worn away in parts.*

treason •NOUN• the crime of not being loyal to your country and possibly causing it harm, for example, by giving away secret information

treasure •NOUN• **treasures** 1 valuable things, especially if they have been hidden: *looking for where the treasure is buried* 2 a precious thing: *the treasures in our museums*
•VERB• **treasures, treasuring, treasured** to think that something is very precious: *Mother treasured all the memories of those family outings for the rest of her life.*

♦ **treasurer** •NOUN• **treasurers** a person who looks after the money of a club or society

♦ **treasury** •NOUN• **treasuries** the part of a government that is responsible for a country's money

treat •VERB• **treats, treating, treated** 1 to deal with someone or behave towards them in a certain way: *I think Debbie treated Steve really badly.* • *You should not treat a mistake like this as a joke.*

2 to give a person who is ill some medicine or medical help: *Our doctors use all the latest methods to treat their patients.*

3 to apply some sort of layer or protection to a surface: *The material is treated with a waterproofing spray.*

4 to pay for something special for someone else: *Dad treated us all to a pizza on the way home.*
•NOUN• **treats** 1 an unexpected present for someone that you pay for: *How would you like a treat?* 2 an enjoyable outing that someone organizes for you: *We went to the theatre as a treat.*

♦ **treatment** •NOUN• **treatments** 1 the way you deal with someone or behave towards them: *Will I get special treatment if I offer to pay more?* **2** the medical care that a patient gets: *My treatment will last for about a month.*

treaty •NOUN• **treaties** an agreement between countries or governments: *a peace treaty*

treble •ADJECTIVE• three times bigger or three times as much: *House prices are treble what they were ten years ago.*
•VERB• **trebles, trebling, trebled 1** to multiply something by three **2** to become or to make something three times as big or as much: *Her pay has trebled over the last year.*
•NOUN• **trebles 1** in music, the treble is the higher range of notes: *Can you turn up the treble any more?*
2 a musical instument with a high tone: *a treble recorder*
3 a boy with a high singing voice

treble clef •NOUN• **treble clefs** a sign (𝄞) that is usually written before musical notes that are higher than middle C

tree •NOUN• **trees** a tall plant with a hard trunk and branches

trek •VERB• **treks, trekking, trekked** to go on a long and difficult journey on foot: *We'll trek over the mountains to the sea.*
•NOUN• **treks** a long hard journey, usually on foot

trellis •NOUN• **trellises** a frame of narrow wooden strips that is used to support climbing plants

tremble •VERB• **trembles, trembling, trembled 1** to shake because you are cold or frightened: *Joe's hand trembled as he dialled the number.* **2** to sound unsteady: *I heard a trembling voice outside the window.*

tremendous •ADJECTIVE• **1** very great: *a tremendous amount of work • travelling at a tremendous speed* **2** very good: *That's tremendous news!*

tremor •NOUN• **tremors 1** a shaking or quivering: *Was there a slight tremor in his voice?* **2** a small earthquake

trench •NOUN• **trenches** a long narrow hole dug in the ground

trend •NOUN• **trends 1** a new fashion: *the*

latest trend in trousers **2** the way things are going or developing: *There's a new trend towards healthier eating at school.*
• **trendy** •ADJECTIVE• **trendier, trendiest** fashionable: *trendy people • trendy clothes*

trespass •VERB• **trespasses, trespassing, trespassed** to enter or go on someone else's land or property without permission: *No trespassing! This is private property.*
• **trespasser** •NOUN• **trespassers** a person who enters someone else's land or property without permission: *Trespassers will be prosecuted.*

trestle •NOUN• **trestles** a wooden suppport with legs that is usually used for holding up the end of a table

tri- •PREFIX• if a word starts with **tri-** it is usually something to do with the number *three*. For example, a *trio* is a group of three

trial •NOUN• **trials 1** a test that you do to make sure something works properly or that someone can do something properly: *We're carrying out trials on new products.* **2** a legal process where a jury decides whether or not a person is guilty of a crime: *a fair trial • The suspect will now have to stand trial.*

triangle •NOUN• **triangles 1** a flat shape with three sides and three angles: *a right-angled triangle* **2** a musical instrument that is a three-sided metal bar that you tap with a short metal stick
• **triangular** •ADJECTIVE• in the shape of a triangle: *a triangular scarf*

triathlon •NOUN• a sports contest that has three events, usually swimming, running and cycling

tribal •ADJECTIVE• belonging to or done by a tribe or tribes: *tribal ceremonies*

tribe •NOUN• **tribes** a group of families who live together and are ruled by a chief

tribesman •NOUN• **tribesmen** a man who belongs to a particular tribe

tribeswoman •NOUN• **tribeswomen** a woman who belongs to a particular tribe

tribulation •NOUN• **tribulations** a great sorrow or great suffering: *a life of tribulation*

tribunal •NOUN• **tribunals** a court or a group

of people whose job is to investigate a particular problem to do with the law

tributary •NOUN• **tributaries** a stream or river that flows into a larger river or lake

tribute •NOUN• **tributes** a speech or action that shows praise, thanks or respect for someone: *The film will be shown as a tribute to its star who died last week.*

trick •NOUN• **tricks** 1 something that you do or say to fool someone: *a nasty trick to get all her money* • *a card trick* 2 a clever special way of doing something: *There's a trick to opening that door quietly.*
•ADJECTIVE• a **trick question** is cleverly worded so that you probably give the wrong answer
•VERB• **tricks, tricking, tricked** to fool someone, especially when you make them do something they do not want to do: *They tricked her into agreeing to help.*
♦ **trickery** •NOUN• using cheating to get what you want
⇒ **tricky**

trickle •VERB• **trickles, trickling, trickled** to flow in a slow, thin stream: *tears trickling down her face*
•NOUN• **trickles** a slow, thin stream of liquid: *The waterfall has become a trickle because there's been so little rain.*

tricky •ADJECTIVE• **trickier, trickiest** difficult to deal with: *a tricky question*

tricycle •NOUN• **tricycles** a vehicle that you pedal, with two wheels at the back and one at the front

tried •VERB• a way of changing the verb **try** to make a past tense. It can be used with or without a helping verb: *I've tried and tried, but I still don't understand.* • *Rita tried not to giggle.*

trifle •NOUN• **trifles** 1 a cold pudding made from sponge, custard, fruit and cream 2 a small amount: *It's a trifle hot in here.* 3 something that is not important or valuable
•VERB• **trifles, trifling, trifled** to **trifle with** someone or something is to deal with them in a light, thoughtless way: *It can be hurtful if someone trifles with your feelings.*
♦ **trifling** •ADJECTIVE• not at all important: *a trifling matter*

trigger •NOUN• **triggers** the small lever that you squeeze to fire a gun
•VERB• **triggers, triggering, triggered** to trigger something or to **trigger something off** is to set it off: *A dusty room always triggers my sneezing off.*

trigonometry •NOUN• a type of mathematics that has to do with calculating the sides and angles of triangles

trill •NOUN• **trills** the repeated sound of two notes next to each other being played or sung alternately
•VERB• **trills, trilling, trilled** to sing repeated high notes: *birds trilling in the high branches*

trillion •NOUN• **trillions** 1 a trillion in Britain and Europe is a million million millions 2 a trillion in the United States and in Canada is a million millions 3 an informal word for a very large number: *There are trillions of things we could do.*

trilogy •NOUN• **trilogies** a series of three plays, novels, poems or operas that have the same subject

trim •VERB• **trims, trimming, trimmed** 1 to cut a little bit off something to make it tidy: *Get your hair trimmed.* • *You'll need to trim that photo to get it into the frame.* 2 to decorate the edges of something: *a coat trimmed with white fur*
•NOUN• **trims** cutting a small amount off something: *Ask the hairdresser for a quick trim.*
♦ **trimming** •NOUN• **trimmings** 1 a ribbon or lace that is used to decorate clothes or furnishings 2 the trimmings are the sauces and vegetables that usually go with a certain meal: *roast turkey and all the trimmings*

trinket •NOUN• **trinkets** a small cheap ornament or piece of jewellery

trio •NOUN• **trios** 1 a group of three people or things, especially musicians 2 a piece of music for three players or singers

trip •NOUN• **trips** a short journey to a place and back again: *a shopping trip* • *a trip to the zoo*
•VERB• **trips, tripping, tripped** 1 to catch your foot on something and fall, or nearly fall over: *Caroline tripped over the edge of the carpet.* • *Mind you don't trip on the step.* 2 to make someone fall or stumble: *One*

of the boys tripped me up.

3 to **trip along** is to walk or run along quickly and lightly

tripe •NOUN• **1** parts of the stomach of a cow or sheep, used as food **2** an informal word for rubbish or nonsense

triple •ADJECTIVE• **1** three times as much or as many: *We had triple the number of entries this year.* **2** made up of three parts: *triple-glazed windows* • *a triple somersault*
•VERB• **triples, tripling, tripled** to become or to make something three times as big: *The number of students learning Latin has tripled this year.*

triplet •NOUN• **triplets** one of three children born to the same mother at the same time

tripod •NOUN• **tripods** a stand with three legs for supporting something like a camera

triumph •NOUN• **triumphs** a great victory or success: *another triumph for the champions* • *a shout of triumph*
•VERB• **triumphs, triumphing, triumphed** to win or succeed: *a man who triumphed over the hardships of a poor background*
♦ **triumphant** •ADJECTIVE• very happy after winning or succeeding: *the triumphant medal-winners*

trivia •NOUN• details and small matters that are not important
♦ **trivial** •ADJECTIVE• small and not important: *You won't lose many marks for a few trivial mistakes.*

trod •VERB• a way of changing the verb **tread** to make a past tense: *Hey, you trod on my toe just then!*

trodden •VERB• the form of the verb **tread** that is used with a helping verb to show that something happened in the past: *A lot of feet have trodden on these steps in the past.*

troll •NOUN• **trolls** an imaginary, ugly, bad-tempered, human-like creature that is either a dwarf or a giant

trolley •NOUN• **trolleys 1** a basket on wheels: *a supermarket trolley* **2** a table on wheels

trombone •NOUN• **trombones** a brass instrument that you blow. You change the notes by pushing a sliding tube in and out

troop •NOUN• **troops 1** a troop is a group of people: *a troop of children on a school outing* **2** troops are soldiers: *troops advancing from the west*
•VERB• **troops, trooping, trooped** to go somewhere in a large group: *tourists trooping around all the art galleries*

trophy •NOUN• **trophies** a prize such as a cup or medal for winning a competition: *Helen won the junior tennis trophy three years running.*

tropic •NOUN• **tropics 1** either of two imaginary circles around the Earth. The **Tropic of Cancer** is 23 degrees north of the equator, and the **Tropic of Capricorn** is 23 degrees south **2** either of the hot regions to the north or south of the equator
♦ **tropical** •ADJECTIVE• to do with, in or from the tropics: *a tropical rainforest*

trot •VERB• **trots, trotting, trotted** to run fairly fast with small steps
•NOUN• **trots** a jogging kind of run
• **on the trot** one after another: *three wins on the trot*
♦ **trotters** •PLURAL NOUN• the feet of pigs or sheep, used as food

trouble •NOUN• **troubles 1** something that gives you a lot of work or problems: *A washing-machine would save you a lot of trouble.* ♦ *You'll have no trouble finding a better job.* **2** your troubles are your worries and problems
•VERB• **troubles, troubling, troubled 1** to trouble someone is to bother or disturb them: *I'm sorry to trouble you, but can you help me please?*
2 to trouble to do something is to make an effort or be bothered to do it: *He didn't even trouble to say where he was going.*
3 to be troubled by something is to worry about it or to suffer from it: *What's troubling you?*
♦ **troublesome** •ADJECTIVE• causing worry or problems

trough •NOUN• **troughs** a long narrow container that animals eat or drink from

trounce •VERB• **trounces, trouncing, trounced** to trounce your opponent is to beat them easily

troupe •NOUN• **troupes** a group of

performers who work together: *a troupe of acrobats*

trousers •PLURAL NOUN• a garment for the lower half of the body that covers each leg separately

trout •NOUN• **trout** or **trouts** a kind of fish that lives in rivers and lakes

trowel •NOUN• **trowels** a tool like a small spade

truancy •NOUN• being absent from school without permission

♦ **truant** •NOUN• **truants** a pupil who stays away from school without permission
• **play truant** to play truant is to stay away from school without permission

truce •NOUN• **truces** an agreement to stop fighting for a while

truck •NOUN• **trucks** 1 a lorry 2 an open railway wagon for transporting goods or animals

trudge •VERB• **trudges, trudging, trudged** to walk with tired, heavy, slow steps: *trudging along in the snow*

true •ADJECTIVE• **truer, truest** 1 real and not invented: *a true story* 2 real and not pretend or supposed: *Are these your true feelings?*
• *a true friend*
⇒ **truly, truth**

truffle •NOUN• **truffles** 1 a kind of chocolate with a soft creamy centre 2 a rare fungus that grows underground and is used as food

truly •ADVERB• really: *Tell me what you truly want to do.* • *I'm truly sorry.*

trump •NOUN• **trumps** trumps are the suit of cards that has been chosen to be worth more than the others in a card game
•VERB• **trumps, trumping, trumped** 1 to trump a card is to beat it by playing a card that has a higher value in that game 2 to **trump something up** is to invent it

trumpet •NOUN• **trumpets** a brass musical instrument that you blow into to make a loud, high, clear sound
•VERB• **trumpets, trumpeting, trumpeted** an elephant trumpets when it makes a loud noise

truncheon •NOUN• **truncheon** a short, thick, heavy stick carried by police officers

trundle •VERB• **trundles, trundling, trundled** to move heavily and slowly along on wheels: *lorries trundling through the empty streets*
• *Gordon trundled the wheelbarrow round to the back of the house.*

trunk •NOUN• **trunks** 1 the main stem of a tree, without its branches or roots
2 an elephant's long strong nose
3 a large box or chest for storing or transporting clothes and other possessions
4 the main part of a person's body, not including their head, arms or legs
5 the American English word for the boot of a car

trunk call •NOUN• **trunk calls** a long-distance telephone call

trunk road •NOUN• **trunk roads** a main road

trunks •PLURAL NOUN• trunks are short trousers or pants worn by men or boys for swimming

trust •VERB• **trusts, trusting, trusted** 1 to believe that someone is honest and loyal: *The colonel picked out ten men he knew he could trust.*
2 to rely on someone to do something properly and not cause damage: *I know I can trust you not to make any mistakes.* • *Can I trust you with my new camera?*
3 to expect and believe that something is so: *I trust that all is well with you?*
•NOUN• 1 the belief that someone is honest and loyal: *It can be difficult to get a new pet's trust.* 2 a responsibility to look after something or do something properly: *The children had been placed in my trust.*
♦ **trusting** •ADJECTIVE• believing that other people are honest and good: *a very trusting person*
♦ **trustworthy** •ADJECTIVE• honest
♦ **trusty** •ADJECTIVE• reliable: *my trusty friend*

truth •NOUN• **truths** 1 what is true and real: *Please try to tell the truth.* • *The truth is that she never really loved him.* 2 being true: *There is no truth in his story.*
♦ **truthful** •ADJECTIVE• 1 a truthful person tells the truth 2 truthful information is not false

Aa Bb Cc Dd Ee Ff Gg Hh Ii Jj Kk Ll Mm Nn Oo Pp Qq Rr Ss **Tt** Uu Vv Ww Xx Yy Zz

• **truthfully** •ADVERB• without lying: *Answer the questions as truthfully as you can.*

try •VERB• **tries, trying, tried** 1 to make an effort or an attempt to do something: *Please try to understand.* • *I'm trying to call John but he's not answering the phone.*

2 to do or use something to see if you like it or if it is good: *Try this powder for a cleaner wash.*

3 to find out if someone committed a crime by hearing all the evidence in a lawcourt: *They will be tried in the European Court of Human Rights.*
•NOUN• **tries** 1 an attempt to do something: *That was a good try. Better luck next time.*
2 in rugby, a successful attempt to put the ball over the other team's goal line
⇒ **trial**

tsar *or* **czar** •NOUN• **tsars** *or* **czars** the male ruler of Russia before 1917

tsarina *or* **czarina** •NOUN• **tsarinas** *or* **czarinas** the wife of the ruler, or the female ruler of Russia before 1917

T-shirt •NOUN• **T-shirts** another spelling of **tee-shirt**

tub •NOUN• **tubs** 1 a round container for liquid or creamy substances: *a tub of ice-cream* • *a tub that will hold 20 litres of water*
2 a bath: *a long soak in the tub*

tuba •NOUN• **tubas** a large brass musical instrument that you blow. It usually plays very low notes

tubby •ADJECTIVE• **tubbier, tubbiest** fat and round

tube •NOUN• **tubes** 1 a long, thin, hollow pipe: *a rubber tube that carries the gas into the other bottle*
2 a long hollow container: *a cardboard tube for storing posters* • *a tube of toothpaste*
3 an underground railway system, especially in London: *We can easily get there by tube.*

tuber •NOUN• **tubers** a swollen plant root that new plants can grow from: *Potatoes are tubers that you can eat or plant again.*

tuberculosis •NOUN• a disease that affects your lungs and makes it difficult to breathe

tuck •NOUN• **tucks** 1 a fold in cloth that is fixed, usually with stitching: *a blouse with tucks down the front* • *We can make a small tuck in the waist to make it fit.* 2 snack foods: *Janie takes tuck money to school every day.*
•VERB• **tucks, tucking, tucked** 1 to hide an edge or loose end inside or under something else to make it firm or tidy: *Tuck your shirt in.* • *Tuck the flap into the envelope and seal it with tape.*
2 to **tuck in** is to eat with enjoyment: *The kids tucked in without waiting for the adults to arrive.*
3 to be **tucked up** in bed is to be snug and comfortable under the bedclothes

tuck shop •NOUN• **tuck shops** a shop in a school where you can buy snack food

Tuesday •NOUN• **Tuesdays** the day of the week after Monday and before Wednesday

ⓘ **Tuesday** comes from the Old English word **Tiwesdæg**, which means *Tiw's day*. Tiw is the Norse god of war and of the sky.

tuft •NOUN• **tufts** a bunch of something, such as grass or hair, that grows from the same place

tug •VERB• **tugs, tugging, tugged** to pull something suddenly or strongly towards you: *Please stop tugging each other's hair.*
•NOUN• **tugs** 1 a sudden hard pull towards you: *I gave Dad's arm a tug and he looked at me crossly.* 2 a short form of the word **tugboat**

tugboat •NOUN• **tugboats** a small powerful boat that is used for towing ships

tug-of-war •NOUN• a contest where the winners are the team that can pull their end of a strong rope over a certain point

tuition •NOUN• teaching or instruction in how to do something: *mathematics tuition*

tulip •NOUN• **tulips** a type of flower with a straight stem and a cup-shaped flower that grows from a bulb in the spring

ⓘ This flower's name comes from a Persian word that means *turban*, because people thought the flower was similar in shape to a turban.

Aa Bb Cc Dd Ee Ff Gg Hh Ii Jj Kk Ll Mm Nn Oo Pp Qq Rr Ss **Tt** Uu Vv Ww Xx Yy Zz

tumble •VERB• **tumbles, tumbling, tumbled** 1 to fall down and over: *The bike skidded and tumbled into a ditch.* 2 to **tumble to** something is to realize or suddenly understand it: *We finally tumbled to the fact that he was lying.*
•NOUN• **tumbles** a fall: *Lucy had taken a tumble over the doorstep.*

tumbledown •ADJECTIVE• falling to pieces

tumbler •NOUN• **tumblers** a large drinking glass with straight sides

tummy •NOUN• **tummies** a word children use for their stomach: *Mummy, my tummy aches.* • *Try to lie still on your tummies.*

tumour •NOUN• **tumours** a lump in or on your body that might make you ill

tumult •NOUN• **tumults** a loud or confused noise made by a crowd
♦ **tumultuous** •ADJECTIVE• noisy and confused: *a tumultuous welcome*

tuna •NOUN• **tuna** a large fish that is used as food: *They went fishing for tuna.*

tundra •NOUN• a large plain with no trees in or near the Arctic

tune •NOUN• **tunes** a series of musical notes that sound nice together
•VERB• **tunes, tuning, tuned** 1 to adjust a musical instrument so that it sounds right
2 to adjust a television or radio to a certain channel or station
3 to adjust an engine so that it works smoothly
• **in tune** 1 a musical note is in tune if it is exactly the right note 2 an instrument is in tune if it produces the right notes
♦ **tuneful** •ADJECTIVE• having a pleasant melody

tunic •NOUN• **tunics** 1 a loose piece of clothing with no sleeves 2 the top half of a policeman's or soldier's uniform

tuning fork •NOUN• **tuning forks** a metal stick with two prongs that rings with a certain note when you hit it

tunnel •NOUN• **tunnels** a long underground passage
•VERB• **tunnels, tunnelling, tunnelled** to make an underground passage: *Will they tunnel under the river or build a bridge over it?*

turban •NOUN• **turbans** a long piece of cloth that is wrapped round and round the head to make a kind of hat

turbine •NOUN• **turbines** a machine or engine that is driven by a flow of water or gas

turbulence •NOUN• disturbance in the water or air that makes ships or aircraft shake
♦ **turbulent** •ADJECTIVE• disturbed or confused: *a turbulent week for the government*

turf •NOUN• short thick grass

turkey •NOUN• **turkeys** a large farmyard bird that is used as food

turmoil •NOUN• a state of worry and confusion: *Her mind was in turmoil but she tried to stay calm.*

turn •VERB• **turns, turning, turned** 1 to move or to move something to face in another direction: *He turned and walked away.*
• *Why have you turned that picture towards the wall?*
2 to spin around or twist: *a turning wheel*
• *Turn the handle to the right.*
3 to change: *She took one look and turned pale.* • *The frog turned into a prince.*
4 to **turn something** or **someone down** is to refuse an offer they make: *He asked her to marry him but she turned him down.*
5 to **turn something down** is to make it less: *Turn that racket down, will you?*
6 to **turn in** is to go to bed
7 to **turn someone in** is to hand them over to the police
8 to **turn out** a certain way is to finish or end up like that: *How did the experiment turn out?*
9 to **turn out** is to come out to see or do something: *Not many people turned out for the local election.*
10 to **turn up** is to appear or arrive: *To our surprise over twenty people turned up.*
11 to **turn something up** is to increase it: *Can you turn the volume up a bit?*
•NOUN• **turns** 1 a curve, bend or change of direction: *Take the first turn on the right.*
2 something that people do one after the other: *It's your turn next.*
3 a short performance in a show: *Jolly Jack*

will be the star turn at the Christmas show this year.

4 a **good turn** is a favour that you do for someone

5 if you do things **in turn**, you do them one after the other

turncoat •NOUN• **turncoats** a person who changes sides in an argument

turnip •NOUN• **turnips** a hard, round, white vegetable that grows under the ground

turnover •NOUN• **turnovers** a small sweet pie made of a piece of folded pastry with a fruit filling

turnpike •NOUN• **turnpikes** a road which travellers pay to use

turnstile •NOUN• **turnstiles** a gate that turns, allowing one person to pass at a time

turntable •NOUN• **turntables** a turning platform

turpentine •NOUN• an oily liquid used for things like making paint thinner and cleaning paintbrushes

turquoise •NOUN• **turquoises** **1** a greenish-blue precious stone **2** a greenish-blue colour

turtle •NOUN• **turtles** a large reptile, that usually lives in the sea with a hard shell and flippers for swimming

tusk •NOUN• **tusks** a long curved pointed tooth that sticks out of the mouth of some animals, such as the elephant and walrus

tussle •NOUN• **tussles** a struggle with someone to get something
•VERB• **tussles, tussling, tussled** to argue or struggle with someone over something you both want

tutor •NOUN• **tutors** **1** a private teacher who teaches individual pupils at home **2** a university or college teacher who teaches students in small groups or gives them advice
•VERB• **tutors, tutoring, tutored** to tutor someone is to teach them
♦ **tutorial** •NOUN• **tutorials** a lesson at a university or college for an individual student or a small group

tutu •NOUN• **tutus** a ballet dancer's dress that has a stiff, sticking-out skirt

TV •NOUN• **TVs** **1** a television set: *We've got a new TV.* **2** television broadcasts: *I think the children watch too much TV.*

tweak •VERB• **tweaks, tweaking, tweaked** to pull with a small jerk: *He tweaked my hair roughly.*
•NOUN• **tweaks** a small pull at something to make a small change: *The tablecloth needs a bit of a tweak.*

tweed •NOUN• **tweeds** thick, rough, woollen cloth that is often used for making outdoor clothing

tweezers •PLURAL NOUN• a small tool for gripping very thin things such as hairs

twelfth •ADJECTIVE AND ADVERB• after the eleventh and before the thirteenth: *the twelfth day of May*

twelve •NOUN• **twelves** the number 12

twentieth •ADJECTIVE AND ADVERB• after the nineteenth and before the twenty-first: *the twentieth day of April*

twenty •NOUN• **twenties** the number 20

twice •ADVERB• two times: *You've done that twice now, so don't do it again.* • *I could eat twice that amount.*

twiddle •VERB• **twiddles, twiddling, twiddled** to twist or twirl something round and round: *Try twiddling some knobs to try to make it work.*

twig •NOUN• **twigs** a small thin piece that grows from a branch of a tree or bush: *We need a pile of dry twigs to start the fire.*
•VERB• **twigs, twigging, twigged** an informal word that means to suddenly realize something: *Then I twigged what he was really talking about.*

twilight •NOUN• the time after the sun sets when it is not quite dark

twin •NOUN• **twins** one of two children born to the same mother at the same time: *Paul and Jo are twins.* • *Yes, I'm a twin.*
•ADJECTIVE• belonging to a pair of things that are very similar: *twin beds* • *a car with twin exhaust pipes*

twine •NOUN• strong string: *a ball of garden twine*
•VERB• **twines, twining, twined** to twist

Aa Bb Cc Dd Ee Ff Gg Hh Ii Jj Kk Ll Mm Nn Oo Pp Qq Rr Ss **Tt** Uu Vv Ww Xx Yy Zz

Aa

around something: *twining a lock of hair round her finger* • *The ivy is twined around the gatepost.*

Bb

twinge •NOUN• **twinges** a sudden unpleasant feeling: *a twinge of toothache* • *a twinge of guilt*

Cc

Dd

twinkle •VERB• **twinkles, twinkling, twinkled** 1 lights twinkle when they glitter brightly: *lights twinkling along the shoreline* 2 someone's eyes twinkle when they are bright with excitement or humour •NOUN• **twinkles** a bright shining light

Ee

Ff

Gg

twirl •VERB• **twirls, twirling, twirled** to turn or spin round quickly: *girls twirling in long skirts* • *The leaders of the parade twirled their batons.* •NOUN• **twirls** a fast turn or spin around

Hh

Ii

Jj

twist •VERB• **twists, twisting, twisted** 1 to wind or turn round: *Her hair was tangled and twisted around the clip.* • *Twist the handle hard and then pull it to open the door.* 2 to turn the top half of your body: *Gregory twisted round in his chair to look at me.* 3 to bend something out of its proper shape: *After twisting my ankle, I developed a bad limp.* • *The front wheel of the bike twisted when it hit the wall.* 4 to wind from side to side: *a road that twists* •NOUN• **twists** 1 a turn round: *Give the lid a good hard twist.* 2 the shape of something that has been turned or wound around: *a twist of wire* 3 a change in the way something happens: *an unusual twist at the end of the story*

Kk

Ll

Mm

Nn

Oo

Pp

Qq

Rr

Ss

Tt

twitch •NOUN• **twitches** a jerky little movement •VERB• **twitches, twitching, twitched** 1 to move jerkily: *Her eyelid twitched* 2 to move something sharply or jerkily: *people twitching curtains to see what was going on outside*

Uu

Vv

Ww

twitter •VERB• **twitters, twittering, twittered** to make a lot of high-pitched noises: *birds twittering in the trees*

Xx

Yy

two •NOUN• **twos** the number 2

Zz

two-dimensional •ADJECTIVE• a two-dimensional shape is flat and has length and width you can measure, but not height or depth

two-faced •ADJECTIVE• not honest or not acting in the same way with everyone

tycoon •NOUN• **tycoons** a rich and powerful businessperson

type •NOUN• **types** 1 a sort or kind of thing or person: *What type of person would write a letter like this?* • *Choose the right type of shampoo for your hair.* 2 letters and figures that are used in printing: *The title should be in bold type.* •VERB• **types, typing, typed** to write using a keyboard on a typewriter or computer: *Type your name and then your password.* ⇒ **typist**

typewriter •NOUN• **typewriters** a machine that you can use to produce printed text

typhoon •NOUN• **typhoons** a violent storm in the western Pacific Ocean

typical •ADJECTIVE• 1 having the usual qualities of a certain type of thing or person: *typical holiday weather* 2 just as you expect from a certain thing or person: *That's typical of Nick.* • **typically** •ADVERB• 1 in most cases: *An insect typically has six legs and two pairs of wings.* 2 as you would expect from a certain person or thing: *Tracy was typically late.*

typist •NOUN• **typists** a person whose job is to type, especially in an office

tyranny •NOUN• **tyrannies** a cruel and unjust way of using power • **tyrannical** •ADJECTIVE• cruel and not fair towards people: *a tyrannical ruler*

tyrant •NOUN• **tyrants** a ruler who has complete power and who uses it unfairly and cruelly

tyre •NOUN• **tyres** a thick rubber ring that is usually filled with air and covers the edge of a wheel: *a flat tyre*

udder • NOUN• **udders** the part like a bag that hangs under a cow and supplies milk

UFO • ABBREVIATION• **UFOs** short for **unidentified flying object**, which is something seen in the sky and nobody knows what it is

ugly • ADJECTIVE• **uglier, ugliest** not very nice to look at: *an ugly man* • *an ugly building*
♦ **ugliness** • NOUN• being ugly

UHT • ABBREVIATION• short for **ultra-heat treated**, which describes a type of milk that you can keep for a long time

ulcer • NOUN• **ulcers** a sore on someone's skin or inside the body

ultimate • ADJECTIVE• happening at the end of a process: *an ultimate aim*
♦ **ultimately** • ADVERB• finally

ultra- • PREFIX• if a word starts with **ultra-**, it means 'very' or 'beyond a particular limit'. For example, *ultra-careful* means 'extremely careful'

ultraviolet • ADJECTIVE• ultraviolet light is light you cannot see

umbilical cord • NOUN• **umbilical cords** the cord that connects a baby to its mother before it is born

umbrella • NOUN• **umbrellas** something you put up and shelter under when it rains, which consists of a frame with cloth over it

ⓘ This word comes from the Italian word **umbrella**, which means *little shadow*. Umbrellas were first used to shade people from the sun.

umpire • NOUN• **umpires** someone who watches a game such as tennis or cricket and makes sure that the rules are not broken

umpteen • ADJECTIVE• an informal word for **many**: *I've told you umpteen times to be quiet.*

un- • PREFIX• if a word starts with **un-**, it means the opposite of its usual meaning. For example, *untidy* means 'not tidy'

unable • ADJECTIVE• not having enough time, strength or skill to do something: *He stood mesmerized, quite unable to take his eyes off the bear.*

unaccustomed • ADJECTIVE• if you are unaccustomed to something, you are not used to it

unanimous • ADJECTIVE• agreed by everyone: *a unanimous decision*
♦ **unanimously** • ADVERB• in a way that is unanimous: *He was elected unanimously.*

unarmed • ADJECTIVE• without weapons: *unarmed combat* • *an unarmed policeman*

unaware • ADJECTIVE• not knowing about something: *We were unaware of the danger.*
♦ **unawares** • ADVERB• when not expected: *Their arrival caught me unawares.*

unbearable • ADJECTIVE• too painful or annoying to deal with
♦ **unbearably** • ADVERB• in a way that is difficult to bear: *It is unbearably hot outside.*

unbelievable • ADJECTIVE• 1 difficult to believe: *an unbelievable excuse.* 2 a word used to emphasize how bad, good or big something is: *an unbelievable success*
♦ **unbelievably** • ADVERB• in a way that is unbelievable: *She's unbelievably rich.*

uncalled • ADJECTIVE• if an action is **uncalled for**, it is not fair or not necessary: *That remark was completely uncalled for.*

uncanny • ADJECTIVE• strange and difficult to explain

uncertain • ADJECTIVE• 1 having doubt about something: *I was uncertain about what to do next.* 2 not definitely known: *The future is uncertain.*

uncle • NOUN• **uncles** 1 the brother of one of your parents 2 your aunt's husband

unclean • ADJECTIVE• dirty or soiled: *unclean clothes*

uncomfortable • ADJECTIVE• not comfortable

Aa
Bb
Cc
Dd
Ee
Ff
Gg
Hh
Ii
Jj
Kk
Ll
Mm
Nn
Oo
Pp
Qq
Rr
Ss
Tt
Uu
Vv
Ww
Xx
Yy
Zz

• **uncomfortably** •ADVERB• in an uncomfortable way: *Tom shifted uncomfortably in his seat.*

uncommon •ADJECTIVE• unusual or rare

• **uncommonly** •ADVERB• extremely: *uncommonly talented*

unconscious •ADJECTIVE• 1 in a state like sleep where you are not aware of what is happening around you, because you are seriously ill or injured: *A brick fell on his head and he was knocked unconscious.*
2 an unconscious feeling is one that you are not aware of having
3 if you are unconscious of something you do not notice it: *He was unconscious of the danger.*

• **unconsciously** •ADVERB• in an unconscious way

• **unconsciousness** •NOUN• being unconscious

uncover •VERB• uncovers, uncovering, uncovered 1 to remove a cover from something 2 to discover something that had been secret: *uncover the truth*

undecided •ADJECTIVE• not able to decide about something

undeniable •ADJECTIVE• true or certain: *It is undeniable that the Earth goes round the sun.*

• **undeniably** •ADVERB• in a way that is true or certain

under •PREPOSITION• 1 below or beneath: *The bag is under the table.*
2 less than an amount: *All the clothes are under £20.*
3 working for someone: *a manager with three members of staff under her*
• **under way** if something gets under way, it starts
•ADVERB• in or to a lower place: *We watched the divers go under.*
• **go under** if a business goes under it fails and has to stop trading

underarm •ADJECTIVE AND ADVERB• an underarm throw is done with your hand kept below your shoulder, moving up and forward

underclothes •PLURAL NOUN• clothes you wear next to your skin and under your other clothes

undercover •ADJECTIVE• working or done secretly: *an undercover police operation*

underdeveloped •ADJECTIVE• an underdeveloped country is not modern and does not have many industries

underdog •NOUN• underdogs the weaker person or team in a competition

underdone •ADJECTIVE• not cooked enough

underestimate •VERB• underestimates, underestimating, underestimated to guess that a cost or amount is less than it really is

underfoot •ADVERB• on the ground where you are walking: *The stones underfoot grew slippery in the rain.*

undergo •VERB• undergoes, undergoing, underwent, undergone if you undergo something you experience it: *He underwent an operation to mend his broken leg.*

undergraduate •NOUN• undergraduates someone who is studying for their first degree at a university

underground •ADJECTIVE AND ADVERB• 1 below the surface of the ground: *Moles live underground.* • *an underground stream* 2 existing or done secretly: *an underground organization*
•NOUN• undergrounds a railway that is under the ground, usually in a large city

undergrowth •NOUN• bushes and plants that cover the ground

underhand •ADJECTIVE• secret and not honest: *underhand business deals*

underline •VERB• underlines, underlining, underlined 1 to draw a line underneath something 2 to emphasize that something is important or true: *She underlined the need to be careful crossing the road.*

undermine •VERB• undermines, undermining, undermined to undermine someone or their plans is to make them weaker

underneath •ADJECTIVE AND PREPOSITION• under something: *Look underneath the table!* • *He was wearing a jumper with a shirt underneath.*

undernourished •ADJECTIVE• someone

who is undernourished does not have enough healthy food

underpants • PLURAL NOUN • underwear that men and boys wear under their trousers

underpass • NOUN • **underpasses** a road or path under another road

underprivileged • ADJECTIVE • having less money and opportunities than other people

undersized • ADJECTIVE • smaller than usual or necessary

underskirt • NOUN • **underskirts** a thin skirt that women and girls wear under another skirt

understand • VERB • **understands, understanding, understood** 1 to know what something means: *I can't understand the instructions.* • *Do you understand German?* 2 to know about something: *Doctors still don't understand how the disease is spread.* 3 to know why someone behaves and feels the way they do: *I'll never understand him.* 4 to think something is true: *I understood that you weren't coming.*
♦ **understandable** • ADJECTIVE • reasonable in a particular situation: *His disappointment at failing the exam was understandable after he had worked so hard.*
♦ **understanding** • ADJECTIVE • able to understand other people's feelings • NOUN • **understandings** 1 the ability to see the meaning of something: *I have no understanding of chemistry.* 2 an agreement: *We have an understanding that we will stand up for each other.*

understudy • NOUN • **understudies** someone who learns the part of another actor so they can play that part if the actor is ill

undertake • VERB • **undertakes, undertaking, undertook, undertaken** to undertake a task is to accept it and do it: *I undertook to make all the travel arrangements.*

undertaker • NOUN • **undertakers** someone whose job is to arrange funerals

underwater • ADJECTIVE AND ADVERB • under the surface of water: *an underwater creature* • *Can you swim underwater?*

underwear • NOUN • clothes you wear next to your skin and under your other clothes

underweight • ADJECTIVE • not heavy enough

underworld • NOUN • 1 in stories, the place where people go when they die 2 the underworld is criminals and the crimes they commit

undesirable • ADJECTIVE • not wanted

undivided • ADJECTIVE • 1 not split into separate parts or groups 2 complete: *You must give me your undivided attention.*

undo • VERB • **undoes, undoing, undid, undone** 1 to open something that is fastened: *He undid his jacket.* 2 to cancel out the effect of something: *She's undone all the good work of the previous manager.*

undoubted • ADJECTIVE • certain: *Ellie has undoubted talent as a singer.*
♦ **undoubtedly** • ADVERB • a word you use to emphasize that something is true: *You are undoubtedly correct.*

undress • VERB • **undresses, undressing, undressed** to take your clothes off
♦ **undressed** • ADJECTIVE • not wearing any clothes: *He was getting undressed.*

undue • ADJECTIVE • more than is necessary: *undue alarm*

unduly • ADVERB • more than is necessary: *He did not seem unduly worried.*

unearth • VERB • **unearths, unearthing, unearthed** 1 to find something by digging in the ground 2 to discover something: *There was always somebody who unearthed the facts which had been hidden.*

unearthly • ADJECTIVE • strange and a bit frightening: *an unearthly sound*

uneasy • ADJECTIVE • slightly worried or unhappy
♦ **uneasily** • ADVERB • in a way that shows you are worried or uncomfortable: *John looked uneasily at his watch, knowing he was late.*
♦ **uneasiness** • NOUN • a feeling of slight worry

unemployed • ADJECTIVE • without a job
♦ **unemployment** • NOUN • 1 the number of

Aa
Bb
Cc
Dd
Ee
Ff
Gg
Hh
Ii
Jj
Kk
Ll
Mm
Nn
Oo
Pp
Qq
Rr
Ss
Tt
Uu
Vv
Ww
Xx
Yy
Zz

people who do not have a job: *Unemployment has risen again.* **2** not having a job

unequal •ADJECTIVE• different in size, amount or position: *an unequal share of money*

uneven •ADJECTIVE• **1** not level or smooth: *an uneven road* **2** not all of the same quality: *Your work has been uneven this year.*
♦ **unevenly** •ADVERB• in an uneven way

unexpected •ADJECTIVE• surprising because you were not expecting it: *an unexpected visitor* • *an unexpected development*
♦ **unexpectedly** •ADVERB• in a way that you were not expecting

unfair •ADJECTIVE• not right or not fair: *an unfair advantage* • *It's unfair to make her pay for everything.*
♦ **unfairly** •ADVERB• in a way that is unfair: *We have been very unfairly treated.*
♦ **unfairness** •NOUN• being unfair

unfaithful •ADJECTIVE• not loyal or not keeping your promises

unfamiliar •ADJECTIVE• not known or seen before: *an unfamiliar feeling* • *an unfamiliar face*

unfasten •VERB• **unfastens, unfastening, unfastened** to open something that was fastened: *She unfastened her coat.*

unfavourable •ADJECTIVE• not good, and likely to cause problems: *The weather was unfavourable for our barbecue.*

unfit •ADJECTIVE• **unfitter, unfittest 1** not suitable or not good enough: *water that's unfit to drink* **2** someone who is unfit is not in good physical condition, especially because they do not do enough exercise

unfold •VERB• **unfolds, unfolding, unfolded 1** to spread out something that was folded **2** to gradually become known or gradually make something known: *The details of what happened began to unfold.*

unforgettable •ADJECTIVE• impossible to forget

unforgivable •ADJECTIVE• unforgivable behaviour is so bad that you cannot forgive the person who has done it

♦ **unforgivably** •ADVERB• in a way that is unforgivable: *You were unforgivably rude to my friend.*

unfortunate •ADJECTIVE• **1** caused by bad luck: *an unfortunate accident* **2** causing regret: *an unfortunate choice of words*
♦ **unfortunately** •ADVERB• a word you use to show that you wish something had not happened: *Unfortunately, I lost the ring.*

unfurl •VERB• **unfurls, unfurling, unfurled** to unfurl a flag is to unfold it

ungainly •ADJECTIVE• not graceful

ungrateful •ADJECTIVE• not showing or saying thanks when someone does something for you or gives you something
♦ **ungratefully** •ADVERB• in a way that is ungrateful

unhappily •ADVERB• **1** in a way that is not happy **2** a word you use to show that something makes you sad or disappointed: *Unhappily, things did not work out as I planned.*

unhappiness •NOUN• being unhappy

unhappy •ADJECTIVE• **unhappier, unhappiest 1** sad: *Ben was unhappy for a long time after his dog died.* **2** not pleased or not satisfied: *We were unhappy with our exam results.* **3** unfortunate: *an unhappy coincidence*

unhealthy •ADJECTIVE• **unhealthier, unhealthiest 1** someone who is unhealthy does not have good health **2** something that is unhealthy is bad for your health: *an unhealthy lifestyle*

unicorn •NOUN• **unicorns** in stories, an animal like a white horse with a horn on its head

ⓘ This word comes from the Latin word **unus**, which means *one* and **cornu**, which means *horn*, because there is only one horn on the unicorn's head.

uniform •NOUN• **uniforms** a set of clothes that someone must wear for school or for their job

unify •VERB• **unifies, unifying, unified** to combine things so they become one

unimportance •NOUN• the fact of not being important

unimportant • ADJECTIVE• not important

uninhabited • ADJECTIVE• an uninhabited place does not have people living in it

unintentional • ADJECTIVE• done by accident and not deliberately

• **unintentionally** • ADVERB• in an unintentional way

uninterested • ADJECTIVE• not interested: I am uninterested in sport.

• **uninteresting** • ADJECTIVE• boring

uninterrupted • ADJECTIVE• 1 not stopped by anything: an uninterrupted conversation 2 an uninterrupted view is not blocked by anything

union • NOUN• unions 1 another word for a **trade union** 2 a group of states or countries that work together

• **unionist** • NOUN• unionists 1 a member of a trade union 2 someone who believes that their country or a part of it should be joined to another

unique • ADJECTIVE• completely different from anyone or anything else

unisex • ADJECTIVE• intended for either men or women: unisex clothes

unison • NOUN• if people do something in **unison**, they all do it together

unit • NOUN• units 1 a single thing, person, or group that can be part of a larger thing: an army unit •The book is divided into ten units.
2 a fixed quantity that is used for measuring something: A metre is a unit of length.
3 a department in a hospital that provides a particular type of treatment: a burns unit

unite • VERB• unites, uniting, united 1 if people or things unite, they join together 2 to unite two or more things is to join them together

universal • ADJECTIVE• something that is universal affects or includes everyone: English may become a universal language that everyone can learn and use.

universe • NOUN• everything that exists anywhere, including the Earth, the sun and all the other planets and stars in space: Somewhere in the universe there might be another world like ours.

university • NOUN• universities a place where you go to study at the highest level after leaving school

unjust • ADJECTIVE• not fair: an unjust punishment.

• **unjustly** • ADVERB• not fairly: He was unjustly punished.

unkempt • ADJECTIVE• not tidy: unkempt hair

unkind • ADJECTIVE• unkinder, unkindest cruel and not kind: It was unkind of you to tease her.

• **unkindly** • ADVERB• in an unkind way: They treated me unkindly.

• **unkindness** • NOUN• being unkind

unknown • ADJECTIVE• 1 not known: The man's whereabouts are unknown. 2 not well known: an unknown actor

unleaded • ADJECTIVE• unleaded petrol does not have lead added to it and therefore causes less harm to the environment

unless • CONJUNCTION• except when or except if: We always go for a walk on Sundays, unless it's raining. •Don't come unless I phone you.

unlike • PREPOSITION• 1 different from: I never saw twins who were so unlike each other. 2 not usual for someone. It's unlike my mum to be so bad-tempered.

unlikely • ADJECTIVE• 1 not likely or expected to happen: It's unlikely that she'll come. 2 probably not true: an unlikely tale

unload • VERB• unloads, unloading, unloaded to unload something such as a ship or vehicle is to remove all the things that it is carrying: After our camping trip, our first job was to unload the car.

unlock • VERB• unlocks, unlocking, unlocked to open something that is locked: Unlock this door now!

• **unlocked** • ADJECTIVE• not locked

unluckily • ADVERB• I am sorry to say: Unluckily, he is injured and can't play football.

unlucky • ADJECTIVE• having, or coming from, bad luck: I never win at cards – I'm very unlucky. •It was an unlucky defeat.

Aa
Bb
Cc
Dd
Ee
Ff
Gg
Hh
Ii
Jj
Kk
Ll
Mm
Nn
Oo
Pp
Qq
Rr
Ss
Tt
Uu
Vv
Ww
Xx
Yy
Zz

Aa
Bb
Cc
Dd
Ee
Ff
Gg
Hh
Ii
Jj
Kk
Ll
Mm
Nn
Oo
Pp
Qq
Rr
Ss
Tt
Uu
Vv
Ww
Xx
Yy
Zz

unmask •VERB• **unmasks, unmasking, unmasked** 1 to unmask someone is to take away their mask or disguise: *The policeman unmasked the robber.* 2 to unmask someone is to show what they are really like: *He was unmasked as a liar and a cheat.*

unmistakable • ADJECTIVE• not able to mistaken for anything else: *What she meant was unmistakable.*
   • **unmistakably** •ADVERB• in an unmistakable way: *It was unmistakably his handwriting.*

unnatural •ADJECTIVE• not natural or not normal: *an unnatural silence*
   • **unnaturally** •ADVERB• in an unnatural way

unnecessary •ADJECTIVE• not necessary or not needed: *It is unnecessary to eat so much.*
   • **unnecessarily** •ADVERB• when it is not necessary: *My dad woke me unnecessarily — it was a school holiday!*

unoccupied •ADJECTIVE• empty and not lived in: *These houses have been unoccupied for years.*

unpack •VERB• **unpacks, unpacking, unpacked** to take things out of a suitcase or bag: *I've unpacked my case.* • *Have you unpacked yet?* • *He still hasn't unpacked his clothes.*

unpleasant •ADJECTIVE• nasty and not pleasant: *an unpleasant smell*
   • **unpleasantly** •ADVERB• in an unpleasant way
   • **unpleasantness** •NOUN• being unpleasant

unplug •VERB• **unplugs, unplugging, unplugged** 1 to unplug something electrical is to take its plug out of a socket 2 to unplug something is to remove a blockage from it: *It will not be easy to unplug the pipe.*

unpopular •ADJECTIVE• not popular or not liked: *His bad behaviour makes him very unpopular with his classmates.*

unravel •VERB• **unravels, unravelling, unravelled** 1 to unravel something is to unwind it or take the knots out of it: *He could not unravel the tangled thread.* 2 to unravel something puzzling is to solve it: *She was determined to unravel the mystery.*

unreal •ADJECTIVE• not actually existing

unreasonable •ADJECTIVE• asking too much, and not fair: *It's unreasonable to expect students to do so much homework.*
   • **unreasonably** •ADVERB• in an unreasonable way

unrest •NOUN• trouble and discontent among people: *unrest all over the country*

unruly •ADJECTIVE• badly behaved and difficult to control: *an unruly child* • *unruly behaviour*

unscathed •ADJECTIVE• without being harmed: *They escaped from the burning building unscathed.*

unscrew •VERB• **unscrews, unscrewing, unscrewed** 1 to loosen or remove something by taking out a screw or screws: *Dad unscrewed the cupboard door.* 2 to loosen or remove something with a twisting action: *Joe unscrewed the lid from the bottle and took a drink.*

unseemly •ADJECTIVE• not suitable or not proper: *unseemly behaviour*

unseen •ADJECTIVE• not seen or not noticed: *He managed to leave the house unseen.*

unselfish •ADJECTIVE• generous and thinking of others
   • **unselfishly** •ADVERB• in an unselfish way: *George unselfishly shared his sweets.*
   • **unselfishness** •NOUN• being unselfish

unsettled •ADJECTIVE• 1 if the weather is unsettled it changes a great deal 2 if a bill is unsettled it has not been paid

unsightly •ADJECTIVE• ugly and not nice to look at: *The new school building is very unsightly.*

unsound •ADJECTIVE• not safe or not reliable: *The bridge is structurally unsound.* • *Her evidence is unsound.*

unspeakable •ADJECTIVE• too bad to describe in words: *unspeakable rudeness*

unsteady •ADJECTIVE• likely to fall and not firm: *After the operation she was very unsteady on her feet.*
   • **unsteadily** •ADVERB• in an unsteady way

unsuccessful •ADJECTIVE• not managing to

do something you have been trying to do:
She tried to find him but was unsuccessful.
♦ **unsuccessfully** •ADVERB• in an
unsuccessful way: *I tried unsuccessfully to
speak to her.*

unsuitable •ADJECTIVE• not right for a
purpose or occasion: *These shoes are
unsuitable for school.*

unsung •ADJECTIVE• not praised or not
recognized: *an unsung hero*

unthinkable •ADJECTIVE• too bad or too
unlikely to be thought about: *It is
unthinkable that he would steal from his
own parents.*

untidy •ADJECTIVE• **untidier, untidiest** not
neat or not well organized: *His room is
always untidy.*
♦ **untidiness** •NOUN• being untidy

untie •VERB• **unties, untying, untied** to
loosen or unfasten something that is tied:
She untied his shoelaces for him.

until •PREPOSITION• up to the time of: *We
waited until ten o'clock.*
•CONJUNCTION• up to the time when: *Keep
walking until you come to the station.*

untimely •ADJECTIVE• happening too soon
or at a time that is not suitable: *his untimely
death* • *her untimely return*

unto •PREPOSITION• an old-fashioned word
for **to**: *The knight came again unto the king.*

untold •ADJECTIVE• **1** not yet told: *the
untold story* **2** too great to be counted or
measured: *untold riches*

untoward •ADJECTIVE• **1** unlucky or
unfortunate: *If nothing untoward happens,
I should be there by lunchtime.* **2** not
appropriate: *untoward rudeness*

untrue •ADJECTIVE• **1** false, not true: *His
story is completely untrue.* **2** not faithful or
and not loyal
♦ **untruth** •NOUN• **untruths** a lie: *You must
stop telling untruths about your friends.*
♦ **untruthful** •ADJECTIVE• not honest: *She
was being untruthful when she said she
didn't care.*
♦ **untruthfully** •ADVERB• in an untruthful
way

unused •ADJECTIVE• **1** that has not been

used: *an unused stamp* **2** if you are unused to
something, you do not know it very well or
have not done it very often: *I'm unused to
spicy food.* • *He was unused to having to
cook his own meals.*

unusual •ADJECTIVE• not normal or not
ordinary: *It's unusual for him to arrive late.*
• *That's an unusual necklace.*
♦ **unusually** •ADVERB• to an unusual
degree: *unusually cold for the time of year*

unveil •VERB• **unveils, unveiling, unveiled**
1 to unveil someone is to take a veil away
from their face
2 to unveil something is to take a cover
away from it as part of a ceremony: *The
Prime Minister unveiled the new statue.*
3 to reveal something: *The headmaster has
unveiled plans for shorter breaks during the
school day.*

unwell •ADJECTIVE• not in good health: *I
feel slightly unwell this morning.*

unwieldy •ADJECTIVE• large and awkward
to carry or manage: *This suitcase is too
unwieldy for me.*

unwilling •ADJECTIVE• not wanting to do
something: *He's unwilling to accept the
money.*
♦ **unwillingness** •NOUN• being unwilling

unwind •VERB• **unwinds, unwinding,
unwound 1** to unwind something is to undo
it from a wound position: *He unwound the
bandage from his ankle.*
2 to unwind is to come undone from a
wound position: *The snake slowly unwound
from the branch.*
3 to relax: *Having a bath is a good way to
unwind.*

unworthy •ADJECTIVE• **1** not deserving: *It's
unworthy of attention.* **2** less good than is
usually expected from someone: *Such bad
behaviour is unworthy of him.*

unwrap •VERB• **unwraps, unwrapping,
unwrapped** to open something that is
wrapped: *She carefully unwrapped the
present.*

unzip •VERB• **unzips, unzipping, unzipped**
to undo the zip of something: *He unzipped
his bag and took out a book.*

Aa
Bb
Cc
Dd
Ee
Ff
Gg
Hh
Ii
Jj
Kk
Ll
Mm
Nn
Oo
Pp
Qq
Rr
Ss
Tt
Uu
Vv
Ww
Xx
Yy
Zz

Aa
Bb
Cc
Dd
Ee
Ff
Gg
Hh
Ii
Jj
Kk
Ll
Mm
Nn
Oo
Pp
Qq
Rr
Ss
Tt
Uu
Vv
Ww
Xx
Yy
Zz

up •ADVERB• **1** towards or in a higher position: *Prices have gone up again.* • *Stand up!*

2 completely, so as to finish: *Drink up your milk.*

3 out of bed: *I got up at five o'clock this morning.*

4 as far as: *He came up to me and shook my hand.*

•PREPOSITION• **1** to or at a higher part of something: *He climbed up the tree.* • *She's up the ladder.* **2** along: *walking up the road*

•ADJECTIVE• **1** going up: *the up escalator* **2** out of bed: *He's not up yet.*

3 ahead: *two goals up at the end of the first half*

4 if the sun is up it has risen

5 finished: *Your time is up.*

6 an informal way of saying 'wrong': *What's up with you today?*

• **up to** **1** if you are up to something you are doing that thing, especially in a secretive way: *My little brother is up to no good again.*

2 if you are up to a task, then you have the ability to do it: *Do you think you are up to winning the race?*

3 if a choice is up to you, then you have to decide what to do or have: *Whether we go swimming or just go home is up to you.*

• **up to date** with all the information or features available just now: *I want to bring my diary up to date.* • *My computer is an old model and not up to date.*

• **ups and downs** good and bad times

upbringing •NOUN• **upbringings** the process of bringing up a child: *We had a strict upbringing.*

update •VERB• **updates, updating, updated**
1 to update someone is to give them the latest information: *Could someone update me on what's been happening here?* **2** to update something is to make it more modern: *I need to update my computer.*

•NOUN• **updates 1** bringing someone or something up to date: *I need an update on what is happening.* **2** an updated version of something: *an update of the news*

upgrade •VERB• **upgrades, upgrading, upgraded 1** to upgrade something such as machinery or a computer is to improve it, especially by adding or replacing parts **2** to

upgrade someone is to promote them

•NOUN• **upgrades** in computing, a newer version of a software program

upheaval •NOUN• **upheavals** a great change or disturbance: *the upheaval of moving house*

uphill •ADJECTIVE• **1** going upwards: *an uphill part of the track* **2** difficult: *This will be an uphill struggle.*

•ADVERB• up a slope: *We travelled uphill for several hours.*

uphold •VERB• **upholds, upholding, upheld** to uphold something such as a decision is to support it or agree with it: *The court upheld his complaint.*

upholstery •NOUN• the coverings and cushions of a seat: *car upholstery*

upkeep •NOUN• **1** the keeping of something, such as a house or car, in good condition **2** the cost of keeping something such as a house or car in good condition

upland •NOUN• high ground

✦ **uplands** •PLURAL NOUN• a region with hills or mountains

uplifting •ADJECTIVE• if something is uplifting it cheers you up and makes you feel more hopeful: *an uplifting song*

up-market •ADJECTIVE• high in quality and price: *an up-market housing estate*

upon •PREPOSITION• a more formal word for **on**: *a high cliff upon which stood a castle*

upper •ADJECTIVE• higher: *the upper floors of the building*

•NOUN• **uppers** the part of a shoe above the sole: *These shoes have leather uppers.*

uppermost •ADJECTIVE• highest: *the uppermost room of the house*

upright •ADJECTIVE• **1** standing straight up: *a row of upright posts* **2** fair and honest: *an upright man*

•NOUN• **uprights** a vertical post or pole, especially one that supports something such as a fence

uprising •NOUN• **uprisings** a fight against a government or a rebellion

uproar •NOUN• **uproars** a noisy disturbance: *The classroom was in an uproar.*

uproot •VERB• **uproots, uprooting, uprooted 1** to pull a plant out of the ground together with its roots
2 to make people move away from their homes: *Thousands of people were uprooted by the war.*
3 to leave your home and go and live in another place: *They uprooted and moved to the country.*

upset •VERB• **upsets, upsetting, upset 1** to make someone sad, angry or worried: *His friend's death upset him very much.*
2 to knock something over: *The dog upset a vase of flowers.*
3 to spoil something: *Her illness has upset our holiday plans.*
•ADJECTIVE• sad, angry or worried: *Are you very upset about failing your exam?*
•NOUN• **upsets 1** sadness or worry: *Her sudden departure caused a lot of upset.*
2 something that causes feelings such as unhappiness and worry: *Losing the match to such a poor team was quite an upset.*
3 a slight disturbance: *a stomach upset*

upshot •NOUN• the final result of something: *The upshot of all of the delays was that we decided not to go at all.*

upside-down •ADJECTIVE AND ADVERB•
1 with the top part where the bottom should be and the bottom part where the top should be: *I knew he wasn't really reading – he was holding the book upside-down.* **2** in or into confusion: *The burglars turned the house upside-down.*

upstairs •ADVERB• to or on a higher floor: *I went upstairs to get the book.*
•NOUN• the higher floor or floors of a building: *The downstairs needs painting, but the upstairs is nice.*
•ADJECTIVE• on a higher floor: *an upstairs bedroom*

upstream •ADVERB• further up a river or stream towards its source, against the direction in which it flows: *Salmon swim upstream to lay their eggs.*

uptake •NOUN• if someone is **quick** or **slow on the uptake**, they are quick or slow to understand or realize something: *He's a bit slow on the uptake, but he's a quick worker when he knows what he's doing.*

uptight •ADJECTIVE• an informal word which means nervous or anxious: *You seem a bit uptight today.*

up-to-date •ADJECTIVE• **1** new or modern: *up-to-date technology* **2** having the latest information: *an up-to-date news story*

upwards •ADVERB• moving or leading towards a higher place or position: *He looked upwards and saw the sun.*
• **upwards of** more than: *Upwards of 200 people came to the meeting.*

uranium •NOUN• a radioactive metal that is used to make nuclear energy

urban •ADJECTIVE• to do with a town or city: *urban life • urban traffic*
♦ **urbanization** •NOUN• being urbanized
♦ **urbanize** or **urbanise** •VERB• **urbanizes, urbanizing, urbanized** to make an area less like the countryside and more like a town: *Many of these small islands are being urbanized.*

urchin •NOUN• **urchins** a dirty child with ragged clothes

urge •VERB• **urges, urging, urged 1** to urge someone to do something is to try to persuade them to do it: *He urged her to drive carefully.* **2** to **urge someone on** is to encourage them to carry on: *He urged his followers on.*
•NOUN• **urges** a sudden feeling of wanting to do something: *I felt an urge to hit him.*

urgency •NOUN• being urgent: *I didn't realize the urgency of the situation.*
♦ **urgent** •ADJECTIVE• needing attention immediately: *I have an urgent message for the headmaster.*
♦ **urgently** •ADVERB• immediately or desperately: *Medical supplies are needed urgently.*

urinate •VERB• **urinates, urinating, urinated** to pass urine out of the body

urine •NOUN• the waste liquid passed out of the bodies of humans and animals

urn •NOUN• **urns 1** a sort of vase for holding the ashes of a dead person who has been cremated **2** a large metal container with a tap, used for heating water or for making large amounts of tea or coffee

Aa
Bb
Cc
Dd
Ee
Ff
Gg
Hh
Ii
Jj
Kk
Ll
Mm
Nn
Oo
Pp
Qq
Rr
Ss
Tt
Uu
Vv
Ww
Xx
Yy
Zz

Aa
Bb
Cc
Dd
Ee
Ff
Gg
Hh
Ii
Jj
Kk
Ll
Mm
Nn
Oo
Pp
Qq
Rr
Ss
Tt
Uu
Vv
Ww
Xx
Yy
Zz

us •PRONOUN• a word you use when you are talking about yourself and at least one other person: *His happy face surprised all of us.* • *Do you want to come with us?*

ⓘ In grammar, **us** and **we** are personal pronouns.
In a sentence in which you (and someone else) are the subject, you use **we** before the verb. You use **us** after the verb or a preposition: *We are going to the cinema. Do you want to come with us?*

usage •NOUN• **usages** 1 treatment: *These chairs have had a lot of rough usage.* 2 the way that the words of a language are used

use •VERB• **uses, using, used** 1 to use something is to put it to a purpose: *Use a knife to open it.* • *Use your common sense!*
2 to **use something up** is to use all of it so that there is none left: *He used up all the milk.*
• **used to** 1 to be used to something is to know it well, or to have done it lots of times: *She soon got used to her new school.* 2 if you used to do something, you did it often or regularly in the past: *We used to go to the seaside every summer.*
•NOUN• **uses** 1 the using of something: *We cannot allow the use of guns.*
2 the purpose for which something can be used: *This knife has a lot of uses.*
3 the value or advantage of something: *Is this coat of any use to you?* • *What's the use of crying?*
♦ **used** •ADJECTIVE• not new: *He sells used cars.*
♦ **useful** •ADJECTIVE• helpful or able to do what needs doing: *She made herself useful by washing the dishes.* • *a useful tool*
♦ **usefulness** •NOUN• being useful
♦ **useless** •ADJECTIVE• having no use, or not doing what it is supposed to do: *This knife's useless – it's completely blunt.* • *I tried to stop the baby crying, but it was useless.*

user •NOUN• **users** a person who uses something: *users of public transport*

user-friendly •ADJECTIVE• easy to use or understand: *Modern computers need to be user-friendly.*

usher •NOUN• **ushers** someone who shows people to their seats in a cinema or theatre
•VERB• **ushers, ushering, ushered** to go with someone and show them the way: *The waiter ushered him to a table.*

usherette •NOUN• **usherettes** a woman who shows people to their seats in a cinema or theatre

usual •ADJECTIVE• done or happening most often: *I took my usual route to school this morning.* • *He was late as usual.*
♦ **usually** •ADVERB• normally, on most occasions: *We usually go on holiday in June.*

utensil •NOUN• **utensils** a tool or container, especially one for everyday use in the home: *knives, pans, and other utensils*

uterus •NOUN• **uteri** a more technical word for the **womb**, the part of a woman's or female animal's body where babies grow until they are born

utility •NOUN• **utilities** 1 usefulness: *a tool of little utility.* 2 a company which supplies gas, electricity, water or another service

utilize or **utilise** •VERB• **utilizes, utilizing, utilized** to make use of: *Old newspapers can be utilized for making recycled paper.*

utmost •ADJECTIVE• greatest possible: *You must take the utmost care.*
• **do your utmost** to make the biggest possible effort: *She has done her utmost to help him.*

utter[1] •VERB• **utters, uttering, uttered** to utter a sound is to make it with your voice: *She uttered a sigh of relief.* • *She didn't utter a single word.*
♦ **utterance** •NOUN• **utterances** something that is said

utter[2] •ADJECTIVE• complete or total: *utter silence*
♦ **utterly** •ADVERB• completely or totally: *I feel utterly exhausted.*
♦ **uttermost** •ADJECTIVE• another word for **utmost**

U-turn •NOUN• **U-turns** 1 a turn in the shape of a U, made by a driver to go back the way he or she has just come 2 a complete change of plan or ideas

vacancy •NOUN• **vacancies 1** a room in a hotel that is available: *Sorry, we have no vacancies.* **2** a job that is available
♦ **vacant** •ADJECTIVE• not being used: *a vacant seat*

vacate •VERB• **vacates, vacating, vacated** to leave a place empty: *He grasped my arms and led me back to the chair I had vacated.*
♦ **vacation** •NOUN• **vacations 1** vacating something **2** an American English word for a holiday: *a two-week vacation*

vaccinate •VERB• **vaccinates, vaccinating, vaccinated** to put a substance into someone's body to protect them from a disease
♦ **vaccination** •NOUN• **vaccinations** the process of vaccinating someone
♦ **vaccine** •NOUN• **vaccines** the substance that is used for vaccinating someone

vacuum •NOUN• **vacuums** a space with no air in it
♦VERB• **vacuums, vacuuming, vacuumed** to clean something using a vacuum cleaner

ⓘ **Vacuum** is a Latin word which means *empty.*

vacuum cleaner •NOUN• **vacuum cleaners** an electrical machine that sucks dust off the floor

vacuum flask •NOUN• **vacuum flasks** a container that has a vacuum between its inside and outside coverings, and which keeps drinks hot or cold

vagina •NOUN• **vaginas** the passage that connects a woman's womb to the outside of her body

vague •ADJECTIVE• **vaguer, vaguest** not very clear or definite: *I have a vague idea where he lives.*
♦ **vaguely** •ADVERB• not clearly or precisely: *He looked vaguely familiar.*

vain •ADJECTIVE• **vainer, vainest 1** too proud of yourself and thinking too much about the way you look **2** useless: *He made a vain attempt to get up.*
• **in vain** without success: *He tried in vain to get out through the bars of the cage.*
♦ **vainly** •ADVERB• without achieving what you want to do: *I tossed about in bed, vainly trying to get comfortable.*
⇒ **vanity**

vale •NOUN• **vales** a valley

ⓘ **Vale** is used mainly in poems.

valentine •NOUN• **valentines 1** a card that you send on Saint Valentine's Day (on 14 February) to show that you love someone **2** the person who you send a valentine to

valet •NOUN• **valets** a male servant who works for another man and looks after his clothes
•VERB• **valets, valeting, valeted** to clean out a car

ⓘ The noun is pronounced va-lay, with a silent t.

valiant •ADJECTIVE• brave. *She made a valiant attempt to rescue the cat.*
♦ **valiantly** •ADVERB• in a brave way

valid •ADJECTIVE• **1** legally or officially acceptable and able to be used: *a valid passport* **2** reasonable and acceptable: *a valid excuse*
♦ **validity** •NOUN• being valid

valley •NOUN• **valleys** a stretch of low land between hills, often with a river running through it

valour •NOUN• bravery or courage, for example in a battle

valuable •ADJECTIVE• **1** worth a lot of money: *a valuable diamond* **2** very useful: *She's a valuable member of the team.*
♦ **valuables** •PLURAL NOUN• things, especially things that you own, that are worth a lot of money

valuation •NOUN• **valuations 1** the act of

deciding how much something is worth **2** an estimated price or value

value •NOUN• **values** 1 the amount that something is worth **2** usefulness and importance

•VERB• **values, valuing, valued** 1 to value something is to think it is important or worthwhile: *I value my free time.* **2** to say how much something is worth: *The jewels were valued at three thousand dollars.*

valve •NOUN• **valves** something that opens and shuts to control the flow of liquid, air or gas through a pipe

vampire •NOUN• **vampires** in stories, a dead person who comes out at night and sucks people's blood

van •NOUN• **vans** a road vehicle, smaller than a lorry, for carrying goods

vandal •NOUN• **vandals** someone who deliberately damages buildings and other things

♦ **vandalism** •NOUN• the crime of deliberately damaging something such as a public building

♦ **vandalize** or **vandalise** •VERB• **vandalizes, vandalizing, vandalized** to deliberately damage something

vane •NOUN• **vanes** 1 a blade that is moved by wind or water and is part of a windmill or mill **2** a pointer, often on top of a steeple, that is moved by the wind and shows which direction it is blowing from

vanilla •NOUN• a flavouring that comes from the pods of a plant: *vanilla ice-cream*

vanish •VERB• **vanishes, vanishing, vanished** to disappear and leave nothing behind

vanity •NOUN• too much pride in the way you look

vaporize or **vaporise** •VERB• **vaporizes, vaporizing, vaporized** to become or make something into a gas: *Water vaporizes to become steam.*

♦ **vaporizer** •NOUN• **vaporizers** a device that sprays liquid very finely

vapour •NOUN• **vapours** a lot of small drops of liquid in the air

variable •ADJECTIVE• changing often and never staying the same

variant •NOUN• **variants** a different form or version of something

♦ **variation** •NOUN• **variations** a change in the amount or level of something: *variations in temperature*

varied •ADJECTIVE• of many different types: *He has varied interests, from reading to outdoor sports.*

variety •NOUN• **varieties** 1 if something has variety, it has many difficult things in it: *I wanted a bit of variety in my life* **2** a type of something that is slightly different from other similar things: *a new variety of rose* **3** a group with different types of the same thing: *The chairs are available in a variety of colours.* **4** a type of entertainment with singing, dancing and comedy

various •ADJECTIVE• different: *There were various things to choose from.*

varnish •NOUN• **varnishes** a liquid that gives a shiny surface to wood
•VERB• **varnishes, varnishing, varnished** to put varnish on to wood

vary •VERB• **varies, varying, varied** 1 to vary is to change: *The weather varies a lot.* **2** to vary something is to change it slightly
⇒ **variable, variant, varied, variety**

vase •NOUN• **vases** a container for flowers that is often kept as an ornament

vast •ADJECTIVE• extremely big: *vast desert lands*

♦ **vastly** •ADVERB• much: *vastly different*
♦ **vastness** •NOUN• being extremely big

VAT •ABBREVIATION• short for **value-added tax**, which is a tax you pay on things you buy

vat •NOUN• **vats** a large container for liquids

vault •NOUN• **vaults** a room underground for dead bodies or for storing valuable things

VCR •ABBREVIATION• short for **videocassette recorder**

VDU •ABBREVIATION• short for **visual display unit**, the screen you use with a computer

veal •NOUN• meat from a calf

Veda •NOUN• the most ancient holy writings of the Hindu religion

veer •VERB• **veers, veering, veered** to change direction: *The car suddenly veered to the left.*

vegan •NOUN• **vegans** someone who does not eat anything that comes from an animal

vegetable •NOUN• **vegetables** a plant that you can eat, especially one that is not sweet: *Potatoes and carrots are vegetables.*

vegetarian •NOUN• **vegetarians** someone who does not eat meat
•ADJECTIVE• not containing meat: *vegetarian foods*

vegetate •VERB• **vegetates, vegetating, vegetated** to lead a dull life
♦ **vegetation** •NOUN• plants, especially plants that grow in a particular area

vehicle •NOUN• **vehicles** something that carries people or goods, for example a car or lorry

veil •NOUN• **veils** a piece of material that covers a woman's head and face

vein •NOUN• **veins** 1 one of the very thin tubes inside your body that carry blood to your heart 2 one of the thin lines on a leaf

Velcro •NOUN• a material made up of tiny hooks and loops that can join together, used to fasten things This word is a trademark

velocity •NOUN• **velocities** the speed at which something moves

velvet •NOUN• a type of cloth with a surface that is covered with short hairs and feels very soft
♦ **velvety** •ADJECTIVE• feeling like velvet

vendetta •NOUN• **vendettas** an angry disagreement that lasts for a long time

vending machine •NOUN• **vending machines** a machine that you can buy things from

vendor •NOUN• **vendors** someone who is selling something: *an ice-cream vendor*

veneer •NOUN• **veneers** a thin layer of wood that is stuck on to something
•VERB• **veneers, veneering, veneered** to put a veneer on something

venerable •ADJECTIVE• someone who is venerable deserves respect because they are old or wise

Venetian blind •NOUN• **Venetian blinds** a blind that consists of long thin pieces of metal, plastic or wood that can be pulled together or turned to let in or keep out light

vengeance •NOUN• punishment that you give to someone who has harmed you
♦ **vengeful** •ADJECTIVE• wanting to punish someone because they have hurt you

venison •NOUN• meat from a deer

Venn diagram •NOUN• **Venn diagrams** a diagram made up of circles which overlap, used in maths to show which members of one set are also members of another set

venom •NOUN• 1 the poison that some snakes produce 2 deep hatred: *letters full of venom.*
♦ **venomous** •ADJECTIVE• poisonous

vent •NOUN• **vents** a small opening to allow air or smoke to pass through
• **give vent to** to express a feeling such as anger

ventilate •VERB• **ventilates, ventilating, ventilated** to let fresh air into a room or building
♦ **ventilation** •NOUN• letting fresh air into a room or building
♦ **ventilator** •NOUN• **ventilators** 1 a machine that helps someone to breathe by pumping air into and out of their lungs 2 an opening or piece of equipment that lets air into a room or building

ventriloquism •NOUN• the skill of speaking without moving your lips and making it look as though a puppet is speaking
♦ **ventriloquist** •NOUN• **ventriloquists** someone who has the skill of ventriloquism

ⓘ These words come from the Latin words **venter**, which means *stomach*, and **loqui**, which means *to speak*. The word used to mean a person who had been taken over by a speaking demon, which is why you would not see their lips move.

venture •NOUN• **ventures** an activity or project: *Our new venture is baking and selling cakes.*
•VERB• **ventures, venturing, ventured** to go somewhere unknown to you, which may be dangerous or unpleasant

Aa
Bb
Cc
Dd
Ee
Ff
Gg
Hh
Ii
Jj
Kk
Ll
Mm
Nn
Oo
Pp
Qq
Rr
Ss
Tt
Uu
Vv
Ww
Xx
Yy
Zz

Verbs

A **verb** is a *doing* word that tells you about an action or a happening.

> digs
> ran
> is shouting

A verb can also be a *being* word that tells you about a process or a state.

> is
> knew
> becomes

There is a verb in every sentence. A sentence cannot make sense without a verb.

Verb forms

Verbs have different forms. These forms have different names and jobs to do.

The **infinitive** is the basic form of the verb, such as **go, make, come, see**. It often has the word *to* in front of it.

> The teacher asked them *to* **sing**.
> Jen did not know which coat *to* **choose**.

Verbs have a **present** and a **past** form (also look at the box called **Tense**).

> I **play**. She **plays**. (present)
> I **played**. She **played**. (past)

Helping verbs

Helping verbs, which are also called **auxiliary verbs**, are short verbs that are used with other verbs. The most common ones are **be** and **have**.

> The children **are walking** to school.
> I **have played** all day.

Do is used with other verbs when you are making questions or saying that something is *not*.

> **Do** you **like** Peter?
> She **did not see** the film.

---

venue • NOUN • **venues** the place where an event takes place

veranda • NOUN • **verandas** an outdoor terrace with a roof, that is built on to the side of a house

verb • PART OF SPEECH • **verbs** the word in a sentence that tells you what someone or something does. For example, *eat* and *speak* are verbs. See the box called **Verbs**

verbal • ADJECTIVE • spoken rather than written: *a verbal promise*

verdict • NOUN • **verdicts** a decision made in a court of law whether someone is guilty or not guilty of committing a crime

verge • NOUN • **verges** the grassy area at the edge of a road
• **be on the verge of** to be almost happening or almost doing something: *Sanjay was on the verge of tears.*

verify • VERB • **verifies, verifying, verified** to

prove or say for definite that something is true

vermin •NOUN• animals or insects such as rats or fleas, which people think are pests

verruca •NOUN• **verrucas** a wart on someone's foot

versatile •ADJECTIVE• 1 useful for many different things: *versatile clothes* 2 able to do many different things: *a versatile actor* ✦ **versatility** •NOUN• being versatile

verse •NOUN• **verses** 1 verse is poetry rather than writing 2 a verse is a set of lines that form one part of a song or poem

version •NOUN• **versions** 1 a description of events from one person's point of view: *I seriously doubt your version of what happened.* 2 a type of something that is slightly different from the original form: *Have you heard the new version of the song?*

versus •PREPOSITION• against. Versus is used when saying who is playing in a sports game: *It's Scotland versus France tonight.*

vertebra •NOUN• **vertebrae** one of the bones that form your backbone

vertebrate •NOUN• **vertebrates** an animal that has a backbone

vertex •NOUN• **vertices** the point on a cone, pyramid, or angle

vertical •ADJECTIVE• standing upright and straight: *vertical lines*

vertigo •NOUN• feeling dizzy because you are in a very high place

verve •NOUN• excitement and energy

very •ADVERB• to a great degree: *I'm very tired.* •ADJECTIVE• exact: *At that very moment, the telephone rang.*

vessel •NOUN• **vessels** 1 a large boat or ship 2 a container for liquids 3 a tube that carries blood through your body

vest •NOUN• **vests** 1 a piece of underwear that covers the top part of your body 2 the American English word for a waistcoat

vestment •NOUN• **vestments** a piece of clothing that a priest or minister wears during religious services

vestry •NOUN• **vestries** the room in a church where the priest or minister puts on clothes for a religious service

vet •NOUN• **vets** someone whose job is to treat animals who are ill or injured

veteran •NOUN• **veterans** 1 someone who has a lot of experience at something 2 someone who fought in a war

veterinary •ADJECTIVE• to do with the care of animals that are ill or injured: *veterinary medicine*

veterinary surgeon •NOUN• **veterinary surgeons** someone whose job is to treat animals that are ill or injured. This is usually shortened to **vet**

veto •VERB• **vetoes, vetoing, vetoed** to stop something from happening: *The president vetoed the plan to lower taxes.* •NOUN• **vetoes** 1 the power to stop a law from being passed or a decision from being made 2 an occasion when someone does not let something go ahead

vex •VERB• **vexes, vexing, vexed** to annoy someone ✦ **vexation** •NOUN• feeling annoyed

VHF •ABBREVIATION• short for **very high frequency**

via •PREPOSITION• travelling through a place: *The train goes to London via Birmingham.*

viaduct •NOUN• **viaducts** a bridge that takes a railway over a road or river

vibrant •ADJECTIVE• 1 exciting and full of life: *a vibrant city* 2 vibrant colours are very bright

vibrate •VERB• **vibrates, vibrating, vibrated** to shake very quickly ✦ **vibration** •NOUN• **vibrations** 1 vibration is shaking very quickly 2 a vibration is a quick shaking movement

vicar •NOUN• **vicars** someone who is in charge of a parish in the Church of England

vice[1] •NOUN• **vices** 1 a vice is a bad habit 2 a vice is behaviour that is bad or not decent

vice[2] •NOUN• **vices** a tool for holding objects firmly while you work on them

vice- •PREFIX• **vice-** at the start of a word tells you that someone is next in importance.

For example, a *vice-president* is someone who is next in rank to a president and takes their place if they are not available

vice versa •ADVERB• the other way around: *I needed his help and vice versa – he needed mine too.*

vicinity •NOUN• the area around a place: *There are no schools in the vicinity.*

vicious •ADJECTIVE• extremely cruel and wanting to hurt people: *a vicious attack*

vicious circle •NOUN• **vicious circles** a situation in which one problem causes another problem which makes the first problem worse

victim •NOUN• **victims** someone who is harmed by a bad situation or bad event: *victims of crime*

♦ **victimize** or **victimise** •VERB• **victimizes, victimizing, victimized** to treat someone in an unfair way and make them a victim

victor •NOUN• **victors** the person who has won a game or competition

victorious •ADJECTIVE• successful in a battle or competition

victory •NOUN• **victories** winning a battle or competition: *victory in the Cup Final*

video •NOUN• **videos** 1 a recording of a film or television programme made on videotape 2 a recording of an event on a videocassette that has been made using a video camera 3 a machine for playing videos •VERB• **videos, videoing, videoed** 1 to record a television programme on to videotape 2 to film an event using a video camera

ⓘ **Video** was taken from the Latin word **videre**, which means *to see*. The -o ending was added so that it would be similar to the word **audio**.

video camera •NOUN• **video cameras** a piece of equipment that you hold and use to record events as they happen on to a videocassette

videocassette •NOUN• **videocassettes** a plastic case that contains videotape

videocassette recorder or **video recorder** •NOUN• **videocassette recorders** or **video recorders** a machine for recording and playing videos

videotape •NOUN• **videotapes** magnetic tape that pictures and sounds can be recorded on

view •NOUN• **views** 1 the things you can see from a place: *There's a fantastic view from the top of the hill.* 2 your ability to see things from a place: *The pillar spoilt my view of the concert.* 3 someone's opinion: *What's your view on the new school uniform?* • **in view of** considering something: *In view of the weather, we have cancelled the game.* • **on view** being shown for people to look at: *Several classic cars will be on view.* • **with a view to** with the intention of: *He's moving to London with a view to finding a job.* •VERB• **views, viewing, viewed** 1 to look at something: *People came from all over the country to view his work.* 2 to think about someone or something in a particular way: *The painting was viewed as very unusual.* ♦ **viewer** •NOUN• **viewers** someone who watches television: *The programme attracted less than a million viewers.*

viewpoint •NOUN• **viewpoints** 1 a place from which you look at something: *a good viewpoint at the top of a hill* 2 a way of thinking about something: *Try looking at what happened from my viewpoint.*

vigil •NOUN• **vigils** a time when people stay awake at night in order to pray, protest or watch someone who is ill

vigilance •NOUN• being careful to notice any trouble or problems ♦ **vigilant** •ADJECTIVE• watching things carefully in order to notice any trouble or problems: *Police have urged people to be vigilant after a series of thefts.*

vigorous •ADJECTIVE• very active or strong: *vigorous defence* ♦ **vigorously** •ADVERB• in an active or strong way: *We argued vigorously.*

vigour •NOUN• strength and energy

vile •ADJECTIVE• **viler, vilest** extremely unpleasant: *a vile taste*

villa •NOUN• **villas** a large house, especially one used for holidays

village •NOUN• **villages** a small place in a country area, which is not as big as a town
 ✦ **villager** •NOUN• **villagers** someone who lives in a village

villain •NOUN• **villains** a bad person or a criminal
 ✦ **villainy** •NOUN• the behaviour of a villain

vindictive •ADJECTIVE• wanting to harm someone because they have been bad to you

vine •NOUN• **vines** the plant that grapes grow on

vinegar •NOUN• a sour liquid used for flavouring food

vineyard •NOUN• **vineyards** a place where grapes are grown to produce wine

vintage •NOUN• **vintages 1** the wine that is produced in a particular year or place **2** the time that something is from
 •ADJECTIVE• typical of a particular time in the past: *vintage clothing*

vintage car •NOUN• **vintage cars** a car made between 1917 and 1930 that is still in very good condition

viola •NOUN• **violas** a musical instrument that looks like a big violin and is played in the same way

violate •VERB• **violates, violating, violated**
 1 to violate a law or rule is to break it
 2 to violate someone's rights is to not respect them
 3 to damage or destroy a special place
 ✦ **violation** •NOUN• violating something

violence •NOUN• behaviour that is rough and intended to hurt someone
 ✦ **violent** •ADJECTIVE• **1** behaving in a rough way that is intended to hurt someone **2** very sudden and strong: *a violent storm*
 ✦ **violently** •ADVERB• in a violent way

violet •NOUN• **violets 1** a small purple flower **2** a purple colour

violin •NOUN• **violins** a musical instrument with four strings, which you hold under your chin and play by drawing a bow across the strings
 ✦ **violinist** •NOUN• **violinists** someone who plays the violin

violoncello •NOUN• **violoncellos** another word for a **cello**

VIP •ABBREVIATION• **VIPs** short for **very important person**

viper •NOUN• **vipers** a small poisonous snake

virgin •NOUN• **virgins** someone who is very pure
 • **the Virgin Mary** the mother of Jesus Christ

virtual •ADJECTIVE• **1** almost a particular thing: *He was a virtual prisoner in his own home.* **2** using computer images that make something seem real: *a virtual tour of the museum*
 ✦ **virtually** •ADVERB• almost: *Virtually all the class can swim now.*

virtual reality •NOUN• pictures and sounds that seem real but are actually created by computer software

virtue •NOUN• **virtues 1** virtue is goodness **2** a virtue is a good quality in a person's character
 ✦ **virtuous** •ADJECTIVE• behaving in a very good way
 ✦ **virtuously** •ADVERB• in a very good way

virus •NOUN• **viruses 1** a germ that causes illnesses such as a cold or chickenpox **2** a computer program that can send itself to many computers, for example by email, and can destroy files on those computers

---
ⓘ **Virus** is a Latin word which means *venom*, the poison made by snakes.
---

visa •NOUN• **visas** a document that you need to travel to and work in some countries

visibility •NOUN• **1** how far and well you can see because of conditions such as the weather: *poor visibility* **2** the fact of being easy to see: *Visibility is important for cyclists.*

visible •ADJECTIVE• able to be seen: *The house is not visible from the road.*
 ✦ **visibly** •ADVERB• in a way that is easy to see: *He was visibly upset.*

vision •NOUN• **visions 1** your ability to see **2** something that you see or imagine might happen: *One ghastly vision after another swam through his brain.*

visit •VERB• **visits, visiting, visited** to go and see a place or person
 •NOUN• **visits** the act of visiting a place or

Aa
Bb
Cc
Dd
Ee
Ff
Gg
Hh
Ii
Jj
Kk
Ll
Mm
Nn
Oo
Pp
Qq
Rr
Ss
Tt
Uu
Vv
Ww
Xx
Yy
Zz

Aa

person: *I'm going to pay him a visit.*
◆ **visitor** •NOUN• **visitors** someone who visits a person or place

Bb

visor •NOUN• **visors** the clear part of a helmet that covers someone's face

Cc

visual •ADJECTIVE• to do with seeing: *The blackboard is a visual aid for teaching.*

Dd

◆ **visually** •ADVERB• in a way that involves your ability to see

Ee

visual display unit •NOUN• **visual display units** a screen that you use with a computer

Ff

visualize or **visualise** •VERB• **visualizes, visualizing, visualized** to form a picture of something in your mind: *I remember his name, but I can't visualize him.*

Gg

Hh

Ii

vital •ADJECTIVE• necessary or extremely important: *vital information*

Jj

◆ **vitality** •NOUN• liveliness and enthusiasm
◆ **vitally** •ADVERB• extremely: *vitally important*

Kk

Ll

vitamin •NOUN• **vitamins** a substance in food that you need to stay healthy: *Oranges contain vitamin C.*

Mm

vivacious •ADJECTIVE• lively and full of energy

Nn

vivid •ADJECTIVE• **1** producing very clear ideas and pictures in your mind: *vivid memories* **2** very bright: *vivid colours*

Oo

Pp

◆ **vividly** •ADVERB• in a very clear way: *I vividly remember meeting him.*

Qq

vivisection •NOUN• doing experiments on animals that are alive, for medical research

Rr

vixen •NOUN• **vixens** a female fox

Ss

vocabulary •NOUN• **vocabularies 1** the range of words that someone knows and uses: *a child with a good vocabulary* **2** words in a particular language: *We're having a test on French vocabulary.* **3** a list of words and their meanings

Tt

Uu

Vv

vocal •ADJECTIVE• to do with your voice
◆ **vocalist** •NOUN• **vocalists** a singer, especially in a band

Ww

Xx

vocation •NOUN• **vocations 1** a job or way of life that you feel is very right for you **2** a belief that you should do a particular job or live in a particular way

Yy

Zz

vodka •NOUN• a strong clear alcoholic drink

vogue •NOUN• a fashion at the moment
• **in vogue** in fashion and popular: *Short trousers are in vogue just now.*

voice •NOUN• **voices 1** the sound you make when you speak or sing: *'Hello!' he said in a loud voice.* **2** your ability to make speaking or singing sounds: *I had a sore throat and lost my voice.*
•VERB• **voices, voicing, voiced** to express an opinion: *Many people have voiced their concerns.*

volcano •NOUN• **volcanoes** a mountain with a hole at the top which hot lava sometimes comes out of
◆ **volcanic** •ADJECTIVE• relating to volcanoes

ⓘ Volcanoes are named after the ancient Roman god of fire, **Vulcan**.

volatile •ADJECTIVE• **1** a volatile person is likely to change their mood very quickly **2** a volatile situation could change very suddenly **3** a volatile liquid changes quickly to a gas

vole •NOUN• **voles** a small animal similar to a mouse or rat

volley •NOUN• **volleys 1** a lot of bullets or weapons that are fired or thrown at the same time **2** in some sports such as tennis and soccer, a volley is hitting the ball before it hits the ground
•VERB• **volleys, volleying, volleyed** in tennis, to hit the ball before it hits the ground

volt •NOUN• **volts** a unit for measuring how strong an electric current is
◆ **voltage** •NOUN• the amount of electrical force something has

volume •NOUN• **volumes 1** the space that something takes up or the amount of space that a container has **2** the amount of sound that something makes: *Can you turn the volume down on the TV, please?* **3** the amount of something: *The volume of trade has increased.* **4** a book, especially a book that is part of a set

voluntary •ADJECTIVE• **1** done by choice and not because you have to **2** done without payment: *voluntary work*

volunteer •NOUN• **volunteers** someone who offers to do something: *Do I have any volunteers to help me tidy up?*
•VERB• **volunteers, volunteering, volunteered 1** to offer to do something: *Dad volunteered to take us swimming.* **2** to give information or make a suggestion without being asked for it

vomit •VERB• **vomits, vomiting, vomited** to bring food back up from your stomach through your mouth
•NOUN• food that a person or animal has brought back from their stomach through their mouth

vortex •NOUN• **vortices** or **vortexes** air or water that spins around and pulls things into its centre

vote •VERB• **votes, voting, voted 1** to choose someone for an official job or choose something by secretly marking a piece of paper or putting your hand up to be counted: *Which party did you vote for?* **2** to decide something by voting: *He was voted best actor.*
•NOUN• **votes 1** a choice you make by marking a piece of paper or putting your hand up to be counted **2** the right you have to vote in elections
• **voter** •NOUN• **voters** someone who votes in an election

vouch •VERB• **vouches, vouching, vouched** to **vouch for** someone or something is to say that they are good or true

voucher •NOUN• **vouchers 1** a piece of paper that can be used instead of money to pay for something **2** a piece of paper that lets you pay less than usual for something

vow •VERB• **vows, vowing, vowed** to promise in a very serious way
•NOUN• **vows** a serious promise

vowel •NOUN• **vowels 1** one of the letters of the alphabet **a, e, i, o** or **u 2** a speech sound you make that does not use your lips, teeth, or tongue to stop the flow of air

voyage •NOUN• **voyages** a long journey by sea or in space

vulgar •ADJECTIVE• extremely rude and having very bad manners

vulgar fraction •NOUN• **vulgar fractions** a fraction that is shown with one number above the line and one number below, for example $\frac{1}{2}$ and $\frac{3}{4}$

vulnerable •ADJECTIVE• weak and likely to be harmed or damaged: *Old people are especially vulnerable.* • *a place that is vulnerable to attack*

vulture •NOUN• **vultures** a large bird that eats dead animals

Aa
Bb
Cc
Dd
Ee
Ff
Gg
Hh
Ii
Jj
Kk
Ll
Mm
Nn
Oo
Pp
Qq
Rr
Ss
Tt
Uu
Vv
Ww
Xx
Yy
Zz

Ww

W •ABBREVIATION• **1** short for **west 2** short for **watt** or **watts**

wad •NOUN• **wads 1** a pad of loose material such as cloth or paper pressed together into one piece: *She cleaned the wound with a wad of cottonwool.* **2** a roll or bundle of bank notes

waddle •VERB• **waddles, waddling, waddled** to walk moving from side to side, like a duck

wade •VERB• **wades, wading, waded 1** to walk through water or mud: *The stream had flooded and we had to wade across.* **2** if you **wade through** something, you find it difficult to do and it takes a long time: *We've been wading through this old exam paper for weeks.*

♦ **waders** •PLURAL NOUN• very high waterproof boots that you wear when you are fishing

wafer •NOUN• **wafers** a very thin flat biscuit, often eaten with ice cream

waffle •NOUN• **waffles 1** a type of pancake with a pattern of squares on it **2** talk that goes on for a long time but does not say anything interesting

waft •VERB• **wafts, wafting, wafted** to float through the air: *The smell of freshly baked bread came wafting out of the window.*

wag •VERB• **wags, wagging, wagged** to move a part of your body or a tail from side to side: *The dog ran backwards and forwards, wagging its tail.* • *Don't you wag your finger at me, boy!*

wage •NOUN• **wages** a wage or wages are money that you are paid for doing your job: *We collect our wages from the office every Friday afternoon.*
•VERB• **wages, waging, waged** to wage a war is to carry it on

wager •NOUN• **wagers** a bet
•VERB• **wagers, wagering, wagered** to make a bet

waggle •VERB• **waggles, waggling, waggled** to move something from side to side or up and down: *Can you waggle your ears?*

wagon or **waggon** •NOUN• **wagons** or **waggons 1** a vehicle or cart with four wheels that is used for carrying heavy loads: *a hay wagon* **2** a type of railway truck with no roof, used for carrying things: *a coal wagon*

waif •NOUN• **waifs** a child who has no home or family, and looks poor

wail •VERB• **wails, wailing, wailed** to cry loudly: *A small child was wailing in the next room.*
•NOUN• **wails** a loud cry or long noise like a cry: *the wail of a siren*

waist •NOUN• **waists** the narrow part of your body between your chest and your hips

waistcoat •NOUN• **waistcoats** a short jacket with no sleeves and usually with buttons up the front

wait •VERB• **waits, waiting, waited 1** to wait or **wait for** someone or something is to stay in a place until they arrive: *Several people were already waiting for the bus.*
2 to wait or **wait until** something happens is to not do an action until that thing happens: *I will wait until it stops raining before I leave.*
3 if someone **waits on** people, they serve them food and drinks: *There are six waitresses to wait on the guests.*
•NOUN• **waits** a delay or period of waiting: *It seemed like an awfully long wait for the show to start.*

waiter •NOUN• **waiters** a man who serves people with food in a restaurant

waiting list •NOUN• **waiting lists** a list of people who are waiting for something: *There's a long waiting list for tickets.*

waiting room •NOUN• **waiting rooms** a room where people can wait, for example in a station or a doctor's surgery

waitress •NOUN• **waitresses** a woman who serves people with food in a restaurant

waive •VERB• **waives, waiving, waived** to give up a claim or right to something

wake[1] •VERB• **wakes, waking, woke, woken** 1 if you wake or **wake up**, you stop sleeping: *She suddenly woke up and looked around.* 2 to wake someone is to make them stop sleeping: *Please don't wake the baby!*

wake[2] •NOUN• **wakes** the strip of disturbed water left behind a moving boat • **in the wake of** happening after or because of something: *Many airlines went bankrupt in the wake of the disaster.*

waken •VERB• **wakens, wakening, wakened** 1 to waken is to stop sleeping 2 to waken someone is to make them stop sleeping: *The sound of the doorbell wakened me.*

walk •VERB• **walks, walking, walked** 1 to move on foot fairly slowly: *The door opened and Simon walked in.* • *I think I'll walk to work today.* 2 to travel on foot because you enjoy it: *We usually go walking on the moors every weekend.* •NOUN• **walks** 1 a journey on foot: *It's just a short walk to the newsagent's.* 2 a way of walking: *I recognised Ann by her walk.* 3 a path that you can walk along for pleasure: *a book of walks in the Lake District*

walkie-talkie •NOUN• **walkie-talkies** a radio that you can carry with you to send and receive messages

walking stick •NOUN• **walking sticks** a stick that you can use to help you walk: *Gran needs to use a walking stick since she fell.*

walkover •NOUN• **walkovers** a game or race that is easy to win: *The score was 3-1 but it was no walkover.*

wall •NOUN• **walls** 1 a structure made of brick or stone that separates or goes around an area: *Hadrian's Wall* • *A high wall surrounds the school.* 2 any of the sides of a room or building: *She hung the new clock on the kitchen wall.* •VERB• **walls, walling, walled** to surround or enclose something with a wall: *a walled garden*

wallaby •NOUN• **wallabies** an animal like a small kangaroo

wallet •NOUN• **wallets** a small folding holder for banknotes and cards that you can put in your pocket: *a leather wallet*

wallflower •NOUN• **wallflowers** 1 a spring flower with a sweet smell 2 someone who does not have a partner to dance with

wallop •VERB• **wallops, walloping, walloped** to hit someone or something hard: *He walloped his head on the door as he came in.* •NOUN• **wallops** a hard hit: *She fell off her bike with quite a wallop.*

wallow •VERB• **wallows, wallowing, wallowed** to roll about in mud or water and enjoy it: *The hippos were wallowing in the mud.*

wallpaper •NOUN• **wallpapers** paper that you can use to cover and decorate the walls of a room

walnut •NOUN• **walnuts** a large nut with a hard, round shell

walrus •NOUN• **walruses** a sea animal like a large seal with very big teeth called tusks

ⓘ This is a Dutch word which means *whale horse*.

waltz •NOUN• **waltzes** an old-fashioned dance for couples, to music with three beats in every bar •VERB• **waltzes, waltzing, waltzed** to dance a waltz

ⓘ **Waltz** comes from the German word **waltzen**, which means *to dance*.

wan •ADJECTIVE• **wanner, wannest** looking pale and sick: *a wan face*

wand •NOUN• **wands** a long thin stick such as the one a magician or fairy uses when doing magic spells or tricks: *The fairy waved her magic wand and turned a pumpkin into a beautiful coach.*

wander •VERB• **wanders, wandering, wandered** 1 to go from one place to another without any definite plan: *We spent the summer wandering all around southern Italy.* 2 to wander or **wander off** is to go

Aa
away from where you should be: *Their little boy had wandered off and could not find them.*

Bb
♦ **wanderer** •NOUN• **wanderers** someone who wanders

Cc

wane •VERB• **wanes, waning, waned**

Dd
1 to become less strong: *Support for the government is waning fast.* **2** if the moon wanes, it seems to become smaller. Look up and compare **wax²**

Ee

Ff
•NOUN• if something is **on the wane**, it is becoming smaller or less powerful: *I think her interest in pop music is on the wane.*

Gg

Hh
wangle •VERB• **wangles, wangling, wangled** to achieve or obtain something by being clever or crafty: *Do you think you could wangle me a couple of free tickets to the concert?*

Ii

Jj

Kk
want •VERB• **wants, wanting, wanted**
1 to wish for something: *Do you want some cake?* • *Someone wants to speak to you.* • *I'll stay here with you, if you want.* **2** to need or lack something: *Your hands want a good wash.*

Ll

Mm
•NOUN• **wants 1** something that you want: *a long list of wants*

Nn
2 the state of being very poor: *families living in severe want*

Oo

Pp
3 a lack of something: *He failed the test, but not for want of trying.*

Qq
♦ **wanted** •ADJECTIVE• **1** someone who is wanted is being searched for by the police: *Pictures of the wanted man appeared in all the newspapers.* **2** loved, needed, and cared for: *Make your pet feel wanted by giving it plenty of attention.*

Rr

Ss

Tt
♦ **wanting** •ADJECTIVE• lacking or missing something

Uu

war •NOUN• **wars** armed conflict between two countries or groups: *the war in Afghanistan* • *War broke out between neighbouring tribes.*

Vv

Ww
•VERB• **wars, warring, warred** to fight in a war: *The two countries have been warring against each other for centuries.*

Xx

Yy
⇒ **warrior**

Zz
warble •VERB• **warbles, warbling, warbled** to sing like a bird

ward •NOUN• **wards 1** a room with beds in it

---

in a hospital: *the children's ward* **2** someone who is looked after by an adult who is not their parent, or by a court of law

•VERB• **wards, warding, warded** if you **ward something off**, you fight to keep it away from you: *He covered his head with his arms to ward off the blows.*

warden •NOUN• **wardens 1** someone who is in charge of a place, for example an old people's home, hostel or caravan site: *All visitors should report to the warden.*
2 someone who is responsible for looking after or controlling something: *a traffic warden* • *a game warden*

warder •NOUN• **warders** someone who guards the prisoners in a prison

wardrobe •NOUN• **wardrobes 1** a tall cupboard that you can hang clothes inside **2** all of the clothes someone owns: *her summer wardrobe*

warehouse •NOUN• **warehouses** a large building where businesses store things: *a furniture warehouse*

wares •PLURAL NOUN• things that are for sale: *The large shop windows are used to display our wares.*

warfare •NOUN• fighting in a war: *modern warfare*

warhead •NOUN• **warheads** the part of a missile that contains the explosive: *a nuclear warhead*

warily •ADVERB• cautiously: *He eyed the guard dog warily.*

warlike •ADJECTIVE• a warlike country or person enjoys fighting

warm •ADJECTIVE• **warmer, warmest**
1 pleasantly hot: *a warm bath* • *As the sun rose we began to feel a little warmer.*
2 warm clothes make you feel warm: *a warm winter coat*
3 kind and friendly: *a warm welcome* • *The school nurse is a warm, kind-hearted person.*
•VERB• **warms, warming, warmed 1** to make someone or something feel warm: *She warmed her hands on the radiator.*
2 to warm or **warm up** is to become warm: *I'll put the heating on and the house'll soon warm up.*

3 if you **warm up for** something, you prepare for it by practising or doing gentle exercises: *The football players were on the pitch, warming up.*

♦ **warmly** •ADVERB• in a warm way: *Make sure you're warmly dressed for the hike.* • *She smiled warmly.*
⇒ **warmth**

warm-blooded •ADJECTIVE• a warm-blooded animal has a temperature that is higher than the air around it

warmth •NOUN• **1** pleasant heat, or the state of being pleasantly warm: *the warmth of the fire* **2** being kind, friendly and affectionate: *the warmth of her welcome*

warm-up •NOUN• **warm-ups** a set of gentle exercises that you do before playing a sport, dancing or running

warn •VERB• **warns, warning, warned** to tell someone that something is dangerous or bad before it happens: *I warned her about the icy roads.*

♦ **warning** •NOUN• **warnings** an event or something that you say to warn someone: *The volcano erupted without any warning.*

warp •VERB• **warps, warping, warped** to become or make something twisted and out of shape: *I his drawer has warped und is hard to open.* • *The wet weather had warped the back door.*
•NOUN• the threads that run along the length of the frame cloth is woven on. Look up and compare **weft**

warpath •NOUN• if someone is **on the warpath**, they are in the type of mood to have an argument or fight with someone: *I'd avoid Mr Bates – he's on the warpath today.*

warrant •NOUN• **warrants** a document that gives the police the right to arrest someone or search their property
•VERB• **warrants, warranting, warranted** to be a good reason or excuse for something: *He was naughty, but it did not warrant such a harsh punishment.*

warren •NOUN• **warrens** a network of tunnels called burrows that rabbits live in

warrior •NOUN• **warriors** a soldier or fighter: *great warriors such as Hannibal*

warship •NOUN• **warships** a ship with a lot of guns used for fighting at sea

wart •NOUN• **warts** a small hard lump on the skin: *The witch had a wart on the end of her nose.*

wary •ADJECTIVE• cautious: *a wary glance* • *I'd be very wary of lending her money.*
⇒ **warily**

was •VERB• the past tense of the verb **be** that you use with **I**, **he**, **she** or **it**: *I was surprised to see Rosie there.* • *Mr Brock was my favourite teacher.*

wash •VERB• **washes, washing, washed 1** to clean something with water and soap: *Wash your hands and face before we eat.*
2 if water washes against something, it flows against it: *Gentle waves were washing against the boat.*
3 if something such as a building, tree or car is **washed away**, the force of the water carries it away: *Whole houses were washed away in the storm.*
4 if you **wash up**, you wash the dishes after you have eaten: *It's your turn to wash up, Adam.*
•NOUN• **washes 1** the act of washing someone or something
2 all the clothes that need to be washed: *Your red shirt is in the wash.*
3 a liquid that you use to wash something: *a bottle of mouthwash*
4 the waves that a boat causes as it moves
5 a thin watery paint
♦ **washer** •NOUN• **washers 1** a flat ring made of metal or rubber that you put under a screw to keep it tightly in place **2** a washing machine
♦ **washing** •NOUN• all the clothes that need to be washed: *a pile of dirty washing*

washing machine •NOUN• **washing machines** a piece of electrical equipment that you wash clothes in

washing-up •NOUN• **1** all the dishes that need to be washed: *How come there's so much washing-up tonight?* **2** the act of washing dishes: *You sit down and relax while I do the washing-up.*

wasn't •SHORT FORM• a short way to say and write **was not**: *Are you sure Mark wasn't joking?*

Aa

wasp •NOUN• **wasps** an insect with a thin black and yellow striped body that can sting you

Bb

waste •VERB• **wastes, wasting, wasted** 1 to use more of something than you need: *I'm trying not to waste any paper.* 2 if you waste time or money, you spend it in a way that is not useful: *You're wasting your time trying to fix the television.*

Cc

Dd

Ee

•NOUN• **wastes** 1 rubbish or useless material: *industrial waste*
2 a bad use of something: *The computer turned out to be a waste of money.*
3 a large area of land that is not cultivated: *the frozen wastes of Siberia*
•ADJECTIVE• 1 waste products or materials are useless and thrown away: *waste paper*
2 waste land has no buildings or crops on it
♦ **wasteful** •ADJECTIVE• involving or causing waste: *It's very wasteful, throwing all these apples away.*

Ff

Gg

Hh

Ii

Jj

Kk

Ll

watch •VERB• **watches, watching, watched**
1 to look at someone or something: *Roy's watching the football match in the other room.*
2 to be careful about something: *Watch you don't trip over that root.*
3 to look after someone or something: *Could you watch the baby for me while I go to the shop?*
•NOUN• **watches** 1 a small clock that you wear on your wrist 2 a time when someone keeps guard: *Two guards kept watch over the prisoners.*
⇒ **watchful**

Mm

Nn

Oo

Pp

Qq

Rr

Ss

watchdog •NOUN• **watchdogs** a dog that is trained to guard a building

Tt

watchful •ADJECTIVE• careful to notice what is happening: *Sue kept a watchful eye on her little sister.*

Uu

Vv

watchman •NOUN• **watchmen** a man whose job is to guard a building: *a night watchman*

Ww

Xx

water •NOUN• a clear liquid with no taste that falls from the sky as rain: *a glass of water*
•VERB• **waters, watering, watered** 1 to water a plant is to give water to it
2 if your eyes water, they produce tears:

Yy

Zz

The thick smoke made her eyes water.
3 if your mouth waters, it produces saliva because you see something good to eat
⇒ **watery**

watercolour •NOUN• **watercolours** 1 a type of paint that is mixed with water, not oil: *a box of watercolours* 2 a painting done with watercolour paints: *a watercolour of a thatched cottage*

watercress •NOUN• a plant that grows in water and has rounded leaves that taste peppery

water cycle •NOUN• the way in which water from the sea evaporates into the air, condenses to form clouds, then falls as rain on to the ground and returns to the sea in rivers and streams

waterfall •NOUN• **waterfalls** a place where a river or stream falls over a high rock or cliff

waterlogged •ADJECTIVE• waterlogged ground is so wet that it cannot take in any more water: *The match was cancelled because the pitch was waterlogged.*

watermark •NOUN• **watermarks** a faint design that you can see in a piece of paper or banknote when you hold it up against the light

watermelon •NOUN• **watermelons** a large round fruit with a hard green skin and red juicy flesh

waterproof •ADJECTIVE• waterproof material does not allow water to pass through it
•NOUN• **waterproofs** a coat or other piece of clothing made of waterproof material: *The fishermen were wearing bright yellow waterproofs.*

watertight •ADJECTIVE• a watertight join or seal does not let liquid in or out

waterway •NOUN• **waterways** a river or canal that a ship can travel along

waterworks •NOUN• a waterworks is a place where water is cleaned and stored

watery •ADJECTIVE• 1 like water: *watery soup* 2 full of water: *watery eyes*

watt •NOUN• **watts** a unit of electrical power. This is often shortened to **W**: *a 60W bulb*

◆ **wattage** •NOUN• electric power measured in watts

wave •NOUN• **waves 1** a moving ridge of water in the sea: *Surfers were jumping into the waves.*
2 a curving shape in your hair: *Your hair has a natural wave.*
3 a vibration that travels through the air and carries something such as sound or light: *radio waves*
4 a movement of the hand to say hello or goodbye or attract someone's attention: *She gave a cheery wave as the train pulled out of the station.*
5 a rush of a feeling or emotion: *The pain seemed to come in waves.*
•VERB• **waves, waving, waved 1** to move your hand backwards and forwards: *Wave bye-bye to granny.*
2 to move in the wind: *flags waving in the breeze*
3 hair that waves or is waved is slightly curly: *Mel's hair waves naturally.*
⇒ **wavy**

wavelength •NOUN• **wavelengths 1** the distance between one point on a radio wave and the next **2** the length of radio wave that a radio or television station uses to broadcast on. These are marked on radios so that you can find them: *Which wavelength is that station on?*

wavy •ADJECTIVE• **wavier, waviest 1** a wavy line goes up and down in gentle curves **2** wavy hair has gentle curls in it

wax[1] •NOUN• **1** the sticky, fatty substance that bees make their cells out of
2 a sticky yellow substance that forms in your ears
3 a substance used to make candles and crayons, which melts when it is hot
4 a substance used to polish furniture
•VERB• **waxes, waxing, waxed** to polish wood with wax
⇒ **waxy**

wax[2] •VERB• **waxes, waxing, waxed** if the moon waxes, it seems to grow bigger. Look up and compare **wane**

waxworks •NOUN• a waxworks is a place where you can see wax models of famous people

waxy •ADJECTIVE• **waxier, waxiest** like wax: *a waxy substance*

way •NOUN• **ways 1** a method or manner of doing something: *She's got a funny way of walking.* • *The best way to make new friends is to join a club.*
2 a road or path: *22 Purley Way*
3 a route or direction: *Could you tell me the way to the cinema?*
4 a distance: *It's quite a long way to the coast.*
• **by the way** you say 'by the way' when you are mentioning another subject: *By the way, I met John in town today.*
• **get your own way** if you get your own way, things happen in the way that you want them to: *You should not let children always get their own way.*
• **in the way** if something is in the way, it is blocking your progress or movement: *Am I in your way if I sit here?*
• **no way** you say 'no way' when you disagree strongly with someone or something: *There's no way that that was a penalty!*

wayward •ADJECTIVE• a wayward person does what they want and does not obey other people

WC •NOUN• a toilet

ⓘ **WC** is short for **water closet**, an old-fashioned word for a toilet.

we •PRONOUN• a word you use when you are talking about yourself and at least one other person: *We left home at about nine o'clock.*

ⓘ In grammar, **we** and **us** are personal pronouns. In a sentence in which you (and someone else) are the subject, you use **we** before the verb. You use **us** after the verb or a preposition: *We are going to the cinema. Do you want to come with us?*

weak •ADJECTIVE• **weaker, weakest**
1 feeble and not physically strong: *His illness has left him feeling very weak.* • *a weak heart*
2 not strong in character: *She's too weak to stand up to her boss.* • *a weak excuse*
3 someone who is weak at a subject or

Aa

activity is not good at it: *I was always weak at maths.*

4 a weak drink or mixture has too much water in it: *a cup of weak tea*

Bb

♦ **weaken** •VERB• **weakens, weakening, weakened 1** to weaken is to become weak: *His determination to leave weakened when Jenny arrived.* **2** to weaken something or someone is to make them weaker: *The bout of flu had weakened her.*

Cc

Dd

Ee

♦ **weakly** •ADVERB• in a way that is not strong or determined: *She smiled weakly at his joke.*

Ff

Gg

♦ **weakness** •NOUN• **weaknesses 1** lack of strength: *the weakness of an argument* **2** a fault or something that you cannot help liking: *Chocolate is my only weakness.*

Hh

Ii

wealth •NOUN• **1** riches: *a businessman of great wealth* **2** a wealth of something is a lot of it: *a sports team with a wealth of talent*

Jj

Kk

♦ **wealthy** •ADJECTIVE• **wealthier, wealthiest** rich: *a wealthy landowner*

Ll

wean •VERB• **weans, weaning, weaned** to gradually start feeding a baby on food rather than only on its mother's milk

Mm

Nn

weapon •NOUN• **weapons** something that you use to fight someone: *weapons of war* • *Our best weapon was surprise.*

Oo

Pp

wear •VERB• **wears, wearing, wore, worn**
1 to be dressed in clothes or carrying something on your body: *Ann was wearing her school uniform.* • *How long have you worn glasses?*

Qq

Rr

2 to arrange your hair in a particular style: *She usually wears her hair in a ponytail.*

Ss

3 to have a particular expression on your face: *Ted wore an angry frown.*

Tt

4 if a material or surface wears, it gradually becomes thinner because of being used or rubbed: *His sleeves had worn through at the elbows.*

Uu

Vv

5 if something wears a material or surface, it gradually makes it thinner: *The pressure of the waves slowly wears away the rocks.*

Ww

Xx

6 if an effect **wears off**, it gradually becomes less: *The anaesthetic should soon wear off.*

Yy

7 if time **wears on**, it passes slowly: *As the day wore on, we got bored.*

Zz

8 if you **wear something out**, it becomes too old or worn for you to use: *Ben seems to*

wear out a pair of shoes every three months.

9 to **wear someone out** is to make them very tired: *Walking so far completely wore me out.*

•NOUN• **1** clothes: *evening wear* **2** damage caused by being used or rubbed: *The carpet was showing signs of wear.*

♦ **wearer** •NOUN• **wearers** someone who is wearing something

weary •ADJECTIVE• **wearier, weariest** tired: *He finally got home, weary after a long day.*

♦ **wearily** •ADVERB• in a weary way: *The old man sighed wearily.*

weasel •NOUN• **weasels** a small wild animal with a long thin body

weather •NOUN• how hot, cold, wet or dry it is outside: *The weather's very warm for October.*

•VERB• **weathers, weathering, weathered 1** to change gradually because of being exposed to the weather: *buildings weathered by the wind and rain* **2** to survive a bad situation safely: *She felt that she had weathered the storm.*
⇒ **weathering**

weatherbeaten •ADJECTIVE• rougher and darker because of being outside in all types of weather: *a weatherbeaten face*

weathering •NOUN• a gradual changing of colour and shape caused by being exposed to all types of weather: *the weathering of the rocks*

weathervane •NOUN• **weathervanes** a piece of metal that swings in the wind to show which direction the wind is coming from

weave •VERB• **weaves, weaving, wove, woven 1** to pass threads under and over each other on a frame called a loom to make cloth **2** to move in and out between objects: *a car weaving through the traffic*

♦ **weaver** •NOUN• **weavers** someone who weaves

ⓘ The past tense of **weave** when it means 'to make cloth' is **wove**: *She wove fine materials.*
The past tense of **weave** when it means 'to move in and out' is **weaved**: *She weaved through the crowd.*

web •NOUN• **webs 1** a spider's web is a type of net it makes to catch insects **2** the Web is the **World Wide Web**
♦ **webbed** •ADJECTIVE• webbed feet have skin joining the toes together

web page •NOUN• **web pages** a page on a website

website •NOUN• **websites** a collection of linked pages on the Web about a subject or an organization

wed •VERB• **weds, wedding, wedded** to wed someone is to marry them
⇒ **wedding**

we'd •SHORT FORM• a short way to say and write **we had** or **we would**: *We'd better hurry up or we'll be late.* • *We'd buy a new car if we had the money.*

wedding •NOUN• **weddings** a marriage ceremony: *I met her at Lucy and John's wedding.*

wedge •NOUN• **wedges 1** a piece of hard material that is thick at one end and thin at the other and is used to hold something in place **2** something shaped like a wedge: *He cut himself a thick wedge of chocolate cake.*
•VERB• **wedges, wedging, wedged** to hold something in place or in a space: *She wedged the door open with a piece of cardboard.*
• *Sally found herself wedged in a corner.*

wedlock •NOUN• the state of being married

Wednesday •NOUN• **Wednesdays** the day of the week after Tuesday and before Thursday

ⓘ **Wednesday** comes from the Old English word **Wodnesdæg**, which means *Woden's day*. Woden is the old German god of war and of wisdom.

wee •ADJECTIVE• an informal word which some people use to mean very small: *a wee boy*

weed •NOUN• **weeds** a wild plant that is growing where you do not want it to: *The garden was overgrown with weeds.*
•VERB• **weeds, weeding, weeded** to remove the weeds from a place: *I offered to weed the garden for my dad.*
♦ **weedy** •ADJECTIVE• **weedier, weediest**

1 full of weeds **2** someone who is weedy is thin and weak

week •NOUN• **weeks 1** a period of seven days, often from Sunday to Saturday: *Debbie teaches aerobics twice a week.* **2** the five days from Monday to Friday when many people go to work: *I don't go out much during the week.*

weekday •NOUN• **weekdays** any of the days from Monday to Friday: *The office is only open on weekdays.*

weekend •NOUN• **weekends** Saturday and Sunday: *We're going to Oxford for the weekend.*

weekly •ADJECTIVE• happening or produced once a week: *a weekly magazine* •ADVERB• once a week: *In those days I used to get paid weekly.*

weep •VERB• **weeps, weeping, wept** to cry tears: *Mother wept when she heard the terrible news.*

weevil •NOUN• **weevils** a small insect that eats grain or flour

weft •NOUN• the threads that run from side to side on the frame called a loom that cloth is woven on. Look up and compare **warp**

weigh •VERB• **weighs, weighing, weighed**
1 to measure how heavy something is by putting it on a scale: *Brenda weighs herself every day.*
2 to have a particular heaviness: *My suitcase weighed 15 kilograms.*
3 if something **weighs you down**, it is heavy or difficult for you to deal with: *I am weighed down with problems.*
♦ **weight** •NOUN• **weights 1** the amount that something or someone weighs: *What weight are you?*
2 a piece of solid material that is used to hold things down or weigh things on scales
3 a load or burden: *Getting a job took a weight off his mind.*
♦ **weightless** •ADJECTIVE• floating in the air because there is no gravity
♦ **weightlessness** •NOUN• being weightless
♦ **weighty** •ADJECTIVE• **weightier, weightiest 1** heavy: *a weighty volume of magic spells* **2** important: *The teachers were discussing weighty problems.*

weir • NOUN • **weirs** a low dam across a river

weird • ADJECTIVE • **weirder, weirdest** strange or mysterious: *a weird light in the sky*

◆ **weirdly** • ADVERB • in a weird way: *weirdly dressed*

◆ **weirdness** • NOUN • being weird

welcome • ADJECTIVE • **1** if someone or something is welcome, you are happy to accept or receive them: *Joe's parents always make us very welcome.* • *a welcome gift* **2** if someone is welcome to do something, you are happy to let them do it: *You're welcome to borrow the car if I'm not using it.* • **you're welcome** something you say after someone has thanked you: *'Thank you for all your help.' 'You're welcome.'*

• NOUN • **welcomes** the way you receive a visitor: *Her fans gave her a warm welcome.*

• VERB • **welcomes, welcoming, welcomed 1** to make someone feel that you are happy to see them: *The whole family turned out to welcome us at the airport.* **2** to accept something gladly: *I would welcome the chance of a different job.*

weld • VERB • **welds, welding, welded** to join together pieces of metal by heating them

◆ **welder** • NOUN • **welders** someone whose job is to weld metals

◆ **welding** • NOUN • the activity of joinnig metal by heat

welfare • NOUN • health, comfort and happiness: *parents concerned for the welfare of their children*

welfare state • NOUN • a system in which a government provides services such as free health care and money for the unemployed

well¹ • ADVERB • **better, best 1** in a satisfactory, successful or correct way: *Janet speaks French very well.* **2** thoroughly: *Mix the butter and sugar well before adding the flour.* • **as well** too: *I'd like an ice cream as well.* • ADJECTIVE • **better, best 1** healthy: *I don't feel well today.* **2** good or pleasing: *All is not well at home.*

well² • NOUN • **wells** a deep hole in the ground where you can get water, oil or gas: *an oil well*

• VERB • **wells, welling, welled** if tears **well up** in your eyes, they begin to flow

we'll • SHORT FORM • a short way to say and write **we will**: *I'm sure we'll meet again.*

well-being • NOUN • health and happiness

wellingtons or **wellington boots** • PLURAL NOUN • high rubber boots that cover your lower leg

ⓘ These boots were named after the Duke of **Wellington**, a British army general who wore boots like them.

well-off • ADJECTIVE • **better-off, best-off 1** rich: *Only the better-off kids had bicycles.* **2** fortunate: *The trouble is, you just don't realize when you're well-off.*

well-to-do • ADJECTIVE • rich: *Our customers are mostly quite well-to-do.*

went • VERB • a way of changing the verb **go** to make a past tense: *Bill went out at about 6 o'clock.*

wept • VERB • a way of changing the verb **weep** to make a past tense. It can be used with or without a helping verb: *I could have wept when I saw the state of the house.* • *A woman wept openly in the corner.*

were • VERB • the past tense of the verb **be** that you use with **you**, **we** or **they**: *We were so relieved to see him.* • *The children were playing in the garden when we arrived.*

we're • SHORT FORM • a short way to say and write **we are**: *We're so pleased you could come.*

weren't • SHORT FORM • a short way to say and write **were not**: *Weren't the acrobats amazing?*

werewolf • NOUN • **werewolves** an imaginary person that changes into a wolf when there is a full moon

west • NOUN • **1** the direction in which the sun sets, opposite to east: *the west of England* **2** the West is a name for the countries in Europe and North America • ADJECTIVE • in, from, or towards the west: *the west coast of America* • ADVERB • to the west: *We travelled west as far as the motorway.*

◆ **westerly** • ADJECTIVE • coming from, or going towards the west

Aa Bb Cc Dd Ee Ff Gg Hh Ii Jj Kk Ll Mm Nn Oo Pp Qq Rr Ss Tt Uu Vv **Ww** Xx Yy Zz

•NOUN • **westerlies** a wind that comes from the west

✦ **western** •ADJECTIVE • belonging to, or coming from the west: *Western Europe*

•NOUN • **westerns** a book or film about cowboys in North America in the past

✦ **westward** *or* **westwards** •ADVERB • to or towards the west: *We travelled westwards.*

wet •ADJECTIVE • **wetter, wettest 1** full of water or covered with water: *wet clothes* • *It's easy to skid on wet roads.*
2 not dried: *wet paint*
3 rainy: *a wet afternoon*
•VERB • **wets, wetting, wet** to wet something is to make it wet: *He wet his hair to flatten it down.*

wet suit •NOUN • **wet suits** a rubber suit that you wear to keep you warm when you swim underwater

we've •SHORT FORM • a short way to say and write **we have**: *We've got something to tell you.*

whack •VERB • **whacks, whacking, whacked** to hit someone or something hard with a loud noise: *He whacked his brother on the head with a book.*
•NOUN • **whack** a hard loud hit: *Jim gave him a whack across the shoulders.*

whale •NOUN • **whales** a very large mammal that lives in the sea

✦ **whaler** •NOUN • **whalers** a ship or person that goes out hunting whales

✦ **whaling** •NOUN • hunting and killing whales

wharf •NOUN • **wharfs** *or* **wharves** a platform where ships stop to be loaded and unloaded

what •ADJECTIVE AND PRONOUN • **1 what** is used to ask questions about things: *What day is it today?* • *What's your brother's name?*
2 you can say **what** in exclamations to emphasize something: *What a beautiful view!*
3 the thing or things: *I hope you find what you're looking for.* • *This bag is just what I wanted.*
• **what if** what will or would happen if: *What if Dad comes back and finds us here?*

whatever •ADJECTIVE AND PRONOUN • **1** any, anything or any amount: *I can give you whatever money you need.* • *Choose whatever you like from the menu.* **2** no matter what: *You know we'll always love you whatever happens.*

whatsoever •ADJECTIVE • at all: *Your problems are nothing whatsoever to do with me.*

wheat •NOUN • a type of grain that is used to make flour

wheatgerm •NOUN • the centre of a grain of wheat

wheedle •VERB • **wheedles, wheedling, wheedled** to beg or persuade someone to do something, often by flattering them: *I managed to wheedle some money out of my dad.*

wheel •NOUN • **wheels 1** one of the round things under a vehicle that turns around as it moves: *The spare wheel is in the boot.*
2 anything that goes around like a wheel: *a potter's wheel*
•VERB • **wheels, wheeling, wheeled 1** to wheel something is to push it along on wheels: *He got a puncture and had to wheel his bike home.*
2 to move in a wide curve: *Vultures were wheeling overhead.*
3 to turn round quickly: *Kay wheeled around when she heard his voice.*

wheelbarrow •NOUN • **wheelbarrows** a small cart with only one wheel at the front and with handles that you use to push it

wheelchair •NOUN • **wheelchairs** a seat with wheels used by people who are ill or cannot walk

wheeze •VERB • **wheezes, wheezing, wheezed** to breathe with a rough, gasping or whistling sound
•NOUN • **wheezes** a rough, gasping or whistling breath

whelk •NOUN • **whelks** a small snail-like sea creature that lives inside a hard shell

when •ADVERB • at what time: *When did you arrive home?*
•CONJUNCTION • **1** at the time at which, or during the time at which: *I was just going out*

Aa Bb Cc Dd Ee Ff Gg Hh Ii Jj Kk Ll Mm Nn Oo Pp Qq Rr Ss Tt Uu Vv **Ww** Xx Yy Zz when the phone rang. **2** in spite of the fact that: *How is it that you don't even have 10p when you've only just got your pocket money?*

whenever •CONJUNCTION• **1** at any time that: *You can borrow my book whenever you want to.* **2** at every time that: *They go swimming whenever they get the chance.*

where •ADVERB• to, from or in what place: *Where are we going?* • *Where did you get that hat?*
•CONJUNCTION• to, from or in what place: *I have no idea where we are.*

whereabouts •NOUN• the whereabouts of a person or thing is the place where they are or it is: *Do you know the whereabouts of your cousin?*
•ADVERB• near or in what place: *Whereabouts in Texas do you come from?*

whereas •CONJUNCTION• but: *They thought he was a bit strange, whereas he was simply quiet and shy.* • *He wanted to go to the cinema, whereas I wanted to go swimming.*

where's •SHORT FORM• a short way to say and write **where is** or **where has**: *Where's the cat?* • *Where's he gone?*

whereupon •CONJUNCTION• at or immediately after which: *His mother told him he couldn't go, whereupon he sat on the floor and started crying.*

wherever •ADVERB AND CONJUNCTION• to, or in, any place or every place: *He follows me wherever I go.* • *Wherever he is, I am sure he will come back soon.*
•ADVERB• a more emphatic way of saying 'where': *The cat's disappeared. Wherever can he be?*

whet •VERB• **whets, whetting, whetted** to whet the blade of a knife is to sharpen it
• **whet your appetite** if something whets your appetite, it makes you want to eat, or it makes you want to do something: *He'd seen a clip of the film, which had whetted his appetite to see more.*

whether •CONJUNCTION• **whether** is used to show that there is a choice between two possibilities: *Whether we like it or not, we have to get up early.*

whey •NOUN• whey is the watery part of

milk that is left after separating out the solid curds which make cheese

which •ADJECTIVE• what one or ones: *Which hand do you think the coin is in?*
•PRONOUN• **1** what one or ones: *Which of these books is yours and which is mine?* **2** you use **which** to talk about the person or thing that has been mentioned in the earlier part of a sentence: *I had eaten four chocolate bars, which made me feel sick.*

whichever •ADJECTIVE AND PRONOUN• that or any one: *Come on whichever day suits you.* • *You can come round on Monday or Tuesday, whichever suits you.*

whiff •NOUN• **whiffs** a smell or scent which you notice as it is carried in the air to your nose: *a whiff of garlic*

while •CONJUNCTION• **1** during the time that: *Will you be going to Disneyland while you are in Florida?* **2** although: *While I understand why you got angry, I think you should try to control your temper.*
•NOUN• a period of time: *We waited inside for a while, but the rain didn't stop.*
•VERB• **whiles, whiling, whiled** to **while away** time is to pass the time doing something: *We whiled away the journey playing 'I spy'.*

whilst •CONJUNCTION• while: *You could look at these magazines whilst you're waiting.*

whim •NOUN• **whims** a sudden idea or a sudden desire to do something

whimper •VERB• **whimpers, whimpering, whimpered** to make a series of low weak crying sounds, showing pain or fear
•NOUN• **whimpers** a low weak crying or whining sound

whine •VERB• **whines, whining, whined 1** a dog or other animal whines when it makes a long high sound **2** a person whines when they talk in a complaining voice
•NOUN• **whines 1** the sound a dog or animal makes when it whines **2** a complaining voice

whinge •VERB• **whinges, whingeing, whinged** to complain in a way that other people find annoying
•NOUN• **whinges** a complaint, especially one made in an irritating way about something unimportant

whinny •NOUN• **whinnies** a gentle series of sounds a horse or pony makes
•VERB• **whinnies, whinnying, whinnied** a horse or pony whinnies when it makes this noise

whip •NOUN• **whips** a piece of leather or cord fastened to a handle and used to hit animals or people
•VERB• **whips, whipping, whipped** 1 to whip an animal or person is to hit them with a whip 2 to whip liquids like cream or eggs is to beat them so that they form a froth or become thick and stiff 3 to **whip something out**, or **whip it away**, is to take it out or take it away very quickly, or in one quick movement 4 to **whip up** something to eat is to prepare it quickly 5 to **whip up** a particular feeling or reaction is to encourage that feeling or reaction in other people

whippet •NOUN• **whippets** a breed of dog with a slim head and body, like a small greyhound

whirl •VERB• **whirls, whirling, whirled** to turn or spin very quickly
•NOUN• **whirls** a very fast turning or spinning movement

whirlpool •NOUN• **whirlpools** a place in a river or in the sea where a current of water swirls round and round and is sometimes strong enough to drag things down

whirlwind •NOUN• **whirlwinds** a column of wind that swirls round and round in a spiral as it moves across the land

whirr •VERB• **whirrs, whirring, whirred** something whirrs when it turns or moves quickly making a buzzing sound
•NOUN• **whirrs** the buzzing sound made by something turning quickly through the air

whisk •NOUN• **whisks** 1 a piece of kitchen equipment made up of loops of wire and used for mixing things like cream or eggs 2 a fast sweeping movement: *With a whisk of his bushy tail, the squirrel was gone.*
•VERB• **whisks, whisking, whisked** 1 to whisk foods like cream or eggs is to beat them with a whisk so that they are well mixed or become thick 2 to **whisk someone**

or **something away** is to take them quickly, or with a quick movement

whisker •NOUN• **whiskers** 1 one of the long stiff hairs that grow on the faces of animals like mice, cats and dogs, and which are sensitive to touch 2 the hair that grows on a man's face is sometimes called his whiskers

whisky •NOUN• **whiskies** a strong alcoholic drink made from grain or barley, especially in Scotland

whisper •VERB• **whispers, whispering, whispered** to talk very quietly under your breath so that only people near you can hear what you are saying
•NOUN• **whispers** a very quiet voice: *She hung her head and answered in a whisper.*

whistle •VERB• **whistles, whistling, whistled** 1 to make a high-pitched sound or a musical note by blowing air through your teeth and lips 2 if something whistles, it makes a high-pitched sound
•NOUN• **whistles** 1 a whistling sound 2 a small device that you blow into to make a high-pitched sound: *The referee blew his whistle.* 3 a simple musical instrument that you blow into and which makes high-pitched sounds

white •NOUN• 1 the very pale colour of milk or snow 2 the white of an egg is the clear substance around the yolk which turns white if it is cooked ⇒ **whiten**

white elephant •NOUN• **white elephants** something that has cost a lot of money but has no useful purpose

white-hot •ADJECTIVE• something that is white-hot is so hot it is glowing with white light

whiten •VERB• **whitens, whitening, whitened** to make something white or whiter

whitewash •NOUN• a thin white liquid, containing lime, used to paint on walls and ceilings to make them white
•VERB• **whitewashes, whitewashing, whitewashed** to paint whitewash on walls or ceilings

Aa Bb Cc Dd Ee Ff Gg Hh Ii Jj Kk Ll Mm Nn Oo Pp Qq Rr Ss Tt Uu Vv Ww Xx Yy Zz

Aa

Whitsun •NOUN• the seventh Sunday after Easter

Bb

whizz •VERB• whizzes, whizzing, whizzed to move very fast
•NOUN• **whizzes** someone who is a whizz at something is an expert at it

Cc

Dd

who •PRONOUN• **1** which person or people: *Who is your favourite pop star?* **2** you use **who** when you want to say something else about a person or people you have just mentioned, or to explain which person you mean: *Emily, who lives next door, is 12 years old.* • *It was Malcolm who told me the news.*

Ee

Ff

Gg

Hh

who'd •SHORT FORM• a short way to say and write **who had** or **who would**: *It was Dad who'd said I could go to the party.* • *Who'd like another biscuit?*

Ii

Jj

whoever •PRONOUN• **1** the person that has done something: *Would whoever it was that left the gate open, please go and close it.* **2** any person: *Bring whoever you like to the party.*

Kk

Ll

whole •ADJECTIVE• all of something: *I couldn't eat a whole bar of chocolate.* •NOUN• a whole is a complete thing, especially one that is made up of different parts: *Two halves make a whole.*
⇒ **wholly**

Mm

Nn

Oo

wholehearted •ADJECTIVE• whole-hearted support or agreement is complete and sincere

Pp

Qq

wholemeal •ADJECTIVE• wholemeal bread or biscuits are made from flour that uses whole grains of wheat

Rr

Ss

whole number •NOUN• **whole numbers** a number like 4, 27 or 375, which is not a fraction and which has no fractions or decimal places after it

Tt

Uu

wholesale •ADJECTIVE• **1** wholesale goods are bought in large amounts by a business which then sells them in smaller amounts to shops or smaller businesses **2** total or complete: *the wholesale destruction of the rain forests.*

Vv

Ww

Xx

wholesome •ADJECTIVE• healthy and good for you

Yy

Zz

who'll •SHORT FORM• a short way to say and write **who will** or **who shall**: *Who'll help me to carry this box?*

wholly •ADVERB• completely: *They were wholly committed to the team.*

whom •PRONOUN• **whom** is used as the object of a verb or preposition, and means the same as **who**: *He phoned his friend Andrew, whom he hadn't seen for years.* • *To whom should I address the letter?*

ⓘ Nowadays, people often use **who** instead of **whom** as the object of a verb, as in: *He phoned his friend Andrew, who he hadn't seen for years.*
However, you should always use **whom** after a preposition:
✗ *To who should I address the letter?*
✓ *To whom should I address the letter?*

whoop •VERB• whoops, whooping, whooped to give a loud shout of joy or excitement

whooping cough •NOUN• a disease which makes it difficult to breathe and causes a painful cough

who's •SHORT FORM• a short way to say and write **who is** or **who has**: *Who's coming for a walk?* • *Who's got the TV guide?*

whose •ADJECTIVE• **1** you use **whose** before a noun when you are asking which person or people something belongs to: *Whose bike is this?* **2** you use **whose** before a noun to mean 'of which' or 'of whom': *the boy whose family owns the castle on the hill*
•PRONOUN• you use **whose** when you are asking or talking about which person or people something belongs to: *Whose is this?* • *It must be someone's dog, but I don't know whose.*

ⓘ Try not to confuse the spellings of **whose** and **who's**.
Whose is the possessive form of **who**, and tells you something belongs to someone: *Whose shoes are these?*
Who's is a short form of two words put together: *Who's in the bathroom?*

why •ADVERB• for what reason: *Why did it have to rain today?*

wick •NOUN• **wicks** the string in a candle or lamp which you light

wicked •ADJECTIVE• **1** very bad or evil: *a*

wicked old witch
2 mischievous: *Don't tip your cup upside-down, you wicked little monkey!*
3 a very informal word for **excellent**: *That's a wicked new haircut you've got there!*

wicker *or* **wickerwork** •NOUN• reeds or strips of cane that have been woven together to make things like baskets

wicket •NOUN• **wickets** in cricket, a set of three upright wooden rods with two horizontal rods across the top in front of which the batsman stands

wide •ADJECTIVE• **wider, widest** 1 measuring a great distance from side to side: *across the wide Missouri river*
2 having a certain width: *The river is nearly a mile wide at some points.*
3 covering a great range or amount: *a wide knowledge of history*
•ADVERB• **wider, widest** 1 with a great distance from top to bottom or side to side: *The tiger opened his mouth wide, showing his enormous fangs.*
2 if you are wide awake, you are completely awake and alert
3 something that is wide of its target is a long distance away from the target
• **far and wide** over a large area: *They travelled far and wide seeking treasure.*
◆ **widely** •ADVERB• something that is widely known or widely admired is known or admired by a lot of people
◆ **widen** •VERB• **widens, widening, widened** to make or cause to be wide or wider
⇒ **width**

widespread •ADJECTIVE• found in a lot of places or among a lot of people: *widespread rumours*

widow •NOUN• **widows** a woman whose husband has died

widower •NOUN• **widowers** a man whose wife has died

width •NOUN• **widths** the width of something is how much it measures from side to side: *This curtain material comes in several different widths.*

wield •VERB• **wields, wielding, wielded** 1 to wield a tool or a weapon is to hold it and use

it: *pictures of Vikings wielding axes and swords* **2** to wield something such as power is to use it

wife •NOUN• **wives** a man's wife is the woman he has married

wig •NOUN• **wigs** a covering of false hair that is worn on the head

wiggle •VERB• **wiggles, wiggling, wiggled** to move from side to side, or backwards and forwards: *Look! I can wiggle my front tooth.*
•NOUN• **wiggles** 1 a movement from side to side or backwards and forwards **2** a line that has lots of bends and curves
◆ **wiggly** •ADJECTIVE• **wigglier, wiggliest** 1 a wiggly line has lots of bends and curves **2** something wiggly moves, or can be moved, by wiggling: *a wiggly tooth*

wigwam •NOUN• **wigwams** a cone-shaped tent that Native American people used as shelter in the past

wild •ADJECTIVE• **wilder, wildest** 1 wild animals or plants live in their natural surroundings and are not kept by human beings: *a wild goat • wild rice*
2 a wild area of land is in a natural state and has not been farmed or built on by human beings
3 wild behaviour is not controlled, and sometimes violent: *The fans went wild with excitement.*
4 wild weather is windy and stormy
5 a wild idea is a bit crazy and isn't very likely to work
6 if you make a wild guess, you guess completely at random
7 if you are **wild about** something or someone, you are very keen on them
•NOUN• **wilds** animals that live in the wild live in their natural environment and are not kept as pets or in zoos

wilderness •NOUN• **wildernesses** a desert or wild area of a country with very few people living in it

wild-goose chase •NOUN• **wild-goose chases** you are on a wild-goose chase if you are searching for something but have no hope of finding it

wildlife •NOUN• wild animals, birds and insects

Aa Bb Cc Dd Ee Ff Gg Hh Ii Jj Kk Ll Mm Nn Oo Pp Qq Rr Ss Tt Uu Vv Ww Xx Yy Zz

wile •NOUN• **wiles** a crafty trick used to deceive people
⇒ **wily**

wilful •ADJECTIVE• 1 a wilful person is determined to do exactly what they want, not what other people think they should do 2 deliberate: *wilful damage*
♦ **wilfully** •ADVERB• in a wilful way

will[1] •VERB• **would** 1 **will** is used to talk about the future: *It will be winter soon.* 2 you use **will** to ask someone to do something, or to tell them to do something, or to ask them what they would like: *Will you hold this for me?* • *Will you please stop making that racket!* • *Will you have tea or coffee?*

will[2] •NOUN• **wills** 1 your will is the control you have over your own actions and decisions 2 your will is what you want to do and your desire or determination to do it 3 a will is a legal document written by someone saying who they want their property and money to be given to after their death
•VERB• **wills, willing, willed** if you will something to happen, you try to make it happen by using the power of your thoughts

willing •ADJECTIVE• if you are willing, you are ready or happy to do what is asked or needed: *a willing helper* • *He's willing to work hard.*
♦ **willingly** •ADVERB• if you do something willingly, you do it happily and eagerly
♦ **willingness** •NOUN• being willing

willow •NOUN• **willows** a tree with long thin branches that often grows near water

willpower •NOUN• willpower is the determination and discipline you need to achieve something

wilt •VERB• **wilts, wilting, wilted** 1 if plants wilt, their stems get weak and hang down towards the ground 2 if a person wilts, they become weak or tired

wily •ADJECTIVE• **wilier, wiliest** crafty

wimp •NOUN• **wimps** someone who is not strong or brave

ⓘ It is not polite to call someone this.

win •VERB• **wins, winning, won** 1 to win is to beat all the others in a competition and get first place or first prize 2 to win something is to get it as a prize 3 to **win someone over** is to succeed in getting them to agree with you or be on your side
•NOUN• **wins** a victory
⇒ **winning, winnings**

wince •VERB• **winces, wincing, winced** to make a small, quick, jerking movement with your face or head in pain or embarrassment: *He winced when I reminded him of his mistake.*

winch •NOUN• **winches** a piece of equipment used for lifting or pulling something heavy by attaching it to a rope which is wound around a cylinder
•VERB• **winches, winching, winched** to winch something is to lift it or pull it using a winch

wind[1] •NOUN• **winds** 1 wind, or a wind, is a strong current of air 2 if someone has wind, they have gas trapped in their stomach, which makes them feel uncomfortable 3 your wind is your breath or your ability to breathe easily 4 the wind instruments in an orchestra
⇒ **windy**

ⓘ This word rhymes with **pinned**.

wind[2] •VERB• **winds, winding, wound** 1 to wind something is to twist it round and round in loops or coils: *A turban is a long piece of cloth that is wound round the head.* 2 to wind or **wind up** a watch or clock is to turn the screw or key that tightens the spring inside and makes it work 3 a road, path or river winds if it twists and turns 4 to **wind down** is to get slower and slower, or less and less active 5 to **wind up** somewhere is to end up in that place or situation, especially one that is unpleasant or uncomfortable 6 to **wind something up** is to finish it or end it 7 to **wind someone up** is to make them believe something is true when it isn't, as a joke or to annoy them

648

♦ **winder** •NOUN• **winders** a key, screw or handle used to wind up a watch, clock or clockwork mechanism

ⓘ This word rhymes with **find**.

windfall • NOUN• **windfalls** something, especially money, that you get without expecting it

wind instrument • NOUN• **wind instruments** an instrument in an orchestra that is played by blowing air into it

windmill • NOUN• **windmills** a building with large sails on the outside which are turned by the wind and provide power for grinding corn

window • NOUN• **windows** 1 an opening in the wall of a building or in a vehicle, with glass fitted in it so that you can see through it, and which can usually be opened to let in air 2 an area on a computer screen where you can view or work with information or a computer file

windpipe • NOUN• **windpipes** the tube that goes from your mouth down your throat and into your lungs

wind power • NOUN• power that is generated by the wind and which can be turned into electricity or used to make machines work

windscreen • NOUN• **windscreens** the clear screen at the front of a car or other vehicle

windshield • NOUN• **windshields** another word for a windscreen, used especially in the United States and Canada

windsurfing • NOUN• the sport of moving across the surface of water standing on a narrow board with a sail attached to it

windswept • ADJECTIVE• 1 a windswept place is exposed to strong winds 2 people look windswept when their hair is untidy from being blown about by the wind

wind tunnel • NOUN• **wind tunnels** a long building or room in which strong currents of air are used to test new designs of things like aeroplanes

windward • ADJECTIVE AND ADVERB• facing into the wind

windy • ADJECTIVE• **windier, windiest** if the weather is windy, there is a wind blowing: *a windy day with the white clouds flying*

wine • NOUN• **wines** an alcoholic drink usually made from grapes, but which can also be made from the juice of other types of fruit

wing • NOUN• **wings** 1 a bird's or insect's wings are the parts of its body that it uses to fly with

2 an aeroplane's wings are the two long flat parts that stick out at either side of its body 3 a wing of a building is a part that sticks out from the main building 4 in games like football and hockey, the wings are the two long sides of the pitch, or the players whose position is at either side of the field: *He's dribbling the ball down the wing.* • *She's the best right wing we've ever had in our team.*

5 a wing of a political party or other organization is a group within it that has its own particular role or its own set of ideas and policies: *the right wing of the Labour Party.*

6 in a theatre, the wings are the areas on either side of the stage that are hidden from the audience

♦ **winged** • ADJECTIVE• having wings: *a winged serpent*

♦ **winger** • NOUN• **wingers** a player in a sports team whose place is on one of the wings

wink • VERB• **winks, winking, winked** 1 to shut one of your eyes and open it again quickly, as a friendly or secret sign to someone 2 lights wink when they twinkle or go off and on again quickly
• NOUN• **winks** a sign you make by closing and opening one of your eyes quickly

winkle • NOUN• **winkles** a small edible sea snail that lives inside a spiral shell
• VERB• **winkles, winkling, winkled** to winkle something out is to get it out with a lot of difficulty and effort

winning • ADJECTIVE• 1 the winning team, entry, shot or goal is the one that wins a competition or match 2 someone who has a winning smile, or winning ways, makes people like them or cooperate with them

Aa
Bb
Cc
Dd
Ee
Ff
Gg
Hh
Ii
Jj
Kk
Ll
Mm
Nn
Oo
Pp
Qq
Rr
Ss
Tt
Uu
Vv
Ww
Xx
Yy
Zz

winnings •PLURAL NOUN• all the money that someone wins from bets or gambling

winter •NOUN• **winters** the coldest season of the year, between autumn and spring
•ADJECTIVE• happening or used during winter: *a warm winter coat* • *the winter months*
♦ **wintry** •ADJECTIVE• cold, like winter

wipe •VERB• **wipes, wiping, wiped 1** to wipe something is to rub its surface to clean it or dry it
2 to wipe a computer disk, or a sound or video tape, is to remove or erase all the information, sound or images on it
3 to **wipe something or someone out** is to destroy them and get rid of them completely
•NOUN• **wipes 1** an act of wiping: *I need to give my glasses a wipe.* **2** a piece of cloth or tissue used to wipe things with
♦ **wiper** •NOUN• **wipers** a piece of rubber on a metal support that moves to and fro and clears water from a vehicle's windscreen

wire •NOUN• **wires 1** metal that has been pulled into a long narrow strand that bends easily **2** a length of wire, or several pieces of it twisted into a cable for carrying electricity or telephone signals
•VERB• **wires, wiring, wired 1** to wire a house is to fit the cables that are needed take electricity to lights and plugs **2** to wire or **wire up** a piece of equipment is to fit it with electrical cables or a plug so that it can be connected to the power supply
⇒ **wiry**

wireless •NOUN• **wirelesses** an old-fashioned word for a radio

wiry •ADJECTIVE• **wirier, wiriest 1** someone who is wiry has a slim but strong body **2** wiry hair is strong and curly

wisdom •NOUN• being able to make sensible decisions about things, based on your knowledge and experience

wisdom tooth •NOUN• **wisdom teeth** your wisdom teeth are the big teeth at the back of your mouth that grow when you are an adult

ⓘ Wisdom teeth are so called because they grow when you are an adult, and so have become wiser.

wise •ADJECTIVE• **wiser, wisest 1** able to make sensible decisions and judgements **2** if you are **wise to** something, you know about it

wish •VERB• **wishes, wishing, wished 1** to want something and hope that it will happen: *I wish it would stop raining.* • *What did you wish for when you blew out the candles on your cake?*
2 to want to do something or want it to be done: *Do you wish to pay now or later?*
3 you wish someone something when you say that you hope they will have it: *We all wish you luck.*
•NOUN• **wishes** something you wish for or want: *Make a wish.*

wishbone •NOUN• **wishbones** the thin V-shaped bone at the top of a chicken's or other bird's breast. The wishbone is often pulled apart by two people, and the person who gets the bigger piece makes a wish

wishywashy •ADJECTIVE• wishywashy colours are pale and uninteresting

wisp •NOUN• **wisps** a wisp of smoke or hair is a long, thin, delicate piece or line of it
♦ **wispy** •ADJECTIVE• **wispier, wispiest** wispy hair or smoke forms wisps

wistful •ADJECTIVE• if you are wistful you long sadly for something that you know you cannot have
♦ **wistfully** •ADVERB• in a wistful way: *He gazed wistfully at the beautiful toy train in the shop window.*

wit •NOUN• **wits 1** intelligence and common sense **2** a clever humour
• **have your wits about you** if you have your wits about you, you are alert and ready to deal with anything that happens
⇒ **witty**

witch •NOUN• **witches** a woman or girl who is supposed to have special magic powers
♦ **witchcraft** •NOUN• the magic and spells that witches do, especially to make something bad happen

witch doctor •NOUN• **witch doctors** a man who uses magic to heal people in his tribe

with •PREPOSITION• **1** in the company of or in the same place as: *Come with me.* • *She keeps her diary on the shelf with her school books.*

Aa Bb Cc Dd Ee Ff Gg Hh Ii Jj Kk Ll Mm Nn Oo Pp Qq Rr Ss Tt Uu Vv Ww Xx Yy Zz

2 using: *We stuck it down with glue.*
3 having: *a house with a green door*
4 going in the same direction: *drifting with the tide*
5 as the result of: *He was doubled up with pain.*
6 against: *They've argued with each other since they were small children.*
7 with is used after verbs about covering, filling or mixing: *He covered the table with a sheet.* • *Mix the dry ingredients with the milk in a large bowl.*
8 with is used after verbs about separating or finishing: *I parted with them at the station.* • *Have you finished with this magazine?*

withdraw •VERB• **withdraws, withdrawing, withdrawn 1** to withdraw is to retreat or move back or away **2** to withdraw something is to remove it or take it back: *I would like to withdraw what I said earlier.* • *He withdrew all his money from his bank account.*
✦ **withdrawal** •NOUN• **withdrawals 1** withdrawing from something or somewhere **2** a sum of money that you take out of your bank account

wither •VERB• **withers, withering, withered** a plant withers when it shrinks and dries up

withhold •VERB• **withholds, withholding, withheld** to withhold something is refuse to give it to someone

within •PREPOSITION• **1** inside: *They felt safe within the castle walls.*
2 in no more than, or less than: *We'll be home within the hour.*
3 not beyond: *A place in the final is within your reach.*
•ADVERB• inside: *The notice on the restaurant window said: 'Waiters wanted. Apply within.'*

without •PREPOSITION• not with or not having: *They left without me.* • *Do you take coffee with or without milk?*

withstand •VERB• **withstands, withstanding, withstood** to withstand something is to bear it successfully: *The buildings are specially designed to withstand earthquakes.*

witness •NOUN• **witnesses 1** someone who sees an event happening and can tell other people about it: *Were there any witnesses to the accident?* **2** someone who is a witness in a court case gives evidence about the facts of the case
•VERB• **witnesses, witnessing, witnessed** to witness something is to see it happening

witty •ADJECTIVE• **wittier, wittiest** a witty person, or a witty comment, is clever and funny
✦ **wittily** •ADVERB• in a clever and amusing way

wives •PLURAL NOUN• the plural of **wife**: *Henry the Eighth had six wives.*

wizard •NOUN• **wizards** a man or boy who is supposed to have special magic powers
✦ **wizardry** •NOUN• **1** magic performed by a wizard **2** clever or surprising things, especially done using machines: *technical wizardry*

wobble •VERB• **wobbles, wobbling, wobbled** to rock or move from side to side unsteadily
✦ **wobbly** •ADJECTIVE• **wobblier, wobbliest** something that is wobbly shakes or moves about unsteadily

woe •NOUN• **woes 1** woe is sorrow, grief or misery **2** a woe is something that causes grief or misery: *He told me all his woes.*
✦ **woeful** •ADJECTIVE• **1** miserable or unhappy **2** feeble or useless: *a woeful attempt to be funny*
✦ **woefully** •ADVERB• miserably or unhappily

wok •NOUN• **woks** a type of pan shaped like a large bowl, used to cook Chinese-style food

woke •VERB• a way of changing the verb **wake** to make a past tense: *He woke with a start.*

woken •VERB• the form of the verb **wake** that is used with a helping verb to show that something happened in the past: *He had woken with a start.*

wolf •NOUN• **wolves** a wild animal like a dog, which lives in family groups called packs
• **cry wolf** to cry wolf is to give a warning of danger when there is no danger
•VERB• **wolfs, wolfing, wolfed** to wolf down food is to eat it very quickly and greedily

woman •NOUN• **women** an adult female human being

♦ **womanhood** •NOUN• being a woman

♦ **womanly** •ADJECTIVE• like a woman or having the qualities people expect a woman to have

womb •NOUN• **wombs** the organ inside a female animal's body where her babies grow until they are ready to be born

wombat •NOUN• **wombats** an Australian animal like a small bear that has dark brown fur and short strong legs

won •VERB• a way of changing the verb **win** to make a past tense. It can be used with or without a helping verb: *We won the cup.*
• *We'd won it for four years running.*

wonder •VERB• **wonders, wondering, wondered** 1 you wonder about things when you are curious about them or cannot decide about them: *I wonder what Jack has bought me for Christmas.*
2 you **wonder at** something when you are surprised by it
3 you use 'I wonder if' when you are asking someone politely about or for something: *I wonder if you could tell me where the post office is?*
•NOUN• **wonders** 1 wonder is the feeling you get when you see something extraordinary or surprising: *The comet filled people who saw it with wonder.* 2 a wonder is something unexpected or extraordinary: *It's a wonder you didn't freeze to death out in that blizzard.*

♦ **wonderful** •ADJECTIVE• extraordinary or marvellous: *a wonderful view of the mountains*

♦ **wonderfully** •ADVERB• in a marvellous way: *The concert went wonderfully.*

♦ **wondrous** •ADJECTIVE• astonishing or impressive: *a wondrous sight*

won't •SHORT FORM• a short way to say and write **will not**: *He won't tell me what he saw.*

wood •NOUN• **woods** 1 wood is the hard material that forms the trunks and branches of trees, and is cut up to make furniture, buildings and paper 2 a wood or the woods is an area of forest or woodland

♦ **wooded** •ADJECTIVE• a wooded area has trees growing on it

♦ **wooden** •ADJECTIVE• 1 made of wood: *wooden toys* 2 a wooden action, expression or behaviour is stiff and unnatural

woodland •NOUN• **woodlands** land covered with trees

woodlouse •NOUN• **woodlice** a small creature similar to a beetle that lives in rotten wood or damp areas

woodpecker •NOUN• **woodpeckers** a wild bird that uses its strong beak to peck holes in trees to find the insects it eats

woodwind •NOUN• the instruments in an orchestra that are made from wood, such as the oboe, clarinet and bassoon

woodwork •NOUN• making objects out of wood, using tools like saws, planes and chisels

woodworm •NOUN• **woodworm** a young form of a type of beetle which eats wood

wool •NOUN• 1 the soft fibre that grows on the bodies of sheep 2 a thread made from this fibre, used for knitting and making cloth: *a ball of wool.*

♦ **woollen** •ADJECTIVE• made of wool: *a woollen blanket*

♦ **woollens** •PLURAL NOUN• jumpers and cardigans made of wool, especially knitted wool

♦ **woolly** •ADJECTIVE• **woollier, woolliest** covered with wool or with hair that is dense and curly like wool

word •NOUN• **words** 1 a unit of language that is written as a group of letters with spaces on either side
2 to get word about something is to get news about it
3 if you give your word, you give your solemn promise that you will do something
•VERB• **words, wording, worded** you word something in a certain way when you choose words to express it

♦ **wording** •NOUN• the wording of something is which words have been used to express it
⇒ **wordy**

word processing •NOUN• using a word processor or a computer to create documents

♦ **word processor** •NOUN• **word**

processors an electronic machine, with a keyboard and a screen, used to type letters and other documents

wordy •ADJECTIVE• **wordier, wordiest** using a lot of words, especially too many words: *a long wordy explanation of what happened*

wore •VERB• a way of changing the verb **wear** to make a past tense: *She wore an old pair of jeans.*

work •NOUN• **works 1** someone's work is their job or employment: *Dad leaves for work about 8 o'clock in the morning.*
2 work is something you do that needs effort: *It was hard work climbing to the top with heavy packs on our backs.*
3 your work is what you create by working
4 a work is something produced by an artist or composer
5 a works is a factory or workshop
6 the works of a machine or clock are the parts inside it that make it operate
7 someone who does good work does good deeds for other people
•VERB• **works, working, worked 1** you work when you do something that needs effort or energy
2 people who work have a job or are employed
3 a machine that works operates properly
4 a plan works when it is successful
5 to work something is to make it operate
6 if something works loose it slackens or becomes loose slowly
7 you **work out** something such as a problem when you think about it carefully until you find the answer
8 something **works out** a certain way when it turns out that way at the end
• **worker** •NOUN• **workers 1** someone who works for a living, especially in a particular industry: *steel workers* **2** a bee, ant, or termite that does the work in the colony, for example feeding the queen and looking after the eggs

working class •NOUN• **working classes** the working class is the people in society who do manual or factory work, or similar jobs

workman •NOUN• **workmen** a man who works with his hands, especially doing building work

• **workmanship** •NOUN• workmanship is the skill that a craftsman has in making things

worksheet •NOUN• **worksheets** a sheet listing work that has to be done or that has been done

workshop •NOUN• **workshops** a place or business where things are built, made or repaired

world •NOUN• **worlds 1** the Earth or all the people living on it: *The whole world is affected by global warming.*
2 a planet: *a creature from another world*
3 an area of life or activity: *the world of antiques*
• **worldly** •ADJECTIVE• **worldlier, worldliest 1** to do with the Earth and life on Earth
2 your worldly goods are all the things that belong to you
3 a worldly person is only interested in things like money and possessions, not in the spirit or the soul

worldwide •ADJECTIVE• everywhere in the world

World Wide Web •NOUN• the World Wide Web is a huge network of computers all round the world where you can find information about almost anything

worm •NOUN• **worms** a small creature with a soft body and no backbone or legs
•VERB• **worms, worming, wormed 1** to worm your way somewhere is to get there by wriggling through small spaces **2** to **worm something out of** someone is to get information from them gradually and with great difficulty

worn •VERB• the form of the verb **wear** that is used with a helping verb to show that something happened in the past: *She had worn the dress before.*
•ADJECTIVE• worn things are damaged by rubbing or wearing: *The carpet is worn and dirty.*
• **worn out** very tired

worried •ADJECTIVE• anxious

worrier •NOUN• **worriers** a person who worries, especially all the time

worry •VERB• **worries, worrying, worried** 1 to worry about a problem is to keep thinking about it in an anxious way because you are not sure how to deal with it or how it will turn out 2 to worry someone is to disturb them and make them anxious or upset •NOUN• **worries** 1 worry is being anxious 2 a worry is something that makes you anxious

worse •ADJECTIVE• **worse** is the comparative form of the adjective **bad**, which you use when you are comparing how bad things are: *My brother's room is a worse mess than mine.* •ADVERB• more badly, or more severely: *It was raining worse than ever.*

♦ **worsen** •VERB• **worsens, worsening, worsened** 1 something worsens when it becomes worse than it was before 2 to worsen something is to make it worse ⇒ **worst**

worship •VERB• **worships, worshipping, worshipped** 1 to honour a god or gods by praising them and praying to them 2 to love or admire someone or something, especially in a way that stops you seeing their faults •NOUN• religious services and other ways of worshipping: *a place of worship*

♦ **worshipper** •NOUN• **worshippers** someone who worships, especially in a church or temple

worst •ADJECTIVE• worst is the superlative form of the adjective **bad**, which you use when you are describing something as the most bad: *It was the worst storm we'd ever seen.* •ADVERB• badly to the greatest degree: *I did worst in the test.* •PRONOUN• the person or thing that is worse than all the others: *His asthma seems to be at its worst on cold mornings.*

ⓘ **Bad** and **good** are two of the adjectives in English that have what are called **irregular** comparative and superlative forms. So something is **bad**, or **worse**, or **worst** (not *bad, badder, baddest*), and something is **good**, or **better**, or **best** (not *good, gooder, goodest*). Remember also that you cannot describe something as *more bad* or *more good*, or *most bad* or *most good*.

worth •NOUN• 1 something's worth is its value or importance 2 someone's worth is their usefulness or value •ADJECTIVE• 1 what something is worth is how much money it is valued at: *The ring is worth £1000.* 2 if something is worth doing or worth considering, it is useful or deserves to be considered

♦ **worthless** •ADJECTIVE• a worthless person or thing has no value or use ⇒ **worthy**

worthwhile •ADJECTIVE• something that is worthwhile is worth doing or getting involved in, because it results in something good

worthy •ADJECTIVE• **worthier, worthiest** 1 to be worthy of something is to deserve it 2 a worthy person, or a worthy cause, deserves to be given respect or support

would •VERB• 1 a way of changing the verb **will** to make a past tense: *She said she would be in touch later.* 2 you use **would** to ask people if they want something or if they will do something: *Would you like a new bike for your birthday?* • *Would you close the door behind you, please.*

wouldn't •SHORT FORM• a short way to say and write **would not**: *She wouldn't go.*

wound¹ •VERB• a way of changing the verb **wind** to make a past tense. It can be used with or without a helping verb: *She wound a long, red, knitted scarf around her neck.* • *He had wound the old grandfather clock in the hall.*

ⓘ This word rhymes with **found**.

wound² •NOUN• **wounds** an injury to a person's or animal's body in which the skin has been damaged by a cut or blow •VERB• **wounds, wounding, wounded** 1 to wound a person or animal is to cause an injury to their body 2 to wound someone is to hurt their feelings

♦ **wounded** •ADJECTIVE• a wounded soldier or animal has been injured by a blow from a weapon

ⓘ This word rhymes with **spooned**.

wove •VERB• a way of changing the verb

weave to make a past tense: *She wove flowers into her hair.*

woven •VERB• the form of the verb **weave** that is used with a helping verb to show that something happened in the past: *The scarves were woven from wool.*

WPC •ABBREVIATION• **WPCs** short for **woman police constable**: *WPC Hobbs*

wrap •VERB• **wraps, wrapping, wrapped** **1** to wrap something, or to **wrap something up**, is to put a covering of paper or other material round it **2** to put something like paper or cloth round another thing to cover it: *She wrapped the bandage round my knee.*
♦ **wrapper** •NOUN• **wrappers** a piece of paper or cardboard that something is wrapped in

wrath •NOUN• great anger
♦ **wrathful** •ADJECTIVE• very angry

wreak •VERB• **wreaks, wreaking, wreaked** to wreak something, such as havoc, damage or revenge, is to cause it

wreath •NOUN• **wreaths** an arrangement of flowers and leaves in the shape of a ring, which is put on a dead person's coffin or grave, or hung up on a door at Christmas time

wreathe •VERB• **wreathes, wreathing, wreathed** one thing is wreathed in another when it is covered or surrounded by that other thing

wreck •VERB• **wrecks, wrecking, wrecked** **1** to wreck something is to damage it or destroy it **2** a ship is wrecked when it is badly damaged, for example by hitting rocks, and can no longer sail
•NOUN• **wrecks** a badly damaged ship or an aeroplane or vehicle that has crashed
♦ **wreckage** •NOUN• the broken or damaged pieces left after something has been wrecked

wren •NOUN• **wrens** a tiny wild bird with brown feathers and a short tail

wrench •VERB• **wrenches, wrenching, wrenched** to pull or twist something very hard so that it comes out of its position
•NOUN• **wrenches** **1** a hard pull or twist **2** a tool used to turn things

wrestle •VERB• **wrestles, wrestling, wrestled** **1** to wrestle with someone is to fight with them by gripping them and trying to throw them over or hold them down on the ground **2** to wrestle with a problem is to try very hard to solve it
♦ **wrestler** •NOUN• **wrestlers** someone who fights by wrestling
♦ **wrestling** •NOUN• the sport of fighting using special holds and movements to throw your opponent to the ground and to hold him or her there

wretch •NOUN• **wretches** a very wicked or very miserable person
♦ **wretched** •ADJECTIVE• **1** very poor and miserable: *They lived in a wretched little shack in the woods.* **2** very annoying: *Where's that wretched cat?*

wriggle •VERB• **wriggles, wriggling, wriggled** to twist about: *Stop wriggling about in your chair and sit still!*
♦ **wriggly** •ADJECTIVE• **wrigglier, wriggliest** a wriggly line has lots of twists and bends in it

wring •VERB• **wrings, wringing, wrung** **1** to twist or squeeze a wet cloth or wet washing so that all or most of the water is forced out **2** to wring something such as someone's hand is to twist or squeeze it hard
♦ **wringer** •NOUN• **wringers** a machine or piece of equipment that squeezes the water out of wet washing

wrinkle •NOUN• **wrinkles** **1** wrinkles are lines and creases that form in your skin as you get older **2** a wrinkle is a crease or ridge in the surface of something
•VERB• **wrinkles, wrinkling, wrinkled** you wrinkle your forehead or your nose when you screw it up so that the skin forms into little creases or lines
♦ **wrinkly** •ADJECTIVE• **wrinklier, wrinkliest** having lots of wrinkles

wrist •NOUN• **wrists** one of the two parts of your body where your arms join your hands

write •VERB• **writes, writing, wrote, written** **1** to form letters and words usually on paper using a pen or pencil **2** you write to someone when you write or type a letter and send it to them

Aa
Bb
Cc
Dd
Ee
Ff
Gg
Hh
Ii
Jj
Kk
Ll
Mm
Nn
Oo
Pp
Qq
Rr
Ss
Tt
Uu
Vv
Ww
Xx
Yy
Zz

3 to write a story, article, play or music is to create it and write it down

4 to **write something off** is think of it as being lost or too damaged to be used again

♦ **writer** •NOUN• **writers** someone who writes books, plays, film scripts or newspaper articles

♦ **writing** •NOUN• **writings 1** writing is forming letters and words on paper or some other surface so that they can be read

2 your writing is the way you write

3 an author's writings are the things he or she has written

wrong •ADJECTIVE• **1** not right or not satisfactory: *Is there something wrong with David? He doesn't look happy.* • *Cheating in examinations is wrong.*

2 not correct: *That was the wrong answer.*

3 not suitable: *He has decided he's in the wrong job.*

•ADVERB• wrongly or incorrectly: *I think I have spelt your name wrong.*

♦ **wrongly** •ADVERB• not correctly or accurately: *The plug had been fitted wrongly so the machine did not work.*

wrote •VERB• a way of changing the verb **write** to make a past tense: *He wrote a letter to his pen friend.*

wrung •VERB• a way of changing the verb **wring** to make a past tense. It can be used with or without a helping verb: *The woman wrung her hands.* • *He had wrung all the water out of the mop.*

wry •ADJECTIVE• **wryer, wryest** a wry smile, comment or sense of humour is one that shows gentle amusement at something that has gone wrong

WWW or **www** •ABBREVIATION• short for **World Wide Web**

Xx

Xmas •NOUN• an informal short spelling of **Christmas**

ⓘ The letter **X** can be a symbol meaning *Christ*, and this is why **Christmas** is shortened to **Xmas**.

X-ray •NOUN• **X-rays** a special kind of photograph that shows the bones inside someone's body

xylophone •NOUN• **xylophones** a musical instrument made up of a set of wooden bars that make different notes when you hit them with hammers

ⓘ This word comes from the Greek word **xylon**, which means *wood*, together with the English ending **-phone**, which means *sound*, because the instrument has wooden keys.

Yy

yacht •NOUN• **yachts** a sailing boat that you use for racing or for pleasure trips

yachtsman •NOUN• **yachtsmen** a man who sails a yacht

yachtswoman •NOUN• **yachtswomen** a woman who sails a yacht

yak •NOUN• **yaks** a type of ox with long hair that comes from Tibet

yam •NOUN• **yams** a root vegetable like a potato that grows in tropical countries

yank •VERB• **yanks, yanking, yanked** to pull something sharply and roughly: *He yanked the book out of my hand.*
•NOUN• **yanks** a sudden sharp pull

yap •VERB• **yaps, yapping, yapped** if a dog yaps, it makes a high-pitched bark
•NOUN• **yaps** a high-pitched bark

yard¹ •NOUN• **yards** a unit of measurement of length, equal to 0.914 metres or 3 feet

yard² •NOUN• **yards** 1 an enclosed area of land used for a particular purpose: *a builders' yard* 2 an American English word for **garden**

yarn •NOUN• **yarns** 1 wool or cotton that

has been spun into thread 2 a story that includes things that are not true: *began the whole story over again, spinning as long a yarn as possible.*

yashmak •NOUN• **yashmaks** a type of veil that some Muslim women wear

yawn •VERB• **yawns, yawning, yawned** 1 to open your mouth very wide and breathe in, because you are feeling tired or bored 2 if a hole yawns, it is wide open: *The mouth of the cave yawned below them.*

ⓘ The word **yawn** comes from an Old English word, **geonian**, which means *to gape widely.*

•NOUN• **yawns** the sound or action of someone yawning

ye •PRONOUN• an old-fashioned word for **you**

year •NOUN• **years** a period of 365 or 366 days, the length of time it takes for the Earth to go around the sun, especially the period from 1 January to 31 December
• **all year round** throughout the year: *The weather's pleasant all year round in Sicily.*
♦ **yearly** •ADJECTIVE• happening every year: *our yearly holiday*

Aa
Bb
Cc
Dd
Ee
Ff
Gg
Hh
Ii
Jj
Kk
Ll
Mm
Nn
Oo
Pp
Qq
Rr
Ss
Tt
Uu
Vv
Ww
Xx
Yy
Zz

yearn •VERB• **yearns, yearning, yearned** to **yearn for** something is to want it very much: *Harry yearned for a guitar of his own.*

yeast •NOUN• a substance that you add to dough to make bread rise

yell •VERB• **yells, yelling, yelled** to shout or scream: *'Let me go!' she yelled.*
•NOUN• **yells** a shout or scream

yellow •NOUN• the colour of the sun or the middle of an egg

yelp •VERB• **yelps, yelping, yelped** if a dog yelps, it makes a short, high sound because it is in pain
•NOUN• **yelps** a short, high sound

yes •ADVERB• a word you say when you agree with someone or something: *'Are these shoes all right?' 'Yes,' I said. 'They're all right.'*

yesterday •NOUN• the day before today
•ADVERB• on the day before today: *We went shopping yesterday.*

ⓘ You can say
✓ *I saw her yesterday morning.*
✓ *I saw her yesterday evening.*
You cannot say
✗ *I saw her yesterday night.*
You say
✓ *I saw her last night.*

yet •ADVERB• **1** by now, by this time: *Have you read her new book yet?* **2** before something is finished, still: *We might win this game yet.*
• **as yet** up till now: *I hope to visit Paris, but I haven't as yet.*

Yeti •NOUN• **Yetis** a hairy creature like a big man who is supposed to live in the Himalayan mountains

yew •NOUN• **yews** a tree with very dark green leaves

yield •VERB• **yields, yielding, yielded 1** to give in or surrender: *The army yielded to enemy forces.*
2 to give way to pressure or force: *The door suddenly yielded and he fell into the room.*
3 to produce an amount of something such as a crop
•NOUN• **yields** the amount of something that is produced: *cows with a high milk yield*

yodel •VERB• **yodels, yodelling, yodelled** to sing in a way that involves changing back and forth between your normal singing voice and a very high voice

yoga •NOUN• a type of exercise in which you stretch your muscles whilst taking deep breaths. Yoga also involves meditation, which is thinking deeply

yogurt or **yoghurt** •NOUN• **yogurts** or **yoghurts 1** a runny food with a slightly sour taste that is made from milk **2** a pot of this food: *a strawberry yogurt*

yoke •NOUN• **yokes 1** a wooden frame that you put around the necks of a pair of oxen when they are pulling a cart
2 something that stops people from being free: *the yoke of slavery*
3 the part of a dress or blouse that fits over your shoulders and neck: *a blouse with an embroidered yoke*
•VERB• **yokes, yoking, yoked** to fasten two things together with a yoke

yolk •NOUN• **yolks** the yellow part in the middle of an egg

Yom Kippur •NOUN• a Jewish religious day when people do not eat. It is also called the Day of Atonement

yonder •ADVERB• an old-fashioned word for 'in that place'
•ADJECTIVE• over there: *Take my sword, and go with it to yonder water side.*

yore •NOUN• an old-fashioned word for **the past**: *times of yore*

you •PRONOUN• a word you use to the person or people that you are talking to: *Do you like pizza?* • *I'll ring you tomorrow night.* • *Max is taller than you.*

you'd •SHORT FORM• a short way to say or write **you had** or **you would**: *You'd better be careful.* • *You'd be sorry if she left.*

you'll •SHORT FORM• a short way to say and write **you will**: *You'll never guess what happened next!*

young •ADJECTIVE• **younger, youngest** not old: *a young boy*
•NOUN• **1** the babies that an animal or bird has: *a sparrow feeding its young* **2** the young are young people

◆ **youngster** •NOUN• **youngsters** a young person

your •ADJECTIVE• belonging to the person or people you are talking to: *Can I borrow your pen?*

ⓘ Try not to confuse the spellings of **your** and **you're**.
Your is the possessive form of **you**, and shows that someone owns something: *I like your shoes.*
You're is short for **you are**: *You're my best friend.*

you're •SHORT FORM• a short way to say and write **you are**: *You're a better singer than he is.*

yours •PRONOUN• a word you use to talk about something belonging to a person or people you are talking to: *Which glass is yours?*
• **Yours faithfully, Yours sincerely** or **Yours truly** words that you write before your name at the end of a formal letter

yourself •PRONOUN• **yourselves 1** you use the words **yourself** or **yourselves** after a verb or preposition when the person or people you are talking to perform an action and are affected by it: *Careful you don't cut yourself on that knife.* • *You'll have to dry yourselves on your T-shirts.*
2 you can use **yourself** or **yourselves** to

show that someone does something without any help from anyone else: *Did you really make that skirt yourself?*
3 you can use **yourself** or **yourselves** to show more clearly who you mean: *You cannot put up the picture yourselves, but you can ask someone else to do it.*

youth •NOUN• **youths 1** the time in your life when you are young: *She spent most of her youth abroad.*
2 a boy aged between about 15 and 20: *a gang of youths*
3 young people as a group: *the youth of today*
◆ **youthful** •ADJECTIVE• young: *a youthful-looking fifty-year-old.*

ⓘ You only use the plural **youths** when you are talking about teenage boys.

youth hostel •NOUN• **youth hostels** a place where people can stay overnight quite cheaply when they are on a walking holiday

you've •SHORT FORM• a short way to say and write **you have**: *You've left the door open again.*

yo-yo •NOUN• **yo-yos** a toy that is made up of a circular object on a piece of string that you have to try to keep spinning up and down

Yule •NOUN• an old-fashioned word for **Christmas**

Aa Bb Cc Dd Ee Ff Gg Hh Ii Jj Kk Ll Mm Nn Oo Pp Qq Rr Ss Tt Uu Vv Ww Xx Yy Zz

Zz

zany •ADJECTIVE• **zanier, zaniest** crazy or funny: *a zany sense of humour*

ⓘ This word comes from the name **Zanni**, who was a clown in old Italian comedy plays.

zap •VERB• **zaps, zapping, zapped 1** to shoot or kill something, especially in a computer game: *You have to zap all the aliens before they catch you.* **2** to move quickly through or between things: *zapping through the TV channels*

ⓘ This is a slang word.

zeal •NOUN• enthusiasm and keenness
♦ **zealous** •ADJECTIVE• very enthusiastic about something: *a zealous supporter of the football team*

zebra •NOUN• **zebras** an animal like a horse with black and white stripes

zebra crossing •NOUN• **zebra crossings** a place where you can cross a road, marked in black and white stripes

zenith •NOUN• the highest point in something: *Scoring those five goals was the zenith of his career.*

zero •NOUN• **zeros 1** nothing or the number 0: *There are six zeros in one million.* **2** the point on a scale where you start measuring things, for example on a thermometer: *It was three degrees below zero.*

zest •NOUN• a lot of enjoyment: *Joe had a great zest for life.*

zigzag •ADJECTIVE• with lots of sharp bends from left to right: *a zigzag pattern*
•VERB• **zigzags, zigzagging, zigzagged** to have a lot of sharp bends from left to right: *The path zigzagged up the hillside.*

zimmer •NOUN• **zimmers** a metal frame that old people sometimes use to help them walk. This word is a trademark

zinc •NOUN• a bluish-white metal

zip •NOUN• **zips** a fastener on clothes or bags that has two rows of metal or plastic teeth that fit tightly together when a sliding piece is pulled along them
•VERB• **zips, zipping, zipped 1** to fasten something with a zip: *Zip up your jacket; it's cold.* **2** to move somewhere very quickly: *The bullet zipped by his head.* **3** to make the information on a computer file fit into a much smaller space, so that it uses up less memory

zip code •NOUN• **zip codes** the American word for **post code**

zodiac •NOUN• in astrology, an imaginary strip in the sky that has 12 parts that are named after constellations, for example *Capricorn* and *Aquarius*

zombie •NOUN• **zombies 1** a dead body that is supposed to come back to life through witchcraft **2** someone who seems to be very slow or stupid

zone •NOUN• **zones** an area or part of a place that people set aside and use for a particular purpose: *a no-parking zone*

zoo •NOUN• **zoos** a place where people keep wild animals to breed them and study them, and where you can go to see these animals

ⓘ The word **zoo** comes from the Greek word **zoion**, which means *animal.*

zoology •NOUN• the study of animals
♦ **zoological** •ADJECTIVE• relating to animals
♦ **zoologist** •NOUN• **zoologists** a person who studies animals

zoom •VERB• **zooms, zooming, zoomed 1** to go somewhere very fast, especially with a loud buzzing noise: *The rocket zoomed up into the air.* **2** if a camera **zooms in**, it makes the thing that is being filmed or photographed look much bigger

zoom lens •NOUN• **zoom lenses** a lens on a camera that can make things look bigger or smaller